International Directory of
COMPANY
HISTORIES

International Directory of

COMPANY HISTORIES

VOLUME 44

Editor
Tina Grant

ST. JAMES PRESS

GALE GROUP

THOMSON LEARNING

Detroit • New York • San Diego • San Francisco
Boston • New Haven, Conn. • Waterville, Maine
London • Munich

STAFF

Tina Grant, *Editor*

Miranda H. Ferrara, *Project Manager*

Erin Bealmear, Joann Cerrito, James Craddock, Steve Cusack,
Kristin Hart, Melissa Hill, Margaret Mazurkiewicz, Carol Schwartz,
Christine Tomassini, Michael J. Tyrkus, *St. James Press Editorial Staff*

Peter M. Gareffa, *Managing Editor, St. James Press*

Library of Congress Catalog Number: 89-190943

British Library Cataloguing in Publication Data

International directory of company histories. Vol. 44
I. Tina Grant
338.7409

ISBN 1-55862-462-7

Printed in the United States of America
Published simultaneously in the United Kingdom

St. James Press is an imprint of The Gale Group

Cover photograph: Istanbul Stock Exchange trading floor
(courtesy: Istanbul Stock Exchange)

10 9 8 7 6 5 4 3 2 1

CONTENTS _____

Company Histories

PREFACE

The St. James Press series *The International Directory of Company Histories (IDCH)* is intended for reference use by students, business people, librarians, historians, economists, investors, job candidates, and others who seek to learn more about the historical development of the world's most important companies. To date, *IDCH* has covered over 5,325 companies in 44 volumes.

Inclusion Criteria

Most companies chosen for inclusion in *IDCH* have achieved a minimum of US$25 million in annual sales and are leading influences in their industries or geographical locations. Companies may be publicly held, private, or nonprofit. State-owned companies that are important in their industries and that may operate much like public or private companies also are included. Wholly owned subsidiaries and divisions are profiled if they meet the requirements for inclusion. Entries on companies that have had major changes since they were last profiled may be selected for updating.

The *IDCH* series highlights 10% private and nonprofit companies, and features updated entries on approximately 45 companies per volume.

Entry Format

Each entry begins with the company's legal name, the address of its headquarters, its telephone, toll-free, and fax numbers, and its web site. A statement of public, private, state, or parent ownership follows. A company with a legal name in both English and the language of its headquarters country is listed by the English name, with the native-language name in parentheses.

The company's founding or earliest incorporation date, the number of employees, and the most recent available sales figures follow. Sales figures are given in local currencies with equivalents in U.S. dollars. For some private companies, sales figures are estimates and indicated by the abbreviation *est.* The entry lists the exchanges on which a company's stock is traded and its ticker symbol, as well as the company's NAIC codes.

Entries generally contain a *Company Perspectives* box which provides a short summary of the company's mission, goals, and ideals, a *Key Dates* box highlighting milestones in the company's history, lists of *Principal Subsidiaries, Principal Divisions, Principal Operating Units, Principal Competitors,* and articles for *Further Reading.*

American spelling is used throughout *IDCH*, and the word ''billion'' is used in its U.S. sense of one thousand million.

Sources

Entries have been compiled from publicly accessible sources both in print and on the Internet such as general and academic periodicals, books, annual reports, and material supplied by the companies themselves.

Cumulative Indexes

IDCH contains three indexes: the **Index to Companies**, which provides an alphabetical index to companies discussed in the text as well as to companies profiled, the **Index to Industries**, which allows researchers to locate companies by their principal industry, and the **Geographic Index**, which lists companies alphabetically by the country of their headquarters. The indexes are cumulative and specific instructions for using them are found immediately preceding each index.

Suggestions Welcome

Comments and suggestions from users of *IDCH* on any aspect of the product as well as suggestions for companies to be included or updated are cordially invited. Please write:

The Editor
International Directory of Company Histories
St. James Press
27500 Drake Rd.
Farmington Hills, Michigan 48331-3535

ABBREVIATIONS FOR FORMS OF COMPANY INCORPORATION

A.B.	Aktiebolaget (Sweden)
A.G.	Aktiengesellschaft (Germany, Switzerland)
A.S.	Aksjeselskap (Denmark, Norway)
A.S.	Atieselskab (Denmark)
A.Ş.	Anomin Şirket (Turkey)
B.V.	Besloten Vennootschap met beperkte, Aansprakelijkheid (The Netherlands)
Co.	Company (United Kingdom, United States)
Corp.	Corporation (United States)
G.I.E.	Groupement d'Intérêt Economique (France)
GmbH	Gesellschaft mit beschränkter Haftung (Germany)
H.B.	Handelsbolaget (Sweden)
Inc.	Incorporated (United States)
KGaA	Kommanditgesellschaft auf Aktien (Germany)
K.K.	Kabushiki Kaisha (Japan)
LLC	Limited Liability Company (Middle East)
Ltd.	Limited (Canada, Japan, United Kingdom, United States)
N.V.	Naamloze Vennootschap (The Netherlands)
OY	Osakeyhtiöt (Finland)
PLC	Public Limited Company (United Kingdom)
PTY.	Proprietary (Australia, Hong Kong, South Africa)
S.A.	Société Anonyme (Belgium, France, Switzerland)
SpA	Società per Azioni (Italy)

ABBREVIATIONS FOR CURRENCY

$	United States dollar	KD	Kuwaiti dinar
£	United Kingdom pound	L	Italian lira
¥	Japanese yen	LuxFr	Luxembourgian franc
A$	Australian dollar	M$	Malaysian ringgit
AED	United Arab Emirates dirham	N	Nigerian naira
		Nfl	Netherlands florin
B	Thai baht	NIS	Israeli new shekel
B	Venezuelan bolivar	NKr	Norwegian krone
BFr	Belgian franc	NT$	Taiwanese dollar
C$	Canadian dollar	NZ$	New Zealand dollar
CHF	Switzerland franc	P	Philippine peso
COL	Colombian peso	PLN	Polish zloty
Cr	Brazilian cruzado	Pta	Spanish peseta
CZK	Czech Republic koruny	R	Brazilian real
DA	Algerian dinar	R	South African rand
Dfl	Netherlands florin	RMB	Chinese renminbi
DKr	Danish krone	RO	Omani rial
DM	German mark	Rp	Indonesian rupiah
E£	Egyptian pound	Rs	Indian rupee
Esc	Portuguese escudo	Ru	Russian ruble
EUR	Euro dollars	S$	Singapore dollar
FFr	French franc	Sch	Austrian schilling
Fmk	Finnish markka	SFr	Swiss franc
GRD	Greek drachma	SKr	Swedish krona
HK$	Hong Kong dollar	SRls	Saudi Arabian riyal
HUF	Hungarian forint	W	Korean won
IR£	Irish pound	W	South Korean won
K	Zambian kwacha		

International Directory of

COMPANY
HISTORIES

Acsys, Inc.

75 14th Street
Suite 2200
Atlanta, Georgia 30309
U.S.A.
Telephone: (404) 817-9440
Toll Free: (877) ACSYSINC
Fax: (404) 815-4703
Web site: http://www.acsysinc.com

Wholly-Owned Subsidiary of Vedior N.V.
Incorporated: 1997
Employees: 574
Sales: $166.3 million (1999)
NAIC: 56132 Temporary Help Services; 56131
    Employment Placement Agencies; 41612 Human
    Resources and Executive Search Consulting Services

Acsys, Inc., headquartered in Atlanta, Georgia, is now a division of Vedior N.V. Located in the Netherlands, Vedior is the largest staffing company in the world. As its subsidiary, Acsys provides professional staffing services throughout the United States. Through 40 offices, it serves 22 major metropolitan markets nationwide. It is the nation's second largest accounting and finance staffing firm among those deriving more than 50 percent of their revenues from accounting and finance staffing services. Among its principal clients are telecommunication, consumer product, healthcare, financial service, industrial, media, retail, technology, and professional service companies, many of which outsource whole portions of their information and finance processing departments to Acsys. A recent trend, outsourcing has increased the demand for the kinds of temporary staffing services that Acsys provides. In 1999, more than 80 percent of the company's business consisted of finance and IT (information technology) temporary staffing services. Until purchased by Vedior's affiliate, Tiberia, in 2000, the company was public and traded on AMEX under the symbol AYS.

1974–97: Acsys, Inc. Is Created

Acsys, Inc. did not actually come into existence until March 1997, when, in effect, a consortium of accounting and finance professional staffing companies agreed to merge into it. Its aim was to build a national specialty staffing business for Fortune 1000 and middle-market companies as well as governmental agencies and nonprofit organizations. Its basic plan was to acquire existing companies that would provide a network of offices in major metropolitan centers across the United States.

Within a brief span, the company acquired seven companies, none of which was very old. They had an average operating history of just 15 years, with the oldest ones dating back 23 years and the youngest just five years. However, Acys, Inc.'s principal lineage can be traced back to 1980, when the chief architect of Acys, Inc., David C. Cooper, formed David C. Cooper & Associates, a company which started up in Atlanta in that year. Cooper founded his firm to provide financial search and staffing services, and from the outset served as its president and CEO. A native of Georgia, Cooper received his education in that state, eventually earning a Bachelors of Business Administration degree at the University of Georgia. In addition to serving in his company's executive posts, for six years Cooper served as president of the American Association of Finance and Accounting (AAFA), a national organization of independently-owned accounting and finance staffing companies. In fact, its was at a 1996 Scottsdale, Arizona, convention of the AAFA that Cooper and his colleagues conceived of the new company that would become a reality as Acys, Inc.

Over the years, Cooper built his company into a very successful temporary and permanent staffing service for clients who were primarily Fortune 1000 and middle-market employers. At the time Cooper & Associates merged with and into Acsys, Inc., the company was producing $7.8 million in staffing service revenues. It also had a subsidiary company, DCCA Professional Temporaries, Inc., which became part of the merger package when Acsys, Inc. was formed.

Three of the first companies making up Acsys, Inc. were a few years older than Cooper's firm. The most senior of the

4   **Acsys, Inc.**

Company Perspectives:

We're a different kind of staffing firm. Our professionals are industry specialists in the fields we serve. Our passion is to understand precisely what our clients want, and use that information to build relationships, not just headcounts. Our personal attention to all of our clients–candidates and companies—is what sets us apart from our competitors. And it's why many of our candidates become our clients.

group were Infinity Enterprises, Inc. and EKT, Inc., both established in 1974. Infinity, which did business as Don Richards Associates of Washington, had offices in Washington, D.C.; Bethesda, Maryland; and Tyson's Corner, Virginia. It brought with it annual revenues from its staffing services of $17.0 million. EKT, which conducted business as Don Richards Associates of Charlotte, had its headquarters in Charlotte, North Carolina. Its revenue had reached $2.8 million in fiscal 1996.

One other company, AcSys Resources, Inc., was also older than Cooper's firm. It dated back to 1977. From its seven offices located in New Jersey, Pennsylvania, and Delaware, AcSys had generated annual revenues of $14.4 million before being merged into Acsys, Inc.

The remaining three companies acquired by Acsys, Inc. in its first half year of its existence were younger than David C. Cooper & Associates. These included C.P.A. Staffing, Inc.; Rylan Forbes Consulting Group, Inc.; and Cama of Tampa, Inc. C.P.A Staffing and its sister companies, C.P.A. Search, Inc. and Career Placement Associates, Inc., based in Atlanta, had a combined revenue of $6.5 million in 1996. These companies were acquired by AcSys Resources and merged into C.P.A. Staffing, Inc. before Acsys, Inc. acquired AcSys Resources. C.P.A. Staffing provided temporary and permanent staffing services to *Fortune* 1000 and middle-market companies. Rylan Forbes, a temporary staffing service with offices in Philadelphia and Edison, New Jersey, was founded in 1992. By the time Acsys, Inc. brought it under its corporate umbrella, Rylan Forbes had reached $1.4 million in annual revenues. Cama of Tampa, Inc., which conducted business as Don Richard Associates of Tampa, was first opened in 1987. Its gross income for 1996 was $2.5 million.

At the time Acys, Inc. was formed in March 1997, it established its headquarters at 2000 Pennsylvania Avenue, N.W., in Washington, D.C. It was there, within the next two months, that it created its core business. The nucleus of Acsys, Inc. initially consisted of the four companies that it acquired in May of 1997: David C. Cooper & Associates; Don Richards Associates of Washington; Don Richards Associates of Charlotte; and Don Richards Associates of Tampa. The ''Don Richards Associates'' name was a registered trademark of Don Richards Associate International, Inc., an unaffiliated company. Acsys purchased the rights to use the name so that the companies could continue to operate under it in the areas where they were already established. However, the right to use the name ''Don Richard Associates of Tampa'' carried a May 1999 expiration date.

1998–99: Acquisitions Spur Company's Growth

By September 1997, Acsys had added the other three companies identified above. The company had also started making plans for going public. It did so in February 1998, but not before it had already operated successfully for almost a year without making any definite commitments to float stock. It had considerable promise, however, and was able to acquire other companies via stock mergers without even providing guarantees that its executives would benefit from a public offering. When floated, the IPO totaled 2.84 million shares of common stock and netted $20.1 million, which helped offset the cost of the company's acquisitions and spurred additional purchases. Altogether, between its formation in March 1997 and September 1998, Acsys acquired 10 other accounting and finance staffing companies.

In September, 1997, in its merger with Acsys Resources, Acsys, Inc. had gained a base on which to build information technology (IT) staffing services. Like the other acquired companies, Acsys Resources provided temporary staffing and permanent placement services to similar clientele, but it also offered IT staffing services. So did another of the company's acquisitions, Icon Search and Consulting Inc., an Atlanta-based IT staffing company that Acsys got in a stock-swap deal in July 1998. That acquisition had also helped build a solid foundation for the company's planned IT staffing area development, an arena it planned to enter before the end of its second year.

By the summer of 1998, in order to further facilitate expansion, the company had moved its CFO, Timothy Mann, Jr., into the position of CEO. Mann, an attorney, was a specialist in mergers and acquisitions, and he brought his previous experience with Alston & Bird, an Atlanta law firm, to the job. Cooper remained the chairman of the company's board. The company also moved its corporate headquarters from Washington, D.C., to Atlanta. Because Acsys was very decentralized structurally, the move required the relocation of only five of the company's top executives. Two of the three chief managers already lived in Atlanta, and, in truth, the firm's business heart was located there. The move did make that city the corporate center for the diversely located offices in Acsys's network of staffing operations. By the time it moved its headquarters, the company had 16 offices in operation across the eastern part of the nation.

In early August of 1998, Acsys purchased Staffing Edge, Inc., a major specialty professional staffing firm headquartered in Des Moines, Iowa. That firm, founded in 1992, had reached an annual revenue rate of about $33 million, with a specialty in placing temporary and permanent professionals in the finance/accounting, IT, legal, engineering and high-end office/clerical and training fields in ten metropolitan markets: Dallas/Fort Worth; Des Moines; Chicago; Denver; Houston; Kansas City; Phoenix, Arizona; San Antonio, Texas; and San Francisco. Terms of the acquisition were not made public.

In 1999, Mann resigned his position as the company's CEO and also relinquished his place on its board. The post was then assumed by Cooper, who also retained his chairmanship of the company's board. By the time Mann stepped down, Acsys had successfully integrated 11 companies. It had also managed an internal growth rate in the top range for all companies in the professional staffing industry.

Key Dates:

1974: Infinity Enterprises Inc. and EKT , Inc. are formed.
1977: Acsys Resources, Inc. is founded.
1980: David C. Cooper founds David C. Cooper & Associates.
1987: Cama of Tampa, Inc. opens its first office.
1992: Rylan Forbes Consulting Group, Inc is created.
1997: David C. Cooper & Associates merges with CPA Search and Staffing, Inc. to form Atlantic division of Acsys.
1998: Company completes IPO and moves headquarters to Atlanta; Acsys also acquires Staffing Edge, Inc. and Icon Search and Consulting, Inc.
2000: Vedior affiliate, Tiberia, buys Acsys.

2000–01: Acsys Inc. Is Acquired by Vedior N.V.

In a *Wall Street Transcript* interview conducted in February 2000, Cooper revealed that about 55 percent of Acsys's revenues came from its accounting and finance staffing services, while about 40 percent came from its information technology services. The IT business segment, which was barely two-years old, had already made tremendous strides. It was made up of two divisions: the first, the local contract group, augmented company staffs and provided an array of familiar computer services; the second, the national products business, augmented staffs for the implementation and support of enterprise resource planning (ERP).

ERP implementation consulting services had become a major part of Acsys's IT business by the end of 2000. Among other things, Acsys had become an SAP National Implementation Partner. SAP, a major software company, specialized in ERP software used to integrate such back-office functions as accounting and distribution. Acsys also was providing implementation support for other applications, including that produced by PeopleSoft, a maker of network-based human resource software; J.D. Edwards, a maker of enterprise and supply-chain management software; and Siebel Systems, a leading maker of customer relationship management (CRM) software which automated the sales and service operations of larger corporations. It was through its strategic alliance with Siebel that Acsys ventured into the high-growth CRM area. Although in 1998 and 1999, Acsys, Inc. had recorded slight losses on the bottom line, its revenues soared, growing from $58.2 million in 1997 to $166.3 million in 1999. Its performance made it a ripe acquisition plum for a larger firm with a similar business focus. The buyout occurred in 2000, when Tiberia B.V. acquired the company through its subsidiary, Platform Purchaser Inc. Tiberia was itself jointly owned by ING Bank Corporate Investments and Amsterdam, Netherlands-based Vedior N.V., the world's third largest staffing company, boasting more than 10,000 employees spread through 2,000 offices in 27 countries. Within that network, Acsys became a member of UK-based Select Appointments (Holdings) Limited. Reportedly, the transaction initially involved the tender of approximately 14.2 million shares of stock, or about 97.8 percent of all of Acsys, Inc.'s outstanding shares.

What impact the change in the company's ownership may have on Acsys, Inc. in the long run remains to be seen. However; the company's autonomy remained intact, and the firm seemed to be doing business as usual through 2000 and into 2001. Starting with its opening of a new office in Reston, Virginia, in January 2000, the company also seemed destined to continue on its expansion course, showing no shift in the focus of its business or a curtailment of its services.

Principal Divisions

Professional Services; Information Technology.

Principal Competitors

Kforce; Manpower, Inc.; Robert Half International Inc.; Interim Services, Inc., Norrell, Inc.; Olsten Corporation; Romac International, Inc.; Accountants, Inc.; Accountants on Call.

Further Reading

"Acsys CEO Outlines Internet Strategy: An Interview with David Cooper," *Wall Street Transcript*, http://www.twst.com/notes/articles/jal602.html.

"ACSY INC.-ACSY," *CDA-Investment Insiders' Chronicle*, March 22, 1999, p. 1.

"Acsys, Inc. Acquires Don Richard Associates of Richmond; Marks Entry into Strong Richmond, Virginia Market," *Business Wire*, March 31, 1998.

"Acsys, Inc. Acquires Staffing Edge, Inc.; Expands Acsys Operations to 10 Key Markets," *Business Wire*, August 4, 1998.

"Acsys, Inc. Announces Move to the American Stock Exchange under Symbol AYS," *Business Wire*, August 31, 1999.

"Acsys, Inc. Chief Executive Officer Resigns," *Business Wire*, December 1, 1999.

Billips, Mike, "National Staffing Firm Sets Up Shop Here," *Atlantic Business Chronicle*, July 10, 1998, p. 1A.

—John W. Fiero

ADT Security Services, Inc.

One Town Center Road
P.O. Box 5035
Boca Raton, Florida 33431-0835
U.S.A.
Telephone: (561) 988-0835
Fax: (561) 988-3601
Web site: http://www.adt.com

Wholly Owned Subsidiary of Tyco International Ltd.
Incorporated: 1901
Employees: 19,000
Sales: $6.08 billion (2000)
NAIC: 561621 Security Systems Services

ADT Security Services, Inc. became part of Tyco International Ltd. in 1998 to ward off a hostile bid made by shareowner Western Resources. Operating as a unit within Tyco's Fire and Security Services division—a division that secured over $6 billion in sales in 2000—ADT is the largest provider of security services to over five million customers, including those in the residential, commercial, and federal sectors. The company provides products and services related to intrusion, fire protection, closed circuit television, access control, critical condition monitoring, and integrated systems. Under the leadership of Tyco, a globally diverse manufacturing and service company with sales of nearly $30 billion, ADT averaged 75,000 new accounts per month in North America during 2000.

Early History: Late 1800s

ADT's beginnings reach back to 1874, when the American District Telegraph Company (ADTC) was founded in Baltimore to deliver telegraph messages. The telegraph was the speediest means of communication known at the time. When a customer wanted to send a message by telegraph, he would write the communiqué and carry it to a local district telegraph agency. (Other customers had call boxes installed in their homes or places of business, which they could use to electronically summon a courier to come and get their message.) At the district telegraph agency, the message was reformatted for swift transmission over the telegraph lines to another agency, which would decode the memorandum and dispatch one of its uniformed messenger boys to deliver it.

The ADTC messenger boy system epitomized the intriguing slice of Americana that was the telegraph system. ADTC maintained rigid standards for its messengers, who attained nearly legendary status in some cities. Paramount among requirements were speed and dependability. According to company annals, one rule stated that "messengers on foot may not take more than one-and-one-half minutes per block." ADTC also required the boys to be in and out of a building in less than two minutes. Some superintendents kept the boys in line by writing regularly to their parents, informing them of their offspring's performance. Worse yet, the racing messengers would reportedly be chased by children on occasion, who jeered "ADT. . . . all day trotters."

ADTC was created by merging 57 district telegraph agencies from different cities into a single, consolidated operation. The resultant organization made it possible for the different agencies to benefit from various economies of scale. Importantly, an improved call box allowed customers in some cities to send different signals that would let the agency know their specific need before the messenger was even dispatched. The result of the new system was that customers were suddenly able to signal their need for the police, a doctor, the fire department, or even a wagon or coach.

Thus, the seeds of ADT security had been planted. By the late 1800s, in fact, a jingle had been written to promote ADTC's services: "A trusty guardian of property . . . day or night protection constantly . . . that's the system, value, and service of ADT." "Way back, they used to have runners," explained ADT Operations Supervisor Dave Roersma in the April 28, 1986 *Grand Rapids Business Journal.* Roersma related: "They'd get signals from different buildings. If somebody had a fire, they'd send a signal down and a runner would grab the message and run down to the fire department. They even used bicycles for a while."

Focus on Security Services: Early to Mid-1900s

ADT's advanced call boxes were installed only in ADT's more populous districts, while traditional messenger services continued to account for about three-quarters of the company's

Company Perspectives:

When you're protected by ADT, you're protected by the largest, oldest, and one of the best security companies in the nation. Throughout its 127 year history, ADT has lead the way in the innovation of security services, from the simple Call Boxes of the early 1900s to the interactive video surveillance of the year 2000. And this expertise is recognized. A significant number of Fortune 500 companies rely on ADT for their security needs, as does the largest residential base in the electronic security industry. Today, and in the future, ADT remains committed to providing peace of mind and unsurpassed customer service in the protection of your home, your business, and the government.

sales through the end of the nineteenth century. By the early 1900s, however, local telephone systems were rapidly displacing the labor-intensive messenger services. To combat telephone competition, ADT scrambled to convert the majority of its messenger systems to electronic signaling in a span of only ten years. The successful transition was partly a result of ADT becoming a subsidiary of Western Union in 1901. Western Union dominated the telegraph industry and was able to help finance ADT's widespread conversion to electronic signaling.

The supremacy of the telegraph system quickly waned after the turn of the century. Emerging communications giant American Telephone and Telegraph Company (AT&T) bought out Western Union, along with ADT, in 1909. Under the auspices of AT&T, ADT's messenger operations were jettisoned, and the company became focused entirely on the signaling business. AT&T took a particular interest in ADT, placing it under the direct leadership of former AT&T President Theodore N. Vail. Vail steered ADT toward an emphasis on security services. Benefiting from AT&T's renowned research and development labs, ADT leapfrogged its potential competitors throughout the 1920s and 1930s with ongoing advancements in theft and fire alarm systems.

A manpower shortage during World War II generated a need for automated alarm systems that were less dependent on humans to signal for help. In response, ADT developed several landmark systems that were considered extremely advanced at the time. Chief among its breakthroughs were the ADT Teletherm (an automatic fire detection system) and ADT Telewave (and automated intrusion detection system). ADT experienced strong growth during the postwar U.S. economic expansion of the 1950s and 1960s. In addition to assuming a leadership role in the U.S. security systems industry, ADT began expanding internationally, particularly in the United Kingdom.

Technology Advances and Rapid Growth: 1970s–80s

ADT broke away from AT&T in 1969 and became a publicly traded company on the New York Stock Exchange. By that time, computer technology was already emerging that would radically change the complexion of communication and security related industries within a few decades. Specifically, semiconductor components began to be incorporated in security and communications equipment, a development that allowed ADT

to begin building components and systems that were smaller, less expensive, and more capable. ADT introduced its first solid-state device in the early 1970s and subsequently developed the first multiplex detection and alarm system, which could simultaneously send multiple messages, or signals, on the same radio frequency or wire.

The advanced semiconductor equipment during the 1970s was significant in that it vastly broadened the potential market for all types of security systems. Prior to the 1970s, security and fire detection systems were purchased almost entirely by businesses or only very wealthy individuals. As the cost of new technology began to fall during the 1970s, though, it became clear to ADT that small businesses and middle-income homeowners would soon be added to the industry's expanding target market. By the late 1970s, in fact, many insurance companies were offering discounted premiums to homeowners who installed security systems.

To take advantage of surging demand, ADT continued to innovate throughout the 1970s and early 1980s. Importantly, ADT launched the first "central station" in the mid-1970s. Central station monitoring represented a major improvement over traditional, locally based fire and intruder systems. From a central station, ADT was able to monitor a large base of customers' premises electronically, round-the-clock, every day of the year. A single monitoring station would eventually be used to protect thousands of homes in a multi-state area. Integrated into ADT's central monitoring systems during the early 1980s were a variety of new components and services, including: Unimode, a fire detection system; CentraScan, a patented computer-based comprehensive security system; and in 1981, SafeWatch, an advanced residential surveillance system.

ADT continued to benefit from improved technology during the 1980s as its base of both commercial and residential customers expanded. The company also prospered as a result of rising crime rates, particularly in major metropolitan areas. By the late 1980s, ADT was serving virtually every Fortune 500 company in some capacity. Furthermore, even though the industry was highly fragmented, ADT's five-plus percent market share was estimated to be at least as great as the combined share of its next three largest North American competitors.

Much of ADT's growth during the 1980s was attributable to residential markets. As consumers became more concerned about crime, and as technology costs dropped, sales of home security systems surged. Instead of tailoring commercial equipment to residential applications, ADT began developing entire product lines specifically for home use. The systems were designed to perform a variety of functions, such as tracking an intruder's movements inside the home, monitoring the home through the telephone, detecting broken pipes, and even noting whether a customer's freezer had stopped operating. A typical basic residential ADT system in the mid-1980s could be installed for under $1,000, with monitoring fees usually running less than $250 annually.

In 1987, ADT, Inc. was acquired by Hawley Group Limited of the United Kingdom. Hawley was a group of diversified companies active in service and other industries, including the electronic security industry. It had begun building its North American security company holdings in 1981 with the purchase

---

Key Dates:

1874: The American District Telegraph company (ADTC) is founded in Baltimore, Maryland, to deliver telegraph messages.

1901: The company becomes a subsidiary of Western Union.

1909: AT&T purchases control of both Western Union and ADT.

1969: ADT becomes a publicly traded company on the New York Stock Exchange.

1974: The firm celebrates its 100th anniversary.

1981: ADT launches SafeWatch, an advanced residential surveillance system.

1987: The company is purchased by Hawley Group Limited of the United Kingdom and renamed ADT Security Systems Inc.

1993: ADT residential customer base increases to 477,000; the firm controls a four percent share of the North American home security market.

1995: Western Resources purchases a 23 percent stake in ADT.

1996: The company changes its name to ADT Security Services, Inc. and moves its headquarters to Boca Raton, Florida.

1998: ADT is acquired by Tyco International Ltd.

1999: The Mobile Security Network system is launched.

2000: QControl, a passenger screening system developed by ADT, is installed in Miami International Airport.

2001: ADT creates a Financial Services and Banking division to capture increased sales in the financial industry.

---

of Electro-Protective Corporation of America in 1981. Between 1982 and 1985, Hawley purchased an assemblage of small security service businesses throughout North America. Its crowning acquisition was ADT. In fact, after the buyout, Hawley changed its name to ADT Limited, and broke its operations into two divisions, the largest of which became ADT Security Systems, Inc.

As a result of the merger with ADT, Inc. and several of Hawley's complementary subsidiaries, ADT Security Systems' sales bolted to about $800 million by the late 1980s. Furthermore, ADT purchased Britannia Security Group PLC, an industry leader in the United Kingdom, in 1990. That purchase, combined with other security company holdings in England purchased by Hawley during the 1980s, helped to boost ADT's aggregate sales to $880 million. Despite general economic malaise in both the United States and Britain, as well as major financial setbacks related to other of ADT Limited's holdings, ADT Security Systems, Inc. continued to perform admirably during the early 1990s.

New Product Development and the Home Security Market: Early 1990s

New product introductions were an important contributor to ADT's expansion during the early 1990s. ADT introduced its popular FOCUS system, which allowed commercial customers to more specifically designate protection zones that could be independently monitored. For example, a perimeter area could be monitored while offices inside the perimeter were left open to employees. ADT also bolstered its line of video surveillance equipment and introduced a slew of home security devices.

By the early 1990s, ADT was offering a full line of advanced security services and systems for the massive upper-middle and middle-income residential market. In most cases, ADT retained ownership of the installed system. The customer paid a one-time installation fee and also agreed to pay an annual service charge for monitoring and maintenance. As new products and services were introduced, ADT expected to make money through system upgrades. The systems, like those designed for commercial use, were commonly configured to detect movement, break-ins, fire, smoke, flooding, and other hazards. ADT could respond by phoning the police, notifying the homeowner, and/or dispatching ADT security personnel to the home.

Besides new products, ADT's growth during the early 1990s was largely a consequence of its newfound emphasis on the booming residential market. After the 1987 acquisition, ADT implemented an aggressive program of consolidation and growth centered on the home security market. The company cut its number of central monitoring stations from 162 to just 30 in North America and Europe, while at the same time significantly boosting monitoring capacity and geographic coverage. The end result was reduced operating costs and system prices. Lower prices, in turn, translated into a larger base of potential customers, particularly homeowners in lower income, high-crime areas.

During the early 1990s, sales of security services and systems to the commercial sector stagnated, squelching sales and income growth in that segment; ADT's base of business customers (customers to which ADT continued to provide monitoring services) wavered around the 385,000 mark. In contrast, residential sales exploded. As a result of savvy marketing and proliferating homeowner concerns about security, ADT boosted its base of residential customers to a record 265,000 by 1991. By 1993, moreover, that base had multiplied to 477,000, representing a leading four percent share of the North American home security market.

As residential sales surged, ADT Security Systems' revenues rose from $880 million in 1991 to $901 million in 1992, and then to a record $937 million during 1993. Net income jumped similarly, to about $150 million in 1993. Adding to ADT's revenues were sales from its related electronic article surveillance business, which featured systems used to tag articles in inventory, such as retail clothing. The tags had to be removed by a special device to avoid setting off an alarm, which was usually located at the facility's exit. Electronic article surveillance equipment registered five percent, or about $44 million, of ADT's sales in 1993.

From a group of 57 telegraph service companies, ADT Security Systems had blossomed into a nearly $1 billion security systems company with over one million customers by the mid-1990s. The subsidiary employed a work force of more than 12,000 and generated more than 20 percent of its revenues from operations outside North America. Steady gains in residential sales and an uptick in commercial markets suggested continued growth in the short term. Likewise, increasing concern about crime in the United States, combined with decreasing technology costs, suggested a bright long-term future for the industry leader.

Indeed by 1996, ADT controlled ten percent of the electronic security market, a $6 billion industry. With a strict focus on its security-related operations, the company continued its growth by purchasing smaller companies and by securing lucrative contracts. In fact, the firm acquired Alert Centre for $93 million in 1996 and also landed a contract with HFS, a franchiser of hotels and real estate brokerage offices. That year, the company changed its name to ADT Security Services, Inc. and moved its headquarters to Boca Raton, Florida.

The Tyco Purchase: 1997–1998

ADT's favorable market position led to increased industry attention during the latter half of the 1990s. In December 1995, Western Resources, a billion dollar utility firm based in Kansas, purchased a 23.4 percent stake in the firm. At the time of the purchase, Western hoped to use the ADT brand name to market security services to its gas and electricity utility customers.

Just a few months later, Republic Industries, led by Wayne Huizenga, offered $4.9 billion for ADT. Republic wanted to sell ADT alarm-monitoring services to customers of its AutoNation USA used-car dealerships. The attempt was blocked in September 1996 however, by Western Resource shareholders. Western then launched a hostile $3.5 billion bid for the firm in December, eyeballing ADT ownership as crucial to its entrance into the security industry. ADT management shunned the offer, claiming it was a "lowball" proposal—one that undervalued the company.

Tyco International Ltd. entered the fray in March 1997, offering a friendly $5.6 billion bid for the security firm. Working together, ADT and Tyco structured the merger to thwart Western's takeover attempts. The deal, in which ADT would actually acquire Tyco, but then allow Tyco to be the surviving company, was highly complex and left Western virtually powerless in its attempts to block the merger. Western finally backed down in July of that year, taking a $710 million profit on its 38 million shares, whose total worth equaled $1.3 billion.

ADT officially became part of Tyco's Fire and Security Services division in 1998. Under its new ownership structure, ADT thrived and continued expansion and new product development. In 1999, the security firm teamed up with retailer Sears to offer Sears HomeCentral customers a program entitled "Sears Home Security by ADT." The company also launched its Mobile Security Network, a mobile security system used to monitor vehicles using Global Positioning Satellite (GPS) technology along with wireless communication technology.

Continued Growth in the New Millennium

ADT entered the new millennium intent on future growth. By 2000, the company was adding 75,000 new accounts per month in North America as a result of aggressive marketing. That year the QControl airport monitoring system began operation in Miami International Airport. Within a year, 15 other airports had signed up for the system, which videotaped images of customers and their baggage before and after going through the airport's X-ray security checkpoint.

Along with new product development, ADT also grew through acquisition. Mach-7 Security, based in Wisconsin, was purchased for over $3 million in 2000. The firm also acquired SCANA Security in 2001 in a $24.5 million deal. During that year, ADT created a Financial Services and Banking division to take advantage of the growing need for security solutions in the financial services and banking industries.

As demand for security systems throughout the residential, commercial, and government sectors continued to be strong, ADT's future looked promising. As a major contributor to a $6.1 billion division, the company appeared to be well positioned for continued growth in the years to come.

Principal Competitors

Pinkerton's Inc.; Allied-SpectaGuard; Ameritech Corp.

Further Reading

"ADT Acquires Mach-7," *The Business Journal-Milwaukee,* June 16, 2000, p. 8.

"ADT Reports Sales and Operating Income Increases for 1992," *PR Newswire,* March 11, 1993.

"ADT Security Welcomes Wendell Thomas To Winston-Salem," *Winston-Salem Journal,* April 7, 1992.

A Brief History of the World Leader in Security for Home and Business, Parsippany, N.J.: ADT Security Systems, 1994.

Elstrom, Peter, "Not in Kansas Anymore," *Business Week,* October 14, 1996, p. 70.

"Fall Monitoring Devices," *Security Management,* April 2001, p. 127.

Fast, Doug, "Security Systems—Just Like Having Clint Eastwood Around," *Grand Rapids Business Journal,* April 28, 1986, p. 5.

Moore, Paula, "ADT Seeks New Home in Aurora," *Denver Business Journal,* July 26, 1996, p. 1A.

"Nothing to Be Alarmed About," *The Economist,* March 22, 1997, p. 84.

Patron, Edward, "ADT: A Safe Bet," *Financial World,* May 20, 1996, p. 22.

Poler, Donna, "ADT Security Systems Introduces the Focus R 55 Commercial Security System," *Business Wire,* June 4, 1991.

Reingold, Jennifer, "A Lollapalooza for Huizenga," *Business Week,* July 15, 1996, p. 29.

"Western Withdraws Offer for ADT," *The Oil Daily,* July 7, 1997.

—Dave Mote
—update: Christina M. Stansell

Alex Lee Inc.

120 Fourth Street S.W.
Hickory, North Carolina 28602
U.S.A.
Telephone: (828) 323-4424
Fax: (828) 323-4435
Web site: http://www.alexlee.com

Private Company
Incorporated: 1992
Employees: 8,500
Sales: $1.69 billion (2000)
NAIC: 42241 General Line Grocery Wholesalers; 44511
    Supermarkets and Other Grocery Stores; 551112
    Offices of Other Holding Companies

Alex Lee Inc. is a holding company that was formed in 1992 to serve as the parent company for three food and food distribution firms in North Carolina. Of the three, the oldest, largest, and original firm is Merchants Distributors Inc. (MDI), a wholesale grocery store distributor serving more than 600 food stores in the Carolinas, Georgia, Tennessee, Virginia, West Virginia, and Kentucky. Among its customers are IGA stores and Galaxy Food Centers. The second, Institution Food House (IFH), also a wholesale food distributor, was rated the 21st largest U.S. food "broadliner" (distributors with the widest range of goods) in 2001. Its customers include restaurants, regional chains, delis and bakeries, public institutions, schools, and those in the healthcare and business industries. Alex Lee's third operating unit, Lowes Food Stores, operates more than 100 supermarkets in the Carolinas and Virginia. Lowes was ranked 46 among the top 75 grocery stores in 2000 by magazine *Supermarket News*. In 1998, Alex Lee established a fourth company called Consolidation Services. The unit was created to provide its customers with warehousing storage space for nonrefrigerated dry products, trucking services, and inventory management systems. Alex Lee Inc. ranked 101 among the top 500 private firms in the United States in 1999 with operations in the Carolinas, Georgia, Florida, Tennessee, Virginia, West Virginia, and Kentucky.

Merchants Distributors Inc.: 1931–59

In 1931, a 27-year-old Lebanese immigrant named Moses George opened a wholesale produce and food distribution business in Shelby, North Carolina, with the goal of becoming a low-cost/low-price middleman between local food processors and the buying public. Although the Depression was quickly becoming more severe than anyone could have predicted, George's enterprise, Merchants Distributors Inc. (MDI), survived on the public's continuing need for basic food goods. George's only concession to circumstance was the relocation of his business a hundred miles north to Hickory, North Carolina, where he reopened MDI from a cramped 2,500-square-foot storefront on the town's Main Avenue.

Throughout the 1920s and 1930s, the U.S. food store industry underwent a radical sea of change. The traditional mom-and-pop grocery store, in which a limited selection of goods was sold from tables and barrels, was giving way to large "self-service" grocery store chains like A&P, Kroger, and Piggly-Wiggly. As grocers began introducing such innovations as merchandise displayed on customer-accessible shelves, price tagging, shopping baskets, and on-the-premises butcher shops, ice cream parlors, and bakeries, the supermarket concept took hold. From the beginning, however, smaller independent merchants saw the threat posed by the chains and began organizing to create the economies of scale that would enable them to compete. In 1926, the Independent Grocers Alliance (IGA) was formed in the Midwest to enable nonchain stores to pool their resources and buy groceries in volume from food distributors; in the East, the Wakefern Cooperative (which later became Pathmark Stores) was founded after World War II to strengthen its members' buying power against the grocery chains of New York and New Jersey.

It was within the battle for survival between the new chain foodstores and the independents that George found his niche. Throughout the 1930s and early 1940s, he positioned MDI to become a leading distributor of food and groceries for the independent supermarkets of North and South Carolina. By the time of his premature death in 1947 he had hired six of the seven men who would lead MDI's explosive growth in the coming years. With George's three children—Alex, Lee, and Josephine—now at the company's helm, MDI continued to expand its territory in the 1950s, shipping flour, corn, meal, salt and pepper, sugar, grits, snuff, shoelaces, milk, potatoes, and a broad range of other food and grocery lines from its Main Avenue facility to customers throughout the Carolinas.

Expansion: 1960–65

By 1960, MDI's 130-plus employees were shipping 11,000 items to more than 400 independent supermarkets in a 100- to 150-mile radius around Hickory, an area encompassing Asheville and Greensboro to the west and east, and the Virginia line and Greenville, South Carolina, to the north and south. With the business quadrupling in a few years, reaching the $16 million level in 1960, MDI (with Alex George now as president) had become one of the largest wholesale food distribution operations in the southeast. A larger facility clearly was needed to house the growing business and in the late 1950s, MDI announced plans for a new million-dollar, four-acre warehouse and office building on Twelfth Street in Hickory.

The new plant, unveiled in March 1960, was state of the art. Eight rail cars and 20 trucks could be unloaded simultaneously at the facility's expansive dock area, 237 boxcars full of food could be stored in the warehouse at one time, and the contents of the entire warehouse could be stocked, sold off to customers, and restocked 17 times a year. One hundred loading carts wound slowly through the warehouse on a chain-pulled system that enabled workers to fill customers' orders with minimal strain; specialized cold storage rooms were maintained for specific perishables like bananas and tomatoes so they could be ripened just before shipment to customers; and an early IBM punch card computer system automated the entire order placement, order fulfillment, product packing, and billing process.

The local Hickory paper celebrated the warehouse's opening with an entire issue, and a "Grand Opening and Food and Specialty Show" was organized to announce MDI's expansion, with more than one hundred food manufacturers, packers, and canners turning out to celebrate the company's growing clout in the regional distribution business. By the mid-1960s, MDI had grown into a full-line grocery wholesaler with a continually growing share of the southeastern food distribution business. Asked in 1960 to account for MDI's success, Alex George enthused to the *Hickory Daily Record* that "our ability to get good men is the secret to the growth of MDI. Take a look at these men. Look how long they have worked with us. Their contribution cannot be overlooked or overestimated."

Institution Food House and Lowes Food Stores: 1966–91

By mid-decade, Alex and Lee George had decided to expand MDI's market from its traditional independent grocery store customer to the institutional food market. The first customers of the resulting operation, MDI Foodservice, were public school systems, but at the 1965 National-American Wholesale Grocers' Association convention in Chicago the George brothers met Norman James, another Hickory food distributor whose James Wholesale Company also sold food to area schools. After exploratory discussions the three agreed to merge MDI Foodservice and James Wholesale as Institution Food House (IFH). By the end of the year, IFH had rented an unused MDI warehouse in downtown Hickory and consolidated the James Wholesale and MDI Foodservice merchandise there.

On January 2, 1966, IFH was officially born with Lee George as president and Norman James as vice-president. Beginning with only 14 employees, IFH took all early orders by hand, building its small customer base into close to $1 million in revenue by the end of its first year. By the summer of 1966, IFH had held the first of its many annual food shows to generate publicity and drum up new customers. Within five years, IFH sales had edged beyond $5 million and it began to expand, acquiring 15 acres for a new warehouse outside Hickory. The 50,000-square-foot facility opened in 1973 and provided IFH with room for 3,000 different items and 15,000 square feet of freezer and cooler space. Like MDI's 1960 warehouse unveiling, the new IFH facility represented the latest in food storage and distribution technology. Products could be easily stored and relocated via a numbered rack system; state-of-the-art materials-handling equipment enhanced storage and order-filling efficiency; a computerized billing and inventory system streamlined paperwork; and all product could be loaded and unloaded inside without exposing personnel or product to the elements.

When Norman James died in the early 1970s, the George brothers bought out his interest in IFH and began to operate it as a subsidiary of MDI. They next merged IFH with the Frosty Acres Brands group (known as F.A.B. Inc.) of Norcross, Georgia, retaining its labels and advertising to maintain brand loyalty. In 1982, *Institutional Distribution* magazine ranked IFH, whose sales had now climbed to $55 million, the 48th largest institutional food distributor in the nation. Its sales area stretched 100 miles around Hickory, its sales force had grown to 30, and its product offerings had increased to 3,500, now including everything from fresh meat and smallwares to chemicals. In 1982, IFH purchased Brothers Foods of Dillon, South Carolina, a $5 million food distributor that expanded IFH's sales region into the South Carolina market.

That same year, CEO Alex George named Dennis Hatchell president of MDI and began laying plans for MDI's second major merger: the purchase of Lowes Food Stores. Lowes traced its origins back to 1921, when Lucius S. Lowe founded the North Wilkesboro Hardware Store to sell general merchandise such as snuff, ladies' shoes, and horse collars to Hickory, North Carolina, residents. When Lucius's son Jim returned from military service in 1946, he joined with his sister's husband, Carl Buchan, to run the business, and Lowe's expanded into groceries, dry goods, notions, and other products. In May of 1954, Jim Lowe decided to open a food store proper, appropriately named Lowes Food Store, but seven months later he sold out to the store's manager, J.C. Faw. While Carl Buchan focused on developing Lowes Hardware into the Lowe's Companies, Inc. home improvement super chain that by 1995 would

Key Dates:

1931: Moses George establishes a wholesale produce and food distribution business, Merchant Distributors Inc. (MDI).

1947: George dies leaving his three children to take over company operations.

1960: MDI opens a state-of-the-art warehouse and office facility; sales reach $16 million.

1966: Institution Food House (IFH) is established.

1973: A 50,000-square-foot warehouse is established for IFH operations.

1982: IFH is ranked as the 48th largest institutional food distributor in the nation; IFH purchases Brothers Foods.

1984: MDI acquires the Lowes Food Store Chain.

1986: Fire destroys IFH's Dillon, South Carolina, facility.

1988: A new 90,000-square-foot facility is erected in Florence, South Carolina, to replace the burned Dillon plant.

1991: IFH purchases 80 percent of the Western Steer Family Restaurant chain.

1992: Alex Lee Inc. is formed as a holding company for Lowes, MDI, and IFH.

1993: Supermarket chain IGA selects MDI as a food wholesaler.

1996: Margaret Urquhart is named president of Lowes; Dennis Hatchell becomes president and chief operating officer of Alex Lee.

1997: Alex Lee acquires Byrd Food Stores Inc.

1998: Consolidation Services is created.

2000: Curtis Oldenkamp is named president of Lowes after Urquhart resigns.

2001: Lowes begins expansion into the northeastern United States and launches its S&H GreenPoints rewards program.

number 350 stores, Faw focused on the expansion of his part of Lucius Lowe's legacy. He opened the second Lowes Food Store in 1960 and in succeeding years progressively expanded the chain before selling it at last to MDI in 1984. Once only a food distributor, MDI now competed head to head with such southeastern grocery store giants as Food Lion and Winn-Dixie. Within five years of the purchase, Alex George had initiated a major expansion program for Lowes, shifting Dennis Hatchell from the presidency of MDI to the lead position at Lowes and relocating Lowes' headquarters from North Wilkesboro to a new facility in Winston-Salem, North Carolina.

In the mid-1980s, the U.S. food distribution industry remained, as *Forbes* magazine described it, "a plodding business with micromargins." Fierce competition was squeezing industry profits, slow growth in food prices was forcing distributors to cut costs and lay off employees, and consolidation seemed to offer the only route to growth for industry firms. Since 1979, the number of U.S. wholesale food operators had dropped by two-thirds to 325, and experts were predicting that the industry would shrink even more, to 100 firms, by 1990. Drastic efficiency measures were needed for industry firms to stay afloat,

and a growing number followed MDI's pioneering lead by increasingly relying on enterprisewide automation and inventory control systems to maintain profitability.

In 1986, MDI's sister firm, IFH, was forced to cope with the aftermath of its decision four years earlier to purchase Brothers Foods. Although the purchase had enabled its volume in the Dillon area to grow to $9 million by 1986 (out of total IFH sales of $96 million), in July of that year a fire destroyed the office, cooler, and some of the dry space area, presenting IFH's new executive vice-president, Robert S. Donaldson, with an opportunity to earn his stripes. Disaster was averted when emergency deliveries of produce and dry groceries from IFH's Hickory facilities enabled IFH-Dillon to fill all its orders without interruption. Working out of trailers installed on the burned-out Dillon plant, IFH's sales reps transmitted customer orders to Hickory, which then flew customers' invoices back to Dillon. Low-temperature produce and grocery trailers were parked at the Dillon site to store customers' goods. IFH held on to its Dillon customers.

Within 18 months of Donaldson's arrival, Alex George had named him president of IFH, making him, at age 33, perhaps the youngest president of a major U.S. food service distributor. Rather than rebuild IFH's Dillon facility on the original Brothers Foods site, George and Donaldson chose to build a new 90,000-square-foot facility in Florence, South Carolina, a few miles south of Dillon. The new site opened in January 1988 and, because of its proximity to Interstate 95, IFH now had ready access to the Myrtle Beach, South Carolina, market as well as direct access to potential customers in Georgia and Florida. Five months after the Dillon fire IFH again expanded by acquiring food service distributor Thomas & Howard of Charlotte, North Carolina. Although IFH had planned to use the Thomas & Howard facility to pursue business with chain store customers, it lost a major chain store account and, unable to replace it, was forced to close the Charlotte facility in January of 1988, transferring its remaining accounts to IFH's facilities in Hickory and Dillon.

Donaldson set about transforming IFH's corporate image, which had been marred by poor truck departure times and low product in-stock rates. He retained a public relations firm to create a new company logo and developed a new mission statement that unambiguously declared IFH's goal to become "a strong regional food service distributor through innovation, development of resources, and by being known for superior customer service and integrity." Donaldson also announced specific goals, known as "IFH Business Values," to improve the company's focus on customers and organizational excellence and to instill a commitment to innovation and integrity. He also initiated a customer feedback program to enhance IFH's responsiveness to customers' needs. By 1991, IFH was selling almost 7,500 different products—dry goods, frozen meat, bakery items, seafood, fruits and vegetables, beverages, and more—to its 3,500 customers, who now included supermarket delis, bakeries, independent full-menu restaurants, and chain restaurants and food stores such as Kentucky Fried Chicken and Piggly-Wiggly, in addition to its original school and healthcare customers.

In an aggressive move to expand its territory, IFH purchased 80 percent of the restaurants in the 150-unit Western Steer

Family Restaurant chain of Claremont, North Carolina, in early 1991. In one fell swoop, a sales territory that had once included only North and South Carolina now spanned 11 states, stretching as far north as Maryland, as far south as Miami, Florida, and as far west as Knoxville, Tennessee, and Cincinnati, Ohio. Aided by Donaldson's commitment to utilizing the latest in electronic data interchange and inventory and transaction software, between 1986 and 1991 IFH's sales had ballooned 90 percent to almost $182 million.

Alex Lee Inc.: 1992–96

In August 1992, the MDI-IFH-Lowes triumvirate was placed under the umbrella of a new holding company structure named Alex Lee Inc., after the first names of Moses George's two sons. The founder's grandson, Boyd Lee George—who had previously held the position of chairman and president of MDI—was named chairman and president of the new entity while staying on as MDI's chairman. In announcing the move, Boyd George described the new corporate structure as "strictly a structural-type" move to streamline the financial structure of the three sister companies and promised that it would have no effect on the three firms' day-to-day operations.

In the early 1990s, the U.S. food industry as a whole continued to be buffeted by consolidation, withering competition, and razor-thin profit margins. The once unquestioned dominance of the supermarket was being dramatically eroded by warehouse food clubs, mass merchants, and deep discount drugstores. In 1992, for example, Albertson's, the fifth largest U.S. grocery chain, announced that it was dropping its traditional food supplier (Super Food Services) in favor of its own distribution network, and in 1993 food wholesalers like MDI lost a major source of income when many food manufacturers began eliminating traditional special-price promotion programs. Food distributors could now no longer profit from the purchase of stockpiles of specially priced goods that could later be resold to supermarkets at higher prices. Moreover, the nation's chain supermarkets—many of which now operated their own distribution networks—were winning the war for market share from the independents on which MDI had traditionally staked its growth.

Alex Lee won a major coup in November 1993, however, when IGA, the third largest supermarket chain in sales in North America, announced that MDI had been selected as one of two food wholesalers to service its distribution system. In October 1995, Alex Lee announced that it would build a brand new $60 million grocery distribution facility (to be completed in late 1997) in Hickory, a few miles north of the site it had occupied since 1960. Local authorities fell over themselves devising the right mix of incentives to land the new facility, and the final decision was made only when an earlier site became the subject of heated annexation disputes, and representatives of Caldwell County and the communities of Hickory and Granite Falls finally offered $5.5 million in economic incentives to win Alex Lee's commitment. In August 1996, Alex Lee floated a $60 million investors' issue to pay for the expansion.

In November, Boyd George named Dennis Hatchell the new president and chief operating officer of Alex Lee and tapped Margaret Urquhart, an experienced supermarket and drug store industry executive, to replace Hatchell as president of Lowes

Food Stores. Only the second woman to run a grocery store chain of 50 or more stores, Urquhart launched a major program to broaden Lowes' share of a market dominated by industry giants. In 1996, she opened two Lowes "FreshSmart" stores, which featured expanded offerings of produce, seafood and meats, prepared and organic foods, and such nonfood services as flower sales and photo processing. She also returned Lowes to the television advertising market after a five-year absence. Under the new company slogan "Quality, Service, the Right Price," she increased Lowes' responsiveness to customer preferences with a toll-free feedback phone line, improved aisle signage, and implemented a "Quick Checkout" policy to speed customers on their way. Buoyed by Urquhart's hands-on campaign to steal the thunder of the big southeastern U.S. foodstore chains, in 1996 Lowes announced plans to build new stores in new markets.

The Late 1990s and Beyond

During the mid 1990s, Lowes had typically opened approximately six stores per year. In an effort to dramatically boost that number, Alex Lee acquired Byrd Food Stores, a 43-store chain based in North Carolina, in 1997. The stores took on the Lowes name the following year as part of a $10 million conversion process. Urquhart also began testing "curbside" supermarket service in some of the Lowes stores. For $4.95, a customer could call ahead, have an employee select their groceries, and have the items hand delivered to their car. In 1999, the company set plans in motion to close 11 stores located in unprofitable locations. To offset the closures, Lowes planned to open nine new stores throughout 1999 and into 2000.

After a successful run as Lowes' president, Urquhart resigned from her post in January 2000 when she was named Krispy Kreme Doughnut Corp.'s executive vice-president and chief operating officer. Curtis Oldenkamp, an Alex Lee executive, took over as president of the growing company. Under his leadership, the regional supermarket chain began aggressive expansion efforts. In 2001, the firm announced a $1.3 billion plan that included the opening of 75 new stores in the northeast including Massachusetts, Pennsylvania, New Jersey, and Maine. As part of the plan, $430 million was earmarked for 25 new superstores in the Boston area. The chain also introduced a reward program in 2001. Entitled S&H GreenPoints, the program entitled customers to ten greenpoints for every dollar spent in a Lowes store. The customer could then redeem their points in the Sperry & Hutchinson Co. catalog or web site.

While efforts to bolster Lowes' sales and image were in progress, Alex Lee was also busy with other business endeavors. In fact, Alex Lee added a fourth company to its arsenal in 1998. Building upon its experience in the food warehousing and distribution markets, the firm created Consolidation Services, a public warehousing company that served both vendors and distributors. The new business provided its customers with dry warehouse storage, inbound and outbound truck broker services, importing and exporting services, and inventory management systems.

As Alex Lee entered the new millennium, it remained determined to position its companies among the leaders in the food industry. To broaden its national exposure, IFH teamed up with the North Carolina Restaurant Association to produce an annual food exposition entitled FoodEx. As part of the five-year contract, IFH also agreed to host training programs. In 2001, IFH joined UniPro Foodservice Inc., the largest distributor buying and marketing group in the United States, and also joined California-based Markon Cooperative Inc., the largest produce group in the nation. As Alex Lee continued to focus on expanding its services, its companies appeared to be well situated for future growth.

Principal Subsidiaries

Merchants Distributors Inc. (MDI); Institution Food House (including Western Steer); Lowes Food Stores; Consolidated Services.

Principal Competitors

Fleming Companies Inc.; SUPERVALU Inc.

Further Reading

"Alex Lee Inc.," *Supermarket News,* October 13, 1997, p. 2.

Ballard, Tanya, "Lowes Foods Sets Up Shop in Reidsville," *Rockingham News & Record,* October 4, 1996, p. 1R.

Bent, Jennifer, "Company President 'Walks the Talk'," *Wautauga Democrat,* September 9, 1996.

Coleman, Zach, "Lowes President Stars in Television Ads," *Winston-Salem Journal,* October 7, 1996.

Dolan, Kerry A., "Food Distributors," *Forbes,* January 1, 1996, p. 13.

"Dream of Long Ago Materializes into Huge Food Distribution Center Here," *Hickory Daily Record,* March 31, 1960, pp. 7, 10.

Eckmann, Katy, "Lowe's First Lady," *AdWeek,* October 7, 1996.

Gomlak, Norman, "Food Distribution Center Set for Caldwell, Reports Say," *Charlotte Observer,* October 3, 1995, p. 1C.

Gutner, Toddi, "Food Distributors," *Forbes,* January 4, 1993, p. 152.

——, "Food Distributors," *Forbes,* January 3, 1994, p. 148.

"Institution Food House," *ID: The Information Source for Managers and DSRs,* July 2001, p. 14.

"Institution Food House: Great Distributor Organization," *Institutional Distribution: The Magazine of Foodservice Distribution,* August 1992.

King, Ralph, Jr., "Food Distributors," *Forbes,* January 12, 1987, p. 130.

Ledbetter, Amy, "Lowes Foods Store Cuts 4,000 Prices," *Statesville Record and Landmark,* June 26, 1996, p. 1.

"Lowe's: Eye on the Future," *Supermarket News,* January 8, 1996, p. 12.

"Lowes Foods Promotes a VP to President," *Winston-Salem Journal,* January 4, 2000.

"Lowes Foods Serves a Modern Classic," *Chain Store Age Executive,* August 2001, p. 93.

"Lowe's to Break into New Territory," *DSN Retailing Today,* February 19, 2001, p. 4.

"MDI Prepares for Big Event," *Hickory Daily Record,* March 29, 1960, p. 1.

"New Lowes FreshSmart Marks Beginning of Grandfather Center Development," *Mountain Times,* September 12, 1996.

"She Bags Top Job at Lowes Markets," *Business North Carolina,* October 1997, p. 104.

"Two Food Retailers Hit Market," *American Banker-Bond Buyer,* August 5, 1996.

—Paul S. Bodine
—update: Christina M. Stansell

Almanij NV

Snydershuis
Keizerstraat 8
B-2000 Antwerp
Belgium
Telephone: (+32) 3-202-87-00
Fax: (+32) 3-23-14-409
Web site: http://www.almanij.be

Public Company
Incorporated: 1931
Employees: 42,809
Total Assets: EUR 19.58 billion ($17.33 billion)(2000)
Stock Exchanges: Euronext Brussels
Ticker Symbol: ALM
NAIC: 551111 Offices of Bank Holding Companies

Almanij NV—short for Algemene Maatschappij voor Nijverheidskrediet (General Company for Industrial Credit)—is one of Belgium's leading financial and insurance holding companies. Almanij operates in the financial services and insurance sectors through majority and controlling shares in a number of more-or-less independently operating companies. With assets of more than EUR 200 billion, Almanij intends to remain a medium-sized and independent player in the rapidly consolidating European financial industry. The primary components of Almanij's holdings are KBC Bank & Insurance Group; KB Luxembourg; Gevaert; Almafin; and Investco. Most of the company's primary holdings are also publicly listed companies. KBC is one of the leading Belgium companies in its sector, with a 20 percent share of the domestic market, and has also built a strong position in the Central European market, notably in Poland, the Czech Republic, Slovakia, and Hungary. Almanij's position totals nearly 73 percent of KBC's shares. KB Luxembourg is 60 percent owned by Almanij and offers private banking services throughout Europe, notably through such subsidiaries as Henry Cooke Group and Brown, Shipley & Co. in the United Kingdom, Urquijo in Spain, sKempf in France, and Merck Finck & Co. in Germany. Investment company Gevaert, formerly part of Agfa-Gevaert and still a major shareholder in that imaging technology company, is 79 percent-owned by Almanij. Almafin is a 100 percent-owned subsidiary that develops specialty financing products, such as leasing products for the leisure and theme parks industry, and other leasing operations, such as those of modular office space and transportation equipment, such as containers. Lastly, Investco, part of KB Luxembourg, operates lending services to the small- and mid-sized business sector. Almanij is itself owned in large part by banking cooperative CERA Holding, which spun off nearly 30 percent of its Almanij shares as the publicly listed Almancora investment vehicle. Almanij is led by chairman Jan Huyghebaert and managing director Ferdinand Verndonck and trades on the Euronext Brussels stock exchange. In 2001, Almanij acknowledged that it was considering a merger with KBC to aid in simplifying the organizational structure of both companies.

Developing Belgium Banking in the Early 20th Century

The Almanij organization entering the 21st century culminated more than 100 years of Belgian banking and insurance history. The holding company was the product of a series of mergers, and particularly the late 1990s mergers of Algemeene Bankvereeniging and Kredietbank with CERA and ABB Verzerkeringen, which formed KBC Bank & Insurance Group.

Kredietbank had its roots in the late 19th century. The bank, which grew into one of Belgium's largest, was originally founded in 1889 as the Volksbank van Leuven as a cooperative partnership operating in Flemish-speaking Belgium. The bank reformed as a limited company after World War I and began to expand throughout the Flanders region. During this period, the Volksbank created a number of subsidiary banks, including the Bank voor Handel en Nijverheid (Bank for Business and Industry) in Kortrijk and the Algemeene Bankvereeniging (General Banking Association) in Antwerp. The Volksbank, which became part of the Middenkredietkas (Central Credit Fund) was also instrumental in financing the setting up of a number of other banks.

The Middenkredietkas had been set up in 1895 as a central savings and investment fund for the growing numbers of Spaar-en Leengilden (savings and loan associations) being formed in

Belgium in the early 1890s following the banking model established by FW Raiffeisen of Germany. As part of its investments, the Middenkredietkas began building up a portfolio of banking groups, such as Volksbank and Algemeene Bankvereening.

The financial crisis of the 1920s, which led to the worldwide depression in 1929, forced the restructuring of much of the Belgian banking industry. The Algemeene Bankvereeniging, which, along with its commercial banking operations, had built up a wide range of financial and industrial assets both in Belgium and abroad, notably in Hungary, restructured its assets into a new holding company, the Algemene Maatschappij voor Nijverheidskrediet—or Almanij, for short. The new company was incorporated in 1931.

Almanij soon became the parent of its own parent company. Throughout the difficult economic climate of the 1920s, Middenkredietkas had been growing steadily, principally through a long series of mergers and acquisitions of smaller banks facing financial troubles. When Middenkredietkas itself nearly collapsed in the mid-1930s, the Belgian government agreed to a vast restructuring of that holding company. The resulting restructuring created a new, independent bank, Kredietbank. As part of the restructuring process, Almanij sold off its industrial assets and in exchange took up a position as Kredietbank's majority shareholder. Kredietbank saw steady expansion throughout the rest of the decade and into the next, becoming a major fixture on the Belgian banking scene.

An offshoot of the creation of the Kredietbank was the launch of what was to become a primary part of CERA Holding. The restructuring had grouped commercial banking operations under Kredietbank. At the same time, the Centrale Kas voor Landboukrediet was formed to take over the Middenkredietkas's central savings and investment fund activities for its network of savings and loan associations. The locally operating Spaar- en Leengilden branches then changed their name to ''Raiffeisenkassen,'' and grew to a network of 800 independent branches.

The third member of the later KBC merger, ABB Verzekeringen, also had its start in the early 1890s. Belgium's Boerenbond (Farmer's Union) began offering fire insurance to its members in 1892, through England's Norwich Union. In 1898, the Boerenbond added accident insurance as well, now through La Belgique Industrielle. At the turn of the century, however, the Boerenbond itself entered the insurance business, setting up its own cooperative policies, Ondelinge Belgische Boerenverzekering, which covered work-related accident insurance, and Landbouwverzekering for other accident insurance coverage, in 1905. The Boerenbond extended its insurance operations in 1917 with the creation of its own fire insurance group. In 1922, the union's various insurance operations were combined into a single limited liability company, Belgische Onderlinge Verzekeringsmaatschappij NV, which was subsequently renamed Verzekeringsmaatschappij van de Belgische Boerenbond to emphasize that the company was part of the farmer's union. At the beginning of World War II, the company changed its name again, becoming Assurantie van de Belgische Boerenbond, or ABB Verzekeringen. ABB later came under the control of CERA, which became a major shareholder.

Postwar Growth

ABB, Kredietbank, and Almanij all enjoyed steady growth during the post-war years as Belgium's economy, largely spared the destruction of the World War II, rapidly returned to steady growth. ABB grew from a relatively small insurance company into one of the country's top four insurers, with more than 1,000 agencies and international activities, primarily in Luxembourg, Hungary and Ireland. Kredietbank expanded to national prominence. Under the motto ''an independent bank for an independent clientele,'' The Almanij-Kredietbank consortium moved beyond its Flanders home base beginning in 1958 to build up a strong share of French-speaking Belgium as well to capture the number three position in the country's banking industry. Kredietbank also turned to the international market, notably with the creation of Kredietbank SA Luxembourg in 1949. That operation, later known as KBL, became one of the four cornerstones of the Almanij group.

Centrale Kas voor Landbouwkrediet changed its name to Centrale Raiffeisenkas in 1970. New legislation at the beginning of that decade, however, led to dramatic changes in the organization. Facing new rules governing the operation of partnerships, the 800 independently operating member partnerships of the Centrale began to reduce their numbers through mergers. This process was stepped up in 1985, and the group changed its name to CERA Bank in 1986.

By then KBL had been launched as an independent company, after Almanij, in part in response to fears that the Belgian banking industry might face a privatization effort akin to its French counterpart, broke off the Luxembourg-based company from Kredietbank in 1978. This move became part of an overall effort to refocus Almanij around three core operations: Kredietbank, KBL, and an increasing interest in insurance companies, notably around subsidiary Fidelitas, and the specialized finance sector.

New rules governing the Belgian banking industry were laid down at the beginning of the 1990s. CERA, which had operated as a savings institution, was now granted the right to convert to full bank status in 1991. At the same time, the new legislation increased the ability of majority shareholders to guide a bank's direction, and Almanij began to take a more active role not only in developing strategy among its banking holdings, but also in raising funds for growth. A primary target for the company became the newly liberated Central European countries.

21st Century Belgium Financial Services Leader

Almanij added a new wing to its holdings in 1997 when it acquired a 79 percent position in Belgian investment company Gevaert. That company had formerly been part of the Agfa-Gavaert firm, founded in 1894 and moved to Germany in 1964.

Key Dates:

1889: Founding of Volksbank van Leuven, which later becomes part of Middenkredietkas.

1892: Boerenbond (Farmer's Union) begins offering fire insurance to its members, forming basis of later ABB Verzekeringen.

1895: Formation of Middenkredietkas as central savings and investment fund.

1931: Middenkredietkas subsidiary Algemene Maatschappij voor Nijverheidskrediet (Almanij), restructures as holding company.

1936: Restructuring of Middenkredietkas creates Kredietbank with Almanij as parent company and spin-off of Centrale Kas voor Landboukrediet.

1949: Almanij forms Kredietbank luembourg (KBL).

1970: Centrale Kas voor Landboukrediet becomes Centrale Raiffeisenkas.

1978: Almanij spins off KBL as independent company.

1986: Centrale Raiffeisenkas becomes CERA Bank.

1991: CERA takes on full bank status.

1998: Almanij, CERA, and ABB Verzekeringen merge to form KBC with Almanij as major shareholder.

2001: Almanij begins considering merger with KBC.

When Bayer acquired the imaging unit of Agfa-Gavaert in 1981, Gavaert was spun off as a separate company, with, Almanij acquiring a strong shareholder position. Gavaert expanded its investment operations throughout the 1980s and 1990s. In 1997, Almanij and majority shareholder Copeba agreed to break up Gavaert into two parts, with Almanij acquiring the Gavaert name and its public listing as well as its expertise in the investment field.

The following year Almanij was catapulted to the top ranks of the Belgian financial world with the announcement of a merger agreement with CERA and ABB Verzekeringen. Almanij joined Kredietbank, as well as Fidelitas and other of its holdings, into the new company, called KBC Bank & Insurance Group, in exchange for a nearly 74 percent share; in return, CERA obtained more than one-third of Almanij's stock. These shares were placed under a newly created entity, CERA Holding. The merger made KBC the leading Belgian banking and insurance group, and a leader in the rapidly expanding Central European market as well.

Almanij now regrouped around three principal holdings, namely Gaveart, KBC, and KBL. As it moved toward a more streamlined organization, Almanij now turned to a number of its smaller holdings, which turned more to specialized finance operations, such as leasing for the theme parks and leisure industries, or the company's specialized Immolease subsidiary. In 1999, these subsidiaries were grouped under a single entity, called Almafin, which remained 100 percent controlled by Almanij.

In April 2000, Almanij—which had been nurturing acquisition ambitions for French banking group Crédit Commercial de France—was taken by surprise when HSBC launched an EUR 11 billion takeover of CCF. Almanij, admitting to being disap-

pointed by the move, sold off its own stake in CCF, which included an 18 percent position held by KBC. KBC quickly bounced back, acquiring Keijser Effecten, a securities company based in the Netherlands, in June 2000, then joining with EDS to set up the Fin-Force joint-venture for the processing of international payment transactions in the new European currency.

At the beginning of 2001, Almanij's major shareholder, CERA Holding, moved to increase the liquidity of its holding, spinning off 25 percent of its shares into a newly created, publicly listed entity, Almancora, which listed on the Euronext Brussels exchange. Almanij was also moving toward a more simplified organizational structure, transferring its Investco subsidiary to KBC. By mid-2001, Almanij began to seek means to correct what many saw as the undervaluing of KBC's stock—a result of the relatively small proportion of free-float shares available. Almanij acknowledged the potential of a merger between Almanij and KBC, most likely in the direction of Almanij acquiring KBC. Such a move would boost the number of free-float shares in the new company above the 50 percent mark, making the stock a more attractive investment. Whether Almanij intended to go ahead with the plan remained to be seen; nonetheless, as the European financial community underwent a wave of mergers at the turn of the century, Almanij remained committed to remaining mid-sized and independent for the new century.

Principal Subsidiaries

Almafin NV; Gavaert NV; Incestco NV; KBC Bankverzekeringsholding NV; Kredietcorp SA; Via KBC Bank: Antwerpse Diamantbank NV (59.11%); Assurisk SA (Luxembourg) (67.81%); CBC Banque SA (67.81%); Centea NV (67.51%); Krefima NV (67.46%); â eskoslovenská Obchodní Banka AS (SOB) (Czech Republic)(55.30%); KBC Finance (Ireland) (67.81%); IIB Bank Ltd. (group)(Ireland)(67.81%); KBC Asset Management NV (67.81%); KBC Asset Management Ltd. (Ireland)(67.81%); KBC Bank NV (67.81%); KBC Bank AG (Germany)(67.36%); KBC Bank Funding LLC & Trust (group) USA 67.81 KBC Bank Nederland NV (Netherlands)(67.81%); KBC Clearing NV (Netherlands)(50.87%); KBC Exploitatie (67.81%); KBC Financial Products (group) (67.81%); KBC International Finance NV (Netherlands Antilles)(67.81%); KBC Lease NV (group) (67.810%); KBC Securities NV (67.81%); KBC Securities France SA (France) (67.81%); KBC Securities Nederland NV (Netherlands)(67.81%); Kereskedelmi és Hitelbank Rt. (K&H Bank) Hungary (49.69%); Patria Finance AS Prague (Czech Republic (62.32%); Kredietbank SA Luxembourgeoise (Luxembourg)(57.55%); Brown, Shipley & Co. Ltd. UK (57.55%); Henry Cooke Group plc UK (57.55%); KB Luxembourg Finance Dublin Unltd. IE (57.55%); KB Luxembourg (Monaco) SA (57.55%); Banque Continentale du Luxembourg SA (Luxembourg; 57.55%); Banque Continentale du Luxembourg—Royal (Private) (Luxembourg; 57.55%); KBL France (57.55%); KBL Beteiligungs AG (Luxembourg)(57.55%); Merck Finck & Co (Luxembourg; 57.55%); Banco Urquijo SA (Spain;40.56%).

Principal Competitors

Berkshire Hathaway Inc. (BRK); Ifi Istituto Finanziario Industriale S.p.A.; Investor AB; Cobepa S.A.; Fortis; ING Groep N.V.

Further Reading

Bollen, Nadine, ''Almancora druk verhandeld op eerste beursdag,'' *De Tijd*, April 4, 2001.

Buckley, Neil, ''KBC Puts a Brave Face on CCF Setback,'' *Financial Times*, April 14, 2000.

Dombey, Daniel, ''KBC's 20% Increase Matches Expectations,'' *Financial Times*, March 6, 2001.

''Fusie Almanij-KBC brengt free float van bankgroep boven 50 procent,'' *De Financieel-Economische Tijd,* July 6, 2001.

Mann, Michael, ''KBC Confident of Profits Increase,'' *Financial Times*, September 4, 2001.

Putman, E., J. Daniëls, and I. Van Thielt, *ABB, een Geschiedenis van Verzekeren*. Leuven, ABB Verzekeringen, 1997, 173 p.

Van Der Wee, H. and M. Verbreyt, *Mensen maken geschiedenis: de Kredietbank en de economische opgang van Vlaanderen: 1935–1985*. Brussel, Kredietbank, 1985, 356 p.

—M.L. Cohen

ALPS

Alps Electric Co., Ltd.

1-7, Yukigaya-Otsuka-Cho
Ota-ku
Tokyo 145
Japan
Telephone: 81(03) 3726-1211
Fax: 81 (03) 3728-1741
Web site: http://www.alps.co.jp

Public Company
Incorporated: 1948 as Kataoka Electric Company
Employees: 4,441
Sales: ¥573.06 billion ($4.62 billion)
Stock Exchanges: Tokyo
NAIC: 334119 Other Computer Peripheral Equipment
    Manufacturing; 333313 Office Machinery
    Manufacturing; 33422 Radio and Television
    Broadcasting and Wireless Communications
    Equipment Manufacturing; 33431 Audio and Video
    Equipment Manufacturing; 336399 All Other Motor
    Vehicle Parts Manufacturing

Alps Electric Co., Ltd. operates as a leading electronic components manufacturer with operations in North America, Europe, Asia, and Japan. Its Electronic Components business is divided into four segments including Components, Communications and Broadcasting Devices, Computer Peripherals, and Car Electronics. Its products—which number in the 1000s—include photo printers, car switches, clock springs used in air bag systems, remote control units, sensors, press toolings, optical communication lens, transceiver units for cellular and cordless telephones, FM/AM tuners, TV-VCR tuners, floppy disk drives, data input devices such as keyboards, liquid crystal displays (LCDs), and magnetic heads for digital media, audio applications, and VCRs. Alps Electronics along with Alpine Electronics Inc. and Alps Logistics Co. make up the core of the Alps Group of companies.

As one of the few secondary manufacturers to remain independent of client companies and other industrial groups, Alps is an oddity in Japanese industry. In order to maintain this independence, the company has had to avoid a "vertical" diversification. Instead of moving from parts manufacturing to finished products, which would have put Alps squarely in competition with its clients, the company expanded "horizontally," developing a wider and more sophisticated array of components and preserving harmony with its customers.

Alps' customers are some of the largest companies in the world; these companies could certainly establish their own parts manufacturing subsidiaries. The fact that they haven't tried to replace Alps testifies to the company's many strengths. It need only be concerned with a very narrow function, and it can benefit from greater economies of scale by selling the same product to several different customers.

Early History

The man behind Alps Electric is Katsutaro Kataoka, a self-styled industrial revolutionary in the mold of Sony's Akio Morita. A displaced war veteran and mechanical engineer, Kataoka worked briefly for Toshiba. He was uncomfortable working for a large firm, so he left Toshiba, borrowed $1,400 from his family, and set up a small manufacturing shop in Ohta, a drab industrial suburb of Tokyo. The company opened for business in November 1948 as the Kataoka Electric Company.

Kataoka's original product line consisted of an unimpressive variety of simple-technology components such as light switches and variable capacitors. He peddled these items to a number of larger manufacturers, offering a reliable product at low unit costs. The company's business grew steadily during the 1950s, but while its volume increased, its technology changed very little.

But as the products manufactured by Kataoka's customers became more complex, these customers began to pressure Kataoka to develop a wider variety of more durable, high-quality parts. Kataoka began investing more heavily in research and development and expanded its operations with new factories. A subsidiary, Tohoku Alps, was established in August 1964, and the following December Kataoka Electric changed its name to the more English-sounding Alps.

Company Perspectives:

Our vision is to create new value in the next era, which we consider the era of symbiosis between humans and earth. We pledge: to conduct our business in pursuit of creating new values; to conduct our business in earth-friendly ways that harmonize with the global environment; to conduct our business so as to learn from customers and respond to their needs; to conduct our business fairly; and to conduct our business as to encourage and take advantage of the enthusiasm of our valued employees.

Extensive Growth: 1960s–80s

Alps Electric began a period of unprecedented growth during the mid-1960s as the Japanese consumer electronics industry took off. Alps components were incorporated into thousands of products, and it established significant market shares in new sectors, such as radio tuners. A technical agreement with General Instrument in 1963 led to Alps' acquisition of UHF television tuner technology; today Alps is the world's leader in TV tuner manufacturing. Eager to capitalize on its profitability and take advantage of promising markets, Alps entered into an agreement to produce car radios with Motorola in 1967. The venture was moderately successful, and it gave Alps a chance to learn about many new technologies developed by Motorola. Alps also established joint ventures with local manufacturers in developing countries, including India (1964), Taiwan (1970), and South Korea (1970).

By 1970, the company was the largest independent component manufacturer in Japan, but it was unable to win the respect usually accorded a company of its size even after listing on the First Market of the Tokyo Stock Exchange in 1967. Because it was limited to producing components, and therefore a captive of its customers' business, analysts and industrialists considered Alps a secondary company, regardless of its sales volume.

In fact, it was Alps and secondary manufacturers like it that made Japan's export-led boom in electronics possible on such a scale. Their billions of simple pieces, produced at very low cost, were essential to final manufacturers. Alps was constantly motivated to maintain its high quality and low prices by the unspoken threat that its customers could find other suppliers.

During the 1970s, Alps established subsidiaries and joint venture companies in the United States, Brazil, and West Germany. It operated a joint venture to produce semiconductors with Motorola from 1973 to 1975, and in 1978 took over Motorola's share of the car stereo venture, changing its name to Alpine Electronics. Alpine subsequently introduced a line of successful upmarket radios under its own name for Honda, BMW, Volvo, Chrysler, and GM.

When exchange rates have depressed the sale of Japanese electronic goods in foreign markets, final manufacturers have often protected their profit margins by demanding lower prices from suppliers such as Alps. While these suppliers were in many cases powerless to argue, Alps began to seize the initiative on several fronts. It began to develop special components, such as automobile electronics devices and to contribute to

research on new end-products. No longer just a supplier but an active participant in the design process, Alps was not in a position to have its prices dictated by its customers anymore.

The company's graduation to a higher position in Japanese industry had an immediate effect on its business. Alps developed computer keyboards for IBM and Apple, and later took over Apple's keyboard and "mouse" plant in Garden Grove, California. Alps began to produce floppy disk drives in 1980 and steadily built market share; its customers include IBM, Apple, and Commodore. By 1985 it was the world's largest producer of floppy disk drives.

That year the company decided to try to exploit certain sectors of the market as a primary manufacturer. The computer market slumped during 1987, however, and the company was compelled to take losses in most of its computer-related product lines.

During the late 1980s, Alps toyed with the idea to reduce its reliance on secondary manufacturing gradually, but at the time, its major products were still secondary: switches (23% of sales), floppy disk drives and printers (21%), car audio sets (19%), and VCR parts, including magnetic heads and cylinders (14%).

As a supplier, Alps had many strengths during the 1980s and 1990s. The company's main plants were located in a rural area of northern Honshu. It had little trouble finding more plant space near existing facilities, and had access to cheaper labor. It made great use of subcontractors, particularly in labor-intensive and marginally profitable processes. Assembly lines were being automated, as were the warehouses.

The 1990s and Beyond

Alps continued expansion into the 1990s. Alps Electric Scotland was established in 1991, along with China-based Ningbo Alps Electronic and Dalian Alps Electronics in 1993, and Alps Electric Manufacturing Mexico S.A. de C.V. That same year, the firm entered the electronic amusement business related to peripheral products.

In 1994, Alps established the Alps Environmental Charter, signaling the firm's commitment to earth-friendly business practices. The company continued its expansion into China the following year, and also established a subsidiary in the Czech Republic.

During the mid-1990s, Alps worked diligently to position itself among industry leaders in the rapidly changing electronics market. Through its subsidiaries, the Alps name continued to grow in popularity both in the U.S. as well as other global markets due in part to its diverse product line that included computer mouse and keyboards, printing mechanisms, pointing devices, touch pads, and magnetic components used in floppy and hard drives. As part of the company's 50th anniversary celebration—the company tagged 1998 as the second founding of Alps—it established a new corporate vision that outlined Alps' business plan for the new millennium. Included in the company's initiatives was a strategy dedicated to focusing on the development of emerging markets.

While relatively untouched by scandal in the past, Alps received a taste of it during 1999 when forced to post a mid-year

Key Dates:

1948: Katsutaro Kataoka establishes the Kataoka Electric Company.
1964: The company changes its name to Alps Electric Co., Ltd.
1967: The firm joins with Motorola to manufacture car radios; Alps-Motorola Inc. is formed.
1970: Alps operates as the largest independent component manufacturer in Japan.
1978: The company takes over Motorola's share of the car stereo venture and Alps Motorola is renamed Alpine Electronics.
1980: Alps begins to manufacture floppy disk drives.
1984: Subsidiary Alps Electric UK is established.
1985: The firm operates as the world's largest producer of floppy disk drives.
1993: Continuing with its international expansion, the company forms Alps Electric Manufacturing Mexico S.A. de C.V.
1998: Alps celebrates its 50th anniversary.
2000: The company's stock is listed on the Nikkei 225 index.

loss after bonds held by two of its subsidiaries proved to be fraudulent. An investigation into Cresvale International Ltd., the agent for the Princeton Fund bonds, led to the allegation that an Alps executive had received "kickbacks" or payments from Cresvale for enticing the company to invest in the fund. The executive resigned from the firm in October of that year amid the investigation.

Alps entered the new millennium intent on continuing its global expansion through product development and strategic partnerships, including a partnership with Immersion Corp., a leading digital touch technology firm. Under the terms of the deal, Alps became a supplier of Immersion's TouchSense-enabled automotive controls. The firm also began construction on several new plants and set plans in motion to develop its Alps Electric U.S. subsidiary into a technological development and marketing base for the company. Despite weakening sales in several of its segments resulting from a faltering American economy, Alps posted a 4.8 percent increase in fiscal 2001 sales as well as an increase of 2.9 percent in operating profit. During that year, Alps was listed on the Nikkei 225 Index.

In order to remain competitive in the future, Alps management remained focused on its growing business segments including communications and broadcasting devices—

responsible for 24.4 percent of electronic sales—and mechatronic devices, which secured 27.1 percent of electronic sales. Kazuya Yoshikoshi, an Alps director, commented on the firm's growth strategy in a 2000 press release, stating that, "Alps is always searching for new, innovative products and technologies designed to fit our philosophy of creating a better, safer environment for our customers and the communities they live in." Under the leadership of president Masataka Kataoka, and with a strong corporate vision in place, Alps appeared to be well positioned for future growth.

Principal Subsidiaries

Tohoku Alps Co., Ltd.; Alpine Electronics Inc.; Alps Logistics Co. Ltd.; Kurikoma Electronics Co. Ltd.; Nishiki Electronics Co. Ltd.; Alps Electric Korea Co. Ltd.; Alps Electric Pte. Ltd. (Singapore); Alps Electric Malaysia Sdn. Bhd.; Alps Electric Hong Kong Ltd.; Dalian Alps Electronics Co. Ltd. (China); Ningbo Alps Electronics Co. Ltd. (China); Wuxi Alps Electronics Co. Ltd. (China); Tianjin Alps Electronics Co. Ltd. (China); Electric (U.S.A.) Inc.; Alps Electric North America Inc.; Alps Electric Manufacturing Mexico S.A. de C.V.; Alps Electric Europa GmbH (Germany); Alps Electric UK Ltd. (England).

Principal Divisions

Components; Communications and Broadcasting Devices; Computer Peripherals; Car Electronics.

Principal Competitors

Toshiba Corporation; Matsushita Electric Industrial Co. Ltd.; Sony Corporation.

Further Reading

Alps Electric Co. Ltd., "History of Alps," Tokyo, Japan: Alps Electronic Co. Ltd., 2001.
"Alps Electric's Quad-Speed Internal CD-ROM Changer Comes With a Four-Disc Magazine," *Information Today,* February 1996, p. 52.
Druce, Chris, "Alps Makes Czech Move Threatening 250 UK Jobs," *Electronics Weekly,* September 5, 2001, p. 5.
"Immersion Signs Strategic Partnership with Alps Electric Co. Ltd.," *Business Wire,* July 30, 2000.
"Japan: Alps Electric to Fall Into Red Over Problem Bonds," *Bernama, The Malaysian News Agency,* September 13, 1999.
"Japan: Cresvale Gave Kickbacks to 4 Other Firms," *Asahi Evening News,* October 22, 1999.
Reis, Chris, "Alps' Micro Dry Printing Process," *Advanced Imaging,* February 1997, p. 39.

—update: Christina M. Stansell

AMCORE Financial Inc.

501 7th Street
Rockford, Illinois 61104
U.S.A.
Telephone: (815) 968-2241
Fax: (815) 961-7544
Web site: http://www.amcore.com

Public Company
Incorporated: 1982 as AmeriCorp Financial Inc.
Employees: 1,400
Total Assets: $4.2 billion (2000)
Stock Exchanges: NASDAQ
Ticker Symbol: AMFI
NAIC: 551111 Offices of Bank Holding Companies;
    52211 Commercial Banking; 52221 Credit Card Issuing

AMCORE Financial Inc. is a Rockford, Illinois-based holding company that includes AMCORE Bank, N.A.; AMCORE Investment Group, N.A.; and AMCORE Mortgage, Inc. In the early 2000s, the company operated more than 60 branches in Illinois, Iowa, and Wisconsin, at which time it administered $4.2 billion in banking assets and more than $4.8 billion in investment assets. In the United States, AMCORE also was rated among the top 150 largest bank holding companies, the top 15 percent of asset management firms, and the top 100 online financial institutions.

1910–29: The Early Years

AMCORE'S roots stretch back to August 1, 1910, when the Swedish-American Bank was founded in Rockford, Illinois. It was located on Seventh Street, which at the time was the hub of Rockford's Swedish immigrant community. The bank's formation was a direct result of the cohesive Swedish community's efforts to create such an institution. In 1909, Rockford had six banks, none of which were located in the Swedish area of Broadway and Seventh Street. That year, some of Rockford's prominent Swedish businessmen decided to organize a national bank. In May, they requested an application form from the comptroller of the currency in Washington, D.C.

As Elizabeth A. Ross explained in *American National Bank and Trust Co.: A History*, "Aside from the ethnocentric desire for a banking house of their own, the Swedes had other reasons for wanting a Swedish owned bank in the Seventh Street area. For one thing, it was not easy for a man who spoke little or no English to get help at a bank where few if any of the employees spoke any Swedish." According to Ross, the ability to speak Swedish was a requirement for those wishing to work at the bank, at least for the first 25 years of its operations. In addition to the bank, the Swedish community also worked to form other noteworthy Rockford institutions, such as nearby Swedish-American Hospital on Charles Street.

After much hard work, the Swedish-American bank was granted a charter. It opened for business on August 1, 1910 in a small storefront. The bank had two teller windows, hardwood floors and, according to Ross, "carefully placed spittoons." Its first president was G. Adolph Peterson, who held the position for two years. Peterson served the bank in many capacities over the course of 32 years, including the role of cashier, vice-president, and chairman.

Swedish-American Bank survived financial crises in 1913 and 1914. During that time, William Johnson was the bank's president, serving from 1913 to 1916. Five years after opening, the bank had outgrown its facilities. Because of this, in 1917 operations moved from the modest one-room office to a five-story building on the corner of Seventh Street and Fourth Avenue. The new building not only met existing needs, but also would accommodate future growth for years to come.

Swedish-American Bank was doing well as the 1920s arrived. The bank's deposits amounted to approximately $855,639 in June of 1916, a figure which climbed to about $2,415,838 four years later. In her history of the bank, Ross described the 1920s as "a period marked by curious inactivity, reflected both within the management of the bank and in the figures from condition statements." Part of this may have been due to the bank's conservative philosophy of "caution, community service, and restraint." However, as it turned out, fiscal conservatism would serve the bank well as the nation fell into the Great Depression during the 1930s.

1930–45: Challenging Times

The Swedish-American Bank weathered some very difficult years during the 1930s and mid-1940s. Besides the economic woes that plagued the nation during the Great Depression from 1931 to 1933, World War II erupted, presenting numerous challenges on many fronts. During the Great Depression, many banks failed throughout the nation. The financial crisis affected the Rockford community just as it did many others. On July 15, 1931 three of the city's banks—Manufacturer's National, People's National, and Security National—closed. By the end of the Depression, only two of the Rockford's eight banks—Swedish-American and Illinois National—remained.

John A. Alden, a local businessman, was Swedish-American's third president. He served in that capacity for 20 years, beginning in 1917, and was responsible for steering the bank successfully through some very difficult times. Although he was known to be a tough, stern individual, his conservative, level-headed, sensible approach was said to have done a great deal for the bank.

One difficult situation that resulted from the Depression was the Reconstruction Finance Corporation's (RFC) involvement with the bank. As Ross explained in her history, the RFC "was empowered by the Emergency Banking Act of 1933 to purchase preferred stock from troubled banks or take such stock as collateral for loans in order that a failing bank might survive." The deputy comptroller of the currency determined that Swedish-American Bank needed the RFC's help, and in February of 1934, the RFC purchased $200,000 of the bank's preferred stock. It thus became the bank's main stockholder and a source of influence over bank operations. Over the years, this influence would result in tension between the bank's administration and the RFC and chief examiner's office. One leading area of disagreement involved the expansion of credit. Alden and the bank saw this as a contributing factor to the Depression, while the less conservative federal government viewed the approach as a tool for economic recovery. In any case, the RFC was able to help the Swedish-American survive during a difficult period in history, and the institution eventually was strong enough to regain local control, although not until May 15, 1945.

By 1936, conditions were improving for the bank. Deposits increased 46 percent over the previous year, resulting in net income of approximately $12,778. The bank began to outgrow its facilities again, and decided to expand into an adjoining building that it already owned. With this expansion also came the installation of dial telephone service.

By the late 1930s, many of the bank's original administrators began to fade from the picture and were replaced with new individuals with equally new ideas. According to Ross' history, "This post depression, or reconstruction, period of the bank's history was a very vital time marked by numerous changes and improvements in both practices and policies."

In 1937, G. Adolph Peterson replaced Alden as president and CEO. The bank's original president, Peterson was called upon to hold the post for a second time, and he did so until 1939. In 1940, Karl K. Plambeck was named president and Harrison A. "Spike" Taylor served as CEO. John Alden died in April 1944, which in one respect signified the end of an era in the bank's history.

1945–56: A Time of Rebirth

On January 22, 1945 the Swedish-American Bank changed its name to American National Bank and Trust Co. This change was partly attributable to the growing sense of patriotism that developed during the war, and was marked by ethnic-based organizations placing less importance on incorporating ethnicity into their names. Interestingly, the name change had been proposed years earlier, in 1915, by one of the city's most well known Swedish residents—Pehr A. Peterson. The "dean" of Rockford furniture manufacturers, Peterson was president of Swedish-American Hospital, as well as more than a dozen firms that played instrumental roles in Rockford's growth. Peterson had written a letter emphasizing that by dropping the word "Swedish" from the bank's name and relying on the greatness of the word "American," the name would have more of an all-encompassing feel.

In July 1945, World War II ended and an optimistic period of expansion and excitement spread throughout the nation. In addition to this, there was another cause for celebration at the bank itself. A few months earlier, the institution finally was able to regain local control by retiring the RFC's stock. At the end of 1945, Plambeck resigned as president and Taylor assumed the role of both president and CEO, a role he would fill through 1956. Taylor had formerly served with Manufacturer's National Bank until it closed in 1931. In many ways, his style of management was similar to Alden's in that he was careful and conservative. Some attributed this to the economic conditions of the Great Depression, which left a lasting mark in the minds of many.

As the 1950s unfolded, American National Bank enjoyed a time of prosperity. Property adjacent to the bank was purchased from the Salvation Army in February 1952 that provided a parking lot for 70 cars. New bookkeeping and accounting equipment was purchased, along with a night depository, and plans for remodeling the bank were finally completed in May 1954. From the standpoint of earnings and growth, the following year turned out to be the best in the bank's history.

1957–69: Modernization

In 1957, Leroy E. Liljedahl replaced Taylor as president and CEO of American National. Liljedahl had joined the bank in 1952 as an auditor. He immediately displayed leadership qualities and was named vice-president within two years, followed by a promotion to executive vice-president in 1956. Liljedahl

---

Key Dates:

1910: Swedish-American Bank founded in Rockford, Illinois, on August first with G. Adolph Peterson as president.

1913: William Johnson named Swedish-American Bank's second president.

1917: Swedish-American Bank operations move from modest one-room office to five-story building; John A. Alden named Swedish-American Bank's third president.

1931: Swedish-American Bank survives when three of the city's banks close on July 15 during a national financial crises.

1934: The RFC purchases $200,000 of the Swedish-American Bank's preferred stock, becoming a major source of influence over operations.

1937: G. Adolph Peterson replaces Alden as president and CEO of Swedish-American Bank.

1940: Karl K. Plambeck named president and Harrison A. "Spike" Taylor named CEO of Swedish-American Bank.

1944: John Alden dies.

1945: Swedish-American Bank changes its name to American National Bank and Trust Co.; American National Bank regains local control from the RFC.

1957: Leroy E. Liljedahl replaces Harrison Taylor as president and CEO of American National Bank.

1964: American National Bank announces plans to build a one-story data processing center near the main bank.

1976: American National Bank unveils a one-ton, 24-square-foot, welded red brass and copper sculpture of an American Eagle to celebrate the American Bicentennial.

1976: CEO Liljedahl and President Robert E. Hitt resign, and David W. Knapp assumes the role of president and CEO.

1982: Holding company AmeriCorp Financial Inc. is formed and goes public the following year.

1985: American National Bank merges with Illinois National Bank, creating AMCORE Bank N.A.; J. Peter Jeffrey becomes president and CEO of AMCORE Bank.

1986: AMCORE Financial is listed on the NASDAQ and assets exceeded $1 billion for the first time.

1989: Robert J. Mueleman named president of AMCORE bank; J. Peter Jeffrey named vice-chairman and CEO.

1990: AMCORE Trust Co. is formed.

1992: AMCORE launches AMCORE Investment Banking and AMCORE Capital Management, and creates the Vintage Family of Mutual Funds.

1994: AMCORE Insurance Group Inc. is formed; assets of AMCORE Bank surpass the $1 billion mark for the first time.

1998: AMCORE rated among the largest 15 percent of asset management firms in the United States, and among the nation's 100 largest bank holding companies.

2000: AMCORE is rated among the nation's leading online financial institutions.

---

came from a family of Iowa bankers, and had previously worked in Chicago in the 7th Federal Reserve District's national banking department. He was active on the boards of many Rockford organizations and was known for his spirit of community service. Liljedahl would lead the bank through a period of modernization until his resignation on July 26, 1976.

During Liljedahl's tenure, the bank celebrated its 50th anniversary. The bank held an open house to celebrate the occasion which was attended by more than 10,000 visitors, including representatives from banks in San Francisco, Detroit, New York, and Chicago. Several major developments unfolded under Liljedahl. One was the expansion of American National's trust department under David Morgan Jr. Another significant development was a similar expansion of the installment loan department. The latter movement signified a new philosophy of less restrictive lending practices. In fact, under the direction of Robert E. Hitt, the installment loan business would be one of the best things that happened to the bank during the 1960s. As Ross explained in her history of the bank, loans increased by almost $38 million over ten years, compared to increasing only $6 million in the first 45 years of the bank's existence.

Other developments during this era included the introduction and expansion of drive-through-banking services, as well as the introduction of computers into the bank's operations. In October 1964, American National announced plans to build a one-story data processing center near the main bank. In 1965, it

purchased an IBM 240 computer system to handle check deposits, and other computerization efforts would follow from that point on.

1970–80: Turbulent Times

During the 1970s, American National sought to improve the physical surroundings near its headquarters. In 1971, the bank demolished five buildings and created a park as part of a neighborhood redevelopment initiative. On July 4, 1976 it unveiled a one-ton, 24-square-foot, welded red brass and copper sculpture of an American Eagle, created by Rockford sculptor Gene Horvath. The new sculpture was part of the bank's Bicentennial contribution to the city, and was affixed to the exterior facade of the bank building.

However, things weren't entirely positive during the 1970s. On July 26, 1976, shortly after the sculpture was introduced, the bank lost two of its leaders when CEO Liljedahl and President Robert E. Hitt resigned. David W. Knapp assumed the role of president and CEO. He had joined the bank at the beginning of the decade as its vice-president and trust officer. An attorney, Knapp was responsible for many developments, including a motor bank at State and Ninth Street, during his tenure.

Knapp was at the helm of American National when it was involved in a nationally publicized lawsuit against Chrysler Corp., which then owed American National $525,000. Although the suit was filed and resolved in 1980, it stemmed from a business relationship that developed during the 1970s. At the time, the auto-maker was in financial trouble and had requested assistance from the U.S. government. In order to qualify for a $1.5 billion bailout program, all of Chrysler's creditors had to agree to a new payment schedule. Instead of joining other banks across the nation, American National instead sued Chrysler and demanded that the auto-maker repay its debt. The bank's initial unwillingness to participate in the federal loan guarantee program meant possible bankruptcy for Chrysler. After the bank was picketed by United Auto Workers Local 1268, which represented workers at a nearby manufacturing plant, and received bomb threats, American National agreed to participate. In the June 20, 1980 issue of the "Rockford Register Star," Knapp explained: "We sense a divisiveness taking place in the community, a community involved with Chrysler Corporation in many ways. Our decision reflects our continuing concern for the community we serve. Second, we are concerned for the safety of our employees and their families. We cannot in good conscience put them at continued risk in this manner."

1980–99: Growth and Expansion

American National Bank began the 1980s by announcing plans for a new motor bank, scheduled to open in December on Sixth Street and Fourth Avenue. However, other developments began to unfold which caused the bank to take on a new look in many ways. On June 1, 1982, a holding company called AmeriCorp Financial Inc. was formed. It became a publicly traded company in 1983, at which time it acquired Carpentersville Savings Bank, American National Bank and Trust Co., Colonial Bank, and First National Bank of Woodstock.

Also in 1983, American National moved into a new, modern, seven-story facility on Seventh Street that replaced the one it had occupied for 67 years. The new building was constructed with technology, security, and future growth in mind. It included a 3,500-square-foot vault, a state-of-the-art fire protection system, and a computerized system that limited access to different areas of the building depending on an employee's ID badge.

Pekin, Illinois-based First National Bank was acquired in 1984. This preceded a monumental merger with Illinois National Bank in November 1985, which was so large it warranted a few name-changes. By combining the $289.3 million assets of Illinois National with the $404.1 million assets of American National, the merger created AMCORE Bank N.A., the eighth largest bank in Illinois and the largest in Rockford. It bumped the bank into a whole new league and increased the holding company's assets to $900 million. At that time, AmeriCorp Financial Inc. became AMCORE Financial Inc. J. Peter Jeffrey, who had served as chairman and president of Illinois National, became president and CEO of AMCORE Bank. David Knapp died shortly after the merger, on December 4, 1985. At the time, Knapp was president of AMCORE Financial, and chairman of AMCORE Bank.

In 1986, Carl J. Dargene succeeded Knapp as president and CEO of AMCORE Financial. A prominent Rockford industrialist, Dargene was a member of AMCORE's board, which asked him to assume the role of CEO following Knapp's death. Also in 1986, AMCORE Financial was listed on the NASDAQ. That

year, its assets exceeded $1 billion for the first time. AMCORE Financial's annual report provided a concise description of the services it was offering by this time:

"All AMCORE banks are full service, commercial banking businesses providing a wide range of banking services throughout the communities they serve. The banks accept demand, savings and time deposits; provide various personal loan services including overdraft protection, installment loans, mortgage loans, personal credit lines and credit card programs. They provide financial services to commercial and governmental organizations including loans, deposits, letters of credit, lease financing, safe deposit box rental, securities safekeeping, foreign currency exchange, as well as lock box and other cash management services. Certain banks administer estates and trusts, including employee benefit plans and estate administration. AMCORE Bank N.A., Rockford provides payroll processing to commercial customers and data processing services to correspondent banks and its subsidiaries. AMCORE Financial Life Insurance Company provides service to the financial industry by underwriting credit life and accident and health insurance."

In 1988, AMCORE announced plans to build a $1 million full-service branch on Mulford Road in Rockford. The following year, it combined AMCORE Bank Colonial with AMCORE Bank Rockford. Robert J. Mueleman was named president and chief operating officer of AMCORE bank in 1989, and J. Peter Jeffrey was named the bank's vice-chairman and CEO. As the company headed into the 1990s, it would experience explosive growth. During that decade, AMCORE acquired many banks and holding companies in nearby communities and expanded its geographic reach in every direction, including north into Wisconsin. Accordingly, AMCORE also opened branches in many communities surrounding Rockford, as well as within locations like supermarkets.

In addition to acquiring other financial institutions, the company formed AMCORE Trust Co. in 1990 and acquired what would become AMCORE Consumer Finance Co. In 1992, the company launched AMCORE Investment Banking and AMCORE Capital Management, and created the Vintage Family of Mutual Funds. AMCORE Insurance Group Inc. was formed in 1994. That year, AMCORE announced its highest-ever first-quarter earnings, with profits of $4.1 million, up 8.1 percent from the previous year. In addition, the assets of AMCORE Bank surpassed the $1 billion mark.

In 1996, Meuleman succeeded Dargene as president and CEO of AMCORE Financial when the latter executive reached mandatory retirement age for CEO. Dargene remained as chairman of AMCORE Financial. Meuleman had joined American National Bank in 1981 as vice-president for investments, and was named president and COO of AMCORE Bank in 1989. He then was named executive vice-president and COO, banking subsidiaries, for AMCORE Financial Inc.

It also was in 1996 that AMCORE's Vintage Equity Fund received a five-star rating from Morningstar for the first time. The fund would continue to receive recognition from Morningstar in subsequent years, as well as from leading financial publications like the *Wall Street Journal* and *Fortune*. By 1998, AMCORE was rated among the largest 15 percent of asset management firms in the United States, and was among the nation's 100 largest bank holding companies.

As the 1990s came to a close, AMCORE implemented a customer-focused strategy to simplify operations through consolidation. In May 1999, it announced that it would consolidate nine bank charters into one. According to Mueleman in the May 3, 1999 *Rockford Register Star*, "To stay competitive, to stay independent, we have to improve the efficiency under which we operate so our shareholders get a better return."

2000–Present: Bright Future

As the new millennium dawned, AMCORE introduced a host of e-banking services for consumers including online bill payment and investment services, as well as features for business customers. In a market where many banks had been continually acquired by larger financial institutions from other cities and states, AMCORE appeared committed to remaining independent. It announced a strategy to consolidate operations in order to geographically focus on its core market. Through fiscal conservatism, hard work, and eventually acquisitions and expansion, AMCORE Financial was able to flourish from the seeds planted by Swedish immigrants in a small storefront some 90 years earlier. The same qualities will likely serve AMCORE well into the new millennium.

Principal Subsidiaries

AMCORE Consumer Finance Co. Inc.; AMCORE Bank N.A.; AMCORE Investment Group N.A.; AMCORE Mortgage Inc.

Principal Competitors

Bank One Corporation; National City Corporation; U.S. Bancorp.

Further Reading

"AMCORE Bank Untouched by Merger Storm," *Rockford Register Star,* February 7, 1999.

"AMCORE Rings in New Year with New Chief. Robert J. Meuleman: The Veteran Executive Who Succeeds Carl J. Dargene, Doesn't Expect Much Change in Direction," *Rockford Register Star,* January 1, 1996, p. 6C.

"AMCORE's New Leader. Bob Meuleman Envisions More Growth for the Bank-Holding Company," *Rockford Register Star,* May 14, 1995, p. 1E.

"Bank to Turn Back Clock for 50th-Year Open House," *Rockford Morning Star,* October 9, 1960.

"Better, Smaller AMCORE," *Rockford Register Star,* May 3, 1999, p. 1B.

"Dargene's 'Clear Choice'," *Rockford Register Star,* May 10, 1996, p. 8A.

Fong, Joe, "Bank Concedes, Joins Bailout," *Rockford Register Star,* June 20, 1980.

——, "Bank Jolts Chrysler's Loan Plan," *Rockford Register Star,* June 17, 1980.

——. "Pressure Mounts Against Suit," *Rockford Register Star,* June 18, 1980.

"John A. Alden Named to New Post by Bank," *Rockford Morning Star,* January 14, 1938.

"Liljedahl to Head American Bank," *Rockford Morning Star,* January 9, 1957.

McKenna, M.A.J. "AMCORE Rises to Big-Time Bank League," *Rockford Register Star,* January 30, 1987, p. 5B.

——, "Rockford Bank's Merge Tuesday," *Rockford Register Star,* November 18, 1985, p. 4C.

"Name Taylor President of American National," *Rockford Morning Star,* January 9, 1946.

"Open House Marks Bank Anniversary," *Rockford Register Republic,* October 13, 1960.

Ross, Elizabeth A., *American National Bank and Trust Co.: A History,* Rockford, Ill.: American National Bank and Trust Co. August, 1980.

Rubendall, Ben, "Carl Dargene Named President of AMCORE," *Rockford Register Star,* January 8, 1982, p. 5C.

——, "Sneak Preview: Inside American's New Bank," *Rockford Register Star,* May 29, 1983.

"Swedish-American National Bank Formally Announces Name Change," *Rockford Morning Star,* January 21, 1945.

"Welcome Public in New Home of East Side Bank," *Rockford Register Republic,* November 24, 1917.

—Paul R. Greenland

American Institute of Certified Public Accountants (AICPA)

1211 Avenue of the Americas
New York, New York 10036-8775
U.S.A.
Telephone: (212) 596-6200
Toll Free: (888) 777-7077
Fax: (212) 596-6213
Web site: http://www.aicpa.org

Private Company
Incorporated: 1887 as the American Association of
    Public Accountants
Employees: 725
Sales: $161.03 (2000)
NAIC: 81392 Professional Organizations

With over 330,000 members, The American Institute of Certified Public Accountants (AICPA) is the premier professional organization for certified public accountants in the United States. As such, it strives to provide its membership with the resources, information, and leadership that enable them to serve the public and clients in a professional manner. Members of the AICPA must have a valid license to practice accounting (having passed the required examinations), be employed in an AICPA-approved institution, and abide by the organization's bylaws. Consisting of a board of directors, a governing council, and a joint trial board, the AICPA institutes programs and policies, while also providing for uniform enforcement of professional standards by adjudicating disciplinary charges against state society and AICPA members. Moreover, the group publishes the monthly *Journal of Accountancy* as well as newsletters—*The Practicing CPA* and *The CPA Letter*—for its membership.

Origins and Early Years: 1887–1934

In 1887, several men, the majority of them Scottish or English chartered accountants who had settled in the United States and started practices there, founded and incorporated the American Association of Public Accountants. Until that time, the profession was vaguely defined; the founding members of the

AICPA set out to ensure that accountancy gained respect as a profession through practicing accountants who acted competently and professionally.

The membership grew to around 30 in the first year and 45 active members were listed in 1896. In 1905 the association merged with the Federation of Societies of Public Accountants in the United States of America, which had been founded in 1902. There were 266 members. The organization began publishing a periodical, *The Journal of Accountancy,* that year. A permanent secretariat for the body was established in 1911. The merged group had retained the name American Association of Public Accountants, but in 1916 it was reorganized as the Institute of Accountants in the United States of America, and shortly after this the name was changed to American Institute of Accountants.

The pre-1916 association essentially had been a federation of state societies; the reorganized body conferred on itself the power to accept applications for membership, prepare its own admissions examination, and draft and enforce a code of ethics for all its members. In the first 10 years after reorganization, the institute grew from 1,150 to 2,064 members. A number of its members formed the American Society of Certified Public Accountants in 1921 to emphasize the importance of the CPA certificate, but this group rejoined the institute in 1936, bringing the membership to 4,890. Thereafter admission was open only to CPAs. The institute eventually stopped giving its examination for admission, accepting members on the basis of what became a uniform CPA examination.

A number of members and state societies contributed in 1917 to an endowment fund in order to establish and support a central library for the accounting profession. This fund enabled the AIA to publish a number of technical books and monographs in the 1920s. During the following decade the institute continued to expand its line, including one of the first efforts to define the principles underlying financial accounting. After World War II, its publications evidenced a strong interest both in detailing practice procedures and expanding the theoretical frameworks supporting the various types of expertise involved in public accounting.

Company Perspectives:

The AICPA is the premier national professional association in the United States. Our employees are a diverse, unified team who: are committed to member service and the public interest, providing the highest quality products, services and support possible; listen and respond to the needs and expectations of members, prospective members, the public and one another; Serve members with excellence; act with the highest ethical behavior, performing with integrity and professionalism; are committed to learning and using new or existing tools and technology to its maximum potential; are responsive to others in a respectful and courteous manner; embrace change and approach challenges with "can do" enthusiasm and creative thinking; constantly seek opportunities to attract and retain members, offer additional products or services, reduce costs, and improve productivity; are empowered to problem-solve and make decisions with the expectation of support by the AICPA.

A strong emphasis on professional ethics had been established by the American Association of Public Accountants, which in 1908 had disseminated five rules on the subject, including a prohibition on members' engaging in incompatible occupations and also of paying commissions to the "laity." During World War I, the AIA proscribed practices such as "touting"—that is, all types of "unprofessional" advertising or soliciting for new business—and unrealistically low bidding and contingent-fee arrangements in pursuit of the same. (These rules were dropped in the 1970s as a result of threatened antitrust litigation by the federal government.) *The Journal of Accountancy* opposed incorporation by accounting firms because they could fall under the control of entrepreneurs who were not members of the profession.

The American Association of Public Accountants resisted efforts by federal government agencies in 1907 and 1914 to introduce uniform accounting rules. At the request of the Federal Trade Commission, the AIA issued, in 1917, a memorandum on balance-sheet audits that became a model for the preparation of financial reports for commercial and industrial enterprises. Such an authoritative statement on acceptable auditing procedures had become necessary because of the growing reliance of banks on audited financial statements for credit purposes. Recognition of the need to standardize accounting rules grew in the 1920s, as the public increasingly bought shares of stock on securities markets.

Seeking to Better Define the Profession: 1934–78

In 1934 the institute, in association with the New York Stock Exchange, issued *Audits of Corporate Accounts,* defining for the first time six accounting principles that firms listed on the stock exchange were required to follow. It also called on accountants not only to certify a company's accounts but also to determine whether or not the system of accounting of a company conformed to acceptable accounting principles. This action was impelled by the establishment of the Federal Securities and Exchange Commission, with jurisdiction over the reporting

of public companies, including the power to define generally accepted accounting principles. Alarmed at this piece of New Deal legislation and fearing that their profession would be drawn into the political pressures they associated with government, accountants won an important concession: public financial statements filed with the SEC would be audited by independent accountants rather than federal employees.

In 1938 the American Institute of Accountants established a committee on accounting procedure (CAP). During the more than 20 years of its existence, the CAP issued 51 accounting-research bulletins defining generally accepted accounting principles. In keeping with its basic philosophy of self-regulation, the SEC traditionally accepted the rulings of this body. Also in 1938 or 1939, in response to a massive fraud case, the AIA formed a committee on auditing procedure to provide guidance on the procedures to be followed in examining financial statements. Fifty-four statements on auditing procedure had been issued by this body through 1972, when it was replaced by an executive committee on auditing standards.

By 1941 the American Institute of Accountants had codified its first rules for members to follow as a means of maintaining the independence of the profession. Among the more important rules adopted in the 1950s with regard to this question was one that incorporated generally accepted auditing standards as an ethical guideline for independent audits, and another prohibiting the expression of opinions on financial statements if a member were a director or officer of a client's concern or had a financial interest in such a concern.

A consensus had grown by 1959 that the CAP was inadequate to deal with new developments in corporate policy, taxation, and government regulation. Accordingly, a new Accounting Research Division was established to publish studies of current problems, and a 21-member Accounting Principles Board (APB) was created to consider the studies and on their basis to publish pronouncements that would be binding on members of the institute, which was renamed the American Institute of Certified Public Accountants (AICPA) in 1957. Authority over tax practice was a considerable source of contention between accountants and lawyers until 1951, when the AIA and American Bar Association jointly approved adoption of a Statement of Principles for Lawyers and CPAs in Tax Practice. Other important actions of the 1950s included the establishment of a committee on management services (1954) and a committee on the economics of accounting practice (1957), as well as the creation of a program of continuing education (1958). A Washington, D.C., office was opened in 1959. By 1961, the institute's staff had grown to 165 and was organized into seven divisions.

The APB labored under a number of handicaps: disagreement within the profession about its basic purposes, a perception that its authority was being undermined by the Securities and Exchange Commission, and mounting criticism of the accounting practices used by some conglomerates during the corporate-merger boom of the 1960s. In 1963 three big accounting firms vowed to ignore a board ruling concerning an investment tax credit and successfully faced down the body. Investment bankers did the same to kill a controversial 1967 ruling on convertible bonds. A central theme voiced by the

APB's critics was that a private professional organization should not have the right to create accounting standards and impose them on businesses. In 1973, this body was replaced by the Financial Accounting Standards Board, whose membership is not confined to accountants. This association is independent of the AICPA.

During the early 1970s, there developed a consensus that the AICPA needed to establish standards for public-accounting firms as well as individual practitioners. A division for CPA firms was established in 1977, with separate membership sections for private-companies practice and SEC practice. Both sections adopted standards for quality-control reviews as requirements for membership. To remain in good standing, member firms were required to periodically undergo peer reviews of their practice policies and procedures. During 1977–78 two new technical committees replaced the prior executive committee on auditing standards, one of them was established to provide guidance principally for compilations and reviews of financial statements of private companies.

The AICPA also was establishing technical standards for tax practice (1964), management advisory services (1969), continuing professional education (1971), accountants' services on prospective financial information (1985), and attestation engagements (1986). As in the case of auditing, these standards defined the minimum levels of acceptable quality that individual AICPA members were required to achieve in those areas of practice.

In 1948, the AIA published an analysis of the financial reports of about 600 leading corporations. This was the first in what became an annual reference work, with comparisons showing trends in the treatment of similar items in the financial statements of different corporations. In 1973, the AICPA established a national automated accounting-research system. The world's largest accounting and auditing database, it enabled users to research the annual reports and proxy statements of over 4,000 public companies.

The AICPA in the 1980s and 1990s

In 1988, AICPA members approved a plan that the organization's president described as the most comprehensive quality-improvement program ever undertaken by any profession, including mandatory quality review of firm accounting and auditing practices. By 1995 about 40,000 firms had participated in an approved-practice monitoring program. The AICPA modified its ethics code to specifically apply to members in industry, who in 1995 constituted 41 percent of the organization's members. Some 283 disciplinary actions for violations of the AICPA code of professional ethics were reported in the 1980s.

The AICPA established three new divisions in the mid 1980s: tax, personal financial planning, and management consulting. An information-technology division was added in 1991. The auditing-standards board issued nine new statements in 1988 and substantially changed the auditor's report to make it more user-friendly. These were the most extensive changes in auditing standards in almost 50 years. In 1992, the organization adopted a bylaw allowing CPAs to practice in any organizational form (including incorporation) authorized by a state. A special committee was appointed in 1994 to provide useful information for decision making.

By the late 1980s the continuing-education division had several hundred offerings in video- and audio-assisted self-study formats, group courses, and seminars. As an outgrowth of a policy objective established in 1968 to end racial imbalance in the accounting profession, the AICPA, in 1985, was providing scholarships to 398 students in order to enable minority students to enter the profession. More than a dozen doctoral students were receiving fellowships. Beginning in 2000, the AICPA required, as a condition of membership, 150 hours of accountancy education.

In 1991 the AICPA moved 650 of its 750 employees from its quarters in Manhattan's Rockefeller Center to Harborside, New Jersey. Association officials estimated that the move would save $125 million over the next 20 years. Barry C. Melancon was appointed president and chief executive officer of the AICPA in 1995, succeeding Philip B. Chenok, who had served in the post since 1980. Olivia F. Kirtley, the first woman to be the organization's chair, held this post in fiscal 1999 (the year ended July 31, 1999). She was also the first chair to be a company employee unaffiliated with an accounting firm.

The AICPA's membership reached 337,454 in fiscal 2000. During the mid-1990s members working in business and industry outnumbered those in public accounting for the first time; the figures for fiscal 2000 were: business and industry, 46.4 percent; public accounting, 39.4 percent; government, 4.2 percent; education, 2.3 percent; and retired and miscellaneous, 7.7 percent.

The AICPA's responsibilities in 2000 included establishing auditing and reporting standards, influencing the development of financial accounting standards underlying the presentation of U.S. corporate financial statements, and preparing and grading the national Uniform CPA Examination for the state licensing bodies. It was conducting research and continuing-education programs and surveillance of practice and was maintaining more than 100 committees, including: Accounting Standards, Accounting and Review Services, AICPA Effective Legislation—Political Action, Auditing Standards, Federal Taxation, Information Technology, Management Consulting Services,

Professional Ethics, Quality Review, and Women and Family Issues. Its publications included *Accounting Trends and Techniques, CPA Client Bulletin, CPA Examinations, CPA Letter, Digest of Washington Issues; The Journal of Accountancy; Practicing CPA,* and *Tax Adviser.*

Principal Divisions

CPA Firms; Information Technology; Management Consulting Services; Personal Financial Planning; Tax.

Further Reading

Chenok, Philip B., ''Fifteen Years of Meeting the Challenges,'' *Journal of Accountancy,* June 1995, pp. 66–70.
Cook, J. Michael, ''The AICPA at 100: Public Trust and Professional Pride, *Journal of Accountancy,* May 1987, pp. 370, 372–74.
Edwards, James Don, and Paul J. Miranti, Jr., ''A Professional Institution in a Dynamic Society,'' *Journal of Accountancy,* May 1987, pp. 22, 24–26, 28–30, 32–34, 36–38.
Penney, Louis H., ''The American Institute of CPAs—Past and Future,'' *Journal of Accountancy,* January 1962, pp. 32–39.

—Robert Halasz

Putting people first.

Astoria Financial Corporation

1 Astoria Federal Plaza
Lake Success, New York 11042-1085
U.S.A.
Telephone: (516) 327-3000
Toll Free: (800) 278-6742
Fax: (516) 327-7461
Web site: http://www.astoriafederal.com

Public Company
Incorporated: 1993
Employees: 2,025
Sales: $1.587 billion
Stock Exchanges: NASDAQ
Ticker Symbol: ASFC
NAIC: 522120 Savings Institutions; 551111 Officers of
   Bank Holding Companies

Astoria Financial Corporation is the holding company formed in 1993 to facilitate the conversion of Astoria Federal Savings and Loan Association from a mutual form of ownership to stock ownership. The Long Island-based institution has since grown via acquisitions to become the second largest thrift in New York State and the sixth largest in the country. Although very much dependent on its traditional family residential mortgage business, Astoria Financial has made recent efforts to diversify by strengthening its retail banking operations. Astoria Financial serves 700,000 customers, with deposits topping $10 billion and total assets of $22 billion. While focused on the sizable Long Island, Brooklyn, and Queens market, Astoria Financial also originates loans through its own offices or brokers in a number of states outside of New York, including Connecticut, Delaware, Florida, Georgia, Illinois, Maryland, Massachusetts, New Jersey, North Carolina, Pennsylvania, South Carolina, and Virginia.

Part of the 1800s Building Association Movement

The history of Astoria Financial dates back to 1888 at a time when mutually owned Building and Loan associations spread across the United States. In essence, people who could not afford to buy or build houses on their own pooled their money in order to receive affordable mortgages. This concept of mutual assistance was akin to the savings bank movement that began in Germany and Switzerland in the later part of the 18th century. Savings banks were formed for the working class in which depositors pooled their money in order to realize higher interest rates. The concept was similar to a contemporary retirement plan, since depositors could withdraw money only when they reached a prescribed age. British progressives seized upon the idea as a way to eliminate poverty, preferring to set up mutual savings plans rather than giving alms, which they believed would simply reward idleness. The first self-sustaining savings bank was established in Scotland in 1810, and the idea spread so quickly that by 1818 the British Isles boasted 465 organizations. The idea then spread to the United States. The first New York mutual savings bank began operating in 1819, and by the time of the Civil War there would be 25 mutual savings banks in Manhattan, Brooklyn, and Queens.

The first mutually owned building association in the United States was the Oxford Provident of Frankfort, established in 1831 in the Philadelphia area to provide housing for the working class. Similar organizations cropped up around the country over the ensuing decades. On December 4, 1888, 16 Queens businessmen pledged $4,000 to create the progenitor of Astoria Financial, the Central Permanent Building and Loan Association, with the stated purpose of promoting thrift and home ownership. Edwin Wooley served as president and G.H. Pierce as secretary. Within a year the association was paying interest on savings accounts.

Like mutual savings banks, building associations evolved into commercial enterprises. In the beginning they were open only several hours a week and often operated out of the offices of insurance or real estate businesses. Mutual savings banks quickly dropped their charitable ties, soon advertising themselves in the newspapers and raising interest rates to lure customers away from rival mutuals. Institutions that had been established to serve the working class eventually fought over the deposits of businessmen. In a similar vein, building associations evolved into contemporary Savings and Loan institutions.

Company Perspectives:

Our mission is to provide a strong return to our share-holders, while recognizing the importance of serving the needs of our customers and the communities in which they reside.

Limited government regulation allowed S&Ls to proliferate, but the Depression of the 1930s would cause a shakeout, and many institutions failed.

With just $600,000 in assets, the Central Permanent Building and Loan Association survived the Depression. In 1936 it changed its name to Astoria Savings & Loan Association. In Washington during the 1930s a spate of New Deal legislation was passed to reform the banking industry, including the creation of federally chartered S&Ls. Astoria Savings received its federal charter in 1937 and duly changed its name to Astoria Federal Savings & Loan Association.

External Growth in 1973

As did the population of Queens, Astoria Federal grew steadily, especially during the building boom that followed World War II. In the 1950s it would become the largest savings association in Queens County and the first city thrift to branch out to adjacent Nassau County on Long Island. In 1973 Astoria Federal took its first steps in external expansion by acquiring Metropolitan Federal Savings, a relatively young thrift that was chartered originally by New York State in 1953 and converted to a federal charter in 1966. By 1977 Astoria Federal boasted assets of $1 billion. In 1983 it acquired another bank, Citizens Savings & Loan Association of New York. Citizens Savings was originally chartered by New York State in 1919 as the Elmhurst Building & Loan Association, then was renamed in 1948 as the Woodside Savings & Loan Association before becoming Citizens Savings in 1974.

Banking in general would see an accelerated move to consolidation in the 1980s, fueled in large part by changes in law that allowed banks from different states to acquire one another. In the highly fragmented thrift sector in the New York City area there was ample opportunity for institutions like Astoria Federal to grow. No single institution controlled as much as 10 percent of area depositors. Moreover, the S&L crisis of the late 1980s resulted in the closing of more than 1,000 thrifts nationwide and pushed hundreds more to the brink of bankruptcy, making the environment even more conducive to consolidation. Federal legislation passed to bail out the industry, however, would have an adverse effect on Astoria Federal. Previously, larger thrifts were encouraged to acquire weaker ones by allowing them to count "supervisory goodwill" (the difference between the purchase price and the actual value of assets) as capital, and thus the amount the government would cushion against loan losses. The 1989 Financial Institutions Reform and Recovery Act (FIRREA) eliminated supervisory goodwill, costing some S&Ls like Astoria Federal hundreds of millions of dollars. The matter would then be litigated and have a further impact on Astoria Federal later in the 1990s.

Astoria Federal's external growth in the 1980s began with the 1983 acquisition of Hastings on Hudson Federal Savings & Loan Association. It was chartered originally by New York State in 1901 as Hastings-on-Hudson Building Co-Op Savings & Loan and converted to a federal charter in 1953. Astoria Federal then acquired Chenango Federal Savings in 1985. Chenango dated back to 1888 when it was chartered by New York State as Chenango Co-Operative Savings & Loan of Norwich, New York. It converted to a federal charter in 1980. Astoria Federal also acquired Oneonta Federal Savings & Loan Association in 1988. It also dated back to 1888 when it was chartered by the state. Oneonta converted to a federal charter in 1981.

In 1989 Astoria Federal changed leadership, which would spearhead the conversion from mutual ownership to stock ownership. Succeeding President and Chief Executive Officer Henry Drewitz, who remained as chairman, was George L. Engelke, Jr., a certified public accountant. After graduating from Lehigh University with a degree in business administration, Engelke was employed by Peat Marwick, Mitchell & Co., concentrating on audit and tax work for thrifts during nine out of his 11 years with the firm. He joined Astoria Federal in 1971 to serve as vice-president and treasurer. He was promoted to executive vice-president in 1974, was named to the bank's board of directors in 1983, and was named chief operating officer in 1986.

Changes in banking laws in the late 1980s made it easier for depositor-owned federal thrifts to convert to shareholder-owned state-chartered savings banks. For acquisition-minded thrifts like Astoria Federal the move was beneficial on two levels. Not only would the bank have stock to use in making purchases, an initial public offering would create a war chest for acquisitions. A mutual converts to stock ownership by creating a holding company, then making a subscription offering to allow depositors, employees, officers, and directors to buy shares in the new corporation at a set price. Half the proceeds generally are used to acquire the bank, and the rest is available for use in growing the institution. Depositors of the mutual stand to gain because the stock of the new holding company is likely to rise substantially, generally spiking 15 percent to 20 percent on the first day of public trading. Through the holding company the bank also can expand into complementary businesses such as insurance, real estate, and financial planning.

On June 4, 1993, Astoria Financial Corporation was incorporated in Delaware to serve as the holding company for Astoria Federal Savings & Loan Association. Then, in November 1993, the holding company sold 13.2 million shares of stock at $25 per share. Astoria was well positioned to take part in the consolidation of New York thrifts that was now heating up. Shortly after New York Bancorp bought Brooklyn's Hamilton Bancorp and the area's two largest thrifts, Dime Bancorp and Anchor Bancorp, agreed to merge, Astoria Financial announced that it had reached an agreement to acquire Long Island-based Fidelity New York for $29 a share in cash. When the transaction was completed in February 1995, the final price would total approximately $157.8 million. As a result of the deal, Astoria Federal increased its assets to nearly $6.5 billion and deposits to $4.4 billion, at the time making it the 14th largest publicly traded thrift in the country. It would have 38 offices in Queens,

Nassau, and Suffolk counties, as well as five branches in upstate New York.

Although he was aggressive in growing Astoria Financial through acquisitions, Engelke remained cautious when it came to the bank's business, electing to concentrate on its traditional residential lending program. In 1996 the U.S. Supreme Court ruled on the supervisory goodwill issue, deciding that the federal government had reneged on incentives to acquire ailing thrifts, setting the stage for Astoria Financial, as well as Dime Bancorp and Long Island Bancorp, to press the U.S. Court of Federal Claims for millions of dollars. Although Dime Bancorp estimated that it lost $700 million, Long Island Bancorp $500 million, and Astoria Financial $160 million, the banks were expected to file for much higher claims. With this potential windfall in new capital, all three institutions appeared poised for even greater growth, but the best acquisition targets had been acquired and others appeared to be overvalued. The situation in the New York metropolitan area was becoming increasingly unpredictable. Although Astoria was eager to buy other banks, it also was making itself an attractive candidate for acquisition.

Engelke, named Astoria's chairman in 1997, began looking to the Brooklyn market, which was similar to Queens and its base of working-class homeowners, especially in the growing immigrant communities. In April 1997, Astoria Financial announced that it would acquire Brooklyn-based Greater New York Savings Bank at a price of $19 per share for a total of $293 million. The acquisition boosted Astoria Financial's assets to $9.8 billion. Its stock price rose to the $40 range, a significant increase over the initial public offering, especially compared with a split-adjusted $12.50 price. Also bidding on Greater New York was North Fork Bancorp, another aggressive player in the area, which would soon contend with Astoria Financial over Long Island Bancorp.

Acquisition of Long Island Bancorp in 1988

Long Island Bancorp was the holding company for Long Island Savings Bank, which had been chartered originally in 1875. It became a prized catch in 1998, due in some measure to the thrift's expected share of the federal supervisory goodwill

settlement. Bidding between rival suitors, which included Dime Bancorp, GreenPoint Financial Corp., and North Fork Bancorp, became so heated that Long Island Bancorp's board traveled to an Orlando, Florida, retreat in order to prevent leaks about the deliberations. North Fork increased its stake in the holding company's stock from 4.5 percent to 9.9 percent and outbid its rivals, but in the end Astoria Financial's $1.8 billion stock swap offer was accepted. Engelke sweetened his offer by agreeing to increase the number of Long Island directors on the combined board from four to five and keep on key executives.

Although the Long Island Bancorp acquisition was regarded as a major coup for Engelke and Astoria Financial, the aftermath of the deal proved to be somewhat rocky. Wall Street expressed concern that the bank had overpaid by bidding down Astoria's stock. Investors were especially dubious about Engelke's plan to make the deal work by cutting 50 percent of Long Island Bancorp's cost structure. He had been able to achieve considerable savings with previous acquisitions, but not to that level. A lower stock price, as a result, hampered Astoria Financial's ability to use its shares for further acquisitions. Moreover, Engelke faced pressure from North Fork, which had positioned itself to become Astoria's largest institutional shareholder through the Long Island Bancorp stock it purchased during the acquisition fight. North Fork's chairman and chief executive, John Adam Kanas, issued a public letter in September, questioning Engelke's plan and threatening to call for a change in management if projected results were not realized. According to *Crain's New York Business,* "It's the type of move that has made Mr. Kanas the most disliked man in local banking, shaking up the otherwise friendly world of savings and loans in the Long Island-New York market. . . . In the past, Mr. Kanas has sought win-win situations in which North Fork buys a stake in a thrift and then pressures it to sell: if the thrift is sold to a competitor, North Fork still collects a tidy profit on its investment." In this case, however, Kanas might have forced Astoria Financial to be sold to an even larger rival, which would severely cripple his chance to emerge in what was rapidly turning into a last-man-standing scenario. Engelke simply wrote back to Kanas to express his confidence that Astoria Financial would indeed meet its projections.

Nevertheless, Astoria Financial was forced to make some adjustments, especially as interest rates rose in 1999. It put further expansion plans on hold and made significant cutbacks on its mortgage-backed securities portfolio. With freed-up capital, it then initiated a stock repurchase program to buy back some 10 percent of its shares. Astoria Financial also looked to diversify its product offerings, in particular establishing an insurance agency, AF Insurance Agency, to market life, health, property, and casualty insurance through its bank branches. It was hardly a ground-breaking move, but one that was long overdue, as was the upgrading of the bank's Internet site. Astoria Financial's stock began to rebound in the fall of 2000, reflecting investors' approval of the changes.

It was a flagging economy in 2001, however, that significantly boosted the prospects for Astoria Financial. A reliance on mortgages, viewed negatively only months earlier, now made thrifts like Astoria Financial a safe haven for investors wary of the stock market. Almost every one of Astoria's residential mortgages were backed by actual property. Moreover, nonperforming assets comprised only 0.2 percent of the thrift's portfolio, compared to rivals with an average of 1.56 percent, according to CIBC World Markets. Commercial banks, on the other hand, stood at 1.75 percent. As a result of these factors, the price of Astoria Financial stock soared. It was now in a position to use its stock for renewed growth. At the same time, however, Astoria Financial became an even more inviting acquisition target for any large outsider looking to make a splash in the New York market. Whichever course lay in store, the days of being a Queens neighborhood thrift were long past for Astoria Financial.

Principal Subsidiaries

Astoria Federal; Astoria Capital Trust I; AF Insurance Agency.

Principal Competitors

Bank of New York; Dime Bancorp; M&T Bank; North Fork Bancorp.

Further Reading

Croghan, Lore, ''Astoria Buy Gives Thrift Greater Clout in Area Market,'' *Crain's New York Business,* May 27, 1997, p. 4.

Elstein, Aaron, ''N.Y. Market Running Out of Takeover Targets,'' *American Banker,* November 12, 1997, p. 26.

Fontana, Dominick, ''New York's Astoria Sticking to Its Thrifty Roots,'' *American Banker,* February 26, 1997, p. 4.

Gabriel, Frederick, ''NY Thrifts Eye Windfall from Ruling,'' *Crain's New York Business,* July 8, 1996, p. 1.

Isidore, Chris, ''Wall St. Jitters Threaten Banks' Acquisition Binge,'' *Crain's New York Business,* July 20, 1998, p. 15.

Murray, Matt, ''Astoria Financial Agrees to Acquire Long Island Bancorp for $1.8 Billion,'' *Wall Street Journal,* April 6, 1998, p. A22.

Talley, Karen, ''Astoria's Chairman Building N.Y. Thrift Empire,'' *American Banker,* May 19, 1998, p. 1.

Wipperfurth, Heike, ''Trimming the Fat for Heartier Stock,'' *Crain's New York Business,* September 4, 2000, p. 15.

—Ed Dinger

Atlantic American Corporation

4370 Peachtree Road N.E.
Atlanta, Georgia 30319-3000
U.S.A.
Telephone: (404) 266-5500
Fax: (404) 266-5702
Web site: http://www.atlam.com

Public Company
Incorporated: 1968
Employees: 249
Total Assets: $351.14 million (1999)
Stock Exchanges: NASDAQ
Ticker Symbol: AAME
NAIC: 524113 Direct Life Insurance Carriers; 524114
    Direct Health and Medical Insurance Carriers; 551112
    Offices of Other Holding Companies

Georgia-based Atlantic American Corporation is a holding company that conducts its large insurance business through its principal subsidiaries: American Southern Insurance Company, American Safety Insurance Company, Association Casualty Insurance Company, Association Risk Management General Agency, Georgia Casualty & Surety Company, and Bankers Fidelity Life Insurance Company. American Southern Insurance and American Safety Insurance, collectively known as American Southern, have historically underwritten automobile and truck liability and physical damage for large commercial policy holders. Association Casualty Insurance Company, originally formed to provide the energy industry's insurance needs, has specialized in workers' compensation insurance, but it has also served the insurance needs of other businesses, primarily in Texas and New Mexico. Association Risk Management General Agency provides workers' compensation insurance coverage through independent agencies. Georgia Casualty provides a wide range of commercial insurance products in the Southeast, including general liability, commercial property, automobile, workers' compensation, and umbrella liability insurance policies. Lastly, Bankers Fidelity, through a nationwide network of independent agents, markets senior-oriented life and health insurance products, including Medicare supplements. Although it is a public entity, Atlantic American remains under the control of its chairman, J. Mack Robinson, and his family, who hold more than a 60 percent interest in the company.

1937–67: Disparate Insurance Companies Merge as Atlantic American

Atlantic American was not incorporated as a holding company until 1968, but it emerged from the gradual accretion of insurance business ventures, two of which can be traced back to 1937. It was in that year that Austin Dilbeck and Dan Dominey pooled their meager resources to found the Dilbeck & Dominey Insurance Company. Between them, they had just $250, but the industrious pair proved able enough to parlay that sum into a going concern. In just a few years, they built their company into one of Georgia's largest writers of workers' compensation insurance. It was also in 1937 that Southern Fire and Marine Insurance Company had its start. Southern, after its transmutation into American Southern Insurance Company, would also play a role in Atlantic American's history.

In 1946, General Casualty & Surety Company, which would later become Atlantic American Life Insurance Company, was chartered in Georgia as a multiple line insurance company. In the next year, Dilbeck, Dominey, and five of their employees formed Georgia Casualty & Surety Company, a firm that began specializing in commercial insurance writing. Meanwhile, on its separate path, General Casualty & Surety grew apace. In 1951, it got its charter amended, allowing it to write life, accident, health, and hospitalization insurance. It also changed its name, becoming General Assurance Corporation. Then, two years later, Dilbeck and Dominey acquired the company. It thus became the first of the many acquisitions that would finally makeup and define Atlantic American Corporation.

Banker Fidelity Life insurance Company, yet another firm to play a vital role in Atlantic American's history, entered the insurance industry in 1955. Also based in Georgia, it began as a legal reserve life insurance company, specializing in marketing life insurance and tax-sheltered annuities to teachers; however, it would eventually focus on providing the insurance needs of senior citizens.

Dilbeck and Dominey also expanded their holdings over the next few years. In 1959, they purchased Royal Life, which was formerly named Whitfield Life of Georgia. During the next year, the Dilbeck and Dominey-owned General Assurance Company purchased Universal American, then changed the acquired company's name to Universal American Insurance Company. It was in 1960, too, that Banker's Fidelity Life paid its first stock dividend and received recognition from *Forbes* as a strong competitor in the insurance field.

In 1962, Atlantic American Life Insurance Company was born from the merger of Universal American and an Alabama-based company, Atlantic National Life. Three years later, in 1965, that surviving company acquired two South Carolina companies: The Sureway Life Insurance Company and The Empire Life Insurance Company. The purchase also brought Atlantic American the charters of two other South Carolina companies: Standard Mutual Life and Life of South Carolina. In addition, Atlantic American acquired Trans South Life, which merged with and into Atlantic.

1968–95: Company Changes Ownership, Expands, and Diversifies

It was in 1968 that Atlantic American Corporation (AAC) was first formed. It was a publicly traded entity created to hold and manage the stock of four Georgia insurance companies: Georgia Casualty & Surety Company; Dilbeck & Dominey Insurance Agency, Inc.; Southeastern Insurance Underwriters, Inc.; and Mortgage Services Company, Inc. Two years later, Atlantic American Life Insurance Company became AAC's wholly owned subsidiary.

Ownership of AAC passed to J. Mack Robinson in 1974, at which time R. Craig Murray was named president and CEO. The corporate headquarters were also relocated that year, moving to The Peachtree Insurance Center in Atlanta. The company's growth continued, starting in 1975, when AAC purchased a controlling interest in Bankers Fidelity Life. By 1984, because of its continued growth, AAC put in motion plans to build a new annex attached to its offices at The Peachtree Insurance Center.

During the 1980s and into the 1990s, Bankers Fidelity Life grew considerably both in its size and services. In 1983, it became one of the first insurance companies to offer a Medicare supplement plan to cover excess Part B charges in Medicare coverage. Then, in 1992, it introduced its Senior Security Service plans, which, in addition to a Medicare supplement, included final (funerary) expense and short-term nursing care coverage. The following year it introduced its proprietary lead generation program which zeroed in on final expense needs and

resulted in a double-digit growth in BFLIC's sales in each succeeding year. In 1998, in recognition of its solid performance, Bankers Fidelity Life was selected as one of only 155 companies to receive charter membership in the Insurance Marketplace Standards Association (IMSA).

Robinson, AAC owner and chairman, had, in 1988, taken on the additional responsibility of serving as its president, and he remained in that post until 1995, when he was succeeded by Hilton H. Howell, Jr. Before that change of guard, AAC had, in 1991, acquired substantially all the stock of Leath Furniture, an Atlanta-based retailer. At the time, that company owned and operated a string of full-line and full-service furniture stores in Florida and the Midwest. However, in 1995, desiring to restrict its focus to insurance, the company sold its 88 percent share in Leath to Mr. Robinson, who continued to operate that company under the Leath name in the Midwest and the Modernage name in Florida. There were other changes at about the same time, including, in 1995, AAC's acquisition of American Southern Insurance Company and its subsidiary, American Safety Insurance Company. The additions to AAC brought the corporation's assets to a hefty $245 million.

1996–99: Company's Growth Leads to Banner Year

In the next year, 1996, Bankers Fidelity Life Insurance Company merged with Atlantic American Life Insurance Company, leaving Bankers Fidelity as the surviving corporate entity. In turn, Bankers Fidelity, in a combination $3.6 million cash and promissory note deal, acquired and consolidated with American Independent Life Insurance Company, a King of Prussia, Pennsylvania-based firm. At the same time, AAC acquired Self-Insurance Administrators, Inc., an Atlantic third-party administrator of public organizations and companies that insure themselves.

In 1998, the performance of the insurance companies making up the AAC group garnered the consortium an AA – rating from Standard & Poor's. By that date, AAC's assets had reached $272.8 million, and the company, through its ongoing acquisitions and restructuring, was approaching a banner year, 1999, when its assets rose to $351.1 million and it undertook further restructuring. In that year, American Independent Life merged with and into Bankers Fidelity, and parent AAC continued its pattern of expansion through major acquisitions and mergers by purchasing Texas-based Association Casualty Insurance Company (ACIC), a firm originally formed in 1978 to fill the unique insurance demands of energy marketers, and its affiliate agency, Association Risk Management General Agency, Inc. In Texas, ACIC had continuously underwritten workers' compensation insurance since its founding, but it had also expanded into other insurance markets. In 1998, it had also begun making its products and services available in New Mexico. As part of the $33.0 million purchase agreement, Association Casualty's founder and president, Harold Fischer, was named to ACC's board.

2000–01: Atlantic American Positions Itself for Further Growth

By 2000, AAC was well positioned to pursue its strategy of aggressive growth through additional acquisitions and the

Key Dates:

1937: Austin Dilbeck and Dan Dominey found Dominey Insurance Agency; Southern Fire and Marine Insurance Company is also established.

1946: General Casualty & Surety Company is granted charter as a multi-line insurance carrier.

1947: Dilbeck, Dominey, and five others form Georgia Casualty & Surety Company.

1951: Company charter amendments permit General Casualty, renamed General Assurance Corporation, to write life, accident, health, and hospitalization policies.

1953: Dilbeck and Dominey purchase General Assurance; Southern Fire and Marine Insurance changes its name to American Southern Insurance Company.

1955: Bankers Fidelity Life Insurance Company starts out as a legal reserve life company.

1959: Dilbeck and Dominey acquire Royal Life.

1968: Atlantic American Corporation (AAC), publicly traded, is organized and incorporated as a stock holding company for four allied Georgia insurance companies.

1970: Atlantic American Life Insurance Company becomes a subsidiary of AAC.

1974: J. Mack Robinson purchases AAC; R. Craig Murray is named AAC's president and CEO, and the company's home office moves to The Peachtree Insurance Center in Atlanta.

1978: Association Casualty Insurance Company is established.

1993: Bankers Fidelity Life Insurance introduces it proprietary lead generation program.

1995: Hilton H. Howell, Jr. is appointed president of AAC, and the company also acquires American Southern Insurance Company.

1996: Atlantic American Life Insurance Company merges into Bankers Fidelity Life Insurance Company; Bankers Fidelity also acquires American Independent Life Insurance Company, and AAC acquires Self-Insurance Administrators, Inc.

1998: Standard & Poor's assigns the AAC group an AA– rating.

1999: American Independent Life merges into Bankers Fidelity; AAC acquires Association Casualty Life and Association Risk Management General Agency.

underwriting of special insurance products. Its total assets over a decade had almost doubled, climbing to $375.8 from $191.3 million in 1991. During that period, through mergers, acquisitions, and restructuring, AAC had developed its panoply of subsidiaries serving the special, well delineated life, health, casualty, and property insurance needs of its customers. Furthermore, its performance had repeatedly won it an AA – rating from Standard & Poor's. According to its own analysis, presented in its historical outline on its Web site, AAC continued to position itself for aggressive growth as an underwriter of niche insurance products in specialty markets. Its strategy called for new acquisitions to complement the services already offered under its corporate umbrella.

Principal Subsidiaries

American Southern Insurance Company & American Safety Insurance Company; Association Casualty Insurance Company & Association Risk Management General Agency; Georgia Casualty & Surety Company; Self-Insurance Administrators, Inc.; Bankers Fidelity Life Insurance Company.

Principal Competitors

Blue Cross and Blue Shield Association; The Prudential Insurance Company of America; The Travelers Corporation.

Further Reading

"Atlantic American Acquires Two Companies," *A.M. Best Newswire*, July 7, 1999.

"Atlantic American Corporation Announces Merger of Its Two Life Insurance Subsidiaries, Bankers Fidelity Life Insurance Co. and American Independent Life Insurance Co.," *PR Newswire*, May 24, 1999.

"Atlantic American Corporation Shows Continued Improved Operations," *PR Newswire*, October 25, 2000.

"Atlantic American Corporation Subsidiary, Georgia Casualty and Surety Company, Appoints New President," *PR Newswire*, May 17, 1999.

—John W. Fiero

Bahlsen GmbH & Co. KG

Podbielski Strasse 11
D-30163 Hannover
Germany
Telephone: (49) (511) 960-0
Fax: (49) (511) 960-2749
Web site: http://www.bahlsen.com

Private Company
Incorporated: 1889 as Hannoversche Cakesfabrik H.
  Bahlsen
Employees: 3,872
Sales: DM 1.04 million ($501.2 million) (2000)
NAIC: 311821 Cookie and Cracker Manufacturing;
  311812 Commercial Bakeries; 31134 Non-Chocolate
  Confectionery Manufacturing

Based in Hannover, Bahlsen GmbH & Co. KG is Germany's leading manufacturer of cookies. The company also makes cakes and granola bars under three major brand-names—Bahlsen, Leibnitz and PiCK UP!—as well as national brands in other European countries such as Austria and France. Bahlsen products are manufactured at eight sites—five in Germany, two in France, and one in Poland. Roughly one third of the company's revenues come from abroad, where Bahlsen maintains a distribution network that serves approximately 80 countries around the world, reaching from its core markets Austria, France, and Poland to the United States and the Middle and Far East. The company is owned and controlled by Werner M. Bahlsen, a grandson of the company founder.

German *Keks: 1889–1919*

Hermann Bahlsen was born in Hannover, Germany, in 1859 into a family of merchants, teachers, priests, and jewelers. After learning the trade of an export merchant, the young Bahlsen worked as an apprentice in Switzerland and England. In England he became involved in the sugar trade, and he saw how popular English biscuits and cakes were manufactured on an industrial scale. Mass-produced baked specialties were almost unknown in Germany at that time, and Bahlsen sensed a business opportunity: to produce these confections at a price every German could afford. To realize this ambition Bahlsen acquired Engl. Cakes and Biscuits, a small factory in Hannover's Friesenstrasse, and renamed it Hannoversche Cakesfabrik H. Bahlsen. Three years later the company moved its operations to a new site in Celler Strasse which remained the company headquarters until the end of the twentieth century. From the very beginning Hermann Bahlsen emphasized making products of high quality which he would be able to sell under a brand name. At a time when brand-name marketing was still in its infancy, it was very common in Germany to name products after well-known personalities. For his first product, the company founder chose the most famous of Hannover's citizens: the philosopher and mathematician Gottfried Wilhelm Leibnitz (1646–1716). Two years after the company's founding, Bahlsen's Leibnitz Cakes were launched throughout Germany. Within four years Bahlsen's sweets were in such demand that the company's number of employees grew from 10 to 100.

A gold medal at the World Exhibition in Chicago in 1893 brought Bahlsen its first international recognition. In 1900 the company expanded its product line to include salty snacks, starting with the company's own version of the American cracker. In 1904 the company started packaging its cakes and cookies in a new dust- and-moisture-resistant package which they called TET. TET was a simplified version of an ancient Egypt symbol that meant "everlasting." Suggested by Hans Bahlsen's friend Friedrich Tewes, a museum director in Hannover, the symbol—a snake over three dots and a semicircle within an oval—as well as the TET signet, became an integral part of the company's logo. Bahlsen also made use of modern production techniques. In 1905 the company was the first in Europe to implement the assembly line method.

With a solid means for mass production in place, Bahlsen's business took off in the following decade. In 1911 Hermann Bahlsen decided to "translate" the English word "cakes" into German, coining the term "Keks," which was pronounced much the same as its English cognate but had a more German appeal. One year after Leibnitz Cakes had become Leibnitz Keks, the company was renamed H. Bahlsens Keksfabrik ("H.

Company Perspectives:

Strong brands as a basis for long-term success. *In times of saturated markets and excessive supply Bahlsen benefits from over a century of expertise in its field. Instead of trying to respond to changing trends, the company develops its own concepts to stimulate new markets. Bahlsen's strategy is based on further developing and improving the company's position as a leading supplier of brand-name cakes and cookies. In order to achieve this goal, the company trusts in three of its major brands—Bahlsen, Leibnitz, and Pick UP!—along with national brands in other countries. With the slogan, ''We sweeten your life,'' Bahlsen conveys the image of a company whose products and services are associated with spoiling oneself and enjoying life.*

Bahlsen's Keks Factory''). The company founder had a passion for the fine arts and sponsored several artists who, for example, designed little stamps with picture stories for Bahlsen's Leibnitz Keks. These commercial artifacts soon achieved the status of collector's items. Later, many of the company's packages, cookie tins, posters, and print ads were designed by various artists. Bahlsen also showed a personal concern for his workers, offering them a company health plan and health care personnel, spacious dining halls, a company library, music room, and roof-top garden. In addition, Bahlsen workers were allowed to take weekly baths during work hours in one of the company's tubs, since most of them could not afford such luxuries in their homes. By 1914 the company had set up national distribution, owning warehouses in 26 German cities. The company employed 1,700 people and Bahlsen's Keks and other sweets were shipped to 31 countries.

Bahlsen's Second Generation

World War I interrupted Bahlsen's growth in 1914, since sweets were not among the goods requested by the German military. Raw materials became scarce, domestic consumers cut back on spending, and the company was cut off from its export markets. By 1918 only one of Bahlsen's 25 ovens was still in operation. After Hermann Bahlsen's death in 1919, three of his four sons entered the business. The first was his oldest son Hans, who had studied at Hannover's Technical College and entered the company in 1919 at age 18. Three years later he was followed by his brother Werner who at the same age became the company's new director while Hans took care of the technical side of the family business. Bahlsen managed to survive the economic turmoil of the 1920s, including hyper-inflation and worldwide economic depression starting at the end of the decade. In 1930 the company founder's youngest son Klaus joined the company at age 22. During the following decade the three brothers struggled to bring Bahlsen back on track. The company's old machines were replaced by modern ones, including the introduction of steel-belt ovens beginning in 1932. Bahlsen also introduced new products to the market. In 1933 the company launched the Express Dose, a one-pound box of wafers which sold for a very low price. The product become a popular item, with about four million boxes sold per year. Despite the very small profit per box, the Express Dose significantly con-

tributed to a steady stream of revenue for the business during the early 1930s, a time of severe economic depression in Germany. Two years later Salzletten, a new salty snack, was launched. Production, marketing, and distribution processes were streamlined during this time. For example, in 1937 Bahlsen reorganized its logistics system. In 1939, the company's 50th anniversary year, Bahlsen had about 2,000 people on its payroll. However, further progress was again interrupted as World War II started in the fall of that year.

During the war, food was rationed and Germans had to use their ''bread stamps'' for cookies. The company also had difficulties securing raw materials, and numerous employees were drafted into the military. Bahlsen ceased all research and development activities and cut its product range down to just eleven—including emergency food supplies for German soldiers. Between 1943 and 1945 the company employed about 200 forced laborers who were working under the same conditions as Bahlsen's German workers and received the same wages and benefits. When Hannover became the target of bomb attacks in 1943, the company established a warehouse in Gera in the southern state of Thuringia. By the end of the war in spring 1945, Bahlsen's production facilities were half destroyed, along with most of the company's warehouses. In April 1945, Bahlsen started making bread for hospitals. Klaus Bahlsen was the driving force behind the company's reconstruction efforts and behind the establishment of a number of new domestic production facilities. Like his father, he also focused his efforts on setting high quality standards. In 1950, Bahlsen established its own laboratories for monitoring product quality. By 1951, the company's work force was back to about 2,200. Bahlsen's second factory was opened in 1954 in Lindau. The third one followed in Barsinghausen in 1957. A fourth factory in Varel started operations in 1963, followed by the opening of a brand-new warehouse in Langenhagen in 1965. Finally, in 1967, Bahlsen's fifth factory started operations.

Four Decades of Growth: 1950–90

After the reconstruction years, Werner Bahlsen was the driving force behind the company's international expansion. Bahlsen was the first German manufacturer of sweets to be issued an export license after the war. In 1950, the first postwar export shipment with Bahlsen products went to Switzerland. Two years later the company began exporting to the United States. By 1956, Bahlsen products were shipped to 74 countries. After the European Common Market had been established, the company started setting up its own foreign sales offices, starting with France and Italy in 1960. During the 1960s and early 1970s, Bahlsen continued establishing subsidiaries in Western European countries, including Austria, Luxembourg, the Netherlands, Belgium, Denmark, Spain, and the United Kingdom. The company's American sales office, Bahlsen of North America, was set up in 1967. In 1972, all Bahlsen subsidiaries abroad were organized under the umbrella of Bahlsen International Holding AG.

Besides growing internationally, Bahlsen expanded its salty snacks division during the 1960s, mainly by acquisitions. In 1963 the company acquired an interest in the Hamburg-based Wilhelm Liebelt company, a maker of nut snacks. In the following year, Bahlsen bought a majority share in potato-chip maker

Key Dates:

1889: Hermann Bahlsen takes over a cakes and cookies factory in the German city of Hannover.
1891: The company launches Leibnitz Cakes, which will eventually become its flagship product.
1919: The company founder dies.
1930: Hermann Bahlsen's son Hans assumes management of the company and is soon after joined by his brother Werner.
1933: The Express Dose, a one-pound box of wafers, becomes a top-selling product for the company.
1952: Bahlsen begins exporting to the United States.
1956: Hans Bahlsen's son Herman enters the family-owned business.
1960: Bahlsen establishes sales offices in France and Italy.
1975: Werner Bahlsen's son Lorenz enters the family business.
1979: Werner Bahlsen's son Werner Michael joins the company.
1980: American Austin Quality Foods Company is acquired.
1988: Bahlsen products are distributed nationally through wholesalers and central warehouses.
1994: Takeover of French cake and cookie manufacturer St. Michel.
1995: Bahlsen takes over the cookie business of its competitor Brandt.
1996: Hermann Bahlsen withdraws from top management position and takes over subsidiary Austin Quality Foods.
1999: Bahlsen launches PiCK UP! bars.
1999: The company is divided into three independent firms with Bahlsen focusing on sweets.

Flessner in Neu-Isenburg. Both of these companies later became fully owned Bahlsen subsidiaries. In 1966 Bahlsen ventured into the market for industrially baked cakes when the company acquired Oldenburg-based firm Brokat. In 1968 the company took over chocolate maker Gubor Schokoladenfabrik located in the Black Forest and expanded its product line again in 1970 to include pre-baked cake layers, which became very popular among German homemakers and working women. Bahlsen acquired additional production capacity outside Germany in 1965, starting with the takeover of Austrian snacks manufacturer Kelly. Nine years later Bahlsen opened its first production facility abroad in Noyon, France. In 1980, the company acquired the American Austin Quality Foods Inc. based in Cary, North Carolina, establishing a commercial foothold in the United States. In that year the number of Bahlsen employees reached an all-time high of 11,200. With the opening of Bahlsen's second factory Nîmes-Grezan in France in 1981 and the start of operations at a state-of-the-art wafer factory in 1982, the company's expansion of its production capacity also reached a high point.

When an economic recession set in around 1982, the company cut down production and reorganized operations to cut costs. Beginning in 1983, Bahlsen's German factories received

flour from only one supplier, the Hedwigsburger Oker-Mühle. In 1985 the company's sales force was reorganized. Two years later production ceased at the company's oldest factory and headquarters in Hannover. In 1988, a modern new plant started operations in North Carolina. Finally the company reorganized its distribution system, and beginning in 1988 Bahlsen products were distributed through wholesalers and central warehouses.

Bahlsen's Third Generation

The 1990s started out with an unexpected growth opportunity when the former German Democratic Republic reunited with its West German counterpart. People in the five new eastern German states were eager to buy the West German brand products that had been unavailable to them for decades—including Bahlsen cookies. In addition, an almost untapped market was waiting to be exploited in Eastern Europe. Bahlsen acquired the Polish firm Unimarex in Poznan in 1992 and cookie maker Skawina near Kraków, with 1,100 employees, one year later. During the 1990s Poland emerged as one of Bahlsen's new core markets from which the company also started venturing into the Czech Republic, Slovakia, Hungary, and Russia, where the company opened its ''House of Bahlsen'' in St. Petersburg in 1993. However, these triumphs were overshadowed by a severe setback when the company had to recall a batch of potato snacks that turned out to contain spices polluted with salmonella. The so-called ''paprika affair'' cost the company almost DM 50 million and contributed to a first-time net loss. The acquisition in the following year of French cake and cookie manufacturer St. Michel-Grellier S.A.—a family business like Bahlsen itself, with roots going back to the beginning of the 20th century—became an important milestone on Bahlsen's way to an international company: 1994 was the first year in which sales abroad exceeded domestic totals. In 1995, Bahlsen took over the cookie business division from Hagen-based competitor Brandt Zwieback-Biskuits GmbH, including cookie and wafer maker Gottena Keks und Waffelfabrik GmbH & Co. KG in Schneverdingen. As a result of this five-year period of expansion the company's sales passed the DM 2 billion mark for the first time in its history.

Alongside the acquisitions and expansions that Bahlsen had made as the 1990s unfolded, the company also faced formidable challenges, including a stagnating German market and the growth of international competition. To complicate matters, tensions between the family members who had so far successfully steered the company surfaced in 1992. The three Bahlsen brothers who managed the company after the war—Hans, Werner, and Klaus—got along well, all of them belonging to the same generation. However, after Hans Bahlsen's early death in 1959, his son Hermann, who had entered the business in 1956, became the junior partner of his uncle Werner while his cousins Lorenz and Werner Michael were just ten and 12 years old. The two sons of Werner Bahlsen entered the family business in the second half of the 1970s when Hermann Bahlsen was already a managing director. Their father Werner Bahlsen died in 1985 and three years later Klaus Bahlsen retired as managing director. By that time, Hermann Bahlsen was established as not only the leading company figure but also as a leader in the industry. When his cousins—20 years his junior—demanded leadership positions, conflict arose.

In 1992 the conflict erupted publicly when Hermann Bahlsen, backed by a prominent advisory board, demanded to bring an experienced manager from outside into the company to lead a business concern which by that time had roughly 10,000 employees. In opposition to this plan, Lorenz and Werner Michael Bahlsen wanted to preserve family control over the business and believed that they were capable of taking over the leadership of the company. In the end, Lorenz and Werner Michael Bahlsen won the battle. Hermann Bahlsen retired from all management responsibilities at Bahlsen and in return took control of the group's American subsidiary, Austin Quality Foods Inc., the maker of Zoo Animal Crackers, which he sold to Keebler Foods Company in early 2000 for an estimated $250 million. The remaining Bahlsen shareholders were Lorenz and Werner M. Bahlsen and their sister Andrea von Nordeck.

In 1993 the company started restructuring its operations: the sweets and snacks divisions were split, first operationally and later legally. In 1995 Bahlsen was renamed Bahlsen KG, which became the holding company for ten domestic subsidiaries. Bahlsen's international firms were organized under the umbrella of Bahlsen International Holding AG. With markets stagnating and competitive pressure rising, the company turned up a loss again in 1997. Finally, in 1999 the family decided to completely spin off the snacks business under the leadership of Lorenz Bahlsen. Brother-in-law Gisbert von Nordeck was handed over control of Bahlsen's Swiss and Austrian subsidiaries. Werner Michael assumed control of Bahlsen, which kept all the brand-name rights and focused on sweets. After the successful launch of Bahlsen's PiCK UP! bars in 1999, the company focused on product innovation in the premium segment and market penetration in Germany and Eastern Europe, as well as fine-tuning its management and sales organization to compete effectively in a consolidating market.

Principal Subsidiaries

Gottena Keks- und Waffelfabrik GmbH & Co. KG; Bahlsen St. Michel SARL (France); Bahlsen Sweet Sp. z o.o. (Poland); Deleben S.A. (Spain); Bahlsen GmbH (Luxembourg); Bahlsen s.r.l. (Italy); Bahlsen Ltd. (United Kingdom); Bahlsen A/S (Denmark); Bahlsen N.V./S.A. (Belgium).

Principal Competitors

Associated British Foods plc; Groupe Danone; Nestlé S.A.; United Biscuits (Holdings) plc.

Further Reading

"Bahlsen: Nach der Neuordnung die Ziele erreicht," *Frankfurter Allgemeine Zeitung*, May 24, 2000, p. 21.
"Bei Bahlsen hat der Familienstreit die Gruppe nicht gesprengt," *Frankfurter Allgemeine Zeitung*, March 13, 1995, p. 25.
"Das Gebäckwerk in Polen bereitet Bahlsen viel Freude," *Frankfurter Allgemeine Zeitung*, September 14, 1999, p. 27.
Fischer, Oliver, "Zwischen zwei Keksen," *Werben und Verkaufen*, January 22, 1999, p. 76.
"H. Bahlsen feiert Geburtstag," *Lebensmittel Zeitung*, November 7, 1997, p. 20.
Kohlbrück, Olaf, and Frank Roth, "Süsswaren; Bahlsen-Marketingvorstand Hans-Jürgen Grabias setzt auf Carpe Diem," *HORIZONT*, January 25, 2001, p. 22.
Schulze, Peter, "Trennung der Geschäftsfelder; Bahlsen will Potenziale für das Saison- und Ganzjahresgeschäft stärker ausschöpfen," *Lebensmittel Zeitung*, December 15, 2000, p. 57.
Sturm, Norbert, "Dynastien, Aussenseiter, Newcomer: Bahlsen KG, Hannover," *Süddeutsche Zeitung*, August 5, 1995.
"Werner Michael Bahlsen; 3 Fragen," *Lebensmittel Zeitung*, June 9, 1995, p. 3.

—Evelyn Hauser

innovators in image processing

Barco NV

President Kennedypark 35
B-8500 Kortrijk
Belgium
Telephone: (+32) 56-262-611
Fax: (+32) 56-262-262
Web site: http://www.barco.com

Public Company
Incorporated: 1934 as Belgium American Radio
    Corporation
Employees: 4,696
Sales: EUR 751.11 million ($707.2 million)(2000)
Stock Exchanges: Euronext Brussels
Ticker Symbol: BAR
NAIC: 333315 Photographic and Photocopying
    Equipment Manufacturing; 334310 Audio and Video
    Equipment Manufacturing; 334510 Electromedical and
    Electrotherapeutic Apparatus Manufacturing

Barco NV has carved out a niche for itself as a world leader in high-technology visualization systems. The Kortrijk, Belgium company operates through three primary divisions: Barco Projections Systems, BarcoView and BarcoVision. Together these three companies combined to generate sales of EUR 751 million in 2000, of which more than 90 percent was made outside of Belgium, and more than 50 percent outside of Western Europe. The North American market accounts for some 30 percent of the company's sales. Barco has also targeted the Asian market for growth since the late 1990s; those markets, including operations in Japan, China, and Singapore, accounted for 20 percent of the company's 2000 revenues. Barco Projection Systems, which represents 42 percent of company sales, develops and manufactures large-image projection systems, include the Barco Control Room system used by television broadcasters. BarcoView manufactures high-resolution display devices for a variety of industries, as well as graphics control devices and related subsystems. BarcoView designs systems for a variety of industries, from military to air traffic control systems to medical imaging systems. This division contributed

EUR 135 million in revenues in 2000. The company's third division, BarcoVision, manufactures optical detection and inspection systems, sorting machines and other computerized viewing systems with such applications as food sorting and other camera-, laser-, and infrared-based sorting machines; measuring systems; and turnkey systems for textile, plastics, and other industries. In addition to its three core divisions, Barco also operates a Specialized Subcontracting division, which develops customized electronic circuit boards, and Electronic Tooling Systems for printed circuit board manufacture. Quoted on the Brussels stock exchange since 1987, Barco has been seeking to spin off or divest some of its operations. Such was the case with BarcoNet, the company's telecom division, which was spun off as an independent public company in 2000. In 2001, the company shed its Barco Graphics division, which was merged into a joint-venture with Denmark's Purup-Eskofot. The company's plan to spin off its other divisions as public companies was put on hold in 2001 because of the prevailing difficult climate for small-scale public companies. The company is led by president and CEO Hugo Vandamme, who is credited with transforming the company into one of Flemish Belgium's strongest high-tech companies since the early 1980s. Chairman Herman Daems also represents the company's largest shareholder, the Flanders region investment group GIMV.

Belgian Radio and Television Pioneer in the 1930s

Barco was founded in 1934 in the town of Poperinge, in the Flemish-speaking region of Belgium. Founder Lucien de Puydt's initial business was to assemble radios from parts imported from the United States—hence the name of his company, the Belgium American Radio Corporation, or "Barco." The company's radios were highly popular in post-war Belgium and Barco's rising sales enabled it to make investments toward entering another highly promising industry, that of television. By the 1960s, Barco's television had become a mainstay in many of Belgium's living rooms. Part of the company's success was based on its willingness to incorporate compatibility with the variety of European broadcasting standards then being developed, and especially the Secam standard adopted by neighboring France, and the PAL standard adopted in various implementations by much of the rest of Europe. In this way, the company's customers were able to tune into broadcasts from the Netherlands, Luxembourg, France, and Germany, as well as from Belgium itself.

While consumer goods were to remain an important part of Barco's business into the 1980s, the company began to diversify into other markets as early as the 1960s. The first of these came in 1965, when the company developed an automated control system for a Belgian maker of weaving looms. This beginning was eventually to lead the company to regrouping around such high-technology niches.

In 1970 the company diversified again, this time adapting its existing television technology to develop a new generation of television studio monitors for Belgium's national television and radio service, the BRT. The success of these monitors gave the company a new niche market and a means to grow into an internationally operating company.

Barco continued to invest in the high-technology sector during the 1970s and especially in the growing electronics field. At the beginning of the 1980s, Barco struck new success with the launch of its BarcoVision large-screen projection system. This product was to form the basis of the company's strongest sales in the years to come. In the meantime, however, the early 1980s nearly spelled disaster for the company. Heavy competition from Japanese television makers, coupled with a Europe-wide recession that caused a drop in television sales combined to depress Barco's own revenues. The rapid rollout of cable television in some of Barco's core European markets, which eliminated the need for multiple-standard compatibility, further crippled the company's television sales. Barco's heavy reliance on its consumer products—which, despite the company's diversification, still generated more than 85 percent of its sales—sent the company skidding toward a collapse.

Barco found rescue in the form of GIMV, an investment company operated by the Flanders regional government. GIMV took over a majority of Barco's shares and placed Hugo Vandamme as head of the Barco group. GIMV also led a breakup of Barco, which was divided into its two core companies, Barco Industries and Barco Electronics in 1981. Barco

Industries took over the company's industrial automation equipment operations, while Barco Electronics took over the company's projection systems and high-end monitor systems. Barco's former mainstay, consumer goods activities were gradually phased out by the end of the decade.

Barco Breaks Up in the 21st Century

Both Barco Industries and Barco Electronics went public, listing on the Brussels exchange in 1986 and 1987 respectively. The GIMV remained the majority shareholder of both companies, however, and, in 1989, the two companies were again combined together under the single Barco name. The newly recombined company now sought to step up its international presence, establishing itself as a worldwide leader in its various operational niches.

Among the company's new activities was the development of pre-press printing systems, which the company built up by acquiring a number of companies starting in 1989, including Disc Graphics. The operations were then grouped under a new division, Barco Graphics. Another growing area of operation was that of printed circuit boards and other microelectronics products, which was stepped up with the acquisition of full control of its Barco Micro Electronics subsidiary in 1994, as well as the purchase of a majority share in Belgium's Silex the following year. Barco meanwhile was achieving a top spot in the growing market for large-screen video projection systems. Among the strongest of the company's performers was its BarcoNet telecommunications unit, which developed and manufactured communications components and systems for television broadcasting, telecommunications, and Internet applications.

The company stepped up its international expansion during this period as well, setting up offices in Singapore, Australia, and elsewhere. By the end of the decade, Barco had developed a global manufacturing and distribution infrastructure, with production facilities in Belgium, Germany, the Netherlands, Norway, Switzerland, the United Kingdom, the United States, the Czech Republic, Japan, and India, while its network of subsidiaries and sales offices grew to include more than 30 countries. Much of the company's growth came through acquisitions, such as those of Loepfe, of Switzerland, boosting the company's automation division, acquired in 1994, and BarcoNet's purchase of RE, based in Denmark, in 1997, enhancing its telecommunications industry capacity. That same year the company acquired Pulsarr, of the Netherlands, and the United States's Electronic Image Systems.

A new acquisition in the United States followed in 1998 when the company acquired Gerber Systems Corp., a subsidiary of Gerber Scientific, which added its computerized plate graphics systems to Barco Graphics. The company also expanded into Taiwan, Australia, and India that year, and boosted its German process control systems operations with the acquisition of that country's Dr. Seufert.

Yet 1998 proved a low point for the company. Sales at its key Projection Systems division plunged after a fire destroyed one of its production facilities. The company's share price, which had peaked at EUR 260 per share, lost half its value by 1999, and dropped to a low of EUR 96 by 2001. At the same time, principal

Key Dates:

1934: Lucien de Puydt founds Belgium American Radio Corporation to assemble radios from American-made components, then enters television manufacturing in the 1950s.
1965: Company diversifies for the first time into automated control systems.
1970: Barco develops professional studio monitors for BRT, sparking new diversification drive into electronics and industrial activities.
1981: Barco splits into two companies, Barco Industries and Barco Electronics; nearly bankrupt, the company is rescued by GIMV.
1986: Barco Industries goes public on Brussels exchange.
1987: Barco Electronics goes public.
1989: Two Barco companies are re-combined as Barco electronics group, ending the company's consumer goods operations. Barco acquires Disc Graphics, then forms new division, Barco Graphics.
1994: The company Acquires Loepfe, of Switzerland.
1997: Barco acquires Denmark's RE, Pulsarr, of the Netherlands, and the United States's Electronic Image Systems.
1998: Barco acquires Gerber Systems Corp, a maker of plate-to-image systems, which is placed under Barco Graphics; fire destroys Projection Systems manufacturing facility, causing drop in sales.
2000: Barco spins off its BarcoNet subsidiary as an independent, publicly listed company, and makes plans to spinoff its four remaining divisions as well.
2001: Company sheds troubled Barco Graphics in merger with Purup-Eskofot, but places the remainder of its divestiture plan on hold.

shareholder GIMV, which retained a 34 percent share in the company, began to grow impatient for signs of improvement and began pressuring Barco to simplify its operations.

Barco responded by splitting the company in two, spinning off BarcoNet as an independent, publicly listed company. Barco chief Vandamme pledged that this spin-off was only the first of many as the company promised to spin off its remaining four divisions as independent companies soon after. Yet the drop in the stock market at the beginning of the new century forced the company to place this plan on hold—if only temporarily. Indeed, the company suggested that it might complete its divestment program by 2005. The company's relatively flat organization, with each division operated more or less autonomously, with its own management structure, helped simplify the prospects for future spinoffs.

In the meantime, the majority of the company's operations returned to revenue and profit group. Only the company's Barco Graphics division remained in trouble, but that was enough to drag down the group's overall profits. By the summer of 2001, the company sought to divest the business and succeeded in doing so in September of that year, when it reached an agreement to merge Barco Graphics with one of its chief rivals,

Denmark's Purup-Eskofot, held by the family behind the Lego Group. The new company, which received the temporary name of BPE, was to be majority-owned by Purup-Eskofot, although Barco retained a 49 percent share of the company.

Barco was now stripped down to three core and highly complementary divisions: Projection Systems; BarcoView, and BarcoVision, each of which attacked a different niche within an overall visualization specialty. The company planned new external expansion efforts, such as the acquisition of a Japanese rival with complementary operations, possibly by the end of 2001. The company also acknowledged its interest in pursuing acquisition targets in the United States, which by then had grown to its single-largest market. Barco expected its business to grow substantially from the end of 2001—the destruction of the World Trade Center in New York was expected to step up demand for many of the company's core specialties, including air traffic monitoring components. At the same time, the company's Intelliroom video long-distance communication and conferencing systems were expected to help fill the gap of business people more reluctant to travel by air.

Principal Subsidiaries

Barco Graphics n.v.; Barco Coordination Center n.v.; AESTHEDES n.v.; Barco Picotron n.v.; Barco Creative Systems n.v.; Barco Silex s.a.; Barco Elbicon n.v.; ELBICON Industries n.v.; Barco Graphics s.a.; Barco s.a.; BarcoView, Texen s.a. (France); Barco Ltd. (UK); Barco Graphics Ltd.(UK); ARTOIS UK Ltd. (UK); BarcoVision Ltd. (UK); OLDOIS Engineering Ltd. (UK); OMNIWARD Ltd. (UK); GERBER Systems Corporation Ltd. (UK); Barco GmbH (Germany); Barco Sedo GmbH (Germany); BAASEL-SCHEEL Lasergraphics GmbH (Germany); Barco CONTROL ROOMS GmbH (Germany); GERBER Systems GmbH (Germany); Barco Graphics GmbH(Germany); ARTIOS Deutschland GmbH (Germany); BarcoView GmbH (Germany); Barco Finance b.v.(Netherlands); PULSARR Industrial Research b.v. (Netherlands); Barco Holding b.v. (Netherlands); Barco b.v. (Netherlands); Barco Electronic Systems s.a. (Spain); Barco Service S.L. (Spain); Barco s.r.l., Via Monferrato (Italy); B&B International s.r.l. (Italy); Barco Loepfe s.r.l. (Italy); Barco s.r.o., Bieblova 19 (CZ); Gebr. Loepfe A.G., Kastellstrasse (Switzerland); Treepoint A.G. (Switzerland); Barco A.G. (Austria); Barco A/S (Denmark); Barco GesmbH (Austria); Barco Sp. z o.o. (Poland); ELECTRONIC IMAGE SYSTEMS, Inc. (USA); BarcoVision Inc. (USA); Barco Electronic Tooling Systems Inc. (USA); BarcoView Inc. (USA); Barco Graphics Inc. (USA); Barco Inc. (USA); Barco Ltd. (China); GERBER Systems Corporation Ltd. (China); Barco Trading Co. Ltd. (China); Barco Electronic Systems Ltd. (Taiwan); Barco Graphics Private Ltd. (Singapore); Barco Pte Ltd. (Singapore); BarcoView Pte Ltd. (Singapore); Barco Hotline Pvt., Ltd. (India); Barco Electronic Systems Pvt., Ltd. (India); Barco Ltd. (Thailand); Barco Ltd. (Korea); BarcoView Ltd. (Korea); Barco Co., Ltd. (Japan); SIS Corporation, Takara Bld. (Japan); Barco Graphics Co. Ltd. (Japan); Barco Sdn. Bhd. (Malaysia); Barco Electronic Systems Ltd. (Israël); Barco Ltda. (Brazil); Barco Systems Pty Ltd. (Australia); Elbicon Pacific Pty. Ltd. Australia); Barco Electronics SA de CV (Mexico); Barco Ltda. (Chile).

Principal Competitors

Wells-Gardner Electronics Corporation; Advance Display Technologies, Inc.; Vidikron Technologies Group, Inc.

Further Reading

"Barco Cancels Further Spin-off Plans, to Retain Existing 3 Divisions," *AFX Europe*, September 7, 2001.

"Barco fuseert deel grafische divisie met Deens bedrijf," *De Financieel-Economische Tijd*, September 8, 2001.

"Barco heeft Japans bedrijft in vizier," *De Financieel-Economische Tijd*, June 19, 2001.

De Witte, René, "Barco en BarcoNet: het begin van een historische ommezwaai," *De Financieel-Economische Tijd*, October 21, 2000.

—M.L. Cohen

BCE Inc.

1000, rue de la Gauchetiere O.
Bureau 3700
Montreal, Quebec H3B 4Y7
Canada
Telephone: (514) 870-8777
Toll Free: (800) 339-6353
Fax: (514) 870-4385
Web site: http://www.bce.ca

Public Company
Incorporated: 1880 as Bell Telephone Company of
   Canada
Employees: 56,608
Sales: C$18.1 billion ($12.06 billion) (2000)
Stock Exchanges: Toronto New York Swiss
Ticker Symbol: BCE
NAIC: 513322 Cellular and Other Wireless
   Telecommunications; 51331 Wired
   Telecommunications Carriers; 51334 Satellite
   Telecommunications; 51312 Television Broadcasting

BCE Inc. operates as Canada's largest communications company with over 22 million customer connections through its content, commerce, and connectivity-related ventures. BCE's core businesses include Bell Canada, in which it owns 80 percent—Ameritech and its parent SBC Communications Inc. owns the other 20 percent—Teleglobe, a connectivity, content distribution and Internet hosting company; Bell Globemedia, whose business ventures include Canadian private broadcaster CTV, newspaper *The Globe and Mail*, and Web portals Sympatico-Lycos and Globe Interactive; and BCE Emergis, an e-commerce product and services provider. BCE also invests in leading technology-based companies including BCI, CGI, Look Communications, and Telesat Canada through its BCE Ventures arm.

Early History

The history of BCE Inc. can be traced to Canada native Alexander Graham Bell's early communications experiments, which eventually led to the formation of Bell Telephone Company of Canada. Chartered by the Canadian Parliament on April 29, 1880, the company, known informally as Bell Canada, would spend the next 100-plus years growing and diversifying into one of Canada's largest and most successful organizations; in fact, by 1983, Bell Canada could be described as both a telecommunications company and a holding company, with controlling interests in more than 80 other organizations. A move to create a new parent company, Bell Canada Enterprises Inc. (BCE), in 1983, left Bell Canada and its other businesses as subsidiaries of a new holding company. The move also changed the course of history for BCE Inc.

The Canadian phone company's history began in the late 1870s, when Canada's first telephone exchange opened in 1878 in Hamilton, Ontario. Toronto's came second, in 1879. In 1881, the company had exchanges in 40 cities. By 1890, the firm was offering long-distance service over 3,670 miles. From early on, the firm used the slogan, ''A telephone business run by Canadians for Canadians.''

Still in its infancy, the telephone industry differed greatly from that which most countries know today. Initially telephone service was offered only during business hours to about 2,100 telephones. Business owners could use the service by buying pairs of instruments to communicate from home to office, from office to factory, or between other pairs of locations. In 1890, the company began to offer evening and Sunday service.

Although United States-based American Telephone and Telegraph Company (AT&T) owned 48 percent of Bell Canada's stock in 1890, Canadians began buying more of that stock as the company grew. In 1895, Bell Canada incorporated its manufacturing arm, Northern Electric & Manufacturing Company Limited, which was partly owned by AT&T's Western Electric.

Early telephone operators were also different from those known today. In *Telephony*, April 28, 1986, one of those early employees recalled her first days as an operator in 1924. They were times characterized by hard, fast, manual work, usually lasting six days a week. The operators worked on Christmas, all summer long, and without paid sick days. For this, starting pay was C$11.50 per week. In 1924, Bell Canada introduced the dial exchange, so users could dial a party directly without waiting for an operator to come on the line.

By 1925, the company was well on its way to living up to its motto, as Canadians owned 94.5 percent of its stock. The late 1920s saw several advances, including a phone service that linked Canada to Britain via the United States; a carrier system; and, in 1931, the formation of the TransCanada Telephone System. The following year the system made possible the first long distance call from Montreal to Vancouver via an all-Canadian route. In 1933, the U.S. federal securities act ended AT&T's right to purchase new shares.

Expansion: 1950s–60s

During the Great Depression, the need for telephone service dropped substantially. Operators worked only three days per week—about half the hours they had put in previously. When World War II began all operators were summoned back to work. Following the war, in 1945, Bell Canada installed its one-millionth phone. In 1954, Bell Canada merged two subsidiaries, Eastern Townships Telephone Company and Chapleau Telephone System. In 1956, the company merged with Kamouraska Telephone Company and expanded once again in 1957, when it acquired Mount Albert Telephone Company Ltd. Also in 1957, Bell Canada acquired most of Western Electric's share of Northern Electric, which Western held through a subsidiary, Weco Corporation. In 1964, it bought the remainder. By 1958, customers in Canada and the United States could dial other telephone users directly, without going through an operator.

Bell Canada acquired Madawaska Telephone Company in 1960. It gained control in 1962 of Avalon Telephone Company Ltd., which would later be known as Newfoundland Telephone Company Ltd. The following year, Bell Canada bought Monk Rural Telephone Company, changing its name to Capital Telephone Company Ltd. in 1966. Also in 1966, Bell Canada gained a new general counsel, A. Jean de Grandpre, who would soon become a major leader in the company's growth and diversification. A Montreal native, de Grandpre graduated from McGill University in 1943 with a degree in law. He brought two decades of experience gained in his own law practice. Under his leadership, the firm grew rapidly through capital expansion and acquisition. In 1970, for example, the firm acquired control of Oxford Telephone Company Ltd. and Caradoc Ekfrid Telephone Company Ltd., as well as an interest in Telesat Canada, a communications satellite operation. The following year saw the founding of Bell-Northern Research Ltd. (BNR) to consolidate the research and development efforts of Northern Electric and Bell Canada. By 1973, de Grandpre had risen to the post of

president of Bell Canada. Three years later, de Grandpre became chairman and chief executive officer.

In 1973, Bell Canada sold a portion of Northern Electric to the public, and in 1976 Northern Electric changed its name to Northern Telecom Limited. Also in 1976, Bell Canada created Bell Canada International Management, Research and Consulting Ltd. (BCI). The firm, which succeeded Bell's Consulting Services Group founded in the mid-1960s, was designed to offer expertise in telecommunications management and technical planning. Based in Ottawa, BCI's clients included common carriers, private corporations, defense companies, contractors, manufacturers, other consultants, and Northern Telecom. In addition, the firm had business dealings across the globe, including Africa, the Middle East, Europe, the Caribbean, South America, Saudi Arabia, and the United States. According to *Telecommunications*, October 1980, BCI "could serve as a case study of transfer of North American technology to other nations, be they underdeveloped, developing, or fully developed." In addition Northern Telecom and Bell Canada formed B-N Software Research Inc. for the research and development of new software. Late in 1978, Bell Canada introduced a fiber-optic system developed by Northern Telecom Ltd. Designed to simultaneously transmit telephony, data, and video, the company introduced the revolutionary new system during a video telephone conference call between Toronto and London. In 1981 the software firm was merged into Bell-Northern Research.

The Formation of Bell Canada Enterprises Inc.

By 1982, Bell Canada controlled nearly 80 other companies. Switching control of the organizations, including Bell Canada, to a new parent company would simplify the business, de Grandpre believed. Consequently in 1983 Bell Canada Enterprises Inc., known since 1988 as BCE Inc., was created to act as a holding company for a corporate family whose assets amounted to $15 billion and included Bell Canada itself. By designating most of the company's businesses as separate BCE subsidiaries, Bell Canada was the only company that remained under the regulatory control of the Canadian Radio-Television and Telecommunications Commission (CRTC). This benefit led many critics to believe that avoiding CRTC supervision was the sole reason for the restructure. Such criticism was well founded, as relations between the phone company and the CRTC were not always smooth. In 1978, for instance, Bell Canada signed a C$1.1 billion contract to improve Saudi Arabia's telecommunications network. Although the contract did not involve any telephone service to Canadians, the CRTC ruled that profits from the venture must be considered when determining Canadian phone rates, which meant smaller rate hikes for Bell Canada. Still, de Grandpre argued that the purpose of the restructure "was to provide the flexibility necessary for Bell to take on major competitors in telecommunications and microelectronics around the world," reported *Maclean's*, February 14, 1983.

In addition to leadership and coordination, BCE provided equity investments to further the development of its various businesses and to finance their growth via new products, markets, internal growth, or acquisitions. Also in 1983, BCE acquired a sizeable percentage of TransCanada PipeLines Ltd. (TCPL), a move described in BCE's 1983 annual report as "a significant commitment by BCE to western Canada and to the

Key Dates:

1880: Bell Telephone Company of Canada is established.
1895: Northern Electric & Manufacturing Company Ltd. is incorporated.
1924: Bell Canada introduces the dial exchange, which allows users to dial a party directly.
1931: The TransCanada Telephone System is formed.
1933: The U.S. Federal Securities Act prohibits AT&T from purchasing new shares of Bell Canada.
1945: Bell Canada installs its one-millionth phone.
1956: The firm merges with the Kamouraska Telephone Company.
1957: Bell Canada acquires most of Western Electric's shares of Northern Electric.
1964: The company purchases the remaining shares of Northern Electric.
1966: A. Jean de Grandpre joins the firm.
1970: Bell Canada acquires the Oxford Telephone Company Ltd., Caradoc Ekfrid Telephone Company Ltd., and an interest in Telesat Canada.
1973: Bell Canada sells a portion of Northern Electric to the public.
1976: Northern Electric changes its name to Northern Telecom Ltd.
1978: Bell Canada introduces a fiber-optic system developed to transmit telephony, data, and video simultaneously.

1983: Bell Canada Enterprises Inc. is created to act as a holding company for Bell Canada and its subsidiaries.
1987: The CRTC forces the company to lower long distance rates in Ontario and Quebec by nearly 20 percent.
1988: The firm officially adopts the name BCE Inc.
1989: De Grandpre retires; Jean C. Monty is named president of Bell Canada.
1994: Competition increases as the long distance phone industry becomes deregulated.
1995: Earnings fall and Bell Canada continues to loose market share due to increased competition; Northern Telecom is renamed Nortel.
1997: Monty is named chief operating officer and president of BCE; the Canadian Radio-television & Telecommunications Commission opens up competition in both the telephone and cable-TV markets.
1998: BCE creates Bell Nexxia and BCE Emergis; Nortel acquires Bay Networks and officially adopts the corporate name Nortel Networks.
2000: BCE purchases CTV Inc. and Teleglobe Inc. and restructures its businesses into four core operating units; Bell Canada distributes 94 percent of its stake in Nortel Networks to shareholders.

resource sector of the Canadian economy.'' Although Radcliffe Latimer, president of TCPL and a personal friend of de Grandpre, cautioned shareholders to ignore BCE's offer of $31.50 per share, BCE still managed to swiftly take over 42 percent of the company. Following the feud, Latimer admitted defeat and commented in *Maclean's*, January 2, 1984, ''We look at Bell as a first class major shareholder.''

BCE's operations then included Bell Canada and several other locally regulated telecommunications operations: Northern Telecom Limited, a telecommunications manufacturer; Bell-Northern Research Ltd., owned by Bell Canada and Northern Telecom Ltd.; Bell Canada International Inc., a consulting firm; Bell Communications Systems Inc.; TransCanada PipeLines Ltd.; Tele-Direct (Publications) Inc., owned by Bell Canada; and Tele-Direct (Canada) Inc.

Aggressive Expansion Leads to Divestiture

BCE's growth spurt continued through the 1980s. In fact its assets jumped from C$14.8 billion in 1983 to C$39.3 billion in 1989. There were investments in energy, real estate, printing and packaging, mobile and cellular communications, and financial services. BCE also became the first Canadian corporation to earn a net income of more than C$1 billion. Despite that success, however, other aspects of BCE's business did not fare as well. One such failure was the firm's venture into real estate in 1985, through BCE Development Corporation (BCED), a new subsidiary. The company's experiments with printing and with oil and gas investments also brought poor reviews from shareholders.

BCE managed to succeed, despite these setbacks and several conflicts with CRTC. In 1986, the CRTC held a six-week hearing to examine Bell Canada's profits from 1985 through 1987. As a result, the CRTC ordered Bell Canada to refund to consumers C$206 million worth of excess payments made earlier that year as well as in 1985. In addition the commission forced the company to decrease its predicted profits for 1987 by C$234 million by lowering long distance rates in Ontario and Quebec by nearly 20 percent.

In 1989, de Grandpre retired as chairman, but remained on the board of directors as founding director and chairman emeritus. J.V. Raymond Cyr, who had been chief executive officer of BCE since May 1988, took the additional post of chairman in August 1989. Bell Canada gained a new president, Jean C. Monty. Cyr faced the monumental task of restoring the faith of BCE's shareholders, who once considered buying stock in the phone company ''as safe as Canada Savings Bonds,'' reported *Maclean's*, July 30, 1990. To do this, the company decided to take a closer look at the types of businesses best suited to its corporate strategy. It was determined that telecommunications would naturally remain as BCE's core business, but the firm's involvement in real estate was dissolved. It chose to concentrate on financial services and acquired Montreal Trustco Inc., an established firm in that field. It was, however, Bell Canada that brought the most revenue to the parent company. With a record year, Bell Canada contributed C$2.75 per share to BCE's 1989 earnings. In addition, BCE stock continued to be the most widely held stock in Canada.

Six years after taking control of TransCanada PipeLines Ltd., which BCE viewed as a solid, long-term investment, the company decided to sell its stake in the energy business. Owning TransCanada PipeLines was simply not consistent with BCE's core businesses in telecommunications and financial services.

In the early 1990s the holding company BCE Inc. owned subsidiaries in three primary areas: telecommunications services, telecommunications equipment manufacturing, and financial services. Although these subsidiaries made crucial contributions to the success of their parent company, many of them were successful enough to warrant widely recognized reputations of their own. While Bell Canada, the country's largest telecommunications company, provided most of the firm's services in that area, for example, Northern Telecom Limited was responsible for the manufacturing end of the business and was the second-largest such company in North America. BellNorthern Research, the largest private industrial research and development organization in the country, also played a vital role in BCE's research and development activities, while financial services were provided by Montreal Trust.

While BCE hurdled a major challenge in its 1983 restructuring, it underwent a series of additional changes in the 1990s as the atmosphere in the telecommunications industry became increasingly competitive. In fact, BCE's earnings in the early 1990s were less than spectacular—they fell dramatically from C$1.2 billion reported in 1994, to C$782 million in 1995. Bell Canada, responsible for nearly 50 percent of the company's earnings at the time, faced increased competition due to deregulation in the long distance phone industry. Its market share had fallen by nearly 22 percent in 1994, as companies, including Sprint Canada Inc. and Unitel Communications Inc., entered the fray, vying for a piece of the Canadian long distance market.

At the same time, Northern Telecom—renamed Nortel in 1995—was also facing increased competition, especially in foreign markets where it hoped to boost sales related to wireless operations. The firm was known however, for its central switches—a market that reached maturity in the late 1980s. While Nortel faced an uphill battle trying to break into the foreign wireless technologies sector, most of BCE's businesses were in similar fights for market share.

A Shift in Focus: Late 1990s and Beyond

In 1996, Rob Osborne, an executive from Maclean Hunter, was named president of BCE after being hired in 1994. Under his leadership and that of CEO and chairman Lynton Wilson, BCE began its turnaround, securing C$1.15 billion in profits in 1996, a substantial increase over 1995 figures. In fact, a 1997 *Canadian Business* article claimed that BCE had been ''overweight, unfocused, and slow to budge'' during the late 1980s and early 1990s, but that ''over the past few years, spurred by new competition, the obese giant has pulled off an amazing transformation.'' The article also stated that ''the newly buff BCE is emerging as the dominant player in areas that range from old standbys such as local phone service and long-distance communications, to nascent gold mines such as Internet access.''

While it cleaned up its image and shed businesses unrelated to its telecommunications focus, BCE also underwent a series of management changes. During 1997, Jean Monty, the CEO of Nortel credited for its rebirth in the 1990s, was named chief operating officer and president of BCE, while Osborne moved over to head up Bell Canada. Then in February 1998, Osborne resigned unexpectedly from Bell to take over operations at Ontario Hydro.

Amidst the management reshuffling, the CRTC decided in 1997 to allow phone companies to enter the cable-TV market, opening up a potentially lucrative market for BCE. In turn, communications firms could now enter the local calling markets. During this time period, the landscape of the telecommunications industry as a whole began to change dramatically due to consolidation and merger activity. Deals including Worldcom Inc.'s purchase of MCI Communications Corp. and Telecport Communications Group Inc.'s acquisition of ACC Corp. threatened Bell Canada's hold on the local calling market in Canada.

As such, BCE forged ahead with its plans to enter the world of Internet and e-commerce. In 1998, the company created Bell Nexxia, a national broadband company, and BCE Emergis, its entrant into the e-commerce arena. Meanwhile, Nortel acquired Broadband Networks Inc., a leading manufacturer of fixed broadband wireless communications network. It also purchased leading IP networking firm Bay Networks in 1998, changing its name to Nortel Networks after the purchase. In order to gain a stronger foothold in North American markets, BCE sold a 20 percent stake in Bell Canada to Ameritech in 1999.

BCE made several key moves during 2000 that signaled the firm's commitment to its telecommunications and e-commerce businesses. It gained a majority ownership in Aliant Inc., a telephone carrier serving Canada's four Atlantic provinces. It also acquired CTV Inc., Canada's leading private 18-channel television network, and then joined with The Thompson Corporation to create Bell Globemedia. This new venture brought under one corporate structure the operations of CTV, the *Globe and Mail*, and Sympatico-Lycos and Globe Interactive, two leading Web portals. The company also acquired Teleglobe Inc., a global data and Internet services provider.

While BCE was beefing up its media and Internet-related holdings, the company decided it was time to let go of its networking business. After over 100 years of operation together, BCE cut Nortel loose in 2000, selling off 94 percent of its stake in the firm to shareholders. Nortel became an independent global company after the sale—a position that management felt would lead to future growth.

By 2001, BCE had reorganized its operations into four operating units including Bell Canada, Teleglobe, Bell Globemedia, and BCE Emergis. Its other interests were combined into BCE Ventures, a unit responsible for equity investments in technology firms including Bell Canada International, CGI Group, and Telesat. Having successfully battled the increased competition brought on by changing regulations in the telecommunications industry, BCE had emerged as a leading communications, media, and e-commerce-based company. While the industry would no doubt continue changing in the future, BCE appeared to be well positioned for growth in its core business sectors.

Principal Subsidiaries

Bell Canada (80%); Bell Globemedia (70.1%); BCE Emergis (66%); Bell Actimedia; Bell Expressvu; Bell Intrigna (33.3%); Bell Mobility; Bell Nexxia; Aliant (52.8%); Manitoba Telecom Services (21.7%); Northern Telephone; Northwestel; Telebec; Teleglobe Inc. (95.4%); CTV Inc.; *Globe and Mail;* Sympatico-Lycos; Bell Canada International; BCI (73.6%); Bimcor; CGI Group (41.4%); Telesat Canada; BCE Capital.

Principal Operating Units

Bell Canada; Teleglobe; Bell Globemedia; BCE Emergis; BCE Ventures.

Principal Competitors

AT&T Canada Inc.; Rogers Communications Inc.; TELUS Corporation.

Further Reading

"Ameritech Takes On U.S. Rivals in Canada With Bell Canada," *Communications Daily,* March 25,1999.

Austen, Ian, "Telecommunications," *Canadian Business,* July 9, 2001, p. 106.

Corcoran, Terence, "The Old Mindset Behind the New BCE," *National Post,* September 16, 2000, p. D11.

Critchley, Barry, "BCE's Nortel Deal Biggest of Its Kind," *National Post,* July 8, 2000, p. C2.

Demont, Philip, "Osborne's Reputation Put to the Test at BCE," *Financial Post,* March 9, 1996, p. 12.

——, "World Turned Upside Down," *Financial Post,* December 27, 1997, p. 48.

Gray, John, "Waiting for the Wave," *Canadian Business,* May 14, 2001, p. 30.

Hardin, Helen, "Bell Canada Marks its 100th Year by Helping Others," *Telephony,* April 28, 1980.

"Jean Monty," *Telecommunications,* October 1999, p. C9.

Onstad, Katrina, "Chomp!," *Canadian Business,* May 1997, p. 56.

Taylor, Peter Shawn, "Here Today, Jean Tomorrow," *Canadian Business,* March 13, 1998, p. 87.

Venetis, Tom, "BCE Drops Bombshell," *Computer Dealer News,* September 21, 1998, p. 1.

Wickens, Barbara, "Tough Times for Ma Bell," *Maclean's,* July 30, 1990.

—Kim M. Magon
—update: Christina M. Stansell

Bell Sports Corporation

6225 North State Highway 161
Suite 300
Irving, Texas 75038
U.S.A.
Telephone: (469) 417-6600
Fax: (972) 871-8676
Web site: http://www.bellsports.com

Private Company
Incorporated: 1953 as Bell Helmets
Employees: 1,677
Sales: $244.5 million (2000)
NAIC: 33992 Sporting and Athletic Goods Manufacturing

The Bell Sports Corporation is the leading manufacturer of bicycle helmets in the United States and one of the top producers of bicycle accessories in North America. The company, which pioneered the first hard shell bicycle helmet in the mid-1970s, is widely recognized for its long tradition of product innovation and safety. It sells a wide range of bicycle helmets for infants, youths, and adults under three brand names: Bell, Bell Pro, and Giro. It also designs, manufactures, and markets a variety of bicycle accessories, such as bike carriers, locks, headlights, pumps, gloves, and racks, under the brand names Bell, Blackburn, VistaLite, and Spoke-Hedz. The company also markets in-line skating, snowboarding, snow skiing, and water sports helmets. Its products are marketed and sold throughout North America, Europe, Australia, and Asia by specialty retailers as well as mass merchandisers such as Kmart and Wal-Mart. In fact, Wal-Mart sales accounted for more than 30 percent of Bell's total sales in 2000.

Early History

Although Bell Sports generates nearly all of its revenue from the bicycle helmet and accessories industry, its origins can be traced to the colorful helmets that have become a familiar part of the auto racing circuit and to the Los Angeles suburb of Bell, a hotbed of high performance racing for more than 60 years. In 1953, three decades before bicycle helmets entered the mainstream, Roy Richter, a race car designer and driver whose Bell

Auto Parts was at the forefront of the latest in high performance technology, began supplying his customers with a new type of fiberglass helmet. The innovative helmets were manufactured using a high-quality, hand-laminated process. They quickly gained favor with the racing community and were worn by such Indianapolis 500 stars as Bill Vukovich.

In 1957, though, an article appeared in *Sports Cars Illustrated*—the forerunner to *Car and Driver*—that would force Richter to redesign his product. According to the research of a Sacramento physician who had set up a small foundation in the name of his friend, Pete Snell, the victim of a fatal auto racing accident, most contemporary helmets, including the Bell "500" model, were useless; some, in fact, increased the trauma to the head during a crash by concentrating force on a single point of the skull. Richter immediately stopped production and, after acquiring the rights to a liner used by a rival company that had fared better in the tests, designed a new helmet, the Bell 500 TX, which became the first helmet to receive Snell Foundation approval. The innovative helmet would serve as the prototype for Bell's state-of-the-art helmets for years to come and would set a company standard for product safety.

At that time, helmets were made primarily of soft rubber. During the late 1950s, however, two professors at the University of Southern California invented the process of using polystyrene, or foam, and Bell again had the forethought to purchase the rights to the more protective substance. The company then established a laboratory—the first of its kind in the United States—to conduct tests on the promising material and build its own foam machines at a cost of just $7,000 a piece. During the 1960s, the company began supplying helmets to the U.S. Ski Team. Bell also found its niche manufacturing motorcycle helmets and evolved into the leader in the industry.

Expansion in the 1970s

The demand for motorcycles exploded in the 1970s, and as many as 55 domestic companies began manufacturing helmets. But success for the vast majority of helmet producers was short-lived. As damages awarded in product liability cases skyrocketed, it became increasingly difficult for companies to obtain insurance. Distributors and dealers were hesitant to carry a

---

Company Perspectives:

Since its beginnings in 1954, Bell has maintained its world-wide leadership position in helmets. We have earned our reputation by insisting on quality in design, workmanship, materials, safety, and performance.

---

product not covered by insurance. Although product liability concerns forced all but around ten companies to stop manufacturing motorcycle helmets by the mid-1980s, Bell solidified its position in the market by establishing an unparalleled reputation for product safety. Although Bell, like its competitors, faced a number of lawsuits, it was forced to pay only one judgment, for $25,000 in 1977. That record of success, a benefit of having its own testing facilities, would continue well into the 1990s, as Bell won 27 straight cases over a 15-year period.

Although Bell focused its attention on motorcycle helmets during the remainder of the decade, it had enough vision to develop other aspects of its business. In 1975, the company quietly introduced a product that would later become its major source of revenue: the Bell Biker, the first hard shell bicycle helmet introduced onto the market. Prior to that introduction, cyclists wore leather helmets, if they wore any protection at all. At this time, though, efforts to market the high-end product were modest; Bell, the nation's largest manufacturer of motorcycle helmets through the early 1980s, attempted to take advantage of the continuing surge in the motorcycle industry.

Despite its preeminent position in this niche market, the $20 million company struggled to make a steady profit. In 1983, Phillip Matthews, a former executive at Wilson Sporting Goods, and two partners acquired Bell Sports. They enlisted the management services of Terry Lee, a Wilson executive in charge of sales and distribution, to help run the company. That same year, though, the motorcycle boom came to a halt and with it the demand for helmets. Matthews's partners wanted out of the deal, and Bell was forced to go into debt to buy back their shares. With nearly every penny of cash flow now going toward debt service, the company could no longer afford to produce new designs, the hallmark of the Bell reputation. What is more, quality slipped: some helmets even left the factory with crooked noses. A better financed Japanese competitor, Shoei, with its superior aerodynamic designs and venting technology at similar prices, began swallowing up some of Bell's U.S. market share.

The New Focus of the 1980s

While the company's motorcycle helmet business was declining, though, bicycle riding suddenly grew in popularity, heightening the demand for helmets and creating an opportunity for the company to return to profitability. Although bicycle helmets comprised only 10 percent of revenues in 1984, sales started growing at 50 percent per year, thanks in part to the introduction of an infant bicycle helmet, the Li'l Bell Shell. Two years later, the company, now producing about 500,000 helmets a year, broadened its product line with the acquisition of its first bicycle accessory company and began manufacturing such items as bicycle pumps, child seats, red flashing safety

lights, and car racks. In 1988, Bell began marketing its products in Europe. That same year the company generated $24 million in revenues, while recording a modest profit, despite the continuing decline of its motorcycle helmet business.

Just before the close of the decade, the company underwent a major restructuring to prepare itself for the changing focus of its business. On November 16, 1989, a group of investors and lenders, including the former management and owners, took over ownership of the company through a leveraged buyout. The Bell Sports Holding Company, as it then became known, consisted of four related businesses engaged in the manufacture and marketing of motorcycle helmets, bicycle helmets, bicycle accessories, and auto racing products.

Changes in the Early 1990s

In 1991, Bell finally ended its 37-year involvement in the motorcycle helmet business, selling its manufacturing and licensing rights to an Italian competitor called Bieffe for an estimated $15 million. "We had to laser-focus on spending the scarce resources we had in the most effective way," Lee told *Forbes* magazine's Zina Moukheiber. Although the motorcycle market did rebound, Lee's strategy proved to be a success. Using the money generated from the sale to reduce debt, the company was now in better position to expand its most promising product lines. Bell, for instance, was now able to market its Li'l Bell Shell aggressively through advertisements in leading parents' magazines. By 1992, the company, with the help of strong expansion in its European markets, was generating $5 million in net profit on sales of $64.5 million, up 36 percent from the previous year.

In an attempt to reduce debt further and generate capital for continued expansion, Lee sold 52 percent of the company in an initial public offering made in April 1992. At that time, the company changed its name to Bell Sports Corporation and was divided into four operating divisions: Bell, a Norwalk, California distributor of the company's premium brand of helmets; Rhode Gear, a Providence, Rhode Island distributor of entry- and mid-level helmets and non-helmet bicycle accessories; BSI, which markets helmets to discount stores and mass merchants such as Wal-Mart, Toys 'R' Us, and K-mart; and, finally, Bell Sports Manufacturing, a Rantoul, Illinois manufacturing and testing facility.

The same year that Bell went public it benefited from legislation that promised to create a boon in its principal market: New Jersey became the first state to require children under the age of 14 to wear bicycle helmets. New York, Connecticut, Georgia, Tennessee, Virginia, and Oregon quickly followed suit. A number of county and municipal governments across the country passed mandatory helmet laws as well. With California and other large states considering similar legislation, the small growth industry appeared ready to explode into a big business.

Bell controlled 50 percent of the bicycle helmet market at the time and, by virtue of its size, was the lowest-cost producer in the industry. The company was in a solid position to take advantage, having established relationships with a number of mass merchants, such as Wal-Mart and Kmart, as well as independent bike dealers. Moreover, Bell was the only vertically on Bell's marketing territory. And, for the first time in Bell Sports history, sales declined.

Key Dates:

1953: Roy Richter begins selling fiberglass helmets at his auto parts store and establishes Bell Helmets.
1957: Richter begins to redesign his product due to safety concerns; Bell establishes the first helmet test laboratory in the United States.
1960: Bell begins supplying helmets to the U.S. Ski Team.
1975: The Bell Biker bicycle helmet is introduced.
1983: Phillip Matthews acquires Bell Sports and partner Terry Lee is named CEO.
1984: The firm launches infant bicycle helmet Li'l Bell Shell; bicycle helmet sales begin growing by 50 percent per year.
1988: Bell begins marketing its products in Europe.
1989: A group of investors and Bell management take over ownership of the firm through a leveraged buyout.
1991: The company sells its motorcycle helmet business.
1992: Bell goes public and changes its name to Bell Sports Corporation.
1994: Revenue climbs to $116 million.
1995: The firm acquires competitor American Recreation Company Holdings, Inc.
1997: Due to weakening demand, the company posts a $18.1 million loss.
1998: Investment firms purchase Bell Sports and take it private; Mary George is named CEO.
1999: Bell restructures and consolidates all manufacturing operations to its Illinois plant.
2000: A management-led recapitalization is finalized; corporate headquarters move from San Jose, California to Irving, Texas.

Aggressive Marketing and Expansion in the Mid-1990s

In an attempt to stay ahead of the competition—which quickly grew to about 50 companies—and regain the confidence of investors, Bell made several strategic moves. First, the company broadened its distribution network, making its BSI helmet, which already was being sold by Wal-Mart and K-mart, available to any store that wanted to carry the line. Whereas supplying discount stores with Bell products may have offended some of the company's regular bike shop customers, it was crucial for the company to further expand its control of the mass merchant market, which in 1994 was responsible for approximately 80 percent of all bicycle helmet sales, compared with only 20 percent three years earlier.

To support this full-scale movement into the mass market, Bell launched its most aggressive advertising campaign to date. The program included a national advertising and promotional campaign on television stations such as ESPN and MTV, as well as on other local and national spots, in magazines written for bicycle and sports/fitness enthusiasts, and in a few general publications. Bell's extensive advertising program was designed not only to promote the quality of the Bell brand name but to educate consumers on the importance of wearing bicycle helmets as well. Another segment of the company's marketing strategy was evident in its continued support of amateur and professional athletics. In 1994, for instance, the company sponsored more than 1,000 cyclists, triathletes, Indianapolis 500 racers, in-line skaters, and wheelchair racers, making the Bell name visible to millions of viewers, spectators, and potential purchasers. At the same time, the company strengthened its commitment to the National SAFE KIDS Campaign, which works to protect children from death and injury by promoting helmet use.

While trying to make the Bell name more visible in the United States, the company also attempted to strengthen its position in the global marketplace. The company began marketing its helmets in Europe in the late 1980s, opening its first European sales office, in Paris, in 1990 and its first European manufacturing facility, in southern France, later that same year. During the early 1990s, Bell also began developing a sales and distribution network in the Asia-Pacific region. The large amount of capital needed to initiate these endeavors, however, combined with the immaturity of these markets, prevented the international divisions of the company from making a substantial contribution to overall corporate profitability. In Canada, though, where mandatory helmet legislation passed in two Canadian provinces in 1995 (covering an estimated 13.4 million adults and children), Bell became the market leader.

In addition to more aggressive marketing and geographical expansion, Bell attempted to improve its performance through acquisitions. Chief among these purchases was the company's 1995 purchase of American Recreation Company Holdings, Inc., the nation's second largest helmet manufacturer at the time, with a 22 percent market share. A distributor of bicycles and bicycle accessories through 2,500 retailers, American Rec-

---

integrated manufacturer in the industry, producing everything from the polystyrene inner lining to the glossy paint on the exterior of its helmets, enabling the company to minimize costs and to monitor product quality. As the only public company in the industry, Bell excited a number of investors on Wall Street; by late 1993 its stock had soared to $49 per share, an increase of more than 225 percent from its original offering of $15. Meanwhile, sales soared to a record $82.6 million and profits moved up to $7 million. Fiscal year 1994 proved to be another banner year as revenue jumped to $116 million and profits jumped to $10.4 million.

The meteoric rise of the company's stock, though, proved to be short-lived. Bell's success quickly attracted a host of competitors. There were few obstacles to entering the market, as bicycle helmets were not difficult to fabricate and plastic and foam were the only materials needed. In fact, the industry as a whole suffered from a slowdown in the passage of mandatory helmet legislation. Expectations for the market were exceedingly high, resulting in an inordinate growth in the market. For Bell, this represented an unprecedented drop in performance. Not only did stock prices fall below the $20 range, but revenue and profits declined as well. For the first time in four years, the company reported a loss as top competitors such as American Recreation, Troxel Cycling, and Giro Sport Designs encroached

reation also marketed Mongoose and Pro Class mountain and road bikes for adults and children through 750 outlets at the time of the deal. The $75 million purchase represented Bell's largest acquisition to date and promised to strengthen its leadership position in North America. Moreover, the combination of complementary products shared by the two companies represented the potential for significant economies of scale and lower production costs.

The Late 1990s and Beyond

As Bell Sports entered the latter half of the decade, its corporate headquarters were moved to Scottsdale, Arizona. Just one year after the American Recreation purchase, Bell made another strategic move and bought former competitor Giro Sport Designs. Bell appeared to be well positioned to make giant strides in the industry after these purchases. At the same time, the actions of state and local legislators also promised to play a key role in the demand for bicycle helmets. In fact, four additional U.S. states and two Canadian provinces passed mandatory helmet legislation in 1996, representing a potential market of more than 22 million adults and children.

In 1997, however, demand related to helmet legislation began to level off and Bell once again faced increased competition. To maintain its hold over the market, Bell was forced to implement price cuts. Although the effort proved to secure its market share, Bell reported a $18.1 million loss for fiscal 1997. During that year, the company divested its Mongoose and SportRack—a Canadian firm it had purchased in 1995—businesses and closed its plant in Memphis, Tennessee.

During 1997, Bell sought out the services of investment bank Montgomery Securities to find buyers for the company in the hope of stabilizing its financial situation. Sure enough, investment management firms Charlesbank Capital Partners LLC and Brentwood Associates Buyout Fund II LP stepped forward to purchase the company in August 1998 for $200 million. Its new owners eyed Bell as a lucrative investment opportunity and set plans in motion to expand the firm's global presence as well as to beef up its existing product line by expanding into helmets and accessories for extreme sports like snowboarding. That year, Bell executive Mary George was named CEO after Lee announced his retirement.

Under new ownership, Bell made several key changes to its business operations. It sold its auto racing helmet business and instead began licensing the Bell brand name for auto racing helmets and automotive accessories. The firm also shuttered its manufacturing plants in Santa Cruz, California, Canada, and Ireland, and sold its facility in France. The move consolidated all manufacturing operations to its Rantoul, Illinois facility and was done in an attempt to control operating costs.

Bell entered the new millennium with additional changes on the horizon. In August 2000, Chartwell Investments purchased a majority interest in the firm from both Brentwood and Charlesbank in a management-led recapitalization of Bell. George, who was named chairman after the deal, commented on the purchase in a 2000 company press release stating, "We have enjoyed a rewarding and productive partnership with Brentwood and Charlesbank. During the two years since Brent-

wood and Charlesbank took the company private, Bell has substantially improved its market position and financial performance." George also added, "With our new partners at Chartwell, Bell Sports continues to be one of the strongest capitalized companies in the industry."

During that year, Bell also moved its corporate headquarters from San Jose, California, to Irving, Texas. The firm's retail operations—those serving mass merchandisers—moved to the new Texas facility while business operations related to specialty retail markets including independent bike shops and Internet sales moved to a company-owned facility in Santa Cruz, California. Although Bell was positioned for growth—it controlled nearly 60 percent of the bicycle helmet market—the industry as a whole experienced a downturn during the first years of the new decade. Whereas sales increased during 2000, the firm expected a decline in fiscal 2001. As such, Bell closed its Canadian distribution facility, discontinued its Rhode Gear and Hydrapak product lines, and announced job cuts. Despite the slowdown in the American economy, Bell management was determined to remain a leader in the cycling and sport helmet industry and eyed these restructuring efforts as key to staying ahead of competition.

Principal Subsidiaries

Bell Sports Inc.; Blackburn Designs Inc.; VistaLite Inc.; Giro Sport Designs International Inc.

Principal Competitors

Trek Bicycle Corp.; Variflex Inc.

Further Reading

"Bell Sports: Hats Off?," *Financial World,* August 2, 1994, pp. 14–15.

Cook, Anne, "Bike-Safety Push a Boon to Rantoul Helmet Maker," *Champaign (Illinois) News-Gazette,* May 8, 1994.

Delaney, Ben, "Bell Sports Shakes Up Organization," *Bicycle Retailer and Industry News,* July 1, 2001, p. 1.

Frothingham, Steve, "Bell Sports Emerges As a Powerhouse," *Bicycle Retailer and Industry News,* March 15, 1995.

Howard, J. Lee, "Living Costs Drive Bell Sports Away," *Business Journal,* June 30, 2000, p. 11.

Moukheiber, Zina, "Mr. Lee, Meet Mr. Murphy," *Forbes,* February 13, 1995, p. 42.

Perez, Christine, "Bell Sports Rolling into Dallas," *Dallas Business Journal,* June 30, 2000, p. 1.

Pressey, Debra, "Bell Sports Hopeful After Lackluster '94," *Champaign (Illinois) News-Gazette,* March 26, 1995.

Tamaki, Julie, "Heady Sales or Hogtied Business?: Motorcycle Helmet Law Runs Up Against Liability, Harley Riders," *Los Angeles Times,* October 28, 1991, p. D1.

Taylor, Dennis, "Bell Sports: Tough Shell Company That Cracked the Gen-X Market," *Business Journal,* March 5, 1999, p. 3.

——, "Investment Firms Acquires Bell Sports," *Business Journal,* August 24, 1998, p. 1.

Wiles, Russ, "Bell Sports Gets OK to Buy Maker of Bikes, Accessories," *Arizona Republic,* June 28, 1995, p. C2.

Yates, Brock, "Reinventing the Wheel," *Car and Driver,* September 1993, pp. 107–12.

—Jason Gallman
—update: Christina M. Stansell

Billabong
International
Limited

Billabong International Ltd.

1 Billabong Place
Burleigh Heads, Queensland 4220
Australia
Telephone: (+61) 75 589 9899
Fax: (+61) 75 589 9800
Web site: http://www.billabong.com

Public Company
Incorporated: 1977 as Gordon & Rena Merchant Pty
  Ltd.
Employees: 500
Sales: A$380.2 million ($196.94 million)(2001)
Stock Exchanges: Australian
Ticker Symbol: BBG
NAIC: 315222 Men's and Boy's Cut and Sew Shirt
  (Except Work Shirt) Manufacturing; 315224 Men's
  and Boy's Cut and Sew Trouser, Slack, and Jean
  Manufacturing; 315228 Men's and Boy's Cut and
  Sew Other Outerwear; 315232 Women's and Girl's
  Cut and Sew Blouse and Shirt Manufacturing; 315233
  Women's and Girl's Cut and Sew Dress
  Manufacturing; 315239 Women's and Girl's Cut and
  Sew Other Outerwear Manufacturing

Billabong International Ltd. markets apparel and accessories designed for surfing, skateboarding, and snowboarding. The company offers more than 2,200 products, including Board shorts; t-shirts; swimwear; shorts, pants, and jeans; fleece tops; "jumpers" or pullover sweaters; jackets; backpacks; sports eyewear; and many other products, primarily for young men and women. Billabong products are sold through licensees or directly from the company and are available in extreme sports shops in over 60 countries worldwide. In the United States, Billabong is among the top three brands of surfing apparel and in its home country of Australia Billabong is the leading brand.

From Kitchen Table Operation to International Brand

Billabong International started at the kitchen table in Gordon and Rena Merchant's small, rented apartment on the Gold Coast of Australia. In 1973, the husband and wife team began to sew and sell knee length Board shorts designed for the rigors of surfing. The Merchants sold their Board shorts to surfing shops on the Gold Coast on consignment for A$4.50 per pair, selling A$5,000 in merchandise the first year in business.

The immediate success of the product and retailer demand persuaded the Merchants to give a name to their company and to add labels inside the Board shorts in 1974. They chose the name "Billabong" because of its uniqueness to Australia, being the aboriginal word often used to mean "oasis." They developed the Wave device logo to create a recognizable representation of the business.

The business continued to grow and Billabong opened its first factory, a 1,000 square-foot space in 1975. By 1977, annual sales reached A$100,000. That year the company failed to get a business loan, but the following year Billabong obtained its first bank loan of A$7,500, allowing the company to relocate to a larger, 7,500 square-foot production facility. With continued innovation and new products designed for the needs of surfers and beachcombers throughout Australia, Billabong reached the milestone of A$1 million in annual sales in 1981.

As surfing developed into a professional sport during the 1970s and 1980s, Billabong positioned its brand products as integral to the surfer lifestyle. Promotions centered on surfer magazines and sponsorship of surfing events and individual surfers. In 1984, Billabong began to sponsor the World Final Surfing Contest, held annually in Hawaii, its largest event to date. The event provided international exposure just as the company started to expand into international markets.

Billabong began to export products to Japan and the United States, particularly Hawaii, in 1979, and the company decided to license its name and product designs in the early 1980s. Licensees sold Billabong products in New Zealand, Japan, and the United States. In 1983, Billy International, co-founded by Bob Hurley, established Billabong in the United States, with a design and production facility located in Costa Mesa, at the center of the surfwear industry in Orange County, California. After a decade in operation, Billy International built Billabong into a nationally recognized brand, with $25 million in annual sales. A 1988 license agreement established Billabong in the United Kingdom as a base for marketing and distribution throughout Europe. In 1992, Billabong took direct control of the European operations, relocating Billabong Europe's headquarters in Hossegor, France, with sales offices in Spain, France, and the United Kingdom, where most European sales originated. Billabong surfwear became available at popular surfing areas in South Africa in 1989, through direct sales, and in Indonesia in 1991 through a licensee.

Billabong's growth as a popular brand and expansion of its product line required new production facilities. The existing facility had been expanded several times to 40,000 square feet by 1989, when the company began operation of an in-house screen-printing shop. In 1992 the company opened a specially designed and constructed, 45,000 square-foot factory and sales showroom. New products at this time attracted crossover board sport enthusiasts in skateboarding and snowboarding. Billabong sold certain items to skateboarders using the "Bad Billy" logo in 1987, but did not target that group much until the mid-1990s. Thin Air, a subsidiary of Billabong formed in the early 1990s, produced jackets for use by surfers, for warming up after riding a few waves, or snowboarders. Thin Air produced snowboard carriers in the form of a backpack. International expansion at this time involved licensees in Brazil (1994); Peru (1995); South Africa (1995); Singapore (1996); and Chile (1997). By the end of fiscal year June 30, 1997 Billabong recorded revenues of A$47.4 million from direct product sales and licensing royalties, the latter at 5 percent to 7 percent of licensee sales. In 1998, Billabong built another, larger production facility and showroom at Burleigh Heads.

Billabong Loses U.S. Licensee in 1998

In June 1998, Bob Hurley of Billy International decided not to renew his license to produce and sell Billabong apparel. Hurley did not want to go in the direction that Merchant planned

to take the company, selling accessories and junior women's clothing, and had decided to start his own line of surfwear. The news caused a wave of trepidation in the surfwear industry as Billabong rated among the top three brands in many surf shops, bringing approximately $70 million in sales to Billy International in 1998. Also, the pending debut of Hurley's line of surfwear raised speculation about new competition for Billabong. The brand was untested in the market, but Hurley had established a strong reputation as a businessman in the industry.

Billabong initially sought to find another licensee, but decided to form its own subsidiary, Burleigh Point Ltd., doing business as Billabong USA. The formation of the subsidiary hinged on the infusion of new capital from a consortium of investors led by Gary Pemberton and Matthew Perrin. Pemberton, who became a non-executive chairman at Billabong, brought experience as chairman of Quantas Airways and leadership in other prominent Australian companies, particularly in the area of international expansion. Matthew Perrin took the position of chief executive officer at Billabong while Gordon Merchant led Billabong USA. The consortium purchased Rena Merchant's 49 percent interest in Billabong for A$24.6 million ($14.3 million) in preparation for taking the company public. In support of the long-term well-being of the company, the investors provided capital to form Billabong USA.

Maintaining a presence in surf and extreme sports shops in the United States was essential for Billabong to expand its market share. Billy International's license expired in June 1999, and Billabong had to act quickly to maintain an uninterrupted flow of merchandise to surf shops. Hurley kept the manufacturing facility in Costa Mesa for his new company, so Billabong had to find a manufacturing facility and prepare it for operation in a matter of months. In November, the company leased an 80,000 square-foot facility in Irvine, California.

Merchant selected Paul Naude, a former executive at surfwear manufacturer Gotcha International, for president of Billabong USA. While Hurley retained many key employees, many chose to remain with Billabong, including national sales manager Richard Sanders and ten of 14 sales representatives. For the sales staff, to stay with Hurley meant a big cut in pay and to sell an unknown brand under Hurley. Naude's reputation in the surfwear industry served to attract top designers and other high profile staff members to Billabong. The hiring process generated controversy and change in the surfwear industry, with several positions being filled by people from competing companies.

When Billabong USA displayed samples of its summer 1999 line at the winter trade shows, it reassured surfwear retailers that the Billabong brand would endure the changes in operations. Billabong found itself in the rather odd position of having Hurley present Billabong surfwear as well, selling the line next to Hurley's debut line of surf apparel. Billabong was pleased with the Hurley's Billabong line and resulting sales. Billabong expected sales in the United States to account for approximately 50 percent of total revenues, as direct control of the market brought product revenues rather than royalties.

Also, in January 1999, Billabong debuted a line of clothing for girls and juniors. With Billabong Girls the company entered a largely untapped, niche market of young women, 16 to 22 years old, who often purchased young men's surf, skate, and snowboarding apparel. The line featured body conscious knits, sheer knits, mesh, unusual floral prints, and bottoms which ranged from hot pants, to Capri pants, to loose, baggy-style pants. Wholesale prices ranged from $15 for a t-shirt to $120 for a jacket. Advertising targeted young women through general magazines, such as *Teen* and *Seventeen*, as well as specialty magazines, such as *Surfer, Surfing,* and *Wahine* (the Hawaiian word for ''girl''). Billabong promoted the line through sponsorship of girls surf and skate meets and of world-class surfers, such as Malia Jones and Layne Beachley, spokeswomen for Billabong and members of the Billabong Girls sports team. Merchant combined Billabong Girls with Billabong USA, operating the two subsidiaries as one division from the facility in Orange County.

Public Offering of Stock Prompts Restructuring in 1999 and 2000

During 1999–2000 Billabong prepared to go public as means to obtain funds that allowed the company to diversify its product line and to expand its reach internationally. With its products being sold in more than 60 countries through licensees, Billabong wanted to obtain direct control over production and distribution. Billabong signed licensing agreements with manufacturers in Israel in 1998 and in Venezuela in 1999. Billabong gained direct control of business in Canada and New Zealand in 1999 and 2000, respectively, where licensees had previously operated. The company also planned to convert Australian Accessories Business, maker of Billabong hats, backpacks, and other accessories, to direct company control in July 2000.

Through direct operation of international operations Billabong sought to improve the marketing and promotion of its products, gaining higher margin income rather than royalty payments. Through management information systems, financial oversight, quality control, and economies of scale through central product sourcing, Billabong hoped to facilitate efficient market expansion as it diversified its product line. The company employed in-store merchandisers and account managers to oversee in-store presentation of its brand merchandise and the international network of commissioned salespeople became direct employees of Billabong with regular pay and sales incentives. Billabong formed a central product sourcing subsidiary in Hong Kong in 1999. While external suppliers existed, 40 percent of licensee sourcing originated with Billabong, allowing the company to reduce costs, provide consistent quality, insure timely delivery, and become flexible with changing market conditions. Also, the company established direct distribution facilities in Victoria and New South Wales, Australia.

At the time of the initial public offering of stock, Billabong products were sold in more than 2,600 surf and extreme sports shops around the world. Revenues at Billabong nearly doubled from A$64.5 million during fiscal year ended June 30, 1998 to A$112.3 million during fiscal 1999 on the strength of the U.S. market. Billabong USA recorded revenues of A$25.6 million in 1999, resulting from three months in sales of men's products, after taking over from Billy International, and six months of sales in young women's products, after the debut of Billabong Girls. Billabong products were distributed through over 900 surf, snow, and skate shops in the USA. In Australia sales to 600 accounts, for a total of 850 retail outlets, reached A$46.3 million in fiscal 1999. In Europe, where the product line included wet suits, accessories, and snowboarding equipment, Billabong products sold through 1,100 independent retail outlets in 25 countries and two company-owned stores in France. European sales generated A$40.4 million in sales. Billabong planned to expand into North Africa, the Middle East, and Asia, to expand its line of snowboard apparel and accessories in the United States, and to launch a line of swimwear for young women.

In July 2000, Billabong initiated the sale of 120.4 million shares of stock, including 11 million shares from oversubscription. Shares sold to institutions at A$2.60 per share and to retail investors at A$2.30 per share, each accounting for about half of stock purchases. The IPO raised A$295 million in capital, exceeding the goal of A$277 million. Strong demand for Billabong stock required the offering to close three days ahead of schedule, with the exchange price rising to more than A$3 per share on the Australian Stock Exchange. The stock offering included half of Gordon Merchant's 51 percent interest in the company, with 60 percent of total company shares sold.

One of the first actions that Billabong took in extending its international reach was to take over the licensee operation in Japan, the fourth largest market for surfwear, after the United States, Europe, and Australia. While the licensee had sold $13 million in merchandise, compared to the leading surfwear brand, Quiksilver, at $43 million, Billabong planned to capture a greater share of the Japanese market. With headquarters in Osaka and a sales office in Tokyo, Billabong began official operation in Japan on January 1, 2001.

In early 2001, Billabong sought to diversify its product line without diluting its brand name by purchasing two apparel and accessories companies, Von Zipper and Element, both based in the United States. Von Zipper specialized in sunglasses and eyewear for extreme sports, such as snow goggles. Von Zipper formed in 1999 and quickly established itself as an up and coming brand. Element, founded in the early 1990s, was considered one of the leading brands of skateboarding apparel and accessories worldwide. Billabong retained key staff at both companies and allowed them to retain their unique identities and independent operations, providing capital resources to expand product lines and distribution to select retailers. News of the acquisitions prompted an increase in Billabong's share price to over A$5.50.

By fiscal 2001, sales at Billabong increased to A$380.2 million, 15 percent higher than projected in the prospectus and 68 percent higher than the previous year, while net profit rose to A$42.1 million, 12.6 percent higher than forecast. Taking direct control of license distribution had a strong impact on revenues as did the formation of Billabong USA. Sales in Australia and Asia increased 26 percent to A$118.8 million, sales in North America increased 50 percent to $179.3 million, and sales in Europe, where distributors in Italy and Belgium were converted to company-controlled operations, sales increased 50 perfect to A$82.1 million. Billabong expected sales to grow approximately 15 percent in Australia/Asia and 25 percent in North America and Europe in 2002. In the United States, Pacific Sunwear, a chain of beachwear clothing stores accounting for

20 percent of sales at Billabong USA, announced plans to double the number of outlets in the United States.

While Billabong has maintained its commitment to surfing throughout its history through sponsorship of events and athletes, in 2001 Billabong initiated a new extreme surfing event, the Billabong Odyssey. This event challenged surfers to a three-year search for the biggest waves in the world, specifically, a search for the never-before surfed 100-foot wave. The idea for the project came as an extension of Project Neptune, an expedition to a surf break 100 miles off the coast of San Diego. The legendary Cortes Bank sea-mount had never been surfed before, but Mike Parsons, a surfer on the Billabong Team, rode a 66-foot wave, winning the Swell XXL for the year's biggest wave. This adventure exhibited new possibilities for mid-ocean surfing by using motorized watercraft to tow surfers farther out to sea, an extreme form of surfing that began in the 1990s. Billabong invited internationally renowned surfers to participate in the event and planned eight expeditions of four to six surfers. Billabong offered a prize of A$1,000 per foot of face height to the surfer who rode the biggest wave each year and an A$500,000 prize to any surfer to ride a 100-foot wave.

Principal Subsidiaries

Burleigh Point Ltd.; Element; Thin Air; Von Zipper.

Principal Competitors

Burton Snowboards; Gotcha International; Hurley International; Quiksilver, Inc.; Rip Curl; Rusty International.

Further Reading

"Australia's Billabong Acquires US-Based Element," *AsiaPulse News*, July 3, 2001.

"Australia's Billabong Acquires US-Based Sunglasses Company," *AsiaPulse News*, March 9, 2001.

"Australia's Billabong Public Offer Closes After Strong Demand," *AsiaPulse News*, July 28, 2000.

"Billabong Founder on the Crest of a Wave as Firm Debuts on ASX," *AsiaPulse News*, August 11, 2000.

"Billabong's Rise Follows Pacific Sunwear," *Los Angeles Times*, March 8, 2001, p. 4.

Earnest, Leslie, "Billabong Fills Three Spots on U.S. Team," *Los Angeles Times*, September 9, 1998, p. 9.

——, "Front Line of Surf-Wear War," *Los Angeles Times*, February 26, 1999, p. 1.

——, "Hurley Rides Enthusiasm for New Styles," *Los Angeles Times*, September 9, 1998, p. 13.

Marlow, Michael, "Bob Hurley Giving Up Billabong's U.S. License," *Daily News Record*, June 10, 1998, p. 4.

Marriner, Cosima, "Billabong Catches Boomer," *Sydney Morning Herald*, August 12, 2000.

——, "Billabong to Drop in on Rival's Wave in Japan," *Sydney Morning Herald*, July 10, 2000.

Rennie, Philip, "Meet the Chairman of the Surfboard," *Business Review Weekly*, December 1, 2000, p. 46.

Williamson, Rusty, "Billabong Catches U.S. Wave," *WWD*, June 3, 1999, p. 21.

—Mary Tradii

CAMBREX

Cambrex Corporation

One Meadowlands Plaza
East Rutherford, New Jersey 07073
U.S.A.
Telephone: (201) 804-3000
Fax: (201) 804-9852
Web site: http://www.cambrex.com

Public Company
Incorporated: 1981 as CasChem, Inc.
Employees: 1,852
Sales: $484.2 million (2000)
Stock Exchanges: New York
Ticker Symbol: CBM
NAIC: 32511 Petrochemical Manufacturing; 32532
   Pesticide and Other Agricultural Chemical
   Manufacturing; 325412 Pharmaceutical Preparation
   Manufacturing; 325998 All Other Miscellaneous
   Chemical Product and Preparation Manufacturing

Cambrex Corporation underwent a major transformation during the 1990s, changing its strategic emphasis from specialty chemicals to serving the life sciences industry. The firm operates as a global supplier of human health and bioscience products, a producer of feed additives and intermediates for the animal and agriculture industry, and a manufacturer of specialty and fine chemicals.

Products related to Cambrex's Human Health segment—the company's largest segment in terms of sales—include over 100 active pharmaceutical ingredients (APIs) and 130 advanced intermediates that are involved in API synthesis. These products are regulated by the FDA and various other government agencies and are sold to the pharmaceutical, nutraceutical, personal care, and medical device industries.

The firm's Biosciences division operates three product groups including Cell Biology, Molecular Biology, and Endotoxin Detection. The Animal Health/Agriculture business manufactures and supplies animal health products, agricultural intermediates, and Vitamin B-3. The Specialty and Fine Chemi-

cals unit produces performance enhancing chemicals as well as polymer systems. Over 78 percent of company sales stem from the operations of its Human Health, Biosciences, and Animal Health/Agriculture business units, while its Specialty and Fine Chemicals operations account for just over 21 percent.

1980s Origins

Cambrex Corporation was established through the efforts of two men, Cyril C. Baldwin, Jr., and Arthur Mendolia. These men had known each other for a long time, having become acquainted through their work in the chemical industry. Ambitious men in their own right, they decided to take advantage of what they perceived as unique opportunities in the specialty chemicals and fine chemicals markets, and they began searching for a company to purchase. In 1981, by means of a leveraged buyout, Baldwin and Mendolia purchased a castor oil company, which manufactured urethanes and castor oil derivatives, from NL Industries. They renamed the company CasChem, Inc. and opened the firm's doors for business.

The strategy pursued by Baldwin and Mendolia involved pursuing and then carving out niche markets in the specialty chemical and fine chemical sectors where CasChem would develop proprietary technology, preferably through the creation of patents over the years. An essential element in this strategy included the acquisition of companies with the appropriate technology that CasChem could adapt and then develop for its own use. Baldwin and Mendolia assumed that making such acquisitions would reduce the time it took CasChem to develop the same technology in-house by at least ten years.

As the company began its business, CasChem was one of the largest purchasers of castor oil in the United States. The company used castor oil in the production of many of its products and, when the market was good, sold large quantities of castor oil derivatives in bulk to other companies within the United States. The purchase price of castor oil by the company was largely determined by the natural changes in weather that affect the castor bean crop. Fortunately, the price of castor oil had remained relatively stable during the early years of CasChem's operations. With China, India, and Brazil the largest commercial producers of castor oil in the world,

CasChem bought directly from organizations in these countries and, as a result, initiated the beginnings of its foreign network.

Acquisitions

The company's second acquisition, spearheaded by Baldwin and Mendolia, was EDT Technology. This company was involved in the manufacture of electronic plating chemicals and was widely regarded by industry analysts as one of the most promising firms in the area of specialty chemicals. Purchased in 1984, EDT Technology did not perform well from the start, but Baldwin and Mendolia decided to keep the company and judge its profitability within a span of three years. The company next acquired Spencer Kellogg, a manufacturer of castor oil derivatives. Bought in 1985, Spencer Kellogg fit in nicely with the already profitable operations at CasChem. During the same year, the company purchased Cosan, a producer of biocides and catalysts for the agricultural chemicals market. One year later, Nepera, Inc. was acquired, a manufacturer of specialty products for the pharmaceutical industry.

With the 1987 acquisition of Wickhen Products, a manufacturer of cosmetic intermediaries, CasChem counted a total of six companies under its management. The strategy of building a business through a process of acquisition led to the implementation of a decentralized management and organizational structure. The company operated each of its businesses as a distinctly separate subsidiary, with its own business manager. Each of the subsidiaries was in complete control of the resources for the manufacture of its products and, consequently, was also totally responsible for its profitability. A holding company, Cambrex Corporation, was set up to coordinate the supervision of all subsidiaries and to provide direct assistance whenever one of the companies was not performing satisfactorily. The holding company also provided services, such as pension and benefits management and advice, which was not directly associated with the financial performance of any of its subsidiaries.

Operating under this decentralized management structure, the company went public in 1987 to raise capital to continue its aggressive acquisitions campaign. At the same time, management decided to sell EDT Technology, admitting that it had misjudged the size of the niche market within which the firm's products were sold. Fortunately, the decentralized organization of the company began to produce results almost immediately. The close association between subsidiary companies and customers allowed Cambrex to meet the needs of the market with greater efficiency. Baldwin and Mendolia were convinced that this type of operating structure more than offset the additional costs incurred by employing duplicate staffs in the areas of research and development, sales, and general management.

In 1987, the Cambrex market mix included the following figures: coatings accounted for 28 percent of the company's business, health and drugs for 15 percent, performance chemicals for 21 percent, agricultural feed additives for 20 percent, and specialty fine chemicals for approximately 16 percent. One year later, however, the bottom fell out of almost all of these highly specialized markets. Competition from the growing number of small niche companies drove prices downward, and companies such as Cambrex, which had previously thrived on their manufacturing flexibility and ability to adapt to the specialized needs of customers, began to feel pressure from environmental regulations imposed by the federal government. As a result, Baldwin and Mendolia decided to pull the company out of its aggressive acquisitions campaign and wait for a more opportune time to make new purchases.

After nearly two years, Cambrex restarted its acquisition campaign with the purchase of Heico Chemical, a manufacturer of inorganic chemicals based in Pennsylvania. Purchased from Humphrey Chemicals, Heico was supposed to propel Cambrex into the market for pharmaceutical intermediaries. Another reason for the purchase was that Heico was working closely with American Cyanamid Company to develop an intermediate for manufacturing a herbicide called Persuit. The collaboration looked like it would produce a certain success in the agricultural chemicals markets. After the purchase, however, management at Cambrex realized that the potential commercial value of the product was offset by the enormously high development expenditures. Consequently, the deal was abandoned and Cambrex was forced to write off the investment at a cost of $9.4 million. To compensate for this loss, in late 1989 Baldwin and Mendolia decided to purchase Heico's parent company, Humphrey Chemicals, to strengthen its base in the fine and specialty chemicals market.

By the late 1980s, Baldwin and Mendolia wanted to retire, and the two men realized that they needed to hire employees that could help them make the transition from an entrepreneurial management team to a professional management team. With this in mind, in 1990 James A. Mack was hired to assume the position of president and chief executive officer. Mack had previously worked as a vice-president at Olin Corporation, one of the largest and most influential manufacturers of chemical products and defense-related items in the United States. At the same time, Peter Tracey was brought in as chief financial officer. Tracey had an extensive background in financial supervision and management at a number of different firms, including Joyce International, Inc., an office products manufacturer, and Robotic Vision Systems, Inc., a maker of automation systems for industrial use.

Under the direction of Mack and Tracey, Cambrex immediately began to clarify its focus and to refine its long-standing acquisition policy. The two most important elements in the company's acquisition strategy included the continuing emphasis on fine chemicals and pharmaceutical intermediaries and the expansion overseas. The company's acquisition criteria were stringent: Mack and Tracey were looking for companies that had highly profitable niche market shares, ranged in size from $10 million to $30 million, did not require any substantial capital investment, and owned patents and proprietary technology that could be used by Cambrex in its already established

Key Dates:

1981: Cyril C. Baldwin, Jr., and Arthur Mendolia purchase a castor oil company and rename it CasChem Inc.

1984: The pair purchase EDT Technology.

1985: Spencer Kellogg and Cosan are acquired by CasChem.

1986: CasChem continues its buying spree and purchases Nepera Inc.

1987: Holding company Cambrex Corporation is formed; the firm goes public.

1989: Humphrey Chemicals is acquired.

1990: James A. Mack is named president and chief operating officer.

1994: Cambrex purchases the Nobel/Profarmaco chemical business from Akzo Nobel.

1997: The firm continues expansion into biotechnology by acquiring BioWhittaker Inc.; strategic emphasis is placed on moving into the life sciences industry.

1999: FMC BioProducts, Irotec Laboratories, and Poietic Technologies Inc. are acquired.

2000: Growth continues with the purchase of Conti BPC, All Line Laboratories' picolinate product line, and LumiTech Ltd.

markets. The two new management leaders thought the best place to look for acquisitions was in the animal health and pharmaceutical industries, where large multinational drug corporations intended to cease specialty chemicals production and focus more on research and end-product manufacturing.

There were two companies that met the criteria established by Mack and Tracey. Salsbury Chemicals was purchased from Solvay's Animal Health division in 1991. Salsbury specialized in the manufacture of bulk intermediates for photo chemicals and pharmaceuticals and conducted high-level research in nitration chemistry. The second company to meet management's strict acquisitions criteria was Zeeland Chemicals, a company that focused on specialty intermediates and on hydrogenation and resolution chemistry. The acquisition of these two companies significantly enhanced Cambrex's presence in the pharmaceutical and photo chemicals markets. Since both Salsbury and Zeeland supplied products for companies in the same market, they began to bring in customers for other companies under the Cambrex umbrella. For example, Polaroid, one of the major purchasers of ethylene maleic anhydride copolymer, a photo chemical made by Zeeland, soon began to transact business with the other companies within the Cambrex operational group.

As the market began to improve steadily for fine and specialty chemicals, Nepera, Inc., one of the Cambrex group companies that manufactured pyridine, began to increase its sales dramatically. Pyridine is used in the manufacture of many important pharmaceuticals and other intermediates such as animal vitamins, and Nepera was one of only four producers of pyridine throughout the world, and one of two manufacturers located in the United States. Nepera's export of 3-cyanopyridine for the production of vitamin B3 shot up 36 percent from 1990 to 1991, largely because of purchases from customers in Taiwan and Korea. In addition,

the company's feed-grade sales also increased rapidly, primarily because of the use of a pyridine-based vitamin that improves weight gain in the raising of poultry for customer consumption. By the end of 1992, more than 25 percent of total sales for the Cambrex group of companies were outside the United States, with Germany and China as the firm's largest export customers.

Continued Growth: Mid-1990s

As the company's operations grew, and sales throughout the world increased, Cambrex continued its growth by acquisition strategy. In January 1994, Cambrex purchased Hexcel Corporation, located in Middlesbrough, England, for a little less than $10 million. Renamed Seal Sands Chemicals, the company manufactured chemical intermediates used in the production of photographic, pharmaceutical, health care, plastics, and water treatment industries. In October of the same year, Cambrex made its most significant overseas acquisition. The company bought the Nobel/Profarmaco chemical business from Akzo Nobel, a large Swedish chemical producer, for just under $130 million. Nobel/Profarmaco was one of the European leaders in the manufacture of intermediates for pharmaceuticals and fine chemicals. The acquisition brought with it the entire operating facilities of Nobel Chemicals AB in Karlskoga, Sweden and Profarmaco Nobel S.r.l. in Milan, Italy, along with an extensive network of sales firms and offices located in the United States, England, and Germany.

These acquisitions, along with the improved performance of other companies in the Cambrex group, began to push revenues upward. In 1994, sales of health care intermediates and pharmaceuticals jumped 34 percent over the previous year, while sales of specialty and fine chemicals shot up 36 percent. Sales of agricultural intermediates and additives increased an impressive 17 percent during this same period. Feed additives that were used to encourage poultry growth and reduce disease were up 25 percent from a year earlier, and sales of pyridine alone increased a hefty 12 percent.

By 1995, Cambrex had become well-known within the specialty and fine chemicals industry as a successful international company. Nearly 40 percent of all of the company's products were manufactured outside of the United States, and approximately 45 percent of all of its products were sold outside of the country where they were originally produced. With the acquisitions of firms in England and Sweden, Cambrex also increased its presence as a major supplier of bulk actives for the generic drug market.

In the mid-1990s, Cambrex management continued to search for companies to add to its impressive and growing list of products. Although sales of feed additives were increasing year after year, management focused on expanding its reach in the life sciences industry as well as its specialty and fine chemicals businesses, which accounted for approximately 65 percent of total sales for the company at the time.

Operating As a Life Sciences Firm: Late 1990s and Beyond

The company's dependence on its specialty and fine chemicals businesses would change dramatically however, as Cambrex began to shift its focus from that segment to life sciences and biotechnology in the latter half of the 1990s. The 1997 purchase of BioWhittaker Inc. signaled the firm's commitment to its new found focus. The $130 million deal was "of significant strategic importance to Cambrex because it gives the company an immediate presence in a field widely considered one of the most promising pharmaceutical frontiers," wrote the *Chemical Market Reporter* in 1997. In fact, both companies claimed that the biotech industry would grow from $9 billion in 1997 to over $75 billion by 2002.

While the Cambrex's focus had shifted, its merger and acquisition strategy remained unchanged. In 1999, the company made several key purchases. The first, Poietic Technologies Inc., was leading supplier of human cells to research laboratories to the academic, biotech, and pharmaceutical industries. The firm also acquired Irotec Laboratories, a Ireland-based supplier of pharmaceutical intermediates. Cambrex also gained control of FMC BioProducts, a molecular biology products manufacturer, for $38 million. In October of that year, Mack was named chairman of the firm.

Cambrex entered the millennium intent on increasing its revenues related to its life science businesses to $1 billion by 2004. Claes Glassell, the company's president and chief operating officer commented on the firm's strategy in a 2000 *Chemical Market Reporter* article, stating, "getting into biotechnology with the BioWhittaker acquisition three years ago gave us broader exposure to what is happening on the biotech scene, and as we learn about these things, we have started making small acquisitions to build up a collection of technologies that we think are going to be very important in the future."

One such purchase was the July 2000 acquisition of LumiTech Ltd., a supplier to the drug discovery market based in the United Kingdom. The company also merged the pharmaceutical intermediates business of Conti BPC NV into its Human Health segment and acquired the All Line Laboratories' picolinate product line. That year, Cambrex formed a partnership with Synthon Chiragenics to develop chiral compounds that are used in therapeutic drugs. Growth continued in 2001 with the purchase of Bio Science Contract Production Corp. The deal gave the firm access to Bio Science's state-of-the-art biopharmaceutical manufacturing facility.

By 2001, Cambrex had successfully transformed itself from a specialty chemicals manufacturer into a leading supplier and manufacturer specializing in the life science industry. Net income in 2000 increased by 30.2 percent over the previous year, and management believed it was on target to achieve future profits. The company's strategic focus was on producing products and services for the innovator and generic pharmaceutical, bioresearch, and biotheraputics markets. Under the leadership of Mack and Glassell, Cambrex appeared to be well positioned for continued success.

Principal Subsidiaries

BioWhittaker Inc.; BioWhittaker Europe s.p.r.l.; BioWhittikar Molecular Applications Inc.; CasChem, Inc.; Chiragene Inc.; Conti BPC NV (Belgium); Cosan Chemical Corporation; Heico Chemicals, Inc.; Irotec Laboratories Ltd.; LumiTech UK; Nepera, Inc.; Nordic Synthesis AB (Sweden); Profarmaco S.r.l.; Salsbury Chemicals, Inc.; Seal Sands Chemicals Limited; Zeeland Chemicals, Inc.; BioWhittaker U.K. Ltd.; Cambrex Chemicals Pvt. Ltd. (India); Cambrex France s.a.r.l.; Cambrex GmbH (Germany); Cambrex Italia S.r.l.

Principal Operating Units

Human Health; Biosciences; Animal Health/Agriculture; Specialty and Fine Chemicals.

Principal Competitors

The Dow Chemical Company; E.I. du Pont de Nemours and Company; Pharmacia Corporation.

Further Reading

"Akzo Nobel Sells Two Units To U.S., German Buyers," *Chemical and Engineering News,* September 26, 1994, p. 16.

"Cambrex Continues on Its Growth Path," *Chemical Marketing Reporter,* August 7, 2000, p. 16.

"Cambrex Corp. Completes Acquisition of the Biopharmaceutical Production Business of Bio Science Contract Production Corp.," *Chemical Business Newsbase,* June 10, 2001.

"Cambrex Corporation," *Wall Street Journal,* January 27, 1995, p. B2.

"Cambrex Corporation," *Wall Street Journal,* July 19, 1995, p. C19.

"Cambrex Links with Synthon," *Chemical Week,* December 6, 2000, p. 5.

"Cambrex: Reinvention As a Fine Art, From Specialties to API's," *Chemical Marketing Reporter,* January 15, 2001, p. 12.

"Cambrex Sees a Turnaround Starting in '92," *Chemical Marketing Reporter,* November 16, 1992, pp. 9–10.

"Cambrex Uses Sharp M&A Strategy to Build New Platforms for Growth," *Chemical Marketing Reporter,* August 9, 1999, p. 5.

Coeyman, Marjorie, "Fine and Custom Chemicals," *Chemical Week,* February 10, 1993, pp. 18–25.

Lerner, Matthew, "Cambrex to Acquire BioWhittaker Marking Push Into Biotechnology" *Chemical Marketing Reporter,* September 1, 1997, p. 5.

Moore, Samuel K., "Cambrex Buys FMC's Biotech Unit," *Chemical Week,* June 16, 1999, p. 30.

Seewald, Nancy, "Cambrex: Thriving on Independence," *Chemical Week,* January 3, 2001, p. 42.

Wood, Andrew, "Cambrex: Acquiring Expertise in Fine Chemical Intermediates," *Chemical Week,* April 5, 1995, pp. 52–54.

—Thomas Derdak
—update: Christina M. Stansell

Caraustar Industries, Inc.

3100 Joe Jenkins Boulevard
Austell, Georgia 30106-3227
U.S.A.
Telephone: (770) 732-3401
Fax: (770) 732-3401
Web site: http://www.caraustar.com

Public Company
Incorporated: 1938 as Carolina Paper Board Corp.
Employees: 6,255
Sales: $963.4 million (2000)
Stock Exchanges: NASDAQ
Ticker Symbol: CSAR
NAIC: 32212 Folding Paperboard Box Manufacturing;
    322213 Setup Paperboard Box Manufacturing; 32214
    Fiber Can, Tube, Drum, and Similar Products Manufac-
    turing; 551112 Offices of Other Holding Companies

Caraustar Industries, Inc. is a leading manufacturer of recycled paperboard and converted paperboard products with more
than 100 facilities in 29 states, Mexico, England, and Canada.
Caraustar's position as a diversified, low-cost producer and
supplier of paperboard and paperboard products has allowed the
company to capture a strong share of each of four key paperboard markets: tubes, cores, and drums; folding cartons; gypsum wallboard facing paper; and other specialty and converted
paperboard products. In the mid-1990s, the company became
the premier supplier of recycled boxboard in the United States
as well as the largest independent supplier of gypsum facing
paper in North America. Additionally, the company is the
nation's second largest supplier of tubes, cores, and composite
containers and is among its top ten carton manufacturers.
Caraustar is the only major paperboard producer to serve each
of its four principal markets, providing the company both stability and flexibility in a traditionally cyclical, commodity-based
industry. The company, which prides itself on its diversification, also produces extruded and injection-molded plastic products to complement its paperboard product lines. Since the early
1980s, Caraustar has pursued an aggressive growth plan
through acquisition and internal expansion, raising net sales
(after freight costs) from $94 million in 1980 to more than
$963.4 million in 2000. Through its long history, Caraustar has
had a nearly unbroken record of sales and income growth.

1938–49: Caraustar Starts Out as a Recycling Pioneer in the 1930s

Caraustar was formed as the Carolina Paper Board Corporation in Charlotte, North Carolina in 1938 by Ross Puette and other
investors. Puette already had more than a decade of experience in
the paperboard industry, beginning his career in the 1920s at
Richmond, Virginia-based Manchester Board and Paper Co.
(which became a subsidiary of Caraustar in 1994). With $25,000
in startup funds, Puette and his partners built North Carolina's first
paper recycling plant, with 45 employees producing 25 tons of
folding carton per day. The company's operations grew quickly:
by 1940, more than 60 employees produced some 8,000 tons of
paperboard, generating sales of $374,000. The choice of loca-
tion—a major urban market with a ready supply of waste paper—
would become a key element of the company's growth strategy.

During the 1940s, Carolina Paper Board branched out, forming affiliated companies in Charlotte and in Greenville, South
Carolina and building two recycled paper processing plants to
supply the company's Charlotte paperboard mill. This move
toward vertical integration, which assured the company a ready
supply of low-cost fiber, would also become a company hallmark. In 1947, the company added forward integration capacity,
when it built a second paperboard mill in Austell, Georgia. In
addition to the paperboard mill, the Austell site featured a
converting facility, serving the folding carton market, and a
recycled fiber processing plant, tapping the low-cost supply of
waste paper in nearby Atlanta. By the end of the decade, Carolina Paper Board's two mills were producing 125 tons per day.
The company's sales grew to $2.3 million on a total volume of
30,000 tons, and its payroll had swelled to 140 employees.

1950–80: Expansion and Steady Growth

The first of the company's strategic acquisitions occurred in
the early 1950s, when Carolina Paper Board purchased a minority

interest in Star Paper Tube, which operated a tube and core converting plant in Rock Hill, South Carolina. By 1958, Carolina Paper Board had gained a majority share of Star Paper Tube and had expanded the subsidiary by building two additional tube and core converting plants, in Danville, Virginia and in Austell, Georgia, serving the textile industry. At the end of the 1950s, Carolina Paper Board's operations had grown to eight facilities, and sales had tripled to $6.4 million on more than 50,000 tons. The company was now represented in three key markets: folding carton, other specialty products, and tube and core.

The booming economy of the 1960s helped Carolina Paper Board increase its production more than 150 percent over the decade to an annual capacity of 128,000 tons. The company opened a third paper mill in 1964 in Greenville, South Carolina. Three years later, spurred by growth in the tube and core market, the company opened a fourth tube and core plant, which in turn prompted the opening of the company's fourth paper mill. In the mid-1960s, Carolina Paper Board also increased its folding carton capacity with the acquisition of Charlotte-based Atlantic Coast Carton Company. With 870 employees, Carolina Paper Board's sales quadrupled to $24.5 million, producing operating profits of more than $3 million. The company's push toward integration was already nearing a 30 percent integration level among its paper mills and converting plants.

The Atlantic Coast Carton acquisition marked a new era of growth strategy for the company. During the 1970s, acquisitions played a major role in Carolina Paper Board's expansion. Between 1970 and 1980, the company acquired one folding carton plant, two recycled fiber processing plants, and eight tube and core converting plants. At the same time, the company continued its internal growth, building five new tube and core converting plants, a recycled fiber processing plant, and a fifth paperboard mill. The new mill also enabled the company to move into a new paper market, the gypsum facing paper market, completing the company's target market areas. Meanwhile, the company was also expanding within the tube and core market, moving beyond its reliance on the textile industry to supply the paper, construction, metal, and film industries. The company

already exhibited another ingredient to its later growth, that of achieving a reasonable balance among its target markets. Many of the company's plants were already capable of converting quickly from one market to another, helping to buffer the company during cyclical downturns in any of its core markets. As the 1970s ended, Carolina Paper Board had continued its strong growth, reaching revenues of $93.8 million and operating profits of $12.8 million. The company's 1,650 employees produced more than 264,000 tons.

1980–89: Company Converts to Caraustar But Slows Growth Near End of Decade

Until 1980, the company had operated as six affiliated corporations, with common management and ownership. In that year, the company consolidated its operations under the holding company, Caraustar Industries, and relocated its headquarters to its 150-acre Austell site. The newly incorporated company continued the internal and external expansion set during the previous decade. Between 1981 and 1986, the company built three tube and core converting plants and acquired two folding carton plants, a plastic extrusion and injection molding plant, three tube and core converting plants, and four recycled paperboard mills. In 1986, however, the company expansion slowed after a leveraged recapitalization added some $300 million to the company's debt. In the late 1980s, Caraustar acquired only one recycled paperboard mill, in Camden, New Jersey. The company also backed into another acquisition, that of Standard Gypsum Corp., a maker of gypsum wallboard, after that company was unable to pay its paperboard bill. In 1996, however, Caraustar sold 50 percent of its interest in Standard Gypsum and relinquished the directorship of that business.

Despite the slowdown in the company's growth, Caraustar managed to post a 187 percent increase in revenues during the 1980s, raising net sales to $141 million by 1990. Operating profits grew still more strongly, gaining 272 percent to reach $47.6 million. The company's 2,567 employees, meanwhile, had increased mill production to 565,000 tons.

1990–96: Company Goes Public and Grows into an Industry Pace Setter

At the start of the 1990s, Caraustar's holdings had swelled to 44 facilities, including 11 paperboard mills located in Texas, North and South Carolina, Illinois, Ohio, New Jersey, and Tennessee. The company had grown to become one of the top ten recycling companies in the United States. The company's Star Paper Tube subsidiary had grown to become the second largest tube and core producer in the country. As the recession of the early 1990s took hold, Caraustar formulated a newly aggressive strategic plan, which called for the company to step up its vertical integration and diversification in its key market areas. Part of that plan included taking the company public, to alleviate the debt load incurred during the 1980s. The company made an initial public offering (IPO) of 11.1 million common shares in December 1992, raising some $90 million.

Part of the funds raised in the company's IPO was earmarked for stepping up the company's acquisition program. Between 1991 and early 1997, Caraustar added some 30 facilities to its recycling empire. During 1992 and 1993, the company

Key Dates:

1938: Ross Puette and other investors found Carolina Paper Board Corporation.

1944: Manchester Board and Paper Co. becomes company subsidiary.

1947: Company builds second paperboard mill in Austell, Georgia.

1964: Carolina Paper Board opens third paper mill in Greenville, South Carolina.

1967: Company builds fourth tube and core plant and opens fourth paper mill.

1980: Company consolidates six affiliated corporations under Caraustar Industries, a holding company with headquarters in Austell.

1992: Caraustar goes public.

1998: Company acquires Chesapeake Paperboard Company.

2000: Caraustar reorganizes, forming four core areas: the Mill Group; the Industrial and Consumer Products Group; the Custom Packaging Group; and the Recovered Fiber Group.

acquired two recycled paperboard mills, Buffalo Paperboard and Manchester Board and Paper, which was renamed Richmond Paperboard Corp. Caraustar bought two tube and core converting plants in Salt Lake City and Phoenix and acquired Federal Packaging Corp., a maker of composite containers using paperboard and injection-molded plastics. The following year, the company added to its folding cartons capacity with the acquisition of Mid-Packaging Group Inc. and that company's two Tennessee-based folding carton plants. While investing in upgrades and maintenance of its existing facilities, Caraustar also built two new tube and core converting plants, in Lancaster, Pennsylvania and in Mexico City, as well as a new production facility for the company's Star-Guard product in Lancaster, South Carolina.

In 1995, the company added GAR Holdings, with two specialty products plants and a folding carton plant, and Summer Paper Tube of Kernersville, North Carolina, with two core manufacturing plants. Summer also manufactured specialty adhesives used in the tube and core and paperboard lamination production processes, helping the company further solidify its diverse operations and integration within the paperboard industry. Toward that end, Caraustar also entered a joint venture with Tenneco Packaging Co., which involved a $114.5 million purchase of an 80 percent interest in Tenneco's clay-coated paperboard mills in Rittman, Ohio and Tama, Iowa, expanding Caraustar's capacity in that high-growth area of the paperboard industry.

By 1996, the company's revenues had almost doubled since 1992 and, at 9.6 percent, had almost reached a double digit profit margin with a net income of nearly $58 million. Its company's flexibility, vertical integration, and diversity had clearly enabled the company to outpace its competitors, many of whom struggled through industry downturns and booming paperstock costs.

By that year, the company was operating 14 paperboard mills in North Carolina, South Carolina, Georgia, New Jersey, Virginia, Illinois, Ohio, Iowa, Tennessee, New York, and Pennsylvania. Its paperboard mills recycled paperstock, reducing it to pulp, then cleaned, refinished, and processed the pulp into various grades of uncoated and clay-coated paperboard. Each of Caraustar's mills had the flexibility of producing paperboard for two or more of the company's four key markets, allowing the company to react quickly to market conditions and maintain high plant productivity rates. Approximately 33 percent of the resulting paperboard was used internally by Caraustar; the remaining 67 percent was sold to other manufacturers of paperboard and related products. External sales of paperboard typically accounted for 36 percent of Caraustar's annual sales.

The company and its subsidiaries operated some 40 converting facilities directly serving Caraustar's primary markets. The company's largest and oldest subsidiary, Star Paper Tube, Inc., operated 28 tube, core, and can converting plants, providing cores for the carpeting, textile, paper, plastic film, and other industries. In 1996 alone, Caraustar produced some 268 thousand tons of tube and core products, which, together with sales of unconverted paperboard to other tube and core manufacturers, represented 36 percent of the company's net sales. In that same years, folding carton operations at ten plants in North Carolina, Ohio, and Tennessee provided 27 percent of Caraustar's net sales. Also, its 13 gypsum wallboard facing paper plants shipped 263 thousand tons, capturing roughly 17 percent of the North American market, for 17 percent of the company's net sales. The company's sales of specialty paperboard products—for the bookbinding, printing, games, puzzleboard, furniture, and other industries—accounted for 14 percent of Caraustar's net sales. Caraustar was then operating five specialty converting plants in Georgia, North and South Carolina, and Texas. Sales of injection-molded and extruded plastics and external sales of paperstock each accounted for approximately three percent of the company's net sales.

Late 1990s and Beyond: Caraustar's Growth and Diversification Continue

Caraustar continued its expansion drive through the rest of the decade and into the next century, resulting in revenues that climbed from $602.7 million in 1996 to $963.4 million in 2000. In the same period, it increased its workforce from 4,048 employees to 6,255. The company's commitment to growth was reflected in the fact that between 1994 and 1999 it was expending an annual average of $33.3 million in capital outlays.

In April 1997, the company reached an agreement to acquire General Packing Service, Inc. of Clifton, New Jersey, adding that company's pharmaceutical, medical, and health, beauty, and personal care packaging products to its product line. In the same year, it purchased all the common stock of Oak Tree Packaging Corporation, whose operations consisted of three folding carton plants located in Versailles, Connecticut; Thorndike, Massachusetts; and York, Pennsylvania. Additionally in 1997, Caraustar and its subsidiary, Star Paper Tube, Inc., acquired substantially all of the assets and business of Baxter Tube Company, a manufacturer of spiral-wound tubes and a subsidiary of Cleveland, Ohio-based The Tranzonic Cos. Baxter Tube's four facilities were located in Ware Shoals, South Carolina; Perrysburg, Ohio; Minerva, Ohio; and Leyland, Lancaster, United Kingdom, where the company operated as Unity Paper Tube, Ltd.

In March of the next year, 1998, the company acquired Chesapeake Paperboard Company and its wholly-owned subsidiary, Chesapeake Fiber Packaging Corporation. Chesapeake, operating in Maryland, processed uncoated recycled paperboard in Baltimore and manufactured folding cartons and specialty corrugated products at its converting facility in Hunt Valley. In the same year, Caraustar purchased all of the outstanding common stock of Etowah Recycling, Inc., which operated recovered fiber plants, one in Canton, Georgia, and the other in Hardeeville, South Carolina. Additionally, the company bought out Tenneco Packaging's 20 percent share of CPI, making Caraustar the sole owner of CPI's operations. Late in 1998, it also acquired all of the outstanding stock of Boxall, Inc., a Birmingham, Alabama, manufacturer of folding cartons. Boxall, which had revenues of $4.5 million in 1997, was slated to operate as a wholly-owned subsidiary and become part of Caraustar's newly-formed specialty packaging group.

Caraustar continued its aggressive growth in the next two years. In 1999, it acquired a handful of small companies, including Carolina Component Concepts, Inc. (a specialty paperboard converting operation), International Paperboard Company's Sprague boxboard mill (a maker of clay-coated recycled paperboard), Halifax Paperboard Company (a producer of uncoated recycled paperboard and a specialty paperboard converter), the Folding Carton Division of Tenneco Packaging, Inc. (a folding carton manufacturer), and Carolina Converting, Inc. (a specialty paperboard converter). This last-named company, the nation's leading manufacturer of jigsaw puzzles and coin folders, reflected Caraustar's ongoing interest in diversification. In addition to outright acquisitions, in 1999 the company entered an equal share venture with Temple-Inland, Inc., with whom it formed Premier Boxboard Limited LLC, a producer of a new lightweight gypsum facing paper and other grades of containerboard.

Early in the next year, Caraustar took steps to build its brand identity by dissolving all of its subsidiaries and renaming them Caraustar groups. For example, one of its principal subsidiaries, Star Paper Tube, was redesignated as Caraustar's Industrial and Consumer Products Group. The net result was that the company organized itself into four groups: (1) the Mill Group, concerned with the manufacturing of recycled paperboard, gypsum facing paper, and laminated paperboard products; (2) the Industrial and Consumer Products Group, concerned with tubing, core, and composite containers; (3) the Custom Packaging Group, concerned with carton and custom packaging; and (4) the Recovered Fiber Group, Plastics and Adhesives, comprised of recovered paper recycling centers, plastics manufacturing, and adhesives production.

The next year, starting in February with the purchase of MilPak, Inc., a contract packager, the company continued its acquisition spree. MilPak, located in Pine Brook, New Jersey, produced blister packaging, cartoning and labeling, as well as other contract packaging for various consumer products.

The company also retrenched, however. It closed down operations at two paperboard mills, first at Baltimore in February, then, in September, at Camden, New Jersey. The first was a permanent move. The second resulted from Caraustar's contract dispute with Georgia-Pacific Corporation, its largest gypsum facing paper customer. Sales to Georgia-Pacific fell by 80 percent in the course of second half of 2000. Caraustar also curtailed the operations of its Buffalo Paperboard Corp. in Lockport, New York, by cutting back its full-time manufacturing to just ten days per month.

During 2000 it had become obvious that, despite sales that continued to grow at a very healthy clip, operating expenses and debt service had begun taking a heavy toll. The company's net income dropped from $41.1 million in 1999 to just $8.1 million in 2000, which called for greater efficiency and, perhaps, a slowing down in capital investments. The result was a kind of balancing act between continued expansion through acquisitions and further cutbacks in the company's operations. For example, in November, after the earlier closure of two plants and the cutbacks at another, Caraustar completed the purchase of Crane Carton Co., the Chicago manufacturer of large folding cartons. The company paid $24.8 million for Crane, which in 1999 had logged revenues of $41 million.

The balancing act continued into the next year. In January 2001, because of a lack of market demand, Caraustar shut down its Chicago, Illinois, uncoated recycled paperboard mill. Although profitable through 1998, by 1999 it had begun to lose money. In March, the company put in effect a plan to combine the operations of its Salt Lake City, Utah, carton plant with those of its Denver, Colorado, carton plant, trimming its work force in the process. Meanwhile, Caraustar was mending some fences and still looking for expansion opportunities. In May, it ended its contract dispute with Georgia-Pacific, with whom it negotiated a new ten-year contract agreement.

Principal Divisions

Custom Packing Group; Mill Group; Recovered Fiber Group; Industrial and Consumer Products Group.

Principal Competitors

Longview Fibre Company; Rock-Tenn Company; Smurfit-Stone Container Corporation; Sonoco Products Company; Weyerhaeuser Company.

Further Reading

"Caraustar, Boxall to Merge Cartons," *Pulp & Paper*, January 1999, p. 25.

"Caraustar Closes Chicago Mill," *Paperboard Packaging*, March 2001, p. 20.

"Caraustar Industries, Inc. Announces Acquisition of MilPak, Inc.," *PR Newswire*, April 7, 2000.

"Caraustar Industries, Inc. Involved in Contract Dispute with Gypsum Facing Customer," *PR Newswire*, September 12, 2000.

"Caraustar Purchases Crane Carton," *Package Printing,* January 2001, p. 78.

"Caraustar to Buy Two Paperboard Mills," *Pulp & Paper*, May 1999, p. 21.

Harte, Susan, "Upward Bound," *Atlanta Journal and Constitution*, May 19, 1996, p. 21G.

Johnson, Jim, "Caraustar, GP Strike Deal," *Waste News,* May 28, 2001, p. 5.

Jones, John A., "Caraustar Diversifies to Outperform Slow Paper Industry," *Investor's Business Daily*, October 7, 1996, p. B14.

Krantz, Matt, "How Flexibility Lets Paper Firm Beat the Cycles," *Investor's Business Daily*, November 5, 1996, p. A4.

Milstead, David, "Rock Hill, S.C., Unit of Atlanta-based Paperboard Firm Getting New Name," *Knight Ridder/Tribune Business News*, January 18, 2000.

Prohaska, Thomas J., "Lockport, N.Y. Mill to Operate Part Time, Lay Off Workers," *Knight Ridder/Tribune Business News*, September 14, 2000.

Shaw, Monica, "Caraustar Industries: Growth Company Focuses on Diversity, Low-Cost Production," *Pulp & Paper*, January 1997, p. 40.

—M.L. Cohen
—update: Jane W. Fiero

Carrier Access Corporation

5395 Pearl Parkway
Boulder, Colorado 80301
U.S.A.
Telephone: (303) 442-5455
Toll Free: (800) 495-5455
Fax: (303) 443-5908
Web site: http://www.carrieraccess.com

Public Company
Incorporated: 1992
Employees: 460
Sales: $148 million (2000)
Stock Exchanges: NASDAQ
Ticker Symbol: CACS
NAIC: 334210 Telephone Apparatus Manufacturing

Carrier Access Corporation is an equipment manufacturer that helps more than 1,800 telecommunications companies enhance service revenue, lower operating costs, and extend capital budgets by providing high-performance access and new service technologies. The company's products and services are used by its customers to provide local and long distance voice, high-speed data and internet services to businesses, government, and other enterprises. The company's digital equipment provides a ''last mile'' solution for the provision and management of high bandwidth services from service providers. Providing connectivity from service provider networks to end-user locations is necessary in order to reach large numbers of businesses and consumers using voice and high speed Internet access. This connectivity is facilitated by the company's central office communications and customer-located voice and data communications equipment. Carrier Access's products enable service providers to connect end-users to their network products in a cost effective manner and decrease transmission equipment and maintenance expenses. At the same time, the company's products enable new service delivery, including integrated voice and high speed Internet access.

1990s Founding

Carrier Access was founded in 1992 when husband and wife Roger Koenig and Nancy Pierce moved to Boulder, Colorado, from IBM and ROLM in Silicon Valley to start a new company selling telecommunications hardware. ''After 16 years in Silicon Valley,'' Koenig stated in a October 2, 1998 interview with the *Denver Rocky Mountain News*, ''we came to get a better business environment, and a better living environment.'' Although an early player in the telecommunications field, the company faced daunting competition from much larger firms. To survive, Carrier Access had to develop and market new products quickly. Initially, chief executive Koenig and Pierce thought they could survive by focusing on increasing their research and development budget. They soon realized, however, that they also had to start acquiring engineering talent and technology.

The company initially focused on making telecommunications products that helped businesses access high capacity phone lines, known as T1s. These lines offered better quality and faster transmission at a lower cost than traditional lines. AT&T originally began providing T1 service ten years earlier for businesses that required higher capacity lines for high bandwidth data applications. Carrier Access was able to establish a successful niche in this market. Not until June 1995, however, did the company introduce its first major product, Access Bank I, which offered digital connections for local and long distance carrier voice and Internet services. Access Bank enabled customers to convert a single T1 line into 12 or 24 standard analog lines for voice, facsimile, modem, and private network connections. The product allowed organizations to increase their phone lines without having to dig up new lines or install expensive new equipment. The Access Bank product was quickly adopted by major telecommunications carriers, utilities, Internet service providers, government entities, and universities to connect to T1 facilities. In 1996, the company worked to refine the Access Bank product solutions, garnering increasing attention from the communications industry. The introduction of this low-cost, highly reliable product quickly positioned the company as the most cost-competitive provider of T1 access solutions.

Company Perspectives:

Carrier Access is a leading provider of broadband digital equipment solutions that meet the rapidly changing needs of communications service providers. Our service provider customers include competitive local exchange carriers, incumbent local exchange carriers, independent operating companies, interexchange carriers, Internet service providers, and wireless mobility carriers. Our products are used by our customers to provide a range of services to businesses, government, and enterprise end-users, including local and long distance voice, high-speed, data, and Internet access.

The company's growth in its first four years led it to relocate three times and increase its staff. In January 1996, Carrier Access moved into a new 38,000-square foot facility in Boulder and doubled its staff to 70 by the end of the year. Demand for high-capacity lines had begun to take off in recent years with everyone from call centers to internet providers using them for networks. At the time, Koenig predicted that connections to T1 lines by businesses would grow by 50 percent in 1996 alone.

The 1996 Telecommunications Act: Change and New Opportunities

The company's opportunities expanded considerably with the 1996 Telecommunications Act, passed by Congress to bring vibrant new competition to the $112 billion market for local phone service and the communications industry. To position itself for the new competitive era and keep pace with rapid demand for its product solutions, the company began adding key executives to its corporate staff. In 1996, the company hired Ken Garrett as vice-president for marketing. Garrett had 17 years of sales and marketing experience with telecommunications and data communications systems. He had held senior-level sales and marketing positions with XEL Communications, US West, and AT&T, and was vice-president for Astarte Fiber Networks. To further bolster its marketing division, the company added a product manager, Bob Wald, who had 14 years of experience in product design, development, and management in the data processing, data communications, and telecommunications industries. Gerry S. Sutton, who held previous marketing communications positions with Storage Technology Corp. and EMASS Inc., was recruited as manager of marketing communications. The company also added a director of strategic accounts, David G. Sant, who had 33 years experience in the computer and communications industry. Timothy Anderson, who had 13 years experience in financial management, was hired as the company's corporate controller.

In addition, in July 1996 Carrier Access announced the addition of Joseph Graziano, former chief financial officer and board member at Apple Computer Inc., to its board. Graziano, who was an investor in Carrier Access, had served as chief financial officer for Sun Microsystems and treasurer of Rohm Corp. In a statement to the Boulder *Daily Camera* on July 16, 1996, Graziano said that he was attracted to Carrier Access because of the company's strong growth potential. "The industry segment they're in is very interesting and fast growing," he said. "Their overall business opportunity is quite optimistic." Graziano's addition to the company's board came just months after another high-profile board appointment. Ryal Poppa, former head of Storage Technology Corp., had agreed to join the company's board in May. Co-founder and chief financial officer Nancy Pierce anticipated that having both Graziano and Poppa on the board would help the company gain respect from Wall Street if the firm decided to make a public offering.

With the new competitive environment unleashed by the 1996 Telecommunications Act, the company concentrated on new product solutions and development. In November 1996, Carrier Access released Access Bank II, which delivered twice the T1 capacity of the Access Bank I in the same size package, enabling service providers to integrate high-speed Internet service with multi-line voice service in a single unit. Access Bank II relied on the same 12-channel telephone line interface circuit cards as the Access Bank I. Nevertheless, each of the two T1 interfaces could accommodate current and future bandwidth requirements to provide a combination of facsimile, modem, high-speed Internet, voice, and PBX telephone services. Service providers came to rely on the flexibility of Access Bank II to provide multi-line voice and high-speed Internet connections to branch offices, small business customers, and medium-sized business locations. In combining voice with digital data over one or two T1 lines, bandwidth could be utilized more efficiently and at less cost.

In November 1997, Carrier Access also introduced its Wide Bank 28 DS-3 Access Multiplexer, enabling the connection of high bandwidth digital T3 (672 telephone line equivalents) network access lines to 28 T1 or 21 E1 service connections. The Widebank 28 allowed communications service providers, Internet service providers, and government customers to consolidate multiple T1s or E1s into T3 services to reduce monthly access costs. According to the company the Widebank 28 answered a tremendous need for multiplexing solutions that provided low-cost, managed access to the growing number of high capacity networks.

In addition, Carrier Access sought strategic development and distribution alliances with other firms to increase industry penetration with its low-cost and highly integrated T1 and T3 access solutions. On April 22, 1997, the company announced a long term alliance with ADC Telecommunications. The alliance allowed ADC to market Carrier Access's line of products, including Access Bank I and Access Bank II T1 voice and data multiplexers, as well as the Widebank 28 access multiplexer. The agreement also entailed a long term collaboration on the development of service delivery systems based on the core technologies of both companies. While Carrier Access represented a leading manufacturer of T1 and T3 network access solutions for the telecommunications and data communications industries, ADC specialized in providing loop access and transport systems to carriers for their delivery of high-bandwidth services to businesses and end-users. On June 30, Carrier Access also signed a North American distribution agreement with Graybar, based in St. Louis, Missouri. The agreement allowed Graybar to market Carrier Access's entire product line to its

---

Key Dates:

1992: Carrier Access founded and incorporated.
1995: The company introduces its first major product, the Access Bank I service.
1996: The company introduces Access Bank II Voice and Data Multiplexer services.
1997: The company introduces Wide Bank 28 DS-3 Access Multiplexer solution.
1998: Carrier Access raises $41 million in an initial public offering of common stock; the company is named fastest growing technology company in Colorado.
1999: Company introduces CACTUS to provide expanded and integrated broadband services to customers.
2000: Carrier Access acquires Millennia Systems, Inc. of Roanoke, Virginia.

---

end-user customer base throughout the United States and Canada. Graybar represented a leading provider of integrated solutions for both the telecom and datacom industries. The distribution agreement enabled Carrier Access to take advantage of Graybar's breadth of telecommunications expertise and its large product distribution network that would help Carrier Access exploit new market opportunities.

To keep pace with its rapid expansion and customer demand, the company added another 13,000 square feet to its corporate headquarters in Boulder in December 1997. In a December 15, 1997 press release reported by *Business Wire*, Chief Financial Officer Nancy Pierce stated that "growth in new carrier equipment purchases has led our company to expand its manufacturing operations twice and significantly increase our engineering and support staffs. The additional facilities expansion is needed to keep pace with demand for our current Access Bank and Wide Bank 28 product lines, as well as to gear up for new products to be introduced in 1998." Indeed, during the previous three years, Carrier Access had successfully established itself as a major supplier of digital access equipment for competitive local exchange carriers (CLECs) and long distance carriers. The company had delivered a steady stream of innovations for the digital "last mile," connections from carriers to customer buildings. At the same time, explosive growth in the use of high-speed DS-3 connections was evidenced in the company's high volume shipments of the Wide Bank 28. These shipments were fueled by the need for managed DS-3 connections for Internet carriers, wireless networks, and the replacement of individual T1 access lines by DS-3. The popularity of the Wide Bank 28 stemmed from filling the need for easily installed, protected, DS-3 connections plus advanced monitoring and testing capabilities.

During 1997, the company also made additional management changes, hiring Shri Dodani as vice-president of engineering and manufacturing. Dodani's experience in high technology was extensive, having held senior positions at Aztek Engineering, Inc. and Nortel Asia South Pacific and Nortel Europe, and at Alcatel NSG. Carrier Access also appointed a new vice-president for marketing, Kevin Leibl, who held the position of general manager with Phillips Communications, where he de-

veloped the company into one the country's leading distributors of wide-area networking and carrier transmission equipment. In addition, the company added Chris Rust as Director of Product Management. Rust had held previous positions with Comcore Semiconductor, where he established their product direction, corporate structure, and business plan, as well as with Sourcecom Corporation and US West Advanced Technologies.

In April 1998, the company introduced another innovation, Access Exchange, comprising the industry's first nodal switching software for optimized T1 access. The product enabled long distance service providers to combine local voice services with long distance and high speed Internet access of their existing switch infrastructure while routing calls to the local exchange carrier for local calling, directory, 911, and other lifeline services. The product made digital access affordable for small and medium size customers by combining local, long distance, and data onto a single optimized T1 circuit.

Late 1990s: Success and Growth

On July 30, 1998, Carrier Access went public, offering 3 million shares at $12 apiece. The initial public offering, which was underwritten by CS First Boston, Hambrecht & Quist and Warburg Dillion Read, left 23.05 million shares outstanding. The company planned to use the $41 million raised by the public offering for general corporate purposes, including product development. The company had been increasingly profitable in the past several years, earning $1.7 million in 1997 and $1.7 million in the first half of 1998. In October 1998, the explosive growth of the company attracted the attention of the accounting firm, Deloitte & Touche, which named Carrier Access the fastest growing technology company in Colorado with a five-year growth rate of 4778 percent.

The company's success was further illustrated by its 1998 year end financial results. Revenue for 1998 had increased to $48.1 million as compared to $18.7 million for 1997, an increase of 157 percent. In addition, net income had increased 773 percent. Roger Koenig—chairman, president, and chief executive officer—stated that revenue growth had exceeded expectations and attributed these results to significant growth in competitive carrier deployments of the company's products. He noted that Carrier Access had started shipping a new product platform, the Access Navigator with GR-303 protocol switching capability. Koenig anticipated that this new host controller and data provisioning product would continue to drive demand for the company's Access Bank products. With this latest product, Carrier Access now offered an end-to-end digital access solution for its competitive carrier customers, with equipment both at the central office and the customer location.

In 1999, Carrier Access continued its pace of introducing new products, including Access Bank II/SDSL, which provided high-speed Internet access to customers' LANs. The availability of the Wide Bank 28/STS-1 offered high-speed STS-1 electrical connectivity directly to SONET Add/Drop Multiplexers and switches to deploy T1 services. As a result, the new Wide Bank product reduced the overall cost of implementing T1 services at carrier switch, co-locations, and on-net building locations. In 1999, the company also introduced the Access

Navigator DCS Service Manager, designed to enable carriers to save local T1 access costs.

With these new innovations and growing demand for the company's products, Carrier Access reported first quarter results of $21.7 million in revenue, an increase of 19 percent over revenue of $18.2 million in the fourth quarter of 1998. Koenig attributed part of this success to demand for the company's new products, particularly the Access Navigator. More impressive was the sky rocketing price of the company's stock. From July 1998, when Carrier Access had gone public with a $12 offering price, its stock had risen by 544 percent by March 1999 to a high of $77.31 per share. Nevertheless, by May 1999 the company's stock price was trading down in the $30 to mid-$40 range. The stock had come under pressure due to announcements by the company's competitors of equipment price reductions by as much as 50 to 60 percent. Although competitors began entering the profitable niche market founded by Carrier Access, the company continued to maintain its lead position in the market. The company's strong market position was verified when Reg King, an equity analyst with Hambrecht & Quist, stated on May 28, 1999 in the Boulder *Daily Camera* that Carrier Access had established itself in a lead position in the market and that it "still has the best product family for competitive carriers." Moreover, despite growing competitive pressure, Carrier Access had increased its workforce from 160 in 1998 to 215 by May 1999. To cope with internal growth, the company also added another 22,000 square feet to its building in Boulder.

In October 1999, Carrier Access was named the second fastest growing technology firm in Colorado in the Deloitte & Touche "Fast 50" program for Colorado—a ranking of the 50 fastest growing technology companies in the area. The company's revenue growth of 6,396 percent over the preceding five years also assured that it was one of the fastest growing firms in the nation. By the end of 1999 the company was staking its future growth on its new Cactus line of products. One of these products, Cactus.lite, allowed customers to upgrade to the next level of telecommunications technology and accommodate an array of fast new transmission interfaces. The company saw the Cactus line of products as taking the telephone networks into the 21st century. Utilizing the Cactus products, however, depended on understanding Carrier Access' array of other products. Up to this point, the company had focused on manufacturing equipment that would allow both established and new telephone companies to concentrate their customers' voice traffic into fewer transmission lines. By condensing customer traffic into fewer T1 lines of up to 24 voice channels each before the transmissions reached the incumbent exchange carrier's regional switch, Carrier Access' customers could save the costs of additional, expensive T1 lines. The savings could be substantial for competitive local exchange carriers—the new telecom service providers that arose after the 1996 Telecommunications Act compelled the regional Bell companies to open their infrastructure for use by competitors. Since 1995, Carrier Access had designed its products to concentrate traffic in several steps. The company's Access Bank T1 multiplexer, for example, digitized up to 24 voice channels and funneled them into one T1 line. The Access Navigator served to concentrate several T1 lines into fewer T1s. Finally, the Wide Bank 28 multiplexor could channel 28 T1 lines into a single T3 line, which could handle 672 voice signals, as the transmission got closer to the service provider's switch.

The company's more current products transmitted signals in the widely accepted Time Division Multiplexing (TDM) format. TDM constituted a traditional circuit-switching technology in dedicating a given circuit to a given transmission for the duration of the transmission. This circuit switching technology, however, was soon expected to yield to more efficient "packet switching" methods. Packet switching technology worked by breaking transmissions into chunks called "packets," transmitting them individually over various circuits, and reassembling the packets in the proper order at the receiving end of the transmission. The packet switching method aimed to enable further concentrations of signals and more efficient use of capacity. Carrier Access had designed its Cactus products to bridge the gap from circuit switching to packet switching. The products would essentially enable carriers to migrate their networks from TDM to transmitting in signals in the packet-switching format known as Asynchronous Transfer Mode (ATM). This would save carriers that still deployed TDM the expense of replacing all their equipment and give them the flexibility of migrating their networks to the ATM format.

The company's continued upward trajectory was reflected in its 1999 end year financial results. Revenue had increased 126 percent to $108,815,000 from $48,133,000 for 1998. Roger Koenig pronounced 1999 an exceptional year, attributing the strong financial results to several accomplishments, including a 300 percent increase in Wide Bank revenue and the successful introduction of the Access Navigator, which contributed $10 million in revenue. He also stated that the company had added a new research and development facility in Tulsa, Oklahoma, which enabled accelerated product development and that Carrier Access had hired well over 100 new employees in 1999.

The company also continued to introduce new innovations as it headed into the year 2000. In February, Carrier Access announced its new Speedway Installation Kit for its Access Bank and Access Exchange products. The product provided everything a user needed to install up to two Access Bank units or Access Exchange switches. The company unveiled the Navigator Valet, designed to provide a graphic user interface that eased the configuration of system parameters and cross connection mappings. Carrier Access also introduced new capabilities for Adit (formerly known as CACTUS), which were aimed at supporting routing and next-generation softswitch applications, making it easier to add new capabilities and evolve with network infrastructure changes. Finally, in January 2001, the company introduced the Broadmore platform, which improved the use of carrier infrastructures by efficiently converting and packing structured circuits into ATM optical connections.

In June 2000, Carrier Access announced that it was expanding its research and development facilities in Tulsa, Oklahoma by 250 people over the next three years. Approximately 120 people were engaged in research and development at the Boulder headquarters, but the company needed another site near educational institutions with a potential pool of skilled employees. The company chose Tulsa because of its proximity to the University of Oklahoma, Oklahoma State University, and the University of Tulsa, which together had established a center of excellence in telecommunications. At the time of this announcement, the company was ranked as the nation's 28th fastest growing company in the May 29 issue of *Business Week* magazine. In just three years, the company's average sales had grown 165 percent, profits had risen 269 percent, and return on capital had increased 15 percent.

In July, Shri Dodani, the company's vice-president of engineering, accepted an appointment as president and chief executive officer at telecommunications start-up VxTel. Dodani's departure came after the promotion of co-founder Nancy Pierce to corporate development officer and Tim Anderson to chief financial officer in May. In her new position, Pierce was to be responsible for strategic planning and ongoing partnership development, in addition to continuing to serve as corporate secretary, treasurer, and director for Carrier Access. Anderson's new position entailed responsibility for all areas of finance, accounting, SEC compliance, and investor relations.

On August 15, 2000, Carrier Access announced its first acquisition with the purchase of Millennia Systems Inc., a Roanoke, Virginia, company that designed communications equipment, for $13 million in stock and cash. Millennia specialized in designing equipment on a contract basis for communications companies, including Carrier Access. Companies hired Millennia if they needed to market their products quickly but did not have the necessary research and development on site, or if they required additional consulting. Koenig, who had hired the firm in April for a short-term project, saw the firm as a complementary operation to Carrier Access. Millennia employed 20 engineers with considerable talent in optics and Internet protocol, plus the company was located in affordable Roanoke, Virginia, only 50 minutes from Virginia Tech University in Blacksburg, known for their computer and communications engineering programs. Although the firm was not for sale at the time, Koenig persuaded the owners to sell in August. Carrier Access planned to triple the Roanoke staff of 22 within the year and to have Mellennia assume control over the company's customer service terminal division, which designed communications equipment located at customer sites. Following the Millennia acquisition, Carrier Access announced in October that it was also acquiring the ATM product line of Litton Network Access Systems of Roanoke, Virginia, after Litton announced that it was going out of business. Roger Koenig believed that the addition of the Litton products together with the additional engineering and technical talent posed a natural fit with the company's acquisition of Millennia Systems. The company planned to move the new product lines into its new Carrier Access Millennia Technology Center in Roanoke by the end of 2000.

In October, Carrier Access was listed as 7th in *Forbes* magazine's 200 Best Companies in America and was named the fastest growing Boulder County firm in the Colorado Technology Fast 50 and third fastest growing statewide. The company had added about 200 employees in 2000 and was planning on moving into additional space in Boulder.

The Telecom Bust: The Company Stumbles

Despite these accolades, however, Carrier Access began to falter. October proved to be a tumultuous month for the company, filled with heady recognition and analyst downgrades. The company warned that its profits would not meet expectations, as sales to communications companies had slipped. As a result, the company's stock dropped from more than $20 to about $14. The company's stock had been earlier trading as high as $60 per share in July, but had tumbled as part of the downturn in the greater telecom market. The company's stock lost another 31.94 percent in value upon announcing lower than expected operating results for the fourth quarter ended December 31, 2000. Although net revenue rose to $148,050,000, compared to $108,815,000 for 1999, revenue growth for the fourth quarter of 2000 had decreased to $25,014,000 from $33,112,000 for the fourth quarter of 1999.

Nevertheless, despite the company's setbacks and the general downturn in the telecom market, the company announced on February 13, 2001 that it was opening an office in Camarillo, California to augment and accelerate its focus on wireless and packet voice infrastructure product development. Roger Koenig stated that the wireless explosion of the past few years had created a large demand for broadband products that provide high bandwidth, increased density, and decreased costs throughout the network. He sought to position the company to produce new capabilities for this market. The Camarillo office was part of the company's ongoing strategy to expand into these target growth areas.

As late as May 2001, Koenig continued to give an upbeat assessment of the company's growth prospects for the near and long term, in spite of the increasing harsh environment in the telecom industry. He believed that the company's main clients, including such customers as Level-3 Communications and Quest Communications, would need to continue investing in access equipment to connect customers to their services. Despite its stock slipping to $8 per share, Koenig believed the company was poised to assist the major service carriers to increase their revenue growth by improving the quality of their services. The investment firm Credit Suisse First Boston estimated that in 2001 $75 billion would be spent on connecting customers to the networks created within the last five years. Carrier Access believed its major opportunity lay in expanding its position by providing this access. Although Carrier Access had recorded a first quarter net loss of $850,000 in 2001 compared to earnings of $7.5 million a year earlier, the company was optimistic that the business environment remained good. The company continued to hire new employees and to invest heavily in research and development, amounting to $15.1 million in 2001—a 111 percent jump from 1999.

Nevertheless, by July 2001 the company began to experience the effects of the telecommunications downturn. The telecommunications equipment sector had fallen on difficult times. In June, for example, Nortel Networks announced that it would lose $19.2 billion in the second quarter alone as demand plummeted for its switches and routers. Level 3 Communications had its first ever layoffs of 1,400 workers. The ratings on the bonds of Lucent Technologies had been cut to junk status by Standard & Poors, a sign that Lucent's survival as an independent company was far from certain. Avaya, another telecom equipment provider, reported that its sales for the rest of the year would fall short of expectations and that it planned to cut 3,000 jobs. Six months previously, demand for the equipment that moves data over telephone lines and across the Internet began a precipitous drop that continued to grow worse. In July, Carrier Access announced that it had to cut 15 percent of its staff, about 80 workers. As with other firms in the telecommunications equipment sector, the harsh economic climate compelled Carrier Access to rein in costs. For the second quarter of 2001, the company reported revenues of $29.4 million, compared with $44.1 million in the same period in the preceding year. In addition, like other telecommunications firms, Carrier Access faced for the first time serious curbs in technology spending. The company also planned to cut other operating expenses by $1 million. As a result of these conditions, the company's stock lost substantial ground over the year, plummeting from a high of $67 to just $4 per share by July 2001.

Indeed, in the first half of 2001, the telecommunications industry had lost 130,442 jobs, a staggering 19 times the amount in the same period in the previous year. The job cuts in the telecom sector accounted for nearly 17 percent of the economy's overall loss of jobs of 777,362. The telecommunications industry, now littered with smaller companies in bankruptcy, nevertheless witnessed a relative resurgence of the larger regional companies. Many of the smaller companies that had gone from explosive growth to bankruptcy blamed their plight on the anti-competitive practices of the regional Bell companies, which were said to have blocked new competitors from accessing their phone lines. The Bell companies argued, however, that the telecom debacle stemmed primarily from bad business plans and over-expansion, not anti-competitive practices by the Bell companies.

In the midst of this environment, Carrier Access switched strategies, from serving small telecommunications companies, which were quickly going bankrupt, to the large regional Bell companies, which remained profitable. In the first quarter of 2001, half of the company's business came from such large incumbent telecoms as Quest and Pacific Bell. As matters stood in the telecommunications industry at the end of 2001, the infrastructure companies had spent billions installing fiber-optic lines. But only 5 percent of the buildings in the United States had been connected to these fiber-optic networks, which appeared to place Carrier Access—especially because its customers included the Bell companies—in an enviable position to provide these "last mile" connections. Nevertheless, because of the telecommunications downturn, capital investment had dried up and some investment analysts anticipated that it would be years before significant growth returned to the sector. Carrier Access, however, remained convinced that customers wanted access to the enormous amount of communications infrastructure already in place. It also saw significant opportunity in entering and introducing products for the wireless market. The company had already begun developing wireless products in 2000, which comprised 6 percent of its total business by the second quarter of 2001. Some of its customers included AT&T Wireless and Verizon.

As a result, the company saw the wireless market as a profitable niche with enormous potential. Rather than lie low during the telecom downturn, Carrier Access decided to pursue the wireless market aggressively. The company employed fully half its workforce in research and development in search of the next innovative product. During the early 2000's, Carrier Access' strategy to weather the telecommunication storm thus lay in switching its customer base primarily to the large and profitable incumbent telecoms and entering the wireless market.

Principal Competitors

Adtran, Inc.; Advanced Fibre Communications, Inc.; Cisco Systems, Inc.; CopperCom; General DataCom Industries, Inc.; Lucent Technologies, Inc.; NEC USA, Inc.; Northern Telecom Limited (Nortel); Paradyne Corporation; Polycom; VINA Technologies.

Further Reading

"ADC and Carrier Access Corporation Plan Alliance for Future Product Development with Signing of OEM Agreement," *Business Wire*, April 22, 1997.

Adams, Duncan, "Electronic Components Supplier to Close Roanoke, Va., Plant," *Roanoke Times*, October 30, 2000.

Branaugh, Matt, "CEO of Boulder, Colo.-Based Broadband Equipment Firm Gives Positive Outlook," *Daily Camera*, May 25, 2001.

"Carrier Access Loses 31.94% On News of Revenue Shortfall," *Canadian Corporate News*, January 3, 2001.

Day, Kathleen and Elboghdady, Dina, "Fear of Telebomb Fallout," *Washington Post*, June 1, 2001.

Demers, Marie Eve, "VXTEL Names Dodani President and CEO," *Electronic News*, July 3, 2000,

Draper, Heather, "Carrier Access No. 7 on Forbes List," *Denver Rocky Mountain News*, October 14, 2000.

Gonzalez, Erika, "Carrier Access Corp. Names Board Member From Apple Computer," *Daily Camera*, July 16, 1996.

——, "Colorado's Carrier Access Corp. Links Firms to Data Transmission Lines," *Daily Camera*, April 16, 1996.

Greim, Lisa, "Fast 50 Tech Firms Share Stellar Profits; At No.1, Carrier Access Corp. Enjoys 4,778% Revenue Jump," *Denver Rocky Mountain News*, October 2, 1998.

Hudson, Kris, "Award-Winning Boulder, Colo., Telecommunications Firm Expands Offices," *Daily Camera*, November 18, 1998.

——, "Boulder, Colo.-Based Telecommunications-Equipment Firm Sees Success," *Daily Camera*, November 28, 1999.

Kelsey, Dick, "Telecom Job Cuts Top 130,000 in 2001," *Newsbytes.com*, July 5, 2001.

Kroll, Luisa, "The Race to Embrace," *Forbes*, October 30, 2000, p 184.

Levy, Larry, "High-Tech Telecommunications Company Expands Tulsa, Okla., Workforce," *Daily Oklahoman*, June 6, 2000.

MacMillan, Robert, "Baby Bells Not Responsible for Telecom Troubles," *Newsbytes.com*, June 27, 2001.

"Maker of Telecom Equipment to Add 250 High-Tech Jobs in Tulsa, Okla.," *Tulsa World*, June 28, 2000.

McDonald, Lisa, "Speculations," *Forbes*, October 10, 2000, p. 266.

Nascenzi, Nicole, "Maker of Telecom Equipment to Add 250 High-Tech Jobs in Tulsa, Okla," *Knight-Ridder/Tribune Business News*, June 28, 2000.

Newman, Richard J., "The Revenge of the Baby Bells," *U.S. News & World Report*, August 13, 2001, p. 34.

Noguchi, Yuki, "Survival of the Biggest," *Washington Post*, June 8, 2001.

Romero, Simon, "Once Bright Future of Optical Fiber Dims," *New York Times*, June 18, 2001, p. A1.

Schnabel, Megan, "Denver Firm Buys, Plans to Expand Roanoke, Va., Communications Equipment Firm," *Roanoke Times*, August 15, 2000.

Springsteel, Ian, "Vultures of the New Economy," *Washington Post*, September 9, 2001.

Stutzman, Erika, "Boulder-Colo.-Based Communications Equipment Firm Acquires Product Line," *Daily Camera*, November 7, 2000.

——, "Boulder, Colo.-Based Telecommunications Firm to Cut 15 Percent of Staff," *Daily Camera*, July 20, 2001.

—Bruce P. Montgomery

Catalytica

Catalytica Energy Systems, Inc.

430 Ferguson Drive
Mountain View, California 94043
U.S.A.
Telephone: (650) 960-3000
Fax: (650) 965-4345
Web site: http://www.catalyticaenergy.com

Public Company
Incorporated: 2000
Employees: 85
Total Assets: $67.77 million (2000)
Stock Exchanges: NASDAQ
Ticker Symbol: CESI
NAIC: 54171 Research and Development in the Physical,
     Engineering, and Life Sciences; 335314 Relay and
     Industrial Control Manufacturing; 325188 All Other
     Basic Inorganic Chemical Manufacturing

Catalytica Energy Systems, Inc. is one of the world leaders in developing and marketing technologies related to the catalytic combustion of fossil fuels. The patented process and materials Catalytica has created—in particular its Xonon catalytic technology—will make possible the production of electrical energy by gas-fired turbines with virtually no polluting emissions. With General Electric (GE), Catalytica operates a large gas turbine equipped with Xonon technology at the Silicon Valley Power Plant near San Francisco. Catalytica is working on similar catalytic systems for motor vehicles and fuel cells. Catalytica plans to ship Xonon to its first commercial customers in late 2001.

1970s–80s: Origins

While Catalytica Energy Systems was founded in 1995 as Catalytica Combustion Systems, and not incorporated as a public company until 2000, its history may be traced to the formation of its former parent, Catalytica Inc. This company was founded in 1974 by Ricardo B. Levy and James A. Cusumano. Until Catalytica began making its breakthroughs in catalytic technology,

Cusumano was perhaps best known as the precocious teenage singer who fronted the Royal Teens when they had their 1950s hit record, "Who Wears Short Shorts?" In the early 1970s Cusumano and Levy were Ph.D. chemists at the Exxon laboratories in New Jersey who shared an interest in catalytic processes. In December 1974 they left Exxon, and with Michele Boudart, a professor of chemical engineering at Stanford University, anted up $10,000 each and founded Catalytica Associates, Inc. Catalytica was a consulting company that served the petrochemical industry. It operated at first out of Levy's small basement but later moved to real offices in Silicon Valley.

By 1980 the company had a staff of 30 and had clients throughout the world. Cusumano and Levy were beginning to gravitate away from pure consulting toward research and development. They hoped to develop catalytic agents that would make possible more efficient energy production with lower pollution, for example in automotive engines and power plant turbines. However, they intended to approach their R&D work differently from other labs. Rather than slow and costly trial and error experiments with various substances, they planned to engineer made-to-order catalysts at the molecular level.

In the early 1980s a Catalytica board member introduced the partners to Tommy Davis, a legendary Silicon Valley-based venture capitalist who founded the Palo Alto-based Mayfield Fund. Davis made a series of investments in Catalytica, about $3 million in 1983 and another $2 million the following year. In October 1984 he helped broker a limited partnership, with Lubrizol Corporation's Catven unit that brought another $20 million to Catalytica. Those investments were meant to finance Catalytica for approximately five years while the company worked on developing marketable technologies.

By 1985, the company was known as Catalytica Inc. and employed 50 people, about half of whom held Ph.D. degrees. In 1988 it stopped consulting altogether to focus entirely on research and development (R&D). It would be some time before Catalytica was able to develop a commercially viable product, but the petrochemical and energy industries expressed interest in its work from the start. In 1989, Catalytica signed an agreement with Koch Industries, a chemical and petroleum refining company. In exchange for a minority interest in Catalytica, Koch invested $10 million and agreed to sponsor specific research projects. Successful technologies would be brought to market jointly by the two partners. Koch's executive vice-president David Koch was given a seat on Catalytica's board of directors.

Helping to fuel interest in Catalytica were the more demanding environmental laws of the late 1980s and early 1990s. Those laws called for significantly lower emissions by electrical power plants of the chemical nitrogen oxide, the primary component of smog and acid rain. Nitrogen oxide is created when fossil fuels are burned at high temperatures. Catalytica was developing processes that would enable plants to generate power by burning fuels at lower temperatures. "Environmental regulations are going to get nothing but more stringent," James Cusumano told Alex Barnum of the *Colorado Springs Gazette Telegraph*. "Besides, we have a moral responsibility to create technology that is cleaner and cleaner."

By 1991, Catalytica's work force had grown to 130, and the company was reporting revenues of approximately $13 million. The company was involved in 14 research ventures with ten different firms. Among its projects was the development of a component of plastics and petroleum refining that would eliminate the use of hazardous chemicals. A 1991 company backgrounder described Catalytica's "three-pronged approach": licensing out the technologies it developed; working with established companies on the production and marketing of those technologies; and, manufacturing and marketing products in Catalytica's own facilities.

Breakthroughs in the 1990s

The year 1992 was significant for Catalytica. In February the company began working with Conoco Inc., a subsidiary of E.I. du Pont de Nemours & Co., and Neste Oy, a Finnish oil company, developing a process to produce gasoline that met the standards of the Clean Air Act without the use of dangerous liquid acids. In July of the same year, the company announced the completion of a pilot program to recover bromine from hydrobromic acid waste. In December it signed a major deal with Japan's Tanaka Kikinzoku Kogyo KK and the General Electric Company to develop processes to eliminate nitrogen oxide emissions in the generation of electricity by gas-fired turbines. Since March 1991 Catalytica had been working on the project with Tanaka, a company that produces and sells prod-

ucts for industrial use in electronics, automotive, catalysis and other applications. The December 1992 agreement brought in the giant GE, whose interest in the new technology stemmed from its position as a leading producer of gas-powered turbines. GE agreed first to fund turbine research at both Catalytica and Tanaka, and then to test any systems that were developed under normal operating conditions. The research on the technology, which Catalytica called Xonon, moved forward rapidly, and the agreement was extended in June 1993.

Catalytica announced another novel production process in January 1993. As part of a project that also involved Petro-Canada and Techmocisco Inc., a Mitsubishi Oil Co. Ltd. subsidiary, a process for making methanol directly from methane was developed. Methanol can be converted into a low-pollution fuel that powers cars, tractors and other motor vehicles. Earlier methods for converting methane to methanol were beset with problems. Highly reactive chemicals used in older processes led to unwanted and hard-to-control reactions. Catalytica's new process utilized methyl bisulfate, a compound more easily controlled. In addition, Catalytica's process was able to convert 43 percent of the methane to methanol compared with a meager 3 percent for other methods.

In late 1993 Catalytica received a patent for one of its Xonon processes. Around that time, *Fortune* reported that Catalytica was closer to creating non-polluting turbine processes than large competitors such as Exxon, Mobil, ICI, or Hoechst. A GE vice president told the magazine "We've been looking for a possibility of clean catalytic combustion with several companies in the past ten years, and Catalytica is the only one that seems to have really strong potential."

1993: Catalytica Goes Public

In December 1992 Catalytica announced an initial public offering of three million shares. The stock first sold in February 1993, was priced at $7 a share, lower than the $9 to $11 Catalytica had hoped for. The company raised just over $28 million, some $10 million of which came from the Mitsubishi Oil Company, Ltd. Despite remarkable progress in its research, none of Catalytica's projects had moved beyond the testing stage to commercial viability. In October 1993 it announced that revenues of $9 million for the previous year had been offset by losses of $7 million; what's more, it predicted even greater losses for the two coming years. Most analysts did not regard this news as a cause for alarm. Based mainly on Catalytica's progress in reducing nitrogen oxide emissions in gas-turbines, they predicted that the company would start showing profits around the 1995–96 fiscal year, and that significant earnings would be achieved in the years following.

By 1993 Catalytica was working on pharmaceutical intermediates, special chemicals used in the manufacture of pharmaceuticals. Catalytica hoped to develop processes that resulted in fewer polluting by-products than standard processes. In the fall of 1993 it was looking for a production facility where it could produce chemicals for drug companies. It found one in December 1993 in East Palo Alto, not far from Catalytica's Mountain View, California headquarters. It purchased the plant from Sandoz Agro, Inc. and began supplying chemicals to Sandoz. Eventually some 40 workers were employed at the facility.

Key Dates:

1974: James A. Cusumano, Ricardo Levy, and Michele Boudart found consulting firm Catalytica Associates, Inc.

1983: Catalytica receives first $3 million in venture capital.

1988: With first work on Xonon technology, Catalytica switches focus from consulting to research and development.

1989: Catalytica signs a $10 million agreement with Koch Industries.

1991: Catalytica begins working with Tanaka Kikinzoku Kogyo KK to develop Xonon technology.

1993: Catalytica receives first Xonon-related patent; makes initial public offering; begins manufacturing ingredients for pharmaceuticals.

1994: Catalytica receives $2 million grant from the Department of Commerce's Advanced Technology Program.

1996: Catalytica makes first sale of Xonon technology to city of Glendale, California.

1999: Turbine equipped with Xonon technology produces a full gigawatt hour of virtually pollution-free energy.

2000: Catalytica Inc. is purchased by DSM N.V.; Catalytica Combustion Systems spun off and renamed Catalytica Energy Systems.

2001: The Environmental Protection Agency announces in February that tests it conducted verified the low emission rates in gas turbines equipped with Xonon.

As expected, Catalytica reported large losses again in 1993, with $8.4 million in revenues, and $9 million in net losses. However, while its financials continued to languish, it continued its progress on both the production and the R&D fronts. It made its first commercial sales ever, $5 million in chemicals produced at its new Palo Alto plant, a success that led the company to look for other strategic partners in the drug industry. In April 1994, it was awarded a patent for its methanol conversion process. Later the same year, Advanced Sensor Devices, a Catalytica subsidiary, had developed a device that continuously monitored nitrogen oxide emissions. The sensor could be mounted directly on exhaust pipes and was not affected by weather conditions. Another sensor developed by Advanced Sensor Devices in 1994 was able to monitor hot wet samples for nitrous oxide or nitrogen oxide and needed only low maintenance.

By the end of 1994, Catalytica took another step toward commercial exploitation of its new technologies. The first was an 18 percent reduction in the company's workforce—approximately 20 workers from throughout the company. "The streamlining was prompted by our desire to focus our financial resources on those programs that promise commercialization in the shortest possible time frame," company president Ricardo B. Levy said in a company statement, "and is part of our transition from a research and development organization to a technology-based commercial business." The reaction of the

markets to the layoffs was initially negative. The day after Catalytica stock dropped a full point to three-and-three-quarters. However, less than three weeks later the company's stock seemed to have recovered completely, its price rebounding by more than 18 percent.

By the mid-1990s, Catalytica's research began to attract money from various granting organizations. In 1994 the Department of Commerce's Advanced Technology Program awarded the company a grant of $2 million for work on the commercial feasibility of nanoscale catalysts—catalysts one-billionth of a meter and smaller—for petroleum and chemical industries. In November 1994 Catalytica's Advanced Sensor Devices division received a three-year grant of $1.2 from the Gas Research Institute in Chicago to develop devices to continuously monitor nitrogen oxide emissions. In August 1996, another Catalytica unit, Catalytica Combustion Systems Inc., was awarded a $3.5 million contract from the Department of Energy's Advanced Turbine System program to fund its research into cleaner, more cost-efficient gas turbines.

Reorganizing in the Late 1990s

Catalytica raised more money in May 1996 when it sold a 15 percent share of its Catalytica Fine Chemicals unit to Pfizer Inc. for $15 million. Catalytica agreed to perform research for Pfizer and to continue to supply chemicals to Pfizer's production division. Just over a month later, Catalytica sold Advanced Sensor Devices to Monitor Labs Inc. for approximately $1 million up front, an undisclosed amount once the company's monitors received final government certification, and royalties once the monitors went into regular production.

With the sale of its sensor division, Catalytica was able to concentrate most of its attention on developing its Xonon turbine systems. In September 1996 it announced the successful conclusion of initial tests on a turbine at General Electric. A spokesman for GE characterized the results as better than expected and expressed the expectation that the technology could be successfully incorporated into GE's line of turbines. At the same time, Catalytica modified the process so it could be used on older turbines. In September 1996, the company, with Woodward Governor Company, formed a joint company called GENXON Power Systems. GENXON retrofitted otherwise unusable turbines with Catalytica technology. Prospects for the new company were good because of plans to deregulate the power industry.

Catalytica was able to sell its Xonon technology for the first time in November 1996. The city of Glendale, California, contracted Catalytica to retrofit an old turbine that, because of pollution restrictions, it was only permitted to run 200 hours a year. The job was experimental in some respects; it would demonstrate whether Catalytica turbines were able to operate under normal conditions on a long-term basis. The contract was an important one for the company. If all went well, Catalytica believed it could look forward to sales to thousands of electric companies throughout the world.

In February 1997, Catalytica Fine Chemicals bought a chemical plant in Greenville, North Carolina, for about $247 million from Glaxo Wellcome. The purchase, and an accompanying $800 million pharmaceutical intermediates production contract with Glaxo, pushed Catalytica's work force up to 1,400 and made it the third largest company in the San Francisco Bay Area. By 1999, Catalytica was producing drug-related products for Glaxo, Warner-Lambert Co., and Eli Lilly & Co.

In another major deal in June 1997 GE agreed to incorporate Catalytica's technology into its line of gas-fired turbines. For Catalytica the news was a sign that its technology would become the industry standard. The market apparently agreed. A definitive deal with GE was signed in November 1998. In April 1998 Pratt & Whitney Canada Inc.'s United Technologies Corp unit placed an order for the Xonon combustion system, the first Catalytica received from an original equipment manufacturer and the first real indication that Xonon was commercially viable. Further evidence came in August 1999 when the company announced that a turbine equipped with Xonon technology had produced a full gigawatt hour of energy with virtually no pollution. In December 1999, Xonon was named the preferred emissions control system in the Pastoria Energy Facility, a power plant Enron Corp. proposed to build on Tejon Ranch land north of Los Angeles. Work on the facility was scheduled to begin sometime in 2001. The Environmental Protection Agency announced in February 2001 that tests it conducted verified the low emission rates in gas turbines equipped with Xonon.

In the summer of 2000, Catalytica took steps to refocus itself on what it saw as its core business, its energy technologies. In August it announced that the Dutch chemical company DSM N.V. would acquire most of its businesses for around $750 million and the assumption of $50 million in debt. DSM retained Catalytica's profitable pharmaceutical-related units, including their production facilities. Catalytica's energy-related operations, Catalytica Combustion Systems and Catalytica Advanced Technologies, were then spun off to form an independent company, Catalytica Energy Systems Inc. Catalytica shareholders received shares in the new company, along with a cash payment from the sale. An advantage of the spin-off for Catalytica was it created an independent company without an initial public offering. Some 85 percent of the shares of Catalytica Energy Systems remained in the hands of the company itself. The deal was approved by Catalytica shareholders in December 2000 and went into effect shortly thereafter.

As Catalytica Energy Systems, the company continued to develop its Xonon Cool Combustion technology. In August 2001 the company made a public offering of five million shares of stock, and in November it opened a new facility in Gilbert, Arizona. With over 40,000 square feet of space, the new plant would house a commercial manufacturing operation expected to begin in 2002.

Principal Subsidiaries

Catalytica NovoTec; Süd-Chemie Catalytica.

Principal Competitors

Exxon Mobil Corporation; Imperial Chemical Industries PLC; Hoechst AG; Farr Company; Mitsubishi Electric Corporation; Siemens AG.

Further Reading

Barnum, Alex, "Firm Cleaning Up on Environmental Problems/ Pollution Laws Create Demand for Catalytica," *Colorado Springs Gazette Telegraph,* December 3, 1989, p. D6.

Bishop, Jerry E., "Scientists Discover Two New Methods to Convert Natural Gas to Alcohol, Fuel," *Wall Street Journal,* January 15, 1993, p. A5.

Bylinsky, Gene, "How To Leapfrog the Giants," *Fortune*, October 18, 1993, p. 80.

"Catalytica Acquires Manufacturing Facility in East Palo Alto," *Business Wire,* December 1, 1993.

"Catalytica Awarded $2 Million Advanced Technology Program Grant From U.S. Dept. of Commerce," *Business Wire,* November 18, 1994.

"Catalytica Streamlines to Focus on Commercialization," *Business Wire,* October 6, 1994.

Galloway, Alice, and Carol Edgarian, "Catalytica Signs $30 Million Equity Funding Agreement With Koch Industries," *Business Wire,* April 3, 1989.

Mantz, Beth, "Catalytica Pres: Pharma Operations Sale, Spinoff Speed Holder Value," *Dow Jones News Service,* August 3, 2000.

Marshall, Jonathan, "Power to the People: Catalytica May Hold Key to Putting Tiny Generators Anywhere," *San Francisco Chronicle,* November 21, 1996, p. D1.

Murphy, Thomas P., "A Winning Bet," *Forbes,* January 14, 1985.

—Gerald E. Brennan

Cendant Corporation

9 West 57th Street
New York, New York 10019
U.S.A.
Telephone: (212) 413-1800
Fax: (212) 413-1918
Web site: http://www.cendant.com

Public Company
Incorporated: 1997
Employees: 57,000
Sales: $3.93 billion (2000)
Stock Exchanges: New York
Ticker Symbol: CD
NAIC: 53121 Offices of Real Estate Agents and Brokers;
   52231 Mortgage and Nonmortgage Loan Brokers;
   72111 Hotels (Except Casino Hotels) and Motels;
   532111 Passenger Car Rental; 81293 Parking Lots
   and Garages

Cendant Corporation was formed in December 1997 when Hospitality Franchise Systems, Inc. (HFS)—led by Henry Silverman—merged with CUC International Inc. Shortly after the $14 billion deal was completed, the company became involved in an accounting scandal, which led to a $2.83 billion settlement of a class action shareholder lawsuit in 1999. Since that time, Silverman has worked diligently to restore Cendant's reputation.

Cendant operates as the world's largest hotel franchiser through its Travel division with over 6,400 locations bearing the names AmeriHost Inn, Days Inn, Howard Johnson, Knights Inn, Ramada Inn, Super 8, Travelodge, Villager, Wingate Inn, and Fairfield Resorts. The company's Vehicle Services division runs the second-largest rental car business in the world through its Avis brand. It also operates National Car Parks, the largest non-municipally owned car park in the U.K. These divisions were responsible for 32 percent of revenues during 2000.

Through its Real Estate Services division—which secured 39 percent of revenues in 2000—Cendant operates Century 21, Coldwell Banker, Coldwell Banker Commercial, and ERA, and also offers mortgage services through Cendant Mortgage. In 2001, one out of every four homes sold or purchased in the United States was done so through a Cendant affiliate. Cendant's Diversified Services division includes the business of Jackson Hewitt Tax Services, the second-largest tax preparation company in the United States, along with business related to insurance and loyalty marketing. This division accounted for 29 percent of revenues during the 2000 fiscal year.

The History of CUC International

In the mid-1990s, CUC International Inc. offered individual consumers access to various services and discounts related to shopping, travel, insurance, automobiles, dining, vacationing, credit card enhancement packages, and various discount and coupon programs. The company offered its services primarily through memberships to clubs and programs. Entering 1996, CUC had about 40 million members who paid $5 to $250 per year. The company was growing rapidly in the mid-1990s through acquisitions and internal expansion.

CUC started out in 1973 as Comp-U-Card (Comp-U-Card of America, Inc.), a company launched to deliver shopping services, including home shopping, using computers and credit cards. The glaring flaw in the strategy—one that the company's founder, Walter A. Forbes, acknowledged in retrospect—was that very few computers, particularly home computer systems, were accessible to shoppers at the time. Thus, Comp-U-Card, far ahead of its time, was destined to struggle in the dawning years of the information age, waiting for technology to catch up with its progenitor's stratagem. Indeed, CUC would languish for a full decade before gradually emerging as a force in electronic commerce.

''It was a silly investment at the time because there were no home computers,'' Forbes conceded in the April 24, 1995 *Forbes.* Nevertheless, he remained committed to the idea and continued to pour money into the flailing venture until its turnaround. Forbes was only 30 years old when he started Comp-U-Card. Only five years earlier he had graduated from the Harvard Business School before taking a comfortable job with a management consulting firm, helping other business

owners and managers to run their companies. Shortly after
going to work for that firm, he came up with his own business
idea: electronic merchandising.

Specifically, Forbes became convinced that there had to be a
better way to get merchandise from the factory floor to people's
living rooms, rather than going through the traditional, torpid,
costly distribution systems that incorporated numerous warehouses, retail stores, and brokers. He believed that computers
could do the job much more efficiently. Buyers could simply
place their order with a credit card using a computer terminal,
which would immediately tell the factory or warehouse where
to send the merchandise. Lower costs and lower prices, among
other advantages of such a system, would effectively obsolete
the traditional retail industry.

Forbes, with the help of several friends, launched Comp-U-
Card in 1973 (they incorporated the business in 1974 as Comp-
U-Card America, Inc.). For three years Forbes and the other
investors dumped hundreds of thousands of dollars into the
venture in an effort to create a sort of electronic retail store.
Meanwhile, Forbes continued to toil at his job and help to
manage Comp-U-Card on the side. Because few people had
access to computers, Forbes decided to try the concept using
television. He tried to create a home shopping network through
which customers could view products, call in with a credit card
number, and have the goods delivered. Forbes later tried
in-store electronic kiosks, which featured pictures of items that
passersby could order electronically. Both the television shopping and kiosk efforts ultimately failed.

By the late 1970s, Forbes and his fellow investors had
dumped about $2 million into Comp-U-Card. The company
showed little promise of returning the investment anytime soon,
if at all. Still, Forbes was convinced of the merit of his concept.
In 1979, in fact, he surprised coworkers when he left his job to
devote all of his energy to Comp-U-Card. Forbes was hoping
that, by the early 1980s, the number of consumers who had
access to home computers would constitute a viable market for
his electronic shopping concept. To that end, in 1979 Comp-U-
Card launched its first online home shopping service, Comp-U-
Store Online.

Forbes was finally forced to accept the fact that the electronic shopping market still had not materialized. By 1982,
Comp-U-Card was generating only a few million dollars in
annual sales and still showed no signs of recovering the millions
of dollars invested since the 1973 start-up. Still undeterred,
Forbes decided to adopt a new strategy. After deciding to focus
on telephone sales, he found that Comp-U-Card was uniquely
positioned to capitalize on a related, emerging trend in the credit
card business—"affinity" programs that offered credit card

customers incentives like memberships in shopping clubs.
Credit card companies began offering memberships or discounts on memberships in Comp-U-Card's discount shopping
services as a lure to attract new customers.

Comp-U-Card's first shopping service was dubbed "Shoppers Advantage." Shoppers Advantage members paid an annual fee (about $40 in the early 1990s), which gave them access
to a toll-free number that they could dial to place orders for
merchandise. Members could purchase brand name items and
have the goods delivered directly to their home. Aside from the
convenience, the service was designed to deliver lower prices in
comparison to typical retail channels. Comp-U-Card paid the
credit card companies a percentage of the membership fees it
collected and benefitted from access to the credit card companies' mailing lists. Everybody involved benefitted, with the
exception of competing retailers.

Comp-U-Card was able to offer low prices on its goods for
several reasons. Aside from bypassing expensive brokers,
Comp-U-Card took bids from numerous distributors. When a
caller would phone in to purchase a pre-selected item, the
Comp-U-Card representative would search the database to find
the lowest bid from hundreds of distributors on the particular
item. Comp-U-Card would effectively award the sale to the
lowest bidder and add a mark-up of about five to ten percentage
points to the price to cover its overhead (i.e. the toll-free phone
call, shipping, and administrative costs). Many manufacturers
initially refused to sell through Comp-U-Card for fear of irritat-
ing their retail customers, but Comp-U-Card was eventually
able to convince most major manufacturers to use the channel,
and the service grew to include more than 250,000 items by the
early 1990s.

Thus, with its telephone shopping club marketed through
credit card companies, Forbes had finally found a winning strategy for Comp-U-Card. Indeed, from about $4 million in 1983,
Comp-U-Card's annual revenue rose past $50 million in 1985.
Realizing the viability of the new strategy, Forbes changed the
company's name to Comp-U-Card International in 1982 and in
1983 took it public to raise expansion capital. Comp-U-Card
followed up with a second offering in 1984. Shortly before the
first offering, moreover, Forbes sold licenses for its shopping
clubs in Europe and Japan for about $6 million. The company's
membership base exceeded one million in 1984, signaling the
beginning of growth that would swell Comp-U-Card's membership ranks to 40 million by the mid-1990s.

By 1986, Comp-U-Card's sales had increased to nearly $90
million. More important, the company was showing healthy
profits by then (net income totaled nearly $30 million between
1986 and 1988). Comp-U-Card's gains were also the result of
complementary programs designed to piggy-back off of the
success of the shopping club program. In 1985, for example, the
company launched Travelers Advantage, a full-service travel
club that guaranteed the lowest price for all travel arrangements
to its members and returned five percent of every dollar spent
through the service. Travelers Advantage eventually became an
important profit center for the company.

As it expanded its membership programs, Comp-U-Card
began diversifying in the mid-1980s as part of an overall strat-

Key Dates:

1973: Walter A. Forbes creates Comp-U-Card, an electronic shopping company.

1979: Forbes quits his day job to focus is efforts on Comp-U-Card; the company launches Comp-U-Store Online.

1982: The company's name changes to Comp-U-Card International.

1983: Comp-U-Card goes public.

1985: The firm launches its Travelers Advantage program.

1986: Revenues reach $90 million upon the success of its telephone shopping club; the company acquires Benefit Consultants Inc. and Madison Financial Corp.

1987: Comp-U-Card officially adopts the name CUC International Inc.

1990: Hospitality Franchise Systems Inc. (HFS) is created by The Blackstone Group and immediately acquires the Howard Johnson franchise system and the U.S.-based Ramada franchise system.

1992: CUC acquires Entertainment Publications; HFS purchases Days Inn of America.

1993: HFS becomes the largest corporate hotel chain operator in the world with the purchase of the rights to Super 8 Motels Inc.

1995: CUC purchases Welcome Wagon International Inc.

1996: HFS purchases Century 21, Knights Inn, Travelodge, Coldwell Banker, Avis Inc., and RCI; CUC acquires Davidson & Associates Inc. and Sierra Online.

1997: HFS purchases CUC for $14 billion; the two companies merge together and form Cendant Corp.

1998: Shareholders file suit against Cendant for accounting irregularities and fraud; negative publicity surrounds the company.

1999: Cedant reaches a $2.8 billion settlement in the shareholder class action lawsuit.

2000: Ernst & Young agrees to pay Cendant shareholders $335 million to settle the accounting fraud suit; Cendant acquires the AmeriHost Inn and Ameri-Host Inn Suites brand names and franchising rights.

2001: Cendant purchases Galileo International and Cheap Tickets Inc.

egy to create a multifaceted marketing organization that profited from technological changes in the marketplace. In 1986, the company acquired two companies: Benefit Consultants, Inc., a marketer of accidental death insurance through credit unions and banks, and Madison Financial Corp. (FISI*Madison), the nation's largest financial marketing organization and a provider of enhancement services (analogous to Comp-U-Card's shoppers club enhancement service) to more than 6,000 financial institutions. The acquisitions helped push Comp-U-Card's sales to $142 million in 1987 (fiscal year ended January 31, 1987), about $9 million of which was netted as income.

Reflecting its growing diversity, Comp-U-Card changed its name in 1987 to CUC International, Inc. It also launched another membership service, AutoVantage, which offered a variety of

products and services for every phase of car ownership. Going into 1988, CUC was boasting about ten million members in all of its clubs combined. During that year, CUC bought a short-notice travel business and opened new satellite centers for its auto, travel, and shopping club services. Those efforts helped the company to boost sales to nearly $200 million in 1988, earning Walter Forbes a spot on the Business Week ''CEO 1000'' list. By the end of the 1980s the company was pulling in sales of close to $300 million and offering a growing diversity of discount products and services to its millions of members.

After rocketing throughout most of the mid- and late-1980s, CUC's stock price lurched downward in 1989, and shortsellers lined up to cash in on what many analysts expected would be a big drop in the company's value. The problem stemmed largely from questions about CUC's accounting methods, which seemed to artificially inflate earnings and emasculate cash flow. CUC executives acknowledged the problem and changed their accounting methods, adding credence to critics' claims that the company risked a downturn in profits if its customers didn't continue to resubscribe to its clubs. The critics had a point. If a significant portion of CUC's members did not resubscribe to its clubs, the company would have to incur huge marketing costs trying to replace them.

In fact, CUC achieved a membership renewal rate of about 70 percent that made it the envy of the industry. That meant that CUC, unlike many other subscriber services, could more easily profit from membership growth rather than maintaining an existing membership base. That benefit was reflected in sustained sales and profit gains; sales rose to $450 million in 1991 and $644 million in 1992, while net income climbed to $16 million annually. That growth was partly the result of more acquisitions and the start of new membership clubs. In 1989, for example, CUC launched Premier Dining, a national discount dining program. In 1991, the company started HealthSaver, which offered discounts on drugs, eyewear, and other health-related merchandise. Incredibly, by 1992 CUC was employing 5,000 workers and operating its network (mostly through licensees) in 36 countries.

During the early and mid-1990s, CUC expanded greatly with significant acquisitions. In 1992, for instance, it acquired the venerable Entertainment Publications, the leading publisher of discount coupon books and promotions in North America. Similarly, in 1995 CUC bought Welcome Wagon International Inc. In addition, the company continued to add new services and membership clubs, including a new Home Shopping Travel Club and PrivacyGuard, which provided access to personal credit rating, driving, medical, and Social Security records. Furthermore, CUC entered into potentially lucrative partnerships to provide services with such big companies as Intel, Time Warner, and American Airlines.

Meanwhile, CUC continued to market its existing clubs geared mostly for shoppers, travelers, and other consumers. Indeed, by 1995 the company was sporting roughly 40 million members in its clubs and still achieving average resubscription rates of more than 60 percent. Interestingly, CUC returned to its roots in 1994 when it purchased the NetMarket Company, a leader in bringing commerce to the Internet. Finally, it appeared as though the interactive market for home shopping by computer was finally emerging as a viable distribution channel, just as Forbes had envisioned it more than 20 years earlier.

CUC sustained its blistering expansion drive into the mid-1990s, doubling revenues from $738 million in 1993 (fiscal year ended January 31, 1993) to $1.4 billion in 1996. During the same period, CUC's net income rose from $25 million to $163 million, making CUC a major force in its niche of the membership/electronic marketing industry. Signaling Forbes's intent to pursue his original dream of electronic commerce, CUC began pitching its clubs on the Internet and various online services in 1995. More important, early in 1996 CUC surprised observers when it announced plans to pay nearly $2 billion to acquire Sierra On-Line and Davidson & Associates, education and entertainment software manufacturers. CUC claimed that the purchase represented its first big move in a bid to become the biggest provider of online content in the world. The deal was completed that year, and CUC went on to purchase RentNet, Ideon, and Book Stacks, an online bookseller. In November 1996, the company paid $86.1 million to acquire software company Knowledge Adventure Inc. In 1997, Berkeley Systems, a screen-saver and game developer, was also purchased.

The History of Hospitality Franchise Systems (HFS)

In the mid-1990s, Hospitality Franchise Systems, Inc., (HFS) was the world's largest hotel franchiser, as measured by number of rooms and properties. Its chief franchise systems included Days Inns, Ramada, Howard Johnson, Super 8, Park Inns, and Village Lodges. It also engaged in the gambling industry and offered various lodging-related fee services. The company's short history was characterized by rampant growth.

HFS was formed in 1990 by The Blackstone Group, a New York-based investment bank. Blackstone hired 50-year-old Henry Silverman, an attorney and investment banker with experience in the lodging industry, to run its merchant banking group. Blackstone formed HFS with the intent of purchasing ailing or undervalued franchise brands or the rights to those chain's brand names. It planned to generate profits by charging its member hotels up-front and annual franchise fees. Rather than own the hotels, it would simply provide marketing, reservation, and other value-added administrative services. In addition, it would target hotels that offered moderate- and low-priced rooms.

To the casual observer, Blackstone's entry into the lodging market may have seemed poorly timed. The U.S. hotel industry had just experienced its greatest period of expansion in history. By the early 1990s, in fact, there were more than three million hotel rooms in the nation, and about 30 percent of those had been built since the early 1980s. By the late 1980s, it was clear to hotel industry participants that the market was quickly fading. Indeed, after increasing at a rate of approximately four percent a year throughout the middle and late 1980s, the number of newly constructed hotel rooms plummeted. By the early 1990s, the growth rate had plunged to less than one percent, and most of the new rooms were built in the Las Vegas area.

The decline of the U.S. lodging industry was the result of several factors. First, the Tax Reform Act of 1986 gradually diminished the tax-favored status of commercial real estate developments, such as hotels, and decreased investment capital for new construction. Second, and more important, was a decline in demand. As the economy slowed in the late 1980s and early 1990s, both business and personal traveling declined. Many hoteliers that had expanded their chains during the 1980s with expectations of high demand and a preferred tax status suddenly found themselves burdened with half-empty, unprofitable properties that they could not sell.

By forming HFS, The Blackstone Group hoped to exploit what it viewed as opportunities amidst turmoil in the lodging industry. Fewer than one-third of all U.S. hotels going into the 1990s were affiliated with a national or regional chain. As a result, their operating costs were generally very high compared to members of national chains, which benefitted from economies of scale. National chains could provide national advertising campaigns, centralized and automated reservation and billing departments, quality assurance programs, administrative support, and management training. Furthermore, HFS believed that the majority of the hotels that were affiliated with a chain could benefit from joining an even larger organization. Because so many hoteliers were strapped for cash by the early 1990s, HFS reasoned that it could sell large numbers of franchised rooms at low prices and profit, despite sluggish demand for hotel rooms.

In July of 1990, HFS made its first acquisitions by purchasing the Howard Johnson franchise system and the rights to operate the domestic U.S. Ramada franchise system. HFS bought the troubled properties from Prime Motor Inns for a scant $170 million. Prime Motor Inns was one of the fastest growing hotel chains in the nation during the 1980s and had accrued an impressive list of holdings by the end of the decade. However, it had also racked up over $500 million in debt, causing it to seek refuge in bankruptcy court when the market finally soured. The profitability of its Ramada and Howard Johnson subsidiaries had deteriorated significantly by 1990— the Ramada chain was even losing money.

With its first purchase, HFS immediately became a major player in the U.S. lodging industry. The Ramada chain brought 472 hotels with more than 77,608 rooms under HFS's corporate umbrella. Howard Johnson added 417 properties with about 51,786 rooms. HFS incurred about $91 million in debt during its first year of operation, but was able to recoup approximately $50 million in franchise fees for a net loss of about $1.9 million—not a bad outcome considering the company's start-up costs. HFS lost about $5 million in 1991 as it bolstered marketing efforts for its chains, began to establish a consolidated infrastructure that could also support future acquisitions, and pared its debt by about 15 percent.

In addition to trying to improve the efficiency of the hotels already in its chain, HFS sought to generate additional profits by adding independent hotels, other chain's hotels, and new construction to the Ramada and Howard Johnson chains. During 1990 and 1991, in fact, HFS added about 22,000 rooms to the two hotel chains. It profited immediately from the additions of these properties because hotel owners that joined the franchises paid HFS an up-front fee, typically around $20,000 to $30,000. In addition, the owners agreed to pay an annual franchise fee of six percent to ten percent of gross receipts. The hotel owners benefitted, of course, from access to a brand name and the reservation and marketing support proffered by HFS.

HFS's initial success prompted its second major acquisition in January of 1992. Also in January of that year it purchased Days Inn of America, Inc., from the troubled Tollman-Hundley Lodging Corp. for $259 million. Days Inn was started by Cecil B. Day in 1970 and had quickly grown into the third largest hotel brand in the world by 1992. It added about 1,220 hotels with about 133,127 rooms to HFS, thus almost doubling HFS's size. The Days Inn purchase proved to be a savvy buy for Silverman and his management team. Although HFS piled up a load of debt, it posted its first profit in 1992—net income (after-taxes) leaped to more than $20 million from revenues of about $200 million. By the end of 1992, HFS's three chains included almost 2,500 hotels with about 300,000 rooms. After fewer than three years of operation, HFS had become one of the largest hotel franchisers in the world.

In addition to praise from many of its investors, Silverman and HFS also drew criticism following their rapid climb in 1992. The Days Inn acquisition represented the third time that a group associated with Silverman had purchased the chain in less than eight years, resulting in a profit of more than $100 million for him and his investors. The first purchase occurred in 1984 by an investment fund headed by Silverman and supported by felons-to-be Ivan Boesky, Michael Milken, and Victor Posner. They sold part of the chain to public investors at a 200 percent profit, bought it back in 1988 following the 1987 stock market crash, and then sold it a year later to Tollman-Hundley for a large profit. Now, Silverman was borrowing heavily, critics said, to buy the chain again.

Although Silverman's deals were all legal, his detractors argued that HFS was engaging in questionable strategies. For example, its practice of growing quickly by lowering franchise fees to attract independent hotels into the chain (instead of building new ones) suggested a possible lowering of chain standards in order to generate short-term royalties. In addition, critics derided HFS's financing strategy, claiming that it bene-fitted certain top executives but reduced the long-term viability of the organization.

Despite criticism from a few analysts, HFS management and investors alike placed faith in the franchiser's growth strategy. The company's success throughout 1992 and into 1993 seemed to support their optimism. In April of 1993, in fact, HFS edged out Holiday Inns as the largest corporate hotel chain operator in the world when it purchased the rights to hotels owned by Super 8 Motels, Inc. Super 8 comprised 971 hotels totaling 59,532 rooms, for which HFS paid $125 million. Super 8 focused on serving government, senior, and family travelers, thus aug-menting HFS's strength in the economy/limited service hotel niche. Because most of its franchises were located in the Mid-west, HFS believed it offered significant potential for expansion into other regions of the United States.

The business strategy adopted by HFS in the early 1990s was to significantly expand each of its franchise systems while maintaining or improving their reputation and to offer high-quality, value-added services to each chain. By accomplishing these goals, HFS expected to continually increase revenues from franchise fees, thus generating capital for new acquisitions and forays into related businesses. An integral component of HFS's overall strategy was its state-of-the-art national reserva-tion systems. Customers that called any of HFS's chains were channeled to one of four national clearinghouses, where an operator would process the hotel reservation and also link cus-tomer travel requests with related services, such as airlines and rental cars. HFS provided each of its franchisees with special-ized reports tracking call patterns and reservation trends, thus allowing them to improve occupancy.

In addition to its reservation system, HFS boosted the value of its franchises through marketing programs. Each of its com-panies had a separate marketing team to research and develop national and regional marketing initiatives, but the teams all benefitted from lower shared costs related to volume purchases of printed materials and media advertising. HFS developed a quality assurance program to complement its marketing efforts by insuring that all franchise members adhered to brand-specific quality controls that created consistency for all hotels within each brand. HFS's training system educated each of its franchi-sees on how to get the most out of its reservation system and marketing programs.

One of the most important means of luring new hotels into its franchise system was its preferred vendor arrangements. Through volume buying, HFS allowed many of its franchise members to slash costs related to goods and services for every-thing from toilet paper to food. HFS also provided telephone support, via toll-free numbers, for each of its franchisees. In addition, it assisted existing hotels that were converting to a franchise with the design and construction services necessary to bring the unit up to its standards. The end result of HFS's various support services was that its hotel owners were typically able to improve occupancy and reduce operating costs, thus improving profitability compared to most independent hoteliers.

In June 1993, shortly after acquiring Super 8, HFS added Park Inn International to its line-up. With 39 properties and 4,683 rooms in 13 states, Park Inn was a relatively small chain. HFS planned to market Super 8 and Park Inn chains separately and hoped to realize strong national growth for both brand names. Its expansion strategy resulted in an increase in the number of Super 8 franchisees of more than 12 percent during 1993, to more than 1,060. Meanwhile, HFS successfully enlarged its other chains, as well. The Ramada chain, for example, swelled to 676 hotels with 107,000 rooms by the end of 1993, and Howard Johnson in-creased to 566 properties with 63,000 rooms. Days Inn grew similarly, expanding to 1,441 hotels with 145,000 rooms.

By the end of 1993, HFS had 3,783 hotels with 383,931 rooms in its systems. Although it had accrued a weighty $350 million in long-term debt, HFS managed to boost sales 27 percent in 1993, to $257 million, as net income climbed 34 percent to $21.5 million. Also during 1993, Silverman and co-managers took HFS truly public, selling all ownership shares held by The Blackstone Group on the stock market. It also increased the average occupancy rate of its hotels and was able to boost royalty fees for new members of its franchises.

HFS continued to grow each of its franchises early in 1994; by April it had about 4,000 hotels sending franchise fees to the home office. Furthermore, the company began branching out into new arenas. It formed several strategic alliances with transportation and food service companies in 1993 and 1994, such as Greyhound, Pizza Hut, and Carlson Hospitality Group, which owned several restaurants and hotels. The agreements provided services to franchise members, such as free in-room pizza delivery and reduced bus rates for HFS franchise guests. Also notable was HFS's entry into the gaming (gambling) market in 1993 and 1994. It began using its existing infrastructure to provide marketing and financing services to casino operators. In addition to those services, HFS was investing in several gambling-related ventures. In late 1994, HFS formed National Gaming Corp. to handle the company's casino and entertainment projects. National Gaming was responsible for the financing, development, and operation of casino gaming and entertainment facilities.

As it entered the mid-1990s, HFS appeared well positioned to benefit from a projected increase in hotel room rates resulting from a dearth of new development in the early 1990s. Silverman continued on an acquisition spree, purchasing Century 21, Coldwell Banker, and ERA Real Estate. HFS also acquired Knights Inn and Travelodge, and the car rental business of Avis Inc. for $800 million in 1996.

The 1997 Merger

During 1996, HFS and CUC began courting the idea of a merger. According to a 1997 *Journal of Business Strategy* article, both companies held beliefs that "merging will allow them to exploit their customer databases more fully, adding an estimated $250 million in annual incremental pretax earnings to their combined balance sheet over the next few years, and allow them to continue their swift growth—25 percent to 30 percent—for longer than either could manage alone." Sure enough, in May 1997, HFS announced its plans to merge with CUC to create a $4.3 billion consumer services powerhouse. CUC was given marketing access to HFS's 80-million customer list, while HFS eyed CUC's Internet businesses as potentially lucrative distribution channels. The deal was completed in December 1997, and the two companies were folded into a new business entity entitled Cendant Corp.

The new company appeared to be well positioned for the growth that both Silverman and Forbes expected from the deal. By January 1998, stock hovered at $33 per share and reached $41 per share just three months later. Disaster struck in April however, when Cendant was forced to admit that 1997 earnings were overstated by $100 million. On April 16, 1998, stock price fell to $19 per share—a market value loss of $13 billion—and then fell to $11 per share in August.

Shareholders filed suit against Cendant for accounting fraud related to years of accounting inaccuracies at CUC. A 1998 audit by Arthur Andersen and law firm Wilkie Farr & Gallagher discovered that CUC had reported overstated revenues and pretax income of over $500 million during the past three years. Cendant then filed suit against accounting firm Ernst & Young, who had been CUC's accountants at the time, claiming that the firm knew about the discrepancies and failed to report the wrongdoing. Ernst & Young put the blame on CUC executives,

including CFO Cosmo Corigliano and Forbes—the pair were fired during the scandal.

In December 1999, Cendant reached a $2.8 billion settlement with its shareholders, the largest recovery awarded in a securities class action case at the time. In February 2000, Ernst & Young agreed to a $335 million settlement with Cendant shareholders. In June of that year, three CUC executives—Corigliano, Casper Sabatino, and Anne Pember—pleaded guilty to accounting fraud. Throughout the entire litigation process, Silverman claimed that HFS knew nothing of CUC's fraudulent accounting practices before the merger. He stated in a 2000 winter edition of *Directors & Boards* that as a firm involved in frequent merger and acquisition activity, "We expect the numbers in financial statements certified by a Big Five accounting firm to be true. We expect management to be aggressive in projecting growth but we don't expect them to lie about the base from which they are growing. We expect optimism regarding the return on capital but we don't expect the capital to be fictitious."

Overcoming the Scandal in the New Millennium

Silverman pledged to restore shareholder confidence in Cendant, not only to boost the company's image, but that of his own. Having spent most of his career as a highly regarded and well respected businessman in financial circles, Silverman spent most of 1999 and 2000 re-establishing Cendant as a leading consumer services firm. During 2000, the company began to resume acquisition activity and purchased the AmeriHost Inn and AmeriHost Inn and Suites brand names and franchising rights. The firm also began to aggressively pursue e-commerce ventures and formed the Cendant Internet Group, which was created to oversee the evolution of Cendant businesses into successful online e-businesses. Despite the company's efforts, share price closed in 2000 at an unremarkable $9.63.

By Spring of 2001 however, there appeared to be a light at the end of Cendant's tunnel. Share price rose by nearly 50 percent. The company made several key moves that year, including the $900 million sale of its Move.com unit to HomeStore.com. The deal left Cendant with a 19 percent stake in HomeStore.com, the largest real estate site on the Web. The company also acquired online travel site Cheap Tickets Inc., ticket reservation system Galileo International, and purchased the remaining shares of Avis Group Holdings.

Just as Cendant appeared to have recovered from the scandal of the past two years, a factor beyond its control shook the travel industry—an industry responsible for over 30 percent of company revenues. The terrorist attacks of September 11, 2001, caused a dramatic slowdown in the travel sector and sent Cendant's share price tumbling back down to the $13 range. The fact that the company was well diversified however, left management confident that it would successfully ride out the economic downturn. With Silverman at the helm, Cendant pledged to continue its growth efforts well into the future.

Principal Subsidiaries

Cendant Mobility; Cendant Mortgage; Century 21; Coldwell Banker; Coldwell Banker Commercial; ERA; AmeriHost Inns

& Suites; Avis; Days Inn; Fairfield Communities; Howard Johnson; Knights Inn; Phh Arval; Ramada; Resort Condominiums International; Super 8; Travelodge; Villager Lodge; Wingate Inn; Wright Express; AutoVantage; Benefit Consultants Inc.; Cendant Incentives; Cims; Fisi-Madison Financial; Jackson Hewitt Tax Service; Long Term Preferred Care; National Car Parks; Privacy Guard; Shoppers Advantage; Travelers Advantage; WixCom.

Principal Divisions

Real Estate; Travel; Diversified Services.

Principal Competitors

The Hertz Corporation; Prudential Financial; Six Continents Hotels Inc.

Further Reading

Adams, Bruce, "Cendant's Moves Reinforce its Internet Strategies," Hotel & Motel Management, March 6, 2000, p. 1.

Braue, Marilee Laboda, "N.J. Hotel Giant Always Has Room for More," Record, January 7, 1993, Bus. Sec.

"Cendant Settles Class Action Suit," United Press International, December 8, 1999.

"CUC to Roll Out Shoppers Adventures," ADWEEK Eastern Edition, September 11, 1995, p. 12.

DeMarrais, Kevin G., "No. 1 in Hospitality," Record, July 7, 1993, Bus. Sec.

DePass, Dee, "Direct-Marketing Firm to Buy Outdoor Club," Star Tribune-Minneapolis, August 25, 1995, p. 3D.

Der Hovanesian, Mara, "Cendant: Ready to Climb Again?," Business Week, March 12, 2001.

Ellis, Junius, "These Internet Stocks Could Get You On-line for 70% Profits in a Year," Money, October 1995, p. 33.

"Entrepreneur of the Year," Fairfield County Business Journal, June 22, 1992, p. 7.

Fink, Ronald, "Hear No Fraud See No Fraud Speak No Fraud," CFO, The Magazine for Senior Financial Executives, October 1998, p. 36.

Heyl, Eric, and Richard Gazarik, "HFS Wants to Be High Roller in Gambling Industry Growth," Tribune Review, April 10, 1994, p. A10.

Hollifield, Ann, "CUC on the Move, Quietly Expanding Operations," Business First-Columbus, September 14, 1987, p. 3.

Holmes, Stephen P., "Hospitality Franchise Systems Reports Record 1993 Results," Business Wire, February 10, 1994.

Lewis, Peter H., "CUC Will Buy Two Software Companies for $1.8 Billion," New York Times, February 21, 1996, p. 1C.

Mannino, Barbara, "Building an Empire," Best's Review—Property/Casualty Insurance Edition, April, 1998, p. 43.

Morgan, Sandra, "CUC International Acquires NetMarket Co.," Business Wire, November 15, 1994.

——, "CUC International Reports Record Year-End and Fourth Quarter Growth," Business Wire, March 21, 1995.

Oliver, Suzanne, "Virtual Retailer," Forbes, April 24, 1995, p. 126.

Pitock, Todd, "HFS and CUC: Perfect Together?," Journal of Business Strategy, July-August, 1997, p. 36.

Plevyak, Laura, CUC International Milestones. Stamford, Conn.: CUC International, Inc., 1996.

Prior, James T., "Hospitality Franchise Systems—A NJ Gem," New Jersey Business, April 1993, p. 22.

Raphael, Steve, "Competitor Buys Entertainment Publishing," Crain's Detroit Business, October 21, 1991, p. 30.

"Regaining Credibility After a Crisis," Directors & Boards, Winter, 2001, p. 24.

Roberts, Jim, "Leguestar Deal Provides CUC with New Market," Fairfield County Business Journal, January 4, 1993, p. 1.

Sloan, Alan, "Once Again, It's Checkout Time," New York Newsday, September 13, 1992, p. 4.

Tsao, Amy, "Cendant: Ascendant Once Again?," Business Week, October 3, 2001.

Woody, Laura, "Econo Lodge to Become Ramada," Stuart News, April 3, 1993, Bus. Sec.

—Dave Mote
—update: Christina M. Stansell

Chicago Pizza & Brewery, Inc.

16162 Beach Boulevard, Suite 100
Huntington Beach, California 92647
U.S.A.
Telephone: (714) 848-3747
Fax: (714) 848-5578
Web site: http://www.bjsbrewhouse.com

Public Company
Founded: 1978
Employees: 1,510
Sales: $52.35 million (2000)
Stock Exchanges: NASDAQ
Ticker Symbol: CHGO
NAIC: 72211 Full-Service Restaurants; 31212 Breweries

Chicago Pizza & Brewery, Inc. operates a chain of restaurants which are run under various names: BJ's Pizza & Grill, BJ's Restaurant & Brewery, BJ's Restaurant & Brewhouse, and Pietro's Pizza. Chicago Pizza & Brewery Inc. has grown steadily during the 1990s, and in 2001 it included 30 restaurants in all in five western states, California, Hawaii, Oregon, Washington, and Colorado. The company expects to continue its expansion and to move into Arizona as well. Chicago Pizza & Brewery restaurants have menus which offer a variety of items, including salads, burgers, pasta, sandwiches, and entrees, but the chain is best-known for its Chicago-style deep-dish pizza. The company also operates microbreweries in six of its restaurants. Those breweries supply the entire chain with a full line of regular and seasonal beers. Beer sales account for about 25 percent of Chicago Pizza & Brewery sales.

Amateur Pizzerias

The history of Chicago Pizza & Brewery is in large part the story of the attractiveness of the restaurant business to outsiders. It began in 1976 when two residents of Ohio, Bill Cunningham, a partner in a brokerage firm, and Michael Phillips, the marketing director for an appliance company, decided to strike out and go into business for themselves. Rather than selecting a business they knew, however, they decided to try their luck in restaurants. Neither partner had any experience whatsoever in

running a restaurant; the deciding factor was that because there would be no accounts receivable or inventory to worry about, the bookkeeping would be simpler. Cunningham and Phillips quit their jobs and moved their families across the country to California where they purchased a Burger King franchise in San Pedro. They were attracted to Burger King primarily by the detailed training the company offered its franchisees. That training provided the basis for the success of their own chain of restaurants. While with Burger King, Phillips and Cunningham hoped eventually to purchase more franchises. They were forced to reconsider that plan, however, when Burger King adopted a new policy that prevented franchisees from owning stores themselves. Instead the partners turned to pizza.

Phillips and Cunningham had no experience in pizza either. They knew what they liked, though, and in their minds, there was a lot of room for improvement in California pizza restaurants. "We didn't think they were very people-oriented," Cunningham once told the *Orange County Register*. "It was: Get in line, order your pizza, put a number on your table. Kids screaming, peanuts on the floor." They made up their minds that pizza could be served just as well in a real restaurant, with wait people and a nice décor. So, in 1978, they founded a company called Roman Systems Inc. and opened the first BJ's Chicago Pizzerias. The first restaurant was located in Santa Ana, California, followed shortly by one in Newport Beach, California. The concept was simple and it worked: traditional Chicago pan pizza, for under $5 per person, served by waiters and waitresses in an attractive restaurant setting rather than amid benches, spilled beer, and sawdust. Through the 1980s, BJ's business increased by about ten percent a year, even during periods of economic recession. When the economy was hit by another recession in the early 1990s, however, even an inexpensive, full service restaurant like BJ's found it was only just holding on—not losing money, but not growing either. The pizza garnered a solid reputation too. By 1991, BJ's had won just about every "Best Pizza" award given in the Los Angeles area.

New Careers in Pizza

By 1991, BJ's had six restaurants, all earning over $1 million annually—about twice the pizza industry average. Cunningham and Phillips began getting inquiries from outsiders

---

Company Perspectives:

BJ's Brewery and BJ's Brewhouse serve markedly superior food and fresh, handcrafted beers in a casual, lively atmosphere. Our employees and experience exude a warm, friendly and energetic spirit that serves to convey a sense of honest value and a commitment to totally exceed the expectations of our guests. To assure the delight and continued loyalty of the guest, we are fanatical about each and every detail: from the use of only quality ingredients and preparation of our product and the well-trained, enthusiastic spirit of our employees to clean premises, a colorful presentation of our image and our on-going community involvement, the BJ's Brand strives to make our guests say "Wow!, I love this place!"

---

interested in opening BJ's franchises. Growth seemed to be in BJ's future and the partners were looking at the addition of 15 new stores in the first half of the 1990s. One of their basic principles was to go slow with growth philosophy until they had adequate experienced staff in place for new openings. By the early 1990s, Cunningham and Phillips were also growing tired of running the business on a day-to-day basis. They were ready to step back and start to enjoy what they had built up. One day the BJ's owners asked their accountants, Paul Motenko and Jerry Hennessey, how to scale back their involvement in the company. Motenko and Hennessey hardly hesitated. They would be willing to take over the management of BJ's. Although they had no experience as restaurateurs, they closed their CPA firm and launched new careers in pizza.

One of Motenko and Hennessey's first decisions was to begin an aggressive expansion of the BJ's chain. They opened a site in Long Beach in 1992, put a second location in La Jolla in 1993, and launched restaurants in Seal Beach, Huntington Beach, and Lahaina, Maui, in 1994. The quick expansion led to losses: in 1994, the company a suffered a $523,000 loss against revenues of $6.5 million, and in 1995 a loss of $1 million against revenues of $6.6 million. Nonetheless, 1995 Motenko and Hennessey were willing to purchase the business outright for about $4 million and stock in the firm, which had been newly incorporated.

Once they owned the firm, Hennessey and Motenko set to work revamping it. Consultants were hired to design a new logo and to create a consistent concept for a chain of restaurants. The results were first incorporated into a restaurant the firm opened in Brea, California, in April 1996. With 10,000 square-feet in floor space, the Brea restaurant was nearly five times larger than most then-existing BJ's. It was also the first store in the chain with a microbrewery. It offered a much larger selection of food, adding pasta, salads, burgers, and sandwiches, and a greatly expanded pizza menu. The Brea restaurant was acquired and running in a remarkably short period of time. The building was first acquired on March 15 and the restaurant was opened on April 1, only two weeks later—after the installation of completely new fixtures, a full renovation, and the hiring and training of 135 new employees.

The opening was not free of problems, however, and the owners spent the next two months getting the restaurant's ser-

vice up to speed. But once the Brea restaurant got on track, it became the flagship store of the BJ's chain. An important part of the new concept was the adoption of a new name for the restaurants: BJ's Pizza & Grill. New stores continued to be opened through the rest of the decade. By October 1996, the BJ's chain was ten stores large, with locations in four states, California, Hawaii, Oregon, and Washington. The growth got an important boost in March 1996 with the purchase of the Pietro's Corp., the owner of a chain of pizza restaurants in the states of Washington and Oregon.

Pietro's was on the verge of bankruptcy at the time and Motenko and Hennessey were able to acquire it for $2.35 million and the assumption of about $500,000 in debt. Four Pietro's restaurants were converted to BJ's format; some others were shut down; in 2000, six were still operating under the old Pietro's name. When Pietro's was acquired, Motenko and Hennessey anticipated that Pietro's might add as much as $11 million in annual sales to their coffers.

Pizza IPO in the Mid-1990s

In the first quarter of 1996, BJ's lost about $367,000 against sales—which had increased by 12 percent—of $1.8 million. Despite the losses, which the owners attributed to the opening of the new restaurants, in October of that year, the firm, under the name of a newly-formed holding company, Chicago Pizza & Brewery Inc., took another major step. It made an initial public offering of company stock, selling 1.8 million shares for $5 a piece. Of the approximately $9 million that the IPO raised for Chicago Pizza & Brewery, nearly $7 million was to go toward the renovation of newly-acquired restaurants and another $1.6 million was to be used for debt reduction. The IPO had one completely unexpected consequence for the firm. Chicago Pizza had floated its offering with a relatively unknown underwriter, the Boston Group of Los Angeles. Not long afterwards, the Boston Group went out of business. From one day to the next, Motenko later said, Chicago Pizza seemed to lose all market support and its shares plunged from their $5 opening price to around $1 where they would hover for much of the next five years.

Despite such unfortunate occurrences, the company had found an effective formula. By the mid-1990s, BJ's was attracting a diverse clientele. The restaurants with their generous portions and low prices drew families, students, and seniors, while the exciting atmosphere of the bars in BJ's drew crowds of singles and young professionals. In March 1997, Chicago Pizza & Brewery announced the opening of its first restaurant in Boulder, Colorado. The site included a restaurant with more than 150 seats and a brewery with a capacity of ten barrels. As 1997 ended, the company boasted 27 restaurants with annual sales of $26 million. In November 1998 the firm announced it would open three more restaurants in the Los Angeles area.

Late 1990s: Outside Interest in Chicago Pizza

In December 1998, La Pizza Loca Inc., one of the largest Latino-owned businesses in California's Orange County, approached Chicago Pizza & Brewery and offered to buy out the company. Pizza Loca's chief executive, Alex Meruelo, who already held a 7.4 percent stake in Chicago Pizza & Brewery

Key Dates:

1978: Bill Cunningham and Michael Phillips open the first BJ's Pizzeria and found Roman Systems Inc.

1991: Cunningham and Phillips turn the management of company over to their accountants, Paul Motenko and Jerry Hennessey.

1992: Motenko and Hennessey begin aggressive campaign of expansion.

1995: Motenko and Hennessey purchase BJ's chain.

1996: Chicago Pizza and Brewery is incorporated as a holding company for the BJ's chain and goes public; company acquires Pietro's Corp. chain of pizzerias in Oregon and Washington states.

1998: A brewery/restaurant in Boulder, Colorado, is opened.

1998: Chicago Pizza & Brewery rejects a takeover bid from La Pizza Loca, Inc.

1999: 1.25 million shares of Chicago Pizza & Brewery stock are sold to ASSI Inc.

2000: Jacmar Inc. obtains majority stake in Chicago Pizza & Brewery.

offered to purchase it for $2 per share, nearly 50 cents above the then-prevailing market price, an offer worth approximately $12.8 million in all. Under the terms of Meruelo's offer, La Pizza Loca would purchase all Chicago Pizza shares except those held personally by Motenko and Hennessey. Those shares would be exchanged for shares in the newly-combined Pizza Loca-Chicago Pizza. Meruelo said he was pursuing the deal because he believed there were strong synergies between the two firms. The owners of Chicago Pizza rejected the offer, however, saying they felt it did not serve the best interests of the company's shareholders.

A little more than two months later, Chicago Pizza & Brewery announced that it was selling 1.25 million shares of its common stock to ASSI Inc., a real estate and hospitality company that had provided funds for the acquisition of the Pietro's chain in 1996. In exchange for the stock, ASSI was to pay Chicago Pizza $1 million and cancel two consulting agreements it had with the company, as well as canceling 3.2 million of Chicago Pizza's outstanding warrants which it held. Those warrants—a kind of stock option certificate which allowed the holder, for a predetermined period of time, to purchase a share of stock at a predetermined price—made up approximately 25 percent of all Chicago Pizza's outstanding warrants. Many saw the deal as linked directly to the retirement of those warrants, which were seen to be depressing the value of Chicago Pizza's stock. Another incentive for Chicago Pizza, however, was the promise of ASSI's real estate expertise as it pursued further expansion. Alex Meruelo, whose La Pizza Loca offer to take over the BJ's chain had been rebuffed in December, immediately filed suit against Chicago Pizza in civil court, alleging that in accepting approximately 80 cents per share from ASSI instead of the $2.00 per share Pizza Loca had offered, Chicago Pizza had acted irresponsibly toward the interests of its stockholders. In March 1999, a California court refused Meruelo's request for a temporary restraining order that would have

blocked the transfer of stock to ASSI. The deal was consummated later in March.

Chicago Pizza earned its first profit under Motenko and Hennessey in 1998, when it reported earnings of $85,000, up from a loss of $315,000 in 1997. The company had 1998 revenues of $30.1 million, up 15 percent from the previous year. In mid-1999 the company announced an executive restructuring with the naming of Ernie Klinger as president. Jerry Hennessey gave up the position and became co-CEO with Paul Motenko. Chicago Pizza denied that the restructuring had anything to do with an attempt by Alex Mereulo, the holder by then of nearly 15 percent of the company's stock, to win a seat on the board of directors.

The year 1999 saw Chicago Pizza's annual sales jump to $37.4 million and same store sales at BJ's restaurants increase by 7.8 percent. In 1999, it also opened new restaurants in Arcadia, Woodland Hills, and La Mesa, California, and planned several other new sites in the coming months. As 2000 began, the company was operating 19 BJ's and eight Pietro's. In spring 2000, Chicago Pizza opened a new restaurant in West Covina, California, which had 12,000 square feet in area as well as the chain's largest microbrewery.

The ownership of Chicago Pizza underwent another change in December 2000, when the Jacmar Cos., one of Chicago Pizza's major restaurant suppliers, agreed to purchase approximately 2.9 million shares of the company's stock. Jacmar had a newly-formed affiliate called BJ Chicago, which had earlier in the year acquired more than 15 percent of Chicago Pizza common stock in open trading. BJ Chicago bought another 2.2 million shares at $4 each from ASSI Inc. and Louis Habash, and co-CEO's Motenko and Hennessey agreed to sell 661,358 of their own shares, about half of their personal holdings, as well. In all, the deal gave Jacmar a 51 percent holding in Chicago Pizza and control of the firm.

Chicago Pizza officials later admitted that debt financing had forced them to make the deal. The Union Bank would only agree to $8 million in loan financing to Chicago Pizza only if the company were able to come up with additional equity. Chicago Pizza & Brewery called 2000 the best year in its history. Four new restaurants were opened in California. It marked the fifth consecutive year of same-store sales increases. Company revenues increased by 40 percent over 1999, reaching $52.35 million.

Principal Divisions

Pietro's Restaurants; BJ's Pizza & Grill; BJ's Restaurant & Brewery; BJ's Restaurant & Brewhouse.

Principal Competitors

T.G.I. Friday's; Chili's Grill & Bar; Claim Jumper; The Cheesecake Factory; California Pizza Kitchen; Pizzeria Uno; Chicago Bar and Grill.

Further Reading

Allar, Bruce, ''LagerHeads,'' *Pizza Today*, July 2000, p. 20.

Barron, Kelly, "Investors Gobble Up Shares Of California-Based Chicago Pizza & Brewery Inc.," *Orange County Register*, October 9, 1996.

"BJ's Pizza, Grill & Brewery Plans 18 Sites in Oregon, Washington," *Portland Oregonian*, September 4, 1997, p. C1.

"Chicago Pizza & Brewery Inc. Announces the Opening of Its Boulder, Colo. Brewery and Grill," *Business Wire*, March 21, 1997.

"Chicago Pizza & Brewery Names Klinger Prexy, Opens Largest Unit," *Nation's Restaurant News*, July 26, 1999, p. 48.

"Chicago Pizza & Brewery to Receive $8M Debt Financing," *Dow Jones News Service*, February 23, 2001.

"Chicago Pizza Announces Agreement With Strategic Investor," *Business Wire*, February 19, 1999.

"Chicago Pizza Trims Losses, Turns Small Profit for '98," *Orange County Register*, April 1, 1999, p. C2.

Crecca, Donna Hood, "By The Numbers," *Chain Leader*, July 2000 pp. 63–70.

Deemer, Susan, "Fast Growth, Slower Profits for Chicago Pizza," *Orange County Business*, Journal, September 6, 1999, p. 4.

Earnest, Leslie, "Chicago Pizza, Assi Complete Stock Deal, *Los Angeles Times*, March 23, 1999, p. C15.

——, "La Pizza Loca Offers to Buy Chicago Pizza for $12.8 Million Acquisitions," *Los Angeles Times*, December 16, 1998, p. C1.

——, "Seeking a Bigger Slice," *Los Angeles Times*, November 11, 1998, p.C7.

Hardesty, Greg, "Chicago Pizza Names Ernie Klinger President," *Orange County Register*, June 22, 1999, p. C2.

——,"No Thanks, BJ's Pizza Says to La Pizza Loca Buyout Bid," *Orange County Register*, December 19, 1998, C2.

Hughes, Paul, "Pizza Push," *Orange County Business Journal*, August 26, 1996, p. 1.

"Jacmar Arm Acquires Chicago Pizza and Brewery," *Nation's Restaurant News*, January 8, 2001, p. 47.

"Jacmar Plans on Controlling Chicago Pizza Food Service," *Los Angeles Times*, December 22, 2000, p. C3.

"La Pizza Loca Blasts 'Sweetheart' Deal and Announces Filing of Lawsuit," *Business Wire*, February 24, 1999.

Morgan, Kitty, "BJ's Pizza Chain Thrives Despite Recession," *Orange County Register*, July 27, 1992, p. D4.

Sheridan, Margaret, "Fast Forward," *Restaurants & Institutions*, August 1, 1998.

—Gerald E. Brennan

Cincinnati Financial Corporation

6200 South Gilmore Road
Fairfield, Ohio 45014-5141
U.S.A.
Telephone: (513) 870-2000
Fax: (513) 870-2911
Web site: http://www.cinfin.com

Public Company
Incorporated: 1950 as The Cincinnati Insurance
  Company
Employees: 3,106
Total Assets: $13.28 billion (2000)
Stock Exchanges: NASDAQ
Ticker Symbol: CINF
NAIC: 524113 Direct Life Insurance Carriers; 524114
  Direct Health & Medical Insurance Carriers; 524126
  Direct Property and Casualty Insurance Carriers;
  52421 Insurance Agencies and Brokerages; 551112
  Offices of Other Holding Companies

With assets of over $13 billion, Cincinnati Financial Corporation was ranked the 17th largest U.S. stock property casualty insurer by *Fortune* magazine in April 2000. This holding company—known in some circles as "Cin-Fin"—controls six subsidiaries. The Cincinnati Insurance Company, founded in 1950, markets property and casualty insurance in 31 states through nearly 1,000 carefully selected independent agencies. The Cincinnati Casualty Company and The Cincinnati Indemnity Company offer business, homeowner, auto, and personal liability insurance. The company markets life, health, long term care, disability income insurance, and annuities through The Cincinnati Life Insurance Company. Cin-Fin's investment-related subsidiary, CFC Investment Company, supports the other subsidiaries and their agents through commercial leasing and financing activities. The company's newest subsidiary, CinFin Capital Management Company, was created in 1999 to provide investment management services to both businesses and individuals.

Historically, Cincinnati Financial's low cost structure, conservative investment strategy, and strong network of agents have enabled it to consistently outperform property and casualty insurance industry averages. In fact, *Barron's* analyst Harlan S. Byrne has characterized Cin-Fin as "one of the best-performing of property-casualty insurance companies." Its revenues increased from $1.05 billion in 1990 to $1.74 billion in 1995, and net income grew from $128.96 million to $227.35 million during the same period.

While able to claim its 40th consecutive year of annual dividend increases in 2000, Cin-Fin was hit hard in the late 1990s and into the new millennium by factors largely outside of its control. Court decisions affecting the auto insurance industry in Ohio, costs related to technology upgrades, losses related to weather conditions, price wars brought on by increased competition, and higher loss costs, all played a part in a 53.5 percent decline in net income posted in 2000. Net income for the year was $118.4 million versus $254.7 million recorded in 1999.

Postwar Origins

The business was chartered as The Cincinnati Insurance Company in 1950 by two brothers, John ("Jack") and Robert Schiff. Jack, the elder of the two, had graduated from Ohio State University in 1938 and started working with Travelers Insurance Company that same year. After serving in the military during World War II, Jack launched an independent insurance agency. His independent insurance agency did not represent any single firm and could therefore sell policies from any number of companies. Robert joined his brother's business in 1946, when he graduated from Ohio State.

It wasn't long before Jack conceived of a new insurance company, one created, owned, and operated by insurance agents themselves. A 1949 meeting with family friend and respected colleague Chester T. Field helped bring the idea to life in 1950. Field and the Schiffs persuaded several local independent agents to join them, including Harry Turner, who became the company's first president. Robert Schiff was the company's first vice-president, while Jack Schiff was named secretary-treasurer, and Chester Field served as a board member. The board raised $200,000 in initial investments and enlisted several independent agents from around the state to begin promoting Cincinnati Insurance Company's fire, auto, and later marine and theft insurance.

The Cincinnati Insurance Company (CIC) was founded on several key concepts, including a conservative investment and growth strategy, low expenses, and a strong agent network. The company kept costs low by hiring agents who either had their own offices or worked out of their homes. This strategy would continue throughout CIC's history; in the early 1990s, expenses were only about ten percent of annual premiums, one of the lowest rates in the industry. The company also kept costs low by carefully choosing its clients as well as its agents, making sure that both were the "cream of the crop."

The firm had two primary constituencies: the independent agents to whom it offered insurance products, and the clients to whom independent agents sold the individual policies. CIC forged strong relationships with its agents by paying high commissions (up to 20 percent of premiums), providing responsive claims service, and encouraging agents to own company stock. In a 1990 *Financial World* article, McDonald & Co. analyst Nancy Benacci noted that Cin-Fin had "a claims person in every town and [made] payments and adjustments fast." A newspaper article written around the time of the company's formation called CIC "the first company owned exclusively by Ohio insurance agents and Cincinnati businessmen." By the early 1990s, company agents owned about one-fifth of its equity. *Financial World's* Adrienne Linsenmeyer noted that in 1990 "70 percent of Cin-Fin's independent agents rate the company tops and book their best business with the company." CIC won over customers by offering guaranteed rates, and policies with premiums that did not increase for up to five years. These factors laid a solid foundation upon which the Schiff brothers and their colleagues built a prosperous business.

Solid Growth in the 1950s and 1960s

Insurance companies typically have two possible profit centers: underwriting (or selling insurance policies) and investing. An underwriting profit is expressed in industry parlance as the "underwriting margin" or "combined ratio." The combined operating ratio compares claims and overhead to premiums collected. A combined operating ratio of 100 or more indicates that a company's expenses equaled or exceeded the premiums that it collected. A ratio of 105, for example, indicates that a company suffered a loss of five percent on underwriting; premiums collected fell short of claims and operating expenses. Beginning in the 1960s, property and casualty insurers in general did not make

money on underwriting. Consequently, any profits made were usually generated through shrewd investment of premiums.

CIC consistently achieved underwriting profits throughout the 1950s and 1960s. By 1955, CIC's roster of products included homeowner's and commercial all-risk plans. From the outset, the firm tailored its policies to small businesses across the Midwest. CIC expanded geographically during its first five years in business, hiring agents in Kentucky in 1955 and Indiana the following year. Gross annual premiums multiplied from $92,000 in 1951 to $928,000 in 1956.

From 1956 to 1971, the company averaged a 9.2 percent annual profit on underwriting. During this period of CIC's history, the company conservatively invested its surplus in government bonds, one of the most low-risk vehicles available. From 1956 to 1968, CIC expanded its reach into six new, primarily Midwest, states: Michigan, Pennsylvania, Florida, Georgia, Alabama, and Tennessee. The company also broadened the types of coverage it offered during this period, adding earthquake, automobile comprehensive and collision, burglary, and robbery options. By 1967, CIC offered 13 types of insurance. Harry Turner served as president until 1963, providing the young company's first decade with what successor Jack Schiff called "wise, conservative management."

Reorganization Brings New Era of Growth

As president of CIC from 1963 to 1975, Jack Schiff ushered in a more aggressive era. In line with a trend that swept the insurance industry in the 1960s, CIC established Cincinnati Financial Corp. as a holding company in 1968. Harry Turner served as the new entity's chairman, while Jack Schiff was president and, starting in 1973, chief executive officer.

The corporate reorganization signaled a period of diversification and rapid growth in revenues and net income. In 1970, Cin-Fin created CFC Investment Company. This segment of Cin-Fin bought and sold commercial real estate for investment purposes. It also provided low cost loans to agents and offered vehicle leases and loans for the agents and their customers.

Public stock floatations in 1971 and 1972 raised about $14 million, $3.5 million of which was used for debt reduction. The remainder went into a fund used in 1972 to acquire The Life Insurance Company of Cincinnati and Queen City Indemnity, a property/casualty firm. Cin-Fin made its biggest purchase ever the following year, merging with Inter-Ocean Corporation, another Cincinnati company and life insurer. The transaction increased Cin-Fin's asset base by almost 60 percent, to $161 million, by the end of 1973. Inter-Ocean Chairman W.G. Alpaugh, Jr., replaced the retiring Harry Turner as Cin-Fin chairman in 1973.

This string of acquisitions helped increase Cincinnati Financial's revenues dramatically, from $19.7 million in 1968 to $96.7 million in 1973, while its net income shot from $1.1 million to $9.8 million. During this time, Cin-Fin's primary profit center shifted from underwriting to investing. From the 1970s through the early 1990s, the insurance industry overall averaged a seven percent annual loss on underwriting. Cincinnati Financial's insurance businesses were more profitable than most, but they still only broke even on average, bringing an increased emphasis on investing.

1950: John and Robert Schiff create The Cincinnati Insurance Company.
1955: The firm begins expansion and moves into Kentucky.
1968: Cincinnati Financial Corporation is established as a holding company.
1970: Subsidiary CFC Investment Company is created to buy and sell real estate for investment purposes.
1973: Cin-Fin merges with Inter-Ocean Corporation, a Cincinnati-based company and life insurer.
1982: Robert Morgan is named CEO.
1984: The company experiences its first decline in profits.
1990: Revenues exceed $1 billion.
1995: The firm expands into Arkansas, Maryland, and Minnesota.
1996: Cin-Fin generates the second-highest profit margin among publicly traded U.S. insurers.
1998: Natural disasters cost the company $93.5 million.
1999: Morgan retires and chairman John J. Schiff, Jr., takes over as CEO; Cin-Fin establishes its sixth subsidiary, CinFin Capital Management.
2000: Two Ohio Supreme Court decisions related to auto insurance force the company to report a 53 percent drop in net income over the previous year.

In 1972, the company hired James Miller as its first full-time investment department employee. According to a late 1995 article in *Forbes* magazine, Miller and Cin-Fin demanded the same performance of its investments that it expected of its own stock: "We want dividends and companies that will increase their dividends." For all its conservatism, by the early 1990s, about half of the insurer's investment portfolio was in common stocks. In fact, nearly 43 percent of the fund was tied up in just two stocks: Fifth Third Bancorp and Alltel, both based in Ohio.

In spite of this fundamental change in its business, Cin-Fin's growth continued unabated through the remainder of the decade. Revenues expanded from less than $100 million in 1973 to over $330 million by 1980, and profits jumped from $9.8 million to $33.4 million during the same period.

Weathering the Storms of the 1980s

Robert Morgan succeeded co-founder Jack Schiff as CEO in 1982. Morgan—who had joined Cincinnati Insurance in 1966, advanced to vice-president and general manager in 1972, and became president in 1976—oversaw a relatively difficult decade for Cin-Fin and other property-casualty insurers. A string of natural disasters highlighted by Hurricane Hugo battered underwriting results, and investment pitfalls including commercial real estate and junk bonds led to the downfall of several insurers. Cin-Fin suffered the effects of both these trends, though not nearly as severely as some of its rivals.

The company experienced its first-ever decline in profits from $68.7 million on $490.6 million revenues in 1984 to $55 million on $596.5 million in 1985. During the mid-1980s,

property-casualty insurers averaged a combined ratio of 116, but in the latter years of the decade, Cin-Fin managed to keep its combined ratio under 100. Revenues increased to $974.4 million and net grew to $111.5 million by 1989, and the dividend nearly doubled from 1986 to 1990.

Cin-Fin's performance won it increased attention from business analysts in the early 1990s, but not necessarily for its insurance activities. To be sure, such observers as *Barron's* Harlan S. Byrne praised the company's "better than average" underwriting results and "tight-fisted control of expenses." But others, including *Forbes'* Thomas Easton, admired the company as "a well-run insurer coupled to a closed-end fund with a superb performance record." Easton noted that the insurer's investment returns had beaten the Standard & Poor's 500 by four percentage points from 1985 to 1995, for example. Cincinnati Financial Corp.'s bottom line bore out these accolades. Having broken the $1 billion revenue mark in 1990, Cincinnati Financial Corp. approached $2 billion in 1995. Net income increased from $128.9 million to $227.4 million during the same period. In 1996, the firm secured the second-highest profit margin among publicly traded U.S. insurers.

While garnering much attention from the business community, Cin-Fin management felt that it lacked adequate attention from investors, especially since its financial performance had a history of being strong. As such, company executives began to target Wall Street analysts in late 1995, touting the company's financial and industry achievements. It was the second time in the firm's history that it aggressively marketed itself to Wall Street. Morgan commented on the strategy in a 1996 *Cincinnati Business Courier* article stating, "We didn't feel we were getting attention from analysts. We wanted to get our story out." The strategy appeared to pay off when in 1997, Cin-Fin's stock was added to the S&P 500 Index. Stock price peaked that year at $141 per share.

Overcoming Challenges: Late 1990s and Beyond

As competition became fierce in the late 1990s, price wars broke out and threatened the company's goal of writing $2 billion of direct premiums on an annual basis. At the time, nearly two-thirds of the firm's policies covered commercial-related lines, a shift from the past when it had focused primarily on personal-related insurance. Due to the increased competition, the company began to increase its emphasis on commercial business, a more profitable segment to write versus auto or homeowners policies.

Cin-Fin also concentrated on expanding to new markets. After moving into Arkansas, Maryland, and Minnesota in the mid 1990s, the firm targeted upstate New York in 1998 and Montana, Idaho, and Utah in 1999. It also began to upgrade its internal technology, which included the development of an intranet that would enable its agents to process claims faster and easier.

During 1999, Morgan retired after over 30 years of services with the company. Chairman John Schiff, Jr., took over as CEO. Along with expanding into new markets, Cin-Fin eyed new business ventures to increase revenues and profitability. In January of that year, the firm created its sixth subsidiary, CinFin

Capital Management, to provide investment management services to businesses and wealthy individuals.

Factors outside of the company's control, however, began to take their toll on the firm's profits. Severe weather, including a tornado that swept through Cincinnati, cost Cin-Fin $93.5 million in 1998. During that year and in 1999, growth slowed to six percent, and the company's stock price began to fall. Share prices fell by 19 percent during 1999, and traded at late 1997 prices.

Despite these setbacks, management remained optimistic about Cin-Fin's future gains. During 1999, the firm's property and casualty premiums grew by seven percent, while the industry average at the time was just 2.3 percent. The firm also began to raise its rates, after nearly ten years of falling prices due to stiff competition. Schiff, Jr., claimed in a February 2000 *Business Courier* article, "We believe our business model gives us strong advantages in continuing to outperform the industry through all kinds of market and economic environments."

While entering the new millennium, however, Cin-Fin again faced challenges beyond its control. During 2000, the company was forced to take a $110 million charge related to two Ohio Supreme Court decisions that affected auto insurers. In the first ruling, Ohio business automobile policies now had to cover employees and family members for injuries caused by uninsured or underinsured motorists, even while on personal—not company—time. The second ruling stated that forms used by insurance companies that allowed Ohio policyholders to decline uninsured motorist coverage were insufficient. Cin-Fin operated as Ohio's largest commercial auto insurer with a 8.4 percent market share, and these new decisions had a negative and dramatic impact on net income for 2000—the company reported a decrease of 53.5 percent over the previous year. The decisions also had the potential to adversely affect results in 2001.

Increased loss costs also played a part in decreasing profits, reflected in its 2000 combined ratio of 110.7 percent (industry average at the time was 110.3 percent). The firm also expected nearly $9 million in losses related to the September 11th attacks on the World Trade Center and the Pentagon. Despite these challenges, Cin-Fin remained confident that it would return to profitability due to its increasing growth rate, especially that of its property/casualty business, which secured a 11.9 percent increase in its net premiums written in 2000. As one of the 20th largest property casualty insurers in the United States, Cin-Fin's long-standing history of success and well-respected position in the industry would no doubt carry it well into the 21st century.

Principal Subsidiaries

The Cincinnati Insurance Company; The Cincinnati Casualty Company; The Cincinnati Indemnity Company; The Cincinnati Life Insurance Company; CFC Investment Company; CinFin Capital Management.

Principal Competitors

The Allstate Corporation; The Progressive Corporation; State Farm Insurance Companies.

Further Reading

Byrne, Harlan S., "Cincinnati Financial Corp.," *Barron's,* January 21, 1991, p. 49.
——, "Cincinnati Financial: Weathering the Storms, Feathering Its Profits," *Barron's,* May 31, 1993, p. 33.
Calise, Angela K., "Cincinnati Financial Moves to Relieve Investor Fears," *National Underwriter Property & Casualty-Risk & Benefits Management,* October 15, 1990, p. 63.
"Cincinnati Financial Suffers Net Loss on Ohio Auto Troubles," *A.M. Best Newswire,* February 6, 2001.
Curry, Robert P., *Prospectus Fulfilled: The Evolution of the Cincinnati Financial Corporation,* Cincinnati: The Cincinnati Financial Corporation, 1984.
De Lombaerde, Geert, "Cincinnati Financial Finds Positives in a Tough Year," *Business Courier Serving Cincinnati-Northern Kentucky,* December 8, 2000, p. 15.
——, "New, Existing Markets to Drive Insurer's Growth," *Business Courier Serving Cincinnati-Northern Kentucky,* May 1, 1998, p. 27.
——, "Tough Conditions Hamper Cincinnati Financial: Expansions Fuel Premium Growth," *Business Courier Serving Cincinnati-Northern Kentucky,* May 7, 1999, p. 29.
Easton, Thomas, "What's in a Name?," *Forbes,* December 18, 1995, p. 294.
Geer, Carolyn T., "Its Agents Do Their Homework," *Forbes,* January 4, 1993, p. 166.
Lazo, Shirley A., "Stressing the Positive: After Loss, Cincinnati Financial Ups Payout," *Barron's,* February 12, 2001, p. 33.
Linsenmeyer, Adrienne, "Cincinnati Financial: Bucking the Trend," *Financial World,* December 11, 1990, p. 14.
Wallace, Bob, "Insurer's Intranet Helps Speed New Business," *Computerworld,* January 12, 1998, p. 39.
Watkins, Steve, "Cincinnati Financial Tells Story to Analysts," *Cincinnati Business Courier,* June 3, 1996, p. 17.
Weinstein, Marc, "Property and Casualty Firms Expected to See Brighter '86; Local Insurers to Follow Industry Trend," *Cincinnati Business Courier,* August 11, 1986, p. 15.

—April Dougal Gasbarre
—update: Christina M. Stansell

Cirrus Design Corporation

4515 Taylor Circle
Duluth, Minnesota 55811
U.S.A.
Telephone: (218) 727-2737
Fax: (218) 727-2148
Web site: http://www.cirrusdesign.com

Private Company
Incorporated: 1984
Employees: 500
Sales: $65 million (2001 est.)
NAIC: 54171 Research and Development in the Physical, Engineering, and Life Sciences; 336411 Aircraft Manufacturing

Cirrus Design Corporation makes advanced piston engine aircraft for the general aviation market. Once a maker of kit planes for home assembly by hobbyists, the company now produces sleek, fast planes selling for as much as $280,000 each. Even at these prices, the company has a long waiting list for its SR20 and SR22 models. Delays in getting its production lines up to speed, however, have made profits elusive. Founders Alan and Dale Klapmeier inevitably draw comparisons to another pair of aerospace pioneers, the Wright brothers. Ever ambitious, from early on they planned to capture half the general aviation market and still are aiming to be the world's largest producer of piston engine aircraft. The company's SR20 was one of the first new designs since the 1950s; pilot enthusiasm for this line of planes suggests the possibility of Cirrus Design attaining its founders' lofty goals.

Dreaming of Flight in the 1970s

The Klapmeier brothers grew up in DeKalb, Illinois. James Fallows writes in the *New York Times Magazine* that a prescription for glasses in the third grade crushed Alan's dreams of becoming a military pilot. Nevertheless, the pair began flying as teenagers after buying a 1947 Cessna 140 for $5,000. In fact, younger brother Dale was flying before he could drive the family car.

The brothers' thoughts soon turned to aircraft manufacture. As early as 1976, as a high school senior, Alan Klapmeier said he wanted to put Cessna out of business. While in college in Wisconsin, the two rebuilt a wrecked 1960 Champion 7GC and put together a kit plane (a Glasair) on the family farm. (Alan took physics and economics degrees at Ripon College; Dale got degrees in business administration and economics from the University of Wisconsin-Stevens Point.)

After this success in aircraft fabrication, they decided to design their own plane. An uncle's Bluewater Marine boat factory in Mora, Minnesota provided a source of both technology and resin. Thus Cirrus Design Corporation was launched in 1984. "Cirrus are fair-weather clouds," explained company president Alan Klapmeier of the name. "And they are the highest and fastest," quoted the Minneapolis *Star-Tribune.* Yet the risks of aviation were always apparent. The same year, Alan Klapmeier survived a two-aircraft collision that killed another pilot.

The brothers borrowed money and started their own factory in Baraboo, Wisconsin. At first they created kit planes for hobbyists to assemble. Traditional general aviation aircraft were made of aluminum; their design had changed little since World War II. The Klapmeiers, however, used the advanced composite materials that had become popular among makers of experimental airplanes. (Experimental aircraft were generally homemade, sometimes from kits, which faced different sales restrictions from factory-built planes.) Cirrus also incorporated NASA-derived formulas for wing design into its planes.

Aloft in 1987

The brothers had begun drafting designs for the VK-30 in 1980. The plane debuted in 1987 and was well received at the annual experimental plane expo at Oshkosh, Wisconsin. They eventually sold 40 VK-30 kits priced between $120,000 and $200,000. The market was limited, though, to people who could afford not only this money but the hundreds or thousands of hours required to assemble the kits. Unlike other kits, the VK-30 could seat four passengers. Sleekly styled, its pusher propeller was located at the rear of the plane. Its fiberglass construction allowed for a more aerodynamic shape than conventional planes.

At the time, the rest of the general aviation industry in the United States was dying, crippled chiefly by product liability lawsuits. Piper was bankrupt and Cessna had stopped building single-engine aircraft. The United States, which had produced 17,000 private planes in 1979, only made 899 in 1992. It was estimated that liability insurance added more than $40,000 to the price of new small planes.

Cirrus began to branch out beyond the kit plane business. Alliant TechSystems, Inc. subcontracted the company to engineer and produce airframe components for the U.S. Army's Outrider reconnaissance drone. The firm also won a $13.4 million contract to develop a prototype of a five-seat turboprop business aircraft for Isaviation, an Israeli-government sponsored project. This plane would become known as the ST50 and was similar in design to the VK-30.

Deadlines in the Isaviation contract put pressure on Cirrus to find a new plant. The University of North Dakota's Center for Aerospace Science helped attract the company to Grand Forks. The Bank of North Dakota agreed to finance part of the company's equipment and building costs. Various state agencies contributed incentives, eager to bring high-paying, high-tech jobs to the area. Initial plans called for the Grand Forks plant to employ about 40 workers, rising to several hundred within a few years. Delays in raising financing, however, caused the company to miss the 1992 building season, which stopped in the winter. The fact that the board of one state development fund failed to raise a quorum at a critical meeting with Cirrus further frustrated the company's plans to open a plant quickly.

Another town under consideration was Oshkosh, Wisconsin, generally considered the Mecca of the experimental aviation community. Ultimately, though, in May 1997 Duluth, Minnesota won out over both Grand Falls and Oshkosh. Cirrus leaders praised its quality of life; government officials, local banks, and private concerns had also assembled a considerable financial package, worth about $3.5 million. Cirrus built a $20 million plant in Duluth and also located its headquarters there. The company brought 35 employees with them and hired another 15 at once.

Liability Reform in 1994

The company first test flew the Cirrus ST-50 in December 1994. It could reach 300 m.p.h. and was to be priced at $1 million each, 60 percent less than its closest competitor.

In the same year, legislation was being passed that would help rescue the small plane industry in the United States. The General Aviation Revitalization Act, which prevented awards for alleged defects in planes or equipment more than 18 years old, passed Congress in 1994. Cessna immediately announced plans to resume manufacture of piston engine planes for the first time in eight years.

At the time, Cirrus also was developing the SR20, a more conventional plane with a projected sale price of about $130,000. It was designed to be stable and forgiving. The landing gear was not retractable. It did have one especially revolutionary feature: a big Kevlar parachute designed to rescue the whole plane in the event of certain emergencies. Ballistic Recovery Systems, a tiny company in St. Paul, Minnesota, supplied the chutes. Avionics were also state-of-the-art, featuring an LCD "moving map" indicating terrain, obstacles, and airports.

Cirrus benchmarked the BMW 500 series of luxury sedans in designing the SR20's spacious interior. Powered by a 200-horsepower Teledyne/Continental engine, the fuel-efficient plane burned about ten gallons an hour, averaging 18 miles per gallon.

In August 1996, Cirrus announced plans to build a plant in Grand Forks after all. A new type under development, the SRX, was to be produced at a 67,500-square-foot facility at Grand Forks International Airport, which was projected to employ 250 people by 1998. North Dakota's tighter product liability limits helped bring Cirrus back to the state. In addition, the city of Grand Forks took $1 million of stock in Cirrus.

Plans for a 106,000-square-foot plant in Duluth were announced in September 1996. The company expected to double its workforce of 100 there after construction of the $4 million plant, which was to fabricate wings for the SR20.

The Federal Aviation Administration approved type certification on the SR20 in October 1998, clearing the way for Cirrus to begin producing and selling the plane. By the end of the year, Cirrus had nonrefundable $15,000 deposits from 200 people for the $168,000 plane, set to begin deliveries in early 1999.

Tragically, Cirrus Design's chief test pilot, Scott Anderson, was killed testing the first SR20 off the production line. The ballistic parachute recovery systems had not yet been shipped. Anderson had joined the company after his predecessor, Robert Overmyer, a former space shuttle astronaut, died testing a new wing for the VK-30 kit plane on March 22, 1996. Anderson also had flown F-16 fighter jets for the Minnesota Air National Guard. The National Transportation Safety Board (NTSB) determined that an aileron jammed in high-stress maneuvers likely caused the crash, and changes were incorporated into the SR20's design.

First SR20 Delivered in 1999

Cirrus pressed ahead after Anderson's death, claiming with justification that its plane was still the safest of its type in the sky. It delivered the first SR-20 on July 20, 1999 (as the U.S. Coast Guard was recovering the remains of John F. Kennedy, Jr.'s famous plane wreck, which occurred in a Piper Saratoga II). The SR20 then had a list price of $179,400; the company sold them only factory direct and had deposits from 324 customers.

The company had raised $60 million by the time of the SR20's launch. Cirrus aimed to deliver 424 aircraft in 2000, thereby producing earnings of $5.2 million on revenue of $92.2 million. By the end of July 2001, however, the company had

Key Dates:

1984: Cirrus Design Corporation is launched.
1987: The VK-30 kit plane is introduced.
1994: The ST-50 business plane makes its first test flight.
1999: The first SR20 is delivered.

delivered a total of only 200 of the SR20/SR22 series planes, although the second hundred planes took only six months to produce, versus 12 months for the first hundred.

The cost of owning the plane was similar to that of owning a luxury RV or car, since airplanes tended to hold their value over 20 or 30 years. By Alan Klapmeier's reckoning, most of the people who bought the 965,000 luxury cars that were sold in the United States in 1997 could have afforded a plane.

Customers were attracted to the planes as a way to opt out of the overcrowded hubs and inevitable delays of the airline industry. This idea had official support in NASA's proposed Small Aircraft Transportation System. Most of the country's air traffic went to only a fraction of the nation's 4,600 airports.

Cirrus's next design, the SR22, was FAA-certified in December 2000. This more powerful plane sold for $280,000, about $100,000 more than the SR20. Unfortunately, the company was not producing SR20s quickly enough to be profitable (it had managed less than half of its projected one-a-day delivery rate), and it laid off 127 of its 639 workers in January 2001. The production rate did continue to accelerate, however.

In August 2001 Cirrus Design announced $100 million in new financing from Crescent Capital, the Atlanta-based subsidiary of the First Islamic Investment Bank of Bahrain. The deal gave Crescent a 58 percent interest in Cirrus.

Principal Competitors

Cessna Aircraft Co.; Kestrel Aircraft Co.; Lancair International Inc.; The New Piper Aircraft, Inc.

Further Reading

"Airframe Parachute Offers Ultimate Insurance Policy," *Design News,* September 7, 1998, p. 40.

Blahnik, Mike, "Cirrus Design to Lay Off 120 in Restructuring," *Star Tribune* (Minneapolis), February 3, 2001, p. 1D.

Campbell, Erin, "Cirrus Breaks Ground for GF Facility," *Grand Forks Herald,* August 27, 1996, p. D5.

Carey, Susan, "If Only They Could Rig a Big Parachute to a Jumbo Jet's Tail," *Wall Street Journal,* December 8, 1998, p. A1.

"Cirrus Lays Off 127," *Grand Forks Herald,* February 3, 2001, p. 1A.

Copeland, Julie, "And the Flights Go On," *Grand Forks Herald,* March 27, 1999, p. 1B.

——, "Cirrus Begins Production of Its SR20," *Grand Forks Herald,* February 13, 1999, p. 1D.

——, "Cirrus Opens 100-150 Jobs," *Grand Forks Herald,* October 23, 1998, p. 1A.

——, "Taking Flight," *Grand Forks Herald,* October 17, 1998, p. 1D.

Cory, Matt, "N.D. Taking Off with Aviation," *Grand Forks Herald,* February 7, 1998, p. 5B.

Cox, Bill, "Cirrus SR20: Single for a New Generation," *Plane & Pilot,* May 1999, pp. 28–35, 96.

——, "Revisiting the SR20," *Plane & Pilot,* August 2000, pp. 27–34.

DeJoy, Christy, "Cleared for Takeoff: A New Site in Duluth for Cirrus Design," *Duluthian,* July 1993, p. 10.

Elmstrom, Dave, "Cirrus Design's Top Gun," *Twin Cities Business Daily,* March 1999, p. 8.

Fallows, James, "The Boys from Baraboo," in *Free Flight: From Airline Hell to a New Age of Travel,* New York: Public Affairs Books, 2001.

——, "Turn Left at Cloud 109," *New York Times Magazine,* November 21, 1999, pp. 84–89.

Gaffney, Timothy R., "Propellers Taking Off, Again," *Dayton Daily News,* September 7, 1997, p. 7B.

Goyer, Robert M., "Revolution," *Flyer,* May 1999, pp. 22–27.

Haines, Thomas B., "Fleet First: The First Cirrus SR20 Finds a Home," *AOPA Pilot,* October 1999, pp. 56–64.

Hanson, Monte, "Exec Brings Chute Firm In for a Soft Landing; Timing, Plan Ended Ballistic's Free Fall," *Star Tribune* (Minneapolis), February 19, 2001, p. 3D.

Huber, Tim, "Cirrus Nears Takeoff," *CityBusiness, The Business Journal of the Twin Cities,* June 29, 1998.

Jones, Mary, "Looking at the Future of General Aviation," *Sport Aviation,* April 1999, pp. 30–34.

Jossi, Frank, "Investor Buzz Helps Cirrus Fly," *Ventures for Growing Twin Cities Companies,* March 1999, pp. 70–71.

Kennedy, Tony, "Cirrus to Move Fuselage Production to Grand Forks," *Star Tribune* (Minneapolis), June 2, 2000, p. 3D.

Oakes, Larry, "Cirrus Design Corp. Plans to Begin Construction Soon on Duluth Factory," *Star Tribune* (Minneapolis), September 19, 1996, p. D3.

——, "Innovation Gets Lifelong Dream Off the Ground," *Star Tribune* (Minneapolis), December 10, 1994, p. B1.

Okerlund, Matthew, "Failed Future Fund Meeting Stuns Grand Forks," *Grand Forks Herald,* Bus. Sec., October 30, 1992.

——, "Who Crashed Cirrus?," *Grand Forks Herald,* Bus. Sec., May 5, 1993.

Phelps, David, "Wisconsin Firm Moving to Duluth," *Star Tribune,* May 5, 1993, p. 3D.

Phillips, Edward H., "Parachute System Tested," *Aviation Week & Space Technology,* July 27, 1998, p. 84.

St. Anthony, Neal, "Taking Flight," *Star Tribune* (Minneapolis), July 25, 1999, p. 1D.

Smith, John Templeton, "Cirrus SR20 Across the Atlantic," *Pilot,* August 2000, pp. 22–27.

Stewart, Don, "Plans for Alternative Aviation System Take Flight," *Tulsa World,* October 8, 2000, p. 1.

Strozniak, Peter, "Growth Takes Flight: How Alan and Dale Klapmeier Took Cirrus Design to New Heights of Aviation Innovation," *Industry Week,* Growing Companies ed., January 1999, pp. 46–50.

Sweetman, Bill, "I Fly," *Popular Science,* June 2000, pp. 52–56.

Tweist, Gabrielle, "Another Chapter in the Cirrus Success Story," *Aviation for Women,* January 2000, pp. 24–26.

Wald, Matthew L., "When the Outlook Seems Bleak, A Parachute for the Plane Itself," *New York Times,* May 6, 1999, p. D4.

Weiman, Dave, "Cirrus Makes Midwest Aviation Community Proud," *Midwest Flyer Magazine,* December 1999/January 2000.

Welbes, John, "Duluth Draws Cirrus with Location, Negotiations," *Grand Forks Herald,* Bus. Sec., May 5, 1993.

Whitson, Steve, "Cirrus Design's SR20: The Aircraft for Everyone," *Private Pilot,* August 1999, pp. 47, 51–53, 91.

Wilson, Jim, "On Angels' Wings," *Popular Mechanics,* October 1999, pp. 72–73.

Wood, Carter, "Absences Jeopardize Plane Plant Prospects," *Grand Forks Herald,* October 28, 1992, p. 1.

——, "Ashley, N.D., Native's Work May Help Ensure Cirrus Success," *Grand Forks Herald,* Bus. Sec., March 12, 1993.

—Frederick C. Ingram

Citrix Systems, Inc.

6400 N.W. Sixth Way
Fort Lauderdale, Florida 33309
U.S.A.
Telephone: (954) 267-3000
Fax: (954) 267-3100
Web site: http://www.citrix.com

Public Company
Incorporated: 1989
Employees: 1800
Sales: $470.4 million (2000)
Stock Exchanges: NASDAQ
Ticker Symbol: CTXS
NAIC: 51121 Software Publishers; 541412 Computer
   Systems Design Services

Citrix Systems, Inc. is the worldwide leader in a niche computer software and services market. Its products enable customers to use a network of computers hooked up to a central server, where the software resides. A large number of employees can have access to the same software and information at the same time using Citrix systems, even if the workers are spread across the country. This solves a number of problems for companies using networks. They do not have to provide all their workers with the same type of computers, and they can use older or cheaper computers. This is called ''thin'' client/server computing. The term ''thin'' implies that a low-powered computer can be made to work as well as a ''fat,'' high-powered, large memory machine with a cutting-edge processor, because the software is at a remote location. Citrix's first chairman, Edward E. Iacobucci, put it simply for *Business Week:* ''We take any application, deliver it to any device, over any network through any bandwidth.'' Iacobucci founded the company and pioneered the thin client/server model. The company's products include Citrix ICA (Independent Computing Architecture), a licensed technology that enhances server computer processing; MultiWin, a process that allows more than one user at a time to connect to the same centralized server software in discrete sessions; the server software MetaFrame; the portal software systems Nfuse and XPS, and others. Citrix also offers train-

ing, maintenance, and support services to its customers worldwide. Citrix users include 99 of the Fortune 100 companies and 90 percent of the Fortune 500. Citrix sells its products and services in over 60 countries. Approximately half of the company's revenue is generated outside the United States.

From IBM to His Own Company

Citrix Systems was founded by Edward Iacobucci, a software developer with a long-standing bent for business. His family hailed from Argentina, and he attended high school in Atlanta. Though he loved mathematics and science, Iacobucci was also fascinated by business early on, and as a teenager was president of a company set up through the Junior Achievement program. He was introduced to computing at Georgia Tech University in the 1970s, and went on to work for IBM. Iacobucci became acquainted with Microsoft's entrepreneurial genius Bill Gates when the two worked together on a joint IBM/Microsoft project to develop the operating system known as OS/2. By 1989, Iacobucci had decided to leave IBM. He was offered a job at Microsoft as chief technical officer of its networking group. But Iacobucci instead gathered capital to go out on his own. He began with $3 million, raised on his vision of a more fluid world of computing, where different machines could run on any kind of software, and perhaps devices like televisions and telephones could be used to connect to powerful central software servers. Iacobucci first set up Citrix in Richardson, Texas, but quickly moved back to Coral Springs, Florida, where he had been living while working for IBM. The company began with five engineers, who also left IBM's Florida offices. The young company's chief executive was Roger Roberts, a veteran of Texas Instruments. Iacobucci was chairman. Citrix spent two years developing its first product, which was called Citrix Multiuser OS/2. Multiuser was to work with OS/2, which Iacobucci had spearheaded for IBM. It would let more than one worker at a time tap into the operating system, through a central server computer. The company went through a second round of financing, another $3 million, in 1990, and by 1991 was ready to bring out its first product. Just days before Citrix was prepared to ship Multiuser, Microsoft announced that it would drop OS/2 in favor of its new operating system, Windows. This was horrific news for Citrix. With OS/2 now an obsolete technology, Multiuser was virtually

Company Perspectives:

As a global leader in application server software and related services, Citrix Systems, Inc. offers innovative organizations the ability to run any application on any device over any connection. With a Citrix solution in place, now everything computes.

useless. Citrix had spent $6 million, and now had little hope of recouping much of this through Multiuser. At a September 1991 board meeting, the members argued about whether to call it quits and shut the company down. But Iacobucci and CEO Roberts were certain that the company's engineers could start over, and make a Windows version of Multiuser, if only Citrix could get more financing.

Some early investors in Citrix were doubtful that the company could keep going. But eventually they agreed to put up more money, if other investors could be rounded up, to spread the risk some. The company came out of its crisis with another $5 million to keep it afloat until it could sell its new Multiuser. Intel was one big new investor, and another was Microsoft. Microsoft bought between 6 and 7 percent of the young company, and put one of its people on Citrix's board. So though Microsoft's ditching of OS/2 had almost capsized Citrix, the software giant then came to the rescue. Over the next four years, Microsoft put a total of $2.4 million into the company. Citrix brought out Multiuser version 2.0 in 1992, and also came out with a network software support service called A + Server Series. Citrix also worked out a licensing agreement with Microsoft for its Windows NT server software. It began working on a new product called WinView for Networks. Revenue for 1992 was $1.8 million, and the company had about 50 employees. By the next year, revenue had jumped to $5 million. For 1994, its fifth year in business, Citrix brought in $10 million, and the word about its thin client/server products was spreading.

There were a variety of ways corporations could network their computers, and the thin client/server model did not seem ideal to everyone. But Citrix products were able to solve certain problems neatly. One user was the giant food corporation Nestle. The company's U.S. headquarters were in Glendale, California, and the office responsible for preparing its U.S. taxes was in Stamford, Connecticut. The Stamford office used Citrix network software to connect with the head office and four regional headquarters. Before using Citrix, each regional office collected its relevant tax information and forwarded it to the Stamford office, often laboriously backing things up on diskettes or CDs. Software upgrades were difficult to coordinate. The Citrix system allowed all the relevant parties access to the same information and same software programs simultaneously, though offices were on the East coast, the West coast, and in St. Louis and Ohio. Many other large corporations found that Citrix could help them with similar situations. By 1995, Citrix had made enough of a name for itself to venture a public stock offering. The company introduced its stock on the Nasdaq exchange in December, 1995, and saw its share price double from $15 to $30 on the first day. The company closed the year with net revenues of $14.5 million.

Working with Microsoft in the 1990s

Citrix's fortunes increased rapidly after its public offering. Its products were unique, and many customers found them invaluable. Citrix launched WinFrame in 1995, which allowed Microsoft's leading Windows software to be distributed through networks. Though not everyone agreed on this, proponents of the thin-client model claimed that Citrix users could save 25 to 30 percent over the cost of owning a similar set-up of standard PCs in a local area network. While some industry analysts claimed the thin-client market was actually quite small, others saw vast possibilities for Citrix as its software caught on. The company forged alliances with a host of other computer companies. It had marketing arrangements with Sun Microsystems and with Netscape, with another leading network company, Wyse, and with hardware makers like Motorola Citrix also worked with software companies like PeopleSoft and dozens of others, so that its network solutions were pushed by a variety of people all through the computer industry.

Citrix's relationship with Microsoft was key to the company's growth. Microsoft's Windows was exceedingly popular, and Citrix allowed network users to run Windows, even if they used Macintosh computers, which had a completely different operating system. The two companies were deeply intertwined. Iacobucci had known Bill Gates for years, Microsoft was a major investor in Citrix, and much of Citrix's growth was due to the demand for access to Windows. But Microsoft shocked Citrix in 1997 when it announced that it was considering building its own version of Windows networking technology, supplanting Citrix with a home-grown Microsoft product. Citrix's stock plummeted on this news, as it did not seem possible for Citrix to survive without Microsoft. Yet in some ways, Microsoft's new plan didn't make sense. At that point, no one besides Citrix made anything like what Citrix made, so there was no chance of Microsoft licensing the technology from another company. And it would take Microsoft some time to develop a comparable program, probably years. Iacobucci flew to Microsoft's headquarters in Redmond, Washington, with a crew of advisors and negotiators and prepared for a long stay. The Citrix team camped out in a suite of apartments and hammered out an agreement with Microsoft over a period of months. Finally Citrix announced that it had signed a new licensing agreement with Microsoft, promising Citrix $75 million immediately, and another $100 million spread over several years. Microsoft would endorse Citrix's Windows networking systems for five more years.

While Citrix proclaimed itself quite happy with the new arrangement with Microsoft, others in the computer industry saw the 1997 licensing agreement as the beginning of the end. There seemed to be nothing to prevent Microsoft from going ahead with its own networking technology, so that sooner or later, Citrix would become obsolete. This was the kind of charge that had been leveled against Microsoft frequently. It was such a big player that it seemed able to dictate who would live and who would die among other companies in the industry. Media reports of Citrix's new agreement were full of doom. The company's success had turned sour, according to a March 17, 1997 article in *Business Week,* and an *InfoWorld* article of May 19, 1997, asked whether Microsoft was "building a partnership or giving Citrix a stay of execution."

Key Dates:

1989: Edward Iacobucci founds company.
1992: Citrix introduces revised new product, Multiuser.
1995: The company makes its initial public offering.
1997: Citrix signs five-year licensing agreement with Microsoft.
2001: Citrix acquires Sequoia Software Corp.

None of this naysaying seemed to prevent Citrix from growing even more rapidly after the 1997 agreement. The company opened new headquarters in Fort Lauderdale in 1997 to house its 300 employees. Revenues for 1997 were $124 million, but the company's market capitalization was enormous, at $2.2 billion. The company had no debt and an expanding market niche as more and more corporations caught on to the thin-client model.

The company was on a rapid upward trajectory. Revenues almost doubled between 1997 and 1998, to $248.6 million, while market capitalization soared to $4.4 billion. Its stock had recovered from its plunge, and by February 1998 was up to $78. The company stepped up its marketing efforts. It hosted a conference on "Thinergy," expounding its thin-client gospel to a global audience in 1998. That year Citrix also licensed its ICA (Independent Computing Architecture) protocol to IBM and to a major keyboard manufacturer, Key Tronics. The agreements with hardware manufacturers put Citrix closer to the goal Iacobucci had always had for it—to run sophisticated software from simple devices. Iacobucci envisioned the next wave of "thin" machine as an "information device" as opposed to a conventional computer. "... you take your keyboard, plug it into a phone jack and a monitor, and that's it," he speculated in a 1998 interview with *Fortune.* Iacobucci was imagining an essential transformation of the computing world. Meanwhile, his company was making real inroads, both in the United States and abroad. By 1999, the company had two development offices in the United States, its Florida headquarters, and international sales offices in England, France, Germany, Japan, Denmark, Ireland, Australia, and in several other countries. The worldwide thin-client market was said to have increased 35 percent over 1997, according to one industry study, and Citrix was doing a large portion of its business abroad.

Up and Down with the Technology Market

The thin-client model seemed to really take off in 1999. Citrix counted the number of customers using its systems as 15 million by 1999, and this was almost double the number of users in 1998. Though Citrix had the leading thin-client technology, it wasn't the only company endorsing the model. IBM, Microsoft, Compaq, Dell, Hewlett-Packard and Sun Microsystems— practically all the big names in computing—came out with thin-client-related products in 1999. Many of these were produced under agreements with Citrix. The new buzz word for 1999 was ASP, for application service provider, which was essentially an Internet-based version of the thin-client idea. ASP technology was only beginning to be viable by 1999, but it seemed like the next big thing, and Citrix was already on top of it.

By early 2000, Citrix shares rode to a high of $122. It had sold its systems to huge, well-known companies such as Sears, Roebuck and AT&T. Its revenue had jumped over 60 percent over 1999, to $403 million, and it seemed poised for a further spurt of growth. The server software market was expected to grow to $60 billion in total sales by 2002, and Citrix already had a 40 percent share of the so-called application management segment of that market. Citrix's CEO, Mark Templeton, predicted that revenue for Citrix would reach $5 billion within five years, as information technology managers increasingly switched to server and Web-based computing systems. Citrix seemed to be in an enviable position. Though it had direct competitors, such as software maker Santa Cruz Operations, Inc., it was by far the best-known and most widely used technology in the market.

The company had been exceedingly optimistic about its prospects. Then in June 2000, Citrix announced that it was revising its earnings estimates downward for the second quarter. The cutback was small and still represented growth compared to the same period a year earlier. But investors were stunned and dropped the stock. From over $100, Citrix shares fell to under $20, and founder and chairman Edward Iacobucci abruptly left the company. CEO Mark Templeton was also asked to resign. It was a strange episode, as nothing had really gone wrong at Citrix. The revised earnings estimate was said to reflect the fact that some sales to large corporate customers took longer to close. So though sales were still growing, profits were taking longer to show up. Less than a year later, Templeton was back at the helm. The company had searched for a new chief executive, hunting in particular for someone with expertise in selling to larger clients. But in the end, it found that Templeton was the best choice, and he was reinstated. In mid-2001 Citrix also completed a major acquisition, buying up the Sequoia Software Corp. for $185 million. Sequoia made what were known as Web-portal software products, which allowed Web sites to be used like corporate databases. Citrix was keen to get in on Web-based technology, and the Sequoia acquisition gave Citrix what it called "the best technology on the market" according to a June 28 article in the *Washington Post.* Citrix was able to post a sizeable profit in the next quarter, showing net income growth of over 50 percent compared to the same period a year earlier. Citrix's stock price remained far lower than it had been in its heyday in early 2000. But this perhaps reflected the uncertainty that afflicted the entire technology sector at the time. The company seemed to be continuing with the business plan it had held for years. In 2001, it came out with a new software, MetaFrame XP for Windows, and it won awards for this and for its Nfuse product. It planned to release a new Web-based software, which it had gained through Sequoia, in early 2002.

Principal Competitors

Microsoft Corporation; Tarantella, Inc.; NetManage, Inc.

Further Reading

Caisse, Kimberly, and Jeff Bliss, "Citrix Beefs Up Thin Clients," *Computer Reseller News,* February 23, 1998, p. 116.
Cope, James, "Citrix Takes a Beating on Wall Street," *Computerworld,* June 19, 2000, p. 29.

DeGeorge, Gail, "Of Mice and Microsoft," *Business Week,* March 17, 1997, p. 36.

Dennis, Kathryn, "Citrix Systems Dances with the Devil," *MC Technology Marketing Intelligence,* May 1998, p. 32.

"Former Chief Executive of Citrix Systems Inc. Is Named CEO Again," *Wall Street Journal,* May 31, 2001, p. B13.

Gibbs, Lisa, "Inside Ed's Head," *Florida Trend,* July 1999, p. 58.

Grzanka, Len, "Citrix Works on Its Image," *Inter@ctive Week,* July 17, 2000, p. 40.

Haddad, Charles H., "The Biggest Share in Shared Computing," *Business Week,* May 22, 2000, pp. 134–36.

Horowitz, Alan S., "Thin on the Inside," *InformationWeek,* November 17, 1997, p. 237.

Jones, Sabrina, "Citrix Blends with Sequoia," *Washington Post,* June 28, 2001, p. E05.

——, "Sequoia's New Owner Posts 53% Profit Rise," *Washington Post,* July 20, 2001, p. E05.

Lee, Jeanne, "Citrix Kicks Some Thin-Client Butt," *Fortune,* February 16, 1998, p. 125.

Petreley, Nicholas, "Is Microsoft Building a Partnership or Giving Citrix a Stay of Execution?" *InfoWorld,* May 19, 1997, p. 134.

——, "The Tale of Two Mantises: Microsoft is Preying, and Now Citrix Is Praying," *InfoWorld,* March 10, 1997, p. 104.

"Still Plenty of Juice in Citrix," *Business Week,* November 24, 1997, p. 168.

"Will Citrix Click After All?," *Business Week,* July 17, 2000, p. 157.

Wilde, Candee, "Citrix Sees Fortunes Rise with Thin-Client Model," *InformationWeek,* November 29, 1999, p. 92.

—A. Woodward

Coal India Ltd.

Coal Bhavan
10 Netaji Subhase Road
Calcutta 700 001
India
Telephone: (33) 220 9980
Web site: http://www.coalindia.nic.in

State-Owned Company
Incorporated: 1975
Employees: 570,000
Sales: Rs 153.98 billion ($3.55 billion) (1999)
NAIC: 212111 Bituminous Coal and Lignite Surface
   Mining; 212112 Bituminous Coal Underground
   Mining; 212113 Anthracite Mining; 213113 Support
   Activities for Coal Mining

Coal India Ltd. (CIL), a holding company, is wholly owned by the Government of India through the Department of Coal and the Ministry of Mines and Minerals. CIL is responsible for 88 percent of coal output in India. In 1999, production was 256.5 million tons of raw coal, up from 250.6 million tons the previous year. However, like many state-owned concerns, CIL's financial performance has been generally poor. During the financial year 2000–2001, CIL reported a loss of Rs 1,400-crore—a crore is equal to 10 million. At the start of the new millennium, the company was under scrutiny by the Indian government for its performance and business practices. Coal provides more than 67 percent of India's energy requirements. However, India's per capita energy consumption is among the lowest in the world. India has vast coal reserves, and these can be mined cheaply, although the coal is generally of poor quality and has a high ash content. In 1998, India's total coal reserves were estimated at 200 billion tons, of which over 69 billion tons were proven reserves. The bulk of India's coal reserves are in the states of Bengal, Bihar, Orissa, and Madhya Pradesh. Due to the structure of the coal mining industry in India, CIL's role is a major one, and its performance and operations very much reflect the policies and priorities of the government of India.

Early History

The Indian coal industry has its origins in the early 19th century, when mining activity became commercial in conjunction with the expansion of the railway network, particularly in the west of the country. The monopoly interests of the British East India Company were revoked in 1813. Initially, the coal fields were operated by a large number of Indian private companies which possessed captive—or company-owned—coalfields to support their iron and steel works. By 1900 there were 34 companies producing 7 million tons of coal from 286 mines. Production continued to grow in the first half of the 20th century, especially during World War I. Demand continued to grow during World War II, and production reached 29 million tons by 1945. By then, the number of companies had increased to 307, and the number of mines to 673. The trend continued for almost a decade after India's independence in 1947. However, India's ambitious economic development plans led to a tremendous demand for energy, and in the absence of alternative sources, coal was targeted as the major source of power for industrialization. Under the government's Second Five Year Economic Development Plan 1957–1961, a target of 60 million tons was set for the end of the plan period. However, government economic planners were convinced that the private sector would be unable to meet this target. Hence, the National Coal Development Corporation (NCDC) was formed, which took the old railway collieries as its nucleus and opened new mines as well. Production of coal increased from 38 million tons in 1956 to 56 million tons in 1961.

During the 1960s, most of India's collieries continued to be operated by the private sector, with the exception of NCDC and the Singareni Collieries, both in the public sector. At the national level, three factors emerged to force the government to consider the nationalization of the coal industry. First, there was a fear that contemporary mining methods were leading to great wastage. Second, the government predicted that future demand for coal would be particularly heavy in view of its industrial development priorities. Finally, during the Third Five Year Plan 1962–1966, as well as the period 1966–1969, despite the increase in production, there was a shortfall in private capital investment in the industry.

During the period 1971–1973, the government carried out a series of nationalizations of the privately owned coal companies in a major effort to increase production and overcome the shortage of coal. At the time of the nationalizations, total coal production in the country was 72 million tons, and the industry had been passing through cycles of shortages and surpluses which prevented effective planning for expansion and modernization. There were over 900 mines in operation, some of which were producing only a few thousand tons of coal a month, and methods of mining were obsolete.

Formation of Coal India Ltd.: 1975

Coking coal mines, with the exception of the Tata Iron and Steel Company, were nationalized in May 1972, and a new public sector company, Bharat Coking Coal Limited (BCCL), was floated to manage them. In May 1973, the non-coking coal mines were also nationalized and brought under the control of the Coal Mines Authority (CMA). The Department of Coal was set up in the Ministry of Energy to oversee the public sector companies. Further reorganization of the industry led to the formation of Coal India Ltd. (CIL), which also absorbed NCDC, in November 1975. The reorganization involved placing the majority of the public sector coal companies under CIL. CIL originally had six subsidiaries. Five of which were involved in production: BCCL, located at Dhanbad; Central Coalfields Limited at Ranchi; Western Coalfields Limited (WCL) at Nagpur; Eastern Coalfields Limited (ECL) at Sanctoria; and North Eastern Coalfields Limited (NECL) at Margherita. The sixth was the Central Planning & Design Institute at Ranchi. Together with the Neyveli Lignite Corporation (NLC), CIL was operated directly by the Indian government through the Department of Coal in the Ministry of Energy. All the subsidiaries of CIL had the status of independent companies, but the authority for framing broad policies and taking administrative decisions rested with CIL.

The structure of the Indian coal industry during the 1970s and 1980s was a reflection of the priorities placed by the government on coal as a source of fuel and energy in economic development. Most of the production was the responsibility of the five subsidiaries of CIL, but there were four other coal producers in the public sector: the Singareni Collieries Limited, the government of Jammu and Kashmir collieries, the Damodar Valley Corporation, and the Indian Iron & Steel Co. Ltd. These last four concerns were responsible for about ten percent of the output. Some two percent of the total output of coal was provided by the captive mines—company-owned mines which ensure coal supplies—of the Tata Iron and Steel Company, the only coal producer in the private sector.

Financially, the subsidiaries of CIL had an average authorized capital of Rs 1.5 billion each during the late 1980s. Each em-

ployed between 100,000 and 180,000 people, and had an annual turnover of between Rs 1.1 and Rs 1.7 billion. Their shares in the total production of coal varied from 25 percent for the Central and Western Coalfields, and about 20 percent for Bharat Coking Coal and Eastern Coalfields. The financial performance of the subsidiaries also varied. BCCL made cumulative losses of Rs 4.5 billion over the five year period 1981–1986. Similarly, Eastern Coalfields made cumulative losses of Rs 3.6 billion over the same five year period. In 1988, BCCL made a loss of Rs 900 million on a turnover of Rs 5.3 billion. However, in the same year the Neyveli Lignite Corporation Limited made a profit of Rs 570 million on a turnover of Rs 1.9 billion.

As a result of the nationalizations, some rationalization took place in the sector. The mines were regrouped and reduced to 350 individual mines. New technology was introduced, and there was a shift from pick mining to blast mining, which resulted in considerable increases in production. The latter totaled 87 million tons in 1975, and 99 million tons in 1976. CIL's share of total production was about 88 percent. Nationalization was intended to provide the basis for modernizing the coal industry, but after the initial increase in production, output stagnated in the period 1976–1980. This was the result of shortages of power and explosives, labor unrest, and absenteeism, excessive employment, technical inefficiencies, and problems of flooding in the western coal fields, as well as fires in the vast Jharia coalfield. During the 1980s, the latter possessed the largest known coking coal reserves in the country and it had been estimated that ongoing fires since around 1931 had accounted for the loss of some 40 billion tons of coking coal. Consequently, CIL'S financial performance was poor during this period. It suffered losses throughout the 1976–1981 period. These losses peaked at Rs 2.4 billion in 1978–1979, but came down to Rs 882 million the following year, and came down even further to Rs 337 million the year after. Total losses for the five year period were almost Rs 6 billion.

Production Problems: Early 1980s

Production picked up in 1980 when it finally exceeded 100 million tons, and increased to 115 million tons by 1983. However, the problems suffered by CIL in particular and the coal industry in general had led to considerable shortages, especially for industrial users. This shortage was compounded by the poor quality of India's coking coal—coal from which the volatile elements have been removed making it suitable as a fuel and for metallurgical purposes—which has difficult washing characteristics and requires the coal preparation plants to run extremely complex processes. The result was that the country had to import coal from abroad, a trend that still persists. The bulk of the imported coal came from the United States, Australia, and Canada, and was significantly more expensive than locally produced coal. This situation had two implications. First, it became feasible for CIL to adopt more expensive mining methods, since they were still cheaper than the imported coal. Second, a need was perceived to improve the coal handling facilities at India's major ports. This need was reflected in the Sixth Five Year Plan, when it was projected that the ports would have to handle at least 4.4 million tons of imported coal by the mid-1980s.

During the Sixth Five Year Plan, coal production grew at 6.2 percent per year, especially in the open-cast mines. Targeted production for the end of the plan period—1984–1985—was for 165 million tons per annum, although actual production fell short at 148 million tons. During the first two years of the plan, CIL made a profit for the first time in its history. This was largely due to the Indian government's increasing the price of coal in both February 1981 and May 1982. The issue of pricing had always been a serious problem for the Indian coal industry and for CIL. Coal prices were administered by the government since 1941, with the exception of a period of seven years, 1967–1974. The pricing formula was based on an Indian industry-wide average with differentials for different grades, but in practice the price was usually set below the industry's average cost. This practice may explain in part CIL's poor overall financial performance.

Coal production in the year 1981–1982 was 125 million tons, above the targeted figure. Total production of coal and lignite was 146 million metric tons in 1983–1984, and 155 million tons in 1984–1985, 162 million tons in 1985–1986, 175 million tons in 1986–1987, 191 million tons in 1987–1988, and 207 million tons in 1988–1989. Despite the increase in production, problems related to operations, such as cost-overruns, poor quality, and low productivity, meant that targeted output was frequently revised downwards. Part of the problem was the high cost of new equipment necessitating new investment, since targeted budgets were overrun. Furthermore, the number of mines, which had been reduced immediately following nationalization, had again increased, to 684 by 1982, thereby negating some of the initial cost reduction benefits of reorganization.

Shifting Demand: Mid- to Late 1980s

Since coal was meeting over 70 percent of the energy requirements of Indian industry, CIL believed the output needed to increase by 25 million tons a year during the 1980s in order to keep up with demand. Demand for coal was projected to reach 165 million tons by 1985, 215 million tons by 1997, and over 350 million tons by the year 2001. The structure of demand for

coal had changed. The railways were no longer the primary source of demand for coal. Rather, demand now lay primarily with the steel plants, other industrial units, and thermal power stations. The reliance on coal-fired thermal power plants for power generation led to a steady increase in the demand for coal throughout this period. To satisfy this demand, CIL relied primarily on the expansion of open-pit mines. Mining coal from shallow seams was financially sound, but it resulted in a steady deterioration of coal quality over time. The Seventh Five Year Plan of 1985 included some important changes introduced by CIL in the structure of its production.

The plan had set a production target of 226 million tons for coal, and by 1988–1989, output for coal alone, excluding lignite, had reached 195 million tons. As a result of the greater need for coal, new opportunities were created for international partnerships in the coal sector throughout the 1980s. CIL signed agreements with the Soviet Union, United Kingdom, Poland, and France, for the construction and development of new mines, and the introduction of new technology. The agreement with the Soviet Union called for investment in the Jayant open cast project with a production capacity of ten million tons a year, as well as a number of other projects. The output from both surface and underground mining was to be increased through additional investment. Open cast—surface—mining was to provide an increased share of total production, from about 30 percent in 1980, to 56 percent in 1990. One of the major factors in increasing underground production was the introduction of additional longwall faces. Longwall mining differs from the traditional board and pillar method of underground mining in that the seams are at a greater depth and the capital costs are higher because of the complexity and greater powered support in the mining.

During the 1990s, a series of new developments occurred in an attempt to increase production of the Indian coal mining industry. In February 1990, CIL decided to invest $250 million in longwall mining over the period 1990–1995. This development was projected to increase the powered support longwall faces from 14 in 1990 to 28 in 1995, and 47 in the year 2000. Longwall coal production, allowing deeper seams to be worked, was also estimated to increase to nine million metric tons by 1995. In April 1990, CIL also approved five additional projects worth some $712 million, as part of its program to increase output to meet the needs of industry into the 21st century. During the 1990–1991 fiscal year, CIL lost Rs 2.5 billion; however by 1992, production began to increase and the company was able to boast a small profit. During the year, CIL began exporting coal to Bangladesh for the first time in its history and secured contracts worth $5 million.

Despite increases in output of almost 9 percent per annum during the duration of the Seventh Five Year Plan, serious coal shortages existed due to CIL's inability to meet specific needs such as the provision of high-quality coking and non-coking coal. CIL's distribution system remained poor, and the Indian Railway system was already heavily overloaded. Consequently there were cost overruns and a buildup of coal reserves at the pit heads. Furthermore, many of the targeted output figures were based on projects sanctioned but not completed by CIL, thus adding to infrastructural and distribution problems. This problem was compounded by poor coal quality, the system of pricing, and it both added to and was affected by CIL's financial position. The Indian government knew that if coal was to be a major source of energy and fuel in the future, CIL had be able to generate sufficient resources internally to meet its investment requirements. In this context, the government continued to show concern about the financial performance of CIL well into the 1990s. About 100 of the 248 corporations owned by the Indian government were heavy loss-makers, and CIL was no exception. As such, CIL was being seriously considered as a candidate for major restructuring during the early 1990s.

Rising Demand Leads to Restructuring: 1990s and Beyond

In 1994, India amended its Coal Mines Nationalization Act allowing foreign companies to hold a 51 percent stake in Indian coal mines. The amendment also enabled foreign and private power companies to operate their own coal mines—since 1973, the government only allowed steel plants to run captive mines in the private sector. Indian officials hoped that the relaxed laws would encourage investment in Indian coal mining, an industry whose demand was growing a rapid clip.

At the same time, the import duty on non-coking coal fell from 85 to 35 percent. The reduction enticed coal-consuming industries to seek out imports, whose coal had a higher calorific value and lower ash content than Indian mined coal. With the threat of increased imports cutting into CIL's production, the company began to petition the government to allow it to fix its coal prices as well as its production targets.

By the late 1990s, the Indian government was fearful that CIL and the entire mining industry would not be able to keep up with the rising demand for coal. India was known for its large amount of coal reserves, but in the past had been unable to keep pace with the demand. In 1997, the country began reforming the industry to further encourage investment and exploration and set plans in motion to deregulate pricing and distribution in the industry. It also requested $1 billion from the World Bank to restructure CIL's operations. The loan was used to purchase new machinery and to build new coal handling plants.

During that time period CIL was also feeling increased pressure from international competition. Major coal producing countries including Australia, South Africa, Indonesia, and Columbia began eyeing the lucrative Indian market as a potential gold mine for their low cost coal. As such, CIL management pleaded with its subsidiaries to cut costs and increase production. Profits, gross sales turnover, and production fell in 1999.

In fact, by 2000 CIL had a poor image throughout the coal industry. Three major subsidiaries including Eastern Coalfields Ltd., Central Coalfields Ltd., and Bharat Coking Coal Ltd., were in financial trouble. The company was also not meeting safety standards when compared with other international coal mining companies. During 2001 the Indian government scrutinized CIL, its subsidiaries, and its management. Allegations ranged from misuse of company finances to illegal mining for profit. CIL's record of project completion also came under fire.

Since nationalization, only 298 out of 401 government sanctioned projects were completed and more than 70 had been delayed.

As CIL neared the end of 2001, its future remained uncertain. The Ministry of Coal was considering merging the seven coal producing subsidiaries of CIL into one unit in order to save nearly Rs 1,000-crore per year in tax related costs. Not knowing what its future would hold, CIL pledged to focus on meeting demand, raising productivity of its coal mining operations, and restoring its subsidiaries to profitability.

Principal Subsidiaries

Bharat Coking Coal Ltd.; Central Coalfields Ltd.; Mahanadi Coalfields Ltd.; Eastern Coalfields Ltd.; Western Coalfields Ltd.; Southeastern Coalfields Ltd.; Northern Coalfields Ltd.; Central Mine Planning & Design Institute Ltd.

Principal Competitors

RAG Coal International AG; UK Coal PLC; BHP Billiton.

Further Reading

Bose, Kunal, "Duty Cut Shocks Indian Coal Industry," *Financial Times* (London), April 22, 1994, p. 30.
"Coal India Gets Funds to Expand," *Power Generation Technology and Markets,* September 26, 1997, p. 1.
"Coal Output Shows Growth of Nine Percent in India," *Journal of Commerce,* August 20, 1991, p. 6B.
"India Eases Restrictions on Coal Mine Ownership," *Journal of Commerce,* November 22, 1994, p. 6B.
"India: Mining," *Cambridge International Forecasts Country Report,* August 1998.
"India: Mining Engineers Told to Cut Costs, Raise Productivity," *Business Line,* July 13, 1999.
"India: Minister Upset With CIL, Subsidiaries," *Business Line,* April 30, 2001.
"India: Whither Coal India?," *Business Line,* October 1, 2001.
Khosla, R.P., "India's Coal Development Plans," *Coal and Energy Quarterly,* Summer 1981.
Laurila, Mel J., "Coal Preparation in India; Prospects for the Future," *Coal Age,* October 1996, p. 38.
"Major Changes in CIL on the Cards," *Statesman* (India), September 13, 2001.
"Move Underway to Improve Efficiency of Coal Companies," *Statesman* (India), August 23, 2000.
Murty, B.S., and S.P. Panda, *Indian Coal Industry and the Coal Mines,* Delhi: Discovery Publishing House, 1988.
"New Projects to Spur Jump in Indian Coal Production," *Journal of Commerce,* March 16, 1992, p. 6B.
Nicholson, Mark, "India Opens Up Coal Mining to Avert Threatened Shortfall," *Financial Times* (London), February 13, 1997, p. 6.
Shafer, Frank E., "A Review of India's Coal Mining Industry," *World Coal,* July 1979.
Varma, S.C., "Coal: Its Extraction and Utilization in India," *World Coal,* July 1979.

—Sarah Ahmad Khan
—update: Christina M. Stansell

Coats plc

2 Fouberts' Place
London W1V 1HH
United Kingdom
Telephone: (+44) 20 7302-2300
Fax: (+44) 20 7302-2340
Web site: http://www.coats.com

Public Company
Incorporated: 1909 as Spirella Company of Great Britain
   Ltd.
Employees: 49,946
Sales: £1.4 billion ($2.3 billion) (2000)
Stock Exchanges: London
Ticker Symbol: CVY
NAIC: 31321 Broadwoven Fabric Mills; 313113 Thread
   Mills; 315222 Men's and Boys' Cut and Sew Suit,
   Coat, and Overcoat Manufacturing; 315224 Men's
   and Boys' Cut and Sew Trouser, Slack, and Jean
   Manufacturing; 315228 Men's and Boys' Cut and
   Sew Other Outerwear Manufacturing; 315232
   Women's and Girls' Cut and Sew Blouse and Shirt
   Manufacturing; 315233 Women's and Girls' Cut and
   Sew Dress Manufacturing; 315234 Women's and
   Girls' Cut and Sew Suit, Coat, Tailored Jacket, and
   Skirt Manufacturing; 315239 Women's and Girls' Cut
   and Sew Other Outerwear Manufacturing

Coats plc—formerly Coats Viyella plc—operates as the world's largest manufacturer of sewing thread with a 22 percent market share. During the late 1990s and into the new millennium, Coats was involved in a major restructuring effort brought on by weakening demand in the U.K. textiles market. As such, Coats divested most of the Viyella division, retaining retail fashion brands Jaeger and Viyella, which are sold in 450 outlets in 15 countries. Coats thread products are used in apparel, footwear, furniture, cars, sporting equipment, and fiber optic cable. The firm also manufacturers needlecraft products

and household sewing thread. In 2000, the majority of the firm's sales stemmed from operations in Europe and North America.

As an entity, Coats plc comprises both the history of much of the United Kingdom's industry and the business career of one man, Sir David Alliance. Alliance came from a Tehran, Iran, family already involved in textiles, arriving in Britain in 1951, at the age of 19. He stayed and eventually presided as chairman over a group that is largely his own creation. At the beginning of the 1980s, there were four large British textile companies—Carrington Viyella, Coats Patons, Courtaulds, and Tootal Group. By the end of the decade two of them had fallen into Alliance's hands and a third was firmly in his sights.

Alliance's Acquisitions: 1950s–70s

The foundations for such growth were laid in the 1950s and 1960s. Alliance's first acquisition, in 1956, was Thomas Hoghton (Oswaldtwistle) Ltd., a firm of cotton goods manufacturers. Many such companies still existed in the so-called junior league of Lancashire textile firms and their acquisition, reconstruction, and turnaround was the substance of Alliance's activities for some years. By the end of the 1960s, he operated through three vehicles—Alliance Brothers, a mail-order and textiles firm, R Greg & Company Ltd., a spinning and fashion fabric firm, and Northern Counties Securities, a finance group.

The pace of growth accelerated in 1968 when Alliance took control of publicly traded Spirella Company of Great Britain Ltd. through a reverse takeover involving R Greg. Spirella was to form the nucleus of what was to become Coats Viyella. In 1969, it became a holding company as Spirella Group Ltd. into which the textile interests of Alliance Brothers were absorbed. Together with his partner Jack Menaged, Alliance reorganized Spirella into three groups—foundation garment manufacture (the business of the original company), textile merchandising and spinning (based on Greg), and household textiles (based on Alliance Brothers).

Spirella soon set off down the road of further acquisition. The foundation garment side of the business was strengthened by the purchase of Richard Cooper & Company (Ashbourne) Ltd. and Leethems (Twilfit) Ltd. A more significant growth area was that of household textiles, particularly towels, where several takeovers were made. John Ainscow & Company Ltd. of Bolton was purchased in 1970, as was WT Taylor and Company Ltd. of Horwich. These two companies were merged with Stott & Smith Ltd., toweling and cotton goods manufacturers, to form the Stott & Smith Group Ltd. Other acquisitions at this time included the Barber Textile Corporation Ltd., Horrockses Ltd., and Dorcas Ltd.

By 1973, Alliance was already contemplating the takeover of another household textiles firm, Vantona Ltd. For Vantona the takeover of 1975 represented a reversal of fortunes, since Spirella had previously been seen as a possible target for Vantona to acquire. The £5 million offer for Vantona was widely seen as shrewdly judged rather than generous and the Vantona board was very publicly split. The industrial logic, however, was undisputed, for while both companies were involved in household textiles, Spirella's strength in towels complemented Vantona's own strengths. The merger, misleadingly billed as the marriage of whalebone and sheets, led to the disappearance of the Spirella name, it being felt that it was too closely connected with corsetry ever to outlive the association. In 1976, the merged company changed its name to Vantona Group Ltd.

Vantona was then the third-largest producer of household textiles in the United Kingdom but still a relatively minor player within the industry as whole. It was all the more remarkable, therefore, that in 1978 Vantona was able to beat off the challenge of both Carrington Viyella and Courtaulds in order to acquire uniform manufacturers J Compton, Sons & Webb Ltd.

The Carrington Viyella Deal: 1982

The next takeover, in 1982, was breathtaking in its scale, for it involved a bid by Vantona for Carrington Viyella, a company eight times its size. Carrington Viyella, a manufacturer of garments, home furnishings, carpets, and fabrics, was a troubled giant, considered by many to be too debt-laden to be an attractive acquisition. It did, however, come with an attractive dowry of brand names including Dorma, Van Heusen, and Viyella itself.

The branded cloth was merely the most famous of a number produced by William Hollins & Company Ltd. (established 1784), the Nottingham-based yarn spinners. The name had been registered as a trade mark in 1894 and was derived from the Via

Gellia, the road linking the Derbyshire villages of Cromford, where Hollins had a mill, and Bonsall. It had become synonymous with quality so that when, in 1961, Hollins became the core of a larger group, it adopted the name Viyella International Ltd. Viyella was to make numerous acquisitions throughout the 1960s before being taken over by ICI Ltd. in 1969 and merged with Carrington & Dewhurst Ltd. the following year.

Skepticism over the wisdom of the Carrington Viyella takeover was perhaps behind Alliance's difficulty in raising the required £50 million, a sum that would soon be made to seem modest. The importance of the Viyella name was again acknowledged when the group became Vantona Viyella plc in February 1983.

The Formation of Coats Viyella: 1986

The year 1985 saw another significant merger, with the Nottingham Manufacturing Company plc, established 1805, after a friendly deal between Alliance and Harry Djanogly of Nottingham Manufacturing. The company was as cash-rich as Carrington Viyella had been debt-laden and brought with it strong links with the retailer Marks & Spencer, to whom Nottingham Manufacturers supplied hosiery and knitwear. This acquisition bolstered the group prior to the climactic merger in the following year with Coats Patons plc.

Coats Patons was itself the result of a 1960 merger between J & P Coats Ltd. and Patons & Baldwins Ltd. J & P Coats had its origins in Paisley, near Glasgow, commencing thread manufacture in 1825. The business was especially successful in the North American market, and its growth culminated in a highly successful public offering in 1890. By the turn of the century, by amalgamation with other thread producers—including its Paisley rivals, Clark & Company—Coats had become the largest textile firm in Britain, with factories worldwide.

Patons & Baldwins derived from two separate concerns—JJ Baldwin & Partners Ltd., established at Halifax in 1785, and John Paton, Son & Company Ltd. of Alloa, established 1813, that merged in 1920. The merged company was a woolen and worsted spinner, specializing in knitting wools, with factories throughout Britain, as well as in Canada, China, and Tasmania.

Early in 1986, Coats Patons was the subject of an agreed takeover bid by a knitwear group, Dawson International plc. Coats had already been identified as a possible long-term target for Vantona Viyella but the proposed Dawson deal precipitated action by them. Dawson was successfully outbid by an offer worth £715 million. In March 1986, Vantona, like Spirella before it, was dropped from the company's name that then reflected its largest components in its new name, Coats Viyella plc.

The Tootal Group Purchase: Late 1980s–91

By 1989, it began to look as if another famous name would have to be accommodated. Tootal Group plc was the descendant of the English Sewing Cotton Company Ltd., incorporated 1897, a sewing thread and yarn producer whose Sylko domestic sewing thread became a household name. As part of the trend towards larger groupings in the textile industry, English Sewing Cotton expanded, acquiring the Manchester-based business of

Key Dates:

1785: JJ Baldwin & Partners Ltd. is established.
1813: John Paton, Son & Company Ltd. begins operations.
1820: JJ Baldwin and John Paton merge.
1825: J&P Coats Ltd. begins manufacturing thread.
1956: Sir David Alliance acquires his first company, Thomas Hoghton Ltd.
1960: J&P Coats and Patons & Baldwins Ltd. merge to form Coats Patons.
1968: Alliance gains control of Spirella Company of Great Britain Ltd.
1975: Spirella merges with Vantona Ltd.
1976: The firm takes on the name Vantona Group Ltd. and operates as the third largest producer of household textiles in the UK.
1982: Vantona acquires Carrington Viyella.
1985: Nottingham Manufacturing Company is purchased.
1986: Vatona acquires Coats Paton; the company officially adopts the name Coats Viyella plc.
1990: Neville Bain is appointed CEO of the firm.
1991: Coats Viyella completes its purchase of Tootal Group plc.
1993: Berghaus International Fashion is acquired.
1996: The firm begins restructuring efforts after reporting losses.
1997: Bain resigns unexpectedly.
1998: Share price falls to a record low; plans are set in motion to divest the Viyella businesses.
1999: Alliance retires; Coats Viyella sells its precision engineering business.
2000: Coats Viyella begins divesting its contract clothing business to focus on its thread operations.
2001: The firm changes its name to Coats plc to reflect its new business focus.

Tootal Broadhurst Lee & Company Ltd., incorporated 1888, in 1963. Five years later, the company changed its name to English Calico Ltd. following the acquisition of the Calico Printers Association Ltd. The change of name was short-lived, and in 1973 the company became Tootal Ltd.

Although one of the "big four" of British textile firms, Tootal's disappointing performance during the 1980s had left it vulnerable to a takeover bid. This duly emerged in the shape of Australian entrepreneur Abe Goldberg, who acquired a 29.9% stake in the company. When he was rebuffed by the Tootal board, Coats Viyella stepped in to acquire Goldberg's shareholding and to agree to terms for a £395 million takeover. The bid lapsed, however, after it was referred to the Monopolies and Mergers Commission (MMC).

Prospects revived after the MMC recommended that Coats divest itself of its U.K. and German sewing thread businesses, a condition with which it was relatively easy to comply. However, when it became clear that Coats was to renew its offer at a much lower valuation, Tootal's resistance grew. Reluctance to be taken over on the cheap, as they saw it, was accompanied by

references to differing management cultures by the Tootal board. The *Daily Telegraph*, compared Tootal's behavior to "... a dowdy Jane Austen heroine: desperate to wed but equally desperate not to look too keen."

Finally, Alliance was persuaded to do what he had never done in all his deals up to this point—launch a hostile takeover bid. An initial offer worth £194 million was raised to £241 million in April and this was sufficient to win the day. Like many previous deals its appeal lay in its industrial logic rather than mere corporate aggrandizement, for while the two groups dominated the international thread market their businesses were largely complementary.

However, the takeover met with reservations on three counts. First, it had been said that the expansion of Coats Viyella had done little more than gather most of the surviving elements of a declining industry under the control of one company. The bid for Tootal succeeded, in this view, not because of Coats Viyella's own performance, which was judged disappointing, but because Tootal's results were even poorer. Fears had also been expressed that the integration of the Tootal businesses might prove difficult and that Coats Viyella's record in this area had not been good. There was additional speculation that, in achieving a dominant position in the industry, Coats Viyella might alienate customers fearful of becoming dependent on such a large supplier, and that they might now be inclined to seek alternatives.

Early indications were that Coats Viyella had appreciated the dangers of imbalance in this area and that through disposals excessive market share in certain areas would be voluntarily relinquished. The appointment of Neville Bain as chief executive in 1990 also increased business confidence. Formerly with Cadbury Schweppes plc, his recognized skills in integrating businesses were matched by the £65 million set aside for integration costs following the Tootal takeover.

Industry Hardships and Change into the 21st Century

While Coats Viyella entered the 1990s a victor in the Tootal deal, the company soon realized that the final decade of the 20th century would perhaps be the most difficult in its history. The U.K. textile industry remained in a downturn and the firm was forced to close plants and lay off employees. In 1992, Coats Viyella cut 566 jobs at two North Ireland manufacturing facilities due to the recession and the increasing amount of cheaper imports that were available. As the European textile economy remained in decline, Bain began to focus on international efforts. A move into the China market signaled the firm's commitment to operations in Asia. Bain stated in a 1993 *Financial Times London* article, "We have already signed six joint ventures and are confident of clinching more shortly. There are enormous opportunities in China; there are 1.2 billion people who are not fully clothed."

While Coat Viyella's profits remained unremarkable, the company continued to acquire and divest certain operations. In 1993, the firm purchased Berghaus International Fashion, a distributor of women's fashion in Western Europe and Russia. It also sold its carpet division to U.S.-based Shaw Industries. By

1995, profits had fallen by 6.4 percent over the previous year, forcing the firm to restructure further. It began to move production from Western Europe and North America to cheaper labor regions including Asia and Eastern Europe. Nearly 3,000 jobs were cut in 1996 as raw material costs increased and demand for thread weakened.

As conditions in the textile industry worsened, Coats Viyella continued to face challenges. In 1997, Bain retired unexpectedly as the firm reported another year of falling profits. Michael Ost was named his replacement. The firm posted record losses in 1998, and it announced a divestiture program that would allow it to focus on thread operations. In February 1999, Coats Viyella sold precision engineering business Dynacast as part of its program. Alliance retired that year, leaving the remains of his textile empire to Sir Harry Djanogly, who took over as chairman of the floundering firm.

Coats Viyella entered the new millennium on weak ground. It continued eyeing its thread business as key to surviving and began to divest its contract clothing, home furnishings, and branded clothing business. As it left the contract clothing market, nearly 2,000 jobs were cut, and it was forced to break ties with Marks & Spencer, with whom it had been doing business for over 70 years. The company reported continued losses in 2000.

In 2001, Martin Flower was named CEO of Coats Viyella. That year, the company announced a name change to Coats plc, reflecting its focus on its global thread business. The firm did however, retain the Jaeger and Viyella fashion brands. While the future of Coats remained uncertain, management was confident that the drastic restructuring of the firm left it in a secure position to compete in the ever-changing global textile industry.

Principal Subsidiaries

Coats Finance Co. Ltd.; Hicking Pentecost Ltd.; Jaeger Holdings Ltd.; Tootal Group Ltd.; Tootal Thread Ltd.; Viyella Holdings Ltd.; Vantona Viyella Ltd.; Coats Deutschland GmbH (Germany); Barbour Campbell Textiles Ltd. (Scotland); Coats Paton Ltd. (Scotland); J & P Coats Ltd. (Scotland); Coats North America Holdings Inc.; Coats Ltd.; Coats Bangladesh Ltd.; Coats Cadena SA (Argentina); Coats Australian Pty Ltd.; Coats Corrente Ltda (Brazil); Coats Canada Inc.; Coats Cadena SA (Chile; 60%); Coats Guangzhou (China; 90%); Guangying Spinning Company Ltd. (China); Jinying Spinning Company Ltd. (China); Coats Sartel SA (France); Coats GmbH (Germany); China Thread Development Company Ltd. (Hong Kong); Coats Hong Kong Limited; Coats Hungary Ltd.; PT Tootal Thread Indonesia (70%); Coats Cucirini SpA (Italy; 72.9%); Coats Tootal Malaysia (51%); Grupo Coats Timon, S.A. de C.V. (Mexico); Cia de Linha Coats & Clark Lda (Portugal); Barbour Threads Ltd. (Scotland); Coats South Africa Ltd.;

Coats Fabra SA (Spain; 98.9%); Coats Thread Lanka (Sri Lanka; 87%); Coats Iplik Sanayii AS (Turkey; 76.1%); Coats American Inc.; Coats & Clark Inc. (U.S.); Coats Tootal Phong Phu Ltd. (Vietnam; 75%); The Jaeger Company Ltd.; The Jaeger Company's Shops Ltd.; William Hollins & Company Ltd.; Pasolds Ltd.; Berghaus BV (Holland); Jaeger Sportswear Inc. (U.S.); CV Home Furnishings Ltd.; Dorma France SA; Madura Coats Ltd. (India).

Principal Competitors

Burlington Industries Inc.; Springs Industries Inc.; Toyobo Co. Ltd.

Further Reading

Armstrong, Paul, "Coats Viyella," *Times* (London),September 9, 1999.

Barker, Thorold, "The Cupboard Is Far from Threadbare," *Financial Times,* September 7, 2000, p. 28.

Barrie, Leonie, "Coats Viyella Closures: A Blow to U.K. Manufacturing Base," *Bobbin,* December, 2000, p. 14.

"Britain's Coats Viyella Delays Demerger, Offers Gloomy Outlook," *Daily Mail,* September 10, 1998.

"Coats Viyella Buys Dutch Firm," *Irish Times,* June 12, 1993, p. 14.

"Coats Viyella Chief Puts His Coat On and Leaves With Much Still to Do," *Irish Times,* July 30, 1999, p. 64.

"Coats Viyella Cuts 566 Jobs in N Ireland," *Financial Times,* April 7, 1992, p. 12.

"Coats Viyella Plans Restructuring," *Irish Times,* March 15, 1996.

"Coats Viyella plc—Statement Re Group Refocus," *Regulatory News Service,* September 6, 2000.

Luesby, Jenny, and Richard Wolffe, "Bains Resigns Unexpectedly as Chief of Coats Viyella," *Financial Times,* March 14, 1997, p. 23.

Murdoch, Bill, "Coats Viyella Sells Carpets Division to US Company," *Irish Times,* December 14, 1994, p. 16.

Patten, Sally, "Coats Viyella Crippled by 'Turn of the Screw'," *Times* (London), September 7, 2000.

Potter, Ben, "Coats Viyella Sees Profits Plummeting Before Split," *Daily Telegraph,* March 12, 1998, p. 30.

Rawsthorn, Alice, "Coats Viyella Buys German Zip Maker," *Financial Times,* June 12, 1989, p. 22.

——, "Coats Viyella Picks New Chief in Strategy Switch," *Financial Times,* September 25, 1990, p. 24.

——, "Unraveling the Fate of the Thread Empire," *Financial Times,* August 29, 1991, p. 17.

Ross, Sarah, "Coats Viyella Losses Highlight Decline," *Financial Times,* March 8, 2001, p. 44.

Rudd, Roland, "Coats Viyella Hits Pounds 63m and Keeps an Eye on China," *Financial Times,* September 10, 1993, p. 24.

Tomkins, Richard, "Coats Viyella Sells Subsidiary," *Financial Times,* December 22, 1989, p. 18.

Wells, Frederick Arthur, *Hollins and Viyella: A Study in Business History,* Newton Abbot: David & Charles, 1968.

—Lionel Alexander Ritchie
—update: Christina M. Stansell

COGNOS®

Cognos Inc.

3755 Riverside Drive
P.O. Box 9707, Station T
Ottawa, Ontario K1G 4K9
Canada
Telephone: (613) 738-1440
Fax: (613) 738-0002
Web site: http://www.cognos.com

Public Company
Incorporated: 1969 as Quasar
Employees: 2,704
Sales: $495.7 million
Stock Exchanges: NASDAQ Toronto
Ticker Symbol: COGN, CSN
NAIC: 51121 Software Publishers

Cognos Inc. is the leading provider of business intelligence solutions that optimize the performance of the world's largest and most successful organizations. Business intelligence (BI) is a category of applications and technologies for gathering, storing, analyzing, reporting on, and providing access to data to help enterprise users make better business decisions. Cognos consistently adds immediate context to business-driving information, aligning decisions and making enterprises more agile. Cognos serves more than 17,000 customers in 120 countries of the world.

1960s Origins

In 1969, computer technology was much different from that of today. It was the era of mainframe computers and terminals. Computers were room sized and information was centralized in one location. The average manager or employee had no contact with computers.

Cognos' forerunner, Quasar Systems Limited, was founded in 1969 by Alan Rushforth and Peter Glenister. The company, consisting of a handful of programmers and consultants, provided information system consulting to the federal government of Canada. In 1972, Michael Potter joined Cognos. He became a partner in 1973 and bought out the co-founders in 1975.

In 1979, Quasar introduced the company's first software product—QUIZ—for Hewlett Packard HP 3000s. QUIZ extracted data from the computer, manipulated and formatted the data, then printed a report or listing. By 1984, sales of QUIZ had reached 2,500 copies at $7,000 each. The same year that Cognos introduced QUIZ, it also introduced a selection of end-user reporting tools for terminal based users.

New Product Development in the 1980s

Three years later, Quasar introduced PowerHouse, a fourth-generation application development tool for the HP mid-range platform. In 1984, Quasar previewed PowerHouse for VAX at the DEXPO West show in Las Vegas. This heralded a new generation of development tools. The success of QUIZ allowed Cognos to expand its sales force and research and development. This, in turn lead to increased development of products based on the PowerHouse computer language. The PowerHouse eventually ported to the major proprietary and Unix platforms. PowerHouse-based packages, such as the new Expert report-writing system, meant that tasks that would have taken weeks to complete using a traditional computer language now could be accomplished in a day or less.

The 1980s were troublesome years for many Canadian software companies. Canada was in a recession and many competitors went under. However, Cognos continued to earn a profit, largely due to its successful switch from the provision of consulting services to the production and sale of packaged software. By the middle of the decade, consultation accounted for only 20 percent of the company's revenues and software for the remaining 80 percent. As Barbara Crook wrote in the *Computer Post:* "This seemingly effortless performance was actually the product of conservative management, strong teamwork, and a hefty chunk of corporate humility." Crook quoted Michael Potter as saying, "We certainly weren't unique in recognizing the importance of packaged software, but I think we were unique in our ability to successfully make that transition from custom to packaged software."

In 1983, Quasar changed its name to Cognos. Cognos is a fragment scissored off the Latin word "cognosco," which means ''knowledge from personal experience.'' Quasar changed the name to Cognos to reflect its growing emphasis on products that provide information and knowledge.

Cognos began concentrating on international markets. By 1984, Cognos had grown to 300 employees across North American, and revenues for fiscal 1983 had topped $18 million. While competitors were turning to third party marketers and value-added resellers, Cognos bucked the trend and continued to utilize a direct sales force. Potter acknowledged that a direct sales force was more costly, but said that having control of the sales effort justified the expense.

In 1984, the company became a key player in artificial intelligence (AI). (AI is the area of computer science devoted to replicating human thought processes.) Cognos headed a $100,000 study by the federal government to determine Canada's priorities in AI research.

Over the previous four years, sales had climbed from $2.1 million to $26.45 million. The *Globe & Mail* reported that in a survey of 437 software companies in Canada, half had sales of less than $500,000. In the early eighties, Cognos had considered going public. However, the market was not right for software companies, and the public listing was put on hold. Cognos had other sources of funds, primarily from the high technology investment arm of the Toronto-based Noranda Inc. Noranda owned 30 percent of the shares, Potter owned 47 percent, and employees owned approximately 25 percent.

In 1985, Cognos opened new headquarters in Canada, the United Kingdom, and the United States. It also opened offices in France and Australia. The expansion was necessitated by a need to find new markets for PowerHouse—which by that time had been adapted to run on several operating systems. The expansion resulted in losses in the first two quarters of the year. Consequently, Cognos made a concerted effort to lower costs by implementing a hiring freeze and cutting back on capital expenditures. Potter was quoted as saying that despite getting ''lean and mean,'' the goal was to support high revenues with the same resources. In the 3rd quarter, the company realized a profit approximately 50 percent of the profit a year earlier.

In 1986, Cognos underwent a major restructuring, commencing with the hiring of Thomas Csathy, formerly of Burroughs Canada, as the new president and CEO. Founder Michael Potter became chairman. Csathy announced his intention to steer Cognos in the direction of software development, believing that software was the way of the future. Csathy also outlined a second objective: to adapt the company's software to

the changing market. Cognos anticipated a changed computer environment within five years, involving the complete ''networking'' of computer systems by major users. Software would have to be compatible and accessible for a whole range of users within an organizational structure

Cognos reorganized in yet another way. In order to respond to its three vendor's distinct markets: Hewlett Packard, Digital Equipment Corp. and Data General Corp. Cognos consolidated product development and sales support along hardware lines. The company replaced separate product development and marketing organizations for each product line with one combined operation. The *Globe & Mail* quoted Potter:'' We have shifted from a functional organization to a product organization.''

As a first step towards developing products for microcomputers, Cognos released a new version of the PowerHouse language. This new version allowed developers to work with relational databases. (Relational databases are collections of data that can be compared and searched by logical relationships.)

Cognos went public in 1986. The share issue allowed the company to retire its million bank debt. However, in 1988, profits dropped dramatically from the previous year, primarily due to increased operating expenses—up 25 percent from 1987. Michael Potter predicted that profits would increase substantially in the coming year, since expenditures had slowed. He attributed the decreased expenditures to planned restraints in spending, lowered product costs and sales commissions. The sales force was now contacting customers by mail and telephone instead of crossing borders to knock on doors in search of prospects. The costly ''face-to-face'' sales approach had been justified when the company was marketing software applications that cost up to $100,000. However, with the switch over to applications for microcomputers, few applications cost more than $2,000. These lower priced applications necessitated a more economical method of conducting sales.

Cognos chairman Michael Potter told shareholders that the new challenge was to broaden the application of software to include giving sales representatives online access to customer information, tailoring software packages to specific customer needs, and helping computer users gain access to the databases of other computers. Potter predicted that information systems, rather than computer languages, would represent the way of the nineties. The company had already begun marketing and developing software in conjunction with other companies to expand its markets.

Cognos increased spending on R&D. The research push was designed to bring the company into new areas of customer demand. Cognos researchers were developing a new generation of software that could write other programs. Potter reported that computer end-users with no programming experience would be able to specify the programs they needed, and the software would do the writing for them.

Despite Potter's optimism, the *Financial Post* reported that analysts were questioning how long it would take Cognos to recover from its growing pains. Analysts linked Cognos's low sales in 1987 to flat HP sales, but commented that 1988 looked more positive. Two years later, in 1989, revenues hit $100 million. The company had become the largest firm in the world devoted to producing software development tools.

The 1990s

In the early years of the nineties, Cognos enjoyed what journalists described as a "spectacular comeback." In 1990, Cognos introduced PowerPlay—a PC Windows-based business analysis tool that set a new standard for ease of use and power in decision support software. The year following, Cognos launched a powerful SQL database query and reporting tool named Impromptu. (SQL or Structured Query Language is a standard interactive and programming language used in the development of some databases.) Impromptu was said to bring corporate data closer than ever to the user. According to corporate documents, Cognos became a leading player in the move toward tools that empower the user.

The early 1990s presented a special challenge to Cognos. Suddenly the market for centralized processing software dwindled, replaced by a rapidly growing interest in computer networks. The movement caught Cognos by surprise. Earnings suffered as the company struggled with the transition to new products and new markets. In 1992, sales dropped to a new low. However, the turnaround was quick to come.

In 1992, Cognos introduced PowerHouse Client for Windows. This software was thought to be a key step in the smooth transition from centralized processing to client/server computing. (Client/server describes the relationship between two computer programs in which one program, the client, makes a service request from another program, the server, which fulfills the request.) Two years later, in 1994, Cognos unveiled the Axiant Developers' Workbench at UNIX Expo.

The next year, 1995, Cognos named Ron Zambonini as chief executive officer. One of Zambonini's strategies was to change the way in which Cognos software was sold. Zambonini advocated that widely different marketing approaches were necessary at different points in a technology's life. He stated that many companies use outdated sales techniques long after the market has shifted.

That same year, Cognos joined the OLAP Council. This was a software industry association established to provide education about the benefits of OLAP technology for business intelligence applications. OLAP refers to on-line analytical processing server technology. In 1996, Impromptu won the Product of the Year award. Also that year, the company announced a three-for-one stock split. Analysts lauded Cognos for cashing in on a lucrative market (i.e. personal computer networks), and stock prices hit a high of $53.50 on the Toronto stock exchange. One year after, in 1997, Cognos acquired Right Information Systems. This acquisition was expected to broaden and extend the business intelligence product family. Likewise that year, a Cognos product, Scenario, won PC WEEK lab analysts choice award.

Nevertheless, problems were arising. The Internet had gained importance, and the *Globe & Mail* reported that Cognos was facing a strategic turning point that threatened to impair its comeback of the last few years. From 1993–97, the company had become one of Canada's three largest software developers, based on the success of its BI products for local area networks (LANS).

However, Internet technologies introduced a new, and more economical type of product—BI software to run on intranets. Intranets are corporate computer networks that use the technology of the Internet. Corporate customers struggled to make decisions between investing in powerful but costly BI software for LANS or the more economical, but less powerful intranet software. Customer indecision resulted in delayed sales. Cognos had expected that Web technology would eventually infiltrate BI technology, but it had not anticipated the speed at which this would occur.

Sales and revenues had been excellent in the past few years. However, Cognos issued a notice to its shareholders that its growth was likely to be moderate over the next few quarters. Investors scrambled to sell and the prices of shares dropped accordingly. For the first time, Cognos turned to acquisitions in a big way to bolster its web technology. As Patrick Brethour wrote in the *Globe & Mail*, "Cognos is being pushed into the unfamiliar role of acquisitor of other firms." Traditionally, Cognos had relied on internal research and development initiatives to acquire new software.

Cognos announced that it had spent $16 million to buy Interweave Software Inc. Interweave's Internet-based information retrieval programs were expected to complement Cognos' main web program, PowerPlay Server Web Edition. This was to be followed by several more acquisitions over the next two years.

In 1998, the company upgraded Interweave's software, renamed it Impromptu Web Query and shipped it. A little later that year, Scenario was named Datamation product of the year. Also, Cognos acquired BI University, which allowed attendees to experience first-hand how BI works in an organization. In

December, Cognos acquired Relationship Matters, including DecisionStream software. And lastly, Cognos received the Software Technical Assistance Recognition award for excellent in automated software support in North America.

PowerPlay Enterprise Service was launched in 1999. This was the only OLAP application server that supported the Web, Windows, Microsoft Excel, and mobile users from a single, centrally administrated server. Also that year, Cognos released Cognos DecisionStream, a dimensional framework to build and implement datamarts to form a fully integrated BI system. (A data mart is a repository of data gathered from operational data and other sources that is designed to serve a particular community of knowledge workers.)

That year, Cognos completed the acquisition of LEX2000 Inc., a developer of financial reporting consolidation, budgeting and forecasting systems, and of Information Tools AG, the Corporation's distributor in Switzerland. Cognos also completed the purchase of the entire outstanding minority interest in the subsidiary in Singapore, Cognos Far East Pte Limited. Also in 1999, Cognos held its first User Conference, Enterprise 99. The conference was held in Orlando, Florida, and was open to all customers and partners.

In 2000, the company released the Cognos platform, an application for building, managing, and deploying BI solutions for enterprise and e-business needs. A little later, Cognos launched a new e-business intelligence applications business unit. *Business Week* magazine named Cognos as one of the world's Top 100 Information Technology companies. It was the only business intelligence software provider named to the list. *DM Review* readers named the company the number one independent business intelligence company in its annual ranking of the industry's top 100 vendors in business intelligence, CRM (Customer Relationship Management), and data warehousing.

Acquisitions continued. In 2000, Cognos acquired Powerstream OY (the distributor in Finland), NoticeCast Software Ltd. (an event management software company), and Johnson and Michaels, Inc. (a provider of business intelligence consulting services).

In June 2001, Cognos announced financial results for the first quarter. Revenue for the quarter was $108.0 million, compared with revenue of $108.7 million for the same period last year. Net loss for the first quarter of fiscal 2002, excluding restructuring charges, was $2.1 million or $0.02 per share. The company attributed the losses to the economic slowdown occurring in the United States and announced a strategy to reduce the cost structure in response to the current economic environment, including a reduction in the work force. On July 3, 2001, Ron Zambonini was listed as the 24th most influential technology industry CEO in the Enterprise Systems Journal Power 100 list.

The Future

Despite economic slowdown in the United States, and the cost-reduction strategies being implemented, the company did not expect its strategic programs to be affected. Cognos has planned a number of product releases for later in 2001— including the fully integrated BI platform and version 5.1 of Cognos Finance.

The high technology industry is volatile and subject to constant and sudden changes. Cognos, like its competitors will always be faced with the need to adjust to changing times and to remain current. Since it has successfully faced such challenges in the past, there is reason to anticipate that it will continue to do so in the foreseeable future.

Principal Subsidiaries

Cognos Corporation (U.S.A.); Cognos do Brasil Ltda. (Brazil); Cognos BC (Sweden); Cognas A/S (Denmark); Cognos Austria HmbH (Austria); Cognos B.V. (Netherlands); Cognos France S.A. (France); Cognos GmbH (Germany); Cognos Limited (U.K.); Cognos N.V./S.A. (Belgium); Cognos OY (Finland); Cognos South Africa (PYT) Limited (South Africa); Cognos S.p.A. (Italy); Cognos (Switzerland) Ltd. (Switzerland); Cognos Far East Pte Limited (Singapore); Cognos PTY Limited (Australia); Teijin Cognos Incorporated (Japan; 50%).

Principal Competitors

Brio Technology, Business Objects, Hyperion.

Further Reading

Becker, Jane, ''Cognos' Chief Thinks Software Is the Place to Be,'' *Globe & Mail,* February 24, 1987.
——, ''Cognos Expects Record Revenue This Year,'' *Globe & Mail,* June 24, 1988.
Brethour, Patrick, ''How a Book Set Cognos Course,'' *Globe & Mail,* March 5, 1997.
——, ''Web Forces Cognos to Change Paths,'' *Globe & Mail,* October, 1997, p. B14.
Carlisle, Tamsin, ''Growing Pains Cramp Earnings at Cognos,'' *Financial Post,* March 14, 1988, p. 39.
''Cognos: Through the Years,'' Ottawa: Cognos, 2000.
Crook, Barbara, ''Transition Pays Off Big for Cognos,'' *Computer Post,* Summer, 1984, p. C17.
''Hard on Software,'' *Free Press,* July 26, 1986.
Howlett, Karen, ''Cognos Credits Its Employees for Software Success,'' *Globe & Mail,* March 10, 1986.
Prentice, Michael, ''The Art of Pottering Around,'' *Province,* August 6, 2000, p. A37.

—June Campbell

Coinstar, Inc.

1800 114th Avenue S.E.
Bellevue, Washington 98004
U.S.A.
Telephone: (425) 943-8000
Toll Free: (800) 928-CASH
Fax: (425) 637-8030
Web site: http://www.coinstar.com

Public Company
Incorporated: 1990
Employees: 552
Sales: $103.1 million (2000)
Stock Exchanges: NASDAQ
Ticker Symbol: CSTR
NAIC: 81299 Miscellaneous Personal Services, Not
    Elsewhere Classified; 33313 Calculating Machines
    Except Computers

Coinstar, Inc., operates a network of automated, self-service coin counting and processing machines that provide customers with a means of converting loose change into cash. The Coinstar units, located in supermarkets, financial institutions, and mass merchants in the United States, Canada, and England, count loose coins and issue vouchers listing the total number, denominations, and dollar value of the coins processed minus an 8.9 percent processing charge. Coinstar also receives handling fees, which amount to about half its revenue, from consumer giants, such as Pepsi, Kraft, and General Foods, whose coupons Coinstar passes along to consumers on printouts. Coinstar is found in more than 8,900 U.S. supermarkets, and the company has turned more than $3.8 billion worth of coins into cash.

1991: The Start of a Unique Service

Jens Molbak came up with the idea for Coinstar in 1988, while he was a graduate student in business at Stanford University. One night, so the story goes, while sitting in his dorm room, thinking about the jar of coins on his dresser, he hit upon the idea to find a way to turn a service into a business. The penny held special significance for Molbak, who, as a ten-year-old, washed 28,011 flowerpots at his Danish immigrant parents' plant nursery in Washington. The $280.11 he collected taught him, so he said in *U.S. News & World Report*, ''that there was real money in coins.''

Molbak's idea was to provide a service to coin hoarders so that for a small fee they would be able to trade their coins in for more useable cash. In 1989, Molbak turned his idea into part of a graduate school project and stood outside Bay Area grocery stores with a clipboard interviewing people as to what they did with their change at the end of the day. ''We talked to 1,500 people, and it turned out that three out of four had coins at home, with an average of about $30 [sitting unused] at any one time,'' Molbak said in a 1997 *Forbes* article. As a result of his research, Molbak estimated that there was about $8 billion worth of change sitting around in jars in the United States. He arrived at this number by subtracting the estimated value of the coins in circulation from the value of all U.S. coins produced during the past 25 years. The remainder, $8 billion, equals a bit more than $30 per adult.

It took Molbak a few years to raise the capital for his private company and to perfect the green and yellow Coinstar machine, which combined ATM-style computer software and Las Vegas slot machine technology. Adapted from the electronic coin counter made by a Swedish company named Scan Coin, it cost about $12,000 and contained a computer, a modem, a video screen, and a printer; its sorting equipment was sensitive enough to kick out key chains, foreign coins, and lint while counting 600 coins per minute. An online network allowed all sorts of information to be transmitted, including how many slugs had been inserted, how much each machine took in by the minute and in what denominations, whether it needed servicing, and when the machine's coffers were full. By the time the machine design was complete, the company held five patents on it.

In 1991, degree in hand, Molbak founded Coinstar. By 1992, Coinstar's machines were installed in four San Francisco supermarkets, each of which received a small portion of Coinstar's fees for promoting the service. In addition, stores benefited from the fact that Coinstar users had to go to a cash register with their machine voucher to collect their money; company surveys showed that three out of four spent part of their voucher in the store. Three years later, in 1995, Coinstar had placed 263 machines in stores. In 1996, the company had about 900 units in use in 18 states, with its largest concentration in Los Angeles; there, 347 machines took in about $5,000 per week and dispensed $4,625 in vouchers—more volume than all the rest combined.

The Late 1990s: Growth through Hard Times

The company began a national rollout of its machines in the late 1990s. Flush with $63 million in loans, which it secured in the fall of 1996, Coinstar had a total of 2,000 machines in 23 states by spring 1997. By year's end, it had increased its presence to about 3,000 machines, in supermarkets and in two new markets—financial institutions and Target stores—nationwide. The company also began its "Coins that Count" campaign, offering customers the chance to donate their change to local non-profits through Coinstar machines.

However, the company had yet to turn a profit, and its annual financial losses had grown since 1991 due to the expense of expanding its business, attributable in turn to the cost of its machines. Between 1995 and 1998, the company lost about $52 million in the United States. In the summer of 1997, Coinstar went public, hoping to net more than $60 million in the deal, but had to settle for $29.3 million, selling one-third fewer shares for $10.50 instead of the originally hoped-for $15. A secondary offering of four million shares took place in July 1999.

The company remained unprofitable despite dramatic increases in revenue mainly because of the high depreciation costs on new machines. In 1998, Coinstar recycled more coins than the U.S. Mint produced—15.84 billion versus 15.81 billion—and revenues doubled to nearly $47.7 million. Still, the company lost $24 million for the year. Although Coinstar's price per share increased to about double its initial price by late 1999, analysts expressed concern about the company's long-term viability when weak third-quarter results—the result of a nationwide shortage of coins—led to a drop in the company's stock price by half—back to about $11.

In 1998, with about 4,900 machines in 37 states, Coinstar began to look overseas toward the potential market in euros. By mid-year, the company had formed a new wholly-owned subsidiary call Coinstar International Inc. in an effort to expand its overseas operations in anticipation of the approximately $23 billion worth of various European currencies needing conversion into the common currency during the next several years. It also raised the transaction fee for its money-changing service to 8.9 percent, turning over 1 percent to supermarkets. In early 1999, the company placed three machines in Toronto stores and signed two separate agreements with British supermarket chains in the United Kingdom. In 2001, the company continued its push into Britain, signing up two more chains.

Turn of the Century: Turning Its Machines Into Marketing Tools

Coinstar also attempted to add to its revenue streams with a turn-of-the-century introduction of its Web site and in-store kiosks. This new service allowed customers to log onto www.my-meals.com and gain access to a recipe center and their grocery list. At the store, they used the kiosk to print out their list and receive grocery coupons. Supermarkets, for their part, could track consumers' shopping patterns.

Finally, in early 2000, Coinstar felt confident it had hit upon a recipe for success. Sales had jumped from $77.7 million in 1999 to $103 million in 2000, while losses stayed fairly constant at somewhere between $21 million and $23 million. Coinstar converted Meals.com into a wholly-owned subsidiary and sold 11 percent of Meals.com's shares to a consortium of investors—a virtual who's who of Seattle's tech scene—for $5.5 million. Daniel Gerrity took over as Coinstar's chief executive, while Molbak assumed the positions of chair and chief executive of Meals.com. However, Gerrity resigned after only nine months in the top job in late 2000.

The company also began plans to make use of its network of machines to let consumers pick up tickets and other printed items ordered over the Internet, implementing a $10 million brand building television campaign using humor to exhort consumers to recycle their coins instead of, as before, the rational benefits of the service.

Coinstar's "Coins That Count" program continued to thrive, providing non-profit organizations with the opportunity to use Coinstar machines to raise money. This philanthropic service offered consumers the choice of making a tax-deductible donation with their coins instead of receiving a voucher for the money they deposited in a Coinstar machine. The non-profit organization received 92.5 percent of the funds collected. In 1998, Coinstar entered into a national relationship with The U.S. Fund for UNICEF as the designated coin processor for their annual Trick or Treat for UNICEF program. During 2000, it initiated a relationship with the American Red Cross to help raise money for disaster relief.

As losses from Meals.com led to increasing losses for the company as a whole, Coinstar continued looking for a way to make it into the black. The firm, which had more than 8,000 machines in 43 states, began working with partners Michigan National Bank and DataWave in 2001 to issue MasterCard-branded plastic to use in its machines as pre-paid cards. Instead of receiving a voucher for coins, customers could opt to have

---

Key Dates:

1991: Jens Molbak founds Coinstar.
1992: Coinstar machines are installed in four supermarkets in San Francisco.
1997: The company holds its initial public offering.
1998: The company forms Coinstar International, Inc.
1999: Coinstar forms Meals.com Inc.; the company's secondary offering of four million shares takes place in July.
2000: Coinstar converts Meals.com into a wholly-owned subsidiary; Daniel Gerrity replaces Molbak as Coinstar's chief executive, and Molbak assumes the positions of chair and chief executive of Meals.com.
2001: Molbak steps down as chairman of the company.

---

the cash applied to the card, which could be used wherever MasterCards were accepted. A five-location trial of this service began with Coinstar machines in Seattle in mid-2001.

Finally, in May 2001, Coinstar announced its first profit of $11,000 for the first quarter from its more than 8,500 machines. The company's net loss had been $24 million in 1998, $21.4 million in 1999, and $22.7 million in 2000. However, the company continued to lose money overall because of the losses of its Meals.com subsidiary. Around that time, Molbak announced his resignation as chair of Coinstar, planning to keep working at Meals.com. The company's ailing Web site had lost $21 million since its inception. As a result, in June, the subsidiary laid off 31 employees, one-third of its work force, and attempted to buy back outstanding shares of Meals.com. The plan was to sell Meals.com in order to focus again on Coinstar's core business.

Coinstar executives still considered the United Kingdom a promising growth area in 2001. Returns from its U.K.-based machines were higher overall than those for its American-based machines. In the United States, Coinstar planned to build its

sales by adding high margin services to its grocery store kiosks—pre-paid phone cards and MasterCards. The company would derive profit from the interest charged on outstanding balances as well as a fee from bank issuers and telecommunications companies. The company also expected to cash in on the country's economic downturn, reasoning that when people feel hard-pressed financially, they are more likely to take the time to turn in their loose change.

However, with a history of sustained operating losses since its inception and the expectation of continued losses, Coinstar itself acknowledged that it might not be able to install a sufficient number of machines or maintain existing levels of customer utilization to allow it to achieve profitability or generate sufficient cash flow to continue to meet its capital and operating expenses and debt service obligations.

Principal Subsidiaries

Coinstar International, Inc.; May Shoppinglist.com, Inc.; Coinstar Ltd. (U.K.); Meals.com, Inc.

Principal Competitors

CoinBank Automated Systems Inc.; Continental Coin Processors; LPS Money Systems Inc.

Further Reading

Flanagan, William G., and Alexandra Alger, " 'It's Found Money': Finally, There's an Easy Way to Cash in All That Extra Change," *Forbes*, February 10, 1997, p. 214.
Stepankowsky, Paula L., "Coinstar Leveraging Coin Machine Network with More Services," *Dow Jones News Service*, July 7, 2001.
Tice, Carol, "Coinstar Adds Services, Plans to Shed Meals.com," *Puget Sound Business Journal*, June 29, 2001, p. 59.
Vogelstein, Fred, and David Brindley, "No More Wrapping and Rolling," *U.S. News & World Report*, April 21, 1997, p. 85.

—Carrie Rothburd

Cookson Group plc

The Adelphi, 1-11 John Adam Street
London, WC2N 6HJ
United Kingdom
Telephone: (+44) (20) 7766-4500
Fax: (+44) (20) 7747-6600
Web site: http://www.cooksongroup.co.uk

Public Company
Incorporated: 1924 as Associated Lead Manufacturers
   Ltd.
Employees: 21,161
Sales: £2.4 billion ($3.7 billion) (2000)
Stock Exchanges: London
Ticker Symbol: CKSN
NAIC: 327112 Vitreous China, Fine Earthenware, and
   Other Pottery Product Manufacturing; 331419 Primary
   Smelting and Refining of Nonferrous Metal (Except
   Copper and Aluminum); 334412 Bare Printed Circuit
   Board Manufacturing; 335999 All Other
   Miscellaneous Electrical Equipment and Component
   Manufacturing

Cookson Group plc is an international materials technology group that provides advanced materials, equipment, and enabling technologies to customers in 100 different countries. The group operates three divisions—Electronics, Ceramics, and Precious Metals. Cookson Electronics, responsible for securing nearly half of the group's sales in 2000, operates as a leading supplier of materials, equipment, process chemistries, and services to manufacturers of printed circuit boards, semiconductor packaging components, and various electronic-related items.

Cookson's Ceramics division manufactures ceramic refractory systems and lining materials, which control and monitor liquid steel, glass, and ferrous and nonferrous metals. This division's products are found in every steel, glass, or foundry market in the world. The company's Precious Metals division supplies precious metals fabricated into wire, sheet, tubing, and chains to the jewelry industry. It also serves the electronics, dental, and electrical industries.

Early History: 1704–1800s

The family was established in Tyneside, England, in 1704 when Isaac Cookson, the son of a brazier from Penrith, Cumberland, moved to Newcastle upon Tyne to seek his fortune. He began operations near South Shields, where the company has had a continuous presence to the present day. The family developed major industrial links in coal mining and the manufacture of iron, salt, and glass, but its direct involvement with a company that came to be part of the present group did not occur until it entered lead manufacturing in the middle of the 19th century.

The earliest direct link with the present group also came in lead manufacture, when in 1778 a Rotherham-based family of ironmasters, the Walkers, began to diversify, and set up its first white lead works at Elswick, Newcastle. White lead—basic lead carbonate—was then the base for virtually all decorative paints and, as the population grew rapidly and the Industrial Revolution gathered pace, the market for white lead and other lead products expanded. Lead, although a long way behind iron, was the second most heavily utilized metal and was to remain so throughout the 19th century, with British firms processing around a quarter of a million tons a year by 1900.

This initial diversification into lead had been made at a propitious time and the Walkers' network of lead works became larger than its original base in iron. By the end of the Napoleonic Wars, the Walkers' partnership was employing a total capital of approximately £500,000 in lead manufacture, with works in London (Islington, Lambeth, and Southwark), Chester, Derby, Liverpool, and Newcastle under Lyme, as well as the original Elswick works. Although some of the smaller works were closed during the 19th century, large smelting and manufacturing sites were purchased at Bagillt and Dee Bank, in north Wales, to work local lead ores, and the Scottish market was supplied by a works in Glasgow.

Although white lead remained important, the output of other lead chemicals—especially red lead, used as the base for protective paints for the increasing output of iron and steel in the

Company Perspectives:

The mission of Cookson is to add value to its customers' businesses by providing materials, equipment, processes, and services that allow them to increase the efficiency, quality, and profitability of their operations. Throughout the world, Cookson companies are known for supplying products that represent the best technology, supported by the best technical service.

country—was developed. The Walkers' partnerships were the first to adopt a new process for the manufacture of lead shot, and built several shot towers at the turn of the 18th century—including one at the Chester works, which is the only early tower still in operation in the United Kingdom. The Walkers' works processed a large amount of blue lead, especially rolled sheet lead and extruded pipe. These products were in great demand as a result of the large increase in both public and private building in the Victorian years, with sheet being used for roofing, and pipe to convey the newly developed water supplies. As a result of these developments, the partnerships—each works was run by a managing partner, and interlocking partnerships between various works provided some overall control—were the largest single force in the British lead manufacturing industry throughout the 19th century.

Despite its large size and considerable potential, the Walkers' partnership lacked initiative and did not dominate the industry in the second half of the 19th century as it might have done. By then the third and fourth generations of partners from the family were managing the firm, and there was evidence that it was suffering the classic symptoms of hardening of the arteries of commercial instinct. Capital employed grew very little over the 19th century; profitability was never high; the innovation of new techniques was left to competitors; and several of the partners became more interested in their country houses and small landed estates than in the fortunes of the firm. A dispute between the partners with regard to profitability led the partnership into the chancery court with the eventual outcome in 1889 that the assets were sold to a newly formed public company, Walkers Parker and Company. The new company experienced even less financial success, with a number of losses in the highly competitive years up to 1914.

Expansion into Lead Manufacture: 1851

In the second half of the 19th century, innovation in the lead manufacturing industry came in large part from newly established firms that were subsequently drawn into what is now the Cookson Group. It was in 1851 that the Cookson family became involved in lead manufacture. In that year, two of the sons of Isaac Cookson III purchased land at Hayhole on the River Tyne in Northumberland, where they built a white lead works. In the mid 1840s their father and his partner had sold the family's glass manufacturing companies, because of increasing competition in this area, and the sons needed to find an outlet for their considerable talents. William Isaac Cookson was a very capable scientist and businessman. At the age of 20 he had spent a year in Michael Faraday's laboratory, and he was later to take out

several patents for improvements to metal-smelting and chemical processes.

Under William Isaac and later his son Norman, Cookson rapidly became a significant force in the British lead manufacturing industry. In 1854, the partners bought from the Hawthorn engineering family a second lead works at Howdon on Tyne, close to the Hayhole works. Since lead smelting and refining and the manufacture of red lead were already in operation at Howdon, the Cooksons had developed the capacity for fully integrated production within less than a decade. Over the next 50 years, the works were expanded and were regularly modernized with the introduction of new processes, the major instance being the first successful British introduction of an alternative to the centuries-old stack process for the manufacture of white lead. In the late 1890s Norman Cookson, like his father an amateur scientist of some distinction with several patents to his name, introduced a German-developed chamber process at Hayhole, which doubled Cookson's output of white lead to some 10,000 tons per annum in the early 1900s, around 20 percent of U.K. output. Cookson's growth brought considerable profitability and, increasingly, leadership of the industry.

By the turn of the 19th century lead manufacturing, like many British industries, was experiencing severe competition, not only from the development of new firms at home but also from imports from continental producers. Most British firms were small family-run companies that were ill-prepared to cope with the competition, although the example of Walkers Parker suggests that the adoption of limited liability status alone was not a satisfactory solution. For most of the companies, salvation was seen in cooperation, common pricing policies, and the formation of cartels. By 1914, there were British conventions of the red, white, and blue lead manufacturers; each of these conventions in its turn negotiating market shares within international, primarily European, conventions.

The Formation of Associated Lead Manufacturers: 1924

Whereas the formation of cartels remained important internationally in the years between World War I and World War II, British manufacturers saw amalgamation as the best way to maintain profitability in the face of increasing competition. The earliest proposals date from World War I but in 1924, under the leadership of Cookson and with Clive Cookson as the first chairman, Associated Lead Manufacturers (ALM) was formed. Two years before Imperial Chemical Industries Ltd. was to perform the same function for the British chemical industry, lead manufacturing had a central focus. The initial merger, with a capital of slightly less than £2 million, was of Cookson and the firm of Locke, Lancaster and W.W.&R. Johnson & Sons, the latter being an earlier amalgamation of several London producers that was now by far the dominant London firm.

ALM thus began its existence with the two major firms in two of the three most significant production areas in the United Kingdom. It lacked a presence, however, in the remaining geographical area of significance, the Northwest, and still faced the regionally diversified competition of Walkers Parker. The first of these deficiencies was overcome rather surprisingly by the 1925 purchase of Rowe Bros. & Company, traditionally a

Key Dates:

1851: The Cookson family becomes involved in lead manufacture.

1924: Associated Lead Manufacturers (ALM) is formed.

1925: Rowe Bros. & Company is purchased.

1929: The firm begins the process of acquiring Walker Parkers and Company.

1930: Paint manufacturer Goodlass, Wall & Company is acquired; Goodlass Wall & Lead Industries is set up as a holding company.

1943: Due to decreasing demand, the firm is forced to begin diversification efforts.

1949: The firm's lead business is reorganized into a single entity, ALM.

1954: Fry's Diecastings is acquired.

1966: The firm adopts the name Lead Industries Group Ltd. (LIG).

1978: LIG purchases the A.J. Oyster Co.

1979: The lead business of NL Industries is purchased; LIG operates as the world's leading producer of lead products.

1983: The firm's name is changed to Cookson Group.

1987: As part of its overseas expansion efforts, Cookson purchases U.S.-based Vesuvius Crucible Company.

1990: Cookson sells its 50 percent interest in Tioxide Group plc.

1992: Economic hardships force Cookson to cut costs and lay off employees.

1995: HTCI, a U.S.-based ceramic filter manufacturer, and SMT, a California-based printing stencil manufacturer, are acquired.

1996: The firm buys Engineered Polymers Corp. and GRP Inc. and sells its organic pigment business.

1998: The company purchases the European Laminates manufacturing business of AlliedSignal Inc.

1999: Cookson sells TAM Ceramics Inc. to Ferro Corp.; the company purchases Enthone-OMI Inc. and Premier Refractories.

2000: The firm focuses on three cores businesses: electronics, ceramics, and precious metals.

builders' merchant and thereby involved in the supply of lead products. Although this purchase would have given ALM an outlet for some of its sheet and pipe production, its true function was to nullify the potential threat of Rowe's growing involvement in lead manufacture. Before World War II, Rowe, in conjunction with Cookson, had purchased the patent rights to a newly invented process for the manufacture of red lead and, perhaps more important, had acquired the Runcorn White Lead Company, which brought with it the plant required for a new "quick" process. Even using Cookson's new chamber process the corrosion period for the production of white lead was almost two months, which involved considerable additional costs as compared with the potential of the as yet little-used quick process, wherein corrosion took only a few days.

ALM continued to act in the predatory way in which it had begun its existence. Within five years of its inception, the company had purchased all of the major lead manufacturers in the country with the exception of the Mersey White Lead Company, which was eventually taken over by ALM in 1972. Although there were significant numbers of small, regional producers of lead pipe—and to a lesser extent of lead sheet—in which scale economies were not essential to the producers' survival, ALM dominated the production of lead chemicals. In 1925, ALM took over the Brimsdown Lead Company, another company with a new white lead process, which had been financed by Ludwig Mond and supported by a research laboratory with a number of impressive young scientists, including Stephen Miall, who was to write what was for a long time the standard history of the chemical industry. This acquisition was followed in the years 1926–28 by the mopping up of several of the smaller Tyneside and London manufacturers and, in 1929, after negotiation had failed, by the aggressive purchase of Walkers Parker shares, which eventually led to an agreed merger.

Formation of Holding Company in 1930

Achieving a dominant position in lead manufacturing was not to be the end of ALM's aims. Not only was there no growth in market size—a result of the Depression during the interwar years and increased foreign competition—there were also new substitutes for lead products. Copper was beginning to make inroads into the market for lead pipe but, more significant, white lead no longer had the virtual monopoly of the paint market. Titanium-based paints and the entry into the market of Imperial Chemical Industries (ICI) with its Dulux brand were to cause ALM increasing problems, although, in large part as a result of the former Brimsdown chemists' work on titanium, the group had a small share in a company set up in the 1930s to produce titanium dioxide. That company, later known as Tioxide Group plc, was jointly owned by Cookson Group and ICI until December 1990 up until which time, as the world's second largest titanium dioxide producer, it made a significant contribution to the Group. In 1930, before the impact of these new paints had become serious, however, ALM purchased Goodlass, Wall & Company (GW) of Liverpool, a large paint manufacturer with retail outlets. Although this might have been a useful diversification, particularly since GW owned the Valspar patents with considerable potential for expansion in the market for varnishes, the merger caused problems. The price paid for GW proved too high in the light of subsequent profits, ALM's capital had to be written down, and GW was never integrated, being run as a separate organization until its sale in 1984.

The ALM board had become distinctly unwieldy in the late 1920s as a result of the appointment of additional directors following the takeover of various family-owned firms. In 1930, Clive Cookson set up Goodlass Wall & Lead Industries (GWLI) as a holding company, and the power of the ALM board withered. The original GW directors were soon pruned from the board of GWLI, and the power of Clive Cookson and his supporters was complete. It is surprising that rationalization was not taken further in the 1930s. A number of lead works closed in London and on Tyneside and production was concentrated geographically to obtain scale economies. The constituent companies essentially remained independent, however, certainly in name (even in the late 1940s at Elswick the switchboard operator had to answer different lines with different company names), and to a considerable extent competed with each other in the market.

Diversification Enforced by World War II

World War II enforced further rationalization. Imports of lead were reduced and controlled by the government, while demand fell, in large part as a result of the almost complete cessation of private building work. The group had to expand several existing businesses, one being the production of solder, as it gradually became clear that diversification away from lead was necessary. After the war, for a number of lead products, there was only limited recovery of demand. White lead was the major casualty, as it was replaced by other bases for paints, and although a new market was found in stabilizers for the plastics industry, the tonnage needed was small. Most of the white lead plant had to be closed. Owing to the motor industry's growing demand for lead in petrol and batteries, total U.K. demand for lead products continued to expand, reaching a peak in the mid-1960s. In this area and in the supply of lead for cables, GWLI faced competition and found the basic lead products business less profitable than its traditional business.

As early as 1943, GWLI had begun to diversify into what Clive Cookson called "some allied field of industry." Fry's Metal Foundries of Merton, Surrey was purchased for £500,000, overlapping with Cookson's existing business in the production of solder but otherwise concentrating on printers' metals and nonferrous alloys. In 1954, another acquisition in this field, Fry's Diecastings, was made. As with the lead side, where a number of plants had been set up overseas during the interwar years to avoid import duties, the purchase of the Fry's companies brought an expansion in foreign holdings. A further area of expansion was at Howdon, where Roland Cookson—nephew of Clive, later to become chairman of the group from 1963 to 1972—added zircon in 1950 to the production of antimony, in which the Cooksons had been involved since the mid-19th century. As with stabilizers for plastics, where GWLI had negotiated for existing U.S. technology through its links with the National Lead Company of the United States, Cookson negotiated a U.K. license to produce zirconium products with TAM Ceramics. These highly refractory materials were beginning to make inroads into the group's existing markets in the ceramics industry and, therefore, offered a sensible diversification, which was to be considerably reinforced in the 1960s with the purchase of two Staffordshire companies—Harrison & Sons (Hanley) Ltd. and E.W.T. Mayer Ltd.—involved in the production of ceramic glazes.

Focusing on Chemicals, Metals, and Paints: 1970s–80s

Although diversification had not taken the group far outside its original activities, it had resulted in a lack of focus. In 1949, the lead business, which included antimony and subsequently zircon, had been reorganized into a single company, ALM, with regionally structured management. This offered little opportunity, however, to concentrate its resources on those products which were most profitable. This problem was exacerbated by the accretion of additional companies and the growing tendency toward inter-company trading below market prices. Gradually, beginning in 1977 with the creation of the antimony and zircon

operation Anzon Limited, the group—which had changed its name in 1966 to Lead Industries Group Ltd. (LIG)—began to adopt a divisional structure. Two years later, ALM was divided into three product divisions: chemicals, metals, and paints.

By this time, it was clear that the lead business was in permanent decline. U.K. consumption had declined by more than 25 percent in the previous ten years, and this had necessitated the closure of several works. Although to some extent offset by the development of new products such as lead-clad steel for buildings, and by overseas expansion in Europe and in the United States, where the lead interests of NL Industries were purchased for $40 million in 1979, making LIG the world's leading producer of lead products, the future of the group clearly lay elsewhere. Already, by the early 1970s ALM accounted for only one-third of group turnover and its contribution to total profits was declining. Further diversification was required.

Changes Under a New Name: Middle to Late 1980s

Fortunately for the group, leadership had moved in the 1970s toward a new set of directors who had only limited links, if any, with the company's traditional lead business and who increasingly recognized the need to reduce those links, not only because of the declining financial returns from lead but also because of its unattractive public image. Leading the new developments were I.G. Butler, group chairman from 1976, and M.J.G. Henderson, his successor in 1990. They recognized that the group was actually less than the sum of its parts, because many of the 100 or so operating subsidiaries, in various parts of the world, did not associate themselves with the name of the group and were directing resources for individual rather than corporate benefit. Since 1983, the change of name from Lead Industries Group to Cookson provided the focus for a new and much more high-profile corporate image for all the subsidiaries worldwide.

A second step was the creation of a clearer divisional structure and the appointment of a chief executive for each division who was responsible for isolating and developing those of its products with major growth potential. The third step was to make further major overseas acquisitions, in recognition of the fact that the U.K. market was not large enough to offer significant opportunity for expansion and profit growth. Among the acquisitions, all by agreed takeover, were A.J. Oster Company in 1978, an American producer of nonferrous metals, and in 1987, Vesuvius Crucible Company of Pittsburgh, a U.S. supplier of ceramics to the steel industry, which was subsequently set up as the Vesuvius Group, with headquarters in Brussels. As a result, the 1980s experienced growth in group turnover from £400 million to £2 billion and in pre-tax profit from £16 million to £183 million. Over the decade, earnings per ordinary share rose from 6.7 to 31.2 pence.

Cookson proved one of the fastest growing British industrial groups during the 1980s. By then, it had established a reputation as supplier of a wide range of specialist products to industry, including nonferrous and precious metals, ceramics and refractories, chemicals, and plastics. The group saw itself as "the name behind many big names of industry." Claiming that its products were almost ubiquitous in daily life—they were incorporated in most things from washing machines to motor cars, flame retardants in children's toys to filaments in light bulbs, and printing on drinks cans to household paint—the group became almost worldwide in its diffusion, with manufacturing plants in more than 40 countries, and 70 percent of its turnover plus 80 percent of profit coming from abroad by the late 1980s.

Acquisition and Divestiture During the 1990s

Cookson spent the majority of the 1990s involved in unloading unprofitable businesses to cut costs. Its first move was the sale of its holding in Tioxide Group plc due to the dismal conditions plaguing the titanium dioxide industry. It also sold its A.J. Oyster brass mill product business and divested its holdings in Cookson Plibrico Ltd. Japan as well as Plibrico's European operations. In 1992, the firm sold its interest in Nanshing Color and Chemical Company, a Far East distributor of materials related to the electronics and plastics industry. That year, the firm was also forced to lay off company employees due to weakening economic conditions.

The group also made certain key acquisitions to strengthen its core operations. In 1991, the firm purchased the dielectric powders business of DuPont, incorporating it into its TAM Ceramics Inc. subsidiary. The following year, Stern Leach, a leading precious metal fabricator, became a wholly owned subsidiary of Cookson. The company also expanded its magnet operations in 1993 by forming a joint venture with New York-based Magnetic Technologies Corp.

Cookson strengthened its hold on the printed circuit board (PCB) industry in 1993 by purchasing the electronic laminates business of Swedish firm Perstorp as well as Brent Electronic Chemicals, a supplier to the PCB market. In 1995, SMT, a California-based printing stencil manufacturer, was acquired. The firm's refractories business, operating under the name Vesuvius, also expanded by acquiring the U.S.-based Technical Ceramics Division of LECO Corp. and the assets of HTCI, a manufacturer of advanced ceramic filters.

By 1996, Cookson's acquisition spree appeared to be paying off. Working with an increased net cash flow of £117 million, the group was able to pay down debt as well as continue expansion and divestiture efforts. As such, Cookson made an $87 million purchase of U.S.-based Engineered Polymers Corp. and bought GRP Inc., a distributor of fused cast refractory materials. In 1996, the group sold its organic pigment business to Hoechst AG. The following year, it sold its antimony products business (Anzon) to Great Lakes Chemical Corp. in a $90 million deal. Stephen Howard, Cookson's CEO, commented on the group's actions in a 1997 *Extel Examiner* article, stating, "Cookson continues to focus management and financial resources on those businesses where it has or is able to achieve leading market and technological positions on a world-wide basis. The sale of the Anzon business completes our exit from the manufacture of plastics additives and releases capital which Cookson will employ in those businesses which are key to its future growth."

Under the leadership of Howard, Cookson continued expanding in the areas deemed profitable. In 1998, the group purchased the U.K. refractories businesses, Flogates Ltd. and KSR International Ltd. It also acquired the European Laminates manufacturing operations of AlliedSignal Inc. and U.S.-based

Matrix, a manufacturer of micron-tolerance precision engineered products.

In 1999, the Plaskon Electronics Materials business of BP Amoco was purchased, along with Premier Refractories International Inc. for $410 million. The group also announced the $503 million purchase of Enthone-OMI Inc., a manufacturer of specialty chemicals used in the electronics, surface metal finishing, and jewelry industries. In 1999, as part of the group's divestiture program, TAM Ceramics Inc. was sold to Ferro Corp.

During the late 1990s, Cookson Group renewed its focus on its core operations: electronics, ceramics, and precious metals. Although sales were up 17 percent in 1999, profits slipped to £149 million from £151 million in the previous year. Management cited the strength of the British pound, the unstable Asian economy, and unremarkable performance in the electronics industry as cause for its lackluster profits.

Cost Cutting and Growth in Key Segments in the New Millennium

During the first year of the new millennium, however, Cookson's profits rebounded, especially in its Electronics division, which reported a doubling of operating profits due to favorable market conditions. The group continued its growth through acquisition policy, acquiring the laminates division of Achem Technology Corp. to bolster its Asian operations in the PCB market. It also disposed of its Neptco, Focas, and Polyflex businesses and planned to continue its divestiture of its Plastic Moldings segment.

Its profit rebound did not last long, however, and in 2001, the electronics industry once again saw a decrease in demand. The U.S. market, as well as the Asian and European markets, experienced a sharp downturn in the industry. Cookson's Ceramics division also came upon hard times as steel production faltered in North America.

Cookson management remained intent on future growth, however, and set forth a strategy dedicated to delivering advanced productivity-driven process solutions to customers, further integration of new acquisitions, and a constant renewal of operations dedicated to changing customer demands. As management continued to cut costs to combat market downturns, Cookson remained well positioned to maintain a leading role as a supplier to the electronics industry.

Principal Divisions

Electronics; Ceramics; Precious Metals.

Principal Operating Units

Polyclad Technologies; Speedline Technologies; Alpha-Fry Technologies; Cookson Performance Solutions; Vesuvius Group; Sterns Metal Group.

Principal Competitors

Asahi Glass Company Ltd.; E.I. du Pont de Nemours; Johnson Matthey plc.

Further Reading

"Alpine Refractories Unit Sold to Cookson," *American Metal Market,* August 10, 1999, p. 1.

"Cookson Buys PCB Laminates," *Chemical Market Reporter,* May 1, 2000, p. 3.

"Cookson Buys Plaskon from BP Amoco and Sells TAM Ceramic Unit to Ferro," *Chemical Market Reporter,* July 19, 1999, p. 7.

"Cookson Group Acquisition," *Extel Examiner,* April 22, 1992.

"Cookson Group Buys Matrix for $13m," *Financial Times London,* September 18, 1998, p. 24.

"Cookson Group Buys U.S. Ceramic Manufacturer HTCI," *Extel Examiner,* July 4, 1995.

"Cookson Group Completes Antimony Products Business Sale for 90 mln USD," *Extel Examiner,* November 4, 1997.

"Cookson Group on Target with 68 Percent Rise Midway," *Financial Times London,* September 6, 1985.

"Cookson Group plc Announces Disposal and Acquisition," *Universal News Services,* August 16, 1991.

"Cookson to Acquire Enthone-OMI," *Machine Design,* April 20, 2000, p. 30.

Debo, David, "Acquisition Strengthens Cookson Presence in WNY," *Business First of Buffalo,* October 28, 1996, p. 5.

Hedley, W.P., and C.R. Hudleston, *Cookson of Penrith, Cumberland and Newcastle upon Tyne,* Kendal: Cookson, 1966.

Jarvis, Paul, "Cookson Plans to Trim 700 Jobs in Cost-Cutting Bid," *Wall Street Journal Europe,* February 12, 1999, p. 8.

John, A.H., ed., *The Walker Family: Iron Founders and Lead Manufacturers 1741–1893,* London: Council for the Preservation of Business Archives, 1951.

Minutes Relating to the Proceedings of the Foundry Co. begun by S. and A. Walker, 1741, and of the Lead Company, begun by Samuel Walker, 1778, Chester, 1879.

Rowe, D.J., *Lead Manufacturing in Britain: A History,* London: Croom Helm, 1983.

"Sales Up at Cookson But Not Profits," *Electronics Weekly,* March 8, 2000, p. 2.

Taylor, Paul, "Cookson Group Builds Laminates Side in Europe," *Financial Times London,* September 1, 1993, p. 20.

—D.J. Rowe
—update: Christina M. Stansell

Cooper Industries, Inc.

600 Travis, Suite 5800
Houston, Texas 77002
U.S.A.
Telephone: (713) 209-8400
Fax: (713) 209-8995
Web site: http://www.cooperindustries.com

Public Company
Incorporated: 1895 as the C. & G. Cooper Company
Employees: 34,250
Sales: $4.45 billion (2000)
Stock Exchanges: New York
Ticker Symbol: CBE
NAIC: 332212 Hand and Edge Tool Manufacturing;
   33251 Hardware Manufacturing; 335311 Power,
   Distribution, and Specialty Transformer
   Manufacturing; 335999 All Other Miscellaneous
   Electrical Equipment and Component Manufacturing

After spending most of the 1990s spinning off businesses and focusing on a few select markets, Cooper Industries, Inc. emerged in the new millennium as a $4.5 billion manufacturer of electrical products, tools, hardware, and metal products with over 100 manufacturing plants across the globe. Its Electrical Products segment—responsible for over 80 percent of company revenues—manufactures thousands of products through seven different divisions involved in the production of support systems for electrical, mechanical, and telecommunications applications; circuit protection products; electrical protection products for the industrial and commercial industry; lighting fixtures; emergency lighting and fire detection systems; equipment and components for the management of electrical power; and wiring devices, switches, and plugs. Cooper's Tools & Hardware segment manufactures electric and pneumatic industrial power tools, and hand tools.

Early History

Brothers Charles and Elias Cooper built a foundry in their hometown of Mount Vernon, Ohio, and called it the Mt. Vernon Iron Works. Soon better known as C. & E. Cooper Company, their first products were plows, maple syrup kettles, hog troughs, sorghum grinders, and wagon boxes. Charles Cooper was the stronger leader. Aggressively anti-slavery and a dedicated prohibitionist, he became a respected community leader, even though many of his views differed greatly from those of his neighbors. When Elias Cooper died in 1848, Charles Cooper took a succession of partners, and with each the company name changed accordingly.

Mount Vernon was linked to the rest of the nation by the railroad in 1851 and the following year Cooper was able to ship its first steam-powered compressors for blast furnaces. Cooper's relationship with the railroad had its difficulties, however. When the Sandusky, Mansfield, and Newark Railway was delinquent in paying for woodburning locomotives from the company, Charles Cooper was driven to chain the wheels of a locomotive to the track, padlock it, and stand sentry until he was paid in full.

By the time of the Civil War, Cooper products included wood-burning steam locomotives and steam-powered blowing machines for charcoal blast furnaces. After Charles Gray Cooper, son of Elias, served in the Union army and attended Rensselaer Institute, he became a partner with his uncle.

In 1869, Cooper became the first company in what was then the West to produce the new, highly efficient Corliss engine. Six years later, it offered the Cooper traction engine, America's first farm tractor. Throughout the rest of the century, the Corliss engine was Cooper's principal product.

The company was incorporated as the C. & G. Cooper Company in 1895, and Frank L. Fairchild, a respected salesman of the Cooper-Corliss engine, was named its first president. Fairchild so enjoyed selling that throughout his 17-year presidency he continued to serve as sales manager.

By 1900, gas was being discovered in new fields and shipped more than 100 miles through primitive pipelines. At the same time, the oil industry was also beginning to develop. Not long after Charles Cooper's death in 1901, it became clear that steam turbine engines were destined to replace the Corliss engine. Cooper management recognized the necessity of focusing on a small segment of the market, and in 1908 it wisely chose to make a gradual change to natural-gas internal-combustion engines, which were being used successfully at the compression stage of pipeline transmission.

Fairchild died suddenly in 1912 and Charles Gray (C.G.) Cooper, took his place. One story describes C.G.'s famous bluntness particularly well: C.G. once visited a procrastinating client and without any preliminary niceties asked, ''Do you want to buy a steam engine?'' The man said he didn't want one just then. ''All right, then you can go to hell,'' C.G. said and stormed out abruptly.

During World War I, Cooper built high-speed steam-hydraulic forging presses for government arsenals, munitions plants, and shipyards, as well as giant gas engines and compressors and triple-expansion marine engines. The company's wartime production demands slowed its transformation from a producer of steam to gas engines, since steam engines were needed for the war effort. But after the war, it became clear that the company had chosen its direction wisely when it set its sights on developing gas internal-combustion engines. The old Corliss was quickly becoming outmoded by competition from steam turbines and gas-powered engines.

In 1919, C.G. Cooper became chairman and Desault B. Kirk, the company's treasurer, became president. Just a year later, Cooper began a long-range program for growth, and the directors elected Beatty B. Williams president. Although he'd married the boss's daughter, few credited Williams's rise to simply marrying into the family. Serving as vice-president and general manager during the war years, Williams was single-minded in his dedication to the company's success and directed Cooper (and subsequently Cooper-Bessemer) with great energy and foresight for 22 years. Always mindful of what he called ''an aloofness'' that could develop between office and factory workers, Williams held conferences in which factory workers were invited to air their views and offered evening courses in production and management in which any employee could enroll.

Natural gas was gaining growing importance in the manufacture of steel and glass and in the emerging petrochemical industry. Cooper field service engineers were often on hand for months at a time to oversee the installation of huge four-cycle Cooper engines and compressors in compressor stations as new pipelines were routed through West Virginia, Louisiana, Arkansas, Oklahoma, and Texas.

The Bessemer Merger

Within just a few years, Cooper became the country's leading producer of pipeline compression engines. Although Coo-

per also produced smaller two-cylinder engines used in natural-gas fields to extract gas as it came from the well, the Bessemer Gas Engine Company of Grove City, Pennsylvania, dominated that field.

Founded in 1897, Bessemer had produced oil-pumping engines for most of its existence and had invested heavily in diesel engine development during the 1920s. While Cooper and Bessemer had some product overlap, their major strengths were in different areas.

By 1929, Cooper needed additional production facilities to meet the mounting orders for large natural-gas engine compressor units. Bessemer, after its lengthy period of diesel development, badly needed new capital. Both companies had posted nearly identical average earnings for the previous three years. The companies negotiated a merger for several months, and the Cooper-Bessemer Corporation came into being in April 1929. The merger made the company the largest builder of gas engines and compressors in the United States. Soon afterward it was listed on the American Stock Exchange.

Cooper-Bessemer's business boom was brief. The company continued the Bessemer line of diesel marine engines, and since most ships were built or converted on the East Coast, Cooper-Bessemer soon decided to open a sales office in New York. The office was opened on October 23, 1929, however, at the very beginning of the Great Depression. Two years later, annual sales had dropped more than 90 percent, reflecting the almost total halt of construction on long-distance pipelines and in American shipyards. Half of all sales that year were for repair parts. Along with thousands of other American companies, Cooper-Bessemer was forced to lay off workers.

Cooper-Bessemer slowly revived in the middle and late 1930s by continuing to improve products and by entering new markets. The company was convinced that the diesel would replace steam-powered railroad engines and it developed one for the new market.

Charles B. Jahnke was elected president in 1940 and Williams moved to chairman of the board, but Jahnke died a year later and Williams returned to the presidency for two more years. Only when Cooper-Bessemer embarked on a wartime production schedule in 1941 did its sales figures surpass their predepression level. The company had sold engines to several branches of the military before the war and was thus in a favored position to receive large orders during World War II. It became a major producer of diesel engines for military vessels of all kinds and also increased production of locomotive engines. At the peak of its wartime production, Cooper-Bessemer had 4,337 employees working in round-the-clock shifts.

In 1941, Cooper-Bessemer's net sales jumped to an all-time high, and just two years later they had more than tripled. The company was listed for the first time on the New York Stock Exchange in 1944. Gordon Lefebvre was elected company president in 1943. He had previously served as vice-president and general manager. Formerly the head of General Motors's Pontiac division, he had a background in engineering and was energetic, likeable, and a tough negotiator.

Key Dates:

1833: Brothers Charles and Elias Cooper build a foundry in Mount Vernon, Ohio.

1852: Cooper ships its first steam-powered compressors for blast furnaces by railway.

1869: The firm becomes the first Western company to produce the Corliss engine.

1908: Coopers begins a gradual shift from Corliss to natural gas internal-combustion engines.

1929: The company merges with the Bessemer Gas Engine Company, forming the Cooper-Bessemer Corp.

1944: The firm lists on the New York Stock Exchange.

1945: Cooper-Bessemer opens its first international sales branch in Caracas, Venezuela.

1951: Sales reach a record $52 million.

1960: The company introduces the world's first industrial jet-powered gas turbine.

1965: The firm changes its name to Cooper Industries.

1970: Cooper branches out into aircraft services with the acquisition of Dallas Airmotive.

1976: The White Superior Engine division of the White Motor Company is purchased.

1979: Cooper acquires the Gardner-Denver Company; sales reach $1 billion.

1981: The firm continues expansion efforts and purchases Crouse-Hinds Company, an electrical products manufacturer, and Belden Corporation, a wire and cable manufacturer.

1985: Cooper merges with McGraw-Edison Co. in a deal that nearly doubles its size and makes it one of the world's largest lighting manufacturers.

1989: The company acquires Champion Spark Plug Co. and Cameron Iron Works.

1992: Cooper purchases Ferramentas Belzer do Brasil, a Brazilian-based handtool maker.

1995: H. John Riley Jr. is named CEO; the firm spins off its petroleum and industrial equipment business.

1997: Cooper completes eight acquisitions throughout the year.

1998: The firm sells its automotive business to Federal-Mogul Corp. for $1.9 billion.

1999: The company—after years of strategic restructuring—operates with two key business segments: Electrical Products and Tools & Hardware.

2000: Cooper acquires Eagle Electric Manufacturing and B-Line Systems.

2001: The company rejects an unsolicited acquisition bid by rival Danaher Corp.

Focus on International Expansion and Product Development

After World War II, Cooper-Bessemer became increasingly interested in selling its products worldwide. It formed an international sales office and announced its first sales-service branch outside the United States, in Caracas, Venezuela, in 1945. Later in the decade, it expanded warehouse facilities in Canada and established a subsidiary sales unit, Cooper-Bessemer of Canada, with three offices, and received its first postwar orders from the Soviet Union.

Cooper-Bessemer had developed its innovative ''turbo flow'' high-compression gas-diesel engine in 1945, and two years later it introduced the GMW engine, which delivered 2,500 horsepower and could be shipped in one assembled unit. In these postwar years Cooper officials began to discuss diversification, which Lefebvre defined as ''finding new markets for old products and new products for old markets, rather than moving into fields with which we are not familiar.''

In 1951, Cooper-Bessemer's sales of $52 million surpassed its wartime high by nearly $10 million. Business that year was boosted by the Korean War; company shipments were almost solely to markets supported by the war effort, such as the petroleum, aluminum, chemical, and railroad industries.

In 1954, a combination of internal and external circumstances led to a startling 38 percent decrease in net sales and Cooper-Bessemer's first net loss since 1938. The company's problems included a seven-week strike at the Grove City plant and a nationwide recession, but the main difficulty was the U.S. Supreme Court's decision in the Phillips Petroleum case, which ruled that producers selling gas to interstate pipelines had to submit to the Federal Power Commission's jurisdiction. This decision produced upheaval and uncertainty among pipeline operators, and therefore for Cooper-Bessemer.

While the company was rebuffing a 1955 takeover attempt by a private investor named Robert New, Lefebvre resigned unexpectedly, and Lawrence Williams, Beatty Williams's son, became president. He served beside his father, who was chairman of the board. Lawrence Williams had already served the company in many capacities and had taken early retirement to pursue other interests; he considered his return a temporary one. The takeover attempt had shaken management. In an attempt to bring an infusion of young talent to the company, Williams made a number of top management changes, including elevating Eugene L. Miller to chief operating officer. Due to revitalized demand, sales bounced back in 1956 to a record high of $61.2 million, but it was becoming increasingly clear that Cooper-Bessemer needed to diversify in order to avoid the cyclical pitfalls of energy-related manufacturing.

In 1957, Gene Miller was elected president. At 38, he was the youngest man to hold the position since the company's original founder. Miller had begun at Cooper-Bessemer in 1946. A year after he became president, the company acquired Rotor Tool Company of Cleveland, the makers of pneumatic and high-cycle electric portable tools.

Over the next few years Cooper-Bessemer struggled to develop an engine to meet the challenge of General Electric's new combustion gas turbine engine, which threatened to supplant several of Cooper's engines in the pipeline transmission market. Its efforts resulted in the world's first industrial jet-powered gas turbine, introduced in 1960.

Under Miller's leadership, the distinction between Cooper-Bessemer administrative and operational management grew more pronounced, as was happening in companies throughout the country. Innovations such as computerization, fluctuations in worldwide monetary exchanges, increased government controls, and changing tax structures had made operating a large business increasingly complicated. In recognition of this, Miller moved the corporate offices from the Mount Vernon plant to offices on the city square to "establish a corporate group capable of administering many relatively independent divisions." Meanwhile, Cooper-Bessemer's international division was also growing. By the end of the 1950s Cooper had sales agents in ten countries, licensees in three, and franchises in two. In 1964 it opened an office in Beirut and also formed a wholly owned British subsidiary, Cooper-Bessemer (U.K.), Ltd.

Diversification Through Acquisition

Cooper-Bessemer was no exception to the trend toward large conglomerates during the 1960s, but it did try to limit its acquisitions to those that could be mutually beneficial. In the early 1960s, it acquired Kline Manufacturing, a producer of high-pressure hydraulic pumps; Ajax Iron Works, which built gas engine compressors and a water flood vertical pump for oil and gas production; and the Pennsylvania Pump and Compressor Company. Between 1960 and 1965, the company's sales grew from $68 million to $117 million.

Cooper had grown into a large, diverse company. To better reflect its nature, it changed its name to Cooper Industries, Inc. in December, 1965. Two years later it moved its corporate headquarters to Houston in order to be more in the geographic mainstream of American business.

Cooper acquired Lufkin Rule Company of Saginaw, Michigan, in 1967. It was the first of many acquisitions for what Lufkin president William G. Rector called a "tool basket"—a high-quality hand tools manufacturing group. Subsequent hand tool-related acquisitions included Crescent Niagara Corporation (wrenches) in 1968, Weller Electric Corporation (soldering tools) in 1970, Nicholson File Company (rasps and files) in 1972, Xcelite (small tools for the electronics industry) in 1973, J. Wiss & Sons Company (scissors) in 1976, McDonough Company's Plumb Tool subsidiary (striking tools) in 1980, and Kirsch Company (drapery hardware) in 1981.

Charles Cooper, the last Cooper family member to be associated with the company, retired in 1968. The grandson of Elias, he had served as a vice-president and board member.

The company branched out into aircraft services in 1970 by acquiring Dallas Airmotive, and later acquired Southwest Airmotive Company in 1973 and Standard Aircraft Equipment in 1975. While these acquisitions performed satisfactorily, the company sold its airmotive segment to Aviation Power Supply in 1981 because it did not see much potential for further growth.

The 1973 oil embargo threw many industrialized nations into an uproar. Cooper's Ajax division struggled to keep up with orders from domestic crude-oil producers and Cooper received a large order for its Coberra gas turbines for the Alaskan pipeline.

After having served as president and chief operating officer since 1973, Robert Cizik was named chief executive officer in

1975. Lured to the company from Standard Oil New Jersey (now Exxon) in 1961, Cizik started his career at Cooper as executive assistant for corporate development.

Cizik stepped up the company's acquisition program. After satisfying a Justice Department challenge, Cooper acquired the White Superior engine division, a heavy-duty engine maker, from the White Motor Company in 1976, and in 1979 Cooper realized a dream of acquiring the Dallas-based Gardner-Denver Company, a company roughly the same size as Cooper. Although *Forbes* described Gardner-Denver as "a company notorious for lack of planning or cost controls," Cooper was confident the company's three energy-related business segments could be successfully merged into its own energy-related manufacturing operations. *Forbes* reported at the time that the merger was one of the ten largest in U.S. history. That year the company passed the $1 billion sales milestone, only three years after it had reached a half a billion dollars in sales.

At the time, Cooper was criticized for handling acquisitions cold-heartedly. After acquiring Gardner-Denver, it closed the company's corporate headquarters, decentralized it, reduced employment, and cut benefits. But many analysts defended these actions, noting that Gardner-Denver had been full of operational problems and was very poorly managed.

Cooper was also known for its manufacturing efficiency and willingness to make capital investments to improve production or market position. For instance, when the last domestic producer of the very hard steel needed to manufacture files stopped making it, Cooper developed a process for making its own steel that was different from the traditional method but still suitable for making files, at half the cost.

Continued Expansion

In 1981, Cooper acquired the highly respected Crouse-Hinds Company of Syracuse, New York, makers of electrical products, after a long battle in which Cooper played white knight, rescuing Crouse-Hinds from Inter-North Corporation. Cooper also acquired the Belden Corporation, a wire and cable manufacturer that Crouse-Hinds had been in the process of purchasing. This acquisition expanded Cooper's size by 50 percent. Shortly after the merger, Cizik explained to *Business Week* that he had entered the electrical components business because "we needed to be in a business that looked beyond the 1980s and even the year 2000 for growth." When demand for gas and oil began to slump in 1981, Cooper's diversification paid off. Sales of the company's energy-related products dropped by 60 percent but its other two divisions were hurt far less.

Cizik continued to look for new acquisitions. Cooper's next bold move was a 1985 merger with McGraw-Edison Company, a manufacturer of electrical energy-related products for industrial, commercial, and utility use. The merger nearly doubled Cooper's size and made the company one of the largest lighting manufacturers in the world. Cooper's 1985 sales passed $3 billion.

After the McGraw-Edison acquisition, most Cooper acquisitions were on a somewhat smaller scale in the 1980s. In 1987 they included the molded rubber products division and the petroleum equipment and products group from Joy Technologies. In 1988, Cooper acquired RTE Corporation, a Wisconsin-based manufacturer of electrical distribution equipment, and

Beswick, a manufacturer of fuses and related products in the United Kingdom. But in 1989, Cooper made yet another major acquisition, of the Champion Spark Plug Company, the world's leading manufacturer of spark plugs for combustion engines. Champion, based in Toledo, Ohio, was also a major producer of windshield-wiper blades. And in late November, 1989, Cooper also acquired Cameron Iron Works, a Houston-based company with annual sales of $611 million. Cameron was a maker of oil tools, ball valves, and forged products.

By the early 1990s, Cooper manufactured more than a million products in 145 plants, 41 of them in foreign countries, and its annual revenues exceeded $4 billion. International expansion continued during this time period. In 1991, three Canadian-based businesses were acquired. The following year, Cooper purchased Ferramentas Belzer do Brasil, a Brazilian-based hand tool manufacturer.

A New Focus: Late 1990s and Beyond

Management began to take a different approach to expansion in the mid-1990s as competition became fierce in many of its markets. In 1995, the firm spun off its petroleum and industrial equipment business, signaling the start of its new strategy. H. John Riley, Jr., was named CEO that year, and under his direction, Cooper began strictly focusing on its Electrical Products, Tools and Hardware, and Automotive Products business segments.

Cooper made eight acquisitions in 1997, the largest being that of the Menvier-Swain Group, an emergency lights and alarm manufacturer. It also divested Kirsch, its window treatment business, along with other units considered to be low-margin and unrelated to the firm's new direction. The company secured a 25 percent increase in net income that year along with the highest share earnings in its history—$3.26.

The company continued with its transformation in 1998, significantly changing its holdings with the sale of its automotive businesses. While this segment secured nearly 35 percent of Cooper's revenues, it was responsible for just 25 percent of earnings. The segment was also in dire need of capital investment to improve performance—an investment that did not fit in with Cooper's strategy. In October of that year, Federal-Mogul Corp. bought up the division for $1.9 billion.

The firm also made 11 acquisitions that year, expanding its power tool business by 50 percent. U.S. power tool manufacturer Intool Inc. was purchased, along with three European-based companies. Cooper's reach in the electrical products market also increased in size that year through several key mergers in the Latin American region.

While market conditions weakened throughout the manufacturing industry—the company claimed the industry was facing the worst economic slowdown it had experienced in the last 20 years—Cooper continued to bolster its two key business segments. During 1999, the firm acquired ten firms and significantly expanded its reach in European markets. In fact, international revenues increased by 17 percent to $1.1 billion that year.

After nearly a decade of restructuring and divestiture, Cooper entered the new millennium a leaner, more focused company. The firm made several key acquisitions in 2000, including the B-Line Systems business of Aldrich Corp. and Eagle Electric Manufacturing, which was incorporated into the company's Wiring and Devices division. By now, Coopers main two business segments—Electrical Products and Tools & Hardware—were securing nearly $4.5 billion in sales, up from $2.8 billion in 1995.

In fact, Cooper held leading positions in many of its markets. That, coupled with its positive revenue and earnings results and its track record of success, made it a takeover target. Sure enough, in August 2001 Cooper turned down an unsolicited offer from rival Danaher Corp., claiming that the proposal undervalued the firm—Danaher had made an undisclosed offer in 1999 and had Cooper taken that first offer, Danaher claimed, shareholders would have realized significant earnings.

While Cooper refused the Danaher offer, the company announced in August 2001 that it would consider the likes of a future merger, acquisition, or strategic alliance in order to increase shareholder value. As its future remained uncertain, the firm's long standing history of growth and its ability to weather fluctuating economic conditions would no doubt position the Cooper name among market leaders in the years to come.

Principal Divisions

Cooper B-Line; Cooper Bussman; Cooper Crouse-Hinds; Cooper Lighting; Cooper Menvier; Cooper Power Systems; Cooper Wiring Devices; Cooper Tools.

Principal Operating Units

Electrical Products; Tools & Hardware.

Principal Competitors

ABB Ltd.; The Black & Decker Corp.; General Electric Company; Danaher Corporation.

Further Reading

Chappell, Lindsay, "Cooper Moves Forward Despite Setbacks," *Automotive News,* June 29, 1998, p. 6.

"Cooper Acquires Crompton Lighting," *Appliance Manufacturer,* December 1999, p. 16.

"Cooper Planning to Slash Jobs," *American Metal Market,* January 4, 1999, p. 6.

"Cooper Rejects Danaher Bid; Looks to Alternatives," *Industrial Distribution,* September 2001, p. 19.

Couretas, John, "Federal-Mogul Completes Buy," *Automotive News,* October 12, 1998, p. 1.

Gallun, Alby, "Acquisition to Help Cooper Expand in Mexico," *Business Journal-Milwaukee,* December 10, 1999, p. 5.

——, "Cooper Power Awaits Word on Cutbacks," *Business Journal-Milwaukee,* January 1, 1999, p. 3.

——, "Cooper Power Systems Poised for Growth in Waukesha," *Business Journal-Milwaukee,* April 17, 1998, p. 1.

Greer, Jim, "Cooper Shuns Suitor as Details of Failed 1999 Deal Surfaces," *Houston Business Journal,* August 10, 2001, p. 2.

Keller, David N. *Cooper Industries: 1833–1983,* Athens: Ohio University Press, 1983.

Papanikolaw, Jim, "Sigma-Aldrich Sells Its B-Line Systems to Cooper Industries," *Chemical Market Reporter,* April 3, 2000, p. 3.

—update: Christina M. Stansell

CORNING
Discovering Beyond Imagination

Corning Inc.

One Riverfront Plaza
Corning, New York 14831
U.S.A.
Telephone: (607) 974-9000
Fax: (607) 974-8091
Web site: http://www.corning.com

Public Company
Incorporated: 1875 as Corning Glass Works Inc.
Employees: 40,000
Sales: $7.1 billion (2000)
Stock Exchanges: New York Zürich
Ticker Symbol: GLW
NAIC: 33429 Other Communications Equipment
   Manufacturing; 33422 Radio and Television
   Broadcasting and Wireless Communications
   Equipment Manufacturing; 33431 Audio and
   Video Equipment Manufacturing; 334418 Printed
   Circuit Assembly (Electronic Assembly)
   Manufacturing; 334419 Other Electronic Component
   Manufacturing

Corning Inc., known as Corning Glass Works until 1989, operates as a global technology firm with three major business segments including Telecommunications, Advanced Materials, and Information Display. Its Telecommunications arm produces optical fiber and cable, optical hardware and equipment, and photonic modules and components. Through this segment, the firm makes nearly 40 percent of the world's supply of optical fiber, making it the largest fiber manufacturer across the globe. The Advanced Materials segment develops specialized products utilizing glass, glass ceramic, and polymer technologies. The firm's Information Display unit operates as a manufacturer of glass panels and funnels for televisions, liquid crystal display glass for flat panel displays, and projection video lens assemblies. Corning, along with its subsidiaries, operates in 20 countries.

Early History: Mid- to Late 1800s

Corning traces its beginnings to 1851 when Amory Houghton purchased an interest in Bay State Glass Company of Cambridge, Massachusetts. Three years later he founded Union Glass Company of Somerville, Massachusetts. After selling Union Glass he and his sons bought the Brooklyn Flint Glass Company of Brooklyn, New York, in 1864. Four years later they moved operations to Corning, New York, renaming the enterprise Corning Flint Glass Company. They chose this western New York location because of its favorable location for transportation as well as for acquisition of coal and wood, then necessary for glass manufacturing.

Amory Houghton, Jr., became president in 1875, the year in which Corning Glass Works was incorporated, and remained in the post until 1911. It was during these years that the firm began to exhibit the technological prowess for which it is known today. The company first called upon scientists at Cornell University in 1877 for help in improving the optical quality of its lenses. In 1880, Thomas Edison asked Corning Glass to make bulbs for his electric lights.

Innovations During the Early 1900s

An important milestone during Amory Houghton, Jr.'s years as president was the establishment of a research laboratory in 1908. It was the fourth such facility in the United States. The laboratory developed a heat-resistant glass, borosilicate, capable of withstanding sudden changes in temperature. One resulting 1912 product was a shatterproof lantern for railway signalmen. Another important borosilicate product, Pyrex, dated from 1915. It found immediate use as laboratory equipment, but it was some years before the company realized its consumer-market potential.

Corning continued to be managed by members of the Houghton family. Alanson B. Houghton succeeded Amory Houghton, Jr., and served until 1919, when he was followed by Arthur A. Houghton, president until 1920.

During World War I, when Corning was able to make glass that others could not produce, the company prospered as a

Company Perspectives:

Corning leads primarily by technological innovation and shares a deep belief in the power of technology. The company has a history of great contributions in science and technology, and it is this same spirit of innovation that has enabled us to create new products and new markets, to introduce new forms of corporate organization, and to seek new levels of employee participation. We embrace the opportunities inherent in change, and we are confident in our ability to help shape the future.

supplier to defense contractors. In the postwar years, demand for Corning products led to the invention of a ribbon machine in 1926, which produced blanks for incandescent lamps at the rate of 2,000 bulbs per minute.

Steuben Glass, a division of Corning, originated in Corning, New York, but did not become part of Corning Glass until 1918. It specializes in fine optical glass as well as fine cut glass. Steuben began producing the crystal for which it became famous in 1933, when Arthur A. Houghton Jr., great-grandson of the founder, became president of the subsidiary. He decided that the company was to sell only quality products of the highest design, and he and a vice-president smashed over $1 million worth of lesser glass in the company warehouse.

Expansion During the 1930s and 1940s

Two presidents served in the decade of the 1920s. Alexander D. Falck was in office until 1928, and Eugene C. Sullivan until 1930. The years of the Great Depression were an era of great expansion for Corning. Under the leadership of Amory Houghton Sr., president from 1930 to 1941, technological innovations continued. Corning built the 200-inch mirror for the Mount Palomar telescope in 1934. It was the largest piece of cast glass up to that time and was the second version of the mirror. The first, which was miscast, is on display at the glass museum in Corning, New York. Corning developed such products as silicones in the early 1930s, electrical sealing in 1938, and 96 percent silica glass in 1939.

During this period, Corning began a policy of joint ventures with other companies. Owens-Corning Fiberglas was organized in 1938—a year after Pittsburgh Corning Corporation began producing glass blocks. Dow Corning was established in 1943 to produce silicones.

The early 1940s brought improvements in optical glass-making. During World War II cathode-ray tubes were mass produced for radar detection systems beginning in 1942. Corning also manufactured a strengthened form of glass tableware for the U.S. Navy. Later advancements in the decade included improved thermometer tubing; ribbon glass as thin as newsprint and used in electronic components; photosensitive glass; and centrifugal casting used primarily for television tubes, which were first automatically produced in 1947.

Glen W. Cole was president during World War II, and was followed by William C. Decker, who served from 1946 until

1961. Amory Houghton Sr. continued to lead as the first chairman of the board, an office created in 1945.

Product Innovations: 1950s–60s

Corning developed electricity-conducting coated glass in 1950 and fused silica in 1952. Color television tubes were introduced in 1953. The process for producing Pyroceram, or glass ceramics, was developed in 1957 and led to the marketing of Corning Ware cookware the following year.

Amory Houghton, Jr., served as president between 1961 and 1964, and then became chairman of the board until his election to the House of Representatives in 1983. During Houghton's tenure as chairman, the presidency was held by R. Lee Waterman until 1971, followed by Thomas C. MacAvoy up to 1983.

Corning made the ceramic heat-resisting reentry shields and the glass windshields for the 1960s Apollo moon program. Cellular-ceramic structures—thin-walled structures used in gaseous heat exchangers—were introduced in 1961 and became key components of automobile catalytic converters beginning in the 1970s. Other developments in the 1960s included chemically strengthened glass in 1964; photochromic glass, which darkens when exposed to light, and fusion sheet glass in mid-decade; and, in the late 1960s, hub machines, used for cutting hot glass into various sizes and shapes, and optical fibers.

During the 1960s, Corning Glass was the undisputed industry leader in glass technology. Sales of bulbs, globes, and panels, Corning Ware, and television-tube blanks grew especially fast in the early 1960s and led to record earnings of $9.28 per share in 1966. Company stock sold at 48 times earnings.

In 1970, Corning's innovations included machinable glass-ceramics and immobilized enzymes. The latter permanently bonded active catalytic materials, such as enzymes, to inorganic substrates, or carriers, leading to the development of radio-immunoassay products for diagnostic testing in 1974. An all-electric melter in 1972, polychromatic glass in 1978, transparent glass-ceramic cookware in 1981, diesel particulate filters in 1986, and dental restorations in 1987 were other breakthroughs.

Problems Arise in the 1970s

Despite these innovations, Corning experienced a decline in earnings in the 1970s. Although over one-third of its products were new, the bulk of its sales came from mature products such as bulbs and television blanks for picture glass, which it sold to other companies. Competition was strong and Corning experienced a decline in market share of these products. Japanese imports of television sets, for example, curtailed the demand for Corning television glass.

Another problem involved Signetics, a semiconductor manufacturer, purchased in 1962. In 1970, Signetics lost $6 million on $35 million in sales. Corning had never developed an expertise in electronics and in 1975 sold Signetics, absorbing a pretax loss of $9.5 million. In 1972, Hurricane Agnes caused a severe flood which cut corporate headquarters off from the outside world for a time and cost the company $20 million. Earnings

Key Dates:

1851: Amory Houghton purchases an interest in Bay State Glass Co.
1864: Houghton and his sons buy the Brooklyn Flint Glass Co.
1868: The glass company is renamed Corning Flint Glass Co.
1875: Corning Glass Works in incorporated.
1880: Thomas Edison asks Corning to make bulbs for his electric lights.
1908: Corning establishes a research laboratory.
1918: Steuben Glass becomes part of Corning.
1938: Owens-Corning Fiberglass is created as a joint venture.
1943: Dow Corning begins operation.
1953: Corning introduces color television tubes.
1958: Corning Ware cookware is marketed.
1972: Hurricane Agnes causes severe flooding, costing the firm $20 million.
1976: Corning files suit against ITT Corp. and the U.S. government for patent infringements.
1987: More than half of the firm's profits stem from joint venture operations.
1989: Company changes its name to Corning Inc.
1992: Subsidiary Dow Corning stops manufacturing silicon breast implants amidst rising controversy over ruptured silicon-gel implants.
1995: Dow Corning declares Chapter 11 bankruptcy.
1997: Corning announces plans to sell its consumer products division.
1998: Earnings fall due to the Asian economic crisis.
2001: Corning operates as the number one producer of fiber optic cable; the firm celebrates its 150th anniversary.

collapsed to $1.76 per share in 1975. In response to these difficulties, Corning closed five plants and eliminated production of domestic black-and-white TV tubes, Christmas ornaments, and acid-waste drain lines. Employment was cut in the 1970s from 46,000 worldwide to 29,000, with an increase in productivity from an industry average of 3 percent per year to 6 percent. Research and development continued, with expenditures of about 5 percent of sales, above the U.S. national average of 2 percent.

Sales volumes fell in 1982 for some consumer products, such as Corning Ware, Pyrex, and Corelle dinnerware. In 1983, Corning halted production of light bulbs. That year leadership changed from president to joint management by group presidents and chairman of the board, James Houghton.

Corelle products designs had not changed in more than a decade, and Corning had not advertised, until 1985, that its products had always been suitable for the microwave oven. The company did not begin market research until 1984. As a result Corning modernized designs of older products and introduced Visions cookware, combining the transparency of glass with the heat-resistant qualities of ceramics.

Focus on Fiber Optics: 1970s–80s

Corning's experience with fiber optics illustrated the problems and the benefits of a company based on research and technology. As a result of Corning's work, glass-fibers, or fiber optics, replaced copper wire in traditional telephone lines. A hair-thin glass fiber could carry as many telephone calls as a four-inch copper wire, using pulses of light to transfer sound. The difficulty was that light could lose its intensity as it moves through the cable. When Corning began working on fiber optics in the middle 1960s, researchers decided that a 99 percent loss over a kilometer was economically viable because it could be boosted at that point. After four years of work, and numerous failed experiments, the research team developed a working product. Physicist Donald Keck recorded the event in his laboratory notebook with the notation "Eureka."

At the time there was no apparent demand for the product. Telephone companies said that they would produce their own fiber when demand made such a step imperative. Although lacking sales, Corning continued improving the product, making the original product obsolete even before it was sold. By 1972, the fiber wire could be extended 20 kilometers without a repeater, five times longer than standard copper wire. Eventually the distance grew to 100 kilometers. These continued improvements resulted in price declines from several dollars to less than 12¢ a meter in the late 1980s.

Corning reacted to the lack of early demand by entering into several joint ventures with European cable companies, believing that local partners would eventually lead to sales to the state-owned telephone monopolies. At the same time, Corning built its own factory in the United States. This move proved successful when deregulation of the telephone industry in the United States led MCI Communications Corporation to order 100,000 kilometers of cable in 1982. Two years later the company spent $87 million on new fiber plant facilities, the largest single Corning investment ever.

By the 1970s, U.S. communication companies were developing and using optical fiber. In July 1976, Corning filed suit against ITT Corporation and its customer, the United States government, charging patent infringements. Five years later, after a countersuit by ITT and much legal conflict, ITT settled, agreeing to pay penalties for patent infringement; a short time later, the government settled with payment of $650,000 for having purchased the fiber. During the next few years, Corning filed similar suits against Valtec Industries and Sumitomo Electric Industries in Japan. These suits too were settled in Corning's favor, in 1984 and 1987 respectively.

Corning's work on laboratory glass instruments led it into laboratory-related services, through the acquisition of other firms. MetPath, a leading clinical testing service in the United States, was purchased in 1982. Hazelton Laboratories, purchased in 1987, became one of the world's leading independent suppliers of services for biological and chemical research. Enseco, acquired in 1989, specialized in environmental testing.

Expansion Through Joint Ventures

During the 1980s, Corning entered into more joint ventures—over two-thirds with foreign firms—than most other

U.S.-based firms. More than half of its 1987 profits came from joint ventures. Dow Corning, with $1.5 billion in revenues, was as large as all of Corning's other joint ventures. The international alliances covered the globe, and included more than 15 joint ventures with companies in Europe, Asia, and Australia, producing such products as optical fiber, specialty glass, ceramics, and cookware. Acquisition of joint-venture partners continued in 1989 and 1990. IBM invested in PCO, an optoelectronics company controlled by Corning. Mitsubishi Heavy Industries, Mitsubishi Petrochemical, and Corning became partners in Cormetech, a pollution-control company. In June 1990, Corning joined with a company in India to form Samcor Glass. Corning entered such relationships to provide instant market penetration and to bring new technologies to the company. In 1989, Corning acknowledged the diversification of its products by changing the company name to Corning Incorporated.

By this time, Corning served as a prototypical "knowledge" firm. While it had always depended on research for new products, it moved even more actively into new products, quality of production, and training. For example, Corning's Total Quality program cut irregularities on a new coating process in fiber optics from 800 parts-per-million in 1986 to none in 1988. By 1991, workers spent five percent of their time in paid training. While many U.S. firms floundered due to Asian competition in the late 1980s and early 1990s, Corning was able to transform itself into one of the world's leading technology companies, while successfully maintaining its strength in manufacturing.

Obstacles and Changes: Mid- to Late 1990s

While operating as a leading technology firm and eventually the top manufacturer of fiber optic cable, Corning was forced overcome many obstacles during the 1990s. In 1992, subsidiary Dow Corning stopped manufacture of its silicon breast implants after controversy erupted over the possible dangers of this product. Hundreds of women filed suit against the firm, claiming Dow Corning hid health risks associated with the breast implants. Corning's earnings were negatively effected by the ordeal and the subsidiary eventually declared Chapter 11 bankruptcy in 1995, after a highly-publicized $4.25 billion class-action lawsuit.

In 1997, Houghton retired naming Roger Ackerman his successor. John W. Loose was elected president of Corning Inc. Under new management, the firm began divesting unprofitable businesses as part of its focus on growth in new business and technology. In 1998, the firm's consumer products division was sold to Borden Inc. By this time, its clinical lab-testing unit had been spun off and over half of the firm's other businesses were scheduled to be divested or sold, signaling Corning's commitment to its communications, environmental, and advanced materials business segments.

During this new focus however, the Asian economy began to falter. The firm supplied fiber optic cable to much of the region and when the crisis put a halt on many Asian telecom ventures, Corning's earnings felt the crunch. In fact, earnings dropped by 44 percent in the first half of 1998 as the firm was forced to lower its fiber prices. Company sales remained flat for the year.

The downturn of Corning's earnings did not last long, however, and Ackerman continued to focus on new technologies.

According to a 1999 Business Week article, "Ackerman began building up other businesses that supplied the almost boundless demand for broadband telecommunications. His goal was to move Corning beyond fiber, by making it a major supplier of photonic components that increase the amount of information a single strand of fiber can carry." The article also stated that Ackerman "spotted double digit growth opportunities in a number of Corning's high-tech niche businesses, from the ultrathin glass used in liquid-crystal displays (LCDs) to the high-purity fused silica that helps etch computer chips."

In 1999, earnings increased by 18 percent. During the year, the firm acquired several firms to strengthen its position in the optical communications market. BICC plc's telecommunications cable businesses were purchased as part of Corning's international efforts. The company also acquired Oak Industries and Siemens AG's global optical cable and hardware businesses.

Corning entered the new millennium on solid ground. The telecommunications, LCD, and advanced materials markets were all experiencing strong growth due to increased demand for bandwidth, the growing number of information display products available to consumers, and tightening environmental regulations. As such, Corning secured revenue gains of 36 percent. Sales increased to $7.1 billion in 2000, a 50 percent increase over the previous year.

While its fiber business continued to thrive, Corning once again faced obstacles in 2001. A slowing economy and a decline in demand for optical components forced the firm to cut 5,900 jobs. It also closed three plants related to its Photonic Technologies division. Corning management however, remained optimistic about future growth. The company's 150-year history of overcoming hardships, remaining on the cutting edge of technology, and strong focus on research and development left both Ackerman and Loose confident that the firm would be able to tackle market downturns.

Principal Subsidiaries

Corning Asahi Video Products Co. (51%); Corning Cable Systems LLC; Corning Cable Systems GMBH & Co. KG (Germany); Corning GMBH (Germany); Corning Japan K.K.; Corning Netoptix Inc.; Corning Noble Park Pty. Ltd. (Australia); Corning Oak Holdings Inc.; Corning Optical Fiber (50%; U.K.); Corning Optical Fiber GMBH & Co. KG (Germany); Corning Precision Lens Inc.; Corning S.A. (France); Intellisense Corp.; Optical Technologies Italia S.P.A. (Italy).

Principal Operating Units

Telecommunications; Advanced Materials; Information Display.

Principal Competitors

Alcatel; Lucent Technologies Inc.; Pirelli S.p.A.

Further Reading

"Ackerman Set to Replace Houghton as Corning Chairman, CEO," Fiber Optic News, February 19, 1996, p. 8.

''Corning Finds Buyer for Housewares Division,'' *Fiber Optic News,* March 16, 1998, p. 1.

''Corning Growth Slows, Battles Asian Flu,'' *Fiber Optic News,* February 16, 1998, p. 6.

Hammonds, Keith H., ''Corning's Class Act,'' *Business Week,* May 13, 1991, p. 68.

Hill Dawn, ''Corning to Divest Consumer Division,'' *HFN,* May 12, 1997, p. 1.

Holstein, William J., ''Dump the Cookware,'' *Business 2.0,* May 2001.

Kerwin, Kathleen, ''On the Firing Line at Dow Corning,'' *Business Week,* May 25, 1995, p. 33.

Magaziner, Ira C., and Mark Patinkin, *The Silent War: Inside the Global Business Battles Shaping America's Future*, New York: Random House, 1989.

Mehta, Stephanie N., ''Can Corning Find Its Optic Nerve?,'' *Fortune,* March 19, 2001.

Non, Sergio G., ''Corning Cuts Jobs, Takes $5.1 Billion Charge,'' *News.com,* July 9, 2001.

''Prescription for Long-Term Success: Continually Reinvent the Company,'' *Machine Design,* September 23, 1999, p. 222.

Skrycki, Cindy, ''Bringing a Bit of City to the Company Town,'' *Washington Post,* August 12, 1990, p. H1.

Symonds, William C., ''Has Corning Won its High-Tech Bet?,'' *Business Week,* April 5, 1999, p. 64.

''Telecommunications/Transportation & Logistics,'' *Forbes,* May 21, 2001.

Weld, Royal, ''Turnaround Tycoons,'' *Industry Week,* November 20, 2000, p. 47.

—Robert E. Ankli
—update: Christina M. Stansell

Quality ceiling fans and lighting.

Craftmade International, Inc.

650 South Royal Lane, Suite 100
Coppell, Texas 75019
U.S.A.
Telephone: (972) 393-3800
Toll Free: (800) 527-2578
Fax: (972) 304-3753
Web site: http://www.craftmade.com

Public Company
Incorporated: 1985
Employees: 131
Sales: $93.5 million (2001)
Stock Exchanges: NASDAQ
Ticker Symbol: CRFT
NAIC: 42122 Home Furnishing Wholesalers

Craftmade International, Inc., based in Coppell, Texas, in the Dallas-Fort Worth area, designs, distributes, and markets ceiling fans and ceiling fan light kits as well as outdoor lighting and bathroom strip lighting and related accessories. Most of Craftmade's products are made outside the United States to Craftmade's specifications. Most are also designed for home use, thus the company markets its various lines through a nationwide network of over 1,600 lighting showrooms and electrical wholesalers who sell such fixtures in the new-home construction and remodeling trades. Craftmade markets over two dozen fan models, ranging in price from the costly to the inexpensive, plus almost 80 different light kits. It is Craftmade's wholly-owned subsidiary, Trade Source International, Inc. (TSI), acquired in 1998, that designs, distributes, and markets the company's bathroom strip lighting and outdoor lighting products, which are sold through mass merchandisers under the Accolade brand name. TSI also makes fan accessories. Craftmade's merger with TSI more than doubled the company's size between 1998 and 1999. In 1999, company founder and CEO James R. Ridings owned an 18 percent or $9.4 million stake in the company.

Ridings and Ivins Found Craftmade in the 1980s

James R. Ridings and James Ivins, two Texas salesmen, co-founded Craftmade International Inc. almost as a fluke. Ridings, a native of Waco, and a Baylor University dropout, had been working as a salesman for a company that sold plumbing supplies and ceiling fans to mobile home manufacturers, but in 1985 he decided to go into business for himself. He teamed up with Ivins, an independent sales representative for Litex Industries, a company that imported and marketed ceiling fans in the United States. Although Ridings and Ivins founded Craftmade as a distributor and marketer of furniture and hardware and plumbing supplies as well as ceiling fans, its chief startup business was the sale of Litex's imported ceiling fans to mobile home makers. However, Litex soon discontinued its mobile home business to concentrate on sales to mass merchandisers like Wal-Mart, a strategy which in effect pulled the rug out from under Ridings and Ivins. They had developed a clientele of 30 mobile home manufacturers, but were left with nothing to sell them.

Their solution was to gather some capital together and go ahead on their own. After raising $30,000, they bought 800 ceiling fans from a Taiwan manufacturer and quickly sold out their stock. They then scrounged together another $45,000, primarily from the sale of property that Ridings owned in Waco, and replenished their supply of fans. They also developed a sales force, in part made up of former Litex representatives, and began moving fans in earnest. Within a year, they had a sales team of 15 and were selling 3,000 fans per month.

Initially, Craftmade was a low-flying operation. Partners Ridings and Ivins handled the company's paper work in the living room of Ivins' apartment in Dallas. Their warehouse and distribution center was a rented 9,000 square foot storage building, operated with a work force of three people. Still, in 1986, its first full year of operations, Craftmade had sales of $1.9 million, earning the new company $50,000. In an effort to increase their sales volume, Ridings and Ivins began selling their fans to lighting showroom companies and electrical wholesalers. They also started designing their own fans, pushing for a better quality product to sell in a higher-margin market. Their success also gave them some clout with their Taiwan manufacturer, whose products they carefully monitored for quality. On one occasion, after receiving complaints from one of their lighting showroom customers, Ivins flew to Taiwan and talked the manufacturer into switching its fan housings from aluminum to steel, thereby improving their screw retention capabilities and making them more reliable.

Initially, Craftmade contracted the manufacture of all of its products rather than make them itself. In 1986, the company entered an arrangement with Fanthing Electrical Corp. of Taichung, Taiwan. Under its terms, formalized in writing in 1989, Fanthing agreed to manufacture ceiling fans to Craftmade's specifications. Later, Craftmade entered a similar agreement with Sunlit Industries, another Taiwan manufacturer. Sunlit made virtually all of Craftmade's light kits for its fans. The outsourcing of its product manufacturing would continue to be a main part of Craftmade's modus operandi; however, in 1990, through an acquisition, the company would also undertake the manufacture of some of its own products.

1990–99 Craftmade Goes Public, Diversifies, and Expands

In that year, Craftmade made two major moves. In February, it went public. Then, later in the year, in exchange for 150,000 shares of Craftmade stock, worth about $450,000, it acquired DMI Products, a struggling, Fort Worth, Texas-based specialty lamp manufacturer that, in 1989, had logged annual sales of about $3.8 million, as compared to Craftmade's $13 million, and had a net worth of about $3 million. Combined, Craftmade and DMI's 1990 sales closed in on $17 million and were expected to exceed $20 million in 1991. Under the terms of the agreement, Craftmade transferred 75,000 shares of its stock to DMI's owners at the closing of the deal and agreed to transfer an additional 75,000 shares on the closing's anniversary. As part of the agreement, DMI's president, Edmond C. Wheeler, was to be retained for two years. An electrical engineer, Wheeler brought design skills to Craftmade, which hoped to create additional electronic products with his help.

In anticipation of the acquisition of DMI, Craftmade moved into a new 118,843 square-foot facility in Grand Prairie, taking

the building so that it could put the combined operations under one roof. In addition to making specialty lighting, DMI, through its GEI division, made computer connections and cables. Altogether, with the DMI purchase, the workforce of Craftmade grew to about 50. Importantly, too, the acquisition diversified Craftmade's product line, a necessary move because sales in the ceiling-fan industry had peaked and stabilized at unit sales levels under those reached in 1983, before Craftmade even entered the business.

During its expansion in the early 1990s, Craftmade earned a reputation as a solid business. Starting in 1992, it made *Forbes* magazine's list of the ''Top 200 Best Small Companies in America;'' and it made the same list over the next two years. The company was, in fact, cruising in overdrive. By 1993, it was marketing its fans in all 50 states, with its biggest sales made in Ohio. At the end of its fiscal year, in June, the company had revenues of $22 million with net earnings of $1.1 million. Altogether, Craftmade had sold over 270,000 fans and 200,000 lamps. Sales would continue to climb the next year, when they reached $32 million and produced a net profit of $2.4 million.

Until 1995, when the company's roster climbed over 100, Craftmade operated on leased property in Grand Prairie. The company also had two subsidiaries: Global Electronics Inc. (GEI), which manufactured computer cables and distributed telecommunications devices to wholesalers; and Durocraft Design Mfg., which made lamps and lighting accessories, primarily for The Bombay Company. In that year, its increased workforce and its need to move into a larger space prompted it to begin building a new 350,000 square foot facility in Coppell, Texas, on property located on the edge of the Foreign Trade Zone at the north end of the Dallas-Fort Worth International Airport.

During the 1990s, under the tutelage of Ridings, Craftmade earned an industry-wide reputation for taking good care of its customers. Its competitive strategy in its highly fragmented market was to offer fans comparable in quality to those of bigger sellers like Hunter and Casablanca at lower costs. As a result, Craftmade seldom had retailers back out of purchase agreements with the company. In order to keep that loyalty, Ridings allowed the company to take some financial hits rather than pass its rising costs onto its customers. For example, in 1996, when the value of Taiwan's currency suddenly inflated, driving up its production costs, Craftmade absorbed losses rather than pass along a 10 percent rate hike to its clients, and, as a result, the company's earnings did not grow that year. In contrast, in 1997, when the Asian economy went into a tailspin, Craftmade passed along an 8 percent savings to his showrooms.

In 1998, Craftmade acquired Trade Source International (TSI), a major purchase that would double the company's revenues. It bought Trade Source, an outdoor lighting company, for $11 million in cash and stock. Like Craftmade, TSI basically designed and marketed its products but outsourced their manufacture. It sold lanterns and post lamps via major home center chains, including Home Depot and Lowe's. Notably, in order to retain the loyalty of his mom-and-pop and small chain customers, Ridings decided against selling Craftmade's better quality fans through these giant outlets. Instead, Craftmade opted to produce a private-brand line for them.

Key Dates:

1985: James Ridings and James Ivins found Craftmade.
1986: Fanthing Electrical Corp. agrees to make Craftmade's fans in Taiwan.
1990: Craftmade goes public and purchases DMI Products.
1998: Craftmade acquires Trade Source International (TSI).

over, the company's net income fell, from $5.7 million to $4.3 million. That slight decline in the company's profit margin was the result of discontinued pricing and promotional programs used to bolster sales in the company's showroom division. In any case, prospects for a significant growth in sales in 2001 looked good. The company recorded a 12 percent increase in its fiscal 2001 first quarter sales over sales from the same period in 2000. Craftmade also expected greater revenue growth from the rollout of a new mix-and-match lamp sales campaign and display developed for Lowe's.

With the acquisition of TSI, Craftmade developed a cross-selling strategy. TSI's customer base consisted largely of home centers and mass merchandisers, while Craftmade's was at least in part made up of independent retailers. Over the next couple of years, Craftmade introduced its established customer base to Trade Source products and began marketing its traditional products through mass merchandising outlets. By 1999, Craftmade was doing business with major home-center chains and some 1,600 mom-and-pop stores across the United States.

That year, it also entered into a partnership agreement with Dolan Design, Inc., lighting designer Patrick Dolan's Portland, Oregon-based firm. Dolan had already designed some of Craftmade's most popular, best selling fans, and under the new arrangement he was to undertake the design of other Craftmade products, including chandeliers, wall pendants, and lighting accessories.

Craftmade's sales jumped from $40.9 million in 1998 to $85 million in 1999, driven in part by the company's acquisitions and the success of its Accolade brand lighting fixtures. The impact of Craftmade's diversification and cross-selling use of its new marketing channels can be seen in the fact that in 1999 ceiling fans only accounted for 32 percent of the company's sales, whereas the year before they had accounted for 68 percent. The huge increase in sales in 1999 was like a shot of financial adrenaline, and while it was in progress it gained Craftmade an important accolade—a 49th ranking on *Forbes* magazine's annual list of the 200 Best Small Companies. It was also featured in that publication's special edition "12 Companies to Watch" section.

2000 and Beyond: New Sales Strategies

The next year, though, Craftmade's sales leveled off at their new plateau, growing by just $500,000 to $85.5 million. More-

Principal Subsidiaries

Durocraft Design Mfg.; Global Electronics; Trade Source International, Inc.

Principal Competitors

Angelo Brothers Company; Casablanca Fan Company; Emerson; The Holmes Group, Inc.; Hunter Fan Company; Quorum International.

Further Reading

Brett, Nelson, "Staying Cool," *Forbes,* November 11, 1999, p. 256.
"Craftmade Announces New Lighting Design Partnership," *PR Newswire*, August 3, 1999.
"Craftmade to Buy DMI, Specialty Lamp Manufacturer," *HFD-The Weekly Home Furnishings Newspaper,* June 18, 1990, p. 31.
"Craftmade Goes Upscale with Orzoco Fans," *HFD-The Weekly Home Furnishings Newspaper,* June 24, 1991, p. 32.
"Craftmade Named to Forbes List of 200 Best Small Companies," *PR Newswire*, October 19, 1999.
"Craftmade Reports Tawain Manufacturing Partner Facility Now Operating," *PR Newswire,* September 28, 1999.
Golightly, Glen, "Competitors' Woes Fan Craftmade's Sales," *Dallas Business Journal,* December 6, 1991, p. 27.
Rodda, Kelli, "Craftmade Acquiring Light Fixture Group," *Business Press,* March 27, 1998, p. 6.
Roth, Steve, "Craftmade Inks Merger Pact, Plans New Manufacturing Site," *Dallas Business Journal,* June 18, 1990, p. 15.
Smith, Frank, "Stock Gurus See High Ceiling for Wall Street Rookie Craftmade," *Dallas Business Journal,* July 16, 1990, p. 2.
Strope, Leigh, "Craftmade Will Build New HQ," *Dallas Business Journal,* April 28, 1995, p. 1.
Sullivan, R. Lee, "Survival Skills," *Forbes,* July 5, 1993, p. 61.

—John W. Fiero

DANISCO

Danisco A/S

Langebrogade 1
DK-1001 Copenhagen
Denmark
Telephone: (+45) 32 66 20 00
Fax: (+45) 32 66 21 75
Web site: http://www.danisco.com

Public Company
Incorporated: 1989
Employees: 17,712
Sales: DKr 23.54 billion ($2.8 billion) (2000)
Stock Exchanges: Copenhagen
Ticker Symbol: DCO
NAIC: 311942 Spice and Extract Manufacturing; 111991 Sugar Beet Farming; 311312 Cane Sugar Refining; 31131 Sugar Manufacturing; 326199 All Other Plastics Product Manufacturing; 325998 All Other Miscellaneous Chemical Product and Preparation Manufacturing.

Danisco A/S has repositioned itself as one of the world's leading manufacturers of food ingredients. The company focuses on high value-added ingredients such as emulsifiers, stabilizers, and flavorings, as well as sugar and other sweeteners, such as xylitol and fructose. Since its acquisition of Finland's Cultor in 1999, Danisco has engaged in a reorganization of its operations, shedding its former foods divisions and most of its packaging division. Danisco Cultor oversees the company's functional ingredients production and holds the world's leading position in that market. Among the division's products are emulsifiers, flavorings, enzymes, starter cultures, antioxidants and antimicrobials, specialty fats, and texture ingredients. Danisco Sweeteners is a world-leading producer of the artificial sweetener xylitol, a leading producer of fructose, and a producer of specialty sweeteners for the baked goods and confectionery industries. Danisco Sugar manufactures sugars and syrups primarily for the industrial market—which accounts for 80 percent of sugar sales—but also for the consumer market, where the company holds a more-or-less monopoly position in the Scandi-

navian market. Through Danisco Sugar, Danisco is the fourth largest sugar producer in Europe, behind Tate & Lyle, Eridania Beghin-Say, and Sudzucker. Other Danisco subsidiaries include Danisco Seed, which develops and produces seed products, such as beets for beet sugar production, but also sunflowers, mustard, rapeseed, and peas; Danisco Venture, a venture capital fund dedicated to investing in new businesses related to the parent company's activities; and a 50 percent share of Genencor International Inc., the Rochester, New York-based biotechnology company. Danisco is traded on the Copenhagen stock exchange and is led by Chairman Jugo Schroder and Chief Executive Alf Duch-Pedersen. In 2000, Danisco posted sales of DKr 23.5 billion ($2.8 billion).

19th Century Sweetness

The Danisco entering the 21st century was the amalgamation of several Danish and other Scandinavian companies, some of which traced their roots to the late 19th century. Three major companies—A/S Danisco, which operated primarily through subsidiary Grindsted Food Products; De Danske Spiritfabrikker, the leading Danish distiller; and Danish sugar monopoly De Danske Sukkerfabrikker—merged in 1989 to form what became known as the ''new'' Danisco. To these were added a decade later another major group, Finland's Cultor, which, apart from controlling Finnsugar, had built itself into one of the world's leading food ingredients companies.

Among the oldest of the Danisco companies was Danske Sukkerfabrikker. This company had been established in 1872 by financier C.F. Tietgen, who also owned Privatbanken. Tietgen invested some five million rix-dollars in equity to start up his own sugar production company. Developments since the middle of the 19th century had enabled the production of sugar from beets—a crop more easily grown in Denmark and the rest of Europe than sugar cane. Tietgen's company began operations by acquiring two existing sugar refineries in Copenhagen, while starting construction on new refineries, including one in Odense, which began construction in 1872. Tietgen's investment capital also went to ensuring a supply of raw beets, supplementing farmers who wished to convert their production to beets. Danske Sukker also began experimenting with breeding and developing its own

Company Perspectives:

Values: We create value. Danisco is managed by principles of value creation. We use our financial and human resources to add value to our customers by supplying innovative products and services based on our in-depth understanding of the customers' needs and requirements. We ensure profitability for our shareholders and strive to increase Danisco's market value. And finally, we want to act as a good citizen in social and environmental respects.

beet seed, but without success. Instead, the Danish beet market relied on international imports for its seeds.

Tietgen's Odense refinery began operations in 1873. By the end of that decade, De Dankse Sukkerfabrikker had added other refineries, including one in Lolland in 1880, originally built by the Frederiksen brothers, Erhard and Johan, who had been among the first Danes to begin sugar beet farming. Dankse Sukkerfabrikker was by then one of the country's leading sugar refiners. Beet sugar production grew in importance throughout the rest of the century. Danske Sukkerfabrikker continued to build a prominent position in the Danish market; by the 1880s the company's production warranted the creation of a dedicated railway network linking beet farmers to refineries.

Danske Sukker's production grew steadily and by 1910 the company was capable of meeting the sugar demand for all of Denmark. The outbreak of the First World War presented the company with a number of difficulties, most notably the inability to import beet seeds. Danske Sukker had dropped its own breeding program in 1903. During the war years, the company turned once again to development of its own seeds. By 1920, the company's seed production had grown sufficiently to create a dedicated subsidiary, which later became known as Danisco Seed. For much of that company's history, however, it was more closely identified with its first major product success, that of the Maribo-N beet variety introduced in 1928. The company's research and development efforts quickly paid off again, this time in 1930 with the development of the world's first polyploid sugar beet—a tetraploid beet seed that was finally launched in 1950 as Maribo-P. The following decade, Danske Sukker invested more than DKr 100 million to convert its operations from split sugar manufacturing and sugar refinery facilities into a network of plants capable of producing finished product through a single combined production process. The development eliminated the need for transporting the raw sugar, which led to the closing of the company's railway system by the middle of the 1960s.

Danske Sukker founder Tietgen's interests extended beyond that industry. In 1881, Tietgen and partner CA Olesen founded a new company, De Danske Spiritfabrikker, uniting several small-scale distillers to form a single company for the production of Danish national drink akvavit, or "water of life," a clear alcoholic beverage similar to gin. De Danske Spirit led a consolidation of the entire Danish distillery sector—at one time the country counted more than 2,500 small independent distillery companies. By 1923, that number had been reduced to just one, as Danske Spiritfabrikker became the sole distiller in all of

Denmark. In 1924, the company went even farther, receiving a monopoly for the production of yeast and all distilled spirits in the country. The company was to hold that monopoly until the early 1970s, when Denmark's entry into the European Community brought the spirits monopoly to an end.

The third major part of the "new" Danisco became part of the "old" Danisco at the end of the 1930s. Grindstedvaerket had been founded in the town of Grindsted in 1924 as a producer of organic chemicals. The company extended its range through the 1930s and gradually came to focus on various food ingredients, such as emulsifiers (useful for preserving the texture of bread, ice cream, and other foods), flavoring agents, and enzymes for processing foods. Danisco took over Grindstedvaerket in 1939 but the food ingredients arm became Danisco's major operation, responsible for the majority of its sales.

Those sales were boosted after World War II with the launch of the company's Cremodan brand of emulsifiers and hydrocolloids, used for the production of ice cream, in 1948. In the 1950s, Danisco began to spread beyond Denmark and the Scandinavian market, establishing a sales subsidiary in Germany. The following decade, Danisco launched another successful product line, Dimodan monoglycerides.

By the late 1970s, industrial production of processed foods had successfully lured vast numbers of the world's consumers with an ever-expanding range of prepared foods. The prepared foods industry's growth was propelled by revolutionary shifts in the work force, as women abandoned traditional roles to pursue their own careers. The growing number of working households left less time for the preparation of meals, and food companies stepped into that breach with new varieties of ready-to-eat foods. Ingredients concerns such as Danisco formed the backbone of the growing processed foods industry, supplying the additives and ingredients that promoted food preservation and enhanced flavor, as well as texturing and color agents to enhance products' appeal to the consumer. The increasingly global scope of the food industry encouraged Danisco to boost its own international activity. A step toward this goal was the renaming of its main Grindstedvaerket to the more international Grindsted Food Products in 1980.

That name change accompanied Danisco's entry into the world's primary market for processed foods, the United States, with the construction of a factory in Kansas. The company reinforced its North American presence with the opening of a factory for the production of pectin, a thickening agent, in Mexico. Over the next several years, Danisco's operations spread around the world. In 1983, the company bought a production facility in France, followed by the purchase of a new plant in Spain in 1985. The company built its own Brazilian operation, an emulsifier plant, in 1986. Another emulsifier facility was constructed in Malaysia in 1990.

Recipe for a Food Ingredients Giant in the 1990s

Despite the loss of its monopoly in 1973, De Danske Spiritfabrikker remained Denmark's dominant distiller throughout the 1980s. De Danske Sukkerfabrikker had also secured the dominant position in the country's sugar industry, both as producer and as distributor, extending its control of the domestic

Key Dates:

1872: CF Tietgen creates De Danske Sukkerfabrikker to produce beet sugar in Denmark.

1881: Tietgen and CA Olesen found De Danske Spiritfabrikker as a leading akvavit distiller and exporter.

1910: Danske Sukker's production is able to meet the entire Danish market demand.

1920: Danske Sukker begins research and development in beet sugar seeds and forms future Danisco Seed.

1923: Danske Spirit acquires Danish distillery monopoly.

1924: Danske Spirit extends monopoly to include all yeast and spirits production; I/S Grindstedvaerket is founded as an organic chemicals concern.

1939: Danisco takes over Grindsted, which is then expanded into food ingredients production and becomes Danisco's main subsidiary.

1954: Danisco opens sales subsidiary in Germany and begins international expansion.

1980: Grindsted changes its name to Grindsted Food Products and opens its first factory in United States.

1981: Danisco opens pectin plant in Mexico.

1983: Company acquires alginate production facility in France.

1989: Merger among Danske Sukker, Danisco, and Danske Spirit creates "new" Danisco; Danisco Sugar acquires the last independent sugar refinery in Denmark.

1992: Danisco Sugar takes over the entire Swedish sugar industry, becoming the fourth largest sugar producer in Europe.

1995: Grindsted changes its name to Danisco Ingredients.

1999: Danisco merges with Finland's Cultor, creating one of the world's largest food ingredients companies.

2000: Danisco begins restructuring, shedding noncore operations (food products; packaging); the company starts production of flavorings in India.

2001: Danisco acquires Australia's Germantown and the United States' Florida Flavors.

market in 1989, when it acquired the country's last remaining independent sugar refinery, Sukkerfabrikken Nykobing.

A number of other key elements of the "new" Danisco also had been undergoing rapid development. One of these was the later Danisco Sweeteners, which had been founded originally in 1976 as a joint venture between Finnsugar—later known as Cultor—and pharmaceuticals maker Hoffman-La Roche to produce the new artificial sweetened Xylitol. This product, which proved to have anti-tartar properties as well, became a widely used ingredient in sugar-free foods and candies, such as chewing gum. Cultor itself was to become a major part of the "new" Danisco; the company was quickly establishing itself as one of Scandinavia's leading food ingredients groups, particularly with such acquisitions as the food ingredients operations from the United States' Pfizer.

Cultor also brought with it its 50 percent interest in another United States-based company, Genencor, founded in 1982, which had built a growing business around its genetically manipulated biotechnology products. Meanwhile, Danisco Seed also had been working in the biotechnology sector during the 1980s; in 1990, the subsidiary's research resulted in the first outdoor planting of a genetically manipulated beet plant.

The 1989 merger of De Danske Spiritfabrikker, De Danske Sukkerfabrikker, and Danisco was one of the largest merger operations ever carried out in Denmark and created one of the company's largest industrial groups. The company's core businesses complemented each other well, creating so-called "cluster" competencies. The three components continued to pursue developments in their own sectors, however, now under the umbrella name of Danisco.

Danisco Sugar proved to be one of the fastest growing components of the new Danisco. After establishing itself as the single remaining sugar producer in Denmark in 1989, the division started its drive to become one of the dominant players in the European sugar market. In 1991, the company acquired eight refineries in what was now the eastern part of the re-unified Germany. The following year, the company took over the entire sugar industry of Sweden, making it the fourth largest sugar company in Europe. Later in the decade, Danisco Sugar continued to expand in its core European market, such as with the 1998 purchases of stakes in sugar refineries in Poland and Lithuania.

The Grindsted Food Products unit changed its name to Danisco Ingredients in 1995, at the same time as it acquired a new pectin plant in the Czech Republic. The company continued to add to its operations through the end of the decade, notably with the acquisition of an emulsifier factory in Sweden in 1996, and the purchase of the United Kingdom's flavorings manufacturer Borthwicks in 1997. The company added another flavorings producer in 1998, Beck Flavors, based in the United States, as well as companies in Germany and Malaysia.

The year 1999 marked a new turning point for Danisco. In that year the company merged with Finland's Cultor, creating one of the world's largest food ingredients groups. As part of the merger, Danisco's ingredients arm took on a new name, Danisco Cultor. The company created the new Sugar and Sweeteners Division, merging Danisco's sugar production with Cultor's sugar arm, Sucros Oy, and its Xylitol and other artificial sweeteners operations. At the same time, Danisco took over Cultor's stake in Genencor, leading the two companies to develop a cooperation agreement in 2000, calling for the development of new biotechnology products for the food ingredients sector.

Following the Cultor merger, Danisco moved to reorganize its operations, focusing on a new core of Ingredients, Sugar, and Sweeteners. The company began selling off its now noncore operations, including Danske Spirit and the company's former frozen foods and other foods subsidiaries, which were jettisoned in favor of the higher-margin ingredients sector. The company also had begun to build up a packaging arm—notably with the acquisition of the United Kingdom's second largest flexible packaging company Sidlay in 1999—but by 2001 Danisco had decided to abandon that sector to focus on its more closely related operations.

Although sugar and sweeteners remained an important part of Danisco's operations, representing, together with Danisco Seed, some 28 percent of the company's sales, food ingredients were claiming a rising share of Danisco's revenues, reaching 25 percent by the end of the company's 2000 year. This unit saw new significant developments at the turn of the century, such as the beginning of flavorings production in India, and the 2001 acquisition one month later of the United States' Florida Flavors, a fruit flavorings supplier to the fruit juice industry. In August 2001, the company paid $100 million for the purchase of the Germantown division of Australia's Goodman Fielder, giving the company a leading position in the worldwide texture agents market. At the same time, Danisco announced its intention to step up its activities in China and the rest of Asia, forecasting that these markets held the strongest promise for growth in the near future. These moves helped confirm Danisco's transition into a worldwide food ingredients leader for the new century.

Principal Subsidiaries

Danisco Sugar; Danisco Seed; Danisco Pack UK; Danisco Foods; Danisco A/S; Danisco Cultor; Danisco Venture; Danisco Sweeteners.

Principal Competitors

Amalgamated Sugar Company LLC; Associated British Foods; Bahlsen GmbH & Co. KG; Eridania Beghin-Say; Imperial Sugar Company; Cumberland Packing Corp.; Ezaki Glico Co., Ltd.; Nippon Beet Sugar Manufacturing Co., Ltd.; Südzucker AG; U.S. Sugar Corporation; Kerry Group; Tate & Lyle plc.

Further Reading

Alperowicz, Natasha, "Danisco Takes Top Spot," *Chemical Week,* March 10, 1999.
"Danisco Beats Forecast Despite Slow Growth," *Reuters,* September 18, 2001.
"Danisco: Cluster Buster," *Economist,* April 15, 2000.
Dyrekilde, Birgitte, "Danisco Sees Sugar Money Funding Food Deals," *Reuters,* May 18, 2001.
Raastrup, Nicolai, "Danisco to Boost Growth in China," *Reuters,* August 8, 2001.

—M.L. Cohen

Darden Restaurants, Inc.

5900 Lake Ellenor Drive
P.O. Box 593330
Orlando, Florida 32809-3330
U.S.A.
Telephone: (407) 245-4000
Fax: (407) 245-5114
Web site: http://www.darden.com

Public Company
Incorporated: 1995
Employees: 128,900
Sales: $4 billion (2001)
Stock Exchanges: New York
Ticker Symbol: DRI
NAIC: 72211 Full-service Restaurants

Operating more than 1,168 units throughout the United States and Canada, Darden Restaurants, Inc. began its existence in 1995 as the world's largest full-service restaurant organization, occupying the casual dining niche between fine dining and quick-service restaurants. Specifically, the company was spun off from General Mills to its stockholders as an independent company, overseeing the restaurant chains Red Lobster, The Olive Garden, and, until late 1995, China Coast.

Founded in 1968 and acquired by General Mills, Inc. in 1970, Red Lobster grew to become the nation's largest seafood and casual dining restaurant chain. Launched in 1982, The Olive Garden became the largest chain of casual but full-service Italian restaurants. China Coast was an unsuccessful ethnic restaurant chain that operated during the 1990s. Darden Restaurants' two newest concepts, Bahama Breeze and Smokey Bones BBQ Sports Bar, were introduced in the late 1990s and together had 30 restaurants in operation by 2001. Controlling nearly 8.5 percent of the $47 billion casual dining market, Darden Restaurants served approximately 3,000,000 meals per year through its restaurant outlets.

The First Red Lobsters in the Late 1960s

William B. Darden, reared in Waycross, Georgia, opened, at the age of 19, a Depression-era Waycross lunch counter that he called "The Green Frog," promising "Service with a Hop." He went on to own some local motel and hotel properties and all or part of about 20 Howard Johnson restaurants. Inspired by the great popularity of seafood in two of his eight restaurants—one in Orlando and the other in Jacksonville—Darden opened his first Red Lobster restaurant in Lakeland, Florida, in 1968. Its manager was Joe R. Lee, a native Georgian who later became chief executive officer of Darden Restaurants.

Darden wanted to market a chain of moderately priced, family-style, full-service seafood restaurants. He chose to open in Lakeland because it was as far from the ocean as possible in Florida, and he wanted to test his concept outside of coastal areas. The first Red Lobster proved a booming success, so much so that Darden and his partners had to work full shifts to meet the objective of getting food to the table within ten minutes of the order.

By 1970, there were three Red Lobsters in operation, all in central Florida, and two more under construction. The three units, which despite their name specialized in the fried fish and hush puppies favored by southerners, averaged $800,000 each in annual sales, and earnings were solid, but the company lacked the cash to grow. For General Mills, a diversified food products giant, acquiring Red Lobster Inns of America made sense because General Mills' fish sales accounted for about $80 million of revenue, or one-ninth of its total sales. Darden was hired to oversee the chain and open a restaurant headquarters in Orlando. He later became a General Mills vice-president and senior consultant, retired in 1984, and died in 1994.

General Mills upgraded Red Lobster into a midpriced seafood dinner house that was a model of corporate efficiency. Lee, who rose to become president of Red Lobster in 1975, carried a slide rule with him everywhere in the early 1970s to calculate prices and portion weights, and to quantify whatever else could be quantified. He also carried a thermometer in order to assure that entrees had been cooked to the proper temperature before being served. In 1971 Red Lobster established an in-house department for purchasing seafood on a worldwide scale. The company also established, long before the rest of the industry, a computerized point-of-purchase system to track how much of any given item was selling where.

Rapid Growth in the 1970s

Red Lobster grew in each year of operation, and it grew rapidly. By the end of fiscal 1971 there were 24 restaurants with total sales of $9.1 million, and by the end of fiscal 1972 there were 47 with sales of $27.1 million. When Lee was named president of Red Lobster in 1975, there were 97 restaurants with 9,500 employees. In 1976 the General Mills subsidiary opened a microbiology laboratory in Orlando to ensure the quality of its products. Red Lobster ended that fiscal year with 174 units in 26 states and total sales of $174.1 million.

Because of higher costs, attributed in large part to increased fuel bills for truck transportation and fishing boats caused by the Arab oil embargo of 1973–74, Red Lobster again felt the need to upgrade in the mid-1970s. It carpeted the floors, re-styled the interiors, and added a few fresh dishes to its predominantly frozen menu, and it sharply jacked up prices to pay for the improvements. The strategy worked. By the end of 1980 Red Lobster, with 260 units and almost $400 million in annual sales, had reached ninth place among fast-food companies and accounted for more than half of total sales by seafood fast-food companies. Although a sit-down chain, frequently with lounges, it was considered ''fast food'' by some analysts because most entree items were delivered frozen.

Alternatively, however, by 1982 Red Lobster was rated as the nation's largest ''dinner-house'' restaurant chain, this being the name for a restaurant offering table service and a full lunch and dinner menu. With an average annual return on invested assets of 22.3 percent before taxes, it was one of the most profitable chains in its field, and its growth had come entirely without franchising.

Wider Choices in the 1980s

Red Lobster provided General Mills with $75 million in operating earnings during fiscal 1982. By early 1983 there were 350 establishments in 36 states. The first of dozens of franchised Red Lobsters in Japan opened in Tokyo in 1982, and the first Canadian unit opened in 1983. Securities analysts attributed the chain's success, in large part, to Red Lobster's position as the only nationwide seafood dinner chain and its extraordinary quality-control measures. According to one of its executives, while seafood could be 16 days old and still legally sold as fresh, Red Lobster's seafood, although frozen, was ''fresh fro-

zen'' at five regional warehouses, each with a quality-control laboratory.

During 1982, however, Red Lobster decided to pursue a new direction. The chain's research, according to Lee, indicated that its customers resented waiting in line yet did not like being hustled out, and wanted a more casual dining experience, with an atmosphere conducive to drinks, appetizers, and finger food to share instead of massive entrees. Accordingly, a prototype unit opened in Kissimmee, Florida, in 1984 was a grazer's delight, with a seafood bar serving up oysters, shrimp, clams, calamari, and other appetizers with drinks, and a glass-enclosed grill where fresh seafood was broiled over mesquite-wood flames. Red Lobster restaurants had deliberately been built without windows so that diners would not take up time seeking a table looking out, but the new unit had picturesque views. Waiters were instructed to relax instead of speeding diners through the dinner cycle.

In 1984, General Mills authorized a $104 million remodeling program for Red Lobster, the largest capital-spending item in the parent company's history. All 370 units were to be overhauled, with the menu 40 percent longer to include such items as seafood salads and pastas, and six or eight fresh fish entrees available, twice as many as in the past. Dinner prices were lowered to draw more customers, with the expectation that patrons would make up for the difference by increased spending on appetizers and alcoholic beverages.

Red Lobster continued to reinvent itself and reward its parent company in subsequent years, passing $1 billion in North American sales during 1988. By then it was General Mills' second largest revenue producer, trailing only the cereals division and accounting for about one-fifth of the parent company's business. A food industry analyst told the *New York Times,* ''They have a concept that works extremely well, but they also constantly refresh their franchise. ... If Cajun food is hot, they'll put five Cajun entrees on the menu. Whatever's hot, they'll do it.''

By this time Red Lobster was offering more than 100 seafood items every day. To supply its units it was buying about 58 million pounds of seafood every year, combing the world's oceans for the latest novelty. These included popcorn shrimp, caught off the shores of Brazil, slipper lobster from Thailand, and Pacific orange roughy, a whitefish from New Zealand to supplement North American standbys from Florida stone crab and Maine flounder to Alaska salmon. By 1995 Red Lobster was purchasing seafood from 44 countries.

The array of options allowed the chain to draw in new customers by featuring bargain specials. Close contact between the chain's buyers and thousands of entrepreneurial fishing operations, and delivery by overnight air express services, enabled much of the catch to reach units daily while still fresh. The price of Red Lobster dinner entrees ranged from about $7 to $19 in 1995. Lunch entrees ranged from about $4.30 to $7. Red Lobster also offered a lower-priced children's menu.

Questionnaires and focus groups also convinced Red Lobster of the importance of good service to securing follow-up trade. It held a four-day training course for servers before each

Key Dates:

1968: William B. Darden opens his first Red Lobster restaurant in Lakeland, Florida.
1970: General Mills, Inc. acquires the Red Lobster chain.
1975: Joe R. Lee is named president of Red Lobster; 97 restaurants are in operation.
1982: General Mills opens its first Olive Garden restaurant in Orlando, Florida.
1984: Red Lobster begins a $104 million remodeling program.
1988: North American Red Lobster sales surpass $1 billion.
1990: The China Coast restaurant chain is launched.
1993: Olive Garden secures $1 billion in sales.
1995: General Mills spins off its restaurant operations as Darden Restaurants Inc.; plans are put in motion to close the China Coast restaurant chain.
1996: Darden Restaurants begins testing its Bahama Breeze Caribbean Grille restaurant concept.
1997: The firm posts a $91.03 million loss; 48 poor performing restaurants are closed.
1998: After successful restructuring efforts, Darden Restaurants secures $102 million in profits.
1999: The company establishes the Culinary Institute of Tuscany in Italy to train Olive Garden chefs; new restaurant concept Smokey Bones BBQ Sports Bar is launched.
2001: Darden Restaurants continues expansion; net income reaches a record $197 million.

restaurant opened and then required the staff to attend follow-up monthly classes. After 1986 waiters and waitresses were encouraged to display individuality in serving customers rather than relying on mechanical recitations of what the restaurant had to offer. The uniform of shirts and slacks was replaced by a maroon apron under which servers wore clothing of their own choice. They also were motivated by Red Lobster's reputation for good benefits, flexible hours, chances for advancement, and the hope of earning more than $100 in tips on good nights.

The Olive Garden: 1982–95

Fearing saturation in the seafood market, however, General Mills had decided years earlier to expand its restaurant group, which included York Steak House as well as Red Lobster. In 1982, following five years of painstaking research and about $28 million for development funds, the company opened the first Olive Garden restaurant in Orlando. By the end of 1985 there were eight such units, and by mid-1989 there were 145, making it General Mills' fastest-growing business and probably the fastest-growing major chain in the United States.

A 1991 *Forbes* article found the dinner portions, averaging only $10, enormous, but called the salad soggy with dressing, the chicken bland, and the fettucine alfredo like something out of a TV dinner. The public, however, flocked to these outlets. Average sales per Olive Garden were $2.8 million that year, compared with $3 million for Red Lobster, and both were high

for the industry. The Olive Garden ended fiscal 1992 with $808 million in sales and 341 outlets. It reached the $1-billion-a-year sales mark in 1993. The menu, in 1995, included not only Italian specialties such as veal piccata, baked lasagna, and chicken marsala but a variety of veal, beef, and seafood dishes. Dinner entree prices ranged from about $7 to $14.25, and lunch entree prices ranged from about $4.25 to $8.75. A limited-menu Olive Garden Cafe concept in food court settings at regional shopping malls was being tested. There were seven such units in late 1995.

Ill-Fated China Coast: 1990–95

The success of The Olive Garden encouraged General Mills to expand its ethnic food format. After three years of development and test marketing the restaurant group launched China Coast in 1990 as the first national Chinese food chain. This eatery opened with an eight-page menu, in *Newsweek's* words, "about as long as the list of emperors in the Ming Dynasty." The interiors were festooned with bamboo, paper lanterns, and Chinese-character wall scrolls, and the servers wore Chinese-style jackets. Eventually the China Coast chain grew to 51, but it failed to thrive and was ordered closed in 1995. During fiscal 1995 China Coast's sales came to only $71 million, and Wall Street analysts estimated that it lost $20 million that year. Thirty China Coast restaurants were converted into Red Lobsters or Olive Gardens.

Forming Darden Restaurants in 1995

General Mills decided in 1995 to spin off its restaurant operations into a new company so that it could concentrate more on its consumer food products. Lee, the chairman and chief executive officer, named the new company Darden Restaurants in honor of his mentor and Red Lobster's founder. Stockholders received one share of Darden Restaurants common stock for each share of General Mills common stock they held. In their last fiscal year under General Mills' auspices, Darden Restaurants' constituent units had combined net income of $108.3 million.

Investors failed to rally around Darden Restaurants, whose stock ended its first day of trading on the New York Stock Exchange below the $12 to $13 a share expected by analysts. One securities analyst said that the restaurants had been accounting for only one-quarter of General Mills' operating profits while absorbing half of the company's capital spending for expansion and renovation. Nevertheless, its market capitalization of $1.8 billion made it second in size only to McDonald's among the nation's publicly traded restaurant companies.

Darden Restaurants indicated in early 1996 that the China Coast experience would not keep it from trying other ethnic formats. In March of that year it began test marketing Bahama Breeze Caribbean Grille, with a menu drawn from Spanish, French, African, Dutch, Indian, and American influences. Entrees, priced between $5 and $15, were to include Bahamian conch chowder, slow-roasted ribs, Caribbean paella, jerk chicken, and rum-glazed yellowtail dolphin, washed down with Caribbean-island beer and other drinks. Lee predicted that, whether Bahama Breeze went into operation or not, Darden Restaurants would add at least two chains to its repertoire by 1998.

Darden Restaurants executives expressed confidence that they were on the right track toward long-term robust growth. Casual dining, according to the company, was the fastest-growing segment of the full-service restaurant market, with sales increasing at more than twice the overall market's rate since 1988 and representing, in 1995, 32 percent of full-service restaurant sales, or $29 billion. The trend toward casual dining, it argued, was reflected in the less formal dress code in the workplace and would continue in years to come. Moreover, the company noted that 40- to 60-year-olds were the most frequent visitors to casual dining restaurants, and that the population aged 45 and older was expected to grow by 40 million through 2010.

At the end of fiscal 1995, Darden Restaurants was operating 1,250 restaurants in every state except Alaska. A total of 73 were in Canada. Red Lobster restaurants were being remodeled, with weathered wood accented by nautical artifacts for a wharfside effect, to be completed by the end of fiscal 1997.

The Late 1990s and Beyond

Despite the company's positive outlook for the future, Darden Restaurants began to experience financial setbacks in 1997 due to market saturation. As such, the company was forced to shutdown some of its poor performing restaurants. Lee commented on the restructuring in a 1997 *Nation's Restaurant News* article claiming, ''There are some situations where we oversaturated and there were some areas where the market changed.'' The article also stated, ''Lee described the closings and write-offs as a strategic move to increase positive cash flow.'' By the end of the fiscal 1997, 48 restaurants were closed—including 26 outlets in Canada—and the firm posted a $91 million loss as a result of the restructuring charges.

Determined to get Darden Restaurants back on track, management focused on reviving the Red Lobster and Olive Garden chains and also eyeballed its Bahama Breeze concept to bolster sales. After its lackluster performance in 1997, the company rebounded and secured profits of $102 million in 1998. The following year, the company established the Culinary Institute of Tuscany in Italy. The facility was created to train Olive Garden chefs in an authentic Italian environment. New Red Lobster restaurants were opened with open floor plans and larger bar areas. Olive Garden restaurants also received a new look and were designed to resemble a Tuscan farmhouse. Darden Restaurants also began testing a new restaurant concept entitled Smokey Bones BBQ Sports Bar and opened its first unit in Orlando in late 1999. The restaurant could seat 300 and had a U-shaped bar in the center. Decorated similar to a mountain lodge, the outlet catered to sports fans with 40 televisions throughout the restaurant and monitors at each table.

Having successfully overcome the sluggish sales of 1996 and 1997, Darden began to actively pursue new store openings. By the end of 1999, there were 669 Red Lobster restaurants, 464 Olive Garden outlets, six Bahama Breeze units, and one Smokey Bones BBQ Sports Bar, and additional store openings were slated for the upcoming year. Profits for 1999 reached $140.5 million on revenues of $3.46 billion.

Darden Restaurants entered the new millennium on solid financial ground. Sales increased 7 percent over the previous year while earnings climbed to $173.1 million. During the year, Red Lobster and Olive Garden achieved their tenth and 23rd consecutive quarter of sales increases, respectively. The company as a whole recorded its 14th consecutive quarter of earnings increases. The company posted its best financial year to date in fiscal 2001. During the year, sales reached $4 billion, while earnings increased to $197 million. The number of Bahama Breeze restaurants rose to 21, while nine Smokey Bones were in operation—national expansion for the sports concept was scheduled to begin in 2002. In addition to its financial gains, the company was named by *Fortune* magazine as one of the top 50 companies for minorities for the third year in a row.

Darden's strategy for 2000 and beyond included a constant reviving of the Red Lobster and Olive Garden chains, expansion of existing new concepts, and the acquisition and development of new concepts. According to Darden, casual dining sales were projected to increase between 6 to 8 percent over the next ten years. Although the American economy began faltering in 2000, the company claimed that historically, the casual dining industry had weathered past economic downturns quite well and that sales had grown during the 1990–91 recession. As such, Darden management remained confident that the company would experience success in the years to come.

Principal Operating Units

Red Lobster; Olive Garden; Bahama Breeze; Smokey Bones BBQ Sports Bar.

Principal Competitors

Brinker International Inc.; Landry's Restaurant Inc.; Metromedia Company.

Further Reading

Carlino, Bill, ''Darden Gives Up on China Coast, Shutters Units,'' *Nation's Restaurant News,* September 4, 1995, pp. 1, 7.

——, ''Darden Is Watching Which Way Bahama Breeze Blows,'' *Nation's Restaurant News,* January 29, 1996, pp. 1, 53.

——, ''Jeffrey J. O'Hara,'' *Nation's Restaurant News,* October 9, 1995, pp. 176, 178.

——, ''William Darden,'' *Nation's Restaurant News,* February 1996, p. 68.

''Darden Expanding Four Chains,'' *Food Institute Report,* June 25, 2001, p. 2.

''Darden Posts FY '97 Loss of $91 Million After Restructuring,'' *Nation's Restaurant News,* June 30, 1997, p. 12.

''Darden Turns Olive Garden and Red Lobster Around,'' *Food Institute Report,* November 8, 1999.

''Darden Ups 2nd-Q Earnings As It Digs Out of Early Slump,'' *Nation's Restaurant News,* January 15, 1996, p. 12.

Gindin, Rona, and Richard L. Papiernik, ''Darden Tests More BBQ Units; Analysts Eye Strategic Growth,'' *Nation's Restaurant News,* March 20, 2000, p. 1.

Harris, John, ''Dinnerhouse Technology,'' *Forbes,* July 8, 1991, pp. 98–99.

Lavecchia, Gina, ''Bahama Mama,'' *Restaurant Hospitality,* November 1998, p. 64.

McGill, Douglas, ''Why They Smile at Red Lobster,'' *New York Times,* April 23, 1989, Sec. 3, pp. 1, 6.

Miller, Annette, and Karen Springen, ''Egg Rolls for Peoria,'' *Newsweek,* October 12, 1992, pp. 59–60.

Papiernik, Richard, ''Darden Faces Up to Its Problems, Finds Its Own Solutions,'' *Nation's Restaurant News,* March 31, 1997, p. 11.

——, ''New Stock Sparks Trades But No Wall Street Fireworks,'' *Nation's Restaurant News,* June 19, 1995, pp. 3–4.

Phalon, Richard, ''Amicable Divorce,'' *Forbes,* May 8, 1995, pp. 70, 74.

Ponti, James, ''A Guy Named Joe,'' *Orlando,* November 1995, pp. 32–39.

''Red Lobster Looking Abroad,'' *New York Times,* February 14, 1983, p. D3.

Romeo, Peter, and Scott Norvell, ''Looking Leeward,'' *Restaurant Business,* November 20, 1995, pp. 40, 44–46.

Saporito, Bill, ''When Business Got So Good It Got Dangerous,'' *Fortune,* April 2, 1984, pp. 61–62, 64.

—Robert Halasz
—update: Christina M. Stansell

Delhaize "Le Lion" S.A.

rue Osseghem 53
Molenbeek-St.-Jean
B-1080 Brussels
Belgium
Telephone: (+32) 2-412-21-11
Fax: (+320) 2-412-21-94
Web site: http://delhaize-le-lion.be

Public Company
Incorporated: 1867
Employees: 152,000
Sales: EUR 18.2 billion ($17.49 billion)(2000)
Stock Exchanges: Euronext Brussels New York
Ticker Symbol: DELB; DEG
NAIC: 445110 Supermarkets and Other Grocery (Except Convenience) Stores

Although based in Belgium, where it is one of that country's leading supermarket groups, Delhaize "Le Lion" SA is also the United States' sixth-largest supermarket group through its publicly listed Delhaize America subsidiary. Indeed, Delhaize America accounts for some 75 percent of the company's sales, which topped EUR 18 billion in 2000. The company operates under various store banners and formats, including nearly 1,200 Food Lion stores in the United States, Belgian banners Delhaize "Le Lion" Supermarket, AD Delhaize, Proxy Delhaize, Delhaize City, and Shop 'n' Go, for a sales network of more than 615 stores. The company is also active in eight other international markets, including Greece, through the Alfa-Beta chain; the Czech Republic and Slovakia, through subsidiary Delvita; Romania, through its part-ownership of Mega-Image; and Thailand, Indonesia, and Singapore. The company's total store holdings reached 2,310 stores at the end of 2000—with plans to open nearly 250 new stores by the end of 2001. Boosting the company's U.S. presence was the July 2000 completion of its acquisition of Hannaford Bros., a $3.3 billion chain operating in Delhaize's own core market of the eastern U.S. regions. Following that acquisition, Delhaize moved to acquire full control of Delhaize America, then listed that company separately on the New York Stock Exchange. The parent company is quoted on the Euronext Brussel exchange, while its Alfa-Beta subsidiary is quoted on the Athens market.

Putting Retail Theory into Practice in the Mid-1800s

Commercial sciences professor Jules Delhaize had developed his own theories about food retailing at the middle of the nineteenth century, and in 1867 he convinced his brother, Edouard and their brother-in-law Jules Vieujant, who were also teachers, to join him in putting his theories into practice. Delhaize was convinced that he could revolutionize Belgium's grocery trade by creating a network of branch stores supplied by a central warehouse, which would enable the company to eliminate the many middlemen involved in the grocery trade and cut down on costs. The company was then able to pass its savings onto its customers. Prices on store items, moreover, were to be clearly marked.

The Frères Delhaize company formed in Charleroi in 1867, adopting Belgium's lion crest as its own symbol. The company's name later incorporated its symbol, becoming Delhaize "Le Lion." The symbol was later to become one of Belgium's most well-known brands. The Delhaize name also contributed to the success of another of the Delhaize brothers, Adolphe, who founded his own network of stores around the same time. In 1883, the company, which had moved to Brussels soon after its founding, changed headquarters for facilities closer to the city's Gare de l'Ouest train station. Featuring then state-of-the-art warehousing facilities, as well as a school and fire brigade, the new site also gave the company a rail link, increasing its distribution capacity. At this time too, the company branched out into manufacturing, producing a range of goods under the Delhaize brand name, including chocolates and biscuits, coffee and spirits, and other products.

By the outbreak of World War I, Delhaize had expanded to a network of some 500 stores throughout Belgium. Following the war, the company sent representatives to the United States, where grocers were steadily introducing new innovations in areas such as store designs, displays, and service. The company's participation in international trade fairs enabled it to

Company Perspectives:

Delhaize will anticipate the wishes of its customers and satisfy them by providing them in each of its companies an easy, convenient and integrated shopping experience. Delhaize is a transnational provider of food and daily items, supplies and services, specialist of self-service, preferred for the quality of its products and retail concepts, recognized for achieving its ambitious goals and respected for the competence of its team and its high sense of ethics.

import new products for its stores. Yet, apart from expanding its network to include the Belgian Congo, the company continued to focus exclusively on its domestic market. The economic crisis surrounding the Depression Era encouraged the company to add a new store banner, Derby, featuring deep-discount products. Despite the troubled economic climate, Delhaize continued to prosper, expanding its branch network to nearly 750 stores at the outbreak of World War II. In addition, the company's strong distribution network and its various production facilities enabled it to build a second network of affiliated, yet independent stores.

Introducing Self-Service in the 1950s

Following World War II, the company shut down most of its manufacturing operations to focus its efforts on its retail and distribution activity. The company updated its wine and spirits warehouses, adopting innovations then being made in France. Delhaize grew externally in 1950, when the grocery chain founded by Adolphe Delhaize was merged into that founded by his brothers. That decade was to mark a revolution in the grocery industry, and the Delhaize company was to become one of the leaders in that revolution in Belgium.

The postwar reconstruction years had rapidly given way to a period of extended economic growth, particularly in Belgium, relatively unscathed by the war. The low unemployment levels, rising wages, growing leisure time, as well as technological innovations, both in the stores and in the home combined to encourage the growth of a new grocery format, the supermarket. More and more consumers were adding refrigerators and freezers at home, making it possible to preserve fresh foods for longer periods. The same was true for the stores themselves, which rapidly added fresh fruits and vegetables, meats and fish, and other perishable items. Delhaize had continued to study innovations being in made in the United States, which had pioneered the supermarket concept, and in 1957 the company opened Europe's first fully self-service supermarket. That supermarket incorporated a number of other features of the American supermarket, such as checkout counters, brightly colored stores, and fluorescent light fixtures.

Delhaize set about converting its network to the new supermarket format, a process that required a new distribution infrastructure, such as cold-storage facilities and the like. In order to finance the company's transformation, it took a listing on the Brussels stock exchange, changing its name to SA Delhaize Frères et Cie "Le Lion" in 1962. In 1963, the company added

chilled warehouse facilities for stocking and handling fresh fruits and vegetables and dairy products. In 1967, the company added its own butchering facilities to supply its new in-store butcher shops.

During the mid-to-late 1960s, the company continued converting its branch network, shutting down a number of its former grocery shops, opening supermarkets, while converting a number of its existing stores to small-format self-service stores. By the middle of the 1970s, the company's supermarket network had grown to 80 stores. Yet the company now faced the first of a series of so-called "padlock" laws that placed severe limits on the number of hypermarkets and supermarkets allowed to open in Belgium. Similar laws had begun to appear elsewhere in Europe, designed to protect small shopkeepers from being crushed by the small number of rapidly growing supermarket giants. Delhaize began developing other retail formats to circumvent the growth laws, launching its own chain of pharmacies and body care stores under the DI banner.

American Expansion in the 1970s

For its supermarket growth, Delhaize turned to a market where such restrictions were unlikely ever to appear—the United States. In 1974, the company made its first entry into that country, buying a one-third share of North and South Carolina-based Food Town Inc., which owned 22 supermarkets but had run out of cash for further expansion. Two years later, Delhaize acquired a majority share in that company. Food Town was to provide a springboard for the company's expansion in the United States. By 1983, the company had grown to more than 225 stores. In that year, Food Town changed its name to Food Lion, bringing it closer under Delhaize's wing.

In 1985, the company, which continued to target expansion in the markets on the eastern coast of the United States, opened its first Cub Foods store in Atlanta. The company later boosted its share of that market with the acquisition of the Food Giant chain. Meanwhile, back home, the company launched a new chain, called AD Delhaize. Rather than being company-owned, the stores affiliated with the new banner remained independent, with Delhaize providing wholesale supply services and management advice.

Delhaize continued to branch out through the end of the 1980s, particularly by launching two new retail formats. The first was Caddy Home, which offered home delivery services. The second was Tom & Co, which took the company beyond supermarkets into a retail pet foods and supplies format. These stores helped expand the company's holdings in Belgium to more than 400 stores—of which nearly 110 were supermarkets. Meanwhile, the company's United States' presence remained its driving force, with over 1,000 supermarkets under Food Lion's control by the beginning of the 1990s.

The 1990s saw Delhaize turn to an even wider international arena for its growth. The collapse of the Soviet Union and the subsequent opening up of the former Eastern Bloc countries presented Delhaize with an opportunity to expand into Central Europe. In 1991, the company launched a new subsidiary in the Czech Republic, Delvita, opening its first supermarket that year. The company's expansion in that country, and neighboring

Key Dates:

1867: Jules Delhaize sets up grocery branch network with brother Edouard and brother-in-law Jules Vieujant.
1871: The company moves to Brussels.
1883: Delhaize opens new state-of-the-art warehouse and headquarters facility.
1930: The company introduces Derby discount retail format.
1950: The company merges with grocery chain founded by Adolphe Delhaize.
1957: The company launches Europe's first fully self-service supermarket patterned after American supermarket concept.
1962: The company lists on Brussels stock exchange as SA Delhaize Frères et Cie.
1974: The company acquires 32 percent stake in Food Town Inc. (USA), with 22 stores in North and South Carolina.
1976: The company acquires majority control of Food Town Inc., begins rapid expansion in eastern United States, and launches DI health and beauty aid shops in Belgium.
1981: In Belgium, the company launches AD Delhaize affiliated store chain.
1983: Food Town renames itself Food Lion Inc., and now boasts 225 supermarkets.
1985: Delhaize opens first Cub Food store in Atlanta.
1989: Delhaize launches Caddy-Home, a home delivery service, and Tom & Co, pet foods and supplies stores in Belgium.
1992: The company acquires Alpha-Beta Vassilopoulos and enters Athens, Greece, market with 15 supermarkets.
1994: The company acquires majority share in France's PG chain, with 38 Shopi and 14 Marché Plus stores.
1996: The company acquires Florida's Kash n' Karry chain.
2000: Delhaize completes takeover of Hannaford; acquires full control of Food Lion Thailand; and acquires 51 percent of Mega-Image (Romania).
2001: Delhaize America becomes first Belgian company to take a listing on New York Stock Exchange.

Slovakia, was rapid—by 1992 the company had opened seven Delvita supermarkets.

Delhaize continued to explore new foreign markets, despite the economic downturn of the period. In 1991, the company acquired a majority share in Greece's Alpha-Beta Vassilopoulos, which operated 15 supermarkets in Athens and surrounding areas. Delhaize next looked to neighbor France, buying a controlling stake in the PG group, which operated supermarkets under the Stoc banner and a network of grocery affiliates under the Marché Plus name. Despite growing PG to 38 supermarkets and 14 affiliates by the end of the decade, Delhaize was forced to withdraw from the bruising competitive climate of the French market, selling out its stake in PG to Carrefour in 2000.

Worldwide Retailer in the 21st Century

The United States, however, continued to provide good fortune for Delhaize. In 1996, the company expanded again, now into the Florida market, with the acquisition of the Kash n' Karry chain. The following year, Delhaize targeted the other side of the world, setting up shop in Thailand and Indonesia. The company imported the Food Lion brand into Thailand, taking a stake in the new Food Lion Thailand and opening 15 stores—including the acquisition of six Sunny's stores—by the end of 1999. The following year, the company acquired full control of Food Lion Thailand. In Indonesia the company stores operated under the Super Indo banner, growing to 14 supermarkets by the end of the decade. At the same time, Delhaize moved into a new Asian market, Singapore, with the acquisition of 49 percent of that country's third-largest supermarket group Shop N Save.

In Central Europe, Delvita established itself as a major retailer in the Czech and Slovakia markets with the acquisition of Interkontakt and its 50 supermarkets. The 2000 acquisition of 51 percent of Romania's Mega-Image allowed the company to expand its presence in the region. In the United States, meanwhile, the company acquired the 28-store chain of Farmer Jack stores before announcing a far larger acquisition at the end of 1999.

That deal, which was closed in July 2000, called for Delhaize to acquire Hannaford Bros., a $3.3 billion company with 152 stores under the Hannaford and Shop N Save banners operating primarily in the northeastern United States but extending as far south as the Carolinas. At the same time, Delhaize announced its was setting up a new U.S. subsidiary company, Delhaize America, to group its growing U.S. holdings, including its 56 percent stake in Food Lion Inc. Hannaford was to remain a separately operating company under Delhaize America, signaling Delhaize's willingness to pursue further growth beyond the Food Lion banner, which, despite growing to nearly 1,200 stores, had been unable to extend its brand beyond its own core southeastern region. The Hannaford deal, which boosted the company's sales to EUR 18 billion by the end of 2000, made it the sixth-largest supermarket group in the United States market.

At the end of 2000, the company announced its intention to buy up full control of Food Lion Inc., a process completed in 2001. At that time, Delhaize America was floated on the New York stock exchange—the first Belgian company to achieve a listing on the NYSE main board. Despite the United States' overwhelming position in Delhaize's balance sheet—accounting for 70 percent of sales and some 85 percent of its cash flow—the company continued to assert itself as a retail leader in its home base. By the end of 2001, the company revealed plans to boost its Belgian presence to more than 650 stores by the year 2006. Supermarket growth, which continued to be tightly controlled by the Belgian government, was to represent only a minor part of that expansion, with just three new supermarkets planned. Instead, the company was banking on the successful rollout of three new small-store formats, the center-city Delhaize City stores; Shop n' Go, typically located next to filling stations and expected to grow to 50 outlets by 2003, and Proxy Delhaize—formerly known as Superettes Delhaize. With a position as a leader in both the United States and Belgium, and growing networks elsewhere, Delhaize seemed certain to carry on its founders' pioneering retail vision.

Principal Subsidiaries

Alfa-Beta Vassilopoulos, S.A. (Greece); Aniserco S.A.; Food Lion Thailand Ltd.; Delhome S.A.; Delanthuis S.A.; Delshop S.A.; Delvita A.S. (Czech Republic); Delhaize America, Inc.; P.T. Super Indo Jl (Indonesia); Super Discount Markets, Inc. (U.S.); Shop N Save Pte Ltd (Singapore).

Principal Competitors

Carrefour SA; Metro AG; Albertsons Inc; Koninklijke Ahold Nv; Aldi AG; Pathmark Stores, Inc; RALLYE S.A.; Safeway Inc.; Auchan Group;Arden Group Inc; Eagle Food Ctrs Inc.; Frsh Fresh Brands Inc; Foodarama Supermarkets Inc; Gristedes Sloans Inc; The Kroger Co; Winn Dixie Stores Inc; Wal-Mart Corporation.

Further Reading

Carreyrou, John, ''Belgium's Delhaize Rises Its Bid to Buy Rest of American Unit It Doesn't Own,'' *Wall Street Journal*, November 17, 2000, p. B6.

''Delhaize 'Le Lion' Buys US Supermarket Chain Hannaford,'' *Eurofood*, August 26, 1999.

''Delhaize wil tegen 2006 650 voodingsverkooppunten,'' *De Financieel Economische Tijd*, June 27, 2001.

Domby, Daniel, ''Belgian Retailer Reports Lower 2000 Profits,'' *Financial Times,* March 16, 2001.

Downey, John, and Lori Johnston, ''Smaller Role for Food Lion in Expansion,'' *Business Journal*, August 20, 1999.

Frederick, James, ''Food Lion Plans Pharmacy Test in Midst of Big Expansion Program,'' *Drug Store News*, March 20, 2000.

Mitchell, Sue, ''Food Lion's Local Links Uprooted by Foreign Buyer,'' *Business Journal*, December 1, 2000.

—M.L. Cohen

Denby Group plc

Derby Road
Denby, Derbyshire DE5 8NX
United Kindgom
Telephone: (+44) 1773 740 799
Web site: http://www.denby.co.uk

Private Company
Employees: 707
Sales: £35.6 million ($50.82 million) (2000)
NAIC: 32711 Vitreous China, Fine Earthenware, and
    Other Pottery Product Manufacturing

Denby Group plc is the holding company for its two subsidiaries: Denby Pottery Company Ltd. and Denby USA Ltd. Denby Pottery, based through its 200-year history in Derbyshire, U.K., is primarily a maker of tableware designed for both casual and formal dining. Because it has included color, shape, and texture in its designs, it has earned a reputation for distinctness and has set itself apart from competitors that only stress pattern in their tableware design. In the UK, Denby operates six Factory Shops at outlet centers spread out from Sterling Mills in Scotland to Clarks Village in Somerset, and at its Visitor Centre in Denby also maintains a complex that, in addition to shops, includes a Cookery Emporium and museum. Denby also has a strong export trade, and in the United States distributes its products through its New Jersey-based subsidiary, Denby USA Ltd. The company, after having undergone several changes in ownership in the 1980s and 1990s, was acquired by its present owners through a 1999 management buyout backed by Phildrew Ventures, one of the U.K.'s leading management buyout specialists. The buyout returned the company to private ownership.

A Maker of Functional and Decorative Stoneware

The history of Denby Pottery begins in 1806, the year in which William Bourne, the company's founder, was called on to examine a large clay deposit unearthed when workers were building a turnpike road between Alfreton and Derby in Derbyshire, a shire in a section of England rich in clay and coal deposits. At the time, London, Nottingham, and Derbyshire were the principal centers of the country's pottery trade, producing both decorative salt glazed stoneware and more common and ordinary utilitarian containers. At the time he examined the new found clay, Bourne was a potter at the nearby Belper Pottery. He at once recognized the high quality and promise of the clay, and he began making plans to open a family pottery at the site of the discovery in Denby.

Bourne set up the new pottery in 1809, but rather than run it himself, he gave the task to his youngest son, Joseph, who was just in his early 20s at the time. The pottery was thus named Joseph Bourne. William's faith in his son was well placed, for Joseph, operating from some small buildings at the clay bed site, soon had the new business thriving. Within a fairly short time, the pottery gained an international reputation for making quality stoneware.

At the time the Bournes founded the business, stoneware was a ubiquitous commodity, in wide use and more common than glass, which was still expensive to make. People used clay pots and other clay containers for holding and storing or preserving foods and such other items as ink and polish. Joseph Bourne was not just a copyist, however; he was an innovator as well, and over the years he patented many of his methods for firing pottery in the salt glazing kilns then in use.

Salt glazing was a common technique used for decorating stoneware in the 19th century. The method involved putting pieces on kiln embers when the maximum temperature was reached. In the process, salt vapor coated the stone ware and produced a glossy brown surface, the sort of coating still seen on earthenware bean pots.

During the next half century, the pottery at Denby continued to grow and prosper. It also remained a family enterprise. Sarah Elizabeth Bourne took charge of the pottery in 1869, when her husband, Joseph Harvey Bourne, died at a fairly early age. She would head the company for the next 30 years. During her tenure, the Denby pottery produced commercial and domestic pottery, still making salt glazed bottles and jars. It was during the later part of the century that glass became much cheaper to produce, making glass bottles less expensive than stoneware

---

Company Perspectives:

Today's entertaining is all about relaxing with friends, and Denby helps you drop the formalities. Distinctive designs and sophisticated colours help you create just the right atmosphere, and reflect your own personal taste. And why shouldn't you have the satisfaction of using quality products everyday? Denby tableware is exceptionally versatile and durable, and safe for use in the dishwasher, oven, microwave and freezer, giving years of continual use.

---

containers. The competition from glass companies forced potteries to diversify, to turn away from such old staples as ordinary earthenware bottles and jugs to produce other kinds of kitchenware as well as ornamental or decorative pieces. One key to the change involved a new technology for making color glazes. Early experiments with such glazes took place at Denby in the 1880s, still under the guidance of Sarah Bourne. In 1886, Denby started producing its Majolica pottery, its first color-glazed line.

Joseph Harvey and Sarah Bourne had no children, but each had a nephew, and upon Sarah's death in 1898, the two nephews assumed control of the business. They jointly managed the pottery through the first few years of the new century.

Denby Adapts to the New Century

After Sarah's nephew withdrew from the business in 1907, Joseph Bourne Wheeler, Joseph's nephew, assumed sole proprietorship and control of the business. Until 1916, he ran it as his aunt and grandfather had before him, but in that year the firm was reorganized into a limited liability company with Bourne as governing director. It was a position he held until his death in 1942.

Because glassware had all but replaced stoneware for the utility of storing both foods and other items, through the first half of the 20th century Denby concentrated on making kitchenware, art, and decorative ware. The company installed new kilns and adapted new glazing techniques. It also developed lines of kitchenware, including Cottage Blue and Manor Green, destined to become classics and remain in production for several decades.

By the 1920s, Denby's was producing functional kitchenware found in homes throughout the British Isles, including everything from pie dishes and jelly molds to colanders and hot water jugs. The company also made "Danesby Ware," decorative vases, bowls, and tobacco jars, all stamped with that trademark. It continued to produce such pieces through the next decade as well, but some of its new lines of kitchenware, like Cottage Blue and Manor Green, had become more colorful. It also produced giftware lines that would later attract collectors, especially Electric Blue and Orient ware.

During World War II, limited in what they could obtain in the way of glazing stains, Denby produced only one line. It was dubbed "Utility Brown," and it turned out many teapots and large bottles for use by servicemen. It also made industrial ware, including telegraph insulators. However, as soon as the war

ended, Denby quickly returned to its peacetime business, making lines of very successful tableware that helped enhance the company's reputation for making quality products. It also made a fine line of jugs, bowls, and chargers called Glynware in honor of their designer.

During the 1950s, the company made some major changes in its product line, becoming primarily a producer of tableware and placing far less emphasis on giftware. Its lines included cups, saucers, and plates. It continued to employ highly skilled designers, who, during the decade, produced such best-selling patterns as Greenwheat and Echo and Ode. Also, for the first time, Denby entered the U.S. market in the 1950s.

In the 1960s, the company continued to turn out excellent tableware sets, including Studio and Arabesque (renamed Samarkand in the United States). At the same time, the pottery placed increasingly less emphasis on giftware, although it would continue to make such items for the next couple of decades. However, through the 1960s, Denby concentrated on tableware design and expansion into overseas markets.

Denby Goes Public and Undergoes Ownership Changes

Denby held to the same focus throughout the 1970s. This period brought a revolution in oven-proof tableware, which allowed items to serve both as cooking and serving containers. The pottery designed and turned out pieces that could withstand high oven temperatures but were also handsome enough to grace most any dining table. Popular designs dating from the early 70s included Gypsy, Romany, and Troubadour Cotswold. During the same period, Denby underwent some significant changes in its organization and marketing strategies. In 1970, for example, it acquired its first U.S. distributing agent. That same year it also went public and floated its first stock offering on the London Stock Exchange.

By the early 1980s, the appeal of casual dining had notably increased in Denby's markets, hence a key to design for its pottery became adaptability to both formal and informal dining. Lines such as Imperial Blue and Regency Green filled that need for flexibility and sold well. However, the 1980s were rough years for Denby. The company made some acquisitions that simply did not pan out, and the result was that Denby faltered, moving in and out of the marketplace three times. What suffered most was the company's U.S. market.

In 1981, Crown House Engineering acquired Denby by purchasing the company's stock. Under its new owners, the company focused primarily on tableware and cookware. In the Crown House group, Denby was just one of several sister tableware companies, including Edinburgh Crystal, Thomas Webb Crystal, Dema Glass, and George Butler Cutlery. Unfortunately for the pottery, Crown House made no significant investment in Denby, and the result was that Denby lost its market leadership and product design initiatives.

Until 1987, Denby Tableware had is own subsidiary in America, but in that year Denby was acquired by Coloroll, another U.K.-based company, and the distribution of its pottery in the United States. was undertaken by Georges Briard, and, thereafter, in the fall of 1989, by Cuthbertson Imports. The

Key Dates:

1806: Clay seam is discovered during road construction at Denby.

1809: William Bourne oversees startup of salt-glazed pottery production and assigns his son, Joseph, the task of running the new business, then known as Joseph Bourne.

1832: Customs & Excise records list Denby as the largest producer of jars and bottles in Britain.

1841: The approximate year in which company is renamed Joseph Bourne & Son.

1860: Joseph's son, Joseph Harvey Bourne, assumes control of the pottery.

1869: Sarah Elizabeth Bourne, widow to Joseph Harvey Bourne, assumes operational control of business.

1898: Sarah's two nephews form a partnership and begin running company after her death.

1907: Partnership dissolves and Joseph Bourne Wheeler assumes sole control of the company.

1942: Joseph Bourne Wheeler dies.

1981: Crown House Engineering acquires Denby.

1987: Coloroll plc. acquires Denby from Crown House Engineering.

1990: Denby's management, backed by three investors, buys out the company as Coloroll goes into receivership; TamCon and Co. is made Denby's exclusive U.S. distributor.

1994: Company goes public and is floated on the London Stock Exchange.

1995: Company acquires Wren, a mug manufacturer.

1998: Company divests Wren.

1999: Another management buyout returns the company to private ownership, and the company is restructured as holding company with two subsidiaries.

confusion that resulted from these changes did not help Denby's reputation.

Denby Undergoes More Changes in Ownership

In June 1990, Coloroll went into receivership and began selling off the companies making up the conglomerate's group. Denby's Tableware was purchased by its own management, backed by 3i, an investment capital group, and was renamed Denby Pottery Co. Ltd. Denby's managing director, Stephen Riley, and three associates, invested £140,000 for a 55 percent stake in the company, while 3i held the balance. At the time, Riley indicated that the company would continue to produce and supply the company's tableware, giftware, and lighting products.

Although it had become an independent company, Denby Pottery had the same management that it previously had while in the Coloroll group. However, Riley believed that the firm's independence would help it improve its service. Among other things, Denby assigned to another company, Morristown, New Jersey-based TamCon and Co., the exclusive U.S. distributorship of its products. Chuck Thompson, who had founded

TamCon to market fine European home furnishing lines in the U.S., was determined to grow the distribution of Denby's line. TamCon began maintaining a large inventory of Denby products in its warehouse in New Jersey for distribution through its dealer network. It also began looking for new marketing channels, targeting upscale department and specialty stores across the country. The company was also renamed Denby Pottery USA, with Thompson at its helm as president and CEO. Its mission statement, provided by the company, has been "to uphold the reputation of Denby Pottery Company in England by supplying the demanding American consumers with quality, innovative, and contemporary casual ware that reflects their changing lifestyle."

In 1994, Denby again went public and floated a public stock offering sponsored by Robert Fleming & Co. By that time, Denby's sales, since the 1990 buyout, had grown at an average annual rate of 25 percent, reaching £17.5 million in 1993. Furthermore, the company's pre-tax profits increased at a rate of 70 percent, and in that same year had grown to £2.75 million. Denby's plan was to use the proceeds from the sale of stock to pay off a £7 million debt, fund capital improvements, and finance overseas expansion. Specifically, the company wanted to expand its sales in North America and France.

By the mid 1990s, Denby Pottery had again emerged as one of the leading makers of casual china. It had also begun expanding not just its markets, but also its product line. In 1995, it purchased Wren Giftware, a five-year-old manufacturer of bone china cups. Denby put up an initial £1.3 million for Wren, which, at its facility in Stoke-on-Trent, employed just over 100 workers. Over the 12 months preceding its acquisition, Wren had reached £1.8 million in sales.

By 1995, Denby's export trade had also grown significantly, reaching £8.13 million or 32 percent of its total sales. Its greatest showing was in the United States, where its sales reached £3.6 million, a 120 percent increase over the previous year. At the beginning of 1996, Denby's lines in the United States were being sold in 873 department-store outlets and 881 independent stores. The company was also doing well in Canada, Australia, and Scandinavia. It had also entered a new market, in Japan, with promising initial sales. By 1996, partly as a result of its increasing foreign sales, Denby held nearly 10 percent of its casual china market niche, a strong showing considering the large number of competitors in that segment. Overall, it ranked fourth in the casual china market, tied with Lenox, but behind Mikasa, the Wedgewood Group, and Noritake.

Denby's performance was in part credited to the superb design and value of its line. It had diligently worked to distance itself from competitors by its quality and lifestyle-conscious design. The company's design signature was the color, shape, and texture of its ware rather than pattern. It also limited its lines to just 10 patterns, unlike competitors that typically introduced upwards of 20 patterns annually. At the same time, Denby did not enter any pricing wars with competitors. Its non-promotional, regularly priced line at retail outlets sold for between $85 and $105 for a five-piece setting, a hefty price tag more typical of formal bone china than casual dinnerware. However, at least in the United States, the cost did not seem to deter upscale department store customers.

Through the remainder of the 1990s, Denby made substantial investments in capital improvements. Among other things, it refurbished its facilities and upgraded equipment. Although still using ''hand-throwing'' techniques and skills, it also adopted state-of-the-art ceramic technology. Adjacent to the pottery, the company also opened its Visitor Centre complex which, in short order, became a major tourist attraction that by the end of the century was hosting 300,000 visitors a year.

However, in the latter part of the decade, sales in the company's market were generally in a slump, and even though Denby's sales were solid, its stock value steadily declined, and Denby had to take some major measures to buoy up its performance. Among other things, in 1998 it sold Wren Giftware to Churchill China for £875,000. Then, in 1999, through another management buyout, the company returned to the private sector and reorganized as Denby Group plc, a holding company with two subsidiaries: Denby Pottery Co. Ltd. and Denby USA Ltd. The MBO was backed by Phildrew Ventures, a British venture capital firm. Towards the close of 2000, in a strategy move designed to update its image, Denby Pottery began a major, £500,000 advertising campaign, featuring a new logo and an upbeat theme: ''Today's entertaining is all about relaxing with friends, and Denby helps you drop the formalities.'' It was hoped that the new push would help restore the company's good reputation and drive its sales to new levels.

Principal Subsidiaries

Denby Pottery Co. Ltd.; Denby USA Ltd.

Principal Competitors

Brown-Foreman Corporation; Mikasa, Inc.; Noritake Co., Limited; The Pfaltzgraff Co.; Waterford Wedgewood plc.

Further Reading

Belmont, David J. ''Denby Targets U.S. with New Products,'' *HFD-The Weekly Home Furnishings Newspaper*, December 26, 1994, p. 38.

''Denby,'' *Investors Chronicle*, December 15, 1995, p. 68.

Hopwood, Irene and Gordon, *Denby Pottery, 1809–1997: Dynasties and Designers*, Ilminster, Somerset, U.K.: Richard Dennis Publishers, 1997.

Hunter-Gadsden, Leslie, ''TamCom Gets Denby Rights: Set As Sole U.S. Distributor of English Stoneware Line,'' *HFN The Weekly Newspaper for Home Furnishing Network*, August 6, 1990, p. 57.

Kehoe, Ann-Margaret, ''Denby Blazing a Path in China: Niche Vendor Grabs Its Share of Casual Market,'' *HFN The Weekly Newspaper for Home Furnishing Network*, September 2, 1996, p. 35.

—John W. Fiero

Dillingham Construction Corporation

5960 Inglewood Drive
Pleasanton, California 94588-8535
U.S.A.
Telephone: (925) 463-3300
Fax: (925) 847-7029
Web site: http://www.dillinghamconstruction.com

Private Company
Incorporated: 1961
Employees: 8,000
Operating Revenues: $1.2 billion (2000)
NAIC: 23321 Single Family Housing Construction;
23322 Multifamily Housing Construction; 23332
Commercial and Institutional Building Construction;
23411 Highway and Street Construction; 23499 All
Other Heavy Construction; 23599 All Other Special
Trade Contractors

Dillingham Construction Corporation operates as a worldwide construction firm involved in the commercial, industrial, heavy civil, and marine industries. Through its subsidiaries, Dillingham provides general construction, design/build, construction management, maintenance, and emergency response services. Its construction projects have included shopping centers, theaters, office buildings, condominiums and subdivisions, power generating plants, water treatment plants, ports and harbors, airports, highways, bridges, dams, tunnels, and rapid transit projects. The firm's customers include AT&T, International Paper Co., Las Vegas Hilton Corp., NASA, Pacific Gas & Electric Co.; San Francisco National Airport, the U.S. Department of State, and the U.S. Navy.

The Dillingham company was established in the Hawaiian islands when they were still an independent kingdom known as the Sandwich Islands. As the Hawaiian economy grew, Dillingham expanded from sugar refining and railroad transportation into construction. By the time the company reverted to private ownership in 1983, it had become one of the largest construction companies in the United States, with numerous projects completed worldwide.

Dillingham in the 1800s

Among the first Americans to settle in the Sandwich Islands were a group of New England missionaries, who arrived in 1820. They established themselves in positions of economic and political power, and began a crusade to convert the Polynesian natives to Christianity. From this group of *haole* (Caucasian) settlers emerged five dominant family-run mercantile companies known as ''The Big Five.'' These five companies established commercial interests in every aspect of the Hawaiian economy.

It was in this environment that Benjamin Franklin Dillingham unexpectedly found himself in 1865. Dillingham, a Cape Cod schooner captain, was stranded in the Sandwich Islands after losing his life's savings in a failed commercial venture to ship bananas to California. Temporarily disabled with a broken leg, Dillingham took a job as a clerk in a local hardware store, and within two years the enterprising seaman had become co-owner of the business.

Dillingham married into the *haole* establishment by taking a missionary's daughter for his wife. Still, he was unable to purchase arable land for an agricultural venture; the Big Five maintained a strict monopoly on land. He did, however, manage to buy a tract of wasteland on the island of Oahu. He organized a group of investors to develop the land for sugar cane cultivation, and built a railroad to connect the inland plantation with a wharf. The Oahu Railway & Land Company, as it became known, was highly successful. The company added more real estate and expanded its trackage—Dillingham even started to transport his competitors' sugar.

The native Queen Liliuokalani was deposed in 1893, and a year later the Republic of Hawaii was established with Sanford B. Dole as its president (Dole's cousin Jim founded the Dole pineapple label in 1898). Dillingham gained greater acceptance in the commercial establishment, and attempted to build a second railway on the island of Hawaii. But construction costs mounted quickly, and soon the company was severely in debt.

Company Perspectives:

Dillingham Construction is an employee-owned, worldwide contractor providing construction and engineering solutions that generate the highest level of customer satisfaction, shareholder returns, and employee opportunities. We strive towards integrity in all business activities, continuous improvement of company and individual performance, respect and care for the environment in which we work, and equal opportunity and empowerment to promote employee performance, growth, and mutually beneficial long-term relationships. Quality is our signature, excellence is our goal.

Benjamin Dillingham summoned his son Walter to interrupt his studies at Harvard and return to Hawaii to manage the crisis.

Development and Expansion: 1902 through the 1950s

Hawaii was annexed by the United States in 1898 and made a territory two years later. The islands' increased exposure to American shipping traffic led Walter Dillingham to establish a new family venture; with a $5000 loan, he founded the Hawaiian Dredging & Construction Company in 1902. The company's first contract called for the dredging of Honolulu Harbor and Pearl Harbor and, by 1910, had generated enough profit to bring the company out of debt. The coral and sediment drawn from the harbors was used to fill a 5000-acre swamp on the island of Oahu, which made possible a Dole pineapple plantation, a tourist development (later known as Waikiki Beach), and, some years later, an airport.

Dillingham's company diversified into pier services, warehousing, barge transportation, and land development. After the Japanese bombing of Pearl Harbor in 1941, the company joined a 14-member consortium of construction companies whose job it was to build air bases on islands captured from the Japanese.

After the war, Dillingham's companies performed construction work in foreign countries. It was involved in widening the Suez Canal, constructing a harbor in Kuwait, and building a variety of structures in Australia. In the United States, Hawaiian Dredging maintained harbors in the Pacific and established a strong presence in the mainland construction industry. The company's principal owner, Walter Dillingham, became one of the richest men in Hawaii by the late 1950's. Dillingham's success, however, did not go unchallenged.

For many years the mainland Permanente Cement Company enjoyed a monopoly in Hawaii. Its proprietor, an outspoken 72-year old entrepreneur named Henry J. Kaiser, had done a great deal of business with Dillingham. But, when Dillingham decided to participate in establishing a local competitor, Kaiser returned the challenge. He announced plans to build a cement plant in the islands and, furthermore, to establish a dredging business in Hawaii. The conflict between Kaiser and Dillingham degenerated into personal attacks, and Kaiser accused Dillingham of disrupting his business with underhanded tactics. Dillingham called Kaiser an "outsider," and maintained that he had no business being in Hawaii.

Dillingham found itself at the fore of a disturbing trend: Hawaiian markets were no longer isolated from mainland interests. The local establishment was forced to adopt more aggressive business strategies in order to maintain its historical competitive advantages. On many levels Hawaiian businesses banded together in self-interest. Walter Dillingham served on the boards of five major companies, including a newspaper and the Bank of Hawaii. Later, he was appointed to the board of American Factors (a Big Five sugar and real estate conglomerate called Amfac). Dillingham opposed statehood for Hawaii because he felt the islands would be dominated by the International Longshoremen's and Warehousemen's Union, which he believed was controlled by communists. (In 1949 the union led a strike which paralyzed the Hawaiian economy for 179 days.) In 1959, as Dillingham began to emerge as the victor in its battles with Kaiser, Hawaii was inducted as the 50th state.

The Dillingham Corporation: 1961

Walter Dillingham gradually relinquished managerial responsibilities to his son Lowell. Only one philosophy course short of a degree from Harvard, Lowell returned to Hawaii in 1934 to learn every aspect of the family business. He was named president of Hawaiian Dredging in 1955, and of the Oahu Railway in 1960. In 1961 he oversaw the merger of his two companies to form the Dillingham Corporation, and the transformation of the family business into a public company.

The company began construction of buildings in 1959. One of its largest projects was the $30 million Ala Moana Center, a large shopping complex which nearly doubled the amount of store space in downtown Honolulu. Having decided that the company should pursue a more global perspective, Lowell Dillingham initiated the "Dilco" plan, under which Dillingham would aggressively seek new projects outside of Hawaii. As a result of the program, Dillingham won contracts to build the 43-story Wells Fargo Building in San Francisco, water works in Vietnam, a large hotel in the Philippines, airfields in Thailand, and numerous other structures in Australia. Dillingham also performed harbor improvements in Iran and established a group of seven subsidiaries in Australia, New Zealand, and Papua New Guinea.

The Dilco plan proved enormously successful—profits had risen from $48 million in 1962 to $325 million in 1968. While the Dillingham family was undoubtedly the greatest beneficiary of this growth (they retained 41% ownership of the company), private investors also found Dillingham an excellent investment. After Dillingham gained a listing on the Pacific Exchange, management strived to expand even further in anticipation of a second listing on the larger New York Exchange.

In order to spur growth through diversification, Dillingham acquired two large California-based construction companies, a supplier of liquefied petroleum gas, and a Canadian tug boat company. Dillingham also entered into joint ventures in mining in Canada and Australia but failed in its attempt to gain control of the United Fruit Company. Herbert C. Cornuelle, a former president of both United Fruit and the Dole Corporation, joined Dillingham as an executive vice-president. Cornuelle later became the first non-family executive to serve as company president.

Key Dates:

1902: Walter Dillingham establishes the Hawaiian Dredging & Construction Company.

1934: Lowell Dillingham becomes involved in the family business.

1959: The company enters the building construction industry.

1961: With Lowell as president, Hawaiian Dredging and Oahu Railway merge to form Dillingham Construction.

1968: Profits rise to $325 million.

1970: At this point in its history, Dillingham has acquired over 30 companies.

1983: Dillingham is taken private in a $350 million leveraged buyout led by Kohlberg Kravis Roberts & Co.

1985: Dillingham secures its first contract from the U.S. State Department.

1986: Kohlberg begins selling off parts of the Dillingham companies.

1987: Shimizu Construction Company Ltd. purchases a 45 percent stake in Dillingham Construction.

1990: Revenues reach $930 million.

1992: The firm partners with Obayashi Corp. to construct part of a $8.3 billion supercollider project in Texas.

1997: Subsidiary Nielsen Dillingham Builders constructs the shell of the building that will house the National Ignition Facility, the world's largest laser.

1998: Subsidiary Dillingham Construction Pacific builds a bilge and oily waste facility at the Pearl Harbor Naval Complex in Hawaii.

2000: Dillingham's sales reach $1.2 billion.

The diversification program encountered problems when it was realized that the company had grown too fast for effective consolidation or efficient management. By 1970, Dillingham had acquired over 30 companies and, while revenues increased 1,000 percent, return on equity fell by 3.9 percent. As president, Cornuelle had the dual task of raising short-term profits while maintaining the company's expansion. He elected to dispense with all marginally performing assets, and to invest the proceeds in more profitable maritime and natural resource ventures—areas more closely related to Dillingham's established operations. While Dillingham was made more competitive as a result of Cornuelle's strategy, because its new profits had not been used to reduce its debt, the company unknowingly became vulnerable to a hostile takeover.

Takeover Attempts and Privatization in the 1980s

A controversial financier named Harry Weinberg announced that he had acquired a 10 percent interest in Dillingham. Weinberg demanded representation on the board of directors, complaining that Dillingham's stock was undervalued and that the company's real estate holdings had been under-exploited. Cornuelle responded by reducing the number of board seats from 15 to three. With the situation deadlocked, Weinberg later agreed to purchase some of Dillingham's most promising real estate. Ownership of these properties, which included the Ala

Moana Center, was transferred to a limited partnership owned by Weinberg and a group of other shareholders. The partnership later split up the portfolio and sold the properties at a substantial premium over its original investment in Dillingham.

Cornuelle's takeover defense was successful, but Dillingham had lost its most profitable division. In order to support the company's share price, Dillingham's other three divisions—construction, maritime operations, and energy—would have to become more profitable. Management was particularly optimistic about expansion of the energy division, which conducted oil and gas exploration, produced liquefied petroleum gas, and transported oilfield equipment.

Share prices, however, remained weak and, as Dillingham was failing to gain the attention of investors on Wall Street, the company became the apparent target of another takeover. Kuo International, a Singapore-based company run by petroleum interests, announced in 1983 that it had increased its holdings in Dillingham to 7 percent. Unable to mount a second defense without seriously dismembering the company, Dillingham turned to the investment banking firm Kohlberg Kravis Roberts & Company (KKR) for advice. KKR recommended that Dillingham return to private ownership; as a private company, it would no longer be subject to hostile takeovers or share performance evaluations. A group of institutional investors was created to purchase all of Dillingham's outstanding shares of $350 million (including $30 million for Harry Weinberg's interest). Dillingham management retained a 12 percent interest in this group and appointed J. Joseph Casey president and chief executive officer. Casey emphasized Dillingham's expertise in construction, and encouraged greater involvement in higher-risk projects. While this shift in emphasis was expected to incur larger debts in the short term, it provided the company with greater operational mobility.

In 1986, however, KKR began selling off the Dillingham companies. The construction business, which was operating at the time as the 15th-largest construction firm in the U.S.—was sold to SC-US Inc., a subsidiary of Japan's largest construction firm, Shimizu Construction Company Ltd. Shimizu took a 45 percent stake in Dillingham and the remainder was sold to the firm's management and employees. The deal was unprecedented for the construction industry; it marked the first time that a Japanese concern had acquired a large interest in a U.S.-based construction firm.

With Donald K. Stager acting as company president, Dillingham began selling off assets to relieve its debt load. During the late 1980s, the firm recorded losses due to a downturn in the industry and unprofitable projects. Its Canadian subsidiary was sold, along with some of its Guam operations. In order to cut costs, the company moved headquarters from San Francisco to Pleasanton, California, and cut 200 jobs.

Overcoming Hardships: 1990s

Dillingham recorded profits in 1990 when revenues reached $930 million and managed to stay in the black the following year when revenues fell to $770 million. A reoccurring downturn in the industry, brought on by a weakening U.S. economy, was named a culprit in the significant drop in revenues. As such,

Dillingham began focusing strong efforts on international growth while continuing to seek out lucrative domestic projects.

In 1992, the firm partnered with Obayashi Corp. to build a 2.7 mile section of the 54-mile, $8.5 billion supercollider project in Texas, which was developed to allow scientists to observe and study subatomic particles. By this time, Dillingham was also involved in a $860 million project to construct a six-lane freeway in Turkey and was beginning to bid on projects in Japan. The firm had become well-known for its construction projects, including the Hyatt in San Francisco, the ValleyCare Medical Center in its hometown of Pleasanton, the Hyatt Regency Waikoloa in Hawaii, the Scripps Clinic in San Diego, and for its work on the Los Angeles Metro Rail project as well as the Hawaii Deep Water program.

While some of Dillingham's subsidiaries won bids for lucrative projects during the late 1990s, others were hurt by a faltering Hawaiian and Asian economy. In 1997, Nielsen Dillingham Builders Inc. landed a contract to construct the framing, metal deck flooring, roofing, and metal siding of the National Ignition Facility, a laser complex home to the world's largest laser. Hawaiian Dredging Construction Company, however, recorded a 36.5 drop in 1997 earnings due to weak demand in Hawaii's construction industry. The subsidiary did manage to secure a $11.1 million contract to build a bilge and oily waste collection and processing facility at the Pearl Harbor Naval Complex. Dillingham's operations in Asia also dropped off, as the economy in that region became unstable.

By the time Dillingham entered the new millennium, the construction company had been involved in projects around the world. Through its commercial construction services, it had erected over 60 shopping centers and retail outlets; 41 theaters, stadiums, and amusement parks; 26 million square-feet of enclosed office space; 95 hotels and resorts; 86 high-rise condominiums and apartment buildings; and 64 single family and townhome residential subdivisions. By way of its industrial construction services, Dillingham had built 100 power generating plants, 43 water treatment plants, 38 industrial storage facilities, and had been involved in ten hydroelectric projects and 95 petroleum industry-related projects. The company had also constructed 120 ports and harbors, secured 42 dredging contracts, built 128 airports and air bases, 546 bridges, 134 miles of tunnels, and 1,500 miles of highway.

Sales in fiscal 2000 reached $1.2 billion, an increase of 4.3 percent over the previous year. While Dillingham's profits were directly related to the strength of the economies in which it operated, the company appeared well positioned to continue its 100-plus year tradition of overcoming hardships while maintaining growth efforts and securing lucrative contracts.

Principal Subsidiaries

Dillingham Construction International Inc.; Dillingham Construction N.A. Inc.; Hawaiian Bitumuls Paving & Precast Company; Hawaiian Dredging Construction Company; Nielsen Dillingham Builders Inc.; Watkins Engineers & Constructors Inc.

Principal Competitors

Bechtel Group Inc.; Peter Kiewit Sons' Inc.; Washington Group International Inc.

Further Reading

Dillingham Construction Corporation, ''About Us,'' Pleasanton, Calif.: Dillingham Construction Corporation, 2001.

''Dillingham Wins $15M Pearl Harbor Contract,'' *Superfund Week*, September 4, 1998.

''Japanese Concern Buying Dillingham,'' *New York Times,* May 29, 1987, p. D4.

''Mitsubishi Cement in Guam Deal,'' *Financial Times London,* July 13, 1990, p. 27.

''Nielsen Dillingham Builders Inc.: Building the Best in San Diego, Western States and Baja California,'' *San Diego Business Journal,* December 18, 2000, p. 35.

Paiva, Derek, ''Arrested Development,'' *Hawaii Business,* November 1998, p. 13.

Pelline, Jeff, ''Pleasanton Builder Goes High-Profile,'' *San Francisco Chronicle,* February 28, 1992, p. B1.

—update: Christina M. Stansell

Drake Beam Morin, Inc.

100 Park Avenue, 11th Floor
New York, New York 10017
U.S.A.
Telephone: (212) 692-7700
Fax: (212) 297-0426
Web site: http://www.dbm.com

Wholly Owned Subsidiary of Thomson Corporation
Founded: 1967 as Drake, Beam and Associates
Employees: 1,100
Sales: $220 million (1999 est.)
NAIC: 62431 Vocational Rehabilitation Services

Drake Beam Morin, Inc. is a world-wide leader in human resource services. The company is best known for so-called outplacement consulting. Firms that are terminating large numbers of employees call on Drake Beam Morin (DBM) to ease the transition and help these employees find new jobs. The company offers career counseling, personal and professional coaching, and provides office space to laid-off workers during their job search. DBM also consults with client companies on other human resource issues, such as employee hiring and retention as well as executive pay. DBM is divided into three main operating divisions. Its Center for Executive Options specializes in job transition and coaching for displaced executives. The division maintains offices in major American cities, including New York, Chicago, Los Angeles, San Francisco, and Dallas. Overseas, the Center for Executive Options works out of major cities across Europe, Asia, South America, and Australia. DBM's second principal division is its Executive Compensation Advisory Services. This division compiles information on executive pay, and consults with client companies on executive pay decisions. The DBM Publishing division puts out books and other materials on an array of human resource topics. DBM was a long-time subsidiary of publishing company Harcourt General. In 2001, DBM was acquired by the Thomson Corporation, a Canadian media and publishing firm, with worldwide sales of $6 billion.

A New Human Resource Service

Drake Beam Morin, Inc. was founded in 1967 as Drake, Beam and Associates. John Drake and Jerry Beam were psychologists in private practice in Boston when they decided to form a human resources consulting firm. The company's first major client was the American Can Company, which retained the new firm to counsel some of its employees that were being laid off. Two years later, Drake, Beam landed another large assignment, handling terminated employees for drug company Warner-Lambert. Through its early work, Drake, Beam more or less invented the human resources field that became known as outplacement.

Outplacement comprises a variety of services to those who are newly unemployed. Drake, Beam offered counseling for those shocked and saddened by losing their jobs. The company helped workers assess their former careers and set goals for the future. Eventually DBM's outplacement services included providing office space, telephones, copiers, fax machines, and clerical help to job hunters. DBM's services were contracted for by the company that was terminating employees. The fee was usually a percentage of the employee's former salary. DBM could often smooth the difficult job of breaking bad news. Terminated workers were often angry and upset, and companies felt it easier to hire a specialist to handle this traumatic situation. Clients hired DBM not only to counsel terminated workers but to ease their anger, possibly reducing wrongful firing law suits. DBM also advised clients on keeping up morale among employees who had been spared the axe, as even those who kept their jobs often suffered while a company was in transition.

In 1974, William J. Morin joined the firm and eventually added his name to the masthead. Morin was not a psychologist but a marketing and human resources expert with in-depth experience working with terminated employees. In his book *Trust Me,* he described an early job he held as a sales manager, where he was told to go out and fire 50 salesmen working under him. The first man to whom he broke the news was so shook up he appeared to be having a heart attack. Morin confiscated the man's company credit cards and company car, leaving him with a severance check for one month's pay. The experience was almost as depressing for Morin as for the man he fired. And

---

Company Perspectives:

DBM is the world's leading provider of strategic human resource solutions that help organizations align their workforces to meet changing business needs. Known for over 30 years for its innovative and effective career transition services, DBM offers in-depth capabilities in transition, retention, development, and selection. Founded in 1967, the company currently has over 200 offices in more than 40 countries.

---

after he had fired 49 other salesmen, Morin himself was let go. When Morin joined Drake, Beam, outplacement became the firm's specialty.

The same year that Morin joined the company, the consulting firm was also acquired by the publishing firm Harcourt Brace Jovanovich. The company became Drake-Beam, Inc., with headquarters in New York. Drake-Beam also opened its first regional offices, starting with one in Chicago and one in Los Angeles. At a time of rapid corporate mergers, downsizings, and realignments, the need for outplacement services grew. The firm opened an office in Paris in 1978, its first outside the U.S. By 1979, Drake-Beam estimated that the number of people receiving outplacement services was doubling annually. William Morin became CEO of the company in 1979, and the name changed to Drake Beam Morin, Inc. The company attracted clients making major changes, such as letting go hundreds of executives at once. DBM began setting up separate offices, which it dubbed Career Centers, near client companies. Terminated workers were usually asked to show up at nine o'clock daily at the Career Center, dressed for work, so that even though they were unemployed, they kept to a business routine. DBM counselors evaluated things like interviewing skills and management style, as well as critiquing resumes. The temporary offices provided the typical executive amenities—coffee, clerical staff, telephones, interaction with peers.

Growth in the 1980s

Drake Beam Morin continued to expand through the 1980s, opening regional offices across the country. It opened an office in Dallas in 1981. This and other southern regional offices grew by as much as 15 to 20 percent a year in the 1980s, following corporate downsizings and revampings, particularly in the energy, banking, and agricultural industries. Corporations were willing to pay fees of between 12 and 17 percent of each terminated employee's salary for DBM's outplacement services. DBM took on a big client in Detroit in 1982, when the J.L. Hudson retailing firm decided to cut one-third of its management. In a consumer-related industry like retailing, public relations were very important, and Hudson retained DBM well before it announced its terminations in order to insure that it didn't lose customer goodwill. The Hudson layoffs involved more than 200 executives. In this case, Hudson actually built DBM a suite of offices adjacent to its headquarters to use during the lengthy outplacement process.

By the mid-1980s, DBM operated around 35 regional offices. The whole field of outplacement was growing, and DBM

was by far the largest company in the field. Revenue in the outplacement industry overall was said to have grown from $35 million in 1980 to $225 million by 1986, and a number of firms crowded the field. By 1988, DBM had annual revenues of around $75 million, with 77 offices worldwide and 500 consultants. Its next closest competitor, Right Associates, of Philadelphia, had sales of just under $30 million, and the other outplacement firms in the top ten all brought in less than $15.5 million. More than 150 firms considered themselves outplacement consultants by 1988, compared to only 43 at the start of the decade. Profit margins could be as high as 50 percent in the field, and it didn't take a formal certification process to set oneself up as an outplacement consultant. The flock of new entrants to the niche brought price cutting. Some firms were driven from the market, such as Mainstream Access, a top-ten outplacement service that filed for Chapter 11 in 1988. But Drake Beam Morin continued to gain market share.

Changing Conditions in the 1990s and Beyond

The outplacement industry continued to grow in the early 1990s. An analyst that tracked the industry estimated that companies would pay over $600 million overall to outplacement firms in 1991. DBM took on a huge job in the early 1990s, handling outplacement for computer giant IBM as it let go 10,000 of its employees. Even DBM, the largest outplacement firm in the business, found its resources stretched by such a large assignment. The company relied on temporary consulting staff to supplement its full-time consulting staff of 500. DBM also expanded its other services while its business grew. It began developing an adjunct program for the special problems of displaced women executives in the late 1980s, and then added a training division. This division offered fuller counseling services for enhancing career management skills for employees who were not necessarily scheduled for termination. The program gave advice on subjects such as retirement planning, career mapping, and management style. By 1992, the training division generated about 15 percent of DBM's annual revenue. DBM also expanded overseas. By 1992, the firm was split about evenly between U.S. offices and offices abroad, with 50 offices scattered across the globe in major cities of Europe, Asia, Australia, and South America. DBM opened an office in Mexico City in 1994, anticipating more business there as passage of the North American Free Trade Agreement heightened competition in the region.

Yet revenue and profits began to shrink for DBM in the mid-1990s. 1994 was an especially low year, and the company's fiscal outlook continued poor over most of 1995. At the end of 1995, the firm announced that its long-time CEO William J. Morin had resigned. Morin claimed in an interview with the *Wall Street Journal* that he had wanted to expand DBM's career management and change management services, against the wishes of other top company executives. Competitors in the outplacement industry also quoted in the *Wall Street Journal* article proposed that DBM's parent, Harcourt General, had wanted to sell the company, and Morin had nixed the deal.

The rumored sale did not take place that year, though in 1996 DBM did take what looked to some to be a sharp turn in its business philosophy. The outplacement industry continued to turn in gloomy revenue figures, at least in North America. In

Key Dates:

1967: The firm is launched in Boston as Drake, Beam and Associates.
1974: William Morin joins company, which is acquired by Harcourt Brace Jovanovich.
1979: The company's name is changed to Drake Beam Morin, Inc.
1988: Annual revenue reaches $75 million
2001: DBM is acquired by Thomson Corp.

May 1996 DBM announced that it was forming a strategic alliance with Manpower, Inc., the world's leading temporary employment service. Manpower would help DBM clients get temporary assignments through its worldwide employment network. DBM claimed this was a realistic way to get laid-off people working quickly, and many temporary assignments did lead to permanent positions. Competitors, however, claimed that temporary work was a merely a band-aid that outplacement counselors should be encouraging clients to avoid. But both DBM and Manpower looked forward to benefiting from the new arrangement. Manpower in particular had been squeezed by consolidation of its competitors in the temporary employment industry. And both companies had extensive networks of overseas offices where some North American workers might be channeled.

By the late 1990s, most of the U.S. economy was booming. This, unfortunately, was not good news for the outplacement industry. DBM decided to close 16 of its 95 North American offices in 1997, laying off some 65 employees. DBM claimed it was still bringing in more and more clients, but its revenue per customer was falling. The massive layoffs of thousands of workers DBM had handled in the 1980s were a thing of the past. Yet the company said its overseas business was still good.

Drake Beam Morin had been the subsidiary of publishing company Harcourt General for most of its life. Rumors of a proposed sale of DBM surfaced in the mid-1990s, when William Morin resigned and competitors noted that DBM was a strange fit for Harcourt, which mostly published academic and trade books. In 2000, DBM's parent was acquired by a large Anglo-Dutch publishing conglomerate, Reed Elsevier, for $4.5 billion plus assumption of $1.2 billion of Harcourt's debt. But Reed Elsevier did not want to take on DBM. As soon as the deal was finalized, Reed Elsevier spun off DBM and two other Harcourt assets to the Canadian media firm Thomson Corp. The arrangement was finalized in July 2001, with Thomson paying Reed $2.06 billion for DBM and the two other units. DBM became part of the larger company's Learning Division. The Learning Division was itself a $2 billion segment, and Thomson had total revenue of around $6 billion. No immediate changes to DBM's business were announced with the sale. By 2001, DBM had grown to a network of over 200 offices worldwide, serving clients in 45 different countries.

Principal Divisions

Center for Executive Options; Executive Compensation Advisory Services; DBM Publishing.

Principal Competitors

Right Management Consultants; Adecco SA; The Murdock Group Holding Corp.

Further Reading

Byrd, Laura, ''Coaching for Life,'' *World and I,* August 2001, p. 122.
Caminiti, Susan, ''Olympic Job Toss,'' *Fortune,* November 27, 1995, p. 42.
Cole, Diane, ''What's New in Outplacement,'' *New York Times,* February 14, 1988, p. F15.
Friedman, Michael, ''Outplacement: Taking Out the Sting,'' *Chain Store Age Executive,* October 1982, pp. 18–20.
Gordon, Jack; Stamps, David; and Zemke, Ron, ''Booming Economy Spells Bust for Outplacement Firms,'' *Training,* September 1997, p. 12.
Lublin, Joann S., ''Drake Beam's Morin Resigns over Strategy,'' *Wall Street Journal,* November 24, 1995, p. B2.
——, ''Manpower Forms Strategic Alliance with Drake Beam,'' *Wall Street Journal,* May 23, 1996, p. A9.
Machan, Dyan, ''Meet the Undertakers,'' *Forbes,* November 11, 1991, pp. 384–88.
Main, Jeremy, ''Look Who Needs Outplacement,'' *Fortune,* October 9, 1989, pp. 85–92.
Milliot, Jim, ''From Harcourt to Reed to Thomson,'' *Publishers Weekly,* July 23, 2001, p. 18.
——, ''Reed Buys Harcourt, Will Sell Parts to Thomson,'' *Publishers Weekly,* October 30, 2000, p. 10.
Morin, William J., *Trust Me* New York: Drake Beam Morin, Inc., 1990.
Morin, William J., and Lyle Yorks, *Outplacement Techniques* New York: Amacom, 1982.
''Outplacement Firms Try Branching Out,'' *Wall Street Journal,* October 13, 1992, p. B1.
Uchitelle, Louis, ''Top Professionals in Layoffs Steered to Temporary Jobs,'' *New York Times,* May 25, 1996, pp. A1, D8.
Vonder Haar, Steven, ''Outplacement Firms Profit with Cuts in Local Workforce,'' *Dallas-Fort Worth Business Journal,* July 27, 1987, p. 2.

—A. Woodward

Dürr AG

Otto-Dürr-Strasse 8
D-70435 Stuttgart
Germany
Telephone: (49) (711) 136-1095
Fax: (49) (711) 136-1716
Web site: http://www.durr.com

Public Company
Incorporated: 1895 as Bauflaschnerei Paul Dürr
Employees: 11,558
Sales: EUR 2.04 billion ($1.92 billion) (2000)
Stock Exchanges: Frankfurt
Ticker Symbol: DUE
NAIC: 333298 All Other Industrial Machinery
    Manufacturing; 335314 Relay and Industrial Control
    Manufacturing; 54133 Engineering Services

A leading vendor in its industry, Durr AG manufactures machinery used in the paint-finishing process for the global auto industry. The company is headquartered in Stuttgart, Germany, and maintains subsidiaries in over 20 countries. Dürr's Paint Systems division accounts for roughly half of the company's total sales and approximately 85 percent of total sales are generated in Europe and North America. The company's other business divisions design and install automation and conveyor systems, industrial cleaning, air cleaning and water purification systems and other industrial services for car makers. Heinz Dürr, a member of the founding family who owns slightly more than half of the company's shares, is Dürr's CEO. The two other major shareholders include EnBW Energie Baden-Württemberg AG which owns a 9.1 percent share and BWK GmbH Unternehmensbeteiligungsgesellschaft which holds 5 percent in the company.

Craftman's Workshop Becomes
Industrial Manufacturer

The roots of the Dürr concern go back to the 19th century. In 1895, 24-year old tinsmith Paul Albert Dürr established his own business, which he called Bau-Flaschnerei Paul Dürr, in the German town of Cannstatt near Stuttgart. With his four apprentices he started making all kinds of metal products used on or in buildings, including stove pipes, ledges and gutters, roof windows and ceiling-mounted ventilators, cornices and roof ornaments made from sheet metal or copper. Paul Dürr was a technology enthusiast and tried to implement new machines to his business early on because they gave him the opportunity to take on more interesting projects. Around the turn of the century, his workshop was among the first that could be reached by phone—under the number Stuttgart 283. From his visit to the World Fair in Paris in 1906 he was inspired to purchase a crankshears two meters long that enabled him to work with larger pieces of sheet metal. Dürr's technical capabilities and high-quality work soon earned him a reputation as a reliable contractor for construction projects in the region. For the next decade or so, he was awarded many contracts for plumbing work in buildings under construction, but mainly for equipping many buildings in the kingdom of Württemberg with copper roofs, including hospitals, churches and industrial buildings. The word about Dürr even spread as far as Austria and Switzerland. In 1911 Paul Dürr and his men finished the roof of Stuttgart's Art Building dome with a majestic stag on top which earned him the title "Tinsmith Master to the Royal Court of Württemberg."

World War I interrupted the company's dynamic growth. Towards the end of the war it became more and more difficult to acquire the necessary raw materials. However, a creative entrepreneur, Dürr bought up thousands of old iron molds for sugar cones from the local sugar factory and started transforming them into buckets, watering cans, ladles, shovels, and other necessary metal utensils. The 1920s brought in new business which in turn made new investments in better machinery necessary. However, before the calculated profits materialized, they were eaten up by spiraling inflation which reached its high point in 1923. Three years later Paul Dürr's 22-year-old son Otto traveled to the Leipzig Fair to find a solution that would pull the company out of trouble. He came back with the idea to replace cast iron with sheet metal in many products the company made, an idea which became the basis of the "light construction" technologies in the following decades. At the same time, the traditional ways of shaping metal parts—casting and riveting—

Company Perspectives:

The Dürr technology group is benefitting from the structural changes in the automotive industry. As a result of the high intensity of competition in this industry, car manufacturers have an increased demand for integrated production systems, thus contributing to better quality, higher productivity, and reduced costs. In order to take full advantage of these opportunities, Dürr has extended its strategic concept and has continued to pursue its systems approach. The Dürr strategy is as follows: *Based on its leading position in automobile painting and industrial cleaning systems, Dürr has extended its range of systems in automobile manufacturing to further areas in the value chain and has established itself as a supplier of manufacturing support services. Apart from a continuous expansion of its traditional business, Dürr is concentrating on the cultivation of new markets and customer groups based on existing technologies. The aim is to achieve growth in earnings on a very much broader market base.*

were replaced by the new welding technology. In 1928, Dürr pioneered the trade by finishing the first aluminum roof. Dürr put roofs on Stuttgart's central railway station and the railway's administrative building, the Hoftheater and the Fangelsbach school, as well as on buildings in other German cities. However, the onset of the worldwide economic depression at the end of the 1920s took its toll. By 1932, the number of people working for Dürr diminished from 40 to a mere seven.

The year 1932 marked the first generation change in the family business when Otto Dürr took over his father's company at age 28. Four years later, Paul Dürr died. Otto Dürr led the company into the era of mass production. Together with his wife Betty he managed the company in a frugal style during the Great Depression, at the same time looking for new business opportunities. A first step was the new production line of heavy machine stands. The sheet metal division started making several types of metal containers for industrial use that were first mass-produced in 1934. In March 1938, Dürr hired the company's first engineer. This was a crucial step that enabled the production of more complicated sheet metal products. It also marked the beginning of Dürr's transition from a manufacturer to an engineering company. With the onset of World War II in 1939, the company was required to make machines and vehicle parts for the German war industry. Construction activities came to an almost complete halt and several of Dürr's tinsmiths were transferred to the sheet metal division. In the later years of the war, raw materials became scarce. Dürr found a way around this situation by inventing technologies that made it possible to use sheet metal that was more than 80 percent thinner than the material used before. In 1943, Dürr's main production facility in Cannstatt was completely destroyed and operations were moved to another site in a neighboring town where the company had set up a workshop seven years earlier.

A Vendor for the Auto Industry after World War II

As after World War I, Dürr started making much needed household products when World War II ended, such as small

stoves, stove pipes, and wash tubs. The company was lucky enough to keep its large machinery which was confiscated in some other firms by the administration of the Allied Forces. With many buildings badly damaged, Dürr's tinsmiths were in high demand once more, repairing and renewing many roofs in the Stuttgart region. In 1947, the company resumed the production of industrial goods. However, Otto Dürr had the vision to make a shift to industrial engineering in the future. A visit to the Hannover Industrial Fair and an informational trip to the United States in 1949 were the background for Otto Dürr's decision to make surface treatment of metal parts a priority. The company had made its first experience with this technology when it was forced to make primed parts for vehicles during the war, and Otto Dürr was convinced that surface treatment with chemicals was a growing market. In 1950, Dürr hired Hubert Schilling, an engineer who had extensive experience with surface treatment technology. In the same year the first Dürr plant for the pre-treatment of wheels with phosphate was handed over to Südrad, a wheel maker in Ebersbach. Soon the new business division became more important than Dürr's traditional tinsmith trade. In 1957, Otto Dürr's son Heinz joined the company and soon became the driving force behind the further expansion of the company's industrial equipment branch. In 1958, Dürr started designing industrial cleaning equipment. These huge ''washing machines'' were often necessary to clean parts the surface of which was chemically treated. They could be manufactured in large series and still be customized according to the customer's specifications. The new product line brought in new business, which resulted in two-digit growth rates during the 1950s, while the number of employees doubled from 100 in 1952 to 205 in 1957.

The postwar economic boom in the 1950s contributed to the rise of the automobile industry in Germany. Due to the company founder's personal acquaintance with engineer Gottlieb Daimler, Dürr had gotten a head start as a vendor for the emerging automobile industry in the mid-1920s. In the 1960s, the company focused its efforts to become a vendor for this dynamically growing market.

In 1962, Dürr took on a project which none of the company's competitors believed was possible for the relatively small company to complete. American car maker Ford needed a new spray painting and pre-treatment facility to be installed—within three weeks. However, pulling all available resources—with everyone from Otto and Heinz Dürr to every apprentice working around the clock—the company managed to get everything done on time. This coup not only earned Dürr a reputation among car manufacturers; it also gave the company's engineers valuable insight and know-how through their cooperation with Ford technicians. Heinz Dürr traveled to the United States again several times. He foresaw the upcoming switch to water-soluble paint in the United States and started experimenting with new technologies in 1963. The company developed a new coating process—the electrophoreic painting process. Ford promptly followed up with a contract to equip a new coating facility in the company's brand-new painting plant in Belgium with the new technology. In the following years the company evolved as the global auto industry's preferred vendor for systems to pre-treat, paint, and clean auto bodies. Dürr's customer list in the 1960s and 1970s included Volkswagen, Seat, Fiat, Volvo, Rover, and Rolls Royce, but also clients from behind the Iron Curtain, in the GDR, Poland, Hungary, and the Soviet Union. As major car

Key Dates:

1895: Tinsmith Paul Dürr establishes his own business near Stuttgart.
1911: Paul Dürr is awarded the title ''Tinsmith Master to the Royal Court of Württemberg.''
1932: The founder's son Otto takes over the business.
1950: The company ventures into surface treatment with chemicals.
1957: With Heinz Dürr the third family generation enters the business.
1958: Dürr starts developing industrial cleaning technology.
1964: The first foreign subsidiary is set up in Brazil.
1968: The environmental business division is established.
1978: Dürr ventures into automation technology.
1989: The company takes over the Behr group and goes public.
1999: Dürr acquires Schenck, Premier, and Alston.
2000: The company's management structure is reorganized.

makers started setting up production plants around the world, Dürr followed their lead. Between 1964 and 1978, Dürr subsidiaries were established in Brazil, Mexico, Switzerland, Austria, the United States, the United Kingdom, South Africa, Italy, Spain, Portugal, and France, followed by new subsidiaries in other countries in the decades after. By the end of the 1960s, over half of Dürr's total sales derived from business with the auto industry.

Changeover: Manufacturing to Engineering after 1970

In 1969, Heinz Dürr became the new CEO of the company which under his leadership changed from an industrial manufacturer to an engineering firm and general contractor for industrial projects. This change was also manifested in the company's name which was changed from Fa. Otto Dürr to Otto Dürr Anlagenbau—Otto Dürr Factory Construction—in 1977 and four years later to Dürr Anlagenbau. In 1968, the company established a new business division that offered environmentally friendly industrial processes for applying chemicals such as paint to metal surfaces and for cleaning chemically treated parts as well as processed air and water. A decade later, Dürr included automation technology to its range of services, offering conveyor systems to, for example, transport car bodies through a painting plant.

The new broadened spectrum of Dürr know-how enabled the company to deliver complete car painting plants to the global auto industry, which had decidedly become its new strategic focus by 1980. While in the beginning Dürr's customers delivered the construction plans after which the facilities were built, this soon began to change with the growing size of the company's research and development department, which enabled Dürr to offer project planning as an additional service. At the same time project management became more important than production as industrial clients were looking for vendors who

were able to ''deliver'' complete plants. The company started cooperating with other vendors, which took over a growing part of the manufacturing while Dürr acted as a general contractor that planned and coordinated the realization of such complex projects. By the mid-1990s, about half of Dürr's workforce were engineers required to go abroad to one of the company's subsidiaries in over 40 countries on all five continents for several months—if need be. To ensure proper communication, English became Dürr's ''official language.'' For the constant stream of technological innovations developed by Dürr engineers the company received several awards in the 1990s, including the ''German Industry Innovation Award,'' the ''German Industry Environmental Protection Award,'' and General Motor's ''Worldwide Supplier of the Year.''

During the 1980s and 1990s, Dürr adjusted its organizational structure according to the changes the company had made in its range of products, services, and clients. In 1985, all German subsidiaries were merged under the umbrella of the new operational unit Dürr GmbH, which also became the parent company for all foreign subsidiaries. To strengthen the company's capital base, the management holding company first set up in 1977 was transformed into a public company named DÜRR Beteiligungs-AG in 1989, followed by the IPO at the Frankfurt and Stuttgart stock exchanges in the same year. From 1980 on, Heinz Dürr, who in the following years took different leading positions in other companies, was replaced as Dürr CEO by non-family managers.

During the 1990s, Dürr expanded its global market reach to Asia and the Middle East, including projects in China, Taiwan, South Korea, Japan, Indonesia, India, and Iran. In the United States the company became the leading vendor for spray painting systems. To strengthen its international position as the leading vendor for car painting plants to the increasingly globally acting auto industry, Dürr made several strategic acquisitions. In 1989, the company took over the Behr Group, the leading manufacturer of varnish coating systems, and merged it with Dürr in 1993. In 1999, the company acquired the internationally leading manufacturer of high-tech systems diagnostic, testing, and automation systems, Germany-based Carl Schenck AG. In the same year Dürr bought French Alstom Automation S.A. and American Premier Manufacturing Services Inc. In 2000, the company's management structure was reorganized into five business divisions: Paint Systems, Automotion, Environmental, Protecs, and Services. Effective in January 2001, Dürr acquired a worldwide license for RoDip, a painting process for the dip painting of car bodies, from Swiss industrial conglomerate ABB Ltd. and took over ABB's development unit for the process located in Butzbach near Frankfurt. Despite excessive production capacities in the auto industry and possible cyclical downturns in the future, Dürr expected a continued demand for its technology because of ongoing pressures caused by tough competition among car makers worldwide. By 2000, car makers accounted for about 80 percent of the company's sales.

Principal Subsidiaries

Dürr Inc. (U.S.); Dürr-AIS Ltda. (Brazil); Dürr Brasil Ltda. (Brazil); Dürr-AIS S.A. (France; 50%); Dürr Ltd. (U.K.); Dürr Systems Spain S.A.; Olpidürr S.p.A. (Italy; 65%); Nagahama Seisakusho Ltd. (Japan; 47%); Shinhang Dürr Inc. (South Korea; 75%); Schenck S.A. (France; 94%); Verind S.p.A. (Italy; 50%); Dürr Paintshop Equipment and Engineering (Shanghai) Co. Ltd. (China); Schenck Shanghai Testing Machinery Corporation Ltd. (China; 47%); Schenck Australia (Pty.) Ltd. (Australia; 69%); Schenck Ash (Pty.) Ltd. (South Africa; 74%); Premier Manufacturing Suppoert Services L.P. (Sweden); Carl Schenck Machines en Installaties BV (Netherlands; 94%); Schenck Vaegt- og Maskinfabrik A.p.s. (Denmark; 94%).

Principal Divisions

Dürr Holding GmbH; Dürr Systems GmbH; Carl Schenck AG (94%); Dürr Automotion GmbH; Dürr Ecoclean GmbH; Inlac Industrie-Lackieranlagen GmbH; Dürr Environmental GmbH; Dürr Ecoservice GmbH.

Principal Competitors

Sames Corporation; Nordson Corporation; Chiyoda Corporation; CLARCOR Inc.; United States Filter Corporation.

Further Reading

''Dürr erhält 100 Mio-Mark-Auftrag von BMW,'' *AFX—TD*, August 29, 2001.

''Dürr erzielt 1999 Umsatzplus von 15%,'' *AFX—TD*, January 26, 2000.

''Dürr-Gesellschaft gründet Joint Venture mit britischem Entwicklungshaus Ricardo plc,'' *AFX—TD*, February 21, 2001.

''Dürr legt beim Ergebnis kräftig zu,'' *Börsen-Zeitung,* January 29, 1998, p. 9.

100 Jahre DÜRR, Stuttgart, Germany: DÜRR GmbH, 1995, 29 p.

—Evelyn Hauser

edel music AG

Wichmannstrasse 4
D-22607 Hamburg
Germany
Telephone: (49) (40) 890-85-0
Fax: (49) (40) 890-85-310
Web site: http://www.edel.com

Public Company
Incorporated: 1985 as "edel" Gesellschaft für
    Produktmarketing mbH
Employees: 1,548
Sales: DM 1.18 billion ($569.6 million) (2000)
Stock Exchanges: Frankfurt
Ticker Symbol: EDL
NAIC: 51222 Integrated Record Production/Distribution;
    51223 Music Publishers

German-based edel music AG sees itself as the largest independent player in the European music industry. With over 90 subsidiaries and affiliations in 15 countries, the company is among the world's largest producers and marketers of classical music as well as rock, pop, and jazz. Edel music operates a state-of-the art CD production facility in Germany and owns an interest in several record labels, including German 45 music, Danish Mega Records, Swedish Playground music, Belgium's Play It Again Sam, and Eagle Rock Entertainment in the United Kingdom. With an 80 percent share in the American music distribution company RED Distribution, edel music also has a strong foothold in the United States. The company's two major divisions, edel records Europe and edel North America contribute about 68 percent to the company's total sales in about equal shares. Another 24 percent comes from Play It Again Sam, a label focusing on cutting-edge progressive and alternative rock as well as club music. The remainder of the company's sales is generated by the company's licensing arm edel media & entertainment, the music publishing division edel publishing, and its production division edel services, which manufactures CDs, CD-ROMs, DVDs, LPs, and MCs. The company's founder and CEO Michael Haentjes owns more than 70 percent of edel music.

Beginnings as a Mail Order Company in 1985

Before Michael Haentjes founded his own company, he engaged in several other occupations, most of them connected in some way with the music industry. In the 1970s Haentjes studied musicology in his hometown Cologne. Previously he had played oboe and keyboards in high-school orchestras and rock bands. However, unlike many of his peers, Haentjes was more interested in music theory and song writing than in performing on stage. After his college years, Haentjes became a music teacher and freelance writer for music magazines. In 1979, he teamed up with Klaus Schulze, a former member of the synth-rock group Tangerine Dream, and co-founded the IC record label, which specialized in electronic music. The label was licensed by the German subsidiary of the major label Wea. Through that connection, Haentjes was hired as the assistant to Wea Germany's Director of Marketing. Later Haentjes took the position of CEO for the German branch of Warner Home Video. For a short time he worked for a Munich-based publisher of computer books before he returned to the music industry, where he took a position at the Hamburg-based record label Teldec.

Finally, in October 1985, Haentjes founded his own business, a marketing firm named Edel Gesellschaft für Produktmarketing. One year later, operating out of his home, Haentjes started selling soundtracks through a mail order catalogue. To Haentjes' surprise the business took off shortly after it went into operation. In its first year the company sold merchandise worth DM 600,000. In 1988 Edel released its first CD and sales started climbing. Haentjes' concept was simple but highly profitable: He acquired licenses for pop hits from other record labels, put them on pop music samplers with such titles as "Party People" and "Best of Eis am Stiel," and sold them through non-traditional marketing channels for much less than record stores were charging. The popularity of the tunes was the main criteria for Edel's music selections, and he drew heavily on material produced for TV. An edel compilation called "Get It" contained the music scores of highly popular TV commercials. Edel also produced CDs with the soundtracks of popular soap operas that aired on German commercial TV stations Sat.1 and RTL. In addition Edel kept producing and selling pop-star-related merchandise such as t-shirts and calendars. A book featuring American pop and movie star David Hasselhoff became the company's first bestseller, lifting the company's sales to DM 6.5 million in 1988.

From National License Merchandiser to International Record Company in the 1990s

In 1990, when a vendor was unable to deliver the number of CDs edel music wanted to order, Haentjes realized that depending on others could significantly his sales—in this case client orders worth DM 800,000. He therefore decided to build his own CD factory. With an investment of DM 12 million edel music's new production facility in the city Röbel, located in the northern German state Mecklenburg-Vorpommern, started operations in January 1992. The investment was only made possible by the continued growth of the company. However, to cover the existing risk Haentjes decided to transform his limited liability company into a corporation. In November 1992, the company became "edel company" music AG and Haentjes prepared to make his enterprise fit for an IPO if the cash flow was sufficient. It was not. In any case, Haentjes was reluctant to bring new shareholders into the empire he had complete control over. Edel's subsidiaries, including the original "edel" Gesellschaft für Produktmarketing, distribution arm "ideal" Vertrieb GmbH, and music production subsidiary "optimal" Tonträger Produktions GmbH, as well as the newly established subsidiaries in Austria and Switzerland, were organized under the new holding.

Besides music recordings edel music also manufactured and marketed textiles such as T-Shirts and sweatshirts with the images of pop stars for which edel music held some 500 licenses. The merchandise was manufactured in the company's production facility in Malchow—also located in Mecklenburg-Vorpommern—and sold in record stores, department stores, and about 150 jeans shops. Textiles contributed about nine percent to the company's total sales, which by 1992 amounted to almost DM 70 million. In 1994, edel music started making CD-ROMS, and this production service soon became a considerable revenue source. The demand grew so strong that the Röbel factory had to be expanded several times. By 1996, the facility's capacity had reached about 40 million CDs per year. The factory employed some 150 people who worked in three shifts. When DJ's from the dance music scene began demanding vinyl LP's again, edel music started manufacturing them after purchasing a used machine in Finland with the capacity to produce about 1 million units annually.

In 1993 edel music acquired a catalogue with about 2,000 titles of classical music from the former East German govern-

ment-owned label Deutsche Schallplatte. The collection included recordings of high profile ensembles, including Leipzig Gewandhaus Orchestra under the direction of Kurt Masur, the Dresden Philharmonic Orchestra, Leipzig's Thomaner Choir, and Dresden's Kreuzchor, which had never been published on CD. In 1994, the company took over Hamburg-based Castle Communications Deutschland GmbH, a company that licensed and marketed oldies. However, Haentjes realized that his company would soon reach its limit of growth if he remained dependent on recordings produced by other companies, which by this point viewed edel music as a competitor to whom they would no longer issue licenses that easily. Therefore, edel music initiated a new strategy that would spur further growth: by signing their own artists and expanding internationally to compensate for the stagnating German market, they became a full-fledged record company.

With favorable contracts and its high-quality recording facilities, edel music attracted first-class artists. Edel music was also able to make a deal with NPG Records, which had signed up The New Power Generation, the band of international pop star Prince, who was looking for a new label after a dispute with his former label. Other recording artists that signed up with edel music included the Irish pop group the Kelly Family and electronic pop dance acts such as Fun Factory, Blümchen, and "happy hardcore" group Scooter, which were especially popular in Germany. On an international level edel music successfully established the teenage star Aaron Carter. The Kelly Family's new album *Over The Hump* and Prince's single "The Most Beautiful Girl in the World" became top hits and edel music's profits soared. The company's artist roster also fueled its sampler business, since it was now able to trade in its own productions in exchange for licenses from other record companies. By 1995 the number of edel music's titles had gone up to 600.

In 1993 edel music acquired a 50 percent share in Swiss Phonag AG which started distributing edel's titles in Switzerland. Edel America Records Inc. was established in North Hollywood to market edel music's products in the United States and to acquire repertoire from American licensees. During the 1990s the company's sales continuously grew by two-digit figures. By 1995 edel music's 350 employees generated DM 170 million in sales. The company sold its products in over 70 countries and sales abroad accounted for roughly 18 percent of their total. Classical music accounted for about two percent.

Going Public and International Acquisitions in 1998

To finance edel music's further expansion, the company went public in 1998 and was renamed edel music AG. Founder and CEO Michael Haentjes, however, was determined to retain control over the company's operations and kept a share of more than 70 percent in the company. The initial stock offering in September 1998 raised over $41 million. Within the first five months of the company's IPO, the value of edel music shares grew eight-fold. In a second stock offering in 1999 the company raised another $108 million.

Michael Haentjes retired from his ten-year involvement in marketing and artist contact and focused on business strategy and development. The CEO used the cash boost for numerous acquisitions in Western Europe and the United States. Edel music bought shares in a number of reputable record labels, including an almost 75 percent in Belgian independent label Play It Again Sam (PIAS). The PIAS group consisted of 16 companies, including French label F-Communications specializing in techno- and house music. The deal also added the pop group Public Enemy to edel music's artist roster. Another acquisition was a 54-percent share in Eagle Rock Entertainment in the United Kingdom and stakes in Danish Mega Records, and Hard'n'Heavy label Roadrunner. Other acquisitions included American K-tel International Inc.'s music subsidiary in Finland and a majority share in the Netherlands-based ABCD/Eddy Ouwens Productions, a special products company experienced in the field of compilations that owned valuable licensing material. With the acquisition of a share in Mega Records edel music also entered the music publishing market through the Danish company's subsidiary Megasong Publishing.

Up until the end of 1999 edel music's products were distributed by Koch International. With revenues of about $7 million in the United States, edel music's California-based subsidiary did not fulfill Haentjes' expectations. He took a major step into the North American market when edel music acquired an 80-percent majority share in the largest independent distribution company in the United States, RED, from Sony Music in November 1999. Sony kept a 20 percent interest in RED, continued using the company for its independent label productions and offering packing, shipping, credit collection, and back-office services for the distributor. Edel music also took over Web-based Talent Net Inc., a firm in New York that ran an online database with over 2,000 music acts that also contained at least three recordings per artist. The site that offered artists free access was intended to strengthen edel music's Artist and Repertoire (A&R) base and was re-branded Broadbandtalentnet.com. Talent Net also had contacts with the Asian Web-site Cybermusic Asia. Edel music also expanded into music TV, one of the industry's major promotion tools.

Besides its aggressive acquisition activities, edel music generated new business through deals with big players in the entertainment industry. In 1998 edel music made a license deal with Buena Vista Music Group, a subsidiary of U.S. entertainment giant Walt Disney, giving edel music the rights to market throughout Europe Buena Vista's catalogue, including Disney's film scores from *Snow White* to *The Lion King,* as well as future productions. In 1999 the company started cooperating with EM.TV & Merchandising AG, a company that owned the rights to about 20,000 half-hour TV programs for children produced by Junior.TV GmbH & Co. KG, a joint venture between EM.TV and the German media concern Kirch Group. edel music's international activities also included a license deal with the firm SWAT Marketing in Asia and a deal with the Australian label Shock Records.

Consolidation: 2000 and Beyond

In the two years after edel music's IPO, as a result of its fast expansion through acquisitions, the company's sales grew significantly. In 2000 alone, edel music's consolidated sales jumped by 260 percent, passing the DM 1 billion mark. However, this did not translate into the expected higher profits. While edel music had turned up profits until it went public, they dropped significantly during 1999, and the company slipped into the red. One of the main reasons, the company announced, was that the release of four new album's of top edel artists Aaron Carter, Jennifer Page, Blümchen, and Sash had been delayed. However, none of the company's German artists had sold 250,000 units yet—which equals the industry's ''gold'' standard—and none of edel's international artists sold over one million units by 1999. On the other hand, CEO Haentjes explained, his company was able to realize higher profit margins from album sales than major record labels, which had to pay their established artists significantly higher royalties. However, industry insiders saw a number of other reasons for edel music's losses. The numerous acquisitions had to be integrated into a functioning whole to realize acceptable profits. Other reasons for the company's losses were the cost of bank loans used to finance the company's investments, external management consultants helping with the company's reorganization, the cost for closing down the company's subsidiary in Argentina, and losses in the U.S. from fixed-price deals with the Dollar gaining in value against the EURO, as well as from investments in less successful artists.

After the company had issued several profit warnings starting in late 1999—at a time when companies listed on the ''Neuer Market,'' the German equivalent to the NASDAQ, crashed in share value by the dozens—the stock market reacted promptly. From an all-time high in 2000 of EUR 67 per share, edel music's value dropped to a mere EUR 3.60 at the end of that year. By January 2001, stock market analysts valued edel stock at less than its own capital base. The first chapter of dynamic expansion was closed by a lack of funds. Next on the agenda came consolidation and corporate restructuring. In 2000, edel music reorganized its operations into business divisions that managed the company's 90 or so subsidiaries and affiliates. The three main divisions were edel records Europe, edel North America, and PIAS, which together generated about 90 percent of the company's total sales. The other three divisions included the company's licensing arm edel media & entertainment, the music publishing division edel publishing, and its production division edel services.

In spring 2001, edel music finished its restructuring program in Germany. The next step was to take the same kind of measures in the company's European operations. The full integration of all business units into a profitable enterprise was edel music's major management challenge. In August 2001, the company announced that it would change its main focus from distribution to developing its own content. Edel sold its 12 percent stake in national music TV channel Viva and terminated its distribution and licensing contracts with Disney. Looking ahead, company founder Haentjes, who still owned over 70 percent of edel music, was planning to strengthen the company's repertoire base, to expand its activities in the music publishing field, and to explore future digital download technologies and business models through its new subsidiary edelNET GmbH. Another strategic focus was to strengthen the company's impact on the British and American markets. Edel music's CEO confirmed his intention to stay independent but did not completely reject the idea to partner up with other companies in the global music business. Michael Haentjes' future vision of his industry, which had been suffering from declining sales in Europe during the second half of the 1990s, was based on the assumption that the Internet would change how the music business was done. He envisioned cooperating with Internet distributors of music content while retaining all of his company's rights. Internet-based ''music platforms'' offering music for free digital download, while charging consumers for the download of top hits from popular artists, seemed to be the most likely development besides traditional CD sales.

Principal Subsidiaries

edel records GmbH; RED Distributions Inc.(U.S.A.; 80%); edel distribution GmbH; edel media & entertainment GmbH; PIAS Group s.p.r.l. (Belgium; 74.9%); Mega Scandinavia A/S (Denmark); Playground Music Scandinavia AB (Sweden; 51%); phonag records AG (Switzerland); edel America Records Inc.; S-Curve Records LLC (51%); Deston Songs LLC (50%); edel classics GmbH; A 45 music GmbH (75%); ABCD Records B.V. (Netherlands); Eagle Rock Entertainment plc (U.K.; 54.58%); Phonag Schallplatten AG (Switzerland); Eddy Owens Productions B.V. (Netherlands; 52%).

Principal Competitors

Zomba Records Limited; BMG Entertainment; EMI Group plc; Universal Music Group.

Further Reading

Brychcy, Ulf, ''Dynastien, Aussenseiter, Newcomer: Michael Haentjes—Prince und Kelly Family singen für die Edel Company,'' *Süddeutsche Zeitung*, May 6, 1995.

Christman, Ed, ''Edel Makes U.S. Move With RED Buy,'' *Billboard,* November 6, 1999, p. 5.

''Deutsche Schallplatte gibt Klassik ab,'' *Frankfurter Allgemeine Zeitung,* May 12, 1993, p. 22.

''Edel Music presst immer mehr Vinyl-LPs,'' *Süddeutsche Zeitung,* January 31, 1996.

''edel music will nach enttäuschendem Jahr wieder durchstarten,'' *dpa,* June 14, 2000.

''Edel will ein eigenes Kuenstler-Repertoire aufbauen,'' *Frankfurter Allgemeine Zeitung,* January 24, 1994, p. 16.

Martens, Rene, ''Cleverer Schund,'' *tageszeitung,* April 22, 2000, p. 25.

''Mit dem Klassik-Repertoire ins Ausland,'' *Frankfurter Allgemeine Zeitung,* November 30, 1993. p. 22.

Pride, Dominic, ''With Investors' Cash, edel Plots Further Expansion,'' *Billboard,* September 18, 1999, p. 72.

Spahr, Wolfgang, ''Edel Plans To Be Global Player,'' *Billboard,* April 15, 2000, p. 8.

Thiede, Meite, ''Edel ist dem Mittelstand zu schnell entwachsen,'' *Süddeutsche Zeitung,* January 22, 2001, p. 29.

——, ''Haentjes liest heute lieber Aktienkurse statt Noten,'' *Süddeutsche Zeitung,* March 6, 1999, p. 25.

——, ''Noch fühlt sich Edel alleine wohler Wachstumspläne,'' *Süddeutsche Zeitung,* April 4, 2000, p. 30.

Udin, Boris, ''Mister Edel ist auf Einkaufstour,'' *HORIZONT,* September 23, 1999, p. 14.

''Umwandlung in Aktiengesellschaft; edel company,'' *Textil-Wirtschaft,* February 11, 1993, p. 190.

—Evelyn Hauser

ERGO Versicherungsgruppe AG

Victoriaplatz 2
D-40198 Düsseldorf
Germany
Telephone: (49) (211) 4937-0
Fax: (49) (211) 4937-1500
Web site: http://www.ergo.de

Public Company
Incorporated: 1997
Employees: 27,489
Total Assets: EUR 12.7 billion ($11.8 billion) (2000)
Stock Exchanges: Frankfurt Düsseldorf
Ticker Symbol: EVG2
NAIC: 524113 Direct Life Insurance Carriers; 524114
    Direct Health and Medical Insurance Carriers; 524126
    Direct Property and Casualty Insurance Carriers;
    524128 Other Direct Insurance (Except Life, Health,
    and Medical) Carriers; 52413 Reinsurance Carriers

ERGO Versicherungsgruppe AG is the management holding company of Germany's second biggest direct insurance group serving more than 25 million customers throughout Europe. ERGO unites under its roof a consortium of four leading groups of insurance companies: the VICTORIA group and Hamburg-Mannheimer which sell a broad range of life and casualty insurance coverage to individuals, groups and businesses; DKV Deutsche Krankenversicherung AG, Europe's number one private health insurance; and D.A.S. which specializes in legal expense insurance and has a leading position in that market in Europe. In addition to 45 domestic subsidiaries, the ERGO group consists of 75 foreign subsidiaries in 22 European countries which contribute roughly 18 percent of total sales. ERGO is majority-owned by the world's largest reinsurance company Munich Re, which owns 91.7 percent of the company's shares. Bavarian bank HypoVereinsbank holds a 5 percent interest. The remaining 3.3 percent are publicly traded at the Frankfurt/Main stock exchange.

ERGO's Roots in 1853

ERGO Versicherungsgruppe AG was created in 1997, when four insurance companies combined their businesses and organized it under the umbrella of a new holding company. These four companies, however, all had a long history of their own before they came together. The oldest of the four was the insurance company VICTORIA, which was incorporated in Berlin in September 1853 as Allgemeine Eisenbahn-Versicherungs-Gesellschaft, a company that offered insurance coverage for possible damage connected with railway transportation such as fire or accidents. In 1861, the company started carrying life insurance, which became its strongest business division. In 1875, the company was renamed VICTORIA zu Berlin Allgemeine Versicherungs-Actien-Gesellschaft, which reflected the broadened focus of a general insurer. By the turn of the century VICTORIA had become the biggest life insurer in Germany and by 1913 the company was unsurpassed by any European life insurance company. In 1904, VICTORIA founded a new subsidiary that offered insurance against fire which was gradually extended to burglary, flood, accident liability, and car insurance. In the 20th century VICTORIA also started expanding its activities geographically, and by 1914 it did business in most European countries, except Great Britain. By 1932, VICTORIA accounted for four-fifths of all foreign premiums collected by German insurance companies. The two World Wars, as well as hyperinflation and the economic depression in between, took a big toll on VICTORIA: its financial assets were devalued, the company was cut off from markets abroad, it lost major markets in eastern Europe, and finally its Berlin headquarters. Hence the company was back to its earlier strength by the time its 100th anniversary rolled around in 1953. With its new headquarters in Düsseldorf, VICTORIA participated in the strong economic growth period of the 1960s, established subsidiaries in Austria, the Netherlands, Spain and Portugal, and kept growing through the 1970s by adding health insurance to its portfolio. In the early 1980s, the company survived a second attempt at a hostile takeover—the first one happened in the 1920s—and at the end of the decade restructured by creating a holding company for its three major operations in life, health, and property insurance. Resisting the industry trend to branch out into financial services, VICTORIA started cooperating with Bayerische Vereinsbank, a major German bank.

Company Perspectives:

ERGO is the No. 1 in health and legal expenses insurance in Europe; in Germany we are the No. 2 in personal accident and life. Expansion in foreign business through acquisitions abroad, especially in growth markets like Italy, Central and Eastern Europe is our goal. ERGO is also gearing towards the growing investment bonds market and has an excellent position with MEAG. With ERGO People & Pensions we have an outstanding position in the market for corporate pension schemes.

It was in 1961 when VICTORIA acquired a majority share in Deutsche Automobil Schutz Allgemeine Rechtsschutz-Versicherungs-AG (D.A.S.), a small insurance company specializing in legal insurance. D.A.S. was founded in Berlin as Deutsche Automobil Schutz AG in 1928 and received a concession as an insurance company in 1935. In 1941, the company started offering legal insurance in connection with transportation, and beginning in 1954 expanded its legal insurance services to other areas. Four years later D.A.S. opened a subsidiary in Austria and was taken over by VICTORIA in 1961. In 1978 the company founded D.A.S. Versicherungs-AG, a subsidiary which started offering other insurance programs besides legal insurance, including car, accident, liability, and different types of property insurance. In 1995, the company set up a legal insurance subsidiary in the Czech Republic before it became part of the ERGO group in 1997.

The third insurance company that became part of the ERGO group was Hamburg-Mannheimer, which was first incorporated as Vita Versicherungs-Actien-Gesellschaft in 1899. In 1902, the Mannheim-based firm received a national concession to sell private insurance. After a decade of sluggish business the company was taken over by Versicherungsgesellschaft Hamburg, another insurer, in 1911. A year later the company moved headquarters to Hamburg and changed its name to Hamburg-Mannheimer Versicherungs-Actien-Gesellschaft. In 1923, due to hyperinflation, the company's assets were almost completely eradicated. Two years later Hamburg-Mannheimer took over health insurance firm Bürgerliche Versicherungs-AG. After the stock market crashed in New York in 1929, Hamburg-Mannheimer's parent company got into financial turmoil and sold its shares in the company to the Swedish reinsurance group Svea in the following year. In 1932, Hamburg-Mannheimer expanded its health insurance activities when the company acquired an 80 percent majority in Berlin-based Deutsche Krankenversicherungs-AG (DKV), the fourth company that would later form the ERGO group. When the German government decided to deny any compensation for war-caused damages for companies over 25 percent foreign-owned in 1942, Svea sold its Hamburg-Mannheimer share packet to the Donner bank. The company's headquarters was left untouched by the war and the business was carried on with little interruption. However, the company changed hands again several times within the next few years until a relatively stable owner structure was achieved in 1951 when the German insurance groups Allianz and Munich Re each acquired a 36.4 percent share in Hamburg-Mannheimer while its old parent company Svea was back as a shareholder with 26.4 percent. In 1957, Hamburg-Mannheimer took over the existing insurance contracts from Hamburg-based life insurer Hansa Lebensversicherung A.G., which was then liquidated. In the booming 1960s, the company's financial assets passed the DM10 billion mark. In 1974 Hamburg-Mannheimer lost its share majority in DKV when the health insurer's capital base was increased by Allianz and Munich Re and ventured into legal insurance in 1979. In the late 1980s, the company acquired a ten percent stake in Austrian insurer Union Versicherungs-AG. In the 1990s, Hamburg-Mannheimer started cooperating with DKV and Dresdner Bank AG in cross-selling financial and insurance products through its new subsidiaries Hamburg-Mannheimer Versicherungs-und-finanzierungs-Vermittlung GmbH (VFV) and Hamburg-Mannheimer Investment Trust. Two years later the company's ownership structure changed again when Allianz lowered its share to 20 percent and Munich Re became Hamburg-Mannheimer's majority owner. In 1993, Munich Re also acquired a 26 percent stake in the company from Swedish Skandia group that was formerly Svea. Five years later the company restructured its operations and became part of the newly formed ERGO group.

DKV was founded in 1927 in Berlin and started out with a solid capital base of 2 million Reichsmark and 15 employees eager to sell health insurance. The company developed a reputation for innovation. In 1936, the company started using sophisticated mathematics to calculate their premiums. In the 1950s, DKV was the first health insurer to introduce health insurance plans with flexible elements that customers could choose from and provided extended security against cancellation for chronically ill patients. In the 1980s, DKV launched ''Medi Card,'' a plastic card that speeded up insurance claim processing with health care providers. In the 1990s, the company developed a program that kept the cost of premiums manageable for older customers. Not least this drive to innovate made DKV Germany's number one health insurer. However, after Germany's leading direct insurer Allianz ceased its distribution cooperation for health insurance with DKV, the company lost roughly one third of its new business.

The ERGO Merger in 1997

The German and European insurance market of the 1990s was characterized by deregulation. Around 1993, the geographical borders fell for the European insurance industry and insurers were allowed to offer their services within the ''common European insurance market'' if certain standards were met. Around the same time the European Common Market superseded the authority of Germany's governmental agency which had approved tariffs and conditions for many insurance products and had rigorously overseen consumer-friendly policies. As a result of the deregulation the market became increasingly competitive, product transparency declined, and prices fell. The European insurance industry reacted with a number of mergers.

On July 4th, 1997, the four insurance companies VICTORIA, Hamburg-Mannheimer, DKV, and D.A.S. announced the formation of a new group—the ERGO Versicherungsgruppe. Despite their considerable size and market share, none of these companies seemed to be in a strong enough position to stay competitive in the European market in the long run. Hamburg-Mannheimer's product portfolio leaned heavily towards life and accident insurance while only ten percent of sales came from

---

Key Dates:

1853: Allgemeine Eisenbahn-Versicherungs-Gesellschaft is founded.

1899: Vita Versicherungs-Actien-Gesellschaft is established in Mannheim.

1927: DKV Deutsche Krankenversicherung AG is founded in Berlin.

1928: Deutsche Automobil Schutz Allgemeine Rechtsschutz-Versicherungs-AG is founded.

1997: VICTORIA, Hamburg-Mannheimer, DKV and D.A.S. form ERGO Versicherungsgruppe AG.

1998: ERGO Versicherungsgruppe AG replaces VICTORIA Holding AG on the German MDAX stock index.

1999: MUNICH ERGO AssetManagement GmbH (MEAG) is established together with Munich Re.

2000: ERGO takes over insurer Alte Leipziger Europa.

---

property insurance. This unbalanced mix made the company more vulnerable to market volatility, and that was even more true for DKV and D.A.S. In addition, their exclusive sales force which marketed only products in their specialized niches—health insurance and legal insurance—increasingly came under cost pressure. VICTORIA had a more diversified product mix and a stronger market position, but was, as a publicly traded company, prone to unwanted takeovers by possible foreign buyers who wanted a strong foothold in the German market.

From that situation, the idea was born to merge the four companies into a new entity. A driving force behind the ERGO merger was reinsurer Munich Re, which held 23 percent in VICTORIA and 80 percent in Hamburg-Mannheimer. However, the merger was carried out in a rather unusual way: by merging the two major holding companies, Hamburg-Mannheimer AG and VICTORIA Holding AG. The result was not—as is most common—the merger of the parties' operative business divisions, but the formation of a consortium of four equal partner companies under the umbrella of the new management holding company ERGO Versicherungsgruppe AG, headquartered in Düsseldorf. Since the four partners had built strong brand names, they were kept in place and every company kept marketing their products under their respective brand. The only visible change for their customers was the additional note: ''A company of the ERGO Versicherungsgruppe'' included under the logo in all correspondence and marketing communication. After the merger had been carried out, ERGO Versicherungsgruppe AG took the place of VICTORIA Holding AG on the German MDAX stock index beginning in February 1998.

Focus on Synergy and International Growth After 1997

Right after the merger, ERGO started reorganizing its operations to create cost-saving and growth-enhancing synergy between its member companies. To synchronize ERGO's policies in similar markets, DKV received a major share in VICTORIA's health insurance subsidiary, while D.A.S. took over a majority share in Hamburg-Mannheimer's legal insurance arm.

The integration of claims management was finalized in 2000 and was done exclusively by VICTORIA for all casualty insurers of the ERGO group. In the same year the group's joint IT services firm, ITERGO, was established. In the mid-term, ERGO's management also expected additional growth from cross selling between the ERGO members.

Another potential area of synergy was financial asset management and investment banking. In the late 1990s, the borders between the insurance and banking markets began to break down. Insurance companies not only had to manage their own financial assets, but realized that offering vehicles for reinvesting paid-out life insurance could be the next step in their value chain. To strengthen the ERGO group's investment power, the company together with Munich Re established MUNICH ERGO AssetManagement GmbH (MEAG) in 1999, in which ERGO held 40 percent. Besides the management of those companies' financial assets, MEAG also offered its services to private and institutional investors. ERGO Trust GmbH, a MEAG subsidiary, offered real estate financing services, mainly to institutional investors.

The second major growth strategy besides creating positive synergy within the ERGO group was international expansion. With the acquisition of Spain's fifth largest private health insurer Previasa S.A. in 1998, health insurance became a second large revenue source abroad, besides legal insurance. ERGO's position in that segment was further strengthened when the company took over Dutch Levob Gezondheidszorgverzekeringen N.V., Spanish NORDICA, and German Alte Leipziger Europa with a strong foothold in Poland and the Baltic, in 2000. A health insurance sales office was also established in China. The takeover of Alte Leipziger Europa, a company that was also active in accident and property insurance, resulted in a foreign sales boost for ERGO in those two areas. Additional ERGO acquisitions included Italian property and casualty insurer Bayerische Assicurazioni and Italian life insurer Bayerische Vita, and a majority share in Lithuania's third largest insurance firm PREVENTA. As a result of the company's international growth efforts, the percentage of foreign sales of the total increased from about eight percent in 1998 to roughly 18 percent in 2000. ERGO expected the introduction of the EURO in 2002 to further increase competition among Europe's direct insurers.

Between 1998 and 2000, ERGO managed to grow faster than the German insurance industry as a whole, which was slowing down. ERGO group's strategic goal was to become Germany's number one direct insurer for individual customers and to increase foreign sales to about 20 percent of the total. A strategic joint venture with German telecommunication leader Deutsche Telekom was established in 2000 to create an online portal for insurance and financial services. Another strategic growth area was the increasing demand for private retirement plans and institutional pension funds. Through a share exchange transaction with Allianz and a public offer to buy ERGO shares, Munich Re was able to increase its share to 91.7 percent in 2001 and made HypoVereinsbank ERGO's exclusive distribution partner.

Principal Subsidiaries

Hamburg-Mannheimer Versicherungs-AG; DKV Deutsche Krankenversicherung AG (99.9%); VICTORIA Versicherung

AG (92.47%); VICTORIA Lebensversicherung AG (99.5%); Hamburg-Mannheimer Sachversicherungs-AG (99.99%); MEAG MUNICH ERGO AssetManagement GmbH (40%); VICTORIA Krankenversicherung AG; VICTORIA Rückversicherung AG; D.A.S. Versicherungs-AG; Vorsorge Lebensversicherung AG; D.A.S. Rechtsschutzversicherungs-AG; Hamburg-Mannheimer Rechtsschutzversicherungs-AG; ERGO Trust GmbH.

Principal Competitors

Allianz AG; AMB Generali Holding AG; AEGON N.V.

Further Reading

''Die Zurückhaltung bekommt Ergo gut,'' *Frankfurter Allgemeine Zeitung*, April 1, 1999, p. 18.

''Ergo und Telekom gemeinsam auf dem Internet-Marktplatz,'' *Frankfurter Allgemeine Zeitung*, April 7, 2000, p. 18.

''Ergo Versicherungsgruppe will sich zunächst intern stärken,'' *Frankfurter Allgemeine Zeitung*, May 14, 1998, p. 23.

''Für eine Victoria-Aktie zehn neue Ergo-Aktien,'' *Frankfurter Allgemeine Zeitung*, October 8, 1997, p. 25.

Janott, Dr. Edgar, ''ERGO-ein anderes Modell für eine Fusion,'' *Aktuelle Fragen der Versicherungswirtschaft,* Karlsruhe, Germany: Verlag Versicherungswirtschaft, 2000, p. 95.

Verschmelzung der VICTORIA Holding AG mit der Hamburg-Mannheimer AG; Kurzfassung des Verschmelzungsberichts, Berlin and Hamburg, Germany: VICTORIA Holding AG and Hamburg-Mannheimer AG, 1997, 12 p.

Weber, Stefan, ''Ergo kauft in Italien zu Erwerb der Bayerischen Vita,'' *Süddeutsche Zeitung*, August 18, 2000, p. 24.

—Evelyn Hauser

Etam Developpement SA

69-73, Boulevard Victor Hugo
93585 Saint-Ouen Cedex
France
Telephone: (33) 1 49-48-70-70
Fax: (33) 1 49-48-70-01
Web Site: http://www.etamdeveloppement.com

Public Company
Incorporated: 1997
Employees: 10,286
Sales: EUR 1.03 billion ($990 million)(2000)
Stock Exchanges: Euronext Paris
Ticker Symbol: TAM
NAIC: 422330 Women's, Children's, and Infants'
    Clothing and Accessories Wholesalers; 448150
    Clothing Accessories Stores

Etam Developpement SA is Europe's leading designer and retail distributor of women's lingerie and ready-to-wear fashions for the women's and young girls' markets. The company operates an international network of more than 1,100 retail stores as Etam and 1,2,3. Etam represents the company's core lingerie and ready-to-wear brand and head of its largest segment of stores—more than 700 company-owned and franchised stores. The 1,2,3 brand offers high-quality, premium-priced ready-to-wear coordinated fashions. This brand has been developed into its own network of more nearly 300 primarily France-based stores. Etam's third brand, Tammy, targets the young girls' market, with sales made through the company's larger-format, ready-to-wear stores. Etam's store formats range from the petite Etam Lingerie shops, at an average sales space of just 90 square meters to its latest mega-store all-in-one stores, with over 1,000 square meters of floor space, as well as its eight-story Parisian flagship stores, the more than 4,000-square-meter ''Cité de la Femme.'' The company has retail operations in Germany, Belgium, China, France, Great Britain, Italy, Lebanon, Luxembourg, Portugal, Reunion, and Saudi Arabia, and Spain, with many of its foreign markets operating through franchise agreements with local partners. More than 40 percent

of the company's sales come from outside of France. Etam Developpement has long pursued a policy of maintaining in-house design staff but outsourcing production to contractors in France and Asia. Etam has been traded on the Paris stock exchange since 1997. The company is led by Pierre Milchior, son of one of the Etam's founders, who himself has acted as chairman for more than 40 years. In 2000, Etam Developpement posted more than EUR 1.1 billion in sales.

Stylish Stockings in the 1920s

Etam was launched by Max Lindemann, a German stockings manufacturer. In 1916, Lindemann decided to venture into the retail arena, launching his own line of lingerie and opening his first store in Berlin. Lindemann chose the name Etam for his retail activity, a name taken from the etamine fabric used in much of his undergarment production.

By the 1920, Lindemann was ready to expand the Etam brand internationally. Rather than risk his fortune by opening company-owned stores in its new foreign market, Lindemann set up a network of local partnerships who in turn developed the Etam franchise in their own markets. As such, the Etam brand was introduced to the United Kingdom in 1923, with a first store opened on London's Oxford Street. Through the rest of the decade, Etam stores opened in other markets, including France, Argentina, the Netherlands and finally Belgium in 1928.

By then, Martin Milchior, founder of Milchior et Cie of Belgium, had launched his own chain of retail lingerie stores. The first Milchior store opened in 1925 and Milchior quickly expanded the store format throughout Belgium. In 1929, Milchior himself went international, opening a boutique in Paris. Over the next 25 years, Milchior's expanded deeper into France and the Milchior family eventually transferred its headquarters to Paris. A major step in this transition came in 1933 when Milchior acquired a chain of 21 stores. The company transformed its new chain of stores into lingerie boutiques, then adopted the Setamil store and brand name in 1941.

Pierre Milchior joined his father's business in 1955 and took over the lead of the company when Martin Milchior died in 1958. The younger Milchior was to prove the chief architect of the company's success, transforming the relatively small company into the European leader in its segment by the end of the century. Meanwhile, Etam had continued to establish itself as an important brand name, especially in the United Kingdom, where, in 1952, Etam Great Britain (Etam GB) launched its first line of ready-to-wear clothing.

Back in France, Setamil and Etam France, operated under parent company Elan SA, were preparing to join forces. This process started in 1961, when Milchior acquired Elan, taking control of the Etam France network. By 1963, Milchior had reached an agreement to merge his operations into Etam parent Max Lindemann, and the two companies began the process of merging the Etam, Elan, and Setamil store brands, resulting in the 49-store Etam chain. At the same time, the newly enlarged company launched a line of Etam-branded ready-to-wear clothing for the French market. Milchior was placed at the head of the company, now known as Groupe Etam, and became its principal shareholder.

The development of the Etam brand remained country-specific, with each local market partner operating as a separate company with operations independent of the largely French-market-focused Groupe Etam. As such, the Max Lindemann family retained control of the Etam Belgium franchise. In the United Kingdom, Etam GB began extending its own operations with the launch of a new brand, Tammy, targeting the young girls' market. That brand was unveiled in 1975 and helped Etam GB extend its network to more than 200 retail stores by the mid-1990s.

In France, Milchior and Groupe Etam continued to develop the Etam network, reaching 120 stores by 1980, with sales of more than Ffr 200 million per year. The company launched a new retail franchise format, Kiosk, that same year. The Kiosk operation led Etam into extending its operations from the retail sphere into the wholesale market. In 1981, Groupe Etam bought out the Lindemann family's stake in Etam Belgium.

Transition to European Leader for the 21st Century

The 1980s marked a transition period for the Etam brand. By 1985, the company had more than doubled its revenues, and by 1990 sales had topped the FFr 1 billion mark. During this time, Etam stopped looking to Hong Kong for its garment manufacture—and instead began contracting for much of its clothing needs from manufacturers in France. This policy enabled the company to react more quickly to fashion trends, while also giving it better oversight on quality. Another important move came with the birth of the company's 1,2,3 store format,

launched in 1983. The 1,2,3 store allowed Etam to branch out from its mid-market position to capture a higher-end lingerie and ready-to-wear clientele. These moves helped Etam outpace its competitors, and by the end of the decade Etam had captured more than 10 percent of the French market for lingerie. Meantime, Etam began extending its brand name into Spain, with the first Etam Lingerie opening in that country in 1983.

Etam GB also enjoyed success through the 1980s. That company went public in 1984 and began building onto its retail network through a series of acquisitions. In 1987, Etam GB acquired the Snob retail chain of 28 stores and the Snob brand name, paying £4 million. That same year, Etam GB paid £6.5 million to acquire Gladesmore Holdings, which operated the Peter Brown retail group. In 1991, however, Etam GB became the target of a hostile takeover by South African group Oceania Investments, which bid some £121 million.

Groupe Etam restructured its organization in 1991, now grouping its operations around its core brands. This restructuring led the company to exit the wholesale market, and switch the Kiosk franchise over to the Etam Lingerie format. From 1992, Etam moved to extend the 1,2,3 store format internationally, opening stores in Germany. The following year, the company acquired complete control of the struggling Etam Belgium group. Etam succeeded in restoring its new subsidiary to profitability, in part through the introduction of the 1,2,3 store brand. Across the Channel, Etam GB was finding success with its newest label, Etam Plus, targeting large-sized customers. Two years later, the France-based Etam brought its brand to China, where the company joined with a local partner to open its first stores in that country. Back home, Groupe Etam prepared a new retail store format, the 1,2,3 Lingerie offshoot of the 1,2,3 retail chain.

By the mid-1990s, however, Etam GB had lost its momentum. The company's sales were slipping and it quickly slid into an extended period of losses. By late 1997, the company acknowledged that is was looking to sell out its operations. Meanwhile, Groupe Etam was preparing to go public. The company had come under pressure from the arrival of a number of foreign clothing groups, notably Sweden's H&M, the United State's Gap, and Spain's Zara, which were attracting growing numbers of Etam's traditional customer base. The public listing, under the name of Etam Developpement, was a step toward achieving Etam's newly developed international expansion goals, which aimed at balancing the company's domestic operations. Despite competitive pressures, Etam remained France's leading women's clothing retailer, posting nearly FFr 4 billion in sales for the 1997 year.

The company seized the leadership position for the European market the following year when it made a friendly takeover offer for Etam GB, paying £93 million for its 215-store 'cousin'. The immediate effect of the acquisition was a slump in Etam's stock price, particularly as the company discovered that Etam GB's financial condition was in worse shape than Etam had initially believed. Instead of the £30 million investment Etam Developpement had counted on making to restore the luster to its new United Kingdom wing, the company's rebuilding of Etam GB was to cost more than twice as much.

Etam GB continued to drag on Etam Developpement's profits through the end of the century. By its 2000 fiscal year, the

Key Dates:

1916: Max Lindemann opens first Etam store.
1923: Etam Great Britain is formed.
1925: Martin Milchior founds Setamil.
1928: Etam Belgium opens.
1933: Milchior acquires 21 stores in France.
1941: Milchior stores adopt Setamil name.
1958: Pierre Milchior leads Setamil.
1961: Etam France is acquired.
1963: A merger with Max Lindemann forms Etam Developpement.
1974: Etam GB launches Tammy brand.
1980: Kiosk franchise is launched.
1983: 1,2,3 brand is launched; Etam GB begins doing business in Spain.
1984: Etam GB lists on London stock exchange.
1991: Reorganization of Etam Developpement occurs.
1993: Etam Belgium is acquired.
1995: Etam Developpement enters Chinese business market.
1997: Etam Developpement lists on Paris bourse.
1998: Etam Developpement acquires Etam GB.
1999: Etam Developpement enters Saudi Arabia, Lebanon, French Antilles, and New Caledonia.
2000: Etam Developpement launches megastore format, and introduces Tammy brand in continental Europe.

company had slipped into losses for the first time. Part of the company's difficulties stemmed from its heavy debt burden, which topped FFr 1.2 billion in 1999. Etam Developpement was also in the process of launching a new large-scale ''megastore'' format, three to four times larger than its traditional format. The company also faced difficulty when fire broke out during the renovation of its new, nearly 4,000-square-foot flagship store on Paris' Rue de Rivoli, which set back that store's opening date several months. Losses on that store alone topped EUR 12 million. Meanwhile, industry observers remained skeptical of Etam's large-scale store format, which depended too heavily on the women's market.

Despite these short-term difficulties, Etam Developpement continued to invest in its long-term growth. In 2000, the com-

pany brought the long-successful Tammy brand to the European continent, with a launch in Belgium. The company also moved into the Japanese market with its Etam Japan subsidiary. Meanwhile, the company added several new foreign markets, notably Saudi Arabia, Lebanon, French Antilles, New Caledonia, and Reunion in 1999.

Etam Developpement continued to roll out its mega-store format at the turn of the century, opening seven megastores in 2000 and planning an additional 15 the following year. Among these new stores was a first mega-store opened in Barcelona, Spain. That country, along with Portugal, became new primary target markets for Etam, which pledged to invest some 900 million pesetas to expand its network of stores in those countries to 100 by 2005.

Principal Subsidiaries

1,2,3 GmbH (Germany); 1,2,3 Luxembourg; Di Carla; Etam SA; Elan SARL; Elan Industries; Etam Belgique; Etamil Bruxelles; Elan Belgium; Etamint (Belgium); E.I.S. (Belgium); Etamil GmbH (Germany); Etam Italie; Etam Japan; Etam Luxembourg; Etam PLC (U.K.); Garnier SA; IFEM (Spain); Intermoda (China; 60%); Modasia Luxembourg (60%); Nortex SA; SARL Entrepôts Compans; S.C.I. Breucq; S.C.I. Sebu; Strasbourg Sélection; Texindia; U.B.O. (India).

Principal Competitors

Abercrombie & Fitch Co.; Arcadia Group plc; Benetton Group S.p.A.; Diesel SpA; Esprit Holdings Limited; Guess?, Inc.; H&M Hennes & Mauritz AB; Marks and Spencer p.l.c.; New Look Group plc; NEXT plc; The Gap, Inc.; Zara SA.

Further Reading

Carr, Miranda, ''Etam Goes to French for Pounds 93m,'' *Daily Telegraph*, November 13, 1997.
Cousteau, Libie, ''Etam: Toujours plus,'' *Enjeux les Echos*, January 1, 1998, p. 42.
Michel, Caroline, ''Etam se rétame,'' *Capital*, February 2001, p. 42.
Peyrani, Beatrice, ''Etam, la marque préférée des lolitas,'' *Expansion*, November 5, 1998, p. 168.

—M.L. Cohen

Express Scripts Inc.

13900 Riverport Drive
Maryland Heights, Missouri 63043
U.S.A.
Telephone: (314) 770-1666
Fax: (314) 702-7037
Web site: http://www.express-scripts.com

Public Company
Incorporated: 1986
Employees: 5,259
Sales: $6.7 billion (2000)
Stock Exchanges: NASDAQ
Ticker Symbol: ESRX
NAIC: 45411 Electronic Shopping and Mail-Order
   Houses; 51421 Data Processing Services

Express Scripts Inc. (ESI) operates as a leading independent pharmacy benefits manager (PBM) in the United States. Headquartered outside of St. Louis, and with facilities in seven states and Canada, ESI provides a full range of PBM services and distributes outpatient pharmaceuticals through retail drug card programs, mail pharmacy services, formulary, and various other clinical management programs. Its clients include health maintenance organizations (HMOs), health insurers, third-party administrators, employers, union-sponsored benefits plans, and government health programs. The company's subsidiary, Practice Patterns Science (PPS), formed in 1994, provides variation analysis and disease management support services. Health Management Services, an ESI division created in 1997, offers demand and disease management support services.

With the rising dominance of managed health care and increasing pressure to contain health care costs, ESI grew rapidly in the 1990s and into the new millennium. The company's sales reached $6.8 billion in 2000 and it secured earnings growth for the 36th consecutive quarter. In 2001, ESI's PBM services covered more than 55,000 pharmacies in the United States—this figure included 99 percent of all U.S.-based retail pharmacies and five mail pharmacy service centers. The firm's member base grew to include 43.5 million customers.

ESI's position as a leading independent among the country's top PBMs has proved to be a strong selling point with its customers. In 2000, *Fortune* magazine ranked ESI as one of the fastest-growing companies in the U.S., and the firm was also named part of the *Fortune* 500 List and the *Forbes* Platinum List.

Origins in the 1980s

Express Scripts was born out of the boom in health management organizations of the late 1970s and early 1980s. In 1983, two employees of McDonnell Douglas, then one of Missouri's largest employers, left that company to start up their own HMO, called Sanus Corp. Health Systems. Backed by major investors McDonnell Douglas and General American Life Insurance Co., the private Sanus grew quickly, expanding into the Dallas, Fort Worth, Houston, and Washington, D.C., markets, as well as in St. Louis, signing up 90,000 members and reaching revenues of $30 million by 1985. One year later, Sanus's membership had swelled to 200,000, and revenues topped $100 million. As Sanus grew, it expanded its range of services as well. Considered innovative at the time, Sanus operated not only an HMO but also a preferred-provider plan, or PPO, and a standard health insurance plan. The expansion of Sanus's services led the company to establish GenCare Health Systems as an umbrella operation for the Sanus plans. By then, Barrett A. Toan had joined the company to serve as executive director.

Toan, who held a bachelor's degree from Kenyon College and a master's degree from the University of Pennsylvania's Wharton School of Finance and Commerce, came to the private sector after years in public service. Early in his career, after a period of working as a high school teacher, Toan served as the assistant director with the office of state planning and development in Pennsylvania, and later as a budget analyst and deputy director for the Illinois Bureau of Budget. In the late 1970s, he was appointed commissioner of the division of social services for the state of Arkansas under Bill Clinton, then in his first term as governor. In 1981, Toan moved to Missouri, where he was named director of that state's department of social service.

As director of social service, Toan was placed in charge of Missouri's Medicaid system, which had seen a 40 percent rise

Company Perspectives:

Our vision is to lead the industry through excellent, innovative, and ethically grounded pharmacy services and through trusted, impartial, and practical counsel that enables our clients to navigate the rapidly changing pharmaceutical landscape.

in costs in the previous year alone. Toan convinced the state legislature to enact major changes in Medicaid, especially in that system's pricing structure. Where previously doctors and hospitals had been allowed to bill Medicaid for services after they were performed, which led to the charging of inflated fees, Toan argued for set fees to be negotiated in advance of treatment. These price caps forced providers to control their own costs, a trend that would lead to the rise of the HMO as the dominant form of health care provision by the mid-1990s.

Toan left public service in 1985, joining GenCare as its executive director, and GenCare, with additional investments from New York Life, expanded into the New York, New Jersey, and Maryland markets. Despite the greater efficiency of managed care over traditional health insurance plans, GenCare found itself paying high prices for its members' prescriptions. Hiring a claims examiner to process prescriptions, however, would not have provided the company greater efficiency. Instead, Toan negotiated with St. Louis-based Medicare-Glaser to process and fill GenCare and Sanus members' prescriptions. Data on prescription orders were then provided to GenCare, eliminating the need for GenCare to enter the data on its own. Medicare-Glaser was, at the time, one of the 25 largest pharmacy chains in the United States, operating nearly 90 pharmacies and full-line drug stores, as well as optical and home health centers, principally in Missouri, but also in Illinois and Connecticut.

Toan quickly recognized that this arrangement had applications beyond the GenCare-Sanus network. In late 1986, GenCare and Medicare-Glaser formed ESI as a joint venture providing mail-order prescription drug and claims processing. Under the agreement, Sanus members in Missouri and Illinois continued to receive their prescription benefit through the Medicare-Glaser pharmacy chain. The remainder of Sanus's 200,000 member network became ESI's initial customers; however, the company quickly began marketing its services to health care providers across the country. Early ESI clients included the cities of Baltimore, Memphis, and San Antonio. Toan became head of ESI, while continuing to lead GenCare.

By 1987, New York Life had begun to increase its investment in Sanus Health Systems, investing more than $50 million in the company and increasing its investment to as much as $75 million in the following year. New York Life was also an early investor in ESI. In 1988, Medicare-Glaser began to stumble as Walgreen's moved to expand aggressively in the former company's core St. Louis market. By early 1989, with losses mounting, Medicare-Glaser announced it was merging with SupeRx of Arizona, Georgia and Alabama Corp., moving its headquarters to Arizona. At the time of the merger, Medicare-Glaser

agreed to sell its 50 percent interest in ESI to Sanus, giving New York Life, which had already gained controlling interest in Sanus, full ownership of both GenCare and ESI. Medicare-Glaser subsequently filed for bankruptcy and closed or sold off all of its stores.

New York Life quickly sold GenCare back to General American, retaining the Sanus HMO and ESI. Toan, however, continued to serve as the head of both GenCare and ESI, both of which were based in St. Louis. Toan remained with GenCare through 1991, when he took the company public. Toan left GenCare in 1992 to turn his full attention to ESI.

Growth in the Early- to Mid-1990s

ESI revenues rose rapidly as it entered the 1990s, from $27.4 million to nearly $72 million by the end of 1991. Membership in ESI prescription plans had also increased to more than 1.5 million. Part of the company's growth could be attributed to the evolving role of PBMs in general, from mail-order prescription drug discounters and claims processors to playing an active role in patient pharmaceutical management. By 1991, less than 80 percent of ESI revenues were achieved through its mail-order sales. PBMs also began to play a more prominent role in health care management: as managed care slowly became the dominant form of health insurance, patient prescriptions became one of the most expensive insurance benefits. PBMs offered not only discounted drugs but also the ability to offer increased data analysis of the care process, working with providers to define cost-effective treatment, offer patient drug education services, and alert providers to potential inappropriate drug treatment stratagems. ESI's services also expanded to provide eye wear and home infusion therapy programs.

Toan took ESI public in 1992, joining a wave of health care-related firms filing initial public offerings in the early 1990s. ESI's IPO, which raised more than $28 million, was made in part to enable New York Life Insurance to maintain control over the company. ESI offered two classes of stock. The class A stock, which accounted for most of the shares being sold, gave shareholders one vote per share. The class B stock, of which New York Life, through its NYLife Healthcare Management subsidiary, controlled nearly 97 percent, gave shareholders ten votes per share. In addition, only the class A stock would be traded on the NASDAQ index. Toan was named CEO of ESI, which by then had more than 220 employees and 1,150 clients. Sanus members, however, continued to account for nearly 55 percent of all ESI sales.

ESI stock rose rapidly, from its IPO of $13 per share to a high of $35.25 per share early in 1993. However, investors grew nervous after the inauguration of President Clinton and his attempted health care reforms. ESI stock slipped to $28 per share and then to $21.50. However, ESI continued to grow, expanding its pharmacy network to 28,000, and membership reached two million customers in 1992. The following year, ESI signed on FHP International Corp. and Maxicare Health Care, both based in California, which together held three percent of the national HMO market. ESI also added such corporate clients as Lockheed Corp., Service Merchandise Co., and Ingersoll-Rand Co. These new clients doubled ESI's customer base, boosting its share of the pharmacy mail-order market to 2.5

Key Dates:

1986: Express Scripts Inc.(ESI) is formed as a joint venture between GenCare Health Systems and Medicare-Glaser.

1989: Medicare-Glaser sells its 50 percent interest in ESI to Sanus Corp., now controlled by New York Life.

1991: ESI revenues reach $72 million; membership increases to 1.5 million.

1992: The company goes public; membership grows to two million customers.

1993: ESI lands FHP International Corp. and Maxicare Heath Care as clients.

1994: The company forms a subsidiary entitled Practice Patterns Science.

1995: Canadian PBM Eclipse Claims Services is acquired.

1996: Membership exceeds nine million after APS Healthcare signs ESI to provide pharmacy benefits.

1997: Health Management Services is created and operates as a new division of ESI.

1998: ESI purchases ValueRx, creating the largest independent U.S.-based PBM (pharmacy benefits manager).

1999: Diversified Pharmaceutical Services is acquired; ESI purchases a 19.9 percent stake in PlanetRx.com Inc.

2000: ESI posts a $9 million loss after writing off the value of its PlanetRx.com stock.

2001: ESI partners with Merck-Medco and AdvancePSC to form RxHub LLC.

percent—behind leader Medco's 50 percent. In 1993, ESI more than doubled its revenues, to $264.9 million for net income of over $8 million. In response to the increase in its West Coast business, ESI opened a second mail-order service facility in Tempe, Arizona.

ESI was also helped by another trend that swept through the PBM industry. In 1993, Merck & Co. paid $6.6 billion for Medco. This acquisition was quickly followed by SmithKline Beecham's $2.3 billion purchase of Diversified Pharmaceutical Services. Then PCS was purchased by Eli Lilly & Co. for $4 billion. Caremark, a division of J.C. Penney with roughly 15 percent of the PBM market, instituted alliances with Pfizer, Bristol-Myers, Rhone-Poulenc, and Lilly in 1994. The last of the large PBMs, Value Health, announced its joint venture with Pfizer in 1995. Distrust of these new relationships—and suspicion that the drug companies would exert too much influence on the PBMs to include their parent companies' drugs in their formularies, that is, the list of drugs approved for their customers' use—proved beneficial to ESI. The company's independent status helped lure FHP as a client—one executive at FHP told the *New York Times:* "Large employers and health plans don't want to get in bed with Lilly or Merck." In 1994, Coventry Corp., a national HMO based in Nashville, also chose Express Scripts as their PBM.

By 1994, ESI had expanded its pharmacy network to 34,000 stores. Its revenues reached $384.5 million, producing a net income of $12.7 million. The company expanded its services by adding workers' compensation prescription services and reinsurance. The company's growth also fueled its stock price, which reached $50.50 per share in April 1994. In that year, the company also began to emphasize computer technology, introducing its RxWorkbench software used for analyzing patient prescription data. By the end of 1994, ESI membership had grown to 5.7 million.

The following year, ESI reached an agreement with San Diego-based American Healthcare Systems Purchasing Partners L.P. to provide for that group's network of 800 hospitals and 100 nursing homes. The company also made a deeper investment in information technology by launching its Practice Patterns Science (PPS) subsidiary in 1994. PPS offered clients the ability to combine medical and pharmaceutical data in order to identify treatment and spending patterns, allowing for improved patient outcomes at lower cost.

ESI's purchase of Canadian PBM Eclipse Claims Services allowed it to move into that market in 1995. Canadian customers included divisions of Aetna, Prudential, and Manufacturers Life insurance companies. The company also instituted an agreement with CIBA Vision Ophthalmics U.S. to form a managed eye care alliance, marketing disease management programs using technology developed by PPS. By the end of 1995, ESI's revenues had increased nearly 42 percent over the previous year to $544 million, with net earnings of over $18 million. The company's pharmacy network increased to 45,000 stores, while its membership swelled to more than eight million people.

ESI's membership jumped past nine million early in 1996 when APS Healthcare—newly formed in a merger among American Healthcare Systems, Premier Health Alliance, and SunHealth Alliance—signed ESI to provide pharmacy benefits. Growth continued the following year, when a contract was signed with RightCHOICE Managed Care, a subsidiary of Blue Cross & Blue Shield of Missouri.

ESI made two key acquisitions in the latter half of the 1990s that would prove to be highly beneficial and position the firm as a leading PBM. In 1998, ESI acquired ValueRx, the PBM business of Columbia/HCA Healthcare Corp. The deal, completed in April of that year, created the largest PBM in the U.S. that was independent of a drug manufacturer.

Just one year later, in April 1999, ESI purchased Diversified Pharmaceutical Services from SmithKline Beecham Corp. The $700 million cash deal secured ESI's position as the third-largest PBM overall in the U.S., managing nearly $10 billion in drug spending. Toan commented on the two purchases in a 1999 company press release, stating, "These acquisitions have not only provided critical mass, but also competitive strength in key markets and scope of capability that translate into value for our customers."

ESI also teamed up with PlanetRx.com in late 1999 to offer ESI members' options for purchasing prescriptions and over-the-counter health products via the Internet. The partnership made PlanetRx.com the exclusive online pharmacy for ESI's growing membership base and ESI received a 19.9 percent stake in the dotcom firm.

ESI published a 1999 Drug Trend Benefit Report which claimed spending on prescription drugs in 1999 rose by 17.4 percent over the previous year, and that average prescription costs rose by 9.6 percent. These trends complemented ESI's bottom line handsomely as revenue for 1999 reached $4.2 billion and net income exceeded $150 million, more than a 250 percent increase over the previous year.

ESI entered the new millennium on solid ground. It was ranked among the top 500 companies in the U.S. by both *Fortune* and *Forbes* and was well positioned to continue its dominance in the PBM industry. During 2000, however, the firm was forced to write off its $165 million relationship with PlanetRx.com when the Internet startup experienced financial difficulties. While the company posted a $9.1 million loss for 2000, management downplayed the deal-gone-bad, claiming it had provided cash for new technology ventures.

One such venture was inked in February 2001, when ESI joined with competitors Merck-Medco and AdvancePCS Inc.—together, the firms were the top three PBMs in the U.S. industry—to create RxHub LLC. The joint venture was designed to develop an electronic exchange that would allow participating physicians to link to PBMs, health plans, and pharmacies. The venture however, was met with concern by pharmacies throughout the industry that were leery about the costs and the flow of information from doctor to pharmacy. There was also fear that the three companies would divert prescription orders to their own mail-order operations versus having them filled at a retail location. Nevertheless, ESI and its partners forged ahead with their plans.

In 2001, ESI predicted that drug spending would increase an average of 15 percent per year for the next five years. While management remained focused on new technology ventures, controlling costs, and growth options, the company's rank as a leading PBM left it in a favorable position to secure positive financial results in the years to come.

Principal Subsidiaries

Practice Patterns Science, Inc.; ESI Canada Inc.; Express Scripts Specialty Distribution Services; IVTx Inc.; Value Health Inc.; Diversified Pharmaceuticals Services Inc.

Principal Divisions

Health Management Services.

Principal Competitors

AdvancePCS Inc.; Caremark Rx Inc.; Merck-Medco.

Further Reading

Chesler, Caren, "Leader's Success," *Investor's Business Daily*, December 20, 1993, p. 1.

"Express Scripts Completes Acquisition of Diversified Pharmaceutical Services," *PR Newswire*, April 1, 1999.

"Express Scripts Completes ValueRx Deal," *Chain Drug Review*, May 25, 1998.

"Express Scripts, PlanetRx Complete Deal," *Chain Drug Review*, November 22, 1999.

"Express Scripts Searches For Ways to Manage Costs," *Chain Drug Review*, March 26, 2001.

Frederick, James, "Pharmacy Leaders Voice Concerns About RxHub Prescribing Concept," *Drug Store News*, May 21, 2001, p. 15.

Jacobson, Gianna, "Independence Creates Niche in Health Care," *New York Times*, July 15, 1995, p. 40.

Lau, Gloria, "Concentrating Drug Purchases to Reduce Costs," *Investor's Business Daily*, April 20, 1994, p. A6.

Manning, Margie, "Express Scripts On a Roll Despite Setbacks in 2000," *St. Louis Business Journal*, March 9, 2001, p. 1.

Roller, Kim, "Express Scripts PBM Reports Record Increase in Drug Spending," *Drug Store News*, August 14, 2000, p. 41.

Steyer, Robert, "Rx for Growth: Express Scripts Pays off Quickly for Investors," *St. Louis Post-Dispatch*, March 1, 1993, p. 12.

—M.L. Cohen
—update: Christina M. Stansell

FAIR GROUNDS RACE COURSE

Fair Grounds Corporation

1751 Gentilly Boulevard
New Orleans, Louisiana 70119
U.S.A.
Telephone: (504) 944-5515
Toll Free: 1-800-262-7983
Fax: (504) 944-2511
Web site: http://www.fgno.com

Public Company
Incorporated: 1941
Employees: 805
Sales: $41.7 million (2000)
Stock Exchanges: OTC
Ticker Symbol: FGRD
NAIC: 711212 Race Tracks; 71329 Other Gambling
Industries

The Fair Grounds Corporation owns and operates the Fair Grounds Race Course in New Orleans, Louisiana. In addition to Thoroughbred horse racing, the company provides off-track betting and video poker gaming both at the track site and in nearby parishes. Besides offering off-track betting at the Fair Grounds, through an affiliate, Finish Line Management Corporation, it also operates five Finish Line off-track betting venues in adjacent parishes. These also offer video poker in addition to parimutuel wagering, as well as food and beverage services. Each year, the Fair Grounds conducts a racing meet or season that normally runs from Thanksgiving to the last Monday in March. Altogether, the company operates over 300 video poker machines and collects additional monies from the 300 plus gaming machines operated by Finish Line. Besides Thoroughbred horse racing, Fair Grounds hosts other events, notably the New Orleans Jazz and Heritage Festival. Although a public company, the Fair Grounds Corporation is largely owned by the Krantz family, which bought controlling interest in the track in 1990.

1852–62: Union Track in New Orleans Is Laid Out

In many ways, the complex history of the Fair Grounds is a story about people and horses, about jockeys and trainers,

legendary Thoroughbreds and their owners, and even some important historical personages who from time to time appear unexpectedly—figures like Jesse James' brother Frank, for example, who in 1902 became betting commissioner for Samuel Hildreth, then the owner of the track's largest racing stable; or Pat Garret, who gunned down Billy the Kid, and who, in 1893, ran a stable of horses in the Fair Grounds' first 100-day meet; or Broadway's infamous ''Diamond Jim'' Brady, who, on January 17, 1906, was in the stands when a 200 to one longshot, North Wind, won the track's feature race.

The Fair Grounds can trace its track's origin back to 1852, when the Union Race Course was laid out on Gentilly Road in New Orleans, the site of the modern track and facility. The Union Course had competition from other tracks, including the Metairie track, which was laid out in 1838. In fact, the Metairie track's competition grew too tough, and the Union track closed down from 1857 to 1859, when it was purchased by the Metairie Trotting and Pacing Club and renamed the Creole Race Course.

1863–79: The Creole Race Track Is Turned into the Fair Grounds

During the Civil War, racing in New Orleans, soon under Union occupation, came to a virtual standstill at first. However, in 1863, the Creole Race Course was transformed into a fair grounds that was leased to promoters of everything from bull and bear fighting and boxing and baseball exhibitions to, yes, some horse racing. By then the site was called the Fair Grounds.

After the war, the Metairie Trotting and Pacing Club was reorganized as the Metairie Jockey Club, which rebuilt and conducted races at the Metairie track from 1867 to 1872. During that time, some of the club's younger members formed a new association, the Louisiana Jockey Club, which, under president Gustav Breaux, renovated the Fair Grounds and began racing there at spring and fall meetings. Meanwhile, the old Metairie track was sold off and turned into a cemetery.

It was on April 13, 1872, that the Louisiana Jockey Club held its first race at the Fair Grounds, a two-mile hurdle with eight jumps. Among other noteworthies who figured in the races held by the Louisiana Jockey Club were General George Armstrong Custer, who owned a horse named Frogtown that raced

---

Company Perspectives:

The Fair Grounds Corporation is a multi-faceted operation that includes a live Thoroughbred racing meet, off-track wagering, and video poker at locations throughout the region and account wagering to local, national, and international customers. As the Thoroughbred racing industry grows and becomes more competitive than ever, Fair Grounds continues to make progress and looks forward to the future.

in two-mile heats, and Grand Duke Alexis of Russia, who attended some of the races.

1880–99: New Louisiana Jockey Club Buys the Fair Grounds

In 1880, after Reconstruction ended, the New Louisiana Jockey Club was formed. Raising $75,000, it bought the Fair Grounds and commenced racing there on March 30 of that year. Notables in the grandstands for that season included Ulysses S. Grant, 18th president of the United States.

In 1886—four years after electric lighting was used in the Fair Grounds' grandstand for the first time—Duncan Kenner became president of the New Louisiana Jockey Club and, in the next year, management of the Fair Grounds was passed over to Caldwell & Lamothe, a partnership. In that same year, 1887, John Campbell opened a jockey school at the track.

Before the century closed, in 1894, the Crescent City Derby was inaugurated. It became the main predecessor of the Louisiana Derby, which in turn became one of the nation's greatest racing events. Two years later, track officials experimented with a new starting gate device that helped insure that all mounts would leave the gate simultaneously. Two years after that, in the summer of 1898, the Fair Grounds was briefly converted into Army Camp Foster for training troops readying for action in the Spanish-American War. Finally, in 1899, the track managers laid out a new steeplechase course.

1900–19: The Fair Grounds Faces Tough Times

Steeplechase racing was short lived at the Fair Grounds, lasting only to 1902, when the course was dismantled. With an enlarged grandstand, the track returned to obstacle-free meets as the only kind of racing. It did face new competition starting in 1905, when City Park opened a winter season and went head to head with the Fair Grounds for clientele. A track war erupted in 1906, but in the next year it was settled when Matt Winn, sent to New Orleans by the American Turf Association, became acting general manager of both tracks. Also in that year, 1907, after betting on horse racing was outlawed in Missouri, the Union Park track in St. Louis was dismantled and sent to New Orleans, where, at the Fair Grounds, it was rebuilt.

Between 1908 and 1915, the so-called Locke Law brought a hiatus to racing in New Orleans. The law had emerged from growing public annoyance with the corrupting influence of bookmakers and a growing disillusion with the sport of kings. When it did start up again in 1915, under the control of the

Businessmen's Racing Association, bookmaking at the Fair Grounds was not allowed. That was only one of its problems, though. In 1917, Jefferson Park, another competing track, opened and, late in 1918, fire destroyed the grandstand at the Fair Grounds. In the next year, the grandstand was rebuilt from the disassembled parts of the grandstand from the defunct City Park racetrack.

1920–41: Parimutuel Betting Is Once More Legalized

Through the early 1920s, the most exciting thing happening at the Fair Grounds was the emergence of Black Gold, one of the all time great Thoroughbreds in the history of racing. In 1926, two years after Black Gold won the Louisiana Derby, Colonel E.R. Bradley, owner of the Palmetto Club, bought the Fair Grounds and ordered the construction of a new clubhouse and stables. Black Gold, which had also won the Kentucky Derby, was put down in January 1928, after going lame in the running of the Salome Purse. The famous horse was buried on the track's infield.

In 1932, Colonel Bradley retired and the Fair Grounds was leased to a group of Chicago investors headed by J.C. Shank. The hard times led the new owners to reduce the race purses, ultimately dropping them in half. Then, in 1934, they sold out to a syndicate headed by Robert S. Eddy, Jr., and Joseph Cattarinich, who were operating Jefferson Park. The syndicate bought the Fair Grounds for $375,000.

Eight years later, on the eve of World War II, under Governor Sam Jones, Louisiana once again legalized horse-race betting and formed the Louisiana State Racing Commission as an oversight agency. However, that same year, 1940, the owning syndicate sold the Fair Grounds to real estate developers, whose plans were to turn the track and grounds into a subdivision. In 1941, at the last possible minute, a group of New Orleans businessmen led by William G. Helis formed the Fair Grounds Corporation and saved the track from destruction. That year also saw the formation of the Fair Grounds Breeders and Racing Association, which oversaw racing at the track.

1942–82: Racing Continues in the War Years and After

Racing continued during the war. Notably, in 1942, Whirlaway, Calumet Farm's famous Triple Crown winning Thoroughbred, won the inaugural Louisiana Handicap. Whirlaway ran at the Fair Grounds as part of a war relief event scheduled by the newly created Thoroughbred Racing Association.

After a brief closure ordered by the War Mobilization Department in January 1945, the Fair Grounds got back in business. For the next several years, it hosted some of racing's legendary mounts and jockeys, including Bill Shoemaker, who in 1950 rode in races during the final month of the track's season. Shoemaker went on to take the national riding title and become the most famous of all jockeys in the sport. Later, in 1958, Tenacious, a very popular Thoroughbred, won the New Orleans Handicap, then won it again the next year.

In 1971, the Fair Grounds, by then very rich in tradition, established its Racing Hall of Fame. In that same year, Jefferson

Key Dates:

1852: Union Race Course is laid out on Gentilly Road in New Orleans.

1857: Competition from Metairie racetrack forces the Union Race Track to close for two years.

1865: The Metairie Jockey Club reorganizes and rebuilds its track, running from 1867 to 1872.

1872: Metairie Jockey Club begins racing at the renovated Fair Grounds track.

1880: Former Metairie Jockey Club members, Robert Simmons and G.W. Nott, form the New Louisiana Jockey Club.

1886: Duncan Kenner becomes president of the New Louisiana Jockey Club at the Fair Grounds.

1887: Caldwell & Lamothe partnership takes over management of the Fair Grounds.

1905: The New Orleans Jockey Club begins winter racing at City Park in direct competition with the Fair Grounds.

1908: The Locke Law ends racing in Louisiana for seven years.

1915: Racing returns to Fair Grounds, but bookmaking is still prohibited.

1918: Fire destroys the grandstand at Fair Grounds but within a year is replaced by the grandstand from the City Park track.

1926: Colonel E.R. Bradley becomes Fair Grounds' new owner.

1932: Bradley retires, and Fair Grounds is leased by a Chicago group.

1934: Syndicate operators of Jefferson Park purchase Fair Grounds.

1940: Fair Grounds owners sell track to real estate developers.

1941: Newly formed Fair Grounds Corporation saves Fair Grounds when developers put it on the auction block.

1971: Fair Grounds Racing Hall of Fame is inaugurated.

1990: Krantz family purchases controlling interest in Fair Grounds from Roussel group.

1994: Rebuilding of grandstand and clubhouse commences but is halted the following year because of gaming industry scandals.

1997: New grandstand and clubhouse facility is opened.

Downs opened at a new location, in Kenner. The old Jefferson Downs was destroyed by Hurricane Betsy. Three years later, Tony Bentley began his 22-year career as Fair Grounds' track announcer. He would go on to call some important races, including the 1975 victory of Master Derby in the Louisiana Derby and the 1982 win by El Baba in the photo finish of that same event.

The middle and late 1980s produced considerable excitement at the Fair Grounds. In the 1983–84 racing season, jockey Randy Romero, a native of Erath, Louisiana, set a record for most wins at the Fair Grounds when riding to his 181st victory. Famous mounts running and winning at the track included, in 1984, Wild Again, eventual winner of first Breeder's Cup Classic; Tiffany Lass, 1986 winner of the Eclipse Award for the country's top three-year-old filly; Risen Star, which in 1988 won the Louisiana Derby and went on to win the Preakness and Belmont Stakes; and Honor Medal, which in 1989 just missed his bid to become the only Thoroughbred to win the New Orleans Handicap three times.

1990–2001: Ownership Changes Usher in Significant Revenue Growth

The Fair Grounds changed ownership again in 1990, when the Krantz family bought a controlling interest in the track and saw the facility through a decade of exciting moments. In 1991, the track hosted the first Louisiana Champions Day, an event dedicated to an all-Louisiana bred, ten-race card. Two years later, in 1993, another legend in the making, Dixieland Heat, completed an unbeaten season of racing. Disaster also struck that year when, on December 17, a fire completely destroyed the grandstand. Racing continued with temporary facilities, and in the next year construction began on a new $27.5 million complex that was finally fully completed and opened in 1997. In the interim, in 1996, Dixie Poker Ace became Louisiana's all-time money-winning Thoroughbred, and Grindstone won the Louisiana Derby before going on to win the Kentucky Derby, becoming the only horse besides Black Gold to accomplish that feat. Also in 1996, the Fair Grounds set an all time single-day record when, on February 3, racing fans plunked down almost $3.85 million in bets.

Towards the end of the 1990s, increases in purses brought status changes and new records. The Louisiana Derby was upgraded to Grade II status in 1998, and two years later, its purse was increased to $750,000. Before that, in 1998, the Louisiana Champions Day had combined purses of $1 million, making it the richest day in Louisiana racing ever. These milestones at the track testified to how well the Fair Grounds was doing. The best year was 1998, when the Fair Grounds' revenues reached $36.8 million and generated a profit of $9.0 million. Its revenue climbed to $41.8 million the next year, but its profits declined to $1.4 million, and in 2000 dropped to $100,000 from gross revenues that had dropped slightly to $41.7 million. Although disappointing after the performance of 1998 and 1999, the income for 2000 was still a long way up from the track's performance in 1994, when the Fair Grounds lost $1.5 million on a gross of only $22.4 million, a sink hole partially created by heavy competition from the gaming industry but one from which the company climbed through the rest of the century.

In the fall of 2000, Fair Grounds stockholders were considering a reverse stock split which would allow the company to revert to the private sector. According to Fair Ground's president, Bryan Krantz, the cost of being a public company was the main consideration. At the time, company stockholders only numbered 413, and the stock traded very thinly. The change was at least deferred, however, and the company was still a public entity in the fall of 2001.

Principal Competitors

The Edward J. DeBartolo Corporation; Harrah's Entertainment, Inc.; Isle of Capri Casinos, Inc.

Further Reading

Brannon, Keith, ''New Orleans Fair Grounds Seeks to Rejoin the Ranks of Private Companies,'' *New Orleans City Business Online*, http://citybusiness.neworleans.com/21.13.7-NewOrleans.html.

''Fair Grounds Corporation Intends to Restate Fiscal 1998 and 1999 Financial Statements,'' *Business Wire*, December 17, 1999.

Finn, Kathy, ''Worried Days at the Races,'' *New Orleans Magazine*, December 26, 1991, p. 84.

''United Gaming Inc., Fair Grounds Corp. Sign Agreement,'' *Wall Street Journal*, March 3, 1992, p. B4.

—John W. Fiero

Flour City International, Inc.

1044 Fordtown Road
Kingsport, Tennessee 37663
U.S.A.
Telephone: (423) 349-8692
Fax: (423) 349-0150
Web site: http://www.flourcity.com

Public Company
Incorporated: 1997
Employees: 1,411
Sales: $70.3 million (2000)
Stock Exchanges: NASDAQ
Ticker Symbol: FCIN
NAIC: 332312 Fabricated Structural Metal Manufacturing; 332321 Metal Window and Door Manufacturing; 332323 Ornamental and Architectural Metal Work Manufacturing; 32799 All Other Miscellaneous Nonmetallic Mineral Product Manufacturing

Flour City International, Inc., based in Kingsport, Tennessee, designs, fabricates, and installs curtainwalls—the non-load bearing wall systems, usually constructed of aluminum frames with glass, granite, or aluminum panels, that comprise building exteriors. Flour City is the only public company that provides curtainwalls with a complete range of service from design and fabrication to installation. The company's focus is on custom curtainwall projects, which represent up to 15 percent of a building's cost. These projects usually involve larger buildings than those faced with standard curtainwalls, ensuring a higher profit margin and less competition. Typically, Flour City works on diverse public and private structures such as mid-rise and high-rise commercial and governmental office buildings. Among other landmark buildings, Flour City fabricated and installed curtainwalls on the Citicorp Center in New York, the First Interstate Bank Tower in Los Angeles, and the Rock and Roll Hall of Fame in Cleveland. The company has operations in several countries, including Australia, China, the Philippines, Thailand, and the U.K. In recent years, much of the growth in the company's revenue has come from its business in the Pacific Rim. As a

modus operandi, Flour City works closely with other companies and firms, including architects, general contractors, and owners/developers. Among others, it has teamed up with such well known architectural firms as Skidmore, Owings & Merrill and Pei Cobb Freed, and such contractors as Bovis, Turner Construction, and Bechtel. Although Flour City is a public company, almost 50 percent of it is held by its chairman, John Tang.

1893–1987: Flour City Begins as an Ornamental Metalwork Foundry

Flour City International took its name from its host city, Minneapolis, Minnesota, which towards the end of the 19th century was popularly known as the flour capital of the U.S. It was there that, in 1893, Flour City was founded as Flour City Ornamental Metal Works. Originally, the company was a foundry that made ornamental metal works, including bronze castings, and manufactured larger units, such as elevator cages and spiral staircases.

During World War I, Flour City began to change its essential business, redirecting its manufacturing focus away from ornamental metal towards military needs. It became a defense contractor, using its manufacturing capacity and industry knowhow to fabricate pieces for strategic use, something it would do again during both World War II and the Korean conflict. For its contributions to the war effort in both those wars it received Defense Department commendations.

During the Great Depression between World Wars I and II, Flour City Ornamental Metal Works gained a certain degree of notoriety when, on September 11, 1934, two young males were killed and 30 others injured when police fired on a crowd supporting striking workers at the company's plant. Publicity surrounding that and other labor disputes that erupted into violence helped unions gain enough public sympathy to emerge as very powerful organizations, especially in such industrial centers as Minneapolis.

In the postwar building boom after World War II, the company began to shift its business in the direction of the fabrication of facing units for large buildings, including the multi-story high rises that technology had made possible in the first half of the 20th century. Among other things, to utilize its expertise and full manufacturing capacity, the company began to make windows and panels for building facades or "curtainwalls."

Basically, curtainwalls are the non-load bearing external walls of modern mid-rise and high-rise structures. They consist of a combination of glazing and cladding elements (windows and panels) and supports necessary to attach them to a building's main structure. They are manufactured from a variety of materials, including glass, aluminum, stainless steel, and diverse natural stones. Essentially, the market has two segments: standard and custom. Typically, standard curtainwalls consist of stock, pre-fabricated components that, because they do not have to be repeatedly designed and engineered, are much less costly than customized curtainwalls. In contrast, custom units require extensive design and engineering work and are more expensive to produce and install. On the average, custom curtainwalls, mostly used in high-rise and monumental buildings, account for between five percent and 15 percent of the overall cost of a building. Once it entered the curtainwall industry, Flour City chose to design and produce custom units.

1988–98: Mergers and Reorganization

Flour City International, Inc. did not take its structural form until the late 1990s. It became the successor to a paper, namesake company that was incorporated in January 1997, also in Nevada, which merged with and into a dormant corporation, International Forest Industries, Inc. (IFI), which, like Flour City International, had been founded and incorporated in Nevada in 1987. IFI then adopted the Flour City International, Inc. name and immediately acquired three companies: Flour City Architectural Metals, Inc. from Armco, Inc.; Hockley International Limited, a British Virgin Islands company; and Kaison Contracting Ltd. Hockley, which was incorporated in 1993, was purchased via a share exchange package and renamed Flour City Architectural Metals (Pacific), a holding company for Flour City's Pacific-Rim operations, which Kaison renamed Flour City Architectural Metals (Asia) and thereafter managed.

1999–2001: Problems and Renewed Growth

Despite taking something of a bottom line pounding in 1999, netting a loss of $2.2 million, Flour City had cause to cheer. A new trade agreement between China and the United States opened up the possibility of a much greater expansion of the company's business in China and Hong Kong. Flour City's 1998 revenues from the Pacific Rim reached 60 percent of the company's total, but during 1999, the figure rose to 70 percent. The good news was that sluggish economies of Pacific Rim

countries, stagnant or recessive for over a decade, had at last started to improve, leading to new contracts for Flour City.

In the summer of 1999, to better deal with the challenges facing the company, Flour City made some high level changes in management. At the top, chairman John W. Tang took on the additional post as CEO, Edward M. Boyle III became president, and Roger Ulbricht filled the slot of executive vice-president. Boyle replaced Michael J. Russo, who resigned and left the company. The shakeup also included changes in lesser executive positions.

Asian market hopes began materializing later in 1999. In October, for example, the company got a $20 million contract to supply over 400,000 square feet of aluminum and glass curtainwall for a 61-story building in the Stubbs Road residential project in Hong Kong, a much sought after plum. Furthermore, Flour City began making progress in the very difficult European curtainwall market, one that had not had a history of welcoming non-European competitors. In January 1999, the company had opened a sales office in London, and during the year it landed contracts for two projects for 2000 totaling $19 million.

In September 2000, Flour City signed a "memorandum of understanding" with Siemens Solar Industries L.P. and Atlantis Energy Inc. The purpose of the agreement was to identify business opportunities for using Building Integrated Photovoltaic (BIPV) modules in new construction projects and jointly develop them. It was a major opportunity for Flour City to expand its use of an important and growing technology–solar energy. The company's research group had already been working closely with Hong Kong University to develop a curtainwall system incorporating Photovoltaic Panels (PV) into the various materials used in curtainwalls and, in April, had filed for a patent for a manufacturing method that eliminated the need to embed a network of wires in curtainwall panels.

Atlantis Energy, a subsidiary of Atlantis Energy Systems, based in Switzerland, is a major manufacturer of BIPV modules, while Siemens Solar is the world's leading producer and supplier of solar cells and modules in the photovoltaics industry. In concert, the three companies agreed to target architects, developers, and contractors wishing to use photovoltaics in their building projects. Although far more costly than other kinds of facades, BIPV modules had a major appeal: used to supplement roof-top solar panels, when installed in windows, walls and sunshades, they could help supply as much as 100% of a building's electrical requirements from solar power alone.

New contracts and alliances were major factors in Flour City's turn around in 2000. Its revenues climbed to $70.3 million, a very strong 64 percent gain over its $45 million from the year before. The company also returned to profitability, with net earnings of $2.5 million. Furthermore, with the new century started, Flour City continued to make significant inroads in foreign markets, including the U.K. In March 2001, it got a $10.4 million contract to design, make, and install the curtainwall for the new MSP (Members of the Scottish Parliament) building to be erected in Edinburgh, Scotland. Scheduled for completion before April 2003 elections, the MSP building would be put up in the historic Holyrood district of Scotland's capital and become an integral part of the new Parliament complex.

Key Dates:

1893: Flour City Ornamental Metal Works is founded.
1997: The company merges with International Forest Industries Inc. (IFI), which changes its name to Flour City International, Inc.; John W. Tang becomes chairman.
1999: Tang assumes post of CEO.
2000: Flour City enters a development arrangement with Siemans Solar Industries L.P. and Atlantis Energy.
2001: Edward M. Boyle III is named CEO and president, but later resigns and is replaced by Tang as CEO and Roger Ulbricht as president; company faces contract terminations.

In July 2001, Edward M. Boyle III succeeded Tang as Flour City's president and CEO. Tang stepped down because of chronic health problems, but he maintained his position as chairman of the company's board. Before joining Flour City in 1998 as COO of Flour City Architectural Metals (Asia), Boyle held various positions in the industry, including a term as director of sales and marketing for Harmon CFEM Facades in the U.K. and Harmon CFEM Facades S.A. He had also been a director of Harmon Sitrarco. Altogether, Boyle brought 17 years of industry experience to his new posts. However, he did not solve some immediate problems faced by Flour City, including the impending cancellation of contracts due to the company's alleged performance defaults. In late August, Flour City announced that some of its project contracts had in fact been terminated. Whether these cancellations were directly responsible or not, Tang re-assumed the company's active leadership as CEO. The company's board appointed Ulbricht president. Ulbricht, a 40-year Flour City veteran, returned from retirement to the take the post. He had previously served as CEO and president of Flour City Architectural Metals and, as indicated above, as executive vice-president of Flour City International.

Altogether, in the summer 2001 debacle, Flour City was terminated as the subcontractor on five major projects, including the Random House Headquarters, Four Seasons Hotel & Tower, Las Olas City, TrumpWorld Towers, and Bronx Criminal Courthouse projects. The company also received default notices on two international projects: the 42D Stubbs Road project in Hong Kong and the Ciro Plaza project in Shanghai. Until that point, Flour City had being doing very well, with revenues that were up 56 percent over the previous year. The company also ranked 216th on *ENR: Engineering News-Record*'s Top 600 Specialty Contractors list and 3rd on its Top 20 list of glazing and curtainwall companies.

In the autumn of 2001, Flour City was busily engaged in damage control through renegotiations with its clients. The contract cancellations were reflected in the company's third-quarter report, which acknowledged that net revenues of $18.6 million for the quarter resulted in a net loss of $17.9 million. At the time, Johnson K. Fong, Flour City's CFO and executive vice-president, announcing the company's displeasure with the financial showing, said, ''While the next few months will be challenging, we believe our longevity, reputation and strong presence within the construction industry will assist management in obtaining the funding necessary for positioning the company to achieve its goals for growth and a return to profitability.''

Chances were that Flour City would iron out its problems. Its business, fed by persistent urban growth needs, is a durable one, and once by the termination difficulties it should be in good shape to regain both its momentum and its reputation.

Principal Subsidiaries

Flour City Architectural Metals, Inc.; Flour City Architectural Metals (Asia) Ltd.

Principal Competitors

Hunter Douglas N.V.; International Aluminum Corporation; James Hardie Industries Limited; Nippon Light Metal Company, Ltd.; Permasteelisa S.p.A.

Further Reading

''Flour City International Expands Worldwide Headquarters to Accommodate Continuing Growth,'' *Business Wire*, June 7, 2000.

''Flour City International Reorganizes Management Team,'' *Business Wire*, August 27, 1999.

''Flour City International to Continue to Strengthen Itself in Its Key Markets: Interview with Edward Boyle,'' *Wall Street Transcript*, September 10, 2001.

''Flour City Ousted from Projects,'' *ENR–Engineering News Record*, September 3, 2001, p. 15.

''New Trade Agreement Between China and U.S. Presents Tremendous New Business Opportunities and Future Growth for Flour City,'' *Business Wire*, November 23, 1999.

''Siemens Solar Teams Up With Flour City International and Atlantis Energy to Offer BIPV Modules in Building Industry,'' *PR Newswire*, September 26, 2000.

—John W. Fiero

Great Harvest Bread Company

28 South Montana Street
Dillon, Montana 59725
U.S.A.
Telephone: (406) 683-6842
Toll Free: (800) 442-0424
Fax: (406) 683-5537
Web site: http://www.greatharvest.com/

Private Company
Incorporated: 1976
Employees: 1,200 (est.)
Sales: $60 million (1999 est.)
NAIC: 53311 Lessors of Nonfinancial Intangible Assets
(Except Copyrighted Works); 311811 Retail Bakeries

Great Harvest Bread Company is known for baking great whole wheat bread and for following unconventional business strategies. There are about 150 franchised Great Harvest bakeries across the United States, and much has been made of the company as a ''learning organization,'' its network of franchisees free to innovate and communicate.

A Business Based on Lifestyle

Great Harvest founders Pete and Laura Wakeman met as children in Durham, Connecticut. As a teenager Pete was sent for two years to finish high school in Deep Springs, California. There he became the school's resident baker, having learned how to make bread from an aunt. Pete and Laura began baking bread for money in 1972 to help pay for college, using an antiquated, water-driven stone mill to grind the wheat. They called the operation ''The Happy Oven,'' Pete recalled in Tom McMakin's book *Bread and Butter*.

The Wakemans' studies at Cornell University were ideal for the career path they would later follow. Pete graduated with a degree in agricultural economics in 1974; Laura earned a degree in nutrition a year later. Pete worked for a year on a dairy farm during his Laura's last year in school. After graduating from Cornell, Pete and Laura married, settling in Montana after

hiking 500 miles between Yellowstone and Glacier National Parks. There they bought an existing bakery in Great Falls, and the unorthodox methods of the Great Harvest Bread Co. began to take shape.

A cardinal rule of conventional baking they abandoned was the early starting hours. After three weeks of getting up at 3:00 a.m., they allowed themselves to work later in the day, which put the sights and smells of making fresh bread in front of the delighted customers. They also addressed the problem of burnout early on by not working weekends and keeping time cards to prevent themselves from working too many hours. However, it was the traditional, even anachronistic baking practices they followed that proved the most effective way of drawing customers. The Wakemans' started with spring wheat from Montana, stone ground every morning. This helped give the bread a shelf life of up to 12 days at room temperature. The dough was kneaded by hand and sweetened with honey or molasses instead of refined sugar.

Franchising in the 1980s and 1990s

To market their bread, the Wakemans gave out samples, warm from the oven. In 1978, someone asked the Wakemans for a franchise, beginning the proliferation of Great Harvest bakeries across the country. In 1982, the couple sold their Great Falls store and moved south to Dillon, a three-hour drive, to live and work as franchisers. After a few years of assisting with all the store openings themselves, the Wakemans hired Ray Potter, who held an M.B.A., in 1988. In early 1992, however, Potter and two other trainers left the company in an event company COO Tom McMakin refers to as the ''great upheaval.'' Great Harvest later sued one of the three for allegedly starting up a competing bakery using the company's trade secrets.

By 1995, Great Harvest had 93 outlets in 33 states. The business was growing an average of 25 percent a year, fueled in part by the habit of giving walk-in visitors a free slice of whole wheat bread—accompanied with butter, if desired. A couple of stores in Wisconsin were giving away 50 loaves of free slices every day. Another store in Kansas gave away more than 700 loaves, one per customer, on its opening day. Bakers also made donations to food banks.

Key Dates

1976: Pete and Laura Wakeman start the first Great Harvest bakery in Great Falls, Montana.
1982: The Wakemans sell their store and focus on franchising.
1996: The number of Great Harvest bread stores reaches 100 nationwide.
2001: The Wakemans sell their company.

Sound business practices were also critical to the chain's survival. Founder Pete Wakeman particularly stressed the importance of remaining as free of debt as possible. Due to his desire for free time, he was also fond of creating checklist-driven systems that allowed the stores to function with a minimum of input from the owners. *Money* magazine reported that at this time, store owners paid an initial $24,000 franchise fee, while setup costs ranged from $100,000 to $300,000. Franchisees were protected from cannibalization (diminution of business by competing franchises) within a 16-mile radius during the first year and a half of operation and an eight-mile radius thereafter. Great Harvest received 7,500 inquiries for the 15 new franchises it signed on in 1994.

Great Harvest insisted that its owners be operators as well in order to insure the quality of the bread. Laura Wakeman told a trade magazine that baking was more difficult than most franchises due to hands-on work and the greater number of variables, since wheat and yeast were living organisms. "They have to have a feel for the bread," she said. New owners, in fact, were bound by a "one-year apprenticeship."

Apart from these requirements, the trade press reported, owners had unprecedented freedom among franchises. "Be loose and have fun," began the company's mission statement. "ANYTHING not expressly prohibited by the language of this agreement IS ALLOWED," read the contract. Some owners operated their stores as delis, while others kept their offerings to the basics. The smallest store—the only one owned by the company—was located in Dillon, Montana, at the 258-square-foot site of a former one-hour photo shop. The microbakery performed nearly all of the functions of a regular store, with the exception that milled flour was shipped in daily. Variations among the products sold by Great Harvest included Oregon Herb, Cinnamon Raisin Walnut, Cheesy Jalapeno Cornbread, Cranberry Orange, and Cracked Pepper Parmesan. Prices ranged from $3 to $5 a loaf. There were also chocolate chip, oatmeal walnut, and oatmeal raisin cookies. Owners often made an effort to inform customers about their products, such as sending recipes and product news to "bread zealots." Such sharing of information may have exposed Great Harvest to the danger of leaks to competitors, noted the *Wall Street Journal;* however, Pete Wakeman believed that due to his group's rapid rate of innovation, "They'll be left holding a blueprint of what Great Harvest was, and we'll be out of view."

Due to the owners' willingness to rapidly implement new approaches—"Innovation happens overnight in our company," said Laura Wakeman in the *Wall Street Journal*—Great Harvest franchises formed a close-knit community connected by an internal e-mail network, a system that served a vital purpose in the chain's support system. In addition, through its Travel Match program, Great Harvest paid for half the travel costs when any franchise owner or employee visited another store in the system.

Tim and Marianne Heeren, owners of two stores in Wichita, Kansas, told a local business journal in 1996 that finding and retaining help was their biggest challenge. Their best answer was to create a relaxed and casual work environment. They played different types of music to accommodate their workers' individual tastes and encouraged creative input from the employees, such as creating new bread recipes. In 1999, a Great Harvest store near Philadelphia was featured in television ads for Microsoft Corp. The owner was shown using the Internet to communicate with his peers and to monitor flour prices.

New Owners in 2001

In June 2000, Great Harvest was testing its first full-service restaurant in a former theater in downtown Butte, Montana. The company aimed to more than double the $450,000 average annual sales of a typical unit before taking the full-service concept national. The most successful Great Harvest shop at the time was taking in $1.3 million a year. Great Harvest received 5,000 inquiries and 150 formal applications in 2000; the company chose only half a dozen to join the elite community of owners. Great Harvest's franchisees' convention that year took place in teepees at Yellowstone Park.

In June 2001, St. Martin's Press published a book of chief operating officer McMakin's reflections, *Bread and Butter,* that became a best seller. Among its advice: make time for yourself first, then money. Tom McMakin, a former Peace Corps volunteer, had moved to Montana with his wife and joined Great Harvest as editor of its newsletter in 1993. He became chief operating officer in May 1997, a position he described to *Franchise World* as the company's sheepdog: "A sheepdog knows the general direction we are supposed to be going and keeps the whole thing moving forward. It runs around the edges and kind of looks out for the whole." He left the company soon after publishing his book.

There were more changes at the top. In spite of founders' emphasis on franchisees running their own stores, and the extent to which Great Harvest Bread Co. reflected their own lifestyles, in June 2001 Pete and Laura Wakeman sold the company to a North Carolina investment group for an undisclosed price. Nido Qubein and William Millis of High Point and Mike Ferretti of Charlotte lead the buyers' group, which pledged to preserve Great Harvest's loose management style. Qubein, owner of a consulting company, became the new chairman, while Ferretti became CEO. Andy Bills, another investor, told the *Greensboro News Record* that the group wanted to create a stronger growth strategy. ''We think there's a sleeping giant here with a lot of untapped potential,'' said Qubein. The company announced its intention to have 500 stores by 2005.

Principal Subsidiaries

Great Harvest Franchising Inc.

Principal Competitors

Breadsmith; Panera Bread Co.

Further Reading

Becker, Denise, ''Group Buys Bakery with Style; New High Point Owners Say They'll Preserve the Great Harvest Bread Co.'s Loose Management Approach,'' *Greensboro News Record* (North Carolina), June 20, 2001, p. B8.

Bishop, Todd, ''Mixing One Part Bread, One Part Microsoft,'' *Philadelphia Business Journal,* June 11, 1999.

Enge, Janet, ''Bakers Enjoy Breaking Bread with Community; Mom-and-Pop Store Donates Day's Profits to Various Charities,'' *Milwaukee Journal Sentinel,* November 9, 1995, p. 11.

''Great Harvest Tests First Full-Service Outlet,'' *Nation's Restaurant News,* June 12, 2000, p. 136.

Hopkins, Michael, ''Zen and the Art of the Self-Managing Company,'' *Inc.,* November 2000, pp. 54–63.

''Introducing the World's Smallest Scratch Bakery,'' *Bakery Production and Marketing,* June 15, 1997, p. 24.

Johnson, Patricia Carroll, ''Generosity Is the Focus of Great Harvest Bread Co.,'' *Intelligencer Journal* (Lancaster, Pa.), July 12, 1996, p. A4.

Kroskey, Carol Meres, ''Age-Old Concepts for the Twenty-First Century,'' *Bakery Production and Marketing,* June 15, 1997, pp. 28–29.

——, ''Keeping the Fun in Fundamentals,'' *Bakery Production and Marketing,* June 15, 1997, pp. 22–25.

Larson, Polly, ''Great Harvest: 'The Best of Both Worlds','' *Franchising World,* January/February 2001, pp. 22–23.

Luciano, Lani, ''Three Franchisors That Make the Grade,'' *Money,* September 1995, p. 116.

McMakin, Tom, *Bread and Butter: What a Bunch of Bakers Taught Me About Business and Happiness,* New York: St. Martin's Press, 2001.

Obiala, Anne Marie, ''Rising Assets: Specialty Bread Shops Sow Seeds of Success,'' *Ft. Wayne Journal-Gazette* (Indiana), November 25, 1996, p. C1.

Petzinger, Thomas, Jr., ''Bread-Store Chain Tells Its Franchisees: Do Your Own Thing,'' *Wall Street Journal,* November 21, 1997, p. B1.

Rotella, Mark, Charlotte Abbott, and Sarah F. Gold, review of *Bread and Butter* by Tom McMakin, *Publishers Weekly,* April 9, 2001, pp. 57–58.

Row, Heath, ''Great Harvest's Recipe for Growth,'' *Fast Company,* December 1998.

Ruthhart, Bill, ''Bread Guru Spreads Recipe for Happiness,'' *Daily Herald* (Arlington Heights, Ill.), June 29, 2001.

Schafer, Sarah, ''Informing Customers,'' *Inc.,* June 1996, p. 114.

Talaski, Karen, ''Bread Goes Premium; Household Staple Becomes a Fashionable Food,'' *Detroit News,* April 18, 2001.

Veltkamp, Ron, ''No Loafing, Rising Profits for Great Harvest Bread Co. Owners,'' *Journal of Alaska Business and Commerce,* February 23, 1998, p. 23.

Wright, Pamela, ''Heerens Keep Work Fun, Casual in Effort to Attract Employees,'' *Wichita Business Journal,* November 29, 1996.

—Frederick C. Ingram

Groupe Fournier SA

42, rue de Longvic
21300 Chenöe
France
Telephone (+33) 3 80 44 70 00
Fax: (+33) 3 80 44 70 66
Web site: http://www.groupe-fournier.com

Private Company
Incorporated: 1880
Employees: 4376
Sales: EUR 689 million ($600 million)(2000)
NAIC: 325520 Adhesive Manufacturing; 322222 Coated and Laminated Paper Manufacturing; 339113 Surgical Appliance and Supplies Manufacturing

Groupe Fournier SA is a minor player among the world's pharmaceutical giants but remains a goliath in its chosen niches. Ranked as the 13th largest French pharmaceutical company—and number 84 in the global market—Fournier has developed a predominant position in the market for lipid-lowering drugs through its discovery and development of fenofibrate-based therapies, notably through its Lipanthyl brand. In addition to its work on cardio-vascular medications, the company also develops drugs for the Uro-gynecology field, including estrogen-replacement systems, and anti-ulcer agents for the gastroenterology specialty. The company has developed its international operations through marketing and distribution partnerships with local companies. International pharmaceutical sales account for more than half of the company's sales in that category. Altogether, Fournier's pharmaceuticals activity accounts for 70 percent of its sales. The company also produces bandages through its Laboratoires Urgo brand, holding the first place in the French first-aid market and a leading position throughout Europe. The company's third division, Plasto Adhesives and Polymers produces a range of products for the healthcare, automotive, electricity and electronics, construction and other industries. Fournier is 100 percent owned by Jean Le Lous through the private Holding Fournier Industrie et Santé. Le Lous's son-in-law, Bernard Majoie, led the company through the 1990s before turning over the CEO spot to former Bristol-Meyers-Squibb executive Bernard Helain in 1999. The company has consistently rejected acquisition approaches from the rapidly consolidating pharmaceuticals industry; in order to protect its position, Fournier invests as much as 16 percent of its revenues in research and development. The company's sales neared EUR 700 million in 2001. Fournier is present in some 29 countries.

Drugstore Origins in the 19th Century

Groupe Fournier traced its beginnings to a drugstore operated in Dijon, home of the famous mustard, in the Burgundy region in France. The pharmacy, operated by Pierre Bon and Eugène Fournier, like many of its counterparts at the time, fabricated many of its own medicines. In 1892, the company built a new facility to house its pharmacy and growing production activity. By the end of the century, Laboratoires Fournier, as the company came to be known, listed some 150 products in its catalog.

The beginning of Fournier's industrial era began in the 1930s, when the company developed its own adhesive tape by adding glue to a strip of cloth. The company's invention soon became a major focus for its activity and a major source of its revenues. Fournier developed its sticking plaster and then a full range of adhesive tapes under the Plasto brand name. The Plasto brand soon captured the leading share in the French industrial adhesives market, and later built up international sales to become the second largest adhesives manufacturer in Europe. In 1952, the company set up a separate subsidiary, Plasto Adhésifs & Polymères. The new subsidiary was backed by a strong client list, including the French army, which contracted the company for supplies of tape for its ammunition crates. Fournier later extended its adhesives operations into the larger plastics sphere, adding products for the automobile industry, but also for the health care, hardware, and construction industries.

The outbreak of World War II proved catastrophic for the Fournier family. By 1941, the company's financial difficulties and lack of raw materials led it to turn to Jean Le Lous, who took over the company and managed to rescue its finances and resume production. If the company had concentrated on its adhesive tape operations since the 1930s, Le Lous placed a new

Company Perspectives:

Groupe Fournier is a diversified international pharmaceutical group, constituted by a conglomerate of French and international companies working in complementary areas and linked under the umbrella of the wholly French-owned holding company Fournier Industrie et Santé.

emphasis on building the company's pharmaceutical product. Under Le Lous, research and development became a primary component of Fournier's activity, and through the war the company began developing new pharmaceutical products based on more readily available raw materials such as saccharine and algae. The company continued to develop its Plasto bandages and tapes as well. By the beginning of the 1950s, Fournier's operations were divided between its pharmaceuticals and adhesives operations. To the Plasto brand of industrial adhesives the company added the Urgo (from *urgent*—French for "emergency") brand of bandages and other first-aid products.

Fournier's breakthrough came in the 1970s. By then the company had been joined by Le Lous's son-in-law Bernard Majoie, who, in 1975, developed a new class of drugs, called fenofibrates, exhibiting lipid-lowering effects. The release of Fournier's new drug, which was given the brand name Lipanthyl, coincided with the developing world-wide understanding of the role of cholesterol, lipids, and hypertension in the incidence of heart disease. The approval of the drug for use in treatment in France and then in Europe placed Fournier, despite its relatively small size, in the front lines among Europe's drug companies.

As research studies continued to validate Lipanthyl's effectiveness, and as researchers discovered new potential for the fenofibrate molecule, Fournier's fortunes rose. By the 1990s, Lipanthyl had become the most-prescribed lipid-lowering medication in Europe. In the United States, however, Fournier's ambitions remained frustrated. Its efforts to introduce Lipanthyl in the United States market, begun in 1984, were successively thwarted by the Food & Drug Administration's tightening drug approval process.

Diversified Conglomerate for the 21st Century

Jean Le Lous turned over leadership of the company to Majoie, who in turn led the company through the 1990s, before retiring in 1999. Le Lous, meanwhile, retained the chairmanship of Fournier's controlling holding company, Holding Fournier Industrie et Santé, which represented the interests of the some 100 members of Le Lous's family. Under Majoie, Fournier stepped up its international expansion in the 1990s. The company extended its sales of Lipanthyl to more than 80 countries. Most of Fournier's international growth came through a series of partnerships with locally operating companies. Many of these partnerships were with Fournier's heavyweight counterparts, such as Glaxo-Wellcome in France, Pfizer in the United Kingdom, and SmithKline Beecham in Italy. Other partnerships were with Byk Gulden in France, Bayer, and, at the end of the 1990s, Abbott in the United States and Grelan/Tekada in Japan.

Fournier invested strongly in its research and development of new products—the company's research and development effort in its pharmaceutical branch represented some 18 percent of total sales, more than the industry average. Among the new products the company worked on were new transdermal drug delivery systems—better known as a 'patch'—which achieved popularity as a smoking cessation aid. Fournier's long experience with adhesives and bandages gave the company a strong position in the developing category. The company combined this expertise with the development of estrogen-replacement therapies for the treatment of menopause symptoms, releasing its Oesclim (Eslcim in the United States) patch.

The company found another strong product with the acquisition of Laboratoires Debat, also based in France in 1993. Debat brought Fournier its research in a new class of drugs for the treatment of benign hypertrophic prostate conditions. Fournier began marketing the new drugs under the Tadenan brand name, which became one of the most widely prescribed medications for that condition worldwide. The addition of Tadenan, and the success of Oesclim and Tadenan helped raise Fournier's sales to more than EUR 490 million by 1996.

Fournier at last received FDA approval for marketing Lipanthyl in the United States in 1994. The company began negotiations to find an American partner to market its drugs and reached an agreement with Abbott Laboratories, which introduced Lipanthyl to the United States in 2000. By then, Fournier had found a partner in Japan as well, with Grelan Pharmaceuticals Co. Ltd., part of the Takeda Group, which began marking Lipanthyl in 1999.

Fournier's international component grew strongly through the 1990s, with new subsidiaries being opened in Germany, Italy, and Spain, a push into Eastern Europe, with offices first opened in Hungary, the Czech Republic, and Slovakia, then in Bulgaria, Russia, and China. The company boosted the share of its international sales from about one-third to more than half by the end of its 2000 year. Important for the company was the development of its international operations beyond Europe.

In 1997, Fournier complemented its Urgo subsidiary with the acquisition of Mobypharm, the French leader in sales of extendible bandages, which marketed its products under the Nylex brand name. That company, which had been founded in 1923, had originally produced curtains and lace products before transforming itself into a medical textiles manufacturer in the 1950s. Mobypharm's success was due to its use of combining nylon and cotton to form its extendible bandages—the company held exclusive rights to its process through the end of the century. Also in 1997, Fournier's Plasto subsidiary formed a joint-venture with the United States' Foamade, called FPA. The joint-venture extended Plasto's growing activity in automobile interior fittings with the purpose of developing and marketing detachable parts for the automobile industry in the United States.

Majoie retired in 1999, replaced by Bernard Helain, forming vice-chairman with Bristol Myers Squibb. That appointment sparked a brief flurry of rumors that Fournier might finally be up for sale to one of its larger competitors—which had long been courting the steadfastly family-controlled company. Fournier quickly dispelled any notion of the company selling, reaf-

Key Dates:

1880: Fournier pharmacy first opens.
1930s: Adhesive tapes are developed.
1941: Jean Le Lous takes over company.
1952: Plasto subsidiary is created.
1975: Lipanthyl is developed.
1993: Laboratoires Debat is acquired.
1997: Mobypharm is acquired.
1999: Lipanthyl is introduced in Japan.
2000: Lipanthyl is introduced in the United States; Selena (Sweden) is acquired.

firming its intention to remain 100 percent private and family-owned.

At the turn of the century, Fournier began looking for new acquisitions to extend its chosen niche activities and to boost its international operations. In 2000, the company acquired Sweden's Selena, a pharmaceutical distributor to the Scandinavian market, which had already been acting as a major distributor for Fournier's products in that region. By the end of that year, the company's sales neared EUR 690 million. Fournier could look back on a century of innovative products and breakthrough medications and to a future of continued growth. The company remained small among the world's global pharmaceutical players, but a giant in its chosen niche.

Principal Subsidiaries

Fournier Hellas (Greece); Fournier Pharma GmbH (Germany); Fournier Pharma SpA (Italy); Laboratorios Fournier SA (Spain); Fournier Pharmaceuticals Ltd. (U.K.); Fournier Pharma Inc. (Canada); Fournier Research Inc. (U.S.); Fournier Group Singapore; Fournier Japan; Plasto Aludec (Spain); Plasto/Foamade Industries (U.S.); Plasto GmbH (Germany); Selena Fournier AB (Sweden); Urgo Healthcare Products Co. Ltd. (Thailand); Urgo Med-Com Spol sro (Czech Republic).

Principal Competitors

Abbott Labs; American Home Products Corporation; Amgen Inc.; AstraZeneca PLC; Aventis; Barr Laboratories, Inc.; BASF AG; Bayer AG; Bristol-Myers Squibb Company; Chiron Corporation; Elan Corporation; Eli Lilly and Company; Genentech, Inc; GlaxoSmithKline PLc; Glaxo Welcom; Hoffmann-La Roche, Inc.; Johnson & Johnson; Merck & Co., Inc.; Mylan Laboratories Inc.; Novartis AG; Novo Nordisk A/S; Pfizer Inc; Sanofi-Synthélabo; Schering-Plough Corporation.

Further Reading

Iskandar, Samer, ''Old Family Business Sticks to Sales Expansion Target,'' *Financial Times*, February 26, 1999.

Jemain, Alain, ''Fournier soigne à Prague et à Bratislava,'' *L'Usine Nouvelle*, July 3, 1997.

''Les Laboratoires Fournier bientôt vendus?'' *L'Expansion*, April, 11, 1999, p. 12.

''Molypharm est repris par le groupe Fournier,'' *Les Echos*, September 2, 1997, p. 21.

Tiller, Alan, ''Niche Drugs Help Fournier Say 'Non','' *European*, November 16, 1995, p. 32.

—M.L. Cohen

Groupe Jean-Claude Darmon

5 rue de Liège
75009 Paris
France
Telephone: (+33) 1-55-07-10-00
Fax: (+33) 1-48-78-80-88
Web site: http://www.darmonsport.com

Public Company
Incorporated: 1969 as Société d'Editions et Promotions
Employees: 83
Gross Billings: FFr 1.14 billion ($165.4 million)(2000)
Stock Exchanges: Euronext Paris
Ticker Symbol: JCD
NAIC: 541820 Public Relations Agencies; 711320
  Promoters of Performing Arts, Sports, and Similar
  Events without Facilities

Groupe Jean-Claude Darmon is France's leading sports marketing group, and founder and chairman Jean-Claude Darmon is widely credited as the force behind the financial coming-of-age of the French professional sports industry. Professional soccer—also known as football—remains Darmon's bread-and-butter: the company handles the advertising, promotions, and public relations for 18 of France's 20 Premiere League teams. The company also has long-standing relationships with the French Football Federation and the National Football League. Darmon has also extended its expertise into other professional sports—including rugby, ice skating and hockey, and tennis—through its ownership of the Tournoi de Toulouse and contracts with the Monte Carlo tennis tournament. Beyond France, Darmon has developed a position in Africa, notably through its contract with the Confédération Africaine de Football and the Fédération Royale Marocaine de Football. Darmon has also launched a satellite channel devoted to football on the African continent. Darmon went public in 1996, taking a listing on the Paris secondary market. In 2001, the company announced its intention to form a new company with Sports Plus, of Vivendi Universal, and Bertelsmann's Ufa Sports, to form the world's leading sports rights group. That merger, expected to clear European Community monopolies scrutiny, will almost certainly result in a name change for the group. Jean-Claude Darmon is expected to remain as chairman of the new company, which will start out with estimated revenues of EUR 570 million.

A New Age in French Sports Marketing

French professional sports, as in most parts of the world, remained a relatively minor business and was often described as amateurish when it captured the imagination of Jean-Claude Darmon. Born in Oran, Algeria, but raised in France since the age of six, Darmon worked as a dockworker in Marseilles while pursuing night school courses. A dedicated soccer fan, Darmon recognized that French soccer had barely developed any kind of self-promotion activities beyond the stadiums, and what little promotion was done was decidedly amateurish.

Darmon came up with the idea of developing a series of "Livre d'Or" commemorative books celebrating the history of France's great soccer teams. Launched in 1968, the series was a success and led Darmon to create his own company, the Société d'Editions et Promotions (SEP). As part of his research for the book on FC Nantes, then at the height of its glory, Darmon paid a visit to the team's aging stadium. At the time, players' jerseys were still free from advertisements—as was the stadium itself for the most part. In 1969 the Nantes team agreed to allow Darmon to commercialize its billboard space, to great success. The following year, Darmon launched the era of advertising-clad uniforms, convincing Michel Axel to pay FFr 15,000 for the right to place its logo on the Nantes team's jerseys.

By the mid-1970s, the same contract was worth more than FFr 400,000—and by the end of the century, companies seeking to place their logos on France's leading teams were expected to plunk down tens of millions of francs for the privilege. Darmon's work for FC Nantes quickly caught the attention of many other French teams. By 1972, Darmon was handling the promotion activities for teams from Nîmes, Reims, and Sochaux. In order to coordinate his growing business, Darmon incorporated as FC Nantes Promotion, with a capital of just FFr 20,000 and three employees.

Key Dates:

1968: Jean-Claude Darmon publishes the "Livre d'Or" series commemorating French soccer clubs.
1969: The group gains first promotional contract with FC Nantes.
1970: The group places first advertisement on players' jerseys.
1972: The group incorporates as FC Nantes Promotions and begins handling rights for other soccer teams.
1976: The group is awarded contract for promotional right for Bastia soccer club at European Cup finals.
1987: The group co-founds POOL television broadcasting rights group.
1990: The group acquires rights to CAF matches.
1992: The group reorganizes operations to create Groupe Jean-Claude Darmon.
1993: The group wins ten-year contract for Cadre Noir equestrian training and sports facility at Saumur.
1996: Groupe Jean-Claude Darmon goes public on Paris stock exchange.
1998: Audiofina acquires 25 percent of the group.
1999: The group forms Club Europe with Canal Plus and teams from Bordeaux, Marseilles, Monaco, Lyon, Paris and Lens.
2000: The group expands into Italy, with rights contracts for five Italian teams.
2001: The group announces its intention to merge with Sports Plus and Ufa Sport.

Darmon's business soon incorporated contracts with many of France's leading teams, including Paris-Saint-Germain, Monaco, and Lyon. The company also was quick to pick up on the potential for television rights. At the end of the 1960s, sports broadcasting occupied a decidedly marginal spot on the French television dial—which sported just three channels. Yet the launch of a new soccer-dedicated program, "Telefoot," on TF1, gave still greater television exposure to France's soccer clubs and opened the way for still more lucrative promotional contracts. In the mid-1970s, also, both the French football federation (FFF) and the French National Football League (LNF) (soccer is called football in France) turned to Darmon to help their organizations build their own promotional activities—a service Darmon provided for free. Yet this recognition of Darmon's expertise served as a strong promotion for his own business, which was flourishing rapidly by the end of the decade. In 1976, Darmon picked up the contract for the public relations and promotions activities surrounding the entry of the Bastia soccer team into the finals of the European Cup—the first time a French team had reached the finals in nearly 20 years.

A New Era in French Sports

When France reached the World Cup in Spain in 1982, Darmon's company was picked to handle the promotional rights for the event. The company now not only held contracts with many of France's major teams, both the FFF and LNF became Darmon customers. Darmon was once again picked to handle the French national teams promotional rights during the 1984

European Cup finals. By the early 1980s, the company's revenues had topped FFr 45 million.

A revolution in sports marketing had been brewing in the meantime. Television rights were set to propel France's professional soccer industry into a new era as a financial heavyweight. Up until the early 1980s, France's three government-owned television stations had shown little regard to sports programming, paying only minor fees for broadcast rights for professional soccer matches. The privatization of TF1, and then the launch of France's first new subscription-based commercial station Canal Plus changed the sports broadcasting landscape.

Darmon once again offered his services free of charge as the FFF and the LNF turned their backs on the French national stations and instead negotiated contracts with the new upstart station. The original deal was for just 20 first division matches per year. Yet these matches helped propel Canal Plus's own growth. The channel quickly surpassed its original expectations of just two million subscribers and doubled that number by the end of the decade, reaching six million subscribers by the late 1990s. Professional soccer's part in that growth helped propel the sport into the ranks of big business. The influx of new money enabled teams to improve their own professionalism and attract more talented players from around the world, which in turn brought still more viewers. If soccer teams initially feared that broadcasting matches might drain their stadiums, the opposite proved true, as the greater television exposure brought still larger numbers of fans to fill the country's stadiums.

Television broadcasting as a new force in the rise of professional soccer—and sports rights—in France was confirmed in 1987 by the World Cup in Mexico, for which Darmon held the promotional rights. At the same time, Darmon helped negotiate a new POOL system, in which both teams and television stations benefited from the growing popularity of European Cup matches. Darmon's company benefited as well, seeing its revenues top FFr 128 million in 1987, then nearly doubling a year later to FFr 235 million. That same year, Darmon looked beyond soccer for the first time, organizing the rugby tournament "Les Villages du Tournoi des V Nations." Yet soccer remained Darmon's dominant activity. The company also ventured outside of France, picking up the management contract for broadcasting rights from the African Confederation of Football.

A Global Sports Rights Heavyweight in the 1990s

With its revenues nearing FFr 340 million in 1990, Darmon stepped up the diversification of his company's activities, such as winning a ten-year contract to handle the marketing rights for the acclaimed Cadre Noir equestrian school of Saumur in 1993. By then, Darmon restructured his businesses, which were regrouped under the new name of Groupe Jean-Claude Darmon. In 1994, Darmon gained the promotional rights contract for the Fédération Française des Sports de Glace, handling broadcasting and advertising rights not only for ice hockey teams but for ice skating competitions as well.

The mid-1990s saw a veritable explosion in the sports broadcasting industry. The arrival of new competition, in the form of satellite broadcasters, greatly increased the price of broadcasting rights. Darmon's revenues reflected this new change, with sales jumping from FFr 352 million in 1995 to FFr 652 million in 1996. In that year, Darmon took his company public, selling 15 percent of his shares on the Paris exchange. Soon after the IPO, Darmon sold another 15 percent of his holding to investor group Henderson Investors. By then, the company had gained the sports rights contracts for 18 of the 20 French first division teams.

In 1997, Darmon reinforced its presence in Africa with the award of the rights contract for the newly created League of Champions of the Confédération Africaine de Football (CAF). The company also moved into the lucrative professional tennis scene, acquiring the Tournoi de Toulouse, and the rights contract for the Monte Carlo tennis tournament. By 1998, sales had topped FFr 835 million.

By the end of the 1990s, Darmon began casting its sights on even bigger contracts. Yet the company, despite sales that grew to FFr 1.14 billion in 2000, remained too small to offer the financial guarantees required for such events as the Olympic Games and the World Cup—the latter's contract was worth more than FFr 12 billion to sports rights leader Leo Kirch. Meanwhile, the sports rights business was growing rapidly and attracting increasingly tough competition from groups with deeper pockets than Darmon.

Darmon had in the meantime begun to interest a number of large-scale media companies. One of these groups was Audiofina, holder of 50 percent of European broadcasting giant CLF-UFA, which acquired a 25 percent stake in Groupe Jean-Claude Darmon in 1998. This investment helped the company win the rights contract for France to host the World Cup in 1999. France's win that year not only boosted French soccer, but also stepped up the growing sports rights industry itself. Darmon formed Club Europe along with Canal Plus and leading soccer clubs Bordeaux, Marseille, Lyon, Monaco, and Paris-Saint-Germain that same year.

In 1999, Darmon turned to soccer-mad Italy in an effort to recreate its French success. In November of that year, the company acquired a 51 percent stake in Bastimo Multimedia. That acquisition provided a foothold for the company in the Italian soccer scene, and by the end of 2000 the company had signed on five professional Italian teams, including one of the country's top teams, Juventus of Turin.

By 2001, Darmon, eager to take part in securing the contracts for the world's biggest sports events, reached an agreement to merge with Sports Plus, the sports rights subsidiary of Canal Plus and ultimate parent Vivendi Universal and Ufa Sports, owned by Bertelsmann through its RTL Group holding. The merger, which absorbed the two larger groups into Darmon in order to gain Darmon's public listing, created the world's largest sports rights group, worth an estimated EUR 570 million in combined revenues. Announced in May 2001, the merger was expected to clear European Commission monopolies inquiries. Jean-Claude Darmon, whose stake in the new group was to be reduced to five percent, was to remain as chairman. Yet his name was not expected to remain—the new global powerhouse was expected to choose a new name by the end of the year.

Principal Subsidiaries

Girosport SA; Société du Palais des Sports de Toulouse SA; Rugby France Promotion SA; Football France Promotion SA.

Principal Competitors

Leo Kirch; News Corp.; International Management Group; WPP Group plc; The Interpublic Group of Companies, Inc.; Clear Channel Entertainment; TBA Entertainment Corporation; Sportsworld Media Group Plc; Havas Advertising.

Further Reading

Belleville, Renaud, "La saga Darmon: Le financier du foot entre en Bourse," *Les Echoes*, November 26, 1996, p. 54.

Garrahan, Matthew, "Sports rights giant unveiled," *Financial Times*, May 21, 2001.

Le Bailly, David, "Les pionniers du sport business passent la main," *La Tribune*, May 23, 2001.

——, "Le marketing sportif surf la vague médiathique," *La Tribune*, October 16, 2000.

"L'Historique de la Société," Groupe Jean-Claude Darmon corporate web site, September 2001.

Meistermann, Nathalie, "Darmon Sees New Heights for Sports Rights Firm," *Reuters* May 22, 2001.

—M.L. Cohen

Grupo IMSA, S.A. de C.V.

Avenida Batallon de San Patricio 111
San Pedro, Garza Garcia, Nuevo Leon 66269
Mexico
Telephone: (528) 153-8433
Web site: http://www.grupoimsa.com

Public Company
Incorporated: 1936 as Industrias Monterrey, S.A. de
   C.V.
Employees: 14,504
Sales: 21.21 billion pesos ($2.21 billion) (2000)
Stock Exchanges: Mexico City; New York (for American
   Depositary Receipts)
Ticker Symbols: IMSA; IMY
NAIC: 331111 Iron & Steel Mills; 331316 Aluminum
   Extruded Products; 332312 Fabricated Structural
   Metal Manufacturing; 332321 Metal Window & Door
   Manufacturing; 32614 Polystyrene Foam Product
   Manufacturing; 32615 Urethane & Other Foam
   Product Manufacturing; 33251 Hardware
   Manufacturing; 335911 Storage Battery
   Manufacturing; 444190 Other Building Materials
   Dealers; 551112 Offices of Other Holding Companies

Grupo IMSA, S.A. de C.V. is a Mexican-based holding company whose four subsidiary holding companies are engaged in diversified manufacturing in the United States and several Latin American countries besides Mexico. It is Mexico's largest intermediate steel processor in terms of sales volume. The company also is the largest automotive starting, lighting, and ignition battery producer in Mexico, the largest producer of fabricated aluminum products in Mexico, and one of the largest producers of prefabricated steel and foam-insulated panels in North America. Extensive operations in the United States, Argentina, Brazil, Chile, and Venezuela have enabled Grupo IMSA to prosper despite the erratic performance of the Mexican economy.

Diversified Manufacturer: 1936–91

The company was founded as Industrias Monterrey, S.A. in 1936 and became known by its acronym (IMSA). A closely held company run by members of the Canales, Clairond, and Reyes families, it interacted with others in Monterrey, the dynamic center of privately owned manufacturing operations in Mexico. IMSA grew significantly as a steel processor during World War II and in subsequent years.

In 1972 Grupo IMSA began manufacturing sophisticated insulated polyurethane and steel sandwich panels for the Multypanel system of modular wall and roof components being used to meet many of Mexico's building needs. Three years later, the company acquired Stabilit, S.A. de C.V., a company producing fiberglass-reinforced plastic panels. Beginning in this decade, the steel and plastic construction-products segment of IMSA—which included value-added steel-processing products such as culverts, guardrails, and steel strapping manufactured by the company since the 1950s—was separated from the steel-processing products segment and established as a separate business within the corporate structure. In 1978, the steel- and plastic-strapping business was incorporated into IMSA Signode, S.A. de C.V., a joint venture between IMSA and the Signode Division of Illinois Tool Works, Inc. Forjas Metalicas, S.A. de C.V. (Formet), a manufacturer of galvanized-steel products mainly for the construction of highways, was established in 1983.

The steel-processing division of IMSA began, in 1986, to produce Galvalume: zinc-aluminum coated sheets made under license from Bethlehem International Engineering Corp., becoming the first in Latin America to manufacture this product. In 1991 IMSA acquired Aceros Planos, the flat-steel division of Fundidora Monterrey, S.A., a company dating back to 1900. Fundidora Monterrey limited itself to making steel bars, rods, rails, wire, and structural profiles until 1956, when it opened Aceros Planos, which quickly became the mainstay of its production. The company fell deeply into debt in the 1970s, however, and was nationalized in 1982. IMSA purchased the Aceros Planos segment of this company with help from Duferco, a Swiss-owned service-center company, and Grupo Villacero, establishing a subsidiary named APM, S.A. de C.V. to operate the facility. The acquisition was especially important because it

Company Perspectives:

Grupo IMSA's mission is to consistently meet the needs of its customers, offering products and services with the best quality, service, and price for the processing, construction, automotive and commercial industries, with the support of highly-qualified human resources and leading-edge technology, contributing to a sustainable development, the promotion of human values in business activities, and involvement with the communities where its subsidiaries operate.

enabled IMSA to assure the availability, and control the quality, of hot- and cold-rolled flat-steel feedstock, the principal raw material for its galvanizing operations, at a reasonable cost.

Grupo IMSA entered the business of automotive batteries and related products in 1987, with the acquisition of Acumuladores Mexicanos, S.A. de C.V. (ACUMEX) and Acumuladores del Centro, S.A. de C.V. EBS de Mexico, S.A. de C.V., a producer of industrial batteries, was acquired the following year. In 1989 IMSA entered the aluminum extrusions business through the acquisition of Cuprum, S.A. de C.V. Through subsequent acquisitions and the establishment of new product lines, Cuprum became a leading manufacturer of fabricated aluminum products. In 1991 Cuprum acquired Davidson Ladders, Inc. and Davidson Manufacturing Corp., manufacturers of wooden ladders and distributors of all types of ladders in the United States, as well as part of the assets of Stapleton Ladders, a manufacturer of wooden attic stairways.

Further Growth in the 1990s and 2000

With the creation of the North America Free Trade Agreement imminent, Grupo IMSA began acquiring more U.S. companies. In 1993, it purchased Advantage Battery Corp., a U.S. distributor of automotive batteries, and also bought controlling interests in manufacturers of automotive and industrial batteries in Argentina, Brazil, and Venezuela. The following year it established Battery Master, a Mexican chain of retail outlets selling all kinds of batteries. At the end of 1994, IMSA acquired full control of Metl-Span Corp., a leading U.S. manufacturer of insulated steel panels for refrigeration chambers in which IMSA had taken a minority interest in 1986. The Metl-Span acquisition, together with the Multypanel subsidiary, brought IMSA into the global market for commercial referigeration equipment. And in 1995, the company acquired Tiendas Alutodo, S.A. de C.V., a Mexican chain of outlets selling aluminum products.

The peso devaluation of late 1994 led to a recession in 1995 that cut into Grupo IMSA's profits. In 1996, however, revenues grew by 12 percent and net income rose more than fourfold, to a record 2.79 billion pesos (about $365 million). The company made its initial public offering on the New York Stock Exchange, raising $142 million in order to reduce dollar-denominated debt and make more acquisitions. Some of this money was also used to buy the remaining shares held by Duferco. By this time Grupo IMSA held 85 percent of the Mexican auto-battery market and

was selling 5 million generic batteries a year in the United States, compared to 1.5 million in 1993.

During 1997, Grupo IMSA spent $12.1 million to buy Guatemala-based Industria Galvanizadora, S.A. (Ingasa), the largest producer of galvanized steel in the fast-growing Central American market. It also, through Stabilit, purchased, for $9 million, Glasteel, Inc., a Memphis-based subsidiary of Alpha Corp. that was producing fiberglass-reinforced plastic panels and steel strip. This acquisition completed a set of seven continuous coated-steel lines in Mexico and the United States, enabling the company to sell in markets throughout Latin America. Also that year, Grupo IMSA raised its interest in Empresas Ipac, S.A., a Chilean steel processor and manufacturer of prefabricated steel and foam-insulated panels, to 50 percent. The remainder of the company was acquired in 1999.

In 1998, IMSA Varco Pruden, S.A. de C.V. was established as a joint venture with Varco Pruden International, Inc., (an indirect subsidiary of The LTV Corp.) for the design and fabrication of low-height metallic buildings for industrial and commercial applications in the Mexican, Central American, and southern U.S. markets. And three joint ventures, with Johnson Controls, Inc. and Varta, AG, were established to produce and distribute batteries throughout the Western Hemisphere. The production capacity of these joint ventures was the largest in Latin America for batteries. Also in 1998, Grupo IMSA and Emerson Electric Co. merged their ladder businesses, establishing a new company, Louisville Ladder Group. Interviewed for *Chief Executive* that year, Eugenio Clariond Reyes, IMSA's CEO, declared, ''We have been able to build our foreign sales and develop operations outside Mexico, which has been the most dynamic part of our growth in the last few years.'' He added, ''We are the largest producer of batteries in Argentina. We are the largest producer of insulated steel and polyurethane panels in the U.S. And we are the second-largest marketer of ladders in the U.S. and Canada.''

Empresas Ipac, the Chilean subsidiary, acquired a Chilean company producing insulated steel panels in 1999. In 2000, Stabilit formed a joint venture with Bayer AG to produce, distribute, and market polycarbonate plastic sheets, a product not manufactured in Mexico before. A new Formet plant in Monterrey began producing metal poles as a joint venture with Valmont Industries. Construction began of a new Industrias Monterrey coated-steel plant that was to include a continuous painting line and a coated-steel processing center.

During 2000, Grupo IMSA made a bid to purchase troubled Altos Hornos de Mexico, S.A. de C.V. (AHMSA), Mexico's largest integrated steel producer. IMSA, which was AHMSA's second-largest customer, offered to buy 60 percent of the company, but the terms were not acceptable to AHMSA. In 1999, AHMSA had sold a galvanizing and painting steel plant to IMSA for $105 million. Later in 2000, IMSA paid $355 million for the U.S. West Coast steel-processing operations of Australian conglomerate Broken Hill Proprietary Co. Ltd. These operations, which became Steelscape, Inc. and IMSA Building Products, consisted of Galvalume, galvanized steel, hot- and cold-rolled steel, pre-painted steel, and seven centers for processing galvanized and pre-painted steel sheeting.

Key Dates

1936: Founding of Industrias Monterrey, S.A. (IMSA).
1972: IMSA adds steel and plastic construction panels to its line of products.
1987: The company begins making automotive batteries.
1989: IMSA adds fabrication of aluminum products to its line.
1991: The company begins producing flat steel for the first time.
1996: IMSA makes its initial public offering on the New York Stock Exchange.
2000: IMSA acquires U.S. West Coast steel-processing operations.

Grupo IMSA in 2000

IMSA ACERO, Grupo IMSA's holding company for steel-processing products, was, in 2000, Mexico's largest producer of galvanized rolled flat steel and cold-rolled flat steel in Mexico. This company was manufacturing and processing steel in three Mexican facilities: Monclava, Monterrey, and San Nicolas de los Garza. The three other production facilities belonged to Ingasa in Guatemala City and Steelscape in Kalama, Washington, and Rancho Cucamonga, California.

IMSA Varco Pruden had a plant in Cienega de Flores, Mexico. Output of steel-processing products came to 1.8 million metric tons. These products included galvanized and pre-painted flat-steel products, galvanized steel shapes, cold-rolled flat steel, hot-rolled coils, and pickled and oiled hot-rolled steel. Coated and non-coated steel each accounted for about the same volume of production.

ENERMEX, the holding company for automotive batteries and related products, was believed to be the lowest-cost manufacturer of automotive starting, lighting, and ignition batteries in Mexico and the only automotive-battery producer in Mexico with recycling operations. Its products included the LTH brand, which had been in production since 1928 and was the best-selling brand of automotive batteries in Mexico. Its Mexican joint venture with Johnson Controls was operating six plants. In all, ENERMEX's production came to 18.83 million batteries, of which 7.2 million were exported. The joint venture with Johnson Controls and Varta was operating a plant in Brazil. GES America was the name of the distribution network established by ENERMEX and Johnson Controls to serve medium and small clients in the United States and Canada.

IMSALUM was the holding company for aluminum and other related products. Its Cuprum subsidiary had three plants in San Nicolas de los Garza, Mexico, and one each in San Pedro, Garza Garcia, and Tlalnepantla. The Louisville Ladder Group had two plants in Kentucky and one each in Arkansas and Tennessee.

IMSATEC was the holding company for steel and plastic construction products for use in the construction and other industries. It was the largest producer of prefabricated steel and foam-insulated panels in Mexico. Other manufactures were translucent and opaque fiberglass-reinforced plastic (FRP) panels, galvanized steel products for the construction industry, steel packaging products, and plastic strapping. Inside Mexico, IMSATEC's Formet subsidiary had plants in Ecatepec and San Nicolas de los Garza, while the Multypanel subsidiary had a plant in Cienega de Flores. Stabil America Inc. had a Tennessee facility, Metl Span had three plants in Texas and Virginia, and Grupo IMSA Chile had three: two in Santiago and one in Talcahuano. The Tiendas Alutodo chain had 23 retail outlets in Mexico.

Grupo IMSA's net sales came to 21.21 billion pesos ($2.21 billion) in 2000, of which IMSA ACERO accounted for 54 percent, ENERMEX, 18 percent; IMSATEC, 14 percent; and IMSALUM, 14 percent. Foreign sales accounted for 34 percent of IMSA ACERO's sales volume, 52 percent of ENERMEX's, 54 percent of INSALUM's, and 56 percent of IMSATEC's. Grupo IMSA expected 50 percent of its total sales volume to come from non-Mexico markets in 2001.

Grupo IMSA's net income was 1.56 billion pesos ($162 million) in 2000. The long-term debt came to 7 billion pesos ($729 million) at the end of the year. The Canales Clariond family group held 14.3 percent of IMSA's capital stock in April 2001. The Clariond Reyes family group held 12 percent. Eugenio Clariond Reyes had been IMSA's chief executive since 1976.

Principal Subsidiaries

ENERMEX, S.A. de C.V.; IMSA ACERO, S.A. de C.V.; APM, S.A. de C.V.; Industria Galvanizadora, S.A. (Guatemala); IMSA Building Products (U.S.); Industrias Monterrey, S.A. de C.V.; Steelscape, Inc. (U.S.); IMSALUM, S.A. de C.V.; Cuprum, S.A. de C.V.; Tiendas Alutodo, S.A. de C.V.; IMSATEC, S.A. de C.V.; Empresas Stabilit, S.A. de C.V.; Forjas Metalicas, S.A. de C.V.; Grupo IMSA Chile; Multypanel, S.A.; Metl-Span Corp. (U.S.); Bayer IMSA (50%); Enertec Argentina (50%); Enertec Brasil (50%); Enertec Mexico (51%); Enertec Venezuela (50%); GES America (50&); IMSA ITW (50.01%); IMSA Varco Pruden (51%); Louisville Ladder Group (51%); Valmont Formet, S. de R.L. de C.V. (51%).

Principal Competitors

Altos Hornos de Mexico, S.A. de C.V.; Cale de Tlaxcala, S.A. de C.V.; Consorcio Industria Valsa, S.A. de C.V.; Gonher de Mexico, S.A. de C.V.; Hylsamex, S.A. de C.V.; Indalun, S.A. de C.V.; Productos Nacobre, S.A. de C.V.

Further Reading

Castellanos, Camila, "Diversify Abroad," *Business Mexico,* Strategies 1999 issue, pp. 50–51.
"Grupo Imsa Acquires U.S. Coated Steel Businesses," *Purchasing,* July 13, 2000, p. 7.
Haflich, Frank, "Good Timing Bodes Well for Imsa Buy," *American Metal Market,* May 31, 2000, p. 1 ff.
"Imsa To Pay Down Debt as Battery Shipments Soar," *Metal Bulletin,* September 16, 1999, p. 15.

Kuster, Ted, ''The Growth in Mexican Steel,'' *New Steel,* December 1997, p. 78.

''Mexico Uses PU Panels To Solve Building Needs,'' *Journal of Commerce,* December 29, 1981, p. 10A.

Millman, Joel, ''Mexican Merger Of Steel Companies Appears to Be Off,'' *Wall Street Journal,* February 25, 2000, p. A15.

——, ''Mexico's Imsa to Buy U.S. Unit Of Broken Hill for $240 Million,'' *Wall Street Journal,* May 26, 2000, p. A19.

''New World Ways: Grupo IMSA: Adventure Capital,'' *Chief Executive,* 1998 Supplement issue, p. 15.

Pozas, Maria de los Angeles. *Industrial Restructuring in Mexico.* San Diego: University of California, San Diego, 1993.

Robertson, Scott, ''Ahmsa Sells Coating Lines to Imsa,'' *American Metal Market,* February 5, 1999, p. 1.

''Sicarta Boost for Mexican Output,'' *Metal Bulletin,* December 3, 1985, p. 27.

—Robert Halasz

GSD&M Advertising

828 West Sixth Street
Austin, Texas 78703
U.S.A.
Telephone: (512) 427-4736
Fax: (512) 427-4700
Web site: http://www.gsdm.com

Wholly Owned Subsidiary of Omnicom Group Inc.
Incorporated: 1971 as AdVantage Associates
Employees: 630
Sales: $86.7 million (2000)
NAIC: 541810 Advertising Agencies

GSD&M Advertising is one of the top 30 advertising agencies in the U.S. The firm's clients include Wal-Mart, Southwest Airlines, Charles Schwab, DreamWorks SKG, and Brinker International and its Chili's restaurant chain. GSD&M's ads are often irreverent and witty, and the company has won many industry awards for work like its "Don't Mess With Texas" anti-littering campaign. The firm was founded in 1971 by six University of Texas graduates, four of whom continue to hold key positions. GSD&M is owned by Omnicom Group, the third largest advertising conglomerate in the world.

Early Years

GSD&M traces its beginnings to the campus of the University of Texas, where in 1970 six friends were tapped by the dean of students to create an orientation film. Calling themselves "Media 70," the six, Roy Spence, Tim McClure, Steve and Bill Gurasich, Judy Trabulsi and Jim Darilek came up with a multimedia presentation that combined references to the Beatles, Janis Joplin, the Vietnam war, and campus mascot Bevo the Longhorn. The group subsequently put on a series of shows both on and off the campus, and upon graduation in 1971 decided to form an advertising agency together. They initially used the name AdVantage Associates, but later changed it to Gurasich, Spence, Darilek & McClure (Judy Trabulsi, believing that she would get married and leave the firm, decided not to be listed).

The partners' first account was Jack Morton's Menswear, but it was lost after six months when a newspaper ad ran too small. Early on the firm also began what would develop into a long association with the Democratic Party when it created ads for senatorial candidate Ralph Yarborough, though his bid for office was unsuccessful. Getting a toehold in the ad business took time, and the company's first years were difficult ones. Roy Spence recalled that during this period he took home just $85 a month and slept on a mattress under an art table in the firm's offices, using a nearby gym to take showers.

The company's first big break came in 1974, when it won the account of the Austin Savings Bank (later NationsBank), which represented $1 million in media billings. For the firm, which had decided to shorten its name to GSD&M, this was a breakthrough into "the establishment," and it soon began to attract other major clients as well. By the end of the decade the company had added to their client list U.S. Home Corp., Pearl Beer, and Church's Fried Chicken, and had opened additional offices in Dallas, San Antonio, and Houston.

Stumbling, then Bouncing Back with Southwest Air

Growth was not proving to be completely healthy for GSD&M as an organization, however, and by the start of the 1980s the company began to falter. In 1981, the firm lost all three of its top accounts, Church's, U.S. Home Corp., and Pearl, which accounted for $10 million in billings and 80 percent of its business. Luckily, a short time later GSD&M was able to win the account of Southwest Airlines, which became the company's first national campaign, worth $4 million in billings. This helped revive the firm's morale, and it soon began to grow once again.

By 1985 GSD&M was working for 80 different clients with combined billings of $76 million. Four of the original founders remained in charge, Jim Darilek and Bill Gurasich having left to pursue other interests. A reevaluation of the agency's priorities previous to this time led to the decision to make creative work the firm's focus, rather than other activities such as media buying. The company soon closed its outlying offices and consolidated its operations in Austin.

Company Perspectives:

Core Purpose: Discover visionary ideas that get our clients where they want to go faster than anyone thought possible. Visionary ideas transform the way we think about things, force us to widen our horizons and view the world differently. They raise the bar and help us win for our clients in the marketplace. And that's the thrill of it all.

In the latter half of the 1980s other major accounts were landed with First Texas Savings, Gibraltar Savings, and the Texas Department of Commerce. GSD&M was also continuing to be allied with Democratic political candidates, having worked on the presidential bid of Walter Mondale, as well as for Texas governor Mark White.

GSD&M campaigns often reflected the input of the company's president, Roy Spence, along with creative director Tim McClure. The colorful Spence declared his company's niche to be "cutting against the grain," and its campaigns frequently refocused a client's image. For Southwest Airlines, which had earlier emphasized its ties to Dallas's Love Field, GSD&M came up with new slogans: "Just Say When" and "The Company Plane." For one Southwest ad, Spence flew to Detroit and spent $150 driving around town with a cabdriver whose input was incorporated into promotions for flights from that city. An award-winning anti-litter campaign called "Don't Mess With Texas" featured entertainers like Willie Nelson and Jerry Jeff Walker making offbeat pitches to keep the state clean.

For a new, national Coors Beer campaign, GSD&M also jettisoned heartthrob actor Mark Harmon and came up with lines like "The First Draft in a Bottle" and "The American Original." Coors, run by a highly conservative family, had stunned the advertising community in 1987 when it shifted its account to a firm which was well-known for working with Democratic politicians. A Coors spokesman commenting on the choice cited GSD&M's "history of sound strategic decisions, excellent production capability, and values at reasonable cost." The firm had previously handled Coors' Hispanic advertising work. The end of the decade saw GSD&M attracting other high profile clients, including *The Wall Street Journal,* Wal-Mart, Brinker International, and CompuAdd Corp. Annual billings topped $150 million by 1989.

Early 1990s Sale to GGT Group

In 1990, GSD&M was sold to Michael Greenlees' GGT Group for approximately $48.5 million, the final total of which would be based on the next five years' revenues. The so-called "earn-out" agreement was requested by GSD&M's partners, who wanted a built-in incentive to continue to grow their business. GGT, a publicly traded advertising and consulting company based in the United Kingdom, had been pursuing a strategy of acquiring regional American ad agencies since 1988. GSD&M's management and independence remained intact after the sale.

Two years later the firm was awarded a contract to produce ads for the Texas state lottery, a move that was protested by a rival agency which alleged improprieties in the pitch it had made for the work. The state comptroller ruled that GSD&M could keep the assignment, however. Also in 1992, the company won the account of Tandy Corp., owner of the Radio Shack electronics chain. That year GSD&M was recognized by industry journal *AdWeek* as its Southwest Agency of the Year.

In 1993, GSD&M gave up a recently won regional contract with Coca-Cola to produce a national image-building campaign for distant third-place cola maker Royal Crown. The $8–10 million program featured RC's first television spots in 20 years. GSD&M's ads, launched the following summer, were characterized by AdWeek as "bizarre," and featured deep-sea fishing boats hooking Coke and Pepsi drinkers, who were reeled in and put on display while a bemused RC drinker looked on. A later campaign for Royal Crown's Kick beverage similarly made fun of rival soda Mountain Dew.

The mid-1990s saw further growth for GSD&M, with clients such as Doubletree Hotels, Fannie Mae, and Advanced Micro Devices added to its roster. In 1994, the company spun off its Hispanic media buying division, which was renamed Amistad Media Group. The next year saw another coup for GSD&M, when the firm won the media buying account of MasterCard, worth $86 million in billings. Though the company had previously bought very little network television time, had no previous credit card experience, and no apparent connections to the client, it prevailed over a number of heavy players to win the work. Speculation in the industry focused on MasterCard CEO H. Eugene Lockhart's 76-year old father, who lived in Austin, as a key player in the deal. Though he proclaimed himself a fan of Roy Spence, the senior Lockhart denied playing a role in the transaction. Whatever the reasons were, the result was a triumph for GSD&M, which was soon rumored to be seeking the creative side of MasterCard's business as well. After the account was won, the firm opened an office in Chicago to coordinate its media buying efforts, which it was seeking to increase across the board.

More New Accounts and a New Headquarters

By 1996, GSD&M was doing work that represented $400 million in ad billings and employing 360 people. New accounts continued to come in, including clothing maker No Fear, Pennzoil/Jiffy Lube, the Yellow Pages, Mobile Systems and Cellular One businesses of Southwestern Bell, the latter worth a total of $60 million in billings. At the end of the year the company also moved to a new 100,000 square foot corporate headquarters in downtown Austin. Dubbed "Idea City," the building utilized a blend of architectural styles and gave secretarial and support staff window views, placing the executives in the center of the building. Different parts of the interior were made up as "neighborhoods," with themes such as Greenwich Village for the area where the company's artists and writers worked.

During 1997, GSD&M, which was now ranked among the top 30 ad agencies in the U.S., landed the accounts of Power Computing and Haggar Clothing Co., as well as the media buying for Bank of America. A pitch to win the work of carmaker Mazda proved unsuccessful, a big disappointment to the firm. January of 1998 saw the company's owner, GGT Group, sold for $235 million to Omnicom Group of New York. Omnicom, the third largest agency conglomerate in the world, had annual revenues of $2.6 billion.

Key Dates:

1971: Six University of Texas graduates found AdVantage Associates in Austin, Texas.

1974: Firm wins first major account, Austin Savings, and is renamed GSD&M.

1978: The company opens an office in San Antonio to facilitate work for Pearl Beer.

1981: GSD&M loses its top three clients, but then wins account of Southwest Airlines.

1986: The company debuts its ''Don't Mess With Texas'' anti-littering campaign.

1987: GSD&M begin working for Coors Beer and Wal-Mart.

1990: The company is sold to GGT Group (United Kingdom) for $48.5 million.

1995: GSD&M wins 86 million MasterCard media buying account.

1996: New Austin headquarters building is completed.

1998: Omnicom Group becomes firm's owner when it acquires GGT Group.

2000: GSD&M top $1 billion in billings and win first auto account for Land Rover.

At about this time GSD&M voluntarily gave up its work for the Texas Department of Highways and Public Transportation, for whom it had created the popular ''Don't Mess With Texas'' spots. The company's ads were credited with a 75 percent reduction in roadside litter since they began in 1986. GSD&M president Roy Spence stated that the move was made to allow other Texas agencies a shot at the job, although some speculated that it had been done to enable the firm to better focus on its corporate accounts.

1998 also saw the enlargement of ''Idea City'' for the company's rapidly growing ranks of employees, now numbering more than 400. GSD&M was lately becoming increasingly interested in the world of entertainment and launched a subsidiary that sponsored screenwriters to write at the company's headquarters, with television productions also planned. The firm began working for the Country Music Association as well, helping promote concerts, compact discs, and books that were part of a public service campaign. During 1998, GSD&M also became the agency of record for telecommunications giant SBC Communications, and opened an office in San Francisco to handle work for Pacific Bell Mobile Services.

A major effort was taking place during this period to win the account of Dreamworks SKG, the new movie studio launched by Steven Spielberg, Jeffrey Katzenberg, and David Geffen. GSD&M and the other finalist for the job, Focus Media, were each given a film to promote, with the final choice to be made after the respective ad campaigns were over. In March of 1999, the company was given the nod and began to handle media planning and buying for Dreamworks' Features, Home Video, and GameWorks divisions, which had total billings of $100 million. Also during the year GSD&M was hired by the U.S. Olympic Committee, the YMCA, Mirage Resorts, and Wenner Media, publisher of *Rolling Stone, Us,* and *Men's Journal*

magazines. Leaping into the dot-com waters, in November GSD&M launched Idea Ventures, a division which traded advertising services for equity in Internet companies.

The firm won more business from SBC in 2000 when that company gave it additional work for its Ameritech subsidiary, worth $100 million in ad billings. GSD&M also won its first automobile account, Land Rover, and was retained by Charles Schwab & Co., as well as by the U.S. Air Force for its recruitment advertising. Billings for the year topped $1 billion for the first time, though the impact of the slowing U.S. economy caused the company to lay off 35 employees in the fall. Also during 2000, GSD&M's newly formed publishing unit, Idea University Press, issued its first title, a children's book written by a staffer.

In 2001, the company began working for the makers of Dial soap, as well as the Kohler Co. Efforts to win the $200 million account of Cingular Wireless, a joint venture of SBC and Bell South, failed, however. In late August the firm celebrated its 30th anniversary with a party in Austin for employees and friends. Starting its fourth decade in business, GSD&M continued on an upward trajectory, its proven ''formula'' of energetic, creative, slightly askew thinking bringing it continued new business and accolades from the advertising industry. Still run by four of its original six founders, the company was looking toward further growth and success in the years to come.

Principal Divisions

Idea Ventures; Idea Studio; Idea University Press.

Principal Competitors

DDB Needham Worldwide Dallas Group; Temerlin McClain LP.

Further Reading

Biesada, Alexandra M., ''The Pitch,'' *Texas Monthly*, March 1, 1998, p. 78.

Breyer, R. Michelle, ''Ad Agency 'Passing the Torch','' *Austin American-Statesman*, February 5, 1998, p. D1.

——, ''Austin's GSD&M, One of the Largest Ad Agencies in the Southwest, Has Achieved Billings of $400 Million by Pushing Clients into New Territory,'' *Austin American-Statesman*, November 5, 1995, p. D1.

——, ''Creative Division Littered With Ads That Joke, Intrigue,'' *Austin American-Statesman*, November 5, 1995, p. D5.

——, ''GSD&M Drives Up Madison Avenue's Alley,'' *Austin American-Statesman*, March 3, 2000, p. D1.

Follette, Daniel, ''GSD&M: The Best Little Ad Shop in Texas,'' *Back Stage*, March 23, 1990, p. 58.

Gleason, Mark, ''GSD&M, Martin Mix High-Tech, Tradition at HQs,'' *Advertising Age*, January 13, 1997, p. 35.

Hill, Dee, ''Dream Factory,'' *Adweek Eastern Division*, January 31, 2000, p. 52.

Krajewski, Steve and O'Leary, Noreen, ''The Austin Bunch,'' *Adweek Eastern Edition*, January 25, 1999.

O'Leary, Noreen, ''How GSD&M Pulled Off Its Surprise MasterCard Win Is the Talk of the Media Town,'' *Adweek Southwest Edition*, August 28, 1995, p. 23.

Robertson, Virginia, ''Big Like Texas,'' *Shoot*, July 12, 1996, p. 39.

Schatz, Amy, "Three Decades Ago, a Group of UT Grads Started Advertising Giant—GSD&M's . . . Excellent Ad Venture," *Austin American-Statesman*, August 26, 2001, p. J1.

"Small Ad Shop is a Mighty Mite," *Fort Worth Star-Telegram*, April 19, 1996, p. 4.

Stanush, Michele, "GSD&M Sold for $48 Million," *Austin American-Statesman*, February 20, 1990, p. A1.

Totty, Michael, "Gray Flannel Suits Are Gone: Next Are Rooms with a View," *Wall Street Journal*, September 18, 1996, p. T1.

Tyson, Kim, "Spence Still Leader of the Pack," *Austin American-Statesman*, February 27, 1989, p. 3.

Weiss, Michael, "Master of the Ad Game," *Dallas Morning News*, April 5, 1988, p. 1D.

Yung, Katherine, "Austin Ad Agency May Have a Big Idea—Firm to Develop Entertainment Programming," *Dallas Morning News*, January 18, 1999, p. 1D.

—Frank Uhle

Gulf Island Fabrication, Inc.

583 Thompson Road
Houma, Louisiana 70363
U.S.A.
Telephone: (504) 872-2100
Fax: (504) 872-9010
Web site: http://www.gulfisland.com

Public Company
Incorporated: 1985
Employees: 875
Sales: $112.1 million (2000)
Stock Exchanges: NASDAQ
Ticker Symbol: GIFI
NAIC: 551112 Offices of Other Holding Companies;
332312 Fabricated Structural Metal Manufacturing;
332313 Plate Work Manufacturing; 23499 All Other
Heavy Construction; 331111 Iron and Steel Mills;
336611 Ship Building and Repairing; 333924
Industrial Truck, Tractor, Trailer, and Stacker
Machinery Manufacturing

Gulf Island Fabrication, Inc., a company headquartered on a 608-acre site in Houma, Louisiana, is a holding company conducting business through its subsidiaries. Chief among these is Gulf Island, L.L.C., a.k.a. Gulf Island Fabrication, which fabricates offshore drilling and production platforms, primarily for use in the oil and gas producing areas of the Gulf of Mexico and, to a lesser extent, in offshore areas of Latin America and West Africa. Specifically, Gulf Island makes jackets and deck sections of fixed production platforms; deck and hull sections of floating production platforms, including tension leg platforms (TLPs); piles; wellhead protectors; sub-sea templates; and other production, compressor, and utility modules. The company also manufactures and repairs petroleum-industry pressure vessels, refurbishes existing production platforms, and fabricates other kinds of steel structures, including warehouses. It also engages in offshore interconnect pipe hook-ups and inshore marine construction. One of Gulf Island Fabrication, Inc.'s two recently acquired subsidiaries, Southport, Inc., specializes in fabricating

living quarters for crews working on offshore platforms. The other, Dolphin Services, Inc., provides off-shore maintenance and staffing services for oil-recovery platforms. Gulf Island claims to be one of only three U.S. companies capable of fabricating fixed offshore production platforms in water depths exceeding 300 feet. Among its principal customers are Texaco and Global Industries, which, together, account for about one third of the company's revenues.

1985–95: Company Begins Operations

Alden J. "Doc" Laborde, Huey J. Wilson, and other investors founded Gulf Island Fabrication Inc. (GIFI) in 1985. Laborde previously had founded Odeco and Tidewater, and has been credited with inventing the offshore oil patch supply boat and the first semi-submersible drilling rig. Wilson was president, CEO and chairman of Wilson's Distributors, a publicly traded company. These two men and the other founding investors would own 100 percent of the company right up until it went public and made its IPO in April of 1997.

At the time the investors created Gulf Island, they bought the assets of Delta Fabrication, then under the guidance of Kerry J. Chauvin, Delta's president. Chauvin had been with Delta since 1973, when he was initially employed as a project manager in charge of new construction. He joined the management team of Gulf Island Fabrication, serving as a board member, COO, and eventually president and CEO.

The company commenced operations at its fabrication yard on the Houma Navigation Canal in south Louisiana, about 30 miles from the Gulf of Mexico. Its property consisted of 608 acres, 261 of which would be developed for fabrication activities, with the remainder held in reserve for future expansion.

Initially, the company fabricated structural components for fixed, offshore petroleum platforms, including jackets (tubular steel, braced structures extending from the seabed mud line to a point above the water surface) and deck sections (the above-sea, multipurpose modules used for everything from drilling and production to quartering offshore crews). A traditional type, the fixed platform was widely used in offshore drilling and production. It answered the needs of client companies operating in sea

Company Perspectives:

The best opportunity for Gulf Island Fabrication is the sale of the MINDOC deep water concept. If one can be sold and prove itself operationally, then the company could secure follow-on contracts from other operators in the deep water area. There are other opportunities to more vertically integrate our company with the industry somewhat in a down cycle. As these opportunities present themselves, the company would seek to develop them through acquisitions or internal expansion. We're constantly looking into situations that would make sense and would add value to our shareholders.

depths of up to 1,000 feet. However, as the industry expanded into deeper waters, Gulf Island also began fabricating hull and deck sections for floating production platforms. In addition, it fabricated piles (rigid tubular pipes that are driven into the seabed to support platforms), sub-sea templates (tubular frames which are placed on the seabed and anchored with piles), wellhead protectors, and an array of production, compressor and utility modules, including pressure vessels capable of withstanding heavy internal pressure loadings.

All in all, 1985 was not a particularly auspicious year in which to start an oil services company. The industry went into a nosedive in the mid 1980s when oil became cheap and plentiful. Crude, which in the early 1980s had risen to $30 per barrel, slipped down as low as $8 per barrel by 1986. That development discouraged new exploration and drilling in the Gulf of Mexico, the company's primary territory. The slump, which continued into the early 1990s, took its toll on Gulf Island, but the company nevertheless gained and maintained profitability from 1988 onward.

The number of active rigs drilling in the Gulf dropped to 60 in May of 1992 before a partial industry resurgence increased that number to more than 150 by 1996, still a far cry from the count of active rigs during the oil boom of the 1970s and early 1980s. Improving prices for both crude and natural gas in part accounted for the rebound, but so did improvements in seismic and drilling technologies and production techniques. These improvements led to renewed activity in and around existing, shallow-water production fields as well as exploration and drilling at water depths previously considered too great for profitable development.

1996–97: Gulf Island Goes Public and Expands through Acquisition

A major contract in a high-visibility project came Gulf Island's way in 1996, when Texaco Corp. and Marathon Oil Co. joined forces in a $400 million plan to develop their deep-water Petronius platform, which was expected to produce an estimated 80 million to 100 million barrels of oil equivalent by the turn of the century. The two partner companies, each owning a 50 percent share, awarded contracts to three other companies, including Gulf Island Fabrication and J. Ray McDermott S.A. Under the terms of its $50 million contract, Gulf Island was to

fabricate and integrate the platform's north and south decks; McDermott's $140 million contract called for the building of the compliant tower platform and all engineering and design work.

Early in 1997, Gulf Island purchased Dolphin Services Inc. and two related inland and offshore fabrication companies. As a group, these operations became a wholly owned subsidiary, which provided interconnect piping services on offshore platforms, inshore structures fabrication, and steel warehouse construction and sales. Dolphin also provided rig refurbishing services.

Gulf Island also went public in 1997. The company filed its IPO on February 14, 1997. The offering, which began trading in April on NASDAQ as over-the-counter stock, consisted of 2 million shares with a reserve of an additional 300,000 shares to allow for over-allotments. The common stock went on the market at $22.50 per share. Gulf Island's principal shareholders, Laborde, 81, and Wilson, 69, decided to make the offering primarily for the diversification of their assets and estate planning.

The Petronius project, a helpful boost in Gulf Island's financial arm, involved one disaster. Late in 1998, while attempting to install Gulf Island's south-deck, 3,800 ton module, J. Ray McDermott's heavy lift vessel, DB-50, accidentally dropped the unit, sending it to the bottom in 1,800 feet of water, where, in all likelihood, it was reduced to scrap by the water pressure and force of the module's impact on the sea floor. Texaco and Marathon decided to abandon the deck, temporarily suspending the Petronius project.

1988–2001: Company Continues Expansion and Diversification

It was also in 1998 that GIFI acquired all the outstanding shares of Southport, Inc., of Harvey, Louisiana, and its wholly-owned subsidiary, Southport International, Inc. The purchase price was $6.0 million in cash, plus additional contingency payments of up to $5.0 million based on Southport's bottom-line performance over the next four years. In order to insure a smooth transition in the ownership of Southport and maintain its quality of service, GIFI elected to retain the management team of its new subsidiary.

Southport had been founded in 1967 as a sister company to Stephen G. Benton Company, Inc., which, at the time, had been in business 14 years. Two years before Gulf Island purchased Southport, the company had completed and put into operation a new, 14-acre facility where it fabricated liftable building modules for both the domestic and international petroleum industries. Southport's chief products included various sized living quarters for offshore oil platforms, custom made to accommodate from four up to 250 bunks.

In 1998, as the offshore oil industry moved into deeper and deeper waters, the company actively moved further into the area of deep-water drilling. Over the course of the next three years, the revenue generated from that sector increased from almost nothing to about 40 percent of the company's total sales. It was in 1998 that, along with four other companies, Gulf Island formed a limited liability company dubbed MinDOC, an acronym for "Minimum Deepwater Operating Concept." The partners created MinDOC, L.L.C. to design, patent, and market a deepwater floating drilling and production concept. In the partnership, GIFI was joined by three engineering firms and a oil field service company. Gulf Island initially owned a one-third share of the new company, with the remainder divided equally among its partners.

In the next year, 1999, GIFI formed Gulf Island MinDOC Company, L.L.C. (GIMCO), a wholly-owned subsidiary created to develop and market deepwater oil and gas production structures, including the MinDOC deepwater floating production company in which GIFI had a proprietary interest. The new subsidiary's headquarters were then established in Houston.

Pursuant to a reorganization plan, on January 1, 2000, all of the operating assets, buildings and properties owned directly by Gulf Island Fabrication, Inc. were transferred to Gulf Island, L.L.C., a newly created and wholly-owned subsidiary formed to conduct all the fabrication and other operations previously conducted by the parent company. Thereafter, Gulf Island Fabrication, Inc. operated as a holding company and began conducting all its operations through its various subsidiaries, including Gulf Island, L.L.C. The purpose behind the change was to improve the management's efficiency and to allow for the further development and expansion of the subsidiaries under the holding company's auspices.

In 2000, the demand for GIFI's services and products hit an all time low, but prospects began to improve during the year as oil and natural gas commodity prices rebounded and started a rapid rise. Despite a 6.7 percent drop in revenue to $112.1 million, the company still turned a net profit and remained debt free. To trim costs somewhat, GIFI decided to relocate Southport operations in Harvey to an idle facility that it owned situated next to Gulf Island, L.L.C.'s main fabrication yard in Houma. The move, scheduled for completion in 2001, would bring three of Gulf Island's facilities within close proximity of each other, thereby cutting operational costs and enhancing efficiency.

In 2000, Gulf Island also completed a replacement module for the Petronius compliant platform owned by Texaco and Marathon Oil. The original module, accidently lost in 1998, had taken 27 months to build; Gulf Island, using over 180 workers for the project, built the new unit in just 12 months. In May, the module, housing crew quarters as well as production and waterflood equipment, was successfully installed by Saipem Ltd. using a derrick barge and a 7,700 ton capacity crane.

In April 2001, Kerry Chauvin, who had served as president and CEO of Gulf Island since 1990, took on the additional responsibility of board chairman. The company's co-founder, Alden "Doc" Laborde, who had been chairman since 1986, stepped down, indicating that his age and health made it necessary to do so. He remained an active board member, however, and was elected to the post of chairman of the board's executive committee.

It has been a point of pride for Gulf Island that it has been profitable every year since 1988, thanks to its focus on controlling costs and providing quality products and services. It has also prided itself on its innovations and its uniqueness, on the fact, for example, that it had developed a deep-water technology that would play a vital role in its growth in the 21st century.

Principal Subsidiaries

Deep Ocean Services, L.L.C.; Dolphin Services, Inc.; Gulf Island, L.L.C.; Southport, Inc.

Principal Competitors

CSO Aker Maritime; Friede Goldman Halter, Inc.; Global Industries, Ltd.; McDermott International, Inc.; UNIFAB International, Inc.

Further Reading

Baltimore, Chris, "Texaco, Marathon Unveil $400 Million Plan to Develop Deep-Water Petronius Platform," *Oily Daily*, September 18, 1996, p. 3.
Chauvin, Kerry J., "Future of Steel for Offshore Work" (excerpt of a speech given at the "Steel in the Sunbelt" forum in Houston on January 20, 1994), *American Metal Market*, February 25, 1994, p. 14.
Furlow, William, "Petronius Project Back on Line," *Offshore*, June 1999, p. 24.
"Gulf Island Fabrication, Inc. Makes Announcement," *Business Wire*, December 16, 1999.
"Gulf Island Fabrication, Inc. Signs Letter of Intent to Reconstruct Petronius South Deck Module," *Business Wire*, April 28, 1999.
"Texaco's Petronius Platform Completed in Gulf of Mexico," *Business Wire*, May 4, 2000.

—John W. Fiero

Guy Degrenne SA

Route d'Aunay
501 Vire Cedex
France
Telephone: (+33) 2-31-66-46-18
Fax: (+33) 2-31-66-45-96
Web site: http://www.guydegrenne.fr

Public Company
Incorporated: 1948
Employees: 2,142
Sales: EUR 142.29 million ($134 million) (2000)
Stock Exchanges: Euronext Paris
Ticker Symbol: GDE
NAIC: 421220 Home Furnishing Wholesalers; 327112
    Vitreous China, Fine Earthenware, and Other Pottery
    Product Manufacturing

Guy Degrenne SA is one of Europe's leading manufacturers and distributors of table service items, including stainless steel cutlery, porcelain, as well as silver and gold jewelry. Cutlery represents some 50 percent of company sales, which include sales in the company's own 15-unit retail store chain, and more than 70 shop-in-shop boutiques. The company, which also sells to hospitals, restaurants, and other institutional customers, is the European leader in the cutlery category and French leader in tableware overall. Guy Degrenne's porcelain items generate nearly 23 percent of sales, while gold and silver goods add a further four percent. The company markets its products under three brand names: Table et Couleurs for the entry level; Guy Degrenne, which targets the mid-range market; and Létang Remy for the high-end sector. The company also operates a subsidiary, Guy Degrenne Industries, that manufactures kitchen equipment and tableware for the institutional market. The company operates production facilities in France, Hungary and Thailand. At the turn of the century, Guy Degrenne has been steadily building its international sales, which account for more than 30 percent of its 2000 sales of EUR 142 million. This effort has been aided by its 2000 acquisition of the cutlery subsidiaries of Austria's Berndorf, the leading manufacturer for the Austrian

and Swiss markets, and by the 2001 marketing and distribution agreement with Hackman Group's Designor, of Finland. Guy Degrenne SA is quoted on the Paris stock exchange and led by CEO and chairman Bertrand Déchery.

From Horseshoes to Flatware in the 1950s

The Degrenne family had a long history as blacksmiths in the Manche area of the Normandy region of France, where cutlery products—especially knives—had been crafted as early as the sixteenth century. The earliest smiths were itinerant craftsman, molding knives and other cutlery items and adding tin-plating services at customers' homes and farms. As craftsmen began to adopt industrial production techniques, the town of Sourdeval became a center of a new ironworks industry.

In 1932, Emile Degrenne, who had been working as a blacksmith, bought a factory in Sourdeval, converting production to the manufacture of iron grillwork, supports for shoeing horses, and other items. Degrenne formed a partnership with Henri-Maris Lorence, the following year. Lorence brought Degrenne a new line of products from his former employer, the Moncel company, and the company converted its production to that of cutlery and other tableware products.

French cutlery production was generally considered of low quality compared to the flatware coming from the Netherlands, Germany, and Belgium. As a consequence of this disparity in quality, the production of Degrenne and Lorence, like other French cutlery makers, was generally limited to finishing activities. The flatware itself was usually manufactured in Belgium, then polished and otherwise finished in France. Rather than compete for the home table service market, Degrenne and Lorence turned to the institutional market, building up a strong customer base among restaurants, cafeterias, and similar outlets.

The outbreak of World War II cut off the company's suppliers. Degrenne and Lorence attempted to fill the gap by adapting new materials, such as iron and copper, launching the company into the full-scale fabrication of cutlery items. At the end of the war, Degrenne and Lorence parted company and Degrenne reformed the company, now bringing in his sons, Guy and Raymond. Degrenne created new tools and equipment using the

Company Perspectives:

We have a vocation: to propose the beautiful and useful for all occasions and place within reach all products that are esthetic, functional, and durable. It is this ambition that leads us to web creativity and industrialization on a daily basis. We have a trade: that of Table Service, that of the refinement of the pleasures of the table. It is this demand that brings us to work with several materials in order to offer the robustness of steel, the brilliance of silver, the colors of porcelain, and the transparency of crystal. We have an objective: to innovate, yet and always, in order constantly to modernize a traditional craft through the talents of our stylists and designers, and also through technology and the care of all our workers in order to guarantee a quality beyond reproach. We have a will: to explore the paths of excellence in all we undertake, to master quality, competitiveness of price, and service at the level expected by our clients, to whom we are loyal. We have a sense of engagement and responsibility. More than 1,000 employees, uniting all of the creative, industrial and commercial expertise of the porcelain and silver crafts, ready to meet the challenges of quick response, flexibility, and respect for deadlines, know that they are working together toward the same goal: to service and satisfy our clients.

armor from the many tanks that had been destroyed during the battle of Normandy. The company was also quick to adopt the new material that was revolutionizing the tableware market, that of stainless steel. The family established itself as Degrenne Fils in 1948. It was oldest son Guy Degrenne who was to lead the company's development—and eventually give it his name.

Forging Market Leadership for the 21st Century

Under Guy Degrenne's leadership, the company began to diversify and innovate. With control of the complete production process, Degrenne was now able to control the quality of its products, establishing a name for itself not only within the institutional circuit, but increasingly in the consumer market as well. By 1958, the company expanded beyond silverware to add more and more flatware and then table service items, and in the early 1960s, Degrenne experimented with new production processes, launching its "monocoque," a single-hull knife, in 1963. The company was steadily imposing itself as one of the leaders in its home market. In order to support its growth, Degrenne built a new factory at Vire, in Calvados, in 1967. At the beginning of the 1970s Degrenne introduced another popular product, champagne buckets.

Degrenne's breakthrough came in the early 1970s. In 1974 the company rolled out its first advertising campaign. The spots featured a history of Guy Degrenne, referring to the company's chief as a "cancre"—French term for school dunce—and describing Degrenne as a student who preferred drawing silverware and tableware designs to listening in class. The campaign proved extremely successful in France, elevating the company to one of the country's best-known brands. The long-running campaign was acknowledged by the award of the 7 d'Or.

Degrenne followed up this success with the launch of a new line of silver-plated cutlery in 1975.

By the early 1980s, Degrenne was one of the top French silverware manufacturers. The company reinforced this position in 1981 with the acquisition of J. Simon, based in Quingey. Three years later, Degrenne acquired new stature with the purchase of Létang et Rémy. That acquisition enabled the company to extend its range into the high-end market. The company went public that same year, listing on the Paris secondary market under the Table de France name. The newly public company not only had newly expanded operations, it also had a new line of products, the Couverts Couleurs line, launched in 1984.

After 40 years at the head of the company, Guy Degrenne sold out in 1987, turning over 98 percent of the company to a FFr 175 million leveraged buyout organized by an investment group headed by Bertrand Dechery and Gérard Zink. The company was renamed Guy Degrenne SA and taken off the public market (the remaining two percent of shares continued to be listed on the Parisian over-the-counter market until 1995).

The new influx of capital brought by Déchery and Zink enabled Degrenne to begin to diversify its product line and pursue an international expansion program. The company's first diversification was into the related porcelain industry, in order to allow Degrenne to offer a more complete range of tableware items, especially for the lucrative wedding-list market. The company first purchased a porcelain works in Limoges, then a second facility in Hungary. In 1988, Degrenne acquired cutlery manufacturer Seed. This purchase gave the company the production volume and expanded product line to enable it to enter France's "hypermarket sector"—the country's largest retail market. The company's new management also helped Degrenne make steady sales gains. From FFr 350 million in 1987, the company sales grew to FFr 540 million by 1990. That year's introduction of a new line of gold-plated and lacquered products gave new boosts to the company's sales, which, despite the long-lasting economic crisis in France, reached FFr 612 million by 1995.

By the end of 1996, Degrenne's management had paid the FFr 175 million debt incurred with the leveraged buyout and prepared to step up the company's further development. Dechery and investment partners had already begun by opening up the company's capital to new investors, notably Consortium de Réalisation (part of Credit Lyonnais) and Lazard, which each acquired 20 percent, and Credit Lyonnais itself, which bought six percent of Degrenne. In December 1996, the company announced its intention to return to the Paris secondary market, selling more than 15 percent of its shares. The new offering was meant not only to allow the leveraged-buyout partners to cash out on their investment, but also to finance the company's newly ambitious growth plans.

As it approached its fiftieth anniversary, Guy Degrenne SA sought not only to continue its investment in its growing porcelain business, but also to continue its diversification into such areas as glassware and decorative tiles. The company also sought to boost its international sales, which, by the mid-1990s, accounted for only about 20 percent of its total sales.

Key Dates:

1932: Emile Degrenne buys foundry and factory in Sourdeval and begins production of grillwork and horse-shoeing equipment.
1933: Degrenne forms partnership with Henri-Maris Lorence and begins production of tableware products.
1948: Degrenne and sons Guy and Raymond incorporate the new company as Degrenne Fils, concentrating on stainless steel silverware production.
1958: The company expands production to include a wider range of tableware items.
1967: The company builds new factory in Vire.
1974: The company's first national advertising campaign is a huge success.
1981: The company acquires J. Simon in Quigley, France.
1984: The company acquires the high-end brand Létang et Rémy, launches its Couverts Couleurs line, and goes public on the Paris stock exchange secondary market.
1987: Guy Degrenne sells company in a leveraged buyout led by Bertrand Déchery, who makes the company private again.
1988: Under its new ownership, the company acquires a porcelain factory in Limoges, the cutlery manufacturer Seed, and reinforces institutional silverware and tableware sales.
1996: The company launches store-in-store boutiques.
1997: The company returns to the Paris stock exchange.
1998: The first company-owned retail store opens.
2000: The company acquires Berndorf Austria and Berndorf Switzerland.

The company was also developing a new distribution concept, the "integrated boutique." Launched toward the end of 1996, the company's "store-in-store" concept presented the company's full line of products in a sales space ranging from 30 to 50 square meters. The company targeted the vast multi-brand wedding gift store market—with more than 1,000 stores in France—for its new boutique. By the end of 1996, Degrenne had already opened six boutiques, with plans to open more than 50 by the end of 1997. This project was given a boost by the successful re-introduction of Degrenne's shares on the public market at the beginning of 1997. The company continued to roll out its network of in-store boutiques, although more slowly than originally planned. By the end of the year, the company had opened 30 store-in-stores. While the company continued to target this market, with plans to open up to 100 boutiques by the end of 1998, it had in the meantime begun developing a new retail concept.

By the second half of the 1990s, the multi-brand boutiques, traditionally located in France's town centers, had seen their sales strength undergo a long decline. If, at the height of the 1980s, this circuit had been valued at some FFr 4 billion in sales per year, most of its sales had been driven by the wedding-list market, which reached a height of 200,000 wedding lists in the mid-1980s. The decline of French interest in weddings, as more and more couples, backed by new legislation, opted to forego

marriage, led to a drop in wedding lists to just 120,000 by the middle of the 1990s. Aggravating this decline was the arrival of new competitors, such as Habitat and Ikea, which, coupled with steady market share gains made by the country's hypermarkets, had captured growing portions of the domestic market.

Degrenne saw a new opportunity to assert itself on the retail scene. "Between the networks like Habitat and the hypermarkets, there is room for a new concept," Dechery explained to *Les Echos*. That new concept was the launch of the company's own retail network of self-standing Guy Degrenne stores. Offering the full range of Guy Degrenne, Table et Couleurs, and Létang et Rémy brands, the new retail stores also gave the company the opportunity to come closer to its customers, particularly with the offering of workshops in creating table settings, painting porcelain, and related subjects. The company tested two 100-square-meter stores in 1997 before proceeding with a full roll out in 1998. By the end of the decade, the company had opened 15 retail stores both in France and throughout Europe.

International sales were meanwhile gaining steadily, reaching 27 percent of the company's sales of FFr 687 million in 1997. Those operations were boosted in 1998 as the company entered a cooperation alliance with famed Christofle to combine their product ranges to pursue the booming hotel and institutional markets in Asia and the rest of the world. The company also began shifting much of its industrial activity outside of France, notably to a production facility in Thailand for its hotel and other institutional production, and to Poland, while converting its home-base Vire facility to value-added products. By 1999, the company's international sales had grown to more than one-third of total sales.

Nearly all of the company's growth had been internal. In 2000, the company moved to generate growth externally. In May of that year, Degrenne acquired the tableware subsidiaries jointly owned by Austria's Berndorf group and retailer Table Center. The purchases, which gave Degrenne control of Berndorf Austria and Berndorf Switzerland—the leading manufacturers of cutlery in those markets—also gave it four Table Center retail stores. With this acquisition, the company cemented its place as Europe's leading cutlery manufacturer. At the same time, its growing porcelain operations had enabled it to capture second place in France's tableware sector, behind leader Bernaudaud.

Degrenne continued to target international sales growth in 2001, expanding its retail branch internationally. In June of that year the company made a new move to assert itself on the European scene when it signed a distribution agreement with Finland's Hackman group and its kitchen utensil subsidiary Designor. The agreement called for Designor to market Degrenne's products in its Scandinavian base, while Degrenne took over distribution for the Scandinavian utensils leader in France. These moves were certain to help prove that the former "dunce" Degrenne had become one of Europe's smartest tableware manufacturers for the twenty-first century.

Principal Subsidiaries

Guy Degrenne Industries SA.

Principal Competitors

ARC International; Brown-Forman Corporation; Christofle Orfevrerie; Mikasa, Inc.; Lifetime Hoan Corporation; Noritake Co. Limited; Oneida Ltd.; Royal Doulton plc; Waterford Wedgwood plc.

Further Reading

Bertouille, Marjorie, ''Guy Degrenne n'envisage pas d'augmentation de capital,'' *La Tribune,* January 10, 1997.

Epinay, Bénédicte, ''Guy Degrenne lance son propre réseau de distribution,'' *Les Echos,* December 9, 1997 p. 10.

Lecoeur, Xavier, ''Guy Degrenne intègre ses dernières acquisitions,'' *Les Echos,* May 22, 2000 p. 18.

——, ''Guy Degrenne prend le contrôle des filiales arts de la table de l'autrichien Berndorf,'' *Les Echos,* February 2, 2000 p. 15.

Le Masson, Thomas, ''Guy Degrenne revient sur le second marché,'' *Les Echos,* December 6, 1996, p. 11.

—M.L. Cohen

H. Lundbeck A/S

Otilliavej 92500
Valby-Copenhagen
Denmark
Telephone: (45) 36301311
Fax: (45) 36301940
Web site: http://www.lundbeck.com

Public Company
Incorporated: 1915 as H. Lundbeck & Co.
Employees: 3,002
Sales: DKK 5.62 billion ($694 million)(2000)
Stock Exchanges: Copenhagen
Ticker Symbol: LUN
NAIC: 3254 Pharmaceutical and Medicine Manufacturing

H. Lundbeck A/S is Denmark's second-largest pharmaceuticals company, behind Novo Nordisk. While a small player in the global pharmaceuticals market, the company is a giant within its specialty of drugs to treat diseases and disorders of the central nervous system. Lundbeck is the only such specialist in the world, and its research and development has propelled it to the number three position in Europe within the antidepressants category and to number six in the world for anti-psychotic drugs. The company's primary product is Cipramil, which has become one of the world's most-prescribed new-generation antidepressants. That drug has been marketed as Celexa in the United States since 1998, where it has captured some 14 percent of the market in just three years. Cipramil alone accounts for some 82 percent of the company's sales, a situation the company hopes to correct in the first years of the new century with an ambitious new-product launch program of a new drug every three-to-five years. One of the company's most promising new medications, the anti-psychotic Serdolect, has been temporarily shelved because of concerns for potential side effects. Lundbeck operates subsidiaries in 29 countries and sales offices in an additional 14 countries; sales in Denmark represent only three percent of the company's nearly DKK 6 billion ($700 million) in revenues in 2000. Europe represents more than 70 percent of sales, while the United States contributes 21 percent

of Lundbeck's sales. The company's main manufacturing facilities are in Denmark, with additional production facilities in the United Kingdom and Italy. The company's research and development facilities are located at its headquarters site in Valby, Denmark. Lundbeck has been traded on the Copenhagen stock exchange since 1999; many of the company's shares are held by the Lundbeck Foundation. The company is led by Erik Sprunk-Jansen, who has been president and CEO since 1989 and has spearheaded the company's strong growth at the turn of the century.

World War I Trading Origins

Denmark's neutral position during World War I placed the country in position to build a flourishing trade with the warring nations in the rest of Europe. With government encouragement, many Danes set up their own import-export businesses. Among them was Hans Lundbeck, who had been trading in butter since the early years of that decade. In 1915, Lundbeck set up a new company, H. Lundbeck & Co., with the purpose of expanding his trading activities to include a wide variety of merchandise. Lundbeck set up a series of agencies to handle the buying and selling of goods which ranged from photographic equipment to production machinery to saccharin and even vacuum cleaners. Most of Lundbeck's operations were conducted from his office in Copenhagen, with no need for warehouse or manufacturing facilities, as Lundbeck acted primarily as a broker.

The revaluation of the Danish currency following the war lowered the price on imports and Lundbeck's business flourished. In 1924, Lundbeck hired Edouard Goldschmidt, who became a partner in the company. Goldschmidt added a new wing to the company, that of importing medicines and medicinal products, and, as such, Lundbeck introduced the Danish market to such products as Anusol, the painkiller Gelonida, laxatives and antiseptics, as well as various over-the-counter medicines. This product led the company to expand into the cosmetics and toiletries market as well.

Restrictions put into place by the Danish government during the Depression years led the company to begin bulk imports, rather than finished products. The company now was responsible for preparing and packaging, as well as marketing its line of medications and cosmetics. Lundbeck then launched into a new field, no longer simply marketing medications, but developing its own. In 1937, the company released its first company-developed medication, Epicutan, designed to aid in healing wounds. This growing activity led the company to relocate from its Copenhagen site to Valby. From there, the company took its first steps into organic research, constructing its own laboratories under the direction of Olof Hübner.

The Nazi occupation of Denmark in 1940 forced Goldschmidt, who was Jewish, to withdraw from the company for the duration of the war. Yet the Lundbeck company was able to continue its work—and open its first foreign subsidiary in neutral Sweden—and soon made its first breakthrough in the pharmaceutical field when it developed the sulphonamide-based Lucosil, which proved effective in combating urinary tract infections. Production of Lucosil, based on hydrazine sulphate, quickly ran into trouble when supplies of the raw material were diverted for use as fuel for the V2 rocket program.

Slippers and Pharmaceuticals in the 1970s

Following the war, Lundbeck procured the rights to develop ketobemidon, a compound that had been created by the Germans then confiscated along with all of the country's patents by the Allies after the war. Lundbeck's laboratories refined the compound into its own brand, Ketogan, a highly effective pain reliever released in 1952. At the same time, the company had been developing its first antibiotic, Neomycin, based on a formula obtained from Nobel Prizewinner Selman Waksman. In the early 1950s, the company built its own microbiology laboratory for the culture of bacteria and development of antibiotics.

By then, both Lundbeck and Goldschmidt had died and the company reincorporated as a limited company in 1950, with Lundbeck's widow, Grete, holding 50.5 percent of the company's shares, and the Goldschmidt family holding the rest. Grete Lundbeck also joined the company's board of directors, together with Olof Hübner, but retired in 1954, setting up the Lundbeck Foundation to control her shares in the company.

The company began placing more and more of its efforts on its pharmaceuticals development. At the end of the 1950s, the company had a new success with the 1958 launch of Truxal, a chlorpromazine-based medication that successfully eliminated that drug's side effects. Truxal, an anti-psychotic useful in the treatment of schizophrenia, marked the company's first foray into its later specialty field of central nervous system (CNS) disorders. In the meantime, however, Lundbeck continued its diversified trading companies, notably in the cosmetics and

toiletries sector, but its product range remained as far-flung as the distribution of slippers.

The success of Truxal gave the company new funds for its research and development work, and through the 1960s the company introduced a number of new pharmaceutical preparations. In order to support its growth, Lundbeck opened new facilities in Lumsås, in the northwestern Zealand peninsula. That factory complex soon took over the company's active compound preparation.

Lundbeck's products had long been marketed on a wider international scale, so that the company's growth was not restricted by the small Danish market. The company's international sales had, since the end of World War II, been handled through agreements with locally based sales agents, with the exception of its Swedish subsidiary. By the mid-1960s, the company's international sales represented 75 percent of its revenues, and the company moved to take its foreign operations into its own hands, setting up subsidiaries and sales offices in most of its foreign market countries.

Grete Lundbeck died in 1965, transferring her shares to the Lundbeck foundation. In 1967, the Lundbeck Foundation moved to purchase the Goldschmidt family's 49.5 percent of the company, giving it full ownership. The company continued to build up its foreign operations, setting up its U.K. subsidiary in 1972, while opening offices in New York and Paris as well. At the same time, the company continued to pursue a wide variety of research projects in both the microbiologic and CNS fields.

In 1975, however, the company reorganized, streamlining its research operations to focus on a more limited area. The company ended its microbiological research, judging its chances of developing new antibiotics as too slender. At the same time, the company began shutting down its toiletries and cosmetics division, and ended its other remaining agency operations left over from its origins as a trading company. Production of many of the company's existing products, which ranged from antibiotics to veterinary products such as cow teat salve, was maintained, however.

The company now placed all of its research efforts into developing new drugs for treating CNS disorders. Yet the long development cycle—the company's most recent marketable drug dated from the mid-1960s—and extensive investments in laboratory upgrades combined to depress the company's profits through the 1980s. By 1987, with sales of nearly DKK 525 million, Lundbeck's profits amounted to just DKK 2 million.

A Better Mood for the New Century

In 1987, Lundbeck hired Erik Sprunk-Jansen as its new managing director. Sprunk-Jansen, who had previously run Greenland's Greenex mining operation, brought new life to the company. A thorough review of the company's operations brought Lundbeck to conclude that its future lay in the development of CNS drugs. The company determined to make this area its specialty and proceeded with a sell-off of its newly non-core activities, shutting down its veterinary products production. In 1991, the company sold off its antibiotics production facility to a Norwegian company for DKK 200 million.

Key Dates:

1915: Hans Lundbeck founds trading company in Copenhagen.

1924: Edouard Goldschmidt joins Lundbeck as partner, adding medicine agencies.

1937: Lundbeck launches the first company-developed medication, Epicutan, designed to aid in healing wounds.

1940: The company opens first foreign subsidiary in Sweden and develops Lucosil urinary infection medication.

1952: The company develops Neomycin and enters antibiotic production.

1954: Grete Lundbeck founds Lundbeck Foundation.

1958: Launch of Truxal, Lundbeck's first CNS (central nervous system) medication.

1967: Lundbeck takes full control of the company by acquiring a majority of shares from Goldschmidt family.

1971: The company opens offices in London.

1975: The company streamlines, ending non-medicine production.

1987: Erik Sprunk-Jansen joins company as managing director.

1989: The company launches Cipramil.

1991: The company ends production of antibiotics and becomes a CNS medication specialist

1993: Lundbeck abandons efforts to introduce Cipramil in the United States through partnerships.

1998: The company's launch of new Serdolect anti-psychotic is suspended; U.S. distribution partnership agreement is signed with Forrest Laboratories.

1999: Lundbeck goes public, listing nearly 25 percent of its shares on Copenhagen stock exchange.

2000: Lundbeck makes its first acquisition, that of Italy's VIS Farmaceutici Spa, and signs Cipramil distribution agreement with Japan's Mitsui Pharmaceuticals.

By then, Lundbeck had launched its first new CNS drug in 20 years. The company's citalopram-based Cipramil had been launched in 1989 in Denmark before being introduced to the worldwide pharmaceutical community. A part of the family of selective serotonin reuptake inhibitors (SSRI), a class that included such competing products as Prozac, Paxil, and Zoloft, Lundbeck's product was to become one of the fastest growing anti-depression drugs in the 1990s—and Lundbeck's core product.

In the meantime, Sprunk-Jansen led Lundbeck through a complete reorganization, trimming management, restructuring the company's organization, and revamping its research and development program. The results—which earned Sprunk-Jansen the moniker of ''Butcher from Greenland''—were a streamlined organization that, despite its relatively tiny size, was able to compete with the world's giant pharmaceutical companies.

Cipramil rapidly gained market share throughout Europe in the early 1990s. Lundbeck then turned to the United States, the world's single-largest market for antidepressant sales. Rather than open its own subsidiary in that country, however, Lundbeck sought to enter a distribution partnership agreement with a local company. But finding the appropriate partner proved difficult. By 1993, after three partnerships had already failed, the company decided to withdraw from the United States. Nonetheless, Cipramil enjoyed steady European success throughout the decade, helping the company achieve strong sales growth, as revenues built to more than DKK 2.3 billion, with profits of DKK 236 million for the year.

Meanwhile, the company stepped up its development of new CNS compounds. In 1998, the company readied the launch of a new drug, Serdolect, considered one of the most promising new medications for treating schizophrenia. Unfortunately for Lundbeck, the company's application for release of Serdolect in the Netherlands was denied because of concerns that the drug might increase the risk of cardiac complications in some patients. The denial effectively ended the company's chances of an immediate launch of the drug in the rest of Europe. The company's hopes of another hit medication, which Lundbeck had expected would have equaled Cipramil in sales, were dashed, at least temporarily.

The year 1998 held its share of good news for the company, however. In that year, the company was approached by the American pharmaceuticals distributor, Forrest Laboratories, which expressed its interest in taking on the marketing and distribution of Cipramil in the United States. An agreement was quickly worked out, and Lundbeck's core product at last entered the United States under the brand name Celexa. The drug quickly caught on in the United States, despite stiff competition from its well-known rivals. By the turn of the century, Celexa had captured some 14 percent of the market, with no signs of slowing down. The United States soon became Lundbeck's principal market, accounting for 20 percent of its sales.

By then, Cipramil/Celexa accounted for nearly 82 percent of Lundbeck's sales, a troubling situation, particularly as the company faced the loss of its patents by 2001. With the continued suspension of Serdolect, Lundbeck was forced to look forward to its product pipeline. Meanwhile, the company continued investing in its laboratory facilities. This effort was helped in part by the company's public listing in 1999, when the Lundbeck Foundation placed nearly 25 percent of the company's shares on the Copenhagen stock exchange. The share listing gave the company increased potential for making acquisitions. And, with the company's value now easily seen from its share price, it became itself a potential takeover target for the right price.

In 2000, Lundbeck made its first acquisition, of Italy's VIS Farmaceutici Spa, a producer of active substances for the pharmaceutical industry. These new operations were converted to production of citalopram, the active ingredient of Cirpramil, which had continued to develop new markets, notably in Turkey, Central Europe, Australia, and, through a partnership agreement with Mitsui Pharmaceuticals at the end of 2000, to introduce Cipramil into the Japanese market. The company's expanded production facilities also enabled it to ready the launch of a new product, Cipralex, a second-generation citalopram-based drug. That drug, originally scheduled for launch in 2001, was instead readied for release by mid-2002. Nonetheless, the results of the company's phase III trials suggested that the drug was still more effective than its predecessor.

Lundbeck remained committed to its CNS disorder specialty as it entered the new century. The company had a promising pipeline, in part through a series of partnership agreements, such as that signed with Canada's Neurochem in 1999 to develop Alzheimer's disease treatments and a partnership with Maxygen signed in 2000 to develop drugs to combat multiple sclerosis. The extent of Lundbeck's recognition among its peers was seen in the variety of its partnerships, which included working with Solvay Pharmaceuticals to develop new antipsychotic medication, and another, signed in February 2001, to join with Teva Pharmaceuticals Industries to develop and market an oral formulation of Copaxone, a multiple sclerosis medication, in Europe and elsewhere. At the same time, the company continued its own development efforts, launching a medication to combat migraine headaches in 2000, and preparing several others for release in the early years of the new century. While Lundbeck remained a small company in a field dominated by multi-billion-dollar corporations, its focus on CNS medications enabled it to compete on an equal level with even the largest of its competitors.

Principal Subsidiaries

Lundbeck Australia Pty. Ltd; Lundbeck Arzneimittel Ges.m.b.H. (Austria); Lundbeck N.V. (Belgium); A/S Lundbeck Overseas (Bulgaria); Lundbeck Canada Inc; H. Lundbeck A/S (Czech Republic); H. Lundbeck A/S (Denmark); OY H. Lundbeck AB (Finland); Lundbeck S.A. (France); Lundbeck GmbH & Co (Germany); Lundbeck Hellas S.A. (Greece); Lundbeck Hungaria Kft. (Hungary); Lundbeck Pharma A/S (Iceland); Lundbeck Japan K.K.; Lundbeck B.V. (Netherlands); H. Lundbeck A/S (Norway); H. Lundbeck AB (Sweden); Lundbeck Limited (U.K.); Lundbeck Inc. (U.S.).

Principal Competitors

Pfizer Inc; GlaxoSmithKline plc; Merck & Co., Inc.; AstraZeneca PLC; Bristol-Myers Squibb Company; Novartis AG; Johnson & Johnson; Aventis Pharmaceuticals Inc.; Pharmacia Corporation; Eli Lilly and Company; Novo Nordisk A/S; CeNeS Pharmaceuticals plc; Orion; Shire Pharmaceuticals PLC; Schwarz Pharma AG.

Further Reading

"Antidepressant Cheers Up Lundbeck Results," *Financial Times*, May 16, 2001

"The History of H. Lundbeck," H. Lundbeck corporate web site, http://www.lundbeck.com, October 2001.

"H. Lundbeck Takes Control of VIS," *European Report*, November 8, 2000.

Jarvis, Lisa, "Antidepressant Market Braces for Change," *Chemical Market Reporter*, August 7, 2000.

"Neurochem and H. Lundbeck Announce Strategic Alliance," *Pharmalicensing*, November 27, 1999.

—M.L. Cohen

HACKMANGROUP

Hackman Oyj Adp

Hameentie 135
P.O. Box 955
00561 Helsinki
Finland
Telephone: +358 204 39 11
Fax: +358 204 39 5708
Web site: http://www.hackmangroup.com

Public Company
Incorporated: 1790 as Hackman & Co.
Employees: 2,610
Sales: EUR 315.8 million ($270 million)(2000)
Stock Exchanges: Helsinki
Ticker Symbol: HACAS.HE
NAIC: 551114 Corporate, Subsidiary, and Regional
Managing Offices; 332211 Cutlery and Flatware
(Except Precious) Manufacturing; 339912 Silverware
and Hollowware Manufacturing; 327112 Vitreous
China, Fine Earthenware, and Other Pottery Product
Manufacturing; 333319 Other Commercial and
Service Industry Machinery Manufacturing

Hackman Oyj Adp, or the Hackman Group, is one of Finland's oldest family-owned firms. The founding family continues to hold more than 54 percent of its listed stock and nearly 90 percent of its K series voting rights stock, although the family is no longer involved in day-to-day operations. Yet Hackman has transformed itself from its historic forest products and stainless steel activities to operate as a holding company focused on two core operations: Hackman Metos, Europe's leading manufacturer of professional kitchen systems and equipment, with operations in more than 20 countries, including neighboring Russia, Latvia, Estonia, but also in France, Italy, the Netherlands and Belgium, and as far away as Japan, Korea and Australia. Metos is the division's main brand, especially in Scandinavia and increasingly in the company's other markets, where it also maintains a selection of regional brands added through various acquisitions. Hackman Metos is the company's largest division, providing nearly half of the company's total sales of EUR 315.8

million in 2000. Designor is the company's second core division, producing housewares featuring Scandinavian design under four main brands: Arabia, Hackman, iittala and Rörstrand, which are sold in ''shop-in-shop'' boutiques through third-party retailers. The company aims to promote the division to a world leader in Scandinavian-inspired houseware products. The company has transferred its remaining holdings—such as its money-losing Hadwaco water filtration subsidiary—to a third division, Other Functions, which also includes administrative operations. Since the late 1990s, Hackman, led by chairman Stig Gustavson and president and CEO Tapio Hintikka, has significantly transformed its holdings, restoring the company to profits and simplifying its structure. Hackman Group is traded on the Helsinki stock exchange.

Trading Trade for Forests in the 19th Century

Johan Friedrich Hackman, native of Bremen and member of a merchant and trading family, went to Vyborg, then part of Sweden-controlled Finland, in 1777. In 1790, at the age of 35, Hackman founded his own trading company, Hackman & Co., importing and exporting goods such as salt, wine, sugar, herring, and other products between Finland and the other Scandinavian countries and European colonies around the world. The company shortly built up its own shipping fleet. Hackman added lumber in 1793, an activity which was to become one of the company's major growth areas in the following century. Already at the very beginning of the nineteenth century, Hackman's company had bought six sawmills in Finland, including one in the town of Sorsakoski. Yet the company was forded to continue without its founder, when Hackman was killed accidentally in 1806.

Led by Hackman's widow, and then by son J.F. Hackman Jr. after 1829, the company continued to prosper, successfully navigating the region's political turmoil—such as Sweden's loss to Russia in 1809, which established Finland as an autonomous region within the Russian empire—and the later Crimean War in the middle of the century. Sorsakoski became a major center of Hackman's activity after 1833, when the company acquired Sorsakoski Manor and began industrial operations there.

Company Perspectives:

We have defined our way of operating on the basis of the following shared values. (1) A strong business ethic. At Hackman we take responsibility for the environment and show concern for the employees. In our operations we adhere to high morals and the principles of sustainable development. (2) Customer orientation. Superior product and service quality are important to us, because that quality is the foundation of customer satisfaction. We collect customer feedback actively and develop our operations on that basis. (3) Openness and participation. At Hackman, openness, interaction and cooperation constitute an essential aspect of everyday life. We consider it important that employees participate in the development of their own jobs and the work community. This increases both motivation and work efficiency. (4) A willingness to change. We are constantly developing our personnel and our organization. We are always striving to anticipate what's ahead and to change in accordance with spirit of the time—without forgetting our strong traditions.

Like many trading companies of the period, Hackman was ever-ready to reinvent itself and adapt to new opportunities. In 1840, for example, the company entered the coffee trade, using its own fleet of ships to transport Brazilian beans. The company continued in coffee trading until the 1920s. Another area of company interest became the nascent public utilities market, as Hackman helped install gas lighting to Helsinki and Vyborg in 1860. At the same time, the company continued to build up its lumber interests, buying up not only four additional sawmills, but also buy an increasingly large area of Finland's large forests.

Another Hackman activity begun during the middle and late 1800s was sugar refining, an area the company did not exit until the 1950s. More lasting was the acquisition of a candle factory located in Vyborg's Havi area. Hackman took Havi as a brand name, adding soap and other household products over time, before selling that division in 1998. Hackman's industrial activities meantime expanded to include production of silverware, knives, and scissors, an activity begun in 1876.

Forest and Steel Magnate in the 20th Century

The next generation of Hackmans took over upon J.F., Jr.'s death in 1879. The new generation included J.F., Jr.'s son, Wilhelm, who took charge of the company's operations, and J.F. Jr.'s son-in-law, Carl-August Ekström, beginning the association of that family name with the company's ownership.

The inauguration of the Finnish Steamship Line, with Hackman acting as a investor, enabled the company to exit the shipping business in 1844, transferring its shipping activities to the new company. The company also transferred its Vyborg-based knife and cutlery production to its Sorsakoski facilities, which began to build up markets throughout Russia and the Baltic region and became the headquarters for the company's growing interests in steel product production in the next century.

Hackman also stepped up its forestry activities near the end of the 19th century, buying up still larger areas of Finland's forests. The company began shutting down its water-based sawmills by then, transferring those operations to a main mill at Pölläkkälä, which was bought in 1893. The company, which also operated a steam-powered mill since 1870, built a new steam-powered mill in 1910, near its eastern Finland forest holdings. That region became the site of a new Hackman activity in 1912, when copper deposits were discovered on company land. Hackman formed a cooperative with the Finnish government to exploit the deposits. Copper mining proved short-lived for the company, and Hackman sold back its share in the venture in 1924.

In the meantime, the company was swept up in the course of world history. During World War I, the company shifted its metal production to making scissors for cutting barbed-wire, bayonets, and other products to support the Russian war cause. The company's celebration of Finland's independence, granted in 1917, was short-lived, however, when the Russian civil war destroyed part of its sawmill operation and a large part of its export lumber stock.

Stainless steel production began in 1924 and helped the company weather the rocky economic climate of the postwar reconstruction period. The following year, after Wilhelm Hackman died, the company's leadership was transferred to his sons, Leo and Henry, while the company's ownership expanded to include the growing numbers of Hackman and Ekström family members. The new leadership expanded the company's operations again, building a pulp mill, then entering the household cleaning products market with the purchase of the Teka brand and production facility near Helsinki.

Diversified Postwar Conglomerate

Finland's war with the Soviet Union at the start of World War II saw the country split in half in 1940. Hackman's possessions, including a large part of its forest holdings, in Vyborg and other parts of the Karelian Isthmus were lost. The company transferred its Havi soap and candle production to its Teka plant, while taking up new headquarters in Helsinki. For the duration of the war, the company turned its production toward supporting the Finnish war effort.

After the war, the company was hampered by materials shortages, but was nonetheless able to expand its production of flatware with the opening of a new production facility. This activity took on greater steam for the company as the region's economy took on steam in the 1950s. The growth of a newly affluent and leisure-rich middle-class during the period stimulated demand for new products. Hackman responded by launching new silverware designs by noted Finnish and Scandinavian designers; by the end of the decade, the company had expanded its production to include a range of houseware products and kitchen utensils.

Hackman's interests in both forestry and lumber products continued, however, as the company modernized its main sawmill at Honkalahti, giving it production volumes of some 4.5 million cubic feet by the beginning of the 1960s. During that decade the company also increased its forest holdings, now

Key Dates:

1777: Johan Friedrich Hackman arrives in Vyborg (formerly in Finland).

1790: Hackman sets up his own trading company, Hackman & Co.

1801: The company begins acquiring sawmills while developing shipping activities.

1833: The company buys manor in Sorsakoski and begins production of cutlery and cookware.

1840: The company begins importing coffee from Brazil.

1866: The company acquires a candle factory in Havi, Vyborg, which forms the basis of the Havi soap and candle division.

1876: Begins production of scissors, knives, and other silverware in Nurmi, near Vyborg.

1884: The company invests in Finnish Steamship Line, which assumes shipping of Hackman's export-import trade.

1890: The company acquires large forest holdings.

1915: Production is converted to barbed-wire scissors and bayonets during World War I.

1924: The company begins stainless steel production, and two years later adds a pulp mill near Vyborg.

1940: The company transfers Havi factory to Riihimäki and moves its headquarters to Helsinki.

1948: The company opens wallboard plant at Honkalahti.

1963: Factory for beam production is built.

1966: The company acquires 50 percent of Terätuote Oy, a maker of blades for sawmills, completing shareholding in 1985.

1969: The company reincorporates as Oy Hackman Ab.

1974: The company acquires share of Harding & Vick (UK), completes shareholding in 1978, and renames subsidiary Hackman UK Ltd.

1981: The company acquires Koltek Oy to enter food-processing equipment industry.

1983: The company buys Dacona Ab (Sweden), a maker of professional kitchen equipment.

1988: The company makes first public offering on Helsinki OTC market.

1989: The company buys Nordtend Ab (Sweden) and Nordtend AS (Norway).

1990: The company acquires Arabia, Gustavsberg (Sweden), Rörstand (Sweden), iitalal, and Nuutajäjarvi to establish new Hackman Tabletop division.

1991: The company exits sawmill sector and begins shifting concentration to cutlery and tableware production, acquiring factory in Hungary.

1993: The company buys Fürst Bestecke (Germany), adding to cutlery production, and establishes Hadwaco, a specialist in water-purification systems.

1994: The company converts shares to listing on Helsinki main board; Hackman family maintains control of 89.9 percent of voting rights.

1997: The company begins rationalization program to focus on Hackman Metos and Hackman Designor divisions.

1998: The company acquires full control of Hackman Metos, Dihr International (Italy), and Frost Team (Norway); it sells off Havi Candles.

2001: The company acquires Nordien Systems (Sweden) and International Catering Systems (Belgium).

capable of supplying 20 percent of the company's own production needs. As an offshoot of its lumber division, Hackman began producing such construction trade products as wallboard and beams. The acquisition of Terätuote in 1966 brought the company into the manufacture of sawmill blades. Another new area of interest was the formation of a piping and related equipment manufacturing plant, formed in 1967 with Nyby Bruk of Sweden. That company, Putkihackman, was fully absorbed by Hackman in 1979.

Now led by Herrick Hackman, son of Henry, and Gunnar Ekström, Hackman continued to diversify in the late 1960s, buying the manufacturing and market rights for Halltek panels in 1969, and opening a purpose-built facility for the production of sinks in 1970. The company also merged its Teka and Havi branches that year, now grouped under the Havi brand.

Hackman converted to limited liability status in 1969, changing its name to Oyj Hackman Ab that year. Three years later, the company hired Heinz Ramm-Schmidt to lead its operations, the first time in its history the company had been led by someone from outside of the Hackman family. The company next looked beyond Scandinavia, buying part of Harding & Vick Ltd., based in England, in 1974, then taking full control in 1978 to establish a new subsidiary, Hackman UK Ltd. Through the rest of the decade the company deepened its interests in the

building products market, notably with the launch of DIY-market products and the development of the Kerrotex-brand of boards. At the same time, Hackman continued to build up its position in the household items sector.

Continuing Change in the New Century

The company's next managing director, Curt Lindbom, took over in 1983 and put the company's tradition of continuous change into overdrive. From its base in silverware and household items, the company now extended its reach into the professional food industry, such as acquiring Koltek in 1983 and adding the company's valves and other food-processing equipment components. This acquisition led the company to enter the market for professional kitchens in 1985, with the acquisition of Dacona Ab. In the second half of the decade, the company made a series of investments in the dairy and other collection systems equipment sector, cheese-making equipment, and other farm-related equipment, such as sack-filling systems. Other acquisitions, including those of Mäntysuopa in 1984 and Nordtend, of Sweden, in 1989, strengthened the company's Havi candle and detergent subsidiary.

Hackman's household products became increasingly international at the same time, with acquisitions in Sweden and Norway especially giving the company a new Nordic region focus. Meanwhile, the company continued to invest in its saw-mill activities, automating its operations in an effort to remain competitive. Yet the company's operations in these areas were quickly outclassed by its far-larger rivals.

Approaching its 200th anniversary, Hackman went public with a listing on the OTC market of the Helsinki Stock Exchange. From silverware, Hackman expanded into tableware in general with the acquisition of porcelain brand Arabia, glassworks brand iitaala, and other porcelain and related facilities in Finland and Sweden in 1990. The company created a new division, Hackman Tabletop that year. The following year marked the end of the company's sawmill operations. Unable to compete against the industry's larger players, the company sold off its last mill in 1991, ending nearly 200 years in that sector. In 1994, Hackman joined the Helsinki exchange's main board. Yet control of the company remained solidly within the Hackman family, which maintained a grip on nearly 90 percent of the company's voting rights, and nearly 55 percent of its stock overall.

Yet in the mid-1990s, Hackman was clearly heading toward a crisis. The company found itself unable to keep up in the increasingly capital-intense forestry sector. At the same time, its holdings in stainless steel production and in the chemicals industry were not strong enough to carry the company. A decision was made to enter new industrial areas and, where possible, extend its existing operations into complementary areas.

The company began a vast expansion program, and by mid-decade it had some 17 divisions and a widely diversified range of industrial production. A new subsidiary was formed as a joint venture when Hackman Professional Kitchens merged with Metos, owned by Instrumentarium, creating Hackman Metos Ltd. Hackman later increased its share from its initial 60 percent to full control. At the same time, the company combined its Hackman Housewares and Hackman Tabletop divisions to form Hackman Designor. Fueling the company's expansion was the sale of its vast forest holdings beginning in 1995.

Yet the intense pace of Hackman's expansion quickly bogged the company down into a new financial crisis. Paying too much attention to adding new operations, the company had begun to neglect its existing operations, many of which slipped into losses toward the end of the decade. By 1997, the company's shareholders—especially the 118-strong Hackman family—voted to replace the company's management and board of directors, including CEO Tapio Hintikka, formerly with Nokia. The new management quickly moved to simplify the company's structure, cutting it back to two new core divisions—those of Hackman Metos and its professional kitchen systems and equipment specialty, fully acquired in 1998, and Designor, its range of tabletop items featuring Scandinavian design. The company sold off most of its other holdings, often in management buyouts, while preparing the sale of others, such as money-losing Hadwaco. As part of this divestment program, the company's Havi subsidiary was sold off in 1998.

By 2000, the newly refocused Hackman Group saw its profits once again on the rise. The company now concentrated on increasing the presence of its two main divisions as international brands. By then, as much as half of the company's sales came from outside of Finland, and an increasing share came from beyond the Scandinavian market. Aiding this development were such acquisitions as that of Dihr International in 1998, which established the Hackman Metos division as one of Italy's leading professional dishwasher producers. That same year, Hackman purchased Norway's Frost Team, a major supplier of professional kitchens to that country, and Pakkaskone, of Finland, which specialized in counters and display units for the restaurant and confectionery markets and held the leading position in the Scandinavian market.

The year 2001 saw continued progress toward establishing Hackman Metos as one of Europe's leading manufacturers of professional kitchen equipment and systems. The company acquired Nordien System AB of Sweden, together with its U.K. subsidiary, in June of 2001, strengthening the company's production of support equipment for professional dishwashers systems. By then, the company had already moved into the Belgian market, with the purchase of International Catering Systems, which focused on marketing and distributing professional ovens. Designor, meanwhile, had also begun to look outside of Scandinavia for further growth. In 2001, that division reached a distribution and cooperation agreement with France's Guy Degrenne, which called for the French tableware maker and retailer to introduce Designor's brands in France.

Hackman Group's rising profits and strong dual focus gave the Hackman family hope to see their company continue to grow at the start of its third century of existence. Yet internal tensions within the extended family, which included opposing strategic viewpoints, and the family's overwhelming grip on both the company's voting rights and its shares, which caused Hackman to remain undervalued on the stock market, suggested that a revision of the company's shareholder base remained a possibility for the near future.

Principal Subsidiaries

Hackman Designor Oy Ab; Hackman Europe B.V.; Hackman Furst AG; Hackman Invest Oy Ab; Hackman Metos Oy Ab; Hackman Prosessi Oy Ab; Hackman-MKT Oy; Hadwaco Ltd. Oy; Kiint Oy Sorsakosken Teollisuustalot; Rondex Oy Ltd.

Further Reading

"Hackman and Guy Degrenne Form Strategic Alliance," *M2 Communications,* June 25, 2001.
"Hackman Improves Result," *M2 Communications,* August 2, 2001.
"The History of the Hackman Group," Helsinki: Hackman Group, October 2001.

—M.L. Cohen

HARIBO

HARIBO GmbH & Co. KG

Hans-Riegel-Str. 1
D-53129 Bonn
Germany
Telephone: (49) (228) 537-0
Fax: (49) (228) 537-289
Web site: http://www.haribo.com

Private Company
Incorporated: 1920 as HARIBO OHG
Employees: 5,000
Sales: not available
NAIC: 31134 Non-chocolate Confectionery
   Manufacturing

HARIBO GmbH & Co. KG, a family firm based in Bonn, Germany, is the market leader for fruit gum and licorice products in Europe with a market share of about 60 percent in Germany. The company's main product is the fruit gum "Gold Bears." In addition, the company makes over 200 other chewy sweets, including fruit gum products, licorice, marshmallow candies, chewing gum, and so-called *Kaubonbons*—chewy candy with the texture of gum that dissolves in the mouth. Besides HARIBO, the company markets the brands "MAOAM," "VADEMECUM," "Bären-Schmidt," and "DULCIA." Manufactured at five factories in Germany and 13 production facilities all over Europe, HARIBO products are sold in about 105 countries. Sales outside Germany account for about 55 percent of the company's total revenues. The firm is owned by the two managing directors Hans and Paul Riegel.

Success for the "Dancing Bear" in the 1920s

Hans Riegel, the son of Peter and Agnes Riegel, was born in Friesdorf near Bonn, Germany, in 1893. Following school he learned how to make hard candies as an apprentice and worked five years for candy maker Kleutgen & Meier in Bonn's suburb Bad Godesberg. After World War I, the candy company Heinen in Kessenich, located in a Bonn suburb, was looking for a qualified hard candy maker. Hans Riegel became a partner and the business changed its name to Heinen & Riegel. However,

only two years later, in 1920, Riegel started his own business which he called HARIBO—short for Hans Riegel Bonn. He set up shop in a courtyard kitchen in Kessenich's Bergstrasse where Riegel established the company's first production facility. With start up "capital" that included a sack of sugar, a marble slab, a stove and a copper pot, Riegel started making hard candies.

In 1921, Riegel got married and his wife Gertrud became HARIBO's first employee, distributing the candy on her bike to their first customers around town. It was in the following year when Hans Riegel came up with the idea that would become HARIBO's flagship product: the "Dancing Bear." Made of fruit gum, the "Dancing Bear" soon became extremely popular. So popular that the couple had to buy a car in the following year to deliver them to HARIBO's rapidly growing customer base. After moving into a small factory in Bonn-Kessenich, HARIBO started making licorice products in addition to hard candy and fruit gums. By 1930, the company already employed 160 people and HARIBO products were distributed throughout Germany. The company invested in a brand new production plant which was built between 1930 and 1933. In the early 1930s, the company founder hired a traveling advertising copy writer to create a memorable slogan. He came up with "*HARIBO macht Kinder froh*" a rhyme meaning "HARIBO makes children happy," which was soon printed on posters for shopping windows, delivery trucks, cartons, and packages.

Based on business contacts between Riegel and the Hansen brothers, the owners of the Danish candy manufacturer Sukkervarenfabrikker Danmark, in the late 1920s, HARIBO's first joint venture abroad was set up in Denmark in 1935. By 1939, HARIBO had grown into a middle sized firm, employing about 400 people producing about ten tons of candy a day. However, that year World War II broke out. Since candy products were not essential for the German war economy, it became more and more difficult for the company to get the raw materials needed. Consequently, HARIBO's output shrunk significantly as did its workforce over time. The number of employees dropped to about 130 in 1943 and less than 20 workers remained on the company's payroll by the end of the war. On March 31, 1945, just a few days before the war ended, company founder Hans

Riegel died at age 52, and his wife managed the company in the first months after the war had ended.

Founder's Sons Take Over the Business in 1946

HARIBO was luckier than other companies—its main production facility was almost left untouched by the war. The company started out again with 30 employees and the main challenge of the time was to find sugar, raw licorice, gum arabic, and aromas—the main ingredients for HARIBO's products. In 1946, the sons of Hans Riegel, Hans Riegel, Jr., and Paul Riegel, took over the company's management. Hans Riegel, at the time 23 years old, would have preferred to study medicine. However, he had promised his father to carry on the family business. After rebuilding HARIBO after the war, Hans Riegel wrote his doctoral dissertation on the role of sugar in world trade and got a Ph.D. in business science at Bonn University. He had a great instinct for business opportunities and took over responsibility for HARIBO's product development and marketing. His brother Paul, three years his junior and a skilled engineer, took over the production and engineering part of the business. Paul's technical expertise was in demand when the two brothers evaluated Hans Riegel's ideas for new products and he developed many of the machines used to make them. One example was a machine for HARIBO's famous "Licorice Wheels," a string of licorice that was curled up like a snail. The "Wheels" were made by hand until Paul invented a machine that curled them automatically. Besides keeping production up and running and technological standards up to date, Paul Riegel was especially concerned with high quality standards. To keep his staff aware of the this aim, walls in production facilities were plastered with posters containing the slogan "Quality Above All."

By 1950, HARIBO's business had grown immensely. Only five years after the war had ended the company employed about 1,000 people. Beginning in the late 1950s, the company started expanding nationally as well as internationally. In 1957, HARIBO acquired the Godesberg-based candy maker Kleutgen & Meier, the company where HARIBO-founder Hans Riegel once learned how to cook hard candy. Under the brand name "Monarch," Kleutgen & Meier sold fruit gums by the piece. In 1961, HARIBO took over the Dutch firm Bonera Industrie en Handelsmaatschappij N.V. which was renamed HARIBO Nederland B.V. Six years later HARIBO acquired a majority in Marseilles-based French candy company Lorette, which was transformed into HARIBO-France S.A. One year later the company bought shares in German sweets manufacturer Dr. Hillers AG based in Solingen.

During the 1950s, HARIBO's "Dancing Bears" underwent a metamorphosis. Their name was changed to "Teddy Bears" and their shape became more compact and round. By the mid-1960s, HARIBO realized that not only children enjoyed the company's chewy sweets. HARIBO's slogan was supplemented by a second line: "HARIBO macht Kinder froh—und Erwachsene ebenso," meaning "HARIBO makes children happy—and adults as well." In 1962, when television was still in its early stages in Germany, a HARIBO commercial aired for the first time. Sung to a simple melody much like a nursery rhyme, the company's slogan was very easily recognizable and soon became immensely popular.

Massive Expansion Into Western Europe in the 1970s–80s

In the 1970s and 1980s, HARIBO kept expanding its market and product range in Germany as well as abroad. National expansion went on in 1971 when the company acquired a majority in the German manufacturer of sweet baked goods and fruit gum products Bären-Schmidt. The company's flagship product were the popular *Lebkuchenherzen*—large, heart-shaped spice cookies. In 1979, HARIBO took over the remaining shares of Dr. Hillers AG and expanded the existing production facilities in Solingen, which were equipped with state-of-the-art machines for making fruit gums, licorice, and chewing gum. In 1986, HARIBO took over Edmund Münster GmbH & Co. KG in Neuss, a company with a long tradition. It's predecessor, the Düsseldorfer Lakritzenwerk, was founded in 1898 and was taken over by entrepreneur Edmund Münster in 1900. At first the company made mostly licorice products, until Münster acquired a license to make the fruity *Kaubonbon* "MAOAM" in 1930. Production started in 1931 and the new product became very popular in Germany in the 1950s. In 1982, the company moved from Düsseldorf to Neuss. The chewy sweet novelty that was not a chewing gum came in fruity flavors such as lemon, pineapple, orange or raspberry and ideally complemented HARIBO's product range.

The company's main focus during the 1970s and 1980s, though, was its massive expansion into Western Europe. In 1972, HARIBO acquired a share in traditional English licorice maker Dunhills. Four years after the Dunhills transaction, HARIBO established a foothold in Sweden by setting up a sales organization in Helsingborg. One year later the company started doing the same in Austria. In 1988, HARIBO took over the Austrian pastries and candy maker Panuli Bonbon Ges.m.b.H. located in Linz on the Danube River and started producing its own product range in Austria. In 1982, HARIBO started selling fruit gums in the United States from its sales offices in Baltimore, Maryland. Starting in 1983, HARIBO intensified its activities in France. In that year the company acquired the French firm Stella based in Wattrelos near Lille. Two years later, HARIBO bought the southern French company Ricqles Zan which was merged with HARIBO France in 1987, resulting in the new company HARIBO RICQLES—ZAN. The company's three production facilities in France supplied the French market as well as other southern European countries with HARIBO products. In 1989, Paul Riegel's oldest son, Hans-Jürgen, became CEO of HARIBO RICQLES—ZAN. The same year HARIBO established a sales office in Oslo, Norway.

Dynamic Growth in the 1990s

After the reunification of Germany, HARIBO took a chance by acquiring East German sweets maker WESA. The com-

Key Dates:

1920: HARIBO OHG is set up in Bonn, Germany.
1922: Company founder Hans Riegel invents the ''Dancing Bear'' figure.
Mid-1930s: The slogan ''HARIBO macht Kinder froh'' is created.
1935: HARIBO's first joint venture is set up in Denmark.
1946: Hans and Paul Riegel take over the company's management.
1960: HARIBO's slogan is expanded to include adults.
1972: HARIBO acquires a share in English licorice maker Dunhills.
1982: The company sets up a distribution subsidiary in the United States.
1986: HARIBO takes over Edmund Münster GmbH & Co. KG and the ''MAOAM'' brand.
1990: HARIBO acquires Italian firm SIDAS DOLCIARIA.
1991: German star entertainer Thomas Gottschalk starts promoting HARIBO products.
1995: HARIBO sets up a production facility in Spain.
1998: A production facility is set up in Ireland and a sales office is founded in the Czech Republic.
2001: The company acquires the majority of Turkish sweets maker Pamir Gida Sanayi A.S.

pany's history reached back to 1898 when entrepreneur Oswald Stengel established a factory for candy, chocolate, and *Lebkuchen* spice cookies in the south-eastern German town Wilkau-Hasslau, near Chemnitz. The son of the founder sold the company to the state of Saxony in 1949 and it was transformed into a government-owned operation.

In 1991, HARIBO began a successful cooperation with German star TV-entertainer Thomas Gottschalk which pushed the level of consumer recognition of HARIBO products up even higher. The sympathetic moderator of several TV shows enjoyed a high popularity among a broad segment of German TV viewers that ideally complemented HARIBO's principal target group from age four to 94. In the early 1990s, a new competitor in HARIBO's core market arose in former East Germany when Peter Kettel, for many years CEO of the firm Petzold und Aulhorn, sold his company to the Van Houten group and founded the Gummi Bear Factory in Boizenburg. The company gained a strong market share of over 25 percent, mainly because of its ''no-name'' production for food retail chains. However, the company was not able to shake HARIBO's leading position which at the end of the 1990s moved closer towards the 60 percent mark in the fruit gum segment. HARIBO's ''Gold Bears'' alone reached a market share of 20 percent for all fruit gum sales in Germany, partly due to a distribution rate of 99 percent, meaning that they were available in almost any store that carried candy. By the mid-1990s, the fruit gum segment accounted for about four-fifths of the company's total sales.

During the 1990s, HARIBO continued to expand into Europe. In 1990, the company took over the Italian firm SIDAS DOLCIARIA, based in Milan, and founded HARIBO Italy. In the following year HARIBO established a sales organization in

Finland based in Helsinki. When German chemicals concern Henkel KGaA acquired the Swedish Barnaengen group, HARIBO took the chance and bought its candy business division, in which Henkel was not interested, in 1993. The deal included the rights to Barnaengen's VADEMECUM brand of chewing gum. As early as 1973 the sugar-free VADEMECUM GUM had been introduced to the European market. By the 1990s, the VADEMECUM GUM line was advertised as a means to keep teeth healthy since the sugar replacement XYLIT had cavity-fighting qualities. In 1994, HARIBO took over the remaining shares of English licorice maker Dunhills, producer of the traditional ''Pontefract Cakes.'' One year later a subsidiary was founded in Spain and a production facility set up. In 1996, HARIBO took over Belgian sweets manufacturer Dulcia Sweet Lines based in Kontich near Antwerp, which specialized in marshmallow sugar products. Two years later, a new production facility was set up in Dublin, Ireland, and a sales office was founded in the Czech Republic in Brno. Also in 1998, HARIBO took over Spanish sweets maker Geldul S.L. in Alicante and the Irish candy company Clara Candy. In 2001, the company acquired the majority of Turkish sweets maker Pamir Gida Sanayi A.S. based in Istanbul, which also specialized in fruit gum and marshmallow sugar products. As a result of HARIBO's growing international activities, the company's sales abroad grew by two-digit figures throughout the 1990s, reaching more than 55 percent of total sales by 2000.

Innovative Products and Conservative Management in the 1990s

During the 1990s, HARIBO enjoyed a dynamic growth which CEO Hans Riegel connected with successful brand management and product innovation rather than with the economic cycle of his industry, which was actually slowing down at the end of the 1990s. Although HARIBO's product range included more than 200 products, new product development had not been delegated to a marketing department. More often than not, Hans Riegel himself generated the constant stream of new ideas needed in an industry in which rapidly shortening product cycles required a high innovation rate. In 1996, an Olympics year, the company launched the ''lucky box'' with fruit gum sports figures. Inspirations for new products also came from children's movies like *Babe,* after which Riegel created the ''*Saure Sau*''—the sour sow. Other Riegel creations included ''red lips'' from wine gum with a cherry taste and a tinge of Menthol; ''kosher'' fruit gums on a solely vegetarian basis for export to Israel, the Middle East, and Moslem countries in Asia; ''Fitness'' fruit gum enriched with vitamins and proteins, and sour fruit gum ''pickles.'' For the younger target groups HARIBO launched the comic figures HARI and BO which shook their clay bodies wildly to the popular Techno music on music TV channels MTV and VIVA. In response to the latest political financial scandals in Germany in the late 1990s Riegel developed a licorice product that looked like coins and that he called ''*Schwarzgeld*''—illegally earned money—which was to be sold in a suitcase-like package. However, not every one of Riegel's new product ideas was successful. When HARIBO launched a fruit gum version of the ''Holy Family'' around Christmas time, the company gave in to protests of the German Catholic church and removed its ''innovation'' from the market. Fruit gum versions of German politicians put on the market around election time got HARIBO a lot of free publicity that did not, however, translate into huge product sales. Other not so successful creations included fried eggs, gum pistols, and punk heads.

As frequently as HARIBO introduced new products, its "Gold Bears" enjoyed a stable and even growing popularity during the 1990s. While the bear's recipe and design didn't change much over the years, consumer's health concerns changed some of its ingredients. When European consumers became aware of the potential dangers of some food colors HARIBO started using natural food colors. When European consumers became concerned about the possible effects of BSE on their health, HARIBO stopped using cattle by-products and switched to gelatin produced from raw material derived from pigs for their fruit gum products.

Not only was Hans Riegel in charge of new product development, his management style had not changed much over the fifty years he had steered the HARIBO enterprise, for which he was criticized by some management consultants and journalists as being patriarchal and old-fashioned. As described by Frank Hornig in the German news magazine *DER SPIEGEL,* Riedel opened every letter addressed to his company to stay on top of things, convinced that otherwise the "bad news" would be hidden from him. Then he would meet one-on-one with each of his directors every day to discuss the issues and tasks of each department based on his findings. Riegel also didn't see the need of modern controlling—until in the mid-1990s one of his directors was caught embezzling HARIBO funds. Another hallmark of Hans Riegel's management style was stability, mainly applied to brand development and finances. While there was a constant stream of new products developed, the advertising and design and slogan for the HARIBO brand remained relatively constant. As a result, HARIBO's brand name and slogan were among the most recognized in Germany in the late 1990s. Due to Hans Riegel's financial conservatism, HARIBO financed its acquisitions with the company's own funds rather than borrowing from banks.

Consequently, despite the criticism of HARIBO's management style, the company was thriving at the beginning of the 21st century. Putting out 70 million "Gold Bears" a year, Hans Riegel was planning HARIBO's next round of expansion with an eye on the United States, Eastern Europe, and the Middle East. Although the company's sales and profits were one of the best-kept secrets besides the "Gold Bear" recipe, insiders estimated the company's sales at roughly DM 2.7 billion in 2000. However, Hans Riegel told *Der Spiegel* that by the beginning of 2000 he didn't think that any of his brother's three sons who all worked at the company were possible successors. His company shares will be inherited by a foundation to promote new talent in the industry.

Principal Subsidiaries

HARIBO of AMERICA Inc.; HARIBO Lakrids OY AB (Finland); HARIBO LAKRITS AB (Sweden); HARIBO LAKRIS A/S (Norway); HARIBO LAKRIDS A/S (Denmark); VAN HARIBO NEDERLAND B.V. (Netherlands); HARIBO UK; Dunhills (Pontefract) plc (United Kingdom); HARIBO BELGIE B.V.B.A. (Belgium); HARIBO LAKRITZEN Hans Riegel Betriebsgesellschaft mbH (Austria); HARIBO RICQLES-ZAN S.A. (France); HARIBO ESPANA S.A (Spain); HARIBO ITALIA S.p.A. (Italy); Pamir Gida Sanayi A.S (Turkey); HARIBO Hungaria Kft.(Hungary).

Principal Competitors

Katjes Fassin GmbH & Co. KG; Gummi Bear Factory GmbH; Wm. Wrigley Jr. Company.

Further Reading

Chwallek, Andreas, "Haribo-Gruppe auf ungebremstem Wachstumskurs," Lebensmittel Zeitung, August 4, 2000, p. 12.
——, "Haribo marschiert international kräftig vorwärts," *Lebensmittel Zeitung,* March 2, 2001, p. 22.
"A Custom-Tailored Global Reach (Vendor Closeups)," *MMR,* October 29, 2001, p. 20.
Fröhlich, Vera Hella, "Mit 75 Jahren soll der Bär die USA und Osteuropa erobern," *Associated Press,* June 17, 1997.
Greimel, Hans, "Hunting New Market, Gummi Bears Go Kosher," *Washington Post,* May 20, 2001, p. A21.
"Haribo auf starkem Expansionskurs," *Lebensmittel Zeitung,* July 5, 1996, p. 16.
"Haribo Extends Collection," *Supermarket News,* October 25, 1999, p. 72.
"Haribo Launches Kosher and Halal Gummies," *Candy Industry,* April 1, 2001, p. 18.
"Haribo Launches Takeover Bid," *Marketing Week,* May 17, 2001, p. 33.
"Haribo legt weiter kräftig im Auslandsgeschäft zu," *Lebensmittel Zeitung,* December 24, 1998, p. 10.
"Haribo Looks to Middle East," *Kid's Marketing Report,* June 5, 2001, p. 2.
"Henkel verkauft Vademecum an Haribo," *Süddeutsche Zeitung,* December 10, 1992.
Hornig, Frank, "König der Gummibärchen," *DER SPIEGEL,* January 24, 2000, p. 97.
"Konkurrenz für Haribo-Gummibären," *Werben und Verkaufen,* March 24, 1995, p. 14.
"Man denkt europäisch," *Lebensmittel Zeitung,* January 29, 1999, p. 60.
"Neues tun - Bewährtes belassen," Lebensmittel Zeitung, August 28, 1998, p. 78.
Telgheder, Maike, "Ein Leben für die Gummibärchen," *HORIZONT,* January 26, 1996, p. 14.
Trauth, Martin, "Haribo will mit 'koscheren' Gummibärchen neue Märkte erobern," *Agence France Presse,* October 4, 2000.
Troester, Christian, "Typen aus der Tüte," *Die Woche,* September 22, 1994, p. 52.

—Evelyn Hauser

Hogan & Hartson L.L.P.

555 Thirteenth Street N.W.
Washington, D.C. 20004
U.S.A.
Telephone: (202) 637-5600
Fax: (202) 637-5910
Web site: http://www.hhlaw.com

Partnership
Founded: 1904
Employees: 1,800
Gross Billings: $320 million (2000)
NAIC: 54111 Offices of Lawyers

With over 800 lawyers, Hogan & Hartson L.L.P. is the largest law firm based in Washington, D.C., and one of the largest in the world. Its practice spans the globe, from Latin America, Europe, and Asia to Africa and the Middle East. It operates branch offices in Tokyo, Berlin, London, Brussels, Paris, Budapest, Prague, Warsaw, Moscow, New York City, Baltimore, Miami, Los Angeles, Denver, Boulder, Colorado Springs, and McLean, Virginia. It provides expertise in virtually all areas of domestic and international law, from antitrust, taxation, and litigation to intellectual property, mergers and acquisitions, and project financing. It continues its historic practice of serving clients in their dealings with federal government agencies. Like other large firms, Hogan & Hartson serves multinational corporations, trade associations, nonprofit groups, and other diverse clients. However, its commitment to pro bono service continues to be rather unusual.

Getting Started and Early Law Practice

Frank J. Hogan, the founder of Hogan & Hartson, was born in 1877 in Brooklyn. In 1902 he received his LL.B. from Georgetown University, was admitted to the District of Columbia Bar, and thus began his long career as a lawyer. One of Hogan's early clients was Theodore Roosevelt. In addition to his private law practice, Hogan lectured on wills, evidence, and partnerships at his alma mater, Georgetown University. He also

wrote articles for legal journals and in 1912 began serving as the advisory editor of the *Georgetown Law Journal*.

For several years Hogan's partnership remained a small practice based in Washington, D.C., where it concentrated on serving clients in their dealings with the federal government that grew from new agencies and laws passed during the Progressive Era. For example, Congress gained the authority to tax incomes with ratification of the Sixteenth Amendment in 1913.

Nelson T. Hartson in 1925 left as the Treasury Department's Internal Revenue solicitor to lead the growing tax practice of the Hogan law firm. Unlike most other early partners who were from the East and had gained their legal education at Georgetown University, Hartson was born in Spokane, Washington, and earned his L.L.B. at the University of Washington.

In the 1932 *Martindale-Hubbell Law Directory*, Hogan, Donovan, Jones, Hartson & Guider, with the five name partners and one associate, described itself as having a "Practice before United States Courts, Bureau of Internal Revenue, Federal Radio Commission, and Government Departments." The 1932 directory stated that the Hogan firm was general counsel for Riggs National Bank and the District of Columbia Bankers Association and counsel for Capital Traction Company, Travelers Insurance Company, and the Evening Star Newspaper Company. The 1940 directory listed Liberty Mutual Insurance Company, Columbia Broadcasting System (CBS), and Crosley Radio Corporation as other clients of Hogan & Hartson. The firm at that time consisted of 13 lawyers. Nevertheless, the nation's largest law firms were headquartered in New York City, the nation's financial and commercial capital. They usually did not have offices in Washington, D.C., until after World War II.

Post-World War II Growth

Hogan & Hartson in 1950 described itself in the *Martindale-Hubbell Law Directory* as practicing "before United States Courts, Bureau of Internal Revenue, Federal Communications Commission, Federal Trade Commission and Government Departments," but by 1960 it said it had a general practice. It also increased from 24 lawyers in 1950 to 36 lawyers in 1960. In the 1960s and 1970s, law firms grew rapidly due to more federal

Company Perspectives:

When you join a law firm, you join a group of people. The people of Hogan & Hartson L.L.P. (Hogan & Hartson) are our greatest strength. We come from across the country and around the world. We are committed to preeminence in a full spectrum of legal services throughout the three major areas of our practice—commercial, litigation, and government regulation. We represent a diverse client base that ranges from local entrepreneurs to Fortune 500 multi-nationals. We believe in contributing to our community through a long-standing and extensive pro bono commitment. We are dedicated to maintaining an environment in which we all work together as a team—in which we respect each other as professional colleagues and enjoy each other's company as friends.

government laws and regulatory bodies, including the 1964 Civil Rights Act and the Environmental Protection Agency. Joseph C. Goulden, in his 1972 book about large Washington, D.C., law firms, estimated that in the previous decade the number of lawyers had increased 25 percent. According to Goulden, the capital had "less than one-half percent of the United States population, and almost five percent of the lawyers." As part of this trend, Hogan & Hartson more than doubled its number of lawyers to reach 76 in 1973.

Lawyer and consumer activist Ralph Nader in 1969 criticized the growing power of corporate law firms. Goulden reported that Nader said "the lobbying infrastructure" slowed the passage of useful consumer laws. In a Senate government operations subcommittee, Nader described firms like Hogan & Hartson as being "eminent specialists in cutting down consumer programs in their incipiency or undermining them if they mature. They are the masters of the ex parte contact, the private deals and tradeoffs, the greasing of the corporate wheels and the softening of the bureaucrats' wills."

Hogan & Hartson in the mid-1970s gained Senator J. William Fulbright as one of its partners after he lost his reelection bid. The Arkansas Democrat was well known for serving five terms in the U.S. Senate from 1945 to 1975, creating the Fulbright scholarships, and being one of the main opponents of the Vietnam War. Fulbright remained with Hogan & Hartson until his death in 1995.

In 1976 Hogan & Hartson was praised in *Verdicts on Lawyers* for having "identified full-time pro bono partners and associates to coordinate the firm's public interest work." Such an example was then and continued to be rather unusual in large corporate law firms. This program was started in 1970 as a way to provide legal services to clients unable to pay regular fees. Over the years thousands of organizations or individuals thus were served, and pro bono work became a significant aspect of Hogan & Hartson's culture. It led to the firm receiving the American Bar Association's top pro bono award in 1991. Hogan & Hartson's example also inspired some other large firms, such as Holland & Knight, Florida's largest law firm, to establish similar programs.

In the 1980s Hogan & Hartson added new offices near its Washington, D.C., headquarters. Its McLean, Virginia office was established in 1985 to serve mainly high-tech companies in Fairfax County. Hogan & Hartson in 1988 became the first large out-of-town law firm to establish a branch office in Baltimore.

The firm's international growth started in 1989 when its partners decided that expansion would be their major goal. "I think many of us believed that for a firm like ours to remain a top-tier firm, we needed to expand our international reach," recalled managing partner Bob Glen Odle in *Legal Times*.

Practice in the 1990s and Beyond

Hogan & Hartson was listed in the 1990 *Martindale-Hubbell Law Directory* as having a total of 278 lawyers at its Washington, D.C., headquarters and also three nearby branch offices in Baltimore; Bethesda, Maryland; and McLean, Virginia. In 1990, it added new offices in London and Prague, its first overseas branches. By 1991, other new offices had been established in Warsaw, Paris, and Brussels.

Hogan & Hartson and several other law firms grew in response to the collapse of communism. In 1989 Germans destroyed the Berlin Wall and soon reunited East and West Germany, and in 1991 the Soviet Union disintegrated into Russia and several other nations. Free market reforms that included new laws and privatizing former state-owned businesses provided new opportunities for foreign corporations and their law firms.

In 1991, the U.S. Agency for International Development (AID) announced it had selected three teams of accountants and law firms to help eastern European nations develop agency-approved regulations and privatize their economies. Hogan & Hartson and KPMG Peat Marwick comprised one of the teams that would receive up to $15 million during a three-year contract. Hogan & Hartson helped the Slovak Republic's Ministry of the Environment and the Czech Republic's Ministry of Agriculture write new regulations. Some critics contended that such work was a conflict of interest because law firms' corporate clients could benefit from favorable laws and regulations. "Hogan & Hartson and the other law firms who represent major ministries have gotten into the business of writing regulations that suit themselves," said Stanley Glod, chair of the Foreign Claims Settlement Commission of the United States, in *The Washington Post*. Started in 1994, the firm's Moscow office illustrated Hogan & Hartson's role in the globalized economy. It helped a United States-based communications company gain a $190 million loan guaranty from a Russian agency. The Moscow office helped clients not only in Russia, but also in the Ukraine, Kazakhstan, the Czech Republic, and other nations in the region.

In 1996 Hogan & Hartson continued its growth in eastern Europe by opening an office in Budapest that focused on industrial and energy privatizations. "I'm very excited," said Bob Glen Odle in *International Financial Law Review*. "Budapest is [a] step in our European strategy of having an office in every major country our client base is interested in." Hogan & Hartson also helped develop eastern Europe's new municipal bond market. Under communism, local governments avoided debt, but by 1996 some municipalities were beginning to see the advantages of long-term bonds to help pay for badly needed infrastructure such as roads, water systems, and airports. Meanwhile, Hogan & Hartson opened new offices in Colorado Springs and Denver in 1994 and Los Angeles in 1996. Its New York City office was started in 1998.

Hogan & Hartson clients in the 1990s included the U.S. Olympic Committee; Genentech Inc., the nation's first biotechnology company; Amgen Inc.; the Biotechnology Industry Organization formed in 1993; and the American Academy of Pediatrics. Jean-Bertrand Aristide, ousted as Haiti's president in 1991, paid the firm $55,000 a month in 1994 to have partner Michael Barnes, a former Maryland congressman, try to get him restored to power. The firm, however, lost a significant client in 1995 when Boston Bancorp replaced it with Boston's Hale & Dorr. Hogan & Hartson had served Boston Bancorp from at least its 1983 debut as a public corporation.

In the 1990s, Hogan & Hartson had close ties to the Clinton administration and the Democratic Party. For example, one of the firm's lawyers served as the Clinton-Gore campaign's general counsel in 1992. Clinton in 1993 chose Hogan & Hartson lawyers to be his deputy national security adviser and his secretary to the cabinet. At the same time, the firm increased its government relations practice by adding 10 new lobbying clients in the first months of the new administration.

In the mid-1990s, a Hogan & Hartson employee delivered a $50,000 donation from Greek citizen George Psaltis' company Psaltis Corporation, a firm client, to the Democratic National Committee (DNC). The DNC later returned the money and said it had not realized Psaltis was not an American citizen and his company had no United States operations. Hogan & Hartson also represented DNC fund-raiser John Huang for alleged improper activities.

Hogan & Hartson continued to have one of the nation's top lobbying practices in the years ahead. For example, in 2000 the firm earned $15.5 million from lobbying, an amount exceeded by only three other law firms and one non-law firm. This was according to Influence, a service owned by American Lawyer Media Inc. Influence published a newsletter and operated www.influenceonline.net to inform the public about lobbying activities. The Hogan & Hartson Political Action Committee donated money to both Republican and Democratic candidates. From 1997 to 2000 it gave between 55 and 64 percent of its contributions to Republicans.

In the November 2000 presidential election, George W. Bush used lawyers from Hogan & Hartson and several other law firms to help him win the struggle over Florida's contested electoral votes. In May 1998, the U.S. Justice Department, 19 states, and the District of Columbia filed an antitrust lawsuit against Microsoft Corporation. Hogan & Hartson, in this much-publicized case, represented the states, the District of Columbia, and also Netscape Communications Corporation, the governments' main witness against the Seattle software developer. Although attempts to split Microsoft were dropped, the legal battle continued in 2001.

Meanwhile, the firm served other clients in antitrust matters. For example, partner Janet L. McDavid represented Mobil Corporation when it merged with Exxon, American Electric Power when it merged with CSW, and also General Dynamics, PacifiCare, American Express, and BT plc in various transactions or investigations.

In July, 2000 Russia's Uneximbank with help from Hogan & Hartson finally reached a settlement on the bank's $1.4 billion bankruptcy. About 75 of the firm's lawyers worked on the 1,600-page settlement document. The authors of an article in the *International Financial Law Review* said, "Uneximbank is important because it was the first Russian credit institution to declare itself bankrupt and the first to then settle its bankruptcy with foreign creditors."

The firm's Prague office represented Radio Free Europe/Radio Liberty when it moved from Munich to Prague, ICF Kaiser International in its Czech steel mini-mill, the Czech and Slovak American Enterprise Fund that aided various businesses, and U.S. West International in a Czech cable television and telephony project.

Hogan & Hartson also counseled Stredoceska Energeticka a.s. in its investment in a power plant near Prague. According to the firm's Web site, the $400 million plant was "the first independent power project in the Czech Republic and probably in Central and Eastern Europe as a whole to raise financing on a non-recourse basis and without the benefit of government guarantees."

In 2000, Hogan & Hartson began an office in Miami as a means to increase its Latin American practice. One of its clients was Petrobras, a company owned by the Brazilian government, as it built and financed a major gas pipeline with Bolivia. Also in 2000, the firm opened a small Tokyo office and worked to absorb 35 lawyers recruited laterally from New York's Davis, Weber & Edwards, the largest acquisition in its history. Hogan & Hartson continued its rapid growth in the new millennium by opening a Berlin office in January 2001 under the name Hogan & Hartson Raue. The 30-lawyer office was the third largest law firm in Berlin, according to *Legal Times*.

In 2001, California businessman Dennis Tito became the first person to buy a flight into space. In addition to paying $20 million to Russia, Tito paid Hogan & Hartson and two other law firms that helped him negotiate with three Russian agencies before he blasted off to visit the International Space Station.

With literally hundreds of new lawyers added in the 1990s, the firm faced numerous challenges. As Hogan & Hartson's first full-time managing partner, Bob Glen Odle traveled to each overseas branch at least twice every year. That personal interaction helped strengthen the firm, which closed no offices during this rapid growth period. Odle stepped down as the firm's chairman at the end of 2000. Since 1979, when Odle became chairman, Hogan & Hartson had grown from one to 18 offices worldwide and more than quadrupled its number of lawyers to over 800. The new chairman was J. Warren Gorrell Jr.

Based on its 2000 gross revenue of $320 million, Hogan & Hartson was the nation's thirty-fifth largest law firm, according to the annual ratings by *The American Lawyer*. The firm's gross revenue increased 22.1 percent from 1999, when it was ranked number 40. With almost a century of experience, Hogan & Hartson had come a long way to become one of the world's largest law firms.

Principal Competitors

Arnold & Porter; Covington & Burling; Akin, Gump, Strauss, Hauer & Feld.

Further Reading

Agovino, Theresa and William R. Long, "East Europe Banks on U.S. Expertise," *Denver Post*, March 24, 1996, p. H1.

Bennett, Tom, "Former Sen. Fulbright of Arkansas, Clinton's Mentor, Dies at 89," *The Atlanta Journal*, February 9, 1995, p. A1.

Blanton, Kenneth, "Boston Bancorp Fires Legal Adviser," *Boston Globe*, March 23, 1995, p. 71.

Blum, Vanessa, "In with the Old," *Legal Times*, June 26, 2000, p. 40.

"Democratic National Committee Returns Second Big Contribution," *Las Vegas Review-Journal*, November 8, 1996, p. 9A.

Fantin, Linda, "USOC Will Release Findings of Scandal Probe to Congress," *The Salt Lake Tribune*, November 11, 1999, p. C4.

"Forty-Three Lobbying Practices Earned $5M+ in 2000," *PR Newswire*, May 16, 2001.

Geyelin, Milo and Alecia Swasy, "Florida's Biggest Law Firm Plans Section Aimed at Pro Bono Work," *The Wall Street Journal*, September 13, 1989, p. 1 [Eastern edition].

Goshko, John M., "Aristide's Government-in-Exile Spends up to $1 Million a Month," *Star Tribune* [Minneapolis], January 31, 1994, p. 16A.

Goulden, Joseph C., *The Super-Lawyers: The Small and Powerful World of the Great Washington Law Firms*, New York: Weybright and Talley, 1972, pp. 8–9, 386.

Grimaldi, James V., "Hearsay: The Lawyer's Column; For David Boies, Working for Gore in Florida Caps a Year of High-Profile Cases," *The Washington Post*, December 25, 2000, p. E3.

Grimaldi, James V. and Carrie Johnson, "Once More Before the Bench as U.S. v. Microsoft Resumes on Appeal—A Guide to the Proceedings," *The Washington Post*, February 25, 2001, p. H1.

"Hogan & Hartson Expands in East Europe," *International Financial Law Review*, June 1996, p. 3.

Kaplan, Sheila, "The Superlawyers Roll East; Big U.S. Legal Firms Elbow for Business Beyond the Elbe," *The Washington Post*, July 21, 1991.

Leonard, John William, *Who's Who in Jurisprudence*, Brooklyn, New York: John W. Leonard Corporation, 1925, p. 709.

MacLachlan, Claudia, "Following the Money," *Legal Times*, March 19, 2001, pp. 31–32.

Maiden, Ben, Daniel Gogek, and Georgy Borisov, "Lawyers Learn to Live in Russia After the Gold Rush," *International Financial Law Review*, October 2000, pp. 33–36.

Nader, Ralph and Mark Green, eds., *Verdicts on Lawyers*, New York: Thomas Y. Crowell Company, 1976, p. 169.

Sarasohn, Judy, "Special Interests; For 3 Lobbyists, a Trio of Challenges," *The Washington Post*, July 27, 2000, p. A21.

Schmidt, Susan and John Mintz, "Florida's Instant Invasion; How Gore and Bush Rushed in Legal and Political Armies," *The Washington Post*, November 26, 2000, p. A1.

Schmitt, Richard B., "Legal Beat: Ties to Clinton Aid Law Firms in Washington," *The Wall Street Journal*, March 12, 1993, p. B1 [Eastern edition].

Somerville, Sean, "A New Legal Landscape in Baltimore . . . ," *The Sun* [Baltimore], December 13, 1998, p. 1D.

Stogner, Amy, "National Law Firm Landing Boulder High-Tech Clients," *Boulder County Business Report*, January 26, 2001, p. 3A.

Torry, Saundra, "Pro Bono Is No Pro Forma Matter for District's Hogan & Hartson," *The Washington Post*, May 20, 1991, p. f05.

"Trip Cost Even More/Beyond $20 Million, Space Tourist Paid Lawyers, Others," *Newsday*, May 4, 2001, p. A28.

"United States: Janet L. McDavid," *International Tax Review*, July 2000, p. 33.

—David M. Walden

Holland Burgerville USA

109 West 17th Street
Vancouver, Washington 98660-2986
U.S.A.
Telephone: (360) 694-1521
Toll Free: (800) 371-1138
Fax: (360) 694-9114
Web site: http://www.burgerville.com

Private Company
Incorporated: 1992
Employees: 1,600
Sales: $50 million (2000 est.)
NAIC: 722211 Limited-Service Restaurants

Holland Burgerville USA is the holding company for the Burgerville USA chain of fast food restaurants, which in 2001 comprised 39 outlets located in Oregon and Washington. The company remains privately held, with President Thomas Mears, son-in-law of founder George Propstra, and his family still majority stockholders. Burgerville has striven over the years to become and remain a Northwest tradition, looking to nurture a strong connection with the communities in which it is located. Specialties, such as fresh strawberry shortcake, raspberry and blackberry sundaes and walla walla onion rings, appear seasonally, in addition to real ice cream milkshakes and fresh halibut fish and chips. Big change came to the company with the closing of the landmark Holland Restaurant in July 2001.

From 1920s Creamery to Family Restaurant

In 1922, Jacob Propstra, a Dutch immigrant who had moved to the United States in 1912, and shortly thereafter took a job at the Old Imperial Creamery in Portland, founded the Holland Creamery in downtown Vancouver, Washington. The butter and egg business evolved into the Holland Butter and Ice Cream Co., and when Sunday visitors stopped by to sample the product, Propstra added cones. In 1928, the business moved to another nearby location. Propstra put in tables and chairs, and, in 1933, he began to offer cheese sandwiches at the newly expanded Holland Restaurant. The average per customer sale at the time added up to about 11 cents.

In 1935, shortly after the restaurant began to offer sandwiches, George Propstra, Jacob's son, who was three months short of completing a college business degree, joined his father in the family business. George Propstra had started out scooping ice cream, washing cans, and wrapping butter as a boy, along with his two brothers—all "part and parcel of being in one of those dairy families," as he described it in a 1982 *Oregonian* article.

In 1956, Jacob Propstra retired and George Propstra assumed control of the business and "realized that the butter, egg, and ice cream businesses were all to be dominated by big outfits. . . . We finally saw the handwriting on the wall," he was quoted as saying in the *Oregonian*. "[A]t the time, we were a one-horse operation." However, there was room to grow in the restaurant business. "We had had a taste of the restaurant business and could see it was a small man's business. You could grow slowly and carefully, opening one restaurant at a time." In 1957, The Holland added a $30,000 bakery addition, located in the restaurant building; the bakery sold Danish and French pastries and all types of cakes.

Burgerville USA Emerges in the 1960s

Under George Propstra's leadership, the company began to grow. In 1961, Propstra opened the first Burgerville USA in Vancouver, and, in 1962, The Holland Gateway in northeast Portland. In the beginning, the Burgerville restaurants featured hamburgers garnished with Burgerville's secret sauce, beverages, and fries, with walk-up service only. Building at a steady rate in Oregon and Washington for the next twenty years, the chain had 22 outlets and was building new executive offices in Vancouver by 1978. Sales at The Holland Restaurants in Portland and Vancouver were $14 million or more in 1979, and the company was interested in advancing its image.

By 1982, there were Burgervilles located throughout the southwest Washington and northwest Oregon—from Centralia, Washington, to Albany, Oregon, and from St. Helens, Washington, to The Dalles, Oregon. In 1979, the company added another

Holland Restaurant in Gladstone. In 1982, it opened Henry's Fish Co., a pet project of George Propstra, north of Vancouver. Propstra was still 85 percent owner of The Holland Inc. with the rest of the stock held by 12 other shareholders, most of them company executives.

In 1981, Propstra began to appear in the company's television ads. The 67-year-old restaurant owner, who had a reputation for getting to The Holland everyday at 6 a.m. to booth hop, for demanding loyalty, and for being blunt to the point of occasionally being brusque, derided national chains for using frozen meat in his unmistakable gravelly voice. Proclaiming Burgerville's adherence to fresh ingredients, he appeared as an angel, a devil, in his nightclothes, and even clutching a squealing pig to advertise Burgerville's bacon burger. In one ad, Propstra slammed a competitor's frozen patty against the side of a truck; in another, he fired a company executive for suggesting the chain compromise on quality. In 1986, as part of its year-long 25th anniversary promotion, the company aired a 3-D commercial, giving away glasses for viewing at all of its stores.

The commercials, despite being low budget, quickly developed a cult following for Burgerville. According to an article in *Portland Business Today* in 1986, the key to the company's success lay in creating an image for itself that differentiated it from other fast food chains and from its newest competition, convenience stores, such as 7-Eleven, which had begun to sell hamburgers. The chain's "inconveniently located" advertising campaign took off a few years later, continuing to emphasize Burgerville's difference from the crowd, taking what might be seen as its disadvantage—its limited market—and turning this into something positive about the company. "We say we're local in a very innovative way," said Pat Klinger, the company's marketing concepts director was quoted as saying in a 1990 *Statesman Journal* article.

Another of Burgerville's attempts to separate itself from other fast food chains came with its introduction in 1983 of salad bars and of its Unburger in 1986. The Unburger, a vegetarian patty served on a hamburger bun with condiments, proved an immediate success, averaging up to six percent of sales throughout the chain. It helped prompt management's decision to increase the number of Burgervilles. The chain, which had been expanding at the rate of up to three new Burgervilles a year, began franchising its establishments in mid-1987.

In fact, Burgerville was unable to compete with McDonald's in attracting the younger crowd, but it had a solid following

among adults, especially women. In 1986, Burgerville enjoyed 14 percent of the fast-service hamburger market in Portland and 40 percent in Vancouver. With close to 30 restaurants, The Holland Inc.'s annual sales were reported as being in the $20 to $30 million range for several consecutive years in the mid-1980s. In 1989, despite unprecedented competition, Burgerville began construction on two new restaurants, part of its move to expand into the area located within a 40-mile radius of Vancouver. The two new buildings were designed to look more like old-fashioned store fronts than fast food outlets.

New Direction and Ownership in the 1990s

However, despite optimism about the company's prospects for growth, all new additions were postponed until 1992 when Tom Mears, Propstra's son-in-law, completed the buyout of The Holland Inc. from George Propstra and became the new head of the business that then included 34 Burgervilles, three Holland Restaurants, 1,200 employees, and revenues of $35 million a year. The company marked the changing of the guard with a giant retirement party for George Propstra to which all employees were invited.

In keeping with the old-fashioned theme, the company opened Burgerville Drive in Portland in 1994, a drive-through only restaurant with trimmed-down menu and lower prices, a return to the drive-in concept of the 1960s. Chickenville, a drive-through and walk-up-only chicken outlet followed later that same year two doors down. Separating the two fast-food outlets was Garden Golf, a miniature golf course also owned by The Holland Inc.

In 1995, The Holland became a joint venture partner in opening the Beaches Restaurant in Vancouver. Located along the Columbia River, the 6,700-square-foot restaurant specialized in serving steaks, seafood, and pasta. At the same time, the company began remodeling many of its Burgerville USA establishments, investing in an $8 million remodeling campaign to give its fast food outlets a 1950s retro look. There were Wurlitzer juke boxes (updated to play CDs instead of records), neon ceiling trim, checkerboard floor tiles, and a bright red, black, and white motif. Along with the remodeling came an expanded menu and a new marketing plan aimed at shifting Burgerville into a niche between fast food and casual dining. Burgerville set up "Great Perks Espresso" bars in the remodeled restaurants, taking its 37 stores into the specialty coffee business.

The remodeling was in part response to competition from the 100 McDonald's, Burger Kings and Wendy's in the Portland area. "As a small, local company competing with major fast food restaurants, we found our market share declining and guest counts declining from the mid-1980s into the 1990s," Tom Mears was quoted in a 1997 *Oregonian* article. The prototype, opened in the summer of 1995, was expected to do about $1.2 million in annual sales, rather than the typical Burgerville's $900,000. It turned out instead to do closer to $1.6 million. "We knew we were onto something," Mears said of this success.

The company built four more restaurants and remodeled eight in the new format within the next two years. When it had

Key Dates:

1922: Jacob Propstra founds The Holland Creamery in downtown Vancouver.

1924: The creamery, now also serving ice cream, moves to a new location in Vancouver.

1933: The Holland begins serving cheese sandwiches.

1935: George Propstra leaves college to begin working at his father's business.

1956: Jacob Propstra retires and George takes over the business.

1961: George Propstra, Jacob's son, starts Burgerville USA in Vancouver.

1982: Tom Mears becomes company president.

1992: George Propstra retires.

2001: The Holland Restaurant closes.

finished all remodels by 2000, it had spent $8 million. In 1997, it added milk shakes, yogurt, and dessert dishes. It reentered the breakfast business it had abandoned earlier in all but six outlets, baking its own bagels on site. All menu items were cooked to order. Revenues from 1996 were $35 million, up 18 percent from $30 million the year before. In 1997, revenues totaled $38 million. The new breakfast business accounted for 7 to 10 percent of the average Burgerville outlet's total revenues.

The so-called "hamburger wars" continued to drive Burgerville to rethink its marketing strategy into 1997. Trying to strategically market itself to each community where it was located, it looked at different residential areas and provided products and services to suit that area. In 2000, it expanded upon its first efforts to advertise its regional nature with promotions of fresh strawberry shakes, shortcake made with fresh biscuits, walla walla onion rings, and burgers.

Big change came to the company with the closing of the Holland Restaurant in July 2001 after the landmark eatery experienced financial struggles. The Holland had been serving traditional family style meals since its opening. George Propstra, who had made it a practice to know the majority of The Holland's customers by name or face, was interviewed in the *Columbian* at the time of the closing; there he was quoted as saying, "Every restaurant has a lifespan. . . . Bodies wear out.

We wear out. Ideas wear out. Today there's a new concept in restaurants that's more pleasing to people." President Tom Mears concurred, adding that "Restaurant styles and consumer food tastes have changed dramatically in the 65 years that The Holland has been in business."

Following the closure, The Holland Inc.'s management gathered to talk about Burgerville's future. The decision was reached to behave more like a Northwest neighborhood eatery and less like a large national chain. The company, which owned the building in which The Holland was located, would also explore various alternatives for its renovation. The future would likely see more Burgerville locations and further changes to the restaurants' appearance and menu, including a smaller version of the restaurant suited to a strip mall setting. However, Holland Burgerville USA, which had had company-wide revenues totaling approximately $50 million at its 38 restaurants in Oregon and Washington in 2000, remained a conservatively run company satisfied with a five to 10 percent annual increase in sales.

Principal Competitors

McDonald's Corporation; Burger King Corporation; Advantica Restaurant Group Inc.; Triarc Companies INc.; IHOP Corporation.

Further Reading

Anderson, Michael A., "Burgerville Aims for Fast Food's Big Three," *Business Journal—Portland*, November 24, 1986, p.1.

Bella, Rick, "Restaurateur's Plans Well Done," *Oregonian*, December 29, 1982, p. B5.

Brenneman, Kristina, "Finding a Niche and Filling It Leads to Fancier Burgervilles," *Business Journal—Portland*, March 31, 2000, p. 3.

Brettmann, Allan, "Executives for Northwest Fast Food Chain to Meet in Portland, Oregon," *Oregonian*, August 7, 2001, p. E1.

Hill, Jim, "Burgerville Beefs Up With Retro Redesign as a Burger Rivalry Heats Up in Portland," *Oregonian*, July 22, 1997, p. C1.

McCullough, Jillyn, "A Taste of Recognition," *Statesman Journal*, May 27, 1990, p. F1.

Pierce, Steve, "Propstra: Failure Is Unthinkable," *Columbian*, July 4, 1978, p. 4.

——, "The Holland Inc.: 22 Restaurants and Still Growing," *Columbian*, July 23, 1978, p. 33.

Rogoway, Mike, "Holland Serves Last Meal: Family Restaurant Closes After Decades in Vancouver," *Columbian*, July 4, 2001, p. A1.

—Carrie Rothburd

Hometown Auto Retailers, Inc.

774 Straits Turnpike
Watertown, Connecticut 06795
U.S.A.
Telephone (860) 945-6900
Fax: (860) 945-4909
Web site: http://www.hometownautoretailers.com

Public Company
Incorporated: 1997
Employees: 386
Sales: $279.8 million
Stock Exchanges: NASDAQ
Ticker Symbol: HCAR
NAIC: 441110 New Car Dealers

Hometown Auto Retailers, Inc. is a publicly traded company that operates ten franchised car dealerships in New Jersey, New York, Connecticut, Massachusetts, and Vermont. It offers a variety of domestic and foreign cars and light truck brands, including Chevrolet, Chrysler, Daewoo, Dodge, Ford, Isuzu, Jeep, Lincoln, Mazda, Mercury, Plymouth, and Toyota. In addition, Hometown is one of the leading suppliers of Lincoln Town Cars and limousines to livery operators through its New Jersey dealership, Westwood Lincoln Mercury. Hometown also sells used cars and replacement parts, offers maintenance and repair services, and provides customer financing. The company owns a minority stake in CarDay, an Internet car auction site it created in 1999. The core of Hometown is comprised of the auto dealerships formerly owned by the Muller, Shaker, and Vergopia families, who retain a controlling interest in the company's voting stock.

From Automotive Repairs to Retail

The Shaker family auto businesses, operating under a holding company called E.R.R. Enterprises, was the acquiring party when Hometown was formed in 1997. The original Shaker business was a Waterbury, Connecticut, automobile repair shop called Shaker Auto Service, established in 1930 by Joseph Shaker. The family did not turn to selling cars until the years after World War II, when it gained franchises for Jeep, Lincoln-Mercury, and Ford. The Shaker holding company would eventually become one of Connecticut's largest dealer groups. Traditionally, auto dealerships have been family-owned, local businesses, but in recent years many have been consolidated into larger, regional concerns that benefit from economies of scale. Despite this trend, large dealerships in the mid-1990s still represented only a small fraction of all franchised dealerships in the United States, as well as total sales revenues of the industry. The densely populated Northeast was more highly fragmented than other regions of the country, a fact instrumental in the Shaker, Muller, and Vergopia families deciding to join forces to create Hometown. Both the Muller Group and Vergopia's Westwood Lincoln Mercury Sales Inc. were located in New Jersey.

Hometown was originally incorporated in New York as Dealerco in March 1997. After the family dealer groups agreed to combine their businesses, the company was reincorporated in Delaware in June 1997 and adopted the Hometown name. Each of the parties, along with the corporation's law firm, received shares of Hometown stock. A temporary corporate headquarters was established in Watertown, Connecticut, with an accounting operation located in Matawan, New Jersey. Salvatore A. Vergopia was named as chief executive officer and chairman of the board; Joseph Shaker as president, chief operating officer, and director; and William C. Muller, Jr., as vice-president and director of New Jersey operations. Immediately the new company agreed to purchase a Vermont dealership, Brattleboro Chrysler Plymouth Dodge, Inc. for $2.7 million and the assumption of debt. A month later Hometown agreed to purchase Leominster Lincoln Mercury, located in Framingham, Massachusetts, for $3 million and the assumption of debt. Both transactions were scheduled to be finalized after Hometown completed an initial public offering of its stock in the following year.

Hometown's strategy was to use its stock in order to acquire small and medium-size dealerships located in the Northeast that generated annual revenues ranging from $20 million to $60 million per location. The goal was to become New England's largest dealer group, in addition to increasing its business in New York and New Jersey and establishing a presence in nearby Mid-Atlantic communities. Management targeted exist-

Company Perspectives:

Hometown's growth strategy is to participate in the recent consolidation trend in the automotive sales and service industry and, through strategic acquisitions, become the largest dealer group in New England and parts of the Mid-Atlantic region and to expand its two "niche" businesses.

ing dealerships that had already gained the trust of local consumers. This belief in the value of "hometown" relationships was the reason the company chose the Hometown name. It also hoped to take advantage of the proximity of dealerships to lower operational costs while increasing sales through coordinated marketing efforts. In addition to new vehicle sales, Hometown dealerships emphasized used vehicle sales, keenly aware that used vehicles generally produce higher gross margins than new vehicles. Moreover, the company looked to provide maintenance and repair services, as well as financing, in order to meet the full range of its customers' needs.

Hometown Goes Public in 1998

Hometown and its predecessors generated combined revenues of $254.2 million in 1997. Most dealership groups that had previously gone public totaled revenues in the $1 billion range, yet Hometown went forward with its initial public stock offering in July 1998, meeting with a less than enthusiastic response. Buying and selling cars, in general, was viewed skeptically by investors, who considered it an unreliable and cyclical business. Hometown planned to offer 2 million shares priced between $9 and $10, eventually opting for the low end of the range and cutting back the number of shares to 1.8 million. Trading on the Nasdaq, Hometown stock quickly sagged below its IPO price. Financial analysts warned that a low stock price would hurt Hometown's ability to use its stock to make acquisitions, predicting that many dealers would be wary of accepting the stock of a small firm with no track record. Hometown, therefore, faced something of a Catch 22 situation: to acquire more dealerships it had to raise its stock price, but in order to raise its stock price it had to acquire more dealerships. Nevertheless, the company was able to use the $16.2 million raised in the IPO to close the two deals it had commenced the previous July. In addition, it purchased Pride Auto Center, Inc. for $925,000, then in December 1998 closed on the acquisition of Boston-area Wellesley Lincoln Mercury, paying $650,000 and assuming certain liabilities. The company also negotiated a $100 million "floor plan" credit facility from GE Capital with which to maintain its new and used car inventories. For the year, Hometown posted revenues of $240.6 million, down by almost $14 million from the previous year. Nevertheless, management touted 1998 as a year of accomplishment, one in which Hometown bolstered its presence in the area west of Boston and in northern New Jersey, and as a result established a base for future growth and a significant increase in revenues. The goal was to reach $500 million in revenues within the next year.

The company's optimism, however, was not borne out by reality in 1999, although the acquisition of new dealerships did increase revenues somewhat. In January, Hometown acquired

Morristown Lincoln Mercury for $500,000. It then added Newburgh Toyota, New York State's leader in Toyota truck sales, paying $2.9 million in cash, plus 100,000 shares of stock and the assumption of liabilities. The acquisition was expected to add $50 million to Hometown's annual sales. In October 1999 Hometown announced an agreement to purchase Wellesley Mazda for $800,000, thereby adding Mazda to the brands the company represented. The dealership would then be "tucked in" with Hometown's nearby Framington business, Bay State Lincoln Mercury, in order to save money by consolidating administrative personnel, sales forces, and service and parts departments. Hometown also announced that it was awarded a Daewoo franchise, which would allow its Westwood Lincoln Mercury dealership in Emerson, New Jersey, to offer the company's 13th different brand of American and Asian automobiles.

Furthermore, Hometown looked to the Internet to increase sales. It launched Cyberlot in January 1999. The Web site was portrayed by the company as an interactive used car salesroom, offering more than 1,000 vehicles from its dealerships. Each listing included a digital photograph of the actual vehicle, rather than a manufacturer's stock picture, as well as pertinent information about the vehicle. Purchased cars could then be delivered to a nearby Hometown dealership or direct to the customer's home. By November 2000, however, Hometown refined its Internet concept by creating a subsidiary called CarDay.com, which it planned to launch in January 2000. CarDay continued to offer vehicles from Hometown's dealerships, which allowed customers a chance for inspection, but differed from Cyberlot by auctioning the vehicles online. CarDay also offered financing and warranties, using Hometown's service facilities to inspect and certify the vehicles. The combination of bricks and clicks proved to be an attractive idea to institutional investors, including Goldman Sachs, Odeon Capital Partners, Sierra Ventures, and Citigroup Investments. CarDay received $25 million in total investments by January 2000. Hometown's stake in the business, as a result, was reduced to 15 percent, which meant any start-up losses would not be included in the company's operating results.

Despite a number of successes in 1999, Hometown fell far short of its lofty financial goals. Instead of reaching $500 million in sales for the year, the company generated just $285 million, albeit an 18.7 percent increase over the previous year. Its net income of $800,000 was significantly less than the $2.3 million posted in 1998. A major part of the shortfall was beyond the control of management; livery operators were dissatisfied with the 1999 Lincoln Town Car, which featured a smaller trunk, and they opted in large numbers not to upgrade their fleets. This situation, however, illustrated Hometown's overdependence on Lincoln sales. More troubling was a computer tracking error that caused Hometown to carry $15 million worth of unnecessary inventory of Town Cars. Management hoped that Newburgh Toyota and Daewoo franchises would help rectify the sales imbalance, and it also began efforts to improve its computer systems. Despite these steps, however, investors were not forgiving and the price of Hometown stock began a steady long-term decline.

In January 2000, as Hometown stock traded in the $4.50 range, the company initiated changes to reassure investors. It

Key Dates:

1997: Incorporation of the company.
1998: Initial public stock is offered by the company.
1999: CarDay.com is formed.
2001: NASDAQ de-lists stock.

centralized its operations, moving into new offices in Watertown, Connecticut. It also added another tuck-in dealership, acquiring the Jeep franchise in Brattleboro, Vermont, for $550,000, plus $269,000 in inventory, which was then added to its Brattleboro Chrysler Plymouth Dodge Dealership. In addition, the Shaker Lincoln Mercury Dealership in Watertown was awarded a Daewoo franchise. In February 2000 Joseph Shaker stepped down as president and chief operating officer in order to focus his attention on the launch of CarDay. He was replaced by his brother, Corey Shaker.

Hometown Stock Begins Steep Plunge in 2000

While the stock price of most publicly traded dealer groups suffered during the first quarter of 2000, Hometown actually increased by some 110 percent, but that bump was fueled by rumors of a possible takeover. When it did not materialize and Hometown reported poorer than expected second quarter results, investor response was harsh. By the end of August, Hometown shares were trading below $1.50. Management could point to its new computerized inventory tracking system that it hoped would help return the company to profitability, as well as announce that managers of under-performing dealerships would be replaced, but clearly what investors wanted from Hometown were major acquisitions. Again, the company's stock price hindered its ability to make a sizeable purchase, despite the fact that Hometown carried no debt. The company then decided to eliminate 12 million of the 24 million shares of stock that Hometown was authorized to sell. While it saved the company $50,000 a year in taxes, it also weakened its ability to use stock in making acquisitions.

After posting disappointing third quarter results, management announced in November 2000 that it would forego plans to expand, which had been the hallmark of Hometown's strategy. Instead, the company would devote its energies to bolstering its existing dealerships. It also looked to take advantage of rising consumer interest in high-end, certified used cars. It purchased a Boston-area dealer of used Mercedes, Porsche, Audi, and Jaguar cars that it incorporated with its Wellesley Lincoln Mercury dealership. Hometown also announced that it planned to cut $2 million in overhead expenses for 2001 and, if necessary, would unload under-performing dealerships. Hometown would also have to line up a new floor plan credit line. Because of its recent losses, Hometown fell short of certain covenants with GE Capital Corp., mostly involving a separate line of credit the company hadn't even touched. Nevertheless, the company's credit line was cut in half and its interest rate increased by 75 percent. When the year was completed, Hometown reported revenues of $279.8 million, almost $6 million less than the year before, with a net loss of $3.6 million.

Hometown stock fell below $1, dipping as low as 31 cents in December 2000, and after trading below the $1 threshold for an extended period was eventually de-listed by Nasdaq and moved to the over-the-counter bulletin board. Even more trouble for the company's image came in February 2001 when Hometown's board of directors voted to remove chairman Salvatore Vergopia and his son, vice-president for fleet operations Edward Vergopia. Corey Shaker took over as the chief executive officer. The two men were accused of fiscal malfeasance involving the sale and transfer of limousine titles to a defaulting customer that cost the company approximately $850,000. They, along with Janet Vergopia, sued Hometown, claiming breach of contract along with age discrimination. They asked for their jobs back, as well as unspecified damages. Several months later, in June 2001, the parties would settle part of the suit. Salvatore and Edward Vergopia dropped their demand to return to their old jobs, and in turn Hometown agreed to allow the men to stand for re-election to the board. Shareholders subsequently retained them as directors. The breach of contract and age discrimination claims, however, remained unresolved.

In 2001, Hometown sold off Morristown Lincoln Mercury, made significant cuts in overhead, and secured a new floor plan credit line with Ford Motor Credit Co. After three consecutive quarters of posting losses, Hometown reported record profits for the first quarter of 2001. Net income stood at $127,000, compared to $38,000 for the same period a year earlier. Revenues were down, in large part due to the sale of Morristown Lincoln Mercury. Nevertheless, management insisted that the company had turned the corner. Investors, on the other hand, would require further proof. In the summer of 2001 the price of Hometown stock edged above $1, but remained well below the level it would need to achieve in order for the company to return to its plan for aggressive growth.

Principal Subsidiaries

E.R.R. Enterprises, Inc.; Hometown Operating Corporation.

Principal Competitors

AutoNation USA; Holman Enterprises; Planet Automotive Group; United Auto Group, Inc.

Further Reading

Hammer, David, ''Hard Times at Hometown,'' *Waterbury Republican-American,* August 20, 2000.
——, ''Hometown Auto Admits Errors at Meeting,'' *Waterbury Republican-American,* August 30, 2000.
——, ''Losses Force Strategy Shift for Connecticut-Based Car Dealer,'' *Waterbury Republican-American,* November 21, 2000.
Harris, Donna, ''New England Chain Issues IPO,'' *Automotive News,* August 2, 1998, p. 8.
Marks, Brenda, ''Family Automotive Group Begins Ride on Wall Street,'' *Waterbury Republican-American,* August 6, 1998.
''Watertown, Conn.-Area Auto Retailer to Position Itself for 2001 Rebound,'' *Knight-Ridder/Tribune Business News,* May 2, 2001.
''Watertown, Conn.-Based Auto Retailer Battles with Two Former Executives,'' *Waterbury Republican-American,* February 12, 2001.

—Ed Dinger

Hughes Hubbard & Reed LLP

1 Battery Park Plaza
New York, New York 10004-1482
U.S.A.
Telephone: (212) 837-6000
Fax: (212) 422-4726
Web site: http://www.hugheshubbard.com

Partnership
Founded: 1904 as Hughes, Rounds & Schurman
Employees: 750 (est.)
Sales: $125 million (1999 est.)
NAIC: 541110 Offices of Lawyers

The New York-based law firm of Hughes Hubbard & Reed LLP boasts an illustrious history, with roots that reach back into the 1800s and connections to many of today's major New York law firms. Its most famous partner was Charles Evans Hughes, whose practice was interrupted by calls to public service. He not only served as Governor of New York, he was also appointed Secretary of State, ran for the Presidency of the United States, and eventually was named Chief Justice of the United States Supreme Court. Hughes Hubbard, though far from the largest law firm, consists of some 300 attorneys who are engaged in 30 specialty practices. In addition to its New York headquarters, Hughes Hubbard maintains offices in Washington, D.C., Los Angeles, Miami, and Paris. A Latin American practice operates out of the Miami office, while the Paris office serves clients throughout Europe, Eastern Europe, Russia, the Middle East, and North Africa. Hughes Hubbard is known for its progressive culture that is especially conducive to the advancement of women to its top ranks. In the 1960s, Hughes Hubbard became the first New York City law firm to name an African-American woman to the partnership, then in 1999 became the first to name a woman as its chair.

1871 Chicago Fire Instrumental in the Firm's Founding

The progenitor of Hughes Hubbard, as well as a number of major New York law firms, was attorney Walter S. Carter. He was born in 1833 in Barkhamsted, Connecticut, the son of a farmer of modest means. He began his study of law in 1850, serving in the office of a Connecticut judge. At the time, even the best law schools were just extensions of law offices in which the teachers were also practicing attorneys. Carter was admitted to the bar in 1855 and began practicing law in Middleton, Connecticut, as well as publishing a newspaper. He then decided in 1858 to move west, relocating to the burgeoning city of Milwaukee, which already boasted a number of distinguished firms and presented more opportunities for a young attorney than did the Northeast. By 1860, he was able to start his own firm, Carter & Whipple, and over the next several years would partner with an assortment of attorneys. In 1869, he moved to Chicago and was admitted to the bar of Illinois. After practicing by himself for a year, he headed the firm of Carter & Becker, which in 1871 became Carter, Becker & Dale. The devastating Chicago fire in October of that year would then result in Carter moving again. Claims from the fire bankrupted 15 fire insurance companies in the East, and Carter went to New York to represent Chicago creditors. It was here that he formed a partnership with attorney Leslie W. Russell, who had studied law in Milwaukee and very likely knew Carter at that time. Carter & Russell was the firm that would evolve into today's Hughes Hubbard.

Although Carter maintained his Chicago partnership until 1876, his heavy workload in New York would lead to his complete relocation to the city. It would also force him to engage help. He turned to the graduates of the new law schools. While other firms provided further training for the aspiring lawyers, Carter paid a salary. He began to keep close tabs on students enrolled in area law schools, and his offices became a place where many turned for advice and employment. A number of "Carter's Kids" became associates who then went on to found important New York law firms, including Paul D. Cravath, Henry Abbott, Henry W. Taft, and George W. Wickersham.

Charles Evans Hughes Joins Firm in 1884

Charles Evans Hughes worked two summers with Carter, Hornblower & Byrne, then upon graduation from Columbia Law School and gaining admission to the bar began a regular clerkship with the firm in 1884. The only child of a minister, Hughes was born in 1862 at Glen Falls, New York. He studied at home until the age of nine and was precocious enough to

Company Perspectives:

Our docket covers the full range of courts and administrative agencies through the U.S., management of litigation in foreign courts and alternative dispute resolution. Our litigation specialties include, among other things, antitrust; insurance damage claims arising from toxic torts, product liability, and mass disasters; and intellectual property and professional liability.

begin college at the age of 14, attending Madison University, now known as Colgate, before transferring to Brown University. He taught school for a year in Delhi, New York, while reading law under a local attorney, then entered Columbia Law School in 1883. Carter, Hornblower & Byrne proved to be a perfect situation for the ambitious young man. The firm had a thriving general practice that exposed Hughes to a wide range of the law as well as the leading attorneys of the day. By 1888 he became a full partner in the firm, which after the departure of Hornblower and Chamberlain became Carter, Hughes & Cravath. Hughes also married Carter's daughter, Antoinette.

Paul Cravath joined the firm after graduating from Columbia Law School. Born in Ohio, he too was the son of a clergyman. After earning a degree from Oberlin College in 1882 he moved to Minneapolis where he intended to study and practice law. Instead he worked as a salesman for an oil company for a year, but he saved enough money to attend Columbia, where he took part in the "quiz classes" that Hughes taught after he graduated from the school. Although Cravath planned to return to Minneapolis, he stayed in New York after he graduated *cum laude* in 1886 and went to work for Carter, Hornblower & Byrne. Cravath brought in significant business from the prolific inventor George Westinghouse, whose chief assistant worked with Cravath's uncle. Westinghouse made his fortune with the invention of the railroad air brake, but also made significant contributions to the commercialization of electricity and other fields. In all, he founded 60 companies. The amount of work that came into Carter, Hughes & Cravath soon required the opening of a branch office, and by 1891 Cravath, by mutual agreement, left the firm, taking the Westinghouse business with him. Cravath would go on to found today's well-known law firm of Cravath, Swaine & Moore.

After Cravath left, Frederick R. Kellogg became a partner and the firm became Carter, Hughes & Kellogg. Hughes' devotion to his work, in the meantime, compromised his health, and he left the firm for two years, teaching at the Cornell Law School before returning to his New York City practice. When Carter died in 1904, Hughes became the senior partner, reorganizing the firm as Hughes, Rounds & Schurman. At this point, Hughes would begin his career of public service that would take him away from the business for long periods of time. He was asked by the state legislature in 1905 to investigate corruption in New York City's utilities. He uncovered a number of irregularities and proposed regulations that were subsequently enacted. He was then enlisted to serve as counsel to an investigation of the insurance industry, which was under attack by city newspapers. Hughes not only exposed questionable business practices, but political corruption as well. He was causing such damage to

New York Republicans that party leaders tried to draft him to run for mayor just to get him off the panel. He refused, continued his work, and, as a result, the reputation of so many Republican candidates were so tarnished that, ironically, he became the Party's only viable hope to win the 1906 governor's race. He then defeated publisher William Randolph Hearst and left his law firm, which now became known as Rounds, Schurman & Dwight.

Hughes served two terms as governor, then in 1910 President Taft named him to the Supreme Court, where he served as the youngest member. After rejecting entreaties to run for the presidency in 1912, he resigned from the Supreme Court in 1916 to run against President Woodrow Wilson, at a time when his party was out of power and a devastating European war threatened to involve the United States. After a decisive defeat that ended his career in elective politics, Hughes once again rejoined his old law firm, which now became Hughes, Rounds, Schurman & Dwight.

Hughes son, Charles Evan Hughes Jr., also joined the firm as a partner after graduating from Harvard Law School in 1912 and worked at the offices of Cadwalader, Wickersham & Taft. When the United States entered World War I, he took a leave of absence to serve as a lieutenant in the Army. The senior Hughes left the firm once again in 1921 when he was named by President Warren Harding to serve as Secretary of State, and once again the firm reverted to the Rounds, Schurman & Dwight name. After serving a year with the Coolidge administration, Hughes returned to his law practice in 1925. His major focus over the next few years was serving as a special master to the Great Lakes water diversion case, in which Chicago was accused of using water from the Great Lakes to flush its sewage into the Mississippi River. This practice caused the level of the lakes to lower, creating a great deal of damage to property as well as hindering navigation on the lakes. Hughes' report would prove instrumental in the Supreme Court's eventual decision that forced Chicago to cease its actions.

In the meantime, the younger Hughes became Herbert Hoover's Solicitor General in 1929, but resigned from the position in 1930 when his father was named the Chief Justice of the United States Supreme Court. Because the son returned to the law practice just as the father was leaving, the firm remained Hughes, Schurman & Dwight, although Richard E. Dwight was now the senior partner and head of the firm. While many law firms devoted to corporate work suffered a severe loss of business during the Great Depression, Hughes Schurman prospered, mostly due to the senior Hughes' emphasis on litigation work. A major client during this period was the Fox Film Corporation, which was reorganizing its studio operations and chain of movie theaters.

In 1937, the firm was dissolved, apparently because Dwight was under attack by President Franklin Roosevelt's Secretary of the Treasury, and the younger Hughes wanted to provide some distance for his father, the Chief Justice. Two groups of partners then formed new law firms. Dwight headed Dwight, Harris, Koegel & Caskey, which is the forefather of today's Clifford Chance Rogers & Wells. Hughes created Hughes, Richards, Hubbard & Ewing, becoming the senior partner of the firm. It opened offices at One Wall Street, assuming an entire floor which had been the headquarters of a financial firm that had

Key Dates:

1871: Chicago Fire litigation sends attorney Walter S. Carter to New York to establish Carter & Russell.
1884: Charles Evans Hughes joins the firm.
1904: Upon Carter's death, Hughes organizes Hughes, Rounds & Schurman.
1906: Hughes leaves firm to serve as Governor of New York, then as a justice on the Supreme Court.
1916: Hughes rejoins firm after failed Presidential bid; Charles Evans Hughes, Jr. also joins firm.
1930: Hughes, Sr. leaves firm to become Chief Justice of the Supreme Court.
1937: Firm splits, and Hughes, Jr. forms Hughes, Richards, Hubbard & Ewing.
1968: Firm becomes known as Hughes Hubbard & Reed.
1999: Candace K. Beinecke named chair.

failed during the Depression. It would remain the home of the firm for the next 50 years, during which time it would grow to occupy four floors, as well as space in other buildings, and the number of lawyers grew from eight partners and eight associates to over 200 lawyers. When the new firm moved into One Wall Street, however, the partners were uncertain of their business prospects, but on the first day, the chairman of Alcoa contacted Hughes about defending his company in an antitrust suit. Aside from providing the firm with the business it needed to launch a prosperous practice, the Alcoa case also entered the annals of legal history. Because so many justices had to disqualify themselves, the Supreme Court lacked a quorum and for the only time in the Court's history, a designated court, the Second Circuit, ruled on the case.

Hughes Dies in 1948

Hughes senior retired from the Supreme Court in 1941, but did not return to private practice, instead devoting his final years to preparing historical records of his life and distinguished career. He died in 1948 of congestive heart failure at the age of 86. Two years later his son would also die suddenly. A Harvard Law School classmate, Allen S. Hubbard, then became senior partner of the firm, now known as Hughes, Hubbard & Ewing. In 1952 the name would change to Hughes, Hubbard, Blair & Reed, and would remain unchanged until 1968. Francis C. Reed would succeed Hubbard as senior partner in 1959.

Reed was responsible for establishing a culture that would endure within the firm. In contrast to the staid atmosphere at most Wall Street law firms, Reed encouraged his lawyers to keep their doors open and address each other by their first names. It was Reed who also oversaw the opening of an office in Paris in 1966, the firm's first office outside of New York. In addition, one of the firm's attorneys, Amalya L. Kearse, became the first African-American woman to be named a partner in a major New York firm. In 1968 the firm became Hughes Hubbard & Reed, then in 1971 Reed was succeeded as senior partner by Orville H. Schell, Jr. A year later, under his leadership, the firm would open offices in Washington, D.C., and Los Angeles. He retired as senior partner in 1975 and would go on to become president of the New York City Ballet and an influential figure in the creation of the Lincoln Center for the Performing Arts.

Jerome G. Shapiro succeeded Schell as senior partner of the firm, which at the time included 105 lawyers. During his tenure, Hughes Hubbard established a Far Eastern Practice. A branch office in Miami was also opened in 1987, the result of the break-up of Sage Gray Todd & Sims, which had been plagued by disagreement among its partners. While a 30-lawyer banking department joined Hughes Hubbard's New York office, Sage Gray's Miami office with its 14 lawyers and international banking law practice was also added. The firm would subsequently organize a Latin American practice, which would be based in the Miami office.

Robert Sisk succeeded Shapiro in 1989 as head of the firm. Charles H. Scherer, who had left the firm to serve as general counsel of Collins & Aikman, returned to become Hughes Hubbard's first full-time managing partner. Under Sisk and Scherer the firm consolidated its New York offices at One Battery Park Plaza. Then in 1999, Sisk was succeeded by Candace K. Beinecke, who became the first woman to chair a major New York law firm, while Scherer remained as managing partner. Beinecke grew up in Patterson, New Jersey. Her father was a practicing attorney and her mother, a radio personality in the 1940s, encouraged her to become a lawyer. After graduating from Rutgers Law School, she joined the firm as an associate in 1970, then made her reputation as an international corporate lawyer.

Despite Hughes Hubbard's reputation as a progressive firm, it suffered some negative effects from its success in a controversial Supreme Court decision in 2000 that upheld the Boy Scouts of American's right to exclude a gay scoutmaster. The firm represented gay and lesbian groups in other litigation, as well as provided benefits for same-sex domestic partners. Moreover, several gay and lesbian groups filed amicus briefs supporting the Boy Scouts' right to association. Yet, Hughes Hubbard was criticized both from within its ranks and from outside. Hughes Hubbard recruiters were regularly asked about the case by law students. It was unlikely, however, that the criticism, which many decried as guilt by association, would cause any long-term damage to the firm's sterling reputation of many years.

Principal Competitors

Baker & McKenzie; Latham & Watkins; Skadden, Arps, Slate, Meagher & Flom.

Further Reading

Carter, Terry, "Sins of the Client," *ABA Journal,* March 2001, p 20.
Goldstein, Matthew, "Making NY Legal History," *Crain's New York Business,* May 24, 1999, p. 31.
Gray, Patricia Bellew, "Sage Gray Todd & Sims Is Making Plans to Split up the Law Firm by March 31," *Wall Street Journal,* March 5, 1987, p. 1.
Hoffman, Jan, "Charm at the Top: It Only Looks Easy, Folks," *New York Times,* June 2, 1999, p. 2.
Koehel, Otto Erwin, *Walter S. Carter, Collector of Young Masters,* New York: Round Table Press, 1953, 491 p.
Puseym, Merlo John, *Charles Evans Hughes,* New York: Macmillan, 1951, 829 p.

—Ed Dinger

Hulman & Company

900 Wabash Avenue
Terre Haute, Indiana 47807
U.S.A.
Telephone: (812) 232-9446
Fax: (812) 232-2397
Web site: http://www.hulman.com;
            http://www.clabbergirl.com

Private Company
Incorporated: 1916
Employees: 100
Sales: $23.7 million (1999 est.)
NAIC: 311999 All Other Miscellaneous Food
    Manufacturing

Although Hulman & Company of Terre Haute, Indiana, is strictly a private, family enterprise, with several business interests, it is principally known as the producer of two brands of baking powder—Clabber Girl and Rumford—either of which can be found in almost any kitchen cabinet in the United States and, increasingly, many overseas cupboards. Recently, it has also developed and begun marketing new products, including baking soda and non-genetically modified cornstarch under both the Clabber Girl and Rumford labels; it has also indicated that in the future it will be adding new products to those two branded lines. In addition, the company produces baking powder under the KC and Hearth Club labels. Collectively, the Hulman brands have about a 65 percent share of the country's retail baking powder market. Although an old, well-established company, Hulman & Co./Clabber Girl has taken to the Internet and launched two e-mail newsletters as part of its fresh initiatives: ''Clabber Girl Club'' for consumers and ''What's Cookin'' for business customers. These are e-mailed directly to subscribers. The Hulman and allied families have owned the company since its founding in the mid-19th century.

Francis Hulman Founds the F.T. Hulman Wholesale Store

The history of Hulman & Co. is intricately bound up in the intriguing history of the Hulman and related families, noted more for their philanthropy and involvement in auto racing than as a business dynasty. The Hulman fortune sprang from a wholesale grocery business started in the mid-19th century. Its wealth greatly increased when Mary Fendrich, heir to a fortune made in an Evansville, Indiana, cigar-manufacturing business, married Anton Hulman, Jr., heir to Hulman & Co. and the grandnephew of Hulman & Co.'s founder, Francis Hulman.

The Hulmans have always acknowledged the role played by John Bernhard Ludowici in the making of their family fortune. Ludowici was born in 1809, in Westphalia, Germany. His family immigrated to the United States and settled in Cincinnati, where he became a grocer. It was there that he met and befriended Francis Hulman, also a German immigrant. Francis had left a Paris bookkeeping job to follow his older brother, Johann Diedrich Hulman, to America. In Cincinnati, with partner Charles B. Meyer, the younger Hulman started importing toys, jewelry, toilet articles, and sundry personal items to that Ohio city, but the trade's instability discouraged him, and he left the business. He then linked up with Ludowici, who convinced him to move to Terre Haute, where, in 1850, he opened a wholesale grocery, tobacco, and liquor store, although exactly where it was located in what was then largely a frontier town remains a mystery.

The partnership was short-lived. Hulman was a more dynamic, less conservative businessman than Ludowici. He was the front man, a drummer, working the store floor, while his partner stayed more in the shadows, among the goods. The pair had a resentful falling out over Hulman's demands that he receive a higher percentage of the profits, and in 1853 they dissolved the partnership. Because he was the major investor, Ludowici kept the store. A few months later, Francis Hulman opened his own operation, naming it the F.T. Hulman Wholesale Store.

In the next year, 1854, Francis' younger half-brother, Herman Hulman, at age 23, joined Francis to work as a salesman. Another brother, Theodore, joined them in 1857. With their help, Francis turned his business into a very successful enterprise, eclipsing that of his former partner and mentor, Ludowici. But then disaster struck. In September 1858, Francis, his wife, and child died when the *Austria*, a ship they were returning on from a European vacation, burned at sea and sank. Thus, at 27, Herman became the proprietor of the family business.

Herman Hulman, the Family Patriarch

During the 1860s, despite the economic ravages of the Civil War and its aftermath, the Hulman business continued to thrive, but not without personal cost. Success prompted Herman, in 1869, to add a storeroom to the store and a spice mill behind it. Then, somewhat later in the year, he merged his business with that of his chief competitor, R.S. Cox, Jr., forming Hulman & Cox. The partners then bought the Alexander McGreggor Distillery, which was destined to become one of the country's largest, though not when owned by Hulman and Cox. Herman sold the distillery in 1875, then repurchased a half interest. Thereafter, in 1878, he traded his share of the distillery to Benjamin G. Cox for his half interest in Hulman & Cox, thereby dissolving that company.

Although Hulman was officially a wholesale grocer, he bought and sold almost anything, from Dr. Gottlieb Fisk's Bitters, which he endorsed, to railway carloads of cigars and coal oil. A major investor, he also bought stock in railroad, telephone, telegraph, water and sewage systems, and gas and electric companies. Not all his ventures succeeded, however. He briefly went into the broom manufacturing business, and, in 1881, even purchased a new factory. But the tough competition in the Cincinnati broom-making business finally drove him out of the market.

Although Herman managed to bear entrepreneurial pressures well, younger brother Theodore did not, and he was forced to retire from the family business in 1879. He took up vegetable farming on land the family would later sell to the government as a site for a large federal penitentiary. Herman's older half-brother, Diedrich, who moved to Terre Haute from Charleston, Illinois, withdrew from the grocery business to raise bees. In 1882, Antonia, Herman's wife, died, leaving him a request to expand a hospital that she had previously encouraged him to fund, the first of many philanthropic ventures of the Hulman family. Herman's two sons, Anton and Herman, Jr., joined their father in his business. Anton, the older of the two, became a junior partner in 1885, but Herman, Jr., never really took a significant role until much later. He eloped and left Terre Haute, only returning after several years. He worked for Hulman & Co. in public relations until his death in 1922.

The main business project in Herman Hulman's life was the construction of a new company building. It was completed and opened in September 1893. Of all the seemingly unlikely persons to do so, Eugene V. Debs gave a laudatory speech at the opening ceremonies. The union activist and future Socialist candidate for the U.S. presidency was, in fact, a close friend of the Hulmans and had for a brief span worked for the company, which, by the time the new building was erected, was called H. Hulman & Company.

Over the years, while developing and expanding the family business, Herman Hulman became intrigued with the problem of trying to produce an effective baking powder. As early as 1879, Hulman & Co. had started making some commercial products, including coffee and baking powder. First, Herman used his spice mill to produce "Crystal" and "Dauntless" double-action baking powders; then, in 1887, under the name "Milk," the company begun marketing another, better baking powder. Hulman continued improving the formula for the baking powder, until, in 1899, under the name "Clabber Baking Powder," Hulman started manufacturing what would become the company's signature product: Clabber Girl Baking Powder. That name change, a new formula, and new packaging did not come until 1923, however.

Before his death in 1913, Herman oversaw the expansion of the family business and the development of additional philanthropic projects. His company's reach expanded beyond Indiana into Kentucky and Illinois. It employed an estimated 50 or more traveling salesman and over 100 others, and it added branches in Mattoon and Paris, Illinois. In 1905, it also built a four-story facility in Evansville and in 1912 purchased a wholesale grocery in the small town of Brazil, both in Indiana. Prior to his death, Herman also set up Hulman & Co. as a partnership with his sons and retired from active control of its operation, but he still spent his days at the company's facility in Terre Haute, conversing with friends and roaming around the building. Upon Herman's death, Anton Hulman became the family patriarch and head of the company.

Company Survives Difficult War Years

Like his father, Anton was something of a workaholic, and World War I put him under considerable strain. Because of the wartime regulations, which restricted businesses to a single base in any given state, Hulman & Co. had to close its Brazil, Evansville, and Paris, Illinois, operations. Moreover, constant price fluctuations forced the company to sell products at very narrow profit margins, adding to Anton's stress. Under doctors' orders, by 1918 Anton had begun putting more of the company's operational control on the shoulders of his brother and the family's associates and began spending more time at his waterfront home in Miami.

The war years were tough on Hulman & Co. It never would reopen its branches in Brazil and Paris, though the operation in Evansville started up again after the armistice. Herman Hulman, Jr., died in 1922, the year before the company perfected its baking powder formula and began producing Clabber Girl Baking Powder, its most successful product. At the time, the company was still struggling to get back on its pre-war footing. It was in the mid 1920s that Anton (Tony) Hulman, Jr., joined the company. Although young Hulman was a Yale graduate, with a degree in administrative engineering, his father insisted that he start in the business at a low rung on the company ladder. That did not phase Tony one bit. In fact, during summers home from Yale, he had been driving company trucks, putting up signs, and calling on customers. He did not live like a low-level employee, however. In 1926, two years after he began full time with Hulman & Co., Tony married Mary Fendrich, heiress to a fortune made by her father in an Evansville cigar-manufacturing business. The family alliance would add greatly to the Hulman family wealth.

Tony's chief task in the 1920s was to help pull the company out of the lethargy into which it had fallen during World War I. He worked hard to change the thinking at Hulman & Co. For a decade, the company had relied on a steady but listless regional trade, with no interest in either expansion or diversification. Tony had more forward-looking ideas, and in 1931, when his father turned over the company's control to him, he put his ideas to work. He immediately launched a decade-long advertising campaign to transform Clabber Girl Baking Powder from a regional into a national product—a household name. He also sent salesmen as far south as Texas, nailing metal Clabber Girl signs on fences and the exterior walls of countless stores and other buildings. In 1932, as the ad campaign started to heat up, Hulman built a six-story baking powder plant that was still in operation at the end of the century. Despite the Great Depression, the campaign worked and Clabber Girl found a prominent place on grocery shelves across the United States.

Tony Hulman Extends the Family Empire

Tony Hulman, like his grandfather, was both a good businessman and a shrewd investor. During his father's lifetime, he extended the family empire by purchasing an office building in Evansville, another in Dayton, Ohio, and two gas companies. When his father died in 1942, Tony and his sister, Grace, inherited the family fortune of over $5 million, and through and after World War II, Tony continued to invest in other businesses. Perhaps his most unusual purchase was made in 1945, when, at the urging of triple Indianapolis 500 winner Wilbur Shaw, he bought the Indianapolis Motor Speedway, the "Brickyard," which was then owned by "Captain Eddie" Rickenbacker, the great World War I fighter ace.

In 1950, Hulman acquired two of its baking powder competitors: the Rumford Chemical Works and the KC Foods Division Plant in North Little Rock, Arkansas. Both were strong sellers

in the East, where Clabber Girl sales were comparatively weak. Located in East Providence, Rhode Island, Rumford was originally a chemical manufacturing company started in 1854 by Professor Eben Horsford and George F. Wilson. The founders named their company after Harvard University's Rumford Chair of the Application of Science to the Useful Arts, which, before his death, had been endowed by Benjamin Thompson, Count Rumford, a man well-known for his contributions to the culinary and dietary fields. Horsford, who derived Rumford's all-phosphate baking powder formula, was awarded the Rumford Chair. Rumford Baking Powder would remain an all-phosphate formula, though its manufacture was shifted to the Hulman plant in Terre Haute, as was the manufacture of KC baking powder. In addition to acquiring proprietary rights to Rumford Baking Powder, Hulman got another branded product from Rumford Chemical Works: Hearth Club Baking Powder. A popular regional brand marketed in the southeastern states, Hearth Club used the same formula as Hulman's Clabber Girl Baking Powder.

Tony Hulman invested extensively in Terre Haute as well. By the mid-1950s, the family had purchased both Terre Haute newspapers, the local television and radio stations, the gas company, and the town's largest hotel. He also invested in the development of the city's first shopping center, The Meadows, as well as the Terre Haute House and Corporate Square, an old high school converted into business offices. Some of the properties were owned by Terre Haute Realty Corp., a wholly-owned subsidiary of Hulman & Co. In 1954, after Shaw died in an airplane crash, Tony Hulman also took over active management of the Indianapolis Motor Speedway.

While Hulman & Co. prospered through the next two decades, family investments continued. In 1965, Tony Hulman purchased the Coca-Cola Bottling Co. of Indianapolis, paying owner James S. Yucker $2 million. He would later buy bottling plants in other Indiana cities, then consolidate the bottling operations in Indianapolis while maintaining warehouses in places where acquired bottling plants had originally been located. The 1960s also brought some retrenchment, though. Hulman & Co. closed its Evansville branch in 1965 and its Mattoon, Illinois branch in 1969. A year earlier, in 1968, it had also closed its spice and coffee mill, an enterprise that Herman Hulman had first got up and going in 1869. A few years earlier, the company had also closed its owned and operated furniture store in downtown Terre Haute.

Meanwhile, under the auspices of the Hulman Foundation, the Hulman family gave much back to the community. Among its many philanthropic gifts were several to what would become the Rose–Hulman Institute of Technology. In all, they would account for $40 million of that institution's $110 million endowment. Gifts to Indiana State University followed, as did a donation of land for a public golf course in Terre Haute.

New Management Oversees Major Business Changes

After a heart attack claimed the life of Tony Hulman in 1977, his widow, Mary Fendrich Hulman, became the family matriarch and head of Hulman & Co. Operational control of the company would probably have passed to Hulman's son-in-law, Elmer George, but after George's wife Mary brought a divorce suit against him, he was killed in a scandalous shootout with his wife's friend, horse trainer Guy Trolinger.

Much of the day-to-day business of Hulman & Co. was handled by Joe Cloutier, who had been Tony Hulman's chief assistant. Mary Hulman became the company's chairwoman. She also became one of the richest women in America, reputed to have been worth $140 million in 1985, when she was named one of the country's 400 richest people by *Forbes*. Although Cloutier succeeded Tony as the Speedway's president, it was Mary Hulman who for the next several years would begin the Indianapolis 500 with the famous words, ''Gentlemen, start your engines.''

Mary followed her husband's basic business strategies, which included a reluctance to dispose of any acquired properties or any other major assets. However, in 1981, the family did sell the Indianapolis bottling company. Also, in exchange for about a 13 percent interest in Indiana Energy, it transferred its ownership of gas companies in Terre Haute and Richmond, Indiana, to that conglomerate. Meanwhile, Hulman acquired other companies, including additional television stations and radio networks in Indiana and Florida. Mary also continued her husband's philanthropic activities, with a special interest in historic preservation.

In 1989, Joe Cloutier died, and his post as president of the Indianapolis Motor Speedway fell to Mary Hulman's grandson, Tony George, who was not at all sure he wanted the job. Tony loved auto racing as a participant, not as top man in the front office. He also carried with him a tinge of notoriety, having gone through a difficult divorce, but he undertook the job and grew with it.

Important changes of another sort were affecting the business of Hulman & Co. Notably, mom-and-pop, independent grocers were waging the last losing battles in a war with supermarket chains that by 1990 had run most of them out of business. The independents had been the mainstay of the wholesale grocery business, including that of Hulman & Co. The company finally succumbed to market realities in 1995 when it closed its wholesale grocery division and let go of 65 of the company's 150 workers, the first mass layoff in its history.

Mary Fendrich Hulman died in 1998, and control of the family affairs passed to Tony George and his mother, Mari Hulman George, who replaced her mother as board chairwoman. The new guard was faced with some pressing problems, not the least of which was the underutilization of some of the company's properties and antiquated equipment, including the machinery in its baking powder plant. Tony George has indicated that somewhere down the line a decision will have to be made about what to do with the plant—as well as what to do with some of the other Hulman holdings, a few of which are located in places that, over time, had become the more decrepit and less desirable areas of Terre Haute. What changes are in the works remain purely speculative, however; Hulman & Co. has not posted any specifics for public inspection.

Principal Subsidiaries

Terre Haute Realty Corp.

Principal Competitors

Kraft Foods Inc.; Tone Brothers, Inc.

Further Reading

''Hulman Dynasty: 1850–1997,'' http://hulman.tribstar.com/INDEX .HTML.

Johnson, Douglas, ''Fast Track,'' *Indiana Business Magazine*, Vol. 36, May 1992, p. 8.

Newcomb, Peter, ''High-Octane Octogenarian,'' *Forbes*, Vol. 136, October 28, 1985, p. 340.

—John W. Fiero

Identix Inc.

100 Cooper Court
Los Gatos, California 95032
U.S.A.
Telephone: (408) 335-1400
Fax: (498) 395-8076
Web site: http://www.identix.com

Public Company
Incorporated: 1982
Employees: 404
Sales: $72.7 million (2000)
Stock Exchanges: American
Ticker Symbol: IDX
NAIC: 335999 All Other Miscellaneous Electrical Equipment and Component and Supplies Manufacturing; 334119 Other Computer Peripheral Equipment Manufacturing; 51121 Software Publishers; 541512 Computer Systems Design Services

Identix Inc. is at the forefront of new developments in the area of electronic security and identification. Identix has developed and marketed proprietary technologies which capture, analyze, and reproduce human fingerprints. While the company produces some hardware products, Identix has established itself as a leader in the area of biometric software—software which measures biological data such as patterns in fingerprints, the hand, and the iris of the eye. Identix products and services are broadly divided into three service areas: Security solutions, imaging solutions, and ANADAC/Government Services. In the area of security, Identix products are used to verify the identity of individuals and to control their access to computer systems, the Internet, intranets, wireless Web networks, e-commerce sites, buildings, secure areas, and the like. Identification is effected by placing a predetermined finger on a touch-sensitive pad connected to a database. The fingerprint of the finger on the touch pad is analyzed and compared with those on file in the database. If there is a match, access is granted. Identix has customers in more than 40 countries for its security applications. Identix imaging applications are used to capture and reproduce forensic quality fingerprints for personal identification and record-keeping. The primary customers for these products are law enforcement agencies. However, they are also used for immigration and employment screening purposes and other kinds of background checks. By 2001, governments in over 30 states and in four foreign countries were using Identix imaging applications. ANADAC/Government Services, administered by ANADAC Identix's wholly owned subsidiary, provides a variety of consulting services to clients in both the public and private sectors. Identix also uses ANADAC's relations with various government agencies as a vehicle for selling its products to federal government clients. Its itrust division provides hardware and software which guarantee secure transaction services for Internet and wireless commerce.

1970s Beginnings

Randall Fowler, the founder of Identix Incorporated, was born in rural Kentucky near Louisville. After his graduation from high school in 1957, he has stated, his grandfather thought he would be unlikely to succeed at anything, "Because I didn't like to plow." Fowler was talented in math, however, and he worked his way through the University of Louisville with jobs at the A&P market, eventually earning a degree in engineering. He went on to get a doctorate in applied mechanics at Stanford University. By the time the 1970s rolled around Fowler was working at TRW Inc., a company that, among other things, developed spacecraft for the government. The company was encountering difficulties establishing the identities of individuals who were using computers to make credit purchases. Fowler became interested in the problem of personal identification, at first on a purely theoretical basis. He started working on it after work in his spare time with books on identification technology from the library. At that early date, he had no inkling that identification technology would become his life's work.

He realized early on that electronic identification of individuals was a problem for biometrics—the measurement of biological data—and the key was fingerprints. They were completely unique and did not change over the course of a lifetime. What's more, fingerprint equipment could be relatively compact. One alternative, retina and iris scanning, was just as accurate, but the equip-

---

Company Perspectives:

Identix, incorporated in August 1982, is the leader in designing, developing, manufacturing, and marketing comprehensive user authentication, security, and identification solutions for the capture and/or comparison of fingerprints. Identix provides solutions for a wide range of applications for markets that include corporate enterprise security, Intranet, extranet, Internet, wireless Web access and security, E-commerce, government, and law enforcement agencies. Identix has more biometric installations worldwide than any other company, and has formed strategic alliances with industry-leaders including Motorola, Compaq, Toshiba, VeriSign, Novell, Dell, Key Tronic, SCM Micro, Cherry, and Unisys.

---

ment was expensive and the process was unpleasant for the person whose eyes the light was analyzing. Another, hand scanners, could be easily tricked. Fowler saw his challenge as the development of a means of reading a fingerprint optically, registering its valleys and ridges and disregarding irrelevant distortions.

Fowler's work eventually attracted the attention of the Federal Bureau of Investigation (FBI) and, as a result, he was awarded a grant by the Law Enforcement Assistance Administration (LEAA), which Fowler used to set up a company. Times worked against the new firm, however. It lost its government support when the Nixon administration cut the LEAA's funding. It did not help that at the time the government was Fowler's only potential customer. The fingerprint technology was extremely expensive, and it would be still years before personal computers would make computers commonplace in homes and offices. Fowler was also becoming aware of the limitations of his knowledge relating to fingerprints, identification, and electronic applications. He closed down the company and went to work for others as a manager and consultant, learning more at each new job. By 1982, he had developed his identification technology to a point where venture capitalists began to see potential. They chipped in $250,000 that year and $2 million in 1983, and Identix was born. The company went public in 1985, despite skepticism from his backers and Wall Street—the entire biometrics industry had rung up only $5 million in sales in all of 1984.

Growth and Expansion in the 1980s

In its first decade Identix focused its energies on developing effective, marketable biometric technologies. An order for a Identix system from the FBI in early 1985 was encouraging, and other orders began to come in gradually as well. In fall 1987, the kingdom of Saudi Arabia purchased 36 computerized fingerprint identification systems to be used in a defense security center near the capital Riyadh. The head of Chicago's Rush Presbyterian-St. Luke's Medical Center's computer center, frustrated by lost or stolen keys and forgotten passwords, ordered some Identix fingerprint identification equipment in late 1989. In June 1990, the California Department of Justice ordered some 600 Identix machines for city and county law enforcement in the state. That contract, which extended over a five year period, was worth nearly $40 million.

The California deal was Identix's largest order to date, by far. It was seen as a turning point for the company. Between 1982 and 1989 the company sold approximately 1,200 of its fingerprint systems, including one to the Pentagon. Nonetheless the firm had lost money every year of its existence. Despite 1989 sales of $1.8 million, the firm lost $2.5 million that year and was running deeply in the red in 1990. One problem for the company was that the admissibility of electronic fingerprints had never been tested in the courts and the FBI had not yet formally endorsed the system, feeling it was not yet accurate enough. That changed in 1991 when the Bureau finally approved Identix products for use by police departments. The police market would soon be Identix's largest.

Identix made a major acquisition in October 1992 when it obtained ANADAC Inc. in a stock deal valued at $5.9 million. ANADAC was an Arlington, Virginia-based contractor that had provided systems integration services to the government since its founding in 1981. Identix selected ANADAC as a takeover target because it was looking for a firm that had both experience with large computer systems and contacts in the government— its major client was the Defense Department, in particular the U.S. Navy. With 158 employees and $17.3 million in sales in 1991, ANADAC was 86th on the list of the 100 largest Washington, D.C., area companies, and some observers found it peculiar that a profitable company such as ANADAC would be taken over by Identix, which had never once turned a profit. However, ANADAC was also seen as a company entering a decline. Defense spending was being cut, and as a result ANADAC's sales were falling. Conversely, the future seemed to hold great things for Identix. Identix also had an investor, Ascom Hasler Ltd. of Switzerland, who was willing to pour money into the company until it hit stride. The acquisition was seen as a good one for stockholders of ANADAC, a company that had few outstanding shares which traded only infrequently. The buyout nearly tripled the value of their holdings. Identix's presence on the American Stock Exchange, it was also felt, would give their stock more visibility. After the takeover, ANADAC became a fully owned subsidiary of Identix.

New Products and Continued Growth in the 1990s

In the mid-1990s, Identix introduced a variety of innovative new products. The firm announced the Identix Gateway for the Automated Fingerprint Identification System (AFIS), produced by NEC Techologies in August 1994. The Gateway provided more efficient communication of fingerprint data from NEC workstations, which were generally found in police departments and other law enforcement offices, and the central AFIS. In October of that year, the company introduced the TouchPrint 600, a system for high resolution recording of fingerprints that exceeded the FBI's requirements for high image quality. After a series of rigorous tests, the system received FBI accreditation in March 1995, the first electronic fingerprint system to be so accredited.

In June 1995, Identix was the defendant in a patent infringement suit brought by Digital Biometrics (DBI) of Minnetonka, Minnesota. The plaintiff, suing for damages which were not reported, alleged that some Identix TouchPrint products violated a DBI patent. Identix fought the suit vigorously, calling it "malicious and frivolous" in statements to the press. Its first Touch

Key Dates:

1982: Randall Fowler founds Identix.
1985: The FBI orders an Identix fingerprint system.
1990: The California Department of Justice places a $40 million order for some 600 Identix Identix machines.
1991: The FBI approves Identix fingerprint systems for use by police departments.
1992: Identix acquires ANADAC Inc.
1994: Identix introduces the TouchPrint 600 system.
1995: The FBI accredits the TouchPrint 600 system.
1997: Identix acquires Biometric Applications and Tecnology Inc.; Identix and Sylvan Learning Systems form joint venture.
1999: Identix acquires Identicator Inc.
2000: Identix introduces its BioLogon software and launches itrust; IDX offers its first itrust product, and Identix is awarded contracts from two major airports.

Print product, the company pointed out, was introduced in 1989, while the Digital Biometric patent was not filed until June 1990. Identix speculated that the suit was an attempt to block an offer to redeem outstanding Identix stock warrants. A year later, in August 1996, a California court ruled that Identix had not infringed the DBI's patent. The case was later dismissed by a California Federal District Court which ruled that no Identix TouchPrint system had violated DBI's patent, a ruling that was upheld by the U.S. Federal Circuit Court of Appeals in 1998.

In 1995, Identix's annual sales reached $27 million and its shares were earning about three cents per quarter. Randall Fowler predicted that sales would grow to $40 million in 1996, and nearly double each in the rest of the decade. In March of 1996, Identix acquired Fingerscan Pty Limited for 6.68 million shares of its stock. Fingerscan was an Asian supplier to Identix and had been integrating Identix technology into its security equipment. The acquisition broadened Identix's marketing presence in Pacific Rim countries. Four months later, the firm purchased Innovative Archival Solutions (IAS) of Springfield, Illinois. IAS, a value-added reseller, was performing fingerprint capture services for various Indiana and Illinois government agencies.

In August 1996, Identix restated its revenues for the previous three quarters, downgrading its second quarter results from earnings of $389,000 to a loss of $4.87 million, and its third quarter from a $4.35 million loss to a $4.87 million loss. The *San Francisco Chronicle* questioned the reasons for the restatement and established that the company had fudged the delivery date of a $1 million order from Marin and Alameda counties in California. Rather than being shipped at the end of March, as publicized, the orders were actually shipped four and a half months later. The paper suggested that the March announcement was timed to push up the price of Identix's slumping stock. At least one Identix shareholder also believed that was the case and instigated a class action suit in U.S. District Court, charging that two officers of Identix had made "false and misleading statements" about the company which led to the price of Identix stock being artificially inflated between January and August 1996. For its part, Identix strongly denied any

wrong-doing. In December 1997 it reached an undisclosed out-of-court settlement with the plaintiff.

In July 1997, Identix acquired Biometric Applications and Technology Inc. (BA&T), a developer of biometric and smart card technology with contracts with the Defense Department and the Federal Aviation Administration. In the deal BA&T shareholders were issued 450,000 shares of Identix stock. A month later, in August 1997, the company announced a joint venture with Sylvan Learning Systems Inc. of Baltimore, Maryland. Under the agreement, Identix would provide fingerprint services at nearly 40 of Sylvan's testing and adult education centers. Before a year had passed the Identix/Sylvan joint venture was also providing fingerprinting services for the Illinois State Agencies, the National Association of Securities Dealers, and United Airlines. Identix imaging systems continued to win new customers. In September 1997, the Immigration and Naturalization Service announced it would buy 400 fingerprint devices. In July 1998, the California state prisons placed an initial order for $1.3 million, and two months later the Detroit Police Department ordered TouchPrint 600 systems worth $1 million.

In May 1998, the firm introduced the Smart-Touch for Unicenter TMG. The Smart-Touch system, developed in cooperation with Computer Associates International Inc., incorporated a point-and-click graphic interface and could be used to access multiple applications in an enterprise with the touch of a finger that lasted less than a second. In October the company introduced a new family of fingerprint verifiers, the TouchSAFE Personal, F3 System Integrator Kit, and TouchNet III. The new readers were developed to operate with personal computer-based desktops and servers. TouchSAFE Personal was a small, compact, and most importantly, affordable device which guaranteed secure access to PCs and networks. The low price made it attractive to a much broader base of business clients.

In April 1999, Identix acquired one of its main competitors, Identicator Inc. of San Bruno California, in a $39.8 million stock deal that included the assumption of $2 million in Identicator debt. Identicator was also a manufacturer of fingerprint verification equipment. It made its first successful inroads into the low-price market when, in 1998, it introduced the first fingerprint reader priced at less than $100. This, in large part, was why Identix decided to make the acquisition—until then it had been unable to crack into the mass market. As a result of the deal, Identix restructured its operations, primarily to reduce duplication.

Challenges in the New Century

In early 1999, Identix and Motorola initiated a cooperative venture to develop products that utilized Motorola chips and Identix technology. The first product of the partnership was released in November of the same year, the DFR 300, an optical fingerprint reader for security applications. In late 2000, when Identix launched a new division for secure transaction services for Internet and wireless commerce, itrust, Motorola invested $3.75 million as a sign of its commitment to the new venture.

The company introduced its BioLogon software in January 2000. BioLogon was a biometric identification system designed to work in conjunction with the Novell Modular Authentication Service and the Novell Directory Service eDirectory. A demonstration of the new software at the launch of Microsoft's Windows 2000 a month later led to a brief run on Identix stock. The following quarter, nonetheless, Identix announced it had suffered greater quarterly losses than anticipated. The company blamed delayed deliveries of a miniature scanner, the DFR300, in April 2000 as a result of quality control concerns. Later that year, in July, the firm closed a facility in Virginia and cut employees by 10 percent. Identix faced further losses in 2000. It said another planned restructuring, which would centralize its marketing, finance, and customer service departments and cut back its Physical Access work, contribute to making the company profitable by 2002.

In June 2001, the itrust division introduced its first product. It was a security platform that controlled access to information sharing and data transfer in open wired and wireless networks. The platform covered the three most important aspects of security, authentication, authorization, and administration. In July 2001, the firm received a contract from Baltimore/Washington International Airport (BWI). Identix was to supply equipment for employee background checks that would enable BWI to comply with the Airport Security Act of 2000. BWI purchased two fingerprint scanners, making it the seventh airport to adopt Identix technology. The others are Washington Dulles International, Ronald Reagan National, JFK International, Boston Logan International, Chicago O'Hare, and Orlando International Airport.

Principal Subsidiaries

ANADA, Inc.

Principal Divisions

itrust.

Principal Competitors

Printrak International Inc.; SAFLINK Corporation; Keyware Technologies; Viisage Technology, Inc.; Ethentica, Inc.; Loronix Information Systems, Inc.; Visionics Corporation.

Further Reading

"Advanced Technology Meets Toughest-Yet Federal Requirement; FBI Awards Image Quality Specifications 'IQS' Accreditation to Identix TouchPrint 600 Live-Scan Fingerprint System," *Business Wire*, March 29, 1995.

"California Company Will Supply Security Systems For Saudi Arabia," *Journal Of Commerce*, September 15, 1987, p. 5a.

Clark, Don, "Futuristic Fingerprinting May Have a Big Future," *San Francisco Chronicle*, June 29, 1990, p. C1.

"Digital Biometrics Inc.: Patent Complaint Is Filed Against Rival Identix Inc.," *Wall Street Journal*, June 5, 1995, p. B2.

Doherty, Kate, "One-of-a-Kind Biometric Identifiers Are Finding Many Security Applications," *Access Control & Security Systems Integration*, September 1, 1997.

"Fingerprint-ID Firm Identix Buys Rival Identicator For $40 Million," *Dow Jones Online News*, November 16, 1998.

Greenberg, Herb, "Now for the Other (Less Glowing) Side of the Identix Story," *San Francisco Chronicle*, February 7, 1996, p. B1.

——, "Why Is Identix Really Restating Its Revenues and Earnings?," *San Francisco Chronicle*, August 27, 1996, p. C1.

Hinden, Stan, "Arlington's Anadac Thinks It's Spied a Good Deal With Identix," *Washington Post*, October 26, 1992, p. F33.

"Keeping A Finger On Security," *St. Louis Post-Dispatch*, January 29, 1990, Pg. 15.

"Motorola, Identix Launch Fingerprint-Based Security Product," *Dow Jones News Service*, November 16, 1999.

"Seventh Major US Airport Selects Identix Live Scan Systems For Employee Background Checks," *PR Newswire*, July 27, 2001.

Sugawara, Sandra, "Calif. Firm Plans to Acquire Arlington Defense Contractor; Deal for Anadac Valued at About $5.9 Million," *Washington Post*, July 15, 1992, p. D3.

"Sylvan, Calif. Company to Form Joint Venture," *Baltimore Sun*, August 6, 1997, p. 1C.

Tracy, Eleanor Johnson, "Biometrics Has A Touch For Spotting Phonies," *Fortune*, April 15, 1985, pp 105.

Ward, Joe, "Ex-Louisvillian Pioneers Access to Computers by Fingerprint," *Courier-Journal Louisville*, July 30, 1999.

Young, Shawn, "Identix And Motorola Link On Fingerprint Security Effort," *Dow Jones News Service*, May 25, 1999.

—Gerald E. Brennan

Integrity Inc.

1000 Cody Road
Mobile, Alabama 36695
U.S.A.
Telephone: (251) 633-9000
Fax: (251) 633-7324
Web site: http://www.integritymusic.com

Public Company
Incorporated: 1987
Employees: 168
Sales: $51.8 million (2000)
Stock Exchanges: NASDAQ
Ticker Symbol: ITGR
NAIC: 334612 Prerecorded Compact Disc (Except
   Software), Tape, and Record Reproducing; 51113
   Book Publishers

Integrity Inc., based in Mobile, Alabama, produces, publishes, and distributes Christian music. Its Christian lifestyle products are designed to entertain and educate as well as enhance worship. Integrity produces works in different formats, including cassettes, CDs, videos, DVDs, and print. It offers praise and worship music in different musical styles designed for a range of audiences. Soundscan tracking has identified Integrity as the nation's leading praise and worship music company, commanding, at the end of 2000, 56 percent of the Christian Bookseller's Association market. The company, which owns rights to about 2,700 songs, distributes its music and videos in retail stores throughout the United States and 161 countries abroad as well as through sales made directly to consumers via mail order catalogs, the Internet, and continuity clubs. It produces various recordings in an array of languages, including Russian, Spanish, Portuguese, French, German, Mandarin Chinese, and Indonesian. Through its new subsidiary, Integrity Publishers, Inc., the company also produces and publishes Christian books. Although public, Integrity is largely owned by the family of Chairman and CEO P. Michael Coleman, who controls the bulk of the company's voting stock

1987–92: Integrity Starts Out as Christian Music, Direct Mail Club

Integrity Music Company, the predecessor of Integrity Incorporated, was founded by P. Michael Coleman in Mobile, Alabama in 1987 after he and an investment partner purchased the music operations of Integrity Communications, Inc., then owned by Charles Simpson Ministries, Inc. Before acquiring the business, Coleman had served as the president of various organizations with the Christian communications industry. From the outset, Coleman directed the company's fortunes as both CEO and president.

Integrity began as a producer of Christian praise and worship music, recorded in a variety of contemporary styles, but it was built on what the company itself termed "a Hosanna! Music mail-order tape program." According to the company's Web site, its mission from the outset was to help people all over the world "experience the manifest presence of God."

Initially, Integrity Music was strictly a Christian music direct mail (CD and tape) club. However, it was the first contemporary Christian music producer to depend on direct marketing techniques, which proved very successful. The company quickly developed a solid customer base that insured its remarkable growth and early entry into new Christian-music market segments. It soon expanded its product line to include young adult and children's music, videos, and instrumental recordings.

To market its labels, Integrity used direct market strategies. For example, to appeal to a young audience, it developed a popular continuity program called "Just for Kids." It also printed a full catalog from which customers could order any of Integrity's CDs and tapes, including its children's label lines: "The Doughnut Repair Club," "Kids Sing-A-Long," and "Songs of Praise." In addition, starting in 1992, Integrity was represented by Rep Sales, which introduced Integrity's top country artist, Susie Luchsinger, into the general market.

Integrity also joined up with Word, Inc.'s Everland label to create an in-store, interactive kiosk program, the first of its kind to be placed in Christian bookstores. In addition, encouraged by the results of its marketing efforts, Integrity took "The Dough-

---

nut Repair Club'' to general markets through direct sales. The line had soon sold over a million units, and its first video in the series went gold very quickly.

1993–97: Integrity's Entry into the Public Sector

By 1993, Integrity's sales had climbed to $29.1 million. Prompted by the company's mercurial rise, and anticipating rapid expansion that would require more working captial, Coleman decided to take Integrity public. After being reincorporated in 1993, the company made its IPO in 1994 and started trading on the NASDAQ exchange.

However, Integrity had a few problems associated with its restructuring and emergence as a public company. In 1996, it laid off 30 of its 145 employees, a necessary belt-tightening measure taken when it experienced lower-than-expected sales. In fact, its revenue fell from $36.3 million in 1995 to $30.4 million in 1996, and in both those years the company had bottom line losses. The slump was of short duration, though, thanks to the successful sale of some key albums, including ''Shout to the Lord,'' ''Let the River Flow,'' ''Shalom Jerusalem,'' and ''Jerusalem Arise.'' Also, sales improved as a result of a partnership that Integrity had formed with Hillsong Music Australia in 1995. Under its terms, Integrity became the exclusive distributor of that company's recordings in the United States. Some analysts also gave credit for Integrity's rebound to COO Jerry Weimer, who joined the company in 1996, and CFO Alison Richardson, both of whom helped the company restructure and pay down its debt.

At the end of 1996, Integrity's label line included ''Integrity Music,'' ''Hosanna! Music,'' ''Integrity Music Just-for-Kids,'' ''Renewal Music,'' and ''FairHope Records.'' It added to the line in 1997, when it inaugurated Vertical Music, a line of church-oriented music produced for the teen and young adult Christian music market. The line represented something of a new direction for Integrity, conjoining as it did praise and worship content with contemporary alternative music.

1998–99: Vertical Music Line, WoW Releases, and Online Store Help Market Performance

The new Vertical Music line helped boost Integrity's sales and return it to profitability from 1997 to the end of the decade, though it was not until 1998, when it revenues rose to $38.8 million, that the company's sales climbed above those reached in

1995. By the end of 1998, Integrity commanded first place and a 29 percent market share in CCLI's Top 500 tracking survey.

One of Integrity's most successful ventures, its WoW double-CD collections, first went into production in 1999. Initially, in 1996, Integrity partnered with EMI Christian Group, Word Entertainment, and Provident Music Group to produce WoW CDs, but it did not actually release any WoW albums until it formed its 1999 partnership with Marantha! Music and Vineyard Music and licensed the WoW trademark from EMI. The WoW albums previously released under other labels had all proved very successful. Each album featured some of the year's highest ranking worship songs taken from the Top 500 list compiled by Christian Copyright Licensing Inc. (CCLI), which annually tracked the use of such songs in about 112,000 North American churches. Very popular, they all achieved platinum status with sales of over 50,000 units within three months after their release. Their stellar performance attracted Integrity and its new partners. The first of the three WoW albums the companies released, *WoW Worship—Today's 30 Most Powerful Worship Songs*, hit the street in June of 1999. It was followed by two more albums in the next two years. The three releases, known within the industry as WoW Worship Blue, WoW Worship Orange, and WoW Worship Green, all were top sellers.

It was also in 1999 that Integrity established a direct sales arrangement with Amazon.com and Crosswalk.com, a Didax Internet site, both of which were already selling Integrity's music but were getting it from third party distributors. Under the new agreement, Integrity began selling its products directly to the two e-commerce businesses. Moreover, encouraged by the success of Internet marketing, Integrity also established its own online store, www.integritymusic.com. It showed promise almost immediately, and the company soon retained InfoMech, a leading Internet developer, to help it improve and expand the company's e-commerce capabilities. From the start, www.integritymusic.com used audio and visual streaming to allow customers to sample Integrity's music and buy its products as well as get information about its artists and worship leaders, appearance itineraries, and scheduled dates for new releases. With InfoMech's help, the revised site added such features as custom recommendations based on an individual buyer's purchase history, customer reviews of products, a more efficient and faster order process, and an intelligent search engine for finding products by category, song title, artist, or description.

With its enhancements, www.integritymusic.com placed in the top seven of all e-commerce music sites in an end-of-the-year survey conducted by BizRate.com, an independent, third-party e-commerce research firm. Integrity, the only Christian music company to participate in BizRate's survey, reached its ranking in competition with such established and successful e-commerce music sites as CDNow, CD Universe, and Tower Records. Coleman noted that the feedback from BizRate's surveys would be valuable for reaching customers and expanding Integrity's market, which, as the CEO also noted, had great sales momentum, growing at a good month-to-month clip.

2000–01: Successful Partnering with Time Life Music

In February 2000, Integrity entered an agreement with Time Life Music to produce Songs 4 Worship, a co-branded series

Key Dates:

1987: P. Michael Coleman organizes and incorporates his company as Integrity Music Company.
1993: The company is reincorporated in Delaware.
1994: Integrity Music goes public.
1995: The company changes name to Integrity Incorporated.
1996: The company begins using television for marketing its music.
1997: Integrity debuts its program, ''Lift Him Up,'' aired twice weekly on the Trinity Broadcasting Network.
1999: Company starts up its online Christian music store but also markets products online through Amazon.com and Crosswalk.com.; in partnership with Marantha! Music and Vineyard Music the company releases first WoW albums.
2000: Integrity's annual revenue surpasses $50 million for the first time; the company partners with Time Life Music to create Songs 4 Worship music series.
2001: Integrity launches Integrity Publishers, Inc., its book publishing subsidiary.

that was eventually slated to grow to 20 volumes. The partnering arrangement linked the world's leader in praise and worship music with its leading television music marketer. The Songs 4 Worship series was to be modeled after Time Life's very successful Songs 4 Life series, which, since its introduction in 1998, had already sold 1.8 million albums. Plans called for the introduction of the series through a Time Life Music direct response television campaign followed by a direct mail campaign conducted by Integrity Direct. Thereafter, Time Life was to make the series available to retailers while Integrity distributed it to domestic Christian retail outlets and through its international sales network.

The marketing campaign worked very well. *Shout to the Lord*, the first double CD volume in the new Songs 4 Worship series, was rolled out late in the company's fourth-quarter, and by the end of the first quarter of 2001, with sales of over one million copies, it had already attained Platinum certification. That first quarter came on top of a strong year for Integrity, one which saw its sales rise from $45.3 million in 1999 to $51.8 million, a 14.3 percent increase. The company's net income also rose, from $1.4 million to $1.7 million. Because of its strong cash flow, Integrity was able to continue paying down its outstanding debt, leaving it in a very good position for both further partnering agreements and growth.

By March 2001, Integrity was searching for a bank that would become its financial partner in the company's long-term growth initiatives. It was also developing strategies for increasing the value of its stock. Clearly, from the success of the first volume in the roll out of the new Songs 4 Worship series, 2001 promised to be even a better year than 2000 had been. Other significant factors would be the strength of Integrity's e-commerce initiative, integritymusic.com; television direct re-

sponse campaigns; and the company's growing continuity club memberships. Combined, in 2000, these marketing outlets delivered a 27 percent increase in consumer-direct sales over the previous year, and were promising to do even better in 2001. Integrity's robust performance seemed unlikely to diminish, even in a cooling economy.

In the summer of 2001, Integrity took a new direction with the creation of book publishing subsidiary. Formed as Integrity Publisher, Inc., with headquarters in Nashville, Tennessee, its purpose, consistent with Integrity's primary mission, was to develop and publish Christian book titles. As president and CEO, Byron D. Williamson was put in position to lead the new subsidiary, bringing years of experience in book publishing to the task. According to Coleman, Integrity Incorporated's CEO, book publishing would begin playing a major role in the parent company's long-term growth strategy. Plans called for selling titles through Christian retail outlets (CBA stores) and general retail stores (such as Barnes & Noble and Borders) as well as direct-to-consumer channels. The addition of publishing to its business brought Integrity's status as a Christian-based media-communications company to its fullest extent.

Principal Subsidiaries

Integrity Publishers, Inc.

Principal Competitors

EMI Group plc; Gaylord Entertainment Company; Provident Music Group; Sony Music Entertainment Inc.; Warner Music Group.

Further Reading

Darden, Bob, ''Christian Labels Sing the Praises of Kids' Entertainment,'' *Billboard*, April 30, 1994, p. 38.

''Integrity Incorporated Joins Two Other Praise and Worship Music Companies in WoW Worship Partnership,'' *PR Newswire*, April 12, 1999.

''Integrity Incorporated Enhances Capabilities of Integritymusic.com,'' *PR Newswire*, February 24, 1999.

''Integrity Incorporated Establishes Direct Selling Relationship with Amazon.com and Crosswalk.com,'' *PR Newswire*, February 24, 1999.

''Integrity Incorporated Opens State-of-the-Art Online Store,'' *PR Newswire*, August 20, 1999.

''IntegrityMusic.com Receives Excellent Rating from e-Commerce Researcher BizRate,'' *PR Newswire*, November 29, 1999.

''Integrity Reports Double-Digit Increases in Revenue and Earnings for 2000,'' *PR Newswire*, March 1, 2001.

''Launch of Songs 4 Worship Proves to Be Largest Direct Response Television Launch in History of Time Life Music and Integrity Music,'' *123Jump*, April 27, 2001.

Price, Deborah Evans, ''Integrity Enters New Phase with Overstreet,'' *Billboard*, February 3, 1996, p. 14.

——, ''Integrity Launches Youth-Targeted Music,'' *Billboard*, August 23, 1997, p. 109.

''Songs 4 Worship The Tour Set for Fall 2001,'' *PR Newswire*, August 9, 2001.

—John W. Fiero

International Olympic Committee

Château de Vidy
Case Postale 356
1007 Lausanne
Switzerland
Telephone: (41 21) 621 61 11
Fax: (41 21) 621 62 16
Web site: http://www.olympic.org

Nonprofit Organization
Incorporated: 1894 as the Comité international des jeux
    olympiques
Employees: 100
Sales: $100 million (1999)
NAIC: 71132 Promoters of Performing Arts, Sports, and
    Similar Events without Facilities; 71211 Museums

The International Olympic Committee (IOC) is the ''supreme authority of the Olympic movement.'' It selects venues and otherwise administers a massive sports festival every couple of years, either the Games of the Olympiad held in the summer or the Olympic Winter Games. About four billion people across the world watch the Summer Games on television, yet former president Lord Killanin once called IOC executive board, filled with aristocrats, ''the most exclusive club in the world.'' The IOC takes in revenues from licensing memorabilia and postage stamps and coins, selling television rights, and selling admission tickets. About a billion dollars a year is taken in; roughly 93 percent of the money is redistributed to the National Olympic Committees, the International Federations that regulate individual sports, and the Organizing Committees from the cities that host the Games.

Olympic Origins

Baron Pierre de Courbertin, a Frenchman, is considered the father of the Olympic Movement. He became interested in sports as an important element in male education, and believed the athleticism he had seen in English public schools could revitalize the rising generations of his home country.

In 1889, Courbertin toured North American schools, gathering evidence to support his promotion of physical education in France. He came to believe that a rebirth of the Olympics of ancient Greece would ultimately increase the acceptance of sport to a point where it could be introduced into schools. At the time, new archeological discoveries in Olympia were being reported in the press on a regular basis, already helping to introduce the idea into popular consciousness.

Courbertin appealed to nationalism to gain support for the Games in France. The team responsible for the excavations in Greece had been German (led by Heinrich Schliemann). Who better than France to resurrect the ceremony of the ancient and noble tradition?

A group of delegates from foreign sports clubs met at the Sorbonne in Paris in June 1894, ostensibly to discuss amateur athletics. Seventy-eight delegates from ten countries attended. Only at the end of the conference was the business of creating a modern version of the Olympic games of ancient Greece introduced. Several important details were worked out on June 23.

A name for the administrative body, the Comité international des jeux olympiques, was decided, and thirteen members were named to its ranks by Courbertin. Its presidency was to change after every Games. Since the first were to be held in Athens (the second, in Paris), Demetrios Vikelas, a wealthy Greek merchant living in Paris, was named the group's first president. The congress also adopted its famous motto, ''Citius, Altius, Fortius'' (swifter, higher, stronger).

One writer, David Young, observes that Courbertin was too busy planning his own wedding to offer much hands-on help to preparations for the first Olympiad. This is flatly contradicted in other accounts. Courbertin is credited with coming up with the famous logo—five interlocked rings in blue, yellow, black, green, and red on a white background—colors found in the flags of all nations across the world.

Among commercial sponsors was Kodak, the photography giant. The 1896 Games were such a success that Greece lobbied to have all future Olympic Games held on its home turf. (It had taken some effort for Courbertin to convince the impover-

Company Perspectives:

Olympism is a philosophy of life, exalting and combining in a balanced whole the qualities of body, will, and mind. Blending sport with culture and education, Olympism seeks to create a way of life based on the joy found in effort, the educational value of good example, and respect for universal fundamental ethical principles. The goal of Olympism is to place everywhere sport at the service of the harmonious development of man, with a view to encouraging the establishment of a peaceful society concerned with the preservation of human dignity. To this effect, the Olympic Movement engages, alone or in cooperation with other organizations and within the limits of its means, in actions to promote peace. The Olympic Movement, led by the IOC, stems from modern Olympism.

ished Greek government to host the games in the first place.) Courbertin and others dedicated to fostering an international spirit in the Olympics successfully countered this proposal. (Further, Greece dropped out of the Games when Turkey declared war on it in 1897.) Vikelas resigned as president after this dispute in late 1896. Courbertin then served as president until 1925, with the exception of a period between 1916 and 1919 when he served in the French military during the World War I. Godefroy de Blonay of Switzerland, a linguist and Egyptologist, was interim president during this time.

Paris in 1900 was the site of intrigues over who would control the IOC, with the IOC claiming its authority over the administration of the Games, which suffered from a lack of organization both in Paris and in St. Louis in 1904.

By the time of the Athens Games in 1896, the IOC had added two members. A postal vote system was initiated for approving new members in 1902. Participating countries had anywhere from one to three representatives on the IOC. Membership criteria were formalized at the IOC's Tenth Session in London in 1908. One of the requirements was that members be conversant in one of the IOC's two official languages, English and French. An executive board, established in 1921, was later tasked with nominating new members. Until 1975, an annual membership fee of 50 to 250 Swiss francs was imposed; those who did not pay were declared *démissionaire*—expelled, in other words.

The 1908 London Games were more successful than the Athens Games, although strained by political disputes between Russia and Finland, and Great Britain and Ireland. The success continued to Stockholm in 1912, when 2,490 athletes from 28 countries participated. The first methodical attempt to license commemorative memorabilia came at these Stockholm Games. In spite of Courbertin's efforts, the truces of the ancient Greeks found no counterpart in modern times, and the next Olympiad, planned for Berlin, was cancelled.

The IOC was headquartered in the Casino de Montbenon in Lausanne, Switzerland, between 1915 and 1921. By 1921, the IOC's archives and museum had outgrown the Casino de Montenon. The Villa Mon-Repos became its home for the period from 1922 to 1968, and that of Courbertin as well. After

Courbertin died in 1937, he was buried in Lausanne, except for his heart, which was buried at the Archaia Olympia, Greece.

In the early 1920s, the IOC began hiring non-members for part-time positions in its secretariat, which handled the organization's daily business. Until this time, the individual members of the board itself carried out such administrative functions as secretary and treasurer.

Comte Henri de Baillet-Latour, a Belgian aristocrat, replaced Courbertin as president in 1925. He had been part of the IOC since 1903. He had helped organize the 1920 Olympics in Antwerp, which had been symbolically chosen due to the invasions Belgium had endured during World World I. Among the issues debated during Baillet-Latour's presidency was whether the women's track and field events introduced at the 1928 Games be allowed to continue. Baillet-Latour unsuccessfully tried to have them eliminated from 1932 Los Angeles on the grounds that athletic competition produced unfeminine women.

Berlin had been awarded the privilege of hosting the 1936 Olympics in 1930, when a congress had been held in that city. After Hitler came to power in 1933, the Olympics presented an unprecedented propaganda opportunity. Despite promises to the contrary, the Nazis banned Jewish athletes from German sports facilities—ostensibly violations of the Olympic code, though officially denied by Hitler. A considerable movement to boycott the Berlin Games arose in North America and Great Britain.

The 1936 Games proceeded even though the Nazis had occupied the Rhineland the previous year. Hitler reportedly left the stadium early to avoid shaking hands with the African Americans who had wrestled gold medals from his Aryan athletes. At a dinner party during the Games, Baillet-Latour corrected one of his German hostesses of any illusions regarding peace and harmony: "We shall have war in three years," he predicted (as quoted in the *New York Times* fifty years later). World War II cancelled the 1940 Winter Games planned for first Sapporo, Japan, and then Garmisch-Partenkirchen, Germany, as well as the Summer Games planned for Tokyo, then Helskini.

Baillet-Latour died in January 1942, shortly after learning his son had died during military exercises in the United States. He was succeeded by Swedish industrialist Sigfrid Edström, who had been the IOC's first vice-president. Edström was a logical successor due to his neutral citizenship.

Edström had played a critical role in the establishment of a separate Winter Olympic Games. In 1924, the IOC helped support the Week of Winter Sports in Chamonix, France, before voting the next year at the Prague Congress to create the Winter Games proper. At the time, Scandinavians opposed this, fearing competition with their own skiing events.

Like other early IOC leaders, Edström opposed compensating athletes with money and resisted efforts to include women. Nevertheless, after Alice Milliat's Fédération sportive feminine internationale produced a popular "Women's Olympics," Edström voted to allow women to compete in five events beginning with the 1928 Amsterdam Games.

Key Dates:

1894: Baron Pierre de Courbertin organizes a committee to promote a revival of the ancient Greek Olympics.

1896: Athens hosts the first modern Olympic Games.

1912: The first official Olympic memorabilia is licensed at the Stockholm Games.

1921: The IOC relocates to the Villa Mon-Repos.

1928: Women's sports included in the Amsterdam Games.

1952: CBS buys TV rights for Squaw Valley and Rome Olympics for about $450,000.

1967: Château de Vidy becomes IOC's new home.

1969: Monique Berlioux, later secretary-general, begins expansion of IOC secretariat.

1974: The word ''amateur'' is removed from the Olympic Charter.

1981: IOC recognized as a nongovernmental, nonprofit organization.

1997: Bribery scandal forces resignations of IOC, Salt Lake officials.

2002: Salt Lake promises the technically most advanced Olympics celebration ever.

Cold War Competitions

At the IOC congress in Vienna in May 1951, Edström defeated motions to prevent delegates from the former Axis powers from remaining in the organization. He referred to some of them as ''old friends.'' The Soviets, who had withdrawn from the games under Lenin, were cleared to participate in the 1952 Helsinki Games. Chinese nationalists on the island of Formosa (Taiwan) boycotted these games; a Chinese team assembled by the mainland Communists arrived too late to compete. East and West Germany, divided by the Cold War, would field a common team from 1956 to 1964 and separate teams between 1968 and 1988.

Edström nominated Avery Brundage as his successor; after 25 rounds of balloting, he was confirmed in 1952. Brundage came from a different background than previous IOC presidents. His origins were working class; his mother ran a boarding house after his father deserted the family. Brundage went on to run a successful construction business in Chicago (Edström had married to a schoolteacher from the Windy City); after becoming a champion handball player, Brundage became an advocate for the United State's participation in the 1936 Games in Berlin. Brundage had helped Edström stay in touch with widely scattered IOC members during World War II.

At the time Brundage took the helm in 1952, the IOC was losing $3,000 a year. The sale of television rights to CBS helped right the balance sheet. CBS paid $50,000 to broadcast the Squaw Valley Winter Games and $394,000 for the Rome Summer Games. These funds helped pay for expenses of the president, who previously had to cover many costs out of his own pocket.

Among the issues the IOC faced during Brundage's tenure was the question of South African apartheid. In 1964 and 1968, Tokyo and Mexico City withdrew their invitations to South Africa, fearing a wholesale boycott from other African nations. After years of debate, the IOC voted to exclude South Africa from the Olympics in 1970.

Meanwhile, the Château de Vidy in Lausanne had become the home of the IOC at the end of 1967. The IOC's secretariat would expand greatly under Monique Berlioux, appointed director of press and public relations in 1969. She also served as de facto secretary-general, a position that was formally given her in 1973. The secretariat tripled in size under Berlioux, reaching 83 employees in 1986.

Sociopolitical violence was beginning to make its way into the Games. In Mexico 1968, students protested the country's disparity of wealth and the amount of money spent on the Olympics there; 267 were killed in an ensuing battle with police. The same Games were boycotted by some African-American athletes.

During the 1972 Munich Games, Palestinian terrorists killed ten Israeli athletes and two bodyguards. Brundage was criticized for not sharing information during the crisis with other IOC members. Brundage's successor, elected before the killings, was Michael Morris, Lord Killanin. A native of Dublin, Killanin had been a journalist, a veteran of D-Day, and a peer in the House of Lords. Although active in athletics at school, it was not sports that drew him into the Olympic family but a desire to help resolve disputes.

Disputes certainly abounded during the eight years Killanin was in charge of the IOC. African nations boycotted the money-losing 1976 Montreal Olympics. The U.S.-led a boycott of the 1980 Moscow Olympics protesting the Soviet invasion of Afghanistan. Also, rules regarding amateurism were relaxed under Killanin. The word ''amateur'' was removed from the Olympic Charter in 1974.

IOC More Corporate in the 1980s

Juan Antonio Samaranch was named president, a full-time position, in 1980. Fond of roller hockey and boxing, he had risen through the ranks as a sporting official in Franco's Spain. After the end of the fascist regime, Samaranch served as Spanish ambassador to the Soviet Union. Under Samaranch, power became more centralized within the IOC. Though some questioned his methods, the movement's fortunes and influence grew greatly during his twenty years at the helm.

In September 1981, the Swiss Confederation recognized the IOC as an international nongovernmental, nonprofit organization, giving it tax relief and allowing it exclusive rights to Olympic trademarks. Under Samaranch, the IOC began selling corporations like Kodak, Visa, and Coca-Cola the rights to display this trademark on their products, which would generate about $300 million in income every four years by 2000.

Though boycotted by the Soviet bloc, the Los Angeles Olympics in 1984 were financially successful; they earned a tidy $225 million profit, observed *Time* magazine. This, in addition to the enormous publicity associated with the Games, intensified the competition among cities eager to host them. As logical as it may seem in retrospect, the IOC did not begin holding Winter and Summer Games on alternate even-numbered years until the

1990s. This greatly increased the value of the TV rights to the Winter Games.

1996 Centennial Games

A special congress was held in Paris in 1994 to mark the organization's 100th anniversary. However, history was not to repeat itself in 1996—the Centennial Games would be held in bustling Atlanta, Georgia, rather than polluted Athens. Eventually, Greece did win the opportunity to host the 2004 Games, while Beijing was picked as the 2008 host city.

Some lamented the growing commercialism of the Olympics. Fast food colossus McDonald's was estimated to have spent $100 million at the 2000 Sydney Games. However, the IOC banned commercial advertising and billboards in Olympic stadiums and venues. It also turned down potentially lucrative satellite and cable revenues to maintain a policy of free-to-air access for Olympic broadcasts.

Allegations of widespread drug use were particularly persistent; occasionally they resulted in medals being stripped from doped athletes after the fact. Still, the Sydney Games were noted for their magnificent spectacle. Samaranch, giving his last closing address as IOC president, declared they were the "best Olympic Games ever." Global television networks reported 3.7 billion viewers during the Sydney Games. The official Olympic Web site logged 8.7 million visitors, while that of NBC counted 15.4 million.

Salt Lake 2002

Salt Lake City, Utah, narrowly lost its bid to host the 1998 Winter Olympics, which instead went to Nagano, Japan. The next time around, the Salt Lake Organizing Committee (SLOC) courted IOC members lavishly, giving them everything from $100 bottles of wine to free travel and medical care, as well as supplying jobs and scholarships for their relatives. Congolese IOC member, Jean Claude Ganga, was particularly well rewarded, earning $60,000 in a Utah land deal. All told, SLOC gave IOC members a total of $1 million in gifts. A major scandal ensued. Ten officials from the IOC and several from the SLOC subsequently resigned (SLOC chairman Tom Welch stepped down in 1997 after being convicted on a domestic battery charge); two SLOC leaders faced criminal charges of fraud. In spite of the scandal, the 2002 Winter Games seemed on track to be the most successful yet. By early 2001, ticket sales, at $160 million, were double those of the previous Winter Games in Nagano, Japan.

Jacques Rogge was named IOC president in July 2001. A champion sailor and orthopedic surgeon, Rogge had lobbied to send a Belgian team to the 1980 Moscow Olympics, which was boycotted by the United States and the rest of its NATO allies over the Soviet intervention in Afghanistan.

Security plans for the 2002 Salt Lake Games were reviewed after the September 11 terrorist attack on New York and Washington, D.C. The last Games to be held in the United States, the 1996 Atlanta Games, had been marred by a bombing held to be the work of an anti-abortion activist. Organizers and athletes remained determined to rally around the Olympic torch, one of the world's greatest symbols of hope and aspiration. An IOC media campaign urged sports fans everywhere to "Celebrate Humanity."

Principal Subsidiaries

Meridian Management SA (25%).

Principal Divisions

Olympic Solidarity Commission; Olympic Foundation; Olympic Museum Foundation.

Principal Operating Units

International Sports Federations; National Olympic Committees; Organizing Committees of Olympic Games; Olympic Solidarity; IOC Commissions and Olympic Movement Efforts.

Further Reading

Abrahamson, Alan, "US Role Is Waning in Politics of the IOC," *Los Angeles Times,* July 21, 2001, p. D1.

Bai, Matt, and Andrew Murr, "Go for the Greed," *Newsweek,* January 25, 1999, pp. 30–33.

Findling, John E., and Kimberly D. Pelle, eds., *Historical Dictionary of the Modern Olympic Movement,* Westport, Conn. and London: Greenwood Press, 1996.

Longman, Jere, "Experienced Helmsman—Jacques Rogge," *New York Times,* July 17, 2001, p. D4.

Paparsenos, Achilles, "Security at Athens 2004," *Los Angeles Times,* February 6, 2001, p. D1.

Payne, Michael, "100 Years of Olympic Marketing," *The IOC Official Olympic Companion 1996,* Searle, Caroline and Bryn Vaile, eds., Atlanta, Ga.: Brassey's Sports, 1996, pp. 469–74.

Rodda, John, "Olympics: Final Curtain for Man Who Made Today's Games," *Guardian* (Manchester, U.K.), Sport Sec., July 16, 2001, p. 16.

Shipley, Amy, "Among Olympic Hopefuls, Athens Has the History," *Washington Post,* August 19, 1997, p. E1.

Verdier, Michèle, "The IOC: A Vast and Complex Global Organization," *The IOC Official Olympic Companion 1996,* Searle, Caroline and Bryn Vaile, eds., Atlanta, Ga.: Brassey's Sports, 1996, pp. 464–68.

Williams, Richard, "Sydney 2000: The Final Workouts: Let the 'Mc-Games' Begin," *Guardian* (Manchester, U.K.), Sport Sec., September 9, 2000, p. 1.

Young, David C., "Demetrios Vikelas: First President of the IOC," *Stadion,* 1988, pp. 85–102.

—Frederick C. Ingram

JetBlue Airways Corporation

80-02 Kew Gardens Road
Kew Gardens, New York 11415
U.S.A.
Telephone: (718) 286-7900
Toll Free: (800) JETBLUE
Fax: (718) 286-7950
Web site: http://www.jetblue.com

Private Company
Incorporated: 1999 as JetBlue Airways Corporation
Employees: 1,800
Sales: $100 million (2000 est.)
NAIC: 481111 Scheduled Passenger Air Transportation

JetBlue Airways Corporation was created by Utah entrepreneur David Neeleman to ''bring the humanity back to air travel.'' It was also a good way to add another chapter to a successful career in budget air travel. Jet Blue was launched with a huge amount capital, brand new planes, and expert personnel in key positions. It grew rapidly as customers flocked to it to escape the steep fares and frequent delays of the major airlines.

Origins

Many small start-up airlines tried the low fare formula in the 1990s. Most, like Kiwi Air Lines and People Express, failed in the face of direct competition from the majors, which were able to withstand fare wars. (In fact, 87 airlines failed between deregulation in 1978 and the end of the century.) Insufficient capital and insufficient management talent were other factors that grounded many of the fledglings.

David Neeleman grew up in Salt Lake City with seven siblings. According to *Time,* a red airplane on his second birthday cake first attracted him to aviation. As a young man, he served in Brazil as a Latter-Day Saints missionary, then studied accounting at the University of Utah. But he dropped out of school before graduating in favor of entrepreneurial pursuits.

Before long, Neeleman was running Morris Air, an innovative, successful low-fare carrier that was the first to offer ticketless reservations. He reportedly earned $20 million when he sold it to Southwest Airlines in 1993. He was just 33 years old at the time. Bound by a five-year non-competition agreement, in 1995 he went left the U.S. to help launch Canadian startup WestJet Airlines.

Neeleman told *Sales and Marketing Management* that it took 30 months of planning to get his next project, dubbed ''New Air,'' in the skies. It also took quite a bit of money. Neeleman raised $130.2 million in start-up capital, an unprecedented amount for a start-up airline, from backers that included Chase Capital Partners ($20 million); two George Soros funds and Quantum and Soros Fund Management ($40 million combined); and San Francisco venture capital firm Western Presidio ($30 million). Banc Boston Ventures, Massachusetts Mutual Life, and Nationsbank Montgomery Securities also invested $10 million each. A group lead by Neeleman invested $10.2 million.

Talented executives were lured from other airlines. President and chief operating officer David Barger had headed Continental Airlines' operations at Newark International Airport. Other executives were recruited from Southwest. Chief financial officer John Owen had been treasurer there when Southwest was buying Morris Air.

The company copied large chunks of Southwest's playbook. Its cabins would have only one class of seats. It did, however, order Airbus A320 narrowbody jets instead of the similar Boeing 737s used by Southwest, and reportedly got a huge discount from the Europeans in the bargain. Its ambitious first order was for 25 brand new jets with options on another 50. On many routes these jets would compete with turboprop-driven planes, deemed less comfortable and perceived as less safe by passengers.

Company Becomes JetBlue in 1999

In mid-July 1999, a new name for ''New Air'' was unveiled at a press conference: JetBlue Airways. ''We're going to bring humanity back to air travel,'' was Neeleman's bold rallying cry. As if that were not enough, JetBlue aimed to undercut other

248

Company Perspectives:

Imagine how you would create an airline if you were building it from scratch. No ridiculous promises of "self-actualization" onboard, no exorbitant airfares, no cattle-train mentality, no hassles. In their place, add simplicity, friendly people, technology, design, and entertainment. JetBlue is a different kind of airline ... younger, fresher, more innovative. We're looking at creative ways to reduce the hassles of flying and simplify the travel experience. So, we're looking for creative, dynamic people to work with us to help develop the airline that brings humanity back to air travel. JetBlue embraces five values that represent the company and create our unique culture: Safety; Caring; Integrity; Fun; Passion. These five values not only differentiate JetBlue's product; they result in a superior customer and crew member experience.

airlines' fares by an average of 65 percent. JetBlue claimed to be primarily aiming to stimulate air traffic like Southwest, rather than stealing existing passengers from the established airlines.

For its base, JetBlue chose John F. Kennedy International Airport (JFK), which was further from Manhattan than LaGuardia but still busier than the out-of-the way airports favored by Southwest. In September 1999, the Department of Transportation awarded JetBlue 75 takeoff and landing slots at JFK. The carrier received an exemption allowing it operate there between the peak hours of 3 p.m. and 8 p.m. (Neeleman observed that the non-peak hours were quite suitable for quick turnarounds.)

Senator Charles Schumer (D-N.Y.), who had pledged to press for better air service to upstate New York in his election campaign, helped JetBlue finagle the slots. "In New York," Neeleman was quoted in *Airfinance Journal*, "people have been ripped off like crazy. There is no low-fare interstate market." Remembering advice from Southwest Airlines chairman Herb Kelleher, Neeleman quickly established a lobbying team for the airline in Washington, D.C.

JetBlue leased gates formerly used by TWA from United Airlines. JFK was undergoing a $10 billion building program that promised to give JetBlue part ownership in a terminal contingent on obtaining financing for it. JetBlue would rely on electronic reservations and ticketing to keep costs down. Neeleman had been CEO of the Open Skies reservation system for four years before it was sold to Hewlett Packard Co. This system allowed passengers to make reservations via Internet or touch-tone phone and could be operated with a tiny information technology (IT) staff, noted *Computerworld*. Within a couple of months of its launch, JetBlue would achieve the second-largest number of Internet bookings in the U.S., after Southwest Airlines.

The company was touted as the first airline launched from scratch in the computer age. Pilots received laptop computers, not manuals, noted *Air Transport World*. A "telemedicine" service from MedAire allowed in-flight consultation with physicians. (Neeleman also maintained a high level of technology at home, where instead of watching television he kept himself and a family of nine children entertained with four networked PCs.)

The in-flight entertainment system boasted 24 channels of live satellite television broadcasts (including A&E, Animal Planet, CNBC, ESPN, the Food Network, Home & Garden, and the Weather Channel, but none of the four major broadcast networks) at every seat, a first among airlines, which usually aired taped shows. LiveTV, a joint venture between the Harris Corporation and Sextant In-Flight Systems, provided the service.

The airline would serve no meals but did offer gourmet blue potato chips and soda. All-leather seats, more legroom, and larger overhead bins were some of JetBlue's other attractive amenities. These and the company's marketing savvy brought it into comparison with Virgin Atlantic Airways, from which the company had in fact obtained some key personnel. One perk JetBlue did lack was a frequent flyer program, so tempting to high-mileage business travelers.

Wheeling in 2000

JetBlue began flying in early 2000 with just two newly leased Airbus A320s. It launched its first route, New York to Fort Lauderdale, Florida, on February 11. Advance-sale, one-way fare was $79. Six days later, the company began service to Buffalo for $49 each way.

Business grew rapidly in JetBlue's first year in the sky. The company's 300 call center employees in Salt Lake City, who had the option of working at home and saving the company overhead, were receiving 12,000 calls a day. Still, the company was booking 40 percent of its business over the Web, according to *Informationweek*.

In December 2000, Neeleman announced JetBlue's millionth customer and third profitable month—an amazing achievement in so short a time for the airline business. (By contrast, rising fuel prices forced startup National Airlines into bankruptcy in 2000.) It reported about $100 million in revenues but no annual profit yet. By this time, the company was flying to ten destinations. In February 2001, JetBlue filled a higher percentage of its seats (79.9 percent) than any other U.S. carrier. Further, the "JetBlue" effect was credited with lower fares and increasing service at other airlines operating in New York.

Flush with initial success, the company aimed even higher. It planned to acquire a new plane every five weeks until 2008. By June 2001, it was operating a fleet of fourteen planes with 76 flights a day through JFK. Most were leased, since Airbus was unable to deliver enough new planes in time. At the Paris Air Show in June 2001, JetBlue announced plans to buy as many as 48 planes for as much as $2.5 billion. At the time, the company had another 68 planes already on order and 15 in service.

The company preferred to increase flight frequency on existing routes rather than quickly expanding the number of markets served. It only planned to add half a dozen destinations in 2001 to the eleven it started in its first year.

A slowdown developing in the general economy worried some analysts; Neeleman countered that low end of the air travel market would be a good position in which to weather a recession. Holly Hegeman, chief executive of PlaneBusiness.com, agreed. "These hard economic times are nirvana for JetBlue," she told the *Seattle Times*. "Nothing makes people

---

Key Dates:

1999: Utah entrepreneur David Neeleman creates JetBlue.
2000: JetBlue begins flying to routes in New York and Florida.
2001: JetBlue opens second base in Long Beach, California.

---

happier than flying on an airline that makes them feel like they are getting a great deal for their money.'' Neeleman was planning to take the company public within two years, reported *Time*.

In July 2001, a new five-year, $60 million lease with the Port Authority of New York and New Jersey gave JetBlue control of its own terminal at JFK. (The airline would then lease a few gates to United.) JetBlue had feared it would soon run out of gate space at JFK by the end of the year, prompting it to open a second base at California's underutilized Long Beach Airport in August 2001. It still had not dared to take on the majors on their own home bases for fear of a price and capacity war.

Principal Competitors

AMR Corporation; Southwest Airlines Co.; UAL Corporation.

Further Reading

Beck, Rachel, ''Bargain Airline Flies High; Blue Skies of Happiness,'' *Seattle Times*, August 7, 2001, p. D1.

Brown, Eryn, ''A Smokeless Herb,'' *Fortune*, May 28, 2001, pp. 78–79.

Deck, Stewart, ''New Low-Fare Airline to Be Quite High Tech,'' *Computerworld*, September 6, 1999, p. 20.

Donnelly, Sally B., ''Blue Skies,'' *Time*, July 30, 2001, 24–27.

Dwyer, Rob, ''Blue Skies,'' *Airfinance Journal*, April 2000, pp. 26–29.

Feldman, Joan M., ''JetBlue Loves New York,'' *Air Transport World*, June 2001, pp. 78–81.

Goetzl, David, ''JetBlue's Growth Strategy: Low Prices and High Loyalty,'' *Advertising Age*, October 23, 2000, pp. 4, 90.

Harris, Elana, ''Undercutting the Competition,'' *Sales and Marketing Management*, November 2000, p. 14.

''Innovators Time 100: The Next Wave: Upstart with a Difference,'' *Time*, January 22, 2001, pp. 64–65.

Kalita, S. Mitra, ''JetBlue Plans Buying Spree, Could More Than Triple Its Fleet'' *Newsday*, June 19, 2001, p. A41.

——, ''JetBlue's Expansion Ready for Takeoff; Kew Gardens Airline Lands 5-Year, $60 Million Lease for Its Own Terminal at JFK,'' *Newsday*, July 31, 2001, p. A37.

Leonhardt, David, ''Live Television, Aloft,'' *New York Times*, June 3, 2001.

L'Heureux, Dave, ''Airport Leader High on JetBlue,'' *The State* (Columbia, S.C.), July 21, 1999, pp. B6, B10.

Lipowicz, Alice, ''Bargain Airline Prepares for Takeoff from Kennedy,'' *Crain's New York Business*, January 24, 2000, p. 4.

Sweat, Jeff, ''Innovators and Influencers 2001: Generation Dot-Com Gets Its Wings,'' *Informationweek*, January 1, 2001, p. 42.

Zuckerman, Laurence, ''Ambitious Low-Fare Carrier Names Itself JetBlue Airways,'' *New York Times*, July 15, 1999, p. 9.

——, ''JetBlue to Expand in West,'' *Deseret News* (Salt Lake City), May 23, 2001.

—Frederick C. Ingram

Kamps AG

Prinzenallee 13
D-40549 Düsseldorf
Germany
Telephone: (49) (211) 530-634-0
Fax: (49) (231) 530-634-34
Web site: http://www.kamps.de

Public Company
Incorporated: 1982 as Kamps GmbH
Employees: 16,188
Sales: EUR 1.50 billion ($1.41 billion) (2000)
Stock Exchanges: Frankfurt
Ticker Symbol: KAM
NAIC: 311811 Retail Bakeries; 311812 Commercial
  Bakeries

Kamps AG sees itself as Europe's largest bakery group with leading market positions in western Germany and the Netherlands. Kamps AG's main revenue source are the company's retail chain bakeries in Germany and the Netherlands, which generate about three quarters of total sales. Kamps AG's German retail bakeries have a market share of about 20 percent in the Rhine and Ruhr areas, Northern Hesse and Hamburg, and about 16 percent in Berlin. About 1,200 sales outlets in Germany belong to the Kamps group, about 80 percent of which are franchises. About three-fifths of them are independent sales branches while 40 percent of them are in shop-in-shop settings such as supermarkets, department stores, and shopping malls. Kamps AG's Wendeln subsidiary is Germany's leading industrial baker which delivers pre-packaged bread and other baked goods to supermarkets through its national distribution network, including the popular brands ''Golden Toast'' and ''Lieken Urkorn.'' The company also has a strong foothold in France through its 49 percent shareholding in the French Harry's group, the market leader in the industrial baked goods segment. Through Harry's, Kamps also has an interest in the Italian baked goods manufacturer Morato Pane. Kamps AG's management owns about 16 percent of the company's shares with founder and CEO Heiner Kamps being the biggest single shareholder.

Founding, Sale, and Management Buy-Out: 1982–1996

The history of Kamps AG reads like a modern fairy tale from Wall Street, but it began in the small Westphalian town of Bocholt, Germany. The company founder, Heiner Kamps, was the oldest son of a baker who ran a small family business in the country. He learned the craft from his father, but didn't want to take over the business from him and was looking for ways to escape small town life. A water sports enthusiast, Kamps took jobs in cities where good water ball was being played, such as Duisburg, Berlin, Würzburg, and Cologne. Besides pursuing his passion, he kept on learning the baker's craft and received his master baker certificate in 1979. He went to business school and finally settled down in Düsseldorf where he took over a small bakery and founded his own retail bakery company under the name Kamps GmbH in 1982.

The success of his shop was partly due to an innovation. So far, it was common in the German bakery trade that everything to be sold that day was baked early in the morning. That's why really fresh baked goods were only available during the morning hours. Kamps had a better idea. He wanted his customers to be able to buy fresh baked goods throughout the day. He put an oven right behind the sales counter and kept it running all day, so customers could see—and smell—the fresh bread, rolls, and sweet snacks coming out of the oven. His idea took off and within a decade became a standard in many German bakeries.

After only ten years, Kamps' enterprise had become Düsseldorf's biggest retail bakery chain, consisting of more than 20 branches, bringing in DM 22 million in sales. However, in 1992 Heiner Kamps decided to sell his company to U.S.-food giant Borden Inc. for DM 22 million. Borden was trying to strengthen its fastest growing European business with sweet snacks and specialty breads. Heiner Kamps became the CEO of Borden's German subsidiary, Wilhelm Weber GmbH, located in Pfungstadt. At that time Weber operated five regional retail bakery chains in Germany, including Nuschelberg, Stefansback, Nur Hier, Lecker Bäcker, and Wriedeler, with a total of more than 300 branches. The company was also among Germany's leading industrial bakeries, supplying packaged baked goods to supermarkets under the brand names ''Weber,'' ''Jaus,'' and ''Golden Toast.'' For four years Heiner Kamps managed and expanded Borden's Weber subsidiary, learning the bakery business U.S. style. He learned about raising venture capital, going public, and management buy-outs. Four years later his turn came again. By 1996, Weber had become Germany's second largest baked goods group. However, Borden's new majority shareholders, investment group Kohlberg, Kravis & Roberts, lost interest in the German market, trying to streamline the company's activities. In 1996, Borden decided to dissolve its German subsidiary. Its industrial baked goods division was sold to Germany's largest industrial baker, the Garel-based Wendeln Grossbäckerei. Heiner Kamps, together with a few management colleagues and equipped with the necessary venture capital provided by Düsseldorf-based bank Bankhaus Lampe and investment firm Apax Partners & Co. in Munich, bought the retail bakery business in a management buy-out.

Kamps AG Goes Public in 1998

The former Weber branches in Hamburg, Stuttgart, Nuremberg, and Weissenfels and the Kamps outlets in Düsseldorf, which altogether generated about DM 320 million per year in sales in 1996, were re-organized at the end of 1996 under the umbrella of a newly founded holding company named BBG Bäckerei Beteiligungsgesellschaft mbH. BBG based in Düsseldorf was by far the largest retail bakery group in Germany. The CEOs of the different chains held a total share of 20 percent in BBG. The two financial investors, Lampe and Apax, held the rest. Heiner Kamps, the new CEO of BBG, and his colleagues were ambitious. In an utterly stagnating market, they were up for growth, but in order to grow they needed more capital.

When Heiner Kamps first approached German stock market analysts, they didn't seem to take him seriously. The argument Kamps got to hear most of the time was that bakeries were not an expanding market and were a rather awkward, old-fashioned industry. However, in order to expand further, Kamps needed more capital and the only way to get it was by going public. The transformation of BBG into the legal form of a public company was only logical. Effective December 23, 1997, BBG became Kamps AG. At the company's first general meeting in March 1998 its capital base was increased to DM 20 million derived from its own funds. The company's capital was again extended by DM 5 million in April 1998, just before Kamps AG went public at the Frankfurt/Main stock exchange, which brought the company a financial boost of DM 166 million. However, after the Initial Public Offering (IPO) on April 8, 1998, the value of Kamps shares did not move much for weeks. At a high time for Internet and telecommunications IPOs, investors didn't seem to

care about specialty breads. However, half a year later investors started to notice and the value of Kamps shares grew by 350 percent.

Further National Expansion After 1998

Encouraged by the success on the German ''Wall Street,'' Heiner Kamps discovered his passion for company-shopping. Within only 15 months, he spent the money the company had raised to acquire several German and Dutch retail bakery chains. The time when Kamps started his consolidation coup was right. The German market for bakery products was stagnating at about DM 26 billion. Many players in the sleepy industry, which was dominated by mainly small family businesses and a few regional chains, were confronted with stagnating or declining revenues and many were struggling to survive. Others had a hard time finding successors who would carry on their business. At the same time, competition had become more fierce. Industry insiders estimated that an independent master baker with one to a handful of local sales outlets needed to attract about 3,000 customers to be profitable. The more cost-efficient regional retail bakery chains needed to attract only half the number of customers to break even. Bakers who wanted to stay in the market were pressed to continuously cut costs by investing in new equipment. However, for the above reasons, the majority had a hard time getting the necessary loans from their banks. In that situation, many bakers were delighted to sell out and hand their businesses over to Kamps.

Kamps' shopping list read like a *Who's Who* of German retail bakeries: Berlin's two competitors Thoben Kuchen with 50 sales outlets and DM 50 million in sales and Ostrowski with 85 shops and DM 42 million in revenues; Dortmund's Klems bakery chain with 75 branches and sales of DM 50 million; Schwalmthaler Backhaus with 175 shops in the lower Rhine region generating DM 100 million in revenues; Ratingen-based Backpartner with 148 outlets in the Ruhr around Cologne and Düsseldorf and DM 80 million in sales; Heilbronn's Weltin bakery with 15 branches and DM 7 million in revenues; as well as smaller chains, including Cologne-based Winkel-Potthoff, Nicolay in Bonn, Kautsch located in Mannheim, and Krefeld-based Berns.

After taking over a new retail chain, Kamps always employed the same pattern. The first step was to hire new management staff. Next, cost-intensive products were eliminated from the shelf. Finally, loss-generating sales outlets were closed down. The integration of the new outlets into Kamps' logistics system also helped cut cost since delivery costs were a big factor for bakeries, estimated at about 30 percent of total costs. The closer together the sales outlets were, the cheaper were the transportation costs between production facility and bakery shops. Another cost-saving factor was that Kamps was able to realize lower prices from producers of raw materials. His integration concept enabled Kamps to boost sales by 20 to 30 percent within only a few weeks of taking over a new regional chain.

Becoming Europe's Largest Bakery in 2000

Kamps had taken the industry by storm. In the 1980s, DM 100 million was believed to be the absolute maximum a large bakery could possibly generate a year. Between 1998 and 1999, Kamps'

Key Dates:

1982: The first Kamps retail bakery branch opens in Düsseldorf.
1992: Heiner Kamps sells his company to US-food giant Borden Inc.
1996: The founder buys his company back in an MBO
1997: Initial Public Offering of Kamps AG in Frankfurt Main.
2000: Kamps AG takes over industrial baker Wendeln Group; the company acquires a 49 percent share in French industrial baker Harry's.

sales doubled from DM 169 million to DM 341 million. The number of the company's production sites went up from 783 to 1,940, and the number of Kamps' employees increased from 3,849 to 6,229 in the same period of time. However, this was not the end of the story. In the following year, Kamps AG acquired the debt-free Wendeln Group, Germany's largest industrial bakery which had taken over part of Borden's Weber subsidiary three years earlier, for an estimated DM 2.1 billion. Wendeln Group manufactured pre-packaged bread, cakes, and pastries in 29 production facilities, and through its 47 distribution centers supplied some 27,000 supermarkets and grocery stores throughout Germany. With about 11,000 employees on their payroll, Wendeln owned the national brands "Golden Toast" and "Lieken Urkorn" and dominated the industrial baked goods segment with a market share of about one-fifth. Wendeln's factory in Günzburg supplied all German McDonald's outlets with hamburger rolls. With this transaction Kamps AG became Germany's largest bakery, but Kamps wanted more.

Kamps' international expansion had begun in 1999 when the company ventured into the Netherlands. In that year Kamps took over the Dutch Bakker Bart Food Group, the market leader in that country's baking trade. Bakker Bart owned more than 720 sales outlets in the Netherlands, about 80 percent of which were stands at markets. Three more acquisitions in the Netherlands followed, including the bakeries Schothius, Quality Bakers, and Bäckerei Vogel, with combined annual sales of about DM 407 million. After Kamps had reached a leading position in the Dutch market, his next target was France. In 2000, the company acquired a 49 percent interest in French industrial bakery group Harry's with an option to the remaining 51 percent. Harry's, however, was not only active in France. The company owned eleven production facilities in seven European countries, generating about DM 900 million in revenues per year. Finally, Kamps—via Harry's—bought Italian baked goods manufacturer Morato Pane. Within just over two years, Kamps had become Europe's largest baker, pushing its sales up twelve-fold to reach almost four billion German Marks.

Explosive Growth Stops in Late 2000

Heiner Kamps' expansion coup did not only cause sympathy. The German baker trade had applauded when Kamps' takeover of the two Berlin rivals Thoben and Ostrowsky suddenly ended a ruinous price war in the capital. But when Kamps took over the Wendeln group, they changed their mind, since

industrial bakeries were the arch-enemy of the family-driven part of the trade. The same happened with Kamps investors. When Heiner Kamps asked them for more money to cover the expenses of integrating the new acquisitions into the group in 1999, they gave him DM 300 million. However, Kamps ran out of money again to finance even more acquisitions. In April 2000 the company raised more money to finance the Wendeln deal through a stock split.

After the mega-deal, many of those who formerly sympathized with Kamps' strategy became more skeptical. While retail bakeries were his field of expertise, industrial bakeries were a subject of their own. Unlike retail bakeries, they relied on the big retail giants to get their products on the supermarket shelves and were able to realize significantly smaller profit margins. Many analysts and investors were afraid that the explosive expansion was a bad move and diminished confidence in the company's future success potential. Not only did Kamps get heavily into debt for the Wendeln and Harry's takeovers but also the company generated a DM 70 million loss which was balanced out with cash reserves in 1999. By mid-2000 it became clear that the integration of the company's purchases would take longer and cost more than expected. The negotiations with big mineral oil concerns about Kamps plan to sell baked goods at 1,000 German gas stations under the "Bakerstreet" brand didn't seem to move forward fast enough. Then, in fall 2000, the Kamps board of directors approved fundamental changes in the company's bookkeeping, which critics saw as a way to manipulate its balance sheets. The stock market's reaction was sudden. After a dynamic upswing between Kamps AG's IPO and February 2000, when Kamps shares grew tenfold in value, reaching a peak of up to EUR 46 a piece, the value of Kamps shares lost over 75 percent of its value within a year, with lows under EUR 10, reaching about EUR 11 in April 2001.

Heiner Kamps seemed to be unimpressed with the spreading skepticism about his strategy. The company announced in July 2001 that due to delays in the realization of the expected synergies Kamps reduced its profit expectations for that year, but didn't question that its ambitious plans would finally materialize. Heiner Kamps used his new position as a public figure to establish "Brot gegen Not," meaning "bread against hardship," a private foundation supported by the UNESCO. Kamps used discarded bakery equipment to set up an educational bakery in Namibia for areas with malnutrition and planned to set up similar facilities in Brazil, Pakistan, and Romania. He shared his vision of the ideal bakery with *Die Woche's* Lutz Spenneberg: the communication center of the neighborhood where packages are delivered for absent neighbors, where kids deposit their fanny packs and mothers their house keys. Even Internet terminals might have a place there, where customers—while sipping their coffee and enjoying a Kamps pastry—could reserve theater tickets or find out what is at the movies. At the beginning of 2001, Kamps was convinced that he had outperformed—or bought up—any potential competitor. He envisioned the yellow pretzel, the company's logo, all over Europe, including France, Spain, Italy, and even Russia. The main question many insiders asked was if Kamps wanted to stay in his niche, or build a food concern and compete with big name multinationals such as Nestlé or Kraft Foods.

Principal Subsidiaries

Kamps Nord GmbH & Co. KG; Kamps Südwest GmbH & Co. KG; Kamps Nordhessen GmbH; Kamps Berlin GmbH; Kamps Rheinland GmbH; Kamps Bonn GmbH; Kamps Niederrhein GmbH; Kamps Westfalen GmbH & Co. KG; Wendeln Brot und Backwaren GmbH & Co. KG; Wilhelm Weber GmbH; Hubert Zimmermann Toastbrotfabrik GmbH & Co. KG (95%); F. Dahlhoff GmbH & Co. KG; Market Food Group (Netherlands); Bart's Retail BV (Netherlands); Kamps International NV (Netherlands); Bakkerij Arie Bertram BV (Netherlands); Bakker Bruinsma BV (Netherlands); Bakkerij Schothius BV (Netherlands); Bakkerij Schothius Niuw-Amsterdam BV (Netherlands); Quality Bakers Europe BV (Netherlands); Harry's SA (France; 49%); Carrs Foods Ltd. (U.K.; 49%); Fresh Cake AS (Turkey; 24.5%); Dan Cake A/S (Denmark; 49%).

Principal Competitors

Harry Brot GmbH; Müller-Brot GmbH; Wiener Feinbäckerei Heberer; Kronenbrot KG.

Further Reading

"Borden Acquires German Retail Bakery Chain," *Business Wire,* October 10, 1992.

Hoffmann, Kurt, "Filialisten auf Einkaufstour," *Lebensmittel Zeitung,* February 27, 1998, p. 38.

"Kamps-Aktionäre ein Jahr nach Going Public mit Vorstand zufrieden," *vwd,* March 30, 1999.

"Kamps expandiert mit Ostrowski," *Lebensmittel Zeitung,* October 16, 1998, p. 22.

"Kamps geht als erste Bäckerei an die Börse," Frankfurter Allgemeine Zeitung, March 26, 1998, p. 29.

" 'Kamps' wird bundesweite Marke," Lebensmittel Zeitung, March 5, 1999, p. 22.

Kerbusk, Klaus-Peter, "Unschuld verloren," *Der Spiegel,* September 13, 1999, p. 124.

Schlitt, Petra, "Grosse Brötchen," *Manager Magazin,* January 1, 2001, p. 116.

Spenneberg, Lutz, "Der grösste Verführer," *Die Woche,* April 27, 2001, p. 14.

"Weber geht an die Wendeln-Gruppe," *Lebensmittel Zeitung,* December 27, 1996, p. 12.

Weber, Stefan, "Kamps backt mehr als grosse Brötchen," *Süddeutsche Zeitung,* September 11, 1999, p. 29.

"Wendeln übernimmt Teile von Weber," *Handelsblatt,* December 20, 1996.

—Evelyn Hauser

Kidde plc

Mathisen Way, Colnbrook
Slough, Berkshire SL3 OHB
United Kingdom
Telephone: 44 (0) 1753 689 848
Fax: 44 (0) 1753 682 572
Web site: http://www.kidde.com

Public Company
Incorporated: 1968 as Walter Kidde & Co., Inc.
Employees: 6,921
Sales: $1.6 billion (2001)
Stock Exchanges: London
Ticker Symbol: KID
NAIC: 334512 Automatic Environmental Control
Manufacturing for Residential, Commercial, and
Appliance Use; 339999 All Other Miscellaneous
Manufacturing

Kidde plc, formed in 2000 by the demerger of Williams plc, is a leading global supplier of fire safety products and services, serving industrial, commercial, aerospace, combustion control, and retail customers. Operating over 50 business units in 20 countries, Kidde's product line includes smoke alarms, carbon monoxide detectors, portable fire extinguishers, breathing systems, industrial explosion protection systems, sprinkler systems, and emission monitoring systems. Kidde's major divisions include North American Fire Protection; European Fire Protection; Aerospace, Specialist, and Emerging Markets; and Residential and Commercial Fire Protection. Walter Kidde began his company in 1900 with only $300 in savings, a degree from Stevens Institute of Technology, and an interest in the construction industry. However, Kidde's business acumen helped push Kidde, Inc. into the ranks of Fortune 500 companies within the United States.

Expansion into the Fire Fighting Industry: Early 1990s

The New York construction company that Walter Kidde established in 1900 grew quickly into another area of interest.

Kidde began to expand into the business of fire fighting, which became the catalyst for his company's rapid growth and development. In 1918, Kidde, Inc., then Walter Kidde & Company, purchased the rights to the "Rich" system for detecting fires on board ships. This method of extinguishing fires by steam had one major flaw, namely, steam caused extensive damage to the ship's cargo. Kidde's answer to this problem was to use carbon dioxide instead of steam as a means of smothering the fire without damaging the cargo.

While Kidde had made advances in solving the problems confronting effective fire fighting, he still faced another major hurdle. The carbon dioxide was not being released quickly enough from its container and therefore the extinguishing process was not completely successful. In 1923, Kidde solved this problem by purchasing the patent rights for a siphon device that allowed quick release of the carbon dioxide. With this new addition to the design of its extinguishers, Walter Kidde & Company achieved two manufacturing firsts: in 1924 the first portable carbon dioxide fire extinguisher was produced, and in 1925 the first built-in industrial system was installed. In addition, the company began winning government contracts. In 1926, Walter Kidde & Company along with the Navy, designed a system to protect airplane engines against fires.

With these new developments in the fire extinguisher aspect of the company, Kidde separated the fire-fighting business from the construction business but kept the original name. This was just the beginning of the multi-interest outlook that was later to become the trademark of Kidde, Inc into the 1980s.

The 1930s were profitable years for Walter Kidde & Company. By 1940, the company had 200 sales agencies in the United States and major cities in Europe, South America, Africa, and Asia. Subsidiary sales companies were also located in Canada, Germany, and Italy, and two factories were producing products in England.

Growth During World War II

In particular, World War II had a significant impact on the growth of the company. Prior to the war 30 percent of the company's extinguisher sales were to the U.S. government. In 1938, Walter Kidde & Company had its best year with sales of

---

Company Perspectives:

Our mission is to make the world a safer place. To do this, we strive to deliver the highest levels of product and service excellence. People and businesses everywhere trust our brands and depend on our expertise to protect what's most valuable to them.

$2 million and a work force of 450. It was in this year that Walter Kidde wondered whether or not he was "smart enough to run a $5 million business," as he pondered the inevitable expansion of his company.

Five short years later, sales far exceeded the $5 million mark. By 1943, Walter Kidde & Company was producing $60 million worth of war equipment and the work force had increased to 5,000. The transition to war-time production was not an easy one; however, once the war began, production and demand for Kidde's products grew rapidly. So rapidly, in fact, that production of war equipment could not meet demand, and the company was often behind schedule. This was in part due to the company's need to adapt their peace time products to war uses.

Although production may have been slower than demand, the products manufactured by Walter Kidde & Company did play an important role in the war. In addition to the fire detection and extinguishing equipment for tanks, planes, and ships, Walter Kidde & Company also manufactured inflation devices for life rafts and safety belts. The company is credited with manufacturing the automatically inflated rubber life boats from which Captain Eddie Rickenbacker, a World War I hero and flying ace, and his seven companions were rescued after spending three weeks in the South Pacific when their airplane ran out of fuel.

Walter Kidde's concern over whether he was capable of running a $5 million business was clearly answered by 1943. The company was headed for a profitable future. While Walter Kidde may have been reticent about his potential as a businessman, his ability to discern future trends and developments assisted him in the growth of his own company. In 1939, he predicted the demand for labor-saving machinery, and the future of the "one-man-push-button-controlled plants" that would create individual working efficiency.

Kidde's ability in the private sector was enhanced by his involvement in the public sector. He was chairman of the board of trustees of Stevens Institute of Technology; a member of the New Jersey advisory board of the Public Works Administration; and president of the New Jersey Chamber of Commerce from 1935 to 1938. He also declined an offer to be the New Jersey Republican candidate for governor in 1927. His interest in making things work was underlined by his success in reorganizing the bankrupt New York, Susquehanna & Western Railroad, of which he was a trustee, and restoring it to a paying basis in 1937. In 1943, the year his company reached peak production figures, Kidde died at the age of 65 from a heart attack, and the company was handed over to his son, John Kidde.

As expected, the drop in production at the end of the war caused a dramatic drop in Walter Kidde & Company sales. In the 1950s the company diversified into areas of machinery and tool manufacturing, siphon devices for consumer and medical uses, and aircraft accessories. Fire extinguishers were still an important part of the company. However, in general, the activity of the company had markedly decreased. In 1959, sales reached the $40 million mark and did not change until 1964 when a new president was brought on board.

Changes Under New Management: 1964–1980s

In January 1964, there were several new changes at Kidde, changes that would affect the size and outlook of a company that had not experienced many since the war. Although Walter Kidde & Company was considered to be a firmly established company with an excellent reputation, it was also considered to be a company that needed direction.

Fred Sullivan, at that time an officer and director of the large conglomerate Litton Industries, was attracted to the idea of "defining" a new direction for the company. Sullivan was so interested in this new opportunity that he succeeded the late Robert L. Dickson, who had been president of the company since 1961.

Sullivan's rise to Kidde's top leadership is a classic story. He began by working as a $14-a-week clerk during the Depression at Monroe Calculating Machine Company, which was then the number one company of its kind. After 10 years at night school, Sullivan earned his BA degree at Rutgers, and a rare MBA at New York University. At the age of 39 he was president of Monroe. When Monroe merged with Litton Industries in 1958, Sullivan became an officer and director of the company until he left in 1964 to assume a new position at Walter Kidde & Company.

From the time Sullivan began his presidency at Kidde, acquisition and growth were elements of his primary strategy. His management style was described by *Forbes* magazine as "no-frills, tight-with-a-buck, keep it lean and liquid." This style meant reducing the work force by 10 percent and reorganizing the entire company upon his arrival at Kidde.

Sullivan's reorganization plans included the need to think in terms of customer markets instead of product lines. Prior to Sullivan's presidency, the company had separate lines for burglar alarms and fire protection services. One of the first initiatives of the company reorganization was to combine these two lines. This new definition of the protection field resulted in acquisitions of lock and safe companies by the close of the 1960s.

Under Sullivan's direction, Kidde quickly grew from a fire extinguisher concern of $40 million in annual revenues in 1964 to $400 million by 1968, when the company was incorporated as Kidde & Company. Inc. Some of the larger acquisitions of the 1960s included Dura Corporation, which manufactures auto parts and testing equipment; Lighting Corporation of America; and Grove Manufacturing Company, which manufactures hydraulic cranes. In particular, Grove became an important acquisition for Kidde because of its lucrative contracts with the U.S. government in the 1980s.

Key Dates:

1900: Walter Kidde establishes a construction company.
1918: Walter Kidde & Co. purchases the rights to a system that detects fires aboard ships.
1926: The firm and the U.S. Navy develop a system to protect airplane engines against fires.
1938: The company's sales reach $2 million.
1943: Walter Kidde dies, and his son John takes over the company.
1964: Fred Sullivan becomes president of the firm.
1968: Company incorporates as Kidde & Company, Inc.
1969: Kidde acquires U.S. Lines.
1980: The firm officially adopts the name Kidde, Inc.
1981: The company moves into the energy industry with the purchase of Oilfield Industries Lines Inc.
1985: Five operating units are sold to compensate for $400 million in losses.
1987: Hanson Industries buys Kidde for $1.7 billion.
1988: Williams Holdings plc purchases Kidde's fire protection business from Hanson.
1990: Subsidiary Walter Kidde Aerospace Inc. expands, creating a Production and Technology Center.
1992: Sullivan is named in an insider trading scandal involving Kidde securities.
1999: Tyco International makes a bid for Williams.
2000: Williams demerges, and Kidde plc is formed and trades independently on the London Stock Exchange.
2001: Kidde acquires Fire Protection Services Ltd.

Kidde's fast rate of growth placed it in a unique position. While most large companies reach the Fortune 500 list after many years of development, Kidde just missed this notable ranking in 1965, a year after Sullivan's move into the company. *Fortune* magazine reported that Kidde was ranked 501 on the list that year and missed being 500 by $60,000, the price of one of Kidde's burglar-alarm systems for a large company. One year later, Kidde not only made it onto the list, but ranked 283.

One of Kidde's most problematic acquisitions was made in 1969 when it purchased U.S. Lines, a major but financially troubled transportation system. Sullivan was later to label this acquisition a "grave mistake." It was an acquisition that resulted in eight years of frustration and litigation. The U.S. Lines acquisition was, at the time, an attractive investment for Kidde because of its future earning potential as a container transportation system.

Although Kidde was apparently looking into the future when it made this acquisition, it did not seem to fit the Kidde formula of buying companies with a "proven record of successful growth faster than the GNP." Kidde competitors looked on in disbelief, feeling sure that Kidde had decided incorrectly. However, Sullivan looked past the operating losses of U.S. Lines and into the future of container transportation, which he believed represented a "major building block in a new kind of transportation system that is coming."

When U.S. Lines lost $1.5 million in 1970, Kidde began to look for a buyer. It was not until 1978 that a sale took place, and even though the shipping company had started to earn money again in the 1970s, Kidde was determined to sell it. The buyer was Malcolm McLean, who had founded Sea-Land Service. Inc., one of the U.S. Lines competitors. U.S. Lines was sold for $111 million, and the general analysis of the sale was that Kidde, and Sullivan, had managed to turn a potential disaster into a profit.

Kidde's sale of U.S. Lines was timely. With the emergence of the recession Kidde found itself in the enviable position of being in good in financial condition. This was also due to Kidde's decentralized approach and the careful acquisitions made in the late 1970s. Overall, Kidde purchased ten businesses in 1979, one of which included Victor Comptometer, which was right behind Sharp Electronics, the leader in sales of desktop calculators.

By 1980, the company had adopted Kidde, Inc. as its title and was making solid profits in its recreational and consumer lines, such as Farberware cookery, Jacuzzi water therapy equipment, Bear archery equipment, and Sargent locks. Sullivan was not concerned that the company was too diversified. He believed that his decentralized approach to managing the Kidde subsidiaries helped to keep the subsidiaries "responsible and profitable." The group managers were considered to be corporate-level executives who had offices at the leading corporation within their group, and not at the New Jersey headquarters. This management style allowed Sullivan to maintain control of the subsidiaries, but it also allowed for decision-making at the local level.

While consumer and recreational products were doing well for the company, Kidde made a move away from this market in 1981 into the energy and industrial markets. Kidde's Grove Manufacturing purchased Oilfield Industrial Lines Inc. that same year and began its oil rig business. Although Kidde was affected when the price of oil dropped in 1982, the company promptly moved into oil and gas exploration as a way in which to establish a market for its own rigs. However, the plan failed, and the blame was placed on the explorers, who were considered to be novices. This failed expansion into oil and gas exploration resulted in the sale of five operating units to compensate for the 1985 losses of $400 million.

While Kidde's entrance into the oil industry was not successful, and its future financial stability was questioned because of such a major loss, the 80 new businesses that had been acquired by the company since Sullivan joined the firm in 1964 had established Kidde as a solid, diversified conglomerate. Even though new developments for Kidde Inc. depended on its ability to recover from the oil and gas exploration setback, management pledged to continue its diversification and growth strategy.

Kidde Falls Under New Ownership: 1987–88

In July 1987, however, Sullivan announced that Kidde was studying options such as reorganization or selling off some or all its assets. Sure enough, in August of that year, Hanson Industries, the U.S. arm of Hanson Trust of the United Kingdom, bought Kidde in a $1.7 billion deal. Sir Gordon White, the chairman of Hanson Industries, commented on the good match of the two groups' operations and said that Kidde would be kept largely intact. Some of Hanson's previous takeovers, however, were paid for in part by disposing of unwanted assets, leaving Kidde's future uncertain.

Hanson's ownership of the diversified conglomerate—at the time of the deal Kidde had over 100 subsidiaries—was short lived. In January 1988, Hanson sold the first of its Kidde holdings, the Computrol manufacturing unit, for $2.2 million. Hanson continued to restructure Kidde operations, selling off bits and pieces of the once highly-diversified group. In August 1988, the firm sold most of the Kidde fire protection business to Pilgrim House Group, a U.K.-based firm involved in electrical products and fire protection. Included in the deal was the Walter Kidde North America Group, Fenwal Inc., and Kidde's Fire Protection Group Europe. Pilgrim House, however, was purchased by Williams Holdings plc, an industrial management firm, during the Kidde acquisition process, leaving Williams ownership of Kidde.

Left with one of its original business focuses, Kidde emerged in the 1990s as a leading fire protection firm. Williams attributed much of its success to its acquisition of both Pilgrim and Kidde, which turned the UK-based conglomerate into global competitor in the aircraft fire detection and suppression equipment industries.

In 1990, subsidiary Walter Kidde Aerospace Inc. opened a Production and Technology Center, spending $4 million to expand its operations to accommodate increasing demand for aircraft, vehicle, and marine fire protection systems. By that time, Kidde products were found in aircraft such as the B-2 Stealth Bomber and 747-700 airliners.

While Kidde experienced renewed growth under new ownership, it did battle with negative publicity during 1992. Sullivan, the former CEO of Kidde, was named in an insider trading scandal that involved Kidde securities. The charges, which claimed that seven men from various companies earned $13 million from 1987 to 1989 on insider trading tips, cast a dark shadow on the Kidde name. Nevertheless, Kidde's parent company continued to focus on its fire protection business.

By 1996, in fact, Williams had sold off many of its interests to relieve its debt load, enabling it to focus on its security and fire-related businesses. The following year, as part of its new direction, Williams purchased Chubb Security plc. The firm continued to divest home improvement subsidiaries, while relying on both Kidde's and Chubb's core businesses to boost its lagging profits.

The profit bolstering plan never reached fruition and in 1998, Williams began merger talks with competitor Tyco International Ltd. Negotiations between the two collapsed that year and again in 1999 after failed attempts to reach an agreement on price.

When profits dropped by 49 percent in 1999, Williams set plans in motion to break up. Like many U.K.-based conglomerates that experienced great success during the 1980s, Williams unraveled during the late 1990s, joining the likes of other failed companies, including Kidde's former owner Hanson as well as BTR and Wassall.

Independent in the New Millennium

On March 7, 2000, Williams officially announced its breakup, leaving Chubb plc and Kidde to operate independently. The firm adopted the name Kidde plc in September 2000, and listed on the London Stock Exchange in November of that year.

Operating on its own for the first time since the 1980s, Kidde focused on its main business of supplying fire and safety products, systems, and services. Without the weight of its parent company, Kidde appeared to be back on track in its first year of independent operation. Its aerospace and industrial fire protection segments reported strong growth in 2000 and management remained optimistic about future growth. CEO Michael Harper stated in a 2001 *AFX European Focus* article that although the firm was concerned with the growth of the U.S. economy, Kidde's "growing strengths in Europe and South America and the influence of regulation in all our markets give us confidence for the year ahead."

Principal Subsidiaries

AB Svenska Tempus (Sweden); Angus Fire Armour Ltd.; Autronica Fire and Security AS (Norway); Chubb Parsi SA (Spain); Detector Electronics Corp. (U.S.); Eau et Feu (France); Fireye Inc. (U.S.); Forney Corp. (U.S.); FSI Mexicana SA de CV; Fyrnetics (Hong Kong) Ltd.; Guardall SrL (Italy); Guardall Ltd. (Scotland); Heien-Larssen A/S (Norway); Incom Explosionsschutz AG (Switzerland); Industrial de Fosfatos SA de CV (Mexico); Kidde Argentina SA; Kidde-Deugra Brandschutzsysteme GmbH (Germany); Kidde-Fenwal Inc. (U.S.); Kidde Fire Protection Ltd.; Kidde Granviner Ltd.; Kidde Technologies Inc. (U.S.); L'Hotellier (France); National Foam Inc. (U.S.); Noha Norway A/S; Pyrene Corp. (Canada); Resmat Parsch Sistemas Contra Incendio Ltda (Brazil); Samtekno OY (Finland); Sai SpA (Italy); Silvani Antincendi SpA (Italy); Societe Industrielle pour le Development de la Securite (France); Kidde Polska SpZoo (Poland); Walter Kidde Portable Equipment Inc. (U.S.); Williams Fairey Engineering Ltd.; Yanes Minas Industria E Commercio Ltda (Brazil).

Principal Divisions

Aerospace, Specialist, and Emerging Markets; Residential and Commercial; North America Fire Protection; European Fire Protection.

Principal Competitors

Européenne d'Extincteurs SA; McWane Corp.; Tyco International Ltd.

Further Reading

Barker, Thorold, and Philip Coggan, ''Williams Shuffles Quietly Off the Stage as its Audience Fades Away,'' *Financial Times*, March 8, 2000, p. 25.

''Hanson Industries to Sell Kidde Fire Protection For Dlrs 265.8 Million,'' *Universal News Services*, August 16, 1988.

Inder, Richard, ''Williams, Tyco Quit Negotiations Regarding Merger,'' *Wall Street Journal Europe*, July 14, 1999, p. 7.

''Kidde Division Sold for More Than Two Million Dollars,'' *Universal News Services*, January 21, 1988.

''Kidde Starts Year With Strong Order Book, Sales Ahead,'' *AFX European Focus*, March 22, 2001.

Larsen, Peter Thal, ''Williams/Chubb: The Key of the Door,'' *Investors Chronicle*, February 21, 1997, p. 12.

——, "Williams Sale Wipes Out Debt," *Investors Chronicle,* December 6, 1996, p. 9.

Oram, Roderick, and Nikki Tait, "Hanson Pays Dollars 1.7 Billion for US Industrial Group," *Financial Times*, August 6, 1987, p. 1.

"Pilgrim Agrees 331m from Williams Group," *Daily Telegraph,* October 11, 1998, p. 23.

"SEC: Inside Traders Netted $13 Million," *USA Today,* June 5, 1992, p. 2B.

Stewart, Robb M., "Williams Unveils Plans for Breakup as Earnings Drop," *Wall Street Journal Europe,* March 8, 2000, p. 4.

Tait, Nikki, "Williams Holdings Leaps to 116 M Pounds," *Financial Times,* March 8, 1989, p. I26.

"Williams Fires on More Cylinders," *London Times,* February 27, 1990.

"Williams PLC," *Industry Week,* August 17, 1998, p. 77.

—update: Christina M. Stansell

Koala Corporation

11600 East 53rd Avenue, Unit D
Denver, Colorado, 80239
U.S.A.
Telephone: (303) 770-3934
Toll Free: (888) 733-3456
Fax: (303) 574-9000
Web site: http://www.koalabear.com

Public Company
Incorporated: 1986
Employees: 400
Sales: $59.7 million (2000)
Stock Exchanges: NASDAQ
Ticker Symbol: KARE
NAIC: 315999 Other Apparel Accessories and Other
    Apparel Manufacturing; 326199 All Other Plastic
    Product Manufacturing; 337127 Institutional Furniture
    Manufacturing; 337215 Showcase, Partition, Shelving,
    and Locker Manufacturing

Demonstrating that necessity is the mother of invention, Koala Corporation is best known for its signature product, the Koala Bear Kare Baby Changing Station, which was developed in response to the increasing acceptance of infants and toddlers in places other than the nursery or the park. Building on its commitment to ''family-friendly'' products, Koala has moved far beyond its initial baby-changing tables; through a series of acquisitions it has branched out into products such as playground equipment and indoor and outdoor play areas. In the years since the Baby Changing Station was introduced, other companies have entered the market—but Koala still has at least half the market share. Its well-known logo—a smiling, diaper-clad koala—is recognized in some 50 countries.

Early Days: A Practical Solution

The history of Koala goes back to 1986, when four Minnesota businessmen formed a company in St. Paul called JBJ Industries. JBJ sold one product—a baby-changing table that

could be attached to walls in public restrooms. Until perhaps the late 1970s, infants and toddlers were not as ubiquitous as they were by the beginning of the twenty-first century. Most families were still the traditional two-parent, one-breadwinner model. Most people would never think to bring their babies with them to shopping malls, restaurants, or other businesses.

As a growing number of families moved into the two-income model, society's view of infants and toddlers in public began to change. People still had to go to stores, and people still wanted to go to movies and restaurants. But they were less willing to leave their children at home. Partly they wanted to have more time with their children, but partly it was no longer as easy to leave toddlers home. Parents hear the phrase ''try finding a baby-sitter'' from their friends as frequently as they hear ''are we there yet?'' from their children.

One of the challenges of going out shopping with an infant is how and where to change diapers. Counter tops in public restrooms were hardly the ideal choice; even those that were clean had limited room. The four St. Paul businessmen, one of whom was medical-device salesman Jeffrey Hilger, came up with the idea of a standalone product—a folding table that could be attached to walls in restrooms. Parents could place their babies on these tables and change them safely and privately. When not in use, the tables would fold flat against the wall.

The result was the Koala Bear Kare Baby Changing Station—a product that is easy to install, easy to use, and easy to maintain. Although the original product evolved over the years, its initial design—molded polyethylene and steel, rounded edges to prevent injury, compact size when folded to accommodate even small restrooms—has remained the same. Among the additions made in later years were safety instructions molded into the station in several languages as well as Braille. Parents who used the Baby Changing Station were both relieved and impressed by the simple and practical application.

JBJ's big break came in 1988, when a fast-food restaurant chain decided to install Baby Changing Stations in its facilities. Before long, Koala Bear Kare tables began appearing in other public restrooms, and within a few years JBJ was developing

Company Perspectives:

Koala Corporation is rapidly building a portfolio of products and solutions that resonate with the values of its brand: convenient, practical solutions for families. Through internal growth and acquisition, Koala has become a full-service provider of these solutions. From its industry leading Baby Changing Station and other parental convenience products to indoor and outdoor modular play equipment, Koala represents one-stop shopping for businesses that cater to families.

related products. The company made "family-friendly" its chief focus.

In 1991, JBJ introduced a child protection seat, a wall-mounted seat with straps. Like the Baby Changing Station, this seat could be attached directly to the restroom wall. The rationale behind this new product was that parents with small children occasionally need to use the restroom themselves. Since parents often carry their children in child pouches rather than wheeling them in strollers, the problem of using a restroom while carrying an infant is obvious. A safe and comfortable seat in which the infant could be placed would have obvious appeal.

JBJ continued to grow, and in 1993 it changed its name to Koala Corporation. It became a public company and began trading on the NASDAQ. A year later, it acquired A&B Booster, a Fort Myers, Florida, company than manufactured booster seats. The product known as the Booster Buddy is designed to allow children who are too old for high chairs but still too small to sit comfortably in adult-sized chairs. Booster Buddy seats allow children to sit at table level in restaurants; they also allow children to sit at eye level in theaters (the seats include recessed cup and snack holders).

A Move and Continued Growth

In 1995, Mark Betker joined Koala as president and CEO. Betker, who had successfully helped grow the industrial cleaning-equipment manufacturer Windsor Industries, became chairman the following year when Hilger retired. In fact, 1996 was a year of significant change for Koala. It acquired Activities Unlimited, a manufacturer of children's play stations for retail stores. This marked the beginning of a new focus for Koala, but one still centered on the family-friendly concept. Also in 1996, Koala moved its corporate headquarters from St. Paul to Denver, Colorado.

The Baby Changing Station was by far the most immediately recognizable Koala product. Koala had made some inroads into diversification with the safety chair and the Booster Buddy, but it was clear that it could move still more aggressively. The trend toward dual-income couples continued, and there was also a rise in single-parent families. Children were increasingly visible in stores, theaters, malls, and even offices. More and more companies, no longer only fast-food restaurants, were looking for ways to become family-friendly.

As other companies began to manufacture their own baby-changing stations, Koala realized that it could not count on its

signature product indefinitely as its cash cow. Even with its strong market share, it was only a matter of time before Koala would be just one of many players. Moreover, there was always the danger that eventually the market would become saturated once baby-changing stations became common in all businesses. Betker thus saw the need for a family-friendly environment in a growing number of venues as the key to Koala's success. In 1997, the company acquired Delta Play, Ltd., a Canadian manufacturer of indoor and outdoor modular play systems, and in 1998 it acquired Park Structures, a manufacturer of outdoor children's play equipment.

The family-friendly approach was adopted by a number of businesses, from small operations to large chains such as Pizza Hut and Outback Steakhouse. Koala's acquisitions and internal developments allowed the company to market everything from simple play-station tables with building blocks to custom-made play units complete with ladders and tunnels. This way, Koala could serve the needs of both individual professionals (such as pediatricians) as easily as it could serve large retail stores. Betker believed that making businesses family-friendly had advantages beyond merely attracting families. Getting a family inside a store is one matter, but keeping the parents from being distracted can be a greater challenge. Betker said as much in 1998 when he told *Forbes:* "No car dealer in the world can compete with a two-year-old."

Thanks in part to its acquisitions, Koala's revenues rose from $8.9 million in 1996 to $19.1 million in 1998. In 1999, Koala acquired Superior Foam and Polymers, Inc., a maker of soft foam play structures. It also acquired Smart Products, a manufacturer of high chairs and grocery cart straps. By year's end, revenues had nearly doubled to $37.1 million.

In 2000, Koala continued to acquire companies that fit its family-friendly focus. March saw the acquisition of SCS Interactive, an interactive play equipment manufacturer. Among SCS's offerings are so-called "water play" products, the sort that would be commonly found in amusement parks and similar venues. One of SCS's most recent projects was the completion of a three-acre theme park inside an existing amusement part. In August, Koala acquired the playground surfacing manufacturer Fibar. Fibar's specialty is protective surfacing, a key concern among playground manufacturers. With safety an issue of constant concern among parents, play areas that minimize the risk of injury have enormous appeal. Also in 2000, Koala signed licensing agreements with La Rue International and Associated Hygienic Products. Under the terms of these deals, the Koala Bear Kare name and logo would appear on such products as disposable diapers, diaper bags, and other infant and child care products.

Koala was working full force to establish its reputation as a supplier of family-friendly products across the board. Whether a family wanted a simple high chair at the local restaurant, a play area to amuse their children at the local mall, or an interactive water slide at a theme park, Koala wanted to be there as well. By the end of the twentieth century, Koala's products had reached such companies as McDonald's. Burger King, Walt Disney World, Target Stores, the Mayo Clinic, and Sony Pictures. Koala finished out the century by being named to *Forbes'* list of the 200 Best Small Companies in America for the fifth year in a row.

Key Dates:

1986: JBJ Industries founded by four Minnesota businessmen who develop wall-mounted baby changing table.

1988: Koala Bear Kare Baby Changing Station makes its debut in fast-food restaurant franchises.

1993: JBJ merges into Koala Corporation and begins trading on the NASDAQ.

1996: Co-founder Jeffrey Hilger retires; Mark Betker is named president. The company relocates corporate headquarters to Denver.

1997: Koala acquires Delta Play, manufacturer of indoor soft play equipment.

1998: Koala acquires Park Structures, modular outdoor play equipment manufacturer.

1999: Koala expands with acquisition of Superior Foam (soft play equipment) and Smart Products (high chairs and grocery cart straps).

2000: Koala announces licensing agreements with La Rue International and Associated Hygienic Products to market child care products under Koala brand.

Striking a Balance

By 2000, Koala had effected a significant shift from the product that had initially put it on the map. Sales of Baby Changing Stations now accounted for less than 15 percent of Koala's sales. This was not a reflection on the Baby Changing Stations, whose sales were still strong in their established markets. Rather, it was because Baby Changing Stations represented a relatively small part of the company's product line. Thanks to its acquisitions, Koala now had a highly diverse product mix.

As the economy began slowing in 2000, Koala felt even more justified that its acquisition strategy was the wisest long-term move it could make. Koala's management was confident that the trend toward family-friendly outings and entertainment would grow. Stores that had seen the advantages of installing child-friendly products, whether baby changing tables or activity/play areas, would obviously want to keep a competitive edge over stores that offered no conveniences for parents or children. Moreover, even the most durable playground equipment wears out, and Koala was banking on revenues generated from replacing existing equipment as well as opening new playgrounds.

By the fourth quarter of 2000, Koala's sales had begun to slow—this after nearly a decade of solid and steady growth. Koala finished out the fourth quarter with $16.6 million in sales—an impressive amount, but short of an anticipated $18 million. The company attributed the unexpected shortfall to several factors, including more competition, higher-than-antici-

pated administrative expenses, and cost overruns in its modular play business.

Revenues for the year were initially set at $61.6 million, up significantly from the year before. In March 2001, the company announced that it was revising those figures downward. The reason: delays in product shipments meant that money credited in the fourth quarter of 2000 would now have to be credited for the first quarter of 2001. As a result, Koala's actual sales for 2000 were $59.7 million. This was still significantly higher than 1999's figure of $37.1 million. Net income for the year, however, was $4.0 million, down for the first time in the company's history (it had been $5.1 million in 1999).

The first quarter of 2001 saw sales 20 percent higher than the previous year—$13.8 million against $11.5 million. Still, sales were lower than expected. Net income for the quarter was $474,930, down from $1.3 million a year earlier. The company attributed the lower-than-expected sales to several factors, including weather-related delays in product shipment and the overall slowing of the economy. Some investment analysts expressed concern over Koala, wondering whether the company may have overextended itself too quickly with so many acquisitions. But Koala said that it remains committed to growing its business through acquisitions that meet its focus and that give it broader access to the market. While the company admitted that it might be suffering from ''growing pains'' in light of its acquisitions, it also said that all of the businesses it had acquired were strong performers with a reputation for high quality and commitment to customers. Koala's outlook for the years ahead is optimistic.

Principal Divisions

Activities Unlimited; Delta Play; Fibar; Park Structures; SCS; Smart Products; Superior Foam.

Principal Competitors

Dorel Industries Inc.; Newell Rubbermaid, Inc.; Evenflo Company Inc.; Landscape Structures Inc.

Further Reading

''Koala Expands Its Offerings,'' *Supermarket News,* August 21, 2000, p. 62.

''Koala Falls Short,'' *Denver Business Journal,* February 14, 2001.

''Koala Marks Ninth Year of Record Earnings,'' *Denver Business Journal,* February 11, 2000, p. 23A.

Lankford, Kimberly, ''Simple Things: Investing in Companies Whose Success Is Based on Simple Product Strategies,'' *Kiplinger's Personal Finance,* July 1997, p. 57.

Palmieri, Christopher, ''Beyond the Bathroom: Koala Expands Product Line,'' *Forbes,* November 2, 1998, p. 210.

Sutherland, Billie, ''Koala Corporation Gets to the Bottom of Problem,'' *San Diego Business Journal,* April 1, 1996, p. 10.

—George A. Milite

Kudelski Group SA

Route de Genève 22
1033 Cheseaux
Switzerland
Telephone: (41) 21 732 01 01
Fax : (41) 21 732 01 00
Web site: http://www.kudelski.com

Public Company
Incorporated: 1968 as Kudelski SA
Employees: 425
Sales: CHF 359.52 million ($223.1 million)(2000)
Stock Exchanges: Swiss
Ticker Symbol: KUD
NAIC: 551112 Offices of Other Holding Companies;
551114 Corporate, Subsidiary, and Regional
Managing Offices; 512290 Other Sound Recording
Industries; 541511 Custom Computer Programming
Services; 3343 Audio and Video Equipment
Manufacturing

Switzerland's Kudelski Group SA is one of the world's leading independent companies specializing in so-called "conditional access" solutions for a growing number of applications, ranging from subscriber-based analog and digital television broadcasting to event ticket purchasing and facilities access, to secure smartcards for online purchasing, interactive services, and health care services. The company also produces, through its original Nagra Audio subsidiary, professional recording equipment for the film and television, security and law enforcement, and other industries, as well as high-end high fidelity equipment for the audiophile community. The company's Nagravision, which produces access systems and software for digital and analog television set-top boxes, is Kudelski Group's largest division, representing 85 percent of the company's sales. The company has been building up its interactive services operations at the turn of the century, such as its Nagracard smart-card subsidiary; the Mediacrypt joint-venture formed with fellow Swiss company Ascom; 54 percent of SportAccess Kudelski, a specialist in "hands-free" ticketing and access systems; and others. Kudelski also operates two subsidiaries in partnership with two of its biggest customers: Nagrastar, in conjunction with the United States' Echostar; and Nagra+, in conjunction with France's Canal Plus. The company, trading on the Swiss stock exchange's blue chip index, is led by André Kudelski, son of founder Stefan Kudelski. The Kudelskis continues to maintain control of the company, holding 35 percent of shares and 64 percent of voting rights; French industrial group Dassault holds a seven percent share of the company's stock. In 2000, Kudelski posted revenues of nearly CHF 360 million ($223 million).

Pioneering Portable Recording in the 1950s

Until the 1950s, recording on location—whether for movies, television, or sporting events—was a difficult endeavor, in particular because of the large bulk and heavy power demands of then-current mobile recording systems. Physics student Stefan Kudelski, who had fled Poland after the Communist takeover, was to revolutionize mobile recording. While studying in Lausanne, at what later became known as the Swiss Federal Institute of Technology, Kudelski began working on a portable audio recording in his garage. Kudelski's first recorder was ready in 1951, a small, all-in-one unit with a wind-up motor for its power supply. Kudelski dubbed the recorder the Nagra and sold one to Radio Geneva, which was then taken on an expedition to Mount Everest. The first Nagra model also saw service in deep-sea dives led by Augustine Piccard. The French radio station Europe purchased a Nagra recorder for its field reporting.

Kudelski released an improved version, the Nagra II, in 1953. Two years later Kudelski added stereophonic recording capacity, and printed circuit boards for greater control of recordings. The recorder's breakthrough came in 1958, when Kudelski introduced the Nagra III. This model was the first to incorporate the new transistor technology. Adding electronic speed control, the Nagra III was capable of recording at quality levels comparable to the large truck-sized and room-sized systems still in use at the time, yet weighed only five kilograms. After adding instrumentation tape recording capability in 1959, the company's sales began to boom. An important moment in the Nagra—and Kudelski's—history came with the 1960 Summer Olympics games in Rome, when the Italian radio and television broadcaster RAI bought 100 Nagra III machines for the event. By then, Kudelski's production had reached nearly 500 machines per year.

Throughout the 1960s, Kudelski continued to improve its technology. A new Nagra model, the Nagra SN (for ''Série Noire''), launched in 1960, was a breakthrough. About the size of a wallet, the SN version was to become widely used among law enforcement agencies as a so-called ''body recorder.'' New technologies were added to the Nagra recordings, including the Neopilot syncronization system, the adoption of silicon transistors, and the incorporation of ''sync'' abilities in the filmmaking process. In 1964, Kudelski's growing sales enabled the company to leave its workshop and build a new production facility at Cheseaux-sur-Lausanne. This factory was ready in 1968; in that year, the company incorporated as a private limited liability company, Kudelski SA. The newly expanded facilities enabled the company to launch a new line of multi-track tape recorders. The addition of the new generation of tape recorders, capable of recording 16 and more audio tracks, was to produce something of a revolution in the recording industry in general.

Kudelski released several new models at the beginning of the 1970s, including the Nagra 4.2, specifically developed for the needs of the moviemaking community, launched in 1971; a stereo model launched the same year; and the Nagra SJ, developed especially for acoustic instruments. The company had also expanded its range of body recordings with the SNN, in 1970, and the SNS, which was low-speed version especially suitable for voice recordings.

In 1977, the company released its Nagrafax system for meteorological applications. That recording quickly became a standard feature on most sea-going vessels. In that same year, the company released a stereo version of its SN body recording, especially prized by law enforcement agencies. In that market, the company's customers included the FBI of the United States.

Recording Debt in the 1980s

By the early 1980s, Kudelski had succeeded in creating a worldwide reputation for the Nagra recorder. Yet the company was beginning to face competition from a new range of competi-

tors, notably Sony Corporation and other Japanese companies, which flooded the world market with lower-priced products. By the middle of the 1980s, Kudelski was starting to struggle to keep up. Despite efforts to enter new territory, such as the launch of its first professional video recorders in 1984, Kudelski began to sink under the competition. Kudelski went public in 1986 in an effort to raise funding; by the end of the decade, however, Kudelski was mired in debt and facing financial collapse.

By then Kudelski's son André had joined the company. The younger Kudelski had completed his own studies at the Swiss Federal Institute of Technology, but had already shown his technological prowess in high school, when, with the help of two friends, he had built his own personal computer. André Kudelski had gone to work in California's Silicon Valley before returning to Switzerland and the troubled family business. The younger Kudelski was convinced that the family company's future lay in the development of specialized software. Yet convincing Stefan Kudelski of this proved more difficult. As André Kudelski told *Forbes,* ''My father didn't think my ideas were very good.''

Kudelski pressed ahead, however, and, soon after joining the company in 1986, received a contract from a Swiss subscriber-based television broadcaster to write billing software for its service. This software caught the attention of France's Canal Plus, which had launched its own encrypted broadcasts that required dedicated set-top boxes to decode the broadcasting signal, in mid-decade. Canal Plus bought Kudelski's software for use with its set-top boxes in 1989.

In 1991, investor pressures forced Stefan Kudelski to step down from the company's lead. The company remained firmly in the family's hands, however, as André Kudelski now took over the company's direction. The younger Kudelski quickly set to work redirecting operations. While Kudelski maintained its founding Nagra Audio division, the company's future was oriented toward the growing market for conditional access systems and products.

The younger Kudelski's efforts had by then already begun to return the company to health. By 1991, more than a million set-top boxes incorporating Kudelski's access-control system had been sold. By 1995, Kudelski's software controlled more than seven million Canal Plus boxes. A joint-venture, Nagra+, sealed the two companies relationship—at least as far as Canal Plus's analog set-top boxes were concerned.

André Kudelski did not merely succeed in turning around the company, he transformed it into one of the world's leading supplier of conditional access systems, capturing a 34 percent market share by the end of the 1990s. The Kudelski company became one of the leaders of Switzerland's small high-technology sector, as its revenues and share price multiplied throughout the decade. By 2001, the company's stock traded at more than 125 times profits—a stunning performance especially in light of the general gloom that had fallen over the high-technology sector during the same period.

21st-Century Interactive Access Specialist

The company's earliest products—both in audio and in television access systems—had been directed toward the analog market. In the early 1990s, Kudelski was quick to begin adapting its products to emerging digital technologies. This included the release of the Nagra-D, in 1992, the company's first digital recorder. Kudelski also began developing conditional access systems for digital broadcasting. While still in its embryonic stages in the early 1990s, digital television showed huge potential—not only in its ability to offer higher-quality image and sound than analog television, but also in its ability to open up new interactive capabilities.

At mid-decade, however, Kudelski stumbled over a new hurdle, when Canal Plus chose to implement its own software system, developed in-house, for its rollout of digital television services. With one of its main customers turned competitor, and the rest of the European market for digital television still in its infancy, Kudelski quickly changed direction, taking its digital technology, dubbed Nagravision, to the United States. In 1995, the company received an order for Nagravision from Echostar, which quickly established North America as the company's primary market. More than 85 percent of sales were now generated in that continent.

Nagravision was well greeted by the industry, which ranked Kudelski's software at the top of the industry. The company received further confirmation of its excellence when it was awarded a special Emmy award for its contribution to the development of digital television. The recognition of Nagravision brought it to the attention of other broadcasters, which helped the company build its market share throughout the rest of the decade. In the meantime, Kudelski continued to innovate in its former core division, launching a number of new Nagra models, including the ARES-C, a portable, solid-state digital recorder. The company's continued development of the Nagra D, including the implementation of 24-bit, 96-Khz functionality, led the company to receive new accolades, such as an Academy Award for the film *The English Patient,* recorded entirely on a Nagra D. The success of the division led Kudelski to take Nagra into the home for the first time, with the launch of a range of extreme high-fidelity components targeting the audiophile market.

The breakthrough of Nagravision in Europe in 1997, however, firmly placed the company's future growth on the rapidly expanding digital television market. The following year, the company entered the U.K. market, adapting its access technology to the cable television market. In that year, the company created its NagraStar joint-venture with main customer Echostar, and also launched its new dedicated smart card subsidiary, NagraCard.

In 1999, the company spotted a new opportunity, with the rise of broadband network systems offering high-speed transmission of a variety of digital content, from music to video. In that year, the company launched the first encryption system for broadband network. At the same time, Kudelski launched a joint-venture, MediaCrypt, in partnership with fellow Swiss company Ascom, using that company's IDEA algorithm for secure digital television and Internet transmission, a market expected to grow exponentially in the initial years of the new century. Another joint venture formed in 1999 was Nagra ID, which, together with partner Thermoplex F. Droz of Switzerland, began producing new generation smart card systems.

The diversification of Kudelski's activities at the end of the decade led the company to reform as a holding company, Kudelski Group. In 2000, the company's strong performance over the past decade was acknowledged with the company's admission onto the Swiss stock exchange's blue-chip SMI index.

In 2001, Kudelski faced a new challenge on the digital television front, when Rupert Murdoch's News Corp. began attempting a takeover of DirectTV—which already used encryption technology made by rival—and News Corp. subsidiary—NDS. Echostar launched a counter-offer for DirectTV, which was backed by an offer for $1 billion in cash from Kudelski itself. That sum, worth approximately one-fifth of Kudelski's paper value, raised eyebrows in the financial community. Yet a possible takeover of DirectTV by News Corp. would end Kudelski's hopes of imposing its software over that of NDS, which had gained a 36 percent share of the worldwide market.

In this light, Kudelski's moves to diversify at the turn of the century were greeted warmly, as the company positioned itself as a more broadly based provider of ''conditional access'' systems. An important component of Kudelski's new strategy came in 2000 with the acquisition of a majority stake in Sports Access, a Swiss-based ticketing systems provider, as well as a majority share of Polirights, which provided e-voting and cyber-administration services. In 2001, the company's acquisitions continued, with the purchase of digital decoder software developer LiveWire; the acquisition of TicketCorner, which was added to Sports Access; the acquisition of Lysis, adding that company's interactive digital television software; and SkiData, which produced software for ski and other facilities access. While the bulk of Kudelski's revenues continued to come from its digital television-based products, its diversification helped to position to the company as a leading independent supplier of next-generation purchasing, ticketing, and access systems.

Principal Subsidiaries

Kudelski SA; Nagracard SA; Nagravision SA; Précel SA; Sportaccess Kudelski SA; (54%); Polirights Political Rights SA (66%); E-Prica SA (50%); Nagrastar Llc (50%); Nagra+ (50%); Mediacrypt Ag (50%); Nagra Id SA (50%); Nagra Kudelski (Gb) Ltd.; Nagra Kudelski Gmbh (Germany); Nagra Italia Srl; Nagra USA Inc.; Nagra France Sàrl; Nagravision North America (USA); Nagravision Brazil; Nagravision Iberica (Spain); Nagravision India; Nagravision China; Nagravision Asia/Pacific (Singapore).

Principal Competitors

ADC Telecommunications, Inc.; Avid Technology, Inc.; CANAL+; DIRECTV, Inc.; Gemplus International SA; Harman International Industries, Inc.; NDS Group plc; OpenTV Corporation.

Further Reading

Echikson, William, ''I-TV's Software Upstart,'' *Business Week International*, February 19, 2001, p. 21.

Hall, William and Peter Thal Larsen, ''Kudelski Offers Echostar Dollars 1bn: Proposal to Back TV Company's Dollars 30bn Bid for Hughes,'' *Financial Times*, August 8, 2001

Hall, William, ''Kudelski Makes Its Mark in Digital TV,'' *Financial Times*, April 19, 2000.

Michelson, Marcel, ''Kudelski in Interactive TV Buying Spree,'' *Reuters Business Report*, May 18, 2001.

——, ''Kudelski Sticks to Guidance,'' *Reuters*, August 21, 2001.

Pitman, John, ''The Next Big Bet,'' *Forbes Magazine*, July 9, 2001, p. 108.

Tomlinson, Richard, and Neel Chowdhury, ''Six Smart Global Bets: Kudelski: Making TVs Secure,'' *Fortune*, December 18, 2000, p. 174+.

—M.L. Cohen

The Longaberger Company

The Longaberger Company

1500 East Main Street
Newark, Ohio 43055
U.S.A.
Telephone: (740) 322-5000
Fax: (740) 322-5240
Web site: http://www.longaberger.com

Private Company
Incorporated: 1973 as JW's Handwoven Baskets
Employees: 8,000
Sales: $1 billion (2000)
NAIC: 321999 All Other Miscellaneous Wood Product
   Manufacturing; 327112 Vitreous China, Fine
   Earthenware, and Other Pottery Product
   Manufacturing

The Longaberger Company is the leading producer of hand-made baskets in the United States. Once the sole product, these baskets made up about half the company's sales in 2000. A network of 70,000 independent sales associates, nearly all of them women, peddles the company's wares at in-home shows à la Mary Kay or Tupperware. The company's staff is also predominantly female; company founder Dave Longaberger named his daughter Tami chief executive in 1998. Using mottoes such as ''handmade to be handed down,'' the company has leveraged a strong sense of nostalgia and an appreciation for quality into a flourishing family legacy. The anachronistic company pays for hardly any advertising for its baskets made by hand by 2,500 non-unionized artisans. In the late 1990s, *Forbes* began listing Longaberger as one of the country's 500 largest private firms; it has been regarded as perhaps Appalachian Ohio's greatest corporate citizen.

Origins

Born in the Ohio town of Dresden, about an hour northeast of Columbus, founder David W. Longaberger coped with a severe speech impediment and epilepsy, both of which hindered his academic career. He failed first grade once and fifth grade

twice, and finally finished high school at the age of 20 at the insistence of his mother. Upon graduation, Longaberger briefly tried door-to-door sales and factory work, then settled into an eight-year stint driving sales and delivery routes for local bakeries.

Longaberger went into business for himself in 1963, when he and his wife bought an ice cream shop in Dresden, a town of less than 2,000 people. Within five years, they were able to purchase a local grocery store. The two businesses—known as ''Popeye's,'' in reference to Longaberger's nickname—were so profitable that he began investigating other ventures in the early 1970s.

Longaberger took particular interest in the resurgent popularity of baskets as decorating elements. Longaberger's family had a basket-weaving heritage dating back to 1896, when his paternal grandfather, John, moved to Dresden and started work at the Dresden Basket Factory. Until the mid-twentieth century, sturdy, utilitarian baskets such as those made at the small town plant were used to transport ceramics within pottery plants in the clay-rich region and by others for everyday chores like egg and vegetable gathering or shopping. Dave's father, JW (for John Wendell), began hand weaving at the basket factory in the late 1910s, and was able to purchase the plant for $1,900 during the Great Depression. He renamed it the Ohio Ware Basket Company, and involved all of his twelve children in some aspect of the business. In the postwar era, Ohio Ware suffered insurmountable competition from modern containers made of cardboard and plastic. In 1955 JW Longaberger closed up shop and went to work at a local paper mill.

The patriarch kept up his craft in the intervening decades, however, selling some baskets for $1.50 and giving others as gifts. So in 1972, when his son asked him to make a few for retail sale, JW agreed. Dave Longaberger soon found that customers would pay $10 and more for the high-quality hardwood baskets. He launched his third business in 1973, calling it JW's Handwoven Baskets for the man who died that spring at the age of 71. Dave hired two weavers to create each basket from thin strips of maple veneer. Promotional materials took pains to assert that ''staples and glue are never used.'' The baskets were fitted with leather hinges, copper rivets, and sometimes maple lids, lightly stained, then initialed and dated by the weaver in a process that remained essentially unchanged throughout the company's history.

Home Sales Start in 1978

Despite his optimism and enterprise, a combination of sluggish retail sales and high startup costs found Longaberger deep in debt by the late 1970s. Instead of abandoning his product, he re-examined his sales method. He related the problem in a 1994 interview with *Columbus CEO* magazine: "I couldn't tell our story in the shops. I had baskets in a couple of shops, and I would go back on Friday and Saturday nights to see how they were doing. I'd watch the expressions on customers' faces as they picked up the baskets and think (about the sales clerk), 'Go on, tell them about Mom and Dad, tell them about the 12 kids, talk about the utilitarian purpose of the baskets, tell them about Dresden.' Well, the clerks didn't know all that, and they didn't really care." In 1978 a friend, Charlene Cuckovich, suggested direct sales. Selling the baskets at Tupperware-style home parties would give salespeople the opportunity to describe the craftsmanship and tradition represented by each basket, she reasoned. Home sales also focused the folksy pitch on the people who were most likely to become customers. Cuckovich became one of Longaberger's first sales consultants.

The new marketing scheme vastly improved sales—within a year, Longaberger had 30 associates and 40 employees. In 1980 the entrepreneur agreed to purchase a veneer factory in nearby Hartville to accommodate his growing materials requirements. He even sold his thriving restaurant in order to raise the necessary capital. But before the purchasing agreement on the veneer factory was complete, the building, which was not insured for its replacement value, was destroyed by fire. Although Longaberger could have walked away from the deal, he instead sold his flourishing grocery store for $300,000, honored his commitment to purchase the property, and rebuilt.

Longaberger's under-capitalized business continued to founder in the mid-1980s. Longaberger later said wryly that "banks almost put me out of business. The IRS [which negotiated a tax payment plan with the struggling entrepreneur] helped look for a way to keep me in." His perseverance finally began to pay off in increasing sales in the late 1980s, with the company selling 1.4 million baskets in 1987 alone. In spite of economic recession, the company began to record growth rates of almost 40 percent annually. In 1989 Longaberger's cash flow was strong enough to buy back his eatery, now known as the Longaberger Restaurant.

Exhibiting a combination of business acumen and altruism, Longaberger began revitalizing the city of Dresden in 1988. The combination of public and private amenities helped make the village both a destination for hundreds of thousands of tourists every year and a more desirable place to live and work. Community investments included the Longaberger Fitness Center, the Swimming Center, the Senior Citizens Center, and an addition to the local public high school. The company designed Dresden's city landscaping—featuring Longaberger baskets, of course—maintained city parks, and even kept up some private property along the town's Main Street. The World's Largest Basket Park (certified by Guinness) featured a 23-foot-high hand-woven maple basket. A former bakery became the Longaberger Museum. Longaberger University, a nineteenth-century schoolhouse, housed corporate training and education programs. Outside the town, Longaberger Farms bred Angus cattle and advocated agricultural education. The company even transformed its weaving plant into a tourist destination, offering "a full mezzanine view of hundreds of crafts people weaving baskets with a centuries-old method," according to a press release.

New Plant, New Products in 1990

In 1990 the company started production at a new plant and opened Popeye's Soda Shop. The addition of fabric liners, wood accessories, and plastic basket inserts added to both the fashion appeal and functionality of the baskets. That year also saw the launch of Woven Traditions Pottery and Dinnerware, a line of earthenware that capitalized on the burgeoning popularity of the hand-crafted baskets. The ceramics featured an embossed pattern that mimicked a basket weave, and, although not hand thrown, appropriated a hand-crafted image with marketing pitches like the following: "traditional pottery-making methods used for centuries," "our own secret [clay] recipe," and "handmade quality."

Upon achieving his own success, Longaberger made "stimulating a better quality of life for customers, associates, and employees" a corporate mission. He sought to manufacture quality products, adopt fair employment policies, support the community, and conserve the natural environment.

Longaberger's magnanimity was evident on the shop floor. In 1994 Vice-President of Corporate Affairs Mike Bennett told *Columbus CEO* that "Dave has an unwritten rule that 25 percent of the day should be dedicated to having fun," which keeps the atmosphere "very relaxed, very professional, [and] very creative." LTV, Longaberger Television, was one outgrowth of that corporate culture. This 70-monitor, closed-circuit network featured company news, music videos, and employee interviews. Programming has even included the wedding of two employees who met at the plant. Employees work 35 hours a week, and their ample benefits plan includes tuition reimbursement. Some weavers, who were paid piece rates, made more than $40,000 per year in the early 1990s. Employees elected their front-line supervisors. Weavers seeking a new challenge or break in the routine could apply to transfer into corporate landscaping and construction crews, one of four local Longaberger restaurants, the company museum, or recreation facilities. In 1993 the company's Weaver Request Program began offering a select few basket weavers the opportunity to travel around the country giving demonstrations of their craft at company sales meetings and events. The employee roll included Dave's daughters, Tami Longaberger Kaido, president of mar-

Key Dates:

1896: John Longaberger begins working at the Dresden Basket Factory.
1955: J.W. Longaberger closes his own basket shop.
1973: Dave Longaberger start JW's Handwoven Baskets.
1978: Longaberger begins direct sales.
1990: Longaberger launches pottery plant.

keting and sales, and Rachel Longaberger Schmidt, president of manufacturing and human resources, as well as seven of Dave's 11 siblings.

By the early 1990s, Longaberger's direct sales team numbered over 25,000 associates, mostly women, in all fifty states. The associates were also some of the company's best customers: a press release noted that some owned more than 800 baskets. According to *Opportunity,* a quarterly company publication, sales associates move up within the organization by bringing new consultants into the group and meeting sales targets. As they progress through the levels of branch advisor, regional advisor, and finally sales director, they cultivate their own sales organizations comprising hundreds of sales associates. Along with the increasing responsibility came progressively greater rewards, with directors earning six figure incomes. Not surprisingly, Charlene Cuckovich became one of the company's first sales directors over the course of her career with Longaberger.

The company's environmental programs included selective harvesting of the maple trees that go into its baskets, the use of water-based stains and recyclable plastics, and the pursuit of relationships with like-minded partners. Longaberger also makes contributions to programs like the International Center for the Preservation of Wild Animals.

Longaberger's philanthropy won both himself and the company national recognition, including the Direct Selling Association's Vision for Tomorrow Award in 1990, the U.S. Department of the Interior's Take Pride in America Award in 1991, *Inc.* magazine's Socially Responsible Entrepreneur of the Year Award in 1992, and the Friend of Education Award and an honor from Childhelp USA in 1994. Longaberger was also named a Central Ohio Business Hall of Fame Laureate in 1994.

Dave Longaberger's confidence in the nostalgia market led him to take the phrase "company town" to a whole new level in 1994, when he announced plans to build Longaberger Village, an "educational theme park" just west of Dresden on a 625-acre campus. Longaberger Village's first phase, Main Street, promised to evoke a "typical" Midwest town of the 1920s. Plans for the complex included a reproduction of the Longaberger home, a soda shop, drug store, and barbershop, as well as gift shops, specialty shops, overnight accommodations, and Longaberger Characters who will "spin tales of the old days."

Dave Longaberger has boiled his company's success down to 18 folksy "Principles of Management," including "you must always be looking on the bank for help and assurance no matter who you are," and "the past is the present; the present is

the future." His plans for the firm's future included venturing into furniture manufacturing and real estate, as well as perpetuating the eccentric charm, financial prosperity, and civic responsibility exemplified by the Longaberger Company for the past two decades.

A Big New Basket in the Late 1990s

Longaberger sold seven million baskets in 1996 and took in revenues of $525 million. Sales rose to $611 million in 1997. The company began using a new sophisticated, computerized sales forecasting system in 1998 to help manage this growth. At the end of 1997, the company's 500 employees moved into their new workplace, a $30 million, seven-story building designed as a replica of a genuine Longaberger basket. Its handles weighed 75 tons; their installation represented a considerable engineering challenge. "People told me, 'Dave, you can't build that basket,'" said Dave Longaberger in *The Wall Street Journal.* "But I said, 'They can put a man on the moon and bring him back. Don't tell me they can't build a basket.'" The unique building gave Dresden something of a tourist attraction and brought Longaberger an untold amount of publicity.

Dave Longaberger, who had contracted cancer in July 1997, died on March 17, 1999. The company he had led, and its related stores, restaurants, and real estate firm, had transformed east-central Ohio. Most of Dresden's 1,581 residents worked at one Longaberger enterprise or another. Before his death, Longaberger dictated a memoir that would became a number-one bestseller, thanks in part to the promotional efforts of the company's 70,000 independent sales consultants. In July 1998, Tami Longaberger, a daughter of the founder, was named president and CEO of the company, while her younger sister Rachel remained president of the Longaberger Foundation.

Ninety-nine percent of Longaberger's clients were white women, mostly from Ohio and neighboring states. In the late 1990s, realizing the potential of a vast new market, the company began a drive to hire sales associates among other ethnic groups, reported local American Cities journal *Business First.* Its designers began incorporating such elements as African Kente cloth into products. Even the mannequins at the new Longaberger Homestead attraction were updated. The push for diversity was important as Longaberger sought to establish new territory: in California, where the company had 1,200 sales associates, minorities comprised half the population. One expert felt that home sales would help Longaberger win minority customers, as it had Avon. The company's U.S. heritage was also expected to appeal to immigrants.

Longaberger was also trying to bring more men into its sales force. It hoped its new $10 million golf course would help. However, the pool of male basket fanatics was relatively small. To appeal to the male buyer, Longaberger introduced functional baskets for shaving supplies and golf balls, etc.

Sales reached $850 million in 1999. The slowing economy prompted Longaberger to cut 400 jobs, five percent of its workforce, in April 2001. Lay offs for another 500 weavers and 300 support staff were announced in July.

The 40,000 baskets Longaberger's Ohio weavers made every day accounted for half the company's $1 billion in revenues for 2000. In May 2001, Longaberger was one of six firms given awards by the Rochester (New York) Institute of Technology and *USA Today* for manufacturing improvements. Three of the company's weavers developed a system to reduce downtime by developing techniques to ensure a more efficient flow of materials to workstations.

Principal Competitors

Euromarket Designs Inc.; Pier 1 Imports, Inc.; Pottery Barn.

Further Reading

Birth of a Basket Company, Dresden, Ohio: The Longaberger Company, 1993.

Echlin, Bill, "State Woman Weaves Basket-Selling Record: Longaberger Co. Honors Her for Posting Annual Sales Topping $75,000," *Detroit News,* December 11, 1998, p. C10.

Ellis, Kristin B., "Basketmania," *York Daily Record,* June 3, 1997, p. 1.

Frazier, Mya, "Too Flimsy a Weave; Longaberger Biography Lacking Depth, His Faults," review of *Longaberger: An American Success Story* by Dave Longaberger, *Plain Dealer* (Cleveland), March 31, 2001, p. 1E.

Gillespie, Charlie, "Longaberger, Maker of Baskets, Tries to Lure Men," *Dayton Daily News,* July 28, 2000, p. 2E.

Gleisser, Marcus, "Longaberger Baskets Founder to Get Memorial," *Plain Dealer* (Cleveland), March 26, 1999, p. 3C.

Goel, Vindu P., "Peer Pressure at Home Parties Helps Sell Baskets and Accessories," *Plain Dealer* (Cleveland), December 6, 1998, p. 5H.

Gorisek, Sue, "Longaberger's Legacy," *Ohio,* September 1, 1998, p. 62.

Hoke, Kathy, "Longaberger Co. Bidding to Weave Ethnic Appeal into Business, Baskets," *Business First* (Columbus, Ohio), July 23, 1999, p. 1.

Jurgelski, Susan, "Basket Belt: Tour Showcasing Longaberger Creations Weaves Through County," *Lancaster New Era* (Pennsylvania), August 17, 2001, p. D1.

Kanner, Bernice, "The Weaver," *Chief Executive,* June 2000, pp. 24–25.

Kiley, David, "Crafty Basket Makers Cut Downtime, Waste; So Far, Changes Saving $3 Million a Year," *USA Today,* May 10, 2001, p. B3.

Longaberger, Dave, *Longaberger: An American Success Story,* New York: HarperBusiness, 2001.

McManamy, Rob, "No Picnic Getting a Handle on It," *ENR,* November 24, 1997, p. 22.

Mangold, Kathy, "Bravura Baskets," *Milwaukee Journal Sentinel,* May 13, 2001, p. 1N.

Maryles, Daisy, "Basket Case," review of *Longaberger: An American Success Story* by Dave Longaberger, *Publishers Weekly,* March 19, 2001, p. 18.

Mentzer, John T. and John L. Kent, "Forecasting Demand in the Longaberger Company," *Marketing Management,* Summer 1999, pp. 46–50.

Nelton, Sharon, "A Basket Maker with Vision," *Nation's Business,* July 1993, p. 14.

Ottolenghi-Barga, Carol, "Dave Longaberger," *Columbus CEO,* October 1994, pp. 12–14.

Philipps, Carole L., "Longaberger Story Told by Basket Mogul," review of *Longaberger: An American Success Story* by Dave Longaberger, *Cincinnati Post,* March 24, 2001, p. 8C.

Quintanilla, Carl, "A Seven-Story Basket Goes Up in the Fields of Ohio," October 15, 1997, p. B1.

Shope, Dan, "Longaberger Agent Breaks Gender Barrier," *Morning Call* (Allentown, Penn.), December 6, 1998, p. D1.

"A Tisket, a Tasket—A 'Basket' Building," *Building Design & Construction,* February 1998, p. 22.

—April Dougal Gasbarre
—updated by Frederick C. Ingram

Life just got easier

Mac-Gray Corporation

22 Water Street
Cambridge, Massachusetts 02141
U.S.A.
Telephone: (617) 492-4040
Fax: (617) 354-3963
Web site: http://www.mac-gray.com

Public Company
Incorporated: 1927
Employees: 525
Sales: $154.3 million (2000)
Stock Exchanges: New York
Ticker Symbol: TUC
NAIC: 81299 Miscellaneous Personal Services, Not
  Elsewhere Classified; 33313 Calculating Machines
  Except Computers

Mac-Gray Corporation provides debit card and coin-operated laundry services and other amenities to multiple housing facilities. Most of its clients are apartment buildings, condominiums, colleges, assisted living communities, military housing, and public housing complexes. The company is the largest provider of laundry services to the U.S. college and university market. Most of the company's laundry equipment is Maytag-brand. Mac-Gray owns and operates about 170,000 washer and dryers in some 30,000 multiple housing laundry rooms across 33 states in the Northeast, Midwest, and Southeast. It also distributes commercial washers and dryers to laundromats, hotels, hospitals, and restaurants; sells a line of combination refrigerators, freezers, and microwaves; and provides vended reprographic services to colleges and libraries.

Origins

In 1927, H.S. (Stewart) Gray left his insurance sales job to found the company that later became Mac-Gray Corporation. Gray, born in 1900, bought a pick-up truck; cut a deal with Maytag, the appliance manufacturer; and began selling wringer washing machines and ice boxes door-to-door in the Boston area. An entrepreneur and risk taker, H.S. Gray remained active in the company into the late 1970s and died in 1994.

Throughout its history, Mac-Gray was a technology leader in its industry. The company leaders tended to be entrepreneurial and creative. In the 1930s, Gray installed coin boxes on washers, pioneering the "pay-as-you-use" laundry service. The company devoted time to redefine or innovate and catch the early wave on industry trends. Examples included adopting European water-efficient technology and leading the change to coinless washers and dryers.

The Great Depression

The biggest challenge faced by the company in its early years was the Great Depression. In the 1920s and 1930s, selling equipment was often a door-to-door business. When the depression hit bottom in 1933, 16 million people (one third of the labor force) were unemployed. People did not have the funds to make a major purchase like an appliance.

This lack of individual sales spurred H.S. Gray to make his appliances available in common areas, put a metering device on them, and allow people to "rent" the washer or dryer by the hour. "At this time, the coin operated laundry business was born out of desperation," explained Stewart Gray MacDonald, Jr., the company CEO in 2001. "That was a major turn of the road where adversity pushed the company in a different direction."

In 1946 H.S. Gray brought in Stewart MacDonald (the father of Stewart Gray MacDonald, Jr.) to help run the company. MacDonald, born in 1925, helped steer the company through a time of rapid change. After World War II, suburban development increased at a rapid rate. The interstate highway system changed the landscape and made the automobile essential to U.S. life. Consumers, whether they lived in apartments, college housing, or their own houses, became enamored with convenience. They were looking for easy access to washing machines and dryers.

1950s: the Leading College Laundry Service Provider

Mac-Gray foresaw that the growing U.S. population, with its movement to the suburbs, would spike the need for public laundromats. In 1952, the company de-emphasized selling appliances to homeowners. It established a store division and helped launch many self-service laundromats. H.S. Gray asked

Company Perspectives:

Unlike every other laundry service provider, Mac-Gray is a public company operating under strict SEC guidelines. That means we're responsible to both customers and shareholders. Our overall approach always reflects the highest ethical standards. The biggest reason for our long-term success is the trust we've established with customers and users. And we won't risk that for anything.

Stewart MacDonald to run the new entity, and they renamed the company "Mac-Gray" to reflect the dual leadership. MacDonald brought creativity, a commitment to customer satisfaction, and a strong work ethic to the job. In the 1950s, Mac-Gray became the leading laundry service provider to colleges and multi-housing communities and New England's top commercial laundry equipment company.

Multi-housing complexes used the services of Mac-Gray to avoid the issues involved in running a laundry service. The company provided liability insurance; purchased, installed, and maintained laundry equipment; and by the 1990s provided coinless systems.

The 1960s brought an expansion of the Cambridge, Massachusetts, corporate headquarters and the introduction of cashless electronic ticket systems, a precursor to Smart Cards. Maytag, the primary manufacturer of nearly all Mac-Gray laundry appliances, created the ticket system. The market embraced this system well into the late 1970s, but it was a limited concept. The ticket system worked well for properties that had on-site managers or someone continually available to sell the tickets to residents. Technology to sell the tickets without human intervention (via vending machines, for example) was not yet perfected.

In the late 1970s, the company left the household market to concentrate on its commercial business. This was also the decade when Mac-Gray began expanding its operations through the acquisition of small companies.

1980s: Water-Efficient Technology

With utility costs rising in the 1980s, Mac-Gray implemented and promoted a new European water-efficient technology. Europeans used a horizontal access (front loading) washing machine as opposed to the common top-loading washer used in the United States. In the European machine the washing drum filled halfway. Rather than having the clothes completely immersed in water, as in the top-loading machines, European models milled the clothes through the water by a horizontal rotation of the drum. This technology conserved water and reduced the amount of electricity needed to heat the water. It also allowed for a faster spin cycle. Clothes came out of the washer with less moisture and needed less time in a dryer. Savings were three-fold: in water, in energy to heat the water, and in energy to run the dryer.

Because Mac-Gray felt that water would become a precious commodity in at least some U.S. markets, the company saw a product niche for a more efficient, front loading washing machine

but none of the U.S. manufacturers were interested in making such a product. That led Mac-Gray to form a relationship with Ipso, a Belgian manufacturer, to produce a front-loading machine for the U.S. market. "We imported the Belgian-made machine and had a nice period of success with it. It filled exactly the niche we had identified," said Stewart Gray MacDonald in 2001.

In 1997, Maytag began manufacturing the Neptune, a washer similar to the European models. It used about 50 percent less water than standard U.S. brands. That year Mac-Gray dropped Ipso to begin selling the Neptune. Twenty years later Mac-Gray still promoted a high-efficiency program designed to cut laundry room operating costs by saving on water, sewer, and energy via the Neptune. Compared to other models available in the United States, the Maytag unit was better for the environment, gentler on clothing, and allowed more people to do more laundry in less time.

Expansion and Acquisitions in the 1980s and 1990s

In 1983, Stewart MacDonald stepped down from his leadership position due to ill health. His son, Stewart Gray MacDonald, joined Mac-Gray in a director position in the early 1980s and accepted an executive position in 1989. He became Chairman and CEO in 1995.

Acquisitions have long been part of the Mac-Gray story, dating back to at least 1983. The company expanded into the southeastern United States in the mid-1980s and into the Midwest in the early 1990s. In 1996, Mac-Gray bought seven smaller competitors. However, the company needed more funding if it was to pursue larger acquisitions and mergers. To raise those funds, the company went public with an initial public offering October 17, 1997. The initial public offering generated sales of 4.6 million shares at $11. Going public made Mac-Gray unique among its competitors, all of whom were private companies. Although 70 years of private ownership ended, Stewart Gray MacDonald and family owned about 50 percent of the company in 2001.

Smart Cards Replace Coins

In the 1990s, Mac-Gray beat its competition in switching to new coinless washers and dryers. After first committing to cashless programs in 1991, Mac-Gray announced what was believed to be the largest cashless washer and dryer program in North America on December 1, 1997. It involved 50,000 Smart Card terminals. A prepaid Smart Card replaced the quarters. Knowing people disliked using quarters, the company saw cashless operating systems as the future.

First developed in France in the 1970s, Smart Cards gained wide use in Europe and Asia, but not in the United States where magnetic strip cards dominated. Smart Cards, plastic debit cards the size of standard credit cards, featured an embedded computer chip. Users added value to the card by inserting money into an ATM-like machine. The computer chip recorded the card's changing value each time cash was added or a purchase was made. The chip was said to make the Smart Card harder to copy than other debit cards.

Smart Cards did more than solve the "no quarters" problem. The cards could reduce laundry room wait times by providing a discount for washing clothes at less busy times. The cards also were used for other purposes like unlocking apartment doors, making photocopies, using vending machines, and providing access to select areas like pools or gyms.

Mac-Gray implemented the cards faster and more widely than any of its dozen or so competitors. The company claimed its cards offered superior security due to advanced encoding it developed via an exclusive relationship with the French company, Schlumberger Danyl. A report by Palmer and Palmer found that properties that switched to Mac-Gray's Smart Card laundry system increased their incomes about 20 percent. One obstacle to the switch away from coin-operated machines was cost. The price tag on implementing the Smart Card system dictated that the switch to coinless operation was only profitable on larger properties.

Combining the card with Mac-Gray's IntelliPass keyless door access system gave housing complex owners greater control of who used their properties. IntelliPass invalidated Smart Cards when they were lost or stolen and when units changed hands. IntelliPass also kept track of who entered the building.

1998 Expansion

In 1998, the company spent $26.4 million in stock and cash to purchase Intirion Corporation, a 48 employee company in Walpole, Massachusetts, that made the MicroFridge. The MicroFridge was a line of compact combination refrigerators, freezers, and microwaves. Colleges and universities, inexpensive hotels, assisted living facilities, and military bases were the markets for the MicroFridge. It was the most popular unit of its kind on college campuses. The purchase of Intirion gave Mac-Gray another major product line for its existing market.

Buying MicroFridge was one step in Mac-Gray's plan to expand both geographically and in its product offerings. The company was trend-spotting and saw the multi-housing industry outsourcing many amenity programs like maintenance and service contracts. Real estate company mergers were another factor leading CEO Stewart Gray MacDonald toward gaining a

presence in the 26 states in which the company had no laundry equipment.

Mac-Gray also acquired Copico in 1998 for $15.1 million in cash and stock. Copico provided reprographic services to colleges and libraries via card and coin-operated copy machines, laser printers, and microfilm machines. It was the leading provider of these services to libraries. The purchase proved ill-timed according to *The Boston Globe*, becoming one factor in a less than banner financial year in 1999. Company earnings fell 63 percent in the second quarter of that year. Throughout the 1998–2000 period, most students began shifting to Internet research and using laser printers to make hard copies on library-maintained printers—often free of charge. As a result, Copico suffered a 25 percent revenue decline in 1999.

"Copico has been a difficult division since we bought it," said Stewart Gray MacDonald in August of 2001. "We had to incur a write-down at the end of 1999 ($8.5 million) in order to reflect what we thought was a diminished value of that division, but we remain cautiously optimistic about it." Another challenging factor in 1999 was an unexpected surge in Mac-Gray's distribution of Maytag and other laundry appliances to laundromats. This portion of the company's business had thinner profit margins than the laundry services.

MicroFridge sales increased 9 percent in 2000. In one change to the business model, Mac-Gray decided to make a gradual, multi-year exit from a segment of the business that rented product directly to students in the academic market, due to low margins. Entering the new century, total company sales continued to grow steadily. Annual sales reached $154 million by December 2000—the fourth straight year of sales growth.

March 2001 brought the announcement an experimental online laundry system. Tested at the Massachusetts Institute of Technology (MIT), the system allowed students in their dorm rooms to log on to a Web site to see if a washing machine was available downstairs in the laundry room. When the student's clothes were washed and dried, the student received e-mail notification. With a history sprinkled with creativity and well calculated risk-taking, Mac-Gray had become a leader in the laundry service business.

Principal Competitors

Coinmach; SpinCycle; Angelica Corporation; Dwyer Group, Inc.; Techsys, Inc.

Further Reading

Ackerman, Jerry, "Globe 100/Bears," *Boston Globe*, May 16, 2000, p. C26.

The Clean and Simple Advances of a Mac-Gray Laundry Program, Cambridge: Mac-Gray Corp, 2001.

Cohen, Joyce, "It's a Dirty Job But Now the Web Offers Help," *New York Times*, March 15, 2001.

Muther, Christopher, "Firm Sees Future in the Cards," *Boston Globe*, February 18, 1998, p. E4.

—Chris John Amorosino

Martin Industries, Inc.

301 East Tennessee Street
Florence, Alabama 35630
U.S.A.
Telephone: (256) 767-0330
Fax: (256) 740-5192
Web site: http://www.martinindustries.com

Public Company
Incorporated: 1974
Employees: 701
Sales: $63.7 million (2000)
Stock Exchanges: NASDAQ
Ticker Symbol: MTIN
NAIC: 333414 Heating Equipment Manufacturing
(Except Electric and Warm Air Furnaces); 335221
Household Cooking Appliance Manufacturing; 336212
Truck Trailer Manufacturing; 337214 Nonwood Office
Furniture Manufacturing

Martin Industries, Inc., based in Florence, situated in the northwest corner of Alabama, manufactures appliances and utility equipment in two industry segments: home heating and leisure and other products. Martin's home heating products, which account for about two-thirds of the company's sales, are produced and sold under the Atlanta Stove, Hunter, Martin Fireplaces, Martin Gas Products, Prime Heat, and Warm Morning brand names. Included are a variety of vented and vent-free gas furnaces and heaters as well as a wide range of gas logs, gas stoves, prefabricated gas and wood fireplaces, and gas inserts. Martin, which manufactures its lines at two plants, one located in Florence and the other in Ontario, Canada, markets its products through a variety of distribution channels in both the United States and Canada. The company's leisure and other products are produced and sold under Broilmaster and NuWay brand names and include gas barbecue grills and utility trailer kits. They are sold in all fifty states as well as in Canada, Mexico, South America, and Europe. An ESOP company since 1992, about a third of Martin is owned by its employees.

1905–41: Martin Brothers Establish Three Companies

It was in 1905, just after the turn of the 19th century, that two brothers, W.H. Martin Sr. and Charles Martin, founded King Stove and Range Company, a small cast iron foundry in Sheffield, Alabama. The foundry made coal and wood heaters, cooking stoves and ranges.

The Martins expanded their business in 1918, when they purchased a financially sinking stove foundry in Florence, just across the river from Sheffield. The brothers incorporated the acquired business as Martin Stove and Range Company, a separate business from King Stove and Range. There they made coal and wood stoves as well as gray iron castings. The foundry also turned out cast hollowware, iron skillets, and clothes-pressing irons known as ''sad'' irons.

The Martins again expanded their holdings in 1939, when they traveled to nearby Huntsville, Alabama, to bid on some machinery being auctioned off at a bankrupt manufacturing plant. They opted to bid on the whole operation, not just the equipment, and their bid won. The Martins turned the operation into their third business, Martin Stamping and Stove Company, which began turning out a small line of unvented gas heaters.

1941–76: Martin-Owned Companies Diversify

During World War II, both of the Martins' foundries manufactured magazine heaters for the Army, and Martin Stamping made bomb crates and other strategic materials. With the end of the war, however, the companies returned to manufacturing their lines of gas, wood, and coal heating equipment. They would add electrical heating equipment in the late 1950s, when Martin Stamping and Stove began making a line of electrical heaters at its facility in Huntsville. Within just few years, demand for its electrical heaters led Martin Stamping and Stove to open a new plant, located in Athens, Alabama. It went into operation, in 1966, as the company's Electric Heater Division. Also located in Athens, the Martin Fireplace Division began rapid growth, thanks in part to the introduction of Martin Firecones in 1968 and zero-clearance fireplaces in 1970.

On January 1, 1974, the three companies making up the Martin holdings merged to form Martin Industries, Inc. Under the reorganization plan, operational control was combined, and in June 1976, the company's executive team set up new central administration offices in Florence. In that same year, also in Florence, Martin Industries established a centralized engineering facility.

1977–90: Martin Expands Its Facilities and Acquires Other Companies

While the reorganization and structural changes were in progress, the Sheffield plant discontinued its foundry operations and was converted into a stamping and fabricating plant. In addition, the Florence plant was retooled into a highly automated foundry to meet Martin Industries' casting demands as well as those of other client companies.

In the late 1970s, the company's need for additional manufacturing space prompted Martin to buy additional facilities. Towards the end of 1977, it bought a plant located in Americus, Georgia, where, in 1978, it began producing its Ashley line of heaters. It also added a 200,000 square foot building in Huntsville. With the addition of that facility, formerly owned by Genesco, Martin's total manufacturing and warehouse floor space reached 1.2 million square feet.

The company's expansion through acquisition continued in the early 1980s. First, in 1980, it purchased the Edison line of dehumidifiers from McGraw Edison. Next, in 1982, it acquired the Sahara line from Hobart Manufacturing, which produced its dehumidifiers for General Electric.

Other changes came later in the decade, notably in 1987, when Martin sold its Florence foundry to several former employees, who entered a long-term agreement with Martin to provide it with its needed cast iron. That same year, Martin purchased the wood and gas divisions of Atlanta Stove, which had been one of Martin's chief competitors for several years. Martin then transferred the manufacture of Atlanta Stove's products to its factories in Huntsville and Athens and moved its sales administration to offices in Florence.

In a calculated strategy to decrease the impact of seasonal sales and thereby achieve a greater and more efficient use of its manufacturing capacity, in 1988 Martin acquired the NuWay line of utility trailer kits and, in 1990, the Broilmaster line of gas barbecue grills. In part, these product lines were purchased because their sales climbed during the warmer months of the year, which contrasted with the company's home heating products, which sold best in the colder seasons.

Martin also diversified into a non-season market, even before acquiring Broilmaster. In 1989, it purchased Filex, Inc., an Ossining, New York company that manufactured and marketed steel office furniture that it sold through major retail outlets. In the third quarter of that year, Martin incorporated production of the Filex desks and filing cabinets into its Sheffield and Huntsville plants. In 1990, Martin also expanded its gas heater lines when, in the same acquisition that brought Broilmaster into its corporate fold, it added the Warm Morning line of vented heaters to its offerings. The purchase included a facility in Washington Park, Illinois, where both Broilmaster barbecues and Warm Morning heaters were made.

1992–96: Martin Establishes ESOP and Goes Public

At the beginning of 1992, Martin instituted an Employee Stock Ownership Plan (ESOP), and in the following year the ESOP purchased a large block of the company's stock which then became available to eligible employees over an extended time. In the next year, the company sold off its manufacturing plant in Americus, Georgia, and its line of dehumidifiers.

Martin Industries finally went public in 1995, making an initial public offering (IPO) of 2.3 million shares of common stock. It entered the public sector in order to obtain funds for further acquisitions, make capital improvements, and develop new products. Among other things, the funds helped finance the company's expansion in Canada. Early in 1996, it completed its acquisition of Hunter Energy and Technologies Inc. and its sister company, Ontario, Inc., by purchasing all the outstanding shares of the two corporations. To buy them, Martin formed a wholly-owned Canadian subsidiary, Ontario, Inc. The total purchase price paid by Martin was about $1.94 million, consisting of cash, promissory notes, and funds paid into escrow. In January 1997, Hunter Energy and Ontario merged to form Hunter Technology Inc. Hunter continued to operate in its 100,000 square foot plant located on a 12 acre site in Orillia, Ontario, manufacturing a line of gas space heaters and pre-fabricated fireplaces.

1997–2001: Company Faces Tough Years at Close of Century

In February 1997, Martin discontinued its manufacture of office furniture, bowing to increased competition and only marginal market success. In June of the next year, it also moved its production of gas grills, gas logs, and free-standing vent-free heaters from its facility in Washington Park, Illinois, to its Athens and Huntsville, Alabama facilities.

In the fall of 1998, Robert L. Goucher replaced William H. Martin III as the company's CEO and president, a move in part made because of Martin Industries' need for some fresh strategic planning. Goucher came over from his positions as president and CEO of StarMark, Inc., a subsidiary of Masco Corporation. Based in Sioux Falls, Idaho, StarMark was a manufacturer of

---

Key Dates:

1905: W.H. Martin, Sr., and his brother, Charles, found King Stove and Range in Sheffield, Alabama.

1918: The Martin brothers purchase a stove foundry located in Florence, Alabama, incorporating it as Martin Stove and Range Company.

1939: The Martins buy a plant in Huntsville, Alabama, which becomes Martin Stamping and Stove Company.

1966: Martin Stamping and Stove Company builds a new plant in Athens, Alabama, for the company's Electric Heater Division.

1968: The company introduces Martin Firecones.

1970: Martin begins manufacturing and marketing zero-clearance fireplaces.

1974: The three companies held by the Martins merge to become Martin Industries, Inc.

1976: Company opens its Central Administration Offices in Florence.

1977: Martin buys a plant in Americus, Georgia.

1980: Company purchases a line of dehumidifiers from McGraw Edison.

1987: Martin sells its Florence foundry to former employees and acquires the wood and gas divisions of Atlanta Stove.

1988: Company acquires NuWay Manufacturing Co.

1989: Martin acquires Filex line of metal office furniture.

1990: Company acquires Broilmaster line of gas barbecue grills and Warm Morning line of vented heaters.

1993: Martin introduces its series of vent-free gas logs and fireplaces; company sells its Americus facility and its dehumidifier line.

1994: Company introduces line of free-standing, vent-free heaters.

1995: Martin goes public with an IPO.

1996: Company acquires Hunter Energy and Technologies Inc. and Ontario Inc.

1998: Martin consolidates its manufacturing by moving part of its operation from Illinois to its plants in Athens and Huntsville.

1999: Martin sells its Ashley solid fuel heating division to United States Stove Company.

---

high-end kitchen cabinets. While at the helm of StarMark, and in previous executive positions he held with Ryobi North America, Goucher's responsibilities included strategic planning as well as operations, sales, business development, and quality control.

The late 1990s proved to be very troubling years for Martin Industries. The company's financial setbacks compelled it to consider stringent counter measures, including the sale of some of its divisions. Martin's net losses for 1998 reached $3.5 million, then ballooned to $6.2 million the next year. Goucher, quoted in an article in *TimesDaily*, indicated that "the year 1999 was very difficult for the company, its employees and stockholders," and further indicated that in 2000 the company was seeking means to restore its financial health. One option was to sell off some or all of its product lines. In fact, it had started to do just that in 1999,

when it sold its Ashley solid fuel heating division. Selling the whole enterprise to a "strategic partner" was also under consideration, a partner who, Goucher said, "Will strengthen our position in the market or possibly bring us new markets, or utilize some of our operational capability."

In 2000, Martin Industries still employed between 150 and 200 people in northwest region of Alabama known as the Shoals, about 400 at its Athens plant, and another 50 at its Canadian operation in Ontario. In that year, as part of its turn-around effort, it expanded its Sheffield operation to allow the plant to assemble gas fireplace log sets and utility trailers. The company also opened a new warehouse, shipping, and distribution center at the Sheffield site, and also upgraded the plant's equipment and began developing new product lines. However, at the same time, it consolidated some operations and closed its plant in Huntsville, and, late in 2000, sold its Washington Park, Illinois, manufacturing plant and some of its equipment.

The year also saw a change at the top when John L. Duncan replaced Goucher as president and CEO. Duncan, who had been a director of the company since 1999, was formerly the president and CEO of Murray Ohio Manufacturing Co. Goucher, although no longer involved in the company's day-to-day operations, was still involved in planning strategic alternatives with the company's investors.

At the end of 2000, Duncan had to face expected but nevertheless very disappointing financial realities. The company reported another net loss, this time climbing to $24.6 million, or $3.19 per share. Sales simply plummeted, falling to $63.7 million, down 29 percent from the company's 1999 sales of $89.2 million. The company's drop in sales in part resulted from its inability to manufacture and ship its hearth products on time because of problems encountered when Martin put in place a new distribution system at the start of 2000. However, with the exception of Broilmaster premium barbecue grills, sales for the company's products fell across the board.

In 2001, Martin, under Duncan's tutelage, took several steps to counteract its sagging sales, including some belt tightening measures. Among other things, it moved its NuWay Trailer Division to its plant in Canada and discontinued assembling both utility trailers and log sets at its facility in Sheffield. The company was also planning some new strategic initiatives, including the option of divesting its Broilmaster Premium Gas Grill line in order to focus more sharply on its Hearth and Heating divisions. It was hoped that such measures would soon return the company to profitability.

In Martin's favor is the fact that it manufactures goods for a solid market with fairly predictable demands. However, each of the industry segments in which the company operates is cyclical, and its sales are affected by general economic cycles, consumer confidence, inflation, and other factors outside its control, such as the demand for new housing and the availability of financing. Furthermore, home heating product sales are seasonal in nature and are directly affected by weather conditions, so the company will always face risks beyond those inevitably imposed by industrial competitors. Part of Martin's difficulties in 1998 and 1999 arose from the fact that sales of its heating equipment declined because those years had very mild winters, some of the warmest ever recorded by the National Oceanic and Atmosphere Administration. Still, Martin is not in a terribly volatile industry and does not face any looming threats from either new technologies or competitive industries. Its chances of getting back on a solid profitability track remained strong at the start of the new millennium, though just how long that might take was uncertain.

Principal Subsidiaries

Hunter Technology Inc.; NuWay Trailer.

Principal Competitors

Barbecues Galore Limited; CFM Majestic Inc.; HON Industries Inc.; Lennox International Inc.; Temtex Industries, Inc.; Weber-Stephen Products Co.

Further Reading

Briner, Russell F., et al., ''Coping with Change at Martin Industries,'' *Management Accounting* (USA), July 1989, p. 45.

''Cooking With Gas,'' *USA Today Magazine,* July 1998, p. 94.

Corey, Russ, ''Sale an Option for Financially Struggling Martin Industries,'' *TimesDaily.com*, March 31, 2000.

''Martin Industries, Inc. Announces Plant Consolidation,'' *Business Wire*, December 9, 1999.

''Martin Industries Inc.-Financial Results,'' *Market New Publishing*, August 16, 2001.

''Martin Industries Names Robert L. Goucher President and Chief Executive Officer,'' *Business Wire*, September 28, 1998.

''Martin Offers a Wide Range of New Fireplace Products,'' *Professional Builder and Remodeler*, January 15, 1992, p. 290.

—John W. Fiero

Mellon Financial Corporation

One Mellon Bank Center
Pittsburgh, Pennsylvania 15258-0001
U.S.A.
Telephone: (412) 234-5000
Fax: (412) 234-9495
Web site: http://www.mellon.com

Public Company
Incorporated: 1869 as T. Mellon & Sons
Employees: 26,000
Sales: $5.9 billion (2000)
Stock Exchanges: New York
Ticker Symbol: MEL
NAIC: 52211 Commercial Banking; 52221 Credit Card
   Issuing; 551111 Offices of Bank Holding Companies

With nearly $2.8 trillion in assets, Mellon Financial Corporation operates as an international financial services firm catering to businesses, institutions, and individuals. Its financial products and services related to businesses and institutions include investment management, trust and custody, foreign exchange, securities lending, contribution services, fund administration, stock transfer, proxy solicitation, employee benefits consulting, and outsourcing for benefit plans and banking services. Mellon also provides services concerning capital markets, venture capital, asset-based lending, loan underwriting, and leasing and real estate finance. The company provides mutual funds, private asset management, electronic brokerage services, and banking services to individuals.

Early History

Born on a potato farm in Ireland in 1813, Thomas Mellon decided at an early age that farming was not his life's calling. When he was five years old, his family moved to Pennsylvania, where he could often be found reading a book as he rode a plow across his father's fields. He became a lawyer in 1839, and although his practice did well, his investments in real estate, construction, and mortgages fared even better. In 1869, Judge

Thomas Mellon retired from public service and founded T. Mellon and Sons, a private banking house at 145 Smithfield Street in Pittsburgh.

The bank prospered during the post-Civil War years, and a second bank, run by Mellon's sons, opened soon after the first. In the Panic of 1873, when half the banks in Pittsburgh failed, the Mellon's never closed either bank. Although Thomas Mellon died in 1908, his sons, Andrew and Richard, were able to build upon their father's foundation to create the giant that would eventually play a key role in fueling industry throughout Pennsylvania and most of the rest of the country.

The Mellon's invested their profits from the bank in other enterprises, such as Alcoa (Aluminum Company of America), originally known as the Pittsburgh Reduction Company, and Gulf Oil Corporation, founded by William Larimer, Thomas Mellon's grandson. Gulf Oil grew to become the world's tenth-largest industrial corporation, and Alcoa became the world's largest aluminum manufacturer. The Mellons' monumental success with Mellon Bank and other such ventures was partly responsible for the long-held belief in Allegheny County, Pennsylvania, that "nothing moves in Pittsburgh without the Mellons."

Four financial institutions founded in the 19th century contributed to the growth and history of Mellon Bank. Besides T. Mellon and Sons, they were: the Farmers Bank of Delaware, established in 1807 by Henry Ridgely; the Harrisburg Bank, founded in 1814 by William Wallace, Robert Harris (son of the founder of the city of Harrisburg), and 11 other Pennsylvania businessmen; and the Girard Savings Institution of Philadelphia, established by Benjamin Wood Richards in 1835. This institution, which eventually came to be known as Girard Bank, was named in honor of Stephen Girard, a multi-millionaire who left $7 million to the city of Philadelphia and lent money to the American government during the War of 1812.

Andrew Mellon Takes Leadership of the Firm: 1882

After serving as president of T. Mellon and Sons from 1869 to 1882, Thomas Mellon retired and turned the bank over to his son Andrew. Under Andrew's leadership, the bank financed the cre-

Company Perspectives:

We have built our company upon a well-defined strategy: provide a breadth of financial solutions to our customers— what they need, when they need them, how they want them delivered. It's the core of our success in the marketplace, the root of shareholder value, our foundation for growth.

ation of Union Transfer and Trust Company; joined the national banking system as Mellon National Bank in 1902; formed its first foreign bureau in 1908 to provide banking services for customer activity outside the United States; and established a long tradition of growth through acquisitions and mergers.

In the late 19th century, goods were often sold with a three- or four-month grace period between delivery and payment due dates. T. Mellon and Sons profited from the common practice of buying at a discount the documents that showed the amount due and holding them until maturity to collect the full value. This business made T. Mellon and Sons the largest private bank between New York and Chicago. The bank soon decided to expand its range of operations, however, to include trust estates and related work, and created the Fidelity Title and Trust Company with the help of other investors. Fidelity was an instant success, so much so that it found itself turning away business in order to avoid conflicts of interest between clients. Consequently, in 1889 it set up its own rival company, the Union Transfer and Trust Company, which became the Union Trust Company not long after. In an effort to consolidate the Mellons' banking interests, the family decided in 1902 that Mellon National Bank should become an almost wholly owned subsidiary of Union Trust. In 1921, Andrew Mellon was appointed secretary of the treasury by President Calvin Coolidge. While he served in Washington, D.C., remaining under presidents Warren Harding and Herbert Hoover, his brother Richard became president of the bank.

Surviving Economic Hard Times: Late 1920s to Early 1930s

Since Mellon National Bank was a federally chartered corporation and Union Trust and Union Savings were state banks, the Mellons were able to take advantage of both banking systems. Together, the banks could finance virtually any enterprise in the country by the 1920s. In 1929, Richard Mellon formed Mellbank Security Company, a bank holding company that helped save numerous smaller banks in western Pennsylvania during the Great Depression. Mellon's knack for giving sound advice to its customers, together with its ability to maintain sufficient liquidity and one of the highest ratios of cash to deposits in the nation, played a major role in the bank's survival through the 1930s. From 1931 to 1932, the combined earnings of Mellon National and Union Trust totaled nearly $12 million. Indeed, since the Mellon name and conservative reputation were well known by the 1920s, many of the panicked customers who withdrew their savings from other banks after the crash flocked to Mellon National. Seeing the crowds team into the bank, Richard Mellon reportedly muttered, ''I told those damn architects to make more room in the lobby.''

After Richard's death in 1933, his son, Richard K. Mellon, took over as president. When Mellon National Bank and Union Trust Company merged in 1946, Richard became chairman of the newly formed Mellon National Bank and Trust Company. Mellon Bank also entered the retail market by expanding its branch network and merging with Mellbank.

By the middle of the 20th century, Mellon began to build a reputation for technological innovation, especially in cash management. The company bought its first computer in 1955, one of the first banks in the nation to do so. In 1958, Mellon established the Mellbank Regional Clearing House, the forerunner of its Datacenter Group, for overnight processing of checks from correspondent banks.

One measure of Mellon's power was the size of its trust assets: in 1967, Mellon Bank controlled a third of all the trust assets in Pennsylvania. That same year, ''outsiders''—people who were not Mellon descendants—first filled the bank's top two positions. Richard K. Mellon became honorary chairman of the board, John A. Mayer, president since 1959, became chairman, and A. Bruce Bowden was appointed president. As president, Mayer had helped Mellon double its savings deposits, nearly double its mortgages holdings, and issue credit cards to 250,000 people. His success was the fruition of a program begun by Richard K. Mellon to expand Mellon's reach from its traditional base of wealthy individuals to all kinds of banking customers.

In 1972, Mellon National Corporation was created as a one-bank holding company to own Mellon National Bank and Trust Company, which officially became Mellon Bank.

By the mid-1970s, Mellon was still one of the most conservative banks in the country, a philosophy that served it well in 1975, when many progressive banks got into trouble with real estate investment trusts, a popular investment item in the 1960s and 1970s. Banks had lent billions of dollars for real estate and construction ventures. With these loans, real estate development companies built so many condominiums, single-family homes, and other buildings that they found themselves short of buyers. Mellon, however, had advised its customers to avoid the real estate investment trusts and was untouched by this crisis.

In 1982, Mellon's assets totaled $19 billion, more than the combined assets of the next three largest banks in Pittsburgh. The company had also become a strong commercial lender with sophisticated credit-accounting techniques, and managed nearly $13 billion in trusts, including many corporate pension and benefit plans. ''It was always easy to identify the leadership in Pittsburgh,'' Joseph Lasala, a former Philadelphia city representative, told *Philadelphia* magazine in 1986. ''There's one of everything. One big industry—steel . . . and one big bank— Mellon.''

Difficulties in the 1980s

On the whole, however, the 1980s were a difficult time for Mellon Bank. Although it nearly doubled its assets between 1982 and 1987, its quick expansion overseas and into ''high growth industries'' such as energy and real estate was poorly timed. Under the leadership of Chairman J. David Barnes, Mellon created an energy lending division and a loan production office in

Dallas, Texas, in 1982—just after oil prices peaked. Foreign operations, which accounted for nearly one-third of Mellon's profits in 1982, caused some of the worst damage. Like many large banks, Mellon's international expansion was poorly timed. Overexposure in Mexico, Brazil, and other Third World nations resulted in many problem loans. Mellon eventually closed almost half of its 20 foreign branches. The company also realigned its international operations to focus on multinational corporate customers rather than overseas borrowers.

The merger of Mellon and Girard Bank in 1982 also exemplified Mellon's eagerness to expand. Girard had merged with the Corn Exchange Bank in 1951, installed its first computer in 1962, and, over the next ten years, pioneered the development of automated retail services in Philadelphia. Its automated bank system would eventually gain industry recognition as state of the art. Girard also acquired the Farmers Bank of Delaware in 1981, renaming it Girard Bank Delaware. Girard's earnings dropped significantly in October 1982, but Mellon finalized the merger anyway, in November, 1982. Girard's growth came to a sudden halt after the merger, and in 1984 the bank's shaky balance sheet—which included a vast portfolio of delinquent

loans—contributed to a 14 percent decline in Mellon's earnings for the year. It also prompted Mellon officers to head to Philadelphia to "Mellonize" things. Their take-charge approach made Girard veterans and customers uncomfortable. In addition to firing several Girard executives, Mellon went so far as to rename Girard Bank Mellon Bank (East), while Girard Bank Delaware became Mellon Bank (DE).

In 1985, Mellon, which had adopted the name Mellon Bank Corporation a year earlier, merged with Commonwealth National Financial Corporation, the Harrisburg-based financial-services holding company formed in 1969 by the merger of the Harrisburg National Bank and Trust Company, Conestoga National Bank, and the First National Bank of York. Mellon also enhanced its integrated banking software and financial data-processing systems through the acquisition of Carleton Financial Computations Inc., in South Bend, Indiana. Also that year, Mellon purchased several subsidiaries of the Fidata Corporation that offered securities transfer, securities pricing, and trust accounting services. By the late 1980s, Mellon was selling its data-processing expertise to some 400 small banks across the country.

Mellon entered the high-growth consumer-banking market in Maryland in 1986, when it bought certain assets of Community Savings and Loan, of Bethesda, and created Mellon Bank (MD). It also opened Mellon Securities Ltd., London, to serve the investment needs of United States-based customers, and added Triangle Portfolio Associates to its eight investment-management subsidiaries.

In 1987, Mellon recorded the first loss in its history, due to increased reserves for Third World loans and for certain domestic credits. When this first-quarter loss was announced, stock shares plummeted and Chairman Barnes resigned. The Mellon family, which held 15 percent of the bank's stock, chose an acting replacement for the CEO and, after an extensive search, approved the appointment of Frank Cahouet. Formerly president of the Federal National Mortgage Association, Cahouet was best known in the finance industry for reviving San Francisco's Crocker National Corporation, although it was sold before he could complete his mission. Cahouet recruited Anthony P. Terracciano, former vice-chairman at Chase Manhattan Corporation, to serve as president and chief operating officer.

Cahouet immediately froze salaries and ordered the 19,500-member staff reduced by 10 percent, to Wall Street's approval. The following year, in 1988, the company formed Grant Street National Bank, a separate entity created solely to clean Mellon's bad-debt slate by liquidating many of its weak domestic loans. The bank was partly backed by Mellon funds and junk bonds, sold to investors who hoped sales of property securing the bad loans would be profitable.

Cahouet's plan was to return the company to its original position as a regional bank by becoming a more niche-oriented institution. During the late 1980s, Mellon concentrated on providing loans and other services to medium-sized companies, breaking its pattern of overextension to large, multinational corporations and foreign governments. This long-term goal to become a super-regional bank, however, put Mellon in direct competition with PNC Financial, the parent company of Pittsburgh National Bank, which had operated very successfully on the middle-market level for years.

Mellon's approach emphasized its service businesses—trust and investment, data processing, and cash management—which showed no signs of slowing down. In 1988, the company acquired Backroom Systems Group, which offered personal computer software designed to automate labor-intensive tasks for financial institutions. Determined to maintain its leadership in the data-processing industry, Mellon also continued to develop BancSource, a data-processing system that would eventually perform all customer loan and deposit processing.

Growth and Expansion in the 1990s

The final decade of the 20th century marked the first time that Pennsylvania allowed true statewide banking; previously, state law governed how many branches a bank could open beyond county borders. The new law allowed banks to offer services where they made sense in terms of market coverage, not physical boundaries.

As such, Mellon spent much of the 1990s strengthening its regional position through strategic acquisitions. In 1990, Mellon purchased 54 Philadelphia branch offices of Philadelphia Saving Fund Society (PSFS) from Meritor Savings Bank. In order to fund the deal, Mellon sold its consumer finance business, Mellon Financial Services Corp., to Associates Corporation of North America. The firm also partnered with Giant Eagle Inc. in Pittsburgh to open its first full-service supermarket office, offering Mellon customers extended banking hours.

The following year, Mellon purchased United Penn Bank for $90.2 million. Cahouet stated in a *New York Times* article that the deal, "[d]emonstrates the corporation's commitment to our home state of Pennsylvania and provides us with a strong presence in one of the few key population centers of the state we do not presently serve." In 1992, Mellon snatched up the remaining PSFS branches from Meritor, after the Federal Deposit Insurance Corp. seized its assets after five years of losses. After the purchase, Mellon PSFS secured the leading position in the five-county Philadelphia region in total deposits, deposit market share, and number of retail offices. By the end of that year, it had also landed the leading position among 28 super-regional banks ranked by *The American Banker* in terms of return on average assets and equity.

In 1993, Mellon acquired The Boston Company, a provider of various institutional banking services, from Shearson Lehman Brothers in a deal worth $1.45 billion. It also purchased AFCO Credit Corp., an insurance premium financing division of The Continental Corporation. At the same time, the firm sold three outsourcing businesses related to its data processing services. In 1992, outsourcing revenues totaled $94 million, falling short of company expectations.

The Dreyfus Purchase: 1994

It was during this time period that mutual funds were becoming increasingly popular. Instead of saving money in traditional bank accounts, many savers opted to put money into investment products such as mutual funds. Mellon acted upon this trend and became the largest bank manager of mutual funds in 1994 with the $1.85 billion purchase of New York-based Dreyfus Corporation. The purchase of Dreyfus, the sixth-largest mutual fund company in the U.S., was the largest mutual fund acquisition in banking history.

While concentrating on its mutual funds business, Mellon also beefed up its retail banking operations. The firm entered the New Jersey market with the purchase of Glendale Bancorporation. The deal allowed Mellon to begin branch banking under the Mellon PSFS name in both traditional banking offices and in supermarkets. In 1994, the firm also partnered with Acme Markets Inc. in a deal that brought supermarket banking to Acme stores in Philadelphia, Delaware, and New Jersey.

Mellon continued its expansion into the mid-1990s. In 1995, the company joined with Chemical Banking Corp. to form Chemical Mellon Shareholder Services, one of the largest shareholder services firms catering to publicly held firms. Mellon also acquired Certus Financial Corp.'s investment management division, renaming the unit Certus Asset Advisors. That same year, the firm formed Mellon Financial Markets Inc., an underwriting subsidiary that provided underwriting, trading, and sales services to investors.

In 1996, Mellon expanded its leasing products and services with the purchase of Chicago-based FUL Inc. and the Business Equipment Finance division of USL Capital Corp. The company also penetrated the Florida market by acquiring Ganz Capital Management Inc., an investment management service provider based in Miami. Mellon also expanded its product line in 1997 by purchasing Buck Consultants Inc., an employee benefits and compensation firm. In order to take advantage of the growing Internet-based brokerage service market, Mellon bought Pacific Brokerage Services Inc. Operating under the name Dreyfus Brokerage Services Inc., the firm catered to online traders.

During late 1990s, the banking industry experienced a wave of consolidation along with corporate takeovers. Mellon's solid reputation made it a prime target. The number of U.S. banks had dropped to 9,500 by 1997, down from 14,000 banks in 1985. A Goldman Sachs banking analyst commented in a 1997 *Fortune* article that Mellon had "collected a group of businesses that major banks want to be in. This is one of the last great trophy franchises out there."

From Traditional Bank to a Financial Services Firm

Cahouet's insistence to keep Mellon intact however, thwarted takeover attempts from the likes of Bank of New York. The firm instead, continued focus on expanding into new, high-growth markets. It acquired Florida-based United Bankshares Inc. and California-based 1st Business Corp. Mellon also focused on international expansion, forming alliances with banks in Brazil, Chile, Hong Kong, Japan, and Singapore. The firm also teamed up with ABN AMRO Bank N.V., a Netherlands-based company. Operating under the name ABN AMRO Mellon Global Securities Services, the joint venture provided custody products and services to financial institutions.

In 1999, Cahouet retired, naming Martin G. McGuinn chairman and CEO of Mellon. In September of that year, the firm changed its name to Mellon Financial Corp. signaling its commitment to operate as a leading financial service company. Management set new strategic initiatives in place that focused on investing in its high-growth, high-return businesses. In order to achieve its new goals, the firm sold its mortgage servicing, credit card, and network services transaction processing businesses.

By the start of the new millennium, Mellon had successfully transformed itself from a traditional commercial bank into an investment service firm. In 2000, the firm acquired the remaining 25 percent of U.K.-based Newton Management Limited (it had already purchased the other 75 percent in 1998.) It also gained full control of ChaseMellon Shareholder Services, a joint venture between Mellon and Chase, and renamed it Mellon Investor Services. Net income for the year grew to over $1 billion for the first time in company history.

A weakening economy in 2001 forced Mellon to cut costs and focus on its most profitable ventures. In July 2001, the firm announced that it planned to sell its retail, small-business, and middle-market banking operations to Citizens Financial Group in a deal worth $2 billion. Eyeing asset management, fund servicing, and private banking as avenues for future growth, Mellon management was confident that the firm would remain a major player in the investment banking industry.

Principal Subsidiaries

Mellon Private Asset Management; Mellon Private Banking; Mellon United National Bank; The Boston Company Asset Management LLC; Certus Asset Advisors Corp.; Dreyfus Brokerage Services Inc.; The Dreyfus Corp.; Dreyfus Investment Services Corp.; Founders Asset Management LLC; Franklin Portfolio Associates LLC; Laurel Capital Advisors LLP; Mellon Bond Associates LLP; Mellon Capital Management Corp.; Mellon Equity Associates LLP; Newton Management Limited; Pareto Partners; Prime Advisors Inc.; Boston Safe Deposit and Trust Company; Buck Consultants Inc.; CIBC Mellon Global Securities Services Co.; CIBC Mellon Trust Company; Dreyfus Retirement Services; Mellon Europe-London; Mellon Fund Administration; Mellon Investor Services; Russell/Mellon Analytical Services; Mellon Bank N.A.; Mellon PSFS; Mellon Bank Community Development Corp.; AFCO Credit Corp.; Mellon Corporate Financing; Mellon Financial Markets LLC; Mellon Ventures Inc.

Principal Operating Units

Wealth Management; Global Investment Management; Global Investment Services; Mellon Global Investment Services and Management Alliances with Non-U.S. Financial Institutions; Specialized Commercial Banking; Large Corporate Banking.

Principal Competitors

FleetBoston Financial Corp.; J.P. Morgan Chase & Co.; PNC Financial Services Group Inc.

Further Reading

Chase, Brett, "Mellon's Departing CEO: We've Had a Great Run," *American Banker,* December 2, 1998.

Dunaief, Daniel, "Analysts See Mellon Reaping Rewards of Dreyfus Purchase," *American Banker,* June 17, 1996, p. 39.

Hersh, Burton, *The Mellon Family: A Fortune in History*, New York: William Morrow and Company, 1978.

Koskoff, David E., *The Mellons: The Chronicle of America's Richest Family*, New York: Thomas Y. Crowell, 1978.

Lappen, Alyssa A., "The Puzzle Called Mellon," *Institutional Investor,* September 1997, p. 55.

Mandaro, Laura, "Decision Expected on Mellon Retail Deal," *American Banker,* July 17, 2001, p. 19.

Massey, Steve, "Mellon Focus of Merger Rumors," *Pittsburgh Post-Gazette,* January 14, 1994, p. B13.

Matthews, Gordon, "Shaky Meritor Props Itself Up With Mellon Deal," *American Banker,* December 6, 1989, p. 2.

McCullough, C.H., *One Hundred Years of Banking*, Herbick and Held Printing Company, 1969.

"Mellon Bank: Competing at the Top," *Magazine of Bank Management,* October 1991, p. 33.

"Mellon Bank in Pact to Buy Glendale BanCorp," *New York Times,* May 7, 1994, p. 41.

"Mellon/Dreyfus: The Lion That Squeaked," *Economist,* December 11, 1993, p. 86.

"Mellon Purchase Now Finalized," *American Banker,* December 8, 2000, p. 8.

"A Merger Chain Reaction," *US Banker,* May 1998, p. 10.

"Meritor Seized After Big Losses," *National Mortgage News,* December 21, 1992, p. 1.

Moyer, Liz, "Mellon, by Splitting Its 2Q Report, Shows New Core's, "Profit Growth," *American Banker,* July 18, 2001, p. 4.

——, "Mellon Tightens Belt for Downturn," *American Banker,* February 27, 2001, p. 1.

——, "Mellon to Scrap 'Bank' from Name for 'Financial'," *American Banker,* September 15, 1999, p. 5.

Padgett, Tania, "Focus Sharpened, Mellon Shifts Sights to Possible Acquisitions," *American Banker,* June 21, 2000, p. 1.

Schwartz, Nelson D., "Takeover Time for the Last Trophy Bank?," *Fortune,* October 13, 1997, p. 26.

Talley, Karen, "Consolidation Is Changing the Face of the Industry," *American Banker,* October 24, 1995, p. 25.

Williams, Terry, "Merger Boosts Mellon's Stature," *Pensions & Investments,* September 28, 1992, p. 2.

—update: Christina M. Stansell

Mitsubishi Electric Corporation

2-3, Marunouchi 2-Chome
Chiyoda-ku
Tokyo 100-8310
Japan
Telephone: (81) 3 33218-2111
Fax: (81) 3 3218-2431
Web site: http://www.mitsubishielectric.com

Public Company
Incorporated: 1921
Employees: 116,715
Sales: ¥4.1 trillion ($33.3 billion) (2001)
Stock Exchanges: London Paris Frankfurt Luxembourg
   Amsterdam Tokyo Osaka Nagoya Fukuoka Sapporo
Ticker Symbol: MIELY
NAIC: 333921 Elevator and Moving Stairway
   Manufacturing; 334111 Electronic Computer
   Manufacturing; 335999 All Other Miscellaneous
   Electrical Equipment and Component Manufacturing;
   33429 Other Communications Equipment
   Manufacturing; 334413 Semiconductor and Related
   Device Manufacturing; 334419 Other Electronic
   Component Manufacturing; 51334 Satellite
   Telecommunications

Even though it shares a name and common heritage with nearly 40 different companies, Mitsubishi Electric Corporation is an independent company with operations in 34 countries. The firm is involved in the manufacture, marketing, and sales of electrical and electronic equipment used in information processing and communications, space development and satellite communications, consumer electronics, industrial technology, energy, transportation, and construction. During the late 1990s and into the new millennium, Mitsubishi was forced to restructure operations due to economic hardships in Japan.

The original Mitsubishi company (the name means ''three diamonds'' in Japanese) was originally founded shortly after the Meiji Restoration in 1868 by Yataro Iwasaki, an enter-prising samurai who gained control of shipping in Tosa prefecture in the first years of Japan's industrial expansion. Japan grew into a major economic and military power in the western Pacific, in many ways as a result of Mitsubishi's ambitious maritime activity. The company connected Japan with foreign markets and succeeded in establishing a shipping monopoly, despite a powerful challenge from rival Mitsui.

Early History: 1910s–20s

By the mid 1910s, Mitsubishi was one of the largest companies in Japan, with diversified interests in heavy manufacturing, mining, real estate, banking, and trading. In order to attract investor capital, the Iwasaki family created several independent companies out of Mitsubishi's subsidiaries. Mitsubishi Electric was one of them, created in 1921.

Mitsubishi Electric originated in 1905 in the parent company's Kobe shipyard as a manufacturer of electrical equipment for ships and mining. Five years later, the division constructed a large-capacity induction motor (the first in Japan) and a turbine generator.

As a victor in World War I, Japan gained recognition as a legitimate naval power in the Pacific. In order to preserve and enhance its position, Japan expanded its navy and merchant marine, creating even greater demand for new ships equipped with generators and other electric devices. As the major shipbuilder in Japan, Mitsubishi engineered a merger between the electric-machinery departments of Kobe Shipbuilding & Engine Works and its own Mitsubishi Shipbuilding company. Shares in the new company, Mitsubishi Electric, were sold to investors, and the capital raised was used to acquire new manufacturing space and equipment.

Mitsubishi Electric, however, was unable to develop devices technologically competitive with those manufactured by foreign companies. Like NEC, which had negotiated an extensive cooperative agreement with Western Electric, Mitsubishi-Electric became closely associated with another American electronics manufacturer, Westinghouse Electric. Their agreement, concluded in 1923, provided Mitsubishi Electric with Japanese marketing and licensing rights for a number of Westinghouse products and designs. As a result, Mitsubishi Electric successfully built a large 2300-kVA vertical-axis-type hydraulic generator.

Mitsubishi Electric remained the favored supplier of large and small electrical devices to all the various Mitsubishi companies while maintaining its expertise in maritime electronics and gaining new strengths in other fields like communication, power transmission, lighting, and consumer appliances. In 1931, Mitsubishi Electric began commercial production of passenger elevators and started exporting fans to China and Hong Kong. Two years later, reacting to greater domestic demand for home appliances, the company began marketing refrigerators.

Difficulties During the 1930s and 1940s

The 1930s were a difficult period for Japan's *zaibatsu* conglomerates like Mitsubishi. The 12 major Japanese companies had become inextricably linked to the government through a 50-year industrial modernization program. But the government had recently been taken over by a quasi-fascist element in the military whose aim was to establish absolute Japanese supremacy in eastern Asia. In their effort to modernize and arm Japan for war, the militarists called upon industrial concerns such as Mitsubishi Electric to provide a vast array of equipment.

While Mitsubishi Heavy Industries eventually became the principal manufacturer of warplanes, particularly the notorious Zero, Mitsubishi Electric developed radio sets for the Zero and other aircraft, and later became deeply involved in additional military projects.

With World War II well under way, Mitsubishi Electric came under increasingly strict control by the government. The company was compelled to follow all military directives and, as a result, in 1944 established a research laboratory whose goal was to develop new instruments for naval and aerial battle management. By August 1945, however, the war was lost, and Japan's battered industries came under the control of government agencies directed by the occupation authority.

Mitsubishi Electric began the enormous task of rebuilding its business after the war. Helped by reconstruction loans but impeded by difficult labor regulations, supply shortages, weak domestic demand, and the dissolution of the *zaibatsu*, Mitsubishi Electric struggled to survive. By 1948, the company had resumed production of consumer and some industrial items, including straight-tube fluorescent lamps. Military production, once the primary source of Mitsubishi's profits, had been banned by the occupation authority.

Entering Foreign Markets: 1950s

Having reestablished marketing agreements with foreign manufacturers, Mitsubishi Electric began selling televisions in Japan in 1953. After completing several successful industrial projects, Mitsubishi resumed foreign operations in 1954 with the completion of a power substation in India.

As a result of the Korean War, the United States government decided to end its extractive, punitive policies toward Japan. Instead, it encouraged the Japanese to build a large and modern industrial infrastructure that would allow Japan to serve as a bulwark against the expansion of communism in the East. Increasingly, in the name of efficient industrial organization, the Japanese government permitted the former *zaibatsu* companies to reestablish ties. The Mitsubishi logo, banned by the occupation authority, was readopted by all the Mitsubishi companies, including Mitsubishi Electric. With the benefit of freer association among the engineering, manufacturing, marketing, and financing wings of the Mitsubishi group, Mitsubishi Electric gained an increased ability to compete in the largely unregulated foreign markets.

The rich U.S. and European markets, however, were already dominated by large electrical-equipment manufacturers like Westinghouse, General Electric, Philips, and GEC. In fact, the Japanese government had passed legislation to protect domestic manufacturers against these companies. Mitsubishi Electric recognized that it could not compete against the large manufacturers until it had first established a stronger base in consumer sales and industrial projects. The increased incomes of Japanese consumers and the ability of Japanese companies to compete on price in middle-technology projects provided Mitsubishi Electric with two important ways to achieve that goal.

Continued International Expansion and Product Innovation: 1960s–70s

In 1960, the company became one of the first in Japan to begin production of color televisions, marking a commitment to maintaining market share in the emerging high end of the market. After production of several electric locomotives for the Japanese railway system, Mitsubishi Electric exported its first one, to the government of India, also in 1960.

During the 1960s, Japanese products gained a reputation for poor quality and simple technology. In electronics, however, the Japanese Ministry of International Trade and Industry (MITI) assisted companies by coordinating technological developments and protecting certain key markets. One of the earliest to show leadership in technological pursuits, Mitsubishi Electric unveiled a computer prototype in 1960, and the following year began production of its Molectron integrated circuit.

In order to reflect both a corporate reorganization and a more international view, the company's name was changed in 1963 from Mitsubishi Electric Manufacturing to Mitsubishi Electric Corporation, or Melco. The company made its first overseas investment in Thailand in 1964, and two years later concluded a sale of electric locomotives to Spain. In communications, Melco completed the first of several antenna designs for satellite earth stations and placed a remote weather station on the summit of Mount Fuji. Mitsubishi's development of communications tech-

Key Dates:

1921: Mitsubishi Electric Manufacturing is formed.
1923: The company forms a licensing agreement with American firm Westinghouse Electric.
1945: The firm comes under control of government agencies directed by the occupation authority.
1948: Production of consumer and industrial items resumes.
1953: Mitsubishi begins selling televisions in Japan.
1963: Company name changes to Mitsubishi Electric Corp.
1966: The firm signs a technical-exchange agreement with Westinghouse.
1973: Sales offices are established in Great Britain, the U.S., Brazil, and Argentina.
1983: An integrated circuit plant is established in the U.S., a cathode ray tube plant opens in Canada, and a VCR manufacturing facility is formed in Britain.
1985: Sales reach ¥2 trillion.
1991: Mitsubishi begins production of the 64Mbit DRAMS.
1993: The company installs the world's fastest elevator in the Landmark Tower in Yokohama.
1994: Mitsubishi joins the General Magic Alliance.
1995: The firm begins constructions on one of the largest color liquid crystal display manufacturing plants in Japan.
1998: The firm reports losses due to a weakening Japanese economy and changing market conditions; Dr. Ichiro Taniguchi is named president.
1999: Mitsubishi completes construction on a satellite assembly and testing plant.
2000: Company forms alliances with both Boeing Company and Toshiba Corp. and is awarded a contract from the Japanese government to supply the Multi-Purpose Transport Satellite-2.

nologies later led to its selection for government projects and electronics work with the U.S. Department of Defense.

Melco funded much of its industrial and high-technology research by cross-subsidizing: taking profits from the consumer and business markets and applying them to government and industrial projects with long lead times but large rewards. Among Melco's successes in the low-ticket markets were air conditioners, color televisions, and small office computers. In order to reduce costs in certain areas of research, Melco revived its technical-exchange agreement with Westinghouse in 1966. In later years, Melco began to sell technology to Westinghouse, marking a significant appreciation in Mitsubishi's status.

The increased quality of Japanese products and the continued production-cost advantages enjoyed by Japanese companies led to tremendous demand overseas. It was at this point, around 1970, that Japan's export-led expansion moved into a new phase of feverish growth. In 1972 and 1973 alone, Melco established sales companies in Great Britain, the United States, Brazil, and Argentina, and yet another was opened in Australia in 1975.

Predicting a gradual deterioration in production-cost advantages in Japan relative to other developing Asian nations, Melco began making substantial overseas investments, building a television plant in Singapore in 1974 and another in Thailand three years later.

Until then, Mitsubishi Electric had been primarily a manufacturer of industrial equipment. The oil crisis of 1973–74, however, critically damaged the company's business in that field and, perhaps more than any other event, convinced Mitsubishi's president, Sadakazu Shindo, that the only way to maintain growth was through expanded consumer sales. One product, aimed directly at the domestic household market, was the futon dryer; 600,000 were sold in 1977 alone.

Melco was one of several companies that elected to develop a home video-recording system based on Matsushita's VHS design. The VHS, although it entered the market a full year after Sony's rival Betamax system, became established as the industry standard. Companies that developed the Beta system—particularly Sony—lost not only a great deal of money in sales but, more important over the longer term, market share. Melco's rising acceptance in the home-video market was complemented by the introduction of such other new products as large-screen projection TVs.

Mitsubishi Electric added sales organizations in West Germany and Spain in 1978, and in Canada in 1980. In order to reduce transportation costs and hedge against rising protectionist sentiment in foreign markets, Melco established television-production facilities in the United States and Britain in 1980, and in Australia in 1982. The following year, Melco opened an integrated-circuit plant in the United States, a cathode-ray-tube plant in Canada, and a VCR plant in Britain. The new plants created thousands of jobs in these countries and revitalized several local economies. By 1985, Mitsubishi Electric's sales had reached ¥2 trillion, double the amount just five years earlier.

Mitsubishi Electric's unusual corporate personality was largely derived from the years Sadakazu Shindo presided over the company. During his presidency, Shindo remained the guiding force at Mitsubishi Electric. Among his strongest legacies were a commitment to frank discussion, honest criticism, and individualism. He was known to have favored the hiring of high school graduates over college graduates, contending that they were only slightly less knowledgeable, but much more willing to ask questions and work in teams.

Diversification and Growth Continues: Late 1980s–Mid-1990s

During the late 1980s, Mitsubishi Electric was well diversified within the electronics industry, deriving approximately equal amounts of profit from communications, consumer products, heavy machinery, and industrial products. In its effort to overtake competitors such as Hitachi and Toshiba, the company concentrated its resources on new-product development. The task of selling the products was handled through Mitsubishi Shoji, its former parent trading company, and much of that sales effort was concentrated in the Middle East in an attempt to retrieve what were called oil yen.

By maintaining close relations with both Westinghouse and General Electric, Mitsubishi Electric bet much of its future success on the integrated microcircuitry that made possible everything from simple industrial robots to artificial intelligence. During the late 1980s, Mitsubishi continued to become more firmly established as an industry leader as it found new applications for these technologies in its existing product lines.

Mitsubishi continued new product development and expansion into the 1990s. The firm purchased the hardware division of Apricot Computers and developed both a 4-megabit static random access memory (SRAM) and a 64-megabit dynamic random access memory (DRAM) chip in order to broaden its reach into the U.S. semiconductor market. In 1992, the firm announced plans to join a U.S. and Canadian telecom project in which it would provide telephones for a new satellite system. The following year, Mitsubishi secured a contract from the Japanese Defense Agency to develop surface-to-air missiles. The company's heavy machinery segment also installed the world's fastest passenger elevator in the Landmark Tower in Yokohama. In 1995, Mitsubishi began production on a color liquid crystal display (LCD) manufacturing plant—one of Japan's largest—in order to take advantage of the growing demand for LCDs.

A major portion of Mitsubishi growth efforts during the mid-1990s was focused towards the American market. In an effort to boost profitability and competitiveness, the company restructured its U.S. subsidiaries, Mitsubishi Electronics America (MELA) and Mitsubishi Consumer Electronics America (MCEA), creating a new company consisting of the audio/video and cellular mobile telephone businesses of both subsidiaries in 1995. The firm also joined the General Magic Alliance, dedicated to developing communication products and services whose membership included Apple, AT&T, France-Telecom, Fujitsu, Matsushita, Motorola, Northern Telecom, Philips, Sony, Sanyo, and Toshiba.

Overcoming Hardships:
Late 1990s into the New Millennium

While continuing its focus on growth, Mitsubishi was forced to overcome hardships during the latter half of the 1990s. In 1995, a devastating earthquake rocked through Kobe and Osaka, Japan. While there were no company fatalities, seven production facilities and four research laboratories were damaged. At the same time, the company began buying finished goods overseas to use in its electric power equipment division in order to combat a strong yen that was wreaking havoc on domestic profits. However, while many Japanese-based firms began moving production overseas, Mitsubishi was able to maintain most of its domestic manufacturing.

In 1997, the firm became part of a public payoff scandal in which sokaiya—corporate racketeers—were paid for their silence during shareholder meetings. In November of that year, Mitsubishi executive Yoshiki Sugiura was arrested for allegedly paying off a sokaiya. According to Tokyo police, the firm had been involved in the payoffs since 1985—its shareholder meetings had lasted an average of 30 minutes with only two questions brought to the table over a ten year time period.

During that same year, the Japanese economy began faltering, and personal consumption declined due in part to the April 1997 rise in Japan's national consumption tax. Semiconductor prices also fell, forcing the firm to report consolidated losses for the first half of 1997—the first consolidated losses ever reported by the firm. As the Asian economy as a whole began to waver, Mitsubishi began to focus on operational efficiency along with new product development.

Losses continued into 1998 as many of the firm's product segments fell victim to falling prices, including the audio visual equipment and air conditioning product lines. Sales fell in the company's industrial machinery and automation equipment division, as well as in the home electronics division. During that year, Dr. Ichiro Taniguchi, a long-time Mitsubishi employee, replaced Takashi Kitaoka as president.

Mitsubishi reported losses in 1999 as well. Japan's economy continued to remain unstable, forcing management to focus on short-term recovery plans. It restructured its foreign subsidiaries involved in the semiconductor, audio-visual, and personal computer industries, while at the same time focusing on securing increased sales and developing new products. Eyeing both the computer and communications industry as growth areas, the firm put plans in motion to divest unprofitable businesses as well as cut nearly ten percent of its work force.

While unfavorable economic conditions continued into the new millennium, Mitsubishi management set forth a strategic plan that consisted of the following goals: to become a prime global manufacturer of satellites and onboard equipment; secure a leading position as a telecommunications infrastructure manufacturer; and to utilize the firm's mobile phone business—it produced 18.5 million handsets in fiscal 2001—as a core for future expansion into the multimedia terminal equipment. The company also focused on its basic operations in electric power equipment, public infrastructure, transportation equipment, building systems, housing equipment, electrical appliances, factory automation, and automotive equipment while divesting businesses deemed unprofitable.

While enduring hardships and trying economic times, Mitsubishi management continually worked towards achieving company goals. As part of its strategic plan, Mitsubishi was awarded a contract from the Japanese government to supply the Multi-purpose Transport Satellite-2 (MTSAT-2) in July 2000. The contract, along with others, secured the firm's position as the leading satellite manufacturer in Japan. The company also formed a partnership with Boeing Co. to develop a high-speed communications network that would enable aircraft to receive online video and two-way Internet communications. An alliance was also formed with Toshiba Corp. that enhanced Mitsubishi's international power transmission and distribution business.

In fiscal 2001, Mitsubishi reported an increase of net income to ¥124.8 billion ($1.01 billion). Intent on remaining a leader in the electronics industry, Mitsubishi management forged ahead with its plans for continued growth and new product development.

Principal Subsidiaries

Mitsubishi Electric and Electronics USA Inc.; Mitsubishi Display Devices America Inc.; Mitsubishi Digital Electronics

America, Inc.; Mitsubishi Electric Automation Inc.; Mitsubishi Electric Automotive America Inc.; Mitsubishi Electric Power Products Inc. (U.S.); Trium/Mitsubishi Wireless Communications Inc. (U.S.); Paceon Corp. (U.S.); Powerex Inc. (U.S.); Diamond Link Inc. (U.S.); Mitsubishi Electric Sales Canada Inc.; Melco de Mexico S.A. de C.V.; MELCO Display Devices Mexico, S. de R.L de C.V.; Melco Argentina S.A.; MELCO-TEC Rep. Com. e Assessoria (Brazil); Fujinor S.A. (Brazil); Melco de Colombia Ltda.; Mitsubishi Electric Automotive Czech s.r.o.; Mitsubishi Electric Telecom Europe S.A. (France); Ascenseurs Mitsubishi France S.A.; Mitsubishi Electric Information Technology Centre Europe B.V. (France); Mitsubishi Semiconductor Europe, GmbH (Germany); Mitsubishi Electric Europe B.V. (Ireland); Mitsubishi Electric Europe B.V. (Italy); Mitsubishi Electric Automotive Europe B.V. (Netherlands); Mitsubishi Elevator Europe B.V. (Netherlands); Mitsubishi Electric Europe B.V. (Portugal); Mitsubishi Electric Europe B.V. (Russia); Mitsubishi Electric Europe B.V. (Spain); Mitsubishi Electric Automotive Europe B.V. (Sweden); Mitsubishi Electric Europe B.V. (UK); Mitsubishi Electric Finance Europe PLC (UK); Mitsubishi Electric Air Conditioning Systems Europe Ltd. (UK); Mitsubishi Electric Information Technology Centre Europe B.V. (UK); Mitsubishi Electric (China) Co., Ltd.; Mitsubishi Electric Dalian Industrial Products Co., Ltd. (China); Mitsubishi Stone Semiconductor Co., Ltd. (China); Beijing Mitsubishi Mobile Communication Equipment Co., Ltd.; Gang Ling Electronic Technology Development(Beijing) Co., Ltd.; Shandong Hualing Electronic Co., Ltd.; Mitsubishi Electric (H.K) Ltd. (China); Bao Ling Trading & Consulting Co., Ltd. (China); Xi Dian Mitsubishi Electric Transmission & Distribution Products Development Co. Ltd. (China); Xi Ling Electric Power Products Manufacturing Co. Ltd. (China); Shanghai Mitsubishi Elevator Co. Ltd.; Shanghai Mitsubishi Electric & Shangling Air-Conditioner and Electric Appliance Co. Ltd.; Mitsubishi Electric (Guangzhou) Compressor Co., Ltd. (China); Mitsubishi Electric (H.K.) Ltd. (Hong Kong); Ryoden (Holdings) Ltd. (Hong Kong); Ryoden Merchandising Co., Ltd. (Hong Kong); Mitsubishi Electric Automotive India Private Ltd.; P.T. Lippo Melco Manufacturing (Indonesia); P.T. Mitsubishi Jaya Elevator and Escalator (Indonesia); P.T. Lippo Melco Electronic Indonesia; Mitsubishi Electric Logistics Corp.; Mitsubishi Electric Information Network Corp.; PacEast Telecom Corp.; Mitsubishi Electric Information Technology Corp.; Mitsubishi Electric Osram Ltd.; Oi Electric Co. Ltd.; LG Industrial Systems Co. Ltd. (Korea); Poscon Corp. (Korea); KEFICO Corp. (Korea); Han Neung Techno Co. Ltd. (Korea); Mitsubishi Electric (Malaysia) Sdn. Bhd.; Ryoden (Malaysia) Sdn. Bhd.; International Elevator & Equipment Inc. (Philippines); Laguna Auto-Parts Manufacturing Corp. (Philippines); Mitsubishi Electric Singapore Pte. Ltd.; Mitsubishi Electric Asia Pte. Ltd. (Singapore); Trium Telecom Asia-Pacific Pte. Ltd. (Singapore); Mitsubishi Electric Taiwan Co., Ltd.; Shihlin Electric & Engineering Corp. (Taiwan); Taiwan Kolin Co., Ltd.; Powerchip Semiconductor Corp. (Taiwan); Kang Yong Watana Co., Ltd. (Thailand); Oriental Electric Industry Co. Ltd. (Thailand); Mitsubishi Electric Consumer Products (Thailand) Co. Ltd.; Mitsubishi Elevator Asia Co., Ltd. (Thailand); Mitsubishi Electric Australia Pty. Ltd.; Melco-Mec Egypt for Elevators & Escalators; Middle East Electric Co. W.L.L., Kuwait; Mitsulift and Equipment S.A.L. (Lebanon); Mitsubishi Electric Saudi Ltd.; Melco Elevator (South Africa) (Pty) Ltd.; M.S.A. Manufacturing (Pty) Ltd. (South Africa); ETA-Melco Elevator Co., L.L.C. (U.A.E.).

Principal Divisions

Energy and Electric Systems; Industrial Automation Systems; Information and Communication Systems; Electronic Devices; Home Appliances.

Principal Competitors

Hitachi Ltd.; NEC Corporation; Toshiba Corporation.

Further Reading

DeTar, Jim, ''While Others Cut Back, Mitsubishi Renews Commitment to the DRAM Market,'' *Electronic News,* May 25, 1998.

Mitsubishi Electric Corp, ''History,'' Tokyo, Japan: Mitsubishi Electric Corp., 2001.

''Mitsubishi Electric Develops 4-Megabit SRAM,'' *Japan Economic Newswire,* February 15, 1990.

''Mitsubishi Electric Final Results,'' *Extel Examiner,* May 26, 1992.

''Mitsubishi Electric Joins Shift Offshore to Fight Strong Yen,'' *Business Times* (Singapore), April 13, 1995.

''Mitsubishi Electric Posts 1st-Ever Group Loss,'' *Jiji Press Ticker Service,* November 27, 1997.

''Mitsubishi Electric to Build Color LCD Plant in Japan,'' *Japan Economic Newswire,* December 27, 1994.

''Mitsubishi Electric Ups Foreign Imports in Bid to Regain Competitiveness,'' *Nikkei Weekly,* May 2, 1994, p. 10.

''Mitsubishi Electric Wins Japanese Missile Development Order,'' *AFX News,* October 6, 1993.

''Mitsubishi Electronic Outlines Consumer Electronics Strategy,'' *AsiaPulse News,* September 14, 2000.

''Mitsubishi Feels Chill,'' *Control and Instrumentation,* January 1999, p. 16.

''Mitsubishi Plans Restructuring,'' *Appliance,* June 1999, p. 16.

Morishita, Kaoru, ''Electronics Makers Entangled in Scandal,'' *Nikkei Weekly,* November 17, 1997, p. 6.

''Quake Fallout May Lead Firms to Spread Risks,'' *Los Angeles Times,* January 30, 1995, p. 1.

—update: Christina M. Stansell

The Montana Power Company

130 North Main Street
Butte, Montana 59701-9331
U.S.A.
Telephone: (406) 497-5100
Fax: (406) 497-5240
Web site: http://www.mtpower.com

Public Company
Incorporated: 1912
Employees: 2,416
Sales: $999.7 million (2000)
Stock Exchanges: New York Pacific
Ticker Symbol: MTP
NAIC: 221122 Electric Power Distribution; 22121
   Natural Gas Distribution

The Montana Power Company is one of the largest utility companies in the Northern Rockies region of the United States. Montana Power also operates properties in non-utility businesses such as coal mining, gas and oil exploration, development and marketing, and technology, including electronic controls and telecommunications. By the early 1990s, the utility's sales had surpassed $1 billion, and its expansion had carried it into four countries, making Montana's only company listed on the New York Stock Exchange a recognizable and formidable force in the U.S. utility industry. With the arrival of utilities deregulation in the 1990s, Montana Power shifted its focus toward its telecommunications business, and by 2001 the company was divesting its utility and energy holdings in order to focus on spinning off its telecommunications interests as Touch America Inc. When the reorganization was complete, Montana Power would be operating as an autonomous subsidiary of the NorthWestern Corporation, while proceeds from the sale would be used to launch Touch America as a publicly-traded telecommunications company.

The Electrification of Montana: 1880–1920

To the sparsely populated area once known as Montana Territory, electricity arrived before statehood, preceding the region's admittance as the 41st state by eight years, when the pioneering denizens of the small silver mining town of Walkerville first received electricity in 1880. The illumination of its famous neighbor, Butte, marked the beginning of the electrification of Montana and spawned a new breed of business competitors; power companies intent on linking major industrial and manufacturing activities to hydroelectric generation on the Missouri and Madison rivers with electrical transmission lines. During the three decades following Butte's historic entrance into the electrical age, 40 small power companies serving sundry small towns gradually joined together to form four regional electric utilities: Butte Electric & Power Co., Madison River Power Co., Billings Eastern Montana Power Co., and Missouri River Electric & Power Co. When these four power companies consolidated in late 1912, the consortium that emerged represented Montana's newest and largest utility, the Montana Power Company.

Chiefly responsible for the merger of the four power companies was John D. Ryan, a prominent Montana businessman with considerable holdings in the region's copper industry. In 1905, he was elected president of Anaconda Copper Mining Company, rising from the position of managing director, a post he had held in several subsidiary companies owned by Anaconda's parent company, Amalgamated Copper Company. Several years later, Ryan would become president of Amalgamated Copper itself, then gain national notoriety by railing against the implementation of anti-trust legislation in the copper industry. However, before doing so, his most notable achievement was the formation of Montana Power, the primary source of the copper industry's power. In the years leading up to Montana Power's formation, Ryan and several business partners purchased power sites along the Missouri river, and then Ryan orchestrated the consolidation of the four hydroelectric utilities. Four days after Montana Power was incorporated, with capital stock amounting to $7.7 million, Ryan was selected as the company's president, on December 12, 1912.

Copper mining at Butte's "Richest Hill on Earth" and processing operations at Anaconda and Great Falls were a major source of Montana Power's early business. Railroad companies were another, with the newly formed utility company providing the power to fuel the electric locomotives that transported people and supplies to and from Montana. To carry current to the railroads and to other customers, dams had to be constructed,

Company Perspectives:

The Montana Power Company is a changing enterprise. We are continuing to move quickly to transform ourselves from a diversified electric and gas utility into a national, high-speed, technologically advanced, broadband fiber-optic products and services transport company under the name Touch America. When this process is complete The Montana Power Company will continue to provide electric and gas services under a new owner, while Touch America will become a publicly-traded telecommunications company.

generating stations needed to be built, and transmission wire needed to be strung, some of which had been accomplished before Montana Power's formation, when small electric utilities populated the state. However, a majority of the construction work would take place after the utility's creation, and much of it under Montana Power's purview. In 1915, Montana Power spent $3.4 million on extending its service area, particularly to include the Chicago, Milwaukee & St. Paul Railroad. The utility registered $4.3 million in revenue that year, up more than 15 percent from 1914's total, and served 32,000 customers.

By extending its service area to accommodate the utility's industrial customers and leasing electric washers and ranges to its residential customers, Montana Power grew, serving 70 towns and cities in Montana by 1922. Two additional dams were brought on line during the 1920s, one at the decade's beginning and the other at its conclusion, giving Montana Power a total of 12 dams from which the utility derived power to generate electricity. Half of these dams were constructed before Montana Power's formation, beginning with Black Eagle Dam in 1890 and ending with the reconstruction of Hauser Dam in 1911. Several of these pre-existing dams were products of Ryan's early power site purchases along the Missouri River, before he coordinated the merger of the four utilities that would form Montana Power, while the six dams constructed after the utility's creation were built under Montana Power's supervision. The first of these dams built by Montana Power was Thompson Falls Dam, which was completed in July 1915. Two more dams were completed that year, the Ryan Dam the following month, and Hebgen Dam two months later in October. The sixth and last dam completed during the decade, Holter Dam, was brought on line in 1918.

Diversification Between the Wars

The 1920s represented a less prodigious period of dam construction, but the decade brought Montana Power into contact with a coal mining operation located at Colstrip, Montana, that would later become an integral contributor to the utility's revenue volume. Montana Power's first association with the coal mines at Colstrip occurred during the construction of Mystic Dam, a dam built to supply electricity to the coal mine's owner and operator at the time, Northern Pacific Railway. Completed in 1927, Mystic Dam enabled Montana Power to supply Northern Pacific with energy to run the railroad company's electrically operated coal mine, which was used to produce boiler fuel. Although it would be roughly 30 years until Montana Power assumed control of the rich Colstrip mines, the

contract to supply Northern Pacific with electricity helped accelerate the utility's growth. Two years after the completion of Mystic Dam, Montana Power earned a profit of $666,390, nearly three times as much as it earned the year before, an increase that was largely attributable to the utility's electricity contracts with large operations in the mining and smelting industries.

Growth continued throughout the 1920s, with annual revenues eclipsing $10 million by 1928, up substantially from the $3 million recorded in 1922. In 1930, another dam was brought on line, the Morony Dam, but the decade would be remembered less for hydroelectric expansion and more for the arrival of a new type of fuel to the region, natural gas. In 1931 Montana Power signed contracts with Anaconda, the copper mining company, that entailed the expenditure of between $10 and $12 million for the construction of natural gas pipelines over the course of the coming year. Constructed chiefly to serve Butte and Anaconda and their industries with natural gas, the pipeline also brought natural gas to other areas included within Montana Power's service area. In July 1931, two months after pipeline construction began, natural gas arrived in Bozeman, Montana, from a separate line origination in south central Montana. A larger, southbound line originating from northern Montana natural gas fields wound through several other Montana towns, arriving in Helena, the state's capital, by the beginning of September and in Butte two weeks later. As it had with electricity, Montana Power offered gas appliances at low costs and initially for free to customers who signed up for gas service, then supported its natural gas service with a fleet of cars and salespeople. By 1932, Montana Power had 9,623 natural gas customers and considerably more electricity customers, giving the utility two foundations from which to further diversify.

The construction of dams did not stop in the 1930s, but progress was slowed appreciably by the debilitative economic conditions characterizing the decade. Construction of Kerr Dam was started in 1930, then halted the following year, resumed in 1936, and finally completed in 1938, as the utility fitfully proceeded through the decade. The 1940s brought few changes to the utility beyond meeting the increasing wartime needs of its residential and industrial customers. The 1950s, however, were replete with significant and sweeping changes that included Montana Power's diversification into non-utility businesses, its adoption of a different form of power generation, and the expansion of its burgeoning natural gas business.

New Forms of Power Generation after World War II

Three signal events occurred early in the decade that dramatically altered Montana Power's future. In 1951, the utility completed construction of the Frank W. Bird plant located on the banks of the Yellowstone River in Billings, Montana. Fueled either by natural gas or oil, the Bird plant represented Montana Power's first fossil-fueled plant and augured the utility's strategic shift away from hydroelectric power to power generation from other fuels. Dwindling opportunities for hydroelectric development—the utility's last Missouri River dam, Cochrane, was completed during the decade—and the mounting energy needs of Montana's residents and businesses compelled Montana Power to begin exploring for alternative energy sources, a decision manifested in the construction of the Bird plant and one that induced the utility to form Western Energy

---

Key Dates:

1912: Montana Power Company is formed.
1915: Construction of Thompson Falls Dam is completed.
1927: Mystic Dam is completed.
1931: Montana Power and Anaconda Copper Mining Company form joint-venture to construct natural gas pipelines.
1951: Frank W. Bird power plant becomes operational.
1957: Altana Exploration Company is formed.
1977: Roan Resources Limited is formed.
1980: North American Resources is formed.
1990: Montana Power acquires Touch America.
1999: Montana Power agrees to sell its electric generation holdings to PP & L Global, Inc.
2000: Montana Power announces intention to sell all utility holdings and to create an independent telecommunications called Touch America.

Company in 1951. Years later in the 1960s, Western Energy would spearhead the utility's movement into coal mining and processing, a fuel Montana Power would rely on heavily to fuel its power generation plants. In 1952, Montana Power began receiving natural gas from Canada, which, in addition to broadening the scope of the utility's natural gas business, led to its diversification into oil and gas exploration in Canada, a venture conducted through Altana Exploration Company, a Canadian subsidiary formed in 1957.

Perhaps the most defining development, however, occurred at the decade's conclusion, when Montana Power secured much of its future fuel supply by purchasing the rights to the Rosebud Coal Mine and other mines located at Colstrip. The Colstrip reserves were vast—the Rosebud mine was regarded as one of the eight largest coal mines in the United States during the 1990s—and Montana Power spent much of the next decade incorporating its new fuel source into the utility's system. By 1968, the utility's first coal-fired generation plant was completed, located 100 miles west of Colstrip in Billings, where the Frank Bird plant was erected.

Efforts to market coal to other utilities were first successful in 1969 and 1970 and provided encouraging results. However, the utility's mainstay continued to be its involvement in supplying electricity, from which Montana Power derived 65 percent of its slightly more than $80 million in annual revenues recorded at the beginning of the 1970s. The balance was derived primarily from the utility's natural gas business, including both the provision and exploration of the fuel. Prospects for the immediate future brightened when one of the utility's major customers, Anaconda, announced plans for a multi-million dollar expansion program to increase its production volume, which for Montana Power meant a heightened need for power. An energy crises during the early and mid-1970s, however, tempered any hopes of widespread industrial expansion in the state and spawned a movement toward energy conservation. Montana Power's management accelerated its natural gas exploration efforts. In 1977, another Canadian subsidiary, Roan Resources Limited, was formed. Roan Resources, Altana (the

other Canadian subsidiary created 20 years earlier), and a U.S.-based company named North American Resources, organized in 1980, made up Montana Power's oil division.

The 1970s also saw the beginning of development of the four Colstrip plants. Units 1 and 2 were 330 megawatt plants owned equally by Montana Power and Puget Sound Power and Light, and Units 3 and 4, at 700 megawatts each, were owned 30 percent by Montana Power, 25 percent by Puget Sound Power and Light, 15 percent by Washington Water Power, 20 percent by Portland General Electric, and 10 percent by PacifiCorp. These four plants represented the second largest coal-fired electric generating complex west of the Mississippi River.

New Ventures: The 1970s and 1980s

After a decade filled with energy construction and conservation measures and widespread federal reform of the utility industry through the promulgation of the 1978 Public Utility Regulatory Act, Montana Power entered the 1980s intending to reposition itself for the future and increase its stake in non-utility ventures. Most of the changes initiated by the utility were organizational in nature and stemmed from developments during the 1970s, as well as from earlier decisions that had steered Montana Power into non-utility businesses. It was the reorganization of these various non-utility businesses that Montana Power began to carry out once power plant construction began winding down in 1983. The following year, the utility formed a new subsidiary named Entech, Inc., which absorbed Western Energy, the company that operated Montana Power's coal properties, as well as the utility's oil exploration businesses, Altana Exploration, Roan Resources, and North American Resources Co. Entech, which essentially became an organizational umbrella under which Montana Power's non-utility interests were grouped, also absorbed two new businesses, Telecommunications Resources, Inc. and Tetragenics Company. Formed in 1982, Tetragenics sold electronic controls, while Telecommunications Resources, organized the following year, was involved, as its name suggested, in telecommunications.

An additional non-utility business, Special Resources Management, was formed in 1985, marking Montana Power's entrance into toxic waste handling and management. Special Resources Management was later sold in 1993. In 1988, the Montana Power completed another organizational move by creating the Independent Power Group (IPG) to manage Montana Power's long-term contracts for the sale of coal produced at Colstrip and to invest in non-utility electric generating plants.

Reshaped during the 1980s, the utility entered the 1990s supported by its three primary business units, Entech, IPG, and its utility division, the heart of Montana Power and the largest contributor to its annual sales volume. The utility registered $823 million in revenues in 1990, more than half of which was generated by its electric and natural gas service. By 1993, revenues had eclipsed the $1 billion plateau, and Montana Power's two newest business units, Entech and IPG, had extended the utility's geographic presence considerably beyond Montana's borders. Entech by this time held an investment interest in a gold mine in Brazil, while IPG maintained a stake in the world's largest co-generation plant in Teesside, England, assumed operational responsibility for a plant in Argentina, and was involved in the development of a coal-fired project in China. In reaching its $1.07 billion in revenues for the year, Montana Power garnered $410.4 million from Entech's various business lines and $120.3 million from IPG's wholesale electricity sales, non-utility electric generation facility operation, and engineering and plant maintenance services.

In 1986, with the completion of the Colstrip Unit 4 and in light of an earlier decision by the Anaconda Company to exit the copper mining and refining business in Montana, Montana Power sold its 30 percent ownership in Colstrip Unit 4, leasing back the power that it has sold outside of Montana on long-term contracts.

As Montana Power charted its future in an industry governed by strict regulatory policies, cause for optimism existed in its enviable and considerable interests in non-utility and, therefore, non-regulated businesses. The coal division operating within Entech stood as one of the 12 largest coal producers in the nation during the mid-1990s, providing sufficient coal to fuel Montana Power's five enormous jointly owned coal-fired electric generating plants while still permitting the sale of coal to other utilities.

Utilities Deregulation at the End of the Twentieth Century

The shift toward electricity deregulation in the mid-1990s forced Montana Power to reexamine its role in the changing utilities industry. While the company had long enjoyed its status as a major regional utility, it became clear that deregulation would attract competition from much larger utilities from other parts of the United States. In response to a notice of inquiry on utility restructuring issued by the Montana Public Service Commission in late 1995, which established guidelines for the transition to a competitive electricity supply market, Montana Power initiated a major corporate realignment program. The plan, which split Montana Power into two primary business units—Energy Supply, and Energy Services and Communications—was designed to streamline the company's power business, while accelerating the development of its non-utility holdings. The Energy Supply Unit maintained the company's traditional focus on electric generation and oil, gas, and coal production, while Energy Services and Communications assumed responsibility for the company's transmission and distribution systems. More significantly, Energy Services and Communications gave Entech's telecommunications operations a more prominent position in Montana Power's overall corporate strategy, making it responsible for advancing the company's position in the communications technology sector.

At the heart of the Energy Services and Communications Unit was a subsidiary of Montana Power called Touch America. A product of the disintegration of AT&T in the early 1980s, Touch America was originally founded in 1983 as a long-distance service provider and supplier business telephone equipment. The company was purchased by Montana Power in 1990, at which point it began developing fiber optic technologies as part of the Entech division. One of Touch America's first projects after the realignment was the creation of a fiber optic network between Billings and Denver. The network, which cost $62 million to complete, became operational in 1997, and ex-

panded the market for the company's telecom business from one to twelve million customers. In September, 1997 Touch America entered into a joint-venture with Enron and the Williams Communications Group to create a major fiber optic network between Portland, Oregon, and Los Angeles, with Touch America providing the construction management for the project. The network was the first to join the two cities using an inland route, extended over 1,600 miles, and linked several other rapidly growing cities in the western United States, including Boise, Salt Lake City, and Las Vegas. With its completion, Touch America total network expanded to 4,600 miles.

Meanwhile, Montana Power's Energy Supply Unit was preparing for deregulation. In July 1996 the company reached a memorandum of understanding with six other Northwest electric companies to create an independent grid operator—IndeGO—which would safeguard the utilities' access to transmission facilities in a competitive market. The time frame for the restructuring of the utilities industry was established in April of the following year, when the Montana State Legislature mandated that electric supply choice be available to all customers by July 1, 2002. A week after this decision, in a move that suggested that the company's interests might be shifting away from electricity generation, Montana Power acquired the oil and gas assets of Vessels Energy, Inc. for $85 million, the largest purchase in the history of the company. In December 1997, a month after Southern California Edison's well-publicized sale of ten generating plants for three times market value, Montana Power announced its intention to sell off its electric supply business. The company's generating operations, comprised of 13 dams and four coal-fired plants, were worth $600 million, and accounted for 25 percent of the company's total assets. A deal was closed in December 1999, when PP&L Global, Inc. of Virginia purchased 13 of Montana Power's generating plants for $1.59 billion.

During this period Touch America continued to expand its network. In February 2000 the company reached an agreement with PF.Net that gave it an additional 5,900 route miles and extended its reach to the Southwest, Texas, Florida, and the East Coast. By 2001 the total length of the company's fiber optic lines exceeded 20,000 miles. The sale of Montana Power's power generation and utility holdings also provided the growing telecommunications business with some much needed investment capital. PanCanadian Petroleum Ltd. purchased the company's oil and gas interests for $475 million in August 2000; in September the company's coal business was purchased by Westmoreland Coal for $138 million, and in October NorthWestern Corporation purchased the power distribution and transmission operations for $1.1 billion. NorthWestern Corporation intended to retain the Montana Power Company name for its energy transmission and distribution services in the state of Montana, while also promising to retain all existing contractual relationships and the work force. The remaining telecommunications business, Touch America, would be debt-free, with over $1 billion to reinvest, and in a position to become a major player in the telecommunications industry.

Principal Competitors

AT&T Corporation; Edison International; Electric Lightwave, Inc.

Further Reading

''Butte to Get Natural Gas,'' *New York Times*, March 7, 1931, p. 32.

''Buys Natural Gas Fields,'' *New York Times*, May 16, 1931, p. 28.

Byrne, Harlan S., ''Montana Power Co.,'' *Barron's*, January 8, 1991, p. 35.

Gannon, Bob, ''The Montana Power Company Perspective,'' *Montana Business Quarterly*, Autumn 1993, p. 11.

Kenworthy, Tom, ''In Montana, a Volt out of the Blue,'' *Washington Post*, March 4, 1998.

''Montana Power Company,'' *Wall Street Transcript*, September 7, 1970, pp. 21, 648.

''Montana Power Earnings,'' *New York Times*, March 22, 1916, p. 15.

''Montana Power Names Engineer to Be Chief,'' *New York Times*, October 2, 1991, p. D4.

''Montana Power's Year,'' *New York Times*, March 20, 1924, p. 28.

''People,'' *Electrical World,* March 1992, p. 22.

Rowe, Bob, and Bob Anderson, ''The Regulatory Compact,'' *Montana Business Quarterly*, Autumn 1993, p. 7.

''Ryan Elected President of Anaconda,'' *New York Times*, June 20, 1905, p. 13.

Setterberg, Diana, ''Montana Disputes Low Ranking in National Tele-communications Survey,'' *Montana Standard*, August 16, 1999.

Stucke, John, ''Touched by Fate,'' *Missoulian* (Montana), April 16, 2000.

—Jeffrey L. Covell
—update: Stephen Meyer

Mt. Olive Pickle Company, Inc.

Corner of Cucumber & Vine
P.O. Box 609
Mount Olive, North Carolina 28365
U.S.A.
Telephone: (919) 658-2535
Toll Free: (800) 672-5041
Fax: (919) 658-6296
Web site: http://mtolivepickles.com

Private Company
Incorporated: 1926
Employees: 800
Sales: $100 million (2000 est.)
NAIC: 311420 Fruit and Vegetable Canning, Pickling,
     and Drying

Mt. Olive Pickle Company, Inc. is America's largest independent pickle company. Each year it packs and sells over 80 million jars of pickles, relishes, and peppers. With its operations located in the small town of Mount Olive, North Carolina (population 5,000), the company is a dominant brand in many Southern states. In large part, pickles are a regional business because the cost to transport the heavy jars puts a manufacturer at a price disadvantage with local packers. Mt. Olive also caters to the tastes of its regional customers by selling sweet pickle cubes, used by southerners in potato salad but an item unfamiliar to most northerners. In a similar way to Duck Head pants, Mt. Olive Pickles has gained sentimental brand loyalty from many southerners. Nevertheless, Mt. Olive has made a long-term effort to expand its distribution. Its products can now be found in 30 states, as far north as New Hampshire and as far west as Texas and Oklahoma.

Company Origins in the 1920s

Compared to Charles F. Cates & Sons of Fiason, North Carolina, Mt. Olive was a latecomer to the pickle business. In 1898 Cates began to produce pickles according to a family recipe. Originally operating out of Swepsonville, the company moved to Faison, just eight miles away from Mount Olive, in order to be closer to its cucumber growers. Mount Olive farmers not only produced cucumbers, over the years they grew tobacco, cotton, and even rice. From 1900 to 1905 the town billed itself as the strawberry capital of the world. It was a bumper crop of cucumbers in 1925 that would lead to the formation of the Mt. Olive Pickle Company. Rather than let the excess cucumbers at the town's major produce market go to waste, a Lebanese immigrant from Goldsboro named Shickrey Baddour wanted to brine the cucumbers, then sell the brine stock to pickle companies. With the blessing of the local chamber of commerce and the assistance of area businessman George Moore, who had previously worked for a North Carolina pickle company, Baddour built a large tank that he filled with water, rock salt, and cucumbers. The newly formed Mt. Olive Pickle Company managed to sell some of the brine stock but not enough to be profitable. Now the company's backers decided to make plans to pack pickles themselves. Rather than sell their cucumbers to Cates, Mt. Olive growers saw a chance to cut out the middleman by gaining a stake in the town's new pickle company.

In 1926, 21 men, all but four of whom lived in Mount Olive, incorporated the Mt. Olive Pickle Company, with a capitalization of $15,875. All the equipment of the original Mt. Olive Pickle Company was turned over to the new corporation in exchange for $5,000 worth of stock. Baddour was also hired as the company's salesman and Moore as the factory superintendent and foreman. In the first year Mt. Olive packed 6,250 cases of pickles, most of which were under the Carolina Beauty label. Within two years annual sales exceeded $50,000. In the beginning everything was done manually by a handful of employees. In 1931, the company brought in an experienced man to serve as plant manager, hiring Harry Kraft away from a Heinz pickle plant in Michigan. During the years of the Great Depression, the company needed help from the Chamber of Commerce and backing from one of its investors, physician C.C. Henderson, to pull it through. Still, the company was large enough to justify the purchase of its first long-distance delivery truck in 1934. It was in the late 1930s that Mt. Olive began to ''fresh pack'' pickles, a process that produced a very crisp product by packing cucumbers only hours after being picked and pickled.

Mt. Olive cracked the $500,000 annual sales mark in 1942. A year later it instituted a profit sharing program for employees, a idea not only progressive for a small town but for the country as a whole. It was one of the first 200 companies in the United States to implement such a plan. By 1947, sales topped $1 million. During these early years Mt. Olive packed pickles under an array of brand names in addition to Carolina Beauty: MOPICO (an abbreviation of Mt. Olive Pickle Company), Little Rebel, Little Mommie, Way Pack, Pick of Carolina, Play Mates, and Plee-Zing. In 1953 the company developed a Mt. Olive label in distinctive script that it began to feature on all of its brands, and which led to the gradual development of a single Mt. Olive brand ahead of similar moves undertaken by its competitors.

In 1955, at the age of 31 and just five years after joining the company, John N. Walker began a run of more than 30 years at the helm of Mt. Olive when I.F. Witherington, who had managed the company since 1928, died of a heart attack. Walker earned an MBA from Harvard, part of the famed class of 1949 that went on to run a number of major corporations. Walker was a serious businessman who was lighthearted about pickles. He became known for his pickle paraphernalia, and pun-laced conversation and correspondence, habitually closing letters with ''Dill then.'' More than anyone he fashioned Mt. Olive's long-time marketing approach emphasizing that pickles are fun, based on his belief that consumers don't view pickles as a staple item but rather require some prompting to take a jar off the shelf.

Technology Improves the Pickle Business in the 1960s

At the same time, Walker was instrumental in Mt. Olive looking to apply whatever technological advances that could be brought to bear on a pickling process that had remained virtually unchanged since it was developed in Mesopotamia over 4,000 years ago. Pickling was always as simple as it was unsightly. Unwashed cucumbers were tossed in uncovered vats of brine, then steeped under sun and rain for as long as two years. No one knew how a little dirt and salt water changed a perishable cucumber into a long-lasting, tasty pickle, and few even asked the question. Mt. Olive began working with research

universities like North Carolina State University in the 1960s to improve the pickle business. In 1966, North Carolina harvested its first fall crop of cucumbers. Until that time, the state produced just a spring crop, ready in June and July, but advances now allowed farmers to plant a second crop that was ready in September and October. In 1969, Mt. Olive became the first food processor in America to replace sugar with fructose corn syrup. Also in the late 1960s researchers at North Carolina State finally discovered a way to control fermentation, the culmination of efforts that began many years earlier. A pilot plant was set up at Mt. Olive, and over the course of the next five years research was conducted that led to improved fermentation methods for the entire pickle industry. Eventually clean cucumbers would be fermented in enclosed fiberglass tanks with designer bacterial cultures.

The pickle industry changed in other ways in the 1960s, as large conglomerates bought up local pickle companies to add to their food holdings. Owned by some 200 shareholders committed to keeping the company locally controlled, Mt. Olive was able to compete. By the mid-1970s, the conglomerates realized that pickles were very much a local, regional affair that had to be run by people who knew how the business worked and were committed to it. They started to sell off their pickle interests. Mt. Olive, in the meantime, continued to grow, reaching the $10 million mark in annual sales in 1974. Ten years later the company would top the $25 million level.

Mt. Olive took a number of steps to improve its business. In 1984, it installed its first piece of computerized technology in its plant, which initiated an on-going effort to upgrade and automate the production process. Eventually computers would become key players from the start of fermentation to the final packing and shipping. In 1991, Mt. Olive would also look to save money by eliminating its ownership of a fleet of delivery trucks, opting instead for a full-service leasing program.

Walker retired in 1990, becoming president emeritus of the company. He was replaced by William H. Bryan, who started working at Mt. Olive in 1985. Raised in the community, Bryan went away to school at the University of Carolina, where he became Phi Beta Kappa and earned a degree in business, then went to work as an accountant in Raleigh, North Carolina. In 1985, he returned home to help with the family plywood business, decided to stay, and went to work for Mt. Olive. After Bryan finally took charge of the company, Mt. Olive soon became the fastest growing brand of pickles in Flordia, Gerogia, Alabama, and the Baltimore-Washington, D.C., market. When North Carolina-based Food Lion grocery stores expanded into Texas, Mt. Olive gained a toehold in that market as well. Moreover, it began to penetrate grocery chains in Tennessee, Louisiana, and Pennsylvania. By 1993, the company was packing 400 million jars of pickled products each year. To accommodate its rapid growth, in 1997 the company opened a new 175,000-square-foot distribution center. In 1998, Mt. Olive reached the $100 million mark in annual sales, after topping the $25 million mark just 13 years earlier.

Mt. Olive Targeted by Farm Workers in 1997

In the late 1990s, Mt. Olive was a thriving enterprise, having become the dominant pickle company in the South. It was its

Key Dates:

1926: The company is incorporated.
1947: The company reaches $1 million in annual sales for the first time.
1966: North Carolina harvests its first fall cucumber crop.
1985: The company reaches $25 million in annual sales.
1998: The company tops $100 million in annual sales.
1999: Farm Labor Organizing Committee initiates consumer boycott of Mt. Olive products.

name recognition, however, that would result in Mt. Olive being targeted by the Ohio-based Farm Labor Organizing Committee (FLOC). In the summer of 1997, FLOC announced that it was beginning a campaign to improve wages as well as living and working conditions for the thousands of migrant workers that harvested North Carolina's cucumber crop. Although Mt. Olive did not hire farm workers but rather contracted for cucumbers from growers, FLOC sought to pressure Mt. Olive into entering a three-way negotiation, in which the company would apply pressure on the growers to make concessions. It was a tactic that had proved successful for the union in the past.

FLOC was established in 1967 by Baldemar Velasquez and other young Chicano activists in the northwestern counties of Ohio, where at the time tomatoes were the primary crop and cucumbers secondary. FLOC first employed its strategy of engaging processors in labor contracts in 1979 when it targeted Campbell's Soup Company, which was a major buyer of local tomatoes. Drawing on support from church and community groups, FLOC organized a boycott of Campbell's products, as well as urging consumers and Campbell shareholders to write letters of protest to management. A drawn-out struggle ensured, highlighted by a 1983 march to Campbell's Camden, New Jersey, headquarters. Finally in 1986, after seven years of struggle, Campbell's took part in negotiations that led to a three-year contract with tomato growers and farm workers. Other contracts were later signed with Campbell's subsidiary Vlasic, as well as Heinz, Dean Foods, and others.

FLOC faced a different landscape in North Carolina, which was a right-to-work state traditionally hostile to unionizing activities. In addition, the migrant worker population was much larger than what FLOC worked with in Ohio, and instead of being families consisted mostly of single males, many of whom were in the country under a government work contract and more reluctant to speak out. Valasquez sought to publicize FLOC's unfolding campaign against Mt. Olive in June 1998 when he led a 70-mile march to the steps of the state capital from the company's main gate. The next step for FLOC was to initiate a formal boycott of Mt. Olive products in 1999. The company maintained that it was being singled out because of its name recognition, and that it had no place in negotiating a contract between growers and laborers, although it would abide by whatever deal the two sides struck. FLOC argued that because Mt. Olive set the price with contractors even before the crop was planted, the company essentially dictated the wages that growers could offer, and was therefore very much a legitimate

part of a labor negotiation. Mt. Olive suggested that the fight was more about FLOC's efforts to bolster the power of its organization than to help North Carolina's migrant workers.

Early support for FLOC's boycott of Mt. Olive Products came from a large number of church groups. Ohio and Michigan were also strong bastions of support, albeit the motive was as much economical as it was moral. Workers in those states were paid $6.10 per 100 pounds of cucumbers, compared to $2.40 for migrants working for Mt. Olive contractors. The FLOC message that cheap North Carolina labor endangered Midwestern jobs and businesses clearly resonated in Ohio and Michigan.

Bryan joined the public relations battle, staunchly defending Mt. Olive and even debating Velaquez on a number of occasions. While continuing to resist being drawn into workers' rights issues, the company did contact growers to make sure housing was up to state standards. The business continued to grow, the boycott seeming to have little effect. Several supermarket chains, mostly located in Ohio, pulled Mt. Olive products from the shelves. The stores claimed that Mt. Olive, new to the market, did not perform well enough to warrant its shelf space. FLOC, on the other hand, attributed the poor sales to the boycott. In any event, the conflict between FLOC and Mt. Olive dragged on. Even if Mt. Olive agreed to enter a three-party negotiation, growers showed no inclination to bargain with FLOC, in many cases vowing to abandon farming altogether. FLOC had already proved to be tenacious and extremely patient, more than willing to devote years to make a boycott work. Velaquez told the press, ''Mr. Bryan can negotiate a contract now, or he can negotiate a contract after a crippling boycott. But he will bargain a contract. We will always have more time than the company has money.'' Only time will tell what effect the boycott will have on the business of Mt. Olive.

Principal Competitors

Vlasic Foods International, Inc.

Further Reading

Coburn, David H., ''Mount Olive, N.C., Pickle Firm Becomes Farm-Labor Group's Latest Target,'' *Charlotte Observer,* April 22, 2000.

——, ''Union Fights Drags On against Mount Olive, N.C.-Based Pickle Grower,'' *Charlotte Observer,* March 9, 2000.

Curry, Kathleen, ''The Green, Green Vats of Home,'' *Charlotte Observer,* July 18, 1993, p. E1.

Howell, Leon, ''Boycotting Pickles,'' *Christian Century,* January 3, 2001, pp. 6–8.

Johnson, Clint, ''You Can Smell the Profits in Pickle Country,'' *Business North Carolina,* October 1987, pp. 33–39.

Morrissey, Marietta, ''The Political Economy of Northwest Ohio Agriculture and Options for Labor Organization,'' *Migration World Magazine,* 1999, pp. 18–22.

McNish, Jacquie, ''They Make Pickles Old-Fashioned Way, and It's Disgusting,'' *Wall Street Journal,* April 15, 1986, p. 1.

O'Neill, Patrick, ''Union Leader Brings Organizing Campaign to Cucumber Pickers,'' *National Catholic Reporter,* July 4, 1997, p. 12.

Sengupta, Somini, ''Farm Union Takes Aim At a Big Pickle Maker,'' *New York Times,* October 26, 2000, p. A22.

—Ed Dinger

Naf Naf SA

6 à 10 boulevard Foch
93807 Epinay sur Seine Cedex
France
Telephone: (+33) 1 48 13 88 88
Fax: (+33) 1 48 13 88 59
Web site: http://www.naf-naf.com

Public Company
Incorporated: 1979
Employees: 158
Sales: FFr 1.25 billion ($166.75 million) (2000)
Stock Exchanges: Euronext Paris
Ticker Symbol: NAF
NAIC: 422330 Women's, Children's, and Infants'
      Clothing and Accessories Wholesalers; 448150
      Clothing Accessories Stores

France's Naf Naf SA is one of France's top ten women's clothing retailers, operating retail boutiques throughout the country and elsewhere in the world. The company's main brand is its Naf Naf line of women's ready-to-wear fashions, targeting the 18-to-25-year-old segment. Naf Naf sales account for 80 percent of all company sales. The company also owns another strong brand, Chevignon, which targets the mid-to-high-end men's sportswear market, and particularly the 25 to 40 year set. Chevignon, representing 18 percent of company sales, has also gained considerable success on the international market. Since 1999, Naf Naf has been building up a third brand, Diapositive, targeting an older, more affluent female consumer. The company owns and operates a retail network of more than 150 stores, including 15 foreign locations, and acts as a wholesale distributor to franchised stores and boutiques around the world, as well as department stores and other retail clothing stores. All manufacturing is contracted out to third parties, principally in Asia. After weathering years of decline during the 1990s—where the company found itself faced with the arrival of heavy competition from such foreign rivals as H&M, Zara, Benetton, The Gap, Esprit, and the like—Naf Naf has fought back, retooling its design concept, rejuvenating its clothing line, refur-

bishing its boutiques, and restructuring its operations, including the closing of a number of its foreign retail outlets. The company has returned to sales growth and profits, nearing EUR 225 million in 2000, with profits of EUR 16 million. Naf Naf has been quoted on Paris' secondary market since 1993; it continues to be controlled and led by founding brothers Gérard and Patrick Pariente.

1970s Origins

Gérard Pariente began his career in fashion in 1973 with the opening of a small boutique, called Influence, in Paris's Sentier garment district. Pariente brought brother Patrick into the business (and later sister Carole as well) and the pair moved to new quarters, creating, in 1976, Influence Pok. The company then turned toward developing its own clothing designs.

Two years later, the Pariente brothers launched their first clothing collection, adopting for their designs the NAFNAF brand (''naf naf'' is a way of writing ''woof woof'' in French). In 1979, the company formally adopted its brand name, incorporating as Naf Naf SA. The Pariente brothers proved complementary business partners, with Gérard taking responsibility for the company's clothing and store designs, and Patrick handling the company's business development.

The NAFNAF label, geared specifically to the young adult market, caught on with in its French market. Through the 1980s, NAFNAF had so successfully imposed itself on the market that for many it came to symbolize French youth fashion. The company recorded a number of milestones during the early 1980s that helped boost it to the ready-to-wear forefront. The first great success came with its launch of the so-called ''boiler suit.'' The design, which featured bright colors and the company's logo at the time (a truck stamped with the company's telephone number) was a huge hit in France, selling more than three million pieces.

The company's breakthrough came one year later. Under the guidance of Franck Davidovici, Naf Naf rolled out a new advertising campaign—and logo—in 1984 that won it that year's Art Director's Club award. Featuring a little pig and sporting the slogan ''le grand méchant look'' (''the big bad

Company Perspectives:

The NAF NAF Group is winning back its clientele with both NAFNAF and Chevignon brands strengthened in France and abroad. The NAF NAF Group is poised to make its mark on fashion in the next millennium.

look''), the advertising campaign propelled Naf Naf to the top ranks of Paris's youth clothing market. Naf Naf quickly took its little pig overseas, where Naf Naf became one of the most popular youth brands. Naf Naf capitalized on its growing fame in 1985 when it launched the first of a wide series of licensed products. The granting of licenses helped the company place its name on a wider variety of products—such as eyeglasses, handbags, shoes, leather goods, and even stationery—and into a wider variety of retail settings, while allowing the company to avoid the risks of developing these products itself. Licensing also enabled Naf Naf to step up its international expansion. In 1986, for example, the company granted a master license to the Japanese market which gave its brand instant access to that rather insular market, while also helping to build the brand name throughout the Asian region.

The year 1986 also marked the Pariente brothers' return to retailing. The company opened its first NAFNAF shop in Paris' rue Passy, and soon followed that opening with more; by 1990, the company owned and operated a chain of 45 retail outlets throughout France. Aiding that expansion was another design success—the launch of the ''puffy jacket'' in 1988 gave the company a new clothing hit and became one of the most popular clothing items of the season.

Encouraged by the success of its brand name, Naf Naf rolled out a new clothing line, NAFNAF Jeans, and then, in 1989, expanded its licensed products range to include swimwear, socks, shoes, lingerie, and even home furnishings such as table settings. Another product, developed in partnership with L'Oréal, was the company's first fragrance line, called ''Une Touche de NAFNAF'' (''A Touch of NAFNAF''). That perfume, which was sold primarily through department stores and other large retail stores, became the top-selling fragrance in its mass-market sector after its 1991 launch.

1990s: Going Public and Expanding

The popularity of its top brand encouraged Naf Naf to ramp up its expansion. By 1992, the company celebrated the opening of its 100th store in France. The company also took control of parts of its foreign distribution activities, setting up subsidiaries in the Netherlands, the United Kingdom, Germany, and Belgium to take control of its growing retail operations in those countries. In the face of a growing economic crisis in the first year of the 1990s, Naf Naf remained one of the healthiest retailers in its sector, owing especially to its policy of relatively low prices. By the time of the company's 20th anniversary in 1993, its sales had topped the FFr 1 billion mark.

Naf Naf went public that same year, taking a listing on Paris' secondary market. The Pariente family nonetheless retained control of more than 70 percent of the company's shares. That

year the company also introduced itself to Canada through a licensing agreement for that country. At home, Naf Naf inaugurated a new, 30,000-square-meter headquarters, warehouse and distribution facility in Epinay-sur-Seine, outside of Paris.

If Naf Naf had successfully established itself as a leading brand name for the young women's market, it had been less successful convincing its customers' male counterparts to sport its little piggy logo. In 1994, Naf Naf took a different tack, acquiring fellow 1980s clothing icon Chevignon. That company had been founded at the end of the 1970s by Guy Azoulay, who began selling ''vintage'' leather designs to emulate the biker look of the American 1950s. The company, incorporated as Charles Chevignon in 1979, became one of the 1980s' hottest-selling brands in France, and its customers eagerly bought up the company's ''American'' designs. Chevignon was to become so closely associated with the United States that by the 1990s it was forced to emphasize to the French market that it was, in fact, a French brand.

In the meantime, Chevignon's sales grew quickly through the 1980s, leading the company to expand into other clothing areas, such as children's clothing, through its Kids and Togs Unlimited brands, launched in 1984. The company also expanded its brand name into other products, through licenses for handbags and accessories. Chevignon, like Naf Naf, also entered the retail arena during the decade. The launch of its Girl line, an attempt to diversify beyond its core young men's market, encouraged Chevignon to launch a new ''mega-store'' retail format in Paris in 1990. The company also launched a line of shoes under license.

Chevignon's international expansion also began to take on speed at the beginning of the 1990s as the company opened a flagship store in New York, then in Tokyo, finally extending its brand name to more than 20 countries worldwide. Back in France, the company achieved a different kind of notoriety when former French tobacco monopoly SEITA launched a new line of Chevignon-branded blond filtered cigarettes (meant to counter the gains of Marlboro and Camel in a French market traditionally dominated by stronger brown cigarettes, such as Gauloises and Gitanes). The linking of cigarettes with the popular youth-oriented clothing brand caused a public outcry and, with the French government threatening to place a ban on all Chevignon advertising, the branded cigarettes were dropped.

Chevignon continued to expand internationally, riding licensing agreements to bring the brand to Argentina, Columbia, Hong Kong, and Turkey. Yet the company was nonetheless facing declining sales as a result of the recession and dampening consumer interest, dropping from a high of more than FFr 600 million in 1990 to just FFr 380 million in 1993. In 1994, Azoulay and the Pariente brothers agreed for Naf Naf to acquire Chevignon.

Despite the opening of two mega-stores in Paris in 1995, Naf Naf itself was shortly to enter a long period of difficulties. The arrival in France of aggressive new competitors such as H&M, Zara, the Gap, Benetton, Esprit, Mandy, and others challenged Naf Naf directly in its core young women's market. Where rivals such as Zara featured constantly rotating clothing designs, Naf Naf proved slower to respond to shifting fashion trends. At

Key Dates:

1973: Gérard Pariente opens retail clothing store, Influence, in Paris.
1976: Gérard is joined by brother Patrick Pariente, and the company opens a new store, Influence Pok.
1978: The Pariente brothers launch a new clothing brand, NAFNAF.
1979: The company incorporates as Naf Naf SA; Guy Azoulay founds Charles Chevignon.
1981: Chevignon launches successful vintage leather line
1983: Naf Naf achieves market success with launch of its "boiler suit."
1984: Naf Naf rolls out its hit advertising campaign, "le grand méchant."
1985: Naf Naf begins licensing NAFNAF brand name.
1986: Naf Naf opens first NAFNAF retail store.
1988: Naf Naf achieves new success with launch of the "puffy jacket."
1989: Chevignon opens the first Parisian mega-store.
1991: Naf Naf and L'Oreal roll out "Une Touche de NAFNAF" fragrance line; Chevignon opens a store in New York.
1993: Naf Naf creates subsidiaries in Spain, the Netherlands, and Germany; Naf Naf goes public on Paris secondary market.
1994: Naf Naf acquires Chevignon.
1998: Naf Naf begins restructuring program.
1999: The company acquires S. Clair (Diapositive) SA.
2001: Naf Naf opens new Chevignon stores in Bordeaux and Toulouse.

the same time, the company began suffering logistics problems that led to sell-outs on its more popular items. A more difficult factor for the company was the loss in popularity of its brand, no longer considered a ready-to-wear fashion trendsetter. Meanwhile, much of the company's international operations were failing, particularly in Belgium and the United Kingdom, where its Naf Naf retail stores were posting losses, dragging down the fortunes of the company as a whole.

Revitalized for the New Century

Naf Naf responded by undergoing a vast restructuring. The company moved to revitalize its image, dropped its longstanding little pig and "grand méchant look" tagline—now considered too "infantile"—and revised its clothing fashions to target a slightly older, 18 to 25-year-old women's market. Accompanying the roll-out of its new advertising and marketing concept, Naf Naf moved to refurbish its retail concept, developing new retail store designs. The company also took the knife to its international retail network, slashing the number of its foreign stores as it worked toward restoring its foreign subsidiaries to profitability.

Naf Naf began to show progress by the end of its 1999 year, reducing losses to just EUR 3 million. By 2000, the company's efforts were beginning to pay off as revenues once again showed steady growth, nearing EUR 225 million, and net profits reached EUR 4 million. The company began to reinforce its growth with a new series of stores openings, now targeting French towns of populations of 50,000 or more. After revitalizing its core brand, Naf Naf turned to Chevignon, adopting a new brand identity of "fighting modern times" and opening new retail stores in Bordeaux and Toulouse. The company also launched a new subsidary, Chevignon Accessories. Meanwhile, Naf Naf was developing a new label, Diapositive, acquired in 1999. Although still a small part of the company's sales, the new brand gave Naf Naf a foothold in the lucrative mid- to high-end women's ready-to-wear market without compromising the image of its more youthful NAFNAF label. These changes combined to give Naf Naf an encouraging vision of its place in the new century. By 2002, the company expected sales to top EUR 300 million for the first time.

Principal Subsidiaries

Diapositive; POK (UK) Ltd.; NAF NAF Boutiques Ltd.; NAF NAF Belgique SA;; NAF NAF Boutiques SA; NAF NAF Group Ltd. (UK); NAF NAF Italia Spa; NAF NAF Int'l. BV (Netherlands); NAF NAF Hellas SA (Greece); NAF NAF Espagne SA; NAF NAF Distribution SNC; NAF NAF Jeans SA; Chevignon Accessories SNC; NNC Production SNC; Chevignon SA; POK Boutiques BV; Ching ON Ltd. (Hong Kong); Jet Top Ltd. (Hong Kong); NCKids SARL; Bava SA; Beral SA.

Principal Competitors

H&M Hennes & Mauritz AB; Groupe André SA; Benetton Group S.p.A.; The Gap, Inc.; Zara SA; Marks and Spencer plc; Esprit Holdings Limited; Diesel SpA; New Look Group plc; NEXT plc; Promod SA; Camaieu SA.

Further Reading

Germain, Isabelle, "Retour aux sources pour NAFNAF," *Le Journal du Textile*, January 8, 2001.
Hamou, Nathalie, "Le groupe Naf Naf voit enfin le bout du tunnel," *LA Tribune*, June 22, 2000.
Le Masson, Thomas, "Naf Naf se lance dans une politique commerciale agressive," *Les Echoes*, June 18, 1998, p. 13.
"Naf Naf confirme son redressement," *Les Echoes*, June 18, 2001, p. 16.

—M.L. Cohen

National Home Centers, Inc.

Highway 265 North
Springdale, Arkansas 72765
U.S.A.
Telephone: (501) 756-1700
Fax: (501) 927-5798
Web site: http://www.nhci.com

Public Company
Incorporated: 1972 as National Lumber Co.
Employees: 448
Sales: $96.6 million (2001)
Stock Exchanges: NASDAQ
Ticker Symbol: NHCI
NAIC: 44411 Home Centers

The brain child of Arkansas native Dwain Newman, National Home Centers, Inc. (formerly National Lumber Co.) is an Arkansas-based lumber company which sells to both home-building professionals and non-professional homeowners, not nationally, but strictly in Arkansas, northeastern Oklahoma, southeastern Kansas, and southwestern Missouri. As of the 2000 fiscal year, approximately 83 percent of National's business was devoted to contractors. Its eight locations combine relatively small retail outlets with 20-acre lumber yards. The company owns roughly 200 delivery vehicles, including 50 vans and pickups, 40 flat-beds, ten 18-wheelers, and 100 other trucks. National received a surge of local press attention from 1993 to 1997, when it aspired to compete with the large home-improvement chains which were flooding the state. In 1994, *Do-It-Yourself Retailing* proclaimed the company "one of the most promising retail chains in the U.S." National has in recent years significantly downsized its operations, cutting retail space by over 400,000 square feet and its overall work force by 600. These actions have decreased revenue but increased the company's profits. Newman, the company's founder and CEO, owns approximately 63 percent of the business. In the fall of 2001 he also tendered an offer to purchase the rest of the company's stock.

1970s Origins as a Building Supply Company for Contractors

Dwaine Newman founded National Home Centers in 1972, initially dubbing it the National Lumber Company. The first outlet, primarily a lumber yard, was located in Springdale, a rural town in Washington County, Arkansas, just north of Fayetteville. Newton, who was 38 when he started the company, had previously been general manager of Gateway Plywood and Door Co., a division of Arizona-based International Forest Products, which had a facility in Springdale.

At first, National's sales were strictly limited to contractors, who accounted for about 95 percent of its revenues. Sales to builders would in fact remain the core business for the next two decades, over which the company developed into a very limited chain of lumber yards and small retail stores serving the northwest portion of Arkansas. The chain remained relatively secure in its business because it did not have any serious competition.

Newman did not begin selling building supplies to do-it-yourself home repair and remodeling customers until 1983, when National started opening retail stores, first in Springdale and then in Little Rock. Their principal purpose was to counteract the financial slumps the company had experienced when high interest rates and a recessive economy curtailed building trade needs. In any case, the business focus through the 1980s and into the early1990s remained on sales to contractors.

Early 1990s: Expansion Runs Into Heavy Competition from Chains

In 1991, Dwain Newman and his board changed National Lumber Co.'s name to National Home Centers, Inc., and began a three-year period of rapidly escalating growth for the business. The company ceased thinking of retail stores as a safeguard, a supplement to its main money-making ventures in the contracting field, and began to consider them an avenue for increased expansion and profits. To help increase business, the company acquired former Wal-Mart buildings in Conway and Russelville, outlets that significantly improved the company's retail traffic. This approach looked very promising at the start,

---

Company Perspectives:

At National Home Centers we are very proud to be Arkansas' own home building supplier. We are headquartered in Northwest Arkansas and have been serving the building materials and home improvement needs of the state for 27 years. We appreciate the loyalty our customers have shown us and we're dedicated to offering quality products at fair prices with knowledgeable service to our fellow Arkansans for years to come.

---

and by 1991 had won National its 35th ranking on *Arkansas Business* magazine's Top 50 private companies list.

By early 1992, National's ambitions had grown, and the company began opening ever-larger retail outlets in an attempt to emulate the "big box" strategies employed by Wal-Mart and the two national chains which would ultimately force the company to bring its business plan full circle: Lowe's and Home Depot. At the start of 1992, the whole chain consisted of just five stores, but within two years had grown to ten stores, and in 1993 alone had increased its sales by 45 percent over the previous year.

National went public in 1993, hoping to acquire the capital necessary for its continued growth. Its first offering, made in May of that year, sold just under two million shares at $10 per share. At that time, founder Dwain Newman already had and would continue to hold a controlling interest in the company. With its capital infusion, National began opening more new stores. Within a year, it had increased its holdings by two retail locations and had broken ground on its largest store built up to that point, a 175,000 square-foot superstore in Fayetteville. Its goals still unmet, National took out a $25 million loan from the First Tennessee Bank National Association in early 1994.

The building of another National superstore was significantly delayed by issues with the Little Rock city government. The store's proposed location on Arkansas Highway 10 conflicted with that city's statutes governing land use. A minor scandal arose when the city director, Joan Adock, who supported National's claim, admitted that the company regularly purchased some of its inventory through her husband, the local sales representative for Newell & Co., window hangings suppliers.

Despite this setback, National moved ahead. In 1993 alone, the company expanded by almost 45 percent in properties and employees. In the 1980s, 70 percent of National's business had been derived from professional contractors. The early 1990s saw the business decrease its contractor sales by 30 percent, with the result that overall the company's revenues were generated from consumer sales of 60 percent and contractor sales of 40 percent. By comparison, the national "big box" chains made 80 percent of their money from amateur home-improvement enthusiasts. Negligible contractor-based sales on the part of the Home Depot and Lowe's juggernauts gave National hope that focusing on versatility would make it a viable competitor in the Arkansas market.

National's continued expansion and increased versatility resulted in an anticipated sales figure for 1994 of $165 million, a three-fold increase from their sales in 1989. By the summer, the company had made plans to build a new factory for their carpentry off-shoot, Cabinet Craft, and a 28,000-square-foot corporate headquarters. However, National was facing a troubled future, largely because by 1994 Lowe's and Home Depot had discovered northwestern Arkansas and had begun making plans for opening outlets there. Like so many other small chains, National had to face the prospect of being crushed by giants whose volume-buying pricing had elsewhere turned them into competitive bulldozers.

Although that competition was still only on the horizon, by 1994 the company was already experiencing some financial problems. Its 1994 fiscal year results fell way short of its expectations. Its sales peaked at $125 million, $40 million shy of the predicted gross. The company's stock value also fluctuated disconcertingly. At one point in 1994, after a few pundits declared National a hot property, the price rose briefly to over $14 a share, but for reasons, as Dwain Newman himself admitted in an interview with *Arkansas Business*, "that had nothing to do with [the company]." As the year ended, the stock dropped to $11. It fell repeatedly thereafter, and would never climb so high again.

Mid-1990s: Company's Growth Leads to Mounting Financial Problems

By the spring of 1995, National was beginning to feel its growing pains in earnest. Newman relinquished his role as the company's president, though he remained CEO and chairman; Danny Funderberg, the COO, assumed the position vacated by Newman. The complexities of running National had grown along with its store base, which had recently grown to ten. Newman no longer wished to handle both the more mundane duties involved in running his business and the constant strategy planning necessary to keep a growing company competitive.

National was spreading itself thin, and industry observers recognized this fact; the 1995 fiscal year ended with the company's stock at $3.81 a share. Though sales had risen to $151.4 million, up considerably from 1994, National had failed to turn a profit. Newman and his fellow executives recognized 1995 as a tough year for staying afloat. They retreated from their aggressive practices, halted expansion, and focused on preparing for the arrival of Home Depot and Lowe's in communities where National had outlets.

Though the company's earnings increased steadily throughout 1996, it was about to be battered from all sides by strong competition. National's home state had attracted a fleet of home improvement superstores far out of proportion to its size. By the end of that year, three Lowe's locations had sprung up in Fort Smith, Russelville, and Conway, attracting customers in droves through their mass merchandise pricing. National still hoped that servicing both contractors and amateur enthusiasts would give it an edge in the market. However, the company would not see a profit for the next three years.

Late 1990s Return to Profitability

In 1997, National began a full retreat. Although the company's aggressive growth and marketing strategies had worked

Key Dates:

1972: Dwaine Newman founds National Lumber Co. in Springdale, Arkansas.

1983: National Lumber begins opening retail stores in an effort to target non-professional home-owners.

1991: National Lumber Co. is renamed National Home Centers.

1993: The company goes public and puts two million shares on the market; Dwaine Newman acquires the controlling share and becomes chairman and CEO; National takes over old Wal-Marts in Conway and Russelville, beginning the chain's investment in "big box"-style retail outlets.

1995: Following a heated competition with national chains, the company begins losing money.

1999: After years of losses and downsizing, National successfully refocuses its attention on contractor sales.

2000: Company returns to profitability.

2001: Newman tenders offer to purchase all outstanding company shares.

to a point, they did not work well enough to pay off the money the company had borrowed. National's debt-to-assets ratio was 42 percent that year, a high proportion which seems even higher when compared to similar figures from other businesses. Lowe's and Home Depot, National's biggest competitors, claimed a debt-to-asset percentage of 20 percent and 11 percent, respectively. Stung by its financial difficulties, the company's stock ended the fiscal year at a new low of $1.50 a share.

In dire need of sound business advice, Newman hired the Senn-Delaney consulting firm to design a new National strategy. The firm made it clear that the key to National's future success would be to reduce its role in the Arkansas retail market. Heeding the firm's instructions, National began shutting down its new stores and putting them on the market, hoping to cut its losses and facilitate debt payments. From October 1997 to the beginning of 1998, the company closed locations in Conway, Little Rock, and Fayetteville. The store at Fayetteville, at 175,000 square feet, had been National's biggest "big box."

In 1997, National put in place four strategic priorities to guide it back to health: it would close under-performing units, recapitalize, reduce its debt, and refocus it business on contractors as its primary customers. Thus, throughout 1998, National closed down and sold off its retail outlets and began a move back to its older business strategy, that of selling to contractors and operating small hardware stores to give added income in bad real-estate market years. In the next year, in order to help sustain its business and pay down its debt, the company entered a credit loan and security agreement, giving it a credit line of $20 million.

By the summer of 1999, the company had reduced its holdings to eight lumber yard/retail store combinations. Although its near 30-year evolution as a company had been reversed, National's management was optimistic about the future. Said Brent Hanby, the firm's CFO, in an interview with *Arkansas Business* in May 1999, "The money tree doesn't grow forever. We're in much better financial shape than we were a year ago."

The next year, 2000, clearly showed the positive results of the strategy put in place in 1997. For one thing, National pulled out of the red, posting a $1.1 million net earnings in 2000. Although its net dropped to $225,840 the next year, it was still logging a profit. In 2001, the company also refinanced its revolving credit line with Wells Fargo Retail Finance, LLC, advancing it to $25 million and extended the credit's term to July 2005 and lowering the lending rate.

Through the first half of 2001, the company was also doing better in sales than it had in 2000, turning in same-store increases that, Dwain Newman observed, were in part attributable to favorable weather conditions, reduced interest rates, and an increase in large building project starts. The improvement was acknowledged by Dun & Bradstreet, which upgraded the company's rating to 4A2, its first upgrade in four years.

Newman's own faith in the company's future was evident in his tendered offer to buy all the company's stock not already under his control. The majority owner, holding 63.49 percent of the stock, Newman first offered to buy the remaining shares at $1.20 per share, then, on October 5, 2001, raised his offer to $1.40 per share. If agreed to by the other stock holders, the sale would result in the return of National to the private sector, a move that Newman has long felt would be in the best interest of the company.

Principal Competitors

Cameron Ashley Building Products, Inc.; The Home Depot, Inc.; Lowe's Companies, Inc.; Sutherland Lumber Company, L.P.; 84 Lumber Company.

Further Reading

"Another Arkansas Winner," Interview with National Home Centers Pres. And CEO Dwain Newman, *Do-It-Yourself Retailing*, July 1994, p. 77.

Bowden, Bill, "National Lumbers Back Into Black," *Arkansas Business*, April 3, 2000, p. 1.

"National Home Centers Rebuilding, Predicts Profits," *Arkansas Business*, May 10, 1999, p. 1.

Shuster, Laurie, "Arkansas Home Center Chain Prepares Its Big-Box Strategy," *Home Improvement Market*, October 1996, p. 16.

Smith, David, "National's Debt Rises Amid More Closings," *Arkansas Business*, December 22, 1997, p. 1.

Waldon, George, "Opponents Land Counterpunch in Rezoning Bout: Controversial Home Center May Be Down for the Count," *Arkansas Business*, April 19, 1993, p. 20.

—Joshua C. Fiero

Nautica Enterprises, Inc.

40 West 57th Street
New York, New York 10019
U.S.A.
Telephone: (212) 541-5757
Fax: (212) 841-7228
Web site: http://www.nautica.com

Public Company
Incorporated: 1966 as Pacific Coast Knitting Mills, Inc.
Employees: 2,850
Sales: $627.7 million (2001)
Stock Exchanges: NASDAQ
Ticker Symbol: NAUT
NAIC: 42122 Home Furnishing Wholesalers; 42232
    Men's & Boys' Clothing and Furnishings
    Wholesalers; 42233 Women's, Children's, and
    Infants' Clothing and Accessories Wholesalers; 44811
    Men's Clothing Stores; 44815 Clothing Accessory
    Stores; 53311 Lessors of Nonfinancial Intangible
    Assets (Except Copyrighted Works)

Nautica Enterprises, Inc. operates as a leading apparel wholesaler and retailer. Its wholesale businesses design, market, and distribute sportswear, activewear, outerwear, the Nautica Jeans Collection, tailored clothing, swimwear, and sleepwear. Nautica opened its 100th retail outlet in 2000, followed by a flagship concept store in Rockefeller Plaza in New York in April 2001. Its merchandise is found in over 1,500 in-store shops in department stores across the United States. Products including Nautica Golf, fragrances, neckware, footwear, watches, hosiery, eyewear, rainwear, leather belts, wallets, gloves, scarves, and home furnishings are also licensed across the globe in over 20 countries. The majority of Nautica's sales stem from operations in its top two markets—the United States and Europe.

California-Based Company: 1966–75

Nautica originated in 1966 as Pacific Coast Knitting Mills, a firm engaged in manufacturing and distributing double-knit

natural and synthetic fabrics in Vernon, California. This company had net sales of $2.1 million and net income of $55,533 in fiscal 1968 (the year ended February 29, 1968). It went public in 1971, offering a minority of its outstanding shares for $8 a share. The company ended fiscal 1972 with $4.1 million in sales but only $44,340 in net income.

In 1972, Pacific Coast Knitting Mills acquired, for $850,000 in cash and notes, almost all the stock of Van Baalen Heilburn & Co., a Rockland, Maine, firm engaged in manufacturing and distributing men's sportswear, swimwear, and robes, generally under the trade name State-O-Maine. Van Baalen, which originated in 1921 in New York, had moved to Maine in the late 1930s to lower its labor costs. At the time of its purchase it was making robes under the Christian Dior name and had long-term contracts with designers John Weitz and Pierre Cardin. The company had net sales of $3 million and net income of $51,880 in fiscal 1971. It was renamed Van Baalen Pacific Corp. after its acquisition.

With Van Baalen in tow, Pacific Coast Knitting Mills raised its sales, but its earnings remained modest. In fiscal 1974, it had record sales of $5.3 million but net income of only $22,000, a circumstance attributed by management to substantial knitting-mill losses. Sales grew to $5.9 million in fiscal 1975, but the company took a $1.5 million loss because of discontinued operations. Its stock quickly fell out of favor with investors, dropping as low as 12 cents a share in 1973 and two cents a share in 1975.

New York-Based State-O-Maine: 1975–83

In June 1975, the knitting-mill business was sold to Stanley Flaster, the president of Pacific Coast Knitting Mills, who renamed it Flastex, Inc. Flaster's wife, who owned the biggest block of Pacific Coast stock, and Myron Herschler, its vice-president and another big investor, sold their shares to Harvey Sanders, the company's chairman, secretary, and treasurer, and Milton Weinick, a director. Sanders and Weinick were partners in a New York City accounting firm that bore their names. Sanders emerged with 41 percent of the stock, and Weinick, named vice-president and treasurer, with 31 percent. The company, renamed State-O-Maine, moved its headquarters to New

Company Perspectives:

Over the past two decades, Nautica has become an international symbol of style, quality, and value. Throughout the years, we have kept pace with changing consumer preferences while staying true to the classic styling and modern sensibility that has given our products such broad appeal. We make it our business to understand consumers and to consistently offer the convenience and comfort that defines a trusted brand. Whether it's for leisure, career, or home, Nautica is recognized as an accessible brand that features innovative designs and quality fabric.

York and won a $725,000 loan from the National Bank of North America, but only on the condition that Sanders also loan the company $225,000. In 1979, Weinick became chairman as well as treasurer, with Sanders as vice-president and secretary. Sanders's rank rose to president in 1983, and he added the title of chief executive officer in 1992.

State-O-Maine made modest profits in the late 1970s but was still shunned by investors. In fiscal 1980, it earned $245,000 on net sales of $12.7 million but ended the fiscal year with a long-term debt of nearly $1 million. Three years later, the company had upped its sales to $19.2 million and its net income to $509,000—steady if unspectacular figures. Customers for its robes and jogging suits included Bloomingdale's, Nordstrom, and Saks. The firm's fortunes advanced that year when a department-store executive introduced Sanders to David Chu, a young, Taiwanese-born clothing designer. Chu and a partner had started a company called Nautica in 1983 and had introduced a collection of brightly colored men's outdoor jackets. They sold well, but the partner did not want to invest the necessary funds for expansion. For a small amount of cash and the assumption of about $1 million in liabilities, State-O-Maine bought out Chu's partner in 1984. Chu later traded his 20 percent interest in the company for State-O-Maine stock.

Nautica's Rise to Prominence: 1984–91

Sanders and Chu devised an expansion plan combining Nautica's products and maritime-based image with State-O-Maine's production and distribution network. This plan entailed selling only to carefully selected high-end stores—only one or two department stores in each market outside New York City—and showcasing Nautica's products as a collection rather than splitting them by categories. These products grew to include men's dress shirts, neckwear, hosiery, belts, suspenders, small leather goods, jewelry, watches, gloves, hats, sunglasses, fragrances, and skin care. Nautica's growth was spectacular, its sales increasing from about $1 million in fiscal 1985 to about $20 million in fiscal 1988, about half-and-half to department and specialty stores. Outerwear accounted for about 45 percent, "activewear" for another 40 percent, and casual sportswear, a line introduced in 1987, for 15 percent. A full collection of women's products was introduced in fall 1988.

Fueled by Nautica's popularity, State-O-Maine became a hot company in the late 1980s. Sales soared from $28.9 million

in fiscal 1986 to $75 million in fiscal 1989, and net income shot up from $1.6 million to $5.4 million. The company's market capitalization grew from $2 million in 1983 to $74 million before the end of 1991. At first about half the company's production was manufactured in Rockland, but this proportion fell to one-third as Nautica established a Hong Kong subsidiary and increasingly outsourced its needs to Far East suppliers. In 1990, State-O-Maine halted production at its Van Baalen subsidiary, restricting the operation to distribution and importing all of its clothing. State-O-Maine opened retail stores in New York City and Newport Beach, California, in 1987 and a Rockland factory outlet store in 1988.

By the end of fiscal 1991, in which Nautica accounted for $63 million of State-O-Maine's $95 million in sales, Chu was a major presence in his field. He maintained total command over the Nautica image, with design control over every style in both the men's and women's clothing lines—now totaling nearly 500 pieces—and also over the licensed products, such as watches and fragrances. He even designed many of Nautica's fabrics. In an interview for a cover story for *Bobbin*, Chu said the Nautica image represented the ''relationship of people to nature. What we try to do is provide functional apparel that is stylish—apparel that can be worn in all kinds of weather and all kinds of nature patterns. . . . The beauty about the textile industry today is the new technologies featuring new fabrics, waterproof fabrics, and microfibers, which make the final product more functional.''

By the spring of 1991, Nautica had established nearly 100 in-store shops, with distinctive deck flooring in certain areas. Its high-end image was fiercely protected by Sanders; when a department store marked down its goods mid-season, the account was dropped. Nautica's carefully crafted marketing plan included advertisements in such magazines as *GQ*, *Esquire*, *Sports Illustrated*, *Vanity Fair*, and *Vogue*, and also sponsorship of sailing competitions, including the United States and international Youth Sailing Championships. For 1992, it created its very own championship in Portugal: the Nautica Cup. That year State-O-Maine opened an expensive new showroom on Manhattan's elegant 57th Street and hired 10 additional designers and merchandising coordinators. However, Nautica's money-losing women's division, which never accounted for more than 15 percent of sales, was discontinued in May 1991.

Continued Expansion and Growth: 1992–96

State-O-Maine added another arrow to its quiver in 1992, when it acquired Bayou Sport for an undisclosed sum. With annual sales volume of about $5 million, this company was manufacturing and marketing men's moderately priced cotton woven and knit shirts, swimwear, slacks, and shorts under its own name. Reflecting the overwhelming presence of the biggest sector of its business, State-O-Maine was renamed Nautica Enterprises in 1994. That year the number of Nautica shops within department stores reached 428. Nautica also had 543 specialty accounts and 18 factory outlet stores. The far-flung number of retail stores licensed abroad under the Nautica name included ten in South Korea and nine each in Mexico and Japan. Licensed products—including boys' and girls' wear, luggage, and even Lincoln-Mercury Villager vans—now made up about 25 percent of sales, which totaled $151 million in the fiscal year.

Key Dates:

1966: Pacific Coast Knitting Mills is established.
1972: The firm acquires Van Baalen Heilburn & Co.
1975: The knitting-mill business is sold to president Stanley Flaster and is eventually renamed State-O-Maine.
1983: David Chu and a partner establish Nautica and launch a line of outerwear.
1984: State-O-Maine buys out Chu's partner and acquires ownership of Nautica.
1987: State-O-Maine opens retail stores in New York City and California.
1988: A full collection of women's products is launched; the company's sales reach $20 million.
1991: The women's division is discontinued.
1994: State-O-Maine changes its name to Nautica Enterprises Inc.
1996: The company launches a sportswear line entitled Nautica Competition.
1999: Nautica launches a Men's Jean line along with a Women's Sleepwear line.
2000: The 100th retail outlet store is opened.

Fiscal 1994 was better yet, with net sales reaching $192.9 million and net income $16.8 million. Sanders—who owned about 11.5 percent of the company—took $6.6 million in salary, according to a trade publication. During the calendar year the number of in-store shops rose to 548. They were averaging 800 square feet in size and $400 in sales per square foot. The number of outlet stores increased to 31; they averaged about 3,000 square feet and $375 per square foot.

In fiscal 1995, Nautica Enterprises advanced once more, its net sales reaching $247.6 million and its net income nearly $24 million. For the 1991 to 1995 period, it posted an average annual gain of 24 percent in sales and 54 percent in net income. The 1995 profit margin of 10.5 percent was the third-highest among the apparel industry's mid- and large-size public firms. That year, the company's accounts grew to 1,100 department stores and more than 500 specialty stores. Sanders announced that he planned to double the size of some of its new in-store shops to an average of 2,200 to 3,000 square feet, compared to the 800- to 1,800-square-foot range of the current ones. In 1996, the company continued its aggressive outlet-store expansion, presented a new Nautica Competition activewear label, announced a licensing deal to sell women's wear under the Nautica label in August 1996, and announced a licensing agreement to market Charles Goodnight robes and loungewear.

Fiscal 1996 was another record-busting year for Nautica Enterprises, its net sales reaching $302.5 million and its net income just short of $32 million. The company opened 146 new shops and expanded 122. In September 1996, it announced its entry into the home-furnishings market with three home-textile licensees: Dan River for sheets and bedroom ensembles; Ex-Cell Home Fashions for shower curtains, bath accessories, and table linens; and Leshner Corp. for bath and beach towels. Company executives estimated Nautica Home would register

about $50 million in retail sales by the end of its first year. The women's line, produced through a licensing agreement with Bernard Chaus, opened in more than 100 new in-store shops. Men's tailored-clothing and infants'/toddlers' lines were also in the works. In 1996, the company announced a joint venture with Financo to distribute the Nautica men's collection throughout Europe, where it would open a showroom in January 1997, a license agreement with Unionbay to design and market a men's denim collection, and a license agreement with Kellwood Co. for dress shirts.

Nautica Enterprises ended fiscal 1996 with 885 in-store shops and saw potential for an eventual 1,500 such shops—a number reached at the start of the millennium. It expanded the size of 159 of its stores in 1996, of which over 40 featured a separate area for the Nautica Competition line. Nautica ended fiscal 1996 with 58 freestanding stores and 145 in-store shops in 30 foreign countries. New openings scheduled for 1996 included Argentina, Brazil, and Beijing, China. Nautica Enterprises had virtually no long-term debt in 1995.

Nautica Enterprises in the Mid-1990s

In fiscal 1996, Nautica International, Inc., a wholly owned subsidiary of Nautica Enterprises, was offering an array of men's sportswear, outerwear, and activewear, primarily targeted to the 25-to-54-year-old age group. Sportswear included sweaters, woven and knit shirts, rugby shirts, pants, and shorts. Outerwear included parkas, bomber jackets, and foul-weather gear. Activewear included fleece and french terry tops, french terry pants and shorts, T-shirts, and swimwear. This clothing came in three principal groups: Anchor, Crew, and Fashion.

State-O-Maine, also a wholly owned subsidiary, was offering Nautica-brand robes and loungewear, sportswear, and swimwear under the Bayou Sports label, apparel designed and sourced for private-label programs—which were first introduced in 1993—and robes and loungewear under the Charles Goodnight label. Except for the Nautica-brand furnishings, these products were more competitively priced and more broadly distributed than the company's other offerings.

Nautica products were being sold primarily to leading department and specialty stores. Its principal customers included Dillard's, May Company Department Stores, Dayton-Hudson's, Marshall Field, Federated Department Stores, Bloomingdale's, Lazarus/Rich's, and Nordstrom. State-O-Maine was selling primarily to department stores, including the first four above, and such national chain-store operators as J.C. Penney and Sears, Roebuck.

Nautica Enterprises maintained a high profile for its products by advertisements in national and regional magazines and through a cooperative advertising program with its retail customers. This effort was being augmented by a series of special events and sponsorships. In fiscal 1996, the company was the official clothing sponsor for the U.S. Sailing Team and the official apparel sponsor for two events on the Senior Professional Golfers' Association tour.

Nautica Enterprises' products were being designed by the company's own staff and manufactured chiefly in Hong Kong, China, the Philippines, Malaysia, Singapore, Saipan, Thailand,

India, and Turkey. The Nautica name and related trademarks were being licensed for sale abroad—both wholesale and through a number of retail stores—by Nautica Apparel, a wholly owned subsidiary.

Nautica Enterprises operated 38 factory outlet stores in fiscal 1996 through another wholly owned subsidiary, Nautica Retail USA, and it maintained flagship stores on Manhattan's Upper West Side and in Newport Beach, California. It was operating three warehouse and distribution facilities in Rockland, Maine, two of which were owned by the company and the third leased. It was leasing administrative and sales offices and a design studio in Manhattan and was also leasing sales offices in Dallas.

Continued Growth and Expansion

Nautica entered the late 1990s on solid ground. In 1997, the firm purchased the E. Magrath Apparel Co., a seller of golfwear under the Magrath and Byron Nelson brand names. The company also expanded its product line with the addition of bed and bath products and plans were set in motion to create a housewares and furniture line. During that year, Nautica introduced a women's swimwear collection.

In 1998 however, Nautica terminated its license agreement with Bernard Chaus—the firm that manufactured the Nautica's women's sportswear line. While Nautica remained a powerful force in men's fashion, the women's sportswear line did little to boost profits. As such, the company focused on launching various different products targeted towards women including a sleepwear line that debuted in January 1999. A December 1998 *WWD* article commented on the strategy claiming that, "although it still is without a women's sportswear collection, Nautica is hoping that other product categories will keep the Nautica brand alive in women's minds."

During fiscal 1999, earnings rose by four percent while sales increased by 14 percent to $552.7 million. As outerware sales faltered due to warmer weather trends in the United States, the company was forced to markdown merchandise to make way for the new season's fashions. Nevertheless, the company continued to strengthen as well as broaden its brands. During 1999, Nautica secured licensing agreements for its Home Accessories, Dinnerware, and Stemware product line. In the fall of that year, the Nautica Jeans Company was created to target consumer between the ages of 16 and 35. Initially the line only included men's jeans; however a women's denim collection was included in fall 2000.

Nautica continued its growth strategy into the new millennium and the company opened its 100th retail outlet. The men's fragrance line, Latitude/Longitude, was launched along with the contemporary designer John Varvatos collection. During that year, the company discontinued its Nautica Sport Tech line after recording several periods of lagging profits due to increased competition and soft retail sales. In May 2001, Nautica purchased Earl Jean Inc., an upscale brand that fit in with management's plan to move into high margin product markets. During that year, the company's major focus was on expanding the Nautica brand into new categories, expanding its brand portfolio, exploring future distribution opportunities, and strategically positioning its global business. Sanders commented on the

firm's direction in a 2001 *Daily News Record* article stating, "Building on the current momentum and capitalizing on the best opportunities that exist, we will focus on the expansion effort on our core markets and scale back operations in less profitable countries."

It was during this time that the apparel retail industry as a whole began to struggle. As the U.S. economy showed signs of weakening, department stores sales fell due to faltering consumer confidence. Nautica however, was convinced that it would continue its tradition of providing products with style, value, and brand appeal. With no long-term debt and with a solid strategy in place, the company appeared to be well-positioned to battle future economic problems.

Principal Subsidiaries

Nautica Jeans Co.; Van Baalen Pacific Corp.; John Varvatos Co.; Nautica Apparel, Inc.; Nautica International, Inc.; Nautica Retail USA, Inc.; Nautica Europe Holdings Ltd.; Earl Jean Inc.

Principal Competitors

Liz Claiborne Inc.; Polo Ralph Lauren Corporation; Tommy Hilfiger Corporation.

Further Reading

Austin, Phyllis, "Taking Care of Business," *Maine Times*, June 3, 1994, p. 2.
Black, Susan S., "Nautica: Its Ship Has Come In," *Bobbin*, May 1991, pp. 52, 54–56.
Brady, Jennifer L., "Nautica to Keep Launching In-Store Shops," *Daily News Record*, October 4, 1996, p. 14.
Curan, Catherine, "Nautica Heads For Deeper Water With New Brands," *Crain's New York Business*, July 16, 2001, p. 4.
D'Innocenzio, Anne, "Nautica Makes a Splash," *WWD*, July 30. 1998, p. 14S.
Esquivel, Josephine R., "Bobbin's Top 40," *Bobbin*, June 1996, pp. 53–54, 63, 68.
"Featuring the Future," *Daily News Record*, February 7, 1994, p. 48.
Furman, Phyllis, "Sailing Ahead in Choppy Apparel Seas," *Crain's New York Business*, November 13, 1984, pp. 3, 46.
Johnson, Sarah, "Nautica Adding Home," *HFN*, September 2, 1996, p. 1.
——, "New Home Ports," *HFN*, March 24, 1997, p. 1.
Lockwood, Lisa, "State-o-Maine Buys Nautica for Undisclosed Amount," *Daily News Record*, August 8, 1984, p. 6.
Monget, Karyn, "Nautica's Bedtime Story," *WWD*, December 28, 1998, p. 9.
"Nautica Completes Magrath Takeover," *Daily News Record*, October 1, 1997, p. 2.
"Nautica, Earl Close Deal," *WWD*, May 4, 2001, p. 13.
"Nautica Earnings Gain 35%; Women's Business 'Just OK'," *WWD*, April 17, 1997, p. 14.
"Nautica Licenses Chaus to Make Women's Wear," *Daily News Record*, September 18, 1995, p. 2.
Ryan, Thomas J., "It's Full Steam Ahead for Nautica's Course," *Daily News Record*, May 16, 1996, p. 5.
——, "Nautica Enterprises to Double Size of Some In-Store Shop Formats," *Daily News Record*, September 14, 1995, p. 2.
——, "Nautica Ent. Planning Major Push in In-Store Shops, Outlet Stores," *Daily News Record*, September 30, 1994, p. 2.
——, "Nautica to More Than Triple Number of In-Store Shops," *Daily News Record*, September 30, 1993, pp. 3, 11.

——, ''New Product Introductions Hurt Nautica Net,'' *Daily News Record,* June 28, 2000, p. 1B.

''Soft Outerwear Sales Cut Into Net at Nautica,'' *Daily News Record,* April 23 ,1999, p. 4.

Temes, Judy, ''Creating an Image Chops State-O-Maine's Earnings, *Crain's New York Business,* October 22, 1992, p. 46.

Weisman, Katherine, ''Kismet on Seventh Avenue,'' *Forbes,* November 25, 1991, pp. 152–53.

—Robert Halasz
—update: Christina M. Stansell

The New Piper Aircraft, Inc.

2926 Piper Drive
Vero Beach, Florida 32960
U.S.A.
Telephone: (561) 567-4361
Toll Free: 1-866-FLY-PIPER
Fax: (561) 778-2144
Web site: http://www.piperaircraft.com

Private Company
Incorporated: 1937
Employees: 1,550
Sales: $290 million (2001 est.)
NAIC: 54171 Research and Development in the Physical, Engineering, and Life Sciences; 336411 Aircraft Manufacturing

The New Piper Aircraft, Inc. builds a wide range of propeller-driven aircraft. The company builds upon the legacy of the original Piper Aircraft, one of the best-known names in general aviation. Virtually no other Western aircraft manufacturer has produced a full range of piston engine planes for as long as Piper.

Birth of a "Cub"

William T. "Bill" Piper was one of the first to apply assembly line techniques to aircraft production, and is often referred to as the Henry Ford of aviation. As W.T. Piper, Jr., described him in a 1970 Newcomen Society address, W.T. Piper was a teetotaler of British stock. After graduating from Harvard with a degree in engineering in 1903, he went into construction and built the first reinforced concrete garage in New York City.

Eventually Piper returned to his native Bradford, Pennsylvania and joined an oil-related partnership. A number of his associates there invested in the Taylor Brothers Aircraft Corporation, which Bradford's chamber of commerce had lured from Rochester, New York, and Piper joined Taylor's board of directors in the early 1920s.

Taylor Brothers Aircraft had been formed to produce a small, two-place, 20-horsepower aircraft that sold for about

$4,000. Steep competition and troubles associated with the Great Depression forced the Taylor Brothers into bankruptcy in 1931. By this time, Piper had become a believer in the future of aviation. Further, company founder C. Gilbert Taylor had already set about designing a low-cost airplane specifically for student instruction—the (E-2) "Cub." The name may be a reference to Piper's commitment to the business—"He had a bear by the tail. . . . He couldn't afford to let go," notes his son. According to W.T. Piper, Jr., the first mock-up of the Cub was constructed of orange crates.

Piper bought the bankrupt company's assets for $600 and arranged for additional financing. According to his son, he then generously gave Gilbert Taylor a half interest in a new entity, the Taylor Aircraft Corporation. After Gilbert Taylor left the company in 1935, he was replaced as chief engineer by Walter Jamouneau, who was responsible for the J-3 version of the famous Piper Cub, which by this time were usually painted their trademark bright yellow. In the years ahead, untold pilots would adore the Cub, an attractive little plane with forgiving flight characteristics. This small, simple, and undeniably cute airplane originally sold for just $999.

In spite of the charm and simplicity of the Cub, the 1930s were hard years for selling small planes. Taylor Aircraft's difficulties were compounded by a fire that wiped out the Bradford plant in 1937. The company then decided to relocate to an abandoned silk mill in Lock Haven, Pennsylvania, renaming itself the Piper Aircraft Corporation in the process.

Piper developed two other models before WWII. The Coupe sat two persons side-by-side. The Cruiser was a three-seater. Production of the Coupe ceased when the war began, but a number of Cruisers were adapted for use as air ambulances.

The L-4 training aircraft was derived from the Cub; eighty percent of U.S. military pilots earned their wings in these planes during the war. Nearly 6,000 L-4s were delivered. Nicknamed "Grasshoppers," L-4s were also used as tactical observation planes and as air taxis for leaders such as Winston Churchill, General George S. Patton, and General Dwight D. Eisenhower.

An erroneous but widely held belief was maintained that after the war Americans would buy up personal airplanes the

307

Company Perspectives:

The New Piper Aircraft, Inc. became a reality in the summer of 1995 when President/CEO Charles Suma and a nucleus of employees took over the assets of the Piper Aircraft Corporation. There were fewer than 100 employees in that first year but they embarked on an exciting assignment. The task was not an enviable one: Take on all the competitors and bring the Piper name back to the forefront of General Aviation. But this cadre of dedicated people was up to the challenges. Engineers were challenged to create an aggressive research and development program to bring new, innovative aircraft to market. Customer service professionals from a variety of industries were tapped to create a system that provides the best service possible to every customer around the world. The organization embarked on a campaign to recruit the best distribution professionals around the globe. And the marketing and sales staff recommitted itself to making New Piper the leader not only in the owner-flown segment of the General Aviation market, but the leader when it comes to supplying the best training aircraft in the world, as well.

same way they would buy new cars and houses in the suburbs. There were, after all, hundreds of thousands of new pilots returning home. Yet, planes required a specific form of infrastructure; they were not nearly as flexible as automobiles. Sales were indeed spectacular, noted Bill Piper, Jr., until 1947, when the market collapsed.

In the early 1950s, Piper adapted its 135-horsepower Pacer by adding a tricycle landing gear (with a steering nose wheel in the front). The resulting Tri-Pacer was easier to maneuver on the ground. Piper decided a market did exist for faster planes than this and the Cub (which some like to say takes off, lands, and cruises all at 65 m.p.h.) with a capacity of seating at least four people.

First Apache Built in 1954

In addition, businessmen needed the reliability and performance of a twin-engine plane in order to fly over weather. In answer to this requirement, Piper debuted its first all-metal plane, the twin-engine Apache, in February 1954. It was priced at nearly $34,000; in spite of the skepticism of its dealers, Piper sold 2,000 of the planes in nine years. The design formed the basis for another successful plane, the Aztec.

The company built a research manufacturing facility at a naval airbase in Vero Beach, Florida, in 1957. One of the first planes developed here was a crop duster dubbed the PA-25 Pawnee. The PA-28 Cherokee, which went into production at the company's expanded Vero Beach manufacturing facilities in January 1961, was to be one of the company's most successful designs. The low-wing design was the basis for numerous models in the next thirty years, including the Warrior, Archer, Dakota, Arrow, Seneca, and Saratoga. The PA-32 Cherokee Six, introduced in 1965, was the earliest derivative and featured a stretched cabin with room for six people and an additional

door in the rear. Eventually, the PA-32 was incorporated into the training fleets of several airlines, training schools, and other operators. Another twin-engine plane, the PA-31 Navajo, was introduced in 1967 specifically as a business aircraft. The Navajo family grew to include the Navajo Chieftain and Mojave, and the Cheyenne, which used turboprop engines. Several airlines used Cheyennes to train their pilots.

Piper's annual revenues passed $100 million in 1969. By 1970, the company had produced 80,000 planes (24,000 of them Piper Cubs); one in every four general aviation planes was a Piper. Piper had added small parts plants near Lock Haven and built a new factory in Lakeland, Florida, bringing total manufacturing space to 1,000,000 square feet.

During most of the 1970s, two companies fought for control of Piper Aircraft Corp. In 1977, Bangor Punta Corp., a $500 million conglomerate, won out over Chris-Craft Industries Inc., known for making yachts. Bangor paid $110 million for Piper and endured years of litigation. Bangor's other subsidiaries produced Smith & Wesson handguns and Starcraft and Jensen boats and campers; its largest unit processed cotton and safflower oil. Piper's revenues were about $270 million in 1977; *Business Week* noted it trailed industry leader Cessna Aircraft Co., which had a 51 percent market share in the general aviation field to Piper's 27 percent.

The PA-44 Seminole, introduced in 1978, was a stretched version of the twin-engine Arrow with a twin tail. Piper's new owners steered the company into an emphasis on larger ''cabin class'' planes for the business market. Sixty percent of Piper's planes were designed for the consumer market, noted *Business Week*.

At Its Peak in 1979

Piper had 8,800 employees at five plants in 1979. Annual sales were $495 million. Unfortunately, high interest rates, high taxes, and exorbitant product liability claims would decimate the piston engine aircraft industry in the 1980s. Shipments of small planes fell from 18,000 in 1979 to less than 10,000 in 1981, according to one estimate. Yet Piper plugged on, introducing its revolutionary PA-46 Malibu in 1983. This was a single engine aircraft featuring a pressurized cabin and other amenities usually found in corporate jets, which had much higher operating costs. A higher-performance version, the Malibu Mirage, was introduced in 1988. (The Malibu was involved a string of in-flight breakups between 1989 and 1992. The National Transportation Safety Board determined ice was forming on the pilot tube, leading to an understated airspeed reading. Blaming the pilots for not switching on the heater for this device, the NTSB urged the Federal Aviation Administration to require high-altitude training for pilots flying at altitudes of 18,000 feet or higher.)

Lear Siegler Inc. bought Piper from Bangor Punta for $290 million in February 1984. Its new owners consolidated Piper's manufacturing operations in a single Vero Beach plant. In 1987, New York buyout firm Forstmann Little & Company acquired Piper. Production had fallen to fewer than 300 planes a year and the company had only 750 employees.

Key Dates:

1947: The aircraft market collapses after World War II.
1954: Piper builds its first all-metal plane, the Apache.
1961: First of the popular Cherokee family debuts.
1977: Bangor Punta acquires Piper.
1983: The Malibu is introduced.
1984: Lear Siegler buys Piper.
1987: Monroe Stuart Millar becomes new owner/CEO.
1991: Unable to finance production, Piper files Chapter 11.
1995: The New Piper Aircraft is launched.
1997: Piper unveils its new flagship, the Malibu Meridian turboprop.

Newport Beach entrepreneur Monroe Stuart Millar then bought Piper (through his Romeo Charlie, Inc. holding company) in May 1987 for a reported $6 million. A former World War II fighter pilot, Millar had taken his first flight in a Cub and reportedly felt it was his destiny to own the company. Millar made several unorthodox moves in attempting to right the troubled company. To stimulate demand, he cut prices 20 percent and introduced new models. He also brought the classic Piper Cub back into production, selling them for $50,000 a piece. The company's Cheyenne 400LS turboprop sold for $3 million. Piper sold hundreds of a new no-frill trainer called the Cadet, designed to lure people into flying.

Most seriously, Millar decided to forgo liability insurance in a highly litigious environment. Under existing law, the company's owner was potentially liable for every plane made by Piper since 1937—a total of 100,000 aircraft. To fend off nuisance suits, the company hired "the meanest bunch of junkyard-dog lawyers," said one company executive. They succeeded in reducing awards against the company from $30 million in 1987 to $8 million in 1989. The company had been paying $25 million a year for product liability insurance with a $15 million deductible. However, few would loan the company money to buy supplies without this coverage.

In one unusual effort to retain loyal customers, Millar paid first-class airfare for 893 patrons while an engine problem with their new $350,000 planes was being fixed. It cost the company $2 million. Sales rose from $50.7 million in 1988 to $90.5 million in 1989, though losses mounted simultaneously. Most of the company's 1,600 employees were furloughed in February 1990 as rumors of bankruptcy circulated. Industry-wide sales were just 1,143 planes in 1989, and Piper's main competitors Cessna and Beech Aircraft had stopped making small piston engine planes.

C. Raymond Johnson was appointed president of Piper in early 1990. Millar ultimately resigned as chairman in May 1992 after selling his stock in the Romeo Charlie Inc. holding company that had owned Piper.

Bankrupt in 1991

The firm went bankrupt in July 1991. Interestingly, the company had a backlog worth $100 million; its assets were $75 million and its liabilities, $47 million. The company simply had no cash. Charles "Chuck" Suma, the company's future president and COO told *Florida Trend,* "We had $1,000 in the bank." (Suma had begun working for Piper in 1976 as a riveter.) No one would lend the company money to operate without product liability insurance. Piper had just 45 employees at the time of its Chapter 11 filing.

While a court weighed Cleveland's Cyrus Eaton Group purchase of its assets for about $46 million, Piper shopped around the U.S. and Canada for a new location in which to rebuild. Ultimately, Eaton did not buy the company. Aerospatiale, the French producer of light planes, also negotiated for its purchase in 1991 but was dissuaded by the product liability issue. Another suitor wanted to relocate manufacturing to a New Mexico Indian reservation to ameliorate this problem, wrote the *Financial Times.*

In 1992, Angus Stone Douglass, a businessman with ties to New Jersey criminal-politicians, bought all of Piper's common stock from Millar for $500,000 cash through his Duck's Nest Investment firm. In his first year in charge, the company shipped 90 planes and reported operating profits of $7 million on revenues of $47 million.

Pilatus then made a controversial bid for Piper. Pilatus was a Swiss company that made single-engine turboprop planes that wanted to emphasize the commercial market more. The problem with Pilatus was that even its civil planes tended to end up in military uses in such unsavory places as Iraq and Angola. Recent sales to Burma and South Africa were freshly controversial. In September 1993, a bankruptcy judge ruled that the Swiss company's $45 million offer would not be enough to pay debts and set up a trust fund for Piper's potential claimants.

The whole U.S. general aviation industry sold only 444 planes in 1994. Piper made 108 of them. However, that year, Congress enacted legislation limiting product liability for planes to 18 years after production. Chief competitor Cessna immediately announced plans to resume production of its small planes.

New Piper in 1995

Suma became CEO in early 1995 after Douglass was forced out of the position over a questionable stock transaction, reported *Florida Trend.* Teledyne (later named Allegheny) and Philly investment firm Dimeling Schreiber & Park bought Piper for $95 million in March 1995, renaming it The New Piper Aircraft, Inc. Piper had been able to pay off its largest secured creditor by selling its Lakeland plant.

In the fall of 1997, Piper announced it was developing a new single engine turboprop, the Malibu Meridian. The first prototype was rolled out in August 1998 and production deliveries began in 2000. New Piper sold 303 planes in 1998 and had revenues of $125 million that year. Revenues were $146 million in 1999 and $181 million in 2000, when Piper sold 395 planes. The industry as a whole sold 2,816 planes worth $8.6 billion in 2000.

In March 2000, Interior Pacific Flight Sytems, based in British Columbia, announced it had bought rights to produce the Piper's classic PA-12 Super Cruiser, a three-seat, fabric-winged plane that had not been built since 1948. Interior Pacific was not allowed to use Piper's name; it would dub its version the Super 12. It would take advantage of the latest avionics and sell for about $113,000; Interior Pacific hoped to be building 36 of them a year within three years.

At the beginning of the millennium, there were rumors of an impending initial public offering. Piper remained a popular brand among pilots; the revived company brought in marketing personnel from Harley-Davidson to promote customer loyalty. The company also had a few enemies; it faced a new spate of litigation that alleged a melting rod bearing in the Mirage's engine caused four crashes in four years.

Principal Competitors

Cessna Aircraft Company; Raytheon Aircraft; Mooney Aircraft Corporation; Cirrus Design Corp.

Further Reading

"Bangor Punta: Steering Piper Toward Growth in Bigger Aircraft," *Business Week*, September 14, 1981, p. 78.

Beauge, John Q., "Piper Plan to Continue on Course," *Northeast Pennsylvania Business Journal*, March 1990, p. 1.

——, "Piper Returns with 600 Jobs," *Northeast Pennsylvania Business Journal*, November 1989, p. 5.

Bhatt, Sanjay, "New Piper Unveils New Plane; Company Touts Six-Seater as 'Bridge to Future'," *Palm Beach Post*, August 14, 1998, p. 1D.

Borfitz, Deborah, "Regaining Altitude," *Florida Trend*, March 1, 1999, p. 64.

Cook, Dan, "Millar Quits as Chairman of Piper Aircraft," *Orange County Business Journal*, May 18, 1992, p. 3.

Daw, James, "Aircraft Firm Studies Move to Canada," *Toronto Star*, October 31, 1991, p. D1.

Field, David, "Old Piper Faces New Competition, Returns to Skies After Bankruptcy," *Washington Times*, August 3, 1995, p. B6.

Francis, Devon, *Mr. Piper and His Cubs*, Eagan, Minn.: Flying Books, 1996.

Glaser, Brian, " 'Lone Wolf' Attempts to Climb Back Into Pilot Seat," *Orange County Business Journal*, August 17, 1992, p. 1.

Hackney, Holt, "Piper Survives a Nose Dive," *Florida Trend*, June 1993, p. 56.

Jordan, Juana, "Plane Maker Markets New Merchandise in Tallahassee, Fla.," *Tallahassee Democrat*, April 21, 2001.

McGinley, Laurie, "Safety Board Clears the Piper Malibu, Citing Pilot Error in String of Crashes," *Wall Street Journal*, July 22, 1992, p. A4.

Martinez, Amy, "Lawsuits Again Threaten Piper Aircraft," *Palm Beach Post*, October 22, 2000.

——, "Piper Aircraft Sued for $75 Million; Plaintiffs Claim Engine Problem Caused 4 Crashes," *Palm Beach Post*, September 26, 2000, p. 5B.

"Piper's New Owner to Run Firm on a Full-Time Basis," *Los Angeles Times*, Bus. Sec., May 23, 1987, p. 1.

Piper, William Thomas, "What Your Town Needs for the Coming Air Age," Lock Haven, Pa.: Piper Aircraft Corporation, 1944.

Piper, W.T., Jr., *From Cub to Navajo: The Story of the Piper Aircraft Corporation*, New York: Newcomen Society in North America, 1970.

Port, Susan T., "Piper Cuts Output from 538 to 489 Planes, But No Layoffs Expected," *Palm Beach Post*, June 15, 2001, p. 11B.

"Pushing Internal Growth After the Piper Victory," *Business Week*, April 10, 1978, p. 108.

Rodger, Ian, and Nikki Tait, "Swiss Group Attempts to Call the Tune at Piper; A Controversial Suitor for the US Producer of Light Aircraft," *Financial Times*, April 28, 1993, p. 28.

Siuru, Bill, "The Piper Cub: Simplicity Takes Flight and Endures," *Mechanical Engineering*, November 1990, p. 48.

"Smaller Piper Plant to Reopen," *Los Angeles Times*, Bus. Sec., August 6, 1985, p. 6.

Valdmanis, Thor, "Six Years After Nearly Collapsing, Piper Takes Off Again," *USA Today*, July 3, 2001, p. B6.

Weiner, Eric, "Piper Aircraft's Rescuer Falters," *New York Times*, March 15, 1990, p. D1.

Weisman, Robert, "Could Piper Aircraft Corp. Fly Up Here?," *Hartford Courant*, October 16, 1993, p. C1.

—Frederick C. Ingram

New World Restaurant Group, Inc.

246 Industrial Way West
Eatontown, New Jersey 07724
U.S.A.
Telephone: (732) 544-0155
Fax: (732) 544-1315
Web site: http://www.nwcb.com

Public Company
Incorporated: 1992 as New World Coffee, Inc.
Employees: 675
Sales: $45.7 million (2000)
Stock Exchanges: OTC
Ticker Symbol: NWCI
NAIC: 722211 Limited-Service Restaurants; 311920
    Coffee and Tea Manufacturing

Originally established in the early 1990s as a chain of coffee bars, New World Restaurant Group, Inc. has evolved into the United States's largest operator of bagel stores. With its corporate headquarters located in Eatontown, New Jersey, New World has approximately 800 outlets that it licenses, owns, or franchises across 34 states and Washington, D.C., operating under such brand names as New World Coffee, Willoughby's Coffee & Tea, Chesapeake Bagel Bakery, Einstein Bros. Bagel, Manhattan Bagel, and Noah's New York Bagels. The combination of bagels, sandwiches, salads, coffee, as well as other food items, allows New World's various brands to attract customers throughout the day, with a particular emphasis on breakfast and lunch. To provide a consistent product, the company supplies its stores with frozen bagel dough, which is then baked on the premises. It also provides cheese spreads and specialty coffees. In November 2001, New World was delisted from the Nasdaq national market, the advisory panel for which cited violations relating to its purchase of the Einstein/Noah Bagel Corporation. The company was appealing that decision while seeking listing on other exchanges.

New World Coffee Established in 1993

New World's founder, Ramin Kamfar, was born in Iran, and emigrated to the United States with his family. He earned an

MBA from the Wharton School of Business, then went to work on Wall Street with investment bank Lehman Bros., where he became a vice president before the age of 30. Despite earning a salary in the range of $500,000 a year, Kamfar had a dream of building his own company. Aware that gourmet coffee chains were spreading rapidly on the West Coast, he decided to apply the idea to the East Coast. Rather than following Starbucks' Italian-style format, in which patrons stood or simply left with their coffee, Kamfar drew on the model of the London coffee-houses and Paris cafés, which served as neighborhood gathering places where people lingered and sat at tables.

In October 1992, Kamfar incorporated New World Coffee in Delaware and soon quit his job. "The people at Lehman thought I was crazy," he recalled in a 1997 *Success* magazine profile. "They reminded me that I was a vice president making a lot of money in the midst of the biggest boom in Wall Street history. They said, 'You'll never get New Yorkers to pay $3 for a cup of coffee.' " While his years at Lehman provided Kamfar with valuable financial knowledge and important contacts, his only retail experience was a spell during college when he worked at a Fotomat. Kamfar didn't even drink coffee, instead preferring tea. Nevertheless, he raised $250,000 from friends and former colleagues, as well as tapping into his savings, and in 1993 opened the first two New World Coffee shops in the West Village of Manhattan, serving a variety of coffees from around the world—Africa and Indonesia in addition to South America. Hence, the New World name.

With the goal of becoming the Starbucks of the East Coast, Kamfar opened new stores at a steady pace during the first three years of New World's existence. By 1996, the company owned 27 stores, and in February of that year Kamfar took the company public in order to raise capital for further expansion. Originally he had planned to sell stock in December 1995, but investor indifference prompted a delay. Even when the offering was made three months later, investors were not especially interested. Starbucks had been the only coffee-bar stock that really captivated the market, while others had enjoyed mixed results. In general, investors viewed New World as a been-there-done-that opportunity. The company had not yet turned a profit, and ambitious plans to open another 40 stores in New York and Philadelphia over the next year were not enough to kindle much enthusiasm. New

---

Company Perspectives:

The thoroughness New World brings to the coffee selection process is unique. After the harvest of each coffee variety, we collect samples of green (unroasted) coffee from our sources. We are only interested in the highest grades, and advise our sources to send us only the best they have. Numerous samples are gathered, sometimes resulting in so many that they cannot be "cupped" in one or two sittings. When all the samples have arrived, our roastmaster roasts and de-identifies each so we can proceed with blind tastings. We do not want to be biased by a coffee's name, reputation, cost or marketing. We are only interested in one thing: which coffee tastes best. This is what we want for our customers. Upon conclusion, the samples' identities are revealed, and we then go to market to acquire the best of the best.

World sold 2.5 million shares at $5.50 per share, grossing some $13.8 million, but by the end of the first week of trading on the Nasdaq the stock fell to 5³⁄₁₆. New World also sold $4 million worth of convertible preferred securities.

Kamfar used the money he raised to expand his business through external growth in 1996. He purchased three Coopers Coffee Bars, an early chain on Manhattan's Upper West Side, for $242,500 in cash and a $770,000 note. He then acquired Willoughby's Coffee and Tea for $3.1 million. Not only did New World add five new locations, it gained Willoughby's New Haven, Connecticut, roasting plant that allowed the company to produce 20 types of coffee. While New World had opened nearly 30 stores in three years, and by the end of 1996 boasted 40 overall, Starbucks was now rolling out 30 new stores each month and acquiring choice locations in the New York City area, often paying above the market rate simply to establish a presence. Starbucks' advantage in economies of scale, as well as its head start, meant that New World could not hope to become the leading coffee bar operator in the metro area. Already it was relegated to fighting for position on a second tier, at the same time the price of its stock was steadily declining. Clearly a change in strategy was in order.

New World Coffee Begins Selling Bagels

In 1996, the bagel business was taking off, with several chains expanding rapidly across the country. Kamfar decided to try selling bagels in two New World stores and was encouraged by the results. While coffee shops like Starbucks enjoyed most of their business early in the day, and bagel shops did well through the lunch hours, New World found that by adding bagels, bagel sandwiches, and pastries it was able to sell all day.

One of the new concept stores located in Manhattan's garment district experienced a 71 percent increase in annual sales, from $500,000 to almost $800,000. By the summer of 1997, Kamfar decided to convert the entire 38-unit chain to the new format, requiring a $50,000 investment in each store to outfit the kitchen with baking ovens, along with proper refrigeration and venting.

To reflect this shift in focus, the company's name was then changed to New World Coffee & Bagels, Inc. in September 1997.

New World also began a transition from a predominantly urban chain to a suburban one, from being entirely company-owned to embracing a franchise system. Kamfar's goal was to open 500 franchises in the next five years. To help him execute this plan, Kamfar hired experienced executives from other franchise operations such as Wendy's and Starbucks. He also invested in a software system to track the daily expenses and incomes of franchises, in order to keep an eye out for weak links in the chain. New World's first franchise opened in 1997. Moreover, the company signed a deal with New York Food Ventures GMBH, a German company, to create a café in Munich and the right to open as many as 100 stores over the next five years. Despite these developments, the price of New World stock continued to sag, dipping as far as $.90 a share. Kamfar spent $27,500 of his own money to purchase shares at $1.25 in order to bolster the price and make a statement about his confidence in the company's long-term prospects. He felt that New World was undervalued by investors because it was overlooked. "I know how those guys on Wall Street think," he told the press in August 1997, "Unless you are doing $30 million a year, they are not interested in you. Because we are relatively small, we are off everyone's radar screen. But we expect that to change in the next six to eight months." Over the ensuing months, New World would post its first profitable quarter and solidify its commitment to bagels by acquiring one of the leading chains, Manhattan Bagel, at a bargain price.

Manhattan Bagel

The founders of Manhattan Bagel, brothers Jason and Andrew Gennusa, were first involved in a Dunellen, New Jersey, take-out chicken restaurant, Chicken Holiday. Looking to enter the breakfast market, while not conflicting with their dinner business, they turned to bagels. At the time they established Manhattan Bagel in 1987 very few bagel shops were to found outside of New York City. When the company embarked on a franchising campaign in the early 1990s, Jack Grumet took over as its chairman and CEO. He had earlier founded Jo-Ann's Nut House, which he built into a 149-unit chain. To fuel Manhattan Bagel's growth, the company made an initial public offering of stock in 1994, selling 900,000 shares at $5 a share. Manhattan grew from a chain of 40, with only three company owned, then spread from Massachusetts to Georgia, increasing to 152 stores in 1995 and almost 300 in 1996. A portion of that growth was accomplished by buying up smaller bagel chains. Unlike New World, Manhattan Bagel caught the attention of investors, who bid up its stock to a high of $29 in June 1996. Bagels were piquing everyone's interest, fueled by studies indicating that the U.S. per-capita consumption of bagels increased from 2.5 pounds in 1988 to 3.5 pounds in 1993 and to 4.5 pounds in 1995. To tap this rising trend, other bagel chains such as Bruegger's and Einstein, and a host of smaller competitors, rolled out new stores at a furious pace, essentially outstripping demand. Moreover, delis and corner stores, as well as non-traditional players like New World Coffee, also began to sell bagels.

The prospects for the bagel business altered dramatically in June 1997 when Dunkin' Donuts announced that its 2,000 stores would begin to sell bagels. This, in one stroke it became

Key Dates:

1992: The company is incorporated.
1993: First New World Coffee shops opened in New York City.
1996: New World begins selling bagels.
1998: Manhattan Bagels is acquired.
1999: Chesapeake Bagel Bakery is acquired.
2001: Einstein/Noah Bagel Corp. is acquired; company's name changes from New World Coffee–Manhattan Bagel to New World Restaurant Group; stock is delisted from NASDAQ.

the largest bagel retailer in the nation. Manhattan Bagel's situation was further complicated by discovered irregularities in the accounting methods of an acquired subsidiary, forcing the company to restate its first quarter revenues. As a result, the company's stock was punished and never recovered. By November 1997, Manhattan Bagel was forced to file for reorganization under Chapter 11. The price of Manhattan Bagel stock dipped below $1 and eventually traded for pennies.

Manhattan Bagel Acquired

In November 1998, New World's reorganization plan for Manhattan Bagel was approved by creditors in federal Bankruptcy Court. The $21.8 million purchase agreement included a $3.5 million payment to First Union National Bank, Manhattan Bagel's only secured creditor, $11.5 million to unsecured creditors, and the assumption of $5 million in debt. Not only did New World add over 300 franchises, it gained two bagel-manufacturing facilities that could supply its New World outlets and a training facility for managers, a so-called "Bagel University." Moreover, New World closed its New York operation and made Manhattan Bagel's less expensive Eatontown, New Jersey, offices its new corporate headquarters. Kamfar, who took over as CEO and chairman of the combined businesses, also quickly moved to acquire Manhattan Bagel's master franchise territories in western New York, Florida, and the region of Maryland, Virginia, and the District of Columbia.

In April 1999, the company changed its name to New World Coffee-Manhattan Bagel Inc. To improve its lunch business it added new specialty sandwiches, available on rolls and wraps in addition to bagels. Coffee-flavored smoothies using New World Coffee extract were also incorporated into the offerings of Manhattan Bagel stores. New World then continued in 1999 to pursue further external growth. In July it acquired Chesapeake Bagel Bakery from AFC enterprises, parent company of Church's Chicken, Popeye's Chicken & Biscuits, Seattle Coffee Co., and Cinnabon. As a result, New World added 89 stores and gained entry into ten new states. In May 2000, the company purchased the assets of New York Bagel Enterprises and its Lots 'A Bagels affiliate, adding approximately 25 stores. By the end of 1999 its 377 units placed New World second among bagel-café operators, trailing only Colorado-based Einstein/Noah Bagel Corp. and its 540 units. New World's focus had clearly shifted from coffee to bagels. In 1999, it sold six outlets to Starbucks and closed three others to reduce the number of

coffee shops to 39. Although Kamfar expressed confidence in the New World brand, he admitted that he saw more opportunities in bagels than coffee.

Kamfar now began talking about a 1,000 bagel store chain. He told the *Wall Street Journal,* "The persons who created the 1,000-store chain will be the Starbucks of the industry." He also felt that it was more economical to buy and convert existing stores than to build. Due to acquisition costs, New World had yet to post an annual profit, but because it had already gone through a restructuring process, Kamfar felt that the company was in a better position than Einstein/Noah to reach the next level. While New World lost $7.5 million in 1998, Einstein/Noah lost $204 million. In October 1998, Einstein/Noah stock was delisted by the Nasdaq for failing to meet financial requirements, and by the end of the year was trading in the $.65 range. Einstein Bagels was created in 1995 by Boston Chicken, which combined four small bagel chains. It then acquired Noah's New York Bagel Inc. and by the end of 1996 boasted 315 stores. The company continued to grow, passing the 500-unit mark, but was simply unable to find the right business model to maintain a chain of that magnitude. By April 2000, it filed for Chapter 11 bankruptcy protection.

Despite New World's relative strength in the bagel industry, and a 1999 profit of $2.42 million, investors continued to show little interest, and the company's stock languished around $2 a share. Restaurant stock in general was faring poorly, and all the major bagel chains had gone bankrupt. Nevertheless, Kamfar was confident that New World had developed a way to make a bagel chain successful, relying in large part on improving margins by manufacturing the chain's own bagel dough and coffee beans. Moreover, the company's franchise approach did not require a significant outlay of capital. The company continued to post improving results, netting $6 million in 2000. In 2001 New World pursued the acquisition of Einstein/Noah, finally making a $190 million winning bid in an auction conducted by the U.S. Bankruptcy Court in Phoenix, Arizona.

A number of Einstein/Noah stores had already been shuttered, but the 460 that remained pushed New World above the 800 unit mark, making it the undisputed leader in the retail bagel industry, more than three times the size of Bruegger's, its closest competitor. Kamfar hoped that New World would soon gain respect from investors. "The Street, I think, doesn't understand us," he told *Nation's Restaurant News,* "But once we start showing our numbers, the Street responds to that. What will be important is to tell our story, and we have an attractive story to tell."

Kamfar now looked to accelerate store openings to become one of the top players in what he called the "fast casual" sandwich business. In order to accomplish this goal he decided to step down as chief executive officer, opting to serve as chairman of the board in order to focus on strategic and financial matters. The new CEO he hired was a former Boston Market and KFC executive, 42-year-old Anthony D. Wedo. Subsequently the company again changed its name, becoming New World Restaurant Group in August 2001. Whether Kamfar would realize his ambitious goals or not, his accomplishment of building a bagel empire out of two Greenwich Village coffee-houses in less than ten years, at the very least, vindicated his decision to quit a lucrative Wall Street career.

Principal Subsidiaries

Einstein/Noah Bagel Corp.; Chesapeake Bagel Franchise Corp.; Manhattan Bagel Company, Inc.; Paragon Bakeries, Inc.; Willoughby's, Inc.

Principal Divisions

New World Coffee.

Principal Competitors

Bruegger's Bagel Bakery; Dunkin' Donuts; Starbucks Corporation.

Further Reading

Berta, Dina, "Einstein Buy Puts Manhattan Bagel on Top of New World," *Nation's Restaurant News,* July 2, 2001, p. 1.

Brown, Heather, "The Bagel Wars—Is the Carnage Over?," *Modern Baking,* May 1998, p. 64+.

Carlino, Bill, "New World Emerging as Biggest Public Bagel Player in 'Last Man Standing' Scenario," *Nation's Restaurant News,* April 10, 2000, p. 11.

Coleman-Lochner, Lauren, "Eaton, N.J., Entrepreneur Seeks 'Bankrupt Bagel Bargains,' " *The Record,* July 29, 2001.

Keenan, Charles, "New World's Hole-Hearted Foray Into Bagel Business," *Crain's New York Business,* June 5, 2000, p. 40.

Lynch, Colum, "Bucking Starbucks," *Success,* October 1997, p. 94.

McGeehan, Patrick, "New World Coffee's IPO Gets Lukewarm Response," *Wall Street Journal,* February 12, 1996, p. C1.

Ordonez, Jennifer, "Food for Thought: Can Einstein Nourish New World?—A Consolidation in Bagel-Chain Business May Now Follow a Rough Period," *Wall Street Journal,* December 7, 1999, p. B4.

Papiernik, Richard, "New World Coffee-Manhattan Bagel Needs Dough to Rise Again," *Nation's Restaurant News,* May 10, 1999, p. 15.

Pate, Kelly, "Einstein Buyout Fills Hole in Owner's Plans," *Denver Post,* July 2, 2001, p. C1.

Prewitt, Milford, "New World Coffee's New Name Means New Game," *Nation's Restaurant News,* August 25, 1997, p. 6.

Silver, Deborah, "New World Order," *Restaurants & Institutions,* March 15, 2000, pp. 71–76.

—Ed Dinger

Nichols plc

Laurel House
3 Woodlands Park
Ashton Road
Newton-le-Willows WA12 OHH
United Kingdom
Telephone: (+44) 1925-222-222
Fax: (+44) 1925-222-233
Web site: http://www.nicholsplc.co.uk

Public Company
Incorporated: 1961 as JN Nichols (Vimto) plc
Employees: 789
Sales: £90.4 million ($135 million)(2000)
Stock Exchanges: London
Ticker Symbol: NICL
NAIC: 312111 Soft Drink Manufacturing

Nichols plc has changed its recipe for success for the 21st century without changing its successful recipe. The creator of the popular (in Northern England and much of the Middle East) soft drink Vimto, now produced and distributed from within its main Nichols Foods subsidiary, Nichols has expanded to include holdings in the food and beverage distribution market, notably through its subsidiaries Cabana, which supplies soft drink dispensing systems to over 6,000 outlets throughout the United Kingdom; Balmoral, the United Kingdom's leading distributor of coffee and hot beverage dispensing systems; and Nichols International, which manufactures and distributes its own and third-party foods and beverages. The company also owns Stockpack, a contract packing company providing co-manufacturing and co-packing services to the food and drinks industries. The company's diversification has enabled it to extend its sales to some 60 countries and boost revenues to more than £90 million. Quoted on the London Stock Exchange, Nichols is led by chairman and grandson of the founder John Nichols, who also holds the family's 20 percent share in the company. Day to day operations are led by managing director Gary N. Unsworth, the first non-Nichols family member to lead the company since its founding.

From Health Tonic to Soft Drink

Chemist John Noel Nichols was a supplier of herbs, herbal preparations, spices, and other substances—such as roots and tree barks—to northern England's flourishing herbalist trade at the beginning of the 20th century. Searching for new formulas, Nichols hit upon a new mix in his warehouse, combining a number of ingredients—including fruit juices such as raspberry and black currant, capsicum, vanilla, horehound, and, according to one source, the edible residue left over from the manufacture of aniline dye to produce a health tonic Nichols dubbed "Vimto," short for "Vim Tonic." Nichols began promoting his new tonic, which was intended to give its imbibers fresh vim and vigor, among herbalists of his Manchester home base. Meanwhile, the recipe for the drink remained a closely guarded family secret.

Herbalists at the time often ran small cafes, where customers were able to consume the herbal preparations. Hot water was often added to the Vimto base, but the drink also became popular with cold flat and carbonated water. During the height of the anti-alcohol movement, Nichols also promoted his cordial among the Manchester area's many teetotaler bars as a healthy alternative to "evil" alcoholic beverages.

Nichols moved to larger facilities in 1910, in Salford, outside of Manchester, where the company increased production to meet the growing demand for its drink. Yet Nichols continued to mix the drink in wooden barrels, which would not be replaced for modern equipment until after World War II. Vimto was not Nichol's only drink product. It was later joined by others, including a powdered milk preparation called "Thump." Yet Vimto was to prove the company's only lasting product.

The next step in Vimto's evolution as a popular, if steadfastly northern, drink came in 1921, when JN Nichols & Co. began supplying syrup to third-party bottlers in England and in Ireland. If no single bottle shape came to represent Vimto during this period, labels supplied by the Nichols company provided the drink with brand awareness. The company encouraged other bottlers to take on Vimto by creating advertising supports, including postcards, displays, and other promotional aids, such as "The Vimto Book of Knowledge," popularized in the post-World War I years.

Vimto had by then expanded beyond the herbalist circuit and was available, through the various bottlers and other agents, in drugstores, cafes, ice cream parlors, grocers, and the like. And by the beginning of the 1920s, Vimto had expanded beyond England as well, as the company's colonial representatives created an overseas demand for the drink. The first international market for the drink was in Guyana; the registration of the Vimto trademark there enabled the company to begin to describe itself as a Whole-sale Export Druggist. A more important market opened up for the company during the 1920s, when a friend of J.N. Nichols, traveling to India, brought along samples of Vimto and helped the company develop a network of bottlers in that country. The large number of British troops stationed in India at the time, or at least the homesick northerners among them, provided a ready market for the drink. The drink was registered as a trademark in India in 1924 and soon began appealing to the local market. From India, Vimto spread to Britain's other colonies in the region, such as the former Burma and Ceylon.

Vimto was released in 1926 in the form of a syrup that allowed consumers to mix up their own Vimto drinks at home. At this time the drink continued to be promoted as a hot beverage, while proving a popular cold soft drink as well. If Vimto remained a decidedly northern England drink—and even became a source of mockery for the country's southern consumers—the health tonic was finding larger markets abroad. During the 1920s, numerous Indians had followed the British colonizers into the Middle Eastern region, and brought Vimto with them. Vimto quickly became somewhat of a traditional drink for breaking the fast of the Islamic holiday of Ramadan. Because of its non-alcoholic nature, Vimto was a popular drink in Muslim markets, such as the region that later became Pakistan.

Back in England, however, the changing tide of public opinion in the 1930s led the company to begin to promote its product as an excellent mixer for alcoholic drinks. This development saw the creation of a number of cocktails with lasting appeal, pairing Vimto with stout, ale, and other alcoholic beverages. The company had by then again expanded its production capacity, moving into to a former laundry building in Old Trafford in 1927. Nichols & Co. also operated their own fleet of delivery vehicles.

World War II forced a suspension of the Vimto brand name, as the British soft drink industry was placed under control of a war time authority. While the company continued to produce its products, Vimto was now marketed simply as a Specialty Flavor Cordial without a brand name. The lack of ingredients, due to rationing at home and the disruption of the import trade, mean-

while, made it impossible for the company to maintain the same level of quality, so it was perhaps just as well that the company was forced to temporarily suspend the Vimto brand name.

Sugar rationing continued to restrict the company's production after the war, although the Vimto brand name reappeared in 1947. The company was not able to step up to full-scale production until 1953. By then, it had modernized its facilities, equipping its production line with modern stainless steel vats as well as machinery for bottling and labeling.

The creation of the new National Health Service (NHS) in 1948 had severe repercussions for JN Nichols & Co. With the advent of NHS, a ban was placed on herbal products promoting themselves as medical aids. At the same time, the creation of the NHS made pharmaceutical products more readily available through the country's drug stores. Vimto was now forced out of its comfortable health tonic category to compete full on with such rapidly growing beverage giants as Coca-Cola, Schweppes, and Pepsi. If Vimto lacked the marketing clout of its rivals, it maintained a strong market in its northern England base, supporting by a first series of television advertisements begun in 1956, and a steadily increasing overseas market. By the middle of the century, Vimto had become a favorite in a variety of markets, not only in the Indian subcontinent and Middle East, but in parts of South America as well. Supplying the countries about the Persian Gulf, notably from ports such as Kuwait and Bahrain, the company began direct shipments from its Salford facility. In order to cut down on transport costs, the Vimto these merchants and bottlers brought was a double-concentrated syrup. And it was this sugary version of Vimto that caught on among Arab customers.

Food and Drink Distributor for the 21st Century

The Nichols family company went public in 1961, adopting the name JN Nichols (Vimto) plc. Founder J.N. Nichols had by then been joined by his sons, Peter and John. John Noel Nichols died in 1966, leaving the company to his sons. At the beginning of the 1970s, the next generation joined on, when the founder's grandson, also named John Nichols, was brought into the company, later to be joined by Simon Nichols in 1983.

By then, the company had begun to market Vimto in cans. Bearing a red-white-and-blue-striped logo evocative of the British flag, the cans, if not altogether aesthetically pleasing, nonetheless became a familiar site in the company's northern base. In 1969, the company began to produce a carbonated Vimto drink, which it canned itself. In 1971, production was transferred to a new plant in South Manchester, which included a full-scale canning and bottling line. For its overseas production, however, the company continued to rely on local bottling and canning partners, while Nichols supplied the Vimto base syrup. The recipe remained a closely held family secret. In 1975, the company signed on a new overseas partner, Solent Canners, which began production of canned, carbonated Vimto for the Kuwait and Saudi Arabian markets. That company was acquired by Nichols in 1980s and then extended its distribution network to include the United Arab Emirates.

The third generation of Nichols began taking over the company's leadership in the 1980s. In 1986, John Nichols was appointed managing director and was soon seconded by Simon

Key Dates:

1908: John Noel Nichols mixes first batch of ''Vimto,'' an herbal health tonic, in Manchester, England.
1910: The company moves production to new facilities in Salford, near Manchester.
1919: The company begins exporting Vimto to Guyana.
1921: The company begins licensing bottling of Vimto to third-party bottlers.
1924: Vimto is registered as a trademark in India.
1927: The company moves to new production facilities in Old Trafford.
1939: Branded production suspended during the World War II.
1947: The company reintroduces Vimto brand; sugar rationing limits production.
1948: Creation of National Health Service forces Vimto to be marketed only as a soft drink.
1953: Full production of Vimto is once again launched.
1961: JN Nichols (Vimto) plc goes public.
1964: Launch of Vimto in cans.
1969: Nichols begins own Vimto canning operations.
1975: Grants canning and distribution license to Solent Canners
1980: The company acquires Solent Canners.
1986: Independent Vending Supplies is acquired to enter vending machines and supplies market, and Cabana Limited, entering draught beverage dispensing market.
1995: Stockpack is acquired to offer co-production and co-packing facilities for third-party food and candy products.
1999: The company acquires Balmoral Limited to begin offering coffee and hot beverage dispensing systems and products.
2000: The company changes its name to Nichols plc.

Nichols, who was named as the company's financial director. The company sought a twofold expansion. Its first move was began seeking ways to break Vimto out of its northern England niche to appeal to the tastes of the country's southern regions. In order to do this the company redesigned its advertising, incorporating a bulldog, named Max, and the tagline ''The Grrreat British Drink.'' The new campaign helped boost sales, but only briefly. As a follow-up to the advertising campaign, the company next hired outside consultants, which led the company to redesign its cans to appear more like beer cans. This too proved a short-lived campaign. By the end of the 1980s, Vimto adopted new labeling that emphasized the relatively high fruit content of its carbonated beverage. During the 1980s, also, Nichols added a new Vimto variant, a sugar-free diet version. These moves did indeed help boost the company's sales in the south of England, while Vimto remained a northern favorite.

Yet Nichols had already been branching out beyond its core soft drink brand and working toward diversifying itself to become a general food and drink distributor. In 1986, the company took a first step with the acquisition of Independent Vending Supplies (IVS). This company had been founded in 1981 and by 1983 had already become a leading manufacturer supplying the vending machine market in the United Kingdom. The IVS acquisition placed Nichols in position to enter the vending machine market; in 1989 the company changed its subsidiary's name to Nichols Foods. Throughout the 1990s, Nichols Foods positioned itself as one of the United Kingdom's leading independent supplier of not only vending machines and systems, but also a wide range of products for its machines, including Vimto, but also third-party products such as Nescafe, PG Tea, and fellow Northern soft drink brand Irn Bru.

Nichols had also ventured into another new, yet related direction in the with the acquisition of Cabana Soft Drinks in 1986. This acquisition positioned Nichols as a major supplier of draught-style soft drink dispensing systems. That operations built up more than 6,000 outlets through the 1990s. In 1995, Nichols made a new acquisition, Stockpack, adding co-manufacturing and co-packing operations, offering the use of its facilities for the production and packaging of third-party food and confectionery products.

Meanwhile, Nichols continued to explore new markets for its core Vimto brand, such as the post-Soviet Union markets, which quickly embraced Vimto as a favorite mixer for alcoholic beverages. Vimto continued to play a driving force in the company's sales; yet Nichols worked steadily on reducing its reliance on this core brand by boosting its operations elsewhere. Nichols' beverage production and distribution operations were reorganized under a new subsidiary, Vimto Soft Drinks, which launched a new drink, Indigo, marketed as a natural energy drink at the end of the 1990s.

In 1999, Nichols expanded its operations again, with the purchase of Balmoral Trading Limited. Founded in 1969, Balmoral had developed into a coffee supply company, offering dispensing equipment and products, throughout the United Kingdom. Balmoral had also correctly guessed the potential for offering more exotic coffee products, such as cappuccino, introduced in the late 1990s.

In 1999, John Nichols stepped up to the position of chairman, turning over the managing director position to Gary N. Unsworth, marking the first time the company's day-to-day operations had been guided by a non-Nichols family member. In 2000, the company, with its acquisition of Balmoral, had sufficiently expanded beyond its former core Vimto beverage product, convincing Nichols to change its name. The company now became known simply as Nichols plc in that year.

Vimto remained a key company product however. At the turn of the century, the company continued to seek new markets for its nearly famous brand name, entering Africa with distribution and bottling contracts in Angola and South Africa. In the Middle Eastern markets, which accounted for about half of Vimto sales, the company launched two new Vimto-branded products, Vimto powder, and Vimto lollipops.

In 2000 and 2001, Nichols was able to boost its Cabana and Nichols Foods operations as well. Both had long been hampered by a lack of major brand names, particularly in the cola segment, making it difficult to compete against the marketing clout of Coke and Pepsi. The addition of two new brands, Sunkist orange drink and especially of Virgin Cola, placed Nichols

Foods in a stronger competitive position. The company also boosted its production and warehousing facilities, notably with the opening of a new purpose-built facility in 1999 and a 25,000-square-foot warehouse extension completed in August 2001. Nichols seemed likely to remain a key player in its U.K. vending and beverage dispensing markets, while the Vimto brand continued to sweeten taste buds around the world.

Principal Subsidiaries

Balmoral Trading Ltd.; Cabana (Holdings) Ltd.; Cabana Soft Drinks Ltd.; Cabana SJ Ltd.; Nichols Foods Ltd.; Stockpack Ltd.

Principal Competitors

Coca-Cola Bottling Co. Consolidated; The Pepsi Bottling Group, Inc.; Cadbury Schweppes plc; Topa Equities, Ltd.; Direct Wines Limited; AG Barr Ltd.

Further Reading

Barrow, Rebecca, "Nichols Diluted by Wet June," *The Daily Telegraph*, August 21, 1997.

Brice, Martin, "Vimto Beats the Bad Weather," *Financial Times*, August 17, 2000.

Cope, Nigel, "Nichols Sales Boosted by August Heatwave," *Independent*, August 21, 1997, p. 18.

Dolan, Siobhan, "Exhibitions: Vim and Vigour," *Independent*, April 1, 1994, p. 24.

Farrelly, Paul, "Vimto's New Fizz," *Observer,* September 24, 2000.

Lee, John, "New Fizz from the Kings of Vimto," *Financial Times*, April 22, 2000.

"Vimto Voices Optimism," *Financial Times*, August 19, 1999.

Windsor, John, "Hard Sell for a Soft, Old Drink," *Independent*, August 13, 1994, p. 32.

—M.L. Cohen

RODENSTOCK

Optische Werke G. Rodenstock

Isartalstrasse 43
D-80469 Munich
Germany
Telephone: (49) (89) 7202-0
Fax: (49) (89) 7202-629
Web site: http://www.rodenstock.de

Private Company
Incorporated: 1877 as Einzelhandelsfirma Optisches
    Institut G. Rodenstock
Employees: 6,712
Sales: DM 979 million ($500 million) (1999)
NAIC: 333314 Optical Instrument and Lens Manufactur-
    ing; 339115 Ophthalmic Goods Manufacturing;
    333315 Photographic and Photocopying Equipment
    Manufacturing

Optische Werke G. Rodenstock is Germany's leading manufacturer of eyeglass lenses. The company also produces and markets eyeglass frames under the NiGuRa, Cerruti 1881, and ENJOY brands. While the eyeglass business accounts for three-quarters of Rodenstock's sales, the company is also involved in the development and manufacturing of ophthalmic equipment, X-ray equipment, and instruments for clinical examination and screening through its subsidiary Rodenstock Präzisionsoptik. The company's subsidiary Docter Optics develops and manufactures optical components for audiovisual slide projectors, overhead projectors, and TV and video projection. Rodenstock's activities in the fields of ophthalmic and precision optics are organized under the umbrella of Rodenstock Technologie Holding, which also includes subsidiaries RODIS and ifa that offer IT services. The company operates production facilities in Germany, the Czech Republic, Thailand and Chile and maintains a growing network of subsidiaries and sales offices on all continents.

Josef Rodenstock Founds Company in 1877

The global optical firm Rodenstock started out as a small workshop in the last quarter of the 19th century. In 1860, at age fourteen, company founder Josef Rodenstock left his parents'

home in the small town Ershausen in Thuringia, Germany. His father, Georg, a former director of a later bankrupt textile factory who—after several failed attempts to get a business off the ground—was struggling to make ends meet for his big family, had given him some loose change and an old travel bag and recommended that he try the life of a traveling salesman. Josef Rodenstock started out selling needles and porcelain buttons, and after a while extended his sales inventory with small technical instruments such as barometers, which he soon started building himself. Always curious about how things worked, Rodenstock began specializing in selling his self-made instruments, including tachometers, scales, measuring instruments, and magnifying glasses. When the young man began making eyeglass frames he had his first encounters with opticians. Rodenstock found optical equipment very fascinating and began teaching himself the underlying principles. His growing business success enabled Josef Rodenstock to financially support his parents and younger siblings. Moreover, he lived a very modest life and was thereby able to put aside a considerable sum which he used as seed capital for his own company.

In late fall of 1877, Josef Rodenstock decided to leave his hometown and moved to Wurzburg, the splendid baroque residence of a prince and a bishop on the river Main. He called himself a physicist and set up a small shop and workshop not far away from the medical department of Wurzburg University. The company which Rodenstock founded the same year was called Einzelhandelsfirma Optisches Institut G. Rodenstock with the "G" referring to his father Georg as a token of the son's appreciation and respect. The new company started out with two employees: Josef Rodenstock's younger brother Michael, whom he took with him to Wurzburg, and another assistant. The small firm manufactured and sold eyeglass lenses, physics instruments, and small chemical equipment, home telegraphs, and even home phone systems. Soon the workshop was extended to house a glass manufacturing and grinding facility to be able to make "diaphragm-glasses." The company's literally "spectacular" new product, spectacle lenses with a black rim that prevented unwanted reflexes at the edges, was invented and patented by Josef Rodenstock. Only two years after the company's founding, the number of employees had jumped to 30. The company's success was supported by an unprecedented economic upswing that Germany witnessed in the late 19th century when groundbreaking technical inventions were made that would fuel the following industrial revolution. Rodenstock's new lenses became a huge commercial success. His company also developed a reputation for high precision craftsmanship and professors from Wurzburg University started asking Rodenstock to make and repair their equipment for mathematical, physical, and chemical experiments. Finally, Rodenstock was awarded the position of university mechanic.

The company founder, however, was obsessed by the idea of somehow figuring out exactly the degree of vision impairedness in different customers. Since he believed that poor vision was not an illness but a minor flaw that could be corrected by custom-shaped lenses, Rodenstock's idea was to deliver customized spectacles to every customer—a revolutionary idea for his time. He developed a ''spectacle-measuring-apparatus'' that opticians could use to determine which lenses would be best for a certain customer—a sensational invention for the trade. Five years after setting up shop, Rodenstock decided to move his business from Wurzburg to Munich, which was emerging as a center for science and technology. In the center of the city, Rodenstock established his Optical-Oculist Institute G. Rodenstock, a shop that offered a novelty to Munich residents: an extra room where eye refraction was determined for each customer. Within only a few years Rodenstock had started what he had once envisioned: he manufactured and sold customized ophthalmic lenses to his clientele.

Soon Rodenstock's production facilities, which at first remained in Wurzburg and the new location in Munich's Colosseumstrasse set up in May 1884, were not able the meet the high demand. In 1886, Rodenstock acquired real estate on the edge of the city. The property on Isartalstrasse, an old gypsum mill close to the river Isar, included several buildings that allowed the industrial production of optical goods, and the nearby water was used to generate electricity. Josef Rodenstock's brother Michael moved the production from Wurzburg to Munich's Isartalstrasse while the company founder marketed his products—including optometers, model eyeglasses, refraction measuring apparatus, barometer scales, and optical lenses for photo cameras—by means of promotional essays and by traveling Europe to establish relationships with potential distributors. Rodenstock's ''Bistigmat'' photo objectives became another huge success. They were not only more powerful than the competition's but also much cheaper, and Rodenstock sold 25,000 of them in only three years. Soon photo optics became a second foothold for Rodenstock and the company started making different kinds of binoculars, telescopes, and theater glasses.

Alexander Rodenstock Joins the Company in 1905

The demand for Rodenstock products was climbing to new heights at the end of the 19th century, stretching the company's production capacity to its limits. However, industrial property in Munich was impossible to find or impossibly expensive. The company founder decided to set up a brand-new factory in Regen, a small town in the Bavarian forest, a traditional center of the glass making industry. Regen was located on the railroad from Munich to Prague—a major transit line at the time. The factory started operations in 1899. However, Rodenstock was waiting in vain for the highly qualified glassmakers to show up at the factory, which consequently started out with 90 farm and forestry workers who had no idea about glass or eyeglass making. In addition, the manager of the new site failed to get the business off the ground. The new factory, which was already a huge financial investment, could only be kept operating with ongoing financial support which soon would have reached the limits of Rodenstock's reserves. Only when Michael Rodenstock—who had been against this venture altogether—took over the management did the business catch on. Five years later the new factory reached its capacity again and another one was set up in the same town. By 1905, Rodenstock employed about 250 employees in Regen. A number of smaller production sites was set up in the following nine years to keep up with demand which was pushed up by a number of Rodenstock innovations, mainly new kinds of ophthalmic lenses with better qualities and functions.

The stressful start-up time had left its mark on Josef Rodenstock's brother Michael. Struggling with health problems, the founder's loyal companion signaled his intention to retire. The founder's oldest son Alexander, who studied physics and economics at Munich's Technical College, was called in to help in the family business. The 22-year-old, who would have preferred to graduate first, followed his father's wish and entered the business in 1905. New ideas and energy were needed in the company since the 59-year-old founder was showing signs of becoming more conservative. After he had gotten an overview of the family operations, Alexander's first endeavor was to strengthen the company's scientific research capabilities—the basis for the constant stream of innovations needed to stay competitive. Since its beginnings, the business had grown from a craftsman's workshop to an industrial enterprise; new organizational structures in production and distribution were needed, as well as new investments in industrial production technology. However, up until 1912 the company founder, with his authoritative, patriarchal style, dominated the operation and made the most crucial decisions. In 1912 the company shares were redistributed and Alexander Rodenstock—as well as his two brothers-in-law—became official shareholders. Seven years later the company founder finally retired and Alexander got to have the final say.

Key Dates:

1877: Josef Rodenstock sets up his Optical Institute in Wurzburg.
1884: The company is moved to Munich.
1898: A new production facility is set up in Regen.
1919: Josef Rodenstock's son Alexander takes over the business.
1953: The founder's grandson Rolf Rodenstock becomes CEO.
1960: A new frame production facility is set up near Munich.
1975: Rodenstock sets up its first subsidiary in the United States.
1978: The company acquires Dusseldorf-based Wernicke & Co. GmbH.
1981: Rodenstock takes over German frame manufacturer NiGuRa.
1989: A lens factory is set up in Thailand.
1990: The founder's great-grandson Randolf Rodenstock becomes CEO.

However, the founder's son took over at a politically and economically turbulent time. When World War I started in 1914, the company's export business broke down completely. The German government administered the country's war economy and boosted Rodenstock's production of different kinds of binoculars with precision optics, which were in high demand in the German army. The economic depression after the war was followed by a temporary upswing which was interrupted by the worldwide economic crisis, a consequence of the Great Depression caused by New York's stock market crash in 1929. High unemployment and the devastating effects of hyperinflation pushed a big part of the German population into poverty—the breeding ground for a radical political turn to the far right. On top of the sluggish domestic market, which shifted to cheaper quality and growing export losses, Rodenstock was threatened by French ophthalmic products, which were less expensive because of lower pay levels in France. Alexander Rodenstock successfully steered the family business through financial hardship caused by the chaotic market and prevented the company from being taken over by German optics giant Carl Zeiss. When the company seemed to run out of financial breath in 1932, Alexander Rodenstock rescued the enterprise once more by securing a big order from the *Reichswehr*, the German army, financed by the Economics Ministry. In the following years the Nazi government started administering the domestic economy again, preparing it for a war. Binoculars and eyeglasses became nationally important products and Rodenstock, under government administration, was pushed to introduce mass production, especially after the company was turned into a vendor of precision optical lenses to be used in the products of other companies. In 1944, the company's factory in Munich was partly destroyed in bombings. However, due to the CEO's intensive efforts, Rodenstock was granted permission to start operations again by the U.S. authorities only three weeks after Germany's capitulation. After another three weeks had passed, Rodenstock's Regen factory, untouched by the war, started production again and supplied objectives for photo cameras and binoculars as well as eyeglass lenses to the Allied forces in occupied Germany.

While leading the company through these turbulent times, Alexander Rodenstock also suffered personally several times due to his continued interest and active participation in politics. As a co-founder of the conservative party Bavarian Volkspartei, he was arrested, taken as a hostage, and condemned to death by political left wing forces who seized power in Munich for a short time during the 1918 German November Revolution. He also had the good fortune to escape a planned assassination attempt. From 1919 on he was active in Munich community politics where he promoted a democratic city charter. During the Nazi years his marriage to a Jewish woman brought him under rising political pressure. However, in the last war years he was awarded the common title "Wehrwirtschaftsführer," ("leader of the defense economy"), as the result of which he temporarily lost his post as Rodenstock CEO during postwar de-nazification. Until he was found innocent in 1947 in a special hearing, the company was led by a trustee.

The Rolf Rodenstock Era Begins After 1945

After the postwar reconstruction years, Germany entered two decades of dynamic economic growth in which Rodenstock successfully participated. This was partly due to the company's continuing efforts to be at the cutting edge of research for new kinds of eyeglass lenses with better capabilities. In the 1950s the company pushed the development of so-called bifocal lenses that unified in one lens sections for long and short distance viewing. They enjoyed growing popularity in the late 1950s and became a huge commercial success in the 1970s. In 1968 Rodenstock started mass-manufacturing lenses for eyeglasses that automatically adopted their color according to changing light conditions. The success of the bifocal lenses led to the development of trifocal lenses, followed by a new generation of progressive lenses that allowed uninterrupted changes of vision from short to far distances. These so-called *Gleitsichtgläser* were introduced to the market in 1980 under the brand name Progressiv. Following the industry trend of plastic lenses replacing the ones made from glass, Rodenstock started making plastic bifocal lenses in 1989. Besides lenses, the company started making frames for eyeglasses in 1960 and ventured further into precision optics which took an upswing with technological progress in laser and satellite technology and space observation programs.

The 1970s saw intensified efforts to expand Rodenstock's global reach. When company founder Josef Rodenstock retired in 1919, he had already built a company with worldwide connections and a strong international reputation, including sales offices in Milan, Brussels, Vienna, London, New York, Chicago, and Moscow. However, the two world wars isolated Germany in the international arena, cutting Rodenstock off from the markets abroad. The first foreign sales offices after World War II were set up in Vienna and Paris in 1965. In 1972, Rodenstock set up a subsidiary in Italy, followed by one in the United States three years later. In 1951, the company started setting up production facilities in other countries with the establishment of Santiago die Industria Optica in Chile. Another factory in Argentina, established in 1958, was closed down when the country got caught up in political and economic turmoil. A frame factory for the United States market was built in Puerto Rico in 1973. In 1989, a Rodenstock lens factory was set up in Thailand. In 1978, the company took over Dusseldorf-based optical manufacturer Wernicke & Co., followed by the acquisition of NiGuRa, a frame maker also located in Dusseldorf, including their production sites on Malta.

The rise of Rodenstock to a globally acting major player in the optical market was mainly driven by Alexander Rodenstock's son Rolf. Rolf Rodenstock entered the family business in 1944. The war had interrupted his studies at Munich University. However, in 1942, after being seriously wounded, Rolf Rodenstock was released from war duties and got his Ph.D. in business administration in 1944. While helping his father rebuild and modernize the company, he felt drawn to the academic life, started teaching, and became a professor at Munich University in 1956. However, after his father passed away in 1953, Rolf Rodenstock decided to turn back to ''real life'' and took over leadership of the family business. Besides his duties as company CEO, he helped set up and chair several industrial trade organizations over the years and impressed the public with his relaxed appearance despite his enormous workload. By the end of the 1980s, Rodenstock had made the transition from a mid-sized business to a global optical firm with 7,000 employees worldwide, generating DM 700 million in sales.

Randolf Rodenstock Takes Over in 1990

The fourth Rodenstock leader took over the family empire in difficult times. Health care reform in Germany, increasing competitive pressures, and globalization were the hallmarks of the 1990s. The founder's great-grandson Randolf Rodenstock studied physics and business administration in Munich and Fontainebleau, France, and—like his father and grandfather—was drawn to academic life, especially in the spirit of the late 1960s when the ''Establishment'' was harshly criticized by the young generation and being an capitalist entrepreneur was greatly out of fashion. However, Randolf Rodenstock decided to put theory into practice and joined the family business in 1976 at age 28. He became a personally liable shareholder in 1983, and took over as CEO in 1990 when he was 42 years old.

In 1987, the German government abolished federal subsidies for prescription eyeglass frames, causing a serious downturn of the German optical industry. Eyeglass consumers put upgrading their lenses on the back burner while doctors became more frugal in prescribing eyeglasses. In the aftermath, sales of the German optical industry dropped by up to one-fifth and Rodenstock slipped into the red in 1989. Randolf Rodenstock took up the challenge of rescuing Rodenstock from a life-threatening downturn. He focused on a tight company restructuring program, product innovation, developing a contemporary design for spectacle frames, and improving the company's public image.

To significantly cut cost, Rodenstock began moving its lens and eyeglass production to Asia, a step that his father Rolf Rodenstock would not have approved. However, it might have been the move that kept the company from extinction. The factory in Bangkok, Thailand, where personnel cost were only 2.5 percent of the cost in Germany, took up the production of plastic lenses. Another production facility was set up in the

Czech Republic in 1994. The main factory in Regen was downsized and became the group's research and development and logistics center, which also developed and built the complex machines needed in lens and frame production. In the mid-1990s the company organized all its industrial business activities, which contributed about 30 percent of sales, under the umbrella of Rodenstock Technologie Holding to be able more easily to enter partnerships and obtain capital from outside the company. The holding included Rodenstock's instruments and precision optics divisions, Wernicke & Co., and the two new acquisitions: ifa Computer system, a software development and training institute for German opticians; and Docter Optics, a vendor of headlight lenses for the German auto industry.

During the same time period, a whole range of new products was introduced to the market, including new generations of progressive and photocromic lenses branded Rodenstock Multigressiv and Cosmolit Office, as well as better quality coatings for plastic lenses and professional photo objectives. The company also became a vendor of ''intelligent'' precision optical elements for manufacturers of systems used in medical, communications, satellite, and military equipment. Within ten years, the number of Rodenstock employees decreased by almost one-quarter. After five years of losses Rodenstock started making a small profit again in 1994.

In the late 1990s, after 15 years of little investment in advertising, the company launched a major image campaign designed to modernize the rather conservative image the public had of Rodenstock. Because of the company's exclusive distribution through opticians and selected retailers, the Rodenstock brand name was almost unknown by consumers. The campaign proved successful and Rodenstock was able to gain a bigger market share in a generally declining market, partly due to its focus on high-quality products with higher profit margins. By the end of the 1990s, Rodenstock focused on its core market—lenses and frames for eyeglasses—where the company saw itself as the German market leader, number two in Europe and number three worldwide. The company had become a truly global firm with half of its sales generated abroad and more than half of its workforce employed outside Germany. With the acquisition of a majority of the American 2C Optics Inc. Rodenstock got access to Individual-Lens-Technology, a patented technology for the production of prescription lenses in just one fabrication step which promised enormous productivity gains, and set up a new production facility in Frankfurt, Germany, for its proximity to a major international airport. However, more than 80 percent of Rodenstock lenses were made in Thailand by 2000, while all frames were manufactured on Malta. To further modernize the company's image, Rodenstock invited Italian fashion designer Cerruti to create a series of fashion frames, developed the ENJOY brand of fashion frames for younger consumers, and entered license production agreements with auto maker Porsche and sports shoes and apparel manufacturer Reebok. On the other hand, Rodenstock sold off the majority of its industrial optics subsidiaries to further consolidate the business and focus on its core market.

Randolf Rodenstock's declared goal at the beginning of the new millennium was to transform the classical industrial enterprise he inherited into an organization that oriented itself strictly to the demands of the market with a less hierarchical structure and more team-oriented work environments. He also emphasized the necessity to broaden the company's capital base, but didn't think his company would go public before 2002. Asked by Martin Schäfer if he saw his son taking over the company one day, Randolf Rodenstock answered: "What would you say if my daughter did that?"

Principal Subsidiaries

NiGuRa Optik GmbH; ERGO Optik GmbH; Rodenstock Beteiligungen GmbH (Germany); Docter Optics GmbH; Rodenstock Italia S.p.A. (Italy); Rodenstock Latina S.P.A. (Italy); Rodenstock France S.A.R.L. (France); London Optical Company Ltd. (United Kingdom); Rodenstock (UK) Ltd.; SUVI B.V. (Netherlands); Rodenstock Nederland B.V. (Netherlands); Rodenstock Instruments Corporation; Rodenstock USA Inc.; Rodenstock Precision Optics, Inc.; Rodenstock Canada Inc.; Rodenstock Norge A/S (Norway); Rodenstock Sverige AB (Sweden); Rodenstock (Schweiz) AG; Ocni optica Klatovy s.r.o. (Czech Republic); Optica Rodenstock Chile S.A.; Rodenstock (Thailand) Co. Ltd.; Rodenstock Australia Pty Ltd.; Optische Werke G. Rodenstock Produktion in Österreich, GesmbH (Austria); Rodenstock Technologie Holding GmbH; RODIS Informationssystems GmbH; ifa Computersysteme.

Principal Competitors

Essilor International S.A.; Hoya Corp.; Carl-Zeiss-Stiftung; Sola International Inc.

Further Reading

"Brillen erstmals vom Maßschneider," *Süddeutsche Zeitung,* June 2, 2000, p. 29.

"Brillenkonzern Rodenstock verkauft zwei Tochterunternehmen," *AFX–TD,* September 3, 1999.

Goslich, Lorenz, "Kein glatter Weg beim Übergang auf die vierte Generation," *Frankfurter Allgemeine Zeitung,* June 14, 1995, p. 25.

Jaitner, Peter, "Starke Brillen," *Werben und Verkaufen,* November 27, 1998, p. 98.

Oberhuber, Nadine, "Ergebniswachstum in 2000-Börsengang nicht vor 2002," *vwd,* May 30, 2000.

"Ohne das Werk Bangkok gäbe es Rodenstock nicht mehr," *Frankfurter Allgemeine Zeitung,* February 2, 2001, p. 27.

100 Jahre Werk Regen, Munich, Germany: Optische Werke G. Rodenstock, 1998, 15 p.

"Rodenstock erhöht Anteil auf dem schwachen deutschen Brillenmarkt," *Frankfurter Allgemeine Zeitung,* June 18, 1998, p. 29.

"Rodenstock fasst Industrieoptik zusammen," *Frankfurter Allgemeine Zeitung,* November 25, 1995, p. 18.

"Rodenstock muss weiter konsolidieren," *Frankfurter Allgemeine Zeitung,* May 31, 2001, p. 26.

"Rodenstock steigert Gewinn deutlich. Umstrukturierung greift," *Süddeutsche Zeitung,* June 18, 1996.

"Rodenstock übernimmt drei Doctor-Optik-Werke," *Süddeutsche Zeitung,* March 14, 1996.

"Rodenstock wettert gegen kurzsichtige Kundschaft," *Süddeutsche Zeitung,* July 29, 1993.

"Rolf Rodenstock 75," *Süddeutsche Zeitung,* June 30, 1992.

Schäfer, Martin, *Josef Rodenstock,* Berlin, Germany: Ullstein Buchverlage GmbH & Co. KG, 1999, 160 p.

"Vorbild in drei Berufen—Trauer um Professor Rolf Rodenstock," *Süddeutsche Zeitung,* February 8, 1997.

—Evelyn Hauser

ORIX Corporation

3-22-8, ShibaMinato-ku
Tokyo 105-8683
Japan
Telephone: (81)3 5419-5000
Fax: (81) 3 5419-5903
Web site: http://www.orix.co.jp

Public Company
Incorporated: 1964 as Orient Leasing Company, Ltd.
Employees: 9,529
Sales: ¥586,149 million ($47.3 billion) (2001)
Stock Exchanges: Tokyo Osaka Nagoya New York
Ticker Symbol: IX
NAIC: 532412 Construction, Mining, and Forestry
   Machinery and Equipment Rental and Leasing;
   532411 Commercial Air, Rail, and Water
   Transportation Equipment Rental and Leasing; 53242
   Office Machinery and Equipment Rental and Leasing;
   53249 Other Commercial and Industrial Machinery
   and Equipment Rental and Leasing; 52231 Mortgage
   and Nonmortgage Loan Brokers; 52421 Insurance
   Agencies and Brokerages

ORIX Corporation began as a Japanese-American joint venture in the mid-1960s, and helped introduce Japanese business to the idea of leasing its equipment instead of owning it. Now a multinational corporation and Japan's largest general leasing firm, ORIX operates as a diverse financial services group involved in leasing, lending, rentals, life insurance, real estate financing and development, venture capital, investment and retail banking, commodities funds, and securities brokerage. The company serves over 500,000 small and medium sized businesses as well as individuals in North America, Europe, Asia, Oceania, the Middle East, and Northern Africa. In 1964, Nichimen Company—later known as Nichimen Corporation—and the United States Leasing Corporation established the Orient Leasing Company (OLC) in Osaka. Backed by the Sanwa Bank, the company began with an initial capital of ¥100 million. At this time, leasing was very new in Japan.

Growth was slow throughout the 1960s as Japanese business adjusted to the idea.

Early Growth: 1970s

OLC spent much of the 1970s establishing itself throughout Asia, developing a pattern of growth either through ties with well-established local businesses or through heavy investment in local companies. In 1970, OLC was listed on the second section of the Osaka Stock Exchange; by 1973 it was on the first section in Tokyo, Osaka and Nagoya. The following year, the company established its first wholly owned subsidiary, Orient Leasing (Asia), in Hong Kong. The subsidiary handles mortgage loans, finances in multiple currencies, and leases major items like ships and planes. In 1972, OLC established its first major subsidiary in Japan, Orient Leasing Interior Company. That same year, Orient Leasing established the Korea Development Leasing Corporation and Orient Leasing Singapore, which leased vehicles, machinery, furniture, medical and dental equipment, and vessels. In 1973, OLC entered Malaysia; in 1975, Indonesia; in 1977, the Philippines; in 1978, Thailand. OLC also established subsidiaries in South America during the 1970s, entering Brazil in 1973 and Chile in 1977. Orient Leasing began to lease commercial aircraft in 1978, when the company purchased a DC-10 from McDonnell Douglas and two Boeing 747 passenger jets for lease to Korean Air Lines. The company purchased another aircraft in the same deal for lease to Thai Airways International. This deal, part of a joint venture with Nippon Shinpan Company, came at a time when American aircraft manufacturers were complaining that limited export funding was making it difficult for them to compete internationally. According to the *Wall Street Journal*, the purchases were arranged in an effort to show genuine Japanese concern for reducing its trade surplus. Later in 1978, OLC purchased two wide-bodied airbuses with C. Itoh & Company for lease to Greece's Olympic Airways.

International Expansion in the 1980s

While Orient Leasing spent the 1970s establishing itself in Asia, the 1980s were a time of expansion in the United States, Europe, and China, one still untapped Asian market. OLC brought leasing to a developing China in 1981. In partnership with two Chinese companies, China International Trust and Investment Corporation and Beijing Machinery and Equipment Corporation, OLC founded the China Orient Leasing Company. Leasing in China boomed in the following years, as state-owned enterprises demanded machinery for their outdated factories. In 1984, China Orient Leasing Company wrote $40 million in contracts, three times the amount it had written just two years earlier, for equipment as varied as plant machinery, film development equipment, and printing presses. In 1982, Orient Leasing opened a representative office in Greece, and in 1983, the company established Orient Leasing (UK) in London, its first step toward an independent presence in Europe. Growth continued in 1986 with the establishment of Lombard Orient Leasing Ltd., a partnership between OLC and Lombard North Central, the largest finance company in the United Kingdom. In 1988, OLC expanded further into Europe when it made an agreement to form a leasing company in Spain to lease Japanese computers and office equipment. In America, OLC set up Orient Leasing USA Corporation in 1981 and Orient-U.S. Leasing Corporation in 1982. In the late 1980s, OLC began to diversify, investing in the Hyatt Group, a hotel chain, and Rubloff Inc., a major Chicago real estate company. With the Hyatt Group, OLC arranged financing for hotels in Chicago, Illinois; Greenwich, Connecticut; and Scottsdale, Arizona. Most of the equity financing came directly from OLC and Hyatt; OLC assembled Japanese investors to cover the rest. In 1987, Orient Leasing entered the American real estate market when it bought a 23.3% interest in Rubloff. Willard Brown, Jr., the chairman of Rubloff, told the *Chicago Tribune*, "(Orient Leasing) has a substantial appetite, and (Rubloff's) job will be to create the right investments for them." OLC entered the housing loan and mortgage security loan markets in the early 1980s. OLC also diversified into securities in 1986, surprising the leasing community with the purchase of Akane Securities Company, Ltd., a small Japanese brokerage firm. Though lease-financing was its core business, through this purchase the company announced its intention to initiate "new operations in related, high-potential fields."

Orient Leasing Renames Itself ORIX Corporation: 1989

As part of its plan to diversify, Orient Leasing renamed itself ORIX in 1989, the company's 25th anniversary. According to company officials, the name ORIX was adopted as an abbreviation of "original," with the "X" added to symbolize a future of "flexibility and diversity." As part of a campaign to increase recognition of its new name, ORIX bought a Japanese baseball team, the Hankyu Braves, and renamed it the ORIX Braves. The leasing business soared in Japan in the late 1980s, fueled by heavy capital investments by Japanese industry. It became such an attractive business, in fact, that many new

companies entered the field, pushing profit margins below one percent even for industry-leader ORIX, according to *The Economist*. The firm's name change signaled the most visible part of the company's move to broaden the financial services it offered in order to decrease its reliance on the leasing business.

Continued Diversification throughout the 1990s

Despite a weakening Japanese economy and instability throughout the entire Asian region, ORIX remained intent on diversification throughout the 1990s. Aiding in its efforts was its status as a leasing company—a status that allowed it to report to Japan's Ministry of International Trade and Industry, while banks and securities brokers were forced to report to the strict Ministry of Finance. The trade ministry's liberal policy enabled ORIX to pursue diverse expansion options. Building upon its 1989 investment in U.S.-based Stockton Holdings Ltd., the company began selling commodities funds in Japan in 1990 and entered the investment management business by creating ORIX Commodities Corp. The firm also purchased outright—rather than financed—74 Airbus Industrie jets from Braniff Airlines Inc. ORIX then sold or leased the jets to different airlines.

In 1993, the company established Shanghai Yintong Trust Co. to operate as one of the first joint consumer credit companies in China. The following year, ORIX teamed up with the Bank for Investment and Development of Vietnam to create ORIX BIDV Leasing Co. Ltd., the first leasing company in Vietnam. The firm also focused on its real estate operations and in 1995, partnered with Daikyo, Inc., an apartment management service company, to expand and develop real estate and lending opportunities. In order to increase its presence in Taiwan, ORIX acquired two leasing credit firms, Sun Leasing Corp. and Sun Credit and Trading Corp., in 1995. Having entered the region in 1990 with the creation of subsidiary ORIX Taiwan Corp., the firm eyed Taiwan as a lucrative market due to the financial deregulation initiated by the Taiwan government that enabled leasing and credit sales firms to embark on lease financing ventures.

As the Asian economy fell under financial crisis in the mid-to-late 1990s, ORIX continued its global expansion efforts. The firm announced plans to enter the Egyptian market in 1997, and continued to take advantage of U.S.-based opportunities. That year, ORIX began a joint venture with Banc One Corp. and formed commercial mortgage firm Banc One Mortgage Capital Markets. In 1998, General Electric Capital Services Inc. entered Japan's leasing market, dramatically increasing competition due to its financial size and expertise in leases related to industrial machinery. While ORIX held an eight percent share of that market and stood as the leader, the firm faced fierce competition and continued to look for ways to bolster profits outside of the leasing arena. ORIX acquired Yamaichi Trust & Bank Ltd. that year, broadening its line of financial services that by now included insurance and brokerage, along with leasing operations.

ORIX also listed on the New York Stock Exchange in September 1998, the first Japanese company to list on the NYSE since 1994. In 1999, ORIX began take advantage of the burgeoning e-commerce world. The firm teamed up with Softbank Corp. and Fuji Bank to create a joint Internet-based leasing venture that offered financial services to small-to-mid-

Key Dates:

1964: Nichimen Co. and the United States Leasing Corp. establish the Orient Leasing Company (OLC).
1970: OLC lists on the second section of the Osaka Stock Exchange.
1972: Subsidiaries Orient Leasing Interior Co., Korea Development Leasing Corp., and Orient Leasing Singapore are formed.
1978: OLC begins leasing commercial aircraft.
1981: The firm enters the Chinese market and forms Orient Leasing USA Corp.
1983: Orient Leasing UK is established.
1986: The company acquires Akane Securities Company Ltd.
1987: OLC enters the U.S. real estate market through a 23.3 percent purchase of Rubloff Inc.
1989: The firm officially adopts the name ORIX Corporation.
1990: ORIX begins selling commodities funds in Japan.
1993: Shanghai Yintong Trust Co. is established as China's first joint consumer credit company.
1994: Company announces plans to set up a joint leasing venture in Vietnam.
1997: ORIX enters the Egyptian market.
1998: ORIX lists on the New York Stock Exchange; it also acquires Yamaichi Trust & Bank Ltd.
2000: The company's management restructures; Yasuhiko Fujiki is named company president and Chief Operating Officer.
2001: The real estate firm Nihon Jisho Corp. is acquired.

sized companies in technology industries. The Japanese government deregulated fixed commissions on stock transactions in October 1999, allowing ORIX to begin online trading. Through its ORIX Securities subsidiary, the firm secured 12,600 online accounts by November of that year.

Focus on Diversified Financial Services in the New Millennium

ORIX entered the new millennium on strong ground. Company management was restructured, leaving Yasuhiko Fujiki as president and Chief Operating Officer, while Yoshihiko Miyauchi remained chairman and CEO. In January 2000, the firm formed an alliance with U.S.-based Enron Corp., allowing it to enter the Japanese retail power market with plans to form new power generation facilities.

In 2001, ORIX continued to develop and diversify its product and service offerings. Real estate firm Nihon Jisho Corp. was acquired, broadening ORIX's reach in the real estate and management industry. The firm also continued to increase its Internet-based offerings with the launch of e-Direct Deposit, allowing its customers to conduct business transactions via the Web. Its auto leasing business also began a program entitled

e-ERG, which allowed leasing customers to manage their accounts online. With a continued emphasis of expanding its financial services product line, ORIX appeared well positioned for future growth.

Principal Subsidiaries

ORIX Alpha Corp.; ORIX Auto Leasing Corp.; ORIX Aircraft Corp.; Sun Leasing Co. Ltd.; ORIX Real Estate Corp.; ORIX Asset Management and Loan Services Corp.; ORIX Estate Corp.; ORIX Rental Corp.; ORIX Rent-a-Car Corp.; X-Rent-A-Car Corp.; BlueWave Corp.; ORIX Credit Corp.; ORIX Club Corp.; ORIX Computer Systems Corp.; ORIX Securities Corp.; ORIX Capital Corp.; ORIX Life Insurance Corp.; ORIX Insurance Services Corp.; ORIX Insurance Planning Corp.; ORIX Interior Corp.; ORIX Investment Corp.; ORIX Commodities Corp.; ORIX Trust and Banking Corp.; ORIX Create Corp.; ORIX Management Information Center Corp.; ORIX Call Center Corp.; ORIX Baseball Club Co. Ltd.; ORIX Investment and Management Private Limited (Singapore); ORIX Leasing Singapore Ltd. (50%); ORIX Car Rentals PTE LTD (Singapore; 45%); ORIX Commodities Singapore PTE Limited; ORIX Asia Ltd. (China); Global Rental Co. Ltd. (South Korea; 26%); ORIX Car Rentals SDN. BHD. (Malaysia; 28%); Infrastructure Leasing & Financial Services Ltd. (India) (20%); Austral Mercantile Collections Pty. Ltd. (Australia) (50%); ORIX Leasing Pakistan Ltd. (57%); ORIX USA Corp.; ORIX Europe Ltd. (U.K.); ORIX Polska S.A. (Poland; 89%).

Principal Competitors

GE Capital Corporation; Mitsubishi Tokyo Financial Group Inc.; Sumitomo Corporation.

Further Reading

''GE Capital Strategy Keys On Acquisition,'' *Nikkei Weekly,* August 3, 1998.

Jarman, Max, ''Banc One, ORIX Form Commercial Mortgage Firm,'' *Arizona Business Gazette,* April 3, 1997, p. 3.

Lau, Shirley, ''ORIX Launch Aimed at Doubling Customer Base,'' *South China Morning Post,* March 14, 2000, p. 2.

''Leasing Company Begins Negotiating to Acquire Yamaichi Trust Bank,'' *Nikkei Weekly,* December 29, 1997, p. 13.

''ORIX Acquires Two Taiwan Leasing, Credit Firms,'' *Japan Economic Newswire,* August 16, 1995.

''ORIX Launches China's First Consumer Credit Business,'' *Japan Economic Newswire,* October 7, 1993.

''ORIX to Enter Investment Management Business,'' *Japan Economic Newswire,* January 31, 1990.

''ORIX to Enter Retail Power Market,'' *Nikkei Weekly,* January 10, 2000, p. 19.

''ORIX to Set Up Vietnam Lease Joint Venture,'' *AFX News,* December 16, 1994.

Plender, John, and Gillian Tett, ''Inside Track: the Shareholder Fundamentalist: Interview Yoshihiko Miyauchi,'' *Financial Times* (London), March 30, 2000, p. 14.

Sterngold, James, ''Japanese Lessor Thrives Under Loose Regulation,'' *New York Times,* July 27, 1990, D1.

—update: Christina M. Stansell

Panera Bread Company

6710 Clayton Road
Richmond Heights, Missouri 63117
U.S.A.
Telephone: (314) 633-7100
Fax: (314) 633-7200
Web site: http://www.panerabread.com

Public Company
Incorporated: 1981
Employees: 2,202
Sales: $151.4 million (2000)
Stock Exchanges: NASDAQ
Ticker Symbol: PNRA
NAIC: 722211 Limited_Service Restaurants; 311812
    Commercial Bakeries

Missouri-based Panera Bread Company operates over 309 bakery-cafés in 29 states, with a principal focus on specialty breads, especially its artisan and sourdough breads. About 68 percent of its bakery-cafés are franchise units, and the remainder are owned by the company. However, Panera Bread does not franchise individual bakery-cafés; rather, it sells multi-store area development agreements. The company maintains 39 of these, with commitments to grow its chain to 733 bakery-cafés through agreements already made. To support its bakery-café network, Panera also operates 11 fresh dough facilities. Although most of the chain's units operate under the Panera name, in the St. Louis area they do business as St. Louis Bread Co. Most of the bakery-cafés, which offer in-house eating as well as take-out service, are in suburban locations, giving the company a strong growth potential and less competition in its specialty market niche. Until 1999, the company was named Au Bon Pain, but in that year it sold off its Au Bon Pain division and adopted its current name from its other principal division. Ronald Shaich, Panera's CEO and chairman, owns approximately 26 percent of the public company.

1976–92: Au Bon Pain and St. Louis Bread Are Founded

Au Bon Pain, which figures importantly in the lineage of Panera Bread Co., started out as a showcase operation for Pavallier BVP SA, a French manufacturer of commercial ovens. In 1976, Pavallier opened the first Au Bon Pain in Boston's celebrated and historic Faneuil Hall Marketplace, the same year in which, after extensive renovations, that facility opened for business. Two years later, Louis I. Kane bought the business and began expanding in the Boston area. In 1981, he was joined by Ronald M. Shaich, and the pair formed Au Bon Pain Co. as a partnership.

Both Kane and Shaich brought diverse experience to the enterprise. Prior to undertaking their joint venture, Shaich was president of Targeting Systems Inc., a political consulting firm. He had also been a regional manager for the Original Cookie Co. Kane had behind him 14 years as an executive officer of Kane Financial Corp., a family-owned finance and investment firm. Following Kane's merger with CNA Financial Corp. in 1969, Kane became chairman and CEO of Healthco Inc., CNA's health-care subsidiary. Kane had also served as a director and executive committee member for Colombo Inc., a yogurt manufacturer and distributor.

In many ways, the new chain was a pioneering undertaking, one of the first to develop a concept that became popular in the next decade: the bakery-café, offering on-site service for sit down customers. Initially, the chain started out as three Boston-area bakeries and a single cookie store that served both cookies and breads and croissants to its customers. It grew very quickly, however, moving into large urban markets in New England and other Eastern states.

During the early expansion of Au Bon Pain, another bakery-café, St. Louis Bread, started up in Kirkwood, Missouri, in 1987. Its founder, Ken Rosenthal, and his wife, ventured into the restaurant business at the insistence of his brother. Rosenthal based his business on that of the sourdough bakeries then popular in San Francisco, where he went to learn the sour dough baking method. The Rosenthals, concerned about quality, ex-

Company Perspectives:

The enjoyment of fresh bread is at the heart of our success. Our talent, expertise, and efforts are directed toward providing our customers a friendly gathering place in which to relax and share the tradition of fresh-baked bread every day, as well as offering ways to extend the tradition to their family table with our take-home bread. In every community, our customers have responded with enthusiastic support and shown us that indeed 'Fresh bread makes friends.'

panded the business fairly cautiously. By 1990, they had grown the company to just five stores, but by 1993, when they first started franchising units, the chain had grown to 20 bakery-cafés. In that year, the company appeared on *Inc.* magazine's list of the 500 fastest-growing companies in the U.S.

Meanwhile, in 1991, Au Bon Pain went public, made its initial public offering (IPO), and continued its growth through expansion of its operations and acquisitions. In 1992, after working out a franchise development agreement in Chile, the company also began branching into foreign markets. It had already tapped deeply into the high-traffic, eastern city markets, and it needed to branch into some fresh markets.

1993–97: Company Acquires the St. Louis Bread Company before Sales Turn Sluggish

A major opportunity came in 1993, when Au Bon Pain acquired the St. Louis Bread Company. At the time the deal was struck, St. Louis Bread had 19 company owned and operated bakery-cafés and one franchised outlet. Thereafter, Au Bon Pain continued to expand the purchased company, introducing the bakery-café concept into new markets. In its home area in Missouri, the new franchised units were opened as St. Louis Bread bakery-cafés, but elsewhere they opened under a different name—Panera Bread. Over the course of its ownership by Au Bon Pain Co., Inc., the Panera/St. Louis Bread division would enter new markets and continue to grow at a solid clip.

By the end of 1996, Au Bon Pain had grown to 231 company-run and 58 franchised bakery-cafés. Of the 231 company-operated units, 177 were Au Bon Pain owned and operated outlets and 54 were Au Bon Pain franchise-operated bakery-cafés. The remaining 54 company-owned bakery-cafés and 10 franchise units were St. Louis Bakery Company units. As concepts, the Au Bon Pain and St. Louis Bakery Company stores were very similar. Both specialized in high quality foods, served for breakfast and lunch. Their menus included fresh baked goods, made-to-order sandwiches, soups, salads, and custom-roasted coffees as well as other beverages. The company's targeted customers were principally urban white-collar workers, suburban residents, and shoppers, students, and travelers with busy schedules to keep. The company's chief strategy was to provide high quality, fresh foods at reasonable prices and with greater variety than its chief market competitors. Most of the bakery-cafés were located in and around major urban centers, including Boston, other New England cities, New York,

Philadelphia, Pittsburgh, Washington, D.C., Columbus, Cleveland, Cincinnati, Chicago, St. Louis, Minneapolis, Los Angeles, Atlanta, and, outside the U.S., Santiago, Chile. For the 1996 fiscal year, total sales generated by the company-owned stores and its franchised units reached approximately $259 million. On the average, company-owned Au Bon Pain bakery-cafés generated about $940,000 each, while the Panera/St. Louis Bakery units generated about $1.1 million per outlet.

It was in 1996, in an effort to enter new markets, that Au Bon Pain began a broad-based franchising program for the Panera/St. Louis Bakery concept and scheduled the first new franchise operated café for a 1997 opening. The company also completed a new $9 million production facility in Mexico, Missouri. The 80,000 square-foot plant tripled the capacity of its older production facility in South Boston. Through the year, the company also continued to test new products and undertook the renovation of some of its stores.

Despite its growth and new strategies, Au Bon Pain faced problems in the mid 1990s, including disappointing, sluggish sales. The rapid expansion of its urban units created operational problems and involved the company in some sour-turning real estate deals. Moreover, the company's competition was rapidly stiffening, thanks to the fact that the bagel and coffee café concept hit its faddish stride at about the same time. By 1995, the company had logged its first net loss, and in 1996 was still struggling to regain profitability. Hoping to turn things around, late in 1996 the company named Robert C. Taft to the newly created position of president. Taft's mission was to direct efforts to improve the operational level of each of the company's 224 units in the company's Au Bon Pain Division.

1998–99: Company Divests Its Au Bon Pain Division

In August 1998, Au Bon Pain entered an agreement to sell to Bruckmann, Rosser, Sherrill & Co. LP., a New York investment firm, its Au Bon Pain Division. The $72 million deal was consummated on May 16, 1999, when Bruckmann, Rosser, Sherrill & Co. took that division its separate way as ABP, Inc., a private company. The sale left the Panera Bread/St. Louis Bakery Company with its group of company-owned bakery-cafés and its related franchise operations. Over the course of its ownership by Au Bon Pain Co., Inc., the Panera/St. Louis Bread Company had entered new markets and continued to grow, opening 51 company owned bakery-cafés and 44 franchise-operated units.

By the end of 1999, a year in which it opened units in 7 new states, the Panera Bread Company, as it was newly named, was operating in 25 states spread from Massachusetts to Florida and Michigan to Texas. For the first time, too, the majority of the 166 units (86) were owned by franchisees; the remaining 80 were company owned. As Panera proudly noted, many of the franchisees were either former owners or owners of major fast foot franchises, including McDonald's, Wendy's, Pizza Hut, and Taco Bell. According to Panera's president, Rick Postle, as reported in a *Knight Ridder/Tribune Business News* release, one of the franchise owners had sold off 45 McDonald's units to

Key Dates:

1976: Pavallier opens first Au Bon Pain in Boston's Faneuil Hall Marketplace.
1978: Louis I. Kane purchases Au Bon Pain bakery-café.
1981: Ronald M. Shaich joins Kane as partner, forming Au Bon Pain Co.
1991: The company goes public.
1993: Au Bon Pain purchases St. Louis Bread Co.
1994: Co-CEOs Kane and Shaich win *Nation's Restaurant News'* Golden Chain Award.
1999: Company sells Au Bon Pain division but retains Panera Bread/St. Louis Bread Co.

invest in Panera. Significantly, Panera no longer had to deal with investors who wanted to open only one or two units. Almost all franchisees agreed to open a minimum of two dozen or so stores, all within a single, entire market area. By November 1999, contractual commitments for opening new stores had reached 600 and were being negotiated.

2000–01: Accelerated Growth Promises a Solid Future for Panera

During 2000, Panera grew at what the *St. Louis Business Journal* termed "a blistering rate." It opened more than 50 new bakery-cafés by the end of the third quarter, and in December announced plans to enter Rhode Island, its 28th state. It was also picking up important franchisees without trouble, an example being Donald Strang III, whose family's hospitality company in Cleveland was then operating 57 Applebee's restaurants. In November, Strang agreed to open 48 Panera Bread bakery-cafés in Pennsylvania, New Jersey, and Delaware.

Panera thus began the new century in fine fettle. Among other things, sticking to some rigorous requirements that all prospective franchisees had to meet, it was positioned to accept only one out of every 400 franchise applicants, a luxury that few companies could afford. However, once teaming up with Panera, a franchised bakery-café was not so tied up by operating regulations that it could not take initiatives to keep its cus-

tomers' loyalty. As reported in a July 15, 2001 article in *Restaurants & Institutions*, the company's number one rule—stipulated by Mike Kupstas, vice president of franchising and brand communications—was "do whatever it takes to satisfy and make customers happy."

By the end of 2000, the company was the clear leader in system-wide sales growth among six bakery-café chains, which included, among others, Corner Bakery and Le Madeleine Bakery & Café. Its sales between 1999 and 2000 had grown by a whopping 73.6 percent, and its number of units in 2000 had grown by 45 percent over the previous year. It ranked a strong third among the top 400 chain leaders in sales growth behind Buca di Beppo and Famous Dave's, and its prospects for continued growth remained excellent.

Principal Competitors

AFC Enterprises, Inc.; Brinker International, Inc.; New World Restaurant Group, Inc.; Starbucks Corporation.

Further Reading

Allen, Robin Lee, "Au Bon Pain Co. Pins Hopes on New President, Image, *Nation's Restaurant News*, December 2, 1996, p. 3.

Battaglia, Andy, "Help Kneaded: St. Louis Bread/Panera to Go Its Own Way, Plans to Rise Without ABP," *Nation's Restaurant News*, February 22, 1999, p.12.

Brokaw, L. "The Mystery-Shopper Questionnaire: How *Au Bon Pain* Boosts Customer Service by Rewarding Employees Who Keep on Their Toes," *Inc.*, June 1991, p. 94.

Faust, Fred, "St. Louis Bread Company Emerges as National Chain," *Knight-Ridder/Tribune Business News*, November 7, 1999.

Hutchcraft, Chuck, "Thinking on Their Feet," *Restaurants & Institutions*, July 15, 2001, p. 97.

Jacobson, Giana, "Let Them Eat Bread, Especially at $4 a Loaf," *New York Times*, November 18, 1995, p. 35.

Powers, Kemp, "Second Rising," *Forbes*, November 13, 2000, p. 290.

Tucci, Linda, "Panera Bread Co. Grows Franchise; Rakes in Dough," *St. Louis Business Journal*, December 11, 2000, p. 3.

Walkup, Carolyn, "Panera Bread Rises as Lagging Bakery-Café Rivals 'Knead' Boost," *Nation's Restaurant News*, July 23, 2001, p. 74.

—John W. Fiero

Payless Cashways, Inc.

800 N.W. Chipman Road
Suite 5900
Lee's Summit, Missouri 64064-8001
U.S.A.
Telephone: (816) 347-6000
Fax: (816) 347-6046
Web site: http://www.payless.cashways.com

Public Company
Incorporated: 1988
Employees: 8,100
Sales: $1.4 billion (2000)
Stock Exchanges: OTC
Ticker Symbol: PCSH
NAIC: 44411 Home Centers; 44413 Hardware Stores;
    44412 Paint and Wallpaper Stores

During the 1990s and at the start of the new millennium, Payless Cashways, Inc. operated as a building materials and finishing products specialty retailer catering to the professional builder, contractor, institutional buyer, and do-it-yourself consumers. The firm's divisions sold thousands of products under the names Payless Cashways, Furrow, Lumberjack, Hugh M. Woods, Knox Lumber, Contractor Supply, PCI Builders Resource, and PCIBuildStreet.com. In 2000, the company operated 128 building materials stores and five PCI Builders Resource locations in 17 states in the Midwest, Southwest, Pacific Coast, and Rocky Mountain regions.

Financial hardships and a large debt load stemming from the 1988 leveraged buyout forced the firm to declare Chapter 11 bankruptcy in 1997. The company emerged the following year, but was unable to recover successfully. In 2001, Payless declared Chapter 11 bankruptcy for the last time and began liquidating its inventory.

Early History: 1930s–40s

The building supplies chain was founded in 1930 by Sanford "Sam" Furrow, who had by that time accumulated 25 years of experience in lumberyards throughout Iowa and South Dakota. With help from sons Sanford and Vernon and a colleague, John Evans, Furrow raised $10,000 to buy a defaulted lumberyard in Pocahontas, Iowa. Although the Great Depression seemed an unfavorable time to go into business, Sam Furrow asserted that he "could not have gotten into the lumber business in a big way if times had been good." Indeed, banks were so desperate to recover any amount of money on foreclosed mortgages that Furrow was able to negotiate low purchase prices on two other lumberyards in the Iowa towns of Early and Webster City by mid-1932, thereby giving each of his sons a business to manage.

Sam Furrow continued to work for the Fullerton Lumber Company, with which he had been employed since 1912, and he named his Pocahontas business Kiefer-Wolfe Lumber Company to conceal the fact of his ownership. When the Fullerton Lumber Company discovered Sam's duplicity in 1933, he quit and went to work at the renamed Pocahontas Lumber Store. The three-store chain carried small selections, focusing primarily on lumber, paint, and builder's hardware in one 80- to 100-square-foot room. Furrow's lumberyards earned steady profits during the 1930s by establishing comprehensive contracts with insurance companies, which repossessed and repaired numerous dilapidated farms during the Depression.

Sam Furrow soon began challenging established business practices in the regional building materials industry, first taking on the Lumber Trust. This amalgamation of businesses was linked by a mutually beneficial price-fixing agreement that helped everyone but the customer. Furrow launched his Webster County Lumber Store in Fort Dodge, Iowa, in 1937 by advertising "Live and Let Live Prices" that were set without regard to the Lumber Trust. Delighted customers flocked to the business, substantiating Furrow's notion that high sales volume, and not the highest margin the market would bear, was the key to success in his chosen field. He gradually increased merchandise selections at his yards, adding plaster board, ceiling tiles, insulation, and asphalt shingles; by the end of the decade, Furrow's stores were offering more than 200 products.

After World War II, John Evans and Sam Furrow split their partnership. Furrow kept all but the Fort Dodge and Webster City yards and, in 1947, he opened a new location in Iowa Falls,

Iowa, to be managed by son Vern. There, Vern first experimented with the "cash-and-carry" policy that would later be applied chainwide. The change reflected shifts in the store's customer base and its terms. Before this time, most customers were professional contractors accustomed to making large orders on credit. After the war, however, many retail suppliers to construction outfits had trouble collecting on accounts receivable; rising lumberyard prices reflected those difficulties. At the same time, increasing numbers of laymen began to circumvent professional repairmen's high rates by tackling their own home repair and improvement projects. Low cash-and-carry prices, as well as more aggressive direct mail advertising, attracted this new class of do-it-yourselfers and bolstered the building suppliers' cash flow.

The loose-knit chain that would become Payless Cashways grew rather spontaneously during these early decades. The family members and long-time colleagues who opened new locations contributed to each new store's start-up costs and, therefore, were entitled to a share of the profits. This arrangement fostered decentralization and self-motivation among individual store managers, considered a major element of the chain's early success. In the 1950s, however, the Furrows instituted several changes that made the loose-knit lumberyards more of a modern retail chain.

Expansion Under a New Name: 1950s–70s

Having suffered a mild heart attack in 1950, Sam Furrow gradually turned the business over to his sons. In 1951, Vern and Sanford, Jr., established a wholesale company, Iowa Lumber and Supply, to pool purchasing and distribution for the stores and thereby achieve economies of scale. Relinquishing management of their lumberyards to take more active roles in the management of the chain, Sanford and Vernon assumed the roles of president and vice-president, respectively, at the new company, which had eight stores by 1954. Within a year, the Furrows brought all of the chain's accounting under one firm and unified advertising and promotion. Under the name Payless Cashways, the stores adopted a logo featuring a curved red arrow and Payless Pete, a caricature of a lumberjack. By the end of the decade, the chain had added stores in Minnesota, Illinois, and Arizona.

When patriarch Sam Furrow and son Sanford died within a year of each other late in the 1950s, Vernon was unexpectedly left to head the chain. The 52-year-old had hoped to retire several years earlier but was instead thrust into a leadership role. In spite of his initial reluctance, Vern led the company's expansion into New Mexico, Colorado, and Nebraska, before taking the company public as Payless Cashways, Inc. in 1969. Vernon was elected chairperson of the 16-store company, and Robert Lincoln, who had served as the company's first chain-wide accountant, became president and treasurer. During its first year as a public entity, Payless recorded sales of $24 million and $.9 million in profits.

Four decades of active family management came to end in 1971, when Vernon Furrow retired. Robert Lincoln became chairperson, president, and chief executive officer. Flush with the infusion of funds from its initial public offering, Payless Cashways focused on growth in the 1970s, concentrating on establishing new stores, expanding and remodeling existing stores, and increasing each location's product line. The company also established its construction division, anticipating dramatic growth in that segment.

Moreover, a new tactic, dubbed invasion, established several stores in a single market for increased impact. Payless "attacked" Dallas and Kansas City, establishing four large-format suburban stores that featured 30,000-square-foot retail areas, 30,000-square-foot warehouses, and massive lumberyards on multiacre sites in each metropolitan area. Automotive and lawn-and-garden supplies were added to the stores' lines, which included more than 13,000 items by the end of the decade. The chain's physical growth was suspended only in 1974, which *Time* magazine called "the year the building stopped." Housing starts declined by more than half that year, and many construction firms failed as a result. By this time, however, Payless catered primarily to do-it-yourselfers, who used the building hiatus to fix up and remodel rather than purchase new homes. That year, the chain's sales and profits actually increased by 34 and 21 percent, respectively.

By the end of the 1970s, Payless boasted 68 stores in 14 states and nine distribution centers. Sites in Texas, Oregon, Missouri, Kansas, Oklahoma, California, and Indiana also were added under the name of Furrow's, due to trademark conflicts in several markets. In 1976, Lincoln abdicated the top position, citing "operational conflicts," and longtime employee Stan Covey was elected chairperson and chief executive officer. The following year, corporate headquarters were moved to Kansas City, Missouri, a more central location. The company's growth was in no way impeded by the management upheaval: sales increased from $24 million to $316.1 million between 1969 and 1979. Profits rose even faster, from less than $1 million to $14.5 million, over the same period. This growth coincided with a six-fold increase in the do-it-yourself market, from slightly less than $6 billion in 1970 to $35 billion in 1980. By 1981, Payless Cashways was the fifth largest chain in the industry, and its annual sales growth in the last half of the 1970s had doubled the industry average.

The 1980s brought the election of a new company president, former attorney and stockbroker David Stanley, who directed a shift from traditional rural markets to more urban and suburban markets in an effort to capture a bigger share of the still-fragmented do-it-yourself market. This change called for an alteration of Payless's store formula, distribution channels and methods, and corporate image. Smaller stores with a more lo-

Key Dates:

1930: Sam Furrow and John Evans buy a lumberyard in Pocahontas, Iowa.

1937: Furrow opens the Webster County Lumber store to compete with the Lumber Trust.

1947: A new location in Iowa Falls is established and run by Vern Furrow.

1951: Sons Vern and Sanford, Jr., establish a wholesale company, Iowa Lumber and Supply.

1955: The store's accounting and advertising procedures become unified under the name Payless Cashways.

1969: The firm goes public; sales reach $24 million.

1971: Vern Furrow retires ending four decades of active family management.

1974: Sales and profits increase despite a downturn in the housing industry.

1981: Payless Cashways operates as the fifth largest chain in the industry.

1984: Sales exceed $1 billion.

1988: David Stanley and a group of investors take the company private to thwart takeover attempts by Asher Edelman.

1993: Payless Cashways goes public once again.

1996: The firm begins a dual marketing approach, catering to both the professional and the do-it-yourself consumer.

1997: The firm files for Chapter 11 bankruptcy, blaming debt related to the leveraged buyout of 1988.

1998: Stanley and Susan Stanton resign and Millard Barron is named president and CEO; the firm emerges from Chapter 11 bankruptcy.

2000: PCI Builders Resource, a wholesale materials and manufacturing company, is created as a new division.

2001: After declaring Chapter 11 bankruptcy again in June, Payless begins liquidating its inventory.

cally targeted inventory would strive to supply "virtually all home building needs," as Stanley told *Business Week* in 1981. Payless's wholesale distribution arm controlled only about 17 percent of the chain's distribution, and managers ordered the remainder of their merchandise directly from vendors. Stanley challenged the persistent autonomy of Payless store managers by directing an increase in the chain's share of cooperative buying to capitalize on previously untapped economies of scale. Payless hoped to transform its corporate image along with its target audience by shifting its appeal from farmers, who had comprised 40 percent of the customer base, to white-collar persons engaged in building projects on the weekends.

One thing Stanley did not change, however, was the growth rate at Payless: the chain doubled in size from 1979 to 1984, adding 39 stores in 1984 alone, including 14 Prime Home Improvement Centers in Colorado and Nevada, as well as Somerville Lumber in Massachusetts. That year, while Payless topped the $1 billion sales mark, profits declined 9 percent from the previous year to $37.4 million. Daniel McConville, an analyst for *Barron's*, attributed the earnings decline to "indigestion."

Taking the Company Private: 1988

Later in the decade, a takeover attempt by Asher Edelman prompted yet another major change at Payless Cashways. In 1988, Stanley marshaled a unique group of investors, under the name PCI Acquisition, to take the company private. The assemblage included Payless executives, financial institutions, and such key suppliers as Masco, a major faucet vendor that contributed more than 20 percent of the $909 million needed for the leveraged buyout. Although highly irregular, the deal with Masco was not considered an infringement on competition because the supplier did not earn an unfair advantage over its rivals for its contribution.

Although the leveraged buyout saved Payless from takeover, it was not an unqualified success. The company did not have a single year of profitability during the five years it was private, as a recession in its core Midwest and Southwest markets, high debt from the buyout, and competition from up-and-coming "category killer" Home Depot, Inc. combined to slow sales growth, weaken margins, and depress operating earnings. With the help of a team of outside consultants, Stanley opted to sidestep competition with Home Depot and return Payless Cashways' focus to professional contractors, a customer group that was growing at a faster rate than do-it-yourselfers.

Stanley and his colleagues formulated a reorganization of everything from distribution and inventory systems to supplier relationships and strategic focus. The new Payless featured separate entrances for contractors, better credit terms than do-it-yourselfers, phone and fax ordering services, delivery, and even free coffee. Moreover, lawn mowers and outdoor furniture were dropped from the merchandise line and were replaced with high-quality—and high-margin—professional tools. In 1992, Payless opened eight Remote Contractor Sales Offices, which offered in-stock, high-demand products and next-day on-site delivery, opening 17 more such offices the following year to access underserved areas within 50 to 75 miles of existing stores.

In 1993, the company experimented with two new formats targeted at the professional homebuilder and remodeler: Home and Room Designs featured kitchen and bath finishing products, and Tool Site offered 6,500 professional tools. Although Payless was not alone in offering many of these services, none of its competitors courted the professional customer so steadfastly. From 1987 to 1993, the company's sales to professionals increased from 25 percent of total revenues to 45 percent, compared with around 20 percent for market leader Home Depot. Sales increased to $2.6 billion in 1993, but the chain remained unable to turn a profit.

Nevertheless, Stanley was able to sell 70 percent of Payless back to the public in 1993, raising $350 million in debt-reduction funds and thereby eliminating almost $80 million in annual interest expenses. Stanley projected the addition of 28 new stores by 1998, and Payless also took advantage of the North American Free Trade Agreement, announcing a joint venture with Grupo Industrial Alfa, S.A. de C.V. to establish 25 stores in Mexico by the turn of the century. The building supplies industry remained fragmented in the early 1990s—the top ten chains comprised only 12 percent of total annual sales—

affording Payless Cashways an opportunity to establish a stable position among the leaders as market consolidation continued.

Financial Difficulties Leading to Bankruptcy: Late 1990s into the New Millennium

The late 1990s proved tumultuous for the firm, however, and it was never able to claim that stable position. In 1996, Payless sold its interest in Total Home de Mexico—the joint venture it had established with Grupo Industrial Alfa. Later that year, the firm announced a new ''dual market'' strategy in which both professional and do-it-yourself consumers were targeted. The new strategy was launched in Phoenix and added 13,000 new products to the store's line.

While sales and profits continued to fall, Stanley, along with Chief Operating Officer Susan Stanton, continued to push the new strategy. The company, however, was forced to declare Chapter 11 bankruptcy in 1997. Stanley stated in a July 1997 *Kansas City Business Journal* article, ''I've admitted that I take responsibility, the management takes responsibility. But the reason we're where we are is because of more than $1 billion of debt from the LBO in '88. This company could no longer handle that debt. Period.''

Investors as well as creditors grew weary of Stanley's and Stanton's aggressive approach and unwavering focus on the dual path strategy. Many blamed them for the company's financial problems and cited the costly marketing approach as a culprit in the firm's faltering bottom line. In 1998, the pair stepped down as Payless emerged from Chapter 11. Millard Barron was named president and CEO of the firm in June of that year.

Barron faced the difficult task of returning Payless to its former status as a leading retailer in the industry among fierce competition from the likes of Home Depot and Lowe's. Although the firm reported three consecutive quarters of earnings in 1998—the first time since 1994—Payless was still burdened by an increasing debt load.

Nevertheless, Barron forged ahead and began to overhaul the stores' merchandise and put the ''dual path'' strategy of serving both the professional and the do-it-yourself markets to rest. Instead, the company began to focus most of its efforts on professional builders, contractors, and institutional buyers.

Eyeing this new focus as key to securing financial gains, Payless began aggressively pursuing its new professional business strategy. In 2000, the company launched a new division entitled PCI Builders Resource, a wholesale outlet catering to professional builders. The firm also converted five Payless Cashways outlets to a Contractor Supply format and adopted a new name for its web site—PCIBuildStreet.com—that offered both the professional and do-it-yourselfer project information and tools, as well as online shopping options.

Despite these new directives, sales in 2000 fell by more than 17 percent while the company posted a $20.6 million loss in net income. A total of 22 stores were closed that year while Barron continued to restructure business operations in hopes of gaining control of the firm's mounting debt and liabilities.

Barron's efforts, however, proved futile. In 2001, the firm closed 42 stores by August after declaring Chapter 11 bankruptcy yet again in June. Never able to regain its edge in the highly competitive industry, Payless Cashways announced in September 2001 that Hilco Merchant Resources LLC, the Ozer Group, and the Nassi Group LLC had been appointed by the U.S. Bankruptcy Court to liquidate the final inventory for the company.

Principal Divisions

Payless Cashways; Furrow; Lumberjack; Hugh M. Woods; Knox Lumber; Contractor Supply; PCI Builders Resource; PCIBuildStreet.com.

Principal Competitors

The Home Depot, Inc.; Lowe's Companies Inc.; Menard Inc.

Further Reading

Cianci, Gary, ''Supplier Sources Fund Payless Cashways' LBO,'' *Chain Store Age Executive,* November 1988, p. 94.

Furrow, Virginia Sugg, *Aged in Wood: The Story of Payless Cashways, Inc.,* Kansas City: Payless Cashways, Inc., 1984.

Gross, Lisa, ''Do It Yourself,'' *Forbes,* October 11, 1982, pp. 102–03.

Haller, Karl, ''Warehouse Stores Lead Home Improvement Push,'' *Chain Store Age Executive,* August 1993, pp. 25A-27A.

Hollar, Katie, ''Payless Cashways Prepares for Liquidation,'' *Business Journal Serving Metropolitan Kansas City,* August 31, 2001, p. 6.

Johnson, Walter E., ''Payless Sets Sights on Future,'' *Do-It-Yourself Retailing,* August 1999, p. 286.

Lambert, Cheryl Ann, ''Payless Cashways Restructures Somerville, Sells Mexican Interest,'' *Chilton's Hardware Age,* January 1996, p. 16.

——, ''Payless Discusses Slow Sales, Redefines Target Customers,'' *Home Improvement Market,* July 1996, p. 13.

——, ''Payless Tests Growth Strategy Despite Weak '96,'' *Home Improvement Market,* February 1997, p. 14.

McConville, Daniel J., ''Lumbering Giant: Payless Cashways Squaring Away Acquisitions,'' *Barron's,* January 14, 1985, pp. 22, 24, 31, 45.

Palmeri, Christopher, ''Remodeling Your Business,'' *Forbes,* August 16, 1993, p. 43.

''Payless Cashways Emerges from Chapter 11 Bankruptcy,'' *Do-It-Yourself Retailing,* January 1998, p. 17.

''Payless: Zeroing in on Suburbia,'' *Business Week,* September 7, 1981, pp. 104–05.

Pike, Helen, ''Think Profit,'' *Computerworld,* April 3, 1989, pp. 18–24.

Trollinger, Amy, ''Payless Cashways CEO Predicts Turnaround Year,'' *Kansas City Business Journal,* April 23, 1999, p. 3.

——, ''Payless Discontent Has Ripple Effect,'' *Kansas City Business Journal,* September 5, 1997, p. 1.

Trollinger, Amy, and Jim Davis, ''Stanley and Stanton Hold Firm to Dual Path,'' *Kansas City Business Journal,* July 25, 1997, p. 1.

—April Dougal Gasbarre
—update: Christina M. Stansell

PDS Gaming Corporation

6170 McLeod Drive
Las Vegas, Nevada 89120
U.S.A.
Telephone: (702) 736-0700
Toll Free: (800) 479-3612
Fax: (702) 740-8692
Web site: http://www.pdsgaming.com

Public Company
Incorporated: 1988 as Progressive Distribution Systems
Employees: 56
Sales: $52.9 million (2000)
Stock Exchanges: NASDAQ
Ticker Symbol: PDSG
NAIC: 522220 Sales Financing; 713210 Casinos (Except Casino Hotels); 713290 Other Gambling Industries

PDS Gaming Corporation (PDS) provides a variety of products and services to casino operators and is licensed for different casino services and operations in more than eleven states and for certain Native American locales. The core business of PDS is the financing and leasing of casino gaming machines and casino-related furniture, fixtures, and equipment. The company reconditions used slot equipment, offering the equipment for sale or lease. PDS owns Digital Card System, a technology being applied to the development of new electronically-based table games, such as Digital 21 blackjack. PDS also owns and operates The Gambler casino in Reno.

From General Leasing to Casino Financing

Husband and wife team Johan and Lona Finley started PDS Gaming in the Minneapolis area in 1988 as Progressive Distributions Systems. Operating under the name PDS Leasing Services, the company handled leasing transactions for vehicles and general equipment. PDS originated the lease transactions and then sold the contracts for immediate profit.

The direction of the company changed in 1991 when Grand Casino, Inc. of Minnesota approached PDS to lease and finance slot machines for Native American casinos then in the initial stages of development. PDS began to finance new gaming operations in Minnesota, Mississippi, Wisconsin, Colorado, and Canada by leasing gaming devices such as slot machines and video games and by financing casino-related fixtures, furniture, including hotel and restaurant furniture and equipment, including computers and office equipment, vehicles, and security and surveillance equipment. To serve these risky new ventures the company formed a new subsidiary, PDS Casinos International, Inc., to handle the transactions. In 1991, 90 percent of the company's business originated with casino-related contracts. By 1993, with all business centered on the gaming industry, PDS revenues and profits reached $4.3 million and $500,000, respectively.

Operating as PDS Financial, the company began to finance larger ventures with the support of its May 1994 initial public offering (IPO) of stock. Through the sale of 1.5 million shares at $5.00 per share, PDS raised $7.5 million. That year PDS financed $110 million in gaming devices and casino-related equipment. The company's new customers included Boomtown, Inc., with PDS providing financing for casinos in Reno, Las Vegas, New Orleans, and Biloxi, entering new and established gaming markets. The IPO allowed PDS to retain more of its financing contracts for recurring revenues, rather than selling them for one-time profit. In 1994, PDS recorded revenues of $8.6 million and pro forma net income of $2.3 million.

In its largest transaction to date, PDS entered into a joint venture, called Maritime Gaming Management, with First Nations Gaming, Ltd. (FNG) in November 1994. PDS entered a new area of business with the venture by financing the construction of Eagles Nest Gaming Palace in Woodstock, New Brunswick, Canada. In exchange for $13.2 million in financing, PDS was to receive a percentage of distributable income from FNG. Under a management contract with First Nation Indian Tribe, FNG received 49 percent of distributable income. Of those fees, FNG agreed to pay PDS 70 percent for the first six years and 50 percent for the next four years.

PDS halted financing in June 1995, however, when FNC did not receive government approval to operate blackjack, roulette, full-fledged slot machines, or video poker. When Eagles Nest opened in July 1995, the project had been reduced in scale,

Company Perspectives:

Our mission is to be the leading diversified gaming company by providing dynamic solutions to our gaming industry customers. We provide value adding proprietary table games, unique slot distribution methodologies, creative financing and leasing alternatives, and niche casino operations. We constantly endeavor to provide our employees a satisfying work environment and strive to build long-term value for our shareholders.

offering high stakes bingo, pull-tabs, and video lottery terminals in a 28,000 square-foot Sprung tent structure. Low attendance exacerbated the problems at the casino. While Eagles Nest seemed to be a good investment—as many casinos in rural, high traffic locations without nearby competition had succeeded in similar circumstances—but industry experts suggested that the investment had exceeded actual financing capacity of PDS. PDS lost $7 million, including interest, closing points, and $4.6 million in financing. Its stock value dropped to $1.87. The failed financing venture resulted in 1995 revenues of $4.6 million and a loss of $4.7 million. The company's own credit line shrank from $50 million to $1 million, inhibiting the company's ability to do business. PDS recovered $400,000 when the company sold its interest in the loans to Dion Entertainment in a stock transaction in summer 1996.

In early 1997, PDS entered into a joint venture, this time with Dion Entertainment, to revive the Eagles Nest gaming enterprise. PDS contributed the amount equal to the loans that Dion purchased and also funded opening costs and operating capital. PDS then owned 80 percent of Transcanada 2 Corporation which reopened the Eagles Nest Gaming Palace under new management in February 1997. PDS purchased Dion's interest in the casino in April 1997.

Seeking Stability in Established Gaming Markets in Mid-1990s

As PDS regained its revolving credit line, which rebounded to $26 million during 1996, the company introduced its Slot Lease program. The program restructured gaming equipment financing by offering operating leases to casino operators for slot machines and other electronic gaming devices. Leasing new machines provided casinos with a cost effective method of obtaining state-of-the-art slot machines while PDS obtained long-term revenues from the transactions. The leases gave customers the option to purchase or return gaming equipment when the lease expired. In June 1996, the company opened a sales office in Las Vegas to market its Slot Lease program in the vicinity of its potential customers, with plans to relocate its administrative offices to Las Vegas the following year. Also, after the difficult situation with FNG, PDS sought to obtain more business from established gaming markets at less risk. At the end of 1996, revenues had increased to $6 million and the company's lease portfolio, those contracts retained for recurring revenues, increased from $6 million in 1995 to $24 million in 1996.

An essential aspect of the company's growth strategy involved obtaining operational licenses from local gaming author-

ities, allowing PDS to receive a percentage of gaming revenues from the equipment it leased. Under these arrangements, PDS retained more leases for long-term income, rather than sell them for immediate profit. PDS obtained equipment sales and distributor licenses in Iowa and Nevada in November 1996, in New Jersey (as a Casino Service Industry license) in 1997, and a manufacturer/distributor license in Colorado in 1997.

PDS continued to regain its borrowing capacity, which rose to $56 million by summer 1997, boosted by the April agreement with Bank of New York for a $20 million revolving credit facility and $10 million from Heller Financial. By October 1997 the company's share value had rebounded to $8.25 per share, compared to $1.75 per share in January 1997. In 1997 the company maintained a lease portfolio value of $24 million, with a total of $84 million in finance originations.

As an extension of the Slot Lease program, PDS introduced its Slot Source program in 1997, offering previously leased, reconditioned slot machines for sale or lease. PDS decided to handle equipment reconditioning in-house and established a reconditioning shop at its new headquarters in Las Vegas. The company restructured some gaming equipment transactions as sales-type leases, designed for reconditioned equipment or equipment purchased at a discount. PDS sold the contracts to remove the equipment as an asset from its balance sheet.

The company marketed reconditioned equipment to small and mid-sized casino operators in Nevada, at Native American reservations, and in the Caribbean. These operators required only standard, spinning-reel slots and video poker games. Slot Source also filled the demand for machines with bill acceptors. While small operators with little capital liked the low-cost program, major casinos, such as Caesar's Palace, also used the service to provide their customers with a wide variety of gaming equipment. Slot Source succeeded from the outset with $2.2 million in sales during the second half of 1997 and $13.1 million in 1998.

By the end of 1997, PDS derived revenues from five distinct sources: equipment sales; sales-type leases; rental revenue on operating leases, with monthly payments and depreciation on equipment; fee income from the sale of lease or notes receivable contracts; and finance income from direct financing of leases or notes receivable that the company retained for ongoing revenues. The company recorded $17.5 million in equipment sales, $14.5 million in sales-type leases, and $11.4 million in rental revenue in 1997. With finance originations at $84.4 million and notes receivable at $3 million, PDS recorded fee income of $1.7 million and finance income of $1.6 million. Total revenues increased nearly 700 percent to $47.4 million, with net earnings at just under $1 million.

While capital leases tended to range in the $500,000 to $2.5 million range, PDS obtained several large contracts in 1998. Sterling Casino Lines contracted for 855 slot machines, valued at $4 million, with shipments taken during spring and summer 1998. By late 1998, PDS obtained $55 million in new business involving $36 million in operating leases and financing commitments for 1998 and 1999. New contracts included $13 million in lease financing with Isle of Capri-Blackhawk LLC and $9 million with Blackhawk Brewery and Casino LLC, both con-

Key Dates:

1991: PDS begins to lease gaming machines to new casino ventures.

1994: PDS IPO raises $7.5 million to fund expansion.

1995: A joint venture in casino construction results in losses.

1996: PDS opens a sales office in Las Vegas to promote its new Slot Lease program.

1997: Slot Source is introduced for the sale and lease of used, reconditioned slot machines.

1999: PDS acquires the rights to the Digital Card System technology for electronic table games.

2001: The Nevada Gaming Commission grants the company its approval to operate a casino.

tracts being for facilities in Colorado, and up to $33 million in contracts with The Resort at Summerlin in Las Vegas. The lease agreements provided slot machines, furniture, fixtures, and equipment. An offering of $11 million in subordinated debentures supported new financing contracts. The company shipped 6,500 gaming devices in 1998, including 3,100 of the high margin, reconditioned units. One customer's delay in shipment of 300 units in late 1998, a $6.4 million value, resulted in a net loss for the fourth quarter, however.

While PDS maintained its five areas of revenue in 1998, the actual sources of revenue shifted. Equipment sales increased to $20.5 million, primarily originating from higher sales of reconditioned equipment. Higher sales of used equipment and higher finance income offset declines in sales of leased assets and in sales-type leases and operating leases. While original financing decreased 29 percent to $60.3 million, a dramatic increase in notes receivable, at $21.9 million, resulted in an increase in fee income to $2.7 million, while finance income nearly doubled to $3 million. Rental revenue declined 41 percent to $6.8 million and sales-type leases declined from $14.5 million to $4 million as PDS decided to offer the leases for reconditioned equipment only. The company experienced a 16 percent increase in interest expense, however, to fund leasing operations and the retention of notes receivable. Total revenues of $36 million reflected a 24 percent decrease and net income dropped by more than half to $356,000.

In an effort to expand its market reach, PDS continued to obtain new gaming licenses. In 1998, the company gained approval for a supplier license from Indiana's licensing commission. In 1999, the company received a manufacturer/distributor license in Mississippi and a supplier license in Illinois, as well as a gaming device manufacturers license from the Nevada Gaming Commission. Under the license Nevada allowed PDS to manufacture certain replacement components for reconditioning slot machines, thus reducing time required for reconditioning process. The license allowed PDS to offer more games, including proprietary games, as well. Also, PDS obtained approval as a slot machine route operator in Nevada. The company did not intend to use the license for operating route, but to offer an alternative financing structure to its gaming equipment customers. This involved lower fixed monthly payments sup-

plemented by sharing in revenue generated by the gaming equipment. Washington became the eleventh state to grant PDS a supplier license, approved in April 2000.

Diversification in the Late 1990s

In September 1999, PDS purchased DigiDeal Corporation's proprietary Digital Card System. The technology utilized high quality graphics to display virtual playing cards to the dealer and players. Intellectual property rights included the Digital 21 Blackjack game and the rights to manufacture and distribute the game in the United States and to sovereign nations within the United States, as well as to apply the technology to other games. PDS established the Table Games Division to handle the new product as well as traditional table games.

PDS began field-testing Digital 21 Blackjack at The Cities of Gold Casino in Santa Fe in February 2000, and at the Sunset Station Hotel and Casino in Henderson, Nevada, outside Las Vegas in June. The Nevada Gaming Commission approved the game for further marketing the following September. PDS began assembly and installation on initial orders immediately. Laboratories Inc. approved the game for operation in California, Iowa, and New Mexico.

Revenues at PDS remained steady in 1999, while the sources of revenue continued to fluctuate. The company's lease portfolio improved with $62 million in leases from $81 million in originated finance transactions. Hence finance income and fee income increased to $5.5 million and $3.7 million respectively. These gains were countered by bad debt, as PDS recorded higher than usual collection and asset impairment expenses of $1.4 million. Equipment sales dropped dramatically, to $6.2 million, as demand for spinning-reel slots declined, resulting in a $609,000 loss from liquidation of excess inventory. Revenues from sales-type leases and operating leases increased to $6.6 million and $12.4 million, respectively. PDS finished 1999 with stable revenues, at $35.5 million, but with a loss of $700,000.

With the slowdown in used equipment sales, PDS expanded it Slot Source program with the acquisition of Casino-SlotExchange.com. The web site listed used slot equipment for sale by casinos, manufactures, and distributors in a "virtual warehouse." After browsing through the inventory a customer chose to buy, lease, and/or finance equipment "as is" or refurbished. The acquisition sales doubled, allowing PDS to maintain sales comparable to 1999. In 2000, PDS sold a total of 5,500 units, compared to 5,300 in 1999. Many customers took equipment in "as is" condition, however, lowering average per unit price. PDS planned to add other casino-related equipment for sale or lease at the site. The company renamed PDS Slot Source to Casino Slot Exchange.

PDS sought to diversify in the ownership and operation of casinos in established gaming markets. Though negotiations for the Four Queens Hotel and Casino in downtown Las Vegas stalled in spring 2000, the following December PDS purchased The Gambler casino in Reno. The company leased the casino back to the owner until it received approval from the Nevada Gaming Commission to operate a casino, in January 2001. The 7,500 square foot gaming hall offered 175 gaming devices. PDS planned to replace one-third of the slot machines with newer models and to redecorate and initiate gaming on the unused second floor of the casino. The company wanted to expand further into casino operations, but had not found appropriate opportunities. PDS explored the possibility of acquiring the PTC Gaming chain of sports bars with betting facilities, but terminated the agreement in July 2001.

The Table Games Division was off to slow start, as few established casinos were willing to lease or purchase Digital 21 Blackjack. Casino operators did not want to relinquish space from a successful table game on the gaming floor to try an unproven game. Sales tended to originate with new casino operations that did not have space dedicated to established games. PDS made some adjustments to the game to make it more appealing. In order to penetrate the market with its technology, PDS formed an agreement with Action Gaming Inc. to develop Digital Card System platforms for Action Gaming's popular Double Play Blackjack and 21 Stud table games. The licensing agreement involved rights to manufacture, market, and distribute the resulting products worldwide. To reflect the company's expansion into game design and production, as well as casino operations, PDS changed its name to PDS Gaming in May 2001.

PDS returned to profitability in 2000 and experienced dramatic increase in business in early 2001. In 2000, revenues reached $52.9 million, with net income of $728,000, bolstered by revenues from sales-type leases that more than tripled in 2000, to $23 million. During the first half of 2001, PDS efforts to increase recurring revenues resulted in spectacular improvements. The company financed $38.2 million in transactions during the first six months, compared to $11.3 million over the same period in 2000. Also shipments of gaming devices doubled compared to the first six months of 2000. PDS continued to seek new markets, seeking licensing in Connecticut, Kansas, and Minnesota, and for Native American tribes in California, Iowa, New Mexico, and North Dakota.

Principal Subsidiaries

PDS Financial Corporation-Nevada; PDS Financial Corporation-Mississippi; PDS Casinos International, Inc.; PDS Financial Corporation-Colorado.

Principal Operating Units

Casino Operations; Casino Slot Exchange; Finance and Lease Division; Table Games Division.

Principal Competitors

Alliance Gaming Corporation; Anchor Gaming; International Game Technology.

Further Reading

Edwards, John G., "PDS Financial Succeeds With Slots Old and New," *Las Vegas Review Journal*, January 26, 1998, p. 1D.
"First Nations Gaming, Inc. Announces Opening of Woodstock Facility," *PR Newswire*, July 7, 1995.
Forster, Julie, "Drawing Aces at PDS Financial," *Corporate Report-Minnesota*, December 1997, p. 16.
Huber, Tim, "PDS completes move of HQ to Vegas After Profits Pick Up," *Minneapolis-St. Paul cityBusiness*, June 26, 1998, p. 3.
"Nevada Gaming Commission Approves PDS Financial Corporation's Digital Card System," *PR Newswire*, September 28, 2000.
"Nevada Gaming Commission Approves PDS Financial Corporation's Operation of The Gambler Casino in Reno," *PR Newswire*, January 25, 2001.
Phelps, David, "Twin Cities Firms Lose on Canadian Gambling," *Star Tribune* (Minneapolis), October 2, 1995, p.1D.
"Spintek Gaming Technologies Signs Agreement with PDS Gaming," *Business Wire*, October 5, 2000.

—Mary Tradii

Philip Morris Companies Inc.

Philip Morris Companies Inc.

120 Park Avenue
New York, New York 10017-5592
U.S.A.
Telephone: (917) 663-5000
Fax: (917) 663-2167
Web site: http://www.philipmorris.com

Public Company
Incorporated: 1919 as Philip Morris & Company Ltd.,
　Inc.
Employees: 178,000
Sales: $80.35 billion (2000)
Stock Exchanges: New York Amsterdam Antwerp
　Australia Brussels Frankfurt London Luxembourg
　Paris Swiss Tokyo Vienna
Ticker Symbol: MO
NAIC: 311513 Cheese Manufacturing; 2111 Cigarettes;
　311941 Mayonnaise, Dressing, and Other Prepared
　Sauce Manufacturing; 311412 Frozen Specialty Food
　Manufacturing; 31192 Coffee and Tea Manufacturing;
　31123 Breakfast Cereal Manufacturing; 311821
　Cookie and Cracker Manufacturing; 311911 Roasted
　Nuts and Peanut Butter Manufacturing; 311942 Spice
　and Extract Manufacturing; 31212 Breweries; 312221
　Cigarette Manufacturing

As a major player in an industry dogged by health concerns, a shrinking domestic market, and widespread investor fears about its future, Philip Morris Companies Inc. (Morris) continued to achieve record-breaking sales and profits during the 1990s, most of them thanks to the enduring appeal of the Marlboro Man. From a position of relative obscurity in the cigarette business in the early 1960s, Philip Morris has ridden Marlboro's success to leadership of the world tobacco market, while battling legal problems surrounding the entire tobacco industry. In 1999, one out of every six cigarettes sold around the globe was a Morris brand. Wanting to limit its dependence on its tobacco sales however, Morris continued to bolster its food-related sales throughout the 1990s and into the new millennium. As the second largest food concern in the world, the company added Nabisco Holding Inc. to its arsenal in 2000, and then led Kraft in the second-largest initial public offering (IPO) in history in June 2001. As litigation in the tobacco industry appeared to be slowing, Morris continued to gain market share in many of its product categories and investor confidence returned. In fact, share price rose over 90 percent during 2000, making Morris the best performer on the Dow Jones Industrial Average for the year.

The Early Years: 1847–1920s

In 1847, an Englishman named Philip Morris opened a tobacco shop in London's fashionable Bond Street area. When British soldiers returning from the Crimean War made the smoking of Turkish-style cigarettes—until then exclusively a habit of the poor—de rigueur, Morris was soon busy as a manufacturer as well as merchant of the newly popular product. He introduced a number of successful cigarette brands, including English Ovals, Cambridge, and Oxford Blues, and continued as one of the leading British tobacconists for many years. Morris's company eventually built a small but stable business in the United States, where its brands sold primarily on the strength of their British cachet. The U.S. market, however, was until 1911 all but owned by the American Tobacco trust, which enjoyed a monopoly in cigarettes comparable to that of John D. Rockefeller's Standard Oil in the oil business.

When the tobacco cartel was dissolved by court order in 1911, a U.S. financier named George J. Whelan formed Tobacco Products Corporation to absorb a few of the splinter companies not already organized into the new Big Four of tobacco—American Tobacco, R.J. Reynolds, Lorillard, and Liggett & Meyers. His first manufacturing acquisition was the maker of Melachrino cigarettes, a company at which Reuben M. Ellis and Leonard B. McKitterick had made names for themselves as outstanding salesmen. Ellis and McKitterick became vice-presidents and stockholders of Tobacco Products Corporation as Whelan considered their amicable relationships with the thousands of tobacco retailers in the New York area an invaluable asset. Whelan purchased the U.S. business of Philip Morris Company in 1919 and formed a new company to manage its

Company Perspectives:

Philip Morris has been guided for many years by a number of fundamental strategies that drive our growth, our profitability, and our vision for the future. Together, these strategies enable us to continue delivering on our promise: to invest in the development, retention, and motivation of our talented employees; to conduct our business as a responsible manufacturer and marketer of consumer products, including those intended for adults; to profitably grow our businesses; to reinvest in our businesses; to pursue a disciplined program of acquisition; to enhance shareholder value; to safeguard our credit rating; and to successfully manage our litigation challenges and play an active and constructive role in regulatory issues.

assets: Philip Morris & Company Ltd., Inc., owned by the shareholders of Tobacco Products Corporation. Ellis and McKitterick thus became part owners and managers of the new Philip Morris brands.

Marlboro Debuts: 1925

While Whelan wheeled and dealed his way toward a financial collapse in 1929, Ellis assumed control of Morris in 1923, at which time the company posted a net income of about $100,000. Ellis's first important move as president was the 1925 introduction of a new premium—20 cents a pack—cigarette called Marlboro, which did well from the beginning and leveled off at steady sales of 500 million cigarettes a year. Industry leaders such as Camel and Lucky Strike sold more than 25 billion a year. Marlboro was originally marketed to women, the wealthy, and the sophisticated, in complete contrast to its 1955 cowboy-image reincarnation. After a seven-year absence, McKitterick rejoined Ellis in 1930 and the two men set about buying Morris's stock from their former employer, now in retreat from the tobacco business. Whelan sold off all of his tobacco interests, allowing Ellis and McKitterick to gain control of Morris by 1931. The company marketed cigarettes mainly under the names of English Ovals, Marlboro, and Paul Jones; handled a modest amount of pipe tobacco as well; and owned a single manufacturing facility in Richmond, Virginia. By any measure, it was a minor competitor in an industry dominated by the remaining pieces of the former American Tobacco trust.

Ellis and McKitterick were both veteran salesmen in the tobacco business, however, which in the 1930s meant that they personally had done business with many thousands of the tobacco jobbers and retailers up and down the East Coast. In a field not yet controlled by the rising mass marketers, such as supermarket chains, those years of handshaking had built for both men a powerful store of goodwill among those who would determine which cigarettes would be pushed at the retail level and which would be allowed to languish. When Ellis and McKitterick launched a new mid-priced cigarette called Philip Morris English Blend in 1933, they could count on the strong support of their jobber network to help them through the difficult introductory period. To further cement their alliance with jobbers, Morris executives let it be known that the company

would refrain from selling to the new mass marketers directly, preventing the latter from retailing English Blend at less than the price of 15 cents set by the jobbers and dealers. The jobbers, already beginning to suffer from price competition with the big chains, readily agreed to Morris's plan—they pushed English Blend at 15 cents after Morris guaranteed that the same package would not end up on supermarket shelves at ten cents.

As experienced marketers, Ellis and McKitterick came up with several novel advertising gambits as additional support for their new product. Morris introduced the use of diethylene glycol as a moisture retentive in its cigarettes, adducing as proof of glycol's milder effect on the human throat a host of more or less scientific evidence gathered by bona fide researchers who were, however, paid for their work by the company. Ellis and McKitterick circulated results of the research among physicians, while settling in their advertisements for the general claim that "scientific tests have proven Philip Morris a milder cigarette." The company kept up this advertising slant for many years despite skepticism voiced by the Federal Trade Commission, among others. Morris's second advertising strategy was the revival of an earlier campaign in which a bellhop was told to fetch a pack of Morris cigarettes. The "call for Philip Morris," slogan used on posters as early as 1919, was updated for radio in 1933 with the recruitment of a bellhop named John Roventini to serve as a living representation of the ad. Roventini, under the name of Johnnie Morris, enjoyed many prosperous years putting in countless appearances in New York and other major cities, while his strident call could be heard every week on radio broadcasts.

Roventini soon earned himself a large fortune, by bellhop standards, and Morris began its long climb to the top of the cigarette world. Sales of English Blend were strong from its introduction in January of 1933, helping Morris to triple its net income—to $1.5 million—in a single year and by 1935 to challenge Lorillard as the fourth-largest cigarette maker in the United States. Ellis and McKitterick were both deceased by 1936, but under new chairman Alfred Lyon the company continued its rise, in that year selling 7.5 billion cigarettes and laying firm hold on the industry's number four spot. Morris was viewed as something of a phenomenon, its combination of marketing expertise and jobber loyalty enabling it to take market share from much larger and wealthier cigarette leaders such as American Tobacco and Reynolds. Lyon personally directed the construction of what quickly became the industry's largest and most effective sales force; although Morris's special relationship with jobbers did not last long—supermarkets proving to be the wave of the future—it remained a company fueled by its expertise in sales and marketing.

By 1939 sales had reached $64 million, and World War II soon put even more pressure on cigarette production. When Morris's sales doubled by 1942, Lyon and company president Otway Chalkey began casting about for some means to expand capacity, especially difficult given the fact that tobacco needed to be cured several years before its use in cigarette production. When Axton-Fisher Tobacco Company of Louisville, Kentucky, was put up for sale in 1945, Morris paid a premium price—$20 million—to win its large stores of tobacco and a second manufacturing plant. The move looked good until the war's end in August of that year precipitated a huge drop in

Key Dates:

1847: Philip Morris opens a tobacco shop in London.
1911: The U.S. tobacco cartel is dissolved by a court order.
1919: George J. Whelan purchases the U.S. business of the Philip Morris Company and forms a new company to manage its assets—Philip Morris & Company Ltd. Inc.
1925: The Marlboro cigarette is introduced.
1931: Reuben M. Ellis and Leonard B. McKitterick gain control of Morris.
1933: The Philip Morris English Blend cigarette is launched.
1936: The company sells 7.5 billion cigarettes and operates as the 4th largest manufacturer in the industry.
1945: The Axton-Fisher Tobacco Company of Kentucky is acquired; cigarette consumption drops after the end of World War II.
1955: The Marlboro brand is reinvented with an "American Cowboy" theme.
1957: Joseph Cullman III takes over management of the company.
1960: George Weissman—credited for making Morris the leading exporter of tobacco products in the U.S.—is named director of international operations.
1970: The company acquires Miller Brewing.

1975: Morris introduces the Merit cigarette brand signaling the firm's entrance into the low-tar market.
1976: Marlboro becomes the leading brand in the U.S.; Morris operates as the largest seller of tobacco in the U.S. and the second largest in the world.
1985: The firm acquires General Foods Corporation in a $5.75 billion deal.
1988: Morris continues to diversify its holdings and purchases Kraft Inc. for $12.9 billion.
1990: Jacobs Suchard, a Swiss maker of coffee and chocolate, is acquired.
1995: Geoffrey C. Bible is named chairman and CEO of Morris.
1997: Stock price plummets amid smoking-related lawsuits and nicotine manipulation allegations.
1998: The tobacco industry forms a settlement with 46 states and agrees to pay out nearly $206 billion over the next 25 years to cover tobacco-related claims and lawsuits; it also agrees to advertising and marketing restrictions related to tobacco.
1999: Morris launches its Web site and admits that smoking can cause lung cancer and other diseases.
2000: The company acquires Nabisco Holdings Corp. for $19.2 billion.
2001: Kraft goes public in the second largest IPO to date.

cigarette consumption, a cut in sales made more painful by Morris's overestimation of peacetime demand. Many of the company's biggest orders in the fall of 1945 were left to grow stale on retail racks, and net income plummeted just as Morris was attempting to float a new bond issue at the end of the year. The company withdrew the offering and suffered a certain amount of embarrassment, but its underlying business was sound and Morris soon bounced back. A massive 1948 advertising campaign claiming that English Blend did not cause "cigarette hangover," a previously unknown disorder, led to a fresh gain in market share and profit.

Repositioning During the 1950s

Despite Morris's success with such advertising claims, the company somehow failed to foresee the most important new development in the cigarette business in many years: the introduction of milder and less harmful filtered cigarettes. Unlike Morris's version of mildness, filtered cigarettes were indisputably less damaging to the throat, and increased public awareness of smoking's real health dangers spurred a rapid shift to filters in the 1950s. Morris was slow to recognize the importance of this innovation, and it was not until 1955 that the company repositioned its old filter entry, Marlboro, as a cigarette with broad appeal by working the myth of the American cowboy into the product's marketing strategy. It took time, however, for the new Marlboro image to take hold, and by 1960 Morris had slipped to sixth and last place among major U.S. tobacco companies, its bestselling entry able to do no better than tenth among the leading brands. It appeared that changing consumer preference had left Morris well out of the new era in tobacco.

Morris had at least three cards yet to play, however. One was the emergence in 1957 of a marketing tactician capable of resurrecting the glory days of Alfred Lyon. Joseph Cullman III took over management of the company in 1957 and guided its amazing growth over the course of the following two decades, much of it earned in the international market. Morris was perhaps the earliest, and ultimately the most successful, U.S. tobacco company to foresee the potential sales growth in the worldwide cigarette business. In 1960, Cullman appointed George Weissman as director of international operations; the company's second greatest resource, Weissman is generally credited with making Morris the United States' leading exporter of tobacco products. The company's ace in the hole was the Marlboro Man, who would prove in the long run to be one of the most successful advertising icons ever created. For whatever combination of reasons—nostalgia for the Old West, clever packaging, tobacco taste—Marlboro almost singlehandedly raised Morris from also-ran to industrial leader during the next quarter century.

While Cullman attended to Morris's resurgence in the tobacco business, he also began the first of many attempts to diversify the company's assets, thereby rendering it less dependent on a product that was gradually becoming known as a serious health hazard. In the mid-1950s Morris bought into the flexible packaging and paper manufacturing trades, and in the early 1960s it added American Safety Razor, Burma Shave, and Clark chewing gum, hoping in each case to use Morris's existing distributor network and marketing experience to sell a wider variety of consumer products. None of these early acquisitions proved to be of great value, with the possible exception of its packaging division, not sold until the mid-1980s. Then, in 1970 the company added Miller Brewing to its holdings. Miller was then only the seventh-largest brewer in the United States, but the combination of a repositioned High Life beer and the introduction of the United States' first low-calorie beer, Miller Lite, brought the company all the way up to number two by 1980. On the other hand, Morris's 1978 purchase of the Seven-Up Company for $520 million was little more than a disaster: after several failed advertising campaigns the soft drink manufacturer was sold in the mid-1980s.

Marlboro's Rise to Superbrand Status: 1960s–70s

In the meantime, the Marlboro Man was running wild, carrying Morris up the ranks of cigarette makers with astonishing speed. Throughout the 1960s Marlboro registered yearly leaps in popularity, especially among the growing segment of younger smokers. By 1973, it was the second most popular cigarette brand in the United States and accounted for roughly two-thirds of Morris's tobacco business. In 1976, it moved past Reynolds's Winston as the leader with 94 billion cigarettes sold that year, helping Morris to become the United States' and the world's second-largest seller of tobacco. In 1961, Morris had controlled 9.4 percent of the market; in 1976 that figure topped 25 percent and continued to rise. With all other competitors in a slump, Morris and Reynolds together controlled well more than half the market. The two leaders thus found themselves in a very comfortable position: growing health concerns about smoking made it unlikely that any new competitor would join the tobacco business, and the need for massive, effective advertising made it difficult for the current competition to maintain its position. The net result was abnormally large profits for the two leaders, especially as their dominance of the market really took hold in the 1980s and they were able to raise prices frequently without fear of being undercut.

Complementing Marlboro's success was the emergence of new fields for Morris. The 1975, introduction of Merit brand signaled Morris's entry into the new low-tar market, a category that would mushroom as U.S. smokers became increasingly concerned with the deleterious effects of inhaling cigarette smoke. The company also began to focus increased marketing dollars on its premium brands, which produced greater profits per pack sold. Meanwhile, under the guidance of Weissman, the company's international business greatly expanded. While the U.S. cigarette market was flat in the 1970s and in retreat by the mid-1980s, international business continued to grow rapidly, and Marlboro soon ranked as the world's bestselling cigarette. That trend would continue through the following decade under the leadership of worldwide tobacco vice president Geoffrey C. Bible.

Morris's response to increasing U.S. controversy over smoking was to sell cigarettes with lower tar, meanwhile promoting all of its brands overseas where relatively less sophisticated consumers cared little about the health risks involved. In 1993, it cut the price of its Marlboro brand in an effort to gain an increased share of a sluggish market. Unfortunately none of these strategies went to the heart of the company's fundamental problem: the association of tobacco with lung disease. By the mid-1990s Morris had become embroiled in the rash of product liability lawsuits spawned by fifth-ranked Liggett's settlement of a class-action

legal action in March 1996. The company was plagued by allegations that it had knowingly suppressed the harmful side-effects of smoking from consumers, and repeatedly made headlines as several former employees—some of them scientists—accused Morris of suppressing knowledge of the addictive quality of nicotine, manipulating levels of the drug in its Marlboro brand, and deliberately courting teenage smokers. In 1996, amid reports of Morris's third-quarter combined tobacco earnings of $2.23 billion and the announcement of a 20 percent increase in its annual stock dividend rate, came the announcement that the FDA planned to regulate the tobacco industry and restrict tobacco-related advertising. While Morris responded with a countersuit in an attempt to block the FDA ruling, the late 1990s were marked by increased litigation and falling share prices as investors grew leery of the tobacco industry.

1985: The General Foods Acquisition

Meanwhile, to ensure its own safety, Morris had begun to diversify its holdings away from tobacco. In 1985, even as it passed Reynolds to become the largest domestic cigarette manufacturer, the company paid $5.75 billion for General Foods Corporation, the diversified food products giant. General Foods was large enough to offer Morris a significant source of revenue apart from the tobacco industry, and its reliance on advertising and an intricate distribution system was similar to Morris's core business; but General Foods was a rather lackluster company in a mature industry, and the acquisition did not kindle great enthusiasm among business analysts. They compared it unfavorably to Reynolds's purchase of Nabisco Brands at about the same time, and predicted that the move would not be sufficient to free Morris of its tobacco habit. In 1987, for example, two years after the General Foods purchase, Morris's total revenue had reached $27.7 billion and its operating income $4.1 billion. The lion's share of that income—$2.7 billion—was earned by the domestic tobacco division, where the slackening of competition allowed a luxurious rate of return on its $7.6 billion in sales. By contrast, General Foods's $10 billion contribution to revenue netted only $700 million in operating income, meaning that it was fully five times as profitable to sell a pack of Marlboros than it was to sell a box of Jell-O or a jar of coffee from General Foods. Indeed, 60 percent of Morris's total profit for 1987 was generated by Marlboro's popularity both at home and abroad.

In 1988, the company took a more decisive step toward reshaping its corporate profile. For $12.9 billion it acquired Kraft, Inc., an even larger and more dynamic food products corporation. Morris chairman Hamish Maxwell merged his company's two food divisions into Kraft Foods, Inc. Under its chief executive officer, Michael Miles, Kraft underwent a successful program of labor cuts and efficiency measures designed to raise its earnings level to something approaching that of the tobacco division. With $27 billion in sales by 1995, and more than 2,800 different product offerings, Kraft ranked as the world's second-largest food company. Within this conglomeration was Post which, as the third-ranking U.S. producer of breakfast cereal, instigated a cereal price war in mid-1996. In a bold attempt to gain market share and stay the rising consumer boycott of pricey breakfast cereals, prices on Post brands were slashed across the board in April, pushing number one producer Kellogg to reluctantly follow suit.

A low inflation rate coupled with an increasing consumer demand for low prices characterized the first half of the 1990s. Such a combination prompted downsizing, loss of jobs, and a search for new markets on the part of many in the food industry. Paralleling its success in expanding its tobacco market, Morris extended its food merchandising infrastructure worldwide. Under its Kraft Foods International division, new markets were established in Europe, South America, and the Asia/Pacific region. Morris also expanded its holdings overseas, buying Jacobs Suchard, a Swiss maker of coffee and chocolate for $4.1 billion in 1990; four years later it purchased confectionery companies in Russia and the Ukraine, as well as making inroads into the Chinese market through several joint ventures. By 1995, international revenues—$32 billion—exceeded North American revenues—$31.4 billion—for the first time in the firm's history.

A World Leader in Packaged Consumer Goods: The 1990s

The success of Kraft and Miller, coupled with Morris's still highly profitable tobacco market, has made Morris the world's largest producer and marketer—as well as the largest U.S. exporter—of packaged consumer goods. In fact, by the early 1990s, substantially more than half of the company's revenue was generated by non-tobacco products. One of the contributors was Miller Brewing's $3.5 billion in sales. Retaining its spot as the second-largest competitor in its field, Miller managed to successfully hold its market share in the face of a changing beer market and a 100 percent increase in the beer tax levied by the U.S. government in 1991. The rise in the number of small-scale "craft" breweries and changing demographics caused a slump in the beer market nationwide; along with number-one ranked Anheuser-Busch and number three-ranked Coors, Miller responded by entering the microbrewery market with its Red Dog and Icehouse brands, as well as by purchasing shares in small breweries in Maine and Texas. Despite heavily marketing its "lite" beers to the Baby Boomer market, Miller's 3rd quarter 1996 income fell 1.7 percent and the company responded by cutting operating costs.

By the close of 1995 Morris's portfolio of brands included 68 that reported sales of over $100 million. Of those 68, six non-tobacco products—Kraft, Miller, Jacobs, Oscar Mayer, Maxwell House, and Post—passed the $1 billion mark. New marketing efforts included revised Marlboro and Virginia Slims merchandise catalogs and a sweepstakes for trips on the "Marlboro Unlimited," a luxury train scheduled to tour Marlboro country in 1998. Although the company's leadership continued to reject plans to divest Morris of its tobacco holdings, because of such successful diversification efforts, Morris planned to continue using the extraordinary cash flow generated by its domestic tobacco sales to finance further moves into the food industry, where the relatively low rate of return could be eventually compensated by means of sheer size.

A Shift in Corporate Image: Late 1990s and Beyond

Indeed, the company's foothold in the food industry continued to become even stronger during the latter half of the 1990s. Under the leadership of Bible—elected chairman and CEO 1995—Morris continued its growth while working diligently to clean up its corporate image. In late 1996, the company agreed to some of the restrictions in marketing and advertising set forth by the FDA, as long as the FDA agreed not to regulate the industry. At the time, the company was involved in nearly 180 smoking-related lawsuits.

The following year, the U.S. tobacco industry reached the Tobacco Settlement Agreement with 46 states in which $206 billion would be paid out over the next 25 years to cover Medicaid-related costs and tobacco-related claims and lawsuits. The settlement also included restrictions on marketing and advertising of tobacco products. In 1999, the company established its Web site on which it stated—for the first time—that smoking could cause lung cancer and various other diseases. The company continued to downplay its tobacco businesses in the media, instead focusing on its Kraft and Miller units. The *United Press International* commented on the strategy in 1999, stating that the moves were "seen as part of the entire tobacco industry's attempts to lessen their legal liabilities. There is an opinion that by admitting to smoking's risks in a public way, future plaintiffs cannot claim they were unaware of the potential dangers of tobacco use." Morris then announced in 2000 that it was pulling more than $100 million in cigarette advertising in more than 50 national publications that had an 18-and-under readership base of over 15 percent. In 1999, Morris accounted for nearly half of all cigarette advertising in magazines.

During the Clinton administration's last year, the Department of Justice filed a healthcare cost recovery suit against the tobacco industry, seeking restitution for expenses related to treating people with problems caused by smoking. In September 2000, however, a federal district judge dismissed a large portion of the case. In fact, when the Bush administration took office in 2001, many analysts felt that the litigation and frequent tax increases would lessen under Republican leadership. Morris also appealed the much-publicized Engle class action case in Florida that delivered a $146 billion verdict and was optimistic that the case would be dismissed due to errors made by the judge during the trial.

While Morris spent much of its effort cleaning up its tainted tobacco image, the company was making giant strides in the food industry. From 1992 to 1997, Kraft's profit margin had increased to 16 percent—one of the highest in the food industry. The unit also controlled 35 percent of the frozen food market, after the successful 1995 launch of DiGiorno Rising Crust pizza, and continued to be the market leader in many of its product segments.

Morris secured its number two position in the global food industry in 2000 with the purchase of Nabisco Holdings Corp. The $19.2 billion acquisition created a $34.9 billion food concern and gave Kraft an entrance into the fast-growing snack foods segment with products like Oreo cookies and Ritz crackers. Management also eyed the deal as a means of reducing costs related to purchasing, manufacturing, distribution, sales, and administration, and expected to save nearly $600 million by 2003. Kraft also acquired Boca Foods and Balance Bar energy and nutrition snack products that year.

In June 2001, Kraft began operating as a publicly traded company when Morris spun off 16 percent of the firm, retaining

84 percent ownership and 98 percent of its voting rights. The public offering generated $8.7 billion and was the second-largest IPO to date. Kraft became the largest publicly traded food company in North America whose brands could be found in over 99 percent of U.S. homes.

After the tough litigation problems of the 1990s, Morris appeared to be stronger then ever in the new millennium. The firm's share price rose over 90 percent in 2000—the best performance in the Dow Jones—signaling that investors who were once leery about the firm were now enticed by the company's strong performance. Morris continued to gain market share in many of its product categories, and while the American economy slowed, company management remained optimistic knowing that Morris had historically performed well during economic downturns. The firm's legal battles seemed to be slowing as well as fewer individual cases were tried during 2000 than in the previous year. As the company looked to be on track for future growth, Morris management remained confident that it would continue its market dominance in the years to come.

Principal Subsidiaries

Philip Morris U.S.A.; Philip Morris International Inc.; Kraft Foods, Inc.; Kraft Canada Inc.; Kraft Foods International, Inc.; Miller Brewing Company; Philip Morris Capital Corporation.

Principal Competitors

Anheuser-Busch Companies Inc.; British American Tobacco p.l.c.; Nestlé S.A.

Further Reading

Fine, Jon, and Ira Teinowitz, "Magazines, RJR Fuming Over Philip Morris Ad Pull," *Advertising Age*, June 12, 2000, p. 3.

Fitzgerald, Nora, "Smoke Filled Rooms," *Adweek Eastern Edition*, July 1, 1996, p. 19.

Gallun, Alby, "Key Ingredient in Kraft's IPO: Philip Morris," *Crain's Chicago Business*, April 2, 2001, p. 1.

Hughes, Alan, "Why Philip Morris' Shares Are Smokin'," *Business Week*, December 27, 2000.

Isidore, Chris, "Lawsuit Settlements Take Toll on Philip Morris Stock Price," *Crain's New York Business*, May 18, 1998, p. 4.

Moore, Paula, "Cigarette Giant Tries to Fix Woes," *Denver Business Journal*, March 28, 1997, p. 3A.

Nulty, Peter, "Living with the Limits of Marlboro Magic," *Fortune*, March 18, 1985.

"Philip Morris & Co.," *Fortune*, March 1936.

"Philip Morris Admits Smoking-Cancer Link," *United Press International*, October 13, 1999.

"Philip Morris Comeback," *Fortune*, October 1949.

"Philip Morris to Acquire Nabisco, Sealing Kraft Foods' Spot As World's No. 2 Food Company," *Food Institute Report*, July 3, 2000, p. 9.

"Philip Morris to Put Its Ad Money Where Its Marlboro Price Cuts Are," *Wall Street Journal*, April 6, 1993.

"Philip Morris Proposes Curbs on Sales to Kids," *Wall Street Journal*, May 16, 1996.

"Philip Morris Realigns Its Int'l Food Business, Unveils Changes," *Nation's Restaurant News*, January 1, 1996, p. 62.

"Philip Morris' Responsible Approach to Tobacco," *Chain Drug Review*, June 19, 2000, p. 228.

Shook, David, "Philip Morris Serves Comfort Food to Investors," *Business Week*, May 22, 2001.

"Tobacco Wars-Blowing Smoke," *U.S. News & World Report*, March 13, 2000, p. 11.

—Jonathan Martin
—updates: Pamela L. Shelton and
Christina M. Stansell

Real learning. Real results.™

Plato Learning, Inc.

10801 Nesbitt Avenue South
Bloomington, Minnesota 55437
U.S.A.
Telephone: (952) 832-1000
Toll Free: (800) 869-2000
Fax: (952) 832-1200
Web site: http://www.plato.com

Public Company
Incorporated: 1989 as The Roach Organization, Inc.
Employees: 376
Sales: $56.11 million (2000)
Stock Exchanges: NASDAQ
Ticker Symbol: TUTR
NAIC: 511199 All Other Publishers

Plato Learning, Inc. is a developer of interactive, computer-based educational and training products for the K-12 and adult markets. The company's courseware, which includes instruction in reading, writing, math, science, life skills, and career skills, is marketed to school systems, colleges, job-training programs, the military, and correctional facilities, as well as to corporations and individual consumers. Its courses are delivered to users via local area networks, intranets, CD-ROMS, or the Internet.

1960s–70s: Roots in Academia

The company that is today called Plato Learning traces its roots back to the University of Illinois. In the early 1960s, at that university's Urbana campus, electrical engineering professor Don Bitzer and physics professor Chalmers Sherwin became intrigued by the idea of using computers for teaching. Operating on grant money from the National Science Foundation, the two men designed and developed the nation's first computer-based education system, which they called PLATO—an acronym for "Programmed Logic for Automatic Teaching Operations." PLATO was a time-sharing program, which meant that multiple users with individual terminals were networked to a central mainframe, allowing for simultaneous use of the system.

The PLATO system soon captured the attention of William Norris, the innovative and progressive leader of Control Data Corp. Norris and a group of associates had founded Control Data in 1957 to design and build extremely powerful, high-speed computers—including the world's first "supercomputer" designed by Seymour Cray. The company, headquartered in Bloomington, Minneapolis, had rapidly diversified into other aspects of the computing industry, designing and producing software and peripheral equipment. When Norris learned about the University of Illinois's research in computer-based learning, he gave the program one of Control Data's large, powerful computers. He also arranged for his company to test the PLATO programs as they were developed.

PLATO continued to evolve throughout the 1960s and 1970s. Whereas the original system could support only a single classroom of users, in the early 1970s PLATO was migrated to a larger-scale mainframe environment that allowed for hundreds of simultaneous users. In addition, in 1973 the system was enhanced by a communications system called Notes. Notes—which allowed students to communicate with each other, both one-to-one and in groups—was the forerunner to today's electronic communities.

In 1976, Control Data obtained the rights to the PLATO system, with plans to sell it to elementary and secondary schools. Such sales failed to materialize, however; at the time, most public and private schools lacked the resources and education necessary to purchase and implement the program. Control Data turned its focus to the adult literacy, remedial learning, job welfare, and job training markets, investing millions of dollars in PLATO to build up the necessary curricula for these new customers. The change in focus produced slightly better results, but still the system never really took off as Norris had hoped.

Late 1980s: Enter Bill Roach

In September of 1989, Control Data sold its training and education group—and along with it, the PLATO system—to William R. Roach. By that time, the business consisted of not only PLATO Education Services, providing K-12 computer-based curricula, but also PLATO Professional Testing & Certification Services, which provided certification services to the real estate, securities, and other industries. Also included was an aviation training business, which provided computer-based training courses to pilots, maintenance staff, and flight crews of commercial airlines and the military.

Plato's new owner, Roach, had previously been president of Applied Learning International, a subsidiary of National Education Corp. Resigning from Applied Learning in 1988, he formed his own company, Edu Corp., to acquire training and education companies. When he purchased the Control Data group for $20 million, he created a subsidiary of Edu Corp. to house it. The subsidiary was called The Roach Organization.

Despite the fact that Control Data had failed to make a go of the PLATO system, Roach had high hopes for it. In an April 1990 interview with the Minneapolis *Star-Tribune*, he said, "We expect to nearly double revenues in our first year, and we're looking for a strong profit as well." Roach believed that PLATO's sluggish sales under Control Data resulted simply from a lack of proper marketing. His opinion was not without a basis; Control Data *had* failed to make good connections with its customer base. When Roach bought PLATO, many potential customers—lacking accurate, current information on the product—wrongly believed that the system was outmoded and outstripped by more modern applications. For example, many believed that the system still ran on a mainframe when in actuality, it had been delivered on PCs, via local area networks, since 1986.

However, The Roach Organization most emphatically did not show a "strong profit" in its first year; rather, it lost some $12 million. This resulted primarily from Roach's decision to invest heavily in the K-12 segment of the business—a move designed to shift the company away from adult literacy and remedial programs and back toward programs that could be integrated into standard school curriculum. This approach was both a huge challenge and a huge opportunity, since PLATO was by no means widely accepted in the mainstream school market. In 1990, the system was installed in only 50 schools.

In 1992, it began to appear that Roach's strategy had been the right one. The company posted a net profit of $3.9 million for that year, even in the face of a severe decline in the testing and certification segment of the business. That same year, the company went public, changing its name to TRO Learning Inc.

Mid-1990s: Difficult Years

Selling off its lagging testing business, TRO continued to be profitable in 1993. The company posted earnings of $4.6 mil-

lion—up 18 percent from the previous year. Encouraged by its success, TRO continued to invest in upgrading the PLATO courseware. The years between 1992 and 1995 were spent redesigning its core curricula. Major changes included a range of instructional improvements; a new user interface with graphics-based function buttons; and new graphics and animation designed to both appeal to the target audience and contribute to learning objectives.

But the mid-1990s ushered in new troubles for the company. Since 1990, the commercial airlines industry—one of TRO's main customers—had been suffering a near-devastating downturn, racking up billions in losses industrywide. Many carriers filed for bankruptcy protection while others cut thousands of jobs in an effort just to stay afloat. As the losses in the airline industry trickled down to its tiers of suppliers, TRO felt the impact. Revenues generated by its aviation training business dropped precipitously—and the company's net earnings followed suit. By 1996, profits were down to $980,000, and in 1997, the company suffered a $20 million loss.

Roach knew drastic measures were in order. One of the first steps he took was to call in help—in the form of John Murray, the head of TRO's UK operation. Murray had been with TRO since Roach formed it; prior to that, he had headed up Control Data Corp.'s London-based training service. When Roach asked him to move to the United States, and subsequently appointed him senior vice-president of operations, it marked the beginning of a restructuring for TRO.

The company made a number of changes over the course of 1997 and 1998, many of them designed to revamp its sales and support operations. By weeding out redundant systems and making better use of order-processing technologies, it was able to reduce its marketing and sales staff by approximately 19 percent. It cut its support staff even more deeply, eliminating around 25 percent of those positions. The company also began offering clients a new fee-based service and support program, which included training, installation, and technical support for the PLATO products. This created a new $2.5 million income stream.

A more drastic restructuring measure came in the fall of 1998, when TRO sold its aviation training business to the United Kingdom-based VEGA Group. This left the company with a single focus: the PLATO education system.

In addition to cost-cutting measures, TRO—which had previously delivered its courses primarily though local area networks or CD-ROMs—began angling for a piece of the growing online learning market. In the spring of 1997, the company partnered with BC TEL Interactive, a British telephone company, to distribute PLATO courseware via the Internet to students in British Columbia. The agreement provided for not just a distribution channel, but a sales channel as well; BC TEL account managers were commissioned to actively market the courseware as part of their Internet service offerings. In late 1997, the company signed a similar agreement with BellSouth, providing for sales and delivery of PLATO courses on the Internet in the nine-state BellSouth service area. Under the arrangement, customers—either individuals or schools—could purchase courses online through BellSouth's Education Gateway site and have them immediately downloaded or shipped in CD-ROM form.

Late 1990s: Turnaround

By the end of fiscal 1998, the company began to show signs of turning around. Demand for the PLATO system had increased, with sales of courseware and related services climbing to $39.4 million—up $8.8 million, or nearly 30 percent, in just three years. The company also managed to post a profit of $3 million—a not insignificant feat, given the previous year's $20 million loss.

Sales continued to increase in 1999, growing to $44.1 million by year-end. The steady growth was partially attributable to a series of strategic partnerships that provided new sales channels. For example, in late 1999, the company partnered with Sylvan Learning Centers to provide PLATO courses throughout the more than 750 Sylvan learning centers. It also partnered with the Provo, Utah-based Brain Garden, a direct seller of nutritional and educational products. The agreement allowed Brain Garden to market PLATO software through its sales network.

Other sales initiatives focused on a newly introduced product: single-topic PLATO courses. The initial single-topic library contained 66 titles, each of which could be purchased individually and delivered either over the Internet or in CD-ROM form. Previously TRO had sold its courseware as entire, integrated curricula. The single-topic courses broadened the company's pool of potential customers considerably, to include individual users who needed reinforcement only in certain academic areas, as well as small, rural school markets who lacked the financing or capability to implement entire curricula. To market these new courses, TRO allied with click2learn.com, a portal site and online catalog dedicated to lifelong learning and education. Simultaneously, the company developed its own e-commerce site through which to direct-sell its single-topic offerings.

The company ended the 1900s on a high note by winning the largest courseware agreement in its history. The deal, finalized in December of 1999, contracted TRO to provide curriculum, along with ten years of professional services, to all the schools in Glasgow, Scotland. One of a consortium of companies—including equipment providers and telecommunications companies—chosen to build the Glasgow network, TRO expected its part of the project to be worth approximately $6 million.

Moving into the New Century

TRO kicked off 2000 with two major announcements—the first involving a change in identity, and the second a change in leadership. On January 5, 2000, the company announced that it would be changing its name to PLATO Learning, to more fully leverage the reputation and recognition of its long-held brand name. Just days later, the soon-to-be-renamed TRO announced the appointment of John Murray to the position of president and chief operating officer. Ten months later, he was also appointed CEO as William Roach retired completely from the day-to-day operations of the company.

More changes were in the offing. In July 2000, PLATO Learning made its first acquisition, buying the Paradise, California-based CyberEd, Inc. for $4.8 million. CyberEd was a provider of science courseware for high schools. With the acquisition, PLATO added approximately 45 new science titles to its library of single-topic courses. The company also planned to integrated CyberEd's course materials into its comprehensive PLATO curricula.

By the end of 2000, PLATO was installed in approximately 5,000 schools—and it was preparing to make a move that would increase its presence by almost one-third. In January 2001, the company announced that it was acquiring Wasatch Interactive Learning Corporation, a Salt Lake City provider of computer-based curricula for K-8 education. Wasatch's products were used in more than 1,500 U.S. schools. It also carried a line of supplementary courseware for the adult education market. When the acquisition was completed in April, the combined companies had more than 10,000 education clients.

Looking Ahead

Midway through the first year of the new century, it appeared that PLATO had positioned itself for future growth and success. With its acquisitions finalized and its expanded customer base solidly in place, the company was turning its focus to what John Murray believed would be the next big thing in computer-delivered education: online, subscription-based products. PLATO had already begun preparing to capture a share of that emerging market. Early in 2001, it had released a web applications platform and simulated test system—products that allowed all of the company's content to be delivered online in a web browser curriculum manager. The company planned to begin offering those two new products to school districts on a subscription basis in order to begin building a subscription-based revenue stream.

The company anticipated that it would remain focused on the K-12 market in the short-term future. In a February 2001 interview with *The Wall Street Transcript*, John Murray said that the company's plan for the ensuing 18 to 24 months was to "continue to sell our core products to the same core markets." As part of its effort to do so more effectively and on a larger scale, in August 2001 PLATO formed a strategic sales group dedicated to pursuing large contracts with states and with the nation's biggest school districts.

Principal Subsidiaries

Lab One Canada Inc.; ExamOne World Wide, Inc.; Systematic Business Services, Inc.

Principal Competitors

Hooper Holmes, Inc.; Laboratory Corporation of America Holdings; Quest Diagnostics Incorporated; American Bio Med-ica Corporation; ChoicePoint Inc.; Employee Information Services, Inc.; Kroll Laboratory Specialists, Inc.; Medtox Scientific, Inc.; PharmChem, Inc.; Psychemedics Corporation.

Further Reading

Cruz, Sherri, "Plato a Happy Not-Com," *Minneapolis Star-Tribune*, October 9, 2000, p. 1D.
"John Murrary, Plato Learning, CEO Interview," *The Wall Street Transcript*, February 19, 2001.
Youngblood, Dick, "Life after CDC: Plato Finds Profit," *Minneapolis Star-Tribune*, April 2, 1990, p. 1D.
——, "TRO Learning Right Itself, Finds Earning Curve," *Minneapolis Star-Tribune*, July 4, 1999, p. 3D.

—Shawna Brynildssen

Poore Brothers, Inc.

3500 South La Cometa Drive
Goodyear, Arizona 85338
U.S.A.
Telephone: (623) 932-6200
Fax: (623) 925-2363
Web site: http://www.poorebrothers.com

Public Company
Incorporated: 1995
Employees: 190
Sales: $41.8 million (2000)
Stock Exchange: NASDAQ
Ticker Symbol: SNAK
NAIC: 42245 Confectionery Wholesalers; 55112 Offices
of Other Holding Companies

Poore Brothers, Inc., with headquarters in Phoenix, Arizona, makes snack, party chips, and dips. and markets them under various brand names: Poore Brothers, Bob's Texas Style, Boulder Potato Company, Tato Skins, and Pizzarias. The company also makes salty snacks under a license from T.G.I. Friday's and produces items for grocery chains in Arizona and California under their store-brand names. In addition, it distributes its own products and those of some other snack-food companies in parts of Texas and throughout Arizona. Its products in its southwestern markets can be bought in food stores and from vending machines.

1986–87: Poore Brothers Foods
Faces Tough Competition

Brothers Don and Jay Poore founded Poore Brothers Foods, in 1986, after selling an interest in a profitable Texas potato chip manufacturing operation, Groff's of Texas, Inc., that they had started in 1983. Before founding Groff's, the brothers had worked over 13 years for Mira-Pak, Inc., a manufacturer of potato chip packaging equipment.

The brothers decided that they again wanted to strike out on their own, opening a new business in Arizona. They had the knowhow for making kettle-cooked potato chips, and they knew a great deal about the chip packaging trade. They also believed that they could parlay their experience into a new and successful business venture.

The Poores opened their Goodyear, Arizona, potato chip factory in December of 1986. They also formed Poore Brothers Texas in 1986, created to provide distribution capabilities for their chips. Convinced that they could succeed by virtue of their product quality, the Poores did not bother to undertake any market or product research. They found it tough going initially, mainly because even their Arizona market, to which they at first restricted themselves, was already flooded with chips made by mass producers of nationally known brands. At the end of their first month, they had only sold $1,500 worth of chips, mostly to Christmas shoppers who were enticed not so much by the Poores' chips, initially marketed under the Arizona Select brand, but by the decorative tins in which the brothers packaged them.

When the initial market shock wore off, the Poores struggled to convince area grocers to carry their line of chips. Their flavors helped some, but it was still very slow going. Sales through the end of 1987 had reached only $340,000, which resulted in a net loss of $100,000, putting the shoestring business at grave risk. The Poores persisted, though, and within a couple of years their company turned the corner financially.

Growth of Company Leads the Poores
to Sell PB Foods

New marketing strategies helped. Late in 1988, the Poores introduced 1-ounce bags of chips for machine vending, a move that produced good results. Sales in 1988 rose to $1.5 million, then increased to $2.15 million the next year. By 1990, the operation was selling about 12 percent of all potato chips marketed in Arizona, ranking fourth behind Frito-Lay Inc., Clover Club, and Laura Scudders. The brothers had also founded Poore Brothers Distributing Co. and considerably expanded their product line to include such flavors as salt and vinegar, barbecue, sour cream and onion, Parmesan and garlic, dill pickle, and chili lemon. Gross sales for that year were expected to reach close to $3 million. Significantly, too, by 1990 the

Company Perspectives:

We will achieve $100 million in revenues by keeping associates, consumers, customers, shareholders, and suppliers reaching for more by continuously improving the quality of our four cornerstones to success. Intensely Different Associates: *We are talented, upbeat team players who thrive on delivering superior results. We come to work everyday to make a difference by embracing and leading constant innovation and positive change.* Intensely Different Brands: *Our key objective is to delight consumers with fun, premium quality brands that are better, different, and special. We contribute to category growth by consistently marketing consumer preferred snacking experiences not found anywhere else.* Intensely Different Customer Service: *We create "raving fans" of our brands and our Company by doing what we say we're going to do with a smile and a thank you! Our Associates strive to build "win-win" business partnerships.* Intensely Different Financial Responsibility: *We invest wisely to pursue rapid revenue and profit growth that enhances shareholder value."*

company had begun extending its market range beyond Arizona, making their product available through distributors in Minnesota, New Mexico, Southern California, and Texas.

In 1993, Mark S. Howells and some associates formed PB Southeast. That company acquired a license from PB Foods to manufacture and market Poore Brothers branded products. In the following year, PB Southeast opened a manufacturing plant in LaVergne, Tennessee, and before the end of year Howells and his directors entered negotiations with the Poores to buy out PB Foods. By 1994, the growth of PB Foods had forced some rethinking about how the company should be managed. Don and Jay Poore had in fact decided that their hands-on style of operating the business was no longer suitable, thus they amicably entered the sale negotiations with PB Southeast. The $4.05 million deal was consummated in May 1995.

Under the new owners, Poore Brothers was reorganized and incorporated. Restructured, it had four operating subsidiaries, all of which were acquired at the time of the sale. Two of the subsidiaries—Poore Brothers Arizona, Inc. and Poore Brothers Southeast, Inc.—were manufacturing companies. The other two—Poore Brothers Distributing, Inc. and Poore Brothers of Texas, Inc.—were distribution companies. Don and Jay Poore continued to work at the Goodyear plant, making sure that the operation ran smoothly and that product quality was maintained.

New Owners Take Company Public before Confronting Financial Woes

In 1996, the company went public and made its initial public offering (IPO) in December of that year, setting the price of its common stock at $3.50 per share. The offering raised approximately $7 million, giving it necessary capital for undertaking both expansion and diversification. The company's chief strategy, reiterated through the next few years, was to grow through acquisitions, but the company also set out to market new prod-

ucts, something it also undertook in 1996. Using a new technology, Poore Brothers launched a new line of fat-free chips. Basing its optimistic expectations on the national mania over fat-free foods, the company anticipated that the line might soon double its annual sales, which, at the time, had reached $17.2 million. However, things did not pan out as planned and the company discontinued the line in 1997.

In February of that year, the company's operational reins were passed on to Eric J. Kufel, who assumed the posts of CEO and president. Just prior to taking those positions, he was serving as the senior brand manager at The Dial Corporation, where he was responsible for the performance of the Purex brand laundry detergent. He also brought other managerial experience from positions he had previously held with Coca-Cola and Kellogg, where he had also specialized in developing marketing plans for both new and established products, the kind of expertise needed to help Poore Brothers develop new markets and expand in its existing ones.

Kufel faced serious problems. Despite going public and developing its growth strategies, including its new products, Poore Brothers suffered financial woes for years after the exchange of ownership. Its annual revenues dropped off and the company operated in the red. In 1997, it lost $3 million on revenues of $15.7 million, and in 1998 it lost $874,090 on revenues of $13.2 million. However, the losses did not prevent investors from backing the company. They saw the company's potential to grow sales and acquire and integrate new business. Accordingly, under Kufel's direction, Poore Brothers set out to purchase other companies, beginning in 1998, when, for an undisclosed amount, it bought Tejas Snacks LP. At the time, that company's Tejas' Bob's Texas Style Potato Chips was a market leader in the $100 million Texas potato chip industry

Growth Through Acquisition, Partnering, and Product Line Extension

Poore Brothers, Inc. continued its growth through acquisition through the next three years. In 1999, it acquired Wabash Foods, LLC, taking over the operation of that company's leased facility in Bluffton, Indiana. There, using a licensed, patented process, Poore Brothers used a sheeting and frying process for turning out its Tato Skins and Pizzarias brand chips. Later it would also produce the salted snacks it makes under license from T.G.I. Friday's.

Like so many other companies, Poore Brothers entered a partnering mode towards the end of 1990s, both to promote its brand awareness and to gain market strength. Among other things, Poore Brothers developed a solid relationship with the Arizona Diamondbacks, a National League baseball franchise. It became one of the team's chief sponsors, and in 1999 started annually producing a commemorative 6 oz. Original Potato Chips honoring the ball club. The arrangement gave the company considerable local exposure and a chance to plan marketing strategies through such techniques as exit sampling, which was conducted at the end of several of the team's home games.

The hometown appeal was one thing, however, and a national appeal quite another. The company got a boost in that direction in February 2000 when it began selling its Tato Skins

Key Dates:

1986: Don and Jay Poore found Poore Brothers Foods and Poore Brothers Texas.
1990: Company forms Poore Brothers Distributing Company.
1993: Mark S. Howells and associates form Poore Brothers Southeast.
1994: PB Southeast opens plant in Tennessee.
1995: Founders sell Poore Brothers Foods to PB Southeast.
1996: Poore Brothers, Inc. goes public and makes IPO; the company also introduces fat-free line of chips.
1997: Eric J. Kufel becomes CEO and president.
1998: Company purchases Tejas Snacks LP.
1999: Poore acquires Wabash Foods, LLC.
2000: The company acquires Boulder Natural Foods, Inc. and the Boulder Potato Co.

brand potato chips in about 200 Sam's Club wholesale stores spread across 17 states, mostly in the east. More importantly, the following May, Poore Brothers teamed up with T.G.I. Friday's. At that time, plans were put in motion to launch of new line of T.G.I. Friday's brand salted snacks to be marketed in supermarkets, club stores, and mass merchandising outlets. In the multi-year agreement, the two companies began with the introduction of T.G.I. Friday's Potato Skins, Fire Bites, and Quesadillas, all made at Poore Brothers' facility in Bluffton.

Poore's revenues reached a record $41.7 million in its fiscal 2000 year, a 79 percent increase over the previous year. The revenue boost largely resulted from the company's acquisitions, which accounted for an additional $13.0 million in sales, plus the fourth-quarter introduction of the T.G.I. Friday's brand of salted snacks in club stores and vending machines. Importantly, it was the second year in a row that Poore's showed a profit, and it was achieved despite the fact that in October 2000 a fire temporarily halted production at the company's Goodyear plant. The fire caused major damage to the roof of the processing area, and it forced Poore Brothers to source products from third-party manufacturers for months; however, workers at the plant were able to season and package the potatoes and other bulk products received from those manufacturers.

By April of 2001, only six months after their introduction, T.G.I. Friday's brand of salted snacks had become Poore Brothers' number one selling brand. Up to that point, distribution had been limited to the eastern region of the country; the company then began distributing the brand into its western region channels. By that time, too, it had resumed full production of its kettle-cooked potato chips at its Goodyear plant and, according to *Business Wire*, its prospects for an accelerated growth in revenue seemed excellent. In fact, Kufel announced, Poore Brothers was "on track to achieve its goal of 30–40 percent revenue growth in fiscal 2001." He also indicated that the company would continue it aggressive spending to improve it capabilities, market its T.G.I. Friday's brand of salted snacks, develop new products, and promote greater awareness of other company brands, pushing what its new "intensely different" catch phrase conveyed, the uniqueness of Poore Brothers' products.

Principal Competitors

Frito-Lay, Inc.; The Hain Celestial Group, Inc.; Golden Enterprises, Inc.; Lance, Inc.; The Procter & Gamble Company.

Further Reading

Gabriel, Angela, "Poore Brothers Bets Chips on Acquisitions for Growth," *Business Journal-Serving Phoenix & the Valley of the Sun*, May 7, 1999, p. 6.

Gonderinger, Lisa, "Poore Bros. Seeks IPO Riches," *Business Journal-Serving Phoenix & the Valley of the Sun*, September 27, 1996, p. 1.

——, "Suit May Dip into Poore Bros. Cash," *Business Journal-Serving Phoenix & the Valley of the Sun*, May 23, 1977, p. 1.

Howell, S. Diane, "Chipping Away at a Niche," *Arizona Business Gazette*, April 27, 1990, p. 16.

"Lawsuit Against Poore Brothers Settled and Dismissed," *PR Newswire*, November 23, 1998.

"Poore Brothers Reports Record Revenue and Profit; T.G.I. Friday's Salted Snacks Become Company's No. 1 Selling Brand; Arizona Plant Resumes Full Production," *Business Wire*, April 26, 2001.

"Poore Brothers Teams Up with the Arizona Diamondbacks," *Business Wire*, March 17, 1999.

"Poore Brothers Teams with T.G.I. Friday's to Introduce an Innovative Line of Salted Snacks," *Business Wire*, May 18, 2000.

Roberts, William A., Jr., "Intended Intensity," *Prepared Foods*, October 2000, p. 17.

Teichgraeber, Tara, "Poore Bros., T.G.I. Friday's Partner," *Business Journal-Serving Phoenix & the Valley of the Sun*, June 2, 2000, p. 5.

—John W. Fiero

PowerBar Inc.

2150 Shattuck Avenue
Berkeley, California 94704
U.S.A.
Telephone: (510) 843-1330
Toll Free: (800) 587-6937
Fax: (510) 843-1446
Web site: http://www.powerbar.com

Wholly Owned Subsidiary of Nestlé USA Inc.
Incorporated: 1986 as Powerfood Inc.
Employees: 250
Sales: $142 million (1999 est.)
NAIC: 31134 Non-Chocolate Confectionary
   Manufacturing

PowerBar Inc. is a leading producer of energy bars. Energy bars are concentrated high-carbohydrate snack bars designed to provide a quick between-meal calorie boost and usually fortified with vitamins and other substances. PowerBar was the first to market such a snack and still retains a leading share of the growing energy bar market. First aimed at runners and other athletes, PowerBars are now distributed through mainstream supermarkets, with ad campaigns targeting people in all walks of life. The PowerBar product line includes its signature bar, known as PowerBar Performance, and two other bars, PowerBar Harvest and PowerBar ProteinPlus. PowerBar Harvest contains whole grains and nuts. The ProteinPlus bar is geared more towards athletes, and contains 24 grams of protein, plus vitamins, amino acids, and L-Glutamine. PowerBar Inc. also markets a product called PowerBar PowerGel, a concentrated carbohydrate gel which is said to deliver a quick burst of energy. PowerBar has two subsidiaries, PowerBar Foods Canada, Inc., in Toronto, and PowerBar Europe GmbH, located in Munich, Germany. In 2000, Nestlé USA bought PowerBar for an estimated $375 million. The company is now a wholly owned subsidiary whose ultimate parent is the Swiss company Nestlé S.A., the largest food company in the world.

A Runner's Niche Product

The PowerBar originated with Brian Maxwell, a world-class marathon runner. Maxwell was born in England and grew up in Toronto. By 1977, Maxwell was ranked third worldwide as a marathoner. He was on the Canadian Olympic team in 1980, although the team did not compete because of his country's boycott of the Moscow games. Maxwell was running a British marathon in 1983 when he suddenly ran out of energy some three-quarters of the way through the race. He became dizzy and weak, and ended the race in seventh place. Maxwell was sure that low blood sugar had contributed to his loss, and he decided to find some way to combat this problem. His idea was to come up with a snack food that he could eat either before, during, or after a race. It would be low in fat, high in carbohydrates, and give the body an energy boost for the extreme stress of distance running. In 1985, Maxwell was still running marathons, supporting himself with a low-paying coaching position at the University of California-Berkeley. There he met Jennifer Bidulph, a 20-year-old sophomore nutrition student and cross-country runner. Maxwell and Bidulph moved in together and began working nights in their kitchen testing recipes for high-energy snack foods. In an interview with *People Weekly,* Maxwell described the product of their first endeavors as "this sort of horrible glop." Maxwell and Bidulph wrapped their homemade bars in plastic and took them to races for runner friends to test. Despite mixed success with their early efforts, Maxwell and Bidulph persevered. By 1986, the couple thought they had perfected the recipe, a mixture of oat bran, maltodextrins, and milk protein sweetened with fructose and fortified with vitamins, minerals, and amino acids.

Now it was time for a serious product launch. Maxwell, Bidulph, and a Berkeley chemist together came up with a business plan which they peddled to potential investors. They asked for backing of $250,000. But people in the food business thought this amount was too low. Maxwell told *Success* magazine that investors advised him to rewrite the business plan and ask for $2 million or $3 million if he wanted serious consideration. Instead, Maxwell raised the money himself. He had appeared in an advertisement for Xerox's Marathon brand copiers and netted $50,000. With this nest egg, plus $5,000 from his parents, Maxwell and Bidulph began producing PowerBars commercially. The couple invested $15,000 in Mylar wrappers and paid a local contractor to make the bars.

Maxwell and Bidulph continued their grass roots marketing efforts, pushing their PowerBars at athletic events. But they had to overcome some difficulties with production. The quality of the bars the contractor produced was quite variable. The bars frequently clogged the machinery, because the low-fat recipe lacked enough oil or fat to keep the equipment lubricated. Maxwell told *People Weekly* that he and Bidulph tried to ease things at the contractor's plant by slipping each of the workers $20 on the days the energy bars were in production.

However, the Maxwells (they married in 1988) were able to afford their own plant within a few years of the product launch. The couple had worked tirelessly to promote PowerBars themselves, passing out samples at races along with coupons and mail-order information. In 1987, the U.S. cycling team in the Tour de France asked PowerBar to sponsor it. The athletes touted the bars on television, and CBS Sports ran a short profile of the young company. The mail-order business took off at that point, as well as sales through cycling shops.

Wider Marketing Efforts in the Early 1990s

By 1989, sales of PowerBars had gone so well that the company was able to afford its own production facility. The new factory used machinery that Brian Maxwell himself designed. This alleviated the sticking problems of the earlier equipment. The company promoted itself primarily through sponsorship of races and other sporting events. It advertised in fitness journals and sold PowerBars at places where athletes shopped.

The company grew by as much as 40 percent a year in the early 1990s. Sales for 1994 were approximately $30 million. The company began to advertise more extensively. It ran ads in about 80 different sports-oriented publications by the mid-1990s. But the product's quick success and widening brand recognition led competitors to bid for the energy bar market as

well. In 1994, Gatorade, well known for its sports drink, brought out a Gator Bar. The much larger company had deep pockets to fund advertising, and it managed to wrest away sponsorship of an amateur athletic competition, the Ironman Triathlon, from PowerBar that year. Many other smaller competitors had also flocked to the market. As the Maxwells knew, anyone with a kitchen and as little as $50,000 could bring out energy bars. Some companies produced imitations of the PowerBar. These were similar bars marketed to athletes under evocative names like BTU Stoker. Others tried to differentiate themselves from PowerBar. The Clif Bar, produced by Kali's Sports Naturals Inc., also of Berkeley, California, described itself as both all-natural and good-tasting, two qualities the PowerBar was not known for. Its originator claimed he invented the Clif Bar after eating five PowerBars on a bike trip and finding he couldn't stand any more.

Competition provoked PowerBar to expand its flavor range. The company put out a berry flavor in the mid-1990s and introduced peanut butter and oatmeal raisin flavors as well. It spent $8.6 million on advertising in 1996. In addition to print ads, the company began airing television commercials in several large urban markets. The TV spots featured football player Steve Young.

As PowerBars gained popularity, the energy bar category began to elbow into other, broader markets. Though the PowerBar was geared toward athletes, by 1996 it was finding its way into mass market distribution channels—supermarkets and drugstores. There it appeared to be a healthy alternative to the candy bar so traditional candy bar makers took note and began putting out their own energy bars. While Hershey Foods Corp. and cereal maker Kellogg Co. were reported to be testing their own energy bars in 1996, giant candy company Mars Inc. began limited marketing of its new player, called VO2Max. Mars distributed it at first only in health food stores and sports shops in California. Print ads in sports magazines claimed VO2Max was clinically proven to supply antioxidants, which helped the body to recover from athletic stress. This seemed to combine the best of two worlds. The energy bar was from a known candy manufacturer, yet it came accredited as an athletic performance booster.

Pressure to Perform in the Late 1990s and Beyond

Sales continued to gallop for PowerBar, reaching an estimated $97 million in 1997, up $15 million from the year previous. But PowerBar's market share fell as competition intensified. The energy bar market niche was exploding. Sales of energy bars in grocery stores grew almost 40 percent over 1997. The entire market was thought to be worth $200 million. In 1996, PowerBar led the energy bar market with a 70 percent share. But a year later, its share had fallen to 52 percent. Surprisingly, its chief competitors were not Mars or Gatorade. Both these companies shelved their energy bars in 1998. The Clif Bar almost doubled its sales over 1997, giving it the number three market spot. And another small company, Bio-Foods Inc., took the number two spot. Its Balance Bar, introduced in 1992, had sales of $42 million in 1997. It marketed its bars with celebrity endorsements and by tying into the faddish high-protein Zone diet.

Key Dates:

1986: PowerBar launched as a company.
1989: The company acquires its own production plant.
1996: PowerBar has 70 percent of the highly competitive energy-bar market.
2000: Nestlé USA buys PowerBar.

The stream of new contenders in the energy bar category whittled away at PowerBar's share. The company tracked a month-by-month decline of its clout and made several marketing decisions to try to turn things around. The Maxwells prepared for possibly taking the firm public, selling a 19 percent share of PowerBar Inc. to two private investment firms. The sale raised about $20 million. Then PowerBar diversified its product line and changed its advertising tactics. In 1998 it brought out a new bar called PowerBar Harvest. This was a crunchier, more granola-like bar, that was advertised with the tag line "for life's daily marathons." The Harvest bar was still aimed at people on the go, but the company promoted it for less grueling activities than biking and marathon running, such as hiking and camping. The Harvest bar's improved texture set it against competitors like the Clif Bar, which was promoted for its appealing taste.

PowerBar brought out another new bar in 1998, the PowerBar Protein Plus. This one was keyed more closely to tough athletics than the original PowerBar. It had increased levels of protein, contained vitamins and minerals, and also had added methionine and so-called free-form glutamine, substances that were said to repair and build muscles. By 1999, the PowerBar product line had expanded to include such products as PowerBar Essentials, which ran under the tag line the "energy bar for mind and body." It contained herbal extracts said to enhance mental performance. PowerBar also brought out some non-bar products. It launched a sports drink in 1999, PowerBar Perform, which came in two bottle sizes. It also marketed Perform Plus, a powdered form of the drink. These came in fruit flavors, fortified with time-released carbohydrates and mineral additives like magnesium and chromium. Its competitors also brought out wider arrays of bars and drinks. Balance Bar, trailing PowerBar in sales by about $20 million, brought out a Total Balance drink in 1999. Its drink, however, was aimed more at people wanting a quick meal or pick-me-up. Like the popular Slim Fast drink, Total Balance was supposed to be able to substitute for a full meal.

In addition to bringing out a wider array of products, PowerBar shelved its earlier ad campaign for something a bit more lighthearted. The company spent at least $12 million on a television campaign with the tag line "don't bonk." The ads were aired in major markets, primarily during sports shows. The spots showed athletes in competition, with the ones eating PowerBars performing effortlessly, while the hapless PowerBar-less competitors tripped, collapsed, or otherwise "bonked"—a runner's term for a sudden loss of energy. PowerBar's market share began to reverse its fall as soon as the ads began running in 1999. The company also continued to advertise in other ways, signing on more sports stars as sponsors, such as Nascar driver Dale Jarrett and the National Basketball Association's rising player Jason Kidd.

PowerBar still claimed the leading spot in the energy bar market into 2000, but it was clear that competition would not ease up. Balance Bar, the number two player, was acquired by the major food company Kraft, and Gatorade declared new plans to launch an energy bar. In early 2000, PowerBar announced that it was being acquired by Nestlé USA, the U.S. subsidiary of Swiss food giant Nestlé S.A. The Glendale, California-based Nestlé USA dwarfed PowerBar, with $8 billion in annual sales and 19,500 employees. Nestlé USA was estimated to have paid $375 million for the small Berkeley company. By 2001, PowerBar was said to have about 40 percent of the energy bar market. This was a pivotal time for PowerBar and for the energy bar market as a whole, as the rapidly growing category sorted itself out into a battle between large and experienced food makers.

Principal Subsidiaries

PowerBar Foods Canada, Inc.; PowerBar Europe GmbH (Germany).

Principal Competitors

Kraft Foods, Inc.; Quaker Oats Co.

Further Reading

Burfoot, Amby, and Marty Post, "Marathon Maestro," *Runner's World,* July 1999, p. 19.

Hays, Constance L., "From Out of the Gym, Into the Grocery Store," *New York Times,* November 22, 1997, pp. D1, D3.

"Market Segmentation Proves Powerful for Bars," *Drug Store News,* June 7, 1999, p. 256.

McNulty, Aidan, "Raising the Bar: How Brian Maxwell Turned a Stomachache into a $50 Million a Year Business," *Success,* August 1998, p. 29.

Mehegan, Sean, "PowerBar Takes to TV sans Young," *Brandweek,* April 7, 1997, p. 8.

Miller, Samantha, "Power Couple: Brian and Jennifer Maxwell Found Their Fortune in a Quick-Fix High-Energy Food Bar," *People Weekly,* August 23, 1999, p. 77.

Mitchell, Russell, "A Marathon Man with Marketing Power," *Business Week,* November 7, 1994, pp. 56–58.

"Nestlé to Purchase PowerBar, Maintain 'Don't Bonk' Line," *Brandweek,* February 28, 2000, p. 14.

Pollack, Judann, "PowerBar Attracts Big Players Hungry for Chunk of Market," *Advertising Age,* November 4, 1996, p. 20.

Pollack, Judann, and Alice A. Cuneo, "Energy Bars Examine Strategy as Entries Hike Competition," *Advertising Age,* November 2, 1998, pp. 3, 56.

Thompson, Stephanie, "PowerBar; Brian Maxwell," *Advertising Age,* June 26, 2000, p. S20.

Weisz, Pam, "The Candy Bar of the '90s?," *Brandweek,* May 29, 1995, p. 21.

—A. Woodward

Preserver Group, Inc.

95 Route 17 South
Paramus, New Jersey 07653-0931
U.S.A.
Telephone: (201) 291-2000
Fax: (201) 291-2125
Web site: http://www.motr.com

Public Company
Incorporated: 1933 as Automobile Association of New
    Jersey
Employees: 185
Sales: $90.1 million (2000)
Stock Exchanges: NASDAQ
Ticker Symbol: PRES
NAIC: 524126 Direct Property and Casualty Insurance
    Carriers

Based in Paramus, New Jersey, Preserver Group, Inc. is a restructured insurance company that grew out of the insurance businesses assembled by the Motor Club of America (MCA). The company provides property and casualty insurance through its five wholly owned subsidiaries, which primarily serve the northeastern United States. Although MCA became involved in the underwriting business by providing car insurance to motor club members in New Jersey, the company in recent years has looked to cut back its involvement in the state, or to abandon it completely, the result of New Jersey's auto insurance regulations that have caused a number of insurers to cease conducting business in the market.

Motor Club Origins in 1926

The Preserver Group's roots reach back to 1926 when three brothers established a motor club. William, David, and Samuel Green were born in Atlantic City, New Jersey, the children of Russian immigrants. William, the second eldest, was the one who took the lead in the motor club business, after having worked a brief time as an accountant. He would serve as chairman of the motor club and its businesses for more than 50 years. As automobiles became more common in the 1920s, drivers looked to pool their resources to provide mutual assistance, leading to the rise of motor clubs that could provide maps and help with emergency repairs and towing. Initially the Greens conducted business in a one-room office in Newark, New Jersey. In short order, they began to sell affordable auto insurance as part of their offerings to club members. In 1933 the company became known as the Automobile Association of New Jersey and moved to a storefront location. The motor club began attracting members beyond New Jersey as it created operations in 13 other states, as far north as Maine, as far south as Florida, and as far west as Ohio, Michigan, and Kentucky.

In the late 1950s the company expanded beyond the automobile business to start Garden State Life Insurance Company. It also began to offer fire and homeowners insurance, as well as expanding on the club's travel services. The company changed its name to Motor Club of America in 1958, and also separated out its insurance businesses by creating Motor Club of America Insurance Company (MCAIC). It subsequently built a five-story headquarters in Paramus, New Jersey, to house the motor club operations and insurance businesses. It created a real estate subsidiary, Fairmount Central Urban Renewal Corp., to own the building and property, and then leased the facilities.

By 1970 the MCA Group consisted of Motor Club of America, three fire and casualty insurance companies, Garden State Life, three insurance sales agencies, two finance companies for car loans, a real estate company, and a travel business. The company in the late 1960s also began an effort to become involved in the hospital services industry by initiating a plan to build the New Jersey Rehabilitation Hospital in East Orange, New Jersey. By running all of these businesses out of one building, the company was able to save on overhead costs. In 1970 MCA enjoyed the most profitable year of its existence, posting net earnings of more than $1.56 million, or $1.41 per share. Premiums from motor club memberships were up by some 27 percent, as were fire and casualty premiums. Garden State Life, with increased sales through the company's fire and casualty agents, was enjoying robust growth. It was now licensed to do business in 49 states, as well as the District of Columbia and Puerto Rico. In 1972 Garden State Life exceeded the $100

Key Dates:

1926: Green brothers establish motor club in New Jersey.
1933: Automobile Association of New Jersey is incorporated.
1958: The name is changed to Motor Club of America.
1972: Insurance unit makes initial public offering of stock.
1986: Green brothers sell interest, turning over control of company to Thrifty-Rent-A-Car System Inc.
1992: Losses from Hurricane Andrew devastate insurance unit.
1999: North East Insurance Co. is acquired.
2000: Mountain Valley Indemnity Company is acquired.
2001: The name is changed to Preserver Group.

million-in-force plateau. To fuel growth in its insurance businesses the company made an initial public offering of the MCAIC unit in June 1972, selling 412,500 shares at $15 each.

Passage of New Jersey's "No Fault" Insurance Laws in 1972

Although most of the company's operations would continue to be profitable, the passage of New Jersey's "no fault" insurance laws in 1972, which went into effect a year later, would soon begin to have an adverse impact on MCA. During the four years from 1976 to 1979, MCAIC endured $27 million in underwriting losses. In addition to the no-fault provisions, the company was hurt by the increased rate of inflation that caused high automobile repair costs. Clearly, the company was overly dependent on New Jersey auto insurance. In 1979 almost 90 percent of MCAIC's net premiums came from New Jersey business, and 77.3 percent of that amount came from automobile premiums. The company sought relief from the state and on January 1, 1980, the New Jersey Insurance Commissioner discontinued assigning high-risk drivers who were distributed among state insurers. The financial state of the company was so compromised by this point that it agreed with both the States of Massachusetts and Connecticut to not write any new insurance or renew policies upon their expiration. MCAIC also withdrew its certificates of authority from several states in which it had yet to begin selling insurance. The company sought additional state relief, including a rate increase and permission to drop certain lines of automobile insurance. Although a general 11 percent rate increase was announced, the Commissioner did not grant any other relief to MCA. In October 1980 the company filed suit against the Commissioner and the State of New Jersey, seeking compensation for the injury caused by the New Jersey regulations.

Other aspects of MCA's business that had been holding up also began to suffer in the early 1980s. Motor Club memberships had enjoyed steady growth, with operations now spreading to include 29 states. Much of this out-of-state growth was fueled by a program with AVCO Financial Services, Inc. With the country enduring higher interest rates, however, the number of loans that AVCO generated dropped significantly, and as a result the opportunity to sell motor club memberships decreased as well. MCA's attempt to enter the healthcare business also

failed to pan out. In 1975 the company's subsidiary, Moderncare Centers of America, Inc., opened the 152-bed New Jersey Rehabilitation Hospital in East Orange, New Jersey. The operation had been modestly profitable in the late 1970s, but in February 1982, MCA sold the hospital for $7 million, receiving a cash payment of $2,650,000 after the purchaser assumed the mortgage. Moreover, in 1982 the company sold Garden State Life to the GEICO Corporation, receiving $15 million in total compensation.

The insurance business rebounded somewhat over the next few years, and the company looked to expand its product offerings by establishing a new subsidiary: Motor Club Fire and Casualty Company. In September 1986 it began to write homeowner coverage for higher valued owner-occupied single family houses. Despite this and other efforts to rebuild the business, the reality was that MCA was still being run by its founders, who were all well into their 80s. In December 1986 the three Green brothers sold 500,000 shares of MCA stock, their entire holdings, to Trac, Inc., the Tulsa, Oklahoma company that owned Thrifty-Rent-A-Car System, Inc. As part of the transaction, Trac gained five of the eight seats on the MCA board. The Green brothers remained directors and officers of the company, but management effectively changed hands.

Alvin E. Swanner served as chairman of the board on an interim basis before Archer McWhorter assumed the role. Both men had been founders of Thrifty, which now enjoyed the benefit of equity ownership in an insurer that could supply the insurance needs of its rental car business. In 1987 MCAIC and Thrifty had five policies in effect. Two of the policies were paid in advance, while three others provided monthly premium payments, based on a percentage of gross revenues generated by Thrifty locations. On the motor club side of the company, MCA looked to expand the selling of service contracts beyond its New Jersey and AVCO efforts. New management also decided to take advantage of the company's licenses to sell insurance in other states, while at the same time cutting back on new business in New Jersey. As a result, net income increased 8 percent to $3.23 million over the previous year.

In 1988 MCAIC began to write homeowner and other property coverage in Florida. Despite efforts to reduce its New Jersey business, however, the company's earnings were undercut by high automobile insurance losses in the state, caused in large part by a major increase in state-mandated assessments, and New Jersey's failure to provide a timely rate increase. Net income for 1988 fell by 67 percent over the previous year to just $1 million. The situation in New Jersey would only worsen for insurers when the state passed new automobile insurance regulations. Not only did insurers now have to pay surtaxes and an assessment to bail out the New Jersey Joint Underwriting Association, a private passenger insurance fund that was $3 billion in deficit, they were required to accept all applicants for private passenger automobile insurance, unless the applicant met a state-mandated definition of a "bad driver." This "take all comers" provision led many insurers to simply abandon the New Jersey market. In March 1990 MCAIC attempted to surrender its Certificate of Authority to sell private passenger automobile insurance in the State of New Jersey, as well as submitting a Plan of Orderly Withdrawal from the state, only to have the state take steps to refuse the surrender of the Certificate of Authority. Subsequently, the company reported its net earnings for 1989, which revealed a further 43 percent drop over the previous year, falling to just $452,000. By 1991 the company was reporting a net loss.

1992: Hurricane Andrew Devastating for MCAIC

Losses in New Jersey were creating a drag on the company's other operations, which were performing fairly well. Management made plans to spin off the automobile insurance unit. Then on August 24, 1992, Hurricane Andrew struck the South Florida coast. MCAIC was essentially wiped out by the losses caused by the storm and placed in receivership. As a result, MCA wrote off more than $23 million in losses. While it canceled its auto insurance spin-off, the company also created a new insurance unit, Preserver Insurance Co., in order to provide coverage for New Jersey customers who had been serviced by MCA Insurance. Also in 1992, two months before Hurricane Andrew, William Green died at the age of 92 in Florida. David Green would then pass away in 1996, and the youngest, Samuel, in 2001.

In addition to the deaths of the Green brothers, MCA lost ties to its original business in 1996 when it sold the longtime motor club to JVL Holding Properties. It now began to reorganize and refashion itself as a commercial insurance company while expanding its business lines outside of New Jersey. A major step in this direction came in January 1999 when MCA and the Maine-based property and casualty insurer North East Insurance Company, incorporated in 1965, agreed to merge. In addition, MCA would acquire North East's American Colonial subsidiary, which had not written any coverage since 1990. By March 1999 the details of the transaction were finalized. North East shareholders were given the choice of accepting $3.30 for each share of North East common stock, one share of MCA common stock for each 5.25 shares of North East common stock, or a combination of cash and MCA stock. The comparative value of the two companies' stock price essentially mirrored the differences in premiums written. For the first nine months of 1998, MCA had net premiums worth $43.6 million, while North East had net premiums of $10.7 million. Following the completion of the merger, MCA named its chief financial officer, Patrick J. Haveron, to the title of chief executive officer, in charge of further mergers and acquisitions to further the company's efforts to diversify beyond New Jersey. He shared the title with Stephen A. Gilbert, who was already serving as the CEO of MCA.

The company's next step in gaining market share in New England came in December 1999 when it announced plans to buy the Mountain Valley Indemnity Co. from Unitrin Inc.

Formed in 1995 as White Mountains Insurance Co., Mountain Valley was based in Manchester, New Hampshire, and wrote $16 million in annual premiums in small and medium-sized commercial lines. Although it conducted most of its business in New Hampshire and Massachusetts, the company also wrote some policies in Maine, Rhode Island, Vermont, and New York. The terms of the deal were finalized in March 2001 when MCA agreed to pay $7.5 million in cash for Mountain Valley.

Because MCA was no longer in the motor club business, in 2001 it changed its name to Preserver Group, Inc. Moreover, the amount of personal auto insurance the company wrote decreased as management focused its attention on expanding its small and midsized commercial lines. In its home state of New Jersey, the company continued to conflict with insurance regulators over the "take-all-comers" requirement. At the very least, Preserver Group would continue to look beyond New Jersey to growing its insurance business in New England, with other small acquisitions a distinct possibility.

Principal Subsidiaries

Motor Club of America Insurance Company; Preserver Insurance Company; North East Insurance Company; American Colonial Insurance Company; Mountain Valley Indemnity Company.

Principal Competitors

21st Century; Farm Family Holdings Inc.; Progressive Corporation.

Further Reading

"Auto Insurer Moves into Maine, Plans Acquisitions," *Insurance Finance & Investment,* February 8, 1999, p 3.

Blumenthal, Robin Goldwyn, "Motor Club Unit Takes Heavy Blow from Storm Claims," *Wall Street Journal,* September 16, 1992, p. A4.

"Motor Club of America to Become Preserver Group," *Insurance Advocate,* May 12, 2001, p. 40.

"Motor Club to Change Name," *Business News New Jersey,* August 14, 2001.

Reid, David, "Paramus, N.J.-Based Insurer Must Abide by Take-All-Comers Law, State Says," *Knight-Ridder/Tribune News,* May 23, 2001.

"Three Auto Insurers Leave New Jersey Over New Legislation," *Wall Street Journal,* March 14, 1990.

"William W. Green, 92: Founded Motor Club," *New York Times Current Events Edition,* June 9, 1992, p. D28.

—Ed Dinger

Printrak, A Motorola Company

1250 North Tustin Avenue
Anaheim, California 92807
U.S.A.
Telephone: (714) 238-2000
Toll Free: (888) 493-3590
Fax: (714) 237-0018
Web site: http://www.printrakinternational.com

Wholly Owned Subsidiary of Motorola, Inc.
Incorporated: 1974
Employees: 561
Sales: $109.91 million (2000)
NAIC: 541512 Computer Systems Design Services;
    561611 Investigation Services

Printrak, A Motorola Company makes automated fingerprint/mug shot identification and data management systems that are used by law enforcement and government agencies throughout the world. Clients include the Federal Bureau of Investigation and New Scotland Yard, as well as many other city, state, and national police agencies. The firm's premier offering is its Digital Justice Solution, an integrated product that can digitize, store, and match fingerprint and photographic images, automate dispatches to officers in the field, and store and organize a wide range of associated data for use throughout the criminal justice system. Originally formed as a division of Rockwell International, in 2000 the company was bought by Motorola, Inc., which intended to integrate its products with those of other subsidiaries that provided wireless communication and information management services to law enforcement agencies.

Early Years

Printrak was formed in 1974 as a division of Rockwell International. The company was created to develop computer programs that could automatically code and match fingerprints for use in law enforcement. Printrak's first major sale came the next year, when the Federal Bureau of Investigation purchased an automated fingerprint identification system (AFIS) from the company. Over the next several years sales also were made to other crime-fighting agencies in the United States.

By 1981, with a total of 11 employees, Printrak was still a small operation. The company seemed lost at Rockwell, which was involved with many larger projects, including the B-1 bomber and the Space Shuttle. At this time the parent corporation decided that Printrak did not fit its overall focus and sold the division to the London-based Thomas De La Rue and Company, Ltd., whose primary business was printing the currency of more than 75 countries. President David Snyder, who had run the firm for Rockwell, was retained, and under its new owners the company (now known as De La Rue Printrak) bloomed. During most of the 1980s growth was strong, with sales made to the New Orleans Police, the State of Florida, the Mexico City Police, and the Royal Canadian Mounted Police, among others. By 1987 the company had grown to employ 250 and was generating annual revenues of $40 million.

Printrak's AFIS system was built on a Digital Equipment Corp. minicomputer that utilized software of the company's own design. Fingerprints were copied onto cards that were scanned into the computer, which then compared the distinctive patterns of lines and whorls with thousands of others that were stored in a database. The system identified as many as ten possible matches, at which point a human expert made the final evaluation.

The automated process greatly sped up print identification. Previously, police could compare a print against perhaps a thousand other sets over a few days, but the Printrak system could run through 100,000 sets in 30 minutes. A satisfied New Orleans police captain told the *Orange County Register* that as many as 90 percent of the perpetrators caught with the Printrak system would not have been found otherwise.

The company's product was one of several on the market at this time, but it controlled an estimated 60 percent of total sales. There were few serious competitors, primarily the Japanese NEC Corp. and Morpho Systemes, a French start-up aligned with IBM. Printrak's goal was to get state governments to buy the system, then have their individual cities follow, assuring compatibility between the different agencies. Although it had made sales to some states, including Florida and Minnesota, it had lost others, including California, to NEC. Prices for a system varied depending on size, ranging from $1 million to as much as $10 million.

Company Perspectives:

Printrak empowers today's law enforcement and public safety agencies by providing the right tools for delivering the right information to the right person at the right time. Printrak has always been the pioneer in public safety and law enforcement, beginning with the introduction of the Automated Fingerprint Identification System (AFIS) to the FBI in 1975. Over a quarter century later, Printrak remains the global leader in positive identification technology with the most sophisticated solutions available to criminal justice, public safety and, civil agencies.

In 1987 Printrak announced creation of Phototrak, a computerized mug shot storage and matching system. Like AFIS, Phototrak could be used for rapid retrieval of photographs of suspects based on a database search that also used information about previous crimes and physical characteristics. Images were taken with a video camera, which sped up the processing time and eliminated the need for physical storage of photographs. Phototrak could work with between 60,000 and 210,000 images that were stored on optical disks, which were potentially more durable than electronic media.

Losses Leading to Management, Ownership Changes in the Late 1980s and Early 1990s

By the end of the decade Printrak was experiencing financial difficulties, due in large part to its over-commitment to too many large contracts, some of which were not fulfilled. In May of 1989 the company reshuffled its leadership, with De La Rue officer Richard M. Giles taking the presidency and David Snyder leaving the company. In the late spring of 1990 more changes took place when company management, led by Giles, Chief Operating Officer Chuck Smith, and Vice-President of Engineering John Hardy, bought the company from De La Rue, which previously had been on the verge of selling to Unisys. De La Rue took a write-off of £55 million in the deal, apparently happy just to divest itself of the money-losing Printrak. The company's annual revenues reportedly had dropped to $20 million, half the figure of just three years earlier. Losses were estimated at $2 million a month, for a total of $90 million since 1987. Once the transfer of ownership was complete, Giles took drastic action and cut the workforce to 150 from 425. Many of the discharged staffers had been hired to work out problems for specific contracts and were not considered essential to the company's overall direction. Following the sale, the company became known simply as Printrak, Inc.

Late 1991 saw the firm reach an agreement with Digital Biometrics, Inc. to use the latter's inkless electronic fingerprinting device as part of its equipment. Printrak also launched a smaller version of its original "Orion" fingerprint matching system, called "Hunter." The latter was priced at between $350,000 and $500,000, less than half the cost of a low-end Orion setup.

During the early 1990s the company made sales to the Czech Republic, the state of Louisiana, and other major clients, and began to recover its financial footing. More competitors were emerging, however, and Printrak lost bids to sell new systems to

the FBI and the state of Ohio. In 1995 Live-Scan 2000 was introduced, the first real-time digital fingerprint and imaging system. The system could communicate with a central computer from a remote location to compare a suspect's photograph or fingerprints in seconds, rather than requiring a paper copy to be scanned in. Each "booking station" unit was priced at about $60,000, with a total system costing considerably more.

Also in 1995, the company began making its component products available for use by outside firms, rather than strictly as part of its own systems. The Los Angeles County Department of Social Services was one of the first to buy such a hybrid, with Printrak's technology used as part of an identification system created by Electronic Data Systems for the agency. The new equipment took the place of an inefficient system that relied on driver's licenses and mothers' maiden names to weed out fraudulent claimants. Within six months of installation, the county was able to catch 8,000 fraudulent welfare recipients, good for annual savings of $12 million. Printrak subsequently began to actively seek sales to this type of end-user.

Initial Public Offering in 1996

In the summer of 1996, Printrak made 2.5 million shares of common stock available on the NASDAQ exchange for about $9 each. The proceeds were earmarked for debt retirement and acquisitions. Chairman, President, and CEO Richard Giles sold 190,000 of his own shares, but remained in control of the firm, retaining 60 percent of its stock. Later in the year the company addressed an issue that had been on the horizon for quite some time, that of compatibility between competing AFIS systems. The firm offered to make its technology available to competitors who wanted to make their equipment compatible with Printrak's. By this time half of the company's clients were overseas, with recent large contracts coming from the Swiss Central Police Bureau, the Amsterdam Police Department, and the Mexican Office of the Attorney General. Research into new technology was ongoing, with nearly 20 percent of revenue plowed back into this area. In addition to earnings from sales of systems, the company also provided a maintenance service, which itself accounted for nearly a fifth of revenues.

In late 1996 Printrak formed a new division, Printrak IDS Solutions, which targeted the growing market for biometrics, or computerized identification of images, fingerprints, and voices. The company also introduced its smallest portable fingerprinting unit, the Single Finger Station 2000, which weighed 2.5 pounds and was powered by batteries. Shortly afterward the firm added its first PC-based AFIS software. Revenues, which had been steadily climbing during the 1990s, reached $52 million for the year.

Growth Through Acquisitions in the Late 1990s

The company made its first acquisition in April 1997 when it purchased TFP, Inc. of Greenville, South Carolina, in a stock swap worth an estimated $19 million. TFP, founded in 1988, produced digital mug shot systems for law enforcement agencies. The move was in keeping with Printrak's strategy of becoming a total solution provider for the crime prevention and identity verification markets. Several months later another company was acquired for $9 million, SunRise Imaging of Fremont, California. SunRise had developed a system that scanned microfilm and

Key Dates:

1974: Printrak is formed as a division of Rockwell International.
1975: The company sells first the automated fingerprint identification system to the FBI.
1981: The company is sold to De La Rue of the United Kingdom; the name is changed to De La Rue Printrak.
1987: Image processing and recognition software debuts.
1989: Mounting losses lead to leadership changes.
1990: De La Rue sells Printrak to management, which cuts staff from 425 to 150.
1996: Printrak goes public.
1997: TFP, SunRise, and the dispatch unit of SCC Communications are acquired.
2000: Emergency Services Group is bought; Printrak is acquired by Motorola.

converted it into electronic images. Its offerings also were expected to be used as part of Printrak's package of law enforcement products. Most of TFP and SunRise's operations were later transferred to Printrak's Anaheim headquarters. During the year the company also purchased the computer dispatch and records management systems unit of SCC Communications Corp. and entered into a joint agreement with Siemens Nixdorf Information Systems AG to develop and market identification systems for use outside the United States. New clients continued to come in, including the governments of Oman, Norway, Sweden, and Denmark, as well as the state of Illinois and the province of Ontario, Canada. Printrak also formed a business unit in Australia to market its products in the far east. Revenues for the year were a record $72 million, though losses totaled $14.5 million due to the acquisitions and subsequent restructuring needed to integrate them.

More large contracts came in during 1998, including a $6 million systems upgrade from the Canadian Mounties and a record $45 million order from the Argentine government to provide an AFIS system for part of that country's national identification program. In the spring of the year the company also reorganized its sales, marketing, and customer support operations into the new Worldwide Sales and Support Division. These had formerly been associated with each product line's operating unit.

The following year Printrak expanded once more by adding a 24,000-square-foot facility near Irvine, California to house its research and marketing employees. The company also was making deliveries of its Digital Justice Solution systems, which combined fingerprint and mug shot handling with document management, computer-aided dispatch, vehicle tracking, and jail management components.

In 2000 Printrak formed a new unit, MetaJustice, which was to offer Internet-based subscription access to software applications for public safety and criminal justice agencies. A British company, Emergency Services Group (a unit of BAE Systems), which marketed computer-aided dispatch systems for fire and police agencies, was acquired in March. The firm also selected a new president, Daniel Crawford, with Richard Giles remaining in the roles of chairman and CEO. Other new contracts were

signed with TRW, Inc., the Western Australia Police Service, and others. Printrak's revenues for the fiscal year leapt to $109.9 million, with net earnings of $7.9 million.

In August of 2000 the company was purchased by Motorola, Inc. for $160 million. Motorola was a longtime provider of telecommunications equipment for law enforcement agencies, and the acquisition was intended to enhance its offerings in this area. Motorola had earlier bought Software Corporation of America, which also made wireless communications equipment for public safety agencies.

Starting its second quarter-century in operation, Printrak was offering its most comprehensive product to date, the Digital Justice Solution, which was a total package of identification and record management products for use by law enforcement, social service, and government agencies. The recent acquisition by Motorola brought the company the deep pockets and powerful marketing abilities of one of the world's leading telecommunications manufacturers. With the world becoming increasingly security conscious, demand for Printrak's products looked certain to remain strong.

Principal Subsidiaries

Printrak Ltd. (U.K.); TFP, Inc.; SunRise Imaging; Printrak International Pty Ltd. (Australia); Printrak de Argentina S.R.L. (Argentina); MetaJustice.

Principal Competitors

NEC Corp.; Groupe SAGEM; Lockheed Martin Corp.; Identix Inc.; Visage Technology, Inc.; Visionics Corp.

Further Reading

Breskin, Ira, ''Sleuthware,'' *Investor's Business Daily,* October 31, 1996, p. A4.

Brown, Ken Spencer, ''Clicks in the Clink: Printrak Offers System to Jails,'' *Orange County Business Journal,* January 31, 2000, p. 49.

Condon, Bernard, ''Prickly Does It,'' *Forbes,* May 5, 1997, p. 66.

Farnsworth, Chris, ''Motorola Lifts Printrak at a 'Steal,' '' *Orange County Register,* August 30, 2000, p. C1.

''Freed from De La Rue Shackle and Shot of Its Debt, Printrak Is Raring to Go,'' *Compugram International,* February 24, 1992.

Hamit, Francis, ''Digital Justice Image Management: Printrak's Integrated Document, Mug Shot, Fingerprint & Dispatch Solution,'' *Advanced Imaging,* March 1, 1999.

Kerber, Ross, ''From Disaster to Profitability—Fingerprint Specialist Printrak Survives Own Identity Crisis,'' *Los Angeles Times,* October 24, 1994, p. 1.

Lyster, Michael, ''OC's Other Fingerprint Firm,'' *Orange County Business Journal,* October 14, 1996, p. 1.

Pietrucha, Bill, ''Ontario Police Capture Fingerprints on PCs,'' *Newsbytes News Network,* August 27, 1997.

Siler, Charles, ''De La Rue Printrak Fingers Criminals,'' *Orange County Register,* June 11, 1987, p. D1.

Taylor, Cathy, ''Track Record Shows Printrak Is the Real Thing,'' *Orange County Register,* May 5, 1996, p. C1.

Van, Jon, ''Motorola to Buy Anaheim, Calif.-Based Software, Services Firm,'' *KRTBN Knight-Ridder Tribune Business News,* August 30, 2000.

Vranizan, Michelle, ''Printrak Managers Buy Company from British,'' *Orange County Register,* June 6, 1990, p. C1.

—Frank Uhle

Public Service Enterprise Group Inc.

80 Park Plaza
Newark, New Jersey 07101
U.S.A.
Telephone: (973) 430-7000
Fax: (973) 623-5983
Web site: http://www.pseg.com

Public Company
Incorporated: 1903 as Public Service Corporation of
New Jersey
Employees: 10,709
Sales: $6.8 billion (2000)
Stock Exchanges: New York Philadelphia London
Ticker Symbol: PEG
NAIC: 221111 Hydroelectric Power Generation; 221112
Fossil Fuel Electric Power Generation; 221113
Nuclear Electric Power Generation; 221119 Other
Electric Power Generation; 221121 Electric Bulk
Power Transmission and Control; 221122 Electric
Power Distribution; 22121 Natural Gas Distribution

Public Service Enterprise Group Inc. (PSEG) operates as an energy and energy services firm with three major subsidiaries including PSE&G, PSEG Power LLC, and PSEG Energy Holdings. During the late 1990s and into the new millennium, PSEG transformed itself from a traditional regulated utility to a diverse global energy firm with over $21 billion in assets. Subsidiary PSE&G operates as a regulated public utility company that provides electric and gas service to more than 3.5 million residential and business customers in New Jersey. Its service area covers a 2,600 square mile area from Bergen to Gloucester counties. PSEG Power acts as a non-regulated independent power producer with generating plants in the Northeast region of the United States. Its three subsidiaries include: PSEG Fossil, which oversees the firm's natural gas, coal, and oil-fired electric generating units; PSEG Nuclear, operator of several nuclear generation stations in New Jersey; and PSEG Energy Resources & Trade, a buyer and seller of electric and gas commodities. PSEG Energy Holdings was created to expand PSEG's international reach and acts as a holding company for three unregulated

businesses. PSEG Global operates and develops generation, PSEG Resources manages energy investments, and PSEG Energy Technologies provides energy-related services related to energy management, operation, maintenance, and finance.

Public Service Corp.'s Early History: Early 1900s

At the beginning of the 20th century New Jersey's utilities were primarily operators of streetcars; secondarily manufacturers and distributors of gas; and minimally producers of electricity, most of which was used to power trolley cars. Streets, homes, and businesses were, for the most part, lighted by gas, and the industrial use of electricity was in its infancy. The utility operators were fragmented into hundreds of small companies, many of which were owned by out-of-state interests, inefficiently run, and poorly maintained. On February 19, 1903, in Newark a streetcar full of high school students skidded down an icy hill onto a railroad crossing and was struck by a train, killing and injuring more than 30 people. A subsequent investigation into the affairs of the car operator and the North Jersey Street Railway Company, revealed shoddy management and extreme financial instability, not only of North Jersey but of many other New Jersey streetcar, electric, and gas companies.

Reform was called for by the public, and by the insurance companies and banks whose utility investments were at risk. One of the largest of these banks, the Fidelity Trust Company of Newark, was managed by a member of a prominent New Jersey family, Uzal McCarter. Uzal's brother, 35-year-old lawyer Thomas Nesbitt McCarter, was the youngest attorney general in the state's history, a director of Prudential Insurance Company, and a director and general counsel of Fidelity Trust. Thomas McCarter saw the opportunity offered by the utility crisis and proposed the creation of a single company that would provide transportation, gas, and electricity services for the entire state. The New Jersey, New York, and Pennsylvania financial and political establishments, with which he was well connected, agreed to McCarter's plan; and he resigned his public office to become president of the new corporation.

With an initial $10 million capitalization to begin its acquisition program, Public Service Corporation of New Jersey (PSC) was incorporated in May 1903. The original shareholders were

Company Perspectives:

We strive to extend our geographic footprint to increase earnings while remaining steadfast in our commitment to provide safe, reliable, high-quality delivery of energy to our customers in New Jersey.

Thomas Dolan, president of Philadelphia's United Gas Improvement Company; John I. Waterbury, president of New York's Manhattan Trust Company; and Thomas McCarter, who in effect represented Prudential Insurance Company and Fidelity Trust. The company clearly originated in the desire of these institutions to secure and re-establish the value of their New Jersey utility investments. Their plan was successful largely thanks to McCarter, who proved to be a strong, skillful manager, especially capable in the financial and political affairs so critical to a growing regulated utility. McCarter served as president for 36 years and as chairman of the board for an additional 6 years, until his retirement in 1945. During this long period he dominated the company's affairs.

PSC began by acquiring the securities of four street railway companies and one electric generating company, the beginning of an acquisition program that eventually brought more than 500 gas, electric, and traction businesses under the control of PSC and its successor companies. Revenues for 1904, the first year of operation, were $8.4 million from street railways, $5.4 million from gas manufacturing and sale, and $3.5 million from electricity.

Along with growth in operations and revenues over time came changes in corporate structure. Until 1907 PSC was a straightforward operating company, acquiring and leasing properties and improving and managing them. State regulation of utilities was institutionalized in 1907, by the creation of the State Railroad Commission, which expanded in 1910 to become the New Jersey State Board of Public Utility Commissioners. In August 1907, PSC was obliged to incorporate the Public Service Railway Company as a wholly owned subsidiary to operate its traction lines. In 1909, PSC formed Public Service Gas Company, also wholly owned, and in 1910 created Public Service Electric Company to generate and distribute electricity. PSC therefore became a holding company for the operating companies. There were further changes for the operating companies. In 1924, the gas and electric businesses were merged to form Public Service Electric and Gas Company(PSE&G), and in 1948, PSC was dissolved and PSE&G became the parent company with the transportation company as a subsidiary.

The Transportation Business: 1916–79

McCarter's original belief that PSC's future lay primarily in the transportation business proved to be erroneous. This business did grow and prosper in the early years, culminating in the opening in 1916 of a magnificent new street railway terminal and office building in Newark. PSC's transportation system grew to carry over 450 million passengers a year. It included street and interurban railways centered around Newark and reaching south to Camden and Trenton, as well as the ownership of amusement parks, ferry lines, cab companies in Newark and Camden, and eventually jitney and bus lines.

The company pioneered the development and use of gas-electric streetcars and buses, and in 1937 began operating the world's first diesel-electric bus fleet. The subsidiary Public Service Transportation Company was formed in 1924 to operate buses, and in 1928, this company and Public Service Railway Company were merged to form Public Service Coordinated Transport Company. The spread of suburban residential areas coupled with the rise of the automobile led to the gradual replacement of the streetcar and the interurban rail by the bus, however, and eventually to declining profitability for all forms of public transportation. The 1960s and 1970s saw a continuation of rising fares and increasing dependence on state subsidies. In 1971, Public Service Coordinated Transport became Transport of New Jersey, largely an operator of buses owned by the state and leased to the company.

In 1979, legislation was passed to permit New Jersey to acquire and operate private bus lines, and PSE&G negotiated the sale of its transport subsidiary to the state.

Unlike the traction companies it acquired, PSC's early gas acquisitions tended to be relatively sound physically and financially, and PSC's goal was to consolidate and expand these properties. In the early years gas was manufactured from coal or oil—natural gas pipelines were in the future—and sold mainly for lighting, cooking, and heating water; electricity use by the public was still minimal. PSC increased its gas sales by aggressively marketing gas stoves and water heaters as well as by increasing its distribution areas. Gas sales grew from 5 billion cubic feet in 1904 to about 20 billion cubic feet by the mid-1920s, then slowed during the 1930s and early 1940s. After World War II, the use of gas for home heating expanded enormously, outstripping the company's gas manufacturing capacity. In 1949, PSE&G began purchasing natural gas from Texas Eastern Gas Corporation and in 1950 from Transcontinental Gas Pipe Line Corporation.

Customers gradually were switched over from manufactured gas to natural gas, a process completed by 1965. During the energy shortages of the early 1970s, PSE&G experimented with plans to purchase liquefied natural gas from Algeria and to produce synthetic natural gas from naphtha. Both projects proved to be impractical because of cost, but gas sales continued to increase, reaching 200 billion cubic feet annually by the late 1970s. In 1972, PSE&G established subsidiary Energy Development Corp. (EDC) to engage in gas exploration and development. PSE&G also continued to expand its gas sales by encouraging home heating conversions from oil, selling gas for electric cogeneration, and experimenting with natural-gas-fueled vehicles. The firm also enlarged its gas supply by initiating purchases of natural gas from Canada in 1990.

Development of Electric and Nuclear Power Generation Plants: Early 1900s–1980s

Electric generating machinery at the turn of the century was still primitive and unreliable, with little residential or industrial use of electricity. When PSC began operations, its 14 generating stations had a capacity of about 40,000 kilowatts, most of which went to power street railways, realizing $3.5 million in electric revenues in 1904. Generator technology improved and electrical use increased tremendously over time. By 1978,

Key Dates:

1903: Public Service Corporation of New Jersey (PSC) is incorporated.
1907: State regulation of utilities becomes institutionalized.
1924: Public Service Electric and Gas Company (PSE&G) is formed.
1927: Agreements are formed with both Philadelphia Electric Co. and Pennsylvania Power & Light Co. for the interconnection and exchange of power.
1937: PSC begins operating the world's first diesel-electric bus fleet.
1948: PSC is dissolved; PSE&G becomes the parent company.
1972: Subsidiary Energy Development Corp. is created.
1974: The firm's first nuclear plant in Pennsylvania begins operation.
1986: Public Service Enterprise Group (PSEG) is formed to act as a holding company.
1989: Enterprise Diversified Holdings is formed to consolidate the firm's unregulated business.
1993: The Federal Energy Regulatory Commission completes deregulation of the supply segment of the natural gas industry; the National Energy Policy Act takes effect.
1994: A PSEG subsidiary signs a joint venture contract to build, own, and operate a power plant in China.
1996: PSEG sells Energy Development Corp.
1997: Energis Resources is created to take advantage of deregulation in the energy services market.
2000: Subsidiary PSEG Power is formed as an unregulated business.

PSE&G operated 13 generating plants with a capacity of 9 million kilowatts and achieved electric revenues of more than $1.5 billion. In 1990, the company's generating capability was 10.1 million kilowatts, and electric revenues were $3.3 billion.

The character of PSE&G's electrical history was shaped by its role as an innovator and pioneer of advanced techniques in power generation. PSE&G began early in this role by installing then-new rotating steam turbines in its Newark and Jersey City plants in 1905 and 1906. These two formerly separate plants acquired by PSC were linked into a single network, increasing the reliability and efficiency of the power system. The idea of linkage was enlarged in 1927 by agreements with Philadelphia Electric Company and Pennsylvania Power & Light Company for the interconnection and exchange of power. This led to the operation of a 230,000-volt transmission ring that was the world's first integrated power pool and that has expanded over the years to become the Pennsylvania-New Jersey-Maryland interconnection.

In 1933, the firm experimented with a 20,000-kilowatt mercury boiler-turbine, the largest unit of its type in the world, but mercury technology proved unsatisfactory. The company was also one of the first utilities to experiment with windpower generation, financing pilot wind-power stations in Burlington, New Jersey, during the early 1930s. Slowing service growth during the Great Depression put an end to this project, however.

The firm pioneered the use of airplane-type jet engines to drive electric generators for periods of peak power requirements. Generating units at the mouths of coal mines and pumped storage generating plants were also built as part of the company's continued search for low-cost power. Tests of solar generating systems were carried out during the late 1970s but proved not to be cost effective.

PSE&G joined with Philadelphia Electric Company, Atlantic City Electric Company, and Delmarva Power & Light Company during the 1960s to plan and build nuclear generating facilities. The first plant, owned jointly with Philadelphia Electric Company, was put in service at Peach Bottom, Pennsylvania, in 1974. Another nuclear plant began operation in 1977 at Salem, New Jersey, and a third went on line at Hope Creek, New Jersey, both in the southern part of the state.

Along with construction cost overruns, the company had other problems with nuclear power, including the temporary closing of the Peach Bottom units in 1987 by the U.S. Nuclear Regulatory Commission because of mismanagement. Among the infractions were workers sleeping on duty. This incident led to financial losses, although Philadelphia Electric, as the operator, was generally held responsible. The firm was also criticized in 1988 because of below average performance of its Salem and Hope Creek facilities. In 1989, the company was required to pay customers a $32 million rebate as compensation for the Peach Bottom shutdown. PSEG made a determined effort to improve its nuclear operations, and in 1990 reported that its nuclear plants had their most productive year ever. The company held a 95 percent interest in the Hope Creek plant, and a 42.5 percent interest in the Peach Bottom and Salem units. In 1990, about 47 percent of PSEG's electricity supplied to customers was provided by nuclear generation.

The period during the mid-1980s was marked by a corporate restructuring and a gradual move to diversify. On May 1, 1986, PSE&G became a subsidiary of Public Service Enterprise Group (PSEG), which also served as a parent of the company's nonutility subsidiaries. In 1989, the nonutility businesses were gathered together into a nonutility subholding company subsidiary, Enterprise Diversified Holdings, Inc. (Holdings). In 1989, PSEG agreed to buy Pelto Oil Corporation from the Southdown Company for about $320 million. Pelto, with substantial oil and gas reserves, operated as a subsidiary of Holdings. PSEG's other nonutility investments included aircraft and utility plant leasing, alternative energy projects, cogeneration, real estate, venture capital, and leveraged buyout funds.

The central motive for this diversification was that the state of New Jersey limited PSE&G's earnings to 13 percent of equity. Like many utilities, PSEG felt it must diversify to grow. E. James Ferland, chairman, president, and CEO since 1986, focused PSEG's efforts on acquiring and forming partnerships with businesses related to the energy industry. The announcement in November 1990 of a joint venture with Brooklyn Union Gas Company to build and operate a $250 million cogeneration plant to produce electricity for Kennedy International Airport near New York City was a step in that direction.

Continued Diversification and Deregulation in the 1990s

The 1990s were marked by continued diversification and change. In 1993, the Federal Energy Regulatory Commission (FERC) completed the deregulation of the supply segment of the natural gas industry. The National Energy Policy Act also went into effect, creating increased competition in the whole-sale electric market. Ferland stated in a 1993 letter to PSEG shareholders, "We, like the telecommunications and airline industries before us, are quickly moving from a relatively safe, secure, and protected field of operations to one of full-bore competition with little time for adjustment in between."

As such, PSEG focused not only on PSE&G operations, but on international expansion and restructuring as well. In 1994, the firm's Community Energy Alternatives Inc. (CEA) subsidiary began a joint venture to build, own, and operate a power plant in China—the first U.S. company to do so. The following year, CEA also began a venture in Venezuela. In 1995, PSEG created a new subsidiary entitled Enterprise Energy Technology Group to act as a energy management services company. As part of PSEG's strategy to pursue the development of new products and new market penetration, the firm sold its Energy Development Corp. subsidiary to Noble Affliates Inc. for $775 million.

Deregulation of the gas and electric utilities industry continued in the late mid-to-late 1990s. In response to increased competition, PSEG formed Energis Resources in 1997 to market energy products and services to business customers. By 1998, PSEG had also invested nearly $3 billion in non-regulated businesses, with almost half in international territories including Brazil, the Netherlands, Argentina, and China. In 1999, PSEG and California-based Sempra Energy announced plans to purchase 90 percent of Chilquinta Energia S.A., a Chilean-based energy firm. That same year, PSEG and Texas-based Panda Energy International Inc. formed a $1.3 billion joint venture to build three power plants in Texas.

As a result of the completion of deregulation in New Jersey, PSE&G's monopoly that controlled power sales to over 2.5 million New Jersey customers came to an end in August 1999. By that time, PSEG had reorganized its operations into operating units that focused on both domestic and international operations.

Operating As a Global Energy Firm in the New Millennium

Despite the increased competition, PSEG entered the new millennium on solid ground. Operating earnings for 2000 increased by eight percent over 1999 results. That year, PSE&G was ordered to transfer its electric generation assets and liabilities to an unregulated business as part of the deregulation order. As a result, PSEG Power was formed. The unregulated business began operation with over 10,000 megawatts of capacity, securing its position as a leading independent merchant energy operator in the United States.

By 2001, PSEG had successfully transformed itself from a traditional utility to a global energy firm. Determined to avoid electric supply problems that had surfaced in states including California, PSEG Power invested in wholesale markets in both New Jersey and New York, and was dedicated to building additional capacity in its home state to ensure adequate power supplies.

Along with its domestic operations, PSEG continued its international expansion in the new millennium. Through PSEG Global, the firm had begun operation of power plants in Texas, India, and China. It had also started construction of plants in California and Poland, and announced plans to purchase the SAESA group of electric distribution firms in both Chile and Argentina.

While eyeing new opportunities in energy services and related markets as key to remaining competitive, PSEG was dedicated to its long-standing tradition of providing gas and electric service to both business and residential customers on the home front. PSEG's successful diversification efforts during the deregulation of the electric and gas industries left management confident that the energy firm would experience continued achievements among its regulated and unregulated subsidiaries.

Principal Subsidiaries

Public Service Electric and Gas Co.; PSEG Energy Holdings; PSEG Global; PSEG Resources; PSEG Energy Technologies; PSEG Power; PSEG Fossil; PSEG Nuclear; PSEG Energy Resources & Trade.

Principal Competitors

Conectiv; GPU Inc.; New Jersey Resources Corporation.

Further Reading

"Chilquinta Deal Inked," *Oil Daily,* June 11, 1999.

Conniff, James C.G., and Richard Conniff, *The Energy People: A History of PSE&G,* Newark, N.J.: Public Service Electric and Gas Company, 1978.

DeMarrais, Kevin G., "Newark, N.J.-Based Utility Company Posts Strong Year Despite Deregulation," *Record* (New Jersey), January 20, 2000.

——, "New Jersey Utilities Expand Overseas," *Record* (New Jersey), September 26, 1998.

Elder, Laura E., "New Jersey Utility Shedding Its Local Energy Development Corp.," *Houston Business Journal,* March 29, 1996, p. 3A.

Gottschalk, Arthur, "Power Players: US Firms Find Global Energy Opportunities," *Journal of Commerce,* September 16, 1994, p. 1A.

Hogan, Rick, "Noble Affiliates Agrees to Buy EDC, Plans to Merge It With Samedan Oil," *Oil Daily,* July 3, 1996, p. 3.

"JFK Gets Power Plant," *Crain's New York Business,* November 12, 1990, p. 57.

"Public Service and Panda Form $1.3 Billion Venture," *New York Times,* April 6, 1999, p. 4.

Robertshaw, Nicky, "Utility's Problems Not Hurting Stock," *Crain's New York Business,* December 2, 1991, p. 43.

Smith, Robert I., *A Cycle of Service: The Story of Public Service Electric and Gas Company,* New York: Newcomen Society in North America, 1980.

Weimer, De'Ann, "Don't Be Shocked by Surges in the Price of Power," *Business Week,* July 27, 1998.

—Bernard A. Block
—update: Christina M. Stansell

R.G. Barry Corporation

13405 Yarmouth Road N.W.
Pickerington, Ohio 43147-9257
U.S.A.
Telephone: (614) 864-6400
Toll Free: (800) 848-7560
Fax: (614) 866-9787
Web site: http://www.rgbarry.com

Public Company
Incorporated: 1947
Employees: 2,600
Sales: $149.4 million (2000)
Stock Exchanges: New York
Ticker Symbol: RGB
NAIC: 316212 House Slipper Manufacturing; 31332
    Fabric Coating Mills; 316219 Other Footwear
    Manufacturing

R.G. Barry Corporation operates as the leading manufacturer and marketer of comfort footwear. Controlling nearly 40 percent of the U.S. slipper market, the firm became well known for brands such as Angel Treads—the first foam-cushioned, washable slipper, created in 1949—Barry Comfort, Dearfoams, EZfeet, Madye's, Mushrooms Slippers, Snug Treds, and Soft Notes. These brands were marketed in department stores, discount stores, warehouse clubs, drug chains, and specialty catalogs, and sold throughout the U.S. and in Mexico, Canada, the United Kingdom, and France. In 2000, over 90 percent of R.G. Barry's sales stemmed from its comfort footwear businesses—Wal-Mart was the firm's largest customer, accounting for nearly 20 percent of sales. Through its Vesture subsidiary, R.G. Barry also manufactures thermal retention technology products under the brands Dearfoams, LavaBuns, LavaPac, MICROCORE, POWERTECH, Quick Heat, and Vesture. In 1998, the firm sued Domino's Pizza, Inc. for patent infringement related to its MICROCORE technology—it had received patent rights earlier in the year. In 2000, Domino's settled the case, agreeing to pay R.G. Barry $5 million. In 2001, the Vesture subsidiary landed contracts with Papa John's International, Inc. and Do-

natos Pizzeria Corp. to supply both companies with heated pizza delivery systems. Having endured volatile swings in profitability and undergoing several reorganizations throughout the 1980s and 1990s, R.G. Barry sought to stabilize its financial path in the new millennium by strengthening its domestic operations as well as increasing its global business.

Early Development of R.G. Barry

The R.G. Barry Corporation was founded in 1945 in a Columbus, Ohio area basement. That is when three partners—Aaron Zacks, his wife Florence, and a colleague, Harry Streim—created Shoulda-Moulders Co., a maker of slippers, bathrobes, and pillows. Two years into the endeavor, the partners changed the company name to R.G. Barry Co., a veiled reference to their three sons. The ''R'' stood for Harry's son Richard, the ''G'' for Aaron and Florence's son Gordon, and Barry referred to his sibling.

Despite his prominence in the company moniker, Barry did not follow his parents into the family business; instead he went on to found the Max & Erma's restaurant chain. It was Gordon who joined the company upon his 1955 graduation from The Ohio State University's College of Commerce. Knowing his son's penchant for learning by doing, Aaron Zacks assigned Gordon to establish a new corporate manufacturing division in New York. Gordon's operation lost money its first year, while the headstrong entrepreneur became acclimated to the intricacies of manufacturing. This ''trial by fire'' would prove vital to the younger Zacks's professional development. In 1957, Gordon was summoned back to R.G. Barry's suburban Columbus headquarters when his father's health began to fail. Aaron Zacks suffered a fatal heart attack in 1965, thrusting his relatively inexperienced 32-year-old son into the company presidency.

After taking a course on corporate management from the American Management Association, Gordon Zacks pared R.G. Barry's interests to Dearfoam slippers, which had been introduced in 1958. He then sought to boost the company's business via acquisitions. Over the course of the 1960s, the firm added operations in Puerto Rico, Tennessee, Texas, North Carolina, and New York, and expanded its family of brands to include

Bernardo brand ladies' imported Italian sandals. The firm went public in 1962 to help fund expansion efforts. In 1971, R.G. Barry acquired Maine's Quoddy Products Inc., retailer of hand-sewn Quoddy moccasins.

This strategy of diversification within the footwear industry was very successful; company sales doubled over the course of Gordon's first five years at R.G. Barry's helm. However, Gordon Zacks's early achievement may have endowed him with a bit of vainglory. In a 1985 interview with *Business First-Columbus*'s Bill Atkinson, he admitted, ''When I think I'm right I have great faith and confidence in my own judgment.'' While admirable to a certain degree, that egoism would later threaten R.G. Barry's fiscal health.

Introduction of Mushroom Brand in the 1970s

Emboldened by his success, Zacks directed the development of a new line of women's comfort shoes. Dubbed Mushrooms, the footwear was five years in the making and was backed by a marketing program that took another three years to fine-tune. Zacks boasted that it was ''one of the most successful marketing programs in the history of the shoe industry.'' Backed by hundreds of thousands in advertising dollars, R.G. Barry's sales and earnings ''mushroomed'' throughout the 1970s, peaking at over $120 million and $3.8 million, respectively, in 1978.

This relatively small central Ohio company's successful diversification out of its traditional house slipper niche caught the attention of U.S. Shoe Corp., a billion-dollar southern Ohio shoemaker and retailer. U.S. Shoe responded to Barry's incursion on its market by developing a competing brand, Candie's, which it supported with a multimillion-dollar advertising campaign. Despite the odds—R.G. Barry had a mere fraction of the financial and market clout of its multifaceted competitor—Zacks struggled to maintain his company's hard-won position in women's shoes. As Barry Zacks commented in Atkinson's 1985 piece, ''[Gordon] began to equate success or failure with his own personal success.'' By the early 1980s, his firm had 22 Mushrooms stores in California, Florida, Michigan, and Washington, D.C. During this period, R.G. Barry also expanded the Quoddy chain to 43 stores. The company supported its greatly expanded retail activities with the addition of three manufacturing plants and a network of warehouses, but Zacks failed to take into account the vagaries of popular taste. His bold growth plan soon began to look more like a hasty overexpansion, especially in contrast to U.S. Shoe's ongoing success. Zacks reflected on his skirmish with U.S. Shoe in the 1985 interview with *Business First-Columbus,* stating, ''We were holding our own, but we were bleeding to death.''

After four years of declining earnings and slipping sales, Zacks conceded defeat in 1982. That year, the company took a $12.5 million loss on the sale of its degenerating Mushrooms chain to none other than U.S. Shoe, which converted the retail outlets to its Candie's format. R.G. Barry incurred an $8.5 million overall loss in 1982. Zacks must have taken some consolation in the fact that his giant rival licensed the Mushroom trademark from his firm for $1 million per year. Barry continued its retreat back to the core Dearfoams slippers with the 1983 spin-off of its Quoddy retail chain to Wolverine World Wide, Inc., manufacturer of Hush Puppies shoes. Two years later, the company sold its Bernardo operations to Jumping-Jacks Shoes, Inc.

Reorganization and Retrenchment in the 1980s

Over the course of the next three years, R.G. Barry worked to pare operating expenses and reinvigorate its neglected slipper line. A 1983 restructuring—one of many to come over the ensuing decade—shuttered three plants and reduced employment by 28 percent, from 3,200 to 2,300. Hoping to take advantage of the lower labor and production costs available overseas, the company launched an import division in 1983 and began moving manufacturing operations from the northeast United States to the Southwest and Mexico. By mid-decade, it had shifted its production ratio from 100 percent domestic to 20 percent domestic and 80 percent foreign.

R.G. Barry also worked to broaden its appeal in the slipper market from a near exclusive emphasis on women to include men and children. A licensing program used the popular Cabbage Patch Kids and Care Bear characters to appeal to children, while Dearfoams developed a line of slippers for men. Other lines with designer names like Oscar de la Renta and Christian Dior commanded higher price points. Barry also redesigned and repackaged its line of women's Dearfoams with particular focus on the product's ''giftability.'' The footwear was such a popular gift that the vast majority, 80 percent, of R.G. Barry's annual sales were concentrated in the fall holiday shopping season. The company emphasized the luxuriousness of its Dearfoams with its first-ever celebrity advertising campaign featuring Zsa Zsa Gabor. In the latter years of the decade, R.G. Barry broadened its retail distribution from its core in department stores to mass merchandisers like Kmart and Wal-Mart. By the end of the decade, CEO Zacks was able to boast that his company had ''fresh and exciting products in every price point.''

These strategies appeared successful. Although sales declined from $141.1 million in 1981 to $86 million in 1986, the company recovered from its loss position to effect a $4.3 million profit in the latter year. Barry's sales increased steadily to $122.8 million by 1989, but its net income fluctuated erratically throughout the latter years of the decade, from a low of only $23,000 in 1988 to $3.7 million in 1989.

Under pressure from increased foreign and domestic competition, the company slid into the red the following year, incurring total losses of $8.3 million in 1990 and 1991. Zacks mandated two ''major restructurings'' in the span of two months in late 1990 and early 1991. The company reduced its inventory, reorganized its sales force, installed an integrated database system, cut its administrative support staff and laid off 370 U.S. employees. Zacks estimated that this ''right-sizing''

Key Dates:

1945: Shoulda-Moulders Co. is established.

1947: The company officially adopts the name R.G. Barry Corporation.

1949: Angel Treads, the first foam-cushioned washable slipper is introduced.

1958: The company launches the Dearfoam brand slipper.

1962: R.G. Barry goes public.

1971: Quoddy Products Inc. is acquired.

1982: The firm is forced to sell its Mushrooms brand to competitor U.S. Shoe Corp.

1983: After posting a $8.5 million loss in the previous year, the company begins restructuring efforts.

1991: R.G. Barry restructures once again due to losses related to increased competition.

1994: Vesture Corp. is purchased.

1995: The firm lists on the New York Stock Exchange; ThermaStor Technologies Ltd. is created as part of a joint venture with Battelle Memorial Institute.

1998: Vesture receives a patent for its MICROCORE pizza/hot food delivery systems; the subsidiary files a lawsuit against Domino's Pizza, Inc. for patent infringement.

1999: Fargeot et Compagnie SA is acquired; the company records its worst year in its history.

2000: The company begins restructuring efforts once again and secures licensing rights for the Liz Claiborne brand name.

2001: R.G. Barry lands contracts with Papa John's International Inc. and Donatos Pizzeria Corp. to supply heat pizza delivery systems to the pizzamakers.

would save the company $6 million to $7 million in operating costs each year. In one of its most surprising moves, R.G. Barry shareholders elected U.S. Shoe Chairman Philip G. Barach to a seat on the board of directors in 1991.

New Products, Global Expansion Pace Mid-1990s Growth

In the midst of these operational shifts, the company also laid the groundwork for the launch of a whole new class of products. In cooperation with Columbus's Battelle Memorial Institute, R.G. Barry developed a flexible, microwaveable pouch that could retain its heat for up to eight hours. Dubbed "ThermaStor," the product won a spot on *R&D* magazine's listing of 1994's top inventions. These units were used in cold-weather accessories like scarves, gloves, and vests as well as household and leisure articles like breadbaskets and stadium seats. The products were offered under the "Heat to Go" brand at mass merchandisers and under the venerable Dearfoams label in department stores. Barry boosted its manufacturing capacity in this segment with the 1994 acquisition of Vesture Corp., whose "MICROCORE" was similar to Barry's own ThermaStor, but utilized a different technology.

Analyst Bart Blout told *Business First-Columbus*'s Carrie Shook that "this technology has far-reaching applications and

hundreds of products will be created with it—from shoes to toys." Not only did this open up a completely new and unique segment of the consumer market to R.G. Barry, but it also held great potential for the development of products for the medical, industrial, commercial, and military segments. In 1995, Barry and Battelle formed a joint venture known as ThermaStor Technologies, Ltd. to explore these opportunities. That same year, the company was first listed on the New York Stock Exchange. Barry also focused on the development of international markets in the mid-1990s, establishing operations in Europe, Asia, Canada, and Mexico.

R.G. Barry's financial performance improved dramatically in the mid-1990s. Sales increased from $101.8 million in 1992 to $136.6 million in 1995; profits grew to a record-breaking $6.3 million in the latter year. In 1996, management assumed that the financial difficulties were in the past and began beefing up manufacturing capacity. Confident that it would continue to secure positive results, the firm began spending to create a strong infrastructure to support the anticipated growth. In 1997, while the firm celebrated its 50th anniversary, R.G. Barry recorded the most favorable financial results in its history.

Further Financial Struggles and Restructuring

The celebration was short-lived however. While 1998 proved to be another successful year, it was followed by one of the worst in the firm's history. In 1999, Sears, J.C. Penney, and Mervyn's began selling private label brand slippers, spelling out disaster for the Dearfoam brand. That year, R.G. Barry lost $8 million in sales related to the department store shift to private label brands. The company also estimated that it lost nearly $6 million in sales due to retail store closings and consolidation in the industry. Management cited several internal factors as culprits in the drastic slide in performance. These included lackluster products, late delivery on holiday slipper styles, manufacturing problems, and weak consumer reception of the company's new Soluna Spa-At-Home collection. Overall, R.G. Barry posted a $13.8 million loss that year.

As such, R.G. Barry entered the new millennium intent on regaining financial stability. The firm announced restructuring efforts in 2000 that included 240 job cuts, a factory shutdown in China as well as North Carolina, closure of its Columbus, Ohio, sample-making plant, and a reduction in manufacturing capacity to adjust with product demand. The firm also focused efforts on reviving its current brands. Ed Bucciarelli, R.G. Barry's comfort division president, stated in a *Footwear News* article, "In restructuring, we've really redefined the needs of the business and responded to those needs. We want to position the brands so that we speak to a more updated consumer as well, a consumer who is more trend oriented. We think by segmenting our line to appeal to these different lifestyles, we'll reach a broader audience and really expand."

Financial results improved in 2000. Sales increased to $149.4 million from $140.1 million recorded in 1999. During that year, the firm secured a licensing contract with Liz Claiborne Inc., allowing the firm to manufacture and sell slippers under the trendy Liz Claiborne brand label. Building upon its 1999 purchase of French-based Fargeot et Compagnie SA, the firm bolstered European operations in 2000 by forming an alliance with the British firm GBR Ltd. The pair formed Barry GBR Ltd. to sell comfort footwear in the UK as well as Ireland.

In 2001, Bill Lenich was named president, chief operating officer, and director of R.G. Barry. Hired to aid the company in a three-year strategic plan, Lenich faced the difficult task of restoring the firm to profitability. The plan, expected to reach completion in 2003, included the following actions: aligning consumer demand with manufacturing capacity, increasing the percentage of products supplied by outside contractors, implementing speed-to-market and cost effective strategies, improving product design and development, and maintaining a firm grasp on expenses. While the entire retail industry was undergoing a decline due to a weakening American economy, Lenich, along with R.G. Barry management, felt confident that the firm would remain a leader among casual footwear manufacturers.

Principal Subsidiaries

Barry de Acuna S.A. de C.V.; Barry de la Republica Dominicana S.A.; Barry de Mexico S.A. de C.V.; Fargeot et Compagnie S.A.; R.G. Barry France Holdings Inc.; R.G. Barry Holdings Inc.; R.G.B. Inc.; R.G. Barry International Inc.; R.G. Barry Texas LP; Vesture Corp.; ThermaStor Technologies, Ltd.

Principal Competitors

Daniel Green Company; Danskin, Inc.; Wolverine Worldwide, Inc.

Further Reading

Atkinson, Bill, "Anatomy of a Mistake," *Business First-Columbus,* November 18, 1985, pp. 12–13, 19.

"Barry Has Quarter, Year Loss Disposing of Mushrooms," *Footwear News,* February 28, 1983, p. 4.

"Barry Quarter in the Chips, As Annual Net Plummets," *Footwear News,* February 25, 1985, p. 48.

"Barry Quarter, Year Profit Up Sharply," *Footwear News,* February 26, 1990, p. 26.

Bell, Thia, "Slipping Ahead; Dearfoams Is Making Strides with Updated Product and New Management," *Footwear News,* April 24, 2000, p. 22.

"Domino's Settles in Delivery Bag Dispute," *Nation's Restaurant News,* April 10, 2000, p. 3.

Foster, Pamela E., "R.G. Barry Moving Some Jobs to Texas," *Business First-Columbus,* February 18, 1991, pp. 1–2.

Jackson, William, "Ohio Sends Manufacturing South: Mexico Wooing U.S. Corporations," *Business First-Columbus,* July 16, 1990.

Kosdrosky, Terry, "Domino's Sued Over Pizza-Warmer Patent," *Crain's Detroit Business,* October 5, 1998, p. 35.

Lenetz, Dana, "R.G. Barry Taps New President, Rethinks Plans," *Footwear News,* February 26, 2001, p. 4.

Lilly, Stephen, "Barry Shareholder Alleges Insider Trading," *Business First-Columbus,* January 16, 1995, pp. 1–2.

Newpoff, Laura, "Zacks Pushing R.G. Barry to Get in Step With New Lines," *Business First-Columbus,* October 29, 1999, p. 4.

"R.G. Barry Initiates Restructuring Program," *Business First-Columbus,* December 24, 1999, p. 34.

"R.G. Barry Lays Off 27; 344 More to Go," *Footwear News,* December 10, 1990, p. 24.

"R.G. Barry Puts Barach on Board," *Footwear News,* August 26, 1991, p. 4.

"R.G. Barry Uses Celebrity, Zsa Zsa Gabor, for First Time in an Ad Campaign," *Columbus Dispatch,* December 20, 1988, p. 3D.

Rieger, Nancy, "Barry Sees Profit Boom," *Footwear News,* April 17, 1989, pp. 2–3.

Seckler, Valerie, "Sickly Retail Scene Seen Affordable Slippers' Boon," *Footwear News,* June 27, 1988, pp. 2–3.

Shook, Carrie, "New Products Heat Up R.G. Barry," *Business First-Columbus,* August 22, 1994, pp. 1–2.

Solnik, Claude, "R.G. Barry to Reorganize Operations," *Footwear News,* January 3, 2000, p. 2.

Wessling, Jack, "Barry Plans to Close or Sell Two Slipper Plants," *Footwear News,* September 3, 1984, pp. 2–3.

——, "Barry Returns to Black in '83," *Footwear News,* July 30, 1984, pp. 2–3.

——, "Barry Sets Designer Slippers," *Footwear News,* May 7, 1990, p. 23.

——, "Critter Pulled in by a Nose," *Footwear News,* February 4, 1991, p. 58.

"Warming Trend," *Women's Wear Daily,* May 31, 1994, p. 22.

—April Dougal Gasbarre
—update: Christina M. Stansell

Reliant Energy Inc.

1111 Louisiana Street
Houston, Texas 77002
U.S.A.
Telephone: (713) 207-3000
Fax: (713) 207-3169
Web site: http://www.reliantenergy.com

Public Company
Incorporated: 1906 as Houston Lighting & Power
    Company 1905
Employees: 15,633
Sales: $29.3 billion (2000)
Stock Exchanges: New York Chicago
Ticker Symbol: REI
NAIC: 221111 Hydroelectric Power Generation; 221112
    Fossil Fuel Electric Power Generation; 221113
    Nuclear Electric Power Generation; 221119 Other
    Electric Power Generation; 221121 Electric Bulk
    Power Transmission and Control; 221122 Electric
    Power Distribution; 22121 Natural Gas Distribution

Reliant Energy Inc.—formerly Houston Industries Inc.—operates among the top five power and natural gas marketers in the United States. With over $32 billion in assets, the company serves nearly four million customers in the southern United States and Minnesota. After the Texas Electric Choice Act was passed in 1999, Reliant Energy rolled its non-regulated operations into Reliant Resources, a majority owned subsidiary with power plants it the United States as well as the Netherlands. Reliant Resources also markets and trades energy in Germany, the United Kingdom, and in the United States. Reliant Energy Communications, an Internet-related division, provides Texans with Internet, data, voice, and other telecommunications services.

Early History

Reliant Energy's earliest predecessor, Houston Electric Light & Power Company (HEL&P), was chartered in 1882 by Emanuel Raphael, a cashier at the Houston Savings Bank and one of several prominent Houston businessmen bent on bringing electric lights to their city. Other investors included Houston Mayor William R. Baker, who ushered the new utility through a franchise agreement with the city, which allowed HEL&P to construct and operate a power plant and electric lines.

HEL&P's policy of charging flat rates, coupled with low electrical usage, spelled early financial problems for the company, and by 1886 the firm had entered receivership. The following year a bankrupt HEL&P was sold to a competing Houston utility, Houston Gas Light Company. In 1889 Citizens' Electric Light & Power Company entered the Houston utility arena and two years later bought out Houston Gas Light's interest in HEL&P.

In late 1897, Citizens' Electric defaulted on bank loans, and in January 1898 the utility was placed under control of another receiver, Houston attorney Blake Dupree. William H. Chapman, a Boston businessman, was soon brought in as general manager of the company and became a stabilizing force, initiating a power line rebuilding program and advocating use of residential lighting.

Shortly after Chapman arrived in Houston, a boiler exploded at the utility's Gable Street power plant during the evening of March 26, killing four men and leaving the city in total darkness. Early the following morning, a fire started in the damaged plant and destroyed everything of value. Vowing to continue operations, Dupree promptly signed a contract with General Electric Corporation for new power plant equipment, and by 1900 a new Gable Street plant was operational.

Citizens' Electric continued to have financial troubles, and in 1901 its assets were transferred to United Electric Securities Company, the investment arm of General Electric and the Houston utility's major creditor at that time. That same year Citizens' Electric was reorganized as Houston Lighting and Power Company (HL&P).

Under United Electric Securities, HL&P established a fully metered system for keeping track of electrical use, and abandoned a flat-rate fee system for one that offered rate incentives for increased usage. Following the discovery of oil in the

Houston area during the year of its incorporation, HL&P changed its boiler fuel from coal to oil.

The discovery of oil also changed Houston, spawning a period of growth and industrialization along the Gulf Coast. General Electric's infusion of cash and electrical generators helped HL&P keep pace, and by 1902 the company's electrical lines were serving nearly all of Houston.

On January 9, 1906, a day after the company declared its first dividend, HL&P was purchased by Isadore Newman & Sons, a holding company based in New York and New Orleans that operated under the name of American Cities Railway and Light Company. That same year the Houston utility was reorganized as Houston Lighting & Power Company 1905, and became part of an electric utility holding company structure that operated a string of southern U.S. properties.

During the first decade of the 20th century, HL&P's sales grew with the area's oil industry. Power lines were extended to oil fields as they sprouted up, as well as the growing number of refiners locating along the Houston Ship Channel. In 1910, the company also began supplying electricity to pipeline firms. In 1911, American Cities Railway & Light Company, renamed American Cities Company, was sold to Bertron Griscom & Company, a holding company with offices in New York, Philadelphia, and Paris. That same year the Bertron Griscom board of directors promoted general manager William H. Chapman to company president.

In 1913, Houston voters approved city charter amendments that empowered Houston to regulate public utilities and establish its own electric utility in the event it was unhappy with HL&P's service. The amendments set in motion a year-long series of negotiations between HL&P and the city, culminating in a profit-sharing agreement, which guaranteed the company a 12 percent rate of return and the city any profits above that return.

Shortly after the profit-sharing agreement was reached in 1914, Chapman retired and the Bertron Griscom board named Edwin B. Parker, an attorney with the firm that represented the company in negotiations with the city, to replace Chapman. Unlike Chapman, Parker served mostly as a figurehead president, who left the day-to-day operations in the hands of Sam

Bertron, who was named general manager a year after Parker's appointment.

By 1914, HL&P was showing a profit for the first time in its history. That same year HL&P began expanding into suburban Houston, acquiring electrical assets in Houston Heights and establishing a franchise agreement to serve the city of Magnolia Park. During the next four years electrical systems were acquired in Sunset Heights, Brunner, and Park Place, with all of the suburbs eventually becoming part of Houston.

After the United States entered World War I in 1917, HL&P was called on to extend its power lines to Camp Logan, a U.S. Army barracks in Houston. The war helped prolong Houston's industrial boom, but during the conflict company finances took a turn for the worse as HL&P struggled to fund additional generating capacity needed to serve the growing area.

The Electric Bond & Share Acquisition: 1922

Financial problems continued for HL&P after the war, and Bertron Griscom, close to receivership itself by 1921, was in no position to help. In 1922 financial help came, as it did 21 years earlier, from a company affiliated with General Electric. In 1922, the Electric Bond & Share Company through its subsidiary National Power & Light Company, acquired HL&P. Electric Bond & Share had been spun off by General Electric as a holding company for public utilities. With the change in ownership, HL&P once again became part of a healthy holding company structure, with operations in 33 states.

Electric Bond & Share put a quick infusion of capital into HL&P's operations, part of which came from an aggressive program of local stock sales beginning in 1922. Among the modernization and construction projects laid out by Electric Bond & Share was a sorely needed modern power plant. In 1923, construction began on the $5 million Deepwater plant along the Houston Shipping Channel, which would more than double the company's generating capacity with the ability to serve two million residents.

By 1924, Deepwater's first two generating units were operational. While the company continued to improve its service system throughout the 1920s with additional generating units, transmission, and distribution line improvements, after Deepwater went on line HL&P turned its focus toward marketing and expansion efforts.

In 1924, HL&P moved from its three-story headquarters into the ten-story downtown Electric Building, where a seven-story lighted sign was hung. HL&P began using the widely visible first floor of the Electric Building to display the variety of electrical appliances it marketed. HL&P also organized sales crews to canvass residential neighborhoods, and demonstrate and sell appliances. With expansion that followed, within a few years HL&P canceled its exclusive merchandise franchises and began encouraging residents to buy appliances from area dealers.

Deepwater's construction allowed HL&P to seek out new industrial as well as residential customers. Rate reductions were offered to attract new business to the area and to bring on line existing industries that had constructed their own generating

Key Dates:

1882: Houston Electric Light & Power (HEL&P) is chartered by Emanuel Raphael.

1887: HEL&P is sold to Houston Gas Light Company.

1891: Citizens' Electric Light & Power Co. takes ownership of HEL&P.

1898: Blake Dupree takes control of HEL&P after Citizens' Electric defaults on bank loans.

1901: Citizens' assets are transferred to United Electric Securities Co.; the firm is reorganized as Houston Lighting and Power Co. (HL&P).

1906: HL&P is purchased by Isadore Newman & Sons, a holding company operating under the name American Cities Railway and Light Company.

1911: American Cities is sold to Bertron Griscom & Company.

1914: HL&P shows a profit for the first time in its history.

1922: National Power and Light Co., a subsidiary of the Electric Bond & Share Co. acquires HL&P.

1932: HL&P workers are forced to take wage reductions as company revenues drop.

1942: The company becomes independent after National Power & Light Co. is forced to sell its interest in order to comply with the 1935 Public Utility Holding Company Act.

1957: The Houston City Council grants HL&P a new 50-year franchise agreement.

1960: The firm requests its first rate increase in order to offset rising costs.

1964: HL&P begins a five-year, $939 million growth and expansion plan.

1973: The company creates subsidiaries Primary Fuels Inc. (PFI) and Utility Fuels Inc. (UFI).

1976: Holding company Houston Industries Inc. (HI) is formed.

1985: HI begins a three-year diversification plan and creates subsidiary Innovative Controls Inc.

1986: HI and Time Inc.'s cable television unit form Paragon Communications; HI forms subsidiary KBLCOM to manage its cable operations.

1987: HI establishes two additional subsidiaries, Development Ventures Inc. and Houston Industries Finance Inc.

1989: PFI is sold and the U.S. cable television system of Rogers Communications Inc. is purchased.

1990: KBLCOM forms KBL-TV to sell advertising on cable channels.

1995: HI sells it cable unit to Time Warner.

1997: The firm completes its $2.5 billion purchase of NorAm Energy Corp.

1999: HI changes its name to Reliant Energy Inc.

2000: The company splits its unregulated and regulated businesses, forming Reliant Resources Inc.

2001: Reliant Resources Inc., the unregulated energy subsidiary of Reliant Energy, raises $1.8 billion in its initial public offering.

facilities during the American Cities Railway era of low-generating capacity.

On the residential side, with its increased capacity HL&P entered nearly 70 Houston-area communities during the 1920s, acquiring existing electrical properties while extending lines into nonserviced areas for the first time. During the second half of the 1920s HL&P also began building a backup power supply, entering into electric system interconnection agreements with neighboring Texas utilities.

Following the death of Edwin Parker in 1930, Sam Bertron, Jr., was promoted to president and Hiram O. Clarke was named vice-president. Despite the Great Depression that began in 1929, HL&P continued expansion efforts through 1931, when it acquired its largest service system to date by purchasing the assets of the Galveston Electric Company.

While the Great Depression never hit Houston as hard as it struck other areas, in 1931 company revenues began to slide and by 1932 workers were forced to take wage reductions to keep their jobs. Revenues bottomed out in 1933, and three years later a financially stable HL&P began a series of rate reductions that stretched through the end of the 1930s. By 1937, the company had resumed construction programs halted earlier in the decade, including a submarine cable to Galveston Island and the addition of a generating unit at the Gable Street plant, which had not been updated since Bertron Griscom controlled the utility.

Expansion as an Independent Company: 1940s–60s

HL&P entered the 1940s with a 5,000-square-mile service area, which included 150,000 customers in 140 communities. In 1942, HL&P also entered a new era, becoming an independent company after National Power & Light Company was forced to sell its interests in the Houston utility in order to comply with the provisions of the 1935 Public Utility Holding Company Act.

After the United States entered World War II, HL&P was called on to construct additional power plants to meet wartime construction needs. In 1943, the first unit of HL&P's third power plant, West Junction, went on line. With concern for power failures, the company also accelerated its interconnection activities during the war and became part of a power-pool arrangement that tied investor-owned utilities in Texas to dams along the state's major rivers.

Following the war, the demands of a petroleum-related industrial boom in the Houston area replaced the war as a motivating factor, and spurred HL&P to increase its generating capacity. Between 1946 and the end of the decade the company placed additional generating units at West Junction, and built a fourth plant, Greens Bayou.

During the first half of the 1950s power plant construction continued at a rapid clip. The company built a fifth power facility, the Webster plant, and added generating units at West Junction and Greens Bayou. In 1950, Hiram Clarke died, and the West Junction plant that Clarke had designed was renamed in his honor. In late 1953 Bertron died, and the following year Walter Alvis Parish, a former company attorney, was tapped to succeed Bertron.

Between 1956 and the end of the decade, the company continued to increase its generating capacity, constructing the Sam Bertron plant, the Smithers Lake plant—later renamed the W.A. Parish plant—and the North Houston plant. In 1957, the Houston City Council granted the company a new 50-year franchise, and HL&P promptly turned to the other 37 incorporated communities it served for similar 50-year franchise agreements.

W.A. Parish was named the company's first chairman in 1958, and Tom H. Wharton, a former executive vice-president, was promoted to president. The following year Parish died, and Wharton assumed the additional post of chairman.

After decades of rate reductions, in 1960 HL&P requested the first rate increase in its history in order to offset the financial effects of its building program and a recession in the Texas economy. The company was granted a $4.1 million increase, half of its $8.2 million request. A year later HL&P faced another setback when Hurricane Carla ripped through its service area, causing $1.6 million worth of electrical system damages.

Despite a slow start, HL&P continued to witness explosive growth in its service area during the 1960s. In response to that growth, three generating units were added to existing plants during the first half of the decade. During the same period HL&P continued building its ''power highway,'' a network of interconnected transmission systems with other electric utilities that would stretch from the Gulf of Mexico to the Red River.

In 1963 P.H. Robinson, an executive vice-president, was promoted to president while Wharton continued to serve as chairman for the next two years. In 1964 Robinson announced the start of a five-year, $939 million growth and expansion plan dubbed Project Enterprise, aimed at doubling the company's generating capacity with the addition of four new generating units, including construction of what would become the P.H. Robinson plant. Project Enterprise's construction projects also included a fully-computerized energy control center, seven new service centers, and a new 27-story corporate headquarters, named the Electric Tower.

Development of Nuclear Power Plants: 1970s

In 1970, Robinson was named to fill the five-year vacancy in the chairman's seat, and Carl Sherman, a former executive vice-president, was promoted to president. By 1971, the company began serious study of nuclear power plants, but those plans as well as other proposals for increased generating capacity during the decade became subject to increasing federal regulations.

HL&P first felt the effects of the changing regulatory environment in 1971, when the U.S. Environmental Protection Agency challenged the location of the company's gas-fired Cedar Bayou generating station, less than a month after the plant had been dedicated. The EPA alleged that Cedar Bayou's discharge of water into Trinity Bay would damage marine life, while HL&P maintained it would improve it. After a two-year legal battle the EPA agreed to end its opposition. In return, the company agreed to reduce its planned number of generating units from six to three, and expand its water-quality monitoring programs.

In 1972, HL&P announced plans for two Austin County, Texas, nuclear power plants, one to be located on Allens Creek and a second plant on the lower Mill Creek. In 1973, Mill Creek plans were scuttled in response to public opposition, and nine years later a series of regulatory hearing delays and escalating construction costs led HL&P to kill the Allens Creek project.

In 1973, HL&P formed a joint venture with the cities of San Antonio and Austin and neighboring Central Power and Light Company to construct a nuclear power plant southwest of Houston along the Gulf Coast. HL&P became managing partner of the venture, owning a 30.8 percent interest in what became known as the South Texas Project (STP). While HL&P was making plans for nuclear plants, during the first half of the 1970s HL&P finished construction of seven gas-fired units at existing plants.

Following the Organization of Petroleum Exporting Countries (OPEC) oil embargo of 1973 HL&P began promoting conservation of electricity. The increasing complexities surrounding fuel supplies also led HL&P to form two wholly owned subsidiaries, Primary Fuels, Inc. (PFI) and Utility Fuels, Inc. (UFI). PFI was created in 1973 to explore for and develop oil and gas reserves along the Texas Gulf Coast. In 1974, UFI was formed to acquire and deliver power plant fuels, with activities initially limited to HL&P fuels and later expanded to serve other companies.

In 1974, Robinson retired as chairman and was replaced by Sherman. Before the year was over Sherman died and in the ensuing corporate reshuffle two former executive vice-presidents took over, with J.G. Reese elected chairman and Don Jordan, at the age of 42, elected the youngest president in the company's history.

Following a corporate restructuring process in 1976, the holding company Houston Industries Inc. (HI) was formed to give HL&P and its affiliates greater financial and organizational flexibility. In 1977, HI became the owner of all HL&P, UFI, and PFI assets. Reese was named chairman of the new holding company and Jordan president. After exactly 50 years of service to HL&P and affiliates, in April 1978 Reese retired, leaving his two chairmen seats vacant.

With increased federal government pressure to abandon oil and natural gas as boiler fuels, during the late 1970s HL&P began converting its generators to coal. UFI played a major role in the gradual transition to coal, negotiating long-term coal-supply contracts and purchasing more than 1,000 railroad cars for coal transportation, which during the following decade led to expansion of UFI's business activities outside of HL&P operations. In 1979, HL&P announced it would construct a power plant in Limestone County, Texas, that would burn lignite, a soft form of coal. Six years later, after escalating costs delayed construction, the Limestone plant began operations.

The South Texas Project also experienced considerable construction delays, and by 1979, three years after building had started, serious questions were being raised about quality control at the construction site. During 1979 and 1980, the company issued several stop-work orders at STP in response to governmental concerns.

With STP just one-third finished, in late 1981 HL&P dismissed Brown & Root, Inc. as construction manager and architect, but asked the firm to retain its assignment to do the actual construction. Brown & Root, however, resigned that post. In moves unprecedented in the construction of nuclear power plants, HL&P changed both its architect and builder, naming Bechtel Corporation as architect-engineer and Ebasco Constructors Inc. as builder. In 1982, HL&P filed suit against Brown & Root charging the firm with breach of contract, and three years later HL&P received a $750 million settlement from its former contractor. Facing the inflationary conditions of 1982, a backlogged construction schedule and heightened public dissent over company rate increases and HL&P's handling of STP, Don Jordan was named chairman and chief executive officer of HL&P, and Don Sykora, a former executive vice-president, was elevated to president and chief operating officer of the utility.

To ease the strain on its generating capacity caused by construction delays, in 1983 HL&P tapped three of its industrial customers and began purchasing power produced through co-generation, the simultaneous production of electricity and thermal energy from the same fuel source. In a move to improve public relations that same year, Jordan created a community services division to provide bill-paying assistance to low-income, elderly, and handicapped customers. In 1983, Hurricane Alicia ripped through Houston, leaving a path of devastation that knocked out 8,000 miles of power lines and left an unprecedented 750,000 customers without electricity, with some customers waiting more than two weeks for power to be restored.

Branching Out Into the Cable Industry: Late 1980s

In 1985, HI began a three-year series of diversification moves and formed the subsidiary Innovative Controls, Inc., to develop and market lightweight security lights. In 1986 HI and Time Inc.'s cable television unit formed Paragon Communications, a 50–50 joint venture to purchase 22 cable television systems serving 550,000 customers, primarily in Texas, Florida, and the Northeast. That same year HI formed the subsidiary KBLCOM Incorporated to manage its cable operations.

In 1987, HL&P formed two other subsidiaries. Development Ventures, Inc., a venture capital organization, was formed to provide start-up financing for small businesses; while Houston Industries Finance, Inc., an unconsolidated subsidiary, was created to purchase accounts receivables of HL&P and other HI subsidiaries to reduce the utility's capital requirements.

In 1988, the South Texas Project was cleared by government bodies of all safety concerns and granted a full operating license, more than 15 years after plans for the plant had begun and after construction costs had risen by nearly 500 percent to $5.5 billion. HL&P also won the first round in a lawsuit brought by the city of Austin, which alleged HL&P had mismanaged the project, leading to the cost overrun. HL&P argued that regulatory changes, not poor management, were responsible, and a state district court agreed. The city of Austin appealed the ruling; its appeal was pending in the early 1990s. The project's co-owners, the city of San Antonio and Central Power & Light,

also alleged HL&P had breached its duties as project manager; these claims were also in arbitration in the early 1990s.

In 1989, HI made the strategic decision to limit its diversified operations, and concentrate immediate expansion efforts on cable television. That same year it sold PFI and acquired the U.S. cable television system of Rogers Communications, Inc. KBLCOM spent more than $1.3 billion on the Rogers Communications purchase, which included more than 550,000 customers in the metropolitan areas of San Antonio and Laredo, Texas; Minneapolis, Minnesota; Portland, Oregon; and Orange County, California.

In 1990, KBLCOM formed KBL-TV to sell advertising on cable channels. The same year HI sold the assets of Innovative Controls, and Development Ventures stopped funding new businesses. As Houston Industries entered the 1990s, it was focused on its cable and utilities operations. HI's plans for the near future did not include major acquisitions, although KBLCOM continued to be interested in expansion of its cable system and services.

Deregulation Leads to Restructuring During the 1990s

These plans changed however, as the utilities industry began to take on a new look during the 1990s due to consolidation and increased competition brought on by deregulation. In fact, the firm sold KBLCOM and its share in Paragon Inc. to Time Warner in August 1995 and instead began to seek out strategic alliances that would position it as a diversified energy firm—a firm that was able to provide customers with a variety of services.

One such move was its acquisition of NorAm Energy Corp. The $2.5 billion deal—completed in 1997—created one of the largest electric and natural gas firms in the United States with assets of $18 billion. Jordan commented on HI's motive behind the deal in a 1996 *The Oil Daily* article, stating that "market and regulatory forces are changing the industry landscape to a more competitive environment. In addition, the electric and natural gas markets are converging, and customers are demanding additional products and service."

In order to better position itself to take advantage of deregulating markets, HI reorganized its company operations into three main segments including HI Power Generation, HI Retail Energy Group, and HI Trading and Transportation Group during 1997 and also named Steve Ledbetter president and chief operating officer of the firm. By 1998, the company had grown from operating as an electric utility serving 1.4 million customers in the Houston area, to a diversified firm with nearly four million customers in the United States as well as a growing customer base abroad. That year, HI acquired its first non-regulated power generation plants in California. It also entered the Ohio and Georgia markets, both of which were in the process of deregulating. The company also expanded its international business in Brazil and purchased three utilities in El Salvador.

A New Name For the New Millennium

In 1999, HI announced that it was changing its name to Reliant Energy Inc. (REI) to better reflect the company's shift from a local utility to a diversified energy services firm. The company once again shuffled its operations into two main groups, Reliant Energy Retail and Reliant Energy Wholesale. Throughout the year, Reliant focused on building its retail group, acquiring assets in the Chicago area as well as in the East Coast region. The company also began aggressive expansion in Florida, eyeing the state as a lucrative growth market. REI also established subsidiary Reliant Energy Trading & Marketing B.V. in the Netherlands, hoping to capture industrial and commercial customers who were able to choose the energy supplier of their choice as part of the Electricity Act of 1998 passed in Europe.

As REI entered the new millennium, Jordan retired leaving Letbetter to take over as chairman, president, and CEO. Under his direction, the company began to shift its focus from its Latin American interests to its European and U.S. businesses. During 2000, it completed its acquisition of the Dutch utility N.V. UNA, expanding its foothold in the European market. The firm also made a $2.1 billion purchase of interests in 21 power plants located in the Mid-Atlantic states, increasing its unregulated power holdings. It also augmented its telecommunications holdings with the purchase of Insync Internet Services, an Internet service and Web hosting provider—REI had entered the telecommunications industry in 1999 as a competitive local exchange carrier.

Reliant came under fire in 2000, however, when it announced that it was paying $300 million for the naming rights to Houston's new football stadium. Just as that news broke, REI reported third quarter earnings that had increased 79 percent over second quarter earnings. At the same time, its HL&P arm requested an increase in electricity rates for the second time that year, angering consumers who felt the price hikes were footing the $300 million bill for the new stadium. Company officials claimed that the price increase had nothing to do with the stadium and that the money used for the deal was from increased revenues and the sale of some of its Latin American holdings.

Meanwhile, REI was preparing to change shape again—a change brought on by the 1999 passing of the Texas Electric Choice Act. Under the terms of the act, REI was required to split its regulated and unregulated businesses into two separate entities in order to create a fair competition environment for new companies entering the electric market. Reliant Resources Inc. was created as a subsidiary responsible for the company's unregulated business operations in the United States and Europe. Its businesses included Reliant Energy Retail Services, Reliant Energy C&I Solutions, Reliant Energy Wholesale Group, Reliant Energy Europe, Reliant Energy Communications, and Reliant Energy Ventures. In 2001, the subsidiary raised $1.8 billion in its initial public offering. That September it announced that it would acquire Orion Power Holdings Inc. for $2.9 billion in order to increase its share of the U.S. power and energy services market.

Having undergone a major transformation over the years, REI stood as a leading energy services firm with positive future prospects. During 2000 revenues increased by over 90 percent while stock price rose by 89 percent during the year. With the Texas electricity market slated to begin full retail competition in January 2002, Reliant Resources also appeared to be well positioned to increase its market share.

Principal Subsidiaries

Reliant Resources Inc.; Reliant Energy HL&P; Reliant Energy Entex; Reliant Energy Arkla; Reliant Energy Minnegasco; Reliant Energy Pipelines; Reliant Energy Retail Services; Reliant Energy C&I Energy Solutions; Reliant Energy Wholesale Group; Reliant Energy Europe; Reliant Energy Communications.

Principal Competitors

Entergy Corporation; TXU Corp.; Utilicorp United Inc.

Further Reading

Beck, Bill, *At Your Service: An Illustrated History of Houston Lighting & Power Company*, Houston, Tex.: Houston Lighting & Power Company, 1990.
Bullion, Lew, "Reliant Shifting Focus From Latin America," *Pipeline & Gas Journal,* January 2000, p. 13.
——, "Reliant Spins Off Unregulated Business," *Pipeline & Gas Journal,* September 2000.
De Rouffignac, Ann, "Houston Industries, Destec Win Bids for California Power Plants," *Houston Business Journal,* November 27, 1998, p. 8.
——, "Moniker Change to Reliant Energy Ends an Era for Houston Industries," *Houston Business Journal,* February 5, 1999.
Fan, Aliza, "Houston Industries to Acquire NorAm in $3.8 Billion Gas-Electric Merger," *Oil Daily,* August 13, 1996, p. 3.
"HI Reorganizes as NorAm Deal Nears," *Houston Business Journal,* January 10, 1997, p. 30.
"Houston Industries Changes Name," *Oil Daily,* February 3, 1999.
Perin, Monica, "Reliant 'Convergence' Has Energy Company Scrambling Over PR," *Houston Business Journal,* October 23, 2000.
——, "Reliant Hastens its European Market Entrance," *Houston Business Journal,* January 7, 2000, p. 5.
"Reliant Energy Expands Retail Business," *Pipeline & Gas Journal,* April 1999, p. 4.
"Reliant IPO Raises $1.8 Billion," *Houston Business Journal,* May 18, 2001.
"Reliant to Buy Bulk of Sithe for $2.1 Billion," *Modern Power Systems,* March 2000, p. 12.
Ryser, Jeffrey, "Serendipity or Savvy Investment? A Cable Investment Pays Off," *Electrical World,* January 1996, p. 55.
"The Power Meltdown in California," *Business Week,* December 6, 2000.

—Roger W. Rouland
—update: Christina M. Stansell

RTL Group SA

R.C. Luxembourg B 10.B07
45 boulevard Pierre Frieden
L-1543 Kirchberg
Luxembourg
Telephone: (352) 421-421
Fax: (352) 421-42-2760
Web site: http://www.rtlgroup.com

Public Company
Incorporated: 1931 as Compagnie Luxembourgeoise de
    Radiodiffusion (CLR)
Employees: 6,930
Sales: EUR 2.85 billion ($2.68 billion) (2000)
Stock Exchanges: London
Ticker Symbol: RTL
NAIC: 51312 Television Broadcasting; 51211 Motion
    Picture and Video Production; 513112 Radio Stations

RTL Group SA reaches some 120 million European TV viewers and radio listeners a day through its 24 commercial ''free TV'' channels and 17 radio stations in 35 countries. The company has achieved leading positions in three of the six largest European media markets, including Germany, France, and the Netherlands. The German RTL Television channel and French TV channel M6, along with its French radio stations, are the group's most important revenue sources. RTL group is one of the world's biggest producers of TV movies and a leading trader of sports broadcasting rights in Europe. It is majority-owned and controlled by the German media conglomerate Bertelsmann.

Becoming the Star of European Commercial Radio in the 1930s

In the 1930s, when Europe's emerging radio landscape was dominated by public broadcasting stations, a group of businessmen engaged in a venture that was designed to change that landscape forever. In 1931, the Compagnie Luxembourgeoise de Radiodiffusion (CLR) was incorporated in Luxembourg and re-ceived a radio broadcasting concession from the Luxembourg government, granting a monopoly for 25 years. The idea of establishing a strong commercial radio station aimed at Western Europe was conceived by radio enthusiast and technician François Anen, ex-radio magazine editor Henri Etienne, and entrepreneur Raoul Fernandez—all Luxembourgians who were joined by several businessmen from Paris. Backed up financially by French capital, the new entity set up the most powerful radio transmitter in Europe: a 100-kilowatt-transmitter with generators powered by two huge 800-horsepower marine diesels. In 1932, the newly established radio station found a home in the Villa Louvigny, a former fort built in the seventeenth century and located in a park in the center of Luxembourg. At first the company rented part of the Villa, and in 1936 bought the whole building which became CLR's headquarters for 45 years. At the Villa Louvigny CLR established a number of studio facilities during the 1930s, including a large studio for a full orchestra, a smaller studio for small orchestras and recitals, four voice studios, a record studio, and a tape recording and dubbing studio.

In early 1933 the station started test transmissions on a long wave frequency, although Luxembourg had no permission to do so from the Union International de Radiophonie (UIR) of which the Grand Duchy was a member. At UIR's Lucerne conference in 1933, the organization reconfirmed its decision to allocate only a medium wave frequency to Luxembourg, which in turn did not sign the resulting treaty. In January 1934, just a day after the new UIR treaty became effective, CLR even seized a long wave frequency that Poland had just abandoned and started using it for its broadcasts.

Radio Luxembourg's long wave programs were broadcast on weekday afternoons and evenings and from 8 a.m. until midnight on the weekend, mainly presenting popular dance music and some symphony music. In the beginning the station broadcast to a different European country every night, including Italy, Belgium, Luxembourg, Germany, the Netherlands, France, and the United Kingdom, with announcements in the appropriate language. In 1933, CLR launched two long wave radio programs: the French program Radio Ondes Longues and Radio Luxembourg for English-speaking listeners. The new programs did not follow any defined framework. The only

Company Perspectives:

The combination of CLT-UFA and Pearson Television created an integrated pan-European company with successful business operations spanning television and radio broadcasting, content and online activities. The directors believe that a shared position at two key points on the value chain, distribution and content, will better place RTL Group to achieve stronger revenue and earnings growth to benefit from consolidation in the world's television market.

guideline for the station was to attract as many listeners as possible at any time of the day. Radio Luxembourg, mainly aimed at the United Kingdom, was able to draw large audiences in the millions very quickly. It presented the most popular music at the time which people wanted to hear but were not able to hear anywhere else. It presented them in a relaxed and fun way—quite different from the more serious fashion of the state-owned radio monopoly British Broadcasting Corporation (BBC). Radio Luxembourg was covering all of the United Kingdom with its powerful transmitter from the less-than 1,000 square miles nestled in between Belgium, Germany, and France that constituted the Grand Duchy of Luxembourg. From the very beginning, BBC tried to fight the "foreign intruder" on its territory by all means imaginable. The BBC tried to put diplomatic pressure on Luxembourg's government through the British government; it offered to pay the station for not going on air; it tried to get on the Board of Directors; it denied the station a cable connection to it's London-based studio; it convinced the British press not to publicize the station's program schedule; it banned announcers and stars that would work for or appear on one of the station's programs—nothing worked. In 1938, the BBC gave up the illusion that it could stop Radio Luxembourg from broadcasting.

Right from the beginning, the business model for CLT was based on advertising revenue from the United Kingdom. For this reason the company's charter included broadcasts in foreign languages, and that is why such a powerful transmitter had to be built. In May 1933, CLT launched an advertising campaign in *Advertiser's Weekly* for "the most powerful broadcasting station in Europe." Since Radio Luxembourg had quickly gained a considerable audience, advertisers jumped at the opportunity to market their products through the new medium. However, because there was no "land line" between Luxembourg and Great Britain, the sponsored programs were produced in London, shipped to Belgium, and put on a train to Luxembourg. By November 1934, the list of advertisers had grown several pages long, including "big names" such as Palmolive, Shredded Wheat, Beecham's Pills, and Rothmans. In the beginning the CLR worked with International Broadcasting Company (IBC), a small radio station based in France that sold commercial advertising, to solicit advertising revenues and produce "sponsored programs." Later a new subsidiary, Wireless Publicity, was founded to sell air time to advertisers, while the J. Walter Thompson advertising agency took on the production part. About 44 different 15 minute long "sponsored programs" were produced at J. Walter Thompson's state-of-the-art London studio every week.

CLR's first radio announcers were "borrowed" from other existing stations such as Toulouse-based Radio Normandy, IBC, and even the BBC in London. Unlike the stiff manners employed by other stations, especially the BBC, Radio Luxembourg's announcers used a very personal style, addressing listeners by name if they wrote a letter to the station, and employed the modern voice-over technique to enliven the program. To further attract listeners Radio Luxembourg started to get as many big name stars into their shows as possible. And with the considerable advertising revenues the station attracted it was able to pay enough for the stars to come, including some big names from the United States, such as Carson Robinson and Morton Downey. By 1937, Radio Luxembourg presented more stars on a single Sunday than the BBC did in a whole week. Later into the 1930s the station started cooperating with Hollywood film makers by broadcasting parts of not-yet-released movies, catering to the curiosity of the huge and growing number of film fans. By the end of 1938, the number of the station's Sunday listeners was 4 million, double the number of the BBC, and Radio Luxembourg charged the highest rates of any commercial radio station anywhere in the world.

In June 1938, CLR started broadcasting its worldwide short wave program. By 1939, the company had established itself as the number one commercial radio station in Europe. However, in that year World War II broke out, causing a major interruption that could have ended CLR's history. German troops occupied the Grand Duchy of Luxembourg in 1940 and immediately took over control of Radio Luxembourg. The German Reich's propaganda minister Goebbels, whose offer to deliver "news" to the station had been turned down in the 1930s, used Radio Luxembourg's powerful transmitter to broadcast Nazi propaganda which was taped in Hamburg throughout Europe. When the Allied forces were approaching Luxembourg toward the end of the war, the Germans tried unsuccessfully to destroy the Villa Louvigny, and the Grand Duchy was liberated by American troops.

Radio Luxembourg Conquering Europe: 1945–70

After World War II had ended, a few determined people decided to build up the radio station again. This was only possible with a great deal of energy and money, but the radio station had become a vital part of Luxembourg's economy, which was otherwise dominated by agriculture and the iron and steel industry. One year after the war had ended, Radio Luxembourg was broadcasting again. However, in the beginning it was tough to produce radio programs since parts of the station's library of recordings had been destroyed and there was not much music being recorded at the time. On the other hand, paying advertisers were as rare in those days as music recordings. However, step by step the radio station was able to gain momentum again and finally regain the success it had in the prewar period.

The postwar decade at Radio Luxembourg was shaped by a man who had joined the station as a DJ in 1946—Geoffrey Everitt. He presented *Swinger Requests,* a show on Sunday afternoons. Later, in 1953, Everitt went back to England where he started working as a radio program producer in the company's London studios. In 1960, Everitt joined CLR's management as Chief Producer and eventually became General Man-

Key Dates:

1931: Compagnie Luxembourgeoise de Radiodiffusion (CLR) is granted a broadcasting license.

1933: CLR launches French program Radio Ondes Longues and Radio Luxembourg for English-speaking listeners.

1954: CLR becomes CLT—Compagnie Luxembourgeoise de Télédiffusion; French-language TV channel Télé Luxembourg starts broadcasting.

1969: Luxembourg-language TV channel RTL Télé Lëtzebuerg goes on air.

1984: Together with Bertelsmann's UFA subsidiary the company launches German TV channel RTL+.

1997: CLT and UFA merge to become CLT-UFA.

2000: CLT-UFA merges with British Pearson TV to form RTL Group.

2001: Bertelsmann becomes the company's majority shareholder.

ager. He first conceived the idea to switch from pre-produced programs to a live format. At the same time Everitt became somewhat disillusioned about the unscrupulousness of some people in the music industry and finally resigned in 1970. He was succeeded by Alan Keen, the former Program Director of the closed down British pirate radio station Radio London. Under Keen Radio Luxembourg made the transition to an all-live format.

During the 1960s, 1970s, and 1980s, commercial radio stations were popping up throughout Europe, most of them with a narrower, local focus. However, Radio Luxembourg was able to defend its position in the increasingly competitive commercial radio market by being sensitive to new music trends and by creating ever new program formats. The British wave was followed by Californian "Flower Power Music" of the late 1960s. In that time period popular music got a huge boost and spurred the growth of the music industry which in turn put out a growing number of recordings. In the late 1960s, the British *Daily Mirror* started supplying news content to Radio Luxembourg and publicized the station's schedules and other information. When independent local radio stations and BBC's local programs started threatening Radio Luxembourg's advertising revenue, the station reacted by inventing new forms of promotion. One of them was the "DJ-Roadshow" which put faces on the immensely popular Radio Luxembourg DJ's voices and brought the radio station into the neighborhood. In the early 1970s, the station spotted the emerging "Teenybopper" wave, promoted their emerging stars such as the Osmonds, and launched the magazine *FAB 208*—208 was Radio Luxembourg's new frequency—that featured the stars of the new scene. When the station found out that advertisers did not think much of it's new teenager audience, it switched to an all-album concept for six months, but moved back to chart music afterwards. In the late 1970s, at the height of the disco era, Radio Luxembourg moved to the disco sound, but finally returned to the successful original format of "the pop hits of the day" mixed with some country and oldies. By the end of the 1970s, the radio programs produced in Luxembourg attracted a total

daily audience of about 40 million in Luxembourg, France, Germany, the United Kingdom, and other European countries and received more press coverage than any other radio station. The company had become Luxembourg's biggest tax payer, unsurpassed by the steel, coal, and banking industries.

Breaking into Television after 1954

A new era arrived for CLT in 1954, when it entered the promising field of television broadcasting. In that year the company launched the French-language TV channel Télé Luxembourg, which started broadcasting to eastern France and southern Belgium during lunch time and from 5 to 11 p.m. To reflect the change the company was renamed Compagnie Luxembourgeoise de Télédiffusion (CLT) in the same year. From then, it took 15 years until CLT's Luxembourg-language TV channel RTL Télé Lëtzebuerg went on the air and another 15 years until television started becoming a real force for CLT in addition to radio broadcasting.

It was in 1984 when CLT together with the German Bertelsmann group's film and TV production subsidiary UFA launched the German commercial TV channel RTL+, in which CLT held 46.1 percent and Bertelsmann 38.9 percent of the share capital. Under the leadership of Austrian executive Helmut Thoma, the Cologne-based station, which was later renamed RTL Television, became CLT's TV flagship and cash cow. Another major launch was the French channel Metropol 6 (M6) in 1987. At the end of the 1980s television replaced radio as CLT's major revenue source.

In 1991, CLT moved company headquarters and its radio unit to Kirchberg on the outskirts of Luxembourg where it soon built new facilities for its growing TV division. By 1991, TV contributed 70 percent to CLT's total sales, and most of that came from RTL. 79 percent of all German households were able to receive RTL through antennas, satellite dishes, or cable, and the channel's share of German TV viewers had reached about 14 percent. One of the most successful RTL projects was the daily soap *Gute Zeiten Schlechte Zeiten*—"good times bad times"—which was produced by UFA and broadcast since May 1992.

As it had happened with commercial radio, a growing number of players entered the European market for commercial television. And as it also happened with radio, the only strategy to keep sales up was diversification. In 1993, CLT became involved in a second German TV channel, RTL2, in which it held about one third of the shares. A third German TV channel, Super-RTL, was created together with the Walt Disney Corporation in 1995. Besides its German TV stations, CLT got involved in TV projects in other countries, including two RTL channels in the Netherlands, the CLT news pool European News Exchange (Enex), and Paris-based Pay-TV program Multivision.

Although CLT was involved in 13 European radio stations, seven TV channels, seven content production firms, and five publishers by the mid-1990s, more than half of the company's revenues of about DM 2.4 billion were generated in Germany. For all these "antennas" as the company's radio and TV channels were called, CLT needed to create a growing stream of content. However, the European content market was dominated by the German Kirch group. In addition to that, advertising-revenue financed "free TV" seemed to have reached its limit of growth. Consequently, license and content acquisition, investments in TV production and the new business model digital pay-TV became CLT's main focus in the second half of the 1990s. Concentrating on television, the company's position in the radio market declined significantly during the 1990s, especially in Germany. By 1996, 22 radio stations contributed ten percent to CLT's total sales while 83 percent were generated from its involvement in 19 TV stations.

A Series of Mergers Begins in 1997

In the late 1990s, consolidation activities of the global media industry accelerated. Further geographical expansion and digital TV technology required significant financial investments and CLT started looking for suitable strategic partners. The cooperation with Bertelsmann had not been without friction. There were disputes over Bertelsmann's policies in connection with Cologne-based TV project Westschiene, where CLT accused the company of being involved in conflicting activities, and the German commercial TV channel VOX, where CLT was left out in favor of Rupert Murdoch's News Corporation. However, after Bertelsmann's successful negotiations with CLT's majority shareholder Audiofina, CLT and Bertelsmann announced their intention to merge CLT with UFA in spring 1996, and the merger became effective in 1997. Half of the new company CLT-UFA was owned by Luxembourg-based holding Audiofina. The other half was held by the German BWTV-Holding in which Bertelsmann had an 80 percent share. The other 20 percent was owned by German newspaper group Westdeutsche Allgemeine Zeitung (WAZ).

The new group got off to a bad start. In its first year CLT-UFA generated a DM 140 million loss. This was mainly due to continued huge investments in the German pay-TV channel Premiere which was launched in 1990 by the Kirch group, Bertelsmann, and French Canal+, and did not take off as soon as expected. The approval of the European Commission was pending and it was clear that further large investments were needed in the future. In a leap of faith Bertelsmann and CLT-UFA—which both had stressed the strategic importance of pay-TV throughout the 1990s—sold all but 5 percent of its shares in Premiere to the KirchGroup for DM 1.2 billion in 1999, and declared commercial "free TV" its main future focus. In April 2000, CLT-UFA announced its merger with British Pearson TV, the TV and movie production arm of the British media group Pearson plc. The companies were merged with CLT's former parent company Audiofina, renamed RTL Group, and listed at the London stock exchange where roughly ten percent of the new group's capital was floated. BWTV held 37 percent in RTL Group's shares; Groupe Bruxelles Lambert S.A. (GBL), the former Audiofina majority shareholder and publicly traded investment Belgian firm controlled by Belgian investors Albert Frere and Paul Desmaris, held 30 percent; Pearson plc held 22 percent; and the rest was publicly traded. In 2001, Bertelsmann gained control over RTL group with an unexpected move. The only way to persuade GBL to sell its share in RTL Group was to offer Bertelsmann shares in exchange. Under the deal GBL received a 25.1 percent share in Bertelsmann which could be offered to the public within three to four years. Bertelsmann received GBL's 30 percent share in RTL Group, making Bertelsmann the new majority owner with 67 percent. Pearson continued to hold its 22 percent package, but was signaling its interest in selling it off.

After the deal was realized, Bertelsmann streamlined RTL's management and Belgian Audiofina manager Didier Bellens was appointed CEO of the new company. The first major task was to cut cost by exploiting synergies within the group's "family" of German TV stations once the company had acquired majority shares in RTL TV and VOX. Rupert Murdoch sold his stake in VOX to CLT-UFA for DM 600 million in 2000. Walt Disney, however, decided to hold on to its stakes in TV channels Super RTL and RTL2 after they started to show profits. In 2001, RTL Group saw its future in raising the percentage of self-produced TV content to 40 percent; launching its own TV news channel and expanding the value chain by acquiring soccer clubs; by implementing new, innovative TV formats in commercial television; by developing new revenue streams from Internet portals through its subsidiary RTL New Media; and by geographical expansion in Europe.

Principal Subsidiaries

RTL Television GmbH (Germany; 99.7%); Metropole TV S.A. (France; 43.8%); RTL2 Fernsehehn GmbH & Co. KG (Germany; 35.8%); VOX Film & Fernseh GmbH & Co. KG (Germany; 99.4%); Channel 5 TV Group Ltd (U.K.; 64.5%); IP Deutschland GmbH (Germany; 99.7%); IP France S.A. (France; 99.6%); Pearson Television Productions Ltd. (U.K.); UFA Film & Fernsehen GmbH (Germany; 99.6%); Trebitsch Produktion Holding GmbH & Co. KG (Germany; 63.8%); RTL Plus S.A. (Luxembourg; 99.7%); RTL4 Beheer BV (Netherlands; 99.6%); RTL Disney Fernsehen GmbH & Co. KG (Germany; 49.8%); M-RTL Rt (Hungary; 48.8%); RTL7 SP. ZOO (Poland; 99.6%); Ediradio S.A. (France; 99.6%); CLT-UFA UK Radio Ltd (U.K.; 99.6%); RTL Radio Deutschland GmbH & Co. KG (Germany; 99.7%); ID (Information et Diffusion) Sarl (France; 99.6%); RTL New Media GmbH (Germany; 99.7%).

Principal Competitors

KirchHolding GmbH & Co. KG; CANAL+; Groupe AB S.A.; The News Corporation Limited; British Sky Broadcasting Group plc.

Further Reading

"Bei RTL plus bald zweites Programm," *Süddeutsche Zeitung*, April 29, 1992.

"Bertelsmann erwirbt Mehrheit an RTL Group—BL neuer Gesellschafter bei Bertelsmann," *OTS Originaltextservice,* February 5, 2001.

"CLT-Ufa schliesst das erste Jahr mit Verlust von 140 Millionen DM ab," *Frankfurter Allgemeine Zeitung*, May 22, 1998, p. 27.

Collins, Rodney (ed.), *Radio Luxembourg 1979,* London: Radio Luxembourg (London) Ltd., 1978, 96 p.

"Die CLT sitzt beim Kommerzfernsehen in der ersten Reihe," *Süddeutsche Zeitung*, October 1, 1992, p. 31.

"Disney ändert seine TV-Strategie," *HORIZONT*, August 5, 1999, p. 4.

Jakobs, Hans-Jürgen, ''Ende einer Ehe,'' *Spiegel,* March 22, 1999, p. 88.

Karepin, Rolf, ''Familienduell,'' *HORIZONT,* July 27, 2000, p. 42.

Lilienthal, Volker, ''Der Riese aus dem Zwergenland,'' *Werben und Verkaufen,* October 28, 1994, p. 117.

Löw, Elke, ''Wo Thomas Gottschalk die Schulbank drückte,'' *Werben und Verkaufen,* July 18, 1997, p. 74.

Nichols, Richard, *Radio Luxembourg—The Station of the Stars: An Affectionate History of 50 Years of Broadcasting,* London: W.H. Allen & Co., 1983, 192 p.

''RTL plant einen Nachrichtenkanal,'' *Süddeutsche Zeitung,* April 28, 2000, p. 30.

Schlosser, Sabine, ''Synergien; Didier Bellens, CEO der RTL Group, über den Rückzug von Pearson, die Kooperation mit Bertelsmann und den Transfer von Erfolgsrezepten,'' *HORIZONT,* September 6, 2001, p. 38.

''Wir waren nicht in die Ecke gedrängt,'' *Süddeutsche Zeitung,* April 6, 1996.

Werb, Andreas, and Andreas Vill, ''Eine Erfolgsstory,'' *Werben und Verkaufen,* August 14, 1998, p. 84.

—Evelyn Hauser

SEMCO ⊛ ENERGY

SEMCO Energy, Inc.

405 Water Street
Port Huron, Michigan 48060
U.S.A.
Telephone: (810) 987-2200
Toll Free: (800) 624-2019
Fax: (810) 987-7286
Web site: http://www.semcoenergy.com

Public Company
Incorporated: 1951 as the Southeastern Michigan Gas
    Company
Employees: 1,850
Sales: $422.59 million
Stock Exchanges: New York
Ticker Symbol: SEN
NAIC: 221210 Natural Gas Distribution; 23491 Water,
    Sewer, and Pipeline Construction

SEMCO Energy, Inc. is a Michigan-based holding company that operates natural gas distribution, infrastructure construction, and information technology subsidiaries, the largest of which is the SEMCO Energy Gas Company, which serves more than 260,000 customers in Michigan. The publicly owned firm, which has been expanding rapidly through internal growth and acquisition, shelved plans to seek new ownership in 2001 when a review concluded that the timing was not right for such a move.

Early Years

SEMCO Energy got its start in February of 1951, when Cecil A. Runyan purchased gas manufacturing and distribution facilities from Detroit Edison and began to run them as the Southeastern Michigan Gas Company. A month later Runyan converted the operation from manufactured gas (produced from heated coal) to natural gas. In 1953, the firm acquired the Albion Gas Light Company, another small Michigan energy provider. Southeastern Michigan Gas continued to operate in this form for the next two decades while steadily growing its customer base.

In 1971, Robert J. Thomson, who had joined the firm as an accountant 13 years earlier, took over as president and CEO. In 1977, the company was restructured, and a new holding company created to serve as parent. This entity was named Southeastern Michigan Gas Enterprises, Inc. Several years later Southeastern Michigan Engine Specialists, Inc. was formed to explore the idea of making automobile engines that ran on natural gas. Eventually, over 200 of the company's vehicles were converted to run on the cleaner-burning fuel.

By 1985, Southeastern Michigan Gas Enterprises was taking in $100 million in revenues, more than 80 percent of which came from the Southeastern Michigan Gas Co. That same year saw the firm acquire the Battle Creek Gas Company for $25 million. Battle Creek served 31,000 customers in and around its home city. Southeastern Michigan Gas Co. was by this time serving 67,000 customers of its own in southeast and south central Michigan.

In 1987, the company purchased the gas distribution operations of Michigan Power Co. of Three Rivers, Michigan for $38 million, renaming it Michigan Gas Co. The purchase boosted Southeastern Michigan Gas Enterprises to a total of 187,000 customers in 20 Michigan counties. In 1989 annual revenues reached a record of more than $226 million, with net earnings of $7.6 million. The company had by this time changed the name of Southeastern Michigan Engine to Southeastern Michigan Financial Services, Inc., and added subsidiaries SEMCO Energy Services, Inc. and Southeastern Michigan Development Co.

In 1990, the firm was ordered to repay customers $1.4 million by the Michigan Public Service Commission because of rules requiring refunds for earnings above pre-established levels. The figure was a compromise from the $2.6 million originally sought. The following year SEMCO Energy Services unit SEMCO Pipeline Co. partnered with three other firms to build the NoArk pipeline system across northern Arkansas. SEMCO Pipeline owned a third of the venture. The company also began construction of an extension to its Eaton Rapids, Michigan pipeline in conjunction with ANR Eaton Co., and started work on a new 18.5 mile pipeline in St. Clair County, Michigan, which would serve a variety of customers including a Detroit Edison power plant.

Company Perspectives:

SEMCO Energy will be a leading diversified energy infrastructure company. We will be a significant regional provider of natural gas services and one of the largest providers of underground engineering and construction services in North America. We will provide high-quality and valued services to our satisfied customers and a total return to our shareholders above the median of our peer group. Our fundamental business is the gas distribution business. The consolidation of gas utility assets occurring in the industry presents opportunities to significantly grow our gas distribution business in attractive areas of the U.S. We will look for opportunities in regions with significant gas consumption or growth, cooperative regulation, and companies offering significant potential cost synergy.

Natural Gas-Powered Vehicles

Continuing to pursue the idea of vehicles powered by natural gas, in 1991 the company built the first fueling station for this purpose in Michigan in the small town of Negaunee in the state's upper peninsula, where the firm's Michigan Gas Company subsidiary provided service. A second station was soon added in the company's home city of Port Huron, with more to follow later. Natural gas yielded 100 to 200 miles per gallon, but cost only two-thirds the price of gasoline. Vehicles could be configured to run on both fuels so that when the natural gas ran out, the engine would automatically switch over to gasoline from a separate tank.

In 1993 president and CEO Robert Thomson retired and his place was taken by executive vice president Ward Kirby. Thomson remained with the firm as board chairman. The following year the company joined with 5 other Michigan gas suppliers to form the Michigan Natural Gas Vehicle Association to promote natural gas-fueled vehicle use. In 1996, CEO Kirby left and William L. Johnson was appointed to the top post by the board. Johnson had a long history in the industry, having most recently served as president and CEO of Northern Pipeline Construction Co. of Phoenix and Kansas City. He had received BS and MA degrees from Central Michigan University, and he and his wife had family ties to the state.

By this time the company's investment in the NoArk pipeline project was proving to be a serious financial drain. The pipeline, which was completed in 1993, had exceeded its original budget of $70 million by almost half and was consistently underutilized. Johnson told securities analysts in September of 1996 that "the dog won't hunt," and declared resolution of the NoArk issue his number one priority. Southeastern Michigan Gas Enterprises was otherwise healthy, reaping above-industry-average returns in the highly regulated gas market for a number of years running.

Reorganization and a New Name

In early 1997, the company shortened its name to SEMCO Energy, Inc. It was simultaneously reorganized into three entities: SEMCO Energy Gas Co., which was a regulated company that consisted of the operations of Southeastern Michigan Gas, Battle Creek Gas, and Michigan Gas; SEMCO Energy Services, an unregulated subsidiary which marketed gas in Michigan, Illinois, New York, Kentucky, and West Virginia; and SEMCO Ventures, which was to manage the company's other capital assets, including production, processing, storage, and transmission facilities. A new marketing agreement was also announced with Itron, Inc., a maker of automated meter reading equipment. Itron products, which were used by gas companies as well as electricity and water providers, would be sold through SEMCO Energy Services in Michigan, Ohio, Illinois, Indiana, and Wisconsin. SEMCO was now focusing on building its brand identity and on pursuing profits from unregulated areas, especially the services sector. CEO Johnson declared his intention to earn $1 billion in revenues or have 1 million gas customers by 2003.

In August the company began implementing a new, aggressive acquisition strategy. The first purchase was Sub-Surface Construction Co. of Comstock Park, Michigan, bought for $15.4 million. Sub-Surface primarily constructed underground natural gas pipelines and related facilities. SEMCO received a favorable ruling from the Michigan Public Service Commission in the fall, when it agreed to allow the company to merge the rate structures and gas cost recovery clauses of Michigan Gas and Southeastern Michigan Gas. The move would raise the bills of its customers by an average of $13 a year. Continuing to focus on services, the company also reached a marketing agreement with General Electric to form SharpService, a repair service for appliances that would be available to SEMCO's 240,000 customers in Michigan.

At year's end, SEMCO acquired Maverick Pipeline Services, Inc., a pipeline consulting and engineering design firm. The $500,000 deal complemented the earlier purchase of Sub-Surface, giving SEMCO a turnkey pipeline design and construction service. Early 1998 saw the nettlesome NoArk situation resolved, when SEMCO sold its interest in the pipeline to ENOGEX Arkansas Pipeline Corporation for approximately $4 million and assumption of debt.

During the winter of 1998, the company completed an early retirement program that reduced its payroll ledger by 101 employees, about a fifth of the total, which helped lower operating costs. SEMCO Ventures also acquired a Michigan-based propane gas company, Hot Flame Gas, Inc., in a stock swap. In May, the company acquired King Energy and Construction, a Tennessee water, sewer, and natural gas construction services firm, while in October an agreement was signed with TransCanada PipeLines to manage SEMCO's pipelines and supply the company with the majority of its gas. The latter move was expected to result in lower costs to consumers.

Another acquisition followed in November of 1998 when Oilfield Materials Consultants was purchased for $15 million in stock and the assumption of $1.1 million in debt. Oilfield Materials, which offered consulting and quality control services, would become a subsidiary of SEMCO Energy Ventures. CEO Johnson described the venture unit's strategy as being "to offer turnkey engineering, design and construction support to a national, if not international, customer base." He anticipated that half of the company's revenues would come from these activities by 2003.

Key Dates:

1951: Charles Runyan founds the Southeastern Michigan Gas Co.
1953: Albion Gas Light Co. is purchased.
1977: Reorganization creates the holding company Southeastern Michigan Gas Enterprises
1985: Battle Creek Gas Co. is acquired.
1987: Michigan Power Co. is purchased.
1997: Firm renamed SEMCO Energy and split into three units; many acquisitions follow.
1998: The company's stake in money-losing NoArk Pipeline venture is sold.
1999: SEMCO Energy Services unit is sold; ENSTAR Natural Gas is acquired.
2000: Aretech Information Services formed to offer secure computer application hosting.

Sale of SEMCO Energy Services

In February of 1999, SEMCO put its Energy Services subsidiary up for sale. The unit was a major revenue source, generating $398 million in earnings in 1998, but it no longer fit the company's business model. A buyer was quickly found in CoEnergy Trading Co., a sister company of Michigan Consolidated Gas Co. In the early summer an accident blamed on human error and incorrect pipeline maps caused high-pressure gas to flow into homes in a Battle Creek, Michigan neighborhood. Two houses burned down and two residents suffered smoke inhalation. Damage was also reported in several dozen other dwellings.

During 1999 SEMCO's acquisitions continued, with K&B Construction, Inc. of Kansas City purchased in February, Iowa Pipeline Associates, Inc. acquired in April, and ENSTAR Natural Gas Co. bought in July. The first two companies built underground pipelines in Iowa, Kansas, Missouri, and Nebraska, while ENSTAR provided natural gas for the city of Anchorage, Alaska. The ENSTAR purchase cost $290 million, making it SEMCO's largest acquisition ever. ENSTAR boosted the company's gas distribution customer base by almost half, to 350,000.

More acquisitions followed in the fall, with Flint Construction Co. of Lawrenceville, Georgia, Long's Underground Technologies, Inc. of Lufkin, Texas, and Drafting Services, Inc. of Monroe, Louisiana all brought on board in September and Pinpoint Locators Inc. of Fort Necessity, Louisiana purchased a month later. The latter two became part of SEMCO's Maverick Pipeline Services, Inc. subsidiary, while the former pair would be operated by SEMCO Energy Ventures.

SEMCO began the millennium with a new stock exchange and ticker symbol, moving from the NASDAQ to the NYSE. New initiatives were now underway to aggressively expand the ENSTAR business in Alaska and to install 100,000 more Itron automatic gas meter-reading devices in Alaska and Michigan. In the latter state, the company's entire customer base would be automated by year's end. In April of 2000, Aretech Information Services was formed to offer computer application hosting ser-

vices for small and medium-sized businesses in Michigan. The new unit would utilize the powerful, secure computer systems that had been built to serve the utility's own needs.

In May, the acquisitions continued when SEMCO bought KLP Construction Co. of East Peoria, Illinois and the construction equipment of a second firm, Lake Area Utilities, Inc. Both would become part of SEMCO Energy Ventures. During the year construction was also started on a $7 million, 7-mile long pipeline in Zeeland, Michigan that would supply natural gas to a Southern Energy electrical plant which was expected to come on line in 2001.

In July of 2000, CEO William Johnson announced that SEMCO was putting itself up for sale, in part because the company's stock price was not rising at a rate consistent with the progress it had been making, and also because the firm's modest size put it at a disadvantage in the rapidly consolidating utility industry. The hope was to find a partner with a "similar strategic bent," but SEMCO was also open to the possibility of separation of assets. After a six month review was conducted by Banc of America Securities, it was concluded that the time was not right for a merger, and the idea was shelved. Johnson subsequently reaffirmed the company's commitment to its previous strategy of expansion through internal growth and selective acquisitions.

February of 2001 saw SEMCO announce it would not seek to raise gas rates in Michigan until April of 2002, while larger rival suppliers Michigan Consolidated and Consumers Power made plans to do so in the near term. The company instead sought state approval for a three-year fixed rate that would ultimately protect its customers by helping them avoid the pricing volatility inherent in the wholesale gas market. SEMCO sought a rate of $4.99 per thousand cubic feet, a 54 percent increase. The offer allowed a limited number of consumers to switch to a different gas provider if they found a lower rate. Consumers and Michigan Consolidated were both moving toward a system that directly reflected market pricing, rather than holding to predetermined fixed rates. SEMCO estimated that the previous 3-year price freeze had saved its customers $112 million in 2000 alone. In June, a new CEO and president, Marcus Jackson, was appointed. He was a member of the company's board.

With its plan to seek a buyer on hold, SEMCO continued to make strides toward diversification. The volatile gas market and continued consolidation of the energy industry were both factors that could impact the company's bottom line, but the continuing need for gas heat in Michigan and Alaska meant there would always be a need for the company's services.

Principal Subsidiaries

SEMCO Energy Gas Co.; SEMCO Energy Ventures; ENSTAR Natural Gas; Alaska Pipeline Company; Aretech Information Services.

Principal Competitors

Michigan Consolidated Gas Co.; Consumers Power Co.; ANR Pipeline Co.; Citizens Fuel Gas Co.; Michigan Gas Utilities.

Further Reading

Bradner, Tim, ''Gas Distributor Plans Major Alaska Expansion Through ENSTAR,'' *Alaska Journal of Commerce*, April 20, 2000, p. 10.

''CEO Interview—Southeastern Michigan Gas Enterprises, Inc.,'' *The Wall Street Transcript*, August 31, 1992.

Gallagher, John, ''Port Huron, Mich., Natural Gas Firm Puts Itself on Sale,'' *KRTBN Knight-Ridder Tribune Business News*, July 26, 2000.

Lane, Amy, ''SEMCO Won't Join Other Utilities in Raising Gas Price,'' *Crain's Detroit Business*, February 26, 2001, p. 25.

Sanchez, Mark, ''SEMCO Proposes Higher Rate, New Three-Year Freeze,'' *Grand Rapids Business Journal*, September 17, 2001, p. 20.

''SEMCO Energy Will Stay the Course, Shuns Possible Combinations for Now,'' *Gas Utility Report*, January 12, 2001, p. 7.

''Southeastern Michigan Gas Sets Lofty Goals Despite Its NoArk Problem,'' *Petroleum Finance Week*, September 2, 1996.

Spiess, Ben, ''Michigan-Based Firm Buys Anchorage, Alaska, Gas Utility,'' *KRTBN Knight-Ridder Tribune Business News*, July 17, 1999.

Winter, Ralph E., ''SEMCO Energy Looking to Become Less Weather-Dependent,'' *Dow Jones Business News*, February 4, 1999.

—Frank Uhle

SL Green Realty Corporation

420 Lexington Avenue
New York, New York 10017
U.S.A.
Telephone: (212) 594-2700
Fax: (212) 216-1785
Web site: http://www.slgreen.com

Public Company
Incorporated: 1980 as S.L. Green Properties, Inc.
Employees: 437
Sales: $230.32 million (2000)
Stock Exchanges: New York
Ticker Symbol: SLG
NAIC: 53112 Lessors of Nonresidential Buildings;
   531312 Nonresidential Property Managers

SL Green Realty Corporation is a self-managed real-estate investment trust (REIT) that owns, manages, leases, acquires, and redevelops Class B office properties, almost all of them in midtown Manhattan. Class B buildings are 25 years or older and rent space to tenants less well-heeled than the big banks, brokerages, and law firms that occupy New York City's trophy buildings. One important asset of SL Green's buildings is desirable location; most of them are within a 10-minute walk from Grand Central Terminal, Pennsylvania Station, or the Port Authority Bus Terminal. SL Green is the largest property owner in the Grand Central area. Substantially all of the company's assets are held by an operating partnership, in which the company is the general partner.

The First 15 Years: 1980–95

A native of Brooklyn, Stephen L. Green was a tax attorney before starting an import-export firm that specialized in human-hair products from Asia. After selling that business he opened a travel company that organized charter trips for skiers. He sold that business, too, and moved to Key West, Florida, to try real-estate development before returning to New York. In 1980, he incorporated S.L. Green Properties, purchasing a Manhattan residential cooperative on Broadway, just south of 14th Street. He next bought three residential condominium properties in the same area.

Frustrated by the rules and regulations governing housing in New York City, Green turned instead in the mid-1980s to commercial properties in an area sometimes dubbed "Midtown South." S.L. Green converted a 12-story loft building at 5 East 12th Street to a commercial condominium. S.L. Green and the periodical *Adweek* purchased, in 1986, a former factory building at 49 East 21st Street, with *Adweek* taking four floors in the 12-story structure. S.L. Green had previously converted a 12-story loft building at 5 East 12th Street into a commercial condominium. In 1988, the company took a 49-year net lease on a 12-story former United Parcel Service warehouse at 333 East 38th Street. A $12-million renovation began the following year, and two years later the building was fully leased. By this time S.L. Green owned and managed ten commercial buildings with a total of three million square feet of space. Green's wife, Nancy Ann Peck, was named president of S.L. Green Real Estate Inc., the design and construction arm of S.L. Green Properties Inc., in 1991. A partnership led by S.L. Green Real Estate purchased a foreclosed office building at 18 East 34th Street in 1992.

Although the 1990–92 recession hit New York City hard, S.L. Green never had a vacancy rate higher than 6 percent in this period and lost only one property to its lenders, an office building in Hempstead, Long Island, which convinced Stephen Green to confine his activities to Manhattan. Since the slump made it impossible to obtain financing in order to buy new properties or even further develop existing ones, the company began marketing itself to banks and other institutional owners, offering to manage distressed properties. The work S.L. Green obtained brought with it such problems as major electrical and plumbing defects, often in violation of building codes. Moreover, at times as many as one-third of the tenants had stopped paying their rent. "It's an immense amount of work," a company executive told Judy Temes of *Crain's New York Business.* "It can be a nightmare."

Appetite for Acquisition: 1997–99

By 1997, Manhattan had entered a new era of prosperity. S.L. Green Properties had disposed of the aforementioned properties but had acquired a new roster of midtown office buildings, mostly between 23rd and 42nd streets. These included 673 First Avenue, 470 Park Avenue South, 1414 Sixth Avenue, 29 West 35th Street, 70 West 36th Street, and 36 West 44th Street. None of these Class B buildings had been constructed later than 1928.

Acquisitions made by S.L. Green Properties in 1997 included landmarked 110 East 42nd Street for $30 million; 1140 Sixth Avenue for $26.5 million; and 1372 Broadway for $52.5 million in midtown, plus the office portion of 17 Battery Place, a Class B downtown building with a magnificent view of New York Harbor, for $65 million. S.L. Green acquired all of the 22-story north tower of this structure and 13 floors of the 31-story south tower. In Midtown South the firm purchased 50 West 23rd Street for $36 million. The company held 12 properties in August 1997, when it went public, raising $228.7 million for the firm by the sale of common stock. Green personally pocketed $27 million and retained a stake of 18 percent in the firm, including operating-partnership units.

Armed with this war chest, SL Green, in February 1998, agreed to pay $165 million for 1466 Broadway, just south of Times Square, plus the long-term leaseholds on 25 West 43rd Street and the Graybar Building at 420 Lexington Avenue. The 31-story Graybar, adjacent to Grand Central Terminal and completed in 1927, was once the largest office tower in the world. After acquiring a 31-year operating sublease on the property, SL Green began a renovation budgeted at $8 million. The Graybar became SL Green's flagship, the site of its headquarters. During the year SL Green marketed big blocks of common and preferred stock, thereby raising another $353 million. By the end of 1998, SL Green had added four more midtown buildings: the 25-story Fashion Gallery Building at 1412 Broadway, for $72 million; 20-story 711 Third Avenue, for $44.6 million; 18-story 440 Ninth Avenue, for $32 million; and 321 West 44th Street, for $17 million.

During 1999, SL Green purchased a 65 percent interest in the 20-story BMW Building at 555 West 57th Street for about $66.7 million. In Midtown South, the firm purchased 286, 290, and 292 Madison Avenue and, with Carlyle Realty, purchased 1250 Broadway for $93 million, taking a 49.9 percent stake in the joint venture. In a joint venture with a Morgan Stanley & Co. fund (in which SL Green took 35 percent), 90 Broad Street, in lower Manhattan, was purchased for $84.5 million. As a public company, SL Green was delivering the kind of financial returns to hearten its stockholders. In 1998, the company had net income of $29.45 million on revenues of $134.55 million. The following year the totals swelled to $42.86 million and $206.02 million, respectively. As a REIT, SL Green exempted itself from certain taxes—most notably the corporate income tax—by distributing 95 percent of its earned income to its shareholders as dividends.

The growing need of tenants for high-quality digital telephone service, e-mail, and direct access to the Internet made it imperative for SL Green Realty to rewire its buildings. "People expect these kinds of services in A buildings," Stephen Green told John Holusha of the *New York Times* in 1999. "Our agenda is to give the same level of service in older, well-located buildings at half the rent." To execute this function, SL Green turned to On Site Access, a company recently organized following the deregulation of local telecommunications service. At the Graybar Building, an unneeded air shaft provided the necessary vertical access needed for wiring. A $2-million renovation at 440 Ninth Avenue also included fiber-optic wiring for high-speed Internet and telecommunications access. Nevertheless, SL Green—able to pick and choose among potential tenants—was reluctant to lease space to new-media or high-technology firms for fear they would be out of business before their leases expired. In order to accommodate such firms, SL Green, plus two partners, established eEmerge Inc., a temporary office-space provider, in 2000. A floor of space established by eEmerge at 440 Ninth Avenue in the summer of 2000 was completely filled less than a month after it first became available.

SL Green in 2000–01

During 2000, SL Green sold most of its downtown properties in order to concentrate on midtown Manhattan, where the company believed the diversity of businesses would enable it to more easily deal with an economic downturn. The firm sold its interest in 90 Broad Street for $60 million and its share of the south tower of 17 Battery Place for $53 million. In midtown, it sold 29 West 35th Street for $11.7 million and 36 West 44th Street for $31.5 million. The company also converted 65 percent of 321 West 44th Street to a joint venture. It took 49.9 percent of a joint venture with Prudential Financial that purchased 100 Park Avenue for $192 million and 180 Madison Avenue for $41.5 million.

In early 2001, SL Green was again buying properties in Midtown South. One Park Avenue, a 20-story office tower built in 1925, was purchased for $233.9 million. The company also bought 1370 Broadway for $56.5 million and took a 35 percent stake in 469 Seventh Avenue for $45.7 million. In June 2001, SL Green purchased 317 Madison Avenue, a 22-story office tower with direct access to Grand Central Terminal, for $105 million. SL Green's average asking rents at the end of 2000 were in the high $30s annually per square foot, compared to as much as $80 in Class A buildings. "We buy older buildings with high ceilings, great floorplates, windows that open and close," Stephen Green told Leslie Jay of *Crain's New York Business*. "Then we create state-of-the-art infrastructure," he added, citing improvements such as broadband wiring and, most recently, lobby upgrades and installation of small television screens in the elevators so that riders could follow headline news.

SL Green's portfolio at the end of 2000 consisted of 19 properties with about 6.7 million rentable square feet of space and one triple-net leased property located in Shelton, Connecticut. This space was about 99 percent rented. The company also had ownership interests in four office properties encompassing about two million square feet of space. In addition, it was managing four office properties, owned by third parties and affiliated companies, with about one million square feet of

Key Dates:

1980: Founding of S.L. Green Properties by Stephen L. Green.
1991: The company now owns and manages 10 commercial buildings.
1997: The company makes its initial public offering of stock as SL Green Realty.
1998: SL Green Realty purchases six midtown Manhattan office buildings.
2001: The company's holdings now include 19 Manhattan commercial properties.

rentable space. The company had net income of $86.22 million in 2000 on revenues of $230.32 million.

Substantially all of SL Green Realty's assets were held by, and all of its operations conducted through, an operating limited partnership of which the company was sole managing general partner. The company owned about 91.4 percent of the economic interests in the operating partnership at the end of 2000. All of the management and leasing operations were being conducted through SL Green Management LLC, an entity wholly owned by the operating partnership. SL Green Realty, through the operating partnership, also held 95 percent of the total equity of S.L. Properties, Inc., which was responsible for the parent company's service operations. Companies run by Stephen Green's son Gary held contracts for custodial and security work. Stephen Green was the principal shareholder of SL Green Realty common stock in March 2001, with 8.9 percent.

Stephen Green's brother, New York City Public Advocate Mark Green, was running in late 2001 for the office held by Mayor Rudolph Giuliani. Reporters noted that the city was SL Green's largest tenant, paying the firm more than $10 million a year in rent to house several agencies, including the Department of Correction and the City University of New York. "SL Green has so many enterprises related to the city government that it retains its own lobbyist who has repeatedly interceded with top city officials to renegotiate leases or seek approvals for renovation projects," wrote Eric Lipton in the *New York Times.* "It routinely files appeals with the Department of Finance challenging tax assessments on its buildings. It has dozens of code violations pending before the Department of Buildings." By August 2001, Stephen Green had raised hundreds of thousands of dollars in campaign donations to his brother from friends and business associates and had helped recruit a team of corporate executives to advise his brother. Wayne Barrett of the *Village Voice* reported that Mark Green had promised "full disclosure" of business interactions between his possible future administration and SL Green Realty, but Barrett also wrote that in a recent *Times* interview the brothers had called inquiries into such interactions "unjustified" and "irrelevant."

Principal Competitors

Reckson Associates Realty Corp.; Vornado Realty Trust.

Further Reading

Bagli, Charles V., "Realtor to Pay $165 Million For 3 Helmsley Office Towers," *New York Times,* February 4, 1998, p. B6.

Barrett, Wayne, "The Green Team," *Village Voice,* August 28, 2001, pp. 20, 22.

Croghan, Lore, "Traditional Landlords Have Suite Tooth for Dot-Coms," *Crain's New York Business,* August 7, 2000, pp. 39, 43.

Dunlap, David W., "For Graybar, Restoring a Lost Luster," *New York Times,* April 1, 1998, p. B8.

Feldman, Amy, "King of B Property at Head of Class," *Crain's New York Business,* September 8, 1997, pp. 3, 44.

Finch, Camilla, "Exec Challenge: Making Difficult Space Appealing," *Crain's New York Business,* March 25, 1991, p. 13.

Garbarine, Rachelle, "All Offices Leased in a Converted East Side Warehouse," *New York Times,* August 14, 1991, p. D15.

Gross, Daniel, "REIT-Shaping NY," *Crain's New York Business,* January 12, 1998, pp. 25+.

Holusha, John, "This REIT's Favorite Lyric, 'We'll Have Manhattan'," *New York Times,* May 10, 1998, Sec. 11, p. 9.

——, "Wiring as the Tip of the Telecommunications Iceberg," *New York Times,* April 11, 1999, p. B9.

Jay, Leslie, "Special Report: Commercial Real Estate," *Crain's New York Business,* January 15, 2001, p. 47.

Lipton, Eric, "Different Lives, Different Politics, But Greens Unite in Mayor's Race," *New York Times,* August 13, 2001, pp. A1, B4.

Rich, Motoko, "Office Owners Grapple With the New Economy," *Wall Street Journal,* June 14, 2000, p. B18.

Rothstein, Mervyn, "On 9th Ave., Upgrading Takes Fringe Out of Area," *New York Times,* April 21, 1999, p. B9.

Temes, Judy, "Brokers Vie for Distressed Property Work," *Crain's New York Business,* April 19, 1993, p. 37.

Vinocur, Barry, "Does Class B Rate an A?," *Barron's,* August 11, 1997, p. 49.

—Robert Halasz

Società Sportiva Lazio SpA

Via di Santa Cornelia 14
00060 Formello, Roma
Italy
Telephone: (+39) 06-90-40-601
Fax: (+39) 06-90-40-00-22
Web site: http://www.sslazio.it

Public Company
Incorporated: 1900 as Società Podistica Lazio
Employees: 110
Sales: EUR 118.23 million ($129.34 million) (2000)
Stock Exchanges: Italian
Ticker Symbol: SSL
NAIC: 711211 Sports Teams and Clubs; 711310
   Promoters of Performing Arts, Sports, and Similar
   Events with Facilities

Società Sportiva Lazio SpA (SS Lazio) is the corporation behind one of Italy's oldest soccer teams, the first Italian soccer team to take a listing on the Milan stock exchange. Based in Rome—the team takes its name from Rome's Lazio region—SS Lazio has long stood at the top of the country's soccer rankings. The company won Italy's first division championship in 2000, marking its 100th anniversary. SS Lazio is majority owned by Sergio Cragnotti, who leads a conglomerate that also owns the country's top tomato sauce and dairy producer, Cirio. Under Cragnotti, SS Lazio has joined the big leagues of European soccer, paying millions in player salaries to boost the team's record. Most of SS Lazio's revenues come from television rights, which stood at 58 percent of sales in 2000. Season ticket sales added another 23 percent that year, while sponsorship contracts combined to form 11 percent of the team's revenues. Cragnotti, whose sold some 41 percent of his holding in the club during its public offering in 1998, owns slightly more than 50 percent of the team and remains its chairman. In 2001, Cragnotti announced his desire to step down as chairman and sell off his holding after enraged SS Lazio fans, protesting the sale of key players, dumped garbage on Cragnotti's front lawn.

Soccer Pioneer at the Turn of the Century

Società Sportiva Lazio came into being in 1900 when a group of friends, led by former Italian army officer Luigi Bigiarelli, founded a cross-country running club in Rome. Another sports club, Roma Gymnastica, had already claimed the city's name; therefore, the new group settled on the name, Società Podistica Lazio, taken from Rome's Lazio region. As team colors, the group chose the white and sky-blue of Olympics homeland, Greece—the club members were later affectionately nicknamed the "biancocelesti" (heavenly whites). Initially Bigiarelli and friends concentrated on running races; in 1902, however, the group discovered soccer, which was only then beginning to be introduced into Italy. Lazio won Rome's first-ever soccer match that same year and quickly dedicated itself to the game, changing its name to Società Sportiva Lazio.

Bigiarelli and company not only became ardent soccer proponents, helping to transform the game into Italy's favorite game, their team was also a consistent winner. By 1907, Lazio remained undefeated in Rome and was ready to move up to interregional competition. That year, Lazio traveled to Pisa to play against regional champions Pisa, Livorno, and Lucca. Lazio swept the series, winning all three games in a single day of competition.

By the outbreak of World War I, Lazio had begun to compete on a national level. In the 1912–13 season, the team qualified for Italy's prestigious championship, Lo Scudetta, reaching the final only to lose to Pro Vercelli. The following year, Lazio inaugurated its new playing field at Rondinella, and then reached the finals of the newly formed national championships, this time losing out to the team from Casale. Despite its inability to go all the way to a national championship, the team maintained its dominance of its home Lazio-Rome region and again reached the national championship finals in 1923. Lazio's consistent record of victories gave it a position in the Series A classification (similar to the United States' baseball major league) formed in the late 1920s.

Lazio's heyday came in the 1930s as the team posted a long string of victories. Joining Lazio during this period was forward Silvio Piola, generally considered the best Italian soccer player

Key Dates:

1900: Luigi Bigiarelli leads a group of friends to form running club Società Podistica Lazio in Rome.

1902: Società Podistica Lazio begins playing soccer, becomes Società Sportiva Lazio (SS Lazio).

1907: SS Lazio wins first interregional match against Pisa, Livorno, and Lucca.

1913: SS Lazio qualifies for Scudetto national championships.

1937: SS Lazio reaches second place position in Series A finals.

1958: The team wins Italian Cup for the first time.

1961: SS Lazio is relegated to Series B division.

1974: SS Lazio wins the Italian championship for the first time in team history.

1987: SS Lazio is near bankruptcy and narrowly avoids being relegated to C1 division.

1992: Sergio Cragnotti buys SS Lazio.

1997: SS Lazio reaches finals of UEFA Cup.

1998: SS Lazio becomes first Italian soccer team to take a listing on the stock market.

2000: SS Lazio celebrates its 100th anniversary and wins the Scudetto national championship.

2001: Cragnotti announces his intention to sell off his shares and step down as company chairman.

of all time and one of the greatest soccer players in the world. Piola helped lead the Italian national team to victory during the World Cup of 1938 and set scoring records for Series A play, with 290 goals, including 143 made for Lazio. Yet even the presence of Piola was unable to boost Lazio to the championship title; the team was not to win the championship until the end of the 1950s.

The outbreak of the World War II and Italy's defeat spelled a new period of struggle for SS Lazio. The team lost its playing field at Rondinella, which was converted to vegetable gardens to help feed Rome's hungry population. In 1953, Lazio found a new playing field, the Stadio Olimpico, which remained its home field for more than 40 years.

From Hard Times in the 1950s to Bankruptcy in the 1980s

The move to Rome's Olympic Stadium corresponded to a long period of decline for the club. In the early 1950s, Lazio struggled to remain in the top four of its division; by the end of the decade, it had slipped to the bottom of the rankings. The only bright spot during the period came in 1958, when SS Lazio captured the title at the Coppa Italia—its first championship in more than 50 years of existence.

The Italian Cup victory was not enough to boost the team's spirit. By 1961, Lazio had slumped so low it was dropped from Series A play and relegated to the Series B. Lazio attempted to rally during the decade that followed, regaining Series A status in 1964. Yet the team was once again dropped in 1967. During this time, meanwhile, Italian soccer was undergoing a transfor-

mation, as more and more teams were being bought up by Italy's political and business elite. Teams such as Inter Milan, bought by the oil-rich Moratti family, Juventus, of Turin, taken over by Fiat's Agnelli family, AC Milan, owned by the right wing's Silvio Berlusconi, and Naples, which found new owners within the Lauros' shipbuilding empire, now had the capital to acquire stronger teams.

Lazio's own position remained shaky throughout the 1970s and 1980s, as the team was once again relegated to Series B play in 1971. In the mid-1970s, however, Lazio seemed to have found a new momentum, as its field, led by former Swansea star Giorgio Chinaglia, not only climbed back into the Series A division, but, with Chinaglia leading league scoring, went on to capture the second place spot in the Scudetto. That record gave Lazio access to the European Cup championships. Yet the team's defeat in the early rounds sparked supporter riots, winning Lazio a one-year ban on European Cup play.

At home, the Chinaglia-led team continued to rack up victories, and the following year Lazio won the 1974 Scudetto, giving Lazio the Italian championship for the first time in the team's history. That victory should have qualified Lazio for a position in the European Cup championship, if not for the team's ban. By the middle of the decade, Lazio seemed once again to have run out of steam. In 1976, Lazio lost its star player when Chinaglia left to go to America to join the newly forming North American Soccer League. One year later, another of Lazio's top players, Luciano Re Cecconi, was killed after pretending to hold up a jewelry store as part of a practical joke.

Lazio's fortunes plunged even lower in the early 1980s when a number of its players were implicated in an insider bettor scandal. The team was once again dropped from Series A play. By the end of that decade, however, even Series B play seemed to be too much for the ailing team. Despite a brief rise back to Series A play in 1983, Lazio appeared to be at the end of its long history. By the 1986–87 season, the team, finishing 16th in its division, found itself facing the possibility of being dropped even from Series B. The threat of relegation to the Series C1, beyond humiliating the once-proud team, seemed certain to sink entirely the near-bankrupt club.

New owners Gianmarco Calleri and Renato Bocchi called back Giorgio Chinaglia, who, now named club president, set out to rescue the team. A single goal enabled Lazio to complete the season and avoid a Series C1 demotion. SS Lazio once again began climbing the ranks toward Series A play. In 1989, however, Lazio faced a new setback when, with Italy slated to host the World Cup, the Stado Olimpico was closed for repairs. Lazio found a new temporary playing field at Stado Flaminio.

Becoming a 21st Century Sports Business

Lazio returned to the refurbished Olimpico in 1990. Soon after, the team found a new owner, when it was bought up by Sergio Cragnotti. The head of Cirio, a leading producer of tomato sauces and dairy products, quickly began to pump money into building up the team. Cragnotti's millions helped attract such talent as Thomas Doll, Aron Winter, Alen Boksic, and Giuseppi Signori, whose top-scoring performances helped the team gain a new, more solid position in Series A play. By

1993 the team ranked fifth in the league, climbing to fourth and third positions as well. Lazio was to remain in the top five through to the new century.

During this time, European soccer was undergoing a radical transformation. The growth of satellite television had created a vast new potential market. In the past, television coverage of soccer matches had remained relatively limited in Europe, in part to encourage home attendance, in part because of soccer's traditional image as a blue-collar sport. Yet satellite broadcasters quickly discovered that the audience for soccer matches was huge, while the soccer teams themselves found that soccer was now able to reach a far wider audience. A number of teams, such as England's Manchester United, even developed world renown.

Relaxation of player trading rules, which enabled players to become free agents in the mid-1990s, led to another revolution—that of huge player salaries. Clubs now were forced to compete on an international scale and were expected to pay sums as high as EUR 65 million to secure contracts for top players. Smaller clubs were faced with a scramble for survival. By the end of the century, Lazio was spending more than 60 percent of its revenues on player salaries. At the same time, the owners of many of Europe's soccer clubs, many of whom had paid very little to acquire their teams, now found their investments skyrocketing.

The mid-1990s saw a wave of initial public offerings (IPOs) as soccer teams transformed themselves into full-fledged businesses. The first IPOs were seen in the smaller market countries, such as Denmark and The Netherlands. The United Kingdom soon took the lead, with more than 20 teams going public by the turn of the century. In 1998, Cragnotti joined the trend, selling more than 41 percent of his holding, and SS Lazio became the first Italian team to go public. Cragnotti, who became chairman of the new company, retained more than 50 percent of its shares. That year, the company moved to new headquarters and training facilities in Formello.

Two years later, Lazio celebrated its 100th anniversary in style, capturing the Series A lead for only the second time in its history, winning the Italian Cup, and reaching the quarterfinals of the Champions League. Lazio scored another trophy in the 2000–2001 season, winning the Super Cup. Yet the team slipped into losses later in the season as its hope for a new championship were dashed when the team lost the Series A championship to arch-rivals—and newly public—AC Roma. Team trainer Sven Goran Eriksson resigned his post, replaced by Dino Zoff in January 2001. Zoff was able to help the struggling team gain a place in the Champions League playoffs.

But in mid-2001, Lazio faced new problems. The team had already been humiliated after racist banners displayed by some of its supporters led to a one-day suspension for the team. The loss of its star player, Argentina's Juan Veron to Manchester United in a deal worth more than EUR 45 million, was followed by the loss of another key Lazio player, the Czech Pavel Nedved, who was wooed away by rival Juventus with a contract for more than EUR 40 million. Outraged Lazio fans stormed Cragnotti's villa, dumping garbage on his front lawn.

In response, Cragnotti announced his decision to sell off his share of Lazio and step down as the company's chairman. Lazio's board, however, rejected Cragnotti's resignation and persuaded him to remain, at least through September 2001. Although Cragnotti claimed to be committed to selling his stake in the team, analysts questioned whether he would be able to find buyers for his stake.

In the meantime, Cragnotti and Lazio went back to the trading table in an effort to rebuild its front line. After acquiring players Gaizka Mendieta, Stefano Fiore, and Giuliano Giannichedda, Lazio completed the summer with an agreement to pay £15.25 million to acquire Jaap Stam from Manchester United. The renewed team quickly suffered a setback when it was eliminated in the early rounds of the Champions League. Cragnotti was forced to sack team trainer, Dino Zoff, replacing him with Alberto Zaccheroni, formerly with AC Milan.

Despite its difficulties in 2001, Società Sportiva Lazio entered its second century as a public company eager to capitalize on the steadily growing European sports market. As broadcasting took on a still greater importance in the soccer world— broadcasting revenues accounted for nearly 60 percent of Lazio's own sales—the company looked forward to continued changes in television and viewing habits. The roll-out of digital television was expected to prompt a new revolution, particularly with the availability of pay-per-view matches. Lazio was now able to recruit new season tickets not only for its stadium seating, but from among the vast television viewing audience throughout Europe.

Principal Competitors

Manchester United Plc; Ajax Amsterdam NV; Newcastle United Plc; Paris Saint Germain SA; Aston Villa Plc; Chelsea Village Plc; FC Porto; Tottenham Hotspur plc; AC Roma SpA; F.C. Internazionale Milano SpA; Juventus F.C. S.p.A; Milan A.C., S.p.A.

Further Reading

Bruce-Ball, Jim, "Cragnotti Cannot Leave Lazio Board Behind, *Guardian,* July 7, 2001.

Buckley, Kevin, "Eternal Rivals Pose Colossal Task for Lazio," *Scotland on Sunday,* Dec 17, 2000.

Coates, Jonathan, "Yesterday's Hero Zoff Now Persona Non Grata at Lazio," *Scotsman,* September 21, 2001.

Gallard, Philippe, "Les patrons du foot font des rêves en or," *L'Expansion,* September 24, 1998 p. 84.

"The Game That Turned to Gold," *European,* August 21, 1997, p. 8.

James, Jennie, "More Money Than Sense," *Time International,* August 7, 2000, p. 60.

Kennedy, Frances, "Lazio Wondering Where It Went Wrong," *Independent,* July 16, 2001.

"The Politics of Italian Football," *Economist,* December 19, 1998.

Schrage, Yael, "Roma AS IPO to Steal Limelight from Rival SS Lazio," *Reuters,* May 15, 2000.

"Soccer and Stockmarkets: Floating Football Clubs Is Often a Good Idea," *Economist,* May 16, 1998.

Sullivan, Ruth, "Tomato Milkshake Unsettles Investors," *European,* April 17, 1997, p. 21.

—M.L. Cohen

Sonesta International Hotels Corporation

200 Clarendon Street
41st Floor
Boston, Massachusetts 02116
U.S.A.
Telephone: (617) 421-5400
Fax: (617) 421-5402
Web site: http://www.sonesta.com

Public Company
Incorporated: 1946
Employees: 3,000
Sales: $184 million (2000)
Stock Exchanges: NASDAQ
Ticker Symbol: SNSTA
NAIC: 72111 Hotels (Except Casino Hotels) and Motels;
  483112 Deep Sea Passenger Transportation

Sonesta International Hotels Corporation owns or operates 25 hotel, resort, and cruise properties in Bermuda, the Caribbean, Egypt, Italy, Peru, and the United States. It caters to upscale business and leisure travelers and distinguishes itself by showcasing the culture and history of each locale. There is no "Sonesta look." Among Sonesta's properties are a tenth-century castle in Tuscany, Italy, and three cruise ships on the Nile. Although relatively unknown in the United States, Sonesta is one of the larger hotel chains in Egypt and the largest international hotel chain in Peru.

Company Founded After "Sonny" Sonnabend Rejected Retirement

Joseph Sonnabend, the father of A.M. (Sonny) Sonnabend, emigrated from Austria to the United States when he was a boy. By age 18, Joseph owned a Boston jewelry store, later adding a pawnshop and another jewelry store. However, he taught his two sons that business was not the most important thing. Joseph told his sons that businesses come and go, but what people always need is houses, stores, and land. Joseph focused on real estate and built up his holdings, turning them over to Sonny in 1918.

Sonny increased the apartment and store holdings to $350,000 by 1927. By World War II, he probably was the leading apartment-house owner in Boston, with some 2,500 apartments. He had also worked his way to millionaire status. At age 49 he told his brother Leopold that he was going to retire.

Then a Boston real estate broker contacted Sonny about an enticing listing. The broker offered Sonnabend the Biltmore and Whitehall hotels, the Palm Beach Country Club, and three Palm Beach, Florida, properties in 1943 for $2.40 million. Sonny said owning hotels would put him in the "Big League." With seven partners he bought the three properties.

His decision proved profitable almost immediately. Conrad Hilton bought the Biltmore from him about a year later for nearly as much as he had paid for all three hotels. Noting that Hilton and Sheraton were both beginning to build chains, Sonny founded Sonnabend Operated Hotels in 1946. A year later he bought the Somerset Hotel on Boston's Commonwealth Avenue. Sonny bought the Edgewater Beach Hotel in Chicago in 1948. Later, rival Conrad Hilton beat him to the punch by adding the Waldorf-Astoria in New York to his holdings. In 1950, Sonny got revenge by buying the Van Sweringen properties in Cleveland with a partner, Royal Little, for $8 million. These properties included the 52 story Terminal Tower, three large office buildings, and the 1,000 room Hotel Cleveland. Three years later he added New York's Plaza Hotel to his properties.

Industry-wide hotel profits climbed in the early 1950s, creating a problem that got Sonnabend's attention—a large taxable income. John Bergen and Irving Felt, partners who controlled the Childs Restaurant Company, presented a solution. In 1956, Sonny sold several hotels to Bergen and Felt in exchange for stock in their money-losing restaurants. The $6 million tax loss helped offset Sonny's hotel profits. He leased the remainder of his hotels to a new entity, the Hotel Corporation of America, which became one of the country's first major hotel companies.

Throughout his career, A.M. Sonnabend benefited from good timing, business acumen, and some luck. In 1930, during the Great Depression, he had protected his apartment holdings by lowering rents for anyone who would sign a long-term lease. His move impressed Boston bankers (who then controlled a

Company Perspectives:

The Mission of Sonesta International Hotels, Resorts & Nile Cruises is to operate outstanding hotels in unique locations in a manner that achieves the following four goals: practice the highest standards of integrity and ethics in the way we conduct our business; value our employees as individuals; exceed customers' expectations; deliver service with passion.

large percentage of the city's commercial real estate) enough that they began offering foreclosed properties to him. After the 1950 Van Sweringen purchase, Sonny recovered the entire down payment because the seller had not looked in the treasuries of the corporation and had left $1 million in surplus cash. However, A.M. Sonnabend earned much of his business reputation on a business move often called the Botany formula.

The Botany Formula Developed in 1954

In 1958, *Fortune* magazine said the Botany formula baffled a lot of people. It was a tax technique Sonny used to buy many profitable companies by using their own excess working capital and future earnings. He then would fold the companies into a corporation with such high losses that it acquired a substantial tax credit. Few businessmen exploited this tax-credit device with greater aplomb than A.M. Sonnabend. He bought more than a hundred companies while supplying no supervision and rarely paying cash.

Sonny devised the Botany formula in the fall of 1954 after purchasing a quarter of the common stock of Botany Mills in Passaic, New Jersey. Credit for the Botany formula belongs at least in part to Bernard Wolfman, a young lawyer who combed the revenue code and discovered an old Treasury regulation. The regulation said a company with subsidiaries that filed consolidated tax returns during a period when it lost money could include newly acquired subsidiaries in its consolidated return. The formula provided Sonny with the advantage of strong incentive for the seller to stay on as manager. Sonny could also offer a generous price since he was guaranteed not to lose money. If the subsidiary showed a loss it was the seller who took on the burden.

Botany Mills was losing money when Sonny came on the scene, but by 1957 it had the highest profit on net worth of any company in the Fortune 500. On a net worth of $14 million Botany made an $8 million profit that year. Success came from an diverse and long list of subsidiaries, including a New York City doll company, an oil-well supply firm in Oklahoma, and a manufacturer of lint-cleaning machinery in Texas. At the height of his business holdings, Sonny controlled Botany, the Hotel Corporation of America, Consolidated Retail Stores, and Artistic Foundations.

1964: Three Sons Take Over

When A.M. Sonnabend's three sons reached adulthood, each joined the business. Sonny started each son high up in the company at young ages. He began devoting much of his time to teaching them the hotel business. The eldest son, Roger, took

the helm of the Nautilus Hotel and Beach Club in Atlantic Beach, Long Island, when he was a 21-year-old MIT graduate. Paul Sonnabend became general manager of Boston's Hotel Shelton after graduating from Cornell's hotel administration school in 1950. The youngest son, Stephen, took an executive position with Childs Restaurants.

When Roger took the reins of the Nautilus he was also about to enter Harvard Business School. He arrived at the hotel, took one look at the less than ideal conditions, and called his father. "What do you want me to do with this relic?" Roger asked. "I want you to manage it!" came Sonny's sharp reply. "She's yours and with her you sink or swim as a hotel man." Sinking seemed a distinct possibility as Roger poured money into the property, raising the eyebrows of his brothers who claimed he spent money "like a drunken sailor." Between his Harvard classes Roger commuted to Atlantic Beach, shopped for chefs, trained staff in courtesy, and interviewed waitresses. He hired painters, electricians, carpenters, and landscape crews. At the end of Roger's first year the Nautilus showed a profit. Roger's brother, Paul also turned red ink to black after a year at Hotel Shelton.

After Sonny's death in 1964, the three sons decided to sell their unprofitable properties and keep the company small. They enjoyed the hotel business, but not the real estate management business. Their decision allowed them to create a hotel management company and maintain personal control over the hotel operation.

The Sonesta Art Collection

One of the first corporate hotel programs dedicated to original art, the Sonesta Art Collection was initiated in the early 1960s. Forty years later the collection included more than 6,000 contemporary paintings, sculptures, original prints, and tapestries by world-renowned artists like Sol Lewitt, Andy Warhol, Frank Stella, and Robert Mapplethorpe. The Sonesta commissioned some works to accentuate the architecture and design of a particular hotel space.

Redefining the Company in the 1970s

The early 1970s proved to be a time of economic recession. The Sonnabends decided to redefine the company as a small, upscale chain. Properties that did not fit into the new, high-end image, or that were not turning a profit (such as the Plaza Hotel New York), were sold. About 30 Charter House motor lodges in Maine, Massachusetts, Ohio, Virginia, Maryland, California, and New York were sold in the mid-1970s. That left Sonesta with three U.S. hotels and three in the Caribbean. In 1979, the brothers renamed the company "Sonesta" after a cattle farm A.M. and his wife owned in New England. The word combined the parents' first names, "Sonny" and "Esther."

Unlike other hotel chains, Sonesta did not stamp its properties with a consistent design or style. For example, in 1995 when it bought the former Casablanca Hotel on Anguilla, it left the North African-inspired architecture with its arches, fountains, and hand-crafted mosaics intact. The company frowned on what it called "cookie cutter" hotel architecture. Instead, Sonesta evaluated the outstanding characteristics of its properties and their locales and emphasized them.

This may be one reason Americans did not have a clear image of Sonesta. "What sets us apart from the competition," President Stephanie Sonnabend said, "is we try to give our guests a true destination experience, not a chain experience. When people think of a Sonesta hotel we want them to think of something a bit unusual or different." Corporate headquarters gave local property managers wide latitude to try new ideas and make their own decisions. Another reason for the public's lack of familiarity with Sonesta was the company's inability to match marketing resources with larger chains like the Marriott and Hyatt. Sonesta marketed only through travel partners like meeting planners and travel agents while some of the competition marketed directly to the consumer. The company also promoted an extended family culture with employees. For example, at its Anguilla resort, Sonesta went as far as buying a van to transport resort employees to and from their homes.

Sonesta Grows a Property Per Year in 1980s

Through the 1980s and much of the 1990s, Sonesta grew at the rate of one property per year. In the 1980s the company opened hotels in Orlando, Florida; Ft. Myers, Florida; and Curacao, Dutch Caribbean. In 1984, the company doubled the size of its flagship property, Royal Sonesta Hotel Boston.

But, most the growth during this time period occurred outside the United States. In 1984, after Sonesta took over a 200-room hotel in Heliopolis, Egypt, the property became the most popular gathering place in town. The improvements made other Egyptian hotel owners take notice and several approached the company about running their properties. By 1997, Sonesta was opening its fifth Egyptian hotel, the Sonesta St. George Hotel Luxor and also had three Nile cruise ships. By 1999, the company had become one of Egypt's largest chains and earned revenues of $101 million in U.S. dollars according to *Hotels* magazine.

Sonesta became much better known overseas than in the United States. Barely 17 percent of its portfolio of properties in 2000 were in the United States. Sonesta failed to grow in the United States less out of neglect than out of a lack of opportunity, according to President Stephanie Sonnabend. She said the company lacked capital, did not pursue capital, and did not need to grow.

It did well financially without U.S. growth. The U.S. hotels performed well. They were not all market leaders, but the Royal Sonesta Hotel in Boston led that city in occupancy rate in 2000. The Royal Sonesta in New Orleans had an 87 percent occupancy rate in 2000. The company as a whole was profitable through most of the 1990s and into the 21st century. In 1986, the stock traded at $13 per share. Fifteen years later it traded at $9.75 after a stock split in 1999. Stockholder equity increased from $19.69 million in 1992 to $29.93 million in 2000.

Family Ownership Continues into 2001

In 2001, Sonesta operated under the leadership of Roger P. Sonnabend, who served as chairman of the Board of Directors, and other members of the Sonnabend family. A.M.'s three sons, Roger, Paul, and Stephen, all had children in executive positions within the company, making them the third generation of the family to operate the hotels. Roger's daughter, Stephanie Sonnabend was president; another daughter, Jacquelyn Sonnabend served as executive vice-president; and his son, Alan Sonnabend, was vice-president and general manager, Sonesta Beach Resort in Key Biscayne, Florida. Stephanie had prepared for her leadership role by earning degrees from Harvard University and MIT's Sloan School of Management.

By early in the 21st century the company announced it was ready to expand in its home country. Sonesta planned to use the success of four U.S. hotels (Royal Sonesta Hotel, Boston; Sonesta Beach Resort, Key Biscayne; Sonesta Hotel & Suites, Coconut Grove (due to open in 2002); and Chateau Sonesta Hotel, New Orleans) to propel its expansion. With an industry consultant, Stephanie sought financial partners and began looking for acquisitions. The plan was to grow around the spoke of Boston with 10 to 12 properties in key cities like New York, Chicago, Toronto, and Washington, D.C. Rather than build, Sonesta sought to purchase existing properties.

Expansion was also planned outside the United States. In 2001, Sonesta signed a master franchise agreement to open as many as 10 hotels in Brazil by 2007. Eventually Sonesta hoped to grow to about 40 properties—still small enough to maintain its individual, personal approach to hotel management.

The company also merged two Aruba properties into one, the Aruba Sonesta Beach Resort in 2000. It began constructing a new property in the Coconut Grove area of Miami that year (to open by 2002) and finalized agreements for the Sonesta Ocean Grande Beach Resort Sunny Isles in North Miami Beach.

Principal Competitors

Accor SA; Four Seasons Hotels Inc.; Starwood Hotels & Resorts Worldwide Inc.; Marriott International Inc.; Hyatt Corporation.

Further Reading

Baraban, Regina S., "Sonesta Hotel: The Quiet Company," *Lodging Hospitality*, November 1997, p. 58.
Hensdill, Cherie, "Sonesta Awakens," *Hotels,* August 2000.
"Men on the Move: The Sonnabend Brothers," *Boston Magazine*, 1963.
Murphy, Thomas P., "Sonnabend's Sackful," *Fortune,* September 1958, p. 133.

—Chris John Amorosino

Spangler Candy Company

400 North Portland Street
Post Office Box 71
Bryan, Ohio 43506-0071
U.S.A.
Telephone: (419) 636-4221
Fax: (419) 636-3695
Web site: http://www.spanglercandy.com

Private Company
Incorporated: 1906 as Spangler Manufacturing Co.
Employees: 450
Sales: $68 million (2001 est.)
NAIC: 31132 Chocolate and Confectionery
    Manufacturing from Cocoa Beans; 31133
    Confectionery Manufacturing from Purchased
    Chocolate; 31134 Nonchocolate Confectionery
    Manufacturing.

The candies of the Spangler Candy Company have been household names in America for decades. Independent and privately owned, Spangler's most famous product is the Dum Dum Pop, a lollipop that is produced in 13 different flavors, including a mystery flavor that changes from batch to batch. With its other lollipops, including rocket-shaped Astro Pops, Saf-T-Pops with the safety loop handle for small children, and Picture Pops, Spangler is the second-largest maker of lollipops in the Untied States. The company also manufactures the popular Circus Peanuts, as well as a full line of candy canes, hard candies, marshmallow candies, and chocolates. The company manufactures and markets licensed products: Jelly Belly Candy Canes, Lemonhead Lollipops, and Atomic Fireball Lollipops. Every day Spangler's 500,000 square foot facility in Ohio produces more than seven million Dum Dums, one million Sat-T-Pops, and 2.5 million candy canes. Spangler celebrates its one hundredth anniversary in 2006.

Early 1900s Origins

The Spangler Candy Company has its origins in the Gold Leaf Baking Powder Company, which Arthur Garfield Spangler purchased for $450 at a sheriff's auction in August 1906. One month later he moved the firm from Defiance, Ohio to Bryan, Ohio, changed its name to the Spangler Manufacturing, and resumed producing the company's earlier line of baking powder, baking soda, laundry starch, spices and flavorings—but no candy. Despite a loyal base of Gold Leaf Baking Powder customers, Spangler found the business hard going at first. He took to selling other products to help make ends meet. One was salted peanuts, which his mother made in her kitchen. At first she was able to make about two pounds of peanuts at a time using her wood stove. When the peanuts proved popular, Spangler bought her a kerosene stove which enabled her to increase her daily quota to about thirty pounds of nuts a day.

Spangler's youngest brother, Ernest, meanwhile was selling candy for a Toledo candy jobber, a company that distributed candy of various manufacturers. Ernest persuaded Arthur to add some candy to the Spangler company's line of goods. It was a success from the first, so much so that in 1908 Ernest sold his interest in the candy jobbing business and joined his brother as a partner. The Spangler company began to grow quickly, aided by Bryan Ohio's prime location on the crossroads of several key rail lines to Chicago, Detroit, Cleveland, and Cincinnati. Before long, the firm's annual sales hit $50,000. Business was so good that Ernest had to give up his position as head of shipping in order to help Arthur with sales. In 1910 Spangler expanded its facilities for the first time, moving to a larger building in Bryan.

The company introduced the Spangler Cocoanut Ball, the first candy it manufactured on its own in 1911. It was based on a recipe that had been developed by a Fremont, Ohio candy maker, whom Spangler hired and brought to Bryan. The Cocoanut Balls were a success, but they required some unusual innovations. In order to remove the tough outer shells of the coconuts, the company arranged to pump into the factory steam from the steam room of a hotel next door. The coconuts were then hacked open by hand with axes. Before long, Cocoanut Balls were being sold as far east as New York City and as far west as Denver. The twenty-five workers making the new candy by hand were completely overwhelmed with work. To relieve them, the company replaced its older machinery with two stirring machines and other power equipment. The age of auto-

Company Perspectives:

We believe an open family atmosphere combined with professional management fosters cooperation and allows each individual to maximize their contribution to the company and realize the corresponding rewards. We believe in complete honesty and integrity in dealing with employees, customers, suppliers, shareholders, and the communities in which we do business. We take a long-term view of performance and will not sacrifice long-term principles for short-term results. We recognize the value of our established brand names and the need to continue to promote and enhance the consumers' awareness and preference for our brands. We believe it is necessary to be a leader in providing reliable, consistent, and accurate service to customers. We invest in technologies to delivery quality product to our customers at a competitive cost. We maintain a conservative financial approach in the deployment and management of our assets. We will remain an independent, privately owned company.

mated candy making had begun. Spangler produced Cocoanut Balls until around 1924.

Later in 1911, Spangler expanded its candy line with chocolates. The firm obtained the recipe for the Cream Peanut Cluster along with the equipment to produce it from another Ohio candy company, Bost Brothers. Because there was no mechanical air conditioning at the time, chocolates were produced in the cool basement of the Spangler facility; production stopped altogether in summertime. By 1913, chocolates were among Spangler's most popular products. The company added new items such as the Hand Roll, a vanilla and chocolate concoction invented by Arthur Spangler's wife Helen, and the Vanilla Jitney, one of Spangler's first chocolate bars. The same year the company moved to its present-day location on North Portland Street in Bryan. A year later, accountant Omar Spangler, a third Spangler brother, became a partner in the company.

Back to Business after World War I

The Spangler company survived World War I in fine shape despite rampant inflation in sugar prices by 1919. After the war ended, competition among candy producers resumed with a vengeance. In 1920 there were over 70 candy manufacturers in Ohio alone. Spangler Cough Drops was one product that gave the firm a leg up. Introduced during the war, the cough drops caught on during the widespread influenza epidemic of 1918. Spangler discontinued them around 1935 when they were no longer cost effective to produce.

As the 1920s began, Spangler was producing nothing but candies—it had even discontinued its once popular baking powder—and in 1920 the firm changed its name to the Spangler Candy Company. Pan Taffy, Lady Fingers, Gypsy Cuts, Wonder Caramels, and Hub Chocolate Drops were among the seventy products then in the Spangler line. The Apple Sucker was so popular that the firm had to introduce a night shift in order to keep up with demand. In 1922, manufacture of Chocolate Cream Peanut Clusters was automated. Spangler formed a

candy wholesaling subsidiary in the Toledo, Ohio, area in 1927. It included a retail store, which was run by Truman Spangler, the fourth Spangler brother who joined the company in 1920. In 1929, partner Ernest Spangler moved to the Toledo area to run the wholesale unit there.

By 1929, Spangler was flourishing. Its annual production had reached 1.25 million pounds of candy. Its most popular item was Bryan Drops, a chocolate-covered vanilla cream. The coming of the Great Depression hurt the company relatively little. Americans were foregoing many of their former pleasures, but they continued to buy candy, which remained relatively inexpensive. Remarkably, the firm's 115 regular workers did not miss a day of work during the Depression, although they were forced to take a pay cut in 1931. The company was even able to make an acquisition at the height of the Depression. In 1931, it purchased the recipe and trademark for Hickok Honeycomb Chips, a popular crunchy toffee and chocolate candy manufactured by C.F. Hickok, another Ohio candy maker. The Honeycomb Chips remained part of the Spangler line until the 1970s.

A New Generation of Candy Makers

The second generation of Spanglers began working for the company during the decade of the 1930s. Ernest Spangler's sons, Norman, Charles, and Albert, entered the firm in 1931, 1933, and 1934 respectively. Omar Spangler's son, Harlan, joined in 1933. Arthur Spangler's son, Theodore, went to work in the factory in 1940. The cousins would eventually take over the management of the Spangler Candy Company after the World War II.

America's entry into World War II brought with it strict rationing of many essential goods; however, wise business decisions made just before rationing began guaranteed it adequate supplies of sugar and chocolate. Spangler had also begun using glucose produced from corn syrup, which was not rationed. Special storage tanks for corn syrup, which were installed at the company in 1941, enabled Spangler to purchase large quantities of corn syrup when it was available on the market and to stockpile it. The war helped create one of Spangler's most successful products of the 1940s. Spangler's Marshmallow Topping, which was made primarily from corn syrup, became popular as a sugar substitute at a time when the real thing was scarce.

1940s–50s: Spangler Incorporates and Expands

When the war was over, Spangler was manufacturing over 300 different products. During the war, the company had also begun to purchase real estate, with the expectation that prices would jump once the conflict had ended. Another subsidiary, Spangler Investments, was founded in 1945 to manage these holdings. Its name was changed to Spangler Properties in 1954. After all the Spangler sons had returned home from the war, in April 1946, the company's structure was changed from a partnership to a corporation. 4,032 shares in all were issued to Ernest Spangler and his sons, the widow of Omar Spangler and their children, and the widow of Arthur Spangler and their children. Omar Spangler had passed away in 1940 after a long illness; Arthur died in a boating accident in 1945.

Expansion had been taking place regularly at Spangler since 1911. After the war, the company's facilities were expanded

Key Dates:

1906: Arthur Spangler purchases the Gold Leaf Baking Company of Defiance, Ohio, for $450, moves it to Bryan, Ohio, and renames it the Spangler Manufacturing Company.

1908: Ernest Spangler joins the company and suggests adding candy to the product line.

1911: Spangler Cocoanut Ball, the first candy manufactured by Spangler, goes into production.

1914: Omar Spangler joins the company.

1920: Truman Spangler joins the company as a salesman; company's name is changed to Spangler Candy Company.

1922: First hard candy and suckers are introduced.

1927: Spangler founds wholesaling subsidiary in Maumee, Ohio.

1931: Spangler acquires Hickok Honeycomb Chocolate of Sydney, Ohio.

1941: Marshmallow Topping is introduced and becomes popular as a sugar substitute during World War II.

1945: Founder Arthur Spangler dies in boating accident.

1953: Dum Dum Pops are acquired from Akron Candy Co. of Bellevue, Ohio.

1954: A-Z Christmas Candy Cane Company of Detroit, Michigan, is acquired.

1957: Ohio Confections Fudge of Cleveland, makers of Pecan Divinity, is acquired.

1962: Shelby Bubble Gum of Shelby, Ohio, is acquired.

1965: American Mint Corp. of New York City is acquired.

1978: Saf-T-Pops is acquired from Curtiss Candy Co. of Chicago, Illinois.

1980: The company acquires Standard the Candy Cane Company of Detroit, Michigan.

1987: Astro Pops brand is acquired from Nellson Candy Co. of Los Angeles, California.

1995: Suck An Egg brand is acquired from Innovative Confections of Idaho Falls, Idaho.

further. A state-of-the-art factory was built in 1947. In 1948, a process was introduced which allowed liquid sugar to be pumped directly from rail sidings into special tanks on the factory's second floor. As a result, cumbersome 100-pound bags of sugar no longer had to be transported, unloaded, and processed. Another 3,400 square feet were added in 1951.

Spangler acquired its best-known product in March 1953 when it purchased the production equipment and trademark for Dum Dum lollipops from the Akron Candy Company. Dum Dums, which had been made since 1924, were said to have been named by Akron Candy's I.C. Bahr for World War I dum-dum bullets. Bahr liked the name because he reckoned any child would be able to say it. At the time of their acquisition by Spangler, Dum Dums were about the fifth largest-selling lollipops in the Midwest. In their first year of production, Spangler turned out more than 84 million Dum Dum suckers.

Just one year later, in March 1954, Spangler made another major acquisition. It purchased Detroit's A-Z Candy Company,

reputed to be the largest maker of candy canes in the United States. A-Z's equipment was transported from Michigan to Bryan, Ohio, and candy canes went into production in fall 1954, just in time for the Christmas rush. In 1955, Montgomery Ward's candy cane giveaway at Christmas gave Spangler sales a boost. Spangler's share of the order amounted to one million canes, which filled ten semi trailers and provided Spangler workers with some 3,500 hours of overtime.

In the 1950s Spangler continued its program of acquiring established candy brands, developing new candies of its own, and expanding its customer base. When Ohio Confections went into liquidation in 1957 Spangler purchased the equipment and recipes for Pecan Divinity Fudge. Spangler was there at the start of the space age in 1958 when it introduced Sputnik Pops, lollipops it produced in two cent and 29 cent sizes. A new Spangler subsidiary, the Gold Leaf Corporation—named for the baking powder company Arthur Spangler had purchased in 1906—was founded in 1959. Based in Cleveland, Ohio, Gold Leaf was formed to sell Spangler candy products to churches, schools, clubs, and other organizations engaged in fundraising activities.

Spangler's successes continued. In the 15 years following World War II, annual sales increased every year and hit $4 million for the first time in 1959. Another milestone was achieved in 1960 when the firm's workers turned out 50 million tons of candy. It acquired another popular penny candy in July 1962 when it purchased the Shelby Gum Company, the maker of Blo-Bubble bubble gum. Spangler added Kraks mints to its product line with the acquisition of the American Mint Corporation in 1965. Dum Dums were advertised for the first time on television in 1966. The test lasted only a short time but it resulted in the adoption of the Dum Dum Drum Man as the mascot of the popular suckers.

As the 1970s began, Spangler's annual sales were reaching all time highs. 1969 sales were $8 million, twice those of ten years earlier. By 1971 they had jumped to $10 million. The continuing automation of the Spangler production processes contributed to the increases. As the seventies went on, however, the economy began to slow, and the prices of both sugar and corn syrup were rising precipitously. By April 1974, costs had risen so much that Spangler could no longer afford to produce one-cent Dum Dum suckers. When a two-cent Dum Dum was introduced that year, an institution ended. For a time, beginning in 1970, the darkening economy caused the Spangler family to consider going public with its enterprise. In spring 1972, the family shareholders met and formed a committee to report on the issue. However despite the economic downturn, the decision was made to keep Spangler a private company, and it is now one of the company's corporate principles to remain privately owned.

1970s: Next Generation Joins the Family Business

As the 1970s progressed, one after another of the second generation of Spanglers retired from the company, first Norman Spangler, then Albert, Harlan, Frank, and Charles. In 1976 C. Gregory Spangler and Dean L. Spangler—the third generation—entered the company's upper management. C. Gregory Spangler was elected president in 1977 and CEO in 1978. Spangler's sales were strong during the seventies, despite rising prices and the sluggish economy. By 1977 Dum Dums were

Spangler's most popular product, accounting for 44 percent of all sales. New products continued to be introduced as well. With consumer interest in sugar-free food on the rise, sugar-free Lite-Mints, introduced in 1978, took off rapidly. The company planned to produce 1,250 cases a month originally. However, within three months of their debut, demand for Lite-Mints reached 11,000 cases a month and additional manufacturing equipment had to be rushed to Bryan from Britain. Later in 1978, Spangler acquired the rights to produce Saf-T-Pops, lollipops with a patented looped handle to make them safe for very young children. The deal gave Spangler the two best-known lollipops in the United States, Dum Dums and Saf-T-Pops, and 1979 sales broke all records, reaching $20 million.

The 1990s and Beyond

Spangler continued to expand its line of candy in the 1980s and 1990s. In 1987 it acquired the Astro Pops Brand from the Nellson Candy Company of Los Angeles California. Astro Pops, rocket-shaped lollipops, were reputed to be the longest lasting lollipop on earth. Spangler next purchased Suck An Egg brand from Innovative Confections of Idaho in 1995.

Spangler reorganized its senior management team in October 1996. C. Gregory Spangler moved from the company presidency to become chairman and CEO. Dean L. Spangler, who had been running the Boren Brick Company, returned to the company to take over as president. In March 2000, the company announced a licensing arrangement with Herman Goelitz, Inc. the maker of Jelly Belly jelly beans. Under the agreement Spangler began producing candy canes in four Jelly Belly flavors for the Christmas season. The candy canes were the largest new product introduction in the company's history. After being named CEO in September 2000, Dean Spangler instituted an aggressive program of product expansion that focused on maximizing the strength of the Dum Dum sucker, the company's flagship brand, as well as pursuing other licensing deals like the successful Jelly Belly candy cane. Spangler struck a deal with the Ferrara Pan Candy Company, makers of Lemonheads and Atomic Fireballs, to produce, market and distribute Lemonhead Lollipops and Atomic Fireball Lollipops. Spangler also announced plans to contract some of its candy cane production out to plants in Mexico. The decision was made partly to free up space in the Bryan factory for lollipop production and partly to respond to increased competition in the candy cane market.

In June 2001, a fire thought to be arson struck a warehouse, destroying some 110,000 cases of Dum Dums, with an estimated value of $6.5 million. The company put an emergency Dum Dum production schedule in force with extended overtime and weekend hours and no interruptions in distribution were anticipated.

Later that year, Dean Spangler was awarded ''Entrepreneur of the Year'' distinction by the *Toledo Business Journal,* which regarded the CEO and president as ''proud and committed to preserving the Spangler family heritage, history and contributions.'' The journal also noted that while the company hoped to expand through acquisitions in the new millennium, it remained for the time ''focused on branding, global expansion and private label growth.''

Principal Divisions

Spangler Wholesale.

Principal Competitors

Tootsie Roll Industries, Inc., Brach's Confections Inc.; Kraft Foods North America Inc.; The Topps Company Inc.

Further Reading

''Entrepreneur of the Year: Dean Spangler, Spangler Candy Company,'' *Toledo Business Journal,* August 1, 2001, p. 40.

Spangler Candy Company, *Fifty Years with the Gold Leaf Trademark,* 1956.

Spangler Candy Company, *Spangler Candy Company at 75,* 1981.

''Spangler Sparkles,'' *Snack Food,* July 1995, pp. 22 + .

''Spangler to Open Operation in Mexico,'' October 23, 2000, *Supermarket News,* p. 81.

''Spangler Unwraps New Promo Efforts,'' *Confectioner,* June 1, 2001, p. 114.

''A Sucker's Born Every Second,'' *Snack Food,* July 1995, pp. 28 + .

''Suppliers Form Candy Alliance in Response to Consolidation,'' *MMR,* May 28, 2001, p. 15.

—Gerald E. Brennan

Speizman Industries, Inc.

701 Griffith Road
Charlotte, North Carolina 28217
U.S.A.
Telephone: (704) 559-5777
Fax: (704) 676-4222
Web site: http://www.speizman.com

Public Company
Incorporated: 1973
Employees: 206
Sales: $115.2 million (2000)
Stock Exchanges: NASDAQ
Ticker Symbol: SPZN
NAIC: 42183 Industrial Machinery and Equipment
    Wholesalers (pt)

Speizman Industries, Inc. is the leading distributor of new sock knitting machines, knitting machines for underwear and other knitted fabrics, and other equipment related to the manufacture of socks, sheer hosiery, and other textile products, principally in the United States and Canada. It is the sole North American distributor for Lonati, the world's largest manufacturer of hosiery knitting equipment through its six companies: Speizman Industries, Inc., Wink Davis Equipment Co., Inc., Todd Motion Controls, Inc., Speizman Yarn Equipment, Inc., Speizman Canada, Inc., and Speizman de Mexico S.A. de C.V. Wink Davis distributes commercial laundry equipment and parts and after sales service. TMC assembles, distributes and services automated boarding and finishing equipment used in the sock knitting industry. Speizman Yarn distributes equipment and related parts used in the yarn processing industry.

From Seller of Secondhand Machinery to a Leader in the Doubleknit Industry

David Speizman, a Jewish Polish immigrant, emigrated from Lodz in 1905, bringing with him his family's experience in spinning, weaving, and finishing fabric. In the early 1920s, he founded the David Speizman Co. in Wilkes-Barre, Pennsylva-

nia, after switching from peddling housewares to selling mill supplies and used weaving machines. In 1936, he sent his son, Morris, south with $2,000 to open a branch of the company in Georgia, where most of the country's weaving was done. However, Morris Speizman settled in Charlotte, North Carolina, with his pregnant wife, Sylvia, who was too tired to move on. Later that same year, he founded the Morris Speizman Company, Inc. and eventually moved into an old textile mill at the corner of North Graham and 5th Streets, an historic green office-factory-warehouse building with needlehooks painted on one outside wall.

Few southern textile mills would deal with a Jewish northerner during the Great Depression, so Morris Speizman started selling sock knitting machines. The machines then weighed about 250 pounds, and to test their quality, buyers sometimes would lift them a few inches and drop them. Originally Speizman's business efforts were focused entirely on the purchase and sale of secondhand hosiery mill machinery. In 1939, Speizman purchased excess equipment—about 700 machines of all types—from a Kenosha, Wisconsin, mill with the help Charlotte's Commercial National Bank. Selling about 30 of the machines to a customer in Canada, Speizman netted about $28,000 on the deal. After World War II, the business expanded to export rebuilt machines to Latin American, Cuba, and Europe. Speizman installed a rebuilding shop and thereby helped to establish the hosiery industry in Peru, Colombia, and Venezuela. During the late 1950s, he expanded operations to include importing new equipment from Europe. In the early 1960s, he opened Morris Speizman Ltd. in Canada.

Lawrence Speizman's, Morris's older son, joined the business in 1958. Under his direction, the company opened the Speizman Knitting Machine Corporation in New York, which handled outerwear textile machinery. Robert Speizman, Morris's younger son, came on board in 1964, after trying out management training for Inland Steel Industries, Inc., in Chicago and selling in New York. Robert "really didn't like the confinement of a large company" and felt that he would do better for himself "making [his] own decisions," according to an article about Speizman Industries in the 1994 *Charlotte Business Journal*. During the late 1960s and into the early

1970s, the company's outerwear division grew more rapidly than the original hosiery division. In 1967, Morris Speizman assumed the role of board chairman and turned operation of the company over to his sons.

Under Robert and Lawrence's aggressive leadership, the firm's annual sales burgeoned from $3 million in 1967 to a high of $41 million in fiscal 1973. Speizman Industries had matured into one of the major companies in the nation's doubleknit industry. "We happened to be in the right place at the right time," recalled Robert Speizman in a 1979, *Charlotte Observer* article. As the distributor for Europe's leading machinery manufacturers, it had three years' worth of orders from textile firms and hosiery manufacturers in hand. It also had branched out to manufacture doubleknit fabric for the Jonathan Logan apparel firm in 1968 as well as producing industrial fasteners and handling air pollution control equipment for textile plants.

1973: Hard Times in the Doubleknit Industry Hurts Speizman

In 1972, the company went public on the American Stock Exchange, trading only on an interdealer basis. However, after the crest of the doubleknit wave in 1972, Speizman's sales and profits decreased, due primarily to the deterioration of the doubleknit industry. "After 1973, the doubleknit industry didn't dip—it died," said Speizman in the *Charlotte Observer*. In the years between 1973 and 1976, revenues dropped to $24 million. The company began to auction off doubleknit machinery to scrap dealers only willing to pay as little as $25 to $100 per machine.

Speizman Industries was in a precarious position since it had sold more than $25 million worth of machines on conditional contracts resold to banks and finance companies and had promised to make good on many of those contracts. Between 1973 and 1976, it paid back more than $12 million on defaulted contracts—more than the company's net worth of almost $10 million. In 1976, sales contracts backed by the company still totaled about $10 million, of which Speizman was liable for about $8 million. In July 1976, it paid financiers $3.2 million to resolve its remaining debt. In all, it repurchased $18 million worth of machines.

In 1977, the company's sales plummeted to approximately $12 million. By 1978, about 70 percent of the firms making doubleknit fabric had folded, and Speizman Industries had a negative net worth of $6.2 million. It had suffered more than $15 million in losses during the past five years, lost its American Stock Exchange listing, closed or sold several facilities, closed offices in Montreal, Zurich, and Mexico City, and cut back from 565 employees to 75.

The company sat down and asked itself, according to Robert Speizman in the *Charlotte Observer* in 1979, " 'What are we and what's our future?' ... We decided our expertise was in hosiery machinery and in specialty knitting areas such as surgical support pads and knit wire for catalytic converters." Management also decided that the company's future lay in manufacturing its own sock and hosiery making equipment rather than simply distributing the equipment of other companies. In 1977, it began to build its manufacturing potential, and by 1979, manufacturing accounted for 40 to 45 percent of its business. Other changes of the late 1970s included selling its fastener division in 1977 and ending its agreement to knit doubleknit cloth for Jonathan Logan. Lawrence Speizman also left the firm to start his own accounting business in New York.

It took several years to turn the company around, but for the year ended June 1979, Speizman Industries once again showed a profit of $629,000. Between 1979 and 1989, Speizman sold 5,000 of its athletic sock knitting machines, named the "Amy" after Robert Speizman's daughter. In 1982, the company began selling sock knitters manufactured by the Lonati Company of Brescia. Lonati was the maker of the most fully computerized sock knitting equipment. Its machines used computer controls to dictate the size and style of the sock being knitted, and were reprogrammed in about 20 seconds, a vast improvement over the needle- and drum-based machines they replaced, which took a skilled technician about a day to rearrange. Speizman ended production of its own lines in 1990, having become Lonati's exclusive North American distributor and the top seller of new sock knitting machines in the United States. In 1989, two years after Morris Speizman died, the company formed a new Montreal subsidiary, Speizman Canada, Inc.

The 1990s Bring a Change of Fortune

In 1991, despite recession, U.S. factories shipped 3.9 billion pairs of socks. About half of that output came from North Carolina where more 40,000 of the nation's 70,000 hosiery workers worked. When the retail industry showed signs of recovering in 1992, Speizman ratched up its visibility with a Nasdaq listing. In 1993, it made $2.4 million in profits, ranking sixth on Nasdaq's list of top performers.

By the late 1990s, Speizman was once again enjoying healthy revenues of $79 million and acquisitions. In 1997, it bought the largest U.S. distributor of laundry equipment, Wink Davis Equipment Company, Inc. and closed its own outerwear dyeing and finishing unit. In 1998, it established Speizman Yarn Equipment Co., Inc., acquired TMC Automation Co., and won the North Carolina Governor's New Product Award for TMC's line of machines that pairs, folds, stacks, and bags socks. It also signed new exclusive agreements with six Italian textile equipment suppliers, to sell machinery in North America. In 1999, the company moved from its original green building to 118,000 square feet of office and distribution space in a building on Griffith Road. The move allowed it to consolidate several other warehouses in Charlotte. 1999 was also the year Lonati revolutionized the way socks are manufactured with the introduction

Key Dates:

1936: Morris Speizman founds the Morris Speizman Company, Inc.
1958: Lawrence Speizman joins his father's business.
1964: Robert Speizman joins the family business.
1971: The company acquires Morris Speizman (Canada) Ltd.
1972: The company is listed on the American Stock Exchange.
1974: The company acquires Beck & Frost Ltd.
1975: Speizman Knitting Machine Corp. merges into the company.
1977: Speizman sells the assets of Mid States Screw & Bolt Co.
1986: The company sells Speizman Industries (U.K.) Ltd.
1987: Morris Speizman dies.
1989: The company forms a new Montreal subsidiary, Speizman Canada, Inc.
1997: The company acquires Wink Davis Equipment Company, Inc.
1998: The company establishes Speizman Yarn Equipment Co., Inc.

of its toe closing machines. Within two months of the introduction, Speizman had 1,200 orders for the machine.

By 2001, sales of seamless garment knitting machines were growing despite the economic slowdown. Speizman believed that the seamless market would continue to grow and get more competitive in terms both of machinery and products. The company was optimistic about its future. It entered into a joint venture with Martint Equipment Company of North Carolina to distribute Braun dye/extracting machines worldwide and opened its own design center in Charlotte with an eye to improving customer service.

Principal Subsidiaries

Wink Davis Equipment Company, Inc.; Todd Motion Controls, Inc.

Principal Competitors

Barmag AG; Burlington Textile Machinery Corp.; Rieter Holding Ltd.; Tapistron International Inc.; Tinque, Brown & Co.; Hirsch International Corp.

Further Reading

Bedwell, Don, ''Turning It Around: Speizman Industries Surviving Doubleknit Disaster,'' *Charlotte Observer*, November, 11, 1979, p. 5B.

Greene, Kelly, ''Speizman Puts New Spin on Family Business,'' *Charlotte Business Journal*, April 11, 1994, p. 17.

Gross, David, ''Seamless Garments: Profitable Alternative for Knitters,'' *Textile World*, January 2001, p. 46.

The Speizman Concept, Charlotte, N.C.: Speizman Industries, 1979.

Speizman, Morris, *The Jews of Charlotte*, Charlotte, N.C.: McNally and Loftin, 1978.

Suchetka, Diane, ''Remnant of Past, Old Cotton Mill, Facing Its Fate,'' *Charlotte Observer*, April 19, 1999, p. 1A.

—Carrie Rothburd

DER SPIEGEL

SPIEGEL-Verlag Rudolf Augstein GmbH & Co. KG

Brandstwiete 19
D-20457 Hamburg
Germany
Telephone: (49) (40) 3007-2869
Fax: (49) (40) 3007-2966
Web site: http://www.spiegel.de

Private Company
Incorporated: 1947 as Spiegel-Verlag GmbH
Employees: 1,106
Sales: DM 691 million ($330 million) (2000 est.)
NAIC: 51112 Periodical Publishers; 51312 Television
  Broadcasting; 51211 Motion Picture and Video
  Production

SPIEGEL-Verlag Rudolf Augstein GmbH & Co. KG publishes *Der Spiegel*. With a circulation of over one million, Der Spiegel is one of Germany's two major weekly news magazines. More than 270 journalists in nine domestic departments and 23 offices abroad deliver content for *Der Spiegel*. Besides its flagship publication, the company puts out four other periodicals: kulturSPIEGEL, Germany's largest cultural magazine; UniSPIEGEL, a magazine targeted at university and high school students published six times a year; SPIEGELreporter, a monthly magazine featuring reports, essays and interviews; and the business monthly *manager magazin* in which publisher Gruner + Jahr AG & Co. has a 24.9 percent share. In cooperation with book publishers and record labels, SPIEGEL-Verlag publishes almanachs, chronicles, CD-ROMs, and audio CD collections. SPIEGEL-Verlag's subsidiary SPIEGEL TV produces TV news shows and documentaries which are broadcast on major German commercial TV channels. The company's Internet activities are organized under the umbrella of SPIEGELnet AG. Employees own one-half of SPIEGEL-Verlag; company founder Rudolf Augstein and Gruner + Jahr each own 25 percent.

Rudolf Augstein Becomes a Journalist
After World War II

Rudolf Augstein's interest in politics reached back to high school. While attending the liberal arts and science-oriented Kaiserin-Auguste-Victoria high school in Hannover in 1941, Augstein, the son of a man in the photography business, questioned in an essay that Germany would be able to win the then-ongoing World War II. After graduation from high school Augstein started out as an apprentice newspaper journalist at the *Hannoverscher Anzeiger*. However, the war interrupted his journalistic career before it even began. In April 1942, Augstein was called up for war service, working as a radio operator and later as an artillery spotter on the Eastern front. Wounded, Augstein became a prisoner-of-war of the U.S. Army for a short time before he returned to his destroyed hometown in the British zone. Augstein applied for an editorial position at the *Hannoversche Nachrichtenblatt*, a newspaper licensed by the British authorities. British Press Officer John Chaloner, exactly one year Augstein's elder, gave him the job after Augstein passed Chaloner's assessment test: Chaloner had requested that every applicant puzzle together a layout from newspaper clippings and write two essays, one about national and one about international politics, which he then evaluated with the help of employees whose German was better than his.

Twenty-two year old Chaloner worked for the British Information Control Unit, whose task it was to establish a brand-new system of print and radio broadcasting media in the British zone. He came up with another idea—to publish a weekly German news magazine. In spring 1946, Chaloner put together an issue of *Diese Woche*—German for "this week"—with the help of two German secretaries who were fluent in English. In the summer he and his co-workers from the Publications Production Unit, lawyer Henry Ormond and glass factory manager Harry Bohrer, who had both escaped from Nazi Germany to Britain because they were Jewish, began to look for people who could put this idea into practice. The first one they approached was Rudolf Augstein. When Augstein asked the three British officers what they meant by a news magazine, they showed him the British *News Review* and said that it was something like that. It wasn't clear at all how much he would get paid and where the magazine would be printed, but Augstein agreed.

From **Woche** to **Der Spiegel**

While Chaloner approached all the British authorities that had to approve his project and Ormond started looking for paper,

Company Perspectives:

DER SPIEGEL is Germany's leading news magazine and the largest in Europe. It is politically independent, being answerable to no one but itself and its readers, and it is not associated with any political party or business group. In the future, our key aim remains to expand and consolidate DER SPIEGEL's market leadership on the editorial, sales, and advertising levels, while at the same time establishing sophisticated, high-quality publications and products in both the new and the old media.

printing ink, rotation presses, and vehicles for distribution, Bohrer gave the prospective writers who had never before seen a news magazine a crash course in more casual writing than they were used to in their newspapers. Based on the writing style of the U.S. *TIME* magazine, Bohrer showed his inexperienced twenty-somethings how to enrich the news stories' essential facts with background information and how to present them in a more personal style. The first two test issues were printed in late October and early November 1946. However, when the British authorities tried to delay the project, Chaloner decided to start in November without their permission. Permission was given after the first issue on November 16—under the condition that the magazine would be censored before publication.

The young editorial crew was inspired by the idea to not bow down before any authority and took it's new job of "objective reporting" very seriously. They reported about extra rations of meat and sweets being distributed in Britain while the Germans were starving; about German prisoners of war who were working in French coal mines; about highly qualified German professionals being shipped to the Soviet Union; and about British companies stealing German patents. Beginning with the third issue, the magazine was censored word for word by British authorities in Berlin. When the other three Allies protested energetically against the "British paper," Chaloner handed the magazine over to Augstein, who was leading the team, along with the request to come up with a new name—literally over night. Augstein came up with *Der Spiegel* and he, together with his colleagues Roman Stempka and Gerhard R. Barsch, received a temporary publishing license from the British authorities. Harry Bohrer told Augstein that the license agreement still contained a censorship clause and encouraged Augstein to request a change. Augstein, who did not speak English, went back to the British Officer, put a pen in the officer's hand and "helped" him cross out the censorship clause. Germany's first news magazine was born. The first 15,000 copies of *Der Spiegel* published on January 4, 1947, sold out quickly. Officially priced at one German Reichsmark, they sold for up to fifteen times that much on the black market. By 1948, the *SPIEGEL* print run was up to 65,000 and reached over 121,000 in the year 1952 when the magazine moved headquarters from Hannover to Hamburg.

Reporting and Causing Scandals in the 1950s and 1960s

Right from the beginning, Augstein's *SPIEGEL* took on as a major task criticism of the postwar West German government led by Christian Democrat Konrad Adenauer. In 1948 Augstein, the publisher and editor-in-chief, started writing an acerbic political column under the pseudonym Jens Daniel. Investigative journalism became one of *Der Spiegel's* hallmarks and the magazine frequently reported about affairs and political scandals. When the magazine reported in 1950 that members of the *Bundestag*, the German parliament, had accepted bribes to vote for Bonn as West Germany's new capital, the whole republic paid attention. Consequently, the Bundestag formed the "SPIEGEL Committee" which tried in vain to shed light on the affair. In the following decade, Augstein's magazine reported about several other domestic political scandals. One of its targets was Franz Josef Strauss, Adenauer's defense minister.

SPIEGEL stories about Strauss covered his many attempts to put his own will above the law and to help some of his friends with positions or references. They also criticized his military politics which were aimed at arming the West German *Bundeswehr* with nuclear weapons. *SPIEGEL's* 41st issue of 1962, which was published on October 8, featured an article titled: "Limited Readiness for Defense." The article reported on the NATO maneuver "Fallex 62," criticized Strauss' military concept, and showed that his army was not in very good shape. The piece was not only based on information from Alfred Martin, a member of the military General Staff, but it had also been checked by Social Democrat's military expert and later-chancellor Helmut Schmidt and even by the German intelligence unit BND.

However, the German chancellor and his defense minister accused the magazine makers of systematic treason for financial gain. On Strauss' order and with the help of the Spanish police, the author of the article, *SPIEGEL* staff writer Conrad Ahlers, was arrested in Spain where he was on vacation. He flew back to Germany afterwards where he was immediately arrested by German police. On the evening of October 26, 1962, about three dozen police officers marched into the *SPIEGEL* offices, sealed them, confiscated documents, and arrested editor-in-chief Claus Jacobi, and other staff. Augstein, who had already left for the day, was warned by his chief economic editor and turned himself in to police on the following morning. Only when it was pointed out to the leading police officer that he might be responsible for a million-Deutschmark loss if the issue the magazine was trying to finish that Friday night did not appear, did he let editors, messengers and printers finish their job. The federal attorneys required upcoming issue number 44 to be inspected by them before publication to prevent another possible "crime."

Unexpectedly, the event caused a sudden wave of solidarity in Germany and was critically commented on by the media abroad. Shortly after the occupation of *SPIEGEL's* offices, other Hamburg-based print media offered their threatened colleagues office space and typewriters. Under chaotic conditions, they kept putting out their magazine. The 700,000 print run of the *SPIEGEL* number 45 sold out shortly after publication. When Chancellor Adenauer refused to accept the protest resignation of Free Democrat Justice Minister Wolfgang Stammberger, the Free Democrats demanded a thorough investigation. For three days at the beginning of November, the affair was discussed in the German parliament. The leading figures gave contradicting testimony while Strauss pretended to know

Key Dates:

1947: The first issue of SPIEGEL magazine is published.
1951: Publisher John Jahr and editor-in-chief Rudolf Augstein become co-owners of SPIEGEL-Verlag.
1962: As the result of a news story critical of the government, German police occupy SPIEGEL offices and arrest staff.
1971: Rudolf Augstein sells a 25 percent share in his enterprise to publisher Gruner + Jahr.
1974: SPIEGEL-Verlag employees become co-owners of the company.
1988: The first *SPIEGEL TV* show is broadcast on the RTL channel.
1994: The *SPIEGEL* magazine goes online.
2000: Internet subsidiary SPIEGELnet AG is established.

nothing. Only bit by bit did the true story emerge. The debate did not get to the truth, but the government was harshly criticized by the German media. As a result of the internal conflict between the people involved, the government dissolved in only a few days time.

The affair that was designed to break the *SPIEGEL* finally fell back on its creator Franz Josef Strauss. The man who had been working hard towards becoming German chancellor not only lost his defense minister post, but was forced out of national politics. At the end of November 1962, the most significant event in the magazine's history was over and *SPIEGEL* operations went back to normal. However, Rudolf Augstein was held in jail until February 1963. Finally, in May 1965, two and a half years after Augstein and his colleagues had been arrested, the law suit against him and Ahlers was called off for insufficient evidence. The last of about 150 of Augstein's Jens-Daniel-columns appeared on April 24, 1967. It was an obituary for Konrad Adenauer.

SPIEGEL Employees Become Co-Owners in 1974

SPIEGEL-Verlag's co-owners changed several times before an enduring structure was established for the company in 1974. Three years later, its co-owners Barsch and Stempka left. Hamburg-based publisher John Jahr stepped in and took over 50 percent of the company's shares. Twelve years later, Jahr sold half of its shares to Richard Gruner who owned a printing business, while Rudolf Augstein bought the other half. In 1969, when *SPIEGEL* moved to its new headquarters in Hamburg's Brandstwiete, Gruner sold his shares back to Augstein for DM 42 million and Augstein became the company's sole owner. (In the meantime, Gruner together with the Jahr brothers formed a new company, Gruner + Jahr, which later became one of Germany's major publishing houses.) In 1971, Augstein (once again) sold a 25 percent share of his business to Gruner + Jahr.

For several years, there had been discussions going on among *SPIEGEL* employees about getting more influence on the company's business. Left-wing liberals and journalists who called themselves socialists especially favored a bylaw that would guarantee certain rights in decision-making. However,

Augstein came up with an even more radical idea. Within the next two years he drafted and promoted a company structure which made *SPIEGEL* employees co-owners of the enterprise. This model not only awarded employees the right to a say in major business decisions, but also a share of the responsibility for their consequences. In 1974, Augstein handed a 50 percent share of the company over to its employees.

Every *SPIEGEL* employee who had worked for the company for at least three years could elect to become a shareholder in the Kommanditgesellschaft Beteiligungsgesellschaft für SPIEGEL-Mitarbeiter mbH & Co. which owned about half of SPIEGEL-Verlag. According to the new organization's bylaws, major decisions among owners required at least three-quarters of all votes, which meant that all three owners had to agree. Such decisions included hiring and firing editors-in-chief and directors of the company, approving annual budgets and balance sheets, changes in the magazine's principal concept and new business ventures. The rights of the employee-owners were represented by five directors elected for a three-year period who fulfilled these duties in addition to their regular jobs for no extra pay. At the end of the business year, every employee-owner received a part of the 50 percent profit share, based on their years of service and annual income. The additional profit-sharing income was mainly seen as a means of saving extra money for retirement since *SPIEGEL* didn't offer a pension plan. Despite several attempts by top managers to get rid of the employee-ownership model, the company's organizational structure endured.

New Print Products and Venturing into TV in the 1980s

As early as 1970, SPIEGEL-Verlag started getting new ventures off the ground. That year the company together with McGraw-Hill founded the new subsidiary manager magazin Verlagsgesellschaft which started publishing *manager magazin*. The new magazine provided business information to top level managers. McGraw-Hill left the partnership in 1973, but the magazine took off and in 1986 Gruner + Jahr joined the venture. By 1989 the magazine's circulation had reached almost 88,000. In a joint venture with *Harvard Business Review*, *manager magazin* contributed to the German version of the *Review*.

In 1988, SPIEGEL-Verlag published the first issue of *SPIEGEL SPEZIAL*, a magazine that provided in-depth reports on a particular subject or theme. Until 1994, SPIEGEL-Verlag published 21 issues of *SPIEGEL SPEZIAL*. From 1994 on, it was published monthly, first as *SPIEGELspecial* and since 2000 as *SPIEGELreporter*. In May 1995, SPIEGEL-Verlag started producing *SPIEGEL Kultur Extra*, a cultural supplement for *SPIEGEL* subscribers. The supplement was designed as a cultural guide to Germany, with reports and interviews; theater, music, movie, and book reviews; and an extensive calendar section. *SPIEGEL Kultur Extra* later became *kulturSPIEGEL* and boosted the number of *SPIEGEL* subscriptions. In 1998, SPIEGEL-Verlag launched another new print title—the *UniSPIEGEL*. The new magazine was published six times a year and covered subjects of interest to high school and university students. Students who subscribed the *SPIEGEL* received *UniSPIEGEL* for free.

When commercial radio and television broadcasting was introduced in West Germany in 1984, SPIEGEL-Verlag took a chance by expanding into the new market through a cooperation with Development Company for Television Programs (DCTP). DCTP offered SPIEGEL-Verlag certain time slots on major commercial TV networks RTL and SAT.1. On May 8, 1988, for the first time, SPIEGEL-Verlag's TV-show *SPIEGEL TV MAGAZIN*, a 40-minute political news magazine, was broadcast on RTL. In 1991, SPIEGEL-Verlag launched TV subsidiary SPIEGEL TV GmbH and one year later the company acquired a share in DCTP. In January 1993, SPIEGEL TV launched a number of new TV formats which were broadcast on the VOX channel. Beginning in 1994, SPIEGEL TV started producing the channel's TV news and developed the news report magazine PRESSE TV for Swiss TV network SF2. In 1996 SPIEGEL TV subsidiary a + i art und information GmbH was founded, a TV production company for programming that didn't carry the SPIEGEL label. In the following years a + i was involved in the production of two successful TV shows: *Wa(h)re Liebe,* a late-night erotic show for VOX and high profile talk show *Johannes B. Kerner Show* for public broadcaster ZDF. In 2000 a + i took over 50 percent of ASPEKT Telefilm-Produktion GmbH, a company that produced movies, reality soaps, and documentaries for TV.

Challenges in the 1990s

After 45 years of a de facto monopoly, *Der Spiegel* was suddenly confronted with a competitor. In January 1993, Munich-based publisher Hubert Burda launched his own weekly news magazine *FOCUS.* Unlike *SPIEGEL*'s lengthy articles, the new magazine featured shorter pieces with plenty of images and graphs. *FOCUS* offered attractive rates to advertisers and soon gained a considerable circulation which by 1996 had reached 800,000. Media experts estimated SPIEGEL-Verlag's 1993 losses in advertising revenues at 15 to 20 percent. Over the years, *FOCUS* gained more and more readers and, according to one media analysis, had caught up with *SPIEGEL* by 1999.

The Internet age began for the *SPIEGEL* on October 25, 1994. On that day the first electronic edition of the magazine was published online. According to SPIEGEL-Verlag, *SPIEGEL* was the world's first online news magazine, launched one day before *Time*'s online version. Subsidiary a + i art und information started working on online editions of *manager magazin* in 1996. In September 2000 SPIEGEL-Verlag founded SPIEGELnet AG as the group's Internet holding company. SPIEGELnet AG organized under its umbrella SPIEGEL ONLINE GmbH, manager magazin ONLINE GmbH, development company portal100 internet GmbH and Quality Channel GmbH, a company that marketed SPIEGELnet's web sites and other sites with high-quality content. In 2000, Rudolf Augstein was awarded the title "Journalist of the Century" by Germany's media trade journal *Medium Magazin*, based on the votes of 100 high-profile journalists.

Principal Subsidiaries

SPIEGEL TV GmbH; manager magazin Verlagsgesellschaft mbH (75.1%); DCTP Entwicklungsgesellschaft für TV-Programme mbH (12.5%); Klassik Radio GmbH & Co. KG (8.1%); a + i art and information GmbH & Co. television productions; ASPEKT Telefilm-Produktion GmbH (60%); STORY HOUSE Productions GmbH (35%); SPIEGELnet AG (86%); SPIEGEL ONLINE GmbH; manager magazin ONLINE GmbH; Quality Channel GmbH; portal100 internet GmbH.

Principal Competitors

Burda Holding GmbH. & Co. KG; Gruner + Jahr AG & Co.; Verlagsgruppe Georg von Holtzbrinck GmbH; Bertelsmann AG; Kirch Gruppe; n-tv.

Further Reading

Augstein, Rudolf, "So fingen wir an, so wurden wir angefangen," *SPIEGEL Sonderausgabe 1947–1997,* Hamburg: SPIEGEL-Verlag, January 16, 1997, p. 6.

Bölke, Peter, "Die Herren im Hause," *SPIEGEL Sonderausgabe 1947–1997,* Hamburg: SPIEGEL-Verlag, January 16, 1997, p. 214.

Geschichte der SPIEGEL-Gruppe, Hamburg: SPIEGEL-Verlag, March 29, 2001.

Hielscher, Hans, "Wollen Sie mitmachen?," *SPIEGEL Sonderausgabe 1947–1997,* Hamburg: SPIEGEL-Verlag, January 16, 1997, p. 10.

Schöps, Hans Joachim, "Ein Abgrund von Landesverrat," *SPIEGEL Sonderausgabe 1947–1997,* Hamburg: SPIEGEL-Verlag, January 16, 1997, p. 56.

—Evelyn Hauser

Standex International Corporation

6 Manor Parkway
Salem, New Hampshire 03079
U.S.A.
Telephone: (603) 893-9701
Fax: (603) 893-7324
Web site: http://www.standex.com

Public Company
Incorporated: 1955 as Standard International Corporation
Employees: 5,600
Sales: $600.2 million (2001)
Stock Exchanges: New York
Ticker Symbol: SXI
NAIC: 333294 Food Product Machinery Manufacturing;
332312 Fabricated Structural Metal Manufacturing;
333995 Fluid Power Cylinder and Actuator Manufacturing; 332919 Other Metal Valve and Pipe Fitting Manufacturing; 332999 All Other Miscellaneous Fabricated Metal Product Manufacturing; 333319 Other Commercial and Service Industry Machinery Manufacturing; 451211 Book Stores

Standex International Corporation operates as a global multi-industry conglomerate that manufactures over 48,000 products in three key areas including Food Service, Industrial Products, and Consumer Products. With over 90 plants in the United States, Western Europe, Canada, Mexico, Australia, Singapore, and Mexico, the company's diverse product line includes items such as ovens and rotisseries used in supermarkets, restaurants, delicatessens, and convenience stores; rolls and texturizing molds used for car interiors; heating and air conditioning ductwork used in homes; Master-Bilt products including cold cases used in the beverage and frozen food industry; hydraulic cylinders used for construction dump trucks; casters and wheels; and pumps used in beverage dispensing machines. Standex also sells bibles, books, music, art, clothing, and church supplies through its Berean Christian Stores outlets and publishes Christian-based material through its Standard Publishing business. The company's Standex Direct business offers unique foods including fruits, vegetables, and salsas through six different catalogs.

Postwar Origins

The origins of Standex International may be traced to shortly after World War II, when Bolta Plastics, a vinyl sheeting company, was founded by John Bolten, Sr.; his son, John, Jr.; Samuel Dennis III; and Daniel Hogan, a former Navy officer and Bolten, Sr.'s son-in-law. In less than a decade, Bolten and his partners grew Bolta from a $1 million-a-year startup to a mature $28 million concern. In 1954, General Tire and Rubber bought the company for $4 million, and within a year Bolten and partners had reinvested the money in Standard Publishing, a Cincinnati-based publisher of religious materials founded in 1866, and Roehlen Engraving, a Rochester, New York-based manufacturer of steel-engraved embossing rollers for creating decorative impressions on tiles, upholstery, and other surfaces. They renamed the business Standard International Corporation; Standard Publishing and Roehlen Engraving later became the core of Standex's Consumer group and Industrial Group, respectively.

Through early acquisitions like Everedy cookware, Lestoil, and Bon Ami cleansing product manufacturers, and Coca-Cola bottling franchises in South America, Standard initiated a strategy of growth that by the mid-1990s had totaled more than 125 acquisitions. In a 1979 interview with *Forbes* magazine, Hogan, who had early on succeeded Bolten, Sr., as company president, described the ''five laws'' that guided Standex's acquisition policy during his tenure: 1. Beware of the time of the hump—when a company inflates its earnings in anticipation of a sale. 2. The price of an acquisition varies inversely with the square of the distance from New York. 3. Companies that have made money for ten years in a row will probably make it again in the eleventh. 4. Companies with loss carryforwards have a demonstrable capacity for losing money. 5. Concentrate on small private businesses that have some sort of proprietary position in their market and which are for sale because of estate problems or lack of professional management.

Almost without exception, all the companies Standex acquired grew at a faster, more profitable rate within the conglomerate than they had on their own. By focusing only on market leaders in basic U.S. industries that were largely unaffected by rapid technological change, Standex immediately positioned itself at the forefront of a new industry segment every time it acquired a company. "If you look at our stable of companies," Hogan told the Boston Globe in 1983, "you'll find that in every case they have a definite niche and a small industry dominant position, in some cases almost a monopolistic position."

Going Public in the 1960s

In 1964, Hogan's management team took Standard International public and began defining the product groups in which it believed the company had the most expertise and around which its acquisition strategy should coalesce. From these early decisions the three basic product groups that would characterize Standex's product identities and market niches for the next three decades were established: industrial products such as pumps, electronic assemblies and switches, and "texturizing" systems for product surfaces; institutional products like restaurant china, casters and wheels, and commercial cooking and refrigeration equipment; and graphics/mail order/consumer products such as religious publications, election forms, mail order food goods, and bookbinding systems.

Early on, Standard adopted a corporate policy of balanced acquisition, ensuring a strong, even cash flow by acquiring cash-generating businesses (like Crest Fruit, purchased in April 1972) at the same time as capital-intensive companies (like Master-Bilt, added in November 1971). Exploiting high inflation rates to largely nullify the four- and five-percent interest charged on the loans it used to fuel its expansion, between January 1967 and June 1968 alone Standard acquired 11 new companies. Standard's growth strategy, however, was coupled with a policy of unceremoniously dumping companies whose profitability or competitiveness in their market niches showed signs of slipping. Through a system of tight financial controls in which all banking matters and cash requests passed through corporate headquarters, Standard focused on unusual requests for cash from it subsidiaries to weed out those potentially ripe for divestiture.

Beyond financial matters, however, Standard encouraged subsidiaries to run their businesses in an independent, entrepreneurial fashion. Indeed, in 1996 Standex's corporate headquar-

ters would consist of only 46 people, managing everything from banking, taxes, and legal affairs to insurance, audits, and investor relations.

Rapid Expansion in the 1970s

Renamed Standex International in 1973, the company continued to fill out its three basic product groups throughout the 1970s and 1980s, adding the firms that would constitute the roughly 25 businesses in its mid-1990s roster of manufacturers. Between 1969 and 1970, Standex acquired Jarvis and Jarvis (now Jarvis Caster Group, Standex's industrial caster and wheel manufacturer), United Service Equipment Co.(now USECO, a manufacturer of food service feeding systems for hospitals, prisons, and schools), and Mason Candlelight (a producer of candles and candle lamps for table top lighting). In 1971, Standex added Spincraft, a Wisconsin firm specializing in the power spinning of metals, and Master-Bilt Refrigeration, a manufacturer of commercial refrigeration equipment ranging from ice cream dipping cabinets to refrigerated warehouses. Within a year, Standex had also added General Slicing Machine Company, a manufacturer of commercial refrigeration equipment, and Crest Fruit Company, a mail-order grapefruit distributor. The company also continued to weed out unprofitable or uncompetitive units—usually at a profit. Of the 25 businesses Standex divested in its first 40-odd years, only one was sold for a loss.

Between 1971 and 1975, Standex's net sales rose from $119 million to $176 million, a 48 percent leap. Industrial products comprised one-third of all sales, followed by consumer products at 28 percent; graphics (i.e., its publishing and printing operations) at 22 percent; and institutional products at 17 percent. In the same period, Standex acquired industrial engraving plants in West Germany, France, and Australia to capitalize on its library of 100,000 industrial embossing master rolls. In 1977, Standex added further to the core of firms with the acquisition of Barbecue King of Greenville, South Carolina (a manufacturer of commercial cooking equipment) and, a year later, the Wire-O Corporation (a producer of wire book binding products), H.F. Coors (a California-based manufacturer of china and cookware), and Williams Manufacturing (a Chicago producer of chiropractic and traction tables that would become the core of Standex's Williams Healthcare Systems operation until the late 1990s).

Standex's strategy of maintaining a mix of varied manufacturers through a rolling series of acquisitions and divestitures amounted to a kind of self-investing diversified mutual fund; the conglomerate could count on the positive performance of any given segment of its product line to offset the shaky performance of any other. Indeed, when appropriate acquisition targets were unavailable or too expensive, Standex literally did invest in itself, choosing to repurchase huge blocks of its own stock rather than invest in other companies. It thus spread the risks of dramatic cyclical downturns throughout the corporation's operations and virtually assured enhanced shareholder value and steadily rising quarterly dividend payments. In fact, through 2000, Standex had increased quarterly dividends 27 times in the past 30 years.

The business press began describing Standex as a "mini-conglomerate" and "one of the best of the small conglomerates," but company management preferred the term "diversified manufacturer," claiming there had never been a "grand

Key Dates:

1955: Standard International Corporation is incorporated.
1964: The company goes public.
1971: Master-Bilt Refrigeration Manufacturing Co. is purchased.
1972: Standard International acquires Crest Fruit Co.
1973: The firm officially adopts the name Standex International.
1977: Sales exceed $200 million; Barbecue King Inc. is acquired.
1984: Management attempts to take the company private.
1985: Daniel Hogan steps down; Thomas L. King is named his replacement.
1986: Federal Industries is purchased.
1988: The firm acquires Custom Hoists Inc.
1991: Standex buys Sapemo S.A.'s multiple ring binding product line.
1995: Edward J. Trainor is named CEO.
1997: The ACME Manufacturing Company is purchased.
1998: Standex completes the sale of its Doubleday Bros. & Co. division; the company begins restructuring efforts.
2001: The company implements a new corporate growth strategy with a focus on its core businesses.

plan'' to create a multinational conglomerate. As Hogan told *Forbes* magazine in 1979, when Standex acquired new companies ''we just thought we were making good investments. Then we found out we were a conglomerate.''

In 1977, Standex's sales broke the $200 million mark for the first time, and in the following year management launched a program of intensive capital spending that by 1981 had topped $70 million. It added commercial food service equipment manufacturer Barbecue King of South Carolina (later renamed BK Industries) to its stable in 1977, acquired the company's British operation in 1979, and opened a manufacturing facility for its Industrial Products Group in Kent, England, that was soon producing more than 20 million reed switches a year for electronic applications.

As the 1970s wound down, Standex's plans for future expansion were centered on a single giant purchase in a new product area or several small acquisitions to its existing business lines. Preferring to pay cash for its new purchases, Standex arranged a four-year, $12 million loan through three banks in 1979, and the following year added James Burn Bindings Ltd., a British book binding operation, to its Graphics/Mail Order Group.

Challenges in the 1980s

A rash of mergers and acquisitions in the 1980s coupled with rising interest rates, however, put a brake on Standex's expansion plans. As Wall Street corporate raiders drove the asking prices for available companies skyward, acquisitive conglomerates, even those who, like Standex, were looking only for long-term investments in niche-leading companies, were branded guilty by association. In contrast to its 30 acquisitions during the 1970s, Standex acquired only 11 firms in the 1980s.

Partly as a result of this inactivity, by 1984 Standex's total debt-to-capital ratio had fallen from 38 percent in the mid-1970s to 20 percent, and it had accumulated $100 million of potential debt capacity for acquisitions. Sales broke the $375 million mark in 1984, and for perhaps the first time in its 30-year history Standex had no money-losing businesses. And for all its emphasis on development-through-acquisition, by 1984 more than 60 percent of Standex's historical expansion growth had come through internal growth. In May, Standex's management joined with a Boston investment firm in an attempt to acquire Standex through a $250 million friendly leveraged buyout. By putting up a percentage of the purchase price and borrowing the rest, with the company itself offered as collateral, Standex's management hoped to buy up its stock and take the corporation private, thereby avoiding the requirement to disclose financial information to the Securities and Exchange Commission and its own shareholders. Within weeks, however, Standex management had withdrawn the offer, citing new uncertainty about the economy. In 1985, Standex nevertheless began aggressively repurchasing its stock on the open market, and by 1996 a total of 17,860,000 shares had been bought back at a cost of over $200 million, reducing the number of outstanding common shares by 57 percent from 1985 levels.

After 37 years at the helm, Daniel Hogan stepped down as president in 1985, leaving the $480 million firm in the hands of Thomas L. King, a Standex veteran of 24 years and, like Hogan, an Ivy Leaguer and former Navy man. King continued to collect the companies' that would comprise Standex's corporate roster in the new millennium. Federal Industries, a Wisconsin-based manufacturer of refrigerated and nonrefrigerated display cases for the food service industry was added to the Institutional Products Group in 1986; and Custom Hoists Inc., a manufacturer of hydraulic cylinders for dump trucks and other vehicles, joined the Industrial Products Group in 1988.

The 1990s and Beyond

In 1991, Sapemo S.A.'s multiple ring binding product line was incorporated into the James Burn International bookbinding operations and, a year later, Standex acquired Toastwell, a St. Louis-based manufacturer of commercial toasters, waffle irons, griddles, and food warmers, for its Institutional Products Group. In mid-1995, Metal Products Manufacturing of Milwaukee, Oregon, was acquired to extend Standex's Snappy Air Distribution product line into the Pacific Northwest. Reflecting the diversity of the product lines Standex sought for acquisition, in 1989 Standex acquired the assets of a massage/traction table manufacturer and two years later bought the entire product line of a Christmas tree stand manufacturer (making Standex, by 1996, the world leader in that market niche).

In June 1995, Tom King retired as Standex's CEO after ten years at the helm, giving way to Edward J. Trainor, a former president of the Institutional Products Group. Standex's prospects for the remainder of the 1990s appeared quite positive. Revenues, net income, earnings per share, return on equity, return on sales, and book value per share all hit record highs in fiscal 1995. Almost half of all sales came from the three components of its Institutional Products Group—Institutional Products, Air Distribution Products, and Commercial Products—and another quarter was generated by the four operations in its Industrial Products Group—Roehlen/Europe, Roehlen/North America, Standex Precision Engineering, and Standex Electronics. In the mid-1990s, Standex added new product lines to its Master-Bilt subsidiary and increased the capacity of its cooler and pipe, duct, and fitting manufacturing operations. Its European subsidiaries, which duplicated its U.S. product lines, experienced renewed growth, and it initiated a marketing campaign in the South American market, expanded the ''quality circle'' program it launched in 1982, and continued to explore potential new acquisitions for the corporate stable. The company's essential identity, however, remained fundamentally unchanged; as former CEO Dan Hogan put it laconically in 1983, ''We manufacture widgets and we sell them and that's all we do.''

Refocusing Company Operations

The late 1990s however, were characterized by a refocus of company operations. Under the leadership of Trainor, Standex began investing in companies that would bolster what would become its new core segments. ACME Manufacturing Company was purchased in October 1997, enabling its Air Distribution group to enter new regional markets in the United States. It also purchased Fellowship Bookstores along with three mail order companies, which included various assets of the Vidalia Onion Store and Salsa Express.

In early 1998, the company's Doubleday Bros. & Co. division was sold, signaling Standex's commitment to divest underperforming, smaller business operations. It was during this time that the firm adopted a strategy of focusing on larger, growth oriented business operations related to its reorganized business segments: Industrial, Consumer, and Food Service. As such, ATR Coil Company Inc., a manufacturer catering to the industrial, automotive, and consumer markets, was purchased, complementing Standex's Industrial unit. The Industrial segment also secured a contract with the Boeing Company worth an estimated $147 million. Standex also expanded its Berean Christian Stores division, which in 1998 operated 23 stores in ten states, as part of its growth efforts in its Consumer division. The firm's new strategy appeared to pay off when sales for 1998 reached a high of $616.2 million.

During 1998, Standex sold its SXI Technologies division along with its Christmas Tree Stand product line. The company completed its restructuring efforts in 1999 with the sale of its Williams Healthcare Systems division. Sales for the year continued to grow and reached $641.4 million.

Standex entered the new millennium operating larger, more focused business units. Sales growth came to a halt however, and while earnings remained strong in the Industrial and Consumer group segments, the Food Service group experienced a decline. Weakening economies in several of Standex's key markets and an unstable stock market were cited as culprits in the decline. As a result, management again looked to a possible restructuring of operations. CEO Trainor stated in a 2001 company press release, ''Standex has reported net income for 46 consecutive years, has paid dividends for 147 consecutive quarters, and has increased its dividend rate 35 times. This record of success demonstrates that our diversity has served us very well; however, we may need to refocus our portfolio of businesses in order to fully capitalize on the changes that are occurring across all of our varied markets.''

Sales for fiscal 2001 fell by 5.8 percent over the previous year. Nevertheless, management remained optimistic about future growth. With a strong focus on new technology, gaining increased market share, operational efficiency, and making key acquisitions, Standex appeared to be on the right track to securing future revenue gains.

Principal Subsidiaries

ACME Manufacturing Co.; B.F. Perkins; BKI; Berean Christian Stores; Crest Fruit Co.; Custom Hoists, Inc.; James Burn International Inc.; Jarvis Caster Group; Standex Air Distribution Products Inc.; Standex Financial Corp.; Standard Publishing; SXI Limited (Canada); Keller-Dorian Graveurs, S.A. (France); S.I. de Mexico S.A. de C.V. (Mexico); Standex International FSC, Inc. (Virgin Islands); Standex International GmbH (Germany); Standex Holdings Limited (U.K.); Roehlen Industries Pty. Ltd. (Australia; 50%); James Burn International Ltd. (U.K.); Standex Electronics Ltd. (U.K.).

Principal Divisions

Food Service; Industrial; Consumer.

Principal Competitors

Hussmann International Inc.; Specialty Equipment Companies Inc.

Further Reading

''BKI, Barbeque King Co. Unveil Merger,'' *Nation's Restaurant News,* November 9, 1998, p. 82.

Cook, James, ''Haphazard Conglomerate,'' *Forbes,* March 19, 1979, p. 38.

Delamaide, Darrell, ''Profits Upturn Underway at Standex International,'' *Barron's,* March 1, 1976.

''Diversified Company Industry,'' *Value Line Investment Survey,* May 10, 1996, p. 1349.

Hebert, Ernest, ''Thomas L. King: Standex International,'' *Business New Hampshire,* July 8, 1987.

Hussey, Alan F., ''Big Fish, Small Ponds: Standex's Winners Range from Electronics to Chiropractor's Tables,'' *Barron's,* November 12, 1984.

''Master-Bilt Announces 60th Year Anniversary,'' *Frozen Food Digest,* December 1998, p. 27.

Pillsbury, Fred, ''Buy Homely Philosophy Has Paid Off for Standex,'' *Boston Globe,* November 29, 1983.

''Standex International Announces Corporate Growth Strategy,'' *Business Wire,* July 18, 2001.

Stein, Charles, ''Officers Bid for Standex,'' *Boston Globe,* May 4, 1984.

——, ''Standex Officers Withdraw Offer,'' *Boston Globe,* June 16, 1984.

Troxell, Thomas N., Jr., ''Acquisitions Spur Gains for Standex International,'' *Barron's,* March 6, 1978, 28 + .

——, ''New Hampshire's Larger Manufacturers Size Up the New Year,'' *New Hampshire Business Review,* December 27, 1991.

——, ''Salem-Based Firm Plies Global Market,'' *New Hampshire Business Review,* March 23, 1990.

Wallace, Glenn, ''Diversification Stands at Standex: Founder's Philosophy to Endure,'' *Manchester Union Leader,* January 20, 1992.

—Paul S. Bodine
—update: Christina M. Stansell

TABCORP Holdings Limited

5 Bowen Crescent
Melbourne, Victoria 3004
Australia
Telephone: (+61) 398682100
Fax: (+61) 398682100
Web site: http://www.tabcorp.com.au

Public Company
Incorporated: 1994
Employees: 6,000
Sales: A$1.62 billion (U.S. $976 million) (2000)
Stock Exchanges: Australian
Ticker Symbol: TABCY
NAIC: 71321 Casinos (Except Casino Hotels); 711212
   Racetracks

TABCORP Holdings Limited offers a variety of gambling products and services, such as sports and race wagering and machine gaming, primarily in the Australian state of Victoria. TABCORP provides and monitors gaming machines to nearly 300 club and hotel venues throughout Victoria, with several venues in Queensland, as well. Wagering on thoroughbred, harness, and greyhound racing is available at over 600 on-course and off-course outlets along with betting on sports such as rugby, tennis, and cricket. Sports and race betting is also available through telephone and Internet wagering. TABCORP owns and operates the Star City casino complex in Sydney, the only such facility in New South Wales.

TABCORP Replaces Government-operated Gaming and Wagering

TABCORP formed under the Gaming and Betting Act of 1994, which privatized government operated gaming and wagering in the state of Victoria. The government entity, the Totalizator Agency Board (TAB), had been in existence since 1961 when it began to conduct off-course totalizator betting on harness and thoroughbred horse racing. ''Totalizator betting,'' a pari-mutuel system, meant that all bets were pooled and redis-

tributed to winning bettors based on final odds when betting closed, less a commission for the bookmaker. In 1992, TAB received a license that allowed it to provide gaming machines to licensed venues, such as nightclubs and hotels, within the state of Victoria.

In preparation for private operation of the wagering division, TABCORP formed a joint venture with VicRacing Pty Ltd. in May 1994. Under the agreement TABCORP owned 75 percent of the joint venture, TABCORP Participant Pty Ltd., and the license for wagering in Victoria. TABCORP agreed to pay fees plus 25 percent of wagering revenues to VicRacing for conducting the thoroughbred, harness, and greyhound races. Wagering took place at 680 on-course or off-course outlets, including PubTabs and ClubTabs, found in clubs and entertainment centers. At this time wagering included fixed-odds betting on sporting events, such as Australian football, tennis, cricket, and golf, under the brand Sportsbet. Telephone betting, called National Sportsbet, allowed bets to be placed from Victoria, all over Australia, as well as from overseas; TABCORP debited and credited prepaid customer accounts according to bets placed and won. Also, at the time of privatization the TAB operated and monitored 7,413 gaming machines in 152 venues under the brand name TABERET.

TABCORP did not begin official operation until August 15, 1994, after it became a public company with a listing on the Australian Stock Exchange in July. The public offering, or ''float'' as it is commonly called in Australia, of 300 million shares sold for A$2.25 to institutional buyers to A$2.70 per share for individual investors. The Gaming and Betting Act restricted stock ownership to a maximum of five percent of voting shares for any one person and an aggregate total of 40 percent of voting shares for non-residents. The company promised a dividend of 5.4 percent, approximately A$0.145 per share. TABCORP encouraged investment from Victoria's citizens by distributing a prospectus through the major daily newspapers, including circulation to 700,000 households throughout Victoria.

With the potential for capitalization of A$810 million, the stock offering raised A$675 million in capital. TABCORP paid A$78 million to acquire the assets, liabilities, and businesses of the TAB and A$597.2 million to the State of Victoria for two gambling licenses. The gaming license allowed the company to license gaming machines and Club Keno. Only one other company in Victoria held a gaming license, Tattersall's. Each licensee was allowed to operate 50 percent of the total games permitted in the state, at 27,500, except for the Melbourne Crown Casino. The wagering license allowed TABCORP to offer totalizator betting for racing and fixed odds betting on sporting events. The two licenses will expire in 2012.

With leadership bringing a mix of experience from the private sector and from involvement with TABs in Australia, TABCORP management applied principles of private enterprise to refine gaming and wagering operations. The company sought to improve customer service and accessibility to its products, to develop new products, to control costs, and through a focus on human resources management, to attract motivated employees. During the first year of operation, TABCORP opened 83 new TABARET venues, for a total of 235 venues, 115 at hotels and 120 at nightclubs.

The company invested A$25 million to add 2,632 gaming machines, for a total of 10,045 machines. The company introduced nine new card games as well as popular slot machines, such as "Hawaii" and "Lightning Strike." The wagering division launched television coverage of harness racing on Saturday evenings to encourage telephone betting from home. TABCORP offered new forms of betting for Sportsbook and planned to introduce betting on more sporting events. The new CrossPay program allowed customers to cash winning tickets at any outlet, regardless of where a customer placed a bet. Also, TABCORP planned to upgrade its wagering computer systems for easier and more effective use by customers and managers.

During the first ten and a half months under TABCORP management, for fiscal year ended July 31, 1995, gaming operations generated A$283.2 million in revenues and wagering operations garnered A$273.8 million in revenues; TABCORP recorded total revenues of A$557 million. Gaming and wagering operations generated A$4.5 billion in betting activity, or "turnover," a 34 percent increase over the same period in 1993–94 under the TAB. Wagering revenues declined due to inclement weather for racing and low participation in Club Keno; however, gaming revenues increased 25.5 percent. TABCORP paid A$134 million in fees and revenue sharing to

the racing industry and $A247.8 million in taxes to the Victorian government. In addition to tax payments, TABCORP contributed to local communities through a variety of assistance programs. While TABCORP recorded revenues and turnover lower than predicted in the prospectus, net profit, at A$63.4 million, was 7.8 percent higher than forecast and 60.5 percent higher than the previous partial year.

An essential aspect of operation as a private enterprise involved the development of a corporate identity. In 1996, TABCORP completed development on new logos for its brand products TABARET, FootyBet, National Sportsbet, and Club Keno, as well as the main, TABCORP logo, a seven-pointed star with an arm swirled around it, as has been used in Australia as a symbol of entertainment.

TABCORP Focuses on Gambling as Part of Entertainment Experience during the Mid-1990s

TABCORP sought to improve all aspects of its gaming products as well as to create a complete entertainment and gaming experience. TABCORP upgraded the atmosphere of its wagering outlets, particularly the PubTabs, opened new ClubTabs and Sportsbet outlets, and integrated wagering into several gaming venues. New wagering outlets, strategically located to attract new customers, offered merchandise and different kinds of betting as well as displayed the results of racing and sporting events on a large screen. TABCORP expanded wagering opportunities as the number of Sunday races increased by 8 days to 24 Sundays and night racing was introduced. Television coverage of horse and greyhound racing continued to expand as well. The company launched Bet Line, a telephone betting service designed to make betting and access to telephone betting account information easier through interactive touchtone or voice response. By the Spring Racing Carnival in 1997 (autumn in the northern hemisphere) the transfer of wagering to a new computer system had begun.

The gaming division initiated the Venue Performance System to provide consistent and high standards of customer service at all gaming venues and to enhance the TABARET atmosphere. TABCORP continued to add new gaming machines and to open new venues. By summer 1997, TABCORP counted 278 venues and 13,004 gaming machines generating daily average revenue of A$150 per machine. In October 1997, TABCORP installed Advanced Gaming Systems, state-of-the-art technology for progressive jackpot networks over a wide area. The system provided management and control software as well. The new Wild Cash jackpot system added a mystery jackpot to generate excitement in the gaming venues. In addition to refurbishing several venues, the company began to systematically replace older and less popular gaming machines and to place new machines in more profitable locations. Also, in early 1998, TABCORP received a gaming license for the state of Queensland, giving the company a new area of expansion as the number of gaming machines allowed in Victoria neared its limit.

Through expansion of gaming and wagering outlets and enhancements to products and services, TABCORP recorded revenues of A$938 million for fiscal 1998. Gaming revenues increased 20.8 percent over 1997, to A$608.7 million, with 13,345 machines in operation. Average revenue per machine increased 12.7 percent to A$168.75 per day. Wagering revenues increased 5.6 percent to A$329.3 million. Both divisions experienced greater operational efficiency with a 25 percent increase in operating profit in gaming at A$146.3 million, and a 13 percent increase in operating profit in wagering, to A$37.5 million. The company recorded a net profit of A$121.3 million, a 20.4 percent increase over the previous year. TABCORP attributed its strong financial position to its growing customer base in an expanding gambling market as well its ability to compete with new gambling outlets. Dividend payments for fiscal 1998 reached A$0.38 per share, including a special A$0.11 per share dividend. Additionally, a return of capital at A$100.4 million paid ordinary shareholders A$0.33 per share. At this time, TABCORP stock was valued at $8.25 per share.

1999 Acquisition of Star City Diversifies TABCORP's Operations and Geographical Range

In 1999, TABCORP made an offer to purchase the Star City Casino in Sydney. The only casino in New South Wales, Star City opened in temporary facilities in 1995 and moved to its permanent location on Darling Harbor in 1997. The casino gaming area provided 1,500 gaming machines and 200 gaming tables, including 45 tables in private gaming room for high rollers. The casino complex contained seven restaurants; nine bars; retail shops; two theaters seating 3,000 people; a 480-room hotel and apartment building; and a conference and banquet facility. Star City held a gaming license valid for 99 years, with exclusive casino gaming in New South Wales until September 2007. With Star City revenues at A$599 million in 1998, TABCORP expected annual revenues of the combined companies to exceed A$1.5 billion. Combined net assets amounted to A$1.4 billion, making TABCORP one of the largest leisure and entertainment companies in Australia.

The initial phase of the offer began in April with an agreement to acquire 110 million ordinary shares at A$1.60 per share, a 19.9 percent interest in Star City Holdings Ltd., from Harrah's Entertainment, Inc. The agreement involved options for 37.4 million unissued ordinary shares. For A$131 million TABCORP acquired an 85 percent interest in the Star City management contract owned by Showboat Australia Pty. Ltd., a subsidiary of Harrah's. Leighton Holdings Ltd., an Australian construction firm involved in the development of Star City, held a 15 percent interest in the contract. According to the three-year contract, Showboat paid its own expenses for managing the complex and TABCORP paid fees based on revenues. Fees comprised a total of 1.5 percent of casino revenue, six percent of casino gross operating profit, 3.5 percent of non-casino revenue and ten percent of non-casino gross operating profit. Depending on which services TABCORP determined that Showboat perform, the contract was valued from A$7 million to A$10 million.

In June TABCORP followed its offer to Harrah's with an offer to Star City shareholders, one TABCORP share plus A$1.49 for eight shares in Star City Holdings. Shifting value of TABCORP's stock prompted the Board of Directors at Star City to reject the bid. TABCORP raised the bid to one share plus A$1.97, an overall increase of A$30 million to the bid, valued at A$1.7 billion. Shareholders accepted the bid and the offer closed in early October. The New South Wales Casino Control Author-

ity approved the merger. Three board directors from Star City, including Philip Satre, Chairman and CEO of Harrah's Entertainment, joined the TABCORP board. TABCORP allocated A$21 million to upgrade facilities at Star City and to develop the complex into a premier entertainment complex. The company earmarked A$2 million for bars and entertainment facilities to be upgraded in time for the Summer Olympics, held in Sydney in September 2000. The addition of 10 gaming tables introduced new baccarat and blackjack games at the casino.

TABCORP Continues Expansion of Products and Services in Late 1990s

TABCORP continued its plan to create a complete entertainment and leisure atmosphere at its wagering outlets and gaming venues. The company opened new wagering outlets, added Sportsbet to services at most of its wagering outlets, and ran Club Keno at more than 100 gaming venues. New coverage of thoroughbred, harness, and greyhound races on Pay TV and Sky Channel led to greater participation in telephone betting. TABCORP added twilight, night, and Sunday racing to attract customers during the more usual leisure times. TABCORP refurbished several gaming venues and replaced 7,400 gaming machines in 2000, introducing 26 new games. Also, in August 1999, TABCORP began to sell books management services for fixed odds wagering on Sportsbet to TABs in Queensland, Tasmania, and Western Australia; accordingly, TABCORP renamed the service TAB Sportsbet. The company completed the last stage of computer system replacement in late 1999. In September TABCORP installed a new wagering system at its retail outlets and in December completed implementation of its gaming machine monitoring system and general management information systems.

TABCORP sought to expand its product offerings with the April 2000 acquisition of Structured Data Systems (SDS), a company that designed and maintained networked wagering systems. SDS products included a games platform, Club Keno systems, and, of particular interest, Trackside. Trackside applied high-resolution graphics and digital sound to create high impact, realistic, simulated racing on a big screen. Before purchasing the company TABCORP field tested Trackside at five locations, obtaining a positive response from customers. TABCORP added Trackside to 70 wagering outlets during the following year, including Star City and Melbourne Crown Casino. TABCORP planned to introduce Trackside to other Australian gaming markets, as well as international markets.

In May 2000, TABCORP introduced sports betting on the Internet, using a betting account like that used for telephone betting. A gaming license in Tasmania allowed TABCORP to offer Internet wagering to residents there. TABCORP planned to add pari-mutuel betting online and to offer self-service wagering at kiosks installed at licensed businesses.

For fiscal 2000, TABCORP reported A$1.63 billion in revenue, including eight and a half months of revenue from Star City. Star City revenue increased 16.5 percent to A$468.3 million, with most new revenue being generated in the main gaming area. TABCORP recorded average daily per table revenue of A$5,457 and average daily machine play of A$296 at Star City. TABCORP reported wagering revenue at A$362.1

million from 588 TAB outlets, and gaming revenue of A$794.4 million from 272 TABARET outlets, with average daily revenue at A$212 per machine. Profit after tax reached A$174.8 million, with taxes to the Victorian government at A$636.8 million. The Victoria state government increased the levy on gaming in April 2001 from A$1,200 per machine to A$1,533 per machine effective for fiscal 2001.

In June, TABCORP suspended the high-roller program at Star City casino due to its instability and low profit margins. High roller programs were very competitive, with offers of rebates and incentives to attract international players from Hong Kong, Taiwan, Singapore, and other countries. These players placed bets in the thousands of dollars, but expected wins often fluctuated wildly. In one extreme example, a player won A$11 million in October 1999. By suspending the program, TABCORP saved A$6 million in annual tax as well as the volatility of such high stakes gambling.

TABCORP continued to improve its products and services. TAB Sportsbet became available at all wagering outlets. The company upgraded Bet Line telephone betting with a speech recognition system that detected subtle nuances of different human voices. TABCORP planned to open new gaming venues and new electronic gaming machines were being added to existing venues.

Principal Subsidiaries

TABCORP Assets Pty. Ltd; TABCORP Manager Pty. Ltd.; TABCORP Online Pty Ltd.; TABCORP Participant Pty Ltd.

Principal Operating Units

Gaming Division; Wagering Division; Star City.

Principal Competitors

Park Place Entertainment Corporation; Tattersall's Holdings Pty. Ltd.

Further Reading

"Australia: No More High-Rollers in Star City," *Australian*, June 29, 2000, p. 21.

"Computer Worries Dog the Vic TAB," *Australian Financial Review*, July 6, 1994, p. 26.

"Harrah's Entertainment and Australia's TABCORP Expand Strategic Alliance," *PR Newswire*, June 28, 2001.

"Harrah's Entertainment to Sell Its Interests in Australia," *PR Newswire*, April 15, 1999.

"Star City's Profit Up as High Roller's Luck Streak Ends," *Global News Wire*, October 14, 1999.

"STCOKWATCH-Tabcorp Higher on Bargain Hunting; Seen Resistant to Downturn," *AFX-Asia*, August 2, 2001.

"TABCORP Acquired SDS," *Australian Financial Review*, April 15, 2000, p. 18.

"TABCORP Bets on Tougher Full Year," *Australian*, March 5, 1996, p. 55.

"TABCORP Extends Offer Period for Star City Bid," *Global News Wire*, July 8, 1999.

"TABCORP Float Aims to Catch the News," *Australian*, July 18, 1994, p. 17.

"TABCORP in $1000m payback," *Australian*, August 21, 1998, p. 39.

"TABCORP's $10M Upgrade," *Australian Financial Review*, November 7, 1996, p. 25.

"TABCORP's Robinson Says Well-Positioned for Future Growth," *AFX-Asia*, October 12, 1999.

"TABCORP to Introduce New Games," *Australian Financial Review*, October 5, 2000, p. 14.

—Mary Tradii

Tata Iron & Steel Co. Ltd.

Bombay House, 24 Homi Mody Street
Fort, Mumbai 400 001
India
Telephone: (91) 033-2882727
Fax: (91) 033-2889881
Web site: http://www.tatasteel.com

Public Company
Incorporated: 1907
Employees: 48,821
Sales: Rs 66.4 billion ($141.41 million)(2000)
Stock Exchanges: Bombay
Ticker Symbol: TISCO
NAIC: 33111 Iron and Steel Mills; 331221 Rolled Steel
  Shape Manufacturing

Tata Iron & Steel Company Ltd. (TISCO) is the iron and steel production company associated with the Tata group of some 80 different industrial and other business enterprises in India, founded by members of the Tata family. TISCO operates as India's largest integrated steel works in the private sector with a market share of nearly 13 percent and is the second largest steel company in the entire industry. Its products and services include hot and cold rolled coils and sheets, tubes, construction bars, forging quality steel, rods, structurals, strips and bearings, steel plant and material handling equipment, ferro alloys and other minerals, software for process controls, and cargo handling services. Through its subsidiaries, TISCO also offers tinplate, wires, rolls, refractories, and project management services.

Tata's Early Beginnings in the 1800s

The story of TISCO is the story of one family or, more accurately, one man whose vision and determination to give India a modern industrial economy helped provide a platform for the country's independence half a century after his death. At the same time, he helped create what was by 1970 India's biggest nonpublic enterprise. Jamsetji Nusserwanji Tata was born into a well-to-do family of Bombay Parsees in 1839. The Parsees, a religious minority group, had carved a niche for themselves in business, in this case in the economy of Victorian India, which was dominated by British interests and was being developed as a client imperial economy. Tata's father was a successful merchant with interests in the cotton trade to Britain. Tata joined the family business after an education at Elphinstone College in Bombay and was sent to Lancashire, England, in 1864 to represent the firm there. This was to be the first of many travels in Europe, North America, and the Far and Middle East during which he formulated his ideas on the best strategy to realize his own ambitions for success in business and to contribute to the economic development of India.

Tata's own background was in cotton production. He believed that mills could function successfully in India in close proximity to the cotton-producing areas in the west of the country, thereby putting them in a strong position to undercut their Lancashire competitors. He obtained air conditioning equipment from suppliers in the United States and the latest cotton spinning machinery installed to provide the optimum climatic conditions for spinning. His early ventures showed promise and in 1874 he founded his first company, the Central India Spinning, Weaving and Manufacturing Company. Three years later, on the same day that Queen Victoria was declared empress of India, he opened the Empress mill in Nagpur.

As Tata was taking his first steps toward establishing a viable cotton spinning business, Indian nationalism also was beginning to find a focus for its aspirations through the Indian National Congress. Tata was present at its inaugural meeting and his devotion to the cause of an independent India was undoubtedly a motivating factor in his own drive for success in business. Cotton was only a start. From his travels in other industrialized nations he had come to identify three essential elements for a modern industrial economy: steel production, hydroelectric power, and technical education. Although he did not live to see any of his schemes in these areas come to fruition, he laid the foundations on which his sons, and then later generations of his family, were able to build to realize his ambitions.

Company Perspectives:

Consistent with the vision and values of founder Jamsetji Tata, Tata Steel strives to strengthen India's industrial base through the effective utilization of staff and materials. The means envisaged to achieve this are high technology and productivity, consistent with modern management practices. Tata Steel recognizes that while honesty and integrity are the essential ingredients of a strong and stable enterprise, profitability provides the main spark for economic activity.

Development of Tata Iron & Steel Company: Late 1800s–1980s

From the mid-1880s, Tata commissioned a series of surveys in India's coal-producing areas, such as Bihar and Orissa in the northeast of the subcontinent, to locate iron ore within easy reach of coal deposits and water, both essential elements in steel production. He visited the United States to seek the advice of the world's foremost metallurgical consultant, Julian Kennedy, and went to Birmingham, Alabama, to study the coking process in action. In England in 1900, he discussed his plans with the secretary of state for India, Lord George Hamilton. In India, the way had been opened for private enterprise with the introduction of a more liberalized mineral concession policy in 1899. With Julian Kennedy's help, American specialists were brought in and began surveying in 1903. After a series of disappointments, rich iron ore deposits were identified in the dense jungle in Bihar at the confluence of two rivers near Sakchi three years after Jamsetji Tata's death in 1904. Also involved in the surveying was Tata's nephew, Shapurji Saklatvala, whose health suffered so much that he was sent to London to recuperate. There, he joined his uncle's London office, which had been established some years earlier to represent the interests of the family cotton business. His energies were soon channeled away from business matters and into politics, and he became Communist member of Parliament for Battersea North in 1922.

Four years after Tata's death, his sons Dorabji and Ratanji began development of the Bihar site. A factory and township were carved from the jungle and named Jamshedpur. A conscious decision was made to retain control within India of the new enterprise, the Tata Iron and Steel Company, by seeking out Indian investors. In the face of warnings that India could not afford a flotation of this size, the Tata brothers set out to raise Rs 23.2 million in shares. Within eight weeks some 8,000 Indian investors came forward and the whole share issue was taken up. The Tatas retained 11 percent of the stock for themselves. There were enormous initial problems in clearing the Sakchi site and, once production began, in ensuring that the coal was of a uniform quality. By 1916, however, production was meeting expectations and during World War I the company exported 1,500 miles of steel rails to Mesopotamia. Rapid expansion to support the Allied war effort was followed by Depression during the 1920s with escalating prices, transport and labor difficulties, and a major earthquake in Japan, by now TISCO's biggest customer. The company had to suspend its dividend for 12 out of 13 years in this period and was on the brink of closing in 1924 when Sir Dorabji Tata had to pledge his personal

fortune to secure the necessary bank loans to keep the business afloat. TISCO emerged from the 1930s, however, as the biggest steel plant in the British Empire. World War II brought a resurgence in demand for Tata products and the company specialized in the manufacture of armored cars, known as *Tatanagars,* which were used extensively by the British Army in the North African desert.

Following six years of almost continuous production to serve the war effort, it became imperative in the late 1940s to begin replacement of the plant. In association with Kaiser Engineering of the United States capacity was expanded and a Modernization and Expansion Program (MEP) was launched in 1951, upgraded four years later to the Two Million Ton Project (TMP) to give TISCO the capacity to produce two million tons of crude steel. This was achieved in 1958 but further expansion was put on hold during the 1960s while the country passed through a period of devaluation and recession. By 1970, however, TISCO employed 40,000 people at Jamshedpur, with a further 20,000 in the neighboring coal mines.

Government attempts to nationalize TISCO in 1971 and 1979 were defeated, in part, it was believed, to retain an efficient private sector yardstick against which the performance of public sector companies could be judged. An ever-increasing range of government legislation to bring private sector businesses into line with national economic planning on the Soviet model, however, hampered Tata's freedom to develop in the postwar period. In 1978, the government restricted TISCO's dividend to 12 percent to force it, as India's only private sector steel producer, to plough money into modernization. Expansion was restricted by a government committed to helping nationalized industry. Further difficulties were created in the late 1970s by chronic shortages of coal, power, and rail transport. An estimated Rs 45 crores of salable steel was lost during 1979–80 because of these shortages. TISCO soldiered on, however, and in the following decade began to benefit from a relaxation of government control as a more pragmatic attitude to the importance of private sector industry emerged. In 1989, the Tata group increased its stake in the steel firm to ward off any attempts by outside shareholders to gain control of the company. By 1990, TISCO remained India's largest nonpublic company, announcing a 30 percent increase in profits against a backdrop of general depression in the Indian economy as a whole.

Growth of the Tata Empire Over the Course of the 20th Century

The growth of Jamshedpur and the involvement of the firm in every aspect of its industrial and municipal life was the subject of several studies. Jamsetji Tata was both a nationalist and a philanthropist. He showed a paternalistic concern for the well-being of his employees, which set the tone for future company policy. The British proponents, pioneers of social reform Sydney and Beatrice Webb, were invited out to India from England to advise the Tatas on the best form of social, medical, and cooperative services for the newly established Jamshedpur and as a consequence schools, recreational facilities, creches, and other amenities were established on site at an early stage. An eight-hour working day had been introduced in 1912, an officially recognized Tata Workers' Union established with Gandhi's associate, C.F. Andrews, as its first president,

Key Dates:

1907: Tata Steel is established by Jamsetji Tata.
1924: On the brink of disaster, Sir Dorabji Tata pledges his personal fortune to secure bank loans to keep the company afloat.
1939: By now, TISCO operates as the largest steel plant in the British Empire.
1951: A Modernization and Expansion Program (MEP) is launched.
1955: The MEP is upgraded to the Two Million Ton Project (TMP).
1970: TISCO employs 40,000 people at Jamshedpur and 20,000 workers in neighboring coal mines.
1978: The Indian government forces TISCO into modernization efforts.
1989: The Tata Group doubles its stake in TISCO to thwart takeover attempts.
1990: TISCO begins expanding and establishes subsidiary Tata Inc. in New York.
1996: The company begins a joint venture with Inland International to build a steelworks facility in India.
1998: TISCO records a 61 percent decline in net income due to a downturn in the steel industry.
2000: TISCO completes a ten-year, $1.5 billion modernization program.

and profit-sharing schemes were brought in in 1934. Against this, it was argued that the Workers' Union operated in fact as a management tool to impose its will on a workforce so heterogeneous by nature that rival unions made little headway. Despite the reputation of the Tata family for concern over workers' rights, there was much unrest among the workforce during the 1920s over wages and conditions and it has been claimed that this, as much as anything, contributed to advances. The commitment of the Indian Trades Union Congress after independence to the same goals as central government—economic self-sufficiency and prosperity—allowed the Tatas a relatively free hand in dictating their own industrial relations policy. Whatever the arguments, TISCO could claim in 1989 that it had not lost a day's work through industrial action in 50 years, and its management illustrated its commitment to the welfare of its employees by commissioning an audit of its ''social performance'' by a team of eminent public figures.

TISCO's success spawned numerous offshoots making use of Tata products, some of them part of the Tata Group. These included the Tata Engineering and Locomotive Company (TELCO). This ripple encouraged other areas of Indian industry to become suppliers of spare parts for new products and by 1970 TELCO had more than 500 Indian ancillary suppliers.

The second element in Jamsetji Tata's plan for India's modernization was the development of a hydroelectric capability. Within reach of Bombay's thriving, basically steam-driven cotton spinning industry lay the monsoon-swollen rivers of the western Ghats. If Bombay's captains of industry could be persuaded to invest in the necessary conversion from steam to electricity, the natural resources existed to provide this new source of power. To encourage the process, the Tatas bought up sufficient mills to create the necessary demand before launching Tata Hydro-Electric Power Supply Company in 1910. By 1915, the required dams and reservoirs, ducts, and pipelines had been laid to feed the new turbines. Two further power stations followed in 1916 and 1919. Between the wars the family had to sell some 50 percent of its stake in the hydroelectric company to a U.S. syndicate to support other less successful firms within the group. By the 1960s, power stations had been supplemented by four thermal installations, which together satisfied Bombay's entire domestic and industrial requirement.

TISCO, TELCO, and Tata Hydro-Electric Power Company were only three parts of the Tata empire that by the late 1970s included 30 separate companies. Together the group accounted for 1.8 percent of India's GNP, with TISCO alone providing 0.4 percent, far more than any single equivalent firm in the United States or United Kingdom. In 1970, the managing agency system that had characterized much of Indian industry since the British period was abolished. Under this system, British investments in the subcontinent were managed by firms of agents who charged commission for their services. Tata Industries Ltd. acted in this capacity for many of the firms in the Tata Group, and until 1970, central control was not difficult. After this date, shares in the 30 or so Tata enterprises were retained by Tata Industries, whose chairman from 1938 was Jehangir Ratanji Dadabhoy Tata, a distant relative of the founder of the Tata industrial dynasty. He was succeeded in 1981 by Ratan Naval Tata, whose father had been adopted by Ratanji Tata's widow in 1917. Following the Monopolies and Restrictive Practices legislation of 1969, which represented the views of a government hostile to large private enterprises, the Tata group was self-conscious within India about the size of its operation and great emphasis was placed on publicizing the independent nature of each of its firms. It was pointed out that 75 percent of the firms' shares was owned by trusts established by the Tata family to promote research and welfare projects. In reality, the Tatas had been adept in holding together their empire with a steady growth in the group's assets, much informal consultation between firms, a recurrence of names in the lists of directors, and a shared head office in Bombay.

The continued prosperity of the group during the difficult postwar years for private sector firms was probably also helped by its refusal to take up an overtly political stance in opposition to prevailing government policy. The only exception was in 1956, when it backed the short-lived Forum of Free Enterprise against a government committed to assigning a dominant role to public sector industry. Government monopoly legislation also restricted diversification into high-profit areas such as fertilizers or pharmaceuticals, an obvious move for a group such as Tata whose traditional staple was high-cost, low-profit industry. There were no restrictions on overseas investment or new technology, however, and inroads into both these areas were made. India needed firms such as TISCO or TELCO if the country was to maintain a viable industrial capability. Therefore, even when government controls officially restricted growth, the Tata Electric Company was given the green light during the 1970s to build privately a new 500-megawatt plant, and sanction was given to TELCO to increase its output from 24,000 to 36,000 vehicles per year.

TISCO developed as one of the independent but interrelated companies within the Tata group. Among the better known of these firms is the Indian Hotels Company, whose centerpiece, the Taj Mahal Hotel, in Bombay, was conceived by Jamsetji Tata and opened in 1913, as the first hotel in the country using electricity. Tata Chemicals was launched in 1939, and its Mithpur plant produced mineral extracts required for glass, ceramic, and leather production. The plant had a checkered history in its early years owing to delays in perfecting the soda ash process. With the support of the Tata group and the usual Tata resourcefulness in times of crisis, however, the company stayed in business. For example, when a drought in 1962 threatened to close the plant, management prevailed upon the local population to ration the domestic consumption of water. This "lakeless week" was a great success and ensured that sufficient supplies of water remained for the company to continue in production. Another venture in 1962 involved joining with James Finlay and Company of Scotland to form the Tata-Finlay Company, which bought Finlay's 53 tea estates and has become the biggest tea producer in the world.

In the field of electronics, Tata joined the Burroughs Corporation of Detroit in 1977 to market the U.S. firm's computer systems and to begin to develop the manufacture of mainframe computers in India. With such an array of experience and expertise, the group entered the consultancy market with the establishment of the Tata Consulting Engineering and Tata Economic Consulting Services. One Tata initiative that slipped through the net was air travel. An air service was inaugurated to carry the mail between Bombay, Karachi, and Madras in the 1930s. In 1946, however, Tata Airlines went public as Air India Ltd, and the company was nationalized in 1953 to form Air India and Indian Airways.

The third requirement of Jamsetji Tata for a successful and independent India was a system of technical education. His scheme to launch a Science University in India in 1898 was opposed by the viceroy Lord Curzon as overambitious and inappropriate for Indian needs. Tata persevered, however, and offered to underwrite the project with an endowment derived from his Bombay properties. He did not live to see the scheme realized. After Curzon's departure, the government of India showed itself more amenable to the proposal, and in 1911, Bangalore was chosen as the site for an Indian Institute of Science with joint funding from the Tata family, central, and provincial governments. The institute produced a number of eminent scientists and became a focus for much pioneering research. Tata funds have gone into other projects such as the Bhabha Atomic Research Center in Bombay, which has developed techniques for more efficient power generation. One of Jamshedji's greatest legacies was a concern for creating better educational opportunities for his countrymen. By the 1920s, one in five of Indian recruits to the Indian civil service had benefited from Tata scholarships.

This commitment to education, welfare, and other humanitarian projects continues today and is part of the Tata distinctiveness. TISCO, for example, took part in a Green Millennium Countdown program and planted 1.5 million trees. In 2001, it also supported the Lifeline Express program that provided healthcare to those living in remote areas. TISCO is also known for providing relief during natural disasters and was awarded the Outstanding Corporate Citizen Award from the *Economic Times*.

The Tata family was often accused of paternalism toward its workers, of an often ill-judged concern for the continued existence of every member of the corporate group irrespective of profitability, and of an over-concentration on traditional high-cost but low-profit industries. TISCO, however, cut its workforce from 78,669 employees in 1993 to 48,821 in March 2001. The management culture of the group as a whole was changing in the new millennium. Tata directors were focused on profitable operations as well as securing leading industry positions for each Tata company.

Since the abolition of the managing agency system in 1970, TISCO and the various Tata companies operated entirely independently, but they retained many personal, family, and business ties. TISCO and most of the larger firms in the "family" shared the same head office in Bombay. The Tata sense of identity survived a postwar period of almost continuous economic and political adversity. At the start of the new millennium, the Tata group included 80 companies involved in various industries including engineering, chemicals, energy, materials, consumer products, IT and communications, and services.

TISCO Operations During the 1990s

During the 1990s, TISCO was faced with trying economic times as it forged ahead with modernization and expansion. During the decade, the steel firm began its fourth stage of upgrades and improvements. As part of the modernization, TISCO planned to increase its annual steelmaking capacity in Jamshedpur to 3.2 million metric tons by 1999, up from 2.7 million tons in 1996.

The steelmaker also broadened its geographic reach. In 1990, a U.S. subsidiary, Tata Inc., was established and the following year, the firm opened offices in Singapore and Dubai. It was during 1991 that restrictions on licensing, price, and distribution were lifted in India, allowing TISCO to expand its capacity. India also began allowing foreign manufacturers involved in such steel-dependent industries as electronics and automobiles to operate in the country. As demand increased, TISCO set plans in motion in 1995 to construct India's largest blast-furnace mill with an eventual annual capacity of ten million metric tons. By 1996, steel consumption in India had grown by ten percent in each of the last four years. That year, TISCO expanded further and teamed up with Inland International Inc. to create Tata-Ryerson, a joint venture that would provide industrial materials management services in India.

During the mid-to-late 1990s, however, India's steel industry and economic climate weakened. Many construction projects in the region were put on hold. As steel demand and prices fell, TISCO's profits plummeted. In 1998, the company reported a 61 percent fall in net income. As such, TISCO began aggressive cost-cutting measures and drastically cut its workforce. While most companies involved in the steel industry reported losses, TISCO was able to keep its bottom line in the black.

Despite the trying economic conditions, TISCO was able to complete its $1.5 billion modernization program in April 2000. It began operation of a 1.2 million metric ton cold rolling mill and also became one of the lowest-cost producers of hot-rolled coils.

During fiscal 2000, TISCO reported earnings of $90.1 million, an increase over $60.2 million earned in the previous year.

In 2001, after 30 years of service, Jamshed Irani, TISCO's managing director, retired, leaving B.D. Muthuraman at the helm. Under a new director, TISCO pledged to continue cutting costs and focus on new growth areas such as making investments in the telecom industries. Although conditions in the steel industry remained uncertain and the economic climate in India remained unstable, TISCO appeared to be well positioned to handle the problematic environment.

Principal Subsidiaries

Tata Refractories Ltd (51%); The Tata Pigments Ltd.; Kalimati Investment Company Ltd.; Tata Korf Engineering Services Ltd. (60.1%); Tata Incorporated; Stewarts & Lloyds of India Ltd.; Tata Technodyne Ltd.

Principal Competitors

Essar Steel Ltd.; Jindal Iron & Steel Co. Ltd.

Further Reading

Bagchi, Pradipta, and Baiju Kalesh, ''TISCO to Invest in Telecom,'' *Times of India,* June 1, 2001.

Datta, Satya Brata, *Capital Accumulation and Workers' Struggle in Indian Industrialisation: The Case of the Tata Iron and Steel Company 1910–1970,* Stockholm: Almquist & Wiksell International, 1986.

Harris, F.R., *Jamsetji Nusserwarji Tata: A Chronicle of His Life,* Bombay: Blackie & Sons, 1958.

Lala, R.M., *The Creation of Wealth. The Tata Story,* Bombay: IBH Publishing Co, 1981.

Mamkoottam, Kuriakose, *Trade Unionism: Myth and Reality. Unionism in the Tata Iron and Steel Company,* Delhi: Oxford University Press, 1982.

Mehta, Harish, ''Tata Iron Plans to Buy Steel Plant in Eastern Europe,'' *Business Times Singapore,* May 15, 1992.

Menon, Aubrey, *Sixty Years: The Story of the Tatas,* Dehra Dun: Tata Industries Ltd., 1948.

Merchant, Khozem, ''Irani Hands On a Rejuvenated TISCO,'' *Financial Times London,* June 4, 2001, p. 17.

Murthy, R.C., ''Record Results for Tata Iron and Steel,'' *Financial Times London,* August 10, 1982, p. 15.

——, ''Tata to Double its Stake in TISCO,'' *Financial Times London,* March 1, 1989, p. 32.

Narayn, N., ''Tata Steel Completes $1.5 Billion Modernization,'' *New Steel,* December 2000, p. 11.

——, ''TISCO Plans Integrated Works, Forms Joint Venture with Inland,'' *New Steel,* September 1996, p. 4.

Raghuvanshi, Vivek, ''TISCO's Earnings Fall 61 Percent,'' *American Metal Market,* August 5, 1998, p. 3.

Rao, N. Vasuki, ''TISCO Looks to Stay Step Ahead of Pack,'' *American Metal Market,* September 18, 1996, p. 15.

Suzuki, Shinichi, ''Tata Iron and Steel to Build India's Biggest Blast Furnace,'' *Nikkei Weekly,* August 14, 1995, p. 21.

—J.G. Parker
—update: Christina M. Stansell

Taylor & Francis Group plc

11 New Fetter Lane
London EC4P 4EE
United Kingdom
Telephone: (+44) 171-583-9855
Fax: (+44) 171-842-2298
Web site: http://www.tandf.co.uk

Public Company
Incorporated: 1804 as R. Taylor & Co.
Employees: 676
Sales: £116.35 million ($173.7 million)(2000)
Stock Exchanges: London
Ticker Symbol: TFG
NAIC: 511120 Periodical publishers; 511130 Book
　　Publishers

The Taylor & Francis Group plc is a fast-growing and leading publisher of scholarly journals, textbooks, and books. Based in London, England, the company operates under several imprints. Taylor & Francis itself has been publishing journals since 1798, when it began printing *Philosophical Magazine*, a title still in print at the beginning of the 21st century, now specialized in the field of physics. The company publishes nearly 200 peer-reviewed journals, ranging from ergonomics to information systems, healthcare, and medicine. Since the 1980s, Taylor & Francis has posted strong growth especially from an aggressive acquisition program—the company has referred to itself as a 'predator'—with major acquisitions including the 1998 purchase of social sciences book publishing group Routledge and the acquisition of Gordon and Breach in February 2001. Other divisions and imprints include Martin Dunitz, a medical books and journals specialist; Spon Press, which focuses on architecture, engineering, and related subjects; Garland Publishing, based in New York, which produces *Molecular Biology of the Cell*, a title that has sold more than 750,000 copies and is now entering its fourth edition; Europe Publications, specialized in directories for the library market, such as the *International Who's Who*; and Carfax, a publisher of more than 250 social science- and humanities-related journals. In all, the Taylor & Francis group publishes more than 800 journals and has a backlist of more than 20,000 book titles. Taylor & Francis is also building a strong Internet-based business, offering online versions of nearly all of its titles. In 2000, the company signed on New York's Versaware Inc. to digitize its entire backlist book catalog. The company has been quoted on the London Stock Exchange since 1998. CEO Anthony Selvey has overseen much of the company's rapid growth in the 1990s: the company's turnover has risen from just £28 million in 1996 to nearly £116.5 million in 2001.

Printing Science in the 19th Century

Richard Taylor, a member of a prominent Norwich family, began his career as an apprentice printer to Jonas Davis in 1797. By 1798, he had taken on an active role in Davis' print shop, which by then had been printing a number of journal titles, including *Transactions*, presenting notes of the Linnean Society. In 1798, Davis took on a new printing order, that of the *Philosophical Magazine*, launched by Alexander Tilloch, which quickly became one of the most prestigious scientific journals in the United Kingdom. *Philosophical Magazine* helped establish the company as somewhat of a specialist in scientific printing and publishing.

Davis's failing eyesight led him to retire to life as a gentleman farmer in 1800. Taylor, then just 20 years old, was not scheduled to complete his apprenticeship until 1804; nonetheless, Davis decided to turn over his business to Taylor. In order to do this, Davis sold his business to Taylor's father, who purchased the print shop in conjunction with another printer Richard Wilks. Richard Taylor therefore became his father's apprentice. Yet, while the elder Taylor was to remain a prime source of funding for the business for many years, Richard Taylor, together with Richard Wilks, took over full responsibility for the shop's operations.

Taylor and Wilks rapidly proved uncomfortable partners. Tensions reached a peak in 1804, when the partners agreed to split the business and dissolve the partnership. Taylor, who in that year became a master printer, continued the business under the name R. Taylor & Co. The company, which shortly thereafter moved to London, kept many of the shop's best customers, notably *Philosophical Magazine.* Taylor himself eventually became co-editor of the journal, then took over Tilloch's role entirely. That journal helped attract a number of other leading scientific works to Taylor's shop, such as the *Introduction to Botany,* published in 1807, William Paley's *Natural Theology* in 1802, and the *Flora Graeca,* compiled by the late John Sibthorp, the first volume of which was published in 1806 and the final volume of which was not published until 1840. Despite the long publishing process, this last work helped establish Taylor's reputation as a leading scientific publisher of the day.

Taylor was joined by other family members in the first half of the 19th century, although none of these partnerships proved fruitful. A more lasting partnership came with the chemist William Francis—who was, in fact, Taylor's illegitimate son. Francis had begun working for his father while a student in Chemistry in Berlin in the 1830s, providing translations of the German science being published at that time. This translation activity led Taylor to launch a side-journal to *Philosophical Magazine,* the series of *Scientific Memoirs,* a seven-volume set of leading papers from France, Germany, Italy, and Scandinavia containing many of the most important discoveries being made at the time in the fields of physics, chemistry, and biology. Begun in 1837, *Scientific Memoirs* proved a money-loser for Taylor, yet helped further enhance his company's reputation. Another prestigious journal was added that same year, when Taylor purchased co-ownership of the *Magazine of Zoology and Botany,* founded by William Jardine, in 1837. After adding another journal, *Magazine of Natural History and Journal of Zoology, Botany, Mineralogy, Geology and Meteorology,* Taylor merged the two journals, creating the prestigious *Annals and Magazine of Natural History,* which remained a leading British biology journal into the 20th century (and was renamed as *Journal of Natural History* in 1967).

William Francis formally joined his father in partnership in 1851, at which time the company's name was changed to Taylor and Francis. Taylor himself resigned the following year, leaving Francis to run the partnership. (Taylor died in 1858.) Yet Francis had long been an active participant in the company's editorial activities, responsible for the launch of such publications as the *Chemical Gazette,* which began publishing in 1840. While not a practicing researcher himself, Francis' background helped him establish strong contacts throughout the British—and European—scientific community, leading to such new printing and publishing contracts as the journals of the Physical Society, formed in 1872; the publication of the *Journal of the Photographic Society,* which was launched in 1859; *Observatory,* which began publication in 1877; and many others. The company's many journal printing contracts led the company to branch out into book printing as well.

Yet journals and printing contracts remained the company's primary activities. By the time of William Francis' death in 1904, Taylor & Francis had become the leading scientific journal printer in the United Kingdom, with the most extensive collection of printing contracts for the nation's most prestigious scientific journals. By then, too, the company had supplemented its journal printing activity—which were not always highly profitable—with printing contracts with many of London's financial firms.

20th Century Publishing Company

Francis was succeeded by sons William Francis Jr. and Richard Taunton Francis. Although initially the more active in the company's operations, particularly as editor of *Philosophical Magazine,* the younger William Francis's poor health led him to retire from day-to-day leadership in the early part of the century. The company, which began to add printing contracts with many of Britain's universities, remained a profitable if somewhat stagnant business.

The demands of the years during and just after World War I—including paper shortages; a drop in research papers, particularly from the important German scientific community; and steadily increasing wages from a workforce in short supply—caused the company to react. In 1917, William Francis sold out his share in the business to younger brother Richard Taunton Francis. The younger Francis had been an apprentice to his older brother and was more familiar with the company's day to day operations. He was also a more aggressive businessman, and, in 1917 arranged the purchase of a larger printing firm, Charles Jones & Co., as well as a number of smaller investments.

Yet the company soon found itself in severe financial difficulties—by 1923, the company was posting losses. Part of the company's troubles, in addition to the prevailing economic climate, was the somewhat faded condition of its flagship publication *Philosophical Magazine,* which was also responsible for a large part of the company's revenues. The journal's editorial board were almost all in their seventies, and therefore less energetic in attracting leading research papers of the day. At the same time, the Royal Society had moved to raise the standards for research papers, which further reduced the available pool of papers. Richard Taunton Francis himself succumbed to the company's financial difficulties, dying in 1931.

Taylor & Francis now entered a brief period under a trusteeship, before converting from a partnership to a private limited company in 1936. Part of the impetus to this change came with the introduction of modern monotype machines—which, being far heavier than the company's old hand presses, required an extensive renovation of the company's offices. Taking charge of the newly incorporated company's operations was Courtney Coffey, who had worked his way up from a position as office boy, the first person to lead the company with no direct experience in printing. Coffey nonetheless showed his skills as a salesman and turned his attention to modernizing much of the company's business practices, which had remained somewhat unchanged since the previous century.

Philosophical Magazine again provided the motor for the company's rescue. The appointment of new editors, and espe-

---

Key Dates:

1797: Richard Taylor becomes printer's apprentice to Jonah Davis in Norfolk, England.
1798: Printing of *Philosophical Magazine* begins.
1804: Taylor takes over printing business, renames it R. Taylor & Co.
1851: Taylor forms Taylor & Francis partnership with son William Francis.
1917: The company acquires Charles Jones & Co printing firm.
1936: Taylor & Francis incorporates as limited liability company.
1948: The company buys printing firm in Peckham, near southeast London, in order to boost printing capacity.
1965: The company launches Wykeham Publications and branches out into book publishing.
1973: The company acquires printing companies Verstage, based in Basingstoke, and Lancashire Typesetting Co., in Bolton, which adds monotype capacity.
1982: The company establishes U.S. subsidiary.
1988: The company acquires Hemisphere Publishing, formerly part of Harper & Row, in U.S., and company is renamed Taylor & Francis Group.
1990: The company sells off its printing operations.
1998: The company goes public and doubles in size with Routledge Group acquisition.
2001: The company acquires Gordon & Breach, raising total number of journals to 800.

---

cially the well-respected researcher Allan Ferguson, in 1939, proved fundamental in the restoring the journal's reputation. Ferguson himself became one of the company's earliest investors and a director of the company. Another important investor was Harry Banister, Ferguson's brother-in-law. The two families were to retain their holdings—nearly 34 percent combined—until the company's public offering in 1998. This move marked a significant moment for the company—where before Taylor & Francis had been run by its family owners, the company's operations were now being overseen by members of the scientific and academic communities.

Yet the outbreak of World War II nearly caused the company to collapse; at one point, Ferguson had to come to its rescue with a personal loan. The bombing of London also threatened the company physically—a massive air raid in 1941 had wiped out most of the city's traditional printing district. But Taylor & Francis' premises, although damaged, were spared, and the firm remained one of the few printers capable of carrying on operations.

Postwar Expansion

Paper and labor shortages, difficulties in obtaining replacement parts for the company's aging machine park kept the company on shaky financial footing in the years just after World War II. The company was faced with the loss of some of its most important customers—in 1950, the Linnean Society, in

fact, switched to new printers after nearly 150 years with Taylor & Francis). The company's largest single customer at that time was the rapidly expanding Physical Society, which, by 1947, was threatening to look elsewhere for its printing needs as well. Taylor & Francis responded to this threat by making its first acquisition since the 1920s, a printing house in Peckham, near southeast London.

Philosophical Magazine had come through the war in order to face new competition from the fast-growing American journal *Physical Review*, which presented Taylor & Francis with a serious rival for English-language papers. The company responded by appointing a new editor, Nevill Mott, who went on to win a Nobel Prize in 1977. Mott restored the company's flagship journal to its former standards of editorial excellence and remained its editor-in-chief until 1970, at which time he was appointed chairman of the company itself. By the 1950s, the magazine, which now focused entirely on the booming physics field, regained its profitability.

The same could not be said for the company's other journals, some of which continued to lose money for the company. Yet the huge expansion in scientific research that began after the war ultimately benefitted the company, as it became involved in a number of new journals, such as *Atomic Scientists News*, and *Advances in Physics*, which presented a forum for very long papers in the United Kingdom.

In the 1950s and 1960s, Taylor & Francis added increasing numbers of new journals, some of which were launched directly by the company itself, such as *Molecular Physics*, in 1958, and *Instrument Abstacts*, in 1960. Other journals, such as the optics journal Optica Acta, were acquired from other publishers. The new journals revealed the company's growing scientific interests, particularly in new and newly emerging fields, such as ergonomics, for which the company launched the journal *Ergonomics* in 1957. Other titles were added by separating formerly closely linked fields—such was the case with the company's *Journal of Electronics and Control*, which was split into two journals devoted to each of the rapidly growing areas.

By the end of the 1960s, the company was producing more than 40 journals. During that decade the company moved also into book publishing, concentrating primarily on works dealing with the physical sciences. For this, the company added a separate subsidiary, Wykeham Publications, which then branched out into the lucrative textbook publishing sector.

The company moved to new quarters in 1970; soon after, it was forced to sell its Peckham plant to the local government. In order to meet its growing printing needs, the company acquired two firms in 1973: Verstage, based in Basingstoke, which had a strong park of linotype presses, and Lancashire Typesetting Co., in Bolton, which added monotype capacity.

During the 1970s, the company became more international, and especially European, as researchers from the European Community countries began to work more closely together. The company bid for and won its first international contract in 1975, when it won the publishing and printing contract for the *SIPRI Yearbook* of the Stockholm International Peace Research Institute. In the mid-1970s, also, the company branched out into education, launching and acquiring a number of journals, such as the *European Journal of Science Education*, in 1976.

Scientific Specialist in the 21st Century

The rising importance of publishing—both journals and books—in the company's revenues caused it to begin cutting back on its printing operations. The company remained one of the few publisher-printers in the United Kingdom until 1990, when it exited printing altogether. By then, Taylor & Francis had achieved rapid growth, particularly internationally. The company's U.S. sales already accounted for some 30 percent of its total; in 1982, the company acquired its first U.S. subsidiary, subsequently moving its U.S. base to Philadelphia. Other U.S. acquisitions followed, such as that of Crane Russak & Co., added in 1985.

Anthony Selvey, who had joined the company in 1963 and was appointed its CEO in 1983 , led the company through its strong expansion throughout the end of the century and into the next. In 1988, Taylor & Francis acquired the U.S.'s Hemisphere Publishing, formerly part of Harper & Row. That year, the company renamed itself Taylor & Francis Group to reflect its growing number of imprints.

Taylor & Francis' strongest growth came during the 1990s, when the company went on an acquisition spree. In 1994, the company bought Accelerated Development Inc., based in the U.S., a psychology specialist. That field took on greater importance for the company with the purchase of Lawrence Erlbaum Associates, in England, and its 14 journals and strong book list. In 1996, the company added UCL Press, of London. By then, the group published some 130 titles. Compared to industry heavyweights Elsevier and Wolter Kluwer, the company remained modestly sized with revenues of just £28 million.

The company's public offering in 1998 enabled it to step up its buying spree, however. In that year, the company acquired Routledge Press, which more than doubled its size, bringing 250 new journals and a back list of over 7,000 books in addition to Routledge's 1,000 new titles per year. The following year Europe Publications was added, specializing in directories, and the international division of Scandinavian University Press. The company suggested that it was on the lookout for new acquisition in the U.S. as well, telling the *Daily Telegraph*, ''We are considered a very serious predator these days.''

The company's new big prey came in February 2001, when Taylor & Francis paid £22.8 million for Gordon & Breach, adding another 250 journals and a number of books, including the best-selling *Molecular Biology of the Cell*. The company had by then also added Martin Dunitz, a specialist in medical textbooks and journals. The Taylor & Francis entering the 21st century had grown to become one of the United Kingdom's leading scientific publishers.

Principal Subsidiaries

Afterhurst Ltd.; Carfax Publishing Ltd.; Europa Publications Ltd.; Falmer Press Ltd.; Martin Dunitz Ltd.; Psychology Press Ltd.; Primal Pictures Ltd. (16%); Routledge Publishing Holdings Ltd.; Scandinavian University Press (UK) Ltd.; Taylor & Francis AB (Sweden); Taylor & Francis AS (Norway); Taylor & Francis Books Inc. (U.S.); Taylor & Francis Books Ltd.; Taylor & Francis Inc. (U.S.); Taylor & Francis Ltd.; Taylor & Francis (Publishers) Inc. (U.S.); Taylor & Francis Publishing Services Ltd.; UCL Press Ltd.

Principal Competitors

The Thomson Corporation; Pearson plc; Reed Elsevier plc; Wolters Kluwer nv; John Wiley & Sons, Inc.; W.W. Norton & Company, Inc.

Further Reading

Brock, W.H., and Meadows, A.J., *The Lamp of Learning: Two Centuries of Publishing at Taylor & Francis*, London: Taylor & Francis Ltd., 1998.

Deshmukh, Anita, ''A Journal of Success for Publisher,'' *Birmingham Post*, March 23, 2001, p. 25.

McIntosh, Bill, ''Taylor & Francis,'' *Independent*, September 20, 2001, p. 21.

—M.L. Cohen

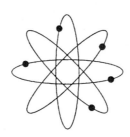

Tech-Sym Corporation

Veritas Capital Fund L.P.
660 Madison Avenue, 14th Floor
New York, New York 10021
U.S.A.
Telephone: (212) 688-0020
Fax: (212) 688-9411
Web site: http://www.veritascapital.com

*Acquired by Veritas Capital's Integrated Defense
    Technologies in August 2000*
Incorporated: 1944 as Western Gold Mines, Inc.
Employees: 1,620 (1999)
Sales: $155.2 million (1999)
NAIC: 334511 Search, Detection, Navigation, Guidance,
    Aeronautical, and Nautical System and Instrument
    Manufacturing; 335314 Relay and Industrial Control
    Manufacturing; 33422 Radio and Television
    Broadcasting and Wireless Communications
    Equipment Manufacturing; 334514 Totalizing Fluid
    Meter and Counting Device Manufacturing; 334419
    Other Electronic Component Manufacturing

When Tech-Sym Corporation was purchased by Veritas Capital Fund L.P.'s Integrated Defense Technologies (IDT) unit in 2000, the firm was operating as a highly diversified electronics engineering and manufacturing firm that designed, developed, and manufactured various products for use in the fields of defense systems, communications, and weather information. Through its principal subsidiary in the defense industry, Metric Systems Corp., Tech-Sym provided airborne training systems, shipboard electronics, and mechanical systems for defense applications. Through subsidiary TRAK Communications Inc., Tech-Sym developed and manufactured highly technological materials and components for the wireless communications industry. Its subsidiary Continental Electronics Corp. operated as a designer and manufacturer of radio frequency transmitters, and subsidiary Enterprise Electronics Corp. was a leading manufacturer of weather information systems. Tech-Sym's operations became part of IDT—owned by Veritas Capital Fund L.P.—after the acquisition.

Early History

Although Tech-Sym had narrowed its focus during the 1980s and 1990s, for a long period of its history the company was a combination of different operations working in different fields. Initially formed and incorporated by a group of investors to take advantage of the uranium and gold deposits still undiscovered in the western part of the United States, from its inception the company was managed by a board of directors who were primarily interested in a return of their investment. This single, overriding interest led the company's management and board of directors to expand its operations. Not satisfied with the small returns garnered from collecting mineral deposits over a period of 15 years, the company began to diversify, among other fields, into the financial services industry and to engage in real estate ventures. The company changed its name to Western Equities, Inc. in 1961 and to Westec Corporation in 1966. The dizzying array of acquisitions made during the early and mid-1960s included Lee Ackerman Investment Company, Arizona Growth Capital, Inc.; Geo Space Corporation, a manufacturer of seismic products and instruments; TRAK Microwave Corporation; Pan Geo Atlas Corporation; Jet Set Corporation, a manufacturer of explosive devices; Engineers & Fabricators, Inc.; Carry Machine Supply, Inc.; Metric Systems, Inc.; and Seacat-Zapata Off-Shore Company, a gas and oil exploration firm.

By 1966, however, the company was suffering from the mismanagement of the past. Flouting such time-honored strategies as economies of scale, management had brought the firm to the brink of financial catastrophe. Many of the acquisitions made during the early part of the decade were losing money, while others had lost their traditional market share. As a result, the company was forced to file a petition in U.S. District Court under Chapter 11 of the Bankruptcy Act. The reorganization immediately went into effect, and the company was required to sell off many of its subsidiaries to pay outstanding debts, including Geo Space Corporation and Pan Geo Atlas Corporation. Other subsidiaries, such as Carry Machine Supply, Inc. and Metric Systems, were reorganized and merged to create more stable and profitable operations. By the time the company changed its name once again, to Tech-Sym Corporation in

Key Dates:

1944: Western Gold Mines Inc. is established.
1961: Company named is changed to Western Equities Inc.
1966: Firm is renamed Westec Corporation during a period of rapid expansion.
1970: During bankruptcy reorganization, the company name is changed to Tech-Sym Corp.
1972: Tech-Sym begins its foray into the lumber industry.
1977: After years of reorganization, the company emerges from bankruptcy.
1989: Seventy-five percent of revenues come from defense contracts.
1990: Tech-Sym acquires Continental Electronics Corp.
1991: Company completes acquisition of Syntron Inc.
1994: Purchases Anarad Inc.
1995: CogniSeis Development Inc. and Symtronix Corp. are acquired.
1996: Firm creates GeoScience Corp. and plans for public spin-off.
1999: Company sells GeoScience Corp. to Sercel Inc.
2000: Tech-Sym is acquired by the Integrated Defense Technologies unit of Veritas Capital Fund L.P.

1970, management seemed to have learned from its past mistakes and had implemented a reorganization strategy that was bringing the company back to profitability.

Yet the road to financial stability was a long and arduous one. With such an extensive history of varied diversification, even the new management at the company continued to delve into widely disparate businesses. In 1972, Tech-Sym purchased All Woods, Inc., a lumber company, and one year later acquired Alexander-Schroder Lumber Company. Later in 1973, management formed Coastal Lumber, S.A., in Costa Rica. These attempts to create a lumber division resulted in the opening of a retail store in Houston, Texas named ''Fine Woods.'' Unfortunately, this foray into the lumber industry did not result in a significant financial improvement. By the late 1970s, management finally decided to focus on an area where profitability and growth were assured—the development and manufacture of electronic products for the United States defense industry.

Growth During the 1970s and 1980s

The first major acquisition during the early 1970s that introduced Tech-Sym to defense industry contracts was E&M Laboratories, a development and manufacturing firm specializing in electronic components for missiles and fighter jets. This purchase, successful both in terms of its amalgamation into the Tech-Sym corporate structure and its highly lucrative product line, helped the company complete its reorganization strategy and emerge from Chapter 11 in July of 1977. As management at Tech-Sym recognized the enormous profitability in procuring defense systems contracts with the United States government, and with other national governments friendly toward America, more attention was paid to possible takeover candidates in the

defense industry. This shift in focus resulted in the sell-off of the company's entire lumber operation.

Although Tech-Sym was firmly established in developing and manufacturing electronic systems for the U.S. Department of Defense by the late 1970s, it was not until the election of Ronald Reagan that the company began to make a name for itself within the industry. President Reagan's commitment to the rebuilding of American armed forces around the world led to numerous contracts for Tech-Sym. During the early 1980s, Tech-Sym filled a huge contract for the development, design, and manufacture of electronic control and monitoring equipment for U.S. Navy ships. But this was only one of its contracts. The company also made airborne weapons systems and electronic countermeasure systems for the U.S. Air Force, microwave components for Navy radar, aircraft, and missiles, radar and missile simulators for training air crews, and a host of computer-based electronic systems used in air and naval defense.

The decade of the 1980s was one of the most successful financial periods in the company's history. As its cash flow continued to improve, management made strategic acquisitions that improved its position in certain fields both within and outside the defense industry. Two of the most important of these purchases included Tecom Industries, Inc. and Enterprise Electronics Corporation. Tecom Industries was a small but important California-based manufacturer of antennas and computer-controlled electromechanical components for aerospace, navigation, surveillance, and command control applications. Tecom had garnered numerous contracts from the U.S. Department of Defense, especially in the area of naval defense systems. On the other hand, Alabama-based Enterprise Electronics Corporation was a designer and manufacturer of highly sophisticated meteorological information systems that detect and display weather patterns and other natural events through the use of Dopplar radars and innovative computer processing. Although Enterprise Electronics was well known as a firm that custom designed and installed meteorological radar systems for countries around the world, Tech-Sym expanded Enterprise's markets to encompass a wider array of customers, such as government agencies, military organizations, and meteorology departments at large universities in the U.S., Europe, and Asia.

Transition and Development after the Cold War

With the end of the Cold War, however, the regular flow of contracts to Tech-Sym and its subsidiaries from the U.S. Department of Defense slowed to barely a trickle. The dissolution of the Soviet Union, and the growing perception within the United States Congress that appropriations for defense systems needed to be decreased, forced many companies that had relied heavily on defense business to alter their market strategy. Tech-Sym was no exception, and management at the company decided to implement a comprehensive diversification program that involved three key elements: acquisitions, new product development, and international expansion.

The transition from being primarily a designer and manufacturer of electronic systems for the defense industry to a more diversified company was not an easy one. Orders from the U.S. Department of Defense began to decline more rapidly than management could switch to commercial ventures. The area of satellite surveillance was especially hard hit and contributed to the company's earnings falling nearly 25 percent in 1991. But management had already made two important acquisitions that would help Tech-Sym ultimately break through the clouds of financial uncertainty. In 1990, Tech-Sym purchased the venerable 45-year-old Continental Electronics Corporation, the world's most famous manufacturer of high-powered radio frequency transmitters. Making transmitters that regularly produced between 500,000 and two million watts, many were used by the Voice of America and Radio Free Europe to broadcast news and various other general information programs throughout the years of the Cold War. Tech-Sym reorganized Continental Electronics and changed its focus from military radars and electronic warfare equipment to a firm that concentrated almost exclusively on manufacturing both high-powered and low frequency transmitters. Tech-Sym then began an intense marketing campaign to sell Continental's high-powered transmitters to foreign countries, including China, which employed the transmitters to broadcast radio shows to more than one billion people in rural areas. In addition, a Catholic organization in Alabama purchased $8 million worth of transmitting equipment to make religious broadcasts to people in South America. Tech-Sym also sold Continental's less powerful transmitters to numerous FM radio stations across the United States.

At approximately the same time, Tech-Sym acquired Syntron, Inc., a manufacturer of highly sophisticated, state-of-the-art seismic instrumentation and equipment. Syntron was one of the first companies in the world to design equipment that made it possible to use three-dimensional computer imaging for identifying gas and oil reserves as much as 25,000 feet below the Earth's surface. Syntron quickly became Tech-Sym's fastest growing and most profitable subsidiary. Based on Syntron's technology, Tech-Sym opened a brand new plant in Singapore in 1992 to take advantage of the growing demand in Southeast Asia for instruments used in the search for gas and oil reserves. Also during the year, the company's Enterprise Electronics subsidiary won a significant contract from the Moroccan government to custom design and install meteorological radar systems in the North African nation, as well as a contract with the Chinese government for the installation of similar radar systems. These acquisitions and sales helped Tech-Sym move away from its traditional reliance upon the defense industry. In 1989, the company derived approximately 75 percent of its total revenues from defense contracts, but by the end of 1992 defense contracts made up only 45 percent of Tech-Sym's revenues.

Diversification in the Mid-1990s

By the beginning of 1993, Tech-Sym was well on its way to succeeding in its strategy to diversify away from the previous heavy reliance on defense industry contracts. Syntron, Inc. was particularly strong, garnering numerous, ever-larger contracts for seismic information systems. One of the largest contracts during this year came from a company working along the Alaskan coastline. Contracts for meteorological radar systems, and for high-powered transmitters, were also growing more numerous, particularly from nations in Europe, Asia, and Africa. In 1994, Tech-Sym made one of its most important acqui-

sitions to date, having purchased Anarad, Inc., an environmental instrumentation firm based in California. The purchase of Anarad was made specifically to take advantage of the impact that the 1990 Clean Air Act would have on manufacturing plants and factories stretching along the Houston Ship Channel in the Texas Gulf. More than 340 factories along the Channel were required to monitor the quality of their emissions into the atmosphere, and each of them needed environmental instruments to measure the amount of contaminated air.

In 1995, Tech-Sym acquired CogniSeis Development Inc., a seismic firm located in Houston, Texas, and Symtronix Corporation, another seismic company. These two firms were then merged with Syntron, Inc. to create GeoScience Corporation. Tech-Sym management brought the three companies together to build a major developer and manufacturer of seismic data acquisition systems used in the oil and gas exploration business. As the demand for three-dimensional data collection grew in the field of oil and gas exploration both on land and offshore, Tech-Sym planned a public spin-off for GeoScience Corporation. Tech-Sym retained solid control of the new company through its 80 percent ownership of GeoScience Corporation stock. With seismic activity continually increasing not only in the Gulf of Mexico but throughout the world, by the end of 1996 the companies that comprised GeoScience were reporting record levels of ever-increasing revenues.

Tech-Sym successfully transformed itself from a company dependent upon defense contracts to a highly diversified firm with growing revenues from markets such as communications, meteorological data systems, and seismic instrumentation and equipment. By the mid-1990s, the company's defense contracts had leveled off at approximately 25 percent of total revenues, with the other 75 percent derived from its diversification activities. With the help of its strategic focus, the company's net income improved from a 25 percent decrease in 1992 to a 20 percent increase by 1995.

Restructuring and Eventual Sale: Late 1990s–2001

Sales for 1996 reached $321 million. Tech-Sym's successes however, were overshadowed by its mediocre stock performance, which management viewed as being undervalued. J. Michael Camp, Tech-Sym's president and CEO, initiated a strategic movement in which the company would simplify its operations and restructure key segments in order to capitalize on high growth markets and lower operating expenses. In 1998, the firm began to restructure its subsidiaries including TRAK Communications and also began to look for a buyer for its GeoScience Corp. The company's new focus rested firmly in its communications products, as well as its defense and weather information systems. Revenue from its restructured units in 1998 was $140.5 million.

In 1999, Tech-Sym initiated a share-repurchase program in an effort to boost share value. At the end of that year, the firm sold GeoScience Corp. to Sercel, Inc., a wholly owned subsidiary of Compagnie Generale de Geophysique, for $53.6 million. The proceeds of the sale were utilized to pay off debt and fund the stock repurchase program. At the time of the sale, Tech-Sym also announced that it had retained an investment firm to review the company's operations. In a company press release CEO

Camp stated, ''we believe our current share price does not accurately reflect our current value or future prospects. Our operating strategy has been to increase the pace of growth of our core businesses while improving financial results and divesting non-core assets.'' Camp also stated that the market had failed to respond accordingly despite positive changes in the company's operating procedures. The company reported a $23.5 million net loss for the year.

Tech-Sym entered the new millennium with an uncertain future. The investment firm that began investigating company operations in 1999 ascertained that the best possible outcome for Tech-Sym would be to sell the firm. A flood of acquisition offers began to surface as a result of the findings, and in June 2000 the company announced that it would be acquired by Integrated Defense Technologies, a portfolio of defense electronics companies owned by Veritas Capital Fund L.P. The $182 million deal was completed in September of that year and was applauded by management for its positive effect on shareholder value. Tech-Sym's outstanding common stock was converted at $30 per share as part of the deal. The firm's operations were then merged into IDT's portfolio of companies. Under IDT, the former Tech-Sym subsidiaries Metric Systems Corporation and TRAK Communications continued to operate.

Further Reading

Byrne, Harlan S., ''Tech-Sym Seismic Line Nears a Payoff,'' *Barron's,* March 8, 1993, p. 44.
Elder, Laura, ''Tech-Sym Goes on Acquisition Spree to Offset Slump in Defense Spending,'' *Houston Business Journal,* July 15, 1994, p. 8.
Marcial, Gene G., ''A Wallflower About to Bloom?,'' *Business Week Online,* June 2, 1997.
Payne, Chris, ''A Farewell to Arms: Defense Firm Comes In From the Cold,'' *Houston Business Journal,* April 26, 1993, p. 1A.
——, ''Diversifying Defense Contractor Reports Strong First Quarter,'' *Houston Business Journal,* May 10, 1993, p. 15A.
Pybus, Kenneth, ''Tech-Sym Spinning Off Seismic Unit,'' *Houston Business Journal,* April 12, 1996, p. 1A.
''Tech-Sym Announces it Has Completed the Sale of GeoScience Corporation,'' *Business Wire,* December 13, 1999.
''Tech-Sym Corporation Announced Fourth Quarter and Fiscal 1999 Results,'' *Business Wire*, February 18, 2000.
''Tech-Sym Corporation Completes Merger,'' *Business Wire,* September 29, 2000.
''Tech-Sym Plans Stock Buyback,'' *Wall Street Journal,* June 26, 1996, p. A6.
''Veritas Capital to Acquire Tech-Sym Corporation for $30.00 Per Share,'' *PR Newswire,* June 27, 2000.

—Thomas Derdak
—update: Christina M. Stansell

TOLLGRADE®

Tollgrade Communications, Inc.

492 Nixon Road
Cheswick, Pennsylvania 15024
U.S.A.
Telephone: (412) 820-1400
Toll Free: (800) 878-3399
Fax: (412) 820-1530
Web site: http://www.tollgrade.com

Public Company
Incorporated: 1986
Employees: 296
Sales: $114.4 million (2000)
Stock Exchanges: NASDAQ
Ticker Symbol: TLGD
NAIC: 513390 Other Telecommunications; 334210
   Telephone Apparatus Manufacturing

Tollgrade Communications, Inc. is devoted to line testing for the telecommunications and cable television industries. Located in the Pittsburgh, Pennsylvania, suburb of Cheswick, the company was originally limited to the manufacture of equipment, but has since grown into a systems developer, providing customers with a total solutions capability. Tollgrade's testing products allow customers to use their existing line tests to monitor systems and diagnose problems from a central office, rather than incurring the expense of dispatching repairmen to test lines on location. Independent telephone companies and the cable television industry have become increasingly more important customers, but Tollgrade's primary customers remain the four regional Bell operating companies: Verizon, BellSouth, SBC, and Qwest. Although more complex lines that are designed to carry high-speed internet service and other data communications are gaining in importance, most of Tollgrade's products are dedicated to plain old telephone service, so-called POTS.

Break up of AT&T in the Mid-1980s Leads to Tollgrade

Richard Craig Allison founded Tollgrade, incorporating it in Pennsylvania in 1986, although the company did not begin oper-

ating until 1988. He was born in Ashtabula, Ohio, raised in Erie, Pennsylvania, and graduated from Gannon University in 1965 with a degree in accounting. He worked as an auditor in the accounting department of U.S. Steel Corporation, then worked in pharmaceutical sales, and established the West Coast division of a radio frequency electronics firm before striking out on his own. Returning to Erie, he founded UTEK, Inc., a construction business that dug ditches and laid pipeline for natural gas utilities. Although the business was successful, it did not fulfil Allison's ambitious nature. He became attracted to the telecommunications business when UTEK began to install high tech gas meters that automatically transmitted data to the utility company.

In the mid-1980s AT&T was broken up into four regional companies, the so-called Baby Bells. Allison sensed that the changing landscape in the telephone industry presented great opportunities for new companies. Because he lacked technical expertise, Allison sought out help. A friend from Erie introduced him to a former Bell of Pennsylvania engineer named Rocco L. Faminio, who had spent 38 years at Bell, managed its Transmission Lab in Pittsburgh, and, despite having retired in 1985, continued to serve as a consultant to the company. The men met for lunch outside of Pittsburgh and agreed to go into business together. The goal was to develop a product that would supply a need in the revised telecommunications landscape. ''We took the Microsoft approach,'' Allison recalled years later. ''We wanted everybody to use it.''

Allison recruited investors, one of the most important being Dr. Richard H. Heibel, a cardiologist. He also began to establish a management team, which included his son, Chris, whose degree in English and background in public relations appeared on the surface to be ill suited to the business, but he also had served as a marketing consultant for high-tech companies during his days as an account executive at Ketchum Public Relations Worldwide. All the new company needed was a name and a product. Flaminio, who was given a free hand on all technology issues, supplied the answer in both instances. The company name was drawn from telephone industry terminology: Only lines that met the highest standard were designated as ''toll grade.'' Thus, Tollgrade was incorporated in 1986. The product that Flaminio knew he wanted to develop was a device that permitted telephone companies to test lines that combined copper and fiber optics, fast becoming the industry standard, with equipment originally designed to test the quality of all-copper telephone lines. What would become the metallic channel unit (MCU) had a ready market in telephone companies, which would now be able to extend the life of their testing equipment and avoid an expensive upgrade. Flaminio had previously attempted to convince Bell Labs to develop his idea, but it proved too complicated and the company elected instead to focus on the manufacture of switches.

Between the time Tollgrade was incorporated and began actual operations in 1988, Flaminio searched for engineers to help in the development of the MCU. Because the man he wanted was under contract, Flaminio interviewed a number of candidates but settled on Fred Kiko, who contacted him in late 1987. Kiko was working in San Diego, but when his contract was up, he didn't want to move back to Chicago. Instead, he agreed to work with Tollgrade when he became available. Work on the MCU would then take place in both San Diego and Pittsburgh, as Flaminio and his team would alternate sites during the development phase. For the first year or so, nobody in the company was paid.

Tollgrade Goes Operational in 1988

As a five-person company during the early years, Tollgrade operated out of the University of Pittsburgh Research Center (U-PARC), which was originally built in the 1930s as the Gulf Oil Corp. Research Center. Following a merger between Gulf and Chevron in the 1980s, the park was donated to the University of Pittsburgh and it served as the incubator for a number of area high tech companies. Tollgrade had a large space at U-PARC that was partitioned into two rooms. Chris Allison had a desk on one side and Flaminio had a lab on the other. They stayed at U-PARC for a year before moving to space across the street when, in order to generate cash, the company developed some less complicated products to sell. Tollgrade produced an upgrade to the high-tech gas meter that UTEK had been installing. The meters were connected to a home's phone line and would dial in daily to the gas company. Unfortunately, the residents were unable to use the phone during these times. Any malfunction, or if the unit's battery went dead, would result in the complete loss of phone service. The Tollgrade device allowed customers to override the meter and obtain a dial tone. The company sold a few units, but made little money because the utility decided to go to a radio frequency system, abandoning phone lines completely. Tollgrade was a bit more successful with its second telecommunications product, the OIU-2E, an enhanced synchronization device. The company then produced a device that would be a precursor to the MCU. It allowed alarms to be relayed from the customer to a central office, despite the mix of fiber optic and copper lines. In effect, it simulated a copper line.

By the end of 1990 Tollgrade was generating some $2 million in revenues, but it was also running out of cash and because Allison wanted to maintain the company's freedom he was reluctant to turn to venture capitalists for funding. The company already had bank financing. Flaminio and Kiko had originally worked as consultants, but it was the bank that insisted they become full-time employees. As a result, Flaminio came out of official retirement, as Allison named him president of the small start-up. When they went back to the bank in the early 1990s in need of funds to put the final touches on the MCU, they met with little enthusiasm. The company was simply too small. Tollgrade had been testing the MCU with Bell Labs, and although it was not quite up to the necessary specifications, Flaminio was confident that his team would have a suitable product in a matter of weeks. In the end, Tollgrade received its bank loan, but it had to be personally backed by Allison, who put up his house, as well as Dr. Heibel. In February 1992, Flaminio's group had produced an MCU that exceeded the Bell Lab's requirements. By May of that year it had made its first sale to New Jersey Bell and began to quickly make the MCU compatible with all major digital loop carrier systems. With the company's flagship product launched, revenues jumped to $5.3 million by the end of 1992.

By now, however, Allison was experiencing serious heart problems. He had had a heart bypass operation at the age of 37, and just before undergoing a second heart bypass operation he turned over the day-to-day responsibilities of the company to his son, who had been serving as Tollgrade's chief operating officer since 1990. With the MCU gaining industry acceptance, Tollgrade saw its revenues increase steadily. In 1994, revenues more than doubled over the previous year, reaching $14.7 million, then grew to $22.3 million in 1995. Net income stood at $2.3 million, a significant improvement over the $114,000 the company earned in 1992. With its business growing, the company was able to move to its present location at Cheswick in September 1994.

In 1995 Chris Allison was named chief executive officer. A short time later, in December 1995, Tollgrade went public, selling 1,485,585 shares of common stock at $12 per share. After underwriting discounts and associated costs of the offering, the company netted approximately $15.8 million, which was earmarked for general corporate purposes. Shares began trading on the Nasdaq. In general the market was cautious about telecommunications stocks, given the move in Congress to deregulate the industry. As much as 97 percent of Tollgrade's business came from the four major Bell companies, and they were reluctant to buy new products until the details of the telecommunications bills in Congress were settled. The Bells were looking to get involved in the long distance business, while long distance carriers were eager to enter the local phone business. Although Tollgrade's immediate prospects were somewhat clouded by the uncertainty in the industry, there was no doubt that once Congress acted, suppliers like Tollgrade would be in a position to experience exceptional growth. Moreover, the rising importance of fiber optics and the need for greater speed because of the emergence of the Internet bode well for the company's prospects. Rather than just rely on the MCU, however, Tollgrade invested generously in a research and development program.

Tollgrade introduced a switching MCU with the ability to communicate with 15 remote terminals instead of just one. It

Key Dates:

1986: The company is incorporated in Pennsylvania.
1988: The company begins operating.
1992: Flagship MCU product is introduced.
1995: The company goes public.
1998: Founder Richard Craig Allison dies.

also developed a fiber loop test product for shorter circuits where MCU was not suitable. Tollgrade also teamed with Encompass software of Buford, Georgia, to develop capabilities of testing the test systems themselves. Although false alarms caused by faulty test equipment only accounted for 2 percent of total alarms, the cost of needlessly dispatching repairmen justified an investment in the product. Because Tollgrade was expanding its product lines, and deregulation was taking effect, the company saw its potential market growing steadily. Cable television companies looking to offer telecommunications services appeared to be a promising target. Typically, cable dispatched repairmen more often than the telephone companies, making them prime customers for less expensive remote testing. In 1997, Tollgrade introduced its LIGHTHOUSE Cable Status Monitoring System, the company's first product specifically designed for the Broadband Hybrid Fiber Coax distribution system used by the cable television industry. Moreover, Tollgrade saw long-term growth possibilities overseas, where the telecommunications testing niche was virtually unfilled. It established a beachhead in Latin America and the United Kingdom.

Stock Surge in 1996 Anticipates Greater Heights

Revenues in 1996 grew by 68 percent over the previous year to $37.5 million, while net income rose by 122 percent to $5.6 million. A year later, revenues reached $45.4 million and Tollgrade was listed by *Forbes* magazine as one of ''The 200 Best Small Companies in America.'' In turn, investors were becoming enthusiastic about Tollgrade. If anything, they worried about the company growing too fast too soon, but were comforted by the fact that Tollgrade's new markets were opening at a manageable pace. The company's stock surged to $31.75 before settling to the $25 range. That movement, however, was only a harbinger of what was to come a few years later.

In 1998 the elder Allison died of a heart attack at the age of 57, leaving his 37-year-old son as chief executive and chairman of the company. Not only was the younger Allison a seasoned executive by now, Tollgrade enjoyed stable management and continued its steady growth. It gained an entry into a new and potentially lucrative market, signing a product development agreement with UT Starcom, an international telecommunications systems developer, which would deploy Tollgrade's MCU technology in the Peoples Republic of China. Also in 1998 Tollgrade announced the development of a new product called DigiTest, its most advance centralized testing solution. It then signed a multi-year, product development, license, and authorized reseller agreement with Lucent Technologies. Tollgrade would adapt DigiTest to work with Lucent's Mechanized Loop Testing operations support system used by the Bell operating

companies. The integrated system would work with Integrated Services Digital Network (ISDN) service, Asymmetrical Digital Subscriber Line (ADSL) service, as well as POTS.

For 1998, Tollgrade showed only a modest improvement in revenues, reaching $46.3 million. Nevertheless, it made the *Forbes* Top 200 list for a second consecutive year. In 1999 Tollgrade would renew its impressive gains in revenues, exceeding $61 million. The following year, however, would prove to be an exceptional year for the company. Not only did it enjoy tremendous results, posting net earning of $27.5 million on revenues of $114.4 million, Tollgrade experienced an extraordinary run-up on the price of its stock. After three years of little movement, shares began to rise in value late in 1999 and continued to move on expectations of robust first quarter results. Then a competitor, Turnstone Systems, went public in February 2000, establishing a benchmark against which to judge Tollgrade. Following its offering, Turnstone had a market capitalization of $2.8 billion, while Tollgrade was valued at just $405 million. Going back the previous four quarters, however Turnstone had earned $4.5 million on $49.4 million in revenues compared to Tollgrade's $14.4 million in net profits on $72.4 million in revenues. Turnstone was experiencing rapid growth, but so was Tollgrade, which had proven that it had the ability to rollout new products suitable to the changing needs of the telecommunications industry. Essentially, the market was rectifying the imbalance between the worth of Tollgrade and Turnstone. In March, a two-for-one split slowed Tollgrade's rising price, but only momentarily. In the autumn of 2000, shares would top out at $168.88, giving Tollgrade a market capitalization of over $2 billion.

The price of Tollgrade stock declined somewhat, but a correction in late 2000 would quickly result in a complete reversal. Despite reporting impressive year-end results, Tollgrade was caught up in the effects of a sour national economy that hindered the growth of the telecommunications industry. Competitive Local Exchange Carriers either went out of business or curtailed investments, cable television slowed the buildouts of hybrid-fiber-coax systems, and the regional Bells were also reluctant to deploy new networks. As a result, Tollgrade's revenues dropped, and investors reacted to the bad news by bidding down the company's stock. In mid-March 2001, it reached a low of $15.25. Tollgrade lost 80 percent of its value in a matter of six months.

At the end of 2000, Tollgrade had record employment of 411, but poor conditions soon forced management to institute cost cutting measures, including the laying off of more than 100 employees. Allison also asked the company's board to cut his salary by 20 percent and to rescind any potential bonus for him for the year. Despite these measures and the gloomy state of telecommunications, Allison considered the downturn to be a temporary setback. In fact, the company began to buy back its stock, which stabilized above $20. As soon as telephone and cable companies began to invest in their infrastructures in order to gain a competitive edge, Tollgrade could be expected to regain its balance. With the rising use of the Internet and the greater demand for high-speed access and the wiring needed to support it, Tollgrade continued to be positioned for substantial long-term growth.

Principal Divisions

Lighthouse; Access Products; DigiTest; Professional Services.

Principal Competitors

Harris Corporation; Spirent plc; Teradyne, Inc.; Turnstone Systems, Inc.

Further Reading

Bahl, Monish, ''TollGrade Communications Inc. (Company Profile),'' *Pittsburgh Business Times,* April 1, 1996, p. 21.

Kovatch, Karen, ''As the Telecom Market Expands, So Do Opportunities,'' *Pittsburgh Business Times,* February 21, 1997.

Mulqueen, John T., ''Telecom Companies Paying a Service Toll,'' *Communications Week,* March 10, 1997, p. 80.

Starzynski, Bob, ''Cheswick, Pa.-Based Telecommunications Firm Pays Off for Its Investors,'' *Pittsburgh Post-Gazette,* June 25, 2000.

——, ''Shares of Cheswick, Pa.-Based Telecom Equipment Maker Sink after Gloomy Report,'' *Pittsburgh Post-Gazette,* January 26, 2001.

Tascarella, Patty, ''Tollgrade Unveils Public Offering,'' *Pittsburgh Business Times,* October 23, 1995, p. 1.

Zapinski, Ken, ''R. Craig Allison Visionary Telecommunications Chief,'' *Pittsburgh Post-Gazette,* April 7, 1998, p. C5.

—Ed Dinger

Tomkins plc

East Putney House
84 Upper Richmond Road
London SW15 2ST
United Kingdom
Telephone: (44) 20 8871-4544
Fax: (44) 20 8877-9700
Web site: http://www.tomkins.co.uk

Public Company
Incorporated: 1925 as F.H. Tomkins Buckle Co. Ltd.
Employees: 52,775
Sales: £4.1 billion ($5.84 billion) (2001)
Stock Exchanges: London New York
Ticker Symbol: TOMK TKS
NAIC: 551112 Offices of Other Holding Companies;
    42183 Industrial Machinery and Equipment
    Wholesalers; 42171 Hardware Wholesalers; 332913
    Plumbing Fixture Fitting and Trim Manufacturing;
    332321 Metal Window and Door Manufacturing;
    333414 Heating Equipment Manufacturing

Tomkins plc is a multinational engineering and manufacturing group, overseeing three major business groups: Air Systems Components, Engineered and Construction Products, and Industrial and Automotive Engineering. After aggressively expanding during the 1980s and throughout the 1990s, Tomkins has been paring back operations in order to focus on its core operations. Leaving its ''guns and buns'' nickname behind—the firm sold gun maker Smith & Wesson and its food manufacturing operations—Tomkins intends to increase shareholder value and return to profitability through its restructuring efforts. Longtime CEO Gregory Hutchings resigned his post in 2000 amid controversy related to company finances.

Tomkins traces its history to the 1925 founding of the F.H. Tomkins Buckle Company Ltd., a manufacturer of buckles and fasteners operating from England's West Midlands. The firm entered the public arena in 1956, listing on the London Stock Exchange. Buckles and fasteners largely remained the company's focus until 1983, when Tomkins underwent a dramatic metamorphosis and emerged as an international conglomerate.

Expansion Under the Leadership of Hutchings: 1980s

The company's sudden change in direction was largely due to the vision of one man, Gregory Hutchings, who in 1983 acquired a 22.9 percent stake in Tomkins. Becoming chief executive of Tomkins in January 1984, Hutchings assembled a management team and set about transforming the company through an aggressive acquisition strategy aimed primarily at companies based in the United Kingdom and the United States. In quick but carefully phased succession, Tomkins acquired Ferraris Piston Service (1984), Hayters, a manufacturer of garden tools (1984), Pegler-Hattersley, a maker of taps, valves, plumbing fittings, and heating control systems (1986), Smith & Wesson, the well-known gun manufacturers (1987), and Murray Ohio, a lawnmower and bicycle company (1988).

During this time, Tomkins was creating and solidifying its careful and conservative approach to business, ''control'' being the company's watchword. Implicit in Tomkins' success as a conglomerate was its unwavering belief that any business, no matter what its end product, would respond to the basic business tenets to which Tomkins subscribed: stringent financial control fortified by tough and realistic budgetary planning; efficient, waste-reducing management procedures; and judicious use of capital as and when dictated by the needs of the business.

The company's acquisition policy also emphasized selectivity. Tomkins favored what it termed ''low-risk'' technology businesses—those that produced and/or distributed products not subject to rapid technological change or frequent development and improvement. Moreover, the company was reluctant to purchase any concern that would hinder the conglomerate's earnings even temporarily; new acquisitions were chosen with the expectation that they would contribute to the firm's profits in their first year. Finally, Tomkins' policy was to fully integrate one acquisition into the company as a whole before moving on to the next. Consequently, Tomkins made only eight major acquisitions between 1983 and 1993.

Company Perspectives:

Tomkins is committed to enhancing shareholder value through increasing the economic value of its businesses by concentrating in product and geographic markets in its chosen sectors where the businesses have sustainable competitive advantage, and which offer prospects for profitable growth.

Each of the companies acquired by Tomkins was afforded considerable autonomy in regards to its management and operations, provided that the company conform to the parent company's strict financial regime. Subsidiaries were expected to strive to become the lowest-priced and most efficient supplier in their particular market. In turn, Tomkins was willing to provide capital for new plants and equipment, product development, management training, advertising campaigns, or whatever was regarded as necessary to achieving that goal.

Seeking to build an empire whose broad base ensures continued profitability even if one sector of the company should suffer a setback, Tomkins also sought to achieve geographical balance among its enterprises. The company's ideal ratio was to have 40 percent of its business based in the United Kingdom, 40 percent in the United States, and 20 percent elsewhere.

Hutchings' strategies proved phenomenally successful. In 1983, Tomkins, wholly reliant on the fastener business, controlled seven companies, employed a work force of 400, and made a pre-tax profit of £1.6 million, mostly in the United Kingdom. In 1994, however, the company boasted 73 companies, supported 45,000 employees, and enjoyed a pre-tax profit of over £257 million garnered from businesses operating in the United Kingdom, North America, Europe, and Australia, with no one product accounting for a disproportionate amount of Tomkins' profits.

In 1994, the company's business fell roughly into five categories: fluid controls; services to industry; professional, garden, and leisure products; industrial products; and Rank Hovis McDougall, a food manufacturer acquired by Tomkins in 1992. The fluid controls business comprised the manufacture and international distribution of water, heating, ventilating, and air conditioning valves, taps, radiators, and plumbing fittings. Tomkins' firms in this category, based in the United Kingdom, the United States, and Canada, included Ruskin, Air System Components, Pegler, and Guest & Chrimes.

The services to industry category, a more varied group, included Totectors, a U.K. supplier of safety footwear; the automotive components distributor Ferraris Piston Service; the Belgian valve and pipeline equipment firms Prometal and Dutch UBEL; as well as U.S. manufacturers of conveyor and material handling systems such as Mayfran and Dearborn Fabricating & Engineering. The services to industry category also included distribution of an array of high specification valves, the supply of fasteners to clients in the United Kingdom and Europe, the provision of spring steel and heat treatment, and the printing of business forms.

The highest-profile business in Tomkins line of professional, garden, and leisure products was the U.S.-based Smith & Wesson, the largest producer of handguns in the world. Another U.S. firm, Murray Ohio, manufactured high-quality lawnmowers and bicycles. Also included in this category was the original Tomkins—F.H. Tomkins Buckle Company—which continued to supply a variety of buckles for both the U.K. and foreign markets.

Tomkins' industrial products were largely low-risk technology products such as plastic and fiberglass moldings, doors, windows, wheels, axles, rubber components, coated textiles, control instrumentation, metal pressings, precision turned parts, industrial disc brakes, clutches, and flexible couplings. Lasco Bathware, Philips Products, manufacturer of aluminum doors and windows for recreational vehicles and manufactured housing, Dexter Axle, Northern Rubber, and Premier Screw were among the Tomkins companies in the industrial products line.

The Rank Hovis McDougall Purchase

Rank Hovis McDougall (RHM), a substantial and controversial acquisition of 1992, made and distributed bread and a range of private-label and other brand-name food products for consumers and for catering and food manufacturing markets in the United Kingdom, Europe, and the United States. Among RHM's well-known brand names were Hovis, Mothers Pride, Mr. Kipling and Cadbury's cakes, Bisto, and Paxo.

Tomkins frequently came under fire for its eclectic acquisition strategy, and never more so than in 1992, when the company bought bread maker and distributor Rank Hovis McDougall. Although it was no surprise that the company should make a bid for a large U.K. concern—at the time only 17 percent of its profits were coming from the United Kingdom, an undesirable ratio to Tomkins—this move "from guns to buns," as the city's pundits delighted in terming it, was viewed by financial analysts and stockbrokers as inexplicable, unwise, and potentially disastrous. To diversify so drastically from Tomkins' usual business was considered a risk, but to diversify into the volatile and oversaturated bread market was regarded as foolhardy.

At the time of the purchase, RHM was in second place in the British baking market, holding approximately 33 percent in comparison to the 36 percent controlled by Associated British Foods, with the remaining market share divided among smaller, independent bakeries. Moreover, although consumption of bread had dropped, production had not, leading to ruthless price wars in the market. In 1989, RHM had pulled a profit of £69 million from milling and baking; by 1992 that figure had dwindled to £20 million. Many analysts saw further cause for alarm in that with this acquisition Tomkins charged the cost to its balance sheet rather than following its usual strategy of writing off the cost in the profit-and-loss account. Stock market doubts were fueled by Tomkins' reluctance to discuss the purchase. Although the company's policy was to keep its own council about a new acquisition until its first full year, no news in this case was seen as bad news, and Tomkins' share price dropped. Even The *Financial Times,* a fairly conservative journal, remarked that it was indeed "perplexing" that Tomkins should invest good money into a "seeming quagmire."

Key Dates:

1925: F.H. Tomkins Buckle Company Ltd. is established.
1956: Tomkins begins trading on the London Stock Exchange.
1983: Gregory Hutchings acquires a 22.9 percent stake in the firm.
1984: Hutchings is named CEO of Tomkins; Ferraris Piston Service and Hayters plc are acquired.
1986: The company purchases Pegler-Hattersley.
1987: Tomkins expands into the United States with the purchase of gun manufacturer Smith & Wesson.
1988: Murray Ohio Manufacturing Inc., a lawnmower and bicycle company, is acquired.
1990: The firm expands further, taking control of Philips Industries Inc.
1992: Food manufacturing group Ranks Hovis McDougall plc is purchased amid controversy.
1995: The company takes over ownership of Colorado-based Gates Rubber Company.
1997: Tomkins acquires Stant Manufacturing Inc., producer of windshield wipers marketed under the Trico brand.
1999: The firm begins restructuring efforts, aligning the group into automotive, construction, and industrial divisions.
2000: The firm sells its European food manufacturing and its garden-related businesses; Hutchings resigns his post.
2001: Tomkins sells Smith & Wesson to Saf-T-Hammer Corp.

Undeterred, Tomkins set out to prove the analysts wrong, instituting a £90 million program of restructuring and rationalization. The company cut RHM bakery capacity by ten percent and well over 2,000 jobs, all without diminishing RHM's market share. Tomkins then instituted an ambitious marketing campaign to reinforce an already-high brand recognition for the new subsidiary's bakery and other food items. Over 300 new food products were developed, including specialty items such as sun-dried tomato bread. Responding to fads popular among children at the time, the bakery also began producing "dinosaur bread" in 1993.

When Tomkins finally lifted its veil of secrecy in 1994, it revealed that while the bakery business remained troubled, it had performed very creditably in the food industry as a whole, better, in fact, than had been expected. Moreover, Tomkins as a whole boasted a 50 percent rise in profits. Nevertheless, the damage to Tomkins' reputation through its purchase of RHM purchase seemed to linger. Financial analysts remained skeptical and wary of Tomkins, and, in 1994, the company's share price had not returned to its pre-RHM high.

Continued Expansion

Some analysts attributed this problem to the fact that Tomkins was out of financial fashion. In the mid-1990s, not only was the food industry regarded as unpromising, but the concept of conglomerates was falling out of favor. "We keep on scoring goals,"

remarked Hutchings, "but still end up bottom of the league." According to the *Guardian,* however, such an experience was "nothing new for Mr. Hutchings, who has had difficulty in the past persuading skeptical investors that he knows what he is doing, is capable of doing it and will go on to do even more."

Nevertheless, Tomkins continued to seek new acquisitions, purchasing the Outdoor Products and Dynamark Plastics businesses of the Canadian Noma Industries in 1994. Tomkins intended Outdoor Products, which made and distributed lawnmowers and snowblowers, to enhance Murray Ohio's range of garden equipment as well as to help balance seasonal sales by offering a product used in the winter months. Dynamark Plastics, an injection molder, was integrated into the company's industrial products sector.

Fortified by a strong cash base, the company appeared set to continue its aggressive but selective acquisition policy. Despite faltering share prices and broker confidence, Tomkins entered the mid-1990s with a record of consistently growing profits every year since 1983, even during the worst of the recession. As Hutchings told Kirstie Hamilton: "There is really no difference between food and lawnmowers. It is about innovation, imagination, attacking costs and introducing new products."

Expansion continued in 1995, with the purchase of Gates Rubber Company based in Denver, Colorado. Gates, the leading manufacturer of rubber belts and hoses, was acquired in a $1.16 billion deal that gave Tomkins an even broader reach in the global market. In turn, the Gates family received a 15.7 percent stake in Tomkins. Profits in 1996 rose to $500 million, an increase of seven percent over the previous year. As such, Hutchings continued planning expansion with a keen interest in global growth in regions including India and China.

Changes in Business Operations

In 1997, Tomkins purchased Stant Manufacturing Inc., an automotive component manufacturer whose products included windshield wipers marketed under the Trico brand name. The firm also purchased Golden West Foods Ltd., a supplier to fast food chain McDonald's, to bolster its presence in the food services industry. That year, Tomkins secured substantial operating profits and began to buy back shares—a move that signaled a change in the company's strategy. Hutchings stated in a 1997 *Milling & Baking News* article, "We have to adapt to market conditions. We are in a bull market and it is harder to get a decent pay-back on a large acquisition, and harder to justify carrying a large amount of cash on the balance sheet."

Along with the repurchase efforts, another significant change in Tomkins' business style emerged in 1999. Since the mid-1990s, conglomerate-type businesses as whole had continued to fall out of favor throughout the United Kingdom, and Tomkins finally gave in to industry and shareholder pressure and began to change its operating structure. That year, the firm announced that it was going to streamline operations and focus solely on its core units in the automotive, construction, and industrial industries. As such, plans were set in motion to divest the firm's food businesses and garden-related units.

Tomkins entered the new millennium amidst radical change. In 2000, it sold its non-core units and continued to buy back shares. Hutchings, who had been at the helm of Tomkins for 17 years, resigned in October of that year after board members questioned his financial past with the company. According the *Wall Street Journal*, investors "hoped that Hutchings' resignation would speed up the company's restructuring efforts."

The disposal on non-core assets continued into 2001. The firm sold its Totectors Ltd. unit and put certain assets of its Gates business up for sale. The company also sold its Smith & Wesson business to Saf-T-Hammer Corp. for $15 million. Tomkins tried to buy back the Gates family interest in the firm as well. Board members eyed the family's partial ownership as a potential threat to restructuring efforts. The company's attempts to purchase the shares however, remained fruitless.

While the American economy was faltering, Tomkins' management remained cautiously optimistic about future gains—a large portion of its business was conducted in North American markets. In fact, over 90 percent of sales from its Engineered & Construction Products segment stemmed from operations in that region. Nevertheless, the company continued to strive to position its newly restructured business segments as leaders in their respective industries. Whether or not Tomkins' efforts would pay off in the future, however, remained to be seen.

Principal Subsidiaries

Air System Components (U.S.); Hart & Cooley (U.S.); Lau (U.S.); Penn Ventilation (U.S.); Ruskin (U.S.); Ruskin Air Management Ltd.; Aquatic Industries Inc. (U.S.); Cobra Investments Ltd. (South Africa); Dearborn Mid-West Conveyor Company (U.S.); Dexter Axle (U.S.); Hattersley Newman Hender Ltd.; Lasco Bathware (U.S.); Lasco Composites (U.S.); Lasco Fittings (U.S.); Mayfran America (U.S.); Mayfran Europe (Netherlands); Milliken Valves Company Inc. (U.S.); Pegler Ltd.; Philips Products (U.S.); Sunvic Controls Ltd.; Fedco (U.S.); Gates GmbH (Germany); Gates Argentina SA; Gates Australia Ltd.; Gates do Brasil Industria e Comercio Ltda; Gates Canada; Gates Europe NV (Belgium.); Gates Formed-Fibre Products Inc. (U.S.); Gates India; Gates Korea; Gates Nitta Belt Company Ltd. (China); Gates Polska (Poland); The Gates Rubber Co. (U.S.); Gates Ltd. (Scotland); Gates Vulca SA (Spain); GNAPCO Pte Ltd. (Singapore); Ideal (U.S.); The Northern Rubber Co. Ltd.; Plews/Edelmann (U.S.); Schrader-Bridgeport International Inc. (U.S.); Standard-Thomson Corp. (U.S.); Stant Manufacturing Inc. (U.S.); Trico Ltd.; Unitta Company Ltd. (Japan).

Principal Divisions

Industrial & Automotive Engineering; Air Systems Components; Engineered & Construction Products.

Principal Competitors

Continental AG; Tenneco Automotive Inc.; United Technologies Corp.

Further Reading

"Bank on Hutchings as Heat Stays on RHM," *Sunday Times* (London), May 16, 1993.

Begin, Sherri, "Tomkins Seeks Growth Through System Supply," *European Rubber Journal,* September 2000, p. 9.

Bögler, Daniel, "Tomkins 50pc Surge Fails to Impress City," *Daily Telegraph,* July 12, 1994.

Bose, Mihir, "Mr. Kipling Goes to War," *Director,* October 1993, pp. 44–48.

"Careful Wording Is Not Enough," *Independent,* May 11, 1993.

Dunham, Robin, "Tomkins: Giving Companies a New Lease of Life," *Accountancy,* May 1989, pp. 130, 132.

Gilchrist, Susan, "Tomkins Defies Critics with 50% Profit Rise," *Times* (London), July 12, 1994, p. 25.

Hamilton, Kirstie, "Hutchings' Dough Fails to Rise," *Sunday Times* (London), July 17, 1994.

"Moving up the Ranks," *Times* (London), July 12, 1994, p. 27.

Pangalos, Philip, "RHM Adds Grist to Tomkins Mill," *Times* (London), July 11, 1994.

"Resilient Tomkins," *Financial Times,* January 12, 1993.

"RHM 'Demerged' by Tomkins," *Food Manufacturer,* August 1999, p. 5.

Sanderson, Michael, "Tomkins Rallies as CEO Announces Decision to Quit," *Wall Street Journal,* October 13, 2000, p. 5.

"Skeptical City Chewing over Tomkins Classic Pudding Mix," *Guardian,* January 11, 1994.

Smith, Brad, "British Company Takes Gates," *Denver Business Journal,* February 16, 1996, p. 8C.

"Tomkins—A Snip," *Independent on Sunday,* March 13, 1994.

"Tomkins Buys Rival Lawnmower Maker," *Independent,* March 12, 1994.

"Tomkins Goes to Mow in Canada," *Evening Standard,* March 11, 1994.

"Tomkins Pre-Tax Profits Increase by a Third; Company to Repurchase Shares," *Milling & Baking News,* July 15, 1997, p. 17.

"Tomkins Profits Gain Bolstered by Food and Milling, Baking Rise," *Milling & Baking News,* July 23, 1996, p. 35.

"Tomkins Slow with Strategy," *European Rubber Journal,* July 2001, p. 8.

"Tomkins Steady in Nervous Times," *Daily Telegraph,* September 18, 1993.

"Tomkins to Wield Axe in Ranks Shake-Up," *Daily Telegraph,* May 11, 1993.

"Tomkins Uses Loaf to Tap Dino-Market," *Birmingham Post,* July 7, 1993.

Wagner, Eileen Brill, "Under the Gun," *Business Journal,* June 22, 2001, p. 1.

—Robin DuBlanc
—update: Christina M. Stansell

DEUTSCHLAND
TUI Group GmbH

Karl-Wiechert-Allee 23
D-30625 Hannover
Germany
Telephone: (49) (511) 567-0
Fax: (49) (511) 567-1301
Web site: http://www.tui.com

Private Company
Incorporated: 1968 as Touristik Union International
    GmbH
Employees: 28,242
Sales: $6.54 billion (2000)
NAIC: 56151 Travel Agencies; 481111 Scheduled
    Passenger Air Transportation; 72111 Hotels (Except
    Casino Hotels) and Motels

TUI Group GmbH, based in Germany, is Europe's largest tourism conglomerate. TUI Group unites over 3,600 travel agencies under one umbrella. Mainly located in Germany, the United Kingdom, the Netherlands, and Belgium, 39 tour operators belong to TUI Group, including the major brands TUI Schöne Ferien!, 1-2-FLY, Arke Reizen, Holland International and JMC, as well as many smaller tour operators specializing in narrower target markets. TUI customers often travel with one of TUI Group's airlines, including German Hapag-Lloyd and British JMC, which own over 60 aircraft with about 14,000 passenger seats. Besides its own 18 incoming agencies, TUI Group offers tour guide services in 69 countries. The company controls over 185 hotels in 19 countries, including the RIU, Grecotel, Iberotel, Grupotel, Dorfhotel, ROBINSON, and the Swiss Inn chains. Most of TUI Group's hotels are located in Spain and other Mediterranean countries. With a major focus on holiday travel, TUI Group is also active in the business travel market. On January 1st, 2000 TUI Group became the tourism division of restructured Preussag AG.

Four German Travel Enterprises Form TUI in 1968

On December 1, 1968, four German tour operators signed the shareholder agreement for a new enterprise in Hannover, Germany: Touristik Union International, in short TUI. The companies that formed TUI included Touropa, Scharnow-Reisen, Hummel-Reisen, and Dr. Tigges-Fahrten. The latter was a company with roots reaching back before World War II, founded in 1928 by husband and wife Hubert and Maria Tigges in Wuppertal. Traveling had been a hobby for city college staff teacher Dr. Hubert Tigges. Finally, in 1928, he decided to take a chance and make it a full-time occupation. Tigges invited his brother-in-law Alois Fischer to join the enterprise. At a time of economic depression, holiday trips were out of reach for many and they had to be cheap for people who could afford to go on vacation. Tigges provided buses that were equipped with a mobile kitchen and that carried tents and collapsible boats to holiday destinations.

Because of Germany's cool climate, German travelers early on developed a preference for warm and sunny holiday destinations. Looking for new places, Tigges was the first German tour operator to "discover" the Balearic Island Mallorca, which belonged to Spain, for organized vacations. The island later became Germany's number one holiday destination. However, when Tigges visited the island with a group of Germans in 1934, it was still mostly untouched by tourism. Tigges and Fischer found a domestic collaborator, hotel owner Luis Rui, and the three men soon became close friends. In the 1950s they developed the idea of offering long-term stays in Mallorca's mild climate during the winter months. The idea was an instant success and opened the door in the early 1960s for year-round international tourism on the Balearic Islands. In the mid-1950s, Tigges also started cooperating with the small Spanish travel agency Utramar-Express on Mallorca which had unprecedented service standards in regards to reliability and high organizational flexibility.

Deeply influenced by the misery of the two World Wars, Tigges and Fischer developed a new vision for a tour operator that was rather unusual at the time. Based on the belief that the experience of foreign countries and cultures and meeting people there could foster mutual understanding, Dr. Tigges-Fahrten started offering study-trips that went beyond the typical sightseeing. This too became a huge success. Supported by the high number of loyal customers, study trips became Dr. Tigges's new hallmark.

Company Perspectives:

Quick success is over quickly. *To ensure the long-term successful existence of our company, we pursue long-term objectives. These enable us to maintain a clear focus in an increasingly complex and complicated environment which is changing ever more quickly. We aim to be the leading leisure company in Europe, offering quality-conscious holiday-makers holiday and leisure experiences all from one single source. It is important for our staff to be familiar with the objectives of the company, because they contribute to setting the targets for their own areas of responsibility.*

The other three tour operators that formed TUI in 1968 were founded in the early 1950s of post-war Germany. With the country still in ruins but with signs of an economic upturn on the horizon, the Germans' desire to go somewhere else for their holidays was awakening. In 1948, the Munich-based travel joint venture DER-Gesellschaftsreisen was founded and three years later transformed to Touropa. In 1957, when people traveled between continents on scheduled ferry lines—a rather boring and time-consuming undertaking—Touropa's CEO Dr. Carl Degener came up with the idea to charter a ship exclusively for cruises—just for fun. Moreover, the cruises ran on a weekly schedule, taking the same route: from Venice to Dubrovnik to Corfu to Delphi and, via Rhodes, back to Piraeus and Athens. The advantage for travelers was that they could interrupt their trip at any harbor, maybe take a trip on land or just stay at a certain place for a week at the beach, and then continue their trip on the next cruise ship.

In 1953, the year when Dr. Tigges offered flights to Mallorca for the first time, two travel operators were founded in Hannover: One was Hummel Reisen which originated from a side business of publisher Axel Springer Verlag in Hamburg and Jochen Stickrodt's Hannover-based travel agency Stickrodt, the other Scharnow-Reisen founded by Willy Scharnow. Three years later the two companies formed a joint venture to be able to carry the higher cost and financial risks of the upcoming air travel. In 1957, Scharnow and Hummel joined forces with Touropa and offered Germany's first air travel catalogue under the label Deutsche Flugtouristik. When Germany's economy picked up speed rapidly in the second half of the 1960s, a strong demand for a broad variety of affordable travel packages developed. Degener and Scharnow recognized that only a larger company with sufficient financial and organizational resources would be able to offer just that on a large scale. In 1966, Touropa and Scharnow-Reisen swapped parts of their shares. One year later, Hummel Reisen joined the group, and Dr. Tigges Reisen followed soon after. In 1968, the year of TUI's founding, the first sales office opened in Berlin. Touropa Austria was established in the same year. By 1969, the number of TUI customers exceeded one million.

New Partners and New Services Spur Growth in the 1970s and 1980s

In 1970, another company joined TUI: airtours international, Germany's biggest tour operator that offered customized air travel with scheduled carriers for educated upscale holiday vaca-
tioners to first class and deluxe hotels around the world. Founded in 1967, airtours served about 140,000 customers in 1970. To be able to deliver adequate service to its well-to-do clientele, the company invested in the travel agencies that carried their catalogue by sending a thousand travel agents a year on "educational trips." In 1971, another big player in the tourism market, TransEuropa-Reisen, was founded as a joint venture between German department store giant Karstadt and the country's largest mail order company Quelle. A year later TransEuropa became part of TUI—for a share in the dynamically growing group. In 1974, TUI's sales reached DM one billion for the first time. In the same year the tour operators that constituted TUI, including Scharnow, Hummel, Dr. Tigges, Touropa and TransEuropa, were transformed into TUI subsidiaries. In 1976, Karstadt gave up its TUI shareholdings so that their planned acquisition of another leading German tour operator, NUR Touristik with its flagship brand Neckermann Reisen, would be approved by the cartel authorities. Department store company Horten AG took over Karstadt's TUI shares in 1977. Beginning in 1979, the headquarters of all TUI subsidiaries were moved to Hannover. Three years later all of the company's divisions, with about 1,000 employees altogether, moved into a brand-new office building on Karl-Wiechert-Allee.

In the 1970s and early 1980s, TUI invested in a number of travel agencies and hotels. The company acquired shares in tour ship operator seetours international: the travel agencies Dr. Degener Reisen in Salzburg; Pollmann's Tours and Safaris Ltd. in Kenya, Africa; and Ultramar Express S.A. in Spain. On the hotel side, Spanish hotel chains Iberotel and RIU became part of the TUI group in the 1970s. TUI also founded their own hotel ventures. In 1971, the company created Robinson Hotel GmbH & Co. KG together with Steigenberger Hotelgesellschaft, a chain of "club hotels." The first Robinson Club was established in the same year on Fuerteventura Island, Spain. In 1981, TUI established the new hotel chain Grecotel with partners in Greece.

In the first two decades after its founding, TUI put a high emphasis on creating a broad portfolio of high-quality services. In 1970, the company created its travel service division TUI Service. Instead of relying on outside vendors, TUI Service staff welcomed their guests at their holiday destinations, gave them tips on how to make the most out of their vacation, helped organize special trips, and took care of problems with other service providers such as hotels. The variety of services offered by the tour operators that comprised TUI were also greatly expanded. The broad spectrum of packaged and individual trips by air, train, car or ship were complemented by new holiday formats ranging from club holidays and stays at country farms to special trips to nude beaches for sunbathers, tennis and sport centers for fitness freaks, and the special youth travel program "twen-tours." In 1971, TUI together with German airline Lufthansa and the government-owned rail company Bundesbahn founded Studiengesellschaft zur Automatisierung für Reise und Touristik, in short START, a joint venture to develop an electronic booking system—a revolutionary idea for the time. By 1979, START GmbH, in which all three shareholders had equal shares, had a working system. In the same year the first TUI trip was booked through a computer, setting off a new age in Europe's travel industry. By 1993, about 90 percent of TUI's bookings, representing approximately 22 million trips, were booked electronically through the START booking system.

Key Dates:

1968: Four German travel enterprises form Touristik Union International (TUI).
1970: German tour operator airtours international becomes part of TUI.
1972: The company expands into Spain by acquiring hotel chain Iberotel.
1981: TUI establishes the new hotel chain Grecotel with partners in Greece.
1989: Franchise system TUI UrlaubCenter is initiated.
1990: TUI holding integrates its tour operators.
1995–96: TUI expands into the Netherlands, Belgium, Austria, and Switzerland.
1998: The company is taken over by the German Preussag Group.
2000: TUI becomes Preussag's tourism brand.

In 1981, TUI took over the marketing for cruise ship *MS Astor*, which a year later became the setting for *Traumschiff*, a popular German TV soap. Cuba became a new TUI holiday destination. In the late 1980s, TUI intensified its activities again when the travel market became more competitive. TUI invested in Dutch tour operator ARKE and Bremen-based Wolters-Reisen and founded tour operator *take off*. Turkey and the Dominican Republic became two major destinations for the company. In 1988, TUI rehashed its corporate design and launched its first national advertising campaign. In cooperation with Bundesbahn TUI introduced the *Autoreisezug*, a train that carried the tourists' own cars to their holiday destination. To raise customer loyalty, TUI issued a card that earned return customers various benefits including discounts and special offers. In 1989, the company launched its own franchise system TUI UrlaubCenter.

Restructuring in 1990 and 1997

By 1990, TUI had grown significantly. In fact, the company had become Europe's largest tour operator. Losses resulting from the Gulf War and violent conflict in Yugoslavia were balanced out by gains from the about 16 million new customers from the reunited eastern part of Germany. Serving more than 3 million guests in business year 1990–91, the company had generated over DM 5 billion in sales. In order to stay on top of things, TUI enacted its first restructuring program. All tour operators were integrated into the TUI holding company, all of which carried the TUI brand in their names, and separate profit centers were established. The offers of the different tour operators were organized and marketed by country under the TUI brand. In 1991, a new three-step distribution concept was introduced: TUI Reisebüro served customers directly through; TUI UrlaubCenter marketed TUI products through their franchise partners; and TUI Profi-Partner served independent travel agencies. The company's next goal was vertical expansion into the hotel and incoming agency business on an international level. Between 1990 and 1993, TUI acquired shares in incoming agencies—travel agencies that served tourists at their holiday destination—in Morocco, Portugal, and Tanzania, Africa. In 1993, TUI together with hotel chain RUI founded a hotel operating company for Spain. In 1995 and 1996, TUI expanded into the Netherlands, Belgium, Austria, and Switzerland, where it founded new subsidiaries.

In 1997, TUI again restructured its organization to make its management more efficient. The company was divided into five business divisions. The first one included tour operators in Central Europe; the second one united tour operators in Western Europe; the third one managed the incoming agencies and guest services and purchasing of hotel capacities at the travel destinations. The new IT division offered central services such as accounting, personnel management, and legal services to all other TUI divisions. The fifth division bundled TUI's own hotel subsidiaries and shareholdings, which numbered more than 120 and which were a main focus of the company's growth strategy. The latter were streamlined in the following years. The Spanish hotel chain Iberotel which had been in financial trouble in 1990 was integrated into the RIU group, which in the meantime had grown to Spain's second largest hotel chain. In Switzerland TUI founded a joint venture together with Swiss tourism groups Imholz and the Charles-Voegele Group. Imholz TUI Voegele (ITV) became Switzerland's second biggest travel company.

The Consolidating Travel Market of the 1990s

In the 1990s, processes of concentration in the German travel industry intensified. Dropping prices drove many smaller, specialized, and even mid-sized companies to the edge of bankruptcy or out of business completely, while the big players were arm wrestling and trying to stay ahead of the crowd. In 1993, the company's 25th anniversary year, a battle for influence over TUI erupted. TUI's shareholders included travel agencies Deutsches Reisebüro GmbH (DER) and Amtliches Bayerisches Reisebüro GmbH (abr), which by then were both owned by Deutsche Bundesbahn; Hapag Lloyd Reisebüro GmbH, owned by airline and logistics company Hapag Lloyd; a holding company that held the shares of mail order firm Quelle and department store chain Horten AG; publisher Axel Springer Verlag; and Walter Kahn Verwaltungs-GmbH & Co. Beteiligungs-KG, a holding company that bundled the interests of 16 smaller TUI shareholders, mainly travel agencies. The Kahn group owned about 30 percent of TUI, Quelle—which was owned by the Schickedanz group—and Horten owned 25 percent, Bundesbahn held a little over 23 percent, Hapag Lloyd owned over 11 percent, and the Springer group another ten percent. When the Kahn shareholders offered to sell their share in 1992, they received a very lucrative offer from Westdeutsche Landesbank, WestLB for short, a large bank that had started to form a tourism concern of considerable size—on behalf of someone else, according to many speculators. Through its own Horten and Hapag Lloyd shareholdings, the bank was connected indirectly with TUI. WestLB also owned part of the LTU group, another big player in Germany's travel market including a holiday charter airline and some major tour operators. The airline, however, had invested too heavily in its fleet of aircraft. Consequently, it had a hard time filling its seats and was craving business.

However, the other TUI shareholders were not so happy with WestLB's plans—they had plans of their own. Schickedanz was planning to make the travel business a second strong business division and to cash in on synergy effects by selling trips through its mail order catalogues. Hapag Lloyd's airline had a major chunk of TUI's flight business and wasn't interested in sharing it with LTU. Bundesbahn hadn't developed any particular concept of its own, but was not interested in letting any more investors in. Besides TUI's old shareholders, two other groups showed a lively interest in more influence over the company: Deutsche Lufthansa and the wholesale and retail giant Metro Group. Lufthansa's subsidiary, charter airline Condor, had the biggest part of TUI's flights and the airline was seeking to secure this business by gaining more influence. The company was planning to raise its 15.5 percent shareholding in Hapag Lloyd by the ten percent share that TUI held. Metro subsidiary Kaufhof, another department store chain, owned shares in two of the country's biggest tour operators, NUR-Touristik and International Tourist Länderreisedienste (ITS), and a minority share in Hapag Lloyd. Kaufhof was also expressing interest in TUI.

When it became clear that WestLB wouldn't have an easy time of it, the bank tried to get in through the back door. In October 1992, a consortium lead by WestLB bought a majority share in Kahn KG. Four months later, Springer Verlag announced it would sell their TUI share to Kahn KG. In the meantime, Horten asked for its voting rights back from Schickedanz to which they had been transferred due to a ruling by the German cartel authorities. With Kahn KG's 40.2 percent and—theoretically—Horten's 12.5 percent, WestLB would have dominated TUI. The other TUI shareholders in turn wanted to exclude Kahn KG from the circle of TUI owners since it had not offered its shares for sale to them first, as required by the company's bylaws. Kahn KG countered by blocking the sale of TUI's ten-percent share in Hapag Lloyd AG to German airline Lufthansa, a deal which the other TUI shareholders had agreed on without Kahn KG. Finally, in October 1993, the dirtiest battle over the power over Germany's largest travel group was completed when the parties involved agreed to a new distribution of the company's shares, while TUI's top management struggled to stay competitive by cutting cost. According to the agreement, WestLB-owned LTU group and Hapag Lloyd held 30 percent each, while Schickedanz-owned Quelle and Deutsche Bundesbahn owned 20 percent each. Horten AG and Kahn KG were no longer TUI shareholders. The nasty battle had a positive side effect for TUI—its brand name recognition jumped suddenly as a result.

In 1997, Karstadt—which meanwhile was partly owned by the Schickedanz group—started talking with Lufthansa about a liaison between the department store's tourism arm NUR Touristic, Germany's number two tour operator, and the airline's charter subsidiary Condor. Lufthansa's Condor had gradually lost more and more of TUI's flight business to LTU and other providers and the two companies were trying to form a new big tour operator that would be able to compete with market leader TUI. It was in that year when German industrial conglomerate Preussag AG, one-third of which was owned by WestLB, announced that it would take over TUI shareholder Hapag Lloyd. In the same year, WestLB transferred the voting rights for its 30 percent share in TUI to Preussag which Preussag passed on to Hapag Lloyd. With the other 30 percent owned by Hapag Lloyd, Preussag had a controlling interest in TUI and announced that tourism would become its number one business. The deal went through after WestLB signed an agreement with the German cartel authorities to sell its interest in LTU. In early 1998, the Schickedanz group, which had formed C&N Condor Neckermann Touristik AG with Lufthansa, sold its TUI share to Hapag Lloyd. The remaining TUI shareholder Deutsche Bahn, however,

did not sell its shares as many insiders had expected. The company took advantage of its stock option and acquired an additional 12.5 percent. After the deal, Hapag Lloyd held a 75 percent majority share while Deutsche Bahn owned 25 percent. In 1999, Preussag acquired Deutsche Bahn's TUI share. One year later, the TUI shareholdings were taken out of the temporary Hapag Lloyd holding company and Preussag formed a new holding, TUI Group GmbH, while TUI became Preussag's new tourism brand.

Principal Subsidiaries

TUI Deutschland GmbH; TUI Beteiligungsgesellschaft mbH; Hapag-Lloyd Fluggesellschaft mbH; TUI Leisure Travel GmbH; TUI interactive GmbH; TUI 4 U GmbH; TUI Austria GmbH; TUI Suisse Ltd; TUI Polska Sp.z.o.o.; Travel Unie International Nederland N.V. (Netherlands; 91%); Hapag-Lloyd Fluggesellschaft mbH; TUI Hellas AE (Greece); TUI Service AG (Switzerland; 85%); TUI International AG (Switzerland; 85%); L'TUR Tourismus AG (51%); airtours international GmbH; TUI Business Travel GmbH.

Principal Competitors

LTU Group Holding GmbH; Thomas Cook AG; REWE Tourism Group; alltours flugreisen GmbH.

Further Reading

"Bahn-Fahrt verlangsamt sich," *Süddeutsche Zeitung*, May 15, 1998.

Berninger, Heiner, "Der Streit bei der TUI verschaerft sich weiter," *Süddeutsche Zeitung*, May 21, 1993.

——, "Die TUI steht vor einer Reise ins Ungewisse," *Süddeutsche Zeitung*, June 27, 1992.

"Die C & N Touristic soll ein Gegengewicht zu TUI und LTU bilden," *Frankfurter Allgemeine Zeitung*, August 22, 1997, p. 16.

"Die grossen Altgesellschafter der TUI wollen die WestLB ausschliessen," *Frankfurter Allgemeine Zeitung*, March 1, 1993, p. 15.

"Die Springer-Gruppe verkauft ihre Anteile an der TUI," *Frankfurter Allgemeine Zeitung*, February 9, 1993, p. 14.

"Die TUI bleibt das Objekt der Begierde," *Frankfurter Allgemeine Zeitung*, October 20, 1993, p. 24.

"Grünes Licht für kleineres rotes Reise-Lager," *Süddeutsche Zeitung*, March 3, 1998.

"Hapag-Lloyd bald mit Mehrheit an TUI," *Frankfurter Allgemeine Zeitung*, June 10, 1998, p. 21.

"Imholz spannt mit Voegele und TUI zusammen," *Neue Zuercher Zeitung*, October 3, 1997, p. 21.

Needham, Paul, "Preussag to Rebrand All Groups Under TUI," *Travel Trade Gazette UK & Ireland*, December 20, 1999, p. 7.

"Neue Organisation für Touristik Union," *Frankfurter Allgemeine Zeitung*, May 21, 1997, p. 21.

"Schickedanz verkauft TUI-Paket an Hapag Lloyd/Preussag," *Frankfurter Allgemeine Zeitung*, March 5, 1998, p. 23.

"TUI-Gesellschafterstreit beigelegt," *Süddeutsche Zeitung*, October 11, 1993.

"TUI saust der Konkurrenz davon," *Süddeutsche Zeitung*, March 27, 1997.

"TUI verbucht einen Rekordumsatz," *Süddeutsche Zeitung*, October 31, 1991.

25 Jahre Schöne Ferien!—Zitat Sachen, Hannover, Germany: Touristik Union International, 1993, 52 p.

Weisshaar, Karen, "TUI strukturiert Hotelportfolio um," *HORIZONT*, September 3, 1998, p. 18.

—Evelyn Hauser

IDEEN FÜR WÄRME

Vaillant GmbH

Berghauser Strasse 40
D-42859 Remscheid
Germany
Telephone: (49) (2991) 18-0
Fax: (49) (2991) 18-2810
Web site: http://www.vaillant.de

Private Company
Incorporated: 1874 as Meisterbetrieb des
    Installationshandwerks von Johann Vaillant
Employees: 5,605
Sales: EUR 855 million ($723.7 million) (2000)
NAIC: 333414 Heating Equipment (Except Warm Air
    Furnaces) Manufacturing; 333415 Air-Conditioning
    and Warm Air Heating Equipment and Commercial
    and Industrial Refrigeration Equipment Manufacturing

Vaillant GmbH is one of Europe's leading manufacturers of heating systems and is based in Remscheid, Germany. The company's flagship products are its wall-hung gas-powered boilers and heaters. Vaillant also makes floor-standing gas-powered boilers and furnaces, combined electricity- or gas-powered water heaters, electric heaters, solar collectors, and aluminum die castings for the auto industry. Wall-hung boilers account for about 60 percent of Vaillant's total sales, floor-standing boilers and furnaces contribute about 13 percent, and electric heating appliances roughly 15 percent. The company maintains production facilities in Germany, Italy, Spain, and the United Kingdom, and sales offices throughout Europe. The acquisition of British competitor Hepburn in 2001 added production sites in France, the United Kingdom, Slovakia, and the Netherlands, and the brands Saunier Duval, Glow-worm, AWB, and Protherm to the Vaillant group.

A Patent and a Logo in the 19th Century

Company founder Johann Vaillant was born in 1851, the tenth child of tailor Franz Theodor Vaillant and his wife Maria, a family with French roots which had moved to the German town of Kaiserswerth in the 18th century. Twenty-three years later the young man moved to Remscheid, near Cologne, and announced in the local newspaper that he had set up shop as a coppersmith and pump maker. At that time, taking a bath was not as common as it later became. Rather, it was considered a luxury for many, and a major undertaking for people who could not afford it. To bathe a family, many pounds of coal had to be carried into the house to heat the necessary amount of water on the kitchen stove. Even for the well-to-do bathing was somewhat troublesome. In the gas-powered "open system" water heaters common at the time, the process gas from burning the fuel dissolved into the bathing water and the water temperature was impossible to control. Johann Vaillant, who made it his principle to maintain close contact with his customers to find out what they really needed, saw a huge business opportunity, and over time developed a completely new kind of gas-powered water heater. In Vaillant's "closed system" water heater, the fuel-burning process was separated from the water tank, in which the water was heated indirectly. This innovation not only made the process more secure and hygienic, it also made it possible to control the water temperature. In 1894, the German *Patentamt* awarded Vaillant a patent for his invention, and his business took off rapidly. By 1897, due the ever-rising demand, increasingly from abroad, production had to be moved from the small workshop to a bigger facility in Remscheid. Vaillant had grown from a craftsman's workshop into an industrial enterprise.

Far ahead of many businesses of his time, Johann Vaillant also had the vision to turn his water heaters into brand name products. For a while the company founder had been looking for a symbol he could use as a trademark. Occasionally he had used an angel, which did not seem to be very original and could not be trademarked. However, one morning around Easter, Vaillant was browsing the monthly Catholic magazine *Alte und neue Welt,* meaning "old and new world," when an illustration caught his eye: an Easter bunny crawling out of an egg that had just broken open. For some reason, the image seemed to be what Vaillant had been looking for. He acquired the rights to the picture from the artist and secured it as a trademark in 1899. Slightly modified in the Jugendstil design style of the time, the Easter bunny soon became the company's easily recognizable logo.

Making Bathing a Luxury for the Masses in the Early 20th Century

At the beginning of the 20th century, apartments very rarely had a separate bathroom and were rather small altogether. Vaillant recognized the demand for an appliance that would take up as little space as possible. He came up with the idea to hang a hot water heater on the wall where it wouldn't take up as much space as the floor-standing models that were common a the time. In 1905, Vaillant introduced the first wall-hung gas water heater to the German market. The new appliance was named ''Geyser'' to evoke the association with the hot springs pouring out of the earth in Iceland. The name was secured as a brand name and became very popular among customers and plumbers, one of the company's main target markets.

Vaillant's annual production at the new factory in Remscheid's Berghauser Strasse reached 10,000 water heaters in 1914. However, preparations to celebrate the company's 40th anniversary were interrupted by the outbreak of World War I. Johann Vaillant's two sons Franz and Max were called to serve in the German army and the government administered what had to be produced for the war economy. A year after the war had ended, in 1920, company founder Johann Vaillant passed away at the age of 68. Karl and Franz Vaillant who had entered the business in 1907 took over after their father's death. Four years later Vaillant engineers developed the company's first gas-powered furnace. The mid-1920s brought about a temporary economic upswing and sales tripled in comparison with 1914. Construction of residential buildings was thriving, taking a bath was becoming a more common pleasure, and Vaillant's ''Volksgeyser''—the people's geyser—was immensely popular. However, in a sudden economic downturn after the ''Black Friday'' stock market crash in New York in 1929, the company's sales dropped by two-thirds in just three years and production was cut in half. It took until the mid-1930s for Vaillant to recover. However, only four years later World War II started. Vaillant was not so much in demand for the war production and it became more and more difficult to organize the necessary raw materials and supplies. Because of these conditions the company moved its operations to the Netherlands. During bombings of Remscheid in 1943, the company's factory was severely damaged and production was ceased.

In these turbulent times Vaillant's marketing underwent many changes as well. The company's first slogan was: ''Warm bath water for everybody.'' Besides its logo the company's most often used images were children and the elegant, busy housewife. The title page of a brochure from 1902 showed a nicely dressed maid giving a shower to four children in a bath tub with water provided from a Vaillant hot water heater in an upscale bathroom. A poster from 1905 showed a horse coach pulling a Vaillant water heater and children following behind, taking a shower under warm water while spectators from different continents and countries watched and applauded from the sides. After the World War I, the company started using the slogan ''Platz ist in der kleinsten Hütte''—there is room in the smallest house—to promote its ''Volksgeyser'' model. In the 1920s, German culture became more tolerant and in 1926 for the first time, a naked female holding a towel up to her hips was portrayed in an ad—of course with her back turned to the viewer. In 1929, the company hired an advertising director for the first time, who synchronized corporate and product design, and the Easter Bunny logo became more stylized. After the Nazis took over political power, there was no place for erotic images anymore. The company began using truck-like automobiles for advertising and promotional tours from house to house, demonstrating different models and offering long term financing. In order to raise customer's sympathy for Vaillant, the company's logo came to life for the first time in 1935 in a comic brochure. In a story called ''Eine königliche Hasengeschichte''—a royal bunny story—the Easter Bunny left his egg and started a trip around the world, convincing everybody he encountered of the advantages of a hot bath.

Post-War Boom Begins in the 1950s

After the end of the Second World War, Vaillant rebuilt its Remscheid factory which had been severely damaged. In May 1947, the factory started up regular operations again. For its first big order after the war, Vaillant manufactured 85,000 ''Kanonenofen'' furnaces. Hans Vaillant, the founder's grandson, led the company through the post-war period and the economic boom years that followed. His son-in-law Franz Wilhelm and nephew Karl-Ernst Vaillant took over in fourth generation. Until the end of the 1980s, the company was led by members of the Vaillant family. In the 1990s the about 40 remaining shareholders form the Vaillant family retreated from operating the business.

In the postwar period, Vaillant focused on product innovation and international expansion. In 1960, the company started making ''Geyser'' water heaters powered by electricity. One year later the company introduced a novelty in the heating market: the wall-hung furnace ''Circo-Geyser.'' Another innovation followed in 1967 when the company launched the ''Combi-Geyser,'' the first heating appliance that could be used both for heating a room and heating water. At the end of the 1960s, the era of Vaillant's comic-bunny began. Dressed in a checked shirt and coveralls, the bunny became synonymous with the friendly and competent handyman who installed Vaillant appliances. In the 1970s the company ventured into sport sponsoring and sponsored German Porsche driver Bob Wollek. ''Always a bunny length ahead'' became the new company slogan.

Before World War II the company exported about ten to 20 percent of its annual output. Hans Vaillant put forward an

Key Dates:

1874: Johann Vaillant sets up his own plumbing business.
1894: The company founder receives a patent for his ''closed-system'' water heater.
1899: The Easter Bunny becomes the company's logo.
1905: The wall-hung gas water heater ''Geyser'' is launched.
1960: The first electric ''Geyser'' model is produced.
1967: A combined appliance for heating air and water is launched.
1970s: Vaillant intensifies international expansion.
1991: The environmentally friendly Vaillant ''Thermoblock'' is introduced.
1997: Vaillant starts making solar collectors.
1999: The company wins the German Quality Award.
2000: The boiler business of Italian manufacturer Bongioanni Pensotti Kalore is acquired.
2001: Vaillant takes over British Hepworth plc.

unprecedented international expansion program starting in the 1970s. Within the next decade, foreign subsidiaries were established in Western Europe including the Netherlands, Austria, Belgium, France, Italy, and the United Kingdom. The economic boom in Germany and the company's international expansion made new production facilities necessary. A new factory for electric water heaters was set up in 1962, and another production facility for foundry and other metal products. In 1981, a production plant for making directly and indirectly heated gas-powered hot water tanks was set up in Bergheim. Two years later a new facility for manufacturing gas- and oil-powered furnaces was build in Hilden. Finally, a new plant was established in Gelsenkirchen for making gas-powered heating appliances. By the mid-1970s the number of Vaillant employees reached about 3,000 and more than doubled in the following two decades. At the onset of the 1990s the company had six production facilities in Germany and 15 foreign subsidiaries.

Focus on Productivity, Quality, and Innovation in the 1990s

Vaillant enjoyed almost continuous dynamic growth until the 1990s. Since the middle of the 1970s sales had grown more than sevenfold, reaching a high of almost DM two billion in 1992. While the rest of Western Europe suffered from a sluggish economy, West Germany's businesses got a huge boost from the reunification with East Germany in 1990. However, stagnation set in after 1992 when the East German households that could afford it had been equipped with new heating appliances. On top of that, the market for heating equipment was swamped by a wave of new competitors pushing into the market. The number of companies competing in the German market for wall-hung heating appliances exploded from just six in 1990 to 50 nine years later. Prices fell significantly, by an estimated 20 percent through the 1990s, and so did Vaillant's profits, since the company had lost most of its technological edge. The strength of the German Deutschmark turned out to be another disadvantage for Vaillant's export business. The fact that newly-built houses were more energy efficient and hence didn't

need to be heated as much anymore was another factor. The only way to stay in the game was to significantly raise productivity levels and to regain the technological cutting edge the company had lost.

To counteract the downward trend of the 1990s, Vaillant started cutting cost by moving part of its production abroad. The manufacture of gas-powered water heaters was moved from Gelsenkirchen to Spain, Europe's largest market for the product, where a joint venture was set up with Spanish competitor Fagor. In 1995, the company streamlined its operations into six decentralized business units working on three major processes, including the innovation, production, and marketing process, staffed with interdisciplinary teams. In addition, Vaillant's top management initiated a comprehensive program of quality management and invested in new product development. Under the ''Vaillant Excellence'' program, assembly lines were replaced by Japanese decentralized production methods. Workers almost completely assembled the product they were responsible for. Every employee agreed on certain goals which were directly connected with their paycheck. In addition, every employee underwent a customized education program, while managers had to select and mentor two potential successors for their position. The rigorous focus on high quality finally paid off. Production cost were cut by 25 percent, reclamation rates went down and development time for new products was cut in half. In 1999, the company won the German Quality Award. The environmentally friendly Vaillant ''Thermoblock,'' a combined furnace and water heater, was introduced in 1991. In 1997, the company started making solar collectors. Vaillant's next cutting edge development project was the fuel-cell heater. First developed as an energy source for space travel, fuel cell technology seemed a promising alternative to burning coal and oil in the late 1990s. In 1997, Korean female executive Seonhi Ro joined the company as project manager for Vaillant's ''fuel-cell heater'' project. Vaillant's vision for its fuel-cell based appliance was to provide not only heat and hot water, but also electricity to residential households with a high energy efficiency and almost no environmental pollution. The company exhibited a prototype of a Fuel Cell Heating Appliance—jointly developed with Latham, New York-based Plug Power, Inc.—in spring 2001 at the International Sanitary and Heating Fair in Germany and was planning to launch its first fuel-cell based product for one- and multiple-family dwellings at the end of the same year.

By the end of the 1990s, the Vaillant group maintained six production facilities and employed about 5,600 people, about one-fifth of whom worked outside Germany. There was no sign that the saturated western European market would pick up speed soon. The only way to grow and stay competitive in an increasingly consolidating market was through acquisitions. Following the company's strategic goal to become the market leader in the major European countries, Vaillant acquired the water heater business of Italian manufacturer Bongioanni Pensotti Kalore in 2000. One year later, the company acquired the majority of leading British competitor Hepworth plc in a friendly takeover. Although faced with a big financial challenge—the deal exceeded Vaillant's own capital by roughly DM 1 billion—the company's top management was confident that in the mid-term this major strategic step would prove to be a success. The two companies of about equal size complemented each other well in their market positions. Vaillant had a strong grasp on the German, Austrian, and Danish markets while Hepburn had strong market positions in France, Spain, and Slovakia. Both of the partners were also well positioned in the Netherlands, Belgium, the Czech Republic and Turkey. With eleven production sites and two joint ventures, including locations in France, the United Kingdom, Italy, Slovakia, the Netherlands, and Spain, and Vaillant's five factories in Germany, the new Vaillant group employed about 11,000 people and generated an estimated EUR 1.8 billion in sales. Hepburn also added new brands to the group's product portfolio, including Saunier Duval, Glowworm, AWB, and Protherm, in addition to the newly acquired Italian brands Bongioanni and Pensotti. Vaillant expected to complete the major steps to integrate Hepburn into the group by the end of 2002 and to cash in on cost synergies in purchasing, procurement, logistics, and research and development as well as through better economies of scale. Vaillant's top management was hoping to be among the winners of the ongoing consolidation process in the European heating technology market which was expected to reduce the number of producers of wall-hung gas-powered heaters from 116 to a mere handful. Whether the company's financial strength would be sufficient to further pursue its acquisition strategy without going public was undisputed by the company's 42 shareholders, all of them relatives of the company founder. However, that remained to be seen.

Principal Subsidiaries

Hepworth plc (U.K.); Bongioanni Pensotti Kalore (Italy); Vaillant Werkzeugbau GmbH (Germany); VAICON Vaillant Consulting GmbH (Germany); Vaillant Ges.m.b.H. (Austria); Vaillant N.V. (Belgium); Joh. Vaillant GmbH u. Co. (Croatia); Vaillant spol. S.r.o. (Czech Republic); Vaillant A/S (Denmark); Vaillant S.A.R.L. (France); Vaillant Hungária Kft. (Hungary); Vaillant S.p.A. (Italy); Vaillant B.V. (Netherlands); Vaillant Sp. z.o.o. (Poland); Vaillant S.L. (Spain); Vaillant GmbH (Switzerland); Vaillant Ltd. (U.K.).

Principal Competitors

Baxi Partnership Ltd., Buderus AG; Viessmann Werke GmbH & Co.

Further Reading

''Auch die Vaillant-Brennstoffzelle wird der Osterhase vermarkten,'' *Frankfurter Allgemeine Zeitung*, March 23, 1999, p. 24.

''Das Unternehmergespräch,'' *Frankfurter Allgemeine Zeitung*, September 21, 1998, p. 24.

''Das Unternehmergespräch,'' *Frankfurter Allgemeine Zeitung*, March 26, 2001, p. 22.

''Die Vaillant Erfolgsstory,'' *Wir beim Vaillant*, October 1999, p. 10.

Eckhard, Martin, ''Vaillant setzt auf Brennstoffzellen-Technik,'' *Die Welt,* March 15, 1999.

''Ein markanter Osterhase,'' *Wir beim Vaillant*, April 1999, p. 10.

''Home Heater Debuts in Germany,'' *Fuel Cell Technology News*, April 2001.

''Processor News: Germany's Vaillant Set to Buy Hepworth,'' *Plastics News,* February 5, 2001. p. 9.

''Vaillant gelingt leichtes Umsatzplus,'' *Frankfurter Allgemeine Zeitung*, May 12, 2001, p. 17.

''Vaillant tritt Entschädigungsfonds bei,'' *AFX—TD,* December 22, 1999.

''Vaillant verlegt Produktion nach Spanien,'' *Frankfurter Allgemeine Zeitung*, September 20, 1996, p. 30.

''Vom ersten Katalog zum emotionalen Commercial,'' *Wir beim Vaillant,* June 1999, p. 8.

Warenweiler, R., ''Quantensprung der Vaillant,'' *Neue Zuercher Zeitung,* May 12, 2001, p. 27.

Weber, Stefan, ''Mit Hilfe des Hasen heizt Vaillant gehörig ein,'' *Süddeutsche Zeitung,* April 6, 1999, p. 28.

—Evelyn Hauser

Vicon Industries, Inc.

89 Arkay Drive
Hauppauge, New York 11788
U.S.A.
Telephone: (631) 952-2288
Toll Free: (800) 645-9116
Fax: (631) 951-2288
Web site: http://www.vicon-cctv.com

Public Company
Incorporated: 1967
Employees: 261
Sales: $74.62 million (2000)
Stock Exchanges: American
Ticker Symbol: VII
NAIC: 33429 Other Communications Equipment
Manufacturing

Vicon Industries, Inc. designs, manufactures, assembles and markets a wide range of video systems and system components used for security, surveillance, safety, and control purposes. Its 700 or so products consist of various elements of a video system, including remote robotic cameras, monitors, recorders, digital video and signal processing units, and motorized zoom lenses. These software-based video systems are typically used for crime deterrence, visual documentation, observation of inaccessible or hazardous areas, enhancing safety, managing personal liability, obtaining cost savings such as lower insurance premiums, managing control systems, and improving the efficiency and effectiveness of personnel. Prices range up to about $100,000 for a large digital control and video matrix switching system. Among the users of Vicon's products are office buildings, manufacturing plants, apartment complexes, retail stores, government facilities, transportation operations, prisons, casinos, sports arenas, healthcare facilities, and financial institutions.

Becoming the Leader in CCTV Accessories: 1967–80

Vicon Industries was started in 1967 by Donald M. Horn, an engineer, in a Long Island garage. It went public two years later

and in fiscal 1971 (the year ended September 30, 1971) was assembling and marketing a group of products related to the surveillance and security industry in connection with the use of closed-circuit television apparatus. These products, manufactured in Farmingdale, Long Island, consisted of securing cameras, silent-panning and remote-control devices, modular video switching units, and the housing and coupling components for same. About 40 percent of sales and profits were under the Vicon name and the remainder under the private labels of other companies. Sales rose from $209,553 in fiscal 1969 to $894,436 in fiscal 1971, when the company turned a profit of $6,523. Sales rose to $1.2 million in fiscal 1972 and $2.15 million in fiscal 1973, when net earnings reached $224,554.

One of Vicon Industries' customers at this time was the city of Philadelphia, which had purchased a system permitting two-way voice and video communication between widely separated offices throughout the city. Vicon's toll-collection surveillance system was in use on two New York City bridges. A street surveillance system in the city's Times Square received nationwide publicity and led to the installation of such a system on the boardwalk in Atlantic City, New Jersey.

Vicon Industries was the largest company in the closed-circuit television (CCTV) accessories market by 1980, when it held about 30 percent of this market, whose value was estimated at $50 million to $60 million (wholesale) per year. The company at this time was making and selling all the items needed to assemble a complete system except for the cameras, monitors, and videotape equipment. Its customers were the manufacturers and/or dealers and distributors of complete systems, who in turn sold to the end user. Sales to dealers and distributors were made under the Vicon name and to more than 40 original-equipment manufacturers on a private-label basis. Its most important private-label customer was RCA Corp.—the largest producer of complete closed-circuit television systems—which accounted for an estimated 24 percent of Vicon's sales in fiscal 1980. The company's net sales had increased each year since fiscal 1971, reaching $13.78 million in 1979. Net income also grew each year in this period, increasing reaching $736,000 in 1979. Vicon raised about $4 million by selling 400,000 shares of common stock at $13 a share in early 1980. Funds from this offering helped finance a 30,000-square-foot addition to its existing 40,000-square-foot manufacturing plant in Melville, Long Island. This factory eventually grew to 110,000 square feet.

Downturn in the 1980s

By mid-1983, Vicon Industries had raised its share of the CCTV accessories market to 35 percent. With the U.S. economy in recession, net income declined for the first time in 11 years during fiscal 1982. There was a rebound the following year, however, and in fiscal 1984 Vicon enjoyed record net income of $1.91 million on record net sales of $29.33 million. Exports were an increasing source of revenue, with the company's British subsidiary accounting for 14 percent of sales in fiscal 1984. In order to be able to offer its clients a complete line of CCTV systems, Vicon added video cameras, monitors, and cassette recorders to its product line in fiscal 1986.

The expansion of Vicon Industries' product line, at a cost of $2 million, eroded earnings, and in 1987 the company lost Burle Industries, Inc. (formerly RCA Corp.) as its principal customer. Although sales continued to climb each year, Vicon lost money in fiscal 1985 and again in fiscal 1987. Vicon's troubles attracted a hostile takeover attempt in 1986 by Sensormatic Electronics Corp., which offered $17.6 million for its common stock. Rebuffing this company's bid for control entailed half a year of distraction and costs of more than $1.2 million in legal and other fees, Kenneth Darby—who later became Vicon's chief executive officer—recalled to Paul Schreiber of *Newsday* in 1998. "That hurt us badly," he told Schreiber. "We got off track. After that, the company struggled. There was a point where I felt as though the company might have to seek [chapter 11 bankruptcy] protection, but fortunately we were able to work through that, primarily with a Japanese trading company, who was our major shareholder at the time, stepping in to provide financing when the banks got nervous."

The Japanese company was Chugai Boyeki Co. Ltd. of Tokyo, which purchased 10.8 percent of Vicon Industries' common stock in 1987 for some $3 million, shortly after obtaining exclusive distribution rights to sell the company's products in Indonesia, Malaysia, Singapore, and Thailand. By late 1989 this company had raised its stake in Vicon to 14.9 percent and received the exclusive right to sell Vicon's products in Japan. As a consequence of this connection, the company's sales abroad reached 26 percent of its total revenue in fiscal 1988. Nevertheless, sales were flat over the next few years, and Vicon lost money in every fiscal year between 1989 and 1993, the loss reaching nearly $4 million in fiscal 1992. During this recessionary period, the surveillance industry began developing digital video systems, and in order to keep pace Vicon had to borrow money to invest in the new technology. To add to its troubles, the company was fined for illegally copying software.

Darby, who succeeded retiring Horn as president in 1991 and chief executive officer in 1992, told Schreiber, "It was real simple. We were guilty, and I'm sure a million other companies around Long Island were, too. It was embarrassing for me. It was embarrassing for the company."

Recovery in the 1990s

In 1993, Vicon Industries made two critical decisions: to cease doing its own manufacturing and to distribute only complete systems rather than components. "One of the reasons the company was struggling so much was that it couldn't be all things to everybody," Darby explained to Schreiber. "We were trying to engineer and design a product, manufacture it, and then market and sell it. And we weren't doing a very good job of any of it." The company subcontracted its manufacturing operations, sending some of the work to South Korea and some to Vermont and Florida. The bulk of the manufacturing, however, was contracted to two Long Island firms: Micro Contract Manufacturing Inc., which made the circuit boards, and Sartek Industries Inc., which assembled Vicon's parts into finished products.

Contracting out manufacturing enabled Vicon Industries to cut its labor force by more than half and to shed its expensive lease on its manufacturing plant. In 1997 the company moved from Melville to a 56,000-square-foot leased building in an industrial park in nearby Hauppauge, Long Island., which it purchased, renovated, and finished in 1998. Much of the building was filled with inventory in the form of finished products and parts. Despite the expense of stocking some $13 million in equipment, Vicon needed the material on hand in order to compete for sales. "Companies anguish over the purchase of [systems] for months and months, years and years," Darby told Schreiber. "Then when they make the decision, they want it the next day."

Vicon Industries was targeting the high end of the market for surveillance systems, estimated at $1.7 billion worldwide, sometimes selling thousands of cameras—as in the case of monitoring a highway—at about $5,000 apiece. The company's new digital video multiplexer allowed users to manipulate a camera for purposes such as zooming in on a person or item. Cameras were activated upon detecting motion, with the images sent to a separate control center. If a camera's cable were cut, an alarm automatically summoned police. Vicon's line of digital detectors "have an outside automatic sensoring level versus the scene stored in memory," company marketing manager Bret McGowan told a reporter for the trade monthly *Security*. "Update of the reference scene can occur every two to five minutes so the current scene is not being compared to an hour ago." Parameters in the digital program that would set off an alarm could be an object's size or the speed at which it moved, or it could be a change in the light level.

A 1998 a *Times* (London) dispatch reported that British aerial reconnaissance photographs of Iraqi President Saddam Hussein's palace complexes and military facilities were being examined in detail each day for evidence of harboring weapons of mass destruction. A British intelligence source said he had studied a high-resolution photograph spread over an area of about 16 square miles that was believed to have been taken by a Royal Air Force bomber equipped with a Vicon high-quality

Key Dates:

1967: Founding of Vicon Industries by Donald Horn.
1980: Vicon leads in the manufacture of closed-circuit TV accessories.
1986: Management beats back a hostile takeover bid.
1993: Vicon Industries loses money for the fifth straight fiscal year.
1998: Now restored to health, the company realizes record earnings.

tactical reconnaissance camera fitted inside a special pod attached to the underside of the plane.

One-third of Vicon's revenue in fiscal 1997 came from exports, principally to Europe and East Asia. The company was seeking more business in Eastern Europe and China; Chinese orders were mostly for surveillance on highways and in prisons and airports.

In the United States, probably Vicon's biggest customer was the Postal Service, which was spending an estimated $9.5 million in 1998 for use of the company's surveillance systems in its major distribution facilities. "Their problem is mail theft," Darby explained to Schreiber. "One of the easiest ways is when merchandise comes into the processing centers. Labels are changed. It's just rerouted to someone's house or a post-office box. Two seconds and you don't walk out the door with anything. We can catch them with some very, very sophisticated techniques." In fiscal 1999 and 2000, indirect sales to the Postal Service under this national supply contract approximated $23 million in each year.

Vicon Industries broke out of the red in fiscal 1994, lost money again the following year, but was profitable again in the next five years, its net income reaching a peak of $5.81 million in fiscal 1998. Revenues grew in each year. In 1998 the company made its first public offering of stock since 1980, raising $10.4 million in order to pay down some of its long-standing, high-interest debt. The company's replenished coffers also enabled it to acquire TeleSite, U.S.A., Inc., a designer, producer, and seller of remote video surveillance systems, in 1999 for $2.1 million. Vikon's increased number of shares, plus its higher share price, made it a more difficult takeover target in Darby's estimation. "I think we're an expensive acquisition for somebody now," he told Schreiber. "You can no longer pick up Vicon for $20 or $30 million. Maybe now it'll cost you $75 or $100 million to try to buy this company. That insulates us a little bit."

Vicon Industries in 2000

Vicon Industries' product line in 2000 consisted of various elements of a video system, including video cameras, display units (monitors), video recorders, switching equipment for video distribution, digital video and signal processing units, motorized zoom lenses, remote robotic cameras, systems controls, environmental camera enclosures, and consoles for system assembly. In addition to selling from a standard catalog line, the company at times was producing to specification or

was willing to modify an existing product to meet a customer's requirements.

Vicon Industries' products were being sold mainly to about 2,000 independent dealers, system integrators, and distributors, both by in-house and independent personnel. Its marketing emphasized engineered video-system solutions that incorporated system design, project management, and technical training and support. Research and development was focused toward the application of digital video technology, specifically toward the compression, transmission, storage, and display of digital video. The company's principal sales offices were located in Hauppauge; Fareham, England; Zaventem, Belgium; New Territories, Hong Kong; and Shanghai. The British subsidiary was in charge of sales for Europe and the Middle East. International sales accounted for 26 percent of consolidated net sales in fiscal 2000, with markets in Europe and the Pacific Rim accounting for about 82 percent of these sales.

Net sales for fiscal 2000 came to $74.62 million, and net income to $961,000, a considerable drop from $4.76 million in fiscal 1999 in spite of a small increase in sales. Darby described the fiscal year as one of investment in product development and technical-support staff needed to meet a growing customer preference for surveillance systems using digital video. The company's long-term debt was $7.09 million at the end of the fiscal year. In December 2000, Chugbai Boyeki (now CBC Co., Ltd.), plus its affiliates owned 11.4 percent of Vicon's common stock. Dimensional Fund Advisors of Santa Monica, California, owned 6.9 percent, and Darby held 5.3 percent.

Principal Subsidiaries

TeleSite U.S.A., Inc.; Vicon Industries Foreign Sales Corporation; Vicon Industries Ltd. (United Kingdom).

Principal Competitors

Checkpoint Systems, Inc.; Panasonic Technologies Inc.; Pelco Sales Co.; Philips Communications and Security Systems, Inc.; Sensormatic Electronics Corp.; Ultrak, Inc.

Further Reading

Breznick, Alan, "Clearer Picture for Video Marker," *Crain's New York Business,* June 22, 1992, p. 39.

Evans, Michael, "Cameras Spy on Saddam's Fortress Palaces," *Times* [London], February 17, 1998, p. 17.

LaFemina, Lorraine, "For Electronic Security Firms, Crime Pays," *LI Business News,"* March 25, 1996, p. 27.

Schreiber, Paul, "Reversal of Fortune," *Newsday,* June 29, 1998, pp. C8–C9.

"Sensormatic Proposes Offer of $17.6 Million for Vicon Industries," *Wall Street Journal,* November 20, 1986, p. 45.

Spindel, Donald I., "Vicon," *Wall Street Transcript,* November 3, 1980, pp. 59, 543–59, 544.

Troxel, Thomas N., Jr., "An Eye on Profits," *Barron's,* April 30, 1984, p. 52.

"Vicon Industries Will Sell Stake to a Unit of Chugai," *Wall Street Journal,* March 24, 1987, p. 4.

"Video Motion Detection Becoming More Reliable," *Security,* June 1997, pp. 26–28.

—Robert Halasz

VICTORIA

Ein Unternehmen der
ERGO Versicherungsgruppe

Victoria Group

Victoriaplatz 1
D-40198 Düsseldorf
Germany
Telephone: (49) (211) 477-0
Fax: (49) (211) 477-4444
Web site: http://www.Victoria.de

Wholly Owned Subsidiary of Ergo Versicherungsgruppe A.G.

Incorporated: 1853 as Allgemeine Eisenbahn-Versicherungs-Gesellschaft

Employees: 10,593

Total Assets: EUR 5.7 billion ($5.3 billion) (2000)

NAIC: 524113 Direct Life Insurance Carriers; 524114 Direct Health and Medical Insurance Carriers; 524126 Direct Property and Casualty Insurance Carriers; 524128 Other Direct Insurance (Except Life, Health, and Medical) Carriers; 52413 Reinsurance Carriers

---

Düsseldorf-based Victoria Group, formerly known as Victoria Holding AG is one of Germany's leading groups of direct all-round insurance companies and is part of the Ergo Group (Ergo Versicherungsgruppe A.G.), the country's second largest direct insurer. The company offers policies for life, accident and health insurance as well as car insurance and pension plans to individuals. Victoria also provides coverage for property damage for individuals and businesses. The company's D.A.S. subsidiary is Europe's leading legal insurer. Victoria policies are sold through the company's exclusive sales network as well as through a network of ERGO affiliates, including a cooperation with Bavarian bank HypoVereinsbank. The group's 26 foreign subsidiaries in 14 European countries contribute about one quarter of its total sales. Victoria's financial assets are managed by ERGO's subsidiary Munich ERGO AssetManagement GmbH (MEAG). Victoria is controlled by German reinsurer Munich Re.

From Railway Insurance to General Insurance in the 19th Century

Victoria is the result of the combination of several insurance companies whose names have changed over more than 135 years.

It became a public limited company on September 26, 1853, under the name of the Allgemeine Eisenbahn-Versicherungs-Gesellschaft (the General Railway Insurance Company). Railway insurance was an innovation introduced by Otto Crelinger, a banker and member of the board of the Berlin-Potsdam Railway Company.

In 1843, Otto Crelinger applied for a royal license to found a railway transport insurance company, claiming that "it is a peculiarity of steam transport that it carries risks which in part cannot be anticipated and in part cannot be avoided, even with the greatest of care, and which are certainly of a more diverse and dangerous nature than those involved in any form of land transport up until now." It was Crelinger's idea to include the insurance charge in the fare and thus to insure all passengers automatically for a sum of between £150 and £450 (1,000 to 3,000 taler).

It took ten years for permission to be granted by King Friedrich Wilhelm IV of Prussia. This delay resulted to some extent from initial fears that insurance of this type might encourage railway companies to neglect safety standards. However, Crelinger's request was granted finally, and he became the first managing director of the company that was later to become Victoria. His company extended coverage for railway transport to related insurance against death, accidents, or fire on the railways, but it remained primarily a transport insurer. Its transport insurance turned out to be very popular and was extended to apply to land and inland waterway transport in 1858.

In 1861, the company became involved in life insurance, introducing the innovative product of a life insurance policy with premium refunds. This policy proved to be a major success. One year after its introduction, the company's total life insurance premium income exceeded one million taler, which was quite a considerable sum. Ever since then, the company's main strength has been in life insurance.

In 1875, the company took the name of Victoria zu Berlin Allgemeine Versicherungs-Actien-Gesellschaft (Victoria of Berlin General Insurance PLC), a step that underlined the company's diversification into general insurance. The premium refunds were extended to various other types of insurance, such as accident insurance in 1883.

Under the leadership of Otto Gerstenberg, Victoria focused its attention still further upon the general public. Gerstenberg's career with the company started in 1873, when he joined as a mathematician. In 1888, he became general manager and from 1913 to 1931 was president of the board. From 1892 onwards, the company offered popular insurance (Volksversicherung) to its customers. This was a type of life insurance new to Germany, a plan that Victoria took from the United Kingdom after studying the Prudential's policies in London. Anyone could take out this type of insurance without the need for a doctor's examination. The insurance payments were low and were collected weekly by 2,600 uniformed employees. This type of popular insurance became extremely successful. The company's particular attachment to popular insurance was to last until the 1970s, when, due to a buoyant economy and the provisions of the welfare state, insurance of this kind became obsolete. Under Gerstenberg's management, Victoria had become Germany's largest life insurance company by the turn of the century and Europe's largest by 1913.

At the same time Victoria branched out further, with the founding of the affiliated Victoria Feuer-Versicherung AG (the Victoria Fire Insurance Company, VFC) in 1904 being of major significance. VFC's activities included insuring not only against fire, but also against burglary, floods, accident, liability, and all kinds of car insurance. It grew quickly and became Victoria's second most important area of business. To this day VFC is Victoria's most important subsidiary with several subsidiaries of its own. Before World War I, Victoria had become a multinational enterprise. It extended its activities to all north, east, and west European countries, excluding the United Kingdom, and to the Balkans. World War I was extremely damaging to Victoria. The losses from the withdrawal of foreign investments were minor compared with those resulting from all the claims made during the war and, worse still, from the hyperinflation that followed.

Economic historians have characterized the interwar period as a time of relative stagnation. This was certainly Victoria's experience. The company had to adapt to new economic conditions. Fearing the negative impact of political events, Victoria acted with characteristic caution. In 1923 it founded two subsidiaries in the Rhine, Victoria am Rhein Allgemeine Versicherungs-Actien-Gesellschaft, offering life insurance, and Victoria am Rhein Feuer- und Transport-Versicherungs AG for fire and transport insurance. In the same year French and Belgian troops occupied the Ruhr district, causing widespread fear that this region would be separated from the rest of Germany. In founding its Victoria am Rhein subsidiaries, the company had safeguarded its interests.

All these changes were time-consuming and expensive to implement. Only by 1927 had Victoria's assets returned to the level at which they had started at the turn of the century. However, Victoria still remained ahead of its competitors. In 1932, it accounted for 80 percent of all the premiums collected from abroad by German insurance companies. This situation was in line with its prewar status. The tradition of popular insurance continued as well and was strengthened in 1939 by the acquisition of Victoria's rival in this field, Vorsorge.

In 1938, after the Treaty of Munich, which brought the Sudetenland in Czechoslovakia under Nazi rule, Victoria took over the activities of a Prague company in that region. World War II, however, caused Victoria major setbacks. Not only did it have to cope with unfavorable conditions in western Germany, but it also lost its main geographical area of activity, central and eastern Germany, as well as its direct foreign investments. Furthermore, Victoria's head offices in Berlin were destroyed.

Cautious Growth after World War II

By its 100th anniversary in 1953, however, Victoria had recovered its standing. During the 1950s, it steadily strengthened its position in the insurance market. Once more, its policy was one of cautious growth. By this stage the company chiefly operated from Düsseldorf, Berlin having become an isolated outpost of the free market economy. Although the company retained an office in Berlin, new offices were built in Düsseldorf in 1952. Four years later, the two affiliated companies of Victoria am Rhein were merged with the two Victoria zu Berlin companies.

The 1960s were years of economic prosperity for West Germany. Victoria showed steady and rapid growth. During the decade, its annual premium income tripled and two important steps were taken. Victoria bought the Deutscher Automobil Schutz Allgemeine Rechtsschutz-Versicherung AG (DAS), a relatively small company specializing in legal expenses insurance. DAS gradually expanded to become Europe's largest company in its particular area of insurance. The second important step for Victoria was a return to overseas expansion. The company made direct investments in the Netherlands, Austria, Portugal, and Spain. Furthermore, Victoria took part in the International Group Program, formulated by the U.S. insurance company John Hancock Mutual Life. The program was aimed at multinational enterprises wishing to offer uniform insurance to all their employees worldwide. A similar scheme, the International Network of Insurance, was started in 1979. Through these ventures Victoria became the leading German insurer in such international insurance networks.

The 1970s saw a further tripling in Victoria's premium income, despite the overall downturn in the world economy. Victoria made little effort to diversify outside insurance. Its acquisition in 1970 of a 25 percent in the paper company Zellstoff AG was sold off a little later. The only investment it retained outside insurance was in a small shipping company. In 1971 Victoria branched out into health insurance. It bought 10 percent of the German Gilde-Versicherung AG from the U.K. Sun Alliance group. Rumors spread that the Sun group would draw Victoria into its orbit. These were vigorously denied by Victoria's chief executive, Heinz Schmöle, who emphasized his group's determination to remain independent.

Past events were remembered and prompted Schmöle's denials when Victoria's shares were subjected to considerable speculation during the winter of 1969–1970. In the 1920s Victoria

Key Dates:

1853: Allgemeine Eisenbahn-Versicherungs-Gesellschaft is founded.
1861: The company introduces life insurance with premium refunds.
1875: The company is renamed Victoria zu Berlin Allgemeine Versicherungs-Actien-Gesellschaft.
1904: Victoria Feuer-Versicherung AG is founded.
1945: The company's Berlin headquarters are destroyed during World War II.
1952: New headquarters are built in Düsseldorf.
1961: Victoria buys a majority in Deutscher Automobil Schutz Allgemeine Rechtsschutz-Versicherung AG (D.A.S.).
1971: The company adds health insurance to its services.
1989: The new holding company Victoria Holding AG is created.
1991: Victoria starts cooperating with Bayerische Vereinsbank AG.
1997: Victoria Holding AG is merged with Hamburg-Mannheimer AG to form ERGO Versicherungsgruppe AG.
1998: The Victoria group launches its first image campaign.
2001: Victoria receives an ''AAA'' Standard & Poors rating for its sound financial standing.

had found itself the object of one of the first German attempts at a hostile takeover bid in Germany. This attempt—by the Michael group—was unsuccessful, but caused anxiety at Victoria. Again in 1983 a group led by two large German competitors, tried unsuccessfully to buy a majority shareholding in Victoria. Although Victoria made a tempting target, chief executive Dr. Jannott stated in 1989 that rumors of takeovers did not worry the company at all. Victoria's shareholders were diverse, with German reinsurance company Münchener Rück being the largest of 8,000 shareholders with a 12 percent stake.

Restructuring in 1989

In 1989, Victoria underwent major restructuring after a decade of careful planning. It was the first restructuring in over 135 years of the group's history and was intended to increase Victoria's competitiveness. Under German law, the Spartentrennungsprinzip prevents life, health, damages, accident, legal, or credit insurance from being offered together by a single company. Insurers wishing to provide cover in these different areas are forced to create a separate company for each, with one company in charge. Victoria was unusual among Germany insurance groups in having a life insurance company at its head, because life insurance had dominated Victoria's activities, especially in its first 60 years. Other insurance groups in Germany were headed either by damages insurance companies, by reinsurance companies, or by holding companies. There was always a danger that with a life insurance company at the head of the Victoria group, it might suffer badly from losses in other group companies dealing with damages insurance or reinsurance, which by their nature carry considerably greater financial risk.

The Victoria group therefore created a holding company, Victoria Holding AG, bringing itself in line with other German insurance groups and allowing itself greater flexibility. Victoria Holding had majority shares in three main enterprises, Victoria Life, Victoria Insurance, and Victoria Health, which in turn held investments in several insurance companies in Germany and abroad.

The restructuring of the group was only one of the steps by which chief executive officer Jannott tried to increase Victoria's competitiveness. On an international level he strengthened Victoria's relationship with Japan's Dai-Ichi Mutual Life and its investment in the United States in the Munich-American Reinsurance Company (MARC) group, in which Victoria had a 10 percent share. The MARC group's capital had increased 11-fold since 1985. In Europe, Victoria occasionally took over small private firms such as the Greek company Olympiaki in 1989.

Focusing on Strengths in the 1990s

By 1991, Victoria's exclusive distribution network consisted of over 10,000 full time and part time salespeople. To expand its reach, the company started cooperating with the Bavarian bank Bayerische Vereinsbank AG. The bank referred its customers to Victoria for their insurance needs and Victoria salesmen recommended the bank's financial services. In addition the two companies founded a joint venture in the area of Bausparen, special savings programs for aspiring homeowners subsidized by the German government, which witnessed a revival after the reunification of the two German states. This cooperation turned out to be very successful for both companies.

While the fall of the Iron Curtain opened up new growth opportunities, it also had a downside. Car theft and burglary as well as claims for car accidents increased significantly. For example, in big cities like Berlin gangs from eastern Europe allegedly smuggled stolen Mercedes and BMW over the Polish border to sell them in Poland and Russia. When its car insurance subsidiary slipped into the red, Victoria started consolidating its business by canceling a number of policies and by being more selective in approving new ones. Another area of concern was fire insurance and building insurance for small and mid-sized businesses where the company dealt with a number of large claims. Fortunately, the losses were neutralized by the company's sales in other markets such as life and health insurance and capital investments where the company reallocated assets from the real estate to the stock market. After five years of expansive growth, the economic recession which had been delayed in Germany because of the reunification, finally left its mark in the mid-1990s when sales started declining in key markets such as life insurance. In response, Victoria focused on cost consolidation and cautious growth under the motto ''profits before growth.'' Although the company invested heavily in new IT technology, Victoria was able to keep administrative cost relatively low. Growth in the second half of the 1990s came from new products in the area of disability and health insurance and private pension plans. The strategy worked very well and as a result Victoria's profits increased significantly despite stagnating sales.

By the mid-1990s, Victoria was one of Germany's top direct insurers. Because of its strong market position and because it was publicly traded, the company was an ideal takeover candidate for foreign insurers who wanted to enter the German insurance market. However, Victoria was committed to remain in German hands and started negotiations with its long-time biggest shareholder Munich Re. Finally, Victoria agreed to merge its holding company with Hamburg-Mannheimer AG, another large direct insurance holding company in which Munich Re held 80 percent, to form the new ERGO Versicherungsgruppe AG. The result was a consortium of equal partner companies. Since Victoria had built a strong brand name, the company kept marketing its products under the Victoria brand. The only visible change for Victoria customers was the additional note ''a company of the ERGO Versicherungsgruppe'' which was included under the logo in all correspondence and marketing communication.

Throughout its history, Victoria never tended to run large advertising campaigns. Instead, it built its success on a reputation for reliability and efficient service. However, to secure the company's position in an increasingly consolidating and competitive market, Victoria launched a DM 25 million image campaign in 1998. Unlike most other German insurance companies, Victoria used neither ''worst case scenarios'' nor ''perfect world'' images to deliver the message that it was a fair partner close to its customers, both with its products and geographically. And unlike its major competitors Victoria used print media, not television, as its main advertising channel. Through a series of magazine ads which stressed Victoria's competence as a problem-solver in day-to-day insurance cases, the company was able to increase its visibility and brand recognition among potential and existing customers.

By the end of the 20th century, Victoria seemed to be well positioned as a part of the ERGO group of insurance companies to defend its position in Germany and to expand internationally in the future. New business by referrals through Hamburg-Mannheimer and DKV was growing and the cooperation with Hypo Vereinsbank had proved valuable. When Germany's federal government enacted new legislation in 2001 that guaranteed government subsidies for certified individual pension plans beginning in 2002, Victoria immediately invested DM50 million in product development, marketing and sales force education to secure a share of this future growth market. Victoria also planned to expand its full-time sales force from 3,900 in 1999 to 4,500 in 2003. Another goal to secure a strong position in the future was to raise the percentage of life insurance customers who would re-invest the money paid after the policy ended through ERGO's investment arm MEAG. Another area of potential future growth was E-business where Victoria Lebensver-

sicherung entered a strategic partnership with BauFinanzierung.direkt AG, a company that offered real estate financing plans through the Internet, in early 2001. In the same year Victoria received an ''AAA'' Standard & Poors rating for its sound financial standing.

Principal Subsidiaries

Victoria Lebensversicherung AG; Victoria Versicherung AG; Victoria Krankenversicherung AG (75%); Victoria Rückversicherung AG; D.A.S. Rechtsschutz-Versicherungs-AG; Victoria International AG; Vorsorge Lebensversicherung AG.

Principal Competitors

Allianz AG; AMB Generali Holding AG; AXA Colonia Konzern AG.

Further Reading

''BauFinanzierung.direkt AG mit neuem strategischen Partner-die Victoria Lebensversicherung AG,'' *OTS Originaltextservice,* January 30, 2001.

''Bei der Victoria ist das Wachstumstempo erlahmt,'' *Frankfurter Allgemeine Zeitung,* November 24, 1995, p. 21.

''BV steigt mit Victoria ins Bauspargeschaeft ein,'' *Süddeutsche Zeitung,* May 18, 1991.

Victoria Versicherung 1853–1928, Berlin: Victoria, 1928.

''80 Jahre Victoria-Versicherung,'' *Victoria Zeitung* Nos. 8/9, 1933.

Die Hundertjahrfeier der Victoria-Versicherung, Berlin: Victoria, 1953.

Hundert Jahre Victoria Versicherung, Berlin: Victoria, 1953.

Im Zug der Zeilen, Düsseldorf: Victoria, 1978.

Jaitner, Peter, ''Sicherheit im Grossformat,'' *Werben und Verkaufen,* December 8, 2000, p. 94.

''1999 war für die Victoria-Gruppe ein Spitzenjahr,'' *OTS Originaltextservice,* April 3, 2000.

''Victoria-Gesellschaften erhöhen wieder die Dividenden,'' *Frankfurter Allgemeine Zeitung*, May 9, 1998, p. 20.

''Victoria Versicherung AG: Wachstumsschub im 1. Halbjahr,'' *OTS Originaltextservice,* August 15, 2001.

''Victoria Versicherung mit Schönheitsfehlern,'' *Süddeutsche Zeitung,* November 24, 1993.

''Victoria wächst überdurchschnittlich,'' *Frankfurter Allgemeine Zeitung,* November 27, 1999, p. 23.

''Victoria: Wir werden nicht jeden Spuk mitmachen,'' *Frankfurter Allgemeine Zeitung,* Novemebr 26, 1994, p. 21.

''Vorsorge; Alles Riester oder was?,'' *Focus Magazin,* June 25, 2001, p. 210.

—Harm G. Schroter
—update: Evelyn Hauser

Williams-Sonoma, Inc.

3250 Van Ness Avenue
San Francisco, California 94109
U.S.A.
Telephone: (415) 421-7900
Fax: (415) 616-8359
Web site: http://www.williams-sonomainc.com

Public Company
Incorporated: 1956
Employees: 22,000
Sales: $1.8 billion (2001)
Stock Exchanges: New York
Ticker Symbol: WSM
NAIC: 45411 Electronic Shopping and Mail-Order
   Houses; 442299 All Other Home Furnishings Stores

Williams-Sonoma, Inc., has become virtually synonymous with home furnishings through its mail-order catalogs and retail stores. In slightly more than 40 years, Williams-Sonoma has grown to a $1.8 billion company, making it a leading U.S. retailer in specialty home furnishings. Retail store sales, through more than 380 stores in the company's four chains—Williams-Sonoma, Pottery Barn, Pottery Barn Kids, and Hold Everything—accounted for 57.2 percent of annual sales in fiscal 2001. Catalog sales, through the *Williams-Sonoma, Pottery Barn, Pottery Barn Kids, Pottery Barn Bed + Bath, Chambers,* and *Hold Everything* catalogs, which ship more than 233 million catalogs each year, accounted for approximately 42.8 percent of sales. In collaboration with Time-Life Books, Williams-Sonoma also publishes the Williams-Sonoma Kitchen Library Series. Published since 1992, the cookbooks in the series feature a single subject, simple recipes, and lavish photographs, and are a best-selling series in the United States.

Each of Williams-Sonoma's divisions is focused on a specialty market. The flagship *Williams-Sonoma* catalog features a range of more than 300 professional, often exotic, products for the kitchen. The more than 200 Williams-Sonoma retail stores, the largest of the company's retail store chains, feature an expanded 3,000-item line of kitchenware, including cookware,

cookbooks, cutlery, dinnerware, and custom-built French stoves. Pottery Barn, the next-largest division, with 136 stores in its retail chain, sells a near-complete line of carpets, lighting, window treatments, furniture, and other home furnishings through its catalogs and retail stores. The company also operates eight Pottery Barn Kids stores and 26 Hold Everything outlets, which offer a unique line of storage and organization products for the home. Williams-Sonoma's home furnishings offerings are rounded out by mail-order catalogs *Chambers,* which offers high-end bed linens and bath products, and *Pottery Barn Bed + Bath,* offering moderately priced items. The company also operates three e-commerce web sites and gift registries. Founder Charles E. (Chuck) Williams, chairman until 1986, continues to guide the company's merchandise selection as vice-chairman.

Starting in 1956 with a Passion for Cooking

After serving as an Air Force aircraft mechanic in North Africa and India during World War II, Charles Williams moved to Sonoma, California, where he worked as a self-taught carpenter. A passionate cook, Williams made a trip to Paris in the early 1950s aboard the famed *Ile de France* cruise ship. While in Paris, he discovered a range of cookware and accessories unknown to the rather bland American kitchen of the period. In 1956, tired of his carpentry career, Williams bought and began to renovate a building in Sonoma that included a failed hardware store. Williams proceeded to dispose of the store's traditional hardware supplies and to stock it instead with the professional quality cooking equipment he had discovered overseas.

The store caught on quickly, becoming popular with many professional and serious cooks. Encouraged by friends such as Julia Child and James Beard—who would be instrumental in sparking an interest in fine cooking in the United States—Williams moved his store to San Francisco, renaming it Williams-Sonoma in honor of its original location. Throughout the next decade, Williams's store prospered, attracting customers from around the country. Williams continued making trips to Europe, discovering new products to bring back to his store.

By the late 1960s, the nature of houseware sales in the United States had changed. Interest in international cuisine was on the rise, generating interest in professional quality cooking equipment. Led by Macy's, department stores were making their kitchenware departments increasingly fashionable. Williams was not impressed by these new departments. "It wasn't that much," he told the *San Francisco Business Times.* Serious cooks continued to flock to the Williams-Sonoma store, and by the early 1970s, Williams, exhausted from shouldering the burden not only of stocking and operating the store, but also from running the business end, began to look for help. One frequent customer and close friend was Edward Marcus of the Nieman-Marcus retail chain. Marcus suggested that Williams either sell his company or expand it himself. Williams decided to expand, and in 1972, Marcus and Williams formed a corporation, Williams-Sonoma, Inc.

Williams continued to handle the purchasing and merchandising, while Marcus brought in a team of executives to guide the company's business end. A second store was opened in Beverly Hills by 1973. In that year, the company brought out its first mail-order catalog. As Williams told Gentry, the catalog was "a learning experience. We found that we could sell items by catalog that wouldn't sell in the stores. We could tell a story that couldn't be explained in the store, especially where the item and its use weren't intuitively obvious." Unlike in the stores, where customers merely saw the products on the shelf, the catalog, called *A Catalog for Cooks,* featured photographs of the products in use. The first mailing of the catalog went to 5,000 people. Sales took off, and the catalog's mailing list quickly went nationwide.

The corporation added stores too. By 1977, the Williams-Sonoma chain had grown to five stores. The following year Marcus, who held one-third of the company, died, and a change in management led the company into trouble. With $4.9 million in sales, the company carried a debt of $700,000 and posted a net loss of $173,000. "[The new management] proceeded to run it the wrong way," Williams told the *San Francisco Business Times.* "In a year's time, the company was in financial difficulty. I decided to sell. If it was going to have these kinds of financial problems, I didn't want it. I'd never had those kinds of problems before. I'd never borrowed money. For years, I never had credit because I paid cash."

New Ownership for the 1980s

In 1978, Williams sold the company for $100,000 to W. Howard Lester, a former IBM salesman and founder of several

computer services firms, and his partner, James McMahan. With the sale came the requirement that Williams remain in charge of selecting merchandise and running the catalog.

Williams-Sonoma turned around quickly under Lester. Within five years, the retail chain grew to 19 stores. Catalog mailings reached 30 million customers by 1983, and catalog sales accounted for more than 75 percent of the company's $35 million in annual revenues. In 1982, the company's catalog sales expanded when it acquired the *Gardener's Eden* catalog, then posting $100,000 in annual sales. To finance further expansion, Lester took the company public in 1983, with an initial public offering (IPO) of one million shares at $23 per share. Lester retained about 22 percent of the company; Williams, who continued to lead the company's catalog, held about 1.9 percent of the company's stock.

With the money raised in its IPO, the company established a new distribution and warehouse facility in Memphis, Tennessee. Over the next three years, the retail chain grew to 31 stores in 14 states, and the company opened a second retail chain, Hold Everything, which would grow to five stores. The company also sought to expand its catalog business, introducing a catalog featuring table settings and a second catalog featuring more exotic cookware, both of which did poorly. Coupled with the catalog losses, the move to Memphis cut heavily into the company's profits, which were down to $445,000 in 1983 from a net of $1.5 million in 1982. By 1984, with sales reaching nearly $52 million, earnings had sunk to a mere $38,000.

This setback proved short-lived. By 1985, sales climbed to $68 million, earning the company a net of $2.4 million. The company continued to expand, adding 14 Williams-Sonoma stores by the end of the following year. Expansion went beyond Williams-Sonoma. In 1986, the company acquired the struggling Pottery Barn, a chain of 27 retail home furnishings stores, from The Gap for $6 million. Pottery Barn also was added to the company's growing line of catalogs, which by then included *Hold Everything* and *Gardener's Eden.* Meanwhile, the retail end was contributing a growing percentage of the company's sales, up to 36 percent by that year. By the end of the 1986 fiscal year, the company's sales climbed past $100 million.

The company continued to grow aggressively, raising the number of Williams-Sonoma stores to 64 in 1988. A joint venture with Tokyo Department Store brought the first Williams-Sonoma store—and the *Catalog for Cooks*—to Japan. The company's sales surged to $136.8 million, and net earnings of $3.4 million, by year-end 1987. To guide this burgeoning empire, Lester brought in former Pillsbury Co. president Kent Larson as Williams-Sonoma president. Under Larson, the company formed a joint venture with Ralph Lauren to open a chain of Polo/Ralph Lauren Home Collection stores. A fifth catalog was added to the Williams-Sonoma ranks in early 1989. This catalog, called *Chambers,* featured bed and both products. By then, retail sales accounted for 53 percent of Williams-Sonoma's sales.

Between 1986 and 1989, the company added an average of 12 stores per year, bringing the total number of Williams-Sonoma, Pottery Barn, and Hold Everything retail units to 102 in the United States, with another unit in Japan. Not all of

Key Dates:

1956: Charles Williams opens a store in Sonoma, California.
1972: Williams-Sonoma, Inc. is formed as a corporation.
1973: A second store is opened in Beverly Hills, California; the company launches its first mail-order catalog.
1978: The company is sold to W. Howard Lester and James McMahan.
1982: The *Gardener's Eden* catalog is acquired.
1983: Williams-Sonoma goes public.
1985: The firm establishes a second retail chain, Hold Everything.
1986: The Pottery Barn chain of stores is purchased from The Gap.
1989: *Chambers,* a new catalog, is mailed to customers.
1992: The company joins with Time-Life Books to create a series of Williams-Sonoma Kitchen Library cookbooks.
1994: The Williams-Sonoma and Pottery Barn stores undergo a series of changes, including a new store format.
1998: The company is listed on the NYSE.
1999: Williams-Sonoma's e-commerce site is launched.
2000: Pottery Barn begins selling merchandise online; first Pottery Barn Kids store is established; *Williams-Sonoma TASTE* magazine begins circulation.

Williams-Sonoma's ventures were successful, however. After one year, the company and Ralph Lauren agreed to dissolve their joint venture partnership. An attempt to establish a Gardener's Eden retail chain also failed, in part because of the inherently seasonal nature of that market. Nevertheless, the company's revenues, led by its growing Williams-Sonoma retail chain, continued to make steady gains, rising from $174 million in 1988 to $287 million in 1990.

Williams-Sonoma's rapid expansion, and the economy's turn into the recession of the early 1990s, badly hurt earnings. The company's $11.2 million net profit in 1990 fell to $1.6 million and $1.8 million in the next two years, while revenues increased slowly, to $312 million in 1991 and $344 million in 1992.

Recovering After the 1990s Recession

Williams-Sonoma's troubles proved short-lived, however. Management was restructured, the company introduced new merchandising strategies and catalog designs, and catalog production was brought in-house. The company also slowed expansion of its retail chains, focusing instead on improving store design and on increasing store square footage. In 1992, the company joined with Time-Life Books to create the first in a series of Williams-Sonoma Kitchen Library cookbooks. Sold initially only through Williams-Sonoma retail stores, the first four books offered simple recipes, clear instructions, and tips on cooking techniques for pasta, pies and tarts, grilling, and hors d'oeuvres. The books sold well, adding to Williams-Sonoma's image as a resource for the serious and even not-so-serious cook.

By year-end 1993, the company had posted a strong turnaround. Revenues rose to $410 million, and earnings again climbed past $11 million. A chief architect of the turnaround was Executive Vice-President Gary Friedman. Friedman introduced major changes throughout the company's retail operations. The *Catalog for Cooks* was redesigned from digest to full size, which, as Lester explained to the *San Francisco Chronicle,* "gives you a lot more punch. You can show bigger recipes and more dramatic photographs on major ideas." The new design spurred an increase of 40 percent on the catalog's sales. Next came a reorganization of the Williams-Sonoma store chain, including grouping in-store promotions around monthly themes—so that, for example, if the theme for the month was pasta, the largest share of in-store displays featured pasta-related merchandise. Within several months, the reorganization helped boost per-store sales by more than 20 percent. For the Pottery Barn division, which had lost more than $5 million in 1992, Friedman introduced even more dramatic changes, including replacing more than 80 percent of the retail stores' merchandise, while increasing square footage in new and future stores. The newly designed Pottery Barn reflected Friedman's own frustration when trying to furnish his home, as he told the *Austin American-Statesman.* "It was a confusing proposition," Friedman said. "I needed a place where I could find everything I needed." To the *Dallas Morning News,* Friedman added: "I wanted a store that would sell me window treatments, lamps, sofas and chairs." The Pottery Barn redesign proved immediately successful and helped spark the division's growth from combined store and catalog sales of $103 million in 1992 to $165 million in 1993.

With total catalog sales rising to $200 million, Williams-Sonoma rolled out new formats for its Williams-Sonoma flagship chain and its Pottery Barn chain. The expanded Williams-Sonoma stores featured professional demonstration kitchens, larger cookbook libraries, tasting bars, and a food hall featuring high-quality foods and the company's own line of private-label foods. The new format for Pottery Barn stores included an average 10,000 square feet—about triple the size of older Pottery Barn stores—featuring a design studio, lighting gallery, and interior finishings shop. The company also started construction on a 300,000-square-foot addition to its 750,000-square-foot Memphis distribution and warehouse facility. The company also entered an agreement with Time-Warner and Spiegel to introduce a 24-hour television shopping network.

With the implementation of these changes, Williams-Sonoma was once again on the fast track. Sales in 1994 reached $528.5 million, for net earnings of $19.6 million. The following year, with the number of Williams-Sonoma, Hold Everything, and Pottery Barn stores topping 200, revenues jumped again, to $644.7 million. That year, the James Beard Foundation awarded Williams with a Lifetime Achievement Award.

E-Commerce and Brand Strengthening: Late 1990s and Beyond

Progress continued into the latter half of the 1990s. In 1998, the firm listed on the New York Stock Exchange and sales reached $1.1 billion. Management began to focus on a multichannel marketing strategy that included its stores and catalogs, as well as a new channel, the Internet. As such, the company began an extensive program aimed at capturing additional sales via the web. CEO Lester commented in a 1999 *HFN The Weekly Newspaper for the Home Furnishing Network* article, ''This is an area of real development for us. We haven't been talking about it that much, but we're really focused in that direction.''

Sure enough, the firm launched the Williams-Sonoma online bridal registry in June 1999, allowing customers to shop online for registry items. Later that same year, the Williams-Sonoma e-commerce web site also became operational. The *Gardener's Eden* catalog was sold in 1999, as part of the firm's new strategy, which focused on its remaining brands and Internet business. The Williams-Sonoma catalog also was revamped to include more information on products as well as special features and tips related to the products. By the end of the decade, more than 311 stores were in operation across the United States.

Williams-Sonoma entered the new millennium determined to remain a leader in the specialty retail and home furnishings market. It upgraded the Williams-Sonoma web site and launched an e-commerce site for Pottery Barn. Focusing on expanding that brand, it began sending customers the *Pottery Barn Bed + Bath* catalog, which featured moderately priced bed and bath items. The company also opened eight Pottery Barn Kids stores after successfully introducing its catalog in the previous year.

The *Williams-Sonoma TASTE* magazine also came to market in 2000, adding yet another publication to the company's arsenal. The new lifestyle magazine focused on food, drink, travel, and entertaining. Plans also were set in motion to develop a new concept entitled Elm Street. The new brand was scheduled to sell lower-end kitchen and housewares items and was designed to complement the Williams-Sonoma and Pottery Barn brands—it was expected to launch in March 2002.

Despite the company's aggressive growth approach and its record revenues of $1.85 billion, a 13.5 percent drop in net income was posted in fiscal 2001. Higher costs related to its catalog and Internet business along with a slowing economy were named as culprits in the decline. In April 2001, Dale Hilpert was named Williams-Sonoma's new CEO. Management looked to his expertise in company infrastructure and growth to aid in the firm's expansion plans.

While the retail sector continued to experience a decline in 2001, Williams-Sonoma pledged to continue posting revenue gains. Its strategic efforts included a focus on its brands, customer satisfaction, channel synergy, vertical integration, and operating efficiency. The company, which emerged successful from the earnings decline in the early 1990s, appeared well positioned to tackle yet another downward trend in the retail industry.

Principal Divisions

Williams-Sonoma; Hold Everything; Pottery Barn; Pottery Barn Kids; Pottery Barn Bed + Bath; Chambers.

Principal Competitors

Bed Bath & Beyond Inc.; Euromarket Designs Inc.; Pier 1 Imports Inc.

Further Reading

Barnett, Frank, and Sharon Barnett, ''Williams-Sonoma's Multi-Channel Marketing Leads to Niche Dominance,'' *Direct Marketing,* March 1999, p. 41.

Breyer, R. Michelle, ''Pottery Barn Bringing New Format to City,'' *Austin American-Statesman,* August 19, 1995, p. D1.

Fisher, Lawrence M., ''A Store for the Gourmet Cook,'' *New York Times,* July 30, 1986, p. D1.

Garry, Michael, ''Upscale Image Reaps $35 Mil for Williams-Sonoma,'' *Merchandising,* September 1984, p. 17.

Halkias, Maria, ''Mending Cracks at Pottery Barn,'' *Dallas Morning News,* July 6, 1995, p. 1D.

Jenkins, Caroline, and Susan Posnock, ''Magazine Taste Test,'' *Folio: The Magazine for Magazine Management,* January 2001, p. 61.

Joss, John, ''The Kitchen God's Life,'' *Gentry,* January/February 1994, p. 61.

Kehoe, Ann-Margaret, ''Team Spirit: Unity of Vision Gives Power Retailer Its Edge,'' *HFN The Weekly Newspaper for the Home Furnishing Network,* April 28, 1997, p. 1 (3).

Marler, Serena, ''Williams-Sonoma Eyes Web for Growth,'' *HFN The Weekly Newspaper for the Home Furnishing Network,* June 7, 1999, p. 5.

Meeks, Fleming, ''Williams-Sonoma,'' *Forbes,* February 18, 1991, p. 60.

Nicksin, Carole, ''Lester Taps Hilpert as CEO of Williams-Sonoma,'' *HFN The Weekly Newspaper for the Home Furnishing Network,* February 19, 2001, p. 1.

Pascale, Moira, ''W-S Cooks Up New Look,'' *Catalog Age,* October 1999, p. 7.

Saeks, Diane Dorrans, ''Williams-Sonoma Net Off Despite Launches in 2000,'' *HFN The Weekly Newspaper for the Home Furnishing Network,* May 28, 2001, p. 41.

Shaw, Jan, ''Williams Learned to Delegate, But He Hasn't Given Up Working,'' *San Francisco Business Times,* December 19, 1988, p. 12.

——, ''Williams-Sonoma Cooks Up Growth,'' *San Francisco Business Times,* November 28, 1988, p. 1.

Springer, Bobbi, ''Cooking on Four Burners,'' *San Francisco Business Magazine,* July 1989, p. 44.

Vincenti, Lisa, ''Williams-Sonoma to Broaden Reach of Home Furnishings,'' *HFN The Weekly Newspaper for the Home Furnishing Network,* October 25, 1999, p. 4.

''Williams-Sonoma Sets Catalog Redeployment,'' *HFN The Weekly Newspaper for the Home Furnishing Network,* January 19, 1998, p. 4.

Yawn, David, ''Williams Sonoma Expanding Distribution,'' *Memphis Business Journal,* April 29, 1996, p. 1.

—M.L. Cohen
—update: Christina M. Stansell

Young Innovations, Inc.

13705 Shoreline Court East
Earth City, Missouri 63045
U.S.A.
Telephone: (314) 344-0010
Toll Free: (800) 325-1881
Fax: (314) 344-0021
Web site: http://www.yiinc.com

Public Company
Incorporated: 1995
Employees: 250
Sales: $51.4 million (2000)
Stock Exchanges: NASDAQ
Ticker Symbol: YDNT
NAIC: 339112 Surgical and Medical Instrument
    Manufacturing; 339114 Dental Equipment and
    Supplies Manufacturing; 339113 Surgical Appliance
    and Supplies Manufacturing; 334517 Irradiation
    Apparatus Manufacturing

Young Innovations, Inc., based in Earth City, Missouri, was organized and incorporated in 1995 as the parent company for subsidiaries that design, manufacture, and market consumable supplies, instruments and other products needed by dental professionals. Their products are primarily used in preventive and restorative dentistry and instrument sterilization, and include prophy products (disposable and metal prophy angles, cups, brushes, and pastes), fluorides, infection control products, dental X-ray equipment, dental instruments, orthodontic supplies, flavored examination gloves, and children's toothpaste and toothbrushes. Young markets its products under its subsidiaries' brand names: Young, Denticator, Panoramic, Athena/Champion, and Plak Smacker. Although Young does sell its products abroad, it markets are largely in the United States, where it has nine locations. In 2000, its international sales accounted for less than 10 percent of its revenues. The family of CEO George Richmond has a controlling interest in Young, owning just over half of the company. His son, Richard, who stepped down as the company's vice-president and secretary at the end of 2000, owns about 3.8 percent.

1900–67: Young Dental Becomes a Revitalized Company after Its Purchase by George Richmond

The modern history of Young Innovations, Inc. began in 1961, when George Richmond purchased Young Dental and quickly began changing its focus to making preventive dentistry products, chiefly the prophy polishing angle, an instrument used in hygienic dentistry. Richmond actually bought the company from his mother. At the time, the firm had only had seven employees and had reached annual sales of only $61,000. It was already a long established company, so it hardly seemed positioned or destined for growth.

Young Dental started manufacturing dental products in the early 1900s. It was just one of several small companies making instruments and supplies for the dental profession, which at that time was still in its infancy, just a few years past an age when dentistry and barberry were synonymous enterprises. Over the next half century, though, the company garnered an excellent reputation for making reliable instruments.

Young's reputation meant a great deal to Richmond. In an article in the *St. Louis Business Journal* of June 22, 2001, Richmond recounted an experience he had once had at a dentistry conference, where a man, explaining why he would love to work for Young, told Richmond that in all his travels as a dentistry salesman, he had found that "whenever dentists complained about their tools not working right they would always recommend Young."

Although it remained a small company in a very fragmented industry, for several decades Young kept pace with the evolution of dentistry by working with academic clinicians and practicing dentists to identify problems in the profession, and, by using its design and manufacturing capabilities, helped solve them. It would continue to do so under a new owner's direction.

1968–89: A Period of Slow but Steady Growth

In 1968, seven years after Richmond bought the company, Young began marketing its Triple Seal prophy angle. Unlike other prophy angles then in use, the Triple Seal angle did not show any significant eroding effects from the abrasive polish

Company Perspectives:

Over the past 100 years, Young has become a true partner in preventive dentistry. For dentists and hygienists, the Young name is synonymous with quality, reliability, and innovation. Building on our strong foundation, Young Innovations has a three-pronged strategy for growth: to continuously improve our manufacturing processes, to develop innovative new products, and to execute strategic acquisitions.

used in cleaning teeth and was made to hold up under repeated sterilizations almost indefinitely. Although significantly more expensive than prophy angles sold by competitors, the durable Triple Seal angle quickly gained a leading share in its U.S. market sector, thanks to its high quality. The company also claimed market front ranking with its prophy cups, which were used in conjunction with the Triple Seal angles.

Still, for the next two decades, Young grew very slowly. It kept its focus on preventive dentistry, however, which the dental profession itself increasingly stressed. Meanwhile, companies that would later play significant roles in the growth of Young got their start.

Rapid Growth Through New Products and Diversification

During the late 1980s and early 1990s, public awareness and concern about infectious disease, including AIDS, became a critical concern of the dental profession and helped ignite a major increase in the number of subscribers to dental health plans. Between 1990 and 1994, that number more than doubled, growing from 7.8 million to 18.4 million. Among others, Young took an active role in establishing standards for infection control in dental care procedures. The new public and professional concern helped boost the sale of the company's metal Triple Seal prophy angle, primarily because of the angle's durability and design. It also led to a new product when, in 1990, Young introduced a disposable Triple Seal angle. The new single-use angle quickly garnered a major share of its particular market, just as the company's older reusable Triple Seal angle had done a dozen years before. In fact, by the end of the decade, the disposable prophy angles would become the largest source of the company's revenue.

The success of Young's prophy angles fueled the company's growth and put it in a financial position both to expand and diversify, something it started to do in 1995. In that year, the company took a significant step forward by acquiring Lorvic Holdings Inc. Lorvic produced a line of infection control products. These included fluoride treatment and application products as well as products for dental equipment sterilization and plaque removal. Also, to position itself for further expansion, Young Dental filed a preliminary prospectus with the SEC. Its plan was to go public and raise up to $25 million in an initial public offering. The move was delayed, however, and the stock issue was not floated until 1997.

Meanwhile, in 1996, using an $18.5 million bank loan from Boatmen's National Bank, the company both paid down its existing debt and purchased Denticator International Inc. of Rancho Cordova, California. Denticator, which produced low cost disposable prophy angles, was in competition with Young, whose angles were somewhat higher in cost. With its acquisition of Denticator, Young both gained 75 percent of the special disposable prophy angle market and broadened its price range within that market. By 1996, between 80 million and 90 million disposable prophy angles were being marketed each year.

Revenues generated by its new acquisitions helped boost Young's gross to $21.6 million in 1996, up from $17.5 million the previous year. It was holding to a pattern of success, which throughout the 1990s showed a steady increase in annual revenues and a corresponding increase in its annual net income. On average, between 1992 and 2000, the company's net profit margin ranged between 15.3 percent and 23.6 percent, which provides a good indication of its excellent financial performance—one that through the 1990s encouraged the company to continue its aggressive growth.

1997–98: Young Goes Public and Continues Expanding

To help spur its sales, in July 1997, Young significantly modified its marketing strategy. Until that time, the company used independent sales representatives who were moving not only Young's products but lines of other companies as well. To improve its domestic marketing efficiency, the company switched to using company employees who represented and sold Young's lines exclusively; however, it did continue to use non-exclusive distributors in overseas markets.

Also, Young at last went public in 1997, making its initial public offering (IPO) of 2.3 million shares on November 10. The sale netted Young $25.2 million, giving the company considerable capital for further expansion. A major acquisition soon followed when, in 1998, Young acquired Panoramic Corporation of Fort Wayne, Indiana. Panoramic, founded in 1986, was created to design, manufacture, and market a panoramic X-ray machine (one allowing dentists to X-ray a patient's whole mouth in one exposure) in the United States and Canada. A highly successful company, Panoramic was unique within the domestic dental equipment market in that bypassing all middle marketers it sold its machines directly to its client dentists. With the purchase of Panoramic, Young picked up that customer database. It also kept its focus on preventive dental care, since panoramic x-rays were widely used for the early detection of dental problems.

Panoramic's founder, Eric Stetzel, had begun selling dental supplies immediately after graduating from college. He jobbed a Japanese panoramic X-ray line and soon became its largest U.S. distributor. In mid-1980s, prompted by the inflating value of the yen, he decided to manufacture a competitive panoramic X-ray machine on his own. Stetzel's new concern reverse-engineered the Japanese product, and by 1988 Panoramic had begun marketing its new product. The company's PC-100, thanks to its high quality, low manufacturing cost, and very competitive price, soon made Panoramic the market-share leader in the United States. When acquired by Young, expectations were that its annual sales would increase by up to 9 percent in 1999.

Key Dates:

1900: Young Dental Manufacturing Company is founded in Missouri.
1953: The Lorvic Corporation is founded.
1961: George Richmond acquires Young Dental.
1968: Young Dental introduces its Triple Seal prophy angle and gains market share leadership in prophy cups and angles.
1986: Eric Stetzel forms Panoramic Corp.
1990: Young introduces the disposable version of its Triple Seal prophy angle.
1995: Young acquires The Lorvic Corporation; Young Innovations, Inc. (YII) is formed as a parent company for Young Dental and other subsidiaries.
1996: YII purchases Denticator International, Inc.
1997: The company goes public and makes IPO.
1998: YII acquires Panoramic Corporation.
1999: Corporation purchases Athena Technology, Inc.
2000: YII acquires Plak Smacker Inc.
2001: Company acquires assets of Biotrol and Challenge from Pro-Dex Corp.

It was also in 1998 that Young completed the transfer and consolidation of most of its Denticator product line manufacturing, moving it from its facility in Sacramento, California, to its facility in St. Louis. Its injection molding production remained at the Sacramento facility. The manufacturing transfer had a slightly negative impact on the company's profit margin, but it was expected to improve Young's earnings in the next and subsequent years.

1999–2001: Continued Growth Through Further Acquisition

Young's growth, fueled by a spending spree, continued through the rest of the decade and into the start of the next century. In 1999, the company acquired Athena Technology, Inc., or Athena/Champion. That company developed, made and marketed handpieces and other related items and supplies for the dental profession. The price tag on Athena/Champion was about $4.9 million, which included Young's assumption of the company's $1 million debt. Young's projections were that the acquisition would add about $4.0 million to its annual sales. In addition, Young bought a one-third interest in Brownsville, Texas-based International Assembly, Inc. (IAI), the company that assembled some of Young's disposable prophy angles at its Maquiladora plant in Matamoros, Mexico. The terms of the agreement included an option, to be exercised before an early date in 2001, which would allow Young to purchase the remaining two-thirds ownership of IAI.

In the next year, Young also bought Plak Smacker, Inc., a Riverside, California-based distributer of a range of dental products for retail consumers and dental professionals, including orthodontic tools and brushes, flavored gloves, and chil-

dren's toothbrushes and toothpastes. Among its products was a cordless, battery-operated flossing device called Floss-o-matic, which the company had introduced in 1996. In addition to marketing its products directly to orthodontists and pedodontists, Plak-Smacker sold its line through mass market outlets. Young bought the company for about $7.0 million, in anticipation of realizing an annual increase in its sales of about $10 million as a result of the acquisition.

Young Innovations, Inc. continued its buying spree in 2001, acquiring both Biotrol International Inc. and Challenge Control Products Inc., two subsidiaries of Pro-Dex Corp., a Louisville, Colorado holding company. Biotrol manufactured infection control products, while Challenge made fluoride gels and whitening products. The cost of the two Pro-Dex subsidiaries was $9.0 million in cash. Their acquisition significantly expanded Young's infection control and preventive product lines, and it was estimated that in tandem they would produce an increase in Young's annual revenue of approximately $8.5 million.

As Young's mission statement indicates, the company's strategy for the new century is to do more of what it was doing at the close of the old one. Plans call for upgrading and expanding its manufacturing capabilities, developing new, innovative products, and making new acquisitions. Its reputation and financial condition argue that the company is very well positioned to execute those plans successfully.

Principal Subsidiaries

Athena Champions Inc.; Denticator International, Inc.; Panoramic Corporation; Plak Smacker Inc.; Young Dental Mfg. Co.

Principal Competitors

DENTSPLY International, Inc.; Henry Schein, Inc.; Milestone Scientific, Inc.; Patterson Dental Company; Sybron Dental Specialties, Inc.

Further Reading

Corey, Andrea, ''Acquisitions Push Young Innovations Closer to $43 Million,'' *St. Louis Business Journal*, November 29, 1999, p. 12.
McLaughlin, Tim, ''Buy Helps Young Dental Polish Off 75% of Market,'' *St. Louis Business Journal*, October 21, 1996, p. 1A.
Sieckmann, Amy, ''George Richmond Young Innovations Inc.,'' *St. Louis Business Journal*, June 22, 2001, p. 36.
Tucci, Linda, ''Richard Richmond Resigns at Young Innovations Inc.,'' *St. Louis Business Journal*, April 20, 2001, p. 5.
''Young Innovations Completes Acquisition of Athena Technology, Inc.,'' *PR Newswire*, April 5, 1999.
''Young Innovations Announces Investment in Maquiladora That Assembles the Company's Disposable Prophy Angles,'' *PR Newswire*, May 18, 1999.
''Young Innovations Completes Acquisition of Plak Smacker, Inc.,'' *PR Newswire*, June 14, 2000.
''Young Innovations, Inc. Acquires Assets of Biotrol and Challenge from Pro-Dex Corporation,'' *PR Newswire*, June 13, 2001.

—John W. Fiero

INDEX TO COMPANIES

Index to Companies

Listings in this index are arranged in alphabetical order under the company name. Company names beginning with a letter or proper name such as Eli Lilly & Co. will be found under the first letter of the company name. Definite articles (The, Le, La) are ignored for alphabetical purposes as are forms of incorporation that precede the company name (AB, NV). Company names printed in bold type have full, historical essays on the page numbers appearing in bold. Updates to entries that appeared in earlier volumes are signified by the notation (**upd.**). Company names in light type are references within an essay to that company, not full historical essays. This index is cumulative with volume numbers printed in bold type.

Altos Hornos de México, S.A. de C.V., **13** 144; **19** 220; **39** 188; **42** 6–8
Altron Incorporated, 20 8–10
Altura Energy Ltd., **41** 359
Aluar. *See* Aluminios Argentinos.
Aluma Systems Corp., **9** 512; **22** 14
Alumax Inc., **I** 508; **III** 758; **IV** 18–19; **8** 505–06; **22** 286
Alumina Partners of Jamaica, **IV** 123
Aluminate Sales Corp, **I** 373
Aluminio de Galicia, **IV** 174
Aluminios Argentinos, **26** 433
Aluminium Co. of London, **IV** 69
L'Aluminium Francais, **IV** 173
Aluminium Ltd., **IV** 9–11, 14, 153
Aluminium-Oxid Stade GmbH, **IV** 231
Aluminium Plant and Vessel Co., **III** 419
Aluminum Can Co., **I** 607
Aluminum Company of America, I 373, 599; **II** 315, 402, 422; **III** 490–91, 613; **IV** 9–12, **14–16**, 56, 59, 121–22, 131, 173, 703; **6** 39; **12** 346; **19** 240, 292; **20** **11–14 (upd.);** **22** 455; **42** 438
Aluminum Company of Canada Ltd., **II** 345; **IV** 10–12, 154
Aluminum Cooking Utensil Co., **IV** 14
Aluminum Forge Co., **IV** 137
Aluminum Norf GmbH, **IV** 231
Aluminum of Korea, **III** 516
Aluminum Rolling Mills, **17** 280
Aluminum Sales Corporation, **12** 346
Aluminum Seating Corp., **I** 201
Alun Cathcart, **6** 357
Alup-Kompressoren Pressorun, **III** 570; **20** 361
Alupak, A.G., **12** 377
Alusaf, **IV** 92
Alusuisse Lonza Group Ltd., **IV** 12; **31** 11
Alva Jams Pty., **I** 437
Alvic Group, **20** 363
Alyeska Pipeline Service Co., **IV** 522, 571; **14** 542; **24** 521; **40** 356
Alyeska Seafoods Co., **II** 578
ALZA Corporation, 10 53–55; **36 36–39 (upd.); 40** 11; **41** 200–01
Alzwerke GmbH, **IV** 230
AM Acquisition Inc., **8** 559–60
AM Cosmetics, Inc., **31** 89
Am-Par Records, **II** 129
Am-Safe, Inc., **16** 357
AM-TEX Corp., Inc., **12** 443
Amagasaki Co., **I** 492; **24** 325
Amagasaki Spinners Ltd., **V** 387
Amagasaki Steel Co., Ltd., **IV** 130
Amalgamaize Co., **14** 18
Amalgamated Chemicals, Ltd., **IV** 401
Amalgamated Dental International, **10** 271–72
Amalgamated Distilled Products, **II** 609
Amalgamated Press, **IV** 666; **7** 244, 342; **17** 397
Amalgamated Roadstone Corp., **III** 752; **28** 449
Amalgamated Sugar Co., **14** 18; **19** 467–68
Amalgamated Weatherware, **IV** 696
Amana Refrigeration Company, **II** 86; **11** 413; **18** 226; **38** 374; **42** 159
Amaray International Corporation, **12** 264
Amarillo Gas Company. *See* Atmos Energy Corporation.
Amarillo Railcar Services, **6** 580
Amarin Plastics, **IV** 290
Amax Gold, **36** 316

AMAX Inc., I 508; **III** 687; **IV 17–19,** 46, 139, 171, 239, 387; **6** 148; **12** 244; **22** 106, 286
Amazon.com, Inc., 25 17–19
Amazôna Mineracao SA, **IV** 56
Ambac Industries, **I** 85
AmBase Corp., **III** 264
Amber's Stores, Inc., **17** 360
Amblin Entertainment, 21 23–27; **33** 431
Ambrose Shardlow, **III** 494
AMC Entertainment Inc., 12 12–14; **14** 87; **21** 362; **23** 126; **35 27–29 (upd.)**
AMCA International Corporation, **7** 513; **8** 545; **10** 329; **23** 299
AMCC. *See* Applied Micro Circuits Corporation.
Amcell. *See* American Cellular Network.
Amchem Products Inc., **I** 666
AMCO, Inc., **13** 159
Amcor Limited, IV 248–50; **19** 13–16 **(upd.)**
AMCORE Financial Inc., 44 22–26
Amcraft Building Products Co., Inc., **22** 15
AMD. *See* Advanced Micro Devices, Inc.
Amdahl Corporation, III 109–11, 140; **6** 272; **12** 238; **13** 202; **14 13–16 (upd.);** **16** 194, 225–26; **22** 293; **25** 87; **40 20–25 (upd.);** **42** 147. *See also* Fujitsu Limited.
AME Finanziaria, **IV** 587; **19** 19
AMEC plc, **I** 568; **36** 322
Amedco, **6** 295
Amer Group plc, 24 530; **41 14–16**
Amer Sport, **22** 202
Amerada Hess Corporation, IV 365–67, 400, 454, 522, 571, 658; **11** 353; **21 28–31 (upd.);** **24** 521
Amerco, 6 351–52
Ameri-Kart Corp., **19** 277, 279
America Japan Sheet Glass Co., **III** 714
America Latina Companhia de Seguros, **III** 289
America Online, Inc., 10 56–58, 237; **13** 147; **15** 54, 265, 321; **18** 24; **19** 41; **22** 52, 519, 522; **26 16–20 (upd.);** **27** 20, 106, 301, 430, 517–18; **29** 143, 227; **32** 163; **33** 254; **34** 361; **35** 304, 306; **38** 269–71. *See also* CompuServe Interactive Services, Inc.
America Publishing Company, **18** 213
America Today, **13** 545
America Unplugged, **18** 77
America West Airlines, 6 72–74, 121
America West Express, **32** 334
America West Holdings Corporation, 34 22–26 (upd.)
America's Favorite Chicken Company, Inc., 7 26–28. *See also* AFC Enterprises, Inc.
American & Efird, Inc., **12** 501; **23** 260
American Agricultural Chemical Co., **IV** 401
American Air Conditioning, **25** 15
American Air Filter, **26** 3–4
American Airlines, I 30–31, 48, 71, **89–91,** 97, 106, 115, 118, 124–26, 130, 132, 512, 530; **III** 102; **6** 60, 81, **75–77 (upd.),** 121, 129–31; **9** 271–72; **10** 163; **11** 279; **12** 190, 192, 379, 381, 487; **13** 173; **14** 73; **16** 146; **18** 73; **21** 141, 143; **24** 21, 399–400; **25** 90–91, 403, 421–22; **26** 427–28, 441; **31** 103, 306; **33** 270, 302; **34** 118; **38** 105. *See also* AMR Corporation.

American Alliance Co., **III** 191
American Allsafe Co., **8** 386
American Amusements, Inc., **III** 430
American Appliance Co., **II** 85; **11** 411
American Arithmometer Company. *See* Burroughs Corporation.
American Asiatic Underwriters, **III** 195
American Association of Retired Persons, **9** 348. *See also* AARP.
American Austin Quality Foods Inc., **44** 40
American Automar Inc., **12** 29
American Automated, **11** 111
American Automobile Insurance Co., **III** 251
American Aviation and General Insurance Co., **III** 230
American Aviation Manufacturing Corp., **15** 246
American Avitron Inc, **I** 481
American Bakeries Company, **12** 275–76
American Bancorp, **11** 295
American Bancshares, Inc., **11** 457
American Bank, **9** 474–75
American Bank Note, **IV** 599
American Bank of Vicksburg, **14** 41
American Bankcorp, Inc., **8** 188
American Banker/Bond Buyer, **8** 526
American Banknote Corporation, 30 42–45
American Bar Association, 35 30–33
American Barge and Towing Company, **11** 194
American Beauty Cover Company, **12** 472
American Beef Packers, Inc., **16** 473
American Beet Sugar Company, **11** 13–14
American Bell Telephone Company, **V** 259; **14** 336
American Beryllium Co., Inc., **9** 323
American Beverage Corp., **II** 528
American Biltrite Inc., 16 16–18; **18** 116, 118; **43 19–22 (upd.)**
American Biodyne Inc., **9** 348
American Biomedical Corporation, **11** 333
American Biscuit Co., **II** 542
American Box Board Company, **12** 376
American Box Co., **IV** 137
American Brake Shoe and Foundry Company, **I** 456. *See also* ABC Rail Products Corporation.
American Brands, Inc., II 468, 477; **IV** 251; **V 395–97,** 398–99, 405; **7** 3–4; **9** 408; **12** 87, 344; **14** 95, 271–72; **16** 108, 110, 242; **19** 168–69; **38** 169. *See also* Fortune Brands, Inc.
American Bridge Co., **II** 330; **IV** 572; **7** 549
American Broadcasting Co., **25** 418. *See also* ABC, Inc. *and* Capital Cities/ABC Inc.
American Builders & Contractors Supply Co. *See* ABC Supply Co., Inc.
American Builders, Inc., **8** 436
American Building Maintenance Industries, Inc., 6 17–19. *See also* ABM Industries Incorporated.
American Bus Lines Inc., **24** 118
American Business Information, Inc., 18 21–25
American Business Interiors. *See* American Furniture Company, Inc.
American Business Products, Inc., 20 15–17
American Cable Systems, Inc. *See* Comcast Corporation.

Cahners Business Information, 43 92–95
Cahners Publishing, **IV** 667; **12** 561; **17** 398; **22** 442
CAI Corp., **12** 79
Cailler, **II** 546
Cain Chemical, **IV** 481
Cains Marcelle Potato Chips Inc., **15** 139
Caisse Commericale de Bruxelles, **II** 270
Caisse de dépôt et placement du Quebec, **II** 664
Caisse des Dépôts, **6** 206
Caisse National de Crédit Agricole, **II** 264–66
Caisse Nationale de Crédit Agricole, **15** 38–39
Caithness Glass Limited, **38** 402
Caja General de Depositos, **II** 194
Cajun Bayou Distributors and Management, Inc., **19** 301
Cajun Electric Power Cooperative, Inc., **21** 470
CAK Universal Credit Corp., **32** 80
CAL. *See* China Airlines.
Cal Circuit Abco Inc., **13** 387
CAL Corporation, **21** 199, 201
Cal-Dive International Inc., **25** 104–05
Cal-Van Tools. *See* Chemi-Trol Chemical Co.
Cal/Ink, **13** 228
Cala, **17** 558
Calais Railroad Company, **16** 348
Calcined Coke Corp., **IV** 402
Calcitherm Group, **24** 144
Calco, **I** 300–01
CalComp Inc., 13 126–29
Calcot Ltd., 33 84–87
Calculating-Tabulating-Recording Company. *See* International Business Machines Corporation.
Calcutta & Burmah Steam Navigation Co., **III** 521
Caldbeck Macgregor & Co., **III** 523
Calder Race Course, Inc., **29** 118
Caldera Systems Inc., **38** 416, 420
Caldor Inc., 12 54–56, 508; **30** 57
Caledonian Airways. *See* British Caledonian Airways.
Caledonian Bank, **10** 337
Caledonian Paper plc, **IV** 302
Calédonickel, **IV** 107
Calgary Power Company. *See* TransAlta Utilities Corporation.
Calgene, Inc., **29** 330; **41** 155
Calgon Corporation, **6** 27; **16** 387; **34** 281
Calgon Vestal Laboratories, **37** 44
Calgon Water Management, **15** 154; **40** 176
Cali Realty. *See* Mack-Cali Realty Corporation.
California Arabian Standard Oil Co., **IV** 536, 552
California Automated Design, Inc., **11** 284
California Bank, **II** 289
California Charter Inc., **24** 118
California Cheese, **24** 444
California Computer Products, Inc. *See* CalComp Inc.
California Cooler Inc., **I** 227, 244; **10** 181
California Dental Supply Co., **19** 289
California Design Studio, **31** 52
California Federal Bank, **22** 275
California First, **II** 358
California Fruit Growers Exchange. *See* Sunkist Growers, Inc.

California Ink Company, **13** 227
California Institute of Technology, **9** 367
California Insurance Co., **III** 234
California Oilfields, Ltd., **IV** 531, 540
California Pacific, **22** 172
California Perfume Co., **III** 15
California Petroleum Co., **IV** 551–52
California Pizza Kitchen Inc., 15 74–76
California Plant Protection, **9** 408
California Portland Cement Co., **III** 718; **19** 69
California Pro Sports Inc., **24** 404
California Slim, **27** 197
California Steel Industries, **IV** 125
California Telephone and Light, **II** 490
California Test Bureau, **IV** 636
California Texas Oil Co., **III** 672
California Tile, **III** 673
California-Western States Life Insurance Co., **III** 193–94
California Woodfiber Corp., **IV** 266
Caligen, **9** 92
Caligor. *See* Henry Schein Medical.
Call-Chronicle Newspapers, Inc., **IV** 678
Callaghan & Company, **8** 526
Callard and Bowser, **II** 594
Callaway Golf Company, 15 77–79; 16 109; **19** 430, 432; **23** 267, 474; **37** 4
Callaway Wines, **I** 264
Callebaut, **II** 520–21
Callender's Cable and Construction Co. Ltd., **III** 433–34
Calloway's Nursery Inc., **12** 200
Calma, **II** 30; **12** 196
Calmar Co., **12** 127
CalMat Co., III 718; **19 69–72**
Calmic Ltd., **I** 715
Calor Group, **IV** 383
Caloric Corp., **II** 86
Calpine Corporation, 36 102–04
Calsil Ltd., **III** 674
Caltex Petroleum Corporation, II 53; **III** 672; **IV** 397, 434, 440–41, 479, 484, 492, 519, 527, 536, 545–46, 552, 560, 562, 718; **7** 483; **19 73–75**; **21** 204; **25** 471; **38** 320; **41** 392–93
Calumatic Group, **25** 82
Calumet & Arizona Mining Co., **IV** 177
Calumet Electric Company, **6** 532
Calvert & Co., **I** 293
Calvert Insurance Co. *See* Gryphon Holdings, Inc.
Calvin Bullock Ltd., **I** 472
Calvin Klein, Inc., 9 203; **22 121–24; 25** 258; **27** 329; **32** 476
Calyx & Corolla Inc., **37** 162–63
Camargo Foods, **12** 531
Camas. *See* Aggregate Industries plc.
CamBar. *See* Cameron & Barkley Company.
Camber Corporation, **25** 405
Cambrex Corporation, 12 147–48; **16 67–69; 44 59–62 (upd.)**
Cambria Steel Company, **IV** 35; **7** 48
Cambrian Wagon Works Ltd., **31** 369
Cambridge Applied Nutrition Toxicology and Biosciences Ltd., **10** 105
Cambridge Biotech Corp., **13** 241
Cambridge Electric Co., **14** 124, 126
Cambridge Gas Co., **14** 124
The Cambridge Instrument Company, **35** 272
Cambridge Interactive Systems Ltd., **10** 241

Cambridge SoundWorks, Inc., **36** 101
Cambridge Steam Corp., **14** 124
Cambridge Technology Partners, Inc., 36 105–08
Camco Inc., **IV** 658
Camden Wire Co., Inc., **7** 408; **31** 354–55
CAMECO, **IV** 436
Camelot Barthropp Ltd., **26** 62
Camelot Group plc, **34** 140
Camelot Music, Inc., 26 52–54
Cameron & Barkley Company, 13 79; **28 59–61**
Cameron Ashley Inc., **19** 57
Cameron-Brown Company, **10** 298
Cameron Iron Works, **II** 17
Cameron Oil Co., **IV** 365
CAMI Automotive, **III** 581
Camintonn, **9** 41–42
Camp Manufacturing Co., **IV** 345; **8** 102
Campbell Box & Tag Co., **IV** 333
Campbell Cereal Company. *See* Malt-O-Meal Company.
Campbell, Cowperthwait & Co., **17** 498
Campbell-Ewald Co., **I** 16–17
Campbell Hausfeld. *See* Scott Fetzer Company.
Campbell Industries, Inc., **11** 534
Campbell-Mithun-Esty, Inc., 13 516; **16 70–72**
Campbell Soup Company, I 21, 26, 31, 599, 601; **II 479–81**, 508, 684; **7 66–69 (upd.)**, 340; **10** 382; **11** 172; **18** 58; **25** 516; **26 55–59 (upd.)**; **33** 32; **43** 121; **44** 295
Campbell Taggart, Inc., **I** 219; **19** 135–36, 191; **34** 36
Campeau Corporation, IV 721; **V 25–28; 9** 209, 211, 391; **12** 36–37; **13** 43; **15** 94; **17** 560; **22** 110; **23** 60; **31** 192; **37** 13
Campo Electronics, Appliances & Computers, Inc., 16 73–75
Campo Lindo, **25** 85
Campofrio Alimentacion, S.A., **18** 247
CAMPSA. *See* Compañia Arrendataria del Monopolio de Petróleos Sociedad Anónima.
Campus Services, Inc., **12** 173
Canada & Dominion Sugar Co., **II** 581
Canada Cable & Wire Company, **9** 11
Canada Cement, **III** 704–05
Canada Cup, **IV** 290
Canada Development Corp., **IV** 252; **17** 29
Canada Dry, **I** 281
Canada, Limited, **24** 143
Canada Packers Inc., II 482–85; 41 249
Canada Safeway Ltd., **II** 650, 654
Canada Surety Co., **26** 486
Canada Trust. *See* CT Financial Services Inc.
Canada Tungsten Mining Corp., Ltd., **IV** 18
Canada Wire & Cable Company, Ltd., **IV** 164–65; **7** 397–99
Canadair, Inc., I 58; **7** 205; **13** 358; **16 76–78**
Canadian Ad-Check Services Inc., **26** 270
Canadian Airlines International Ltd., **6** 61–62, 101; **12** 192; **23** 10; **24** 400
Canadian Bank of Commerce, **II** 244–45
Canadian British Aluminum, **IV** 11
The Canadian Broadcasting Corporation (CBC), 37 55–58

Greaseater, Ltd., **8** 463–64

Great Alaska Tobacco Co., **17** 80

Great American Bagel and Coffee Co., **27** 482

Great American Broadcasting Inc., **18** 65–66; **22** 131; **23** 257–58

Great American Cookie Company. *See* Mrs. Fields' Original Cookies, Inc.

Great American Entertainment Company, **13** 279

Great American First Savings Bank of San Diego, **II** 420

Great American Life Insurance Co., **III** 190–92

Great American Lines Inc., **12** 29

Great American Management and Investment, Inc., 8 228–31

Great American Reserve Insurance Co., **IV** 343; **10** 247

Great American Restaurants, **13** 321

The Great Atlantic & Pacific Tea Company, Inc., II 636–38, 629, 655–56, 666; **13** 25, 127, 237; **15** 259; **16** 63–64, **247–50 (upd.); 17** 106; **18** 6; **19** 479–80; **24** 417; **26** 463; **33** 434

Great Bagel and Coffee Co., **27** 480–81

Great Beam Co., **III** 690

Great Eastern Railway, **6** 424

Great 5¢ Store, **V** 224

Great Halviggan, **III** 690

Great Harvest Bread Company, 44 184–86

Great Lakes Bancorp, 8 232–33

Great Lakes Bankgroup, **II** 457

Great Lakes Carbon Corporation, **12** 99

Great Lakes Chemical Corp., I 341–42; 8 262; **14 216–18 (upd.)**

Great Lakes Corp., **IV** 136

Great Lakes Energy Corp., **39** 261

Great Lakes Pipe Line Co., **IV** 400, 575; **31** 470

Great Lakes Steel Corp., **IV** 236; **8** 346; **12** 352; **26** 528

Great Lakes Window, Inc., **12** 397

Great Land Seafoods, Inc., **II** 553

Great Northern, **III** 282

Great Northern Import Co., **I** 292

Great Northern Nekoosa Corp., **IV** 282–83, 300; **9** 260–61

Great Northern Railway Company, **6** 596

Great Plains Software Inc., **38** 432

Great Plains Transportation, **18** 226

Great Shoshone & Twin Falls Water Power Company, **12** 265

The Great Universal Stores plc, V 67–69; 15 83; **17** 66, 68; **19 181–84 (upd.); 41** 74, 76

Great-West Lifeco Inc., III 260–61; 21 447. *See also* Power Corporation of Canada.

The Great Western Auction House & Clothing Store, **19** 261

Great Western Billiard Manufactory, **III** 442

Great Western Financial Corporation, 10 339–41

Great Western Foam Co., **17** 182

Great Western Railway, **III** 272

Great World Foods, Inc., **17** 93

Greatamerica Corp., **I** 489; **10** 419; **24** 303

Greater All American Markets, **II** 601; **7** 19

Greater New York Film Rental Co., **II** 169

Greater Washington Investments, Inc., **15** 248

Greb Industries Ltd., **16** 79, 545

Grebner GmbH, **26** 21

Grede Foundries, Inc., 38 214–17

Greeley Beef Plant, **13** 350

Greeley Gas Company, **43** 56–57

Green Acquisition Co., **18** 107

Green Bay Food Company, **7** 127

The Green Bay Packers, Inc., 32 223–26

Green Capital Investors L.P., **23** 413–14

Green Cross K.K., **I** 665

Green Giant, **II** 556; **13** 408; **14** 212, 214; **24** 140–41

Green Island Cement (Holdings) Ltd. Group, **IV** 694–95

Green Line Investor Services, **18** 553

Green Mountain Coffee, Inc., 31 227–30

Green Power & Light Company. *See* UtiliCorp United Inc.

Green River Electric Corporation, **11** 37

Green Thumb, **II** 562

Green Tree Financial Corporation, 11 162–63. *See also* Conseco, Inc.

The Greenalls Group PLC, 21 245–47

The Greenbrier Companies, 19 185–87

Greene King plc, 31 223–26

Greenfield Healthy Foods, **26** 58

Greenfield Industries Inc., **13** 8

Greenham Construction Materials, **38** 451–52

Greenleaf Corp., **IV** 203

Greenman Brothers Inc. *See* Noodle Kidoodle.

GreenPoint Financial Corp., 28 166–68

Greensboro Life Insurance Company, **11** 213

Greenville Insulating Board Corp., **III** 763

Greenville Tube Corporation, **21** 108

Greenwell Montagu Gilt-Edged, **II** 319; **17** 325

Greenwich Associates, **19** 117

Greenwich Capital Markets, **II** 311

Greenwood Mills, Inc., 14 219–21

Greenwood Publishing Group, **IV** 610

Greenwood Trust Company, **18** 478

Gregg Publishing Co., **IV** 636

Greif Bros. Corporation, 15 186–88

Grenfell and Colegrave Ltd., **II** 245

Gresham Insurance Company Limited, **24** 285

Gresham Life Assurance, **III** 200, 272–73

GretagMacbeth Holdings AG, **18** 291

Gretel's Pretzels, **35** 56

Grey Advertising, Inc., I 175, 623; **6 26–28; 10** 69; **14** 150; **22** 396; **25** 166, 381

Grey United Stores, **II** 666

Grey Wolf, Inc., 43 201–03

Greyhound Corp., I 448–50; II 445; **6** 27; **8** 144–45; **10** 72; **12** 199; **16** 349; **22** 406, 427; **23** 173–74; **27** 480; **42** 394

Greyhound Lines, Inc., 32 227–31 (upd.)

Greyhound Temporary Services, **25** 432

Greylock Mills, **III** 213

GRiD Systems Corp., **II** 107

Griesheim Elektron, **IV** 140

Grieveson, Grant and Co., **II** 422–23

Griffin and Sons, **II** 543

Griffin Bacal, **25** 381

Griffin Land & Nurseries, Inc., 43 204–06

Griffin Pipe Products Co., **7** 30–31

Griffin Wheel Company, **7** 29–30

Griffon Corporation, 34 194–96

Griffon Cutlery Corp., **13** 166

Grigg, Elliot & Co., **14** 555

Grimes Aerospace, **22** 32

Grindlays Bank, **II** 189

Gringoir/Broussard, **II** 556

Grinnell Corp., III 643–45; 11 198; **13 245–47**

Grip Printing & Publishing Co., **IV** 644

Grisewood & Dempsey, **IV** 616

Grist Mill Company, 15 189–91; 22 338

Gristede's Sloan's, Inc., 31 231–33

GRM Industries Inc., **15** 247–48

Grocer Publishing Co., **IV** 638

Grocery Store Products Co., **III** 21

Grocery Warehouse, **II** 602

Groen Manufacturing, **III** 468

Grogan-Cochran Land Company, **7** 345

Grolier Inc., IV 619; 16 251–54; 43 207–11 (upd.)

Grolier Interactive, **41** 409

Groot-Noordhollandsche, **III** 177–79

Groovy Beverages, **II** 477

Gross Brothers Laundry. *See* G&K Services, Inc.

Gross Townsend Frank Hoffman, **6** 28

Grosset & Dunlap, Inc., **II** 144; **III** 190–91

Grosskraftwerk Franken AG, **23** 47

Grossman's Inc., 13 248–50

Grossmith Agricultural Industries, **II** 500

Grosvenor Marketing Co., **II** 465

Groton Victory Yard, **I** 661

Ground Round, Inc., 21 248–51

Ground Services Inc., **13** 49

Group Arnault, **32** 146

Group 4 Falck A/S, 42 165–68, 338

Group Health Cooperative, 41 181–84

Group Hospitalization and Medical Services, **10** 161

Group Lotus, **13** 357

Group Maintenance America Corp. *See* Encompass Services Corporation.

Group Schneider S.A., **20** 214

Groupe AB, **19** 204

Groupe AG, **III** 201–02

Groupe Air France, 6 92–94. *See also* Air France *and* Societe Air France.

Groupe Ancienne Mutuelle, **III** 210–11

Groupe André, 17 210–12

Groupe Axime, **37** 232

Groupe Barthelmey, **III** 373

Groupe Bisset, **24** 510

Groupe Bollore, **37** 21

Groupe Bruxelles Lambert, **26** 368

Groupe Bull, **10** 563–64; **12** 246; **21** 391; **34** 517. *See also* Compagnie des Machines Bull.

Groupe Casino. *See* Etablissements Economiques de Casino Guichard, Perrachon et Cie, S.C.A.

Groupe Castorama-Dubois Investissements, 23 230–32

Groupe Danone, 14 150; **32 232–36 (upd.)**

Le Groupe Darty, **24** 266, 270

Groupe Dassault Aviation SA, 26 179–82 (upd.); 42 373, 376

Groupe de la Cité, IV 614–16, 617

Groupe de la Financière d'Angers, **IV** 108

Groupe DMC (Dollfus Mieg & Cie), 27 186–88

Groupe Fournier SA, 44 187–89

INDEX TO INDUSTRIES

Index to Industries

BEVERAGES

BIOTECHNOLOGY

CONSTRUCTION

ENGINEERING & MANAGEMENT SERVICES

ENTERTAINMENT & LEISURE

FINANCIAL SERVICES: BANKS

FINANCIAL SERVICES: NON-BANKS

FOOD PRODUCTS

FOOD SERVICES & RETAILERS

HEALTH & PERSONAL CARE PRODUCTS

HEALTH CARE SERVICES

HOTELS

INFORMATION TECHNOLOGY

INSURANCE

MATERIALS

MINING & METALS

PAPER & FORESTRY

PERSONAL SERVICES

PETROLEUM

PUBLISHING & PRINTING

REAL ESTATE

RETAIL & WHOLESALE

RUBBER & TIRE

TELECOMMUNICATIONS

TEXTILES & APPAREL

UTILITIES

GEOGRAPHIC INDEX

Geographic Index

Montgomery Ward & Co., Incorporated, V; 20 (upd.)
Moog Inc., 13
Moore Medical Corp., 17
Moore-Handley, Inc., 39
Moran Towing Corporation, Inc., 15
Morgan Stanley Dean Witter & Company, 33 (upd.)
Morgan Stanley Group Inc., II; 16 (upd.)
Morgan, Lewis & Bockius LLP, 29
Morris Communications Corporation, 36
Morris Travel Services L.L.C., 26
Morrison Knudsen Corporation, 7; 28 (upd.)
Morrison Restaurants Inc., 11
Morse Shoe Inc., 13
Morton International Inc., 9 (upd.)
Morton Thiokol, Inc., I
Morton's Restaurant Group, Inc., 30
Mosinee Paper Corporation, 15
Mossimo, Inc., 27
Motel 6 Corporation, 13
Mothers Work, Inc., 18
Motley Fool, Inc., The, 40
Motor Cargo Industries, Inc., 35
Motorola, Inc., II; 11 (upd.); 34 (upd.)
Motown Records Company L.P., 26
Mountain States Mortgage Centers, Inc., 29
Movado Group, Inc., 28
Movie Gallery, Inc., 31
Movie Star Inc., 17
Mr. Coffee, Inc., 15
Mr. Gasket Inc., 15
Mrs. Baird's Bakeries, 29
Mrs. Fields' Original Cookies, Inc., 27
Mt. Olive Pickle Company, Inc., 44
MTS Inc., 37
Mueller Industries, Inc., 7
Multimedia Games, Inc., 41
Multimedia, Inc., 11
Murdock Madaus Schwabe, 26
Murphy Family Farms Inc., 22
Murphy Oil Corporation, 7; 32 (upd.)
Musicland Stores Corporation, 9; 38 (upd.)
Mutual Benefit Life Insurance Company, The, III
Mutual Life Insurance Company of New York, The, III
Muzak, Inc., 18
Mycogen Corporation, 21
Myers Industries, Inc., 19
Mylan Laboratories Inc., I; 20 (upd.)
Nabisco Foods Group, II; 7 (upd.)
Nabors Industries, Inc., 9
NACCO Industries, Inc., 7
Nalco Chemical Corporation, I; 12 (upd.)
Nantucket Allserve, Inc., 22
Nash Finch Company, 8; 23 (upd.)
Nashua Corporation, 8
Nathan's Famous, Inc., 29
National Amusements Inc., 28
National Association for Stock Car Auto Racing, 32
National Association of Securities Dealers, Inc., 10
National Audubon Society, 26
National Auto Credit, Inc., 16
National Beverage Corp., 26
National Broadcasting Company, Inc., II; 6 (upd.); 28 (upd.)
National Can Corporation, I
National Car Rental System, Inc., 10
National City Corp., 15
National Convenience Stores Incorporated, 7
National Discount Brokers Group, Inc., 28
National Distillers and Chemical Corporation, I

National Envelope Corporation, 32
National Football League, 29
National Fuel Gas Company, 6
National Geographic Society, 9; 30 (upd.)
National Grape Cooperative Association, Inc., 20
National Gypsum Company, 10
National Health Laboratories Incorporated, 11
National Hockey League, 35
National Home Centers, Inc., 44
National Instruments Corporation, 22
National Intergroup, Inc., V
National Media Corporation, 27
National Medical Enterprises, Inc., III
National Patent Development Corporation, 13
National Picture & Frame Company, 24
National Presto Industries, Inc., 16; 43 (upd.)
National Public Radio, 19
National R.V. Holdings, Inc., 32
National Railroad Passenger Corporation, 22
National Record Mart, Inc., 29
National Rifle Association of America, 37
National Sanitary Supply Co., 16
National Semiconductor Corporation, II; VI, 26 (upd.)
National Service Industries, Inc., 11
National Standard Co., 13
National Steel Corporation, 12
National TechTeam, Inc., 41
NationsBank Corporation, 10
Natural Wonders Inc., 14
Nature Conservancy, The, 28
Nature's Sunshine Products, Inc., 15
Nautica Enterprises, Inc., 18; 44 (upd.)
Navarre Corporation, 24
Navistar International Corporation, I; 10 (upd.)
Navy Exchange Service Command, 31
Navy Federal Credit Union, 33
NBD Bancorp, Inc., 11
NBTY, Inc., 31
NCH Corporation, 8
NCNB Corporation, II
NCO Group, Inc., 42
NCR Corporation, III; 6 (upd.); 30 (upd.)
Nebraska Public Power District, 29
Neff Corp., 32
Neiman Marcus Co., 12
NERCO, Inc., 7
Netscape Communications Corporation, 15; 35 (upd.)
Network Associates, Inc., 25
Neutrogena Corporation, 17
Nevada Bell Telephone Company, 14
Nevada Power Company, 11
New Balance Athletic Shoe, Inc., 25
New Dana Perfumes Company, 37
New Piper Aircraft, Inc., The, 44
New Plan Realty Trust, 11
New Street Capital Inc., 8
New UK Business Services, Inc., 18
New UK Confectionery Co., 15
New UK Electric System, V
New UK Mutual Life Insurance Company, III
New Valley Corporation, 17
New World Restaurant Group, Inc., 44
New York Daily News, 32
New York Life Insurance Company, III
New York Restaurant Group, Inc., 32
New York State Electric and Gas, 6
New York Stock Exchange, Inc., 9; 39 (upd.)

New York Times Company, The, IV; 19 (upd.)
Newcor, Inc., 40
Newell Co., 9
Newhall Land and Farming Company, 14
Newman's Own, Inc., 37
Newmont Mining Corporation, 7
Newport News Shipbuilding and Dry Dock Co., 13
Newport News Shipbuilding Inc., 38 (upd.)
News America Publishing Inc., 12
Nextel Communications, Inc., 10; 27 (upd.)
NFO Worldwide, Inc., 24
NGC Corporation, 18
Niagara Corporation, 28
Niagara Mohawk Power Corporation, V
Nichols Research Corporation, 18
NICOR Inc., 6
NIKE, Inc., V; 8 (upd.); 36 (upd.)
Nikken Global Inc., 32
Nimbus CD International, Inc., 20
Nine West Group, Inc., 11; 39 (upd.)
99¢ Only Stores, 25
NIPSCO Industries, Inc., 6
NL Industries, Inc., 10
Nobel Learning Communities, Inc., 37
Noble Affiliates, Inc., 11
Noble Roman's Inc., 14
Noland Company, 35
Noodle Kidoodle, 16
NordicTrack, 22
Nordson Corporation, 11
Nordstrom, Inc., V; 18 (upd.)
Norelco Consumer Products Co., 26
Norfolk Southern Corporation, V; 29 (upd.)
Norrell Corporation, 25
Norstan, Inc., 16
Nortek, Inc., 34
North Face, Inc., The, 18
North Star Steel Company, 18
Northeast Utilities, V
Northern States Power Company, V; 20 (upd.)
Northern Trust Company, 9
Northland Cranberries, Inc., 38
Northrop Corporation, I; 11 (upd.)
Northwest Airlines Corporation, I; 6 (upd.); 26 (upd.)
NorthWestern Corporation, 37
Northwestern Mutual Life Insurance Company, III
Norton Company, 8
Norton McNaughton, Inc., 27
Norwood Promotional Products, Inc., 26
NovaCare, Inc., 11
Novell, Inc., 6; 23 (upd.)
Novellus Systems, Inc., 18
NPC International, Inc., 40
Nu Skin Enterprises, Inc., 27
Nu-kote Holding, Inc., 18
Nucor Corporation, 7; 21 (upd.)
Nutraceutical International Corporation, 37
NutraSweet Company, 8
Nutrition for Life International Inc., 22
NVR L.P., 8
NYMAGIC, Inc., 41
NYNEX Corporation, V
O'Charley's Inc., 19
O'Melveny & Myers, 37
O'Reilly Automotive, Inc., 26
O'Sullivan Industries Holdings, Inc., 34
Oak Industries Inc., 21
Oak Technology, Inc., 22
Oakley, Inc., 18
Oakwood Homes Corporation, 15
Occidental Petroleum Corporation, IV; 25 (upd.)
Ocean Spray Cranberries, Inc., 7; 25 (upd.)

NOTES ON CONTRIBUTORS

Notes on Contributors

AMOROSINO, Chris John. Connecticut-based freelance writer.

BRENNAN, Gerald E. Freelance writer based in California.

BRYNILDSSEN, Shawna. Freelance writer and editor based in Bloomington, Indiana.

CAMPBELL, June. Freelance writer and Internet marketer living in Vancouver, Canada.

COHEN, M. L. Novelist and freelance writer living in Paris.

DINGER, Ed. Brooklyn-based freelance writer and editor.

FIERO, Jane W. Freelance writer and editor.

FIERO, John W. Freelance writer, researcher, and consultant.

FIERO, Joshua C. Student in Creative Writing at Louisiana State University with plans to continue his studies in graduate school and to work as a professional writer.

GREENLAND, Paul R. Illinois-based writer and researcher; author of two books and former senior editor of a national business magazine; contributor to *The Encyclopedia of Chicago History* (University of Chicago Press) and *Company Profiles for Students.*

HALASZ, Robert. Former editor in chief of *World Progress and Funk & Wagnalls New Encyclopedia Yearbook*; author, *The U.S. Marines* (Millbrook Press, 1993).

HAUSER, Evelyn. Researcher, writer and marketing specialist based in Arcata, California; expertise includes historical and trend research in such topics as globalization, emerging industries and lifestyles, future scenarios, biographies, and the history of organizations.

INGRAM, Frederick C. Utah-based business writer who has contributed to *GSA Business, Appalachian Trailway News,* the *Encyclopedia of Business,* the *Encyclopedia of Global Industries,* the *Encyclopedia of Consumer Brands,* and other regional and trade publications.

MEYER, Stephen. Freelance writer based in Missoula, Montana.

MILITE, George A. Philadelphia-based writer specializing in business management issues.

MONTGOMERY, Bruce P. Curator and director of historical collection, University of Colorado at Boulder.

ROTHBURD, Carrie. Freelance technical writer and editor, specializing in corporate profiles, academic texts, and academic journal articles.

STANSELL, Christina M. Freelance writer and editor based in Farmington Hills, Michigan.

TRADII, Mary. Freelance writer based in Denver, Colorado.

UHLE, Frank. Ann Arbor-based freelance writer; movie projectionist, disc jockey, and staff member of *Psychotronic Video* magazine.

WALDEN, David M. Freelance writer and historian in Salt Lake City; adjunct history instructor at Salt Lake City Community College.

WOODWARD, A. Freelance writer.